Lecture Notes in Artificial Intelligence 1114

Subseries of Lecture Notes in Computer Science
Edited by J. G. Carbonell and J. Siekmann

Lecture Notes in Computer Science
Edited by G. Goos, J. Hartmanis and J. van Leeuwen

Springer
Berlin
Heidelberg
New York
Barcelona
Budapest
Hong Kong
London
Milan
Paris
Santa Clara
Singapore
Tokyo

Norman Foo   Randy Goebel (Eds.)

PRICAI'96: Topics in Artificial Intelligence

4th Pacific Rim International Conference on Artificial Intelligence
Cairns, Australia, August 26-30, 1996
Proceedings

Series Editors
Jaime G. Carbonell, Carnegie Mellon University, Pittsburgh, PA, USA
Jörg Siekmann, University of Saarland, Saarbrücken, Germany

Volume Editors

Norman Foo
School of Computer Science and Engineering
University of New South Wales
Sydney, NSW 2052, Australia

Randy Goebel
Department of Computer Science, University of Alberta
Alberta, Canada T6G 2H1

Cataloging-in-Publication Data applied for

Die Deutsche Bibliothek - CIP-Einheitsaufnahme

Topics in artificial intelligence : proceedings / PRICAI '96, 4th Pacific Rim International Conference on Artificial Intelligence, Cairns, Australia, August 26 - 30, 1996. Norman Foo ; Randy Goebel (ed.). - Berlin ; Heidelberg ; New York ; Barcelona ; Budapest ; Hong Kong ; London ; Milan ; Paris ; Santa Clara ; Singapore ; Tokyo : Springer, 1996
(Lecture notes in computer science ; Vol. 1114 : Lecture notes in artificial intelligence)
ISBN 3-540-61532-6
NE: Foo, Norman [Hrsg.]; PRICAI <4, 1996, Cairns>; GT

CR Subject Classification (1991): I.2

ISBN 3-540-61532-6 Springer-Verlag Berlin Heidelberg New York

Printed in Germany

Typesetting: Camera ready by author
SPIN 10513348 06/3142 – 5 4 3 2 1 0 Printed on acid-free paper

Preface

The Fourth Pacific Rim International Conference on Artificial Intelligence (PRICAI'96) held in Cairns, Australia, is the successor to three earlier PRICAIs held in Nagoya, Seoul, and Beijing in the years 1990, 1992, and 1994 respectively. The gradual realization that the Pacific Rim is one of the most dynamic regions in the world has contributed to the recognition that it is not only an eager consumer of modern technology but increasingly also an innovator. That this is so in the area of industrial robotics was evident in Japan for over two decades, but the newer areas of AI like neural nets and knowledge representation are finding commercial applications for the first time in a number of Asian countries. PRICAI was set up to facilitate and stimulate the exchange of AI research, information, and technology in this region while also functioning as a sister conference to its North American and European counterparts, the AAAI and ECAI. PRICAI'96 has formalized this cooperation by canvassing for papers to be jointly submitted to it and its sister conferences, and by obtaining logistic support from them. By hosting PRICAI'96, Australia is making a statement that it, together with the western seaboard of the Americas and New Zealand, is proudly part of this Pacific Rim. It is fitting that Cairns, with its new convention centre, is the site of PRICAI'96 as it is often the arrival point of many Asian guests in Australia.

PRICAI'96 received over 175 paper submissions from 16 countries, including a good number from outside the Pacific Rim. From these, 56 were accepted for presentation (included in this volume) and another 10 for posters published separately. Most papers were refereed by three reviewers selected by members of the Program Committee, and a list of these reviewers appears on pages XI – XIII.

The technical program comprised two days of workshops and tutorials, followed by paper sessions, invited plenary speakers, and panels on Robotics and on AI and Telecommunications. The invited speakers, Juzar Motiwalla, Marvin Minsky, and Joerg Siekmann need no introduction. The Robotics Panel, chaired by Jane Hsu, included Shin'ichi Yuta, Rodney Brooks, and Ray Jarvis. The AI and Telecommunications Panel, chaired by Rye Senjen, was sponsored by Telstra Australia and included Andrew Jennings, Bhavani Raskuti and Kim Horn. As a measure of PRICAI's maturing status, even the workshops and tutorials had prominent AI researchers as speakers, including Rodney Brooks, John Sowa, and Henry Kyburg, to complement well-known AI researchers from the Pacific Rim listed in the Workshop and Tutorial Summaries.

The preparation for PRICAI'96 was the joint effort of many people and institutions from many countries. Generous financial support of PRICAI'96 was

given by a number of organizations and companies, and sister conferences and learned societies offered cooperation. Their names appear on page VII.
We thank Springer-Verlag and its Computer Science Editor Alfred Hofmann for efficient assistance in publishing these proceedings of PRICAI'96 as a volume in its Lecture Notes in Artificial Intelligence series.

August 1996

Norman Foo and Randy Goebel
Program Co-Chairs

Sponsors

PRICAI-96 gratefully acknowledges financial support from the following sponsors:

The Artificial Intelligence and Expert Systems Committee of the Australian Computer Society
The Australian Artificial Intelligence Institute
The Australian Tourist Commission
Continuum Ltd
The CRC for Advanced Computational Systems
The CRC for Intelligent Decision Systems
CSIRO Division of Information Technology
Defence Science and Technology Organisation
Digital Equipment Australia Pty Ltd
Distributed Systems Technology CRC Pty Ltd
Griffith University
The Institute of Electrical and Electronic Engineers, Region 10
The Institute of Systems Science NUS
The Queensland Government Department of Tourism, Small Business and Industry
Sun Microsystems Australia Pty Ltd

Cooperating Organizations and Conferences

PRICAI'96 is held in cooperation with:

The Institute of Electrical Engineers (IEEE) Asia-Pacific Region
The American Artificial Intelligence Institute (AAAI)
The Australian Computer Society (ACS)
The Japanese Society for Artificial Intelligence (JSAI)
The International Society for Applied Intelligence (ISAI)
The European Conference on Artificial Intelligence (ECAI)
The International Joint Conference on Artificial Intelligence (IJCAI)
The Canadian Society for the Computational Studies of Intelligence (CSCSI)

PRICAI Standing Steering Committee

Chair:

Jin-Hyung Kim	Korea Institute of Science & Technology

Committee:

Michael Georgeff	Australian Artificial Intelligence Institute
Randy Goebel	University of Alberta
Se June Hong	IBM TJ Watson Research Laboratories
Juzar Motiwalla	Institute of Systems Science
Zhongzhi Shi	Chinese Academy of Sciences
Wai Kiang Yeap	University of Otago
Benjamin Wah	University of Illinois

Conference Committee

General Co-Chairs:

Michael McRobbie	The Australian National University
Robin Stanton	The Australian National University

Program Co-Chairs:

Norman Foo	University of Sydney
Randy Goebel	University of Alberta

Local Arrangements Chair:

Abdul Sattar	Griffith University

Local Arrangements Co-Chairs:

Shyam Kapur	James Cook University
Geoff Sutcliffe	James Cook University

Workshop Co-Chairs:

Pavlos Peppas	Macquarie University
Scott Goodwin	University of Regina

Tutorial Co-Chairs:

Peter Eklund	University of Adelaide
Ingrid Zukerman	Monash University

Conference Secretariat:

Susan Dickey	Finn Aussi Conference Services

Program Committee

Leopoldo Bertossi	Universidad Catolica de Chile
Francisco J. Cantu	ITESM, Center for Artificial Intelligence
David Dowe	Monash University
Phan Minh Dung	Asian Institute of Technology
Peter Eklund	University of Adelaide
Norman Foo	University of Sydney
Randy Goebel	University of Alberta
Scott Goodwin	University of Regina
Se June Hong	IBM T.J. Watson Research Center
Jenq-Neng Hwang	University of Washington
David Israel	SRI International
R.A.Jarvis	Monash University
Alex Kean	Hong Kong University of Science & Technology
Jin Hyung Kim	Korea Institute of Science and Technology
Young-Bin Kwon	Chung-Ang University
Younghwan Lim	Soong Sil University
Dekang Lin	University of Manitoba
Juzar Motiwalla	Institute of Systems Science
Hiroshi Motoda	Osaka University
Seung Soo Park	Ewha Womans University
Pavlos Peppas	Macquarie University
Claude Sammut	University of New South Wales
Zhongzhi Shi	Chinese Academy of Sciences
Tatsuhiko Tsunoda	Kyoto University
W.K. Albert Yeap	University of Otago
Chengqi Zhang	University of New England
Hong Zhang	University of Alberta
Ingrid Zukerman	Monash University

Administrative Support

Kyle Dean	University of Sydney
Amanda Erbacher	CRC for Advanced Computational Systems
Aditya Ghose	University of Sydney
Helen Harris	The Australian National University
Rex Kwok	University of Sydney

Brendan McCane	James Cook University
Maurice Pagnucco	University of Sydney
Joe Thurbon	University of Sydney
Denise Vercoe	Griffith University
Deidre Whitelaw	The Australian National University

Programmers

Markus Buchhorn	The Australian National University
Michael Lawley	Griffith University
Timothy Nicholson	University of Sydney
Rattana Wetprasit	Griffith University

Workshop Organizers

Leila Alem	CSIRO Div. of Info. Technology
Grigoris Antoniou	Griffith University
Lawrence Cavedon	RMIT
Dominique Estival	University of Melbourne
Srinivas Padmanabhuni	University of Alberta
Dickson Lukose	University of New England
Rye Senjen	Telstra Research Labs

Tutorial Presenters

Grigoris Antoniou	Griffith University
Rodney Brooks	MIT
Robert Dale	Microsoft Institute
Aditya K. Ghose	University of Sydney
Abhaya C. Nayak	University of Sydney
Anand S. Rao	Australian AI Institute
Claude Sammut	University of New South Wales
John F. Sowa	SUNY Binghamton

PRICAI'96 Reviewers

PRICAI'96 is indebted to the following reviewers:

Jose Julio Alferes
Roy Anderson
Grigoris Antoniou
Chid Apte
Mauricio Ayala
Michael Bain
Chitta Baral
Mathias Bauer
Rohan Baxter
Peter van Beek
Leopoldo Bertossi
Michael Boshra
Ramon Brena
Andrew Burrow
Y.T. Byun
T. Caelli
Michael Cameron-Jones
Francisco J. Cantu
Lewis Chau
Teo Seng Cheam
Sung-Bae Cho
Hyung-Il Choi
Jong S Choi
Man-Hoi Choy
Chin Seng Chua
KyuSik Chung
Richard Cole
Paul Compton
Dan Corbett
Stephen Cranefield
Honghua Dai
Shiyong Dai
Robert Dale
Fred Damerau
John Debenham
Hendrik Decker
Peter Deer
Marc Denecker
Simon Dixon
Patrick Doherty
David Dowe
Phan Minh Dung
Ed Durfee
H. Durrant-Whyte
Kim Fairchild
Graham Farr
George Ferguson
Marcus Frean
Pascale Fung
Peter Gardenfors
Hector Geffner
Chris Geib
Aditya Ghose
Roberto Giacobazzi
Laura Giordano
Roderick Girle
Rajeev Gore
Paul Gorman
James Gray
Ian Green
Jim Greer
Edna Grossman
Lindsay Groves
Kamal Gupta
Michael Bonnell Harries
Fumio Hattori
Nevin Heintze
Achim Hoffman
Masahiro Hori
Jonathan Hosking
Ken Hotz
Scott B. Hunter
M. Inaba
Makoato Iwayama
Mark d'Inverno
Ken Jackson
Sanjay Jain
Margaret Jefferies
Hong Tae Jeon
Eric Jones
Antonis Kakas
Hoon Kang
Hirofumi Katsuno
Alex Kean
Ray Kemp
MinKoo Kim
Soo Dong Kim
Ross King
Takashi Kiriyama
L. Kleeman
Igor Kononenko
Hyung Joon Kook
R. Kotagiri
Ina Kraan
Phil Kremer
C. Ronald Kube
Kok Fung Lai
E. Lamma
Mark Lauer
Chris Leckie
Christopher Lee
Dik Lee
Jimmy Ho-man Lee
Jong-Hyeok Lee
Ho Soo Lee
Sang-ho Lee
Seong-Whan Lee
Soo-won Lee
Mun Kew Leong
Neil Leslie
Ho-fung Leung

Jonathan Lever
Qing Li
Yunfeng Li
Joo Hwee Lim
Young-hwan Lim
Dekang Lin
Fangzhen Lin
A. Lipton
Dayou Liu
Ling Liu
John Lloyd
Jorge Lobo
Fred Lochovsky
Boon Toh Low
Helen Lowe
Michael Luck
Dickson Lukose
Nicole Malloy
J. Mathews
Eric Mays
Gordon McCalla
Ricky McConachy
Kathleen McCoy
Joao Meidanes
Paola Mello
Alberto Mendelzon
Tim Menzies
Rob Miller
Guy Mineau
Grisha Mints
Riichiro Mizoguchi
Chunghua Mo
Leora Morgenstern
David Morley
Juzar Motiwalla
Hiroshi Motoda
Seshashayee Murthy
Karen Myers
Sivakumar Nagarajan
Hideyuki Nakashima
Yoshio Nakatani
Abhaya Nayak
Raymond Ng
Teow Hin Ngair
Heinrich Niemann
Toyoaki Nishida
Chris Nowak
Masayuki Numao
Jon Oliver
Paek Eun Ok
Maurice Pagnucco
Rae-Hong Park
Young Tack Park
Srinivas Palthepu
Wanlin Pang
Dan Patterson
Judea Pearl
Edward Pednault
Pavlos Peppas
Nigel Perry
Charles Petrie
Javier Pinto
Martin Purvis
Hae-Chang Rim
V Ram Kumar
Anand Rao
Bhavani Raskutti
Greg Restall
Robert Rist
Chris Robertson
Simon Ronald
Barry Rosen
Francesca Rossi
Enrique Ruspini
R.A. Russell
Pablo Saez
Claude Sammut
Ken Satoh
Marshall Schor
Lenhard Schubert
Luis Serra
Arun Sharma
Y. Shirai
Andreas Shotter
Guillermo Simari
Gurminder Singh
John Slaney
Mark Stickel
Pablo Straub
Peter Stuckey
Jiping Sun
Toshiharu Sugawara
Tatsuhiko Tsunoda
Ah Hwee Tan
Toshikazu Tanaka
Ahmed Tawfik
Takao Terano
Gil Tidhar
Kaiming Ting
Kentaro Torisawa
J. Trevelyan
Andre Trudel
George Tsiknis
Eric Tsui
Hiroshi Tsuji
Katsuhiko Tsujino
Takehito Utsuro
Manuel Valenzuela
Henk Vandecasteele
S. Venkatesh
Jacques Wainer
Chris Wallace
Jun Wang
Xian-chang Wang
Tony Weida
Kay Wiese
Mary-Anne Williams
Andrew Wilson
Wayne Wobcke
Dekai Wu

Jian Kang Wu
Beat Wuthrich
Qianq Yang
Wai Kiang Yeap
Seo Jung Yun
Minjie Zhang
Chengqi Zhang
Xindong Wu
Yang Xiang
Xin Yao
Kennichi Yoshida
A. Zelinski
Nevin Zhang
Tatjana Zrimec
Zhibiao Wu
Seiji Yamada
Meng Ye
Xinghuo Yu
Jian Zhang
Yan Zhang
Ingrid Zukerman

Contents

Machine Learning I

Interactive Systems

Knowledge Representation I

Reasoning About Change

Neural Nets And Uncertainty I

Natural Language

Constraint Satisfaction And Optimization

Qualitative Reasoning

Machine Learning II

Automated Reasoning

Neural Nets And Uncertainty II

Knowledge Representation II

Nonmonotonic Reasoning

Intelligent Agents

Planning

Pattern Recognition

A General Framework for Mechanizing Induction Using Test Set

Adel BOUHOULA

INRIA Lorraine & CRIN
Campus Scientifique
615, rue du Jardin Botanique - B.P. 101
54602 Villers-lès-Nancy Cedex, France
E-mail: bouhoula@loria.fr

Computer Science Laboratory
SRI International
333 Ravenswood Avenue, Menlo Park
California 94025, USA
E-mail: bouhoula@csl.sri.com

Abstract. We present in this paper a test set induction procedure which is refutationally complete for conditional specifications (not restricted to Boolean specifications), in that it refutes any conjecture which is not an inductive theorem. Previously, we could only compute a test set for a conditional specification if the constructors were free. Here, we give a new definition of test sets and a procedure to compute them even if the constructors are not free. The method uses a new notion of provable inconsistency and induction positions (that need to be instantiated by induction schemes) which allows us to refute more false conjectures than with previous approaches. We also present an algorithm to compute all the induction positions of a conditional specification. The method has been implemented in SPIKE. Computer experiments show the superiority of SPIKE concerning mutual induction over explicit induction based systems.

Keywords: Automated reasoning, Theorem Proving, Logic and Formal Verification.

1 Introduction

Nowadays, computer science is applied in an increasing numbers of safety critical systems. Consider for example, the supervision of nuclear power stations or anesthetic control devices. Therefore, the safety of computer systems is vital. However, such systems may in general contain errors, and to ensure that they work safely, we must use a battery of tests. Unless we can perform an infinity of tests, we run the risk of not detecting some mistakes which will be discovered in exceptional cases. The use of formal methods can be considered as a remedy. What are formal methods? Typically they use mathematically based notions.

In this context, equational reasoning plays a critical role in many computer science and artificial intelligence applications, in particular, in program verification and specification of systems. The use of equations is motivated by the existence of an initial model, and proof methods for this model are usually based on an induction scheme such as the one on the structure of terms. Many approaches have been developed to prove a theorem by induction. The first one applies explicit induction arguments on the structure of terms. The Nqthm system [7] was developed in this framework and is considered as one of the most powerful theorem provers. Many of the heuristics in Nqthm have been rationally reconstructed in the prover Clam [8]. RRL [20] is another theorem proving system that supports a *cover set* method which is closely related to Boyer and Moore's approach. Within the last decade, the proof by consistency approach which is based on rewriting and completion techniques has been developed in [16] and refined in several ways in [12, 13, 11, 1]. However, both approaches have many limitations. Indeed, guiding a proof by explicit induction requires some skill in finding the right axioms or hypotheses to apply. On the other hand, the proof by consistency technique does not require guidance from the user since the generation of lemmas is performed automatically through the completion procedure. However, the completion often misses *good* lemmas and fails where explicit induction succeeds. More recently, a new approach has been proposed which combines the full power of explicit induction and proof by consistency [15, 19, 5, 6]. As in explicit induction, we use explicit induction schemes called *cover sets* or *test sets* so that we have more control on the generation of lemmas. As in proof by consistency, we do not require the construction of a hierarchy of lemmas to be proved. We have developed the system SPIKE [1] [4] on this principle. SPIKE has proved several interesting theorems using a minimum of interaction with the user. For instance, it has proved the Gilbreath Card Trick using two user lemmas [6] while classical induction provers like COQ [10], Nqthm, and RRL require no less than fifteen lemmas. However, the SPIKE system is restrictive, because the computation of test sets is done only if the constructors are free, and the strategy is refutationally complete only with respect to Boolean specifications. Note also that the set of false conjectures that can be refuted is very limited and the correctness proof of the procedure is long and delicate.

In this paper, we present a procedure of proof by test set induction which is refutationally complete for conditional specifications (not restricted to Boolean specifications), in that it refutes any conjecture which is not an inductive theorem. This procedure relies on the notion of *test set*, which can be seen as special induction scheme. Our definition of *test set* is more general than the previous one given in [15, 6]. This new definition together with a new notion of provable inconsistency and induction positions (these positions are an extension of *inductively complete positions* [11] for conditional specifications) permit us to refute more false conjectures than our previous definition [15, 6], particularly when the axioms are not sufficiently complete. Previously, we could only compute a test set for a conditional specification if the constructors were free. Here, we give a procedure to compute them even if the constructors are not free. We give also an algorithm to compute all the induction positions of a given conditional specification. This computation is carried out only once for a given specification and permits us to determine whether a variable position in a conjecture is an induction variable or not. Then we guarantee the efficiency of the method because it is not necessary to consult the axioms several times in order to select the induction variables of a conjecture. Finally, we present a new notion of inductive rewriting which permits us to use induction hypotheses and conjectures not necessarily proved as well as axioms, during the simplification. This

[1] SPIKE is available via anonymous ftp from ftp.loria.fr, in the directory /pub/loria/protheo/softwares/Spike

rule allows us to prove more conjectures than with previous approaches [19, 6, 5]. Our method does not need any hierarchy for managing the subgoals. This point is crucial for handling mutually recursive definitions. Recently, we have noted that our approach has some advantages concerning this problematic aspect of explicit induction techniques [2].

The paper is organized as follows. In Section 2, we introduce the basic notions about term rewriting and inductive theory. We present in Section 3 algorithms to compute induction positions and test sets even if the constructors are not free. Inductive rewriting is a fundamental tool for proving inductive theorems; in Section 4 we generalise the notion of inductive rewriting given in [6, 5]. The strategy can be embedded in a correct set of inference rules described in Section 5. When the axioms are ground convergent and the functions are completely defined over free constructors the strategy is proved refutationally complete. A computer experiment with SPIKE is discussed in Section 6. This example shows the superiority of SPIKE concerning mutual induction over explicit induction based systems such as Nqthm.

2 Terminology and Notation

We assume that the reader is familiar with the basic concepts of rewriting and induction. We introduce notation and refer to [9, 17] for a more detailed presentation.

A many sorted signature Σ is a pair (S, F) where S is a set of *sorts* and F is a finite set of function symbols. For short, a many sorted signature Σ will simply be denoted by F. We assume that we have a partition of F into two subsets: the first one, $\mathcal{C}$, contains the *constructor symbols* and the second, $\mathcal{D}$, is the set of *defined symbols*.

Let X be a family of sorted variables and let $T(F, X)$ be the set of well-sorted F-terms. $Var(t)$ stands for the set of all variables appearing in t and $\sharp(x, t)$ denotes the number of occurrences of the variable x in t. A variable x in t is *linear* if and only if $\sharp(x, t) = 1$. We use *lin_var(t)* to denote the set of linear variables of t. If $Var(t)$ is empty then t is a *ground* term. By $T(F)$ we denote the set of all ground terms. From now on we assume that there exists at least one ground term of each sort. A *constructor term* is a term built only from constructors. We say that a sort $\mathcal{S}$ is *finitary*, if the set of ground terms of sort $\mathcal{S}$ is finite.

Let N^* be the set of sequences of positive integers. For any term t, $occ(t) \subseteq N^*$ denotes its set of positions and the expression t/u denotes the *subterm of t at position u*. We write $t[s]_u$ (resp. $t[s]$) to indicate that s is a subterm of t at position u (resp. at some position). The top position is written ε. Let $t(u)$ denote the function symbol or the variable in t at position u. A position u in a term t is said to be *a strict position* if $t(u) = f \in F$, a *linear variable position* if $t(u) = x \in X$ and $\sharp(x, t) = 1$. We use $socc(t)$ to denote the set of strict positions in t. If u is a position, then $|u|$ (the *length* of the corresponding string) gives us its *depth*. If t is a term, then the *depth* of t is the maximum of the depths of the positions in t and denoted *depth(t)*. The symbol $\equiv$ is used for syntactic equality between two objects.

An F-substitution assigns F-terms of appropriate sorts to variables. Composition of substitutions σ and η is written by $\sigma\eta$. The F-term $t\eta$ obtained by applying a substitution η to t is called an *instance* of t. If η assigns every variable of its domain to a ground term, then we say that η is a ground substitution. If $t\eta$ is ground then it is called a ***ground instance*** of t. A term t unifies with a term s if there exists a substitution σ such that $t\sigma \equiv s\sigma$.

A *conditional* F-equation is a formula of the form: $s_1 = t_1 \wedge \cdots \wedge s_n = t_n \Rightarrow s_0 = t_0$ where $n \geq 0$ and for each i: $s_i, t_i \in T(F, X)$ are terms of the same sort. An F-clause is a formula of the form: $\neg(s_1 = t_1) \vee \neg(s_2 = t_2) \vee \cdots \vee \neg(s_n = t_n) \vee (s'_1 = t'_1) \vee \cdots \vee (s'_m = t'_m)$. When F is clear from the context we omit the prefix F. In the following, we consider a clause as a term in an extended alphabet. Let c_1 and c_2 be two clauses such that $c_1\sigma$ is a subclause of c_2 for some substitution σ, then we say that c_1 subsumes c_2. Let H be a set of clauses and C be a clause, we say that C is a logical consequence of H if C is valid in any model of H. This will be denoted by $H \models C$.

In what follows, we suppose that $\succ$ is a transitive irreflexive relation on the set of terms, that is Noetherian (there is no infinite sequence $t_1 \succ t_2 \succ \cdots$), monotonic ($s \succ t$ implies $w[s] \succ w[t]$) and stable ($s \succ t$ implies $s\sigma \succ t\sigma$). The multiset extension of $\succ$ will be denoted by $\gg$.

A conditional equation $a_1 = b_1 \wedge \cdots \wedge a_n = b_n \Rightarrow l = r$ will be written as $a_1 = b_1 \wedge \cdots \wedge a_n = b_n \Rightarrow l \rightarrow r$ if $\{l\sigma\} \gg \{r\sigma, a_1\sigma, b_1\sigma, \cdots, a_n\sigma, b_n\sigma\}$ for each substitution σ; in that case we say that $a_1 = b_1 \wedge \cdots a_n = b_n \Rightarrow l \rightarrow r$ is a *conditional rule*. The term l is the *left-hand side* of the rule. A set of conditional rules is a *rewrite system*. Let c be a constructor symbol. If for any rule $\mathcal{R} \in R$, the top of the left-hand side of $\mathcal{R}$ is different from c, then we say that c is a free constructor. A rewrite rule $c \Rightarrow l \rightarrow r$ is *left-linear* if l is linear. A rewrite system R is *left-linear* if every rule in R is left-linear. The ***depth of a rewrite system*** R, denoted *dep(R)*, is defined as the maximum of the depths of the left-hand sides of R.

A conditional rule is used to rewrite terms by replacing an instance of the left-hand side with the corresponding instance of the right-hand side (but not in the opposite direction) provided that the conditions hold. The conditions are checked recursively. Termination is ensured because the conditions are smaller (w.r.t. to $\succ$) than the left-hand side. A set of conditional rules is called a conditional rewrite system. Now we introduce the notion of term rewriting (w.r.t. $\succ$) with conditional rules:

Definition 1 Conditional Rewriting. Let R be a set of conditional rules. Let t be a term and u a position in t. If there is a substitution σ and a conditional rule $\bigwedge_{i=1}^{n} a_i = b_i \Rightarrow l \rightarrow r$ in R such that: *for all* $i \in [1 \ldots n]$ there exists c_i such that $a_i\sigma \rightarrow_R^* c_i$ and $b_i\sigma \rightarrow_R^* c_i$, where $\rightarrow_R^*$ denotes the reflexive and transitive closure of $\rightarrow_R$. Then, we write: $t[l\sigma]_u \rightarrow_R t[r\sigma]_u$.

A term t is *R-irreducible* if there is no term s such that $t \rightarrow_R s$. A term t is *strongly R-irreducible* if none of its non-variable subterms matches a left-hand side of R. We say that two terms s and t are joinable if $s \rightarrow_R^* v$ and $t \rightarrow_R^* v$ for some term v. he rewrite relation $\rightarrow_R$ is said to be *ground convergent* if the terms u and v are joinable whenever $u, v \in T(F)$ and $R \models u = v$. An operator $f \in \mathcal{D}$ is *sufficiently complete* if and only if for all $t_1, \cdots, t_n$ in $T(C)$, there exists $t \in T(C)$ such that

$f(t_1, \cdots, t_n) \rightarrow^*_R t$. If every $f \in \mathcal{D}$ is sufficiently complete, then we say that R is sufficiently complete.

The case analysis used in this paper simplifies a conjecture with conditional rules where the disjunction of all conditions is inductively valid.

Definition 2 Case analysis. Let R be a set of conditional rules and let C be a clause. Case-analysis$(C[g\sigma]_u) = \{p_1\sigma \Rightarrow C[d_1\sigma]_u; \cdots; p_n\sigma \Rightarrow C[d_n\sigma]_u\}$ **if** $\forall i \in [1 \cdots n] : p_i \Rightarrow g \rightarrow d_i \in R$ **and** $R \models_{ind} p_1\sigma \vee \cdots \vee p_n\sigma$.

where $\models_{ind}$ is written for inductive consequence w.r.t. the initial model.

3 Selection of Induction Schemes

To perform a proof by induction it is necessary to provide induction schemes. In our framework, these schemes are defined first by a function, which, given a conjecture, selects the positions of variables where the induction will be applied (induction variables) and second by a special set of terms, called a *test set*, with which these variables are to be instantiated. Let us first consider the problem of choosing induction variables.

Definition 3 induction variables. Let R be a conditional rewrite system and let C be a clause. The set of induction variables of C, denoted by $ind\_var(C)$, is the smallest set satisfying the following conditions:

1. if x is a variable of a *finitary* sort then $x \in ind\_var(C)$.
2. if x is a variable which appears in a non-variable subterm t of C at position u $(t(u) \equiv x)$ and there exists a rule $\wedge_{i=1}^n g_i = d_i \Rightarrow g \rightarrow d$ in R such that t is unifiable with g and:
   (a) u is a strict position of g or;
   (b) $g(u)$ is a non linear variable in g or;
   (c) $g(u) \in (\bigcup_{i=1,n}\{ind\_var(g_i),\ ind\_var(d_i)\})$.

Then $x \in ind\_var(C)$.

Note that this definition is more general than the one given in [6] and allows us to refute more false conjectures (see Example 2), particularly when the axioms are not sufficiently complete.

To compute induction variables we start by the computation of induction positions of function symbols. This computation is done only once and permits us to determine whether a variable in a clause C is an induction variable or not. Then we guarantee the efficiency of the method because it is not necessary to consult the axioms several times in order to select the induction variables of a conjecture. The algorithm presented in Figure 1 computes for all functions $f \in F$, the set of induction positions of f, denoted by $ind\_pos(R, f)$. We can easily prove that the algorithm terminates since F is a finite set of function symbols and there are only a finite number of rules in R. The following proposition gives us a sufficient criterion to compute induction variables without the use of unification.

- **Input:** a rewrite system R.
- **Output:** induction positions of function symbols.

For all $f \in F$:
 - S_f := $\{s \mid$ there exists $\wedge_i u_i = v_i \Rightarrow g \to d \in R$ and s is an element of $\{u_i\}_i \cup \{v_i\}_i \cup \{g\}$ such that $s(\varepsilon) = f\}$.
 - $pos_0(f)$:= $\{u \mid \exists s \in S_f$ and $u \in (socc(s) \setminus \{\varepsilon\})$ or $s(u) \notin lin\_var(s)\}$

i := 0; *saturation* := *false*;
While $\neg$ *saturation* **do**
 - For all $f \in F$:
   For all $\wedge_i u_i = v_i \Rightarrow g[x]_u \to d$ in R such that $g(\varepsilon) = f$ and $x \in lin\_var(g)$:
   - E_{hv} := $\{(h, v) \mid \exists$ a subterm s of $\{u_i\}_i \cup \{v_i\}_i$ that contains x at position v and $s(\varepsilon) = h\}$
   - If there exists $(h, v) \in E_{hv}$ such that $v \in pos_i(h)$
     then $pos_{i+1}(f)$:= $pos_i(f) \cup \{u\}$
     else $pos_{i+1}(f)$:= $pos_i(f)$
 - If for all $f \in F$: $pos_{i+1}(f) = pos_i(f)$
   then for all $f \in F$: $ind\_pos(R, f) := pos_i(f)$; *saturation* := *true*
   else $i := i + 1$

End.

Fig. 1. Computing induction positions

Proposition 4. *Let C be a clause containing a variable x of sort s. We say that x is an* induction variable *of C if s is* finitary *or if x occurs at a position $u.v$ of C such that v is an induction position of $t(u)$.*

Our method is based on the notion of *test sets*. Let us introduce first the following definition:

Definition 5 weakly irreducible term. Let R be a conditional rewriting system. A term t is *weakly R-irreducible* if for all subterms s of t, if there exists a rule $p \Rightarrow g \to d$ in R and a substitution σ with $s = g\sigma$, then $p\sigma$ is unsatisfiable for R (i.e. for all ground substitution τ: $R \not\models p\sigma\tau$).

Definition 6 test set. A set of terms TS is a *test set* for a conditional rewriting system R if:

1. For all ground R-irreducible term s, there exist a term t in TS and a ground substitution σ such that $t\sigma \equiv s$.
2. Given n terms $t_1, \cdots, t_n$ and a test substitution [2] σ such that for each i: $t_i\sigma$ is weakly R-irreducible, there exists a ground substitution τ such that $t_i\sigma\tau$ is ground and R-irreducible for each i.

Test sets can be considered as refined induction schemes, they allow us to avoid the failure of the procedure of proof by induction in many cases. Test sets also permit us to refute false conjectures by constructing a counterexample. We propose a new criterion to reject conjectures that are not inductively valid.

[2] We say that σ is a test substitution of C if it maps every induction variable of C to an element of TS of the same sort and whose variables have been renamed.

Definition 7 provably inconsistent. Let R be a conditional rewriting system and let TS be a test set of R. Let $C \equiv \neg(a_1 = b_1) \vee \cdots \vee \neg(a_n = b_n) \vee (c_1 = d_1) \vee \cdots \vee (c_m = d_m)$ be a clause. C is provably inconsistent if and only if there exists a test substitution σ such that:

1. for all i, $R \models_{ind} a_i\sigma = b_i\sigma$.
2. for all j, $c_j\sigma \not\equiv d_j\sigma$ and the maximal [3] element of $\{c_j\sigma, d_j\sigma\}$ w.r.t. $\prec$ is weakly R-irreducible.

If C is *provably inconsistent* and the axioms are ground convergent, then C is not an inductive theorem. This result can be proved by the construction of a ground substitution which gives a counterexample.

Theorem 8. *Let R be a conditional ground convergent rewriting system. If a clause C is* provably inconsistent, *then C is not an inductive theorem.*

Our notion of provably inconsistent clause allows us to refute more false conjectures than previous methods [15, 6, 5]. In particular, we can now refute false conjectures even when the axioms are not sufficiently complete.

Example 1. Consider the following conditional specification which defines the predicate $\leq$ on the natural numbers and the predicate *ordered* which checks whether a list is ordered: $\{0 \leq x = true,\ s(x) \leq 0 = false,\ s(x) \leq s(y) = x \leq y,\ ordered(cons(x, nil)) = true,\ x \leq y = false \Rightarrow ordered(cons(x, cons(y, z))) = false\}$. The predicate *ordered* is not sufficiently complete and the equation $ordered(cons(0, cons(0, y))) = false$ is *provably inconsistent*. Indeed, $ordered(cons(0, cons(0, y)))$ does not contain any induction variable and is *weakly R-irreducible* since $0 \leq 0 = false$ is unsatisfiable in R. With the methods [15, 5, 6], this equation is not *provably inconsistent* since $ordered(cons(0, cons(0, y)))$ is not strongly R-irreducible. ♦

Example 2. The following axioms define *odd* and *even* for nonnegative integers: $\{even(0) = true,\ even(s(0)) = false,\ even(s(s(x))) = even(x),\ even(x) = true \Rightarrow odd(x) = false,\ even(s(x)) = true \Rightarrow odd(x) = true\}$, the predicate *odd* is not sufficiently complete. Consider the conjecture $odd(x) = true$, x is an induction variable w.r.t. Definition 3. Instantiating x by 0 yields $odd(0) = true$ which is simplified by R into: $false = true$, which is *provably inconsistent*. We conclude that $odd(x) = true$ is not an inductive theorem. Now, with the method [6], x is not an induction variable, on the other hand $odd(x) = true$ is not provably inconsistent since $odd(x)$ is not strongly R-irreducible. Therefore, the method [6] fails to refute the conjecture $odd(x) = true$. ♦

The computation of test sets for equational specifications is decidable (see [14]). Unfortunately, no algorithm exists for the general case of conditional specifications. However, in [5, 6] some methods are described for computing test sets for conditional specifications over a *free set of constructors*. The following proposition gives us a procedure to compute a test set even if the constructors are not free. We first recall

[3] If $c_j\sigma$ and $d_j\sigma$ are incomparable, then both $c_j\sigma$ and $d_j\sigma$ must be weakly R-irreducible.

that a term t is inductively reducible by a rewrite system R if every ground instance of t is reducible. Plaisted [18] proved the decidability of inductive reducibility for finitely many unconditional equations.

Proposition 9. *Let R be a conditional rewrite system. Assume that R is left linear and sufficiently complete. Let $\mathcal{T} = \{t \mid t$ is a constructor term of depth $\leq \text{dep(R)}$ where variables may occur only at depth $\text{dep(R)}\}$. Then, the subset of $\mathcal{T}$ composed of terms that are not inductively reducible by R, is a test set for R.*

If the constructors are specified by a set of unconditional equations, then we can decide inductive reducibility of constructor terms and therefore, we obtain an algorithm to compute test sets.

4 Inductive Rewriting

To simplify goals, we generalize the inductive rewriting relation defined in [6], so that we can use induction hypotheses and other conjectures not necessarily proved as well as axioms, during the simplification. In the following, we suppose that $\prec_c$ is a well-founded ordering on clauses (see [6]).

Definition 10. Let R be a conditional rewrite system and let W be a set of conditional equations. Consider a clause $C[s\sigma]$. We write: $s\sigma \overset{C}{\longmapsto}_{R<W>} t\sigma$, if there exists a conditional equation $\mathcal{R} \equiv \bigwedge_{i=1}^{n} a_i = b_i \ \Rightarrow s = t \in R \cup W$ such that:

1. if $\mathcal{R} \in W$, then $\mathcal{R}\sigma \prec_c C$ and $\{C\} \gg \{a_1\sigma,\ b_1\sigma,\ \cdots,a_n\sigma,\ b_n\sigma\}$.
2. $\forall i \in [1 \cdots n]\ \exists c_i$ such that $a_i\sigma \overset{C}{\longmapsto}{}^{*}_{R<W>} c_i$ and $b_i\sigma \overset{C}{\longmapsto}{}^{*}_{R<W>} c_i$.

Definition 11 Inductive rewriting. Let R be a conditional rewrite system and let W be a set of conditional equations. Consider a clause C. We write: $C[a]_u \longmapsto_{R<W>} C[a']_u$ if and only if $a \overset{C}{\longmapsto}_{R<W>} a'$ and $C[a]_u \prec_c C[a']_u$.

The set W in the definition is intended to contain induction hypotheses and conjectures which are not necessarily proved, in the proof system described below. This rule allows us to prove more conjectures than previous approaches.

Example 3. Consider a specification with the only axiom $s(s(0)) = 0$, then the proposition $s(s(x)) = x$ is an inductive property. The methods of [19, 6, 5] fail to prove this conjecture if we consider the cover set $\{0,\ s(x)\}$. Indeed, the instantiation of x by $s(y)$ gives us the equation $s(s(s(y))) = s(y)$ which cannot be simplified by the axiom. Now, thanks to the new inductive rewriting, $s(s(s(y))) = s(y)$ can be simplified into $s(y) = s(y)$, using the conjecture $s(s(x)) = x$ in spite of its not being yet proved, since $s(s(y)) = y \prec_c s(s(s(y))) = s(y)$. ♦

5 A proof procedure for Conditional Theories

Now we present a test set induction procedure which, as opposed to the method given in [6], is refutationally complete even when we have a non Boolean specification. Let us first introduce the following definition: A term t is *quasi-irreducible* by a

generate: $(E \cup \{C\}, H) \vdash_I (E \cup (\cup_\sigma E_\sigma), H \cup \{C\})$
if for all TS-substitutions σ of C:
either $C\sigma$ is a tautology and $E_\sigma = \emptyset$
or $C\sigma \mapsto_{R<H \cup E \cup \{C\}>} C'$ and $E_\sigma = \{C'\}$
otherwise $E_\sigma = case\_analysis(C\sigma)$.

case simplify: $(E \cup \{C\}, H) \vdash_I (E \cup E', H)$
if $E' = case\_analysis(C)$.

simplify: $(E \cup \{C\}, H) \vdash_I (E \cup \{C'\}, H)$
if $C \mapsto_{R<H \cup E>} C'$.

positive decomposition: $(E \cup \{f(\mathbf{s}) = f(\mathbf{t}) \vee r\}, H) \vdash_I (E \cup (\cup_i \{s_i = t_i \vee r\}), H)$
if f is a free constructor.

negative decomposition: $(E \cup \{\neg f(\mathbf{s}) = f(\mathbf{t}) \vee r\}, H) \vdash_I (E \cup \{\vee_i \neg(s_i = t_i) \vee r\}, H)$
if f is a free constructor.

positive clash: $(E \cup \{f(\mathbf{s}) = g(\mathbf{t}) \vee r\}, H) \vdash_I (E \cup \{r\}, H)$
if f and g are two distinct free constructors.

eliminate trivial equation: $(E \cup \{\neg(s = s) \vee r\}, H) \vdash_I (E \cup \{r\}, H)$

subsume: $(E \cup \{C\}, H) \vdash_I (E, H)$
if C is subsumed by another clause of $R \cup H \cup E$.

delete tautology: $(E \cup \{\vee_{i=1}^n \neg(x_i = t_i) \vee r\}, H) \vdash_I (E, H)$
if for all i : $x_i \notin var(t_i)$ and $r\sigma$ is a tautology where $\sigma = \{x_i \leftarrow t_i \mid i \in [1 \cdots n]\}$.

occur check: $(E \cup \{\vee_{i=1}^n \neg(x_i = t_i) \vee r\}, H) \vdash_I (E, H)$
if there exists i such that $x_i \not\equiv t_i$, $x_i \in var(t_i)$ and t_i quasi irreducible.

negative clash: $(E \cup \{\neg f(\mathbf{s}) = g(\mathbf{t}) \vee r\}, H) \vdash_I (E, H)$
if f and g are two distinct free constructors.

refute: $(E \cup \{C\}, H) \vdash_I$ *Refutation*
if no other rules are applied to C.

Fig. 2. Inference System J

rewriting system R if for all ground R-irreducible substitution σ, $t\sigma$ is R-irreducible. Let $f \in F$ be a sufficiently complete function symbol. If for all rules $p_i \Rightarrow f(\mathbf{t}_i) = d_i$ whose left-hand sides are identical up to a renaming μ_i, we have $R \models_{ind} \bigvee_i p_i\mu_i$, then f is strongly complete w.r.t. R. We say that R is strongly complete if any function symbol is strongly complete w.r.t. R. Note that the transformation of a sufficiently complete rewriting system into another one which is strongly complete is obvious if the functions are sufficiently complete over free constructors.

Let R be a conditional rewriting system and let TS be a test set for R. Our procedure is defined by a set of transition rules (see Figure 2). The *generate* rule allows us to derive subgoals. The *case simplify* rule simplifies a conjecture with conditional rules where the disjunction of all conditions is inductively valid. The ***simplify*** rule reduces a clause C with axioms from R, induction hypotheses from H, and other conjectures which are not yet proved. Note that ***simplify*** permits mutual simplification of conjectures. This rule implements simultaneous induction and is crucial for efficiency. The rules ***positive (resp. negative) decomposition***, ***positive clash*** and ***eliminate trivial equation*** take advantage of the fact that constructors are free to simplify clauses [4]. The rules ***subsume***, ***delete tautology***, ***occur check*** and ***negative clash*** delete redundant clauses. The ***refute*** rule is applied to (E, H) if no other rule can be applied to $C \in E$. An I-derivation is a sequence of states: $(E_0, \emptyset) \vdash_I (E_1, H_1) \vdash_I \ldots \vdash_I (E_n, H_n) \vdash_I \ldots$. An I-derivation is *fair* if the set of persisting clauses $(\cup_{i \geq 0} \cap_{j \geq i} E_j)$ is empty.

The inference system J is refutationally complete; this result is expressed by the following theorem:

Theorem 12. *Let R be a ground convergent rewriting system that is strongly complete over free constructors. If a derivation issued from $(E_0, \emptyset)$ terminates by application of the rule* refute, *then $R \not\models_{ind} E_0$. Conversely, if $R \not\models_{ind} E_0$, then all fair derivations issued from $(E_0, \emptyset)$ terminate by application of the rule* refute.

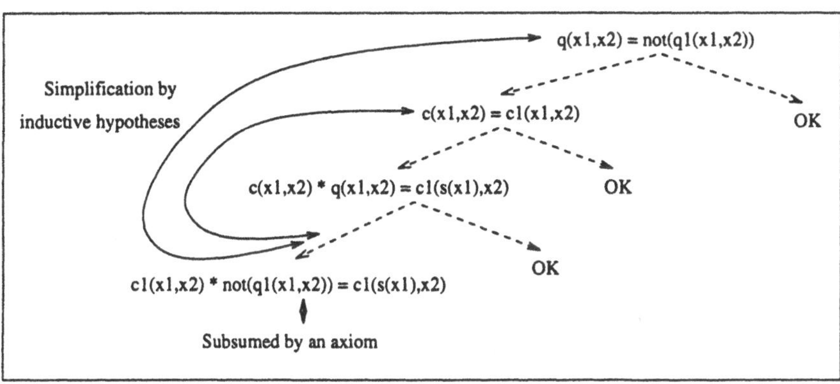

Fig. 3. The proof scheme

6 Computer Experiment

Consider the following set of axioms which specifys a *forward counter* and a *backward counter*: $\{c(0,t) = input(t),\ c(s(i),t) = c(i,t) * q(i,t),\ q(i,0) = init(i),\ q(i,s(t)) = q(i,t) + c(i,t),\ c_1(0,t) = input(t),\ c_1(s(i),t) = c_1(i,t) * not(q_1(i,t)),\ q_1(i,0) = not(init(i)),\ q_1(i,s(t)) = q_1(i,t) + c_1(i,t),\ not(not(x)) = x,\ not(x+y) = not(x) + y\}$. The set of constructors $\mathcal{C}$ contains: $\{0,\ s,\ +,\ -,\ true,\ false,\ input,\ init\}$. The theorem to be proved is: $q(i,t) = not(q_1(i,t))$. This problem cannot be proved by

[4] Inference rules for free constructors are necessary to guarantee the refutational completeness of the inference system I.

Nqthm (without modifying the axioms) due to the presence of mutually recursive operators. Note also that the specification is not sufficiently complete and the function *not* is not defined over constructors ($not(not(x)) = x$). The scheme of the proof generated by SPIKE is presented in Figure 3.

7 Conclusion

We have proposed a new proof procedure by test set induction for conditional specifications. The main arguments in favor of our method are:

Well-founded ordering: The well-founded ordering on which induction is based is exactly the termination ordering used to orient the axioms into rules. Therefore, the numerous mechanical tools that were designed to prove termination of rewrite systems are readily available for suggesting good induction orderings.

Induction schemas: Schemas are defined first by a function which, given a conjecture, selects the positions of variables where the induction will be applied (induction variables) and second by a special set of terms called a *test set* with which these variables must be instantiated. The computation of induction positions is carried out only once for a given specification and determines whether a variable position in a conjecture is an induction variable or not. Then we guarantee the efficiency of the method because it is not necessary to consult the axioms several times to select the induction variables of a conjecture.

Generation of lemmas: The lemmas are generated by replacing the induction variables of a conjecture by test sets or cover sets and applying inductive rewriting or case analysis.

Mutual induction: Conjectures are processed in a non-hierarchical order. New subgoals to be proved are simply added to this list. Therefore, mutual induction is automatically handled by our technique. This point is also crucial for handling mutually recursive definitions. Recently, we have noted that our approach has some advantages concerning this problematic aspect of explicit induction techniques [2].

Case analysis: With test set induction, case analysis can easily be simulated by term rewriting. Divergence problems are avoided by applying conditional rules.

Refutation: We can refute false conjectures when the axioms are presented by a ground convergent conditional rewrite system. A conjecture is rejected whenever an inconsistency appears. We have proposed a new notion of provable inconsistency which allows us to refute more false conjectures than with previous approaches. Our strategy is also refutationally complete, in that it refutes any conjecture which is not valid in the initial model provided that the axioms are ground convergent and the functions are strongly complete over free constructors (not restricted to Boolean specifications).

Our test set induction procedure is implemented in the prover SPIKE. In contrast to the majority of current proof systems that construct their proofs step by step and require frequent user intervention, not to say a great expertise on the part of the user, SPIKE has proved several interesting problems with a minimum of interaction with the user [3].

We plan to enhance the system with generalization techniques for suggesting lemmas and we hope to prove more challenging problems with a minimal number of lemmas provided by the user.

Acknowledgement: I am grateful to José Meseguer and Michaël Rusinowitch for their valuable comments.

References

1. L. Bachmair. Proof by consistency in equational theories. In *Proceedings 3rd IEEE Symposium on Logic in Computer Science, Edinburgh (UK)*, pages 228–233, 1988.
2. A. Bouhoula. The challenge of mutual recursion and mutual simplification in implicit induction. Invited talk at the International Workshop on the Automation of Proof by Mathematical Induction, June 1994.
3. A. Bouhoula. *Preuves Automatiques par Récurrence dans les Théories Conditionnelles*. PhD thesis, Université de Nancy 1, March 1994.
4. A. Bouhoula. Using induction and rewriting to verify and complete parameterized specifications. *Theoretical Computer Science*, 170, December 1996.
5. A. Bouhoula, E. Kounalis, and M. Rusinowitch. Automated Mathematical Induction. *Journal of Logic and Computation*, 5(5):631–668, 1995.
6. A. Bouhoula and M. Rusinowitch. Implicit induction in conditional theories. *Journal of Automated Reasoning*, 14(2):189–235, 1995.
7. R. S. Boyer and J. S. Moore. *A Computational Logic*. Academic Press inc., New York, 1979.
8. A. Bundy, F. van Harmelen, C. Horn, and A. Smaill. Rippling: A heuristic for guiding inductive proofs. *Artificial Intelligence*, 62:183–253, 1993.
9. N. Dershowitz and J.-P. Jouannaud. Rewrite systems. *Handbook of Theoretical Computer Science*. Elsevier Science Publishers B. V. (North-Holland), 1990.
10. G. Dowek, A. Felty, H. Herbelin, G. Huet, C. Paulin-Mohring, and B. Werner. The Coq Proof Assistant. User's guide, INRIA-CNRS-ENS, 1991.
11. L. Fribourg. A strong restriction of the inductive completion procedure. *Journal of Symbolic Computation*, 8(3):253–276, September 1989.
12. G. Huet and J.-M. Hullot. Proofs by induction in equational theories with constructors. *Journal of Computer and System Sciences*, 25(2):239–266, October 1982.
13. J.-P. Jouannaud and E. Kounalis. Automatic proofs by induction in theories without constructors. *Information and Computation*, 82:1–33, 1989.
14. E. Kounalis. Testing for the ground (co-)reducibility property in term-rewriting systems. *Theoretical Computer Science*, 106:87–117, 1992.
15. E. Kounalis and M. Rusinowitch. A mechanization of conditional reasoning. In *First International Symposium on Artificial Intelligence and Mathematics, Fort Lauderdale, Florida*, January 1990.
16. D. R. Musser. On proving inductive properties of abstract data types. In *Proceedings 7th ACM Symp. on Principles of Programming Languages*, pages 154–162. 1980.
17. P. Padawitz. *Computing in Horn Clause Theories*. Springer-Verlag, 1988.
18. D. Plaisted. Semantic confluence and completion method. *Information and Control*, 65:182–215, 1985.
19. U. S. Reddy. Term rewriting induction. In *Proceedings 10th International Conference on Automated Deduction*, *LNCS* 449, pages 162–177. 1990.
20. H. Zhang, D. Kapur, and M. S. Krishnamoorthy. A mechanizable induction principle for equational specifications. In *Proceedings 9th International Conference on Automated Deduction*, *LNCS* 310, pages 162–181. 1988.

Inductive Equational Reasoning

Michael Bulmer

Department of Mathematics, University of Tasmania,
GPO Box 252C, Hobart, 7001, Australia
Michael.Bulmer@maths.utas.edu.au

Abstract. We present a simple learning algorithm for equational reasoning. The Knuth-Bendix algorithm can produce deductive consequences from sets of function equations but cannot deduce anything from grounded equations alone. This motivates an inductive procedure which conjectures function equations from a given database of grounded equations.

1 Introduction

Equational systems, together with the Knuth-Bendix procedure [5], give a framework for *deductive* reasoning. For example, from the equational system

$$\mathsf{wife\ husband} = \mathsf{i}, \quad \mathsf{wife\ John} = \mathsf{Jill},$$

where i is the identity function, we are able to deduce that $\mathsf{husband\ Jill} = \mathsf{John}$. In this paper we give a procedure for *inductive* equational reasoning, so that from the system

$$\mathsf{wife\ John} = \mathsf{Jill}, \quad \mathsf{husband\ Jill} = \mathsf{John}$$

we may conjecture that $\mathsf{wife\ husband} = \mathsf{i}$. We have evidence for this new fact since whenever we apply the composite function $\mathsf{wife\ husband}$ to a person we get the same result as applying the identity function i. This observation leads to an induction procedure for learning general equations from a database of ground knowledge.

In Section 1.1 we give a brief overview of the term language with which we represent our equational knowledge. It should be noted that this language is variable-free, placing the emphasis on function evaluation rather than the predicate unification of standard ILP. Section 2 presents the induction algorithm and states an important termination result. The behaviour of the algorithm is then illustrated using a dialogue with a prototype reasoner in Section 3 and then with a larger example in Section 4. Our ultimate interest in this work lies in the things we can then say about the pragmatic and philosophical notions of consistency and changing belief. We touch briefly on this aspect in the example dialogue.

1.1 Language

Our language will be that of a ground (i.e. variable free) term algebra T_Σ generated by a signature Σ. We typically view T_Σ as a category with terminal object Ground, products, and set constructors. We call the objects of the category the *sorts* of T_Σ and say that an arrow from σ to τ is a *term* of *type* $\sigma \to \tau$. The number of single arrows in a composite arrow f is the *length*, $\delta(f)$, of f. For example, $\delta(\mathsf{wife\ husband}) = 2$.

A term $f : \sigma \to \tau$ has *domain* $\mathrm{dom}(f) = \sigma$ and *codomain* $\mathrm{cod}(f) = \tau$. If a term f is of type Ground $\to \sigma$ we write $f \in \sigma$ and say that f is *grounded*. If a term is not grounded it is called a *function*. For each sort σ there are two distinguished operators, the *identity* $\mathsf{i} : \sigma \to \sigma$ and the *erasing* operator $! : \sigma \to$ Ground. For any terms f and g we have the structural rules $f\ \mathsf{i} \to f$, $\mathsf{i}\ f \to f$, and

$$f\ !\ g \to \begin{cases} f, & \text{if } \mathrm{dom}(g) = \mathsf{Ground}; \\ f\ !, & \text{if } \mathrm{dom}(g) \neq \mathsf{Ground} \end{cases}$$

The set constructor we use is a special instance of a boolean affine combination [3] where the coefficients of the combinations are suppressed. For every collection of terms $f_1, f_2, \ldots, f_n$ with common type $\sigma \to \tau$ we can form the *set* $\{f_1, f_2, \ldots, f_n\}$ with type $\sigma \to \tau$.

The basic structural rules for T_Σ are given in [8]. Structural rules for sets are inherited from the boolean affine combinations, giving the following:

$$\begin{aligned} &f\ \{g_1, \ldots, g_n\} \to \{f\ g_1, \ldots, f\ g_n\}, \\ &\{f_1, \ldots, f_n\}\ g \to \{f_1\ g, \ldots, f_n\ g\}, \\ &\{\ldots, f_k, \{g_1, \ldots, g_m\}, f_{k+1}, \ldots\} \to \{\ldots, f_k, g_1, \ldots, g_m, f_{k+1}, \ldots\}, \\ &\{f, f, g_1, \ldots, g_n\} \to \{f, g_1, \ldots, g_n\}. \end{aligned}$$

Sets are important in rewrite-based reasoning as they give a means of capturing multi-valued functions, as in the example of Section 4, and recursive definitions.

We represent knowledge as equations between terms in T_Σ. For example, to capture the statement that 'Alice's father is John' we introduce to Σ the sort Person and the function father : Person $\to$ Person and grounded words Alice, John $\in$ Person. Then we can assert the equation father Alice $=$ John. A negative predicate statement such as 'Alice is not male' is represented by male Alice $=$ False.

If F is a set of equations then we write $F \Rightarrow (f = g)$, or $f =_F g$, if the equation $f = g$ is a deductive consequence [1] of F.

If f arises from a single arrow in Σ, i.e. $\delta(f) = 1$, then f is called a *Σ-word.* Grounded Σ-words may be declared to represent an *entity* in the modelled world. For example, we represent the two classical notions of truth as the grounded words True, False $\in$ Sentence, or three different people as Alice, John, Paul $\in$ Person. We call such declared words the *Σ-entities* of Σ.

The important property is that these entities are distinct. Having declared a collection of Σ-entities we implicitly require that any system F contains the inequation $a \neq b$ for all Σ-entities a and b with $a \not\equiv b$. Thus if we declare True and False to be Σ-entities then every system will contain True $\neq$ False. A system

F is then *inconsistent* if $a =_F b$ for some distinct entities a and b. We will usually declare grounded words to be entities by writing them with an uppercase letter (reflecting the similarity with a proper noun).

An equation between two grounded terms (such as the above $\mathsf{father\ Alice} = \mathsf{John}$) is called a *grounded equation*, or a *datum*, and a set of such equations is called a *database*. An equation which is not grounded is called a *function equation*.

As noted in [5], the Knuth-Bendix completion procedure applied to a database will never use critical-pair deduction to produce new information. Our initial motivation for looking at induction is to find a notion of reasoning which does produce new information from a database.

2 Induction Method

The induction procedure IND takes a complete set of rewrite rules Δ (the *database*) and returns a set of function equations (the *conjectures*). These function equations will be of two kinds; facts and conjectures.

Definition 1 (Fact). A *fact* from a database Δ is a function equation $f = g$ such that $\Delta \not\Rightarrow (f = g)$ and $fx =_\Delta gx$ for all Σ-entities $x \in \mathrm{dom}(f)$.

Definition 2 (Conjecture). A *conjecture* from a database Δ is a function equation $f \simeq g$ such that $\Delta \not\Rightarrow (f = g)$ and $fx =_\Delta gx$ for at least one Σ-entity $x \in \mathrm{dom}(f)$ and there is no Σ-entity $y \in \mathrm{dom}(f)$ such that $\Delta \Rightarrow (fy \neq gy)$.

That is, a fact is a function equation which holds when applied to any entity of appropriate type. A conjecture is an incomplete fact, a function equation which holds for at least one entity and is not falsified by any other entity. A conjecture is not a fact because information is absent in Δ about the meaning of the composition of one of the functions and some entity.

This illustrates well why we don't adopt a closed-world assumption. We instead take the scientific view that the truth of some equations may simply be unknown. Truth or falsity, if not the deductive consequence of a system of beliefs, can only be established by carrying out new experiments.

From these definitions it is clear that facts can never produce new database information, capturing only truth that is always present. In this sense, a fact represents *summative* induction, the equation summarizing the complete information we have about the data. Although a fact can generate no new data, it can be used to compress the database by eliminating data which are implied by it. This process is equivalent to an axiomatization of the system [11].

If a conjecture is accepted by a reasoner it can then produce new database information by essentially filling in the gaps which prevented it from being called a fact in the first place. A conjecture is a form of *ampliative* induction, the equation providing new information and thus amplifying our knowledge [4]. Conjectures will be our main focus as they have close and interesting parallels with scientific method.

Proof by consistency [9] can be used to *prove*, rather than merely conjecture, that an equation is an inductive consequence of system in the sense of *mathematical* induction. The following two results give a concrete relationship between our inductive process and such inductive theorems, that is, between scientific and mathematical induction.

Theorem 1. *A fact from a system Δ is an inductive theorem of Δ.*

Theorem 2. *If Δ gives rise to a conjecture then Δ is ambiguous.*

This second result is perhaps our "fundamental theorem". If a system is ambiguous then we are unable to prove an inductive theorem by consistency. Thus a conjecture can be simply characterized as an inductive theorem that cannot be proved.

2.1 Algorithm

Let Σ_σ denote the vector (ordered set) of all Σ-entities of type σ and let $\Sigma^n_{\sigma\to\tau}(\Delta)$ denote the set of all Δ-normal forms of Σ-functions with type $\sigma \to \tau$ and length at most n.

For a function term f, a vector of entities $X = \{x_i\}$, and a given rewrite system Δ, define $fX \downarrow_\Delta$ to be the vector $\{n_i\}$, with each n_i defined as follows:

$$n_i = \begin{cases} s \text{ if } fx_i \to^*_\Delta s \text{ for some entity } s \\ * \text{ otherwise} \end{cases}$$

The condition that s is an entity in the first case will correspond to the requirement that we must have complete knowledge about the function value before we make any conjecture. The special term $*$ in the second case indicates that no complete information is present in Δ about the value of the function for that particular entity.

Finally, for vectors S_1, S_2 from $T_\Sigma \cup \{*\}$ having equal length, we say $S_1 = S_2$ if S_1 and S_2 are identical at each position and both are free of the element $*$. We write $S_1 \simeq S_2$ if S_1 and S_2 are identical at each position where neither has a $*$ and there is at least one such position.

With these definitions, we can now give the following definition of IND:

procedure IND(Δ, n)
  $E_{\Delta,n} := \phi$
  for each sort σ
    for each $f, g \in \Sigma^n_{\sigma\to\tau}(\Delta)$, $f \not\equiv g$,
      if $f\Sigma_\sigma \downarrow_\Delta = g\Sigma_\sigma \downarrow_\Delta$ then $E_{\Delta,n} := E_{\Delta,n} \cup \{f = g\}$
      if $f\Sigma_\sigma \downarrow_\Delta \simeq g\Sigma_\sigma \downarrow_\Delta$ then $E_{\Delta,n} := E_{\Delta,n} \cup \{f \simeq g\}$
  IND := $E_{\Delta,n}$
end.

For each Σ-sort σ we look at the set of parallel Σ-functions with domain σ, reduced by Δ. We take pairs of distinct f, g from this set and apply each of them to the vector of all entities with codomain σ. These applications are then reduced by Δ, using $*$ for any whose normal form is not an entity. If the reduced lists are free of $*$ and identical then we generate $f = g$ as a fact. If they are identical at each element where neither list has $*$, and there is at least one such element, then we generate $f = g$ as a conjecture, written $f \simeq g$.

In an implementation of the procedure there are many efficiency improvements that can be made to reduce the number of functions to be considered and the number of normal form reductions to be performed. For example, if we have found the normal form $f_n f_{n-1} \cdots f_1 x \to y$ then the normal form of $g f_n \cdots f_1 x$ is obtained by reducing gy. In general though, the number of functions to be considered grows exponentially with n, the maximum function length. To work with this we apply the induction algorithm iteratively. Starting with $\Delta_1 = \mathrm{IND}(\Delta, 1)$, we evaluate $\Delta_{j+1} = \Delta_j \cup \mathrm{IND}(\Delta \cup \Delta_j, j+1)$, the conjectures arising from the result of induction for length j being used to reduce the candidate functions of length $j+1$. We then say that the result of the induction of Δ is then set Δ_∞. The following result shows that Δ_∞ is finite.

Theorem 3. (Termination). *For a given database Δ there exists some K such that $\Delta_k = \Delta_K$ for all $k > K$.*

Even though this theorem shows that the inductive knowledge will be finite, the number of conjectures of general length can be quite large. This is especially so early on in a series of experiments when often many wild conjectures appear before later being refuted by further observations. In most cases we concentrate on finding $\mathrm{IND}(\Delta, 2)$ only, conjecturing simple relationships between functions. In essence this is Occam's razor at work; we first look for simple explanations of the data and only if we cannot find any do we search for more complex hypotheses.

3 Dialogue

We illustrate the induction process with a simple dialogue from an implementation of a reasoner which uses the algorithm presented in Section 2.1. This reasoner takes simple sentences from an external oracle and converts them into equational beliefs. Each time the reasoner's belief set is enlarged or revised we apply IND to the corresponding canonical rewrite system (which needs to be generated in establishing consistency). The resulting conjectures may in fact be inconsistent with the given beliefs [1]. If this is the case we can view the maximal subsets that are consistent with the beliefs as *competing theories*, different explanations of the observed data [2]. We use Popper's falsifiability criterion [10] to choose a single working set of *conjectured beliefs* from these theories.

For compactness, at each stage of the dialogue we only give newly declared beliefs, rather than repeating the whole set of beliefs. Whenever the belief set changes we additionally give the resulting set of conjectured beliefs, although in practice this need only be generated when a question is asked of the reasoner.

When asked a question the reasoner attempts to find an answer based on its given beliefs, such as 'Yes' if the question corresponds to an equational consequence of the belief system. If it cannot find such an answer, it then looks for an answer by augmenting its beliefs with the working set of conjectures. If, for instance, the question is then a consequence of the augmented system, it responds with 'Yes, I think so' to indicate the answer is based on tentative information.

The dialogue in Tables 1 and 2 involves competing theories in the reasoner's conjectures. When asked a question, the answers which rely on conjectures are augmented by requests for the results of any *experiments* the reasoner determines will resolve the inconsistency.

Human	**Reasoner**	**Belief Set**
Peter is male.	Okay.	male Peter = True male ≃ True !
Peter is Paul's father.	Okay.	father Paul = Peter male father ≃ True ! male ≃ True !
Is Alice's father male?	Yes, I think so.	
John is Alice's father.	Okay.	father Alice = John male father ≃ True ! male ≃ True !
Is John male?	Yes, I think so.	
Peter is not female.	Okay.	female Peter = False male father ≃ True ! male ≃ True ! female father ≃ False ! female ≃ False !
Alice is not male.	Okay.	male Alice = False male father ≃ True ! female father ≃ False ! female ≃ False !
Is Paul male?	I don't know.	
Is Paul female?	No, I don't think so.	

Table 1. Example dialogue with the implemented reasoner

Here an inconsistency arises when told 'The not of False is True'. Table 3

Human	Reasoner	Belief Set
The not of True is False.	Okay.	not True = False male father ≃ True ! female father ≃ False ! female ≃ False ! not male ≃ female not male ≃ False ! not ≃ False !
The not of False is True.	Okay.	not False = True male father ≃ True ! female father ≃ False ! female ≃ False ! not female ≃ True ! not not = i
Is Paul male?	I don't know.	
Is Paul female?	No, I don't think so, but it would be useful to know if Alice is female.	
Alice is female.	Okay.	female Alice = False not male ≃ female not female ≃ male female father ≃ False ! male father ≃ True ! not not = i
Is Paul female?	I don't know.	

Table 2. Example dialogue (continued)

shows the two competing theories and their predictions. The theories disagree on the prediction for female Alice and so it is suggested as an experiment. Meanwhile the strongest theory, the one making the most predictions, is taken as the working set of conjectured beliefs.

4 Comparison

A larger example comes from trying to learn the structure of family trees. This was first given by Hinton [7] as an example of learning using a neural representation, and then by Quinlan [12] as a comparison for FOIL. The aim is not just to learn definitions but to learn definitions from incomplete data and use them

Conjectures	Predictions	Falsifiability
not not = i	female Alice = False	0.9375
female $\simeq$ False !	female John = False	
not female $\simeq$ True !	male John = True	
female father $\simeq$ False !	female Paul = False	
male father $\simeq$ True !		
not not = i	female Alice = True	0.875
not male $\simeq$ female	female John = False	
not female $\simeq$ male	male John = True	
female father $\simeq$ False !		
male father $\simeq$ True !		

Table 3. Competing theories from the dialogue in Tables 1 and 2

to predict the missing information.

The family trees in Figure 1 give information about twelve family relationships: wife, husband, mother, father, daughter, son, sister, brother, aunt, uncle, niece, and nephew. We represent this knowledge as an equational database with rules such as wife Marco = Lucia. Multivalued functions, such as aunt and uncle, are expressed using the set constructor, so that aunt Sophia = {Gina, Angela}, etc.

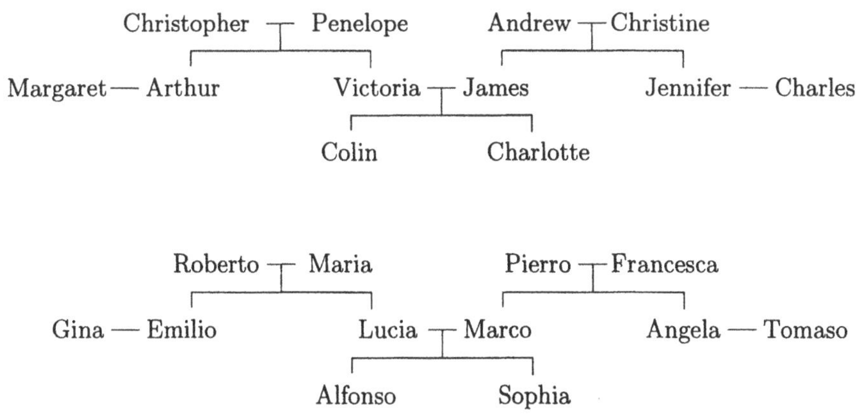

Fig. 1. Two family trees

In both FOIL and the neural representation of Hinton, it is necessary to give negative information, usually in the form of a closed world assumption. For instance, we would include that the mother of Penelope is not Sophia since it is not specified by the tree. For equational induction we only use positive information, assuming that we simply have no knowledge about unspecified function values. This can lead to some wild conjectures but such conjectures are often the basis of scientific progress, and indeed in this example we find they help in recovering missing information (while at the same time producing much spurious information).

The two trees in Figure 1 specify 104 data equations. Hinton used 100 of these as a training set and then tested to see if the remaining 4 relationships could be found by the trained network. Doing this twice he recorded 7 successes out of 8. Quinlan performed the same experiment 20 times and recorded 78 successes out of 80. Repeating these 20 trials with equational induction, all 80 missing relationships were recovered.

We can repeat this comparison for smaller training sets, where instead of removing just 4 data, we remove 10, 20, 30, ..., 90 of the data. Testing each case 8 times for both FOIL and equational induction gave the proportions of recovered data presented in Figure 2. The obvious balance is in the efficiency of the two methods. The additional conjectures generated by equational induction are expensive. As a rough estimate of this difference, running FOIL on a SparcStation 10 to learn rules for the complete family tree took 3.5 seconds, while the current implementation of IND (in LISP) required 22.9 seconds.

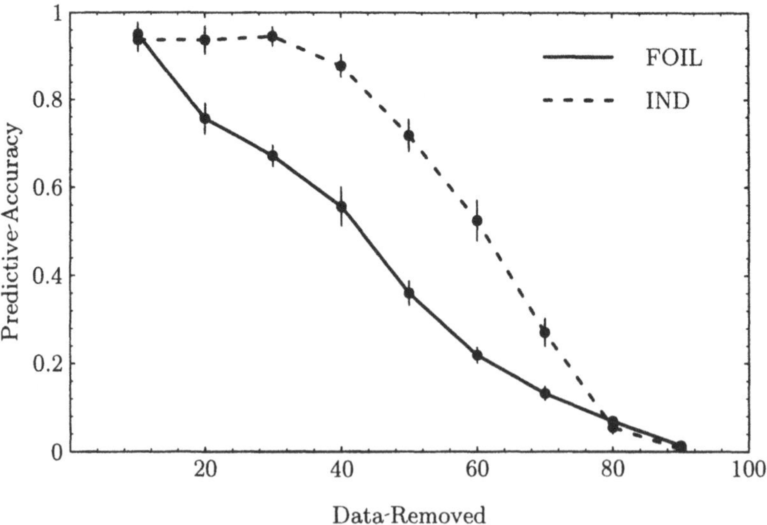

Fig. 2. Predictive performance of FOIL and equational induction.

5 Concluding Remarks

As seen in the dialogue of Section 3, notions of consistency and belief dynamics arise immediately from the induction procedure. The implementation of the reasoner has provided an empirical means of exploring these notions, some of which are summarized in [2]. Standard ideas from scientific philosophy, such as Popper's falsifiability criterion, are found to have simple expressions in equational terms and obvious relations to pragmatic reasoning.

Here we have assumed that the belief system we are making conjectures from is provided by a consistent oracle. However the issue of noise is somewhat meaningless for the induction algorithm, whose main interest is in the reduction of function applications to normal forms. If, through noisy data, the reasoner has more than one value for a given function application then its beliefs will be inconsistent. The task of resolving the inconsistency is deductive, rather than inductive, as described in [6] and [1].

References

1. M. Bulmer. *Reasoning by Term Rewriting*. PhD thesis, University of Tasmania, 1995.
2. M. Bulmer. Inductive Theories from Equational Systems. Submitted for publication, 1996.
3. M. Bulmer, D. Fearnley-Sander, and T. Stokes. Towards a Calculus of Algorithms. *Bulletin of the Australian Mathematical Society*, 50(1):81–89, 1994.
4. L. J. Cohen. *An Introduction to the Philosophy of Induction and Probability*. Oxford University Press, 1989.
5. N. Dershowitz. Completion and its Applications. In H. Aït Kaci and M. Nivat, editors, *Resolution of Equations in Algebraic Structures*, volume 2, pages 31–85. Academic Press, London, 1989.
6. P. Gärdenfors. *Knowledge in Flux: Modelling the Dynamics of Epistemic States*. MIT Press, 1988.
7. G. Hinton. Learning Distributed Representations of Concepts. In L. Erlbaum, editor, *Program of the Eight Annual Conference of the Cognitive Science Society*. Amhearst, MA, 1986.
8. G. Huet. Cartesian Closed Categories and Lambda-Calculus. In G. Huet, editor, *Logical Foundations of Functional Programming*, pages 7–23. Addison-Wesley, Reading, Mass., 1990.
9. D. Kapur and D. R. Musser. Proof by Consistency. *Artificial Intelligence*, 31:125–157, 1987.
10. K. Popper. *Conjectures and Refutations - The Growth of Scientific Knowledge*. Routledge and Kegan Paul, London, 1974.
11. K. Popper. *The Logic of Scientific Discovery*. Hutchinson, London, 1974.
12. J. R. Quinlan. Learning Logical Definitions from Relations. *Machine Learning*, 5:239–266, 1990.

Cost-Sensitive Specialization

Geoffrey I. Webb

Deakin University,
School of Computing and Mathematics,
Geelong, Vic, 3217, Australia.

Abstract. Cost-sensitive specialization is a generic technique for misclassification cost sensitive induction. This technique involves specializing aspects of a classifier associated with high misclassification costs and generalizing those associated with low misclassification costs. It is widely applicable and simple to implement. It could be used to augment the effect of standard cost-sensitive induction techniques. It should directly extend to test application cost sensitive induction tasks. Experimental evaluation demonstrates consistent positive effects over a range of misclassification cost sensitive learning tasks.

1 Introduction

Most research into machine learning has considered all misclassifications to have equivalent cost. However, for many applications this assumption will not be justified. For example, when diagnosing diseases, the cost of failing to diagnose some diseases will be low, because the symptoms will eventually become more pronounced, enabling suitable diagnosis. In contrast, failure to diagnose other diseases will have high cost, as irreparable damage will occur before adequate diagnosis is eventually obtained. Similarly, mis-diagnosis of a disease will in some cases have low cost—the patient receives unnecessary treatment with few side-effects; but in others will have high cost, such as undesirable side-effects.

Previous approaches to misclassification-cost sensitive induction can be considered to fall into four main categories. The first of these divides the training data into subsets on which inductive experiments are performed in order to infer a learning bias that will minimize misclassification costs [11, 14]. The selected bias is then employed to learn a classifier from the full set of training data.

The *better safe than sorry* strategy [10] considers for high misclassification cost classes only rules with high empirical support (that cover large numbers of training examples) while rules with lower empirical support are considered for low misclassification cost classes. The classification rules are learnt independently from one another. However, on application they are considered in order from lowest to highest misclassification cost.

A number of approaches alter the empirical bias of the learning system [1, 2, 5, 8, 9]. An empirical bias is a learning bias that selects between hypotheses on the basis of how they perform on the training data. This is modified so as to provide different weights to different types of misclassification.

The final category employs background knowledge to provide biases toward suitable hypotheses [3].

This paper presents the cost-sensitive specialization strategy. This strategy was inspired by the theorem of decreasing inductive power [15]. This theorem predicts increases in the proportion of false positives to true positives on previously unseen cases when a classifier is generalized without altering empirical support. (The empirical support for a classifier is evidence based on its performance on the training data.) In the context of learning with variable misclassification costs, this theorem suggests that elements of a classifier associated with high misclassification costs should be specialized (so as to minimize the proportion of false positives to true positives). In the context of classifiers that cover all of the instance space (classifiers that never respond *I don't know*), specializing one element of the classifier requires generalization of another. As the generalized elements are expected to have higher proportions of false positive to true positives, they should be selected from those with low misclassification cost. (The misclassification cost of a class is taken herein, except where specifically indicated otherwise, to mean false positive misclassification cost—the cost of incorrectly assigning the nominated class to an object.)

In the context of learning decision trees, this translates into a strategy of generalizing leaves for classes with low misclassification costs and specializing leaves for classes with high misclassification costs. In the context of learning decision rules, this translates into generalizing rules for classes with low misclassification costs and specializing rules for classes with high misclassification costs.

However, this general strategy can be justified without recourse to the theorem of decreasing inductive power. If there are cases where, without altering the expected error rate, the leaves or rules associated with high misclassification costs can be specialized in favor of leaves or rules with lower misclassification costs then such a change will decrease expected total misclassification costs as there can be expected to be a transfer from errors with high cost to those with low cost without any change in the numbers of those errors.

This paper presents a theoretical analysis of the cost-sensitive specialization strategy and evaluates a modification to the C4.5 [12] decision tree induction system that supports cost-sensitive specialization.

2 Cost sensitive specialization

Consider a region of the instance space to which one is considering assigning a single class in an n class classification learning task. This will be the case with the region associated with a single classification rule or decision tree leaf. Let p_i = the expected proportion of objects belonging to class i that will be encountered in this region of the instance space. Let c_{ij} = the expected cost of classifying an object belonging to class i as belonging to class j. We assume that $\forall i : c_{ii} = 0$ (correct classifications have no cost).

Let t_i be the total expected misclassification cost if the region is assigned class i. $t_i = \sum_{j=1}^{n} p_j.c_{ij}$. The empirical bias approaches to misclassification cost sensitive induction [1, 2, 5, 8, 9] seek to minimize t_i but do not consider areas of the instance space that are occupied by no training objects. These are treated as if they make no contribution to the total expected misclassification cost.

Consider the case where there is no evidence relating to the distribution of classes within a region. In such a case one should not distinguish between classes with respect to the expected proportion of objects for that class. It follows that $\forall i, j : p_i = p_j$. In this case p_i can be considered to be a constant. From this it follows that t_i will be minimized for the class for which $\sum_{j=1}^{n} c_{ij}$ is minimized. In other words, when one has no prior knowledge about the distribution of classes within a region of the instance space, expected misclassification costs will be minimized by assigning to that region the class for which the average of misclassifications to that class is minimized.

So far we have considered the case of a complex misclassification cost function, where the misclassification cost is a function of the correct class for an object and of the class assigned to that object. Two less complex forms of cost function are worth considering. A false positive misclassification cost function is one where misclassification costs are a function of the class assigned to an object—$\forall i, j, k : i \neq j \wedge i \neq k \rightarrow c_{ji} = c_{ki}$.. A false negative misclassification cost function is one where misclassification costs are a function of the class of an object—$\forall i, j, k : i \neq j \wedge i \neq k \rightarrow c_{ij} = c_{ik}$..

For a false positive misclassification cost function, $\sum_{j=1}^{n} c_{ij}$ is ordered on the relative false positive misclassification cost for a class. For a false negative misclassification cost function $\sum_{j=1}^{n} c_{ij}$ is ordered in the reverse of the order of the false negative misclassification cost for a class.

To summarize, in general one should seek to minimize the expected misclassification cost function. Where there is no evidence as to the relative frequencies of alternative classes for a region of the instance space, expected misclassification costs are minimized by selecting the class for which the mean expected cost of misclassifications is lowest. For false positive misclassification cost functions this is the class with the lowest false positive misclassification cost. For false negative misclassification cost functions this is the class with the highest false negative misclassification cost.

Where one has available an empirical bias that is able to minimize expected errors, the above analysis suggests that between alternatives that maximize that empirical bias, one should favor classifiers for which classes with high mean expected misclassification cost are as specific as possible and classes with low mean expected misclassification costs are as general as possible. This is because if the empirical bias gives equal weighting to the two classifiers, on the assumption that it agrees with respect to the expected error rates for regions of the instance space for which the two classifiers agree, then it does not in general distinguish between the expected error rates for the classes involved in regions of the instance space which are associated with different classes by the two classifiers. As the above analysis shows, associating such regions with classes with low mean expected misclassification costs minimizes total expected misclassification costs. Cost-sensitive specialization is a bias toward specializing aspects of classifiers associated with high expected misclassification cost where such specialization is neutral with respect to the other learning biases. Such specialization has the associated effect of generalizing aspects of classifiers that are associated with low expected misclassification cost.

3 C4.5CS

C4.5CS is a decision tree post-processor that is used in conjunction with C4.5. This post-processor implements cost-sensitive specialization by seeking to specialize leaves for high misclassification cost classes in favor of leaves for low misclassification cost classes. The current implementation of C4.5CS assumes a false positive misclassification cost function.

The decision trees learnt by C4.5 have different forms of decision nodes for discrete and continuous attributes. For continuous attributes C4.5 selects a cut value and generates two branches. A test is generated of the form $v \leq cut$. Objects for which this test succeeds pass down one branch while those for which it fails pass down the other.

With respect to branches on continuous attributes that lead directly to leaves, it is straight forward to specialize the leaf for the higher misclassification cost class. This is achieved by moving the cut to the most extreme value that specializes the branch for the higher misclassification cost class. C4.5 sets the cut at the greatest value for an object from the training set that passes down the $\leq$ branch. It is therefore not possible to further specialize the $\leq$ branch without affecting the empirical support for a classifier. The method employed herein to specialize the $>$ branch is to set the cut to the least value of a training object that passes down that branch and to alter the test to $<$. This ensures the greatest possible specialization without affecting the empirical support for the classifier.

However, not all branches lead directly to leaves. Relaxing the condition attached to a branch will generalize all leaves below that branch. This will in general only be desirable when all leaves below that branch are associated with classes with costs no greater than the lowest misclassification cost of a class for a leaf below the alternative branch. To this end, a split on a continuous attribute with $\leq$ branch l and $>$ branch g is changed to a $<$ test if and only if $max\,(cost(x) : leaf(x) \wedge below(l, x)) \quad \leq \quad min\,(cost(y) : leaf(y) \wedge below(g, y))$ where $leaf(x)$ is true if and only if node x is a leaf; $below(x, y)$ is true if and only if node y is below branch x; and $cost(x)$ = the false positive misclassification cost associated with the class for leaf node x.

For discrete attributes C4.5, by default, generates a branch for each value. (An optional technique for grouping multiple values to a single branch is not considered herein but could be treated by separating out values that apply to no training objects.) It is not possible to directly generalize or specialize any of these branches by altering the test. However, when no objects from the training set follow a branch, C4.5 constructs a leaf node for the class that dominates the node from which the branch descends. As such an assignment has only weak empirical support, it might be possible to change the class for such a leaf with

Table 1. UCI data sets used for experimentation

Name	No. of Attrs.	% continuous	No. of objects	No. of classes
audiology	69	0	226	24
autos	25	44	205	7
breast cancer Slovenia	9	4	286	2
breast cancer Wisconsin	9	100	699	2
Cleveland heart disease	13	46	303	2
credit rating	15	40	690	2
echocardiogram	6	83	74	2
glass	9	100	214	3
hepatitis	19	32	155	2
house votes 84	16	0	435	2
Hungarian heart disease	13	46	295	2
hypothyroid	29	24	3772	4
iris	4	100	150	3
lymphography	18	38	148	4
new thyroid	5	100	215	3
Pima indians diabetes	8	100	768	2
primary tumor	17	12	339	22
promoters	57	0	106	2
soybean large	35	0	307	19
tic-tac-toe	9	0	958	2

little risk of increasing expected errors. Changing the class to that with the lowest misclassification cost leads to generalizing the proportion of the instance space associated with that class and specializing that associated with higher misclassification cost classes.

C4.5 develops two types of decision tree—pruned and unpruned trees. C4.5CS post-processes both types of tree. It identifies and performs all of the types of generalization described above for each tree to which it is applied.

4 Experimental evaluation

To evaluate the efficacy of this approach, C4.5CS was applied to the twenty data sets from the UCI repository of machine learning databases described in Table 1. For each data set this table lists the number of attributes by which each object is described, the proportion of these that are continuous, the number of objects in the data set and the number of classes into which these objects are divided. These data sets were selected with the intention of exploring as wide a cross-section of attribute-value machine learning tasks as possible. In the absence of true cost functions for a wide range of learning tasks and in the interest of exploring as wide a range of different types of misclassification cost sensitive task as possible, a range of different false positive misclassification cost functions were randomly generated for each data set.

For each data set, 100 runs were performed. For each run—

Table 2. Errors

	Unpruned trees				Pruned trees			
Data Set	C4.5	C4.5CS	p	Ratio	C4.5	C4.5CS	p	Ratio
audiology	11.3±0.3	11.8±0.3	0.000	1.06	10.7±0.3	11.1±0.3	0.000	1.04
autos	10.6±0.4	10.8±0.4	0.032	1.02	10.8±0.4	11.0±0.4	0.022	1.02
breast cancer Slov.	21.6±0.4	21.6±0.4	0.708	1.00	17.1±0.4	17.1±0.4	0.530	1.00
breast cancer Wisc.	8.3±0.2	8.4±0.2	0.132	1.01	7.2±0.2	7.2±0.2	1.000	1.00
Cleveland heart dis.	16.6±0.3	16.6±0.3	0.744	1.00	16.1±0.3	16.1±0.3	0.770	1.00
credit rating	25.0±0.5	25.3±0.5	0.011	1.02	21.4±0.4	21.5±0.4	0.193	1.01
echocardiogram	4.0±0.2	3.8±0.2	0.013	0.97	3.8±0.1	3.6±0.1	0.000	0.96
glass	13.7±0.3	13.8±0.3	0.734	1.00	13.8±0.3	13.8±0.3	1.000	1.00
hepatitis	6.9±0.2	6.8±0.2	0.028	0.99	6.5±0.2	6.4±0.2	0.032	0.98
Hung. heart dis.	14.0±0.3	13.9±0.3	0.140	0.99	12.9±0.3	12.8±0.3	0.195	0.99
house votes 84	5.0±0.2	5.1±0.2	0.074	1.04	4.5±0.2	4.6±0.2	0.198	1.01
hypothyroid	4.1±0.2	4.1±0.2	1.000	1.01	4.1±0.2	4.1±0.2	0.083	1.01
iris	1.5±0.1	1.5±0.1	0.368	1.00	1.5±0.1	1.5±0.1	0.250	1.00
lymphography	8.1±0.3	8.1±0.3	1.000	1.00	8.0±0.3	8.0±0.3	0.158	1.00
new thyroid	4.0±0.2	4.0±0.2	0.549	1.03	4.1±0.2	4.1±0.2	0.558	1.03
Pima indians diab.	46.2±0.5	46.0±0.5	0.107	1.00	43.0±0.5	42.9±0.5	0.235	1.00
promoters	5.4±0.2	5.5±0.2	0.566	1.03	5.4±0.2	5.4±0.2	0.664	1.03
primary tumor	40.8±0.5	40.8±0.5	0.045	1.00	40.7±0.4	40.7±0.4	0.083	1.00
soybean large	15.5±0.5	16.0±0.5	0.000	1.03	15.3±0.6	15.3±0.6	0.259	1.03
tic-tac-toe	29.6±0.7	29.5±0.7	0.101	0.99	31.9±0.7	31.7±0.7	0.030	0.99
Mean ratio				1.01				1.00

1. the data was randomly divided into training (80%) and evaluation (remaining 20%) sets.
2. misclassification costs were assigned to classes as follows.
   (a) The classes were randomly ordered from 0 to $n-1$.
   (b) Each class was assigned the misclassification cost $i.\frac{99}{n-1}+1$ (truncated to the closest integer) where i is the rank order of the class.

   This ensured that the minimum cost was 1, the maximum cost was 100 and that the remaining costs were evenly spaced between those extremes.
3. Both C4.5 and C4.5CS were applied to learn decision trees from the training set. Both pruned and unpruned decision trees were learnt by C4.5 and post-processed by C4.5CS.
4. All decision trees were applied to the evaluation set and the total number of errors and total cost of misclassifications calculated.

Table 2 presents the means and standard errors for the numbers of errors per run in these experiments. For each of unpruned and pruned trees this table presents the mean and standard error of each treatment followed by the result of a two-tailed t-test comparing these means and the ratio of total numbers of errors (C4.5CS/C4.5). The bottom row presents the mean ratio of numbers of errors for C4.5CS against C4.5. This is the mean of the ratio for each run.

Post-processing had a variable effect on the total error rate. While C4.5CS is seeking to perform specializations that will not affect total error rate, for

Table 3. Costs

	Unpruned trees				Pruned trees			
Data Set	C4.5	C4.5CS	p	Ratio	C4.5	C4.5CS	p	Ratio
audiology	560±18.7	507±18.8	0.000	0.90	536±17.6	489±17.4	0.000	0.91
autos	543±31.3	519±31.6	0.000	0.95	552±29.9	539±30.1	0.001	0.97
breast c. Slov.	1139±46.5	1124±45.6	0.001	0.99	925±58.8	923±58.3	0.330	1.00
breast c. Wisc.	408±21.1	407±21.3	0.350	0.99	329±18.1	329±18.1	1.000	1.00
Cleve. heart dis.	836±30.1	808±29.0	0.000	0.97	800±28.3	781±27.7	0.000	0.98
credit rating	1210±33.6	1155±33.2	0.000	0.96	1041±32.9	1014±32.1	0.000	0.98
echocardiogram	205±13.9	184±13.9	0.000	0.91	188±11.4	169±11.3	0.000	0.91
glass	665±28.2	641±27.5	0.000	0.96	658±28.4	633±27.2	0.000	0.96
hepatitis	330±17.7	317±17.6	0.000	0.95	320±18.3	310±19.0	0.004	0.96
Hung. heart dis.	727±31.9	706±31.8	0.000	0.97	668±33.4	652±33.0	0.000	0.98
house votes 84	261±18.6	251±17.6	0.013	0.98	227±19.9	222±20.0	0.028	0.99
hypothyroid	191±12.8	189±12.9	0.265	1.00	183±12.3	183±12.5	0.975	1.00
iris	79±7.8	78±7.7	0.338	1.00	78±7.6	77±7.4	0.341	1.00
lymphography	359±21.6	346±21.0	0.000	0.97	350±21.6	343±21.4	0.005	0.98
new thyroid	186±16.4	176±16.5	0.011	1.00	190±16.9	179±16.7	0.010	1.00
Pima ind. diab.	2353±48.6	2266±48.4	0.000	0.96	2221±50.1	2154±50.7	0.000	0.97
promoters	274±17.0	236±15.3	0.000	0.90	264±17.3	236±16.1	0.000	0.91
primary tumor	1971±38.0	1969±38.0	0.112	1.00	1956±39.6	1956±39.6	0.083	1.00
soybean large	798±34.2	741±31.4	0.000	0.94	784±41.8	757±39.2	0.037	0.97
tic-tac-toe	1618±80.4	1558±80.5	0.000	0.96	1713±98.9	1673±99.4	0.000	0.97
Mean ratio				0.96				0.97

unpruned trees it is averaging 1% more errors than C4.5. For pruned trees the overall difference in error rates is negligible. On a treatment by treatment basis the effect varied from an increase in total errors of 6% for the audio data set with unpruned trees to a decrease in total errors of 4% for the echocardiogram data set with pruned trees.

It appears that the effect of C4.5CS is smaller for pruned trees than unpruned trees. Of the 592 occasions on which the number of errors for a C4.5 unpruned tree differed from the C4.5CS unpruned tree, in 219 cases there was no difference between the corresponding pruned trees. In comparison, of the 406 occasions on which the number of errors for a C4.5 pruned tree differed from the C4.5CS pruned tree, in only 33 did the unpruned trees not also differ. A binomial sign test indicates that this difference in numbers of unique effects is significant (p=0.000). It is hardly surprising that C4.5CS has more frequent effect for unpruned than for pruned trees as pruned trees have fewer nodes and hence fewer opportunities for C4.5CS to make a change. In particular, pruning frequently deletes the leaves associated with no training items. These leaves provide the only mechanism relating to discrete attributes that C4.5CS can apply.

Table 3 presents the means and standard errors for the misclassification costs per run. This table follows the format of Table 2 and ??.

Despite the slight increase in errors apparent in Table 2, Table 3 shows that there is a marked decrease in misclassification costs. For 37 of the 40 treatments there is a decrease in mean misclassification costs. The only exceptions are the

Wisconsin breast cancer data set with pruned trees for which both systems had identical costs for all 100 runs; the hypothyroid data set for pruned trees for which the mean costs to 2 decimal places are C4.5: 183.58 and C4.5CS: 183.61 and the primary tumor data set for pruned trees for which the mean costs to 2 decimal places are C4.5: 1956.43 and C4.5CS: 1956.46. These small differences are not statistically significant. On average, misclassification costs were reduced by 4% for unpruned trees and by 3% for pruned trees. Decreases of 8% or more occurred for the audio, echocardiogram and promoters data sets for both pruned and unpruned trees. In the case of unpruned trees for the promoters data set, the decrease was 10%.

The effect appears smaller for pruned trees than unpruned. Of the 725 occasions on which the total costs differ for the unpruned C4.5 and C4.5CS trees, on 236 occasions there is no difference between the corresponding pruned trees. Of the 511 occasions on which the pruned C4.5 and C4.5CS trees differ, the corresponding unpruned trees fail to differ in only 22. A binomial sign test indicates that this difference in numbers of unique effects is significant (p=0.000). This can be explained by the decrease in opportunities for post-processing with pruned trees.

Table 4 presents the results of binomial sign tests comparing the numbers of times each system obtained a higher value than the other for each measure. With respect to unpruned decision trees, C4.5 had fewer errors significantly more often than did C4.5CS. With respect to pruned decision trees, C4.5 had fewer errors more often than did C4.5CS, but this difference was not statistically significant. For both pruned and unpruned trees, C4.5CS had lower misclassification costs significantly more often than did C4.5.

Table 4. Summary comparison

Measure	C4.5 > C4.5CS	C4.5 < C4.5CS	p
Unpruned Errors	251	341	0.0001
Pruned Errors	196	210	0.2594
Unpruned Costs	472	253	0.0000
Pruned Costs	332	179	0.0000

These experimental results demonstrate that C4.5CS can significantly reduce misclassification costs for a wide range of learning tasks. The numbers of errors that were observed demonstrate that this effect cannot be attributed to a reduction in the numbers of errors.

5 Extension to complex cost functions

C4.5CS is restricted in application to situations in which the relative misclassification costs of the classes can be ordered. Note that it is not dependent upon the assignment of accurate misclassification costs or ratios between costs. The only information that it utilizes is the order of these costs.

It can be utilized with orderings either by the costs of false positives or of false negatives. While the above work has considered misclassification costs to relate to false positives (the cost is a function of the class that is incorrectly assigned to the object) the techniques are equally applicable to situations where the misclassification costs relate to the costs of false negatives (the cost is a function of the class to which the misclassified object belongs). In the latter context, classes with high misclassification costs should be generalized (to minimize a chance of a false negative) and those with low misclassification costs should be specialized.

C4.5CS could be extended to more complex cost functions by considering at each branch on a continuous attribute the greatest cost of misclassifying an object of any class as belonging to a class represented by a leaf on the $\leq$ branch and comparing this to the minimum cost of misclassifying an object of any class as belonging to a class represented by a leaf on the $>$ branch.

A default class i for leaves that cover no objects in the training set could be selected on the basis of minimizing the mean cost of incorrectly classifying an object of another class as belonging to i.

While the modifications made by C4.5CS depend upon the relative ordering of misclassification costs but not their relative magnitude, the size of the effect of its application will depend upon the magnitude. The greater the difference in magnitude of misclassification costs for different classes the greater the expected reduction in total misclassification costs resulting from its application.

6 Increasing the degree of specialization

The cost-sensitive specialization strategy espoused by this paper involves the specialization of aspects of a classifier relating to high false positive or low false negative misclassifications and generalization of those relating to low false negative or high false positive misclassifications where those specialization and generalization actions have low impact on expected accuracy. This has been evaluated in the context of two specialization/generalization operators for C4.5 decision trees, one relating to tests on continuous attributes and the other to tests on discrete attributes.

For these operators the degree of reduction in misclassification costs is small but consistent. Where greater reductions are sought, more powerful specialization/generalization operators should be employed. Candidate operators for decision trees include the generation of characteristic leaves [4] and cuts based on evidence for neighboring regions of the instance space [16]. A variety of potentially useful specialization and generalization operators for classification rules have been described elsewhere [15].

This research deliberately avoided the use of these more powerful operators as they are likely to also improve predictive accuracy. Operators that did not improve predictive accuracy were used in order to provide clear cut support for the predicted effect without the possibility that costs were reduced simply by a reduction in errors.

7 Relationship to previous approaches

Unlike approaches based on altering the empirical bias, the cost-sensitive specialization approach does not require accurate misclassification costs. All that is required is a relative ordering of the misclassification costs. Nor does cost-sensitive specialization require additional background knowledge.

It is distinguished from approaches that use induction to select learning biases by avoiding the problem of induction and the subsequent risk that the inferred bias will turn out to be inappropriate.

Cost-sensitive specialization can be seen as a more specific statement of the *better safe than sorry* policy. In this light, the two types of mechanism that Provost and Buchanan [10] propose can be seen as techniques for specializing high misclassification cost rules and generalizing low misclassification cost rules. Relative ordering of rules does this by implicit conjunction of the conditions for subsequent rules with negations of the conditions for preceding rules. Allowing rules with lower empirical support to be developed for low misclassification cost classes has the effect of generalizing the total classifier with respect to those classes.

Cost-sensitive specialization could be applied in conjunction with alternative approaches to misclassification cost sensitive learning in the expectation of further boosting the effect of those approaches.

8 Other types of classification cost

While cost sensitive specialization has been presented as a means of minimizing misclassification costs, the same technique could also be employed to minimize other costs such as the costs of applying tests [6, 7, 13, 14]. In the context of a decision tree, specialization of branches leading to high cost tests will reduce the average cost of applying the tree as those tests will be applied less frequently. Where such specialization is neutral with respect to expected misclassification rate, there will be a reduction in expected application costs with no effect to expected accuracy.

9 Conclusion

Cost-sensitive specialization is a generic technique for cost sensitive induction. This technique involves specializing aspects of a classifier associated with high costs and generalizing those associated with low costs. It

- is widely applicable;
- is simple to implement;

- requires only relative ordering of costs rather than precise ratios between costs;
- is based on a simple intuitive principle; and
- has demonstrated consistent positive effect on a wide range of learning tasks.

While it has been implemented herein as a post-processor for an existing machine learning system, cost-sensitive specialization could also be employed directly during initial tree induction. The technique should extend in a straight forward manner to sensitivity to costs of test application. It should be emphasised that the implementation of the technique herein has been intended solely as proof-of-concept. To this end, specialisations that may be expected to increase predictive accuracy, such as has been investigated elsewhere [16] have been avoided. The magnitude of gains could be expected to rise if such specialisations were included.

It should also be noted that these techniques would be best applied to augment other cost sensitive induction techniques [1, 2, 3, 5, 8, 9, 10, 11], with which they are fully compatible. Cost sensitive specialisation could be applied to augment any induction technique that relies primarily upon empirical support for selecting between alternative hypotheses.

Acknowledgements

This research has been supported by the Australian Research Council.

I am grateful to Foster Provost for comments on an earlier draft of this paper.

The following data sets were compiled and donated by the corresponding donors—breast cancer Slovenia, lymphography and primary tumor: Ljubljana Oncology Institute, Slovenia; breast cancer Wisconsin: Dr. William H. Wolberg, University of Wisconsin Hospitals, Madison; audiology: Prof. Jergen, Baylor College of Medicine. Thanks to the UCI Repository, its maintainers, Patrick Murphy and David Aha, and its donors, for providing access to the data sets used herein.

References

1. L. Breiman, J. H. Friedman, R. A. Olshen, and C. J. Stone. *Classification and Regression Trees.* Wadsworth, Belmont, Ca, 1984.
2. B. A. Draper, C. E. Brodley, and P. E. Utgoff. Goal-directed classification using linear machine decision trees. *IEEE Transactions on Pattern Recognition and Artificial Intelligence*, 16:888–893, 1994.
3. D. Gordon and D. Perlis. Explicitly biased generalization. *Computational Intelligence*, 5(2):67–81, May 1989.
4. R. C. Holte, L. E. Acker, and B. W. Porter. Concept learning and the problem of small disjuncts. In *Proceedings of the Eleventh International Joint Conference on Artificial Intelligence*, pp. 813–818, Detroit, 1989. Morgan Kaufmann.
5. U. Knoll, G. Nakhaeizadeh, and B. Tausend. Cost-sensitive pruning of decision trees. In F. Bergadano and L. De Raedt, editors, *Proceedings of the Eighth European Conference on Machine Learning, ECML-94*, pp. 383–386, Catania, Italy, 1994. Springer-Verlag.

6. S. W. Norton. Generating better decision trees. In *Proceedings of the Eleventh International Joint Conference on Artificial Intelligence, IJCAI-89*, pp. 800–805, Detroit, MI, 1989. Morgan Kaufmann.
7. M. Nùñez. The use of background knowledge in decision tree induction. *Machine Learning*, 6:231–250, 1991.
8. M. J. Pazzani, C. Merz, P. Murphy, K. Ali, T. Hume, and C. Brunk. Reducing misclassification costs. In *Proceedings of the Eleventh International Conference on Macine Learning*, pp. 217–225, New Jersey, 1994. Morgan Kaufmann.
9. F. J. Provost. Goal-directed inductive learning: Trading off accuracy for reduced error cost. In *Proceedings of the AAAI Spring Symposium on Goal Directed Learning*, pp. 94–101, 1994.
10. F. J. Provost and B. G. Buchanan. Inductive policy. In *Proceedings of the Tenth National Conference on Artificial Intelligence (AAAI-92)*, pp. 255–261. AAAI Press, 1992.
11. F. J. Provost and B. G. Buchanan. Inductive policy: The pragmatics of bias selection. *Machine Learning*, 20(1/2):35–61, 1995.
12. J. R. Quinlan. *C4.5: Programs For Machine Learning.* Morgan Kaufmann, San Mateo, 1993.
13. M. Tan. Cost-sensitive learning of classification knowledge and its applications in robotics. *Machine Learning*, 13:7–33, 1993.
14. P. D. Turney. Cost-sensitive classification: Empirical evaluation of a hybrid genetic decision tree induction algorithm. *Journal of Artificial Intelligence Research*, 2:369–409, 1995.
15. G. I. Webb. Generality is more significant than complexity: Toward alternatives to Occam's razor. In C. Zhang, J. Debenham, and D. Lukose, editors, *AI'94 – Proceedings of the Seventh Australian Joint Conference on Artificial Intelligence*, pp. 60–67, Armidale, 1994. World Scientific.
16. G. I. Webb. Syntactic complexity is not predictive of predictive accuracy: Experimental evidence against Occam's razor. To be published in *Journal of Artificial Intelligence Research*, 1996.

Efficient Multiple Predicate Learner Based on Fast Failure Mechanism

Xiaolong Zhang and Masayuki Numao

Department of Computer Science, Tokyo Institute of Technology,
1-12-1 Oh-okayama, Meguro, Tokyo 152, Japan
Email: {zxl, numao}@cs.titech.ac.jp

Abstract. We present a multiple predicate learner (MPL-Core) which efficiently induces some Horn clauses from example sets of multiple predicates and relative background knowledge. Core, a single predicate learning module, has a fast failure mechanism, and can select refinement operators based on the learning task. By means of GPC, an efficient pruning method, Core effectively prunes unpromising branches in a search tree, making the search space a rational volume. MPL-Core employs both the intensional and extensional learning style in the induction of target predicates. Furthermore, our system with the fast failure mechanism gives a distinct improvement over the existing multiple predicate learning systems in the computational complexity.

1 Introduction

Inductive logic programming (ILP) is envisaged as a blossomed field which focuses on theories, methods and applications of machine learning in first order logic representation. Multiple predicate learning (MPL) is worth research in inductive logic programming. The notation of MPL was first used in [2]. The potential applications of MPL are automatic logic program synthesis, scientific discovery and intelligent database design.

Existing MPL systems, such as Rx [10], MTL [1] and FORTE [8], are irregular ones. Rx only refines some faults in the concept and its subconcepts in special forms of Horn clauses rather than common Horn clauses. MTL assumes some tasks share some substructure in the representation and only tackles the concepts in propositional description. FORTE depends on the order of processing the examples and prefers having a prior approximate domain theory. The system constructed by De Raedt et al. [2], is a regular multiple predicate learning system. However, it suffers from the computational complexity and is not an efficient MPL system.

Some single predicate learning (SPL) systems, such as FOIL [7] and GOLEM [6], induce a target predicate using background knowledge only in ground atom form. If an MPL system applies one of them as its SPL module, it requires that all the multiple predicate examples be completely given and all the constants appearing in the arguments of the examples come from the same constant range. Such an MPL system is impractical one. Furthermore, if an SPL module has no fast failure mechanism and learns from insufficient background knowledge, then it always costs long time to recover from failure induction, thus, the MPL system with this SPL module is inefficient. We advocate that when an MPL system is based on an SPL module in inducing a target predicate (also call it target), it requires that its SPL module has the capability of applying background knowledge in Horn clause form, and has a fast failure mechanism.

Our system named MPL-Core employs Core[1] as a single predicate learner. Core is a top-down learning style with complete refinement operators and an efficient failure-recovery function. Its heuristic function is similar to that of CHAM [4]. MPL-Core randomly selects a target and calls Core to learn the selected target. If the selected target is learned then the learned results are added into the system as new background knowledge ready for learning the other targets, else it fails quickly and MPL-Core selects another target to be induced. If the given example sets of all the predicates and relative background knowledge are complete, MPL-Core correctly learns targets. As mentioned in [2], an MPL system tackles the learning tasks in which one target definition may depend upon the other targets.

In section 2, the fast failure mechanism is the main content. The algorithm of MPL-Core and the procedure of Core are described in section 3. Section 4 shows the results of comparing MPL-Core with MPL-CHAM, where MPL-Core employs Core as its SPL module and MPL-CHAM employs CHAM as its SPL module. Section 5 contains some evaluation of interesting problems in the MPL systems. Final section concludes this paper and points out the demerits of our system for future research.

2 Fast failure mechanism

One of the most important problems in an MPL system is how to make the system fail quickly when there is not proper or sufficient background knowledge for the current target to be induced. This problem does not appear so important in the SPL systems. In fact the failure-recovery mechanism has been employed in some systems. For example, CHAMP [5] is also based on a failure driven mechanism, where a clause is not specialized further when the clause-bits of a clause exceeds positive-example bits. If there are not any resultant clauses from CHAM, CHAMP invents new predicates.

Merit in CHAM [4]: The heuristic *merit* in CHAM consists of two parts, one is the *gain* similar to that of FOIL, and the other is the *likelihood*:

$$merit(C) = gain(C) + likelihood(C)$$

and $gain(C) = T_C^+ \times (I(T_0) - I(T_C))$; $likelihood(C) = T_C^+ \times \Gamma(C)$; $I(T_0) = -\log_2(T_0^+/(T_0^+ + T_0^-))$ and $I(T_C) = -\log_2(T_C^+/(T_C^+ + T_C^-))$, where C is a partial clause, and T_0^+ and T_0^- are the number of the positive and negative examples in the current training set T_0 respectively. T_C^+ and T_C^- are the number of the positive and negative examples that satisfy C respectively.

[1] Core is abbreviated from Complete refinement operators.

$$\Gamma(C) = \frac{\sum_{i=1}^{m}\sum_{j=1}^{n}\sum_{k,l}\gamma(VIn_{i,k}, VOut_{j,l})}{\sum_{i=1}^{m}\sum_{j=1}^{n}\sum_{k,l}\sigma(VIn_{i,k}, VOut_{j,l})}$$

where m is the number of input and intermediate variables in the clause C and n is that of output variables, $VIn_{i,k}$ is a value of each input and intermediate variables enumerated by $\sum_{i=1}^{m}$, and $VOut_{j,l}$ is that of each output variables enumerated by $\sum_{j=1}^{n}$. If a variable instantiated by several values, then all of these are enumerated by $\sum_{k,l}$. The values used for calculation of *likelihood* come from the current seed example. $\gamma(v1, v2)$ and $\sigma(v1, v2)$ are determined by:

1. Variables are lists:

$$\gamma(list1, list2) = \frac{max(length\ of\ matched\ sublists)}{max(length\ of\ list1,\ length\ of\ list2)}; \quad \sigma(list1, list2) = 1$$

2. Variables are atoms:

$$\gamma(atom1, atom2) = \begin{cases} 1 \text{ if atom1=atom2} \\ 0 \text{ otherwise} \end{cases}; \quad \sigma(atom1, atom2) = 1$$

3. If $v1$ and $v2$ have different variable types then $\gamma(v1, v2) = \sigma(v1, v2)$=0.

GPC constraints: We propose GPC constraints employed in the effective failure-recovery mechanism and used to limit the search space. We first give some definitions and then explain the GPC.

Definition 1. A clause P is called a parent clause of a clause Q if there exists a downward refinement operator ρ in a quasi-ordered set $\langle S, \succeq \rangle$, if $\forall P \in S$: $\rho(P) \subseteq \{Q \in S \mid P \succeq Q\}$.

Definition 2. Suppose G, P and C are clauses, G is a grandparent clause of C if G is the parent clause of P and P is the parent clause of C, where C is called a current clause.

Definition 3. The *normalized merit* of a clause C is $\overline{merit}(C)$:
$\overline{merit}(C) = (gain(C) + likelihood(C))/T_C^+ = \overline{gain}(C) + \overline{likelihood}(C)$
T_C^+ is the number of the positive examples covered by the clause C.

Definition 4. Suppose there are a current clause C, its grandparent clause G and its parent clause P. The normalized merit values of them are represented as $\overline{merit}(G)$, $\overline{merit}(P)$ and $\overline{merit}(C)$. The GPC constraints are:

$$\overline{merit}(C) \geq \overline{merit}(P) \tag{1}$$

$$\overline{merit}(C) > \overline{merit}(G) \tag{2}$$

The normalized merit of a clause is independent of the number of examples covered by the clause. GPC suggests that when a literal is added to a partial clause C, the $\overline{merit}(C)$ of the partial clause should never decrease. A partial clause C containing a literal which hardly offers any normalized merit is discarded. But GPC also takes into account the non-discriminating literals in the induction process.

Explanation of GPC: The normalized merit of a clause C is composed of two parts in terms of definition 3, that is, $\overline{merit}(C) = \overline{gain}(C) + \overline{likelihood}(C)$.

Core initiates from a most general clause (a clause with a *true* body), adds a literal to a partial clause C and tries to make the partial clause cover as many positive examples as possible and cover as less negative examples as possible in the same time. If the partial clause C with the adding literal covers large number of positive examples and less number of negative examples, $\overline{gain}(C)$ increases. The worst case is that a non-discriminating literal L_p (zero gain literal) is added to the partial clause C and makes the gain of the partial clause be equal to the gain after adding the zero gain literal. In order to increase the possibility for a promising zero gain literal L_p to be added into the body of the partial clause, we use $\overline{likelihood(C)}$. $\overline{Gain}(C)$ does not increase after adding the literal L_p. Provided that $\overline{likelihood}(C)$ increases after adding L_p, then, it is still possible for our system to select the clauses with the literal L_p in the next induction. Moreover, in order to incorporate a literal, whose normalized gain and likelihood are both zero, into a partial clause, we allow $\overline{merit}(C) \geq \overline{merit}(P)$, where clause P is the parent clause of clause C.

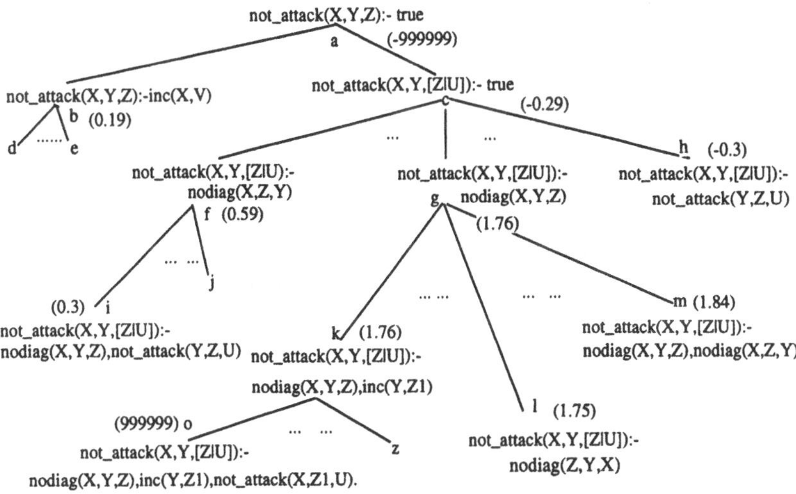

Fig. 1. The Part of Refinement Graph of not-attack(X,Y,Z)

The refinement graph in Fig. 1 shows the GPC constraint relations among the refinement nodes (clauses). All the specialized nodes have their values of normalized merits denoted in the parentheses. The root node begins with a large negative value of normalized merit (-999999). Let us consider the node l as a current node (clause), then its grandparent node is node c and its parent node is g. According to GPC constraints, we should have $\overline{merit}(l) \geq \overline{merit}(g)$ and $\overline{merit}(l) > \overline{merit}(c)$. From the Fig. 1, we know that $\overline{merit}(l) = 1.75$, $\overline{merit}(g) = 1.76$, thus the current node l is discarded. Similarly, node h and node i are also discarded by GPC. However, node k would not be discarded by GPC, though node k is specialized from node g by adding a non-discriminating literal *inc(Y,Z1)*, because $\overline{merit}(k) = \overline{merit}(g) = 1.76$. In fact, the partial clause *not_attack(X,Y,[Z|U]):- nodiag(X,Y,Z),inc(Y,Z1)* at node k is a candidate resultant clause of this problem.

Fast failure mechanism: The fast failure mechanism used in our system is:

- If there are not specialized clauses that cover positive examples, Core fails
- If a partial clause does not meet the GPC, it is deleted
- If the number of bits encoded a partial clause exceeds the number of bits encoded the positive examples covered by the partial clause, the partial clause is deleted, we call this constraint *code constraint (CC)*

The fast failure mechanism is also a recovery mechanism from failure, thus we also call it failure-recovery mechanism. The third constraint CC in the mechanism stems from FOIL [7]. Actually, it is not efficient that our system only applies the CC in failure-recovery mechanism. The CC does not prune a partial clause before the encoding bits of the partial clause exceeds the encoding bits of the positive examples covered by the partial clause. The increment of the bits of a partial clause is not a short process and can be time consuming. We put forward the GPC, an additionally constrained method, to enhance the abilities of the failure mechanism.

3 MPL-Core algorithm

MPL-Core was developed to test the behavior of learning multiple predicates. The input of MPL-Core is example sets of all the targets, background predicates which are in either ground atom form or first order logic (Horn clause) form, and mode declarations of all the targets and background predicates. The output of MPL-Core is some Horn clauses induced from the given targets. In order to denote the order of the learned targets, we use *learning level* to reveal the successful orders of the induced clauses for all the targets in a learning task. Every learned clauses has its *learning level.* It is possible that a target learned in a high level depends on some targets learned in low levels.

Algorithm of MPL-Core: MPL-Core described in Fig. 2 randomly selects a target and calls the procedure Core to induce the selected target. If it is learned, the resultant clauses are sorted and added to the system as new background knowledge. If the current target is not induced, it is marked as a failure target and suspended until all the predicates on which it depends are induced. There is a phenomenon that, even the correct resultant clauses of a learned target are added into the system as background knowledge, they sometimes could not be correctly used by the system, because the order of these resultant clauses stored in the system does not obey those in Prolog. In Prolog, a clause takes priority over the others when the clause is stored before the others, even though all the heads of these clauses are the same. Our system can sort the learned clauses in terms of the orders in Prolog.

Our system directly employs these learned clauses to induce other targets. This is called an intensional learning style. In contrast, that the system employs the background knowledge in ground atoms is called extensional. When a target is learned, the learning level *LEVEL* increases by 1 and all the marked targets can be selected again for learning. The marked targets are those targets which had been selected to learn but failed to obtain correct or complete resultant clauses.

Procedure of Core : Core, described in Fig. 3, is a procedure called by MPL-Core. Core induces *LearnedClauses* from the example set of a target predicate *Target* and the current background predicates. Before specialization, Core selects a refinement type[2] according to the mode declaration of *Target*. There are an outer loop and an inner loop in this procedure.

The outer loop repeats the steps until there are not positive examples to be covered: Core selects a seed example, and calls the inner loop to obtain an resultant clause. If the inner loop is successful, Core adds the resultant clause into *LearnedClauses* and removes the positive examples covered by the resultant clause. If the inner loop fails, this *Target* fails to be learned.

The inner loop iterates the process until there exist some partial clauses covering no negative example: Core employs the selected refinement type to specialize a partial clause into some special ones by adding background predicates to the body of the partial clause; calculates the merits of all the partial clauses, filters all the partial clauses with GPC and CC constraints, and selects better merit partial clauses in terms of the beam width. If there exist partial clauses covering no negative example, the inner loop returns with *LearnedClauses*; if there are no partial clauses that can be specialized further, the inner loop fails.

4 Experimental results

MPL-Core learns Horn clauses from a learning task in which some targets depend on the others. For example, in the Dutch flag problem, target *dutch(X,Y)* depends on target *append(X,Y,Z)*. The examples and background knowledge are given as follows.

```
  The examples of dutch(X,Y)         The examples of append(X,Y,Z)
--------------------------------   ----------------------------------
(dutch([r,w,b],[r,w,b]),true).     (append([1,2],[3],[1,2,3]),true).
(dutch([r,b,w],[r,w,b]),true).     (append([1],[3],[1,3]),true).
(dutch([w,r,b],[r,w,b]),true).     (append([2],[1],[2,1]),true).
        ...   ...                              ...   ...
(dutch([r,w,b],[r,b,w]),false).    (append([3,1],[3,1],[3,2]),false).
(dutch([r,b,w],[r,b,w]),false).    (append([3,2],[3],[1,2,3]),false).
        ...   ...                              ...   ...
```

The definition of the background predicate *distribute(X,Y,Z,W)* is:

```
distribute([],[],[],[]).
distribute([r|Xs],[r|Rs],Ws,Bs):-distribute(Xs,Rs,Ws,Bs).
distribute([w|Xs],Rs,[w|Ws],Bs):-distribute(Xs,Rs,Ws,Bs).
distribute([b|Xs],Rs,Ws,[b|Bs]):-distribute(Xs,Rs,Ws,Bs).
```

[2] MPL-Core has four refinement types, each of them containing some refinement operators.

```
Algorithm MPL-Core
  Input: several example sets of targets and relative background predicates
  Output: Horn clauses of all the targets in different learning LEVEL
    Begin
      NumOfGoal := the number of targets;
      While there exist some targets not induced Do
        choose randomly a target Target from the existing targets;
        call Core(Target, LearnedClauses);
        If the return of Core(Target, LearnedClauses) is success Then
          sort the learned clauses LearnedClauses ;
          add the sorted results into the system as background knowledge;
          LEVEL increase 1;
          remove the marks from the marked targets
        Else
          mark Target that cannot be induced in this LEVEL
      endWhile
      If LEVEL< NumOfGoal Then exit some targets not induced
    End.
```

Fig. 2. The MPL-Core Algorithm

```
Procedure Core(Target, LearnedClauses)
  Input: Background predicates, positive ⊕ and negative ⊖ examples of Target
  Output: Horn clauses LearnedClauses of the predicate Target
  Begin
    select the refinement type based on the mode declaration of Target;
    While some ⊕ examples not covered Do
      select a seed example and get a most general clause MGC;
      insert the MGC into a candidate clause set Q;
      While all the candidate clauses in Q still cover ⊖ examples Do
        the partial clause set for further specialization SP= {};
        specialize all the partial clause of Q into Q1;
        evaluate Q1 into Q2;
        delete the redundant partial clauses in Q2;
        filter Q2 into SP in terms of GPC and CC;
        If SP={} Then
          LearnedClauses :={};
          return failure
        select best N partial clauses and put in Q (N is the beam width)
      endWhile
      select a clause that does not cover ⊖ examples but cover ⊕ ones with the
      largest number;
      assert the clause into LearnedClauses;
      remove all the ⊕ examples covered by this clause
    endWhile
    return success
  End.
```

Fig. 3. The Procedure of Core(Target, LearnedClauses)

learning task	learning level	learning results of target predicates
	1	append([],X,X):- true.
sort	1	append([X|Y],Z,[X|V]):- append(Y,Z,V).
with	2	sort([],[]):- true.
append	2	sort([X|Y],Z):- sort(Y,V),part(X,V,Y1,Z1),comp(X,Z1,W1), append(Y1,W1,Z).
	1	mult(X,Y,X):- zero(X).
factorial	1	mult(X,Y,Z):- dec(X,V), mult(V,Y,Y1),plus(Y,Y1,Z).
with	2	fac(X,X):- one(X).
mult	2	fac(X,Y):- dec(X,U),fac(U,W),mult(X,W,Y).
	1	brother(X,Y):- father(Z,Y),son(X,Z).
	2	sister(X,Y):- father(Z,Y),daughter(X,Z).
nephew	3	nephew(X,Y):- wife(Z,Y),brother(V,Z),son(X,V).
relation	3	nephew(X,Y):- husband(Z,Y),sister(V,Z),son(X,V).
in Hinton	3	nephew(X,Y):- brother(Z,Y),son(X,Z).
family	3	nephew(X,Y):- sister(Z,Y),son(X,Z).
	1	member(X,[Y|Z]):- member(X,Z).
union	1	member(X,[X|Z]):- true.
two lists	2	union([],X,X):- true.
with	2	union([X|Y],Z,U):- union(Y,Z,U),member(X,Z).
member	2	union([X|Y],Z,[X|V]):-union(Y,Z,V),not-member(X,Z).
	1	append([],X,X):- true.
Dutch	1	append([X|Y],Z,[X|V]):- append(Y,Z,V).
flag	2	dutch(X,Y):-distribute(X,U,V,W),append(U,V,Z1),append(Z1,W,Y).
	1	member(X,[Y|Z]):- member(X,Z).
	1	member(X,[X|Z]):- true.
making	2	not-member(X,[]):- true.
a list	2	not-member(X,[Y|Z]):- not-member(X,Z),not-equal(X,Y).
no	3	no-doubles([X|Y],[X|U]):-no-doubles(Y,U),not-member(X,Y).
double	3	no-doubles([X|Y],Z):- no-doubles(Y,Z),member(X,Y).
elements	3	no-doubles([],[]):- true.
	1	not-attack(X,Y,[Z|U]):- nodiag(X,Y,Z),inc(Y,Z1),not-attack(X,Z1,U).
	1	not-attack(X,Y,[]):- true.
	2	select(X,[Y|Z],U):- select(X,Z,X1),comp(Y,X1,U).
	2	select(X,[X|Z],Z):- true.
N-queens	3	queen([],X,X):- true.
problem	3	queen(X,Y,Z):-select(U,X,W),comp(U,Y,V),queen(W,V,Z), not-attack(Y,U).

Table 1. The learning tasks and results with non-failure learning

In the Dutch flag problem, the constants {1,2,3} appearing in the examples of *append(X,Y,Z)* are different from those {r,w,b} in *dutch(X,Y)*. Our system induces this learning task depending on the intensional learning style.

In order to compare our SPL module Core with CHAM in the MPL system, we design two kinds of learning orders in the experiment. In the first kind of learning order, no targets fail in the induction process (called non-failure learning); in the second one, some targets fail in the induction process (called failure-recovery learning).

MPL learning tasks: The learning tasks used to test MPL-Core are listed in Table 1. All the targets in the same problem are learned in different *Learning level*. The head of clause is a target in that problem. All the literals not occurring in the heads are background predicates. The results listed in Table 1 are just those results induced under the non-failure learning orders. We discuss learning orders in detail in section 5.

	total/pos.	width	hypothesis spaces		qualified nodes		time(second)	
targets	examples	of beam	Core	CHAM	Core	CHAM	Core	CHAM
sort	40/23							
append	71/47	2	823/43	1188/70	170	500	32.2	42.4
factorial	69/8							
mult	23/12	3	1814/81	NO	227	NO	47.8	NO
nephew	168/7							
brother	144/6							
sister	144/4	2	1585/93	NO	238	NO	57.0	NO
union	175/25							
member	41/22	2	202/47	365/70	64	143	2.2	13.7
dutch	48/5							
append	71/47	2	557/30	743/30	184	279	52.0	174.5
no-double	19/11							
member	41/22							
not-member	41/19	3	219/51	310/68	51	87	0.9	1.6
not-attack	97/18							
select	41/22							
nqueens	48/7	3	2218/146	NO	298	NO	19.3	NO

hypothesis spaces: the number of generated/visited nodes in the learning problem.
total/pos. examples: (the total examples)/(the positive examples).
NO: no result in this term.

Table 2. The results of non-failure learning

Non-failure learning: All the problem results in Table 2 are learned without failure. Table 2 compares the results from the MPL separately employing Core and CHAM as its SPL module. We test the parameters like the hypothesis spaces, the qualified nodes and the learning time. The time (in seconds) is for SICStus prolog 2.19 on a Sun SPARC station 20/61. All of the targets in a problem have the same beam width. In the hypothesis spaces, the generated nodes (partial clauses) are the total nodes produced for learning all the targets in the same problem. Some of these nodes which do not cover the seed example are discarded. The visited nodes are those nodes which are specialized at least one time. Actually, most of them are the critical nodes occurring in the specialization paths from the most general clause to the resultant clause. The qualified nodes are those nodes whose merits are calculated by Core. *NO* denotes no results, which is because of a large search space or promising partial clauses cut by a limited beam width.

Failure-recovery learning: The results in Table 3 are from the same problems as given in Table 2, but with some target failures in the induction process. Besides the listed results in Table 3, We have tested all the possible learning orders of the listed problems with MPL-Core, and all of them are correctly learned. In the MPL systems, it is a normal situation that some targets fail in the induction process, because these targets employ the results of the other targets which are not yet induced. And these targets should recover from failure by adopting the failure-recovery mechanism. If the failure-recovery process is

targets	MPL-Core				MPL-CHAM			
	hyp.space target fail	time(sec.) target fail	total hyp.space	total time	hyp.space target fail	time(sec.) target fail	total hyp.space	total time
sort*	381	26.0			2227	158.4		
append			1721	55.6			8219	312.9
factorial*	81	3.3			***	***		
mult			2330	50.7			***	***
nephew*	60	0.7			439	27.5		
brother								
sister			2277	61.1			***	***
union*	71	1.0			199	31.0		
member			415	3.5			961	21.1
dutch*	74	1.9			415	30.9		
append			816	52.2			2035	205.5
no-double*	39	0.1			127	1.0		
member								
not-member			700	1.6			1352	5.9
nqueens*	1544	10.1			466	10.8		
select								
not-attack			11946	60.6			***	***

target with *: a target which first fails in learning.
***: no result.
hyp.space target fail: the number of nodes produced by the failure target.
time target fail: the number of seconds cost by the failure target.
total hyp.space: all the generated nodes in that problem.
total time: the total time (in seconds) for learning the targets in that problem.

Table 3. The results of failure-recovery learning

inefficient, the system needs much long time to recover from failure induction. The worst situation is that the system cannot recover from the failure and cannot obtain any results, which can be found in MPL-CHAM listed in Table 3.

5 On evaluation

In this section, we discuss the shift of biases and learning orders. We also compare the computational cost of MPL-Core with that of the system constructed by De Raedt et al. [2]. Learning order is not a problem in SPL systems but is important in MPL systems.

Shift of biases: From the bias point of view mentioned in [3], Our system applies reasonable procedural biases which are embodied in selecting subset of refinement operators to form the efficient and specific hypothesis space and in sharply diminishing the search spaces by means of GPC. Our system employs the learned clauses to induce the other targets, which is a kind of shift of hypothesis language. This weakens the bias by adding the learned clauses to hypothesis language so that the weaken bias becomes correct, and target predicates thus can be learned.

Effect of different learning orders: In an MPL system, there exits the phenomena that different learning orders to a certain extent lead to different learned results. In our system these differences are the *learning level* of the learned clauses, the volume of the *hypothesis space* and *time* cost. The extreme situation is that, in some learning problems, the different learning orders of the targets may produce totally different results. This is because when the learning order is changed, the newly added background predicates, i.e., the contents of the learned clauses, may be different.

Computational complexity: Suppose that p is total number of background predicates, a is the the largest arity in any literals, and m is the total number of the variables existing in a clause. If there are n clauses to be induced in a multiple predicate learning system and the average length of every clause (the number of literals) is l, in terms of [9], the cost of one clause is $pl(m+a-1)^a$. According to the algorithm in [2], let us call it MPL-93, and we assume all the checks of the globally complete and consistent of learned clauses do not fail. The main procedure in MPL-93 employs a sub-procedure *Findbest* to find one best learned clause by refining all the n heads of the target clauses simultaneously, with the cost $npl(m+a-1)^a$; then to find the second best clause by refining all the $(n-1)$ heads with the cost $(n-1)pl(m+a-1)^a$; this process iterates until $n=0$. Hence, the total cost of MPL-93 is $\sum_{i=1}^{n} ipl(m+a-1)^a$. However, having employed the fast failure mechanism, MPL-Core learns these n clauses with cost $npl(m+a-1)^a$. From the results of this analysis, with increasing the target predicates n, the cost of MPL-93 raises with the sum of $\sum_{i=1}^{n} i$, which can be intractable for MPL-93. In contrast, the cost of MPL-Core increases in proportion to n. Thus, MPL-Core is more efficient than MPL-93.

6 Conclusion

We have described a multiple predicate learner MPL-Core. It employs both the intensional and extensional learning styles when it induces target predicates. With the described fast failure mechanism, MPL-Core successfully learns the multiple predicate learning problems with reduced search space and time. Particularly, some background predicates are irrelevant background predicates while learning a target, which can enlarge the hypothesis space and can sometimes obstruct the system from correctly learning. Our system also makes use of GPC to keep away irrelevant background knowledge in induction. However, MPL-Core learns in serial style and learns only one target even though more than one target can be induced in the same learning level; it also cannot reuse the partial clauses already constructed by failure induction when the system re-learns the failure target predicates. We will extend it to overcome these drawbacks.

Acknowledgments

We would like to thank Tsuyoshi Murata, Einoshin Suzuki and C. Rahman Mofizur for the remarks and discussion about this research. Also, many thanks to the anonymous reviewers for their helpful comments on the initial draft of this paper.

References

1. R. A. Caruana. Multitask learning: A knowledge-based source of inductive bias. In *Proc. of 10th International Conference on Machine Learning*, pages 41–48. Morgan Kaufmann, 1993.
2. L. De Raedt, N. Lavrač, and S. Džeroski. Multiple predicate learning. In *Proc. Thirteenth International Joint Conference on Artificial Intelligence*, San Mateo, CA, 1993. Morgan Kaufmann.
3. D. F. Gordon and M. Desjardins. Evaluation and selection of biases in machine learning. *Machine Learning*, 20:5–22, 1995.
4. B. Kijsirikul, M. Numao, and M. Shimura. Efficient learning of logic programs with non-determinate non-discriminating literals. In *Proc. Eighth International Workshop on Machine Learning*, pages 417–421, San Mateo, CA, 1991. Morgan Kaufmann.
5. B. Kijsirikul, M. Numao, and M. Shimura. Discrimination-based constructive induction of logic programs. In *Proc. Tenth National Conference on Artificial Intelligence*, San Mateo, CA, 1992. Morgan Kaufmann.
6. S.H. Muggleton and C. Feng. Efficient induction of logic programs. In *Proc. First Conference on Algorithmic Learning Theory*, pages 368–381, Tokyo, 1990. Ohmsha.
7. J.R. Quinlan. Learning logical definitions from relations. *Machine Learning*, 5(3):239–266, 1990.
8. B. L. Richard and R. J. Mooney. Automatic refinement of first-order horn-clause domain theories. *Machine Learning*, 19:95–131, 1995.
9. G. Silverstein and M. Pazzani. Relational cliches: Constraining constructive induction during. In *Proc. of Eighth International Conference on Machine Learning*, pages 203–207. Morgan Kaufmann, 1991.
10. S. Tangkitvanich and M. Shimura. Refining a relational theory with multiple faults in the concept and subconcepts. In *Proc. Ninth International Conference on Machine Learning*, pages 436–444, San Mateo, CA, 1992. Morgan Kaufmann.

Acquiring User Preferences for Information Filtering in Interactive Multi-Media Services*

Bhavani Raskutti and Anthony Beitz

Telstra Research Laboratories
Clayton, Victoria 3168, Australia

Abstract. The increasing availability of a large number of interactive multi-media information services means that users have a large and diverse collection of choices open to them. One method of assisting users to navigate through this large collection is to use *information filtering* to extract only the information relevant to an end-user according to his/her long-term preferences. In this paper, we describe a mechanism to acquire a user's long-term preferences (*user profile*), and then show how the acquired profile may be used to suggest selections that may be of interest to the user. The profile is acquired on the basis of a user's habits using a Heuristic-Statistical approach, and is used to create *selection indices*. Our mechanism has been incorporated into an experimental Video On Demand service that is implemented using a client-server architecture.

1 Introduction

The wide acceptance of computer-network-based information services in recent years is likely to lead to an explosion of Interactive Multi-Media Services (IMMS), such as, Video On Demand (VOD), electronic directories and home shopping. The huge amount of information available through these services and the diversity of choices open to customers can easily lead to an *information overload* that dissuades customers from using such services. One method of alleviating this information overload and assisting end-users to navigate through large and diverse collections is to use automatic personalised information filtering to extract the information of interest to a user.

In this paper, we describe a mechanism for acquiring the characteristics of information of interest to a user (*user profile*) and then show how this profile may be used to filter information. Our mechanism has been designed for use in IMMS, and hence the following factors are taken into account:

- *Portability*: The benefits gained from profile implementation is cost-effective only if the cost of incorporation of profiling into new services is low.
- *Useful for end-users and vendors*: The benefits of profile implementation can be increased if profiling information is used both to assist end-users find relevant information and to supply vendors, such as video providers, with information for effective market penetration.
- *Non-intrusive profile acquisition*: Since IMMS users are typically casual users of services, they are not likely to accept profile acquisition methods that involve extensive interactions, such as those in GRUNDY [Rich 1979]. Hence, a user's preferences must be learnt implicitly, i.e., by observation of the user's

* The permission of the Director of Telstra Research Laboratories, to publish this work is gratefully acknowledged.

habits. Further, reactions to user choices, whether solicited or volunteered, must be obtained without much intrusion.

- *Profile acquisition from a small number of samples*: Since IMMS user population will include a large number of casual users, a user's preferences must be learnt from a small number of past selections. Hence, machine learning techniques that require a large training set are not suitable.
- *Information filtering in real-time*: In the context of IMMS, information filtering must be done in real time, and hence it is essential to avoid the use of computationally intensive methods of assessing each item in the information source against a complex matching criteria during on-line interactions.

The first two issues of portability and dual use are discussed in [Raskutti & Beitz 1996], while this paper focusses on profile acquisition for information filtering in IMMS. Profile acquisition from a small number of samples (usually between 10 and 20) is achieved by using a Heuristic-Statistical approach (Section 2). The acquired profiles are then used to create indices that can select items from the information source, thus avoiding the computationally intensive process of assessing each item for matching (Section 3). The profile acquisition and index creation processes are performed off-line, while suggesting selections for user viewing is done on the basis of these indices during online interactions. User feedback for profile acquisition is in the form of a single selection rather than extensive interactions with the service and is obtained during online interactions (Section 4). Our mechanism for profile acquisition and filtering has been incorporated into an experimental Video On Demand (VOD) service that is implemented using a client-server architecture. The profile acquisition and filtering components are incorporated into a VOD server on a multi-tasking machine, while the VOD user interface resides on a personal computer (Section 4).

2 Profile Acquisition

A user profile contains summary information about the characteristics that affect a user's evaluation, along with an indication of our confidence regarding these inferences. This summary is then used to select *items* of interest from a large *collection*. Each item in the collection is described by a set of *attributes*, eg., attributes genre, director and producer in a VOD service, and the value(s) of each attribute that are applicable to this item, eg., value "Action" for attribute "genre" for the movie item titled "Die Hard".

The user profile is acquired on the basis of a number of knowledge sources, such as the habits of the user in the form of past *selections*, i.e., items from the collection that were selected by the user; his/her reactions to these selections; the features[2] of the selections; and how these selections were chosen.

The profile creation is performed off-line using a Heuristic-Statistical approach. This is done when a new selection is made by the user and the addition of this selection to the user's habits provides sufficient samples of user selections (usually between 10 and 20). The created profile is then used to build selection

[2] In this paper, the term *feature* is used to denote an attribute-value pair, eg., movie "Die Hard" has the feature that it is of "Action" genre.

indices that may be used to select items during on-line interactions. Each index consists of a conjuction or disjunction of features, and attempts to emulate the user's decision-making process when choosing items from the collection.

2.1 Constituents of a Profile

The user profile contains information from which the profiler may personalise a user's interface to a service. One way of personalising a service is to filter data from large collections such that the selected data is likely to be of interest to the user[3]. Such filtering may be done on the basis of a user profile that contains a summary of the features that affect a user's evaluation along with an indication of our confidence regarding these inferences. For example, if the user indicates that s/he enjoyed the books ***The hound of the Baskervilles*** and ***The return of Sherlock Holmes*** enormously, then the user profile may hold the inference that the user likes the author ***Arthur Conan Doyle.*** Clearly, this inference is not certain since other features of these books, namely, that it is a mystery thriller, may have contributed to the user evaluation of these books. These other features are also noted in the user profile, along with their certainties.

In order to model both a user's likes and dislikes, a user profile contains both a positive profile to mirror a user's likes as well as a negative profile that holds information about the user's dislikes. A positive profile is derived on the basis of the selections liked by a user, while the negative profile is derived on the basis of selections disliked by the user. The positive profile is used to choose features that make up a selection index for filtering, while both the positive and negative profiles are used to determine the suitability of the index (Section 3).

Clearly, each of the profiles needs sufficient samples (typically around 10 each) to draw inferences, and there may be situations where a user profile contains only one of the profiles due to insufficient samples of the other kind. From our experiments with users, we believe that a profile consisting of only the positive part is more likely than the one consisting of only the negative part.

A feature that is common between both liked and disliked selections has an entry both in the positive and negative profiles, and the combined rating is then used to determine if this feature is useful in determining user preferences. This separate representation of likes and dislikes enables us to properly apportion impact when there are equal like and dislike ratings for a particular feature, but the certainty of one of the ratings is much higher than that of the other.

An example of a user profile for the VOD service is shown in Table 1. This profile is part of the positive profile of Anthony, constructed on the basis of his selections. Anthony's profile does not include a negative profile since his selections did not include sufficient negative samples. The negative profile, when present, contains similar information except that the rating is negative and represents user dislike. For each attribute that significantly affects user evaluations, the profile holds all the values of relevance, i.e., the values for which an inference

[3] Other means of personalising navigational interfaces are to (1) sort the data selected such that the preferred ones are listed first, and (2) highlight the preferred ones. While our profile may be used to do filtering, sorting and highlighting, our current focus is on filtering.

Table 1. Positive Profile for Anthony for Video On Demand service

Attribute	Value	Rating	Certainty
genre	Drama	+4.86	0.33
	Action	+3.14	0.33
rating	M	+8.57	0.33
	PG	+1.43	0.33
director	John McTiernan	+1.71	0.50
	Rob Reiner	+0.85	0.33
producer	Mace Neufeld	+0.85	0.33
	Ivan Reitman	+0.85	0.33
year	1991	+2.0	0.33
	1988	+2.0	0.33

could be drawn regarding user evaluations (column 2 in Table 1), e.g. "Drama" and "Action" for the attribute genre are included for Anthony's profile since they influence his choice. Values for which an inference could not be drawn are not included in the profile. For instance, Anthony's profile does not include information about the genre "Science fiction". Similarly, there is no information regarding attributes that are not considered for profiling, e.g., title, as well as attributes that have little impact on user choice (eg., uniform distribution of values perhaps). For each relevant value of each attribute, the profile contains:

- *Rating for this value of the attribute* (column 3 in Table 1): Rating varies from 0 (indicating indifference) to +10 (indicating total liking) in positive profiles and -10 (indicating total dislike) to 0 in negative profiles.
- *Certainty of inference* (column 4 in Table 1): This represents the degree of confidence in our judgement regarding this preference of the user. The representation of certainty is useful when creating an index to retrieve information from the database since the system could perform approximate/inexact matches depending on the certainty. For instance, since Anthony likes John McTiernan and the certainty of this inference is high, if there are no John McTiernan films available, the system could choose to present films that are similar to those by John McTiernan. In addition, indices may be constructed to ignore preferences that are inferred with low certainty.

2.2 Information Used for Profile Acquisition

The profiler uses the following information to contruct a personal profile:

A user's past habits in the form of user's selections and his/her reactions to these selections: Our system uses user reactions HATED, DISLIKED, INDIFFERENT, LIKED and LOVED, and assigns values -2,-1,0,+1 and +2 respectively to these reactions. If the user does not provide any feedback regarding his/her selections, then it is assumed that s/he LIKED the selection, since the very fact of this choice indicates a possible positive reaction to it. Our preference for quantized reactions as opposed to a number from 0 to 10 as used in [Karunanithi & Alspector 1995] or a rating scale as used in [Kay 1995], arises from the fact while people find it difficult to place a quantitative value on how much they liked/disliked a selection, they can readily identify their qualitative reaction to a selection.

The features of these selections: The attributes of relevance include genre, director and producer for a VOD service, and attributes such as author, publisher, genre and series for a book selection service.

Information about how a selection is chosen: The method of choice may indicate how a feature influenced a user's evaluation, and thus contributes to the strength of evidence, i.e., certainty. For example, if the user explicitly requested for a movie starring X, and then disliked it, then it is likely that it was not X but other factors that caused the dislike. In contrast, if the user liked the film starring X, it is likely that the cast member was a factor in the user liking the movie. Currently the possible methods of choice are CHOSEN_BY_USER, FROM_PROFILE and INCIDENTAL, and these respectively represent situations (1) when the user explicitly requests a selection with a feature, (2) when a selection is made on the basis of the user's profile, and this feature from the profile is used in the selection process, and (3) when a selection chosen by other means happens to have this feature. Our future research directions include the ability to integrate volunteered natural language feedback, such as, "I liked the film because it had actor X in it" and assign greater certainty to evidence from direct user input and inferences from such input [Elzer, Chu-Carroll & Carberry 1994].

The number of possible values for each attribute of relevance: This information is usually obtained once only during service creation. It is primarily used to determine if user selections are uniformly distributed across all values of an attribute, and if this is the case, then that attribute has little or no impact on this user's preferences. In some situations, it is possible to obtain only an approximate figure regarding the number of possible values, e.g., attributes such as director and actor in a VOD service.

2.3 Constructing a User Profile

At the early stages of service usage, the profiler usually does not have sufficient information about the user's habits to construct a personal profile. Hence, the system must use general information about the user, such as his/her age, sex and occupation, in order to determine the user's preferences. General information about user may be used to assign to a user either (1) a stereotypical profile or (2) the profile of a user who is likely to have similar tastes Currently, our profiler uses the first option during initial service usage. A library of stereotypical profiles itself is created by the profiler over time on the basis of the profiles it has created for its user base. The assignment of the profile of another user with possibly similar tastes is a research issue.

At later stages of service usage, profile creation is achieved using the following Heuristic-Statistical approach:

First, for each value of each attribute, numbers are accumulated to reflect a user's like rating for the positive profile, and the user's dislike rating for the negative profile, as well as the certainties of ratings. The user rating is dependent on the features of the items selected by the user and his/her reactions to these items. The positive profile is built up from the selections that the user liked/loved, and the negative profile is created on the basis of selections the user disliked/hated. The certainty is based on how selections are chosen, and the reactions of the user to the selections.

Next, each attribute is examined to see if they influence the user's evaluation, and those attributes with little or no impact on the user's evaluation are eliminated. The numbers for the remaining attributes are then normalised and the features with the most influence are retained.

Accumulation of User ratings and Certainties $AccRating_{pos}$, the accumulation for rating in the positive profile for each value of each attribute is done using the following formula:

$$AccRating_{pos} = \sum_{i=1}^{N} f(i) \times Reaction_i \times Pos_i \tag{1}$$

where N is number of selections of the user that have been maintained for learning the user's preferences, $f(i)$ is a weighting function to take into account user's taste changes as described below, $Reaction_i$ is a number between -2 and 2 and indicates the user's reaction to this selection and Pos_i ensures that the summation is over only those selections where this attribute value occurs and to which the user had a positive reaction. Hence Pos_i is 1 when this value occurs for the particular attribute in this selection and the user's reaction to the selection is positive, and is 0 otherwise.

$AccRating_{neg}$, the accumulation for rating in the negative profile for each attribute-value pair is done similarly using the following formula:

$$AccRating_{neg} = \sum_{i=1}^{N} f(i) \times Reaction_i \times Neg_i \tag{2}$$

where N, $f(i)$, and $Reaction_i$ are as defined for equation(1), and Neg_i ensures that the summation is over those selections where this attribute value occurs and to which the user had a negative reaction. Hence Neg_i is 1 when this value occurs for the particular attribute in this selection and the user's reaction to the selection is negative, and is 0 otherwise.

The weighting function $f(i)$ may be used to model a user's taste cycles, such as the fact that a user is not likely to go to the same restaurant two days in a row, or that a user's habits have been slowly changing, so information from last year is no longer relevant. Ideally, this function $f(i)$ itself is learnt by the profiler. However, in our current implementation, the system uses one of the functions from the following to model user's taste cycles: (1) the unity function to weight all of the user selections equally, (2) a trapezoidal function to assign greater weight for the selections in the middle, and lesser weight to those selections in the distant past or those that were selected in the immediate past, and (3) a scaling function that gives greater weight to selections in the immediate past, i.e., incorporating decay. The profiles described in this paper have been created using the unity function, while use of other functions is being researched.

The accumulation for certainty for each value of each attribute takes into account both the user's reaction to a selection as well as how the value was chosen, thus assessing the strength of evidence for updating the user's rating.

Table 2. Effect based on user's reaction to selection and method of choice

	Method Used for Choosing the Value for the Attribute		
User's Reaction	CHOSEN_BY_USER	FROM_PROFILE	INCIDENTAL
Positive	3	2	1
INDIFFERENT	0	0	0
Negative	1	2	3

$AccCertainty_{pos}$, the accumulation of certainty in the positive profile is calculated using the following formula:

$$AccCertainty_{pos} = \sum_{i=1}^{N} f(i) \times Effect_i \times Pos_i \tag{3}$$

where N, $f(i)$, and Pos_i are as defined for equation(1), and $Effect_i$ determines how likely it is that this value of the attribute contributed to the user's reaction. The value for $Effect_i$ is determined based on the user's reaction to the selection and the method by which the value was chosen in accordance with the entries in Table 2. The entries in Table 2 take into account the fact that if a user explicitly requested for a movie starring X, and then disliked the movie enormously (i.e., there was a negative reaction), then it is likely that it was not X but other features that caused the dislike, and hence only a small weight is added to the certainty. In contrast, if the user liked the film starring X (i.e., there was a positive reaction), then it is likely that the cast member was a factor in the user liking the movie, and hence a larger weight is added to the certainty. Such explicit specification of evidence also ensures the ability to use better feedback techniques in future, such as a user explicitly specifying that s/he liked a movie because of actor X, and assigning greater certainty to this fact.

$AccCertainty_{neg}$, the accumulation of certainty in the negative profile is calculated in a similar manner using Neg_i instead of Pos_i.

Normalisation and Determining Influence The numbers accumulated in the previous stage have an entry for each value of each attribute that might have had a positive or negative influence on the user's evaluation. In order to determine which of these values really influence user choice, the negative and positive profiles are examined and processed as follows. First, the number of selections to which the user had a positive reaction is checked and a positive profile is formed only when there are sufficient[4] positive samples. Similarly a user's negative profile is formed only when there are sufficient samples to which the user had a negative reaction. Our experience with the current profiler is that the negative profile is created long after the positive profile, since users often choose items which they expect to have a positive reaction to, and thus, there are more positive samples than negative ones. Also, the positive profile is more useful during information filtering since it is able to constrain the collection better than the negative profile.

[4] Currently, sufficiency is determined on the basis of a configurable threshold of minimum samples.

Next, the accumulated numbers for the values in each attribute in each of the constructed profiles is examined, and those attributes with uniform distribution are eliminated[5]. This is because all of the possible values of the attribute in question are rated equally by the user, and hence, this attribute has little or no impact on this user's evaluation of selections. Further since positive and negative profiles are accumulated separately, it is possible that an attribute has impact on user dislikes but not on his/her likes or vice versa.

The ratings for the remaining attributes are normalised to [-10,0] range for the negative profile, and [0,10] range for the positive profile. $NormRating_{pos}$, the normalised ratings in the positive profile is calculated using the following formula:

$$NormRating_{pos} = \frac{AccRating_{pos} \times 10}{\sum_{i=1}^{N} f(i) \times Reaction_i \times PosReaction_i} \quad (4)$$

where N, $f(i)$, $Reaction_i$ and $AccRating_{pos}$ are as define for equation(1), and $PosReaction_i$ ensures that the summation is only over those selections to which the user had a positive reaction. It differs from Pos_i in that it is independent of whether the attribute value appeared in the ith selection. $PosReaction_i$ is 1 when $Reaction_i$ is greater than 0 and 0 otherwise. Hence, the normalisation using equation(4) would assign a rating of 10 to an attribute value if all the selections to which the user had a positive reaction included this attribute value.

The normalisation in the negative profile is carried out similarly so that a rating of -10 is assigned to an attribute value if all the selections to which the user had a negative reaction included this attribute value.

The certainty that the normalised ratings are indeed correct is determined by normalising the accumulated certainties. The certainties in the positive profile are normalised using the following equation to yield $NormCertainty_{pos}$:

$$NormCertainty_{pos} = \frac{AccCertainty_{pos}}{\sum_{i=1}^{N} f(i) \times MaxEffect \times Pos_i} \quad (5)$$

where N and $f(i)$ are as defined earlier, $AccCertainty_{pos}$ is the accumulated certainty of the attribute value in the positive profile, and Pos_i, as defined in eqaution(1), is 1 when this value occurs for the particular attribute in this selection and the user's reaction to the selection is positive, and is 0 otherwise. $MaxEffect$ is the maximum effect a single selection may have on the certainty of an attribute value. In the current implementation, it is 3 and occurs when the user's reaction is positive and the attribute value is CHOSEN_BY_USER or the user's reaction is negative and the attribute value choice is INCIDENTAL (Table 2). In future implementations, we propose to have other sources of evidence, such as explicit user feedback and inferences based on such user input, and in this case the effect of explicit feedback would be $MaxEffect$.

The certainties in the negative profile are similarly normalised using the contents of the negative profile of the user.

---

[5] Uniform distribution is checked by determing if a profile contains all of the possible values for an attribute, and whether the accumulated numbers for user ratings for these values are uniformly distributed (by measurement of their standard deviation).

This normalisation ensures that an attribute value in a profile has a certainty of 1, when every contributing evidence is strong. For instance, if an attribute values occurs in 3 selections to which a user had a positive reaction, and in all 3 instances the attribute value was CHOSEN_BY_USER, then this attribute value has a normalised certainty of 1. Further, if many attribute values in a profile have strong supporting evidence, then each of these have a high certainty. Thus, one attribute value having high certainty does not automatically preclude the presence of another with high certainty.

The normalised ratings and certainties are then used to determine N_{best} (=3 currently, but may be altered after experiments) values for each attribute in each profile, i.e., the features that have the greatest impact on user evaluation. This determination is done by examining the combined rating of an attribute value. *CombRating*, the combined rating is calculated on the basis of $NormRating_{pos}$ and $NormCertainty_{pos}$, the normalised rating and certainty of an attribute value in the positive profile, and $NormRating_{neg}$ and $NormCertainty_{neg}$, the normalised rating and certainty of the same attribute value in the negative profile, using the following formula:

$$CombRating = \frac{\sum_{i=pos,neg} NormRating_i \times NormCertainty_i}{\sum_{i=pos,neg} NormCertainty_i} \quad (6)$$

According to this equation, if an attribute value has nearly equal positive and negative rating but the certainty for positive rating is significantly higher than that of the negative rating, then the combined rating reflects the fact that the impact of positive ratings is greater due to the stronger evidence. Clearly, if only one of the two profiles is constructed (as has often been the case during our experiments) or an attribute value is present in only one of the profiles, then the combined rating is this single rating.

The attribute values in each attribute in each profile are ordered according to their combined rating, and all but N_{best} values from each attribute of each profile are eliminated. Since combined ratings are taken into account, it is likely that only those values with clear positive or negative influence will be retained.

3 Information Filtering

In order to present suggestions to the user during on-line interactions, the profiler may use the acquired profiles (1) to create a set of indices off-line, and then use these indices during on-line interactions to select items from the collection, or (2) to perform extensive checking of each item in the collection for compatibility/ranking against the profile during on-line interactions. The second option is time consuming, and hence, is not useful in the context of IMMS where real-time response is required.

In order to provide a varied set of suggestions to the user, and to cater for varied requirements during real-time interactions (such as number of items that can be handled by the terminal interface), a number of indices (currently 10) of sufficient utility are created during the off-line index construction process. The utility of each index reflects how likely it is that this index will model the user's preferences, while at the same time constrain the items selected from the data collection. It is based on the following parameters:

- *The ratings and certainties for attribute values*: The higher the rating and certainty of the features that make up the index, the greater the utility. The rating and certainty used are those from the positive profile, since the suggestions are primarily determined on the basis of user's likes.
- *The priorities of the attributes*: The priority depends on how likely it is that an attribute affects user selections in general. The greater the likelihood that an attribute or combination of attributes is used for selection, the higher the utility of using it for extracting data.
- *The coverage achieved over the user's selections using this index*: An index that covers a larger fraction of the user's positive selections is preferable to one that has little coverage.
- *The ability to discriminate*: An index that is likely to constrain the collection, and hence offer a smaller set of suggestions to the user is preferred. Hence, an index that covers a small percentage of collection has higher utility.
- *Suitability of items selected by index*: An index that selects items that are compatible with the user's profile (both likes and dislikes) is preferable. Suitability is determined by computing a rating based on the user's positive and negative profiles for each of the items selected by the index, and then computing an average based on these ratings.

The constructed indices are used to select items from the database to provide suggestions during on-line interactions. In the current implementation, the items selected by the first index that satisfies user interface requirements are presented to the user. In future implementations, disjunctions of indices of high utility will be used to yield a more varied set of suggestions.

4 Implementation in VOD service

The profiler described above has been incorporated into a VOD service. The user interface to the service resides on a personal computer on a data network, and communicates with a VOD server residing on a multi-tasking machine on the same network. The server performs profiling and accesses the movie information database. The database contains 500 movies with information about a movie's title, plot, genre(s), release year, censor rating, director(s) and producer(s).

The user interface offers the ability to navigate through the movie database by using commands to view top 10 movies, new releases, catalog search and suggestions based on stored indices. When a movie is selected for viewing, a brief clip/plot of the movie is displayed, and the user is asked to provide feedback. This request for feedback is in the form of 5 cartoon faces depicting great satisfaction, satisfaction, indifference, dissatisfaction and great dissatisfaction. The user provides feedback by clicking on one of these faces.

Our VOD implementation was qualitatively assessed as follows: the habits of 6 users were monitored, and personal profiles for these users were created using only the selections for which they had a positive reaction. On the basis of these profiles, users were offered suggestions, and asked if these suggestions were acceptable. Of the 6 users, 5 found the suggestions acceptable while the sixth user indicated displeasure. An analysis of the movies suggested to the displeased user indicated that due to the simplicity of features selected for profiling, the commonality of movies viewed by this user had not been correctly captured. While this shortcoming can be overcome by better choice of features, our belief is that extensive knowledge engineering for particular domains should be avoided whenever possible, and non-domain-specific methods explored to improve learning.

5 Related Work

User preferences may be acquired explicitly by user specification or implicitly. Implicit acquisition may be done either by assigning a user to a stereotypical group or by learning personal preferences from user habits.

Explicit profile acquisition is done either by users providing a set of keywords that specify their interests [Houseman & Kaskela 1970], or by users creating rules based on keywords to filter information [Mackay et al. 1989]. While explicit profiles mirror users' requirements correctly, both explicit profile acquisition methods often fail in obtaining relevant information. Profiles by keyword specification fail because words are often used ambiguously, i.e., a single word has more than one meaning (e.g., ball - plastic or dance), or when a single concept can be expressed by many different words (e.g., user model, customer profile). Filter specification by rules is useful only when the collection of information is structured or semi-structured (as in email), and the evolving multi-media information infrastructure lacks the structure that makes rule specification useful.

Stereotypical profiles have been used in Grundy to suggest novels that may be of interest to a user [Rich 1979]. A stereotypical profile in Grundy contains information about different facets, such as, Thrill, Motivations etc., and their corresponding ratings. Novels in the database are similarly annotated for comparison. While our mechanism also uses facets (attributes) and ratings, it differs from Grundy in that our system uses the attributes that are already in the data collection, thus avoiding expensive knowledge engineering of collections. In addition, our focus is on learning a personal profile on the basis of habits, while Grundy's focus was on adaptation of stereotypes.

Implicit personal profiles are created when a user's long-term preferences are determined on the basis of the user's habits. Implicit profiles have been used for information filtering by using (1) a similarity measure, such as overlap of nouns in news items, between past news items read and a new item to determine if this item may be of interest [Allen 1990], (2) memory-based learning to see if a new situation is similar to any of the past memorized situations [Maes 1994], and (3) a feature-based neural network for filtering news articles [Jennings & Higuchi 1992] and for determining a new movie's rating based on the user's ratings of earlier movies [Karunanithi & Alspector 1995].

Each of the implicit methods mentioned including Grundy require that every item in the collection that is to be filtered be checked for compatibility, and hence, they are not suitable for filtering information in the context of IMMS, where the collection size can be huge. In addition, the neural-network based movie selector requires a large number of examples (typically 350) to train on, and this requirement is unrealistic in the context of IMMS owing to the possibility of a large number of casual users of services. In our system, extensive computation during online interactions is avoided by creating indices of good utility off-line, and then using these indices to select items from the collection.

LyricTime, a personalised music system, performs information filtering in an IMMS in order to present users with a smaller set of songs from a collection of 1000 songs [Loeb 1994]. However, it does not perform profile acquisition. Instead it uses a stored profile acquired by other means.

6 Conclusion

In this paper, we have described a mechanism to acquire a user's long-term preferences and then show how the acquired profile may be used to suggest selections that may be of interest to the user. The mechanism has been designed for use in Interactive Multi-Media Services. The user profile is acquired on the basis of a user's habits using a Heuristic-Statistical approach, and is used to create selection indices. Our mechanism is incorporated into an experimental Video On Demand service. Our implementation was qualitatively assessed for its usefulness, and the assessment indicates that our approach is worth pursuing.

References

Allen, R. B. 1990. User Models: Theory, Method and Practice. *International Journal of Man-Machine Studies*, 32: 511-543.

Elzer, S.; Chu-Carroll, J.; and Carberry, S. 1994. Recognizing and Utilizing User Preferences in Collaborative Consultation Dialogues: In Proceedings of the Fourth Internation Conference on User Modeling, 19-24.

Houseman, E. M.; and Kaskela, D. E. 1970. State of the Art of Selective Dissemination of Information. *IEEE Transactions on Engineering Writing and Speech III*, 2: 78-83.

Jennings, A.; and Higuchi, H. 1992. A Personal News Service Based on a User Model Neural Network. In IEICE Transactions on Information and Systems, Vol. E75-D, No. 2, pp. 198-209.

Karunannithi, N.; and Alspector, J. 1995. A Feature-Based Neural Network Movie Selection Approach: In Proceedings of the International Workshop on the Applications of Neural Network to Telecommunications 2, 162-169.

Kay, J. 1995. The UM Toolkit for Cooperative User Modeling. *User Modeling and User Adapted Interaction*, 4(3): 149-196.

Loeb, S. 1992. Architecting Personalized Delivery of MultiMedia Information. *Communications of the ACM*, 35(12): 39-48.

Mackay, W. E.; Malone, T. W.; Crowston, K.; Rao, R.; Rosenblitt, D.; and Card, S. K. 1989. How do Experienced Information Lens Users Use Rules? In Proceedings of ACM CHI '89 Conference on Human Factors in Computing Systems, 211-216.

Maes, P. 1994. Agents that Reduce Work and Information Overload. *Communications of the ACM*, 37(7): 31-40.

Raskutti, R.; and Beitz, A. 1996. Customer Profiling in Interactive Multi-Media Services. Forthcoming.

Rich, E. 1979. User Modeling via Stereotypes. *Cognitive Science* 3: 329-354.

The Development of an Interactive Fault Diagnosis Expert System for Telecommunication Applications

Ming Zhao, Chris Leckie

Artificial Intelligence Systems Section
Telstra Research Laboratories
770 Blackburn Road, Clayton, 3168, Australia
{m.zhao, c.leckie}@trl.oz.au

Abstract

This paper presents work on an interactive fault diagnosis expert system for telecommunication applications. A new knowledge representation and inference algorithm is proposed to suit the characteristics of the application environment, namely: (1) no parallel event exists in human fault reporting, (2) the diagnostic sequence is unpredictable, and (3) the inference engine is passive in an event-driven environment. A lattice data structure is used for knowledge representation, which is generated automatically from a script of decision rules. The inference engine works in a transaction-like style by prompting and responding to the user according to the knowledge in the lattice. It can explicitly guide the inference sequence, as well as respond to ad hoc input from the user.

Keywords: Expert System, Fault Diagnosis, Industrial Application

1 Introduction

With significant progress in telecommunication technologies and the merging of computing and communication, telecommunication products are becoming more and more complex. It becomes crucial for a communication company to deploy an intelligent, flexible, and easy-to-use helpdesk system to improve the quality of customer services. Fault diagnosis and reporting is one important component of a helpdesk system. Without such a support, the operator can only record the fault symptoms the customer reported and pass it to a customer service expert. The expert then analyses the symptoms and makes the necessary tests, decides what the problem is, and sends a repair request to appropriate area. This process is awkward as the information collected by an operator is often incomplete and thus the expert has to call the customer back to acquire more information. The result is a delay in fault repair and reduction of customer satisfaction.

A helpdesk system has been developed at TRL for one of Telstra's business units. This is an integrated service system dealing with all inbound customer calls, including payments, bill inquiries, service requests, fault reports, disputes, and so forth. An interactive fault diagnosis expert system has been developed as one module of the helpdesk system to support customer fault reporting. As it runs in a heavily-loaded front-end system and deals with a three-way dialogue (customer, operator, and expert system), the expert system must be compact in size, flexible in operation, and resourceful in providing context sensitive information.

We studied several popular expert system development shells and found none of them satisfies the requirements of an interactive front-end expert system. Therefore we decided to develop our own expert system, code-named IES (Interactive Expert System). The main contributions of IES to the interactive application of expert systems are its lattice knowledge representation data structure, the event-driven inference algorithm, and a very compact inference engine. At the time of writing, IES has been fully implemented and tested. A pilot system has been running in a Telstra business unit for a few months supporting 60 users, and the national roll out has been scheduled. The concept and architecture of IES have proved advantageous in the interactive environment. It has also been accepted by another Telstra business unit in the Public Switched Telephone Service (PSTS). A new project has been started using IES as a kernel of a front-end system to support a range of PSTS products.

This paper presents the design and implementation of IES and describes its development as a sub-system for a helpdesk application for telecommunication services. A lattice knowledge representation data structure is proposed to suit the interactive, event-driven computing environment. The knowledge base is automatically generated from a script of transition statements. The inference engine reasons on the lattice, and works in a transaction-like style. It accepts user input, executes the appropriate actions triggered by that input, and hands the control back to the user interface. The inference engine can respond to input to any decision node in the lattice. Thus it can provide a structured diagnosis with the user, as well as being reactive to unexpected information from the user working in an event-driven environment. Section 2 of this paper discusses the issues raised in the development of the event-driven diagnosis expert system, and the design principles of IES. Section 3 introduces the major components of system. Section 4 presents the implementation of the fault diagnosis system. Section 5 concludes the paper.

2 Interactive Fault Diagnosis in an Event-Driven Environment

The helpdesk described in this paper has been designed as a front-end system to support a CSR (Customer Service Representative, the user of the helpdesk system) in handling all inbound customer calls. The front-end computer is connected to the back-end server in a typical client-server configuration. The server provides the clients with customer and system data, network status, and line test facilities. With the helpdesk, a CSR can pick up a customer phone call, activate an appropriate system component corresponding to the customer request, and solve the problem following the guidance of the helpdesk while the customer is on-line. This greatly enhances the efficiency of customer service.

Fault diagnosis is one important aspect of telecommunication customer services. Because of its technical complexity, an ordinary CSR can only record the fault symptoms that the customer reported and send the fault report to the customer support or network service area, where the experts will diagnose, locate, and repair the fault. Since the availability of experts is limited and the fault report may not have all the necessary information, fault diagnosis is impeded by the need to call the customer for more information. An interactive fault diagnosis expert system helps to alleviate this difficulty (Sassen, Buiel and Hoegee 1994, Vale, Goncalves and Vale 1993). The objectives of IES are to:

1. guide a CSR to ask relevant questions to a customer when he/she reports a fault,
2. identify the possible source of the fault,
3. collect all necessary information for further analysis, and
4. direct the fault to the appropriate service area depending on the fault category.

Whenever the answer to a question can be retrieved or computed from the available system data, the system will try to get it without asking the question to the CSR. The system also advises the CSR to find relevant information from other resources, in case they are not connected to the helpdesk system.

A critical factor in the design of IES is how the user will interact with the system (Berry 1994, Suh and Suh 1993). From our knowledge acquisition sessions, a few unique characteristics of interactive fault diagnosis via telephone conversations were observed which strongly influenced the architecture of our expert system.

No parallelism: In a typical rule based expert system application, the kernel of the system is an inference engine which works on a set of working memory elements and a set of production rules. The significant advantage of this approach is its parallelism in dealing with multiple instances. In contrast, we have found that in our application the diagnosis is driven by a mostly sequential flow of questions to the customer or CSR (we don't expect that a human will work in parallel in this circumstance). Therefore, it is not necessary for us to adopt a multi-instance matching structure like RETE (Forgy 1982).

Unpredictable diagnostic sequence: Two factors prohibit us from simply adopting a sequential structure like a decision tree. First is the usability of the system to the CSR. In fault diagnosis, the expert system presents the relevant questions on the screen. It is visually more sensible if the questions are presented together on the screen, not one after another. Since all questions are presented, we have to allow access to them in any order; otherwise, it would be frustrating for the CSR to use. The second factor is due to the scenario in which a customer could voluntarily provide information about the fault he/she has experienced. In our application, the CSR records the relevant fault description while listening to the customer. In this situation, it is not possible to predict how a customer would describe the fault.

Passive inference operations: The helpdesk works in an event-driven style. It responds to the events generated from the graphical user interface. This affects the way the control structure is organised for the inference engine. Though a modern programming environment provides full support for event-driven programming, there is no place for a centrally controlled inference engine to play the driver's role (Dumas 1988). Therefore, all the inference functions of the inference engine have to be provided in the form of event handling procedures to be activated by the triggering of certain events.

Two additional characteristics particular to a large service company are the high turnover rate of the CSRs and the frequent introduction of new products. If the system is easy to use and can provide guidance to inexperienced CSRs, it will considerably reduce the costs of training. The frequent introduction of new products requires a generic, flexible system architecture to reduce the cost of using it for a new product.

The above characteristics clearly indicate that a new type of knowledge base and inference algorithm is needed to achieve good performance, high efficiency, and greater flexibility. We also realise that it would be beneficial if the inference engine can support the manipulation of the graphical display as a GUI (Graphical User Interface) has become a standard component of an interactive application environment.

3 The Design of IES

Through contact with the experts in the customer service areas, we find they often use flowcharts to describe the process of fault diagnosis, as shown in Figure 1. This motivated us to use a similar structure to represent the knowledge. A lattice is a natural choice. We have defined a lattice data structure in which each node is used to hold decision knowledge, as well as the information collected during the diagnosis (from either humans or on-line databases).

To avoid the problem of having to code the knowledge into the data structure (McLaughlin and Christie 1994), the expert knowledge is represented as a set of rules similar to those used in a rule-based system. The rules are stored in a script file, and then are read by a script compiler to generate the lattice knowledge base.

To address the problem of unpredictable input sequences, we need to design the inference engine in such a way that it will accept input to any of the decision nodes at any time and act accordingly, while it will highlight the question which the inference engine recommends next. Therefore, an experienced CSR can answer questions in any order, as in the order the customer narrates the fault symptoms, while an inexperienced CSR can carry on a diagnostic session by simply following the highlighted questions.

Finally, to suit the event-driven application environment, a transaction-like control style is adopted. The engine is designed as a passive program module. It executes only one rule at each interaction. After initialisation during the loading stage, the inference engine stays idle. When the CSR makes a selection or types information to

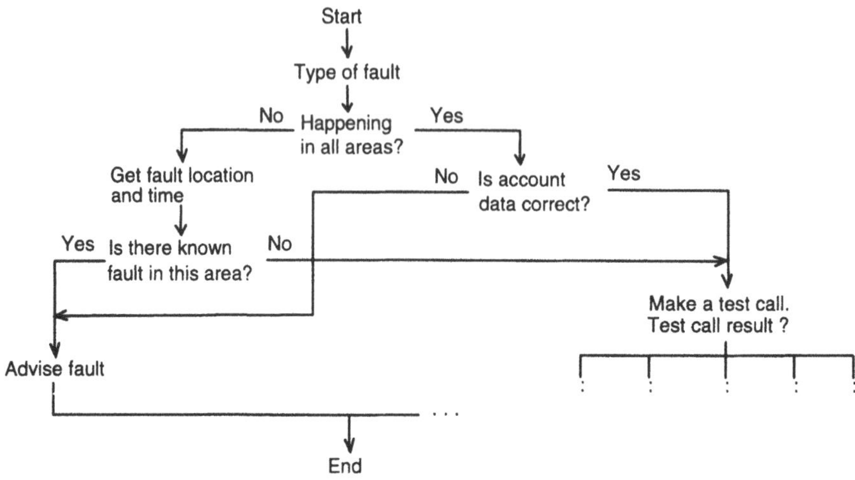

Figure 1. A segment of the expert diagnostic flowchart (simplified)

the helpdesk screen, the GUI activates the engine. The engine does one step of reasoning, then hands the control back to the interface, waiting for the next input.

3.1 The Architecture

As shown in Figure 2, the Inference Engine is the central block of the fault diagnosis expert system. Its interface with the user is through the Helpdesk Screen, where the CSR makes input to the Inference Engine, and reads the output on the screen. The knowledge is edited by the knowledge engineer in a Script, which is compiled by the Script Compiler to form the Lattice Knowledge Base. A node in the lattice can take certain actions when it is visited, like the action part of a rule. The Inference Engine reasons on the knowledge base, based on the CSR input and the result of the node's action. If the inference passes across the boundary of a form, the Inference Engine will send a request to the Form Manager to update the active form. The information required from and delivered to other systems is managed by the Inference Engine by calling a set of communication commands which are developed elsewhere in the helpdesk.

3.2 The Script Language

A script language is designed to code the domain expert knowledge and the script is later compiled into the lattice knowledge base. The main body of the script is a series of statements in the format:

if <present_node> [= <condition>] **next** <next_node>

The statement defines a transition (branch) from the present lattice node to the next node on satisfaction of the condition. [= <condition>] is optional. If it is absent, the transition will be unconditional. <condition> can be a constant value the

<present_node> can possibly have, or the key word **Other** which represents any value other than those explicitly listed. Notice that although the statement looks like a production in a rule-based system, it specifies a transition, not a condition-action relationship.

Four kinds of nodes are defined in the script language as the lowest level components. Q (questioning) and E (executable) nodes are operational nodes for information gathering and decision making, while S (sub-block) and C (control) nodes are functional nodes to provide structural control.

Figure 3 is the script definition of the expert diagnostic flowchart of Figure 1. In Figure 3, *sub*General is a mnemonic text string for the name of the block, *frm*General is the name of the form to appear on the screen, *qai*FaultType is the start node of this block, and *con*Exit is the end node. A sequence of transition statements define the reasoning logic of this block.

A simple naming convention is introduced in defining names of various nodes. The first character of a name indicates its category, that is, *q*, *e*, *s*, or *c*. The second character denotes the type of the node: *a* for a simple node (*a* field), or *f* for a node of multiple fields(*f*). The third character defines the data type of the node, *i* for integer, *s* for text string, etc. If the node is not expected to carry any value, *z* is used instead. For example, *qai*TestCall is a simple Q node with an integer value for decision making. *qfz*FaultLocation is composed of three text strings and one drop-down list for collecting location information. The naming convention applies only to Q and E nodes. For S and C nodes, the leading characters are always *sub* and *con*, respectively.

The full script definition of the knowledge base is composed of several blocks which can appear in any order. There must be one and only one main block, denoted by a key word **main** after the key word **block**. All other blocks are sub-blocks. The statements within a block can also appear in any order. The inference engine will find a match on this order. Therefore in a group of statements with the same

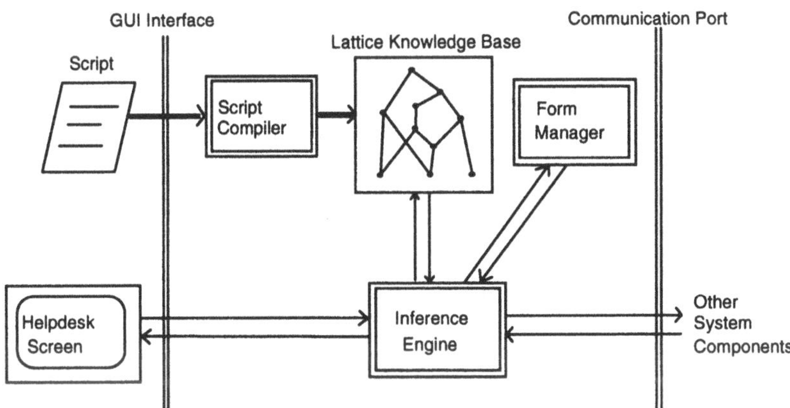

Figure 2. The IES architecture

<present_node>, the unconditional statement, or statement with condition **Other**, must be the last one. Comments are accepted in the script. Anything after ' (single quotation mark) until the end of the line is treated as a comment.

3.3 The Management of Interaction

The control of interaction is complex in an event-driven environment. The inference engine, though the subordinate force in this environment, has to ensure the correct flow of the inference sequence, the integrity of data storage, and the appropriate presentation of different windows.

The inference engine processes the four kinds of script nodes differently. A Q node has a corresponding visual object on the helpdesk screen to collect CSR input for diagnosis. When an input is received, the engine will not initiate a visit to the corresponding Q node again. Only manual input to the node can bring the engine back to it, so modification at any time to any input node is allowed.

An E node is associated with a developer defined function for arbitrarily complex operations, normally a database access, or a computation on existing data. There are two visiting types for the E nodes. "Once off", the node is visited only once during inference; or "always", whenever the inference passes through the node. The former is for the computation that needs to be done only once whatever the inference result will be, for example, to get the account details of the customer.

An S node in a script statement works like a function call in a programming language. When an S node is visited during inference, the node is replaced by the

```
block subGeneral
        form frmGeneral                     'name of the form
        entry qaiFaultType                  'start node of the block
        exit conExit                        'end node of the block

        if qaiFaultType                     next qabEverywhere
        if qabEverywhere = Yes              next eabAccountCorrect
        if qabEverywhere = No               next qfzFaultLocation
        if qfzFaultLocation                 next qfzFaultTime
        if qfzFaultTime                     next qabKnownFault
        if qabKnownFault = Yes              next qazAdviseCustomer
        if qabKnownFault = No               next qaiTestCall
        if eabAccountCorrect = Yes          next qaiTestCall
        if eabAccountCorrect = No           next qazAdviseCustomer
        if qaiTestCall = Answered           next ...
        ... ...
        if qazAdviseCustomer                next conExit
        ... ...
end block
```

Figure 3. An excerpt of a knowledge base script

body of the corresponding sub-block, and the inference engine needs to activate the form manager to bring the corresponding form onto the screen. We add the restriction that only one entry node and one exit node are allowed for a sub-block.

A C node is used to facilitate the control of the interaction. It is not an operational node, that is, not to be used to collect information. Normally a C node is placed at the end of a sub-block to serve as a uniform exit point, and is associated with a command button, often the Next button. An event subroutine can be associated with the C node to analyse the inference sequence within this sub-block, decide the condition on exit, and generate the diagnostic description. The inference engine always stops at a C node when the inference passes through it. This gives the CSR a chance to review the present screen before clicking on the Next button to advance to another screen.

The inference engine interacts with a CSR only on a Q or C node. E and S nodes are processed without the CSR's intervention. The inference engine maintains a history list of the nodes it has visited. When an input event happens, the engine checks if it is on a node in the history list. If it is, that means it has been processed before, but for some reason the CSR does the operation again, probably to make a correction. In this case, the engine traces back to that node, renews the data storage, and starts inference from that node. If the input is on the node of present attention, the inference engine records it in the history list, stores the data, and starts inference from the node. Otherwise, the input is to a node that has not yet been processed. The engine simply records the data, and stays idle. Next time when the inference comes through this node, the engine will not stop at the node. It reads the stored data, makes a decision, and continues the inference on to the next node.

In the script definition, each block is associated with a form. The form manager's role is to make sure the present screen form includes controls for the present node. Each time an S node is processed, its form is loaded. The form manager provides a form navigation capability through a set command buttons. The CSR can use Previous or Next buttons to move back and forth among consecutive forms.

3.4 The Inference Algorithm

As discussed before, since there cannot be a centralised control program in an event-driven environment, the control algorithm of the inference engine is broken into single step operations. The working state is recorded in an inner data structure to maintain the trace of inference. A CSR input event, such as typing a text string or clicking on an option button, will activate the inference engine. The engine stores the value for the input node, advances to one of its next nodes according to the condition provided by the input, highlights it as the present node, and ends. Figure 4 is a brief description of the inference algorithm. The two parameters to the algorithm are supplied by the calling event subroutine. *Name* is the name of the node the CSR has operated on, and *Value* is the value the node is to obtain. For example, in the GUI screen, if the CSR clicks on the option button "Cannot call out", the click event will trigger a call Inf_Engine("*qai*FaultType", NoCallOut), where NoCallOut is a constant value associated with the button clicked.

PresentNode is a pointer which always points to the present inference node. Initially it is set to the entry node of the main block. When it reaches the exit node of the main block, that is the end of the inference. The inference algorithm also keeps a history record which is a list of all nodes visited previously. Via the pointer and the history record, the inference engine knows if a call is to the past, present, or future node, and processes it accordingly.

The algorithm first records *Value* to the memory of the node *Name*. Then it checks if *Name* is in the history record. If it is, the inference engine resets PresentNode to

```
Inf_Engine ( Name, Value )
    Record Value for Name
    If Name equals name of history record i Then
        Set PresentNode to hist(i)
    End If
    If Name equals PresentNode.name Then
        Find matching next node on condition Value
        Set PresentNode to the next node
    Else
        Return
    End If
    While PresentNode is an S node, or a no-stop Q or E node already has a Value'
        If PresentNode is an S node Then
            Expand the S node to connect the sub-block
        Else
            Find matching next node on condition Value'
        End If
        Advance PresentNode to the next node
    End While
    If PresentNode is a Q node Then
        Highlight the corresponding label on screen
        Return
    ElseIf PresentNode is a C node Then
        Return
    ElseIf PresentNode is an E node Then
        Set Value' to ExeUserFunc(PresentNode)
        Set Name' to PresentNode.name
        Call Inf_Engine (Name', Value')
    End If
    If PresentNode reaches the end of the lattice
        Call Post_Processing
    End If
End Sub
```

Figure 4. The inference algorithm

that node, which makes the condition of the next If statement always true. The second If statement checks if *Name* is the present node. If not, the engine does nothing more, and returns control back to the user interface.

After recording the present node, the engine advances PresentNode to the next node according to the *Value* parameter. The following While loop connects the sub-block definition for an S node, and finds the next node for a Q or E node if the node has been visited before. The value of the node (*Value'*) saved in previous operation is used to decide the next node. The connection of a sub-block is very simple. It assigns next-node links of the S node to the corresponding links of the exit node, and sets the PresentNode to the entry node. This forward linking guarantees a smooth return to one of the next nodes of the S node when the inference within the sub-block has been finished. Because the withdrawal to a previous node is not managed on the lattice knowledge base, no backward linking is needed.

Finally, when coming out of the While loop, the present node must be a "fresh" Q or E node to acquire an input, or a C node. For a Q node, the engine highlights the corresponding label on screen, reminding the CSR it is the recommended input node, and ends itself. The control is handed back to the user interface, assuming the CSR will activate it again. For an E node, the engine calls a function associated with the node (ExeUserFunc), and resumes inference. The difference from processing a Q node is that in processing an E node, there cannot be an input event to activate the inference engine. Therefore, the engine has to retain the control. It appears in the algorithm description as a recursive subroutine call. In the implementation, it is replaced by a Do loop based on the standard tail-recursion eliminating procedure (Aho, Sethi and Ullman 1986). For a C node, the engine just ends.

When the inference engine reaches the end of the lattice, the interaction with the CSR on fault diagnosis is complete. Two sources of diagnostic data are available at this stage. One is the data stored for each individual node, and the other is the inference history record. Analysing these two data structures, the inference engine can decide what the possible fault is and conduct corresponding post processing, like fault reporting, advising, and logging.

This inference algorithm is a highly efficient one due to the use of the lattice knowledge base. Each lattice node has a reference to the node memory, so both its search and data storage have linear complexity. The matching of the node during reasoning also has linear complexity. The inference engine first checks the history record, and then the present inference node. If not found, the process on this node is delayed until the node is passed through.

4 Expert System Implementation

The fault diagnosis expert system is implemented as a module of a helpdesk system which integrates services for all inbound customer calls. The system was developed in Visual Basic under MS Windows environment. The expert system is composed of several components: the script compiler, the inference engine, the fault diagnosis forms, and the collection of E node functions. The source code for the script compiler is 27K. The source code for the inference engine and form manager is 73K. A script file of 16 blocks and 330 rules has been defined for the helpdesk application which creates run time tables of 2200 entries. The inference engine needs another 100 dynamic table entries in its execution. There are 16 fault forms. The source code for E node functions is 28K. The compactness in system architecture makes it very easy to run the expert system on a heavily loaded CSR front-end PC.

Though the system has grown very large and is written in Visual Basic, which is not intended for efficient execution, the only noticeable delay in fault diagnosis is the loading of a new form, which is the normal overhead of using a GUI.

The fault diagnosis expert system provides various kinds of support to the CSRs. It presents relevant questions on screen, accesses system data, calls system functions when they are needed, provides help information to assist CSRs to access other application systems, and highlights the recommended next question to guide the diagnosis. The last feature is particularly welcome by the inexperienced CSRs, which makes training significantly simpler. The expert system alleviates the memory burden on CSRs, shortens the training period for the fault diagnosis process, reduces the effort required by CSRs to access other application systems, and guarantees the collection of all necessary fault symptoms required for fault repair.

During operation, a CSR can shift freely between different components of the system, or any other systems loaded on the desktop. The system development has been completed and the software is under field-trial. A pilot version is running in a real business environment supporting 60 CSRs. National roll out has been scheduled and will be implemented shortly.

The IES concept appears very attractive to another major Telstra business unit in the Public Switched Telephone Service (PSTS). A new project has been started to develop a customer fault service system for PSTS products. IES is used to build the front-end of a client-server system. As the new system will support more CSRs and a range of PSTS products, its compactness in size and ability to quickly define new rules and screens make IES the most suitable candidate for this application environment. One design principle of the new system is to let the business unit edit the rules and screens, while the system kernel is owned by the IT unit and is not to be changed. Thus greater flexibility is provided to the business unit when business rules have to be changed or a new product is to be introduced.

5 Conclusions

This paper presents a new knowledge representation and inference algorithm for interactive fault diagnosis in a GUI environment. We propose the lattice knowledge base data structure which is very efficient both for memory requirements and for searching during inference. The script compilation avoids the disadvantage of hard-coding knowledge into data structures. The transaction-like inference algorithm is designed for an interactive application environment. It provides flexibility to experienced users, as well as guidance to inexperienced users, while still providing an efficient inference mechanism.

The fault diagnosis expert system has been developed as a sub-system of a helpdesk system for a telecommunications application. It alleviates the memory burden on CSRs, shortens the training period for the fault diagnosis process, simplifies CSR access to other application systems, and guarantees the collection of all necessary fault symptoms required for fault repair. The system development has been completed and the software is under field-trial. The response to the field-trial is very encouraging. National roll out has been scheduled and will be implemented shortly. A new application of the expert system is being undertaken to support multiple products and more CSRs.

Acknowledgment

The author would like to thank Muriel de Beler for her contribution in knowledge acquisition and system design. The permission of the Director of Telstra Research Laboratories to publish this material is hereby acknowledged.

References

Aho, A. V. Sethi, R. and Ullman, J. D. (1986) *Compilers Principles, Techniques and tools*, Reading, Mass: Addison-Wesley.

Berry, D. C. (1994) Involving users in expert system development, *Expert Systems*, **11**(1), 23-28.

Dumas, J. S. (1988) *Designing User Interfaces for Software*, Prentice Hall.

Forgy, C. L. (1982) Rete: a fast algorithm for the many pattern/many object pattern match problem, *Artificial Intelligence*, **19**(1), 17-27.

McLaughlin, L. and Christie, R. D. (1994) Are expert system rules really easier to modify?, *International Journal of Engineering Intelligent Systems for Electrical Engineering and Communications*, **2**(4), 263-272.

Sassen, J. M. A. Buiel, E. F. T. and Hoegee, J. H. (1994) A laboratory evaluation of a human operator support system, *International Journal of Human-Computer Studies*, **40**, 895-931.

Suh, C. K. and Suh, E H. (1993) Using human factor guidelines for developing expert systems, *Expert Systems*, **10**(3), 151-156.

Vale, A. A. Goncalves, M. J. and Vale, Z. A. (1992) Improving Man-machine interaction in control centres, *IEEE Power Engineering Society 1992 Summer Meeting*, SM 602-3, USA.

An Intelligent Education System Which Supports Scientific Thinking: *Galileo*
- Philosophy And Basic Architecture -

Kumiko Ishino[1], Katuo Sugai[2] and Riichiro Mizoguchi[3]

[1] Industrial Technology Center of WAKAYAMA Pref.
60, Ogura, Wakayama-City, 649-62, Japan

[2] Faculty of human sciences, Osaka University
1-2, Yamadaoka, Suita-City, 565, Japan

[3] The Institute of Scientific and Industrial Research, Osaka University
8-1, Mihogaoka, Ibaraki-City, 567, Japan

Abstract. This paper discusses, Galileo, an Intelligent Education System which facilitates learners' scientific thinking. In the discussion we will focus on the concepts behind the designing of Galileo, and the guidance that it provides. First, we will discuss how to support scientific thinking. For this purpose, we will discuss naive knowledge which has been formed through learner's daily experiences. A learner who has naive knowledge cannot think about a given situation scientifically because the naive knowledge interferes with the appropriate understanding of the situations. Next, we present a design of Galileo focusing on teaching interaction and the learner models that enables it.

1 Introduction

In order to build a system which adaptively supports learners' scientific thinking to the learners' comprehension, it is important to consider how humans understand a phe -nomena. Moreover, it is also important to understand in-depth how to support such learning from the psychological point of view. Galileo[9][10][11][12][13][14] is proposed by modeling the understanding of a learner based on the results obtained in pedagogy and psychology, and by describing the support method.

First of all, we will pay a close attention to naive knowledge, which learners have before they study. This naive knowledge is vague and is often not compatible with scientific knowledge. It is based on daily experiences. Even university students who have been educated in Engineering have naive knowledge[22], and they use formalized knowledge like physics laws only when they solve school type problems in examinations[21]. This is mainly caused by the conventional teaching methodology which tries to transfer formalized knowledge without considering the naive knowledge which learners already have. Therefore, it is important to help learners build formalized knowledge by expanding naive knowledge. In order to do this, the existence of the naive knowledge has to be taken into consideration in designing the system. With the help of the system, learners can build important basic knowledge to understand quantitative knowledge[5]. By quantitative knowledge we mean the knowledge which can be described as the parameters of physical equations and a kind of the formalized knowledge. By basic knowledge we mean the knowledge which is also a kind of the formalized knowledge, but which is tightly connected with daily experience and is consistent with scientific knowledge.

Galileo aims to provide such supports, although it is a challenging goal. However as we can find typical patterns in naive knowledge[2], careful analysis of the factors which make learning difficult and some extending the factors would enable us to realize such support. For this, not a few available factors in human science will be analyzed.

Because naive knowledge is easily affected by something the learner perceives, we also investigated human recognition systems.

This paper, mainly discusses how Galileo presents a phenomena to learners and builds a learner model of a comprehension state of the learner who has naive knowledge.

The targeted knowledge domain of Galileo is the motion of an object.

In the next section, after the discussion of the support to facilitate of scientific thinking, the obstruction factors against scientific thinking are investigated, and, effective ways of support are considered, taking human recognition systems into account.

Section 3 presents the details of Galileo.

Section 4 discusses the future work.

2 Support of scientific thinking

We define scientific thinking as building concepts of the world by understanding phys -ical laws through extending the world model based on the formalization of intuitive comprehension of causality[8][9].

In other words, it requires many important activities such as recognition of facts, consideration and comprehension of causal relations, formalization of concepts and facts, consideration and comprehension of relation among the physical laws, verbaliza -tion and graphical representation of the laws, recognition of the facts which cannot be explained, generation of hypotheses, consideration of the experiment environments and tools for hypothesis verification, setting up appropriate environments, experiment, validation and verification of hypotheses, and extension of the world model.

Next, let us investigate science education methods. In science education, learners are usually provided environments in which they can conduct experiments, in order to facilitate learning through experience. Such learning is well-accepted by many in the field. We basically agree with this learning style, but, when a learner is provided only an environment in which he/she conducts experiment without any guide, it is often hand for him/her to understand the phenomena only by observation[20], and he/she cannot discover anything teacher wants him/her to learn[15][24]. Even worse, the environment often strengthen naive knowledge rather than modifying his/her incorrect knowledge[7][18]. In addition, learners are often ignorant of their comprehension state, so, a simple message indicating their contradiction cannot make them notice their misconceptions[23]. This is also because the learners who have inappropriate naive knowledge cannot extend the world model properly. This difficulty is deeply related to the human recognition systems.

2.1 Naive knowledge

As mentioned before, we will pay a close attention to naive knowledge, which learners have before they study. This naive knowledge is vague and is often not compatible with scientific knowledge. It is based on daily experiences such as follows:

- Objects fall straight downward [17]
- Every moving object receives force [6]

:

The naive knowledge is easily affected by what it also and how learners perceive, and depends on their causal understanding[3][19].

The factors which make learning difficult include:

- Learners are ignorant of their naive knowledge.
- The application range of the naive knowledge is narrower than that of the formalized knowledge[4].
- Because the naive knowledge prevents learners from proper understanding of phenomena, they cannot comprehend or extend physical laws.

This analysis suggests the necessity of the following supports:

- Allow learners to recognize their naive knowledge.
- Allow learners to extend their naive knowledge.
- Allow learners to comprehend the situation properly.
- Get learners motivated to analyze and investigate the difficulties they have.

The support methods which allow learners to recognize their naive knowledge include:

- Presentation of situations and to allow learners to predict their outcome.
  This is effective because naive knowledge changes with causal understanding depending on the situation(s).
- To allow learners to recognize the causal relations of the predicted outcome.
- To allow learners to define related concepts.

:

Support methods we need in addition to the above are ones which let this naive knowledge extend:

- Presenting learners events they cannot explain using their naive knowledge and to allow them to compare the events with those they understand.
- To allow learners to generate a hypothesis about the situation.
- To allow learners to set up an experiment environment where they can confirm the hypothesis.
- To allow learners to recognize events in the simulation.
- To allow learners to recognize the difference between conflicting events.
- To allow learners to understand the causality of the events they observe.
- To allow learners to formulate laws explaining the events which they observe.

:

2.2 Human recognition systems

On the other hand, the following are known as facts concerning human recognition systems. When humans perform a task which requires them to recall visual images, it is easier for them to simultaneously perform verbal level thinking than to simultaneously perform another visual level process, on the other hand, when they are involved in recalling verbal information, it is easier for them to simultaneously process visual information than to perform another verbal task[1]. In summary, human recognition systems have two different systems related to visual and verbal processing. And it is known that the two systems complimentarily act with each other[16].

Typical interactions between the two in the understanding of phenomena include:

- Recognition of the phenomena presented verbally.
- Recalling various images associated with the phenomena.
- Verbal explication of the image recalled.
- Verbal recognition of causality.

:

Proper understanding of phenomena requires these operations.

Support for augmentation of the capability of these include:

- Verbal presentation of situations reflecting the learners' understanding state and the education goal, etc.
- Presentation of a situation generated by simulation of the phenomena for learners who cannot understand it at the verbal level.
- The support which allow learners to envision the situation presented at the verbal level.
- The support for describing and verbalizing of learners' images.
- The support for setting up conditions for a simulated environment.
- The support to recognize causality in the situation presented by visualization.

: [11][13]

Therefore, in order to support scientific thinking, Galileo has to be able to provide verbal and nonverbal supports and be able to recognize the difference in contexts between the learner's comprehension states induced by verbal stimuli and those induced by image level stimuli generated by simulation. Furthermore, Galileo should consider the difference in effects of many types of supports[11][13] in generating educational supports.

3 The design of Galileo

3.1 Overview

On the basis of the above discussion, we designed Galileo so that it could dynamical-

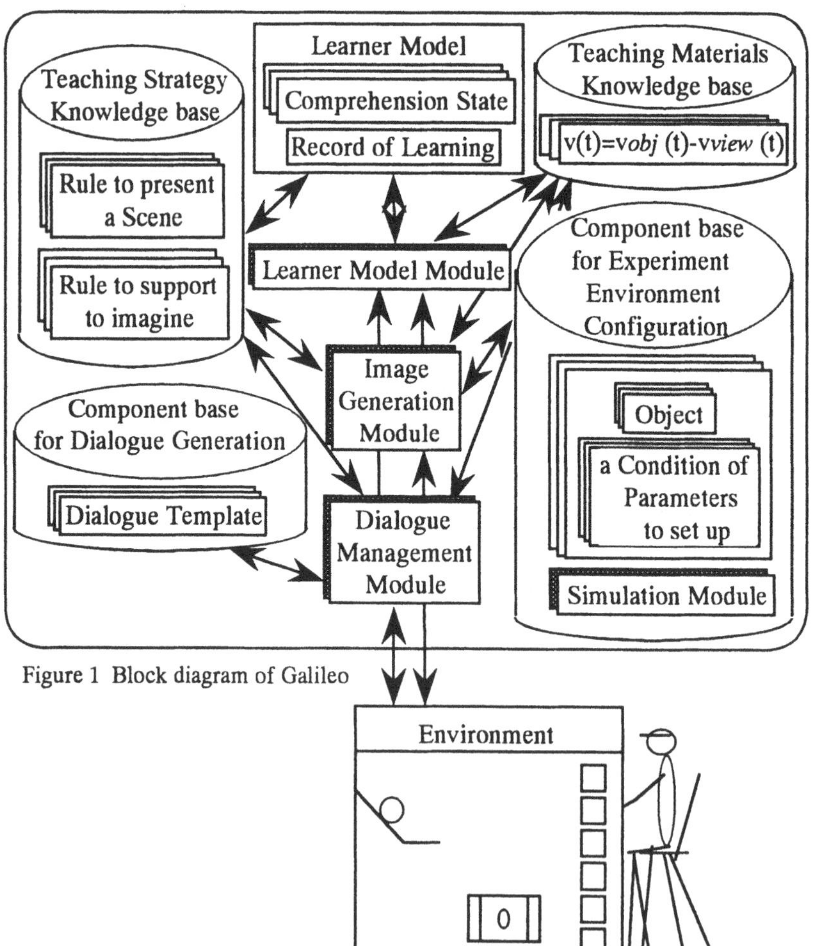

Figure 1 Block diagram of Galileo

ly generate environments compatible with the learner's comprehension state and provide suitable guides and simulation. To do this, information about learners and the supports that Galileo performs have to be effectively organized in the system by investigating of the constituents of the learners' models and presenting factors of learners' scientific thinking together with their grain size of the primitives used for describing concepts and relations among them[12][14].

Fig.1 shows the block diagram of Galileo. It consists of the learner model module, the teaching strategy knowledge base, the component base for experiment environment configuration, the component base for dialogue generation, which consists of dialogue templates, the dialogue management module which organizes dialogue, the image generation module which presents visual images, and the teaching material knowledge base which consists of equations as shown in Fig.2 which shows physical laws.

$l(t)=(l_x(t),l_y(t),\ldots)$ ↑ **object's location to be displayed**

$v(t)=(v_x(t),v_y(t),\ldots)$ ↑ **object's velocity to be displayed**

$l(t)=l(t-\Delta t)+v(t-\Delta t)\cdot\Delta t$

$v(t)= v_{obj}(t) - v_{obs}(t)$

$v_{obj}(t)$ ↑ **object's velocity**; $v_{obs}(t)$ ↑ **observer's velocity**

$v_{obj}(t)= v_{obj}(t-\Delta t) + F_{obj}(t-\Delta t)\cdot\Delta t/m_{obj}$

$v_{obj}(t-\Delta t)$ ↑ **object's velocity at (t-Δt)**; $F_{obj}(t-\Delta t)\cdot\Delta t/m_{obj}$ ↑ **the velocity which has added to the object during Δt**

$v_{obs}(t)= v_{obs}(t-\Delta t) + F_{obs}(t-\Delta t)\cdot\Delta t/m_{obs}$

$v_{obs}(t-\Delta t)$ ↑ **observer's velocity at (t-Δt)**; $F_{obs}(t-\Delta t)\cdot\Delta t/m_{obs}$ ↑ **the velocity which has added to the object to observe during Δt**

$F_{objx}(t)= +\kappa\cdot m_{obj}\cdot v_{objx}(t) + f_{ax}(t)$

$\kappa\cdot m_{obj}\cdot v_{objx}(t)$ ↑ **friction by medium**; $f_{ax}(t)$ ↑ **other force e.g. reaction**

$F_{objy}(t)= -m_{obj}\cdot g + \rho\cdot g\cdot V_{obj} + \kappa\cdot m_{obj}\cdot v_{objy}(t) + f_{oy}(t)$

$m_{obj}\cdot g$ ↑ **gravity**; $\rho\cdot g\cdot V_{obj}$ ↑ **buoyancy by medium**; $\kappa\cdot m_{obj}\cdot v_{objy}(t)$ ↑ **friction by medium**; $f_{oy}(t)$ ↑ **other force e.g. reaction**

:

Figure 2 Formulas and parameters

3.2 Teaching strategy knowledge base

The teaching strategy knowledge base consists of the rules for presenting experimental environments and those for instructive interactions.

The former rules are classified into three kinds as follows:

1. Verbal presentation
2. Setting up the parameters' conditions
3. Selection of components for the environment configuration

The latter are fired responding to the education goals, the learner's naive knowledge, the learner model, the learning history, the learner's response time, the contents presented.

Such rules include:

4. Suggesting simulation
5. Getting learners motivated to analyze the problems
6. To allow learners to compare the phenomena they comprehend with those they do not
7. To allow learners to envision the phenomena from the verbal presentation
8. To allow learners to verbalize their visual image
9. To allow learners to draw their image visually
10. To allow learners to verbalize the state of their recognition what they observe
11. Explaining the phenomena that learners are observing
12. Suggesting points learners should watch
13. Suggesting methods which make it easier for learners to interpret the phenomena they observe
14. To allow learners to define the causal relations in the phenomena they imagine

:

In naive knowledge, visual factors strongly affect visual image formation[1]. In order to allow learners to recognize their naive knowledge more effectively, Galileo first presents a phenomenon verbally (1.), then allows them to envision the verbal stimulus (7.), to verbalize it (8.), and to define the causal relation (14.).

3.3 Component base for Dialogue Generation

The component base for Dialogue Generation consists of templates for units of dialogue. Some examples are shown below. $...$ shows variables which are instantiated according to the context.

Setting up a situation:

• Assume a person is observing an $object$ is released from a rocket $transportation's state$ $the state of transportation's velocity$ $place$ through a monitor. (a)

:

Support for envision point:

• How does this $object except transportation$ move ? (b)

:

Support for verbalization:
• Choose one from: $patterns of responses$, I don't know. (c)

:

Support for defining the causal relation:
• What causes $the parameter of education goal$ to change $a scene (t>t1)$? (d)

:

When the teaching strategy rule fired suggests that verbal interaction is appropriate in the context, the dialogue management module selects a dialogue template and organizes the dialogue according to the scene selected at that time in the environment, the educational goal in the teaching materials knowledge, and the learner model, and finally presents the dialogue on the screen.

Now, let us explain the scene which will be presented in the next section. If strategy 1. "Verbal presentation" is fired, the dialogue management module selects dialogue template (a) from component base for dialogue generation, and determines the words according to the parameters set in 3.4 as follows:

$transportation's state$:←flying <(1)>
$the state of the transportation's velocity$:←at a constant velocity <(1)>
$place$:←in a space <(3)>

:

The number in parentheses shows those attached to formulas which will be discussed in 3.4.

The words are thus specified and the sentence shown in Fig.3 is presented.

Galileo: Assume a person is observing an object is released from a rocket flying at a constant velocity in a space through a monitor.

Figure 3 Presentation of scenes by language

The dialogue template will be used in the order of (b), (c), (d)...

3.4 Representation of learner model

The knowledge representation of the learner model, which is a foundation of knowledge expression in the Intelligent Education System, will be considered below.

3.4.1 The model at the parameter level

First, we organize the knowledge in the formalized world which rules the motion of objects, that is, the equations of motion will be put in order, parameters necessary for the purpose are identified, and the concepts of motion which our system treats will be put in order. The various state of learners' comprehension of the motion concepts are analyzed, first. Then, based on the result of the analysis, the levels of description are determined. We also adapt concepts which are related to the object's motion observed in the daily life, such as situation, velocity, acceleration, inertia, time, mass, volume, the velocity of the observing point, gravity, viscosity, buoyancy, reaction and friction[10] (see Fig.2). The component base for environment configuration consists of the parts which are presented in the scenes. In other words, it consists of objects to present, the conditions of parameters which specify the motion under consideration (this can be described by using parameters shown to Fig.2.), the tools for changing the conditions of parameters, the tools for executing simulation, and the response pat -terns of learner.

Using these components, the motion of objects in the various scenes can be simulated[10].

An example can be set up as follows:

The objects to present and the condition of related parameters:

- a rocket: velocity $v_r(t)$=constant (1)
- an object: velocity(t<t1) $v_{obj}(t)=v_r(t)$ (2)

:

The setting of other parameters:

- place : gravity g=0 , density $\rho=0$, coefficient of viscosity $\kappa=0$ (3)
- observer : the point of observation : $v_{obs}(t) = 0$ (4)

:

The pattern of responses (t>t1):

$$(v_x(t) > 0,\ v_y(t) = 0),\ (v_x(t) > 0,\ v_y(t) > 0),\ (v_x(t) = 0,\ v_y(t) = 0) \quad (5)$$

3.4.2 The model of naive knowledge level

If we take the view that humans understand motion on the basis of this formulation, then Fig.2 presents the parameter level primitives to express the concept construction of humans.

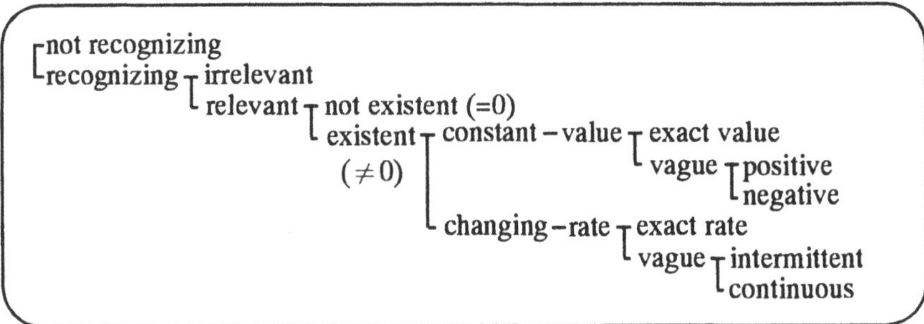

Figure 4 The recognition states of parameters

Learner models can be expressed in terms of the above parameters, the recognition state of them (Fig.4), the causal relations, and the context. We can identify several rec

-ognition states for each parameter which is organized as shown in Fig.4. At the top level, there are two states such as "recognizing" and "not recognizing" the exist -ence of the parameter. The former is further divided into two states: the learner recognizes the relevance of the parameter or not. The positive state is divided into two states, one is, the learner recognizes that the parameter is zero. This means that the quantity of the parameter represents does not exist. The other is that the learner understands the quantity of the parameter exists($\neq 0$). This state is further divided into two states: 1) the parameter is constant. 2) the parameter is changing. In the first case, the value that the learners recognize can be exact, that is, it can be vague, the learners recognize the value only as positive or negative. In the second case, the rate that the learners recognize can be exact, or it can be vague, in which case, they recognize it only as intermittent or continuous.

3.5 Building a learner model

The learner model is built on the assumption that humans think logically. Accordingly, learner's understanding through visual interaction and that through verbal interaction are separately modeled using the supports practiced and the context. This enables the system to alter the teaching behavior.

If contradictions occur between the two models, verbalization of the visual image and the visualization of the verbal comprehension of the phenomena can be the educational goals.

Also, the learner model building is done at the level deeper than v(t)=0 used by the dialogue, as investigated in 3.4. The learner model building at the level of "v(t)=0" can be done by describing the typical response pattern corresponding to the scene. The learner's concept construction at the deeper level also can be inferred from the description of a scene and the educational goal which are selected, and the learner model which is represented in terms of parameters which are indicating the motion of the ob -ject, the causal relations, and the recognition states of parameters. The learner model building is discussed below.

Now, assume that rule 7. fires and dialogue template (b) for supporting visualization is selected, after that, rule 8. to verbalize fires, then dialogue template (c) is selected.

Then, the sentence is presented in Fig.5. If a learner answers "still" to this ques-

Galileo: How does this object move ?

:

Galileo: Choose one from: linear motion, parabolic motion, still, I don't know.

Figure 5 An example of verbal interaction

tion, it means the parameter's state is constant.

And the learner model is expressed

$$v(t)=0 \qquad ...(A).$$

This is an inappropriate comprehension state. It means "$v_{obj}(t)-v_{obs}(t)$" is constant (zero) (See Fig.2). The Fig.6 help us understand the state of learners' recognition of the each parameter. In the Fig.6, states of parameters are represented by binomial formulas, for example, x of "x=y+z". And the "First" in Fig.6 means the states of the first parameters like y in the equation, then the "Second" means the states of the second parameters like z in the equation. For instance, if the first and the second parameters are positive (>0), it is positive (>0) because the first parameter is added to the second one.

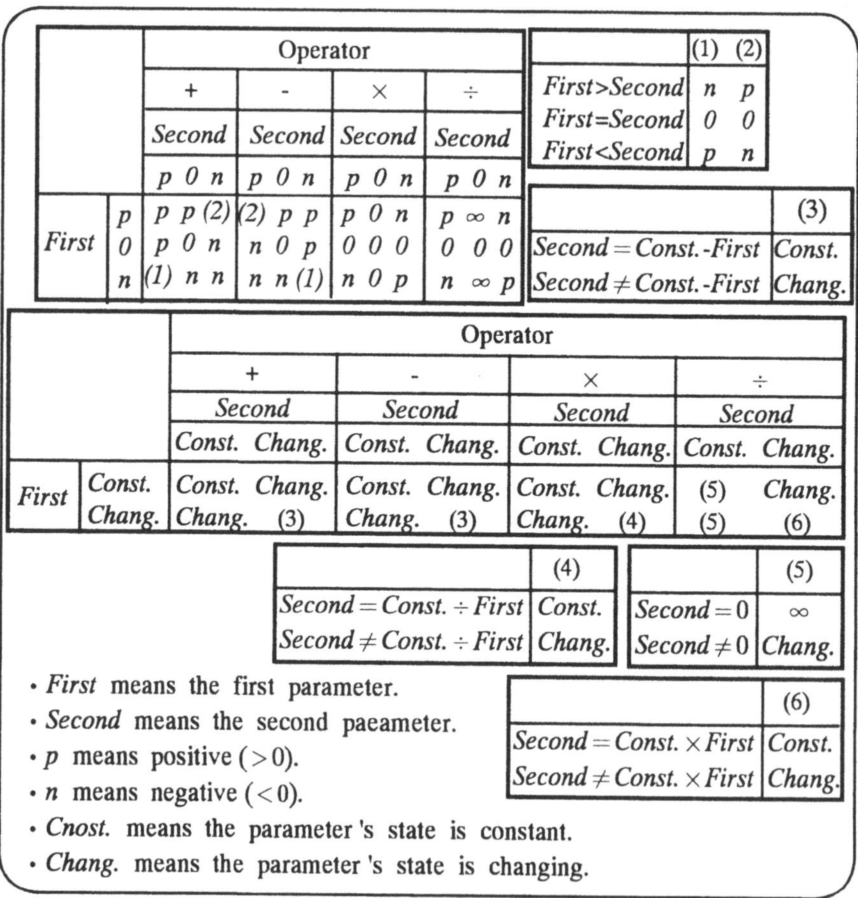

		Operator +			Operator -			Operator ×			Operator ÷		
	Second	p	0	n	p	0	n	p	0	n	p	0	n
First	p	p	p	(2)	(2)	p	p	p	0	n	p	∞	n
	0	p	0	n	n	0	p	0	0	0	0	0	0
	n	(1)	n	n	n	n	(1)	n	0	p	n	∞	p

	(1)	(2)
First>Second	*n*	*p*
First=Second	*0*	*0*
First<Second	*p*	*n*

	(3)
Second = Const.-First	*Const.*
Second ≠ Const.-First	*Chang.*

		Operator +		Operator -		Operator ×		Operator ÷	
	Second	*Const.*	*Chang.*	*Const.*	*Chang.*	*Const.*	*Chang.*	*Const.*	*Chang.*
First	*Const.*	*Const.*	*Chang.*	*Const.*	*Chang.*	*Const.*	*Chang.*	(5)	*Chang.*
	Chang.	*Chang.*	(3)	*Chang.*	(3)	*Chang.*	(4)	(5)	(6)

	(4)
Second = Const. ÷ First	*Const.*
Second ≠ Const. ÷ First	*Chang.*

	(5)
Second = 0	∞
Second ≠ 0	*Chang.*

	(6)
Second = Const. × First	*Const.*
Second ≠ Const. × First	*Chang.*

- *First* means the first parameter.
- *Second* means the second paeameter.
- *p* means positive (>0).
- *n* means negative (<0).
- *Cnost.* means the parameter 's state is constant.
- *Chang.* means the parameter 's state is changing.

Figure 6 The recognition states of parameters which are represented by binomial formulas

Because when parameter v(t) is constant in (A), we can know that these two parameters $v_{obj}(t)$ and $v_{obs}(t)$ are constant, or that the both parameters are changing (not con

-stant) and the second parameter $v_{obs}(t)$ is equal to the result of the subtraction of the first parameter $v_{obj}(t)$ from the constant value. We can also know that because the parameter v(t) is zero in the equation (A), the two parameters are zero, or the value of the first parameter is same as that of the second parameter. (In this case the value is not zero.). Other cases that we can think of are 1) learners cannot recognize these parameters or one of them, 2) they cannot recognize the relevance of the parameters (/a parameter) to the phenomenon (See Fig.4). To identify the learner's comprehension state, rule14. fires to allow the learner to define the causal relationship in the phenom -ena that they imagine, and the corresponding dialogue templates are selected in the component base for dialogue generation. The following as an example of dialogues could be generated by the system. The learner model can be expressed by the dialogue of Fig.7 as shown below.

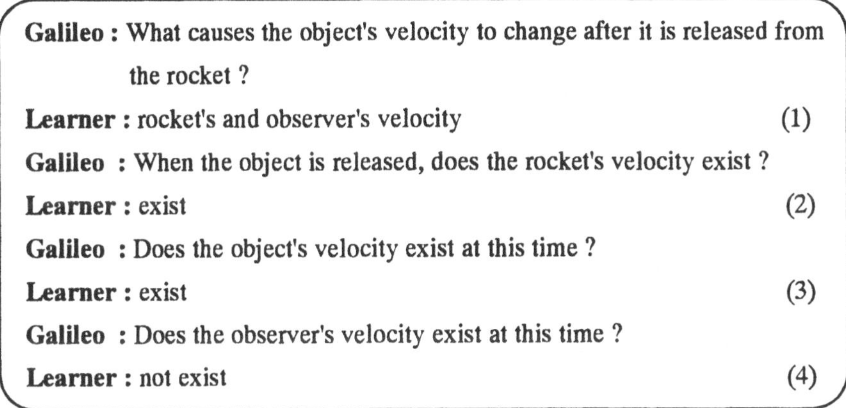

Galileo : What causes the object's velocity to change after it is released from the rocket ?
Learner : rocket's and observer's velocity (1)
Galileo : When the object is released, does the rocket's velocity exist ?
Learner : exist (2)
Galileo : Does the object's velocity exist at this time ?
Learner : exist (3)
Galileo : Does the observer's velocity exist at this time ?
Learner : not exist (4)

Figure 7 Support to define causal relation

by (1) in t>t1
$v_{obj}(t)$__$v_r(t)$: relevant ...(B)
$v_{obj}(t)$__$v_{obs}(t)$: relevant ...(C)

by (2) $v_r(t1) \neq 0$ (appropriate) ...(D)
by (3) $v_{obj}(t1) \neq 0$ (appropriate) ...(E)
by (4) $v_{obs}(t1) = 0$ (appropriate) ...(F)

But if (A) and (E) are right, (F) is inappropriate. And if (A) and (F) are right, (E) is inappropriate. This learner's vision images(A) contradicts verbal comprehension (B), (C), (D), (E), and (F). He/she may have the naive knowledge that the observer's veloc -ity is equal to the object' velocity. Or he/she may be imagining the situation that the rocket's velocity is zero. So it is more effective to set educational goals for him/her which allow him/her to draw from the image he/she visualized allow him/her to make a formula based on his/her visual image or verbal comprehension, or allow him /her to verbalize or draw an image from the formula.

But if the learner only says "rocket's velocity" at (1), and gives the same "exist" at both (2) and (3), and "I don't know." at (4), he/she does not recognize the concept of the observer's velocity. And he/she has the naive knowledge that the observer's velocity is equal to the rocket's velocity. It is effective to set educational goals for this learner which allow him/her to recognize the concept of $v_{obs}(t)$, that it is equal to zero, and the causal relation between $v_{obj}(t)$ and $v_{obs}(t)$.

If a learner imagines the environment on the earth, he/she responds to the parabolic motion in Fig.5. In this case, it is effective to set the educational goal to allow him/her to recognize the difference between being on earth and in space.

The models for other learners can be built in the same way as above.

4 Concluding Remarks

The supports to facilitate learners' scientific thinking have been discussed and Galileo is proposed. Among Galileo several features, we focused on the presentation schema, including verbal and/or visual presentations, learner's comprehension of them, and the building of a learner model. In chapter 2, the design of the system which considers hu -mans recognition systems was proposed, but in the system, at this stage, it cannot judge whether the learner is thinking visually or verbally. But the system can understand how learners comprehend the phenomena and learner the physical law behind them when they were provided visual support, verbal support or both. Further study is necessary to acquire more detail information concerning the state and process of learner's thinking. Other supports not mentioned in this paper because of the space limitation were described in other papers[9][10][11][12][13].

References

1. Brooks L., Spatial and verbal components of the act of recall', Canad. F. Psychol., 22, pp.349-368, 1968
2. A. Caramazza, M. McClosky, B.Green, 'Naive beliefs in "sophisticated" subjects: misconceptions about trajectories of objects' , Cognition, 9, pp.117-123, 1981
3. J. Clement, ' Students' preconception in introductory mechanics ' , American Journal of Physics, 50 (1), pp.66-71, 1982
4. Erickson G. L., 'Children's Conceptions of heat and temperature', Science Education, 63(2), pp.221-230, 1979
5. R. Gamble, 'Simple equations in physics' , EUR. J. EDUC., Vol.8, No.1, pp.27-37, 1986
6. I. Galili and V. Bar, 'Motion implies force : where to expect vestiges of the misconception ?' , INT. J. SCI. EDUC., Vol.14, No.1, pp.63-81, 1992
7. Gunston R. F. and White R. T., 'Understanding of Gravity', Science Education, 65(3), pp.291-299, 1981
8. K. Ishino, 'The consideration of physics education for example electromagnetism' , Osakakyouiku University Thesis, 1989
9. K. Ishino, M. Ikeda and R. Mizoguchi 'Conceptual design of an intelligent tutoring system which promotes scientific thinking from plural view points' , Proceedings of

the 7th Annual Conference of Japanese Society for Artificial Intelligence, pp.721-724, 1993

10. K. Ishino, M. Ikeda and R. Mizoguchi, 'Design of an intelligent education system which supports scientific thinking', Proceedings of the 18th Annual Conference of Japan Society for CAI, pp.67-70, 1993
11. K. Ishino and R. Mizoguchi, 'Support strategies of Galileo: Intelligent Education System which supports comprehension', Proceedings of the 8th Annual Conference of Japanese Society for Artificial Intelligence, pp.761-764, 1994
12. K. Ishino and R. Mizoguchi, 'Concepts Network of Galileo: Intelligent Education System Which Supports Comprehension', Proceedings of the 9th Annual Conference of Japanese Society for Artificial Intelligence, pp.573-576, 1995
13. K. Ishino, K. Sugai and R. Mizoguchi, 'Discussion about an intelligent education system which supports scientific thinking', Japanese Society for Information and Systems in Education Report of research, Vol.95, No.2, pp.19-28, 1995
14. K. Ishino, K. Sugai and R. Mizoguchi, 'An Intelligent Education System: Galileo which supports scientific thinking -Guidance and modeling through verbal indication of situation-', Transactions of Japanese Society for Information and Systems in Education, Vol.13, No.1, 1996
15. Koertge N., 'TOWARD AN INTEGRATION OF CONTENT AND METHOD IN THE SCIENCE CURRICULUM', Curriculum Theory Network, 4, pp. 26-44, 1970
16. M.Denis, 'LES IMAGES MENTALES', Presses Universitaires de France, 1979
17. M. McCloskey, A. Washburn and L. Felch, 'Intuitive Physics: The Straight -Down Belief and Its Origin', Journal of Experimental Psychology: Learning, Memory and Cognition, Vol.9, No.4, pp.636-649, 1983
18. Rowell J. A. and Dawson C. J., 'Laboratory counter examples and the growth of understanding in science', EUR. J. SCI. EDUC., Vol.5, No.2, pp.203-215, 1983
19. Elaine Reynoso, H., Enrique Fierro, H. and Gerrdo Torres, O., 'The alternative frameworks presented by Mexican students and teachers concerning the free fall of bodies', EUR. J. SCI. EDUC., Vol.15, No.2, pp.127-138, 1993
20. Sere. M. - G., 'A study of some frameworks used by pupils aged 11 to 13 years in the interpretation of air pressure', EUR. J. SCI. EDUC., Vol.4, No.3, pp.299-309, 1982
21. Solomon J., 'Learning about energy : how pupils think in two domains', EUR. J. SCI. EDUC., Vol.5, No.1, pp.49-59, 1983
22. Viennot L., 'Spontaneous Reasoning in Elementary Dynamics', EUR. J. SCI. EDUC., Vol.1, No.2, pp.205-221, 1979
23. S. Vosniadou, 'Fostering Conceptual Change : The Role of Computer-Based Environments, Computer-Based Learning Environments and Problem Solving', NATO ASI Series, Series F : Computer and Systems Sciences, Vol.84, pp.149-162, 1992
24. Wellington J. J., 'What's supposed to happen sir ? : some problems with discovery learning', School Science Review, 63, pp.163-173, 1981

Acknowledgement

We'd like to thank Mr. Kouji Kimura for helping us with Fig.6., and also thank Ms. Hiromi Taniguchi for her helping us with improve English.

A Unified Approach to Handling Uncertainty During Cooperative Consultations*

Bhavani Raskutti[1] and Ingrid Zukerman[2]

[1] Telstra Research Laboratories, Clayton, VICTORIA 3168, AUSTRALIA
[2] Department of Computer Science, Monash University, Clayton, VICTORIA 3168, AUSTRALIA

Abstract. In this paper, we present a unified approach to handling uncertainty during plan inference in cooperative consultations. This approach assists with the following aspects of the plan inference process: inferring a user's intentions among a number of possibilities, deciding whether to admit an unlikely interpretation of the user's request or to actively acquire information from the user, determining whether a perceived ambiguity in a user's request is to be resolved by heuristics or by soliciting information from the user, and deciding whether a recognized intention is sufficiently detailed so that a plan may be proposed to satisfy it. We define an information-theoretic measure which allows us to determine the amount of information in an interpretation of a user's request, and show how this measure is combined with probabilities of interpretations to give preference to interpretations that are better defined. Our approach is implemented as part of a computerized consultant that operates as a travel agent.

1 Introduction

Consider the query "`Can I drop numerical analysis?`" from a student to a course advisor. In order to provide a helpful response to the student, the course advisor must make a number of decisions. Firstly, the course advisor (the consultant in this situation) must infer the user's intention from a number of possibilities. Secondly, if the advisor cannot infer an intention at all (e.g., the advisor believes that this student has not registered for this subject), then s/he must decide between admitting an unlikely interpretation of the user's request (e.g., accepting that the user may be referring to a different subject) and active acquisition of information from the user. Thirdly, if the advisor is unable to choose between two or more possible intentions (e.g., s/he is not sure if the student wants to drop the subject because s/he wants to avoid failing or because s/he does not like the lecturer), then s/he must determine whether the ambiguity is to be resolved by heuristics or by soliciting information from the user. Lastly, when a unique intention is inferred (e.g., the advisor has determined that the student is dropping the subject because s/he is not interested in it), the advisor must decide if the inferred intention is sufficiently detailed so that a plan may be proposed to satisfy it (e.g., is there enough information about the student's degree aspirations to determine if dropping the subject is a valid plan?).

* The permission of the Director of Telstra Research Laboratories to publish this work is gratefully acknowledged.

The first of these processes, namely inferring intentions, has been addressed by a number of researchers [10, and references therein]. The incorporation of intention inference capabilities into computerized consultants has enabled a range of cooperative behaviours, such as supplying more information than what is explicitly requested [1] and responding to ill-formed queries [5]. The second process, namely dealing with intention recognition failures, has been addressed in [7]. The third process, namely acquiring information to resolve plan ambiguity, has been discussed in [12, 16, 17]. The fourth process, namely determining whether an intention is sufficiently detailed, has not been addressed.

In this paper, we present a unified approach to the execution of these processes. To this effect, we define an information-theoretic measure to assess the amount of relevant information in an interpretation of a user's requirements (Section 2), and show how this measure may be combined with probabilities of interpretations to assist in choosing the interpretation intended by a user (Section 3). This measure is also used to determine if the selected interpretation is sufficiently detailed to attempt planning (Section 4), and, if the interpretation lacks detail, it assists in making a decision regarding whether to pose a query to acquire additional details and what the content of the query should be (Section 5). Our approach is implemented as part of a computerized consultant that operates as a travel agent.

2 The Information Content Measure

In order to assess the amount of information in an interpretation of a user's requirements, it is first necessary to define an interpretation. An interpretation, in the context of cooperative consultations, consists of a sequence of action instances, where each action instance specifies a domain action with a number of instantiated parameters. For example, the interpretation that John intends to fly to Sydney on the 1st of January 1995 consists of one action instance that specifies the domain action of TAKE-PLANE. The parameters *destination*, *departure-date* and *departure-time* of this action are instantiated.

The amount of relevant information, i.e., the *information content* of an interpretation, needs to reflect both our knowledge and our ignorance about this interpretation. Our knowledge about an interpretation depends on two factors: (1) what we know about the interpretation, and (2) how certain we are about what we know. Our ignorance is taken into account only to the extent the things we do not know affect our ability to perform the task at hand.

2.1 Information Content of a Parameter

The information content of a parameter in an action instance must reflect (1) our knowledge about the parameter, (2) our certainty that this knowledge has been correctly inferred, and (3) how our ignorance of this parameter (if any) affects our information regarding the action instance. These observations are implemented by defining the information content of a parameter in terms of the following factors: (1) its *specificity*, which is defined as the reciprocal of the number of values assigned to this parameter; (2) its *strength* or *certainty*, which depends on the source of information from which this parameter was obtained; and (3) its *significance*, which depends on the importance of this parameter's definition (or our lack of ignorance about this parameter) for the overall definition of the action instance. Borrowing from Information Theory [14], the information content of a parameter p, $IC(p)$, is defined as follows:

$$IC(p) = \begin{cases} \log_2 \frac{S(p)}{N(p) \times Sig(p)} & \text{if } N(p) \neq 1 \\ \log_2 S(p) & \text{otherwise,} \end{cases} \tag{1}$$

where $N(p)$, $S(p)$ and $Sig(p)$ are defined below.[3]

$N(p)$ is the number of values assigned to p. It is 1 when a parameter's value is inferred exactly. Otherwise, it is the number of possible values that can be assigned to the parameter given the information at hand. The greater the value of $N(p)$, the less we know about this parameter, and hence the lower the information content of this parameter. For parameters with specific values, this is exactly the number of values inferred, e.g., if the destination is known to be either Melbourne or Sydney, then $N(p)$ is 2. For parameters within a range, $N(p)$ is determined on the basis of $N_u(p)$, the $N(p)$ of an uninstantiated parameter. $N_u(p)$ is an estimate of the number of values that could be assigned to an uninstantiated parameter p if nothing is known about it, e.g., 120 for departure time, since 120 flights depart from the airport every day.[4] Now, if the departure time is inferred to be between 3 p.m. and 6 p.m., then $N(p)$ is calculated as a fraction of $N_u(p)$ as follows:

$$N(p) = \frac{120 = N_u(p)}{\left(\frac{24 = (\text{Number of hours in a day})}{3 = (6\,\text{pm} - 3\,\text{pm})}\right)} = 15.$$

$S(p)$ is the strength or certainty associated with p. It is a measure of our certainty that the values inferred for this parameter are indeed correct. The strength of a parameter is the strength of the inference that was used to derive the value of the parameter. It is proportional to the reliability of the information source on which this inference is based [12]. Thus, inferences based on reliable sources have a higher strength than inferences based on unreliable sources. Inferences based on a user's statements have the greatest strength, namely 1, and the least reliable inferences, which are based on common-sense notions, have the lowest strength.

$Sig(p)$ is the significance of the parameter p. It measures the effect of our lack of knowledge regarding this parameter on the overall information content of an action instance. It is proportional to the importance of the parameter's definition for the definition of the action instance. The significance of a parameter is domain dependent. For example, while a travel agent cannot book a trip if its destination is not exactly specified, s/he can proceed with a booking if the time

[3] For the information content to be proportional to the log of the inverse of the number of values of a parameter, these values must have a uniform prior probability distribution. This is a reasonable initial assumption in the absence of any prior information.

[4] This method effectively discretizes continuous parameters by accepting as valid only certain points in the continuum. In this example, time, which is continuous, has been converted to the space of valid flight times.

is inexactly specified. Thus $Sig(p)$ must be determined on the basis of domain knowledge. For example, in our system, which operates in the travel domain,

$$Sig(origin) = Sig(destination) = 8$$

$$Sig(departure/arrival\ time) = Sig_{least}(=1) < Sig(departure/arrival\ date)(=3).$$

The information content measure ranges over the non-positive values. For example, if the departure date of a trip is directly inferred from a user's statements to be between the 9th and the 15th of May 1995, then the information content of this parameter is $\log_2 \frac{1\{=S(p)\}}{(7\{=N(p)\}\times 3\{=Sig(p)\})} = -4.39232$.

According to Equation (1), undefined parameters have the least information content, since they can take on all possible values in the domain. Inexactly defined parameters of high significance, e.g., origin, have a lower information content than inexactly defined parameters of low significance. This is based on the observation that ignorance about a significant parameter contributes more to the lack of definition of an interpretation than ignorance about an insignificant parameter. Since there is no lack of knowledge when a parameter is exactly defined, i.e., $N(p) = 1$, the parameter's significance is not taken into account when computing its information content. Hence, in this case, $IC(p) = \log_2 S(p)$. Thus, a parameter inferred exactly from a reliable source, i.e., $S(p) = 1$, has a maximum information content, which is 0 according to Equation (1).

2.2 Information Content of an Action Instance

The information content of an action instance is defined as the sum of the information content of the parameters that are *necessary* for the definition of the action instance. Two factors affect the determination of these parameters:

- *An action instance may have several sets of necessary parameters.* For instance, *(origin, destination, departure-date, departure-time)* is one such set for the action instance consisting of the operator TAKE-PLANE, and *(origin, destination, arrival-date, arrival-time)* is another set. The instantiation of the parameters of one set automatically determines the instantiations of the parameters of the other sets. Hence, in order to compute the information content of an action instance, the system must first determine which set of necessary parameters to consider.
- *The set of parameters that are necessary for defining an action instance is not static.* For example, in order to determine the cost of travel between two places, it may not be necessary to know the exact day of travel. Similarly, if there is only one flight a day between a specified origin and destination, then the departure/arrival time need not be specified by the user. Thus, elements of the set of necessary parameters are determined by (1) the purpose of the query, i.e., whether it is a preliminary exploration query or a request for assistance in achieving a goal, and (2) the instantiations of other parameters.

The first factor is taken into account by determining in advance the various sets of necessary parameters for each operator type, and selecting for the computation of the information content of an action instance the set of necessary parameters that yields the highest information content for this action instance. The second factor can be taken into account either by using inference rules (Section 4.2) or by interacting with the planning process (Section 4.3).

Once the set of necessary parameters is determined, the information content of an action instance Act_j is determined by the following formula:[5]

$$IC(Act_j) = \beta_j \times \left(\sum_{\{\text{parameters } p_i \text{ in } Act_j\}} IC(p_i) \right), \tag{2}$$

where $IC(p_i)$ is the information content of parameter p_i in action instance Act_j, and β_j is a constant whose value is determined on the basis of the inference that leads to the recognition of Act_j, i.e., whether Act_j is inferred from a user's statements or postulated by the system. An example of a postulated action is a trip which returns to the place of origin, when the user has asked only for a trip to a particular destination. Postulated action instances have a lower certainty, and hence a higher value of β_j, than action instances that are inferred from a user's statements. β_j accounts for the reliability of the inference that leads to the recognition of an action instance, while the information content of the individual parameters reflects the strength of the inferences that give rise to the particular instantiations of these parameters (Equation (1)).

2.3 Information Content of an Interpretation

The information content of an interpretation, $IC(I)$, is defined as the sum of the information content of each action instance in the interpretation. It is calculated using the following formula:

$$IC(I) = \sum_{\{\text{action instances } Act_j \text{ in } I\}} \beta_j \times \left(\sum_{\{\text{parameters } p_i \text{ in } Act_j\}} IC(p_i) \right) \tag{3}$$

The information content measure is additive over multiple action instances and it ranges over non-positive values. The maximum value for the information content of an interpretation is 0, and it is achieved when all the parameters in a set of necessary parameters of the action instances of the interpretation have a maximum information content, i.e., 0.

3 Calculating Probabilities

During intention inference, our information content measure is used to modify the probabilities of interpretations so that interpretations with more relevant information are given preference over those with less relevant information. This is because during cooperative consultations, such as those occurring at a travel agency, the user wants his/her intentions to be understood by the consultant, hence interpretations with a higher information content are more probable. The initial probability of an interpretation is determined by our plan inference mechanism on the basis of a number of factors, such as the coherence of the dialogue, the amount of relevant information in the interpretation, and the practicality of the plan proposed in the interpretation [12].

---

[5] The information content of the parameters can be added to obtain the information content of an action instance if the information sources are independent. This is not always true of action instances. However, the dependence between parameters is limited by the requirement that the necessary set of parameters should include only parameters that cannot be defined by means of other parameters in the set.

The information content measure calculated using Equation (3) ranges over non-positive values. In order to use it to calculate *Prob*(I), the probability of an interpretation I, the information content measure is mapped to the (0,1] range. The calculation of *Prob*(I) is performed by means of the following formula:

$$Prob(I) \leftarrow Prob(I)\left(1 - \frac{IC(I)}{IC_{normalize}}\right). \tag{4}$$

The impact of the information content measure on the probabilities of the interpretations can be varied by judicious choice of a value for $IC_{normalize}$. In the current implementation, $IC_{normalize}$ is a multiple of the sum of the information content of all the interpretations under consideration. This value allows the information content of an interpretation to have a substantial influence on its probability. A low information content reduces substantially the probability of an interpretation, while a high information content reduces this probability only slightly. Such an influence is desirable during plan inference in cooperative consultations, since in such consultations the interpretation intended by the user is likely to contain sufficient relevant information to enable the consultant to be helpful. The resulting probabilities are then used as follows.

If there are multiple interpretations, the probabilities are used to prune the set of interpretations by dropping all the interpretations whose probabilities fall below a relative rejection threshold. The pruning is done after normalizing the probabilities of the inferred interpretations so that the sum of these probabilities is 1. $Prob(I_{retain})$, the probability of an interpretation that is retained, satisfies the following condition:

$$\frac{Prob(I_{retain})}{Prob_{max}} \geq Threshold, \tag{5}$$

where $Prob_{max}$ is the maximum of all the normalized probabilities, and *Threshold* is a number in the [0,1] range. This calculation ensures that interpretations with a low probability relative to the most probable interpretation are dropped. For example, if *Threshold* is 0.5, an interpretation with probability 0.3 is dropped if there is another interpretation with probability 0.7. In contrast, if there are three interpretations with probabilities 0.4, 0.3 and 0.3, then all three are retained. By judicious choice of a value for *Threshold* the system may be tailored to consider different numbers of possibilities.

If no intention is recognized, then the probabilities in combination with the value of *Threshold* are used to determine whether interpretations that were previously rejected should be re-admitted. If *Threshold* is high (0.5 in our system), then the value of *Threshold* is lowered (to 0.05 in our system), thereby allowing the inference process to consider additional (less plausible) interpretations that may have been dropped with the earlier threshold. If *Threshold* is already at the lower value, then the user is asked to rephrase his/her request.

If there is ambiguity regarding a user's intentions, the probabilities in combination with the decisions made by the system during plan inference are used to determine whether a query should be posed, and what the actual content of the query should be. This is done by taking into account two factors: (1) *nuisance factor* – the annoyance caused to the user from a query that does not pertain to the user's intentions, and (2) *estimated queries* – the number of additional queries that the system expects to generate as a result of posing the chosen query. These factors, which depend on the probabilities, are combined in order to generate disambiguating queries that minimize both of them jointly [12, 13].

4 Checking Completion of Plan Recognition

During the plan recognition process, the information content measure is used as an *informative stopping rule* [4] to determine whether the inference process should be discontinued. Discontinuation happens under the following conditions:

- At least one complete interpretation, i.e., an interpretation with sufficient information content, is inferred (Section 4.1).
- No new inferences can be drawn on the basis of existing evidence, i.e., the information content of all the interpretations cannot be increased further.

4.1 Determining Sufficiency of Information

An interpretation has sufficient information for plan generation when its information content exceeds a threshold denoted $IC_{complete}$, where $IC_{complete}$ ranges over the non-positive values. The value chosen for $IC_{complete}$ affects the interaction between the user and the consultant during the planning process.

Since $IC_{complete}$ determines the threshold at which a consultant accepts an intention for planning, the input to the planning process is well defined when $IC_{complete}$ is high, and not so when $IC_{complete}$ is low. This input in turn affects the results of the planning process. If the value of $IC_{complete}$ is high then the interpretation may contain specifications that cannot be satisfied simultaneously. Hence, it may not be possible to find a plan to achieve the user's intentions. If the value of $IC_{complete}$ is low then the interpretation may not have specifications for some of the necessary parameters of an action instance. Hence, there may be several plans that achieve the user's intentions. In both situations, the system must initiate a negotiation process. In the first case, the purpose of the negotiation is to relax some of the extra specifications, and in the second case, it is to determine a preferred plan among the formulated ones.

In our system, the value of $IC_{complete}$ is chosen so that an interpretation is accepted as complete for plan formulation when all the necessary parameters of high significance are specified exactly, and some of the necessary parameters of low significance are partially specified. Thus, in the travel domain, our system will usually accept those interpretations where the origin, destination and departure/arrival dates of the action instances are known exactly. Since information content is additive, an interpretation may be accepted as complete when a single significant parameter is not known exactly and all the other parameters are known exactly. However, due to the use of $Sig(p)$ in the computation of the information content, this situation is not likely to occur.

Even with the use of significance for computing the information content of an interpretation, it is still possible to consider an interpretation to be incomplete when in fact it is complete, and accept it as complete when it is incomplete. This happens when the actual instantiation of a particular parameter determines whether an interpretation is complete. For example, the goal inferred from the statement "`I need a repair shop for my Ford`" is incomplete and hence under-constrained, since a location still needs to be specified. But if the car's make was Ferrari, then the recognized goal may very well be complete, since there are only a few Ferrari shops in a city. Further, if the user were to specify a location, then the goal may be over-constrained since there may not be a Ferrari shop in the specified location.

Thus, the amount of information that is sufficient for planning often depends on the context of the inferred interpretation. Context may be taken into account either by using inference rules or by interacting with the planning process.

4.2 Using Inference Rules

Inference rules take context into account by modifying the set of necessary parameters that is used to compute the information content of an action instance in an interpretation. For instance, a rule that alters the set of necessary parameters to exclude the suburb information when the make of the car is uncommon essentially increases the information content of the interpretation generated from the statement "`I need a repair shop for my Ferrari`". Similarly, a rule that excludes the departure time of overseas flights from the set of necessary parameters performs the same function in the travel domain.

However, the use of inference rules to alter the information content of an interpretation may not work all the time. Consider a situation where there are multiple flights scheduled to an overseas location, and there is only one flight servicing a remote domestic location, e.g., Darwin. The above rule would then fail to fire with respect to Darwin, thereby requiring that the departure time to Darwin be known, when in fact it is not necessary. In principle, this problem can be overcome by defining destinations which are unusual, and stipulating that unusual destinations do not require the specification of a departure time. However, the list of unusual destinations depends on the point of departure, e.g., there may be only one flight per day from Bombay to Trichy, but many more from Madras to Trichy. Hence, the use of inference rules in this case would require that an exception list be maintained for each city.

4.3 Interacting with the Plan Generator

Another way of taking context into account is by interacting with the planning process to determine whether an interpretation is sufficiently detailed. This is done by initially setting $IC_{complete}$ to a particular value, performing the planning process if appropriate, and then based on the results of the planning process, modifying $IC_{complete}$ and the information content of the interpretation.

The initial setting of $IC_{complete}$ is determined using the considerations discussed in Section 4.1. If the system infers a single interpretation whose information content is greater than the initial setting of $IC_{complete}$, then it attempts to generate a plan that achieves the recognized user intentions. Otherwise, the user is queried for additional information (Section 5). Depending on the number of plans generated, the consultant decides whether $IC_{complete}$ should be altered, and the direction of the alteration, if any.

- If the planning process yields no plans at all, then the goal expressed by this interpretation is over-constrained. Hence, some of the specifications in the interpretation must be relaxed.

- If the planning process yields exactly one plan, then the interpretation has exactly the relevant details and no more. In this case, $IC_{complete}$ is left unaltered, and the user is informed of the formulated plan.
- If the planning process yields many alternative plans, then the goal expressed by this interpretation is under-constrained. Hence, additional specifications must be added.

To illustrate this approach, consider a situation where there is only one daily flight scheduled to Darwin. If the initial setting of $IC_{complete}$ accepts an interpretation without a departure/arrival time specification, planning is attempted, and the planning process yields a unique plan. Thus, the interpretation is correctly determined to be sufficiently detailed. In contrast, if there are many flights scheduled to an overseas location, additional information is sought from the user because there are many plans that can satisfy the user's requirements. Thus, this approach has the advantage that details are filled in only if necessary. Hence, it is the approach taken in our system.

Relaxing Specifications. If the planning process yields no plans at all, then some of the specifications in the interpretation are relaxed as follows. First, the value of $IC_{complete}$ is lowered so that an interpretation with a lower information content may be considered complete. Next, a specification in the interpretation, such as the departure time of a particular trip, is retracted. The inference process is then re-applied in order to yield a new interpretation where the values of parameters that depend on the retracted information have been altered, and planning is attempted once more. This process of planning, followed by an appropriate modification of $IC_{complete}$ and of the interpretation is repeated until a plan is formulated or $IC_{complete}$ becomes smaller than a lower bound. If the relaxation process yields a valid plan, then the user is informed of it. Otherwise, the user is informed of the failure in planning.

To illustrate the relaxation process, consider the following request "**`Get me a ticket to Sydney departing tomorrow`**". The consultant infers that the user wants to fly from Melbourne to Sydney. Suppose that this request cannot be satisfied because there are no flights from Melbourne due to a strike at the airport. In this case, the relaxation process first lowers $IC_{complete}$, and then retracts the specification that the mode of transport is flight (on the basis of the information obtained during planning). The inference process is then performed to retract any inference based on this mode of transport, thus yielding an interpretation without a mode of transport. If this interpretation can be planned for, then the user is informed of the formulated plan and of the retractions performed. Otherwise, $IC_{complete}$ is lowered again and other specifications are retracted. This process continues until either a plan is generated or the lower bound for $IC_{complete}$ is reached.

Adding Specifications. If the planning process yields many plans, then the consultant must obtain additional specifications so that a unique plan may be determined. Depending on the number of plans formulated, these specifications may be obtained either by means of inferences or by querying the user.

If a large number of plans is formulated, then it is impractical to present all of them to the user. In this case, additional specifications are obtained by means of inferences as follows. First, the value of $IC_{complete}$ is increased, and then additional specifications are added by means of inferences from existing information to yield an interpretation with a higher information content. If this information content exceeds the new value of $IC_{complete}$, then planning is attempted. Otherwise, the user is queried to acquire additional information (Section 5). This process of planning followed by an appropriate modification of $IC_{complete}$ and of the interpretation is repeated until a unique plan is formulated or $IC_{complete}$ exceeds an upper bound. Since the upper bound in our system is 0 (the maximum information content of an interpretation), it is unlikely that the number of plans is still large when the upper bound is reached.

If only a few plans are formulated, then the consultant may either (1) choose the plan that is most likely to be favoured by the user and present it to him/her, or (2) present all the formulated plans and leave the choice to the user. In our system, the second option is chosen. This is because analysis of transcripts at travel agencies indicates that when there are a few means of satisfying an inferred goal, human consultants present all the available options to the user and leave the choice to him/her. For instance, when there are several possible departure times, the user is asked to choose from a list of options.

5 Completing an Interpretation

When an interpretation has insufficient details, i.e., its information content is less than $IC_{complete}$, and additional inferences do not increase its information content, then it is necessary to elicit additional information from the user by means of queries. This process is directed at increasing the information content of an interpretation so that it is greater than $IC_{complete}$. The information content of an interpretation may be increased by generating (a) *confirmation queries* to increase the strength of some inferences that led to the interpretation, and/or (b) *information-seeking queries* to obtain specifications for parameters that are unspecified or inexactly specified. The style of the interaction and the number of query/answer turns needed to complete an interpretation are influenced by the approach used to select parameters for querying.

When the interaction is to be kept short, a useful approach is one which maximizes the gain in the information content of the interpretation achieved with each query. In this approach, the consultant poses a query with respect to the parameter with the highest potential contribution to the information content of the interpretation. This parameter is selected as follows. First, the action instance with the least information content is chosen. Next, the set of necessary parameters that yields the highest information content for the chosen action instance is selected as the set that must be specified. The parameter with the least information content in this set is then selected for querying.

This approach is effective for keeping interactions succinct. However, the queries generated with it do not conform to the expectations of hierarchy and sequence in the travel domain. Thus, a modified version of this approach which takes into consideration these expectations is used in the travel domain [12], while this approach is best suited to the following situations: (1) in domains where a single action instance is considered, e.g., retail consultation where the user intends to buy a single item, and domains where the information is not organized hierarchically and sequentially, e.g., car repair assistance; and (2) during preliminary consultations in any domain, where $IC_{complete}$ is set to a low value.

6 Discussion

The requirement that computerized consultants deal with the uncertainty inherent in plan inference has been widely recognized, and several approaches have been used to plan inference when only partial and/or approximate information is available to the consultant. These approaches have been mainly used to choose between multiple possibilities and/or explanations (i.e., the first of the four processes discussed in Section 1), and no attempt has been made to define an approach that is useful during all stages of a cooperative consultation. These approaches to handling uncertainty may be broadly classified as either non-numeric or numeric.

Non-numeric approaches may be categorized as (1) those that maintain only the best possible explanation or plan [15], and (2) those that determine all possible explanations [9, 11]. These approaches do not rank the various possibilities that are maintained, and cannot choose between a normal explanation for the observed events and an abnormal one. This has led to several approaches based on numerical methods for ranking explanations based on evidence for and against an explanation, such as probabilistic modeling [8], weighted abduction [2] and the Dempster-Shafer theory of evidential reasoning [3, 6]. Three of these systems [2, 3, 8] are not concerned with cooperative consultations, hence they have no need to develop a framework for making the decisions discussed in Section 1. The fourth system [6] chooses between alternatives during a cooperative consultation, but it is not used for the other processes mentioned in Section 1.

When no intention is recognized, Eller and Carberry use a rule-based approach to relax the constraints under which a user's utterances were originally interpreted [7]. When there is plan ambiguity, Wu uses a decision-theoretic approach to decide whether active acquisition of information is warranted [17]; van Beek and Cohen address the same issue using a rule-based mechanism [16].

Thus, there have been several approaches to handling different aspects of the problems faced by computerized consultants, but there has been no unified framework to cope with all the decisions required during plan inference in cooperative consultations. Our research is a step towards rectifying this omission.

The framework described in this paper has been implemented as part of a computerized consultant that operates as a travel agent. Our consultant was tested on 8 different types of requests in the travel domain. The performance of our system was evaluated by means of surveys to assess (1) the interpretations it selects on the basis of these requests, and (2) the disambiguation, confirmation and information-seeking queries it generates to arrive at the correct interpretation. This evaluation indicates that the interpretations selected by our system and the queries generated using our information content measure are consistent with what is expected of human travel agents [12, 13].

References

1. Allen, J.F. and Perrault, C.R., Analyzing Intention in Utterances. *Artificial Intelligence* **15**, 143-178, 1981.
2. Appelt, D.E. and Pollack, M.E., Weighted Abduction for Plan Ascription. *User Modeling and User Adapted Interaction* **2(1–2)**, 1–25, 1992.
3. Bauer, M., Acquisition of User Preferences for Plan Recognition. In *UM96 Proceedings – the Fifth International Conference on User Modeling*, 105-112, Kona, Hawaii, 1996.
4. Berger, J.O. and Berry, D.A., The Relevance of Stopping Rules in Statistical Inferences. In Gupta, S.S. and Berger, J.O. (Eds.), *Statistical Decision Theory and Related Topics IV*, **Vol. 1**, Springer Verlag, 1988.
5. Carberry, S., Modeling the User's Plans and Goals. *Computational Linguistics* **14(3)**, 23-37, 1988.
6. Carberry, S., Incorporating Default Inferences into Plan Recognition. In *AAAI Proceedings – the Eighth National Conference on Artificial Intelligence*, 471-478, Boston, Massachusetts, 1990.
7. Eller, R. and Carberry, S., A Meta-Rule Approach to Dynamic Plan Recognition. *User Modeling and User Adapted Interaction* **2(1-2)**, 27-53, 1992.
8. Goldman, R. and Charniak, E., A Probabilistic Model for Plan Recognition. In *AAAI Proceedings – the Ninth National Conference on Artificial Intelligence*, 160-165, Anaheim, California, 1991.
9. Kautz, H. and Allen, J.F., Generalized Plan Recognition. In *AAAI Proceedings – the Fifth National Conference on Artificial Intelligence*, 32-37, Philadelphia, Pennsylvania, 1986.
10. Kobsa, A., *User Modeling and User Adapted Interaction* **1(4)**, **2(1-2)**, 1991-2.
11. Konolige, K. and Pollack, M.E., Ascribing Plans to Agents. In *IJCAI-89 Proceedings – the Eleventh International Joint Conference on Artificial Intelligence*, 924-930, Detroit, Michigan, 1989.
12. Raskutti, B. (1993), Handling Uncertainty during Plan Recognition for Response Generation. Ph.D. Thesis, Department of Computer Science, Monash University.
13. Raskutti, B. and Zukerman, I., Acquisition of Information to Determine a User's Plan. In *ECAI-94 Proceedings – the European Conference on Artificial Intelligence*, 28-32, Amsterdam, The Netherlands, 1994.
14. Shannon, C.E. (1948), A Mathematical Theory of Communications. *Bell System Technical Journals*, October 1948.
15. Sullivan, M. and Cohen, P.R., An Endorsement based Plan Recognition Program. In *IJCAI-85 Proceedings – the Ninth International Joint Conference on Artificial Intelligence*, 8-23, Los Angeles, California, 1985.
16. van Beek, P. and Cohen, R., Resolving Plan Ambiguity for Cooperative Response Generation. In *IJCAI-91 Proceedings – the Twelfth International Joint Conference on Artificial Intelligence*, 938-944, Sydney, Australia, 1991.
17. Wu, D., Implications of Active User Model Acquisition for Decision-Theoretic Dialog Planning and Plan Recognition. *User Modeling and User Adapted Interaction* **1(2)**, 149-172, 1991.

Declarative Program Theory with Implicit Implication

Vilas WUWONGSE and Ekawit NANTAJEEWARAWAT

E-mail: {*vw,ekawit*}*@cs.ait.ac.th*
Computer Science and Information Management Program
School of Advanced Technologies, Asian Institute of Technology
GPO Box 2754, Bangkok 10501, THAILAND

Abstract. In order to provide a general framework for deductive object-oriented representation systems, Akama's declarative program theory is extended under the assumptions that there exists implicit implication among elements of an interpretation domain and that this implicit implication can be represented by a preorder on the domain. Under the consequent constraint that every interpretation must conform to the implicit implication, an appropriate model-theoretic semantics as well as its corresponding fixpoint semantics for declarative programs is described. Based on Köstler *et. al.*'s foundation of fixpoint with subsumption, it is shown that if the implicit-implication relation is further assumed to be a partial order, then the meaning of a program can be determined more efficiently by the application of an immediate-consequence operator which involves only the reduced representations, basically consisting only of their maximal elements, of subsets of the interpretation domain.

1 Introduction

As an axiomatic theory of logic programming, DP theory (the theory of declarative programs)[1] [1, 2, 3, 4] generalizes the concept of conventional logic programs and provides a unified theoretical foundation for many declarative knowledge representation systems and programming languages including extensions of Prolog, constraint logic programming, context-free grammars and typed unification grammars. An extension of DP theory as a general framework for deductive object-oriented representation systems is attempted in this paper.

In DP theory, programs and their semantics are formulated on an abstract structure called *specialization system* which comprises four basic components — a domain of atoms, a subset of the domain called *interpretation domain*, a set of specialization parameters and a specialization operator — together satisfying some simple axioms. The atoms in a specialization system are inherently interrelated by means of specialization operation — an application of the specialization operator with a certain parameter to some atom may yield another atom. The interpretation domain plays the role of the Herbrand base in the conventional

[1] DP theory was previously called the theory of generalized logic programs.

theory in discussing the semantics of programs. In most knowledge representation systems, the atoms in an interpretation domain are ground, *i.e.*, they are not changed by any specialization, and, thus, unconnected with each other.

In deductive object-oriented systems, however, the atoms in an interpretation domain are usually interrelated in an additional way, *i.e.*, some atom may implicitly imply others, based on their structures, their intended meanings and class/subclass information. In particular, in the systems which separate taxonomic schema declarations from data definitions,[2] such an interrelation can generally be predetermined. For example, in a conceptual graph language [7, 8, 9, 10], when generalization lattices of concept types, relation types and markers are provided, non-redundant atomic conceptual graphs can be partially ordered into a generalization hierarchy in which a graph logically implies each of its more general ones. This kind of implication is implicit in the sense that it need not be declared by definite clauses in application programs, but is embodied in the systems.

This paper first assumes that there exists predetermined implicit implication among the atoms in an interpretation domain and that this implicit implication can be described by a binary relation on the domain. By the characteristics of implication, such a relation is typically a preorder (also called a quasi-order), *i.e.*, it is reflexive and transitive. Under the assumption, an interpretation is required to be closed with respect to the preorder. An appropriate model-theoretic semantics together with its corresponding fixpoint semantics for declarative programs is developed accordingly. Thereafter, a stronger assumption that the implicit-implication relation is a partial order is considered. With the partial-order structure, a legitimate interpretation can be represented equivalently by its reduced version which, intuitively, consists only of its maximal elements with respect to the order. In addition, based on the foundation of fixpoint iteration with subsumption provided by [12, 13], the reduced representation of the meaning of a program can be directly computed by an immediate-conseqence operator on a quotient set of the reduced interpretations.

In order to make this paper self-contained, the basic part of DP theory is reviewed in the next section. Section 3 explains the motivation of the paper in more detail and discusses the model-theoretic semantics and the fixpoint semantics of a declarative program under the primary assumption. Section 4 recalls some definitions and results related to subsumption ordering from [12, 13] and applies them to provide a more elegant fixpoint semantics under the stronger assumption. Section 5 concludes the paper. Due to space limitation, the proofs of all results are omitted. They are included in the full version of the paper [15].

2 DP Theory

In order to introduce DP theory, the notion of specialization system will be reviewed first. Then, the concepts of declarative programs, their minimal model

[2] In other words, in the systems in which taxonomic information (*e.g.*, class/subclass relation and class population) cannot be conditionally defined by rules.

semantics and least fixpoint semantics, which are based on a specialization system, will be presented. Procedural semantics for declarative programs [2] and inference rules in DP theory [4] are beyond the scope of this paper and not included in this section.

2.1 Specialization Systems

From the viewpoint of DP theory, the usual concrete definitions of atoms and substitutions restrict the applicability, complicate the concepts and thus obscure the full power of logic programming. Atoms in DP theory, on the other hand, can have any forms, and variable-substitution operation on atoms are generalized into specialization operation. They are defined, not by syntactic characterization, but, by axiomatic characterization on an abstract structure called specialization system, which is described as follows:

Definition 1. [4] **(Specialization System)** A *specialization system* is a 4-tuple $(\mathcal{A}, \mathcal{G}, \mathcal{S}, \mu)$ of three sets $\mathcal{A}, \mathcal{G}$ and $\mathcal{S}$, and a mapping μ from $\mathcal{S}$ to *partial_map*$(\mathcal{A})$ (*i.e.*, the set of all partial mappings on $\mathcal{A}$), that satisfies the following conditions:

1. $(\forall s', s'' \in \mathcal{S})(\exists s \in \mathcal{S}) : \mu s = (\mu s'') \circ (\mu s')$,
2. $(\exists s \in \mathcal{S})(\forall a \in \mathcal{A}) : (\mu s)a = a$,
3. $\mathcal{G} \subseteq \mathcal{A}$.

The elements of $\mathcal{A}$ are called *atoms*; the set $\mathcal{G}$ is called the *interpretation domain*; the elements of $\mathcal{S}$ are called *specialization parameters* or simply *specializations*; and the mapping μ is called the *specialization operator*. A specialization $s \in \mathcal{S}$ is said to be *applicable* to $a \in \mathcal{A}$, iff $a \in dom(\mu s)$. □

For the rest of this section, let $\Gamma = (\mathcal{A}, \mathcal{G}, \mathcal{S}, \mu)$ be a specialization system. A specialization in $\mathcal{S}$ will often be denoted by a Greek letter such as θ. When there is no danger of confusion, a specialization $\theta \in \mathcal{S}$ will be identified with the partial mapping $\mu\theta$ and used as a postfix unary (partial) operator on $\mathcal{A}$, *e.g.*, $(\mu\theta)a$ will be written as $a\theta$.

2.2 Declarative Programs

A declarative program on Γ is defined as a set of definite clauses constructed out of atoms in $\mathcal{A}$. Every logic program in the conventional theory can be regarded as a declarative program on some specialization system.

Definition 2. [5] **(Definite Clause and Declarative Program)** Let X be a subset of $\mathcal{A}$. A *definite clause C on X* is a formula of the form:

$$A \leftarrow B_1, \ldots, B_n$$

where $A, B_1, \ldots, B_n$ are atoms in X. The atom A is denoted by *head*(C) and the set $\{B_1, \ldots, B_n\}$ by *Body*(C). The set of all definite clauses on X is denoted by *Dclause*(X). A *declarative program* on Γ is a (possibly infinite) set of definite clauses on $\mathcal{A}$. □

Let $C = (A \leftarrow B_1, \ldots, B_n)$ be a definite clause on $\mathcal{A}$. A definite clause C' is an *instance* of C, iff there exists $\theta \in \mathcal{S}$ such that θ is applicable to $A, B_1, \ldots,$ B_n and $C' = (A\theta \leftarrow B_1\theta, \ldots, B_n\theta)$. Denote by $C\theta$ such an instance C' of C and by $Instance(C)$ the set of all instances of C. Given a declarative program P on Γ, denote by $Gclause(P)$ the set

$$\bigcup_{C \in P} (Instance(C) \cap Dclause(\mathcal{G})).$$

2.3 Model-Theoretic Semantics

In order to discuss the model-theoretic semantics of a declarative program on Γ, an interpretation assigning truth values to the atoms in the interpretation domain $\mathcal{G}$, the truth value of a definite clause on $\mathcal{A}$ with respect to a particular interpretation, and a model of a declarative program on Γ are defined.

Definition 3. [5] **(Interpretation)** An *interpretation* is a subset of $\mathcal{G}$. A definite cluase C on $\mathcal{A}$ is true with respect to an interpretation I, iff

$$(\forall C' \in Instance(C) \cap Dclause(\mathcal{G})) : ((head(C') \in I) \text{ or } (Body(C') \not\subseteq I)). \quad \square$$

Definition 4. [5] **(Model)** An interpretation I is a *model* of a declarative program P on Γ, iff all definite clauses in P are true with respect to I. $\square$

As in the conventional theory, the model intersection property also holds for declarative programs on Γ and the semantics of a declarative program P on Γ is defined as the intersection of all models of P, which is called the minimal model of P and denoted by $\mathcal{M}_P$.

Proposition 5. [5] **(Model Intersection Property)** *The intersection of more than one model of a declarative program P on Γ is also a model of P.* $\square$

Theorem 6. [5] *Every declarative program P on Γ has the minimal model $\mathcal{M}_P$, which is the intersection of all models of P.* $\square$

2.4 Fixpoint Semantics

Throughout this subsection, let P be a declarative program on Γ. Associated with a declarative program P on Γ are the mappings T_P and K_P on the complete lattice $(2^{\mathcal{G}}, \subseteq)$. Their least fixpoints are both equal to the minimal model of P.

Definition 7. [5] For each $X \subseteq \mathcal{G}$,

$$T_P(X) = \{head(C) \mid C \in Gclause(P) \ \& \ Body(C) \subseteq X\}. \quad \square$$

Definition 8. [5] For each $X \subseteq \mathcal{G}$, $K_P(X) = T_P(X) \cup X$. $\square$

Proposition 9. [3] *T_P and K_P are $\subseteq$-continuous.* $\square$

Theorem 10. [3] *Let I be an interpretation. Then*

1. *I is a model of P, iff $T_P(I) \subseteq I$,*
2. *I is a model of P, iff $K_P(I) = I$.* $\square$

Theorem 11. [3] $\mathcal{M}_P = lfp(T_P) = lfp(K_P)$. $\square$

3 DP Theory with Implicit Implication

When a generalization taxonomy of types or classes is provided, an implication relation among the atoms in an interpretation domain can often be determined by examining their structures and their intended meanings. For example, in a conceptual graph language [7, 8, 9, 10], as the intended meaning of an atomic conceptual graph $[t : o] \rightarrow (r) \rightarrow [t' : o']$ is "there exist individuals o of type t and o' of type t' such that o and o' are related by a relation r", the atomic conceptual graph [woman : mary] → (father) → [man : john] implicitly implies the atomic conceptual graph [person : mary] → (father) → [person : john], provided that the types man and woman are more specific than the type person. Likewise, in F-logic [11], as the intended meaning of a signature expression[3] $c[m \Rightarrow c']$ is "if a method m for an object of class c is defined or derived, then it must return an object of class c'", the signature expression person[father ⇒ man] implicitly implies the signature expression woman[father ⇒ person], provided that the id-terms man and woman are subclasses of the id-term person. In most deductive object-oriented systems, this kind of implication is not required to be declared by definite clauses in application programs, but is incorporated directly into their reasoning apparatuses.

A specialization operator is not a proper means to capture such an implicit-implication relation, inasmuch as it may cause undesired side effects on the meanings of programs. To illustrate, let a, a', a'', b and b' be atoms in an interpretation domain such that a implicitly implies a', a' in turn implicitly implies a'', and b implicitly implies b', and let P be a definite program $\{a', b \leftarrow a\}$. Since a' implicitly implies a'', it is readily seen that the expected meaning of P with respect to the implicit implication is $\{a', a''\}$. Now suppose that the above implicit implication is realized by means of specialization operation, *i.e.*, $a\theta_1 = a'$, $a'\theta_2 = a''$ and $b\theta_3 = b'$ for some specializations θ_1, θ_2 and θ_3. Suppose further that there exists a specialization θ such that $a\theta = a\theta_1$ and $b\theta = b\theta_3$.[4] Then, according to Definitions 3 and 4, the definite clause $(b \leftarrow a)\theta = (b\theta_3 \leftarrow a\theta_1) = (b' \leftarrow a')$ must be satisfied in every model of P. Consequently, the minimal model of P contains b', contradicting the expected meaning above.

This section assumes that the implicit implication among the atoms in an interpretation domain can be predetermined and represented by a preorder on the domain. More precisely, in the sequel, assume that $\Gamma_{\sqsubseteq} = (\mathcal{A}, \mathcal{G}, \mathcal{S}, \mu)$ is a specialization system and $\sqsubseteq$ is a preorder on $\mathcal{G}$ such that for any $g, g' \in \mathcal{G}$, $g \sqsubseteq g'$, iff g is implicitly implied by g'. Under the constraint that every interpretation must conform to the implicit implication, an appropriate model-theoretic semantics for declarative programs with respect to $\sqsubseteq$ along with its corresponding fixpoint semantics is developed.

---

[3] A signature expression in F-logic is considered as an atom in DP theory.

[4] Such a specialization θ usually exists. For example, let a and b be atomic conceptual graphs [woman : mary] → (father) → [man : john] and [man : tom] → (sister) → [woman : mary], respectively, and θ_1 and θ_3 be concept substitutions {[woman : mary]/[person : mary], [man : john]/[person : john]} and {[woman : mary]/[person : mary], [man : tom]/[person : tom]}, respectively. Then, θ could be $\theta_1 \cup \theta_3$.

3.1 Model-Theoretic Semantics

In the original DP theory, an interpretation arbitrarily assigns truth values to the atoms in an interpretation domain, and, therefore, every subset of the domain can serve as one possible interpretation. Under the established assumption, by contrast, the truth values of the atoms must be consistent with the implicit implication described by the preorder $\sqsubseteq$ and thus cannot be randomly assigned. Accordingly, not all of the original interpretations, but only those which are closed with respect to $\sqsubseteq$ will be used henceforth to discuss the model-theoretic semantics for declarative programs on $\Gamma_{\sqsubseteq}$.

Definition 12. ($\sqsubseteq$-Closed Interpretation) An interpretation I is said to be *$\sqsubseteq$-closed*, iff

$$(\forall g \in I)(\forall g' \in \mathcal{G}) : (g' \sqsubseteq g \Longrightarrow g' \in I). \quad \square$$

The truth value of a definite clause on $\mathcal{A}$ with respect to a $\sqsubseteq$-closed interpretation is still defined as in the original DP theory (see Definition 3). A *$\sqsubseteq$-closed model* of a declarative program P on $\Gamma_{\sqsubseteq}$ is straightforwardly defined as a $\sqsubseteq$-closed interpretation which is also a model (according to Definition 4) of P. The meaning with respect to $\sqsubseteq$ of a declarative program P on $\Gamma_{\sqsubseteq}$ is then defined as the intersection of all of its $\sqsubseteq$-closed models, which is also its $\sqsubseteq$-closed model (see Proposition 14), called its *minimal $\sqsubseteq$-closed model* and denoted by $\mathcal{M}_P^{\sqsubseteq}$.

Lemma 13. *The intersection of more than one $\sqsubseteq$-closed interpretation is also a $\sqsubseteq$-closed interpretation.* $\square$

Proposition 14. ($\sqsubseteq$-Closed-Model Intersection Property) *The intersection of more than one $\sqsubseteq$-closed model of a declarative program P on $\Gamma_{\sqsubseteq}$ is also a $\sqsubseteq$-closed model of P.* $\square$

Theorem 15. *Every declarative program P on $\Gamma_{\sqsubseteq}$ has the miminal $\sqsubseteq$-closed model $\mathcal{M}_P^{\sqsubseteq}$, which is the intersection of all $\sqsubseteq$-closed models of P.* $\square$

3.2 Fixpoint Semantics

In order to provide fixpoint characterization of the $\sqsubseteq$-closed model semantics, the $\subseteq$-continuous mapping $K_P^{\mathcal{E}}$ on the complete lattice $(2^{\mathcal{G}}, \subseteq)$ is associated with a declarative program P on $\Gamma_{\sqsubseteq}$. An important virtue of this mapping is that each of its fixpoints determines a $\sqsubseteq$-closed model of P (Theorem 21). Therefore, the minimal $\sqsubseteq$-closed model $\mathcal{M}_P^{\sqsubseteq}$ can be obtained by computing its least fixpoint (Theorem 22). To start with, the notion of expanded version of a subset of $\mathcal{G}$ with respect to the preorder $\sqsubseteq$, which will be used in the definition of the mapping $K_P^{\mathcal{E}}$, is introduced.

Definition 16. (Expanded Set)[5] Let $X \subseteq \mathcal{G}$. The *expanded version* of X, denoted by $\mathcal{E}(X)$, is defined as follows:

$$\mathcal{E}(X) = \{g \in \mathcal{G} \mid (\exists x \in X) : g \sqsubseteq x\}. \quad \square$$

[5] This definition is an adaptation of that of expanded set with respect to a partial order on a basic set given in [13].

The next proposition links the notion of $\sqsubseteq$-closed interpretation up with that of expanded version of an interpretation.

Proposition 17. *An interpretation $I \subseteq \mathcal{G}$ is $\sqsubseteq$-closed, iff $\mathcal{E}(I) = I$.* □

For the rest of this subsection, let P be a declarative program on $\Gamma_{\sqsubseteq}$. It is important to note that $\mathcal{M}_P^{\sqsubseteq}$ is in general not equal to the expanded version of the minimal model $\mathcal{M}_P$ and, hence, $\mathcal{M}_P^{\sqsubseteq}$ cannot be obtained simply by expanding the least fixpoint of K_P. Next, the mapping $K_P^{\mathcal{E}}$, the least fixpoint of which equals $\mathcal{M}_P^{\sqsubseteq}$, is presented.

Definition 18. The mapping $K_P^{\mathcal{E}}: 2^{\mathcal{G}} \rightarrow 2^{\mathcal{G}}$ is defined as follows: for each $X \subseteq \mathcal{G}$,

$$K_P^{\mathcal{E}}(X) = K_P(\mathcal{E}(X)). \quad \square$$

Proposition 19. *$K_P^{\mathcal{E}}$ is $\subseteq$-continuous and $\sqsubseteq$-monotonic.* □

Theorem 20. $lfp(K_P^{\mathcal{E}}) = K_P^{\mathcal{E}} \uparrow \omega$. □

Theorem 21. *Let I be an interpretation. Then $K_P^{\mathcal{E}}(I) = I$, iff I is a $\sqsubseteq$-closed model of P.* □

The next theorem is the main result of this subsection.

Theorem 22. $M_P^{\sqsubseteq} = lfp(K_P^{\mathcal{E}})$. □

4 DP Theory with Partially-Ordered Interpretation Domains

As illustrated at the begining of the previous section, the implicit implication among atoms in a particular system, where their intended meanings are clearly known, can generally be decided by examining their forms and the generalization relationship between the types or classes occuring at the corresponding positions in them. Since a generalization hierarchy of types or classes commonly has a partial-order structure, the implicit-implication relation is often also a partial order.

This section further assumes that the implicit-implication relation on the interpretation domain is a partial order, *i.e.*, the preorder $\sqsubseteq$ in the previous section is additionally assumed to be antisymmetric as well. Under this stronger assumption, it applies the results on fixpoint iteration with subsumption provided by [12, 13] (Subsection 4.1) to describe a more elegant fixpoint semantics for declarative programs with respect to the implicit implication (Subsection 4.2).

Formally, throughout this section, let $\Gamma_{\sqsubseteq} = (\mathcal{A}, \mathcal{G}, \mathcal{S}, \mu)$ be a specialization system and $\sqsubseteq$ a *partial order* on $\mathcal{G}$ such that for any $g, g' \in \mathcal{G}$, $g \sqsubseteq g'$, iff g is assumed to be implicitly implied by g'. All definitions and results in the previous section are applicable in this section.

4.1 Basic Definitions and Results

This subsection recalls some definitions and results from [12, 13], which will be used in the next subsection.[6]

Based on the partial order $\sqsubseteq$ on $\mathcal{G}$, the binary relation $\sqsubseteq$ on $2^{\mathcal{G}}$ is defined as follows: for any $X, Y \subseteq \mathcal{G}$,

$$X \sqsubseteq Y \iff (\forall x \in X)(\exists y \in Y) : x \sqsubseteq y.$$

This relation is a preorder on $2^{\mathcal{G}}$, but not necessarily a partial order.[7] Based on it, the equivalence relation $\sim$ on $2^{\mathcal{G}}$ is defined by

$$X \sim Y \iff X \sqsubseteq Y \ \& \ Y \sqsubseteq X,$$

for any $X, Y \subseteq \mathcal{G}$. The preorder $\sqsubseteq$ on $2^{\mathcal{G}}$ is extended to the quotient set of $2^{\mathcal{G}}$ modulo $\sim$ (*i.e.*, $2^{\mathcal{G}}/{\sim}$) by

$$[X] \sqsubseteq [Y] \iff X \sqsubseteq Y,$$

for any $[X], [Y] \in 2^{\mathcal{G}}/{\sim}$. This extended relation is a partial order on $2^{\mathcal{G}}/{\sim}$.

Next, the notion of reduced version of a subset of $\mathcal{G}$ is described.

Definition 23. [13] **(Reduced Set)** Let $X \subseteq \mathcal{G}$. Let $\mathcal{C}$ be the set of maximal (with respect to set inclusion) chains[8] of X. For each $C \in \mathcal{C}$, let $max_{\sqsubseteq}(C)$ denote the maximum (with respect to $\sqsubseteq$) element, if exists, of C. The *reduced version* of X, denoted by $\mathcal{R}(X)$, is defined as follows:

$$\mathcal{R}(X) = \bigcup_{C \in \mathcal{C}} R_C,$$

where

$$R_C = \begin{cases} \{max_{\sqsubseteq}(C)\}, & \text{if } max_{\sqsubseteq}(C) \text{ exists,} \\ C, & \text{otherwise.} \end{cases}$$

Denote by $2^{\mathcal{G}}_{\mathcal{R}}$ the set of all reduced subsets of $\mathcal{G}$, *i.e.*, the set $\{\mathcal{R}(X) \mid X \in 2^{\mathcal{G}}\}$. □

For each $X \subseteq \mathcal{G}$, the maximal chains in X without maximum elements[9] are left unchanged in $\mathcal{R}(X)$, while those with maximum elements are reduced to their maximum elements in $\mathcal{R}(X)$. Thus, if X is a finite set, then $\mathcal{R}(X)$ consists only of the maximal elements of X. The next proposition interrelates reduced sets, expanded sets, set inclusion, and the relations $\sqsubseteq$ and $\sim$ on $2^{\mathcal{G}}$.

[6] It should be noted that all results presented in this subsection still hold without the condition that the partial order $\sqsubseteq$ represents an implicit-implication relation on $\mathcal{G}$.

[7] This preorder on $2^{\mathcal{G}}$ is usually called Hoare's ordering.

[8] The maximal chains of a partially ordered set X are the totally ordered subsets of X that are maximal with respect to set inclusion. For example, let $X = \{a, b, c, d\}$ be partially ordered by $a \sqsubseteq b \sqsubseteq c$ and $a \sqsubseteq d$. Then the maximal chains of X are $\{a, b, c\}$ and $\{a, d\}$.

[9] Only infinite chains may have no maximum elements.

Proposition 24. [13] *Let* $X, Y \subseteq \mathcal{G}$. *Then*

1. $X \sim \mathcal{R}(X) \sim \mathcal{E}(X)$,
2. $X \sqsubseteq Y \implies \mathcal{R}(X) \sqsubseteq \mathcal{R}(Y)\ \&\ \mathcal{E}(X) \subseteq \mathcal{E}(Y)$. □

It is shown in [13] that $(2^{\mathcal{G}}_{\mathcal{R}}/\sim, \sqsubseteq)$ is a complete lattice, where the top element is $[\mathcal{R}(\mathcal{G})]$, the bottom element is $[\emptyset]$ and $lub\{[X_i]\}_{i \in I} = [\mathcal{R}(\bigcup_{i \in I} X_i)]$. The main theoretical results on fixpoint iteration on this complete lattice provided by [13] are next recalled. In the sequel, let $F: 2^{\mathcal{G}} \to 2^{\mathcal{G}}$.

Definition 25. [13] If F is $\sqsubseteq$-monotonic, then the mappings $F_{\mathcal{R}}$ and $F^{\sim}$ are defined as follows:

1. $F_{\mathcal{R}}: 2^{\mathcal{G}} \to 2^{\mathcal{G}}$ such that $F_{\mathcal{R}}(X) = \mathcal{R}(F(X))$, for each $X \subseteq \mathcal{G}$,
2. $F^{\sim}: 2^{\mathcal{G}}_{\mathcal{R}}/\sim \to 2^{\mathcal{G}}_{\mathcal{R}}/\sim$ such that $F^{\sim}([X]) = [F_{\mathcal{R}}(X)]$, for each $[X] \in 2^{\mathcal{G}}_{\mathcal{R}}/\sim$.[10]
□

Theorem 26. [13] *If* F *is* $\sqsubseteq$*-monotonic, then* $F^{\sim}$ *has a least fixpoint.* □

Theorem 27. [13] *If* F *is* $\sqsubseteq$*-monotonic and* $\subseteq$*-continuous, then*

1. $lfp(F^{\sim}) = F^{\sim} \uparrow \omega$,
2. $[\mathcal{R}(F \uparrow n)] = F^{\sim} \uparrow n = [F_{\mathcal{R}} \uparrow n]$, *for any* $n < \omega$,
3. $[\mathcal{R}(lfp(F))] = lfp(F^{\sim}) = lub\{[F_{\mathcal{R}} \uparrow n] \mid n < \omega\}$. □

4.2 Fixpoint Semantics Based-on Partially-Ordered Interpretation Domains

Under the assumption of this section, it follows from Propositions 17 and 24 that, for every $\sqsubseteq$-closed interpretation I, $\mathcal{E}(\mathcal{R}(I)) = \mathcal{E}(I) = I$, *i.e.*, every $\sqsubseteq$-closed interpretation can be recaptured from its reduced version by expansion. This suggests that $\sqsubseteq$-closed interpretations can be equivalently represented by their reduced versions. Moreover, for any declarative program P on $\Gamma_{\sqsubseteq}$, as $K^{\mathcal{E}}_{P}$ is both $\sqsubseteq$-monotonic and $\subseteq$-continuous (Proposition 19), $K^{\mathcal{E}}_{P}$ determines the mapping $(K^{\mathcal{E}}_{P})^{\sim}$ on the complete lattice $(2^{\mathcal{G}}_{\mathcal{R}}/\sim, \sqsubseteq)$ (see Definition 25), and, it follows from Theorem 22 and 3 of Theorem 27 that

$$[\mathcal{R}(\mathcal{M}^{\sqsubseteq}_{P})] = [\mathcal{R}(lfp(K^{\mathcal{E}}_{P}))] = lfp((K^{\mathcal{E}}_{P})^{\sim}).$$

This means, if $lfp((K^{\mathcal{E}}_{P})^{\sim}) = [A]$, then, by 2 of Proposition 24, $\mathcal{E}(A) = \mathcal{E}(\mathcal{R}(\mathcal{M}^{\sqsubseteq}_{P}))$, and, as $\mathcal{M}^{\sqsubseteq}_{P}$ is $\sqsubseteq$-closed, then, $\mathcal{E}(A) = \mathcal{M}^{\sqsubseteq}_{P}$. Therefore, the minimal $\sqsubseteq$-closed model $\mathcal{M}^{\sqsubseteq}_{P}$ can be obtained by expanding any representative of the least fixpoint of $(K^{\mathcal{E}}_{P})^{\sim}$.

As $(K^{\mathcal{E}}_{P})^{\sim}$ is a mapping on a quotient set of the reduced subsets of $\mathcal{G}$, computing $\mathcal{M}^{\sqsubseteq}_{P}$ by the application of $(K^{\mathcal{E}}_{P})^{\sim}$ is appealing. However, it should be noted that, by Definition 25, for any equivalence class $[X]$ in $2^{\mathcal{G}}_{\mathcal{R}}/\sim$,

$$(K^{\mathcal{E}}_{P})^{\sim}([X]) = [\mathcal{R}(K^{\mathcal{E}}_{P}(X))] = [\mathcal{R}(K_{P}(\mathcal{E}(X)))]. \tag{1}$$

[10] It is shown in [13] that $F_{\mathcal{R}}$ and $F^{\sim}$ are well defined and are $\sqsubseteq$-monotonic.

Therefore, if $(K_P^{\mathcal{E}})^{\sim}([X])$ is evaluated directly according to Equation (1), *i.e.*, by means of the mapping K_P, then the reduced set X must be expanded and the merit of computing on reduced sets will be lost. It will be shown next that, instead of following Equation (1), $(K_P^{\mathcal{E}})^{\sim}([X])$ can be computed in another way, which does not involve the expanded version of X, by using another mapping called $K_P^{\sqsubseteq}$.

In the sequel, let P be a declarative program on $\Gamma_{\sqsubseteq}$. The next definition associates with P a mapping $T_P^{\sqsubseteq}$, based on which the mapping $K_P^{\sqsubseteq}$ is defined.

Definition 28. The mapping $T_P^{\sqsubseteq}: 2^{\mathcal{G}} \to 2^{\mathcal{G}}$ is defined as follows: for each $X \subseteq \mathcal{G}$,

$$T_P^{\sqsubseteq}(X) = \{head(C) \mid C \in Gclause(P) \ \& \ Body(C) \sqsubseteq X\}. \quad \square$$

Definition 29. The mapping $K_P^{\sqsubseteq}: 2^{\mathcal{G}} \to 2^{\mathcal{G}}$ is defined as follows: for each $X \subseteq \mathcal{G}$,

$$K_P^{\sqsubseteq}(X) = T_P^{\sqsubseteq}(X) \cup X. \quad \square$$

Lemma 30. *Let $X \subseteq \mathcal{G}$. Then*

1. $T_P(\mathcal{E}(X)) = T_P^{\sqsubseteq}(X)$,
2. $K_P^{\mathcal{E}}(X) \supseteq K_P^{\sqsubseteq}(X)$,
3. $K_P^{\mathcal{E}}(X) \sim K_P^{\sqsubseteq}(X)$. $\square$

Proposition 31. *$K_P^{\sqsubseteq}$ is $\subseteq$-continuous and $\sqsubseteq$-monotonic.* $\square$

As $K_P^{\sqsubseteq}$ is always both $\subseteq$-continuous and $\sqsubseteq$-monotonic (Proposition 31), the mapping $(K_P^{\mathcal{E}})^{\sim}$ on the complete lattice $(2^{\mathcal{G}}_{\mathcal{R}}/{\sim}, \sqsubseteq)$ is well-defined by Definition 25 and has all the properties listed in Theorem 27. Theorem 32 below illuminates the equality between the mappings $(K_P^{\mathcal{E}})^{\sim}$ and $(K_P^{\sqsubseteq})^{\sim}$. As a result, given an equivalence class $[X]$ in $2^{\mathcal{G}}_{\mathcal{R}}/{\sim}$, $(K_P^{\mathcal{E}})^{\sim}([X])$ can be computed through the mapping $K_P^{\sqsubseteq}$ by the following equation:

$$(K_P^{\mathcal{E}})^{\sim}([X]) \;=\; (K_P^{\sqsubseteq})^{\sim}([X]) \;=\; [\mathcal{R}(K_P^{\sqsubseteq}(X))]. \tag{2}$$

Observe that, in the evaluation of $K_P^{\sqsubseteq}(X)$, X is not expanded, but directly compared with $Body(C)$, based on the preorder $\sqsubseteq$ on $2^{\mathcal{G}}$, for each $C \in Gclause(P)$.

Theorem 32. $(K_P^{\mathcal{E}})^{\sim} = (K_P^{\sqsubseteq})^{\sim}$. $\square$

The next theorem is the main result of this section.

Theorem 33. $[\mathcal{R}(\mathcal{M}_P^{\sqsubseteq})] = [\mathcal{R}(lfp(K_P^{\mathcal{E}}))] = lfp((K_P^{\sqsubseteq})^{\sim})$. $\square$

5 Conclusions

Atoms in an interpretation domain normally serve as basic statements which describe relationships among objects. When class/subclass information is provided, there usually exists an implicit-implication relation among the atoms, which is determined by considering their forms and their intended meanings. In a system which regards subclass relationship as schema information, this kind of implicit-implication relation does not depend on any particular interpretation and can usually be determined in advance.

This paper first assumes that the implicit-implication relation among the atoms in an interpretation domain is predetermined and described by a preorder $\sqsubseteq$ on the domain. An appropriate model-theoretic semantics with respect to the implicit implication for declarative programs together with its corresponding fixpoint semantics is discussed. Afterwards, it further assumes that the implicit-implication relation $\sqsubseteq$ is a partial order and shows that, under this stronger assumption, the meaning of any program P can be computed more elegantly by expanding any representative of the least fixpoint of the immediate-consequence operator $(K_P^{\sqsubseteq})^{\sim}$ on a quotient set of reduced subsets of the interpretation domain.

Nevertheless, it should be remarked that the basic assumption that the implicit-implication relation can be determined beforehand is not always admissible. In systems which treat classes as objects and uniformly manipulate subclass relation and other object relations (*e.g.*, F-logic [11]), atoms are also used to describe class/subclass information and, consequently, different interpretations would determine different implicit implications. Another extension of DP theory which accounts for a declarative semantics for programs with respect to such interpretation-dependent implicit implication is discussed in a companion paper [14]. The authors believe that this paper and [14] together provide a solid axiomatic foundation for deductive object-oriented systems with monotonic inheritance. A more general foundation for systems with nonmonotonic inheritance based on Dung's argumentation framework [6] is also in progress.

References

1. K. Akama. Declarative Semantics of Logic Programs on Parameterized Representation Systems. Technical report, Hokkaido University, Sapporo, Japan, 1990.
2. K. Akama. Generalized Logic Programs on Specialization Systems and SLDA Resolution. Technical report, Hokkaido University, Sapporo, Japan, 1990.
3. K. Akama. Declarative Semantics of Logic Programs on Parameterized Representation Systems. *Advances in Software Science and Technology*, 5:45–63, 1993. A revised version of [1].
4. K. Akama. Sufficient Conditions of Inference Rules for Declarative Programs. Technical report, Hokkaido University, Sapporo, Japan, 1994.
5. K. Akama. Logical Formalization of Problems Using Declarative Programs. Technical report, Hokkaido University, Sapporo, Japan, 1995.

6. P. M. Dung. On the Acceptability of Arguments and Its Fundamental Role in Nonmonotonic Reasoning, Logic Programming and *N*-Person Games. *Artificial Intelligence*, 77(2):321–357, September 1995.
7. B. C. Ghosh and V. Wuwongse. Declarative Semantics of Conceptual Graph Programs. In *Proceedings of the Second Workshop on Peirce held in conjunction with the First International Conference on Conceptual Structures (ICCS'93)*, Quebec City, Canada, August 1993.
8. B. C. Ghosh and V. Wuwongse. Inference Systems for Conceptual Graph Programs. In W. M. Tepfenhart, J. P. Dick, and J. F. Sowa, editors, *Proceedings of the Second International Conference on Conceptual Structures (ICCS'94)*, volume 835 of Lecture Notes in Artificial Intelligence, pages 214–229, College Park, Maryland, USA, August 1994. Springer-Verlag.
9. B. C. Ghosh and V. Wuwongse. A Direct Proof Procedure for Definite Conceptual Graph Programs. In G. Ellis, R. Levinson, W. Rich, and J. F. Sowa, editors, *Proceedings of the Third International Conference on Conceptual Structures (ICCS'95)*, volume 954 of Lecture Notes in Artificial Intelligence, pages 158–172, Santa Cruz, CA, USA, August 1995. Springer-Verlag.
10. B. C. Ghosh and V. Wuwongse. Conceptual Graph Programs and Their Declarative Semantics. *IEICE Transactions on Information and Systems*, E78-D(9):1208–1217, September 1995.
11. M. Kifer, G. Lausen, and J. Wu. Logical Foundations of Object-Oriented and Frame-Based Languages. *Journal of the Association for Computing Machinery*, pages 741–843, July 1995.
12. G. Köstler, W. Kießling, H. Thöne, and U. Güntzer. The Differential Fixpoint Operator with Subsumption. In S. Ceri, K. Tanaka, and S. Tsur, editors, *Proceedings of the Third International Conference on Deductive and Object-Oriented Databases (DOOD'93)*, volume 760 of Lecture Notes in Computer Science, pages 35–48, Phoenix, Arizona, USA, December 1993. Springer-Verlag.
13. G. Köstler, W. Kießling, H. Thöne, and U. Güntzer. Fixpoint Iteration with Subsumption in Deductive Databases. *Journal of Intelligent Information Systems*, 4(2):123–148, March 1995. A revised and extended version of [12].
14. V. Wuwongse and E. Nantajeewarawat. Declarative Program Theory with Interpretation-Dependent Implicit Implication. Technical report, Computer Science Program, School of Advanced Technologies, Asian Institute of Technology, Bangkok 10501, Thailand, September 1995.
15. V. Wuwongse and E. Nantajeewarawat. Declarative Program Theory with Implicit Implication. Technical report, Computer Science Program, School of Advanced Technologies, Asian Institute of Technology, Bangkok 10501, Thailand, April 1996.

Knowledge Decomposition: An Analysis

John Debenham
Key Centre for Advanced Computing Sciences, University of Technology, Sydney,
PO Box 123 Broadway, NSW 2007, Australia.
debenham@socs.uts.edu.au

ABSTRACT

Items are a uniform framework for modelling the data, information and knowledge in a knowledge-based system. If two items share an unstated sub-item between them then any changes to that unstated sub-item will require that both of those two items should also be modified; this situation constitutes a maintenance hazard. Knowledge decomposition reduces each item to a form in which it contains no sub-items and thus prevents such maintenance hazards from occurring. An analysis of different forms of knowledge decomposition is developed. Knowledge decomposition can be applied equally to items which represent knowledge or information, or to items which represent combinations of knowledge and information.

1. INTRODUCTION

The terms 'data', 'information' and 'knowledge' are used in a rather idiosyncratic sense. The *data* in an application are those things which could be represented naturally as simple variables, the *information* is those things which could be represented naturally as relations, and the *knowledge* is those things which could be represented naturally in some rule language. In [1] we have proposed 'items' as a uniform framework for modelling the data, information and knowledge in a knowledge-based system. Further in [2] we have defined a single rule of decomposition for items.

Here we briefly describe the notion of an item and its decomposition. We develop a taxonomy of decomposition as a set of 'decomposition forms'; part of this taxonomy is a direct, but non-trivial, generalisation of the 'classical' normal forms for database. All of our decomposition forms may be applied to knowledge as well as to information. We also derive a decomposition form which is *not* a generalisation of the classical normal forms for database. Examples are given which illustrate the application of the various decomposition forms. The goal of these decomposition forms is to ensure that two items do not share a possibly unstated 'sub-item'. Applied to knowledge, the rationale is that if two chunks of expertise do share a sub-chunk then this situation presents a serious maintenance hazard; note that if the expertise within the sub-chunk should change then both of the chunks will have to be modified to preserve correctness.

A complete design methodology for knowledge-based systems has been developed. One goal of this design methodology is to generate a conceptual model which is both easy to understand and easy to maintain [3]. If a conceptual model contains the duplicate representation of things buried within that model then it will be unnecessarily hard to understand and to maintain. Knowledge decomposition removes such duplications; this is achieved by a single decomposition rule. This single rule is expressed in terms of 'items'; items are a formalism which can represent the traditional database construct the 'relation' (or 'information') as well as the essential knowledge-based construct the 'rule' (or 'knowledge') [1]. This single rule thus applies equally to the knowledge (ie "rules") and to the information [4] (ie "relations") in a knowledge-based system.

The maintenance of knowledge-based systems is concerned with two key problems. First the problem of engineering the basic structure of the knowledge base so that it is inherently maintainable [2] [8]; matters to be considered here include the choice of predicates, or relations, for expressing knowledge and the way in which knowledge is represented in terms of those predicates. Second, once the basic structure of the knowledge base has been engineered, the problem of presenting the represented expertise so that it can readily be modified within that structure in response to changes in circumstance; see for example [5] [6] [7]. The approach reported here addresses the first problem. A *first generation methodology*, developed in a collaborative research project between the University of Technology, Sydney and the CSIRO Division of Information Technology, is described in [9]. That methodology was supported by a Computer Assisted Knowledge Engineering tool, or CAKE tool. An experimental version of this tool was trialed in a commercial environment. A *second generation methodology* supporting the construction of systems that are inherently easy to maintain is described here. In addition knowledge constraints [8] may be used to further protect knowledge-based systems against the introduction of update anomalies.

2. ITEMS

Items are a formalism for describing the things in an application; they are described in detail in [1]. They have two important properties: items have a uniform format no matter whether they represent data, information or knowledge things [10]; items incorporate two powerful classes of constraints. The key to this uniform representation is the way in which the "meaning" of an item, called its *semantics*, is specified. Items may be viewed either formally as λ-calculus expressions or informally as i-schema. The λ-calculus view provides a sound theoretical basis for the work; it is *not* intended for practical use. The i-schema view enables the approach to be employed as a practical modelling tool. Thus the work is practical and has a sound theoretical basis [11].

Items have a name which by convention is written in italics. The semantics of an item is a function which *recognises* the members of the "value set" of that item. The value set of an information item at a certain time τ is the set of tuples which are associated with a relational implementation of that item at that time; for example, the value set of the item named *part/cost-price* could be the set of tuples in the "part/cost-price" relation at time τ. Knowledge items have value sets too. This idea of defining the semantics of items as recognising functions for the members of their value set extends to complex, recursive knowledge items. Items thus provide a uniform framework for describing all of the things in the application [12].

Formally, given a unique name A, an n-tuple $(m_1, m_2, \ldots, m_n)$, $M = \sum_{i=1}^{n} m_i$,

if:

- S_A is an M-argument expression of the form:

  $\lambda y_1^1 \ldots y_{m_1}^1 \ldots y_{m_n}^n \bullet [S_{A_1}(y_1^1, \ldots, y_{m_1}^1) \wedge \ \ldots\ldots \wedge S_{A_n}(y_1^n, \ldots, y_{m_n}^n) \wedge J(y_1^1, \ldots, y_{m_1}^1, \ldots, y_{m_n}^n)] \bullet$

  where $\{A_1, \ldots, A_n\}$ is an ordered set of not necessarily distinct items, each item in this set is called a *component* of item A;
- V_A is an M-argument expression of the form:

  $\lambda y_1^1 \ldots y_{m_1}^1 \ldots y_{m_n}^n \bullet [V_{A_1}(y_1^1, \ldots, y_{m_1}^1) \wedge \ \ldots\ldots \wedge V_{A_n}(y_1^n, \ldots, y_{m_n}^n) \wedge K(y_1^1, \ldots, y_{m_1}^1, \ldots, y_{m_n}^n)] \bullet$

  where $\{A_1, \ldots, A_n\}$ are the components of item A, and
- C_A is an expression of the form:

  $C_{A_1} \wedge C_{A_2} \wedge \ldots \wedge C_{A_n} \wedge (L)_A$

  where L is a logical combination of:
  - Card lies in some numerical range;
  - $\mathrm{Uni}(A_i)$ for some i, $1 \leq i \leq n$, and
  - $\mathrm{Can}(A_i, X)$ for some i, $1 \leq i \leq n$, where X is a non-empty subset of $\{A_1, \ldots, A_n\} - \{A_i\}$.

then the named triple $A[\, S_A, V_A, C_A]$ is an n-adic *item* with *item name* A, S_A is called the *semantics* of A, V_A is called the *value constraints* of A and C_A is called the *set constraints* of A. "Uni(a)" is a *universal constraint* which means that "all members of the value set of item a must be in the value set of item A", "Can(b, X)" is a *candidate constraint* which means that "the value set of the set of items X functionally determines the value set of item b", and "Card" means "the number of things in the value set". The subscripts indicate the item's components to which that set constraint applies [2].

For example, an application may contain an association whereby each *part* is associated with a *cost-price*. This association could be subject to the "value constraint" that parts whose part-number is less that 1,999 will be associated with a cost price of no more than $300. This association could also be subject to the "set constraints" that every part must be in this association, and that each part is associated with a unique cost-price. This association could be represented by the information item named *part/cost-price*; the λ-calculus form for this item is:

$$\begin{aligned}&\textit{part/cost-price}[\ \lambda xy \bullet [S_{part}(x) \wedge S_{cost\text{-}price}(y) \wedge \mathrm{costs}(x, y)] \bullet,\\ &\quad \lambda xy \bullet [\ V_{part}(x) \wedge V_{cost\text{-}price}(y) \wedge ((x < 1999) \rightarrow (y \leq 300))\ ] \bullet,\\ &\quad (\mathrm{Uni}(\mathrm{part}) \wedge \mathrm{Can}(\mathrm{cost\text{-}price}, \{\mathrm{part}\}))_{part/cost\text{-}price}\ ]\end{aligned}$$

The λ-calculus form is not intended for practical use. Figure 1 shows the i-schema format for the *part/cost-price* item. The '∀' represents a universal constraint; the horizontal line and the 'o' represents a candidate constraint.

item name	*part/cost-price*	
item components	*part*	*cost-price*
dummy variables	x	y
item semantics	costs(x,y)	
item value constraints	$x<1999 \rightarrow y \leq 300$	
item set constraints	∀	
	------------	o

Figure 1 i-schema format for the item '*part/cost-price*'

[part/sale-price, part/cost-price, mark-up]		
part/sale-price	*part/cost-price*	*mark-up*
(x, w)	(x, y)	z
$\rightarrow (w = z \times y)$		
$\rightarrow w > y$		
∀	∀	
------------------------------------		o
o	------------------------------------	
----------------	o	----------------

Figure 2 i-schema for *[part/sale-price, part/cost-price, mark-up]*

Rules, or knowledge, can also be defined as items. The i-schema for the knowledge item *[part/sale-price, part/cost-price, mark-up]* is shown in Figure 2; this i-schema has four set constraints. The λ-calculus form for this item is:

$$
\begin{aligned}
&[\textit{part/sale-price, part/cost-price, mark-up}][\\
&\quad \lambda x_1 x_2 y_1 y_2 z \bullet [(S_{\textit{part/sale-price}}(x_1, x_2) \wedge S_{\textit{part/cost-price}}(y_1, y_2) \wedge \\
&\qquad S_{\textit{mark-up}}(z)) \wedge ((x_1 = y_1) \rightarrow (x_2 = z \times y_2))] \bullet, \\
&\quad \lambda x_1 x_2 y_1 y_2 z \bullet [V_{\textit{part/sale-price}}(x_1, x_2) \wedge V_{\textit{part/cost-price}}(y_1, y_2) \wedge \\
&\qquad V_{\textit{mark-up}}(z)) \wedge ((x_1 = y_1) \rightarrow (x_2 > y_2))] \bullet, \\
&\quad (\text{Uni}(\textit{part/sale-price}) \wedge \text{Uni}(\textit{part/cost-price}) \\
&\qquad \wedge \text{Can}(\text{part/sale-price}, \{\textit{part/cost-price, mark-up}\}) \\
&\qquad \wedge \text{Can}(\textit{part/cost-price}, \{\textit{part/sale-price, mark-up}\}) \\
&\qquad \wedge \text{Can}(\textit{mark-up}, \{\textit{part/sale-price, part/cost-price}\}) \\
&\quad)_{[\textit{part/sale-price, part/cost-price, mark-up}]}]
\end{aligned}
$$

3. ANALYSIS OF ITEM DECOMPOSITION

In [2] the "item join" operation is defined; item join provides the basis for item decomposition. Given items *A* and *B*, the item with name $A \otimes_E B$ is called the *join* of *A* and *B* on E, where E is a set of components common to both *A* and *B*. When two items are joined on the component set which consists of *all* of their common components we omit the subscript of the join operator.

The rule of composition ⊗ enables knowledge items, information items and data items may be joined with one another regardless of type. For example, the knowledge item:

$$[cost\text{-}price,\ tax]\ [\lambda xy\bullet[x = y \times 0.05]\bullet,\ \lambda xy\bullet[x < y]\bullet,\ C_{[cost\text{-}price,\ tax]}]$$

can be joined with the information item *part/cost-price* on the set {*cost-price*} to give the information item *part/cost-price/tax*. In other words:

$$[cost\text{-}price,\ tax] \otimes_{\{cost\text{-}price\}} part/cost\text{-}price =$$
$$part/cost\text{-}price/tax[\ \lambda xyz\bullet[\text{costs}(x,y) \wedge z = y \times 0.05]\bullet,$$
$$\lambda xyz\bullet[((1000<x<1999) \rightarrow (0<y\leq 300)) \wedge (z<y)]\bullet,$$
$$C_{part/cost\text{-}price/tax}\ ]$$

Using the rule of composition ⊗ items may be joined together to form more complex items. Alternatively, the ⊗ operator may form the basis of a theory of decomposition in which each item may be replaced by a set of simpler items. An item I is *decomposable* into the set of items $D = \{I_1, I_2,..., I_n\}$ if:

- I_i has non-trivial semantics for all i,
- $I = I_1 \otimes I_2 \otimes ... \otimes I_n$, where
- each join is *monotonic*; that is, each term in this composition contributes at least one component to I.

If item I is decomposable then it will not necessarily have a unique decomposition. We now give one rule of decomposition: "Given a complete set of items discard any items which are decomposable". This rule applies to all items. For example, this rule requires that we discard the item *part/cost-price/tax* in favour of the two items *[cost-price, tax]* and *part/cost-price*.

Item decomposition will now be analysed at two levels on the basis of:

- the number of components in the item, and
- the candidate constraints present in the item.

An item of two components has only trivial decompositions. Items of three or more components have interesting decomposition forms.

4. DECOMPOSITION OF THREE COMPONENT ITEMS

The functional dependencies between sets of components in an item are represented by the candidate constraints. For three component items there are five different decomposition forms each determined by a different candidate constraint structure. Coincidentally these five decomposition forms are non-trivial generalisations of the 'classical normal forms' for relational database. The *classical normal forms* for the relational data model are those normal forms referred to as first, second, third, fourth, fifth and Boyce-Codd normal forms [4]. If item I has two component sets:

$$D = \{D_1, D_2,.., D_p\} \quad \text{and} \quad E = \{E_1, E_2,.., E_q\}$$

then we use the notation Can(D, E) to denote the set of candidate constraints Can(D_i, E) for all i = 1,..,p. If an item contains a candidate constraint Can(d, E) then we say that the item contains a *functional dependency* from E to d. For example if the constraint Can(Z, {X, Y}) is valid then that item contains a functional dependency from {X, Y} to Z.

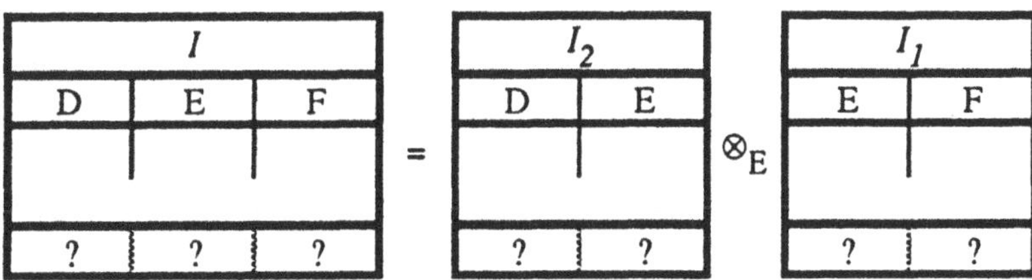

Figure 3 Decomposition [D3.2]

Suppose that item I has the three component sets D, E and F; we denote this by I(D, E, F). Consider the different ways in which the item $I = I(\text{D, E, F})$ can be decomposed into two sub-items I_1 and I_2 by:

$$I(\text{D, E, F}) = I_2(\text{D, E}) \otimes_{\text{E}} I_1(\text{E, F}) \qquad \text{[D3.2]}$$

The different ways in which item I can be decomposed are categorised by the different ways in which candidate constraints are present in the set constraints of I; there are three different cases:

- there are no candidate constraints in I;
- the candidate constraints in I are only between pairs of D, E and F, and
- there is at least one candidate constraint in I of the form Can(Z, {X, Y}).

Consider the first case, if there are no candidate constraints in I at all then:

$$C_I = \emptyset \;;\; C_{I_1} = \emptyset \;;\; C_{I_2} = \emptyset \qquad \text{[4NF]}$$

and the decomposition [D3.2] is a generalisation of classical *fourth normal form*.

Consider the second case when the candidate constraints in I are only between pairs of D, E and F. Removing unnecessary duplications and deleting trivial decompositions, this may occur in one way only:

$$C_I = \{\text{Can(F, D), Can(F, E), Can(E, D)}\};$$
$$C_{I_1} = \{\text{Can(E, D)}\}; \quad C_{I_2} = \{\text{Can(F, E)}\} \qquad \text{[3NF]}$$

This is a generalisation of classical *third normal form* and is illustrated in Figure 4.

Consider the third case in which I contains at least one candidate constraint of the form Can(Z, {X, Y}). Removing unnecessary duplications and deleting trivial decompositions, this may occur in two different ways:

$$C_I = \{\text{Can(E, \{F, D\}), Can(D, E)}\};$$
$$C_{I_1} = \{\text{Can(D, E)}\}; \quad C_{I_2} = \emptyset \qquad \text{[BCNF]}$$

and

$$C_I = \{\text{Can(D, \{E, F\}), Can(D, E)}\};$$
$$C_{I_1} = \{\text{Can(D, E)}\}; \quad C_{I_2} = \emptyset \qquad \text{[2NF]}$$

[BCNF] is a generalisation of classical *Boyce-Codd normal form*. [2NF] is a

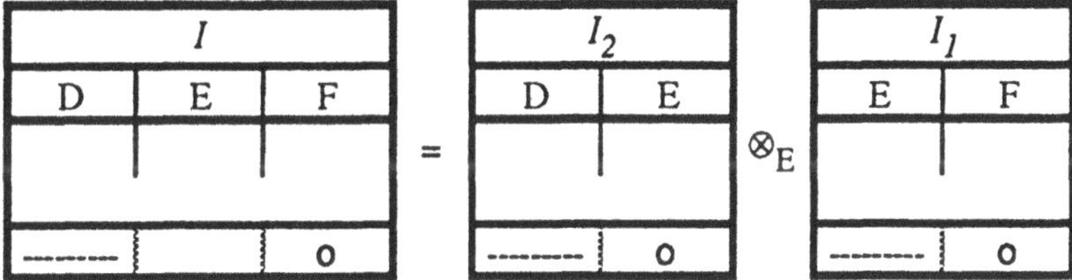

Figure 4 Classical third normal form for items

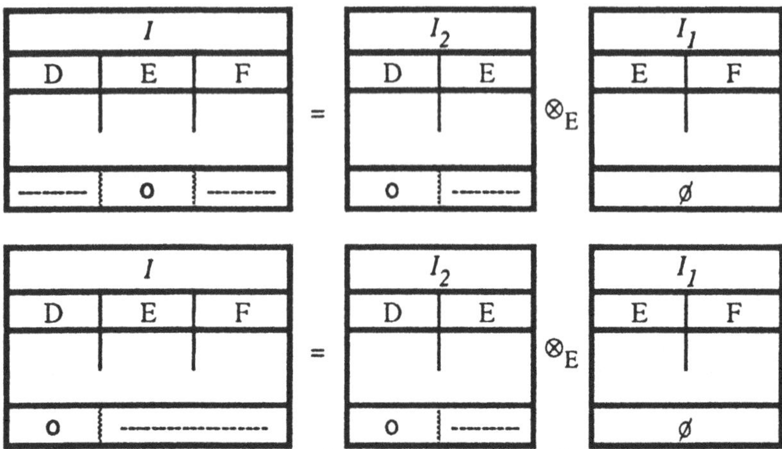

Figure 5 Classical Boyce-Codd and second normal forms for items

generalisation of the classical *second normal form.* [BCNF] and [2NF] are illustrated in Figure 5.

The only other way in which an item of three component sets can be decomposed is by:

$$I(\text{D, E, F}) = I_3(\text{F, D}) \otimes I_2(\text{D, E}) \otimes I_1(\text{E, F}) \qquad \text{[D3.3]}$$

If there are no candidate constraints present in I then this decomposition becomes:

$$C_I = \emptyset; \ C_{I_1} = \emptyset; \ C_{I_2} = \emptyset; \ C_{I_3} = \emptyset \qquad \text{[5NF]}$$

which is a generalisation of the classical *fifth normal form.* Further if there *are* candidate constraints present in I then it may be shown that the decomposition [D3.3] reduces to one of the above. Thus we see that these five generalisations of the five classical normal forms provide a complete characterisation of the ways in which an item of three component sets may be decomposed [13].

4.1 APPLICATIONS

We now apply the decomposition forms [BCNF], [2NF], [3NF] and [4NF], derived in the previous section, to some examples. Our general rule of decomposition may be applied to any item. In particular it may be applied to the decomposition of knowledge.

First consider the decomposition form [BCNF]. Consider the following example: "An organisation is staffed by 'persons (pers)'. Each person will hold one of three 'jobs (job)': 'General Manager (GM)', 'Department Manager (DM)' or 'Worker (W)'. A person who holds the job of DM or W is an 'employee (emp)'. Employees work in 'departments (dep)'. There is one GM, and each department has one DM. Each employee has a 'supervisor (super)': the GM supervises the DMs, and each DM supervises the Ws who work in that DM's department." The wisdom in this example can be expressed in terms of four information items *emp/super*, *pers/job*, *emp/dep* and *dep/man*. Expressed in logic programming, if:

emp/super(x, y) ← pers/job(x, 'W'), emp/dep(x, z), dep/man(z, y)
emp/super(x, y) ← pers/job(x, 'DM'), pers/job(y, 'GM') [A]

and:

item1		
P	*Q*	*R*
(x,v)	(x,y)	(z)
→ v = x × y		
∅		
∀		
o	------------------------------	

item2	
P	*Q*
(x,v)	(x,y)
→ v = x × y	
∅	
∀	
o	--------------

Figure 6 Form [2NF] applied to items

pers/job(x, 'GM') ← emp/super(y, x), emp/super(z, y)
pers/job(x, 'DM') ← emp/super(y, x), emp/super(y, z)
pers/job(x, 'W') ← emp/super(x, y), emp/super(y, z)

then [A] breaches decomposition form [BCNF] and should be replaced by:

emp/dep(x, y) ← dep/man(y, x)
emp/dep(x, y) ← emp/super(x, z), dep/man(y, z) [B]

In general when the Boyce-Codd normal form is applied to conventional relations dependencies may be lost. The same is true when the decomposition form [BCNF] is applied to knowledge. Note that if [A] is deleted in the above example then neither of the two groups of clauses which remain enable emp/super to be derived.

Second consider the decomposition form [2NF]; this form applied to knowledge objects states, for example, that *item1* shown in Figure 6 should be replaced by *item2*.

Third consider the decomposition form [3NF]; this form applied to logic programming states, for example, that if we have the clause:

part/sell(x, y) ← part/cost(x, z), part/type(x, v),
type/m-up(v, w), y = (z × w) [C]

where "m-up" stands for "mark-up-factor". Suppose that buried within this clause is the sub-rule that "the mark-up factor for a spare part is the mark-up factor associated with that spare part's type". This sub-rule could be represented as:

part/m-up(x, y) ← part/type(x, z), type/m-up(z, y) [D]

and clause [C] breaches the form [3NF]. [C] should be replaced by [D] and by the following third clause:

part/sell(x, y) ← part/cost(x, z), part/m-up(x, w),
y = (z × w) [E]

Note that [C] can be re-generated from [D] and [E] by resolution. The item form of this decomposition is shown in Figure 7.

Fourth consider the decomposition form [4NF]; this form is applied to the item *[P, Q, R]* shown in Figure 8; this item breaches decomposition form [4NF] and should be replaced by the items *[P, Q]* and *[P, R]*.

5. DECOMPOSITION OF FOUR COMPONENT ITEMS

In the previous section we analysed the decomposition of items with three component sets. In this section we apply the single rule of decomposition to items of four components. In this way we derive a new, "non-classical" decomposition form for items [14].

[part/sell, part/cost, part/type, type/m-up]			
part/sell	*part/cost*	*part/type*	*type/m-up*
(x, y)	(x, z)	(x, v)	(v, w)
→ (y = z × w)			
∅			
∀			
o	--		

=

[part/m-up, part/type, type/m-up]		
part/m-up	*part/type*	*type/m-up*
(x, y)	(x, z)	(z, y)
∅		
∅		
∀		
o	------------------------	

⊗

[part/sell, part/cost, part/m-up]		
part/sell	*part/cost*	*part/m-up*
(x, y)	(x, z)	(x, w)
→ (y = z × w)		
∅		
∀		
o	------------------------	

Figure 7 Form [3NF] applied to items joined on {*part/m-up*}

Suppose that item *I* has the four component sets A, B, C and D. We now consider the different ways in which this item *I*(A, B, C, D) can be decomposed which do not reduce to the classical decomposition forms. The decomposition of *I* into two sub-items may be achieved in a number of ways; in particular it may be achieved by:

$$I(\mathrm{A, B, C, D}) = I_1(\mathrm{A, B, C}) \otimes_{\{\mathrm{B,C}\}} I_2(\mathrm{B, C, D}) \qquad \text{[D4]}$$

[P, Q, R]		
P	*Q*	*R*
(v, w)	(v, x)	(y, z)
(x = w × 1.2) ∧ (y = v+w) ∧ (z = w × 1.7)		
∅		
∀	∀	∀

=

[P, Q]	
P	*Q*
(v, w)	(v, w)
(x = w × 1.2)	
∅	
∀	∀

$\otimes_{\{P\}}$

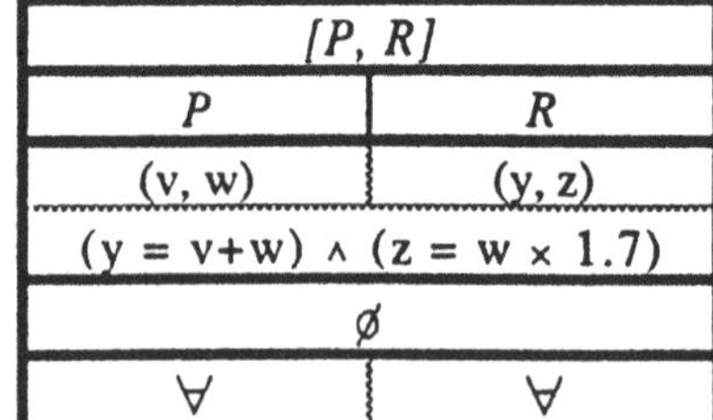

[P, R]	
P	*R*
(v, w)	(y, z)
(y = v+w) ∧ (z = w × 1.7)	
∅	
∀	∀

Figure 8 Form [4NF] applied to items

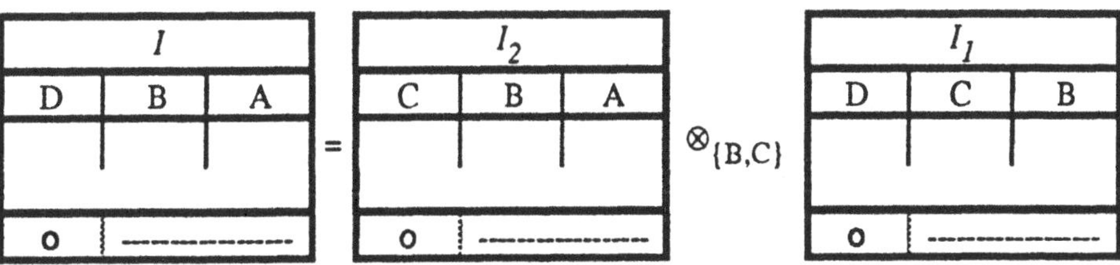

Figure 9 Form [xNF] for items

The different ways in which this rule of decomposition can be employed may be categorised by the different ways in which candidate constraints are present in I. We identify three different cases:

- there are no candidate constraints in I;
- the candidate constraints in I are only between pairs of A, B, C and D, and
- there is at least one candidate constraint in I of the form Can(Z, {X, Y}).

The first and second of these cases reduce to classical decomposition forms. However consider the third case when the candidate constraint Can(D, {B, A}) is present in I; if this candidate constraint is present in I then one way in which candidate constraints may be present in I_1 and I_2 is:

$$C_I = \{\text{Can}(D, \{B, A\}), \text{Can}(D, \{C, B\}), \text{Can}(C, \{B, A\})\};$$

$$C_{I_1} = \{\text{Can}(C, \{B, A\})\}; \qquad C_{I_2} = \{\text{Can}(D, \{C, B\})\} \qquad \text{[xNF]}$$

This rule of decomposition is not equivalent to any of the classical forms introduced above. The structure of the decomposition [xNF] is illustrated in Figure 9.

[part/profit, part/cost, part/m-up]		
part/profit	*part/cost*	*part/m-up*
(x, y)	(x, w)	(x, u)
→ (y = w × (u - 1))		
∅		
∀		
o	------------------------	

=

[part/profit, part/sell, part/cost]		
part/profit	*part/sell*	*part/cost*
(x, y)	(x, z)	(x, w)
→ (y = z - w)		
∅		
∀		
o	------------------------	

⊗

[part/sell, part/cost, part/m-up]		
part/sell	*part/cost*	*part/m-up*
(x, y)	(x, z)	(x, w)
→ (y = z × w)		
∅		
∀		
o	------------------------	

Figure 10 Form [xNF] applied to items joined on {*part/sell, part/cost*}

5.1 APPLICATIONS

We now apply the decomposition form [xNF]. Applied to logic programming this form advises us that if the clause:

part/profit(x, y) ← part/cost-price(x, w),
part/m-up(x, u), $y = w \times (u - 1)$ [F]

has buried within it the sub-rule that "the sale price of a part is the cost price of that part multiplied by the mark-up-factor associated with that part" then clause [F] should be decomposed. This sub-rule could be represented as the clause:

part/sale-price(x, y) ← part/cost-price(x, z),
part/m-up(x, w), $y = (z \times w)$ [G]

Clause [F] also has buried within it the sub-rule that "the profit of a part is the difference of the sale price of that part and the cost price of that part". This sub-rule could be represented as the clause:

part/profit(x, y) ← part/sale-price(x, z),
part/cost-price(x, w), $y = z - w$ [H]

In other words, decomposition form [xNF] requires that clause [F] should be replaced by clauses [G] and [H]. The item form of this decomposition is shown in Figure 10. The join in this decomposition involves two components each of which plays a different role in the candidate constraints. Note that this decomposition is not equivalent to the example illustrated in Figure 7; in that example the join was effected on just one component.

6. CONCLUSION

Chunks of raw knowledge may contain duplicate representations of, possibly unstated, unstated sub-rules; further any changes to a sub-rule will require that all knowledge chunks containing that sub-rule should also be modified. This situation can constitute a maintenance hazard. Knowledge decomposition removes the representation of sub-rules and thus removes these maintenance hazards. Knowledge decomposition is expressed in terms items. In all of the decomposition forms described above, with the exception of classical Boyce-Codd normal form, the decomposition of a given item is a set of items which may be joined to reconstruct the given item. Thus, with the exception of the Boyce-Codd normal form, no knowledge is lost by applying the decomposition forms described. Applying knowledge decomposition usually relies on continual reference to the knowledge source and thus decomposition can be an expensive process.

REFERENCES

[1] J.K. Debenham, "Integrating Knowledge Base and Database", in *proceedings 10th ACM Annual Symposium on Applied Computing SAC'96*, Philadelphia, February 1996, pp28-32.

[2] J.K. Debenham, "Normalising Knowledge Objects", in *proceedings Second International Conference on Information and Knowledge Management*, Washington, November 1993, pp335-343.

[3] H. Katsuno and A.O. Mendelzon, "On the Difference between Updating a Knowledge Base and Revising It", in *proceedings Second International Conference on Principles of Knowledge Representation and Reasoning, KR'91*, Morgan Kaufmann, 1991.

[4] C.J. Date, "*An Introduction to Database Systems*" (4th edition) Addison-Wesley, 1986.

[5] B. Kang, W. Gambetta, and P. Compton, "Validation and Verification with Ripple Down Rules", *International Journal of Human Computer Studies* Vol 44 (2) pp257-270 (1996).

[6] F. Coenen and T. Bench-Capon, "Building Knowledge Based Systems for Maintainability", in *proceedings Third International Conference on Database and Expert Systems Applications DEXA'92*, Valencia, Spain, September, 1992, pp415-420.

[7] F. Lehner, H.F. Hofman, R. Setzer, and R. Maier, "Maintenance of Knowledge Bases", in *proceedings Fourth International Conference DEXA93*, Prague, September 1993, pp436-447.

[8] J.K. Debenham, "Understanding Expert Systems Maintenance", in *proceedings Sixth International Conference on Database and Expert Systems Applications DEXA'95*, London, September 1995.

[9] J.K. Debenham, "*Knowledge Systems Design*", Prentice Hall, 1989.

[10] H. Ito "Interface for Integrating a Knowledge-Based System and Database Management System Using Frame-Based Knowledge Representation", in *proceedings Expert Systems World Congress*, J. Liebowitz (Ed), Pergamon Press 1991.

[11] N. Tayar, "A Model for Developing Large Shared Knowledge Bases" in *proceedings Second International Conference on Information and Knowledge Management*, Washington, November 1993, pp717-719.

[12] J.K. Debenham, "A Unified Approach to Requirements Specification and System Analysis in the Design of Knowledge-Based Systems", in *proceedings Seventh International Conference on Software Engineering and Knowledge Engineering SEKE'95*, Washington DC, June 1995, pp144-146.

[13] P.M.D. Gray, "Expert Systems and Object-Oriented Databases: Evolving a New Software Architecture", in "*Research and Development in Expert Systems V*", Cambridge University Press, 1989, pp 284-295.

[14] J.K. Debenham, "Characterising Maintenance Links", in *proceedings Third World Congress on Expert Systems*, Seoul, February 1996.

The Concept Classification of a Terminology Extended by Conjunction and Disjunction

Gerd Stumme

Technische Hochschule Darmstadt, Fachbereich Mathematik
Schloßgartenstr. 7, D–64289 Darmstadt, stumme@mathematik.th-darmstadt.de

1 Introduction

At the two conferences KRUSE '95 ([6]) and ICCS '95 ([7], [8]) held at Santa Cruz in August 1995 researchers on description logics, conceptual graphs, and formal concept analysis came together and discovered common interests and tasks. A fruitful discussion revealed that these three disciplines should integrate their research. Therefore common developments were considered. In one of the presented papers ([2]), for instance, F. Baader demonstrated how a classification algorithm providing more information can be built by combining a subsumption algorithm of description logics with a knowledge acquisition tool of formal concept analysis. In this paper we show how a classification algorithm providing still more information can be obtained by choosing another acquisition tool of formal concept analysis.

Much work has been done to develop algorithms for computing the subsumption hierarchy for knowledge representation systems based on description logics (also called KL-ONE like systems, terminological knowledge representation systems; cf. [1]). In [2], F. Baader describes how this computation can be extended to all conjunctions of concepts given in a terminology (TBox). He applies *attribute exploration* [9], an exploration tool of formal concept analysis (cf. [22], [10]) which is usually used as an interactive procedure to interview efficiently a human expert about a certain domain of knowledge. Instead of computing only the partially ordered set of the concepts in the TBox with the subsumption ordering, he obtains the complete semi-lattice of all possible conjunctions of concepts in the TBox. Since every complete semi-lattice is in fact a complete lattice, the existence of suprema (i. e., least common superconcepts) is asserted. However they generally differ from the disjunction – unlike the infima which are always equal to the conjunction of concepts. This paper describes, how the complete lattice of all possible combinations of conjunctions and disjunctions (and negations) of concepts in the TBox can be computed by applying another exploration tool of formal concept analysis, namely *distributive concept exploration* [17], instead of attribute exploration.

As in [2] we restrict ourselves to the description logic language $\mathcal{ALC}$, but the results can be generalized to other languages. The basic notions of $\mathcal{ALC}$ are recalled in the next section. There we also give a short introduction into formal concept analysis.

2 Description Logic and Formal Concept Analysis

In this section we briefly recall the basic notations of the description logic $\mathcal{ALC}$ and of formal concept analysis. For a more detailed introduction we refer to [14] and [1] for $\mathcal{ALC}$, and to [10] and [22] for formal concept analysis.

2.1 The Description Logic $\mathcal{ALC}$

The *syntax* of $\mathcal{ALC}$ is built from a set of *concept names* and a set of *role names*. *Concept descriptions* are defined recursively:

- The concept names (which are assumed to contain two particular names $\top$ and $\bot$ for the *top* and the *bottom concept*) are concept descriptions.
- If C and D are concept descriptions and R is a role name, then $C \sqcap D$ (*conjunction*), $C \sqcup D$ (*disjunction*), $\neg C$ (*negation*), $\exists R.C$ (*existential restriction*), and $\forall R.C$ (*value restriction*) are concept descriptions.

A *terminological axiom* is a pair $A{=}D$ where A is a concept name different from $\top$ and $\bot$ and D is a concept description. A *terminology* (*TBox*) is a finite set $\mathcal{T}$ of terminological axioms such that there are no cyclic and no multiple definitions. The concepts A appearing in an axiom $A = D$ on the left side are called *defined concepts*, otherwise they are called *primitive concepts*.

Next we describe the *semantics* of $\mathcal{ALC}$: An *interpretation* $\mathcal{I}$ consists of a set $\text{dom}(\mathcal{I})$ and of a function $(\,)^{\mathcal{I}}$ which maps every concept name to a subset of $\text{dom}(\mathcal{I})$ ($\top$ has to be mapped to $\text{dom}(\mathcal{I})$ and $\bot$ to the empty set) and every role name to a binary relation on $\text{dom}(\mathcal{I})$. This mapping is recursively extended to concept descriptions by

- $(C \sqcap D)^{\mathcal{I}} := C^{\mathcal{I}} \cap D^{\mathcal{I}}$,
- $(C \sqcup D)^{\mathcal{I}} := C^{\mathcal{I}} \cup D^{\mathcal{I}}$,
- $(\neg C)^{\mathcal{I}} := \text{dom}(\mathcal{I}) \setminus C^{\mathcal{I}}$,
- $(\exists R.C)^{\mathcal{I}} := \{x \in \text{dom}(\mathcal{I}) \mid \exists y \in C^{\mathcal{I}} \colon (x,y) \in R^{\mathcal{I}}\}$,
- $(\forall R.C)^{\mathcal{I}} := \{x \in \text{dom}(\mathcal{I}) \mid \forall y \in \text{dom}(\mathcal{I}) \colon (x,y) \in R^{\mathcal{I}} \Rightarrow y \in C^{\mathcal{I}}\}$.

A *model* of a TBox $\mathcal{T}$ is an interpretation $\mathcal{I}$ which satisfies the equality $A^{\mathcal{I}} = D^{\mathcal{I}}$ for all terminological axioms $A{=}D$ in the TBox $\mathcal{T}$.

We say that a concept description D *subsumes* a concept description C *with respect to* a TBox $\mathcal{T}$ ($C \sqsubseteq_{\mathcal{T}} D$), if the inequality $C^{\mathcal{I}} \subseteq D^{\mathcal{I}}$ holds for all models $\mathcal{I}$ of $\mathcal{T}$.

In [14], a *subsumption algorithm* is described which computes for given concept descriptions C and D whether C is subsumed by D with respect to a TBox $\mathcal{T}$. In [2], it is shown that, if C is not subsumed by D then the algorithm can provide a "counterexample", i.e. a model $\mathcal{I}$ of $\mathcal{T}$ and an individual $c \in \text{dom}(\mathcal{I})$ with $c \in C^{\mathcal{I}} \setminus D^{\mathcal{I}}$.

2.2 Formal Concept Analysis

Formal concept analysis is based on the philosophical understanding of a concept as a unit of thought consisting of two parts: the extension contains all objects belonging to the concept and the intension contains all attributes valid for all these objects (cf. [21]). Formal concept analysis starts with a *formal context* (G, M, I) which consists of two sets G and M and a relation $I \subseteq G \times M$. The elements of G and M are called *objects* and *attributes*, respectively, and $(g, m) \in I$ is read as "the object g has the attribute m".

Now, the *formal concepts* of the context (G, M, I) are all pairs (A, B) with $A \subseteq G$ and $B \subseteq M$ such that (A, B) is maximal with the property $A \times B \subseteq I$. The set A is called the *extent* and the set B is called the *intent* of the formal concept (A, B). The set $\mathfrak{B}(G, M, I)$ of all formal concepts of a formal context with the ordering $(A_1, B_1) \leq (A_2, B_2) :\iff A_1 \subseteq A_2$ is always a complete lattice which is called the *concept lattice* of the context (G, M, I) (cf. [22]). The ordering reflects the subconcept-superconcept-relation.

Next we introduce the two derivations $A' := \{m \in M \mid \forall g \in A\colon (g, m) \in I\}$ for $A \subseteq G$, and $B' := \{g \in G \mid \forall m \in B\colon (g, m) \in I\}$ for $B \subseteq M$. The fact that (A, B) with $A \subseteq G$ and $B \subseteq M$ is a formal concept is equivalent to $A' = B$ and $A = B'$. The smallest formal concept having an object g in its extent is $\gamma g := (\{g\}'', \{g\}')$, the largest formal concept having an attribute m in its intent is $\mu m := (\{m\}', \{m\}'')$. In the concept lattice, infima and suprema are calculated as follows:

$$\bigwedge_{t \in T} (A_t, B_t) = (\bigcap_{t \in T} A_t, (\bigcup_{t \in T} B_t)''), \quad \bigvee_{t \in T} (A_t, B_t) = ((\bigcup_{t \in T} A_t)'', \bigcap_{t \in T} B_t)$$

Every complete lattice can be viewed as a concept lattice: The Basic Theorem of Formal Concept Analysis (cf. [22]) shows that a complete lattice L is isomorphic to the concept lattice $\mathfrak{B}(L, L, \leq)$. We say that a complete lattice L is *represented* by a formal context (G, M, I) if $L \cong \mathfrak{B}(G, M, I)$. If L is a finite lattice then it is also isomorphic to the concept lattice $\mathfrak{B}(J(L), M(L), \leq)$ where $J(L)$ is the set of all join-irreducible elements and $M(L)$ is the set of all meet-irreducible elements of L. The context $(J(L), M(L), \leq)$ is said to be *reduced*. It is (up to isomorphism) the unique minimal context which represents L.

Since description logics and formal concept analysis have been developed independently, the notations are slightly different (see [27] for an extensive discussion): The concepts in description logics are understood as unary predicates. Hence they correspond more to the attributes in formal concept analysis than to the formal concepts, which have no direct counterpart in description logics. The conjunction of concepts in description logics correspond directly to the infimum of attribute concepts in formal concept analysis. In [11] and [15], concept formations like negation and disjunction are discussed for formal concept analysis, since they are important for the handling of incomplete knowledge (cf. [4], [11], [25], [26]) in *conceptual knowledge systems* [26]. For her dissertation, U. Priß is working on adding existential and value restriction (cf. also [12]).

Description logics have a strict distinction between the TBox containing purely intensional definitions of concepts and roles, and the ABox providing information about individuals. In formal concept analysis, extension and intension are understood as two aspects of a concept which cannot be treated separately.

3 Extending the Concept Classification of a Terminology

It is efficient to provide the subsumption relationships of the concepts in a terminology explicitly as a partially ordered set for further computations. The computation of the ordering, called *classification*, is done by repeatedly applying a subsumption algorithm. For two given concepts C and D the subsumption algorithm computes whether C is subsumed by D with respect to a terminology. In [14], the first sound and complete subsumption algorithm for $\mathcal{ALC}$ is given.

Although the classification gives important information about a terminology, there are hierarchical dependencies between the concepts that cannot be described. In [2] (where also the subsumption algorithm of [14] is described), F. Baader gives as example the terminology

Male = ¬Female, Human = Male ⊔ Female, Parent = ∃child.Human,
NoDaughter = ∀child.Male, NoSon = ∀child.Female,
and NoSmallChild = ∀child.¬Small

where Small and Female are primitive concepts. In the ordering resulting from the classification, the three concepts NoDaughter, NoSon and NoSmallChild are incomparable. The subsumption NoDaughter ⊓ NoSon ⊑ NoSmallChild cannot be deduced from the partially ordered set.

For including information about the subsumption-relationship between conjunctions, the classification can be extended with all conjunctions of the concepts of the terminology. Instead of testing all pairs of conjunctions for subsumption (which would not be effective, since in the worst case the number of concepts built by conjunction is exponential in the size of the terminology), Baader applies *attribute exploration* ([9], see also [10], [3]), an exploration tool of formal concept analysis. Attribute exploration produces questions of the kind "Is $C_1 \sqcap \ldots \sqcap C_n$ subsumed by $D_1 \sqcap \ldots \sqcap D_m$?" which are answered by the subsumption algorithm. The set of all suggested subsumptions being accepted by the subsumption algorithm is a minimal representation (called *Duquenne–Guigues–Basis*) of the semi-lattice of all possible conjunctions of the concepts in the TBox. Additionally this algorithm provides a list of "counterexamples" $(\mathcal{I}, c)$ for all subsumptions that do not hold with respect to the terminology: For every pair $C_1 \sqcap \ldots \sqcap C_n$, $D_1 \sqcap \ldots \sqcap D_m$ of conjunctions of concepts of the TBox with $C_1 \sqcap \ldots \sqcap C_n \not\sqsubseteq_{\mathcal{T}} D_1 \sqcap \ldots \sqcap D_m$ there is a pair $(\mathcal{I}, c)$ in the list such that $c \in (C_1 \sqcap \ldots \sqcap C_n)^{\mathcal{I}} \setminus (D_1 \sqcap \ldots \sqcap D_m)^{\mathcal{I}}$.

Since every complete semi-lattice is also a complete lattice, we can compute suprema in the resulting ordering. For instance, the supremum of Male and Female is Human in our example. Unfortunately, this does not imply Human = Male ⊔ Female (but only Human ⊒ Male ⊔ Female), since the supremum in general does not correspond to the disjunction.[1] The subsumption Human $\sqsubseteq$ Male $\sqcup$ Female cannot be deduced from the classification of all conjunctions alone, although it follows directly from the definition of Human in the TBox.

By replacing attribute exploration by *distributive concept exploration* ([17], [5]), the classification algorithm computes the complete lattice of all combinations of conjunctions and disjunctions of the concepts in the TBox. In particular, the supremum in the resulting lattice will correspond to the disjunction. The lattice will be represented by a minimal formal context (which can be stored for further computations). As in the previous case, the algorithm provides a list of counterexamples for all non valid subsumptions.

4 Computing the Conjunction-Disjunction-Lattice

The algorithm for the computation of the conjunction-disjunction-lattice generated by the concepts of a terminology uses the fact that this lattice is isomorphic to a suitable quotient lattice of the free bounded distributive lattice generated by the concepts. Hence the main task is to determine the corresponding congruence relation. Since free bounded distributive lattices grow exponentially, the algorithm does not calculate in this lattice, but splits up the task of determining the congruence relation. Therefore the tensor product for complete lattices ([23], see definition below) which is the coproduct in the category of completely distributive complete lattices is used. The equation $\mathrm{FBD}(\{x_1, \ldots, x_i\}) = \mathrm{FBD}(\{x_1, \ldots, x_{i-1}\}) \otimes \mathrm{FBD}(\{x_i\})$ allows an iterative computation.

Starting with $i = 1$ the algorithm determines a lattice L_i that is isomorphic to the conjunction-disjunction-lattice generated by the first i concepts $C_1, \ldots, C_i$ of the terminology. The lattice L_i results from L_{i-1} by $L_i := (L_{i-1} \otimes \mathrm{FBD}(\{C_i\}))/\Theta_i$, where L_0 is the two element lattice $\bot < \top$. The congruence relation Θ_i is determined by applying the subsumption algorithm. The lattice $L_{i-1} \otimes \mathrm{FBD}(\{C_i\})$ is the lattice which respects all hierarchical dependencies between the first $i-1$ concepts, but no relationships to the concept C_i. The congruence Θ_i is then describing these relationships. Both congruence relations and tensor products can be defined by formal contexts representing the lattices. This allows an effective computation.

4.1 Tensor Products and Congruence Relations of Complete Lattices

The *tensor product* of two complete lattices L_1 and L_2 is defined to be the concept lattice $L_1 \otimes L_2 := \mathfrak{B}(L_1 \times L_2, L_1 \times L_2, \nabla)$ with $(x_1, x_2)\nabla(y_1, y_2) :\Longleftrightarrow (x_1 \leq y_1 \text{ or } x_2 \leq y_2)$. We define the *direct product* of two contexts $\mathbb{K}_1 := (G_1, M_1, I_1)$ and $\mathbb{K}_2 := (G_2, M_2, I_2)$ to be the context $\mathbb{K}_1 \times \mathbb{K}_2 := (G_1 \times G_2, M_1 \times M_2, \nabla)$ with the incidence $(g_1, g_2)\nabla(m_1, m_2) :\Longleftrightarrow ((g_1, m_1) \in I_1 \text{ or } (g_2, m_2) \in I_2)$.

[1] The supremum always subsumes the disjunction; in general the inverse does not hold.

The tensor product of two concept lattices is (up to isomorphism) just the concept lattice of the direct product of their contexts: $\underline{\mathfrak{B}}(\mathbb{K}_1)\otimes\underline{\mathfrak{B}}(\mathbb{K}_2) \cong \underline{\mathfrak{B}}(\mathbb{K}_1 \times \mathbb{K}_2)$ (cf. [23]).

We say that a context is *distributive* if its concept lattice is distributive. All contexts in the following will be distributive reduced finite contexts. The direct product of distributive reduced contexts is again a distributive reduced context.

In reduced finite contexts every *congruence relation* corresponds to a *compatible subcontext*: A context (H, N, J) is called a *subcontext* of a context (G, M, I) if $H \subseteq G$, $N \subseteq M$ and $J = I \cap (H \times N)$. It is called *compatible* if for every concept (A, B) of (G, M, I) the pair $(A \cap H, B \cap N)$ is also a concept of the subcontext. Every compatible subcontext of a distributive reduced context is again a distributive reduced context (cf. [10]).

Factorizing a concept lattice is equivalent to deleting suitable rows and columns in the context (which generates a compatible subcontext). The rows and columns that have to be deleted can be described with the $\swarrow\!\!\nearrow$-*relation*: For $g \in G$ and $m \in M$ we write $g \swarrow\!\!\nearrow m$ if γg is minimal in γG with $\gamma g \not\leq \mu m$ and μm is maximal in μM with $\gamma g \not\leq \mu m$. In a distributive reduced finite context the $\swarrow\!\!\nearrow$-relation is a bijection between the set of objects and the set of attributes, and the compatible subcontexts are exactly those of the form $(H, N, I \cap (H \times N))$ where $g \swarrow\!\!\nearrow m$ implies $g \in H \iff m \in N$. The following theorem (cf. [17]) describes the correspondence between the compatible subcontexts and the congruence relations:

Theorem 1. *Let (G, M, I) be a distributive reduced finite context, $g \in G$ and $m \in M$ with $g \swarrow\!\!\nearrow m$. Then $(A_1, B_1)\Theta(A_2, B_2) :\iff A_1 \setminus \{g\} = A_2 \setminus \{g\}$ ($\iff B_1 \setminus \{m\} = B_2 \setminus \{m\}$) defines the congruence relation on $\underline{\mathfrak{B}}(G, M, I)$ that is generated by the pair $(\gamma g, \gamma g \wedge \mu m)$ (i. e., by forcing $\gamma g \leq \mu m$). The corresponding compatible subcontext is*

$$(G \setminus \{g\}, M \setminus \{m\}, I \cap ((G \setminus \{g\}) \times (M \setminus \{m\}))) \ .$$

For determining the congruence relation we have thus to compute for every pair $g \swarrow\!\!\nearrow m$ if the subsumption $\gamma g \leq \mu m$ holds. For the computation of the $\swarrow\!\!\nearrow$-relation, the algorithm uses the fact that the relation is inherited to compatible subcontexts, and that for every direct product of contexts the equivalence $(g_1, g_2) \swarrow\!\!\nearrow (m_1, m_2) \iff (g_1 \swarrow\!\!\nearrow m_1$ and $g_2 \swarrow\!\!\nearrow m_2)$ holds.

4.2 Classifying with Distributive Concept Exploration

In this subsection we explain the algorithm via the example given above. First we list the concepts of the terminology: $C_1 :=$ Female, $C_2 :=$ Male, $C_3 :=$ Human, ..., $C_8 :=$ NoSmallChild. The concepts $\top$ and $\bot$ are considered in the first step of the computation.

The algorithm starts with the free bounded distributive lattice FBD($\{C_1\}$) which is the three element chain shown in Fig. 1. For the two $\swarrow\!\!\nearrow$ in the context the subsumptions $\top \sqsubseteq$ Female and Female $\sqsubseteq \bot$ are tested with the subsumption

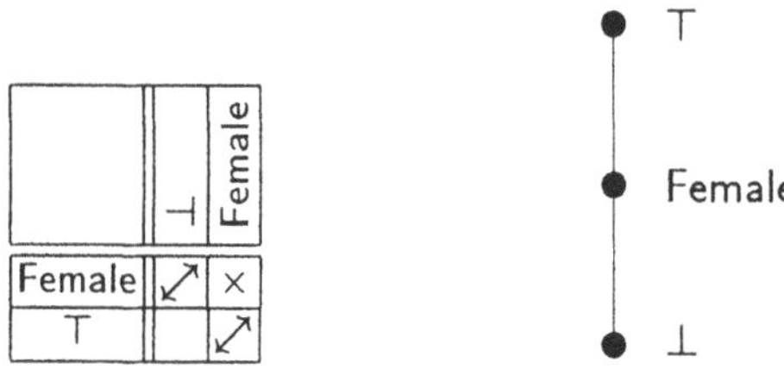

Fig. 1. The free bounded distributive lattice $\mathrm{FBD}(\{C_1\})$ and its context representation

algorithm. The algorithm denies both and provides the two counterexamples $(\mathcal{I}_1, c_1)$ and $(\mathcal{I}_2, c_2)$:

$(\mathcal{I}_1, c_1)$
$\mathrm{dom}(\mathcal{I}_1) := \{\mathrm{Otto}\}$
$\mathsf{Female}^{\mathcal{I}_1} := \emptyset$
$\mathsf{Small}^{\mathcal{I}_1} := \emptyset$
$\mathsf{child}^{\mathcal{I}_1} := \emptyset$
$c_1 := \mathrm{Otto}$

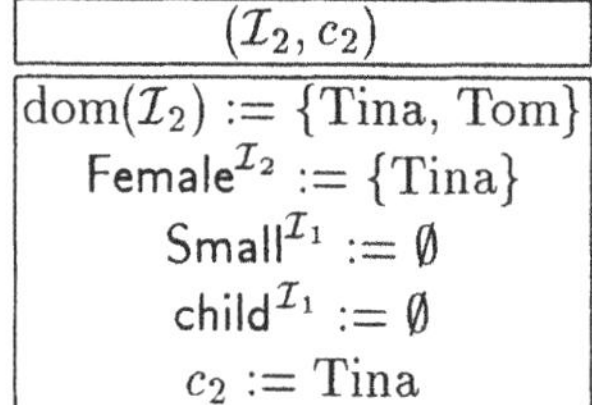

$(\mathcal{I}_2, c_2)$
$\mathrm{dom}(\mathcal{I}_2) := \{\mathrm{Tina, Tom}\}$
$\mathsf{Female}^{\mathcal{I}_2} := \{\mathrm{Tina}\}$
$\mathsf{Small}^{\mathcal{I}_1} := \emptyset$
$\mathsf{child}^{\mathcal{I}_1} := \emptyset$
$c_2 := \mathrm{Tina}$

Hence there are no rows or columns to delete. We obtain the lattice L_1 describing the subsumption relationships between the three concepts $\bot$, $\top$, and Female. The lattice and the representing context $\mathbb{K}_1$ are shown in the upper left of Fig. 2. At the left of the context the counterexamples are listed.

Now the tensor-product of L_1 with $\mathrm{FBD}(\{C_2\})$ is computed (see Fig. 2). The computation is only done on the context level, the line diagrams are only displayed for a better understanding. For the two counterexamples $(\mathcal{I}_1, c_1)$ and $(\mathcal{I}_2, c_2)$, now the algorithm tests (by finite model-checking) whether $c_1 \in \mathsf{Male}^{\mathcal{I}_1}$ and $c_2 \in \mathsf{Male}^{\mathcal{I}_2}$. The answers "Yes" and "No", resp., determine the place to put the counterexamples in the context $\mathbb{K}_1'$. In the context we write Female ⊓ Male for the object (Female, Male) and Female ⊔ Male for the attribute (Female, Male), since this is exactly the interpretation of the relation ∇ in the definition of the direct product.

Next the congruence relation that describes the subsumption relationships of the concept Male to the three already computed concepts $\bot$, $\top$, and Female is computed. For two of the four $\swarrow\!\!\!\nearrow$ there are already counterexamples. For the other two $\swarrow\!\!\!\nearrow$, the subsumption algorithm is asked the questions "Does Female ⊓ Male $\sqsubseteq \bot$ hold?" and "Does $\top \sqsubseteq$ Female ⊔ Male hold?". This time both subsumptions are accepted, since the subsumption algorithm is not able to provide a counterexample. Hence the corresponding two lines and two columns have to be deleted. The resulting lattice is shown at the bottom of Fig. 3.

In this way the classification continues. The next step, for instance, with $C_3 =$ Human, discovers that $\top =$ Human, since the subsumption algorithm accepts the two subsumptions Male $\sqsubseteq$ Female ⊔ Human and Female $\sqsubseteq$ Male ⊔ Human.

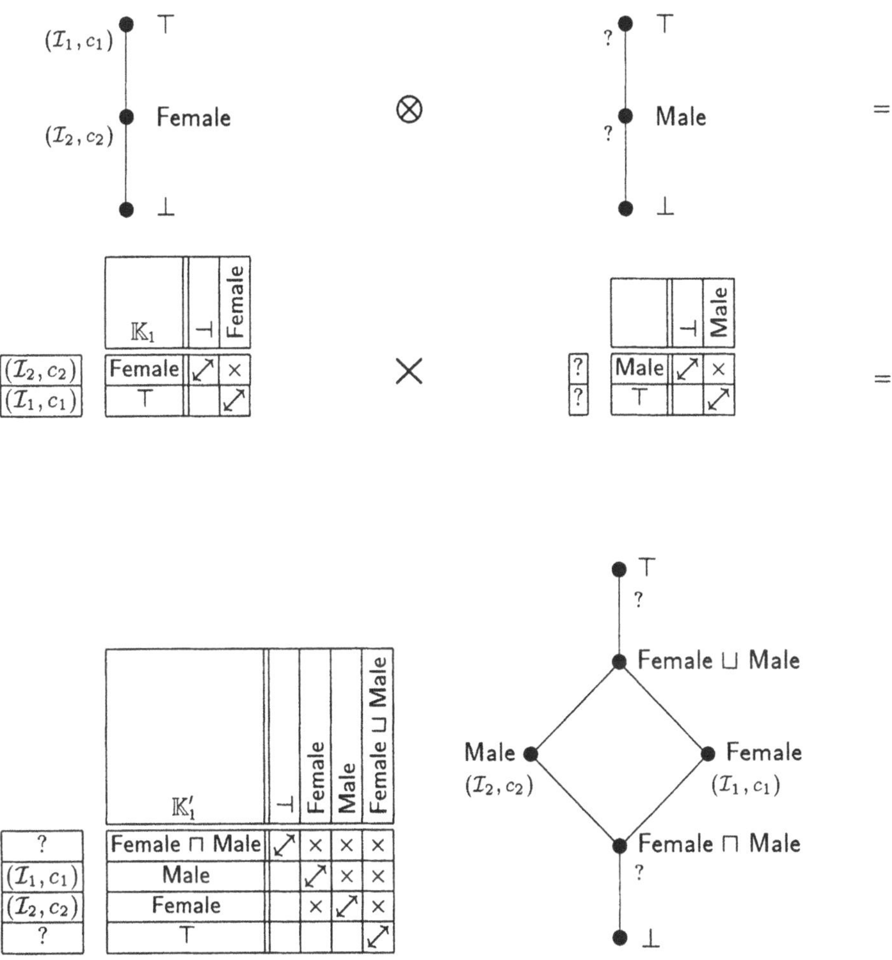

Fig. 2. The tensor-product

Hence the fact that every individual of a model of the terminology is a Human can directly be read from the result of the classification. The computation for our example ends with the eighth concept NoSmallChild. The result is a formal context with 44 objects and 44 attributes, and a list of 44 counterexamples.

5 Outlook

The algorithm can easily be modified such that it computes the Boolean lattice of all combinations of conjunctions, disjunctions, and negations of the concepts in the terminology, since the tensor-product is also the coproduct in the category of completely distributive complete Boolean algebras. In that case the free bounded

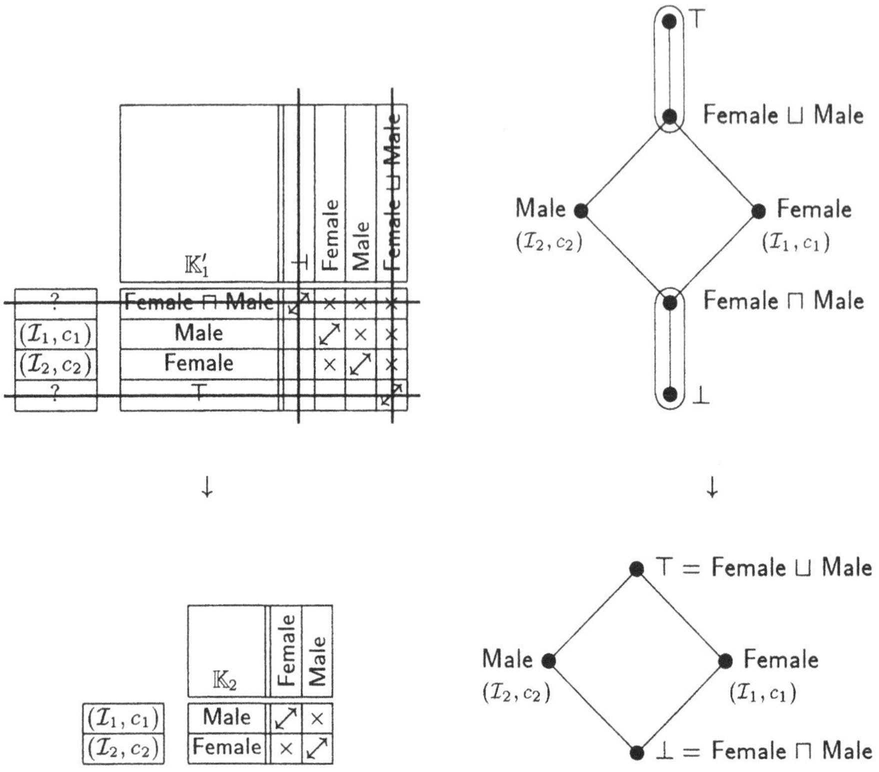

Fig. 3. Factorization of the tensor-product

distributive lattice FBD($\{C_i\}$) has to be replaced by the free Boolean algebra FBA($\{C_i\}$) (see Fig. 4). An interesting question is whether the classification can be extended further by existential and value restriction. There one encounters with new problems: The free algebra is infinite, and hence the desired result may be infinite, too. This could be overcome by restricting the length of the concept descriptions to be considered. Secondly these algebras have less algebraic structure than semi-lattices, lattices or Boolean algebras; and the quantifiers are less related to the subsumption ordering than conjunction, disjunction and negation.

The inference mechanisms presented in the last section and the one described in [1] show that combining techniques of description logic and formal concept analysis can provide interesting results. A further extension of these combinations seems desirable, especially for the development of conceptual knowledge systems. While description logics are more sophisticated in knowledge representation and inference, tools of formal concept analysis focus more on knowledge acquisition (cf. [16], [24]) and communication (cf. [20]). All four aspects

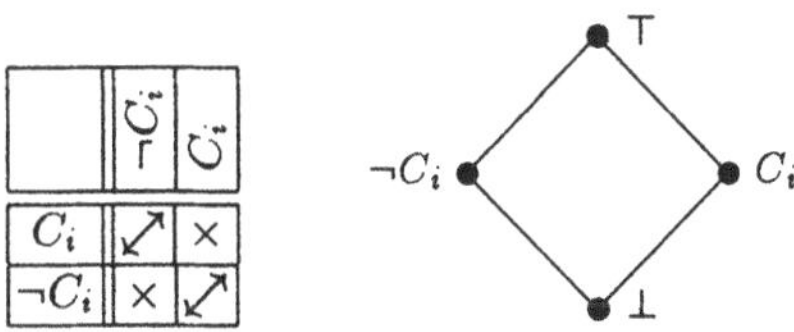

Fig. 4. The free Boolean algebra FBA($\{C_i\}$) and its context representation

play a crucial role for conceptual knowledge systems. The management system TOSCANA ([20]) for *conceptual data systems* ([13], [19]) provides techniques for knowledge representation and communication. It is promising to examine how this system can be extended with a terminology in order to increase expressiveness and to treat incomplete knowledge.

References

1. F. Baader: Logische Methoden in der Wissensrepräsentation am Beispiel terminologischer Repräsentationssprachen. Preprint
2. F. Baader: Computing a minimal representation of the subsumption lattice of all conjunctions of concepts defined in a terminology. In: G. Ellis, R. A. Levinson, A. Fall, V. Dahl (eds.): *Proceedings of the International KRUSE Symposium: Knowledge Retrieval, Use and Storage for Efficiency.* Santa Cruz, CA, USA, August 11–13, 1995, 168–178
3. P. Burmeister: ConImp – Programm zur formalen Begriffsanalyse einwertiger Kontexte. TH Darmstadt 1987 (latest version 1995)
4. P. Burmeister: Merkmalsimplikationen bei unvollständigem Wissen. In: W. Lex (ed.): *Arbeitstagung Begriffsanalyse und Künstliche Intelligenz,* Informatik-Bericht 89/3, Universität Clausthal-Zellerfeld, 1988, 15–46
5. B. Groh: Distributive Concept Exploration for Windows, TH Darmstadt 1995
6. G. Ellis, R. A. Levinson, A. Fall, V. Dahl (eds.): Proceedings of the International KRUSE Symposium: Knowledge Retrieval, Use and Storage for Efficiency. Santa Cruz, CA, USA, August 11–13, 1995
7. G. Ellis, R. A. Levinson, W. Rich, J. F. Sowa (eds.): Conceptual Structures: Applications, Implementation and Theory. Third International Conference on Conceptual Structures, Santa Cruz, CA, USA, August 14–18, 1995, Springer, Berlin – Heidelberg – New York 1995
8. G. Ellis, R. A. Levinson, W. Rich, J. F. Sowa (eds.): Supplementary Proceedings of the Third International Conference on Conceptual Structures, Santa Cruz, CA, USA, August 14–18, 1995
9. B. Ganter: Algorithmen zur Begriffsanalyse. In: B. Ganter, R. Wille, K. E. Wolff (eds.): *Beiträge zur Begriffsanalyse.* B. I.-Wissenschaftsverlag, Mannheim, Wien, Zürich 1987. 241–254
10. B. Ganter, R. Wille: Formale Begriffsanalyse: Mathematische Grundlagen. Springer, Heidelberg 1996

11. P. Luksch, R. Wille: A mathematical model for conceptual knowledge systems. In: H.-H. Bock, P. Ihm (eds.): *Classification, data analysis and knowledge organization.* Springer, Berlin 1991, 156–162
12. U. Priß: The formalization of WordNet by methods of relational concept analysis. In: C. Fellbaum (ed.): *WordNet: An electronic lexical database and some of its applications.* MITpress 1996 (to appear)
13. P. Scheich, M. Skorsky, F. Vogt, C. Wachter, R. Wille: Conceptual data systems. In: O. Opitz, B. Lausen, R. Klar (eds.): *Information and classification.* Springer, Heidelberg 1993, 72–84
14. M. Schmidt-Schauß, G. Smolka: Attribute concept descriptions with complements. Artificial Intelligence **48**, 1991, 1–26
15. G. Stumme: Boolesche Begriffe. Diplomarbeit, TH Darmstadt 1994
16. G. Stumme: Exploration tools in formal concept analysis. In: *Proceedings of the International Conference on Ordinal and Symbolic Data Analysis*, Paris, June 20–23, 1995, Springer, Heidelberg 1996, 31–44
17. G. Stumme: Knowledge acquisition by distributive concept exploration. In: G. Ellis, R. A. Levinson, W. Rich, J. F. Sowa (eds.): *Supplementary Proceedings of the Third International Conference on Conceptual Structures*, Santa Cruz, CA, USA, August 14–18, 1995, 98–111
18. G. Stumme: Attribute exploration with background implications and exceptions. In: H. H. Bock, W. Polasek (eds.): *Data analysis and information systems. Statistical and conceptual approaches.* Studies in classification, data analysis, and knowledge organization **7**, Springer, Heidelberg 1996, 457–469
19. F. Vogt, C. Wachter, R. Wille: Data analysis based on a conceptual file. In: H.-H. Bock, P. Ihm (eds.): *Classification, data analysis, and knowledge organization.* Springer, Heidelberg 1991, 131–140
20. F. Vogt, R. Wille: TOSCANA – A graphical tool for analyzing and exploring data. In: R. Tamassia, I. G. Tollis (eds.): *Graph Drawing '94*, Lecture Notes in Computer Sciences **894**, Springer, Heidelberg 1995, 226–233
21. H. Wagner: Begriff. In: H. M. Baumgartner, C. Wild (eds.): *Handbuch philosophischer Grundbegriffe.* Kösel Verlag, München 1973, 191–209
22. R. Wille: Restructuring lattice theory: an approach based on hierarchies of concepts. In: I. Rival (ed.): *Ordered sets.* Reidel, Dordrecht–Boston 1982, 445–470
23. R. Wille: Tensorial decomposition of concept lattices. In: *Order* **2**, 1985, 81–95
24. R. Wille: Knowledge acquisition by methods of formal concept analysis. In: E. Diday (ed.): *Data analysis, learning symbolic and numeric knowledge.* Nova Science Publisher, New York, Budapest 1989, 365–380
25. R. Wille: Local completeness of conceptual knowledge systems. In: E. Diday, Y. Lechevallier (eds.): *Symbolic-numeric data analysis and learning.* Nova Science Publisher, New York–Budapest 1991, 347–356
26. R. Wille: Concept lattices and conceptual knowledge systems. In: *Computers & Mathematics with applications* **23**, 1992, 493–515
27. M. Zickwolff: Begriffliche Wissenssysteme in der künstlichen Intelligenz. FB4-Preprint 1506, TH Darmstadt 1992

Extending Partial Orders for Sort Reasoning

Andrew Fall*

School of Computing Science, Simon Fraser University
Burnaby, B.C. V5A-1S6, Canada
email: fall@cs.sfu.ca

Abstract. Although mathematically elegant, partial orders limit the representation of taxonomic knowledge to subsort-supersort (or *isa*) relationships. We cannot, for example, directly state that two sorts are incompatible or define one sort as the intersection of a set of other sorts. This poses problems for specifying more complete taxonomic relationships as well as for denotational semantics in sorted logic. Research on many sorted logics has addressed this issue by expanding the expressive power of relationships among sorts. In this paper we propose the extraction of sort reasoning from the application, whether this is within a logic, a programming language or a knowledge representation system. This specialized sort reasoner is given information about sorts in the form of assertions and can be called upon to answer queries regarding the sort structure specified. We develop a sound and complete propositional *sort logic* with which the sort reasoner operates. Unfortunately, general sort reasoning is NP-Complete, and in some applications it may be important to preserve tractability. We suggest some ways to limit the expressiveness of sort reasoning to gain polynomial time operation.

1 Introduction

Partial orders have been used to represent hierarchically related information, from organization in ecology and biology [6, 14] to representations of lexicons in linguistics [15], but they have been most extensively utilized in sorted logic (e.g. [3, 4]) and AI (e.g. description logics [17], machine learning [13], computational linguistics [12], conceptual structures [7, 9], and logic programming [2]). The mathematical basis of partial orders has been exploited in taxonomic knowledge representation and reasoning, and research on taxonomic encoding has provided techniques for efficient management of partial orders (e.g. [1, 8]). Unfortunately, the simple structure of a partial order limits the taxonomic knowledge that can be represented. At the other extreme are description logics (e.g. the KL-ONE family [17]) in which taxonomic relationships among sorts are specified using a logic language, but the taxonomy itself must be derived through *classification* (which may or may not be NP-Hard, depending on the logic). We feel that explicit maintenance of a taxonomy is important for efficiency, but that additional information may be represented by extending taxonomic specification.

* This research was supported by the author's ECO-Research Doctoral Fellowship and by V. Dahl's NSERC Research Grant 31-611024 and NSERC Infrastructure and Equipment Grant given to the Logic and Functional Programming Lab, in whose facilities this work was developed. We are also thankful for the use of facilities provided to us by the School of Computing Science at Simon Fraser University.

Research on integrating additional forms of taxonomic knowledge into partial orders is scarce. Most notable, work by Cohn [4] proposed a generalized form of taxonomic specification within a sorted-logic framework. In [10] we proposed some extensions to partial orders to integrate machine learning [13] and systemic classification [12]. We extend these proposals in an attempt to develop a taxonomic knowledge representation system that is both flexible and parsimonious. For example, we may wish to define an element to be the intersection (union) of another set of elements (e.g. $woman = human \cap female$). Although this may hold coincidentally through meets (joins), such a restriction ensures that any changes must also respect this constraint. As another example, every element in a taxonomy must normally be specified, but there may be cases when this is both unnecessary and inefficient. Suppose we wish, e.g., to view people along lines of religion (e.g. Catholic, Jewish, Muslim, etc.), nationality (e.g. Canadian, Belgian) and occupation (e.g. student, prof, miner). Currently, we need to specify all possible combinations (i.e. the *cross-product*) of these facets to produce all sorts of people (e.g. a Belgian Catholic student). It would be cleaner if we could specify these lines separately, and infer the cross-product when needed.

After outlining partial order essentials, we formalize sorts and sort hierarchies, and identify the relation between lattice and set operations. We then propose the *sort reasoning problem* as the fundamental problem for a sort reasoner, and discuss how sort relations can be specified in two expressive, but equivalent ways. In section 4 we develop a three-valued propositional logic for sort reasoning and introduce the notion of a *sort context*. Using this logic, we show that, although resolution provides and sound and complete mechanism for sort reasoning, it is NP-Complete. The focus of section 5 is to identify tractable subcases of sort reasoning. Finally, we discuss some implementation issues.

2 Partial Orders

A *partial order* is a pair $(P, \leq)$, where $\leq$ is a reflexive, transitive and anti-symmetric binary relation called *subsumption* defined on a set P. If $x \leq y$ or $y \leq x$, then we say that x and y are *comparable*, and if $x \leq y$ but $x \neq y$, we write $x < y$. We say that x is a *child* of y, or y is a *parent* x, if $x < y$ and $x \leq z < y$ implies that $x = z$. For more details see [5]. Ordered sets can be shown diagrammatically, as exemplified in Figure 1.

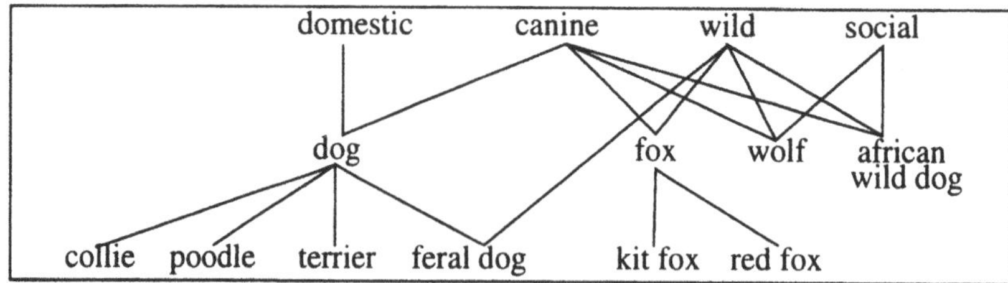

Fig. 1. Example ordered set

If P has a greatest (least) element, we call it *top* (*bottom*), denoted $\top$ ($\bot$). An element $x \in P$ is an *upper (lower) bound* of a subset Q if $q \leq x$ ($q \geq x$) for every $q \in Q$. If the set of all upper (lower) bounds of Q has a least (greatest) element x, then x is called the *join* or *least upper bound* (*meet* or *greatest lower bound*) of Q, denoted $\sqcup Q$ ($\sqcap Q$). If $Q = \{x, y\}$, this may be written $x \sqcup y$ ($x \sqcap y$). The meet $x \sqcap y$ may fail to exist because x and y have no common lower bound or because they have no *greatest* lower bound. In the former case we call x and y *meet incompatible.* For a subset Q of an ordered set P, we call the set of minimal upper bounds of Q the *join base* and the maximal lower bounds of Q the *meet crest.* By abuse of notation, we denote lower bound, or meet, crests the same as meets (and upper bound, or join, bases the same as joins), although the result is a set, not a single element. In Figure 1, neither $dog \sqcap fox$ nor $dog \sqcup wild$ exist, but $wild \sqcap social = \{wolf, african\ wild\ dog\}$ and $fox \sqcup wolf = \{canine, wild\}$. A *lattice* is a non-empty ordered set for which joins and meets exist for every $x, y \in L$. An example of a lattice is 2^X for a set X, ordered by set inclusion.

3 Sort Reasoning

Sorts represent sets of individuals grouped according to common features. Intuitively, a sort p_1 is a *subsort* of p_2 provided that every individual in p_1 is also in p_2 (e.g. *collie* is a subsort of *dog*). We don't require that sorts denote unique sets of individuals, so two sorts p_1 and p_2 may be *aliases* for the same set (e.g. *car* and *automobile*), or that a sort be non-empty (e.g. *unicorn* is an empty sort). As we describe below, subset information on sets of aliases forms a partial order.

- Let $\mathcal{U}$ be the domain of discourse (i.e. the set of individuals).
- Let $\mathcal{P}$ be a set of *base* sorts, notated using letters p and q. $\forall p \in \mathcal{P}$, p represents a subset of $\mathcal{U}$. $\mathcal{P}$ contains an implicit element: $\top_{\mathcal{P}}$, representing $\mathcal{U}$.
- Then $\subseteq$ forms a preorder relation on $\mathcal{P}$ (i.e. $\subseteq$ is reflexive and transitive).

From $\mathcal{P}$ we can specify the *literal* sorts: $\mathcal{P}_{\mathcal{L}} = \{p, \neg p | p \in \mathcal{P}, \neg p = \mathcal{U} - p\}$, notated using greek letters α, β, etc. We can derive an implicit literal sort $\bot_{\mathcal{P}} = \neg \top_{\mathcal{P}}$ that represents $\emptyset$. We can also extract two relations:

- The *sort equivalence relation*, $=_{\mathcal{P}}$: for $p_1, p_2 \in \mathcal{P}$, $p_1 =_{\mathcal{P}} p_2$ if and only if $p_1 \subseteq p_2$ and $p_2 \subseteq p_1$. We denote the set of equivalence classes of $\mathcal{P}$ as $\mathcal{P}_=$, and each equivalence class as $[p]$, where p is a *representative* for the class.
- The *sort (partial) order*, $(\mathcal{P}_=, \leq_{\mathcal{P}})$: for $[p], [q] \in \mathcal{P}_=$, $[p] \leq_{\mathcal{P}} [q]$ if and only if $\forall p_i \in [p], q_j \in [q]$, $p_i \subseteq q_j$. Clearly $\leq_{\mathcal{P}}$ is reflexive and transitive. To show anti-symmetry, consider two classes $[p]$ and $[q]$. If $[p] \leq_{\mathcal{P}} [q]$ and $[q] \leq_{\mathcal{P}} [p]$, and $p_i \in [p], q_j \in [q]$, then $p_i \subseteq q_j$ and $q_j \subseteq p_i$. Thus, $p_i =_{\mathcal{P}} q_j$, so it must be the case that $[p] = [q]$.

For simplicity of notation, we omit the brackets surrounding alias classes. We now describe the relationship between taxonomic and set operations.

- If $p_1 \sqcap p_2 = p_3$, then $p_1 \cap p_2 \supseteq p_3$. For example, if $p_1 \sqcap p_2 = \bot$, we cannot infer that there is no element in $\mathcal{U}$ that is in both p_1 and p_2. We can only infer that there is no known sort that represents such elements. However, if we know that $p_1 \cap p_2 = p_3$ then we can infer $p_1 \sqcap p_2 = p_3$. For non-singleton meet crests, if $p_1 \sqcap p_2 = \{q_1, \cdots, q_k\}$, then $\forall q_i, 1 \leq i \leq k, p_1 \cap p_2 \supseteq q_i$.
- If $p_1 \sqcup p_2 = p_3$, then $p_1 \cup p_2 \subseteq p_3$. However, if we know that $p_1 \cup p_2 = p_3$ then we can infer $p_1 \sqcup p_2 = p_3$. For non-singleton join bases, if $p_1 \sqcup p_2 = \{q_1, \cdots, q_k\}$, then $\forall q_i, 1 \leq i \leq k, p_1 \cup p_2 \subseteq q_i$.

Thus, it is not always possible to perform sort inferences using taxonomic operations. This issue was the focus of the lattice completion proposed in [4]. Figure 2 shows the above relationships using Venn diagrams. Our goal is to exploit both the complete and incomplete knowledge in a sort hierarchy for a sort reasoning system. This requires a general means of specifying, maintaining and reasoning with information that relates sorts.

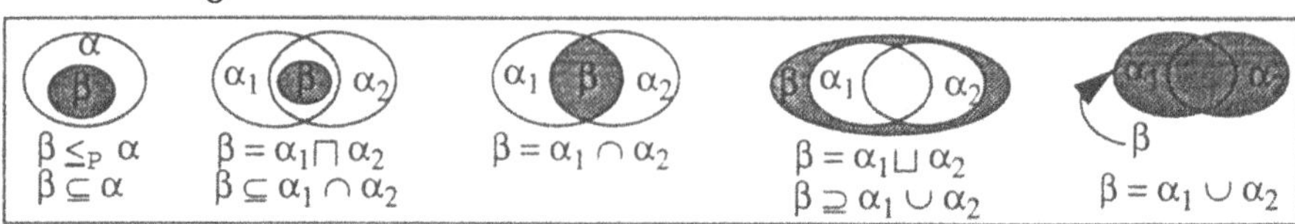

Fig. 2. Relation between taxonomic and set operations

3.1 Generalizing Sort Reasoning

Definition 1. Suppose we have a set $\mathcal{P}$ of n *base* sorts.

- An *atomic* sort is a sort s obtained by intersecting, for every sort $p \in \mathcal{P}$, either p or its complement $\neg p$.
- A *derived* sort is a set of atomic sorts.
- A *conjunctive* sort is intersection (conjunction) of a set of literal sorts.
- A conjunctive sort s is *consistent* if and only if it does not contain both a base sort and its complement. A consistent conjunctive sort is a derived sort.

In a Venn diagram of all possible combinations of sorts, each distinct region is an atomic sort of which there are 2^n. Taxonomic information may reduce the number of non-empty atomic sorts (e.g. if $p_1 \leq p_2$ then an atomic sort with p_1 but not p_2 is empty). A derived sort is obtained by selecting 0 or more atomic sorts, and corresponds to the union of distinct regions in a Venn diagram. In the worst case (no taxonomic constraints) there are 2^{2^n} non-empty derived sorts.

To illustrate, consider the specifications: (i) $francophone \leq person$ and (ii) $canadian \leq person$. Although sorts $francophone$ and $canadian$ are incomparable, there is no information that indicates they are disjoint. Combining them results in the derived sort $canadian\_francophone$. In general, conjunctive sorts can be denoted by juxtaposing their constituent sort labels (lexicographically to ensure uniqueness, although any total order on the sort labels could be used). Automatic derivation of conjunctive sorts can be contrasted with LIFE in which the same combination will result in failure, since their coincidental meet is $\perp$.

For conjunctive sorts, we can specify an *intrinsic* ordering ($\preceq$): for two conjunctive sorts s_1 and s_2, we know that $s_1 \subseteq s_2$ if s_1 contains a superset of the literals in s_2. For example, $p_1 \wedge \neg p_2 \wedge p_3 \preceq \neg p_2 \wedge p_3$. Taxonomic information provides further *extrinsic* ordering among conjunctive sorts. Thus, for conjunctive sorts s_1 and s_2, $s_1 \preceq s_2$ implies that $s_1 \subseteq s_2$, but not necessarily the converse.

Clearly there is potential for a combinatorial explosion in the number and size of derived sorts. In [4], completeness in a many-sorted logic setting is required, and so the entire derived sort space must be handled. Unfortunately, this leads to the possibility of a sort structure of exponential size. Our goal is to produce a general sort reasoner which minimally retains polynomial space, and so we choose to restrict the set of derived sorts to conjunctive sorts.

Conjunctive sorts are natural in that they group together individuals in $\mathcal{U}$ that share attributes. They provide for monotonic sort reasoning, since the set of individuals denoted by a partially specified sort cannot increase as new constraints are applied. These are the types of sorts produced in LIFE [2] through unification. Conjunctive sorts have a natural representation using a three-valued logic by selecting for each base sort $p \in \mathcal{P}$ either *true* (include sort p), *false* (exclude sort p) or *uncertain*. Thus, there are at most 3^n different consistent conjunctive sorts, although constraints may reduce this number. Conjunctive sorts have a simple and efficient implementation using logical terms (section 6).

Our problem can now be described succinctly as follows:

Definition 2. Sort Reasoning Problem (abstract): Given a set of base sorts $\mathcal{P}$, a set of assertions $\mathcal{A}$ which specify the emptiness or non-emptiness of zero or more conjunctive sorts, and a conjunctive sort s. Can we infer that s is empty or non-empty?

We show that interesting sort reasoning problems can be characterized as special cases of this problem, and we describe general methods of specifying the assertions. We develop a *sort logic* (not a sorted-logic, but a logic for sort reasoning) which has a sound and complete reasoning strategy. We also show that this problem is NP-Complete, so we explore tractable subsets of sort reasoning.

The assertions $\mathcal{A}$ partion the conjunctive sorts into three groups: *empty* sorts, *non-empty* sorts and *possibly empty* sorts. If a conjunctive sort s_1 is empty, and $s_2 \preceq s_1$, then s_2 must also be empty. Dually, if s_1 is non-empty, and $s_1 \preceq s_2$, then s_2 must be non-empty. Thus, sort reasoning can be viewed as classifying conjunctive sorts into these groups based on the current set of assertions.

3.2 Clausal Taxonomic Specification

In [4], a suggestion is made for clausal specification of taxonomies: $\forall x, p_1(x) \vee \cdots \vee p_m(x) \vee \neg q_1(x) \vee \cdots \vee \neg q_n(x)$, where the p_i and q_j are base sorts. A number of special cases are worth noting:

1. $m = 0, n = 2$: q_1 and q_2 are incompatible.
2. $m = 0, n > 2$: $q_1, \cdots, q_n$ cannot simultaneously hold.
3. $m = 1, n = 1$: $q_1 \subseteq p_1$.
4. $m > 1, n = 0$: $p_1, \cdots, p_m$ decompose $\top$ (i.e. $\bigcup\{p_1, \cdots, p_m\} = \top$).

The usefulness of these clausal specifications is not explored in [4]. In light of the sort reasoning problem, such a specification can be viewed as asserting that a certain conjunctive sort is empty. The universally quantified form is equivalent to $\not\exists x, \neg p_1(x) \wedge \cdots \wedge \neg p_m(x) \wedge q_1(x) \wedge \cdots \wedge q_n(x)$ (i.e. conjunctive sort $\neg p_1 \wedge \cdots \wedge \neg p_m \wedge q_1 \wedge \cdots \wedge q_n$ is empty). We propose to also allow dual specifications: $\exists x, \neg p_1(x) \wedge \cdots \wedge \neg p_m(x) \wedge q_1(x) \wedge \cdots \wedge q_n(x)$, which permit asserting that a certain conjunctive sort is not empty. Duals of the above special cases are:

1. $m = 0, n = 2$: q_1 and q_2 are compatible.
2. $m = 0, n > 2$: $q_1, \cdots, q_n$ can simultaneously hold.
3. $m = 1, n = 1$: $q_1 \not\subseteq p_1$.
4. $m > 1, n = 0$: $p_1, \cdots, p_m$ do not decompose $\top$.

With these two forms, we have the ability to fully specify any instance of the sort reasoning problem, so we can dispense with the quantification, and limit our focus to propositional logic. Universally quantified assertions (or *universal sorts*) are global in that they must all simultaneously hold, but not existentially quantified assertions (or *existential sorts*), which may specify different individuals in $\mathcal{U}$. Figure 3 shows the set relationships imposed by these specifications.

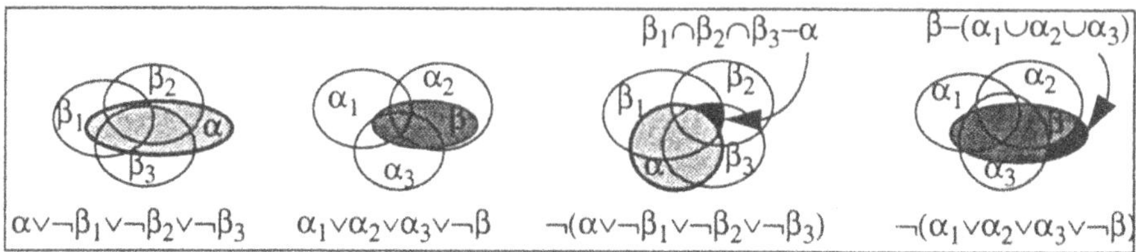

Fig. 3. Venn diagrams of clausal taxonomy specification

3.3 Definitional Specifications

As an alternative to clausal specifications, a number of natural relationships can be constructed using sort definitions. Some possibilities are described below and shown in Figure 4, and formed the basis of *extended description spaces* [10].

Conjoined Sort Definition: We may want to *define* a sort as precisely the intersection of a set of other sorts. For example, we may want to define *woman* as the intersection of *person* and *female*. We can denote this using set intersection: $p = \alpha_1 \cap \cdots \cap \alpha_k$, where the α_i are sort literals. Such definitions are equivalent to the clauses: (i) $p \vee \neg\alpha_1 \vee \cdots \vee \neg\alpha_k$; and (ii) $\neg p \vee \alpha_i$ for $1 \leq i \leq k$. Partial orders only permit the second set of clauses, and so we may only say: $p \subseteq \alpha_1 \cap \cdots \cap \alpha_k$.

Sort Decomposition: Sometimes we know that a set $\{\alpha_1, \cdots, \alpha_k\}$ of (possibly overlapping) sorts *decomposes* another sort p. That is, $p = \alpha_1 \cup \cdots \cup \alpha_k$. For example, we may wish to define a sort *university_course* = *grad_course* ∪ *undergrad_course* (where some courses may be cross-listed as both). Such a declaration is equivalent to the clausal specifications: (i) $\neg p \vee \alpha_1 \vee \cdots \vee \alpha_k$; and (ii) $p \vee \neg\alpha_i$, for $1 \leq i \leq k$. Every conjoined sort definition $p = \alpha_1 \cap \cdots \cap \alpha_k$ induces a dual sort decomposition $\neg p = \neg\alpha_1 \cup \cdots \cup \neg\alpha_k$, and vice versa.

Sort Partitioning: We may have even stronger information that a set Q decomposes a supersort p and every pair of elements in Q is disjoint. For example, we may want to say that the sort *person* is partitioned into *woman* and *man*. We can denote this using disjoint set union: $p = \alpha_1 + \cdots + \alpha_k$, where + is interpreted as union with the constraint that each pair of sorts on the right-hand side must be disjoint. Such assertions are equivalent to the clauses: (i) $\neg p \vee \alpha_1 \vee \cdots \vee \alpha_k$; (ii) $p \vee \neg\alpha_i$ for $1 \leq i \leq k$; and (iii) $\neg\alpha_i \vee \neg\alpha_j$, for $1 \leq i < j \leq k$.

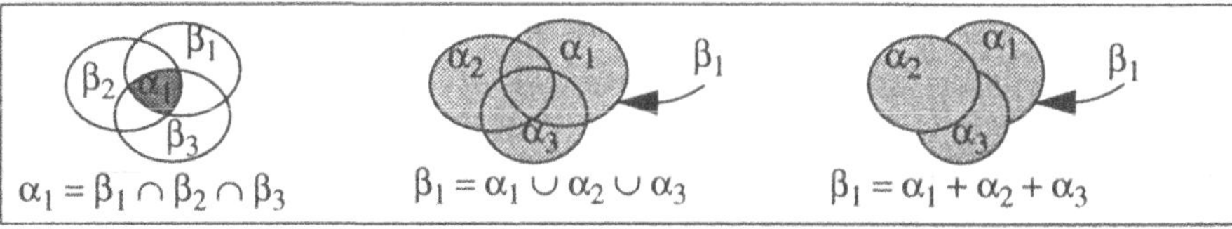

Fig. 4. Aggregate specifications

We can specify the dual of these assertions, by replacing equal signs by strict subsets. We may, e.g., state that *wild* and *canine* is insufficient to define *wolf* as $wolf \subset wild \cap canine$ (i.e. the sort $\neg wolf \wedge wild \wedge canine$ is non-empty).

Interestingly, definitional and clausal specifications are equivalent. A universal assertion: $p_1 \vee \cdots \vee p_m \vee \neg q_1 \vee \cdots \vee \neg q_n$ can be specified as: (i) $q' = q_1 \cap \cdots \cap q_n$; (ii) $p' = p_1 \cup \cdots \cup p_m$; and (iii) $q' \cap p' = q'$ (or $q' \leq p'$). An existential assertion: $\neg(p_1 \vee \cdots \vee p_m \vee \neg q_1 \vee \cdots \vee \neg q_n)$ can be specified as: (i) $q' = q_1 \cap \cdots \cup q_n$; (ii) $p' = p_1 \cup \cdots \cup p_m$; and (iii) $q' \cap p' \subset q'$ (or $q' \not\leq p'$).

4 Sort Logic

Definition 3. A *sort context* is a triple $\Sigma = (\mathcal{P}, \mathcal{E}, \mathcal{N})$, where

- $\mathcal{P}$ is a set of sort symbols, and $\mathcal{P}_{\mathcal{L}}$ is the corresponding set of sort literals.
- $\mathcal{E}$ is a set of universal sort assertions, where for every $\epsilon \in \mathcal{E}$, $\epsilon = \alpha_1 \vee \cdots \vee \alpha_k$ and each α_i, $1 \leq i \leq k$, is a sort literal. Conjunctive sort $\neg\epsilon$ is in the same sort equivalence class as $\perp_{\mathcal{P}}$ (i.e. $\neg\epsilon$ is empty).
- $\mathcal{N}$ is a set of existential sort assertions, for every $\eta \in \mathcal{N}$, $\eta = \alpha_1 \wedge \cdots \wedge \alpha_k$ and each α_i, $1 \leq i \leq k$, is a sort literal. Conjunctive sort η is in a different sort equivalence class from $\perp_{\mathcal{P}}$ (i.e. η is non-empty).

Since existential sort clauses are local (i.e. they implicitly existentially quantify an individual), we cannot use them indiscriminately: we only allow at most one to appear in a proof. Our sort logic has three truth values: T (*true*), F (*false*) and U (*unknown* or *uncertain*). For example, the answer to the query $dog \wedge cat = \emptyset$? may be *true*, whereas the answer to the query $student \wedge plumber = \emptyset$? may be *uncertain*. We also have one rule of inference, resolution, which we can formalize as follows (where the α_i and β_j are sort literals, and $\neg\neg p = p$):

$$(\gamma \vee \alpha_1 \vee \cdots \vee \alpha_j) \wedge (\neg\gamma \vee \beta_1 \vee \cdots \vee \beta_k) \vdash \alpha_1 \vee \cdots \vee \alpha_j \vee \beta_1 \vee \cdots \vee \beta_k$$

Using a standard resolution process, we finish when either the empty clause is derived, or no more resolution is applicable. The empty clause is derived only if both α and $\neg\alpha$ can be derived, which clearly indicates inconsistency.

A sort context Σ is *consistent* if for every conjunctive sort s resulting from $\mathcal{P}_{\mathcal{L}}$, we cannot infer that s is both empty and non-empty. Since resolution is sound and *refutation complete* [11], determining if a sort context is inconsistent using resolution is sound and complete. We do not assume complete knowledge, however, so it may be the case that we cannot infer that s is empty or non-empty. In this case, following Cohn [4], we call s *possibly-empty*.

Queries can be dealt with as follows:

Empty Sorts: To check if a conjunctive sort $s = \alpha_1 \wedge \cdots \wedge \alpha_k$ is empty, we assert that it is not empty by adding s as an existential sort, and attempt to derive the empty clause through resolution. If we derive the empty clause, then s must be empty, and $\neg s$ must be a universal sort (i.e. the sort context $(\mathcal{P}, \mathcal{E}, \{s\})$ is inconsistent). If not, then s may be either non-empty or possibly-empty. Note that we only use elements of $\mathcal{E}$, but not of $\mathcal{N}$, for this.

Inferring Sorts: We may be interested in the sorts which can be inferred from s. These can be produced as a side product of the above resolution process. If s is an empty sort, then every sort is derivable.

Non-empty Sorts: To check if s is non-empty, we assert that it is empty (i.e. add $\neg s$ as a universal sort), and attempt to derive the empty clause through resolution. We do this by finding a non-empty sort $\eta \in \mathcal{N}$ with which we can derive the empty sort (i.e. the sort context $(\mathcal{P}, \mathcal{E} \cup \{\neg s\}, \{\eta\})$ is inconsistent). Note that this is akin to *skolemizing* the existential sort η.

We can now restate the sort reasoning problem in more definite terms.

Definition 4. Sort Reasoning Problem (concrete): Given a sort context $\Sigma = (\mathcal{P}, \mathcal{E}, \{s\})$. Is Σ consistent?

The Sort Reasoning Problem is NP-Complete, as we prove formally in the full paper. This can be demonstrated by modeling an instance of 3-SAT using sort definitions, as shown in Figure 5, where a conjunctive normal form formula with ternary clauses $f = c_1 \wedge \cdots \wedge c_k$, where $c_i = l_{i,1} \vee l_{i,2} \vee l_{i,3}$, $1 \leq i \leq k$ can be represented using one intersection definition for f and one union definition for each of the clauses. In diagrams, we denote intersection (resp. union) definitions by connecting the parent (resp. child) subsumption arcs with a horizontal line.

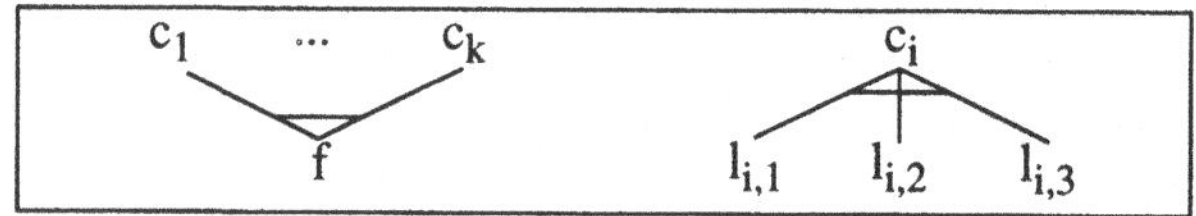

Fig. 5. Using sort definitions to represent an instance of 3-SAT: $f = c_1 \wedge \cdots \wedge c_k$, where $c_i = l_{i,1} \vee l_{i,2} \vee l_{i,3}$, $1 \leq i \leq k$

From a logical standpoint, intractability is of no concern, provided the logic is sound and complete. Also, some systems may prefer to retain expressiveness and assume that the worst-case will rarely, if ever, occur. Even so, there is some sort structure maintenance that we may perform to reduce the cost of sort reasoning. If we determine that a sort s is empty or non-empty, then we can assert this information in the sort context. We refer to this as *sort memoing*, since it is akin to memoing in OLDT resolution [16]. If sort reasoning is performed in localized areas of the sort structure, then this enhancement may result in improved performance at the cost of additional storage (in the worst-case, one conjunctive sort is added to the context for any query).

5 Tractable subcases

Many knowledge representation systems are concerned with tractable reasoning strategies, so it is important to identify subcases of the sort reasoning problem with polynomial solutions. As intractability results from empty sort assertions and queries, there is no need to restrict the form of non-empty sort assertions.

Positive literal sorts. A simple way to achieve tractability is to avoid negated sorts by only allowing assertions which involve positive literals. In LIFE [2], only subsumption (i.e. $p \leq q$) assertions are permitted in specifying a sort hierarchy. However, if the meet crest $p_1 \sqcap \cdots \sqcap p_k$ happens to be $\{q_1, \ldots, q_n\}$, there is an implicit assertion of the form $p_1 \wedge \cdots \wedge p_m = q_1 \vee \cdots \vee q_n$.

Horn sorts. Another possibility is to restrict specification to Horn clauses (i.e. clauses with at most one positive literal). This leads to tractable resolution if we restrict each base sort to be a positive literal of at most one clause.

5.1 Containing Sort Reasoning Complexity

Both cases above impose unnecessarily strict limitations on the expression of taxonomic knowledge. To achieve more flexibility while retaining tractability, we can either restrict the form of assertions or the form of queries. We choose a combination. The basic form of universal sort assertions we allow are (i) binary clauses, which can define a partial order among the literal sorts (i.e. $p \vee q, p \vee \neg q$ or $\neg p \vee \neg q$); (ii) intersection (conjoined sort) definitions: $p = \alpha_1 \wedge \cdots \wedge \alpha_m$; and (iii) union definitions (sort decomposition): $p = \alpha_1 \vee \cdots \vee \alpha_m$.

Sort contexts can be described as $(\mathcal{P}, \mathcal{A}, \mathcal{N})$, where $\mathcal{A}$ is a set of definitional assertions which satisfies the above forms. Such assertions could be reduced to clausal form, but such definitional assertions can be maintained in a partial order structure on the literal sorts, augmented with notation for the intersection and union definitions. $\mathcal{N}$ is a set of existential conjunctive sort assertions as before.

Note that asserting a binary clause imposes two constraints: $\alpha \vee \beta$ asserts $\neg\alpha \leq \beta$ and $\neg\beta \leq \alpha$. Asserting an intersection or union definition, also asserts the dual. The intersection definition, $p = \alpha_1 \wedge \cdots \wedge \alpha_m$ also asserts $\neg p = \neg\alpha_1 \vee \cdots \vee \neg\alpha_m$. The union definition $p = \alpha_1 \vee \cdots \vee \alpha_m$ also asserts $\neg p = \neg\alpha_1 \wedge \cdots \wedge \neg\alpha_m$.

Without restrictions, of course, we have full sort reasoning power with the above assertion forms. Even limiting sorts to have at most one definition may lead to intractable behaviour, as shown in Figure 5. Our solution is to limit the extent of intractability. First we need to define several notions.

Definition 5. Let $s = \alpha_1 \wedge \cdots \wedge \alpha_k$ be a conjunctive sort. The *expanded* form s^* of s is the fixpoint of the following construction (i.e. there exists a $k \geq 0$ for which $s_{k+1} = s_k = s^*$): (i) $s_0 = \{\alpha_1, \ldots, \alpha_k\}$; (ii) $s_{i+1} = s_i \cup \{\beta | \exists\gamma \in s_i$ such that $\gamma \leq \beta\} \cup \{\beta | \beta = \gamma_1 \wedge \cdots \wedge \gamma_m$ is an assertion in $\mathcal{A}$ and $\gamma_j \in s_i, 1 \leq j \leq m\}$

Thus, given a conjunctive sort s, its expanded form is the set of all sort literals which may be directly inferred from s.

Definition 6. Let $s = \alpha_1 \wedge \cdots \wedge \alpha_k$ be a conjunctive sort, and s^* be its expanded form. The set of *potential conjunctive inferences* $\mathcal{C}(s)$ associated with s is defined recursively as the fixpoint of the following construction (i.e. there exists a $k \geq 0$ for which $s_{k+1} = s_k = \mathcal{C}(s)$): (i) $s_0 = s^*$; (ii) $s_{i+1} = s_i \cup \{\beta | \beta = \gamma_1 \wedge \cdots \wedge \gamma_m$ is an assertion in $\mathcal{A}$, and $\gamma_j \in s_i$ for some $1 \leq j \leq m\}$

Definition 7. Let $s = \alpha_1 \wedge \cdots \wedge \alpha_k$ be a conjunctive sort, and s^* be its expanded form. The set of *unresolved disjunctions* $\mathcal{D}(s)$ associated with s is defined as: $\mathcal{D}(s) = \{\{\beta_1 \vee \cdots \vee \beta_k\} | (i) \alpha = \beta_1 \vee \cdots \vee \beta_k$ is an assertion in $\mathcal{A}$; (ii) $\alpha \in s^*$; and $(iii) \not\exists\gamma \in s^*$ such that $\gamma \leq \beta_i$ for some $i, 1 \leq i \leq k\}$.

Thus, $\mathcal{D}(s)$ is the set of union definitions for which the left-hand side sort, but none of the right-hand side sorts, is in s^* (so the disjunction is implied but not satisfied by s).

Definition 8. Let $s = \alpha_1 \wedge \cdots \wedge \alpha_k$ be a conjunctive sort. A *locally consistent* selection of literals from the unresolved disjunctions $\mathcal{D}(s)$ is a set $Q = \{\beta_1, \ldots, \beta_m\}$ of at least one sort literal from each disjunction in $\mathcal{D}(s)$ where the expanded sort s_1^* ($s_1 = \alpha_1 \wedge \cdots \wedge \alpha_k \wedge \beta_1 \cdots \wedge \beta_m$) is consistent.

The existence of a locally consistent selection is necessary but not sufficient to show that sort s is not provably empty. Unresolved disjunctions may *cascade* due to a locally consistent selection - $\mathcal{D}(s_1)$ may contain unresolved disjunctions.

In order to determine if s is provably empty or not (provided s^* is consistent), we need to show that every possible way of resolving the set of disjunctions $\mathcal{D}(s)$ leads to inconsistency. This problem may be intractable in two dimensions. First, even making a locally consistent selection from $\mathcal{D}(s)$ may be NP-Complete (cfr. 3-SAT problem). Second, the potential cascading effect of unresolved disjunctions may lead to an exponential search space, even if determining locally consistent selections can be done in polynomial time. The following set of restrictions attempts to curtail both of these sources of intractability, while retaining a degree of power that makes sort reasoning useful:

1. Positive literal sorts may not subsume negative literal sorts, and no set containing negative literals may imply a positive literal. This is achieved by enforcing the following syntactic constraints on assertions: (i) Subsumption assertions must have the form $p \vee \neg q$ (i.e. $q \leq p$ and $\neg p \leq \neg q$) or $\neg p \vee \neg q$ (i.e. $p \leq \neg q$ and $q \leq \neg p$); (ii) The sorts on the right-hand side of intersection and union definitions must be positive literals.
2. For a given conjunctive sort $s = \alpha_1 \wedge \cdots \wedge \alpha_k$, limit the number of unresolved disjunctions (union definitions) containing positive literals associated with s to a constant $n_{\cup}$. This ensures that we can determine in polynomial time if there is a locally consistent selection of literals from the unresolved disjunctions $\mathcal{D}(s)$. If $\mathcal{D}(s)$ is empty or contains only disjunctions with negative literals, then a locally consistent selection can be done in linear time.
3. Limit the cascade of unresolved disjunctions by imposing constraints on the relation of positive sorts involved in one union definition $p = q_1 \vee \cdots \vee q_k$ to other union definitions. If $s_i = \mathcal{C}(q_i)$, $1 \leq i \leq k$, then $\mathcal{D}(s_i)$ can only contain disjunctions with negative literals. Note that if q_i is not subsumed by any sorts on the right-hand side of an intersection definition, then this reduces to the constraint: $\mathcal{D}(q_i)$ can only contain disjunctions with negative literals. This restriction ensures that, for a conjunctive sort s, any locally consistent selection from $\mathcal{D}(s)$ can be checked for global consistency in polynomial time since cascading disjunctions can only contain negative literals (and no selection of negative literals can result in a positive literal being derived).

The first and third restrictions are purely syntactic. The second affects both assertions (i.e. the conjunctive sorts on the right-hand side of intersection definitions) and queries, and depends largely on the current sort structure. It can, however, be checked quickly given any conjunctive sort. If it is not satisfied in a query, we can notify the client and provide the option to attempt a potentially costly answer. Together these restrictions permit us to specify a polynomial time algorithm for determining if a conjunctive sort s is provably empty:

1. Construct s^*. If s^* is inconsistent then s is provably empty.
2. Determine $\mathcal{D}(s)$ and check if there is a locally consistent selection. If none exists, then s is provably empty.
3. Attempt to expand each locally consistent selection to a globally consistent selection. If this is not possible, then s is provably empty.

The first step in the algorithm is performed automatically and efficiently using lattice operations and the logical term implementation described in the following section. Due to the second restriction above, the second step of the algorithm can be accomplished in polynomial time, and due to the third restriction, checking if there exists at least one globally consistent selection (in which case s is not provably empty) also takes polynomial time.

6 Implementing Conjunctive Sorts

For a simple logical term encoding of sort orders, that is fast to compute and flexible to update, we assign terms in which each element has one position and use a variant of a top-down transitive closure encoding [1]. For any element $p \in \mathcal{P}$, position i of the code $\tau(p)$ may have one of three values: (i) If $p \leq p_i$ then position i will contain a 1; (ii) If $p \leq \neg p_i$ then position i will contain a 0; (iii) Otherwise position i will contain an anonymous variable (denoted "_").

We can extend our logic and implementation to four values: *true* (1), *false* (0), *uncertain* (_) and *inconsistent* (!). Inconsistency in a sort position could be used as an explanatory feature to identify the base sort at the root of an inconsistency. It could also be used as a basis for extending our sort logic to include default and non-monotonic reasoning - an inconsistent value for a base sort p would indicate that somehow both p and $\neg p$ have been acquired. Our proposal does not provide a means of resolving this inconsistency, but does give a framework upon which a default or non-monotonic logic system can be built.

7 Conclusion

Taxonomic knowledge representation is a complex, yet intuitive and pervasive problem. By separating sort constraints into a sort reasoner, specialized techniques can be used to manage the sort relations arising in a system. We have argued that, although mathematically elegant, partial orders are unwieldy for representing all the relations desired in a system. Although sort reasoning can be plunged into a partial order (in fact, a boolean lattice), the size of this partial order is extraordinary - given n base sorts, the lattice can be as large as 2^{2^n}. We showed that the typical use of partial orders for sort reasoning, in which each base sort is an atom (i.e. plunging the sort structure in a boolean lattice of size 2^n), leads to either the inability to state certain relations (e.g. sort *woman* is the intersection of sorts *person* and *female*) or to unjustifiable conclusions.

We proposed extending partial orders to more efficiently handle sort processing. By restricting attention to *conjunctive sorts* (sorts which consist of conjunctions of positive and negative base sorts), the scope of the problem is reduced to the interesting case which is most apparent in current logic programming systems (e.g. LIFE [2]). We defined the *sort reasoning problem* as the problem of inferring whether a given conjunctive sort s is provably empty, provably non-empty or neither, given a particular sort context. We extended a clausal sort specification notation introduced in [4] to include the specification of existential sort assertions, the dual of universal sort constraints. We also developed a definitional specification notation, in which many important taxonomic relations can be asserted (e.g. sort *univeristy_student* is defined as the union of sorts *grad_student* and *undergrad_student*). Although the two forms are equivalent in power, the latter may be more intuitive for some constraints.

Using the set of base sorts, and the existential and universal sort relations, we defined a *sort context*, and formalized the sort reasoning problem. Sort reasoning is NP-Complete in general, and for many-sorted logics this is of little concern, since sound and complete resolution strategies can be used. A main contribution of this paper is the identification of a tractable subcase of sort reasoning, which is important for practical many-sorted systems. We identified a number of restrictions which achieve a polynomial-time sort reasoning algorithm, while retaining a relatively high-level of expressive power. This goal is not easily obtained, due to the many ways in which intractability may creep into a sort structure.

References

1. H. Aït-Kaci, R. Boyer, P. Lincoln, and R. Nasr. Efficient implementation of lattice operations. *ACM Transactions on Programming Languages*, 11(1):115–146, 1989.
2. H. Aït-Kaci and A. Podelski. Towards a meaning of LIFE. *Journal of Logic Programming*, 16(3/4):195, 1993.
3. A. G. Cohn. Many sorted logic = unsorted logic + control? In M. Bramer, editor, *Research and Development in Expert Systems III*. 1987.
4. A. G. Cohn. Completing sort hierarchies. *Computers and Mathematics with Applications*, 23(2-9):477–491, 1992.
5. B. A. Davey and H. A. Priestley. *Introduction to Lattices and Order*. Cambridge University Press, Cambridge, England, 1990.
6. R. Dawkins. Hierarchical organisation: a candidate for ethology. In P. Bateson and R. Hinde, eds., *Growing Points in Ethology*. Cambridge Univ. Press, 1976.
7. G. Ellis. Efficient retrieval from hierarchies of objects using lattice operations. In *Proc. First Int. Conf. on Conceptual Structures*, Quebec, Canada, 1993.
8. A. Fall. The foundations of taxonomic encoding. Technical Report 94-20, Simon Fraser University CSS/LCCR, 1994.
9. A. Fall. Spanning tree representations of graphs and orders in conceptual structures. In *Proc. Third Int. Conf. on Conceptual Structures*, Santa Cruz, CA, 1995.
10. A. Fall and V. Dahl. Integrating description identification and systemic classification. Technical Report 93-12, Simon Fraser University CSS/LCCR, 1993.
11. M. R. Genesereth and N. J. Nilsson. *Logical Foundations of Artificial Intelligence*. Morgan Kaufmann Publishers, Palo Alto, CA, 1987.
12. C. Mellish. Implementing systemic classification by unification. *Computational Linguistics*, 14(1):40–51, 1988.
13. C. Mellish. The description identification problem. *Artificial Intelligence*, 52(2):151–167, 1991.
14. R. V. O'Neill, D. L. DeAngelis, J. B. Waide, and T. F. H. Allen. *A Hierarchical Concept of Ecosystems*. Princeton University Press, Princeton, New Jersey, 1986.
15. C. Pollard and I. Sag. *Information-Based Syntax and Semantics*. CSLI Lecture Notes No. 13. Stanford, CA, 1987.
16. J. A. Robinson. Logic and logic programming. *Communications of the ACM*, 35(3):40–65, March 1992.
17. W. A. Woods and J. G. Schmolze. The KL-ONE family. *Computers and Mathematics with Applications*, 23(2-5):133–177, 1992.

An Update Procedure for
A Probabilistic Deductive Database

Angelo C. Restificar
Department of Computer Science
Assumption University, Huamark
Bangkok 10240, Thailand
Email: angelo@science.s-t.au.ac.th

Abstract
A sound and complete view update procedure for a probabilistic deductive database is formulated using SLDp derivation trees introduced by Ng & Subrahmanian in [9]. In order to reduce the number of valid translations that can satisfy an update request a preference criteria is proposed. Moreover, we introduce a method called *Δ-factor* to minimize the change effected by updates in the database.

1. Introduction

A deductive database that supports the expression of probabilities is very useful in representing information when the data is not always certain. Studies have been made to provide for quantitative deduction in logic programming. These works include that of [3][12][6]. However, these frameworks do not facilitate the use of probabilistic information. Subrahmanian and Ng in [9] presented a probabilistic framework which supports subjective and conditional deductive databases.

When information is added or removed from the database there is a need for a correct procedure to do it and at the same time maintain the probabilistic consistency of the database. In this paper, we present a procedure to delete and insert views in the database. Moreover, we present a preference criteria based on the inherent characteristic of the probabilistic database as a method to choose from among the minimal translations. We generalize the concept of minimal translation in [2][4] to translations involving probabilities.

Intuitively, we prefer explanations that are more specific in terms of certainty. This means that explanations in which we are less ignorant are more preferable to those in which we are less sure of our knowledge. The tighter the estimate the more preferable the explanation. *The measure of our ignorance is the difference between upper and lower bounds of our estimated fact.* In a probabilistic deductive database, the probability range of a base predicate is an estimate of its certainty.

The update procedure in this paper consists of two parts: the deletion procedure and the insertion procedure. The procedure for deletion finds a minimal translation that would effect the deletion of a view. On the other hand, the insertion procedure gives the first-minimal translation after checking inconsistencies that may occur when the insertion will be performed.

Methods are also provided to cut down the number of minimal translations that can be generated. We introduce the notion of *Δ-factor*. This will allow us to choose base predicates to be used in the update translations that would affect less views.

2. Overview of the Probabilistic Framework

This section presents the framework in [9] where we base our update procedure. Let L be a language generated by finitely many constant and predicate symbols without ordinary function symbols. L contains a different function called *annotation function* defined as

Definition 1 : For c,d such that $0 \leq c,d \leq 1$, let a closed interval[c,d] be the set $\{x \mid c \leq x \leq d\}$. Let C[0,1] denote the set of all closed sub-intervals of the unit interval [0,1]. An *annotation function* f of arity n is a total function $(C[0,1])^n \rightarrow C[0,1]$.

L also contains two different variables: the *object variables*, which is the normal variables in first order logic and the *annotation variables* whose values only range between 0 and 1 and which appear only in annotation terms.

Definition 2 : $[\rho_1,\rho_2]$ is called an annotation term ρ_i $(i = 1,2)$ if (1) it is either a constant in [0,1] or an annotation variable in L, or (2) is of the form $f(\mu_1, \ldots, \mu_n)$, where f is an annotation function of arity n and $\mu_1,\ldots,\mu_n$ are annotation terms.

An annotation which does not contain any annotation variable is called *c-annotation*, otherwise it is called *v-annotation*. Let B_L denote the Herbrand base of L. It is finite since it does contain function symbols. A *basic formula* is defined as follows:

Definition 3: A *basic formula*, not necessarily ground, is either a conjunction or a disjunction of atoms. A disjunction and conjunction cannot occur simultaneously in one basic formula. Let $bf(B_L)$ denote the set of all basic formulas by using distinct atoms in B_L ,i.e., $bf(B_L) = \{ A_1 \wedge \ldots \wedge A_n \mid n \geq 1$ and $A_1,\ldots,A_n \in B_L$ and for all $1 \leq i,j \leq n$, $i \neq j \rightarrow A_i \neq A_j \} \cup \{ A_1 \vee \ldots \vee A_n \mid n \geq 1$ and $A_1,\ldots,A_n \in B_L$ and for all $1 \leq i,j \leq n$, $i \neq j \rightarrow A_i \neq A_j \}$, where all A_i's are all ground atoms.

Definition 4 : If $F_0,\ldots,F_n$ are basic formulas, and $\mu_0,\ldots,\mu_n$ are annotations such that all the annotation variables that appear in μ_0, if any, also appear in at least one of $\mu_1,\ldots,\mu_n$, then the clause $F_0{:}\mu_0 \leftarrow F_1{:}\mu_1 \wedge \ldots \wedge F_n{:}\mu_n$ is called a *pf-clause*. A probabilistic logic program, *pf-program*, with annotated formulas is a finite set of pf-clauses.

Intuitively, $F{:}[c_1,c_2]$ where $[c_1,c_2]$ is a c-annotation means : "the probability of the basic formula F must lie in the interval $[c_1,c_2]$". A formula function defined below assigns a probability range to each ground basic formula.

Definition 5: A formula function is a mapping $h: bf(B_L) \rightarrow C[0,1]$.

The notion of world probability density function relates a formula function and a probabilistic interpretation. The concept of worlds and world probability functions here are similar in essence to the "possible worlds" of [10].

Definition 6: Let a world W be a Herbrand Interpretation. A *World Probability Density Function* WP : $2^{B_L} \rightarrow [0,1]$ assigns to each world $W_j \in 2^{B_L}$ a probability $WP(W_j)$ such that for all $W_j \in 2^{B_L}$, $WP(W_j) \geq 0$ and $\sum_{W_j \in 2^{B_L}} WP(W_j) = 1$. To simplify the notation, we use p_j instead of $WP(W_j)$.

Definition 7: Let h be a formula function. A set of linear constraints denoted by LC(h) is defined as follows. For all $F_i \in bf(B_L)$, if $h(F_i) = [c_i,d_i]$, then the inequality $c_i \leq \sum_{W_j \models F and W_j \in 2^{B_L}} p_j \leq d_i$ is in LC(h). In addition, LC(h) contains the following 2 constraints: (1) $\sum_{W_j \in 2^{B_L}} p_j = 1$ and (2) $\forall W_j \in 2^{BL}$, $p_j \geq 0$. Let WP(h) denote the solution set of LC(h). Note that each solution WP $\in$ WP(h) is a world probability density function.

To compute the probabilistic truth value of a formula F, the probabilities of all possible worlds in which F is true is added. A ground instance of a pf-clause C is a clause obtained by replacing the object variables in C by members of the Herbrand Universe. Let *grd*(P) denote the ground instances of the clauses in a program P.

Definition 8: A probabilistic interpretation $I_{WP} : bf(B_L) \rightarrow [0,1]$ is defined as follows: $I_{WP}(F) = \sum_{W_j \models F and W_j \in 2^{B_L}} p_j$ for all basic formulas $F \in bf(B_L)$.

Definition 9: Let I be a probabilistic interpretation and let $F_0,\ldots,F_n$ be in $bf(B_L)$, and $[c_0,d_0],\ldots,[c_n,d_n]$ be closed sub-intervals of [0,1]. Furthermore, let C be a pf-clause, and let x and V denote an object and annotation variable, respectively.

1) $I \models_p F_1 : [c_1,d_1]$ iff $I(F_1) \in [c_1,d_1]$;
2) $I \models_p (F_1:[c_1,d_1] \wedge \ldots \wedge F_n:[c_n,d_n])$ iff for all $1 \leq j \leq n$, $I \models_p F_j:[c_j,d_j]$;
3) $I \models_p F_0:[c_0,d_0] \leftarrow F_1:[c_1,d_1] \wedge \ldots \wedge F_n:[c_n,d_n]$ iff $I \models_p F_0:[c_0,d_0]$;
or $I \not\models_p (F_1:[c_1,d_1] \wedge \ldots \wedge F_n:[c_n,d_n])$;
4) $I \models_p (\exists x)(C)$ iff $I \models_p (C(x/t))$ for some ground term t, where C(x/t) denotes the replacement of all free occurrences of x in C by t;
5) $I \models_p (\forall x)(C)$ iff $I \models_p (C(x/t))$ for all ground terms t;
6) $I \models_p (\exists V)(C)$ iff $I \models_p (C(V/c))$ for some $c \in [0,1]$; and
7) $I \models_p (\forall V(C)$ iff $I \models_p (C(V/c))$ for all $c \in [0,1]$ such that $\mu(V/c) \neq \emptyset$, where V occurs in annotation term μ.

A program P probabilistically entails a formula F iff I $\models_p$ F for all probabilistic interpretation I that satisfies each clause in P. Finally, the notion of query processing in this framework is presented below:

Definition 10: θ is a unifier of $(A_1 \wedge \ldots \wedge A_n):\mu_1$ and $(B_1 \wedge \ldots \wedge B_m):\mu_2$ iff $\{A_i\theta \mid 1 \le i \le n\} = \{B_i\theta \mid 1 \le i \le m\}$. Similarly, θ unifies $(A_1 \vee \ldots \vee A_n):\mu_1$ and $(B_1 \vee \ldots \vee B_m):\mu_2$ iff $\{A_i\theta \mid 1 \le i \le n\} = \{B_i\theta \mid 1 \le i \le m\}$. Given θ a unifier of C_1, C_2, let $[\theta]$ denote $\{\gamma \mid \theta \le \gamma$ and $\gamma \le \theta$ and γ unifies $C_1, C_2\}$. We say that $[\theta_1] \le [\theta_2]$ iff there exists γ such that $[\theta_1] = [\theta_2\gamma]$, and that $[\theta_1] < [\theta_2]$ iff $[\theta_1] \le [\theta_2]$ and $[\theta_1] \ne [\theta_2]$. Furthermore, θ is a max-gu (maximally general unifier) of C_1 and C_2 iff θ is a unifier of C_1, C_2 and there does not exist another unifier θ_1 such that $[\theta] < [\theta_1]$.

Definition 11: Let P be a finite but non-empty set of ground clauses, i.e. $P=\{C_1, \ldots, C_n\}$, where for all $1 \le i \le k$, C_i is of the form $F_i:[\delta_i, \rho_i] \leftarrow Body_i$. (1)Define a set LP(P) of linear constraints in the following way. For all $1 \le i \le k$, the inequality $\delta_i \le \sum_{W_j \models F and W_j \in 2^{B_L}} p_j \le \rho_i$ is in LP(P). In addition, LP(P) contains the 2 constraints: : (a) $\sum_{W_j \in 2^{B_L}} p_j = 1$ and (b) $\forall W_j \in 2^{BL}$, $p_j \ge 0$. (2) Define the closure of P, denoted by cl(P), as follows. Let cl(P) = P $\cup$ $\{F:[\delta_F, \rho_F] \leftarrow Body_1 \wedge \ldots \wedge Body_k \wedge Con_{sol} \mid F \in bf(B_L)$, $\delta_F = \min_{LP(P)} \sum_{W_j \models F and W_j \in 2^{B_L}} p_j$ and $\rho_F = \max_{LP(P)} \sum_{W_j \models F and W_j \in 2^{B_L}} p_j$ and Con_{sol} denotes the conjunction of constraints on the annotation terms for LP(P) to have solutions.$\}$

Definition 12: Let P be a pf-program. Define (1) *redun*(P) = $\{F:[0,1] \leftarrow \mid F \in bf(B_L)\}$ and the compiled version of P, *com*(P) = $\cup$ cl(Q) for each subset Q of *redun*(P) $\cup$ *grd*(P).

Definition 13: A *query* is a formula of the form $\exists(F_1:\mu_1 \wedge \ldots \wedge F_n:\mu_n)$ such that for all $1 \le i \le n$, F_i is a basic formula not necessarily ground, and $\mu_i = [\delta_i, \rho_i]$ where δ_i, ρ_i are either constants in [0,1] or annotation variables in L. A *constrained query* Q is of the form $\exists(F_1:\mu_1 \wedge \ldots \wedge F_n:\mu_n \wedge Con_Q)$ where the query part of Q is $F_1:\mu_1 \wedge \ldots \wedge F_n:\mu_n$ and the constraint part Con_Q is a conjunction of constraints on the annotation terms.

Definition 14: An *SLDp-deduction* of a constrained query Q_1 from a pf-program P is a sequence $\langle Q_1, C_1, \theta_1 \rangle, \ldots \langle Q_r, C_r, \theta_r \rangle, \ldots$, where for all $i \ge 1$, C_i is a renamed version of a clause in *com*(P) and Q_{i+1} is an SLDp-resolvent of Q_i and C_i via a maximally general unifier θ_i. An SLDp-refutation is a finite SLDp-deduction where the query part is empty and the constraint part is satisfiable.

If the linear constraints in P does not have a solution then it does not have a probabilistic model hence inconsistent. The following set of clauses P is inconsistent because the solution set LP(P) is empty:

Example 1. $r(X):[0,0] \leftarrow b_3(X):[V_1,V_2]$
$b_2(t):[0.90,0.95] \leftarrow$
$b_2(t):[0.50,0.75] \leftarrow$ □

The update procedure which will be presented in the later sections will be in the context of pf-compact programs defined as follows.

Definition 15: A pf-compact program is a set of pf-clauses such that $\forall F \in bf(B_L)$ $\exists$ an integer $k < \omega$ such that $\forall F$ $lfp(T_p)(F) = T_p \uparrow k(F)$.

3. Semantics of the Update

Consider a pf-program D as defined in Definition 4. The pf-clauses in D can be partitioned into two classes: The *pf-extensional database definition* (pf-edb) and the *pf-intensional database definition* (pf-idb) defined below.

Definition 16: The head of a pf-clause with a non-empty body is called a *pf-intensional database predicate*. All predicates in pf-ddb that are not pf-intensional database predicates are called *pf-extensional database predicates.*

Definition 17: A collection of pf-clauses having the same pf-intensional database predicate is called a *view definition*. A view is a pf-intensional database predicate logically implied by a pf-program D.

Where no confusion will arise we interchangeably use base predicates and pf-edb predicates. The following illustrates the partition in our deductive database:

Example 2 pf-idb: $p(X,Y):[0.95,1] \leftarrow s(X):[1,1], q(Y):[V_1,V_2]$
$t(X)):[0.80*V, 0.80*V] \leftarrow r(X):[V,V]$
pf-edb: $s(a):[1,1] \leftarrow$
$q(e):[0.80,1] \leftarrow$
$r(e):[0.90,0.90] \leftarrow$ □

We restrict pf-edb to contain only ground unit clauses whose annotations are constant and whose interval assignment is unique, i.e., for all base predicates b_i there is only one interval to which b_i is mapped. This allows us to extend to our framework the concept of minimal translations w.r.t. set inclusion. Note that pf-edb $\cup$ pf-idb = pf-ddb. Pf-idb contains pf-clauses whose bodies are nonempty and whose annotations may be nonground. Direct insertion or direct deletion of a view is not allowed. We have to procedurally change the view through the pf-edb which contain our facts. An update translation T, chosen to satisfy an update request, only contains elements of the pf-edb.

Definition 18: A *strictly ground instance of a pf-clause* C, SGI(C), is a ground instance of a pf-clause whose annotations are constants c $\in$ C[0,1]. Let SGIU(C) denote a strictly ground instance of a unit pf-clause C. A fact F $\in$ pf-edb is an SGIU(F). An update of a fact F is denoted as INS(F) for inserting F and DEL(F) for deleting F. An update *translation* T is a set of updates.

Definition 19: Let D be a pf-ddb and U(pf-ddb) denote an updated pf-ddb. After a deletion update on fact F, U(pf-ddb) $\not\models_p$ F. After an insertion update, U(pf-ddb) $\models_p$ F. A *valid* translation is a set of updates applied to the deductive database that satisfy an update request.

The problem of whether it is possible to rank alternative valid translations according to some criteria independent of the domain and task, has drawn discussions among researchers. Since no logical criterion can be used to support the choice [11][8] we exploit the probabilities inherent to our domain to rank our alternatives and thus reduce the number of valid translations. This can be achieved by using the notion of *Δ-factor* and *measures of ignorance*. The lower and upper probabilities enable us to distinguish between situations in which our beliefs can be described by a single probability value and those in which we have less information. It is thus imperative to differentiate between beliefs which contain more information and beliefs which contain less.

Definition 20: Let b:[d,r] be an annotated base predicate. The *measure of ignorance* of the base predicate b, denoted as $m_{ig}(b)$, is equal to the absolute value of the difference of d and r. Thus for any base predicate b_j:[d_j,r_j], $m_{ig}(b_j) = | d_j - r_j |$. The measure of ignorance for a set S of base predicates, denoted as $m_{ig}(S)$, is the sum of all $m_{ig}(b_i)$ for each $b_i \in S$.

When a unique probability range is assigned to each base predicate in the pf-edb, the notion of minimality w.r.t. set inclusion [2][12][4] can be generalized to the level of probabilistic satisfiability. For example, { b_1:[0.5,1], b_2:[1,1] } $\models_p$ {b_1:[0.5,1] } generalizes { b_1 } $\subseteq$ { b_1, b_2 }. Moreover, it is also true that given two sets of updates E and E', E $\models_p$ E' iff E $\models$ E'. This follows since each base predicate is assigned a unique probability range. A set of updates is considered *minimal* iff there does not exist another set of updates such that the latter is probabilistically implied by the former. More formally,

Definition 21: Given update translations T and T', T' > T iff T' $\models_p$ T. Let $T_1,\ldots,T_m$ be a finite sequence of translations s.t. $\forall i$ ($T_i > T_{i+1}$), then the translation T_m is said to be a *minimal translation.*

4. Procedure for Deletion

View update restricts application of an update request only to pf-edb predicates. We assume that our deductive database is pf-compact. The update request is a ground root of an SLDp refutation. Intuitively, this means removing from the pf-edb all the ground pf-edb predicates such that the view is no longer implied by the database.

The number of minimal translations can be greatly reduced by rule annotations [13] or by pruning derivation trees as in [2]. We complement their techniques by exploiting the probabilities in our framework to reduce the number of candidate translations. We only need to consider those base predicates that support the update request. Thus, we need the notion of support sets for deletion which is similar to the extensional dependency set in [13].

Definition 22: A *support set for deletion* (*SSD*) is a set of elements of the pf-edb such that these elements appear as input clauses in a successful branch of a derivation tree rooted at the update request. A view is *dependent* on a pf-edb predicate if the pf-edb predicate is in the body of the view.

The framework represents negation through the notion of impossibility, e.g. A:[0,0], which means that "A will not happen". Thus, unlike updating procedures for normal logic programs[7] where negation-by-failure is to be handled, our procedure derives solution from only one SLDp tree. Furthermore, when deleting (resp. inserting) information in the database it is desirable to choose a translation such that the loss (resp. addition) of information is minimized (resp. maximized). The notion of *Δ-factor* will help us to choose those translations (see Example 3).

Definition 23: Let L be the total number of view dependencies on the pf-edb predicates in pf-idb. Then the *Δ-factor* of a pf-edb predicate B, denoted as $\Delta(B)$, is the ratio of the number of views that depend on B to L. Hence $\Delta(B) = n / L$, where n is the number of views dependent on a base predicate. If k is the number of base predicates in the pf-idb then $\Sigma\ \Delta(B_i) = 1$ for all $i = 1, \ldots, k$.

Definition 24:(*Preference Criteria For Deletion*) Let T be a translation of an update request. Choose the minimal sets and order the elements of T in the following manner: (1) The smaller the *Δ-factor* the higher the preference; (2) Among equal values in (1), the larger the $m_{ig}(b)$ of each base predicate the higher the preference. This means that we prefer to delete information which we are less certain.

The preference criteria can also be applied to a candidate set in case it is not singleton by adding the values in each base predicate in the candidate set. We abuse the word "best" to mean the first element of the queue. The best translation for deletion, denoted as T_b, is the first element in a translation queue, ordered according to the *Preference Criteria For Deletion*. Next, we present the procedure for deletion. If no translation is obtained using the first step, then the process is incremented to the second step. The first step, therefore, serves as a sieve to reduce the number of candidates whenever possible.

Procedure For Finding A Translation For Deletion

Let k be the number of SSDs in a SLDp derivation tree rooted at the delete request. An element e of SSD_i is redundant iff $\exists\ e' \in SSD_i,\ e,e' \in T_b$.

STEP1: Let CSD be the $\cap$ SSD_i
IF CSD $\neq \emptyset$ then
begin
order(CSD)
T_b = *first*(CSD)
return T_b
end
ELSE
STEP2: *order*(SSD_i) i = 1,..,k
T_b := { collection of all first elements of each SSD_i s.t.
no element is redundant }

The function *first* returns the first element in the ordered set CSD while the procedure *order* arranges the entire set according to the preference criteria.

Example 3: Consider the following probabilistic deductive database where the preferred base predicate is the base predicate $b_2(X)$.:

pf-idb: $a(X):[V_1,V_2] \leftarrow b_1(X):[V_1,V_2], h(X):[1,1]$
$a(X):[1,1] \leftarrow b_3(X):[1,1], q(X,X):[0,0], b_2(X):[0.70,0.70]$
$q(X,Y):[0.60,0.70] \leftarrow b_1(X):[1,1], b_3(Y):[1,1]$
$h(X):[0.75,0.75] \leftarrow b_3(X):[0,0]$
pf-edb: $\emptyset$
The following table shows the *Δ-factor* of each of the base predicates:

base predicate	dependent views	*Δ-factor*
$b_1(X)$	a(X),q(X,Y)	0.33
$b_2(X)$	a(X)	0.17
$b_3(X)$	q(X,Y),a(X),h(X)	0.50
TOTAL	L = 6	1.00

The following lemma shows that if one pf-extensional database predicate is taken out from the set of all predicates that make up a refutation branch for any view then that branch can no longer succeed.

Lemma 1: Let b $\in$ SSD_i, i = 1,...,n of a view F. If b is deleted from an SSD_i, then $\{SSD_i \backslash b\}$ is no longer a successful branch for F.

A *valid deletion set S* for a view F is a set of translation for deletion such that if {pf-ddb \ S } $\not\models_p$ F.

Lemma 2: If the candidate translation set for deletion contain at least one element of all SSD_i, i = 1,...,n then the candidate translation set is a valid deletion set.

Lemma 3: If a candidate translation set is a valid deletion set of distinct elements and it is the case that each SSD_i has exactly one representative element in the CSD then CSD is a minimal translation.

Theorem 1: (*Correctness Theorem For Deletion*) Let DELETE(F) be an update request to delete the view F, T_b be the translation for deletion generated by the above defined procedure for deletion and D be a compact pf-ddb, then U(D) $\not\models_p$ F.

Theorem 2: (*Completeness Theorem For Deletion*) Let DELETE(F) be an update request to delete the view F and D be a compact pf-ddb, then there exist a T_b s.t. U(D) $\not\models_p$ F.

5. Procedure for Insertion

The insertion of a view into the database is the process by which we make the SLDp-tree succeed, making at least one branch succeed. The derivation tree could become very large so that a very large amount of computing time is needed to construct all possible successful branches. [1] argues that it is not always possible to find the best translation. Here we present a procedure which can be stopped at anytime to yield the best (at a given time) translation so far generated. Again there could be more than one best translation. We shall refer to this procedure as first-best.

Insertion updates in pf-ddb is *nonmonotonic*, since the addition of a view in the probabilistic deductive database may result to a deletion of some views held as true in the current state of the database. Also, there is a need for the insertion procedure to detect probabilistic inconsistency before it inserts a view in the pf-ddb. The procedure traverses the tree by expanding a set in the queue with the highest precedence and adds into the ordered set of generated translations the translations generated at each level. *The threshold for the measure of ignorance and that of the Δ-factor may be set to a user-satisfiable value which can be used to prune the tree.* In cases where a variable needs to be grounded or a probability range needs to be provided, which may happen during the insertion procedure, we assume that the data is provided by an external system separate from our update procedure. While traversing the tree, the candidate translations for insertion are queued up in the *partial priority translation queue* according to the *Preference Criteria For Insertion*. If all the elements of a candidate translation are already pf-edb predicates.then they are placed into the *full priority translation queue*.

Definition 25:(*Preference Criteria For Insertion*) Let T be a set of translations. Choose the minimal sets and order T in the following manner: (1) The smaller the sum of the $m_{ig}(b)$ of each base predicate in T the higher the preference. This means that we prefer to insert information in which we are more certain. (2) Among equal values in (1)the larger the sum of the *Δ-factor* the higher the preference.

After criterion (2) there may still be equally-valued sets, we assume that an external system be forced to choose from among the possible translations. Let PTQ be a family of a set of predicates ordered by the *Preference Criteria For Insertion.* The set PTQ is called a *partial priority translation queue* iff every set in PTQ contains at least one view predicate or a non-ground pf-edb predicate used as input clause in a successful branch for an SLDp-tree of a view V. Also, let FTQ be a set of translations ordered by the *Preference Criteria For Insertion.* The set FTQ is called a *full priority translation queue* iff every translation in FTQ contains ground pf-edb predicates used as input clauses in a successful branch for an SLDp-tree of a view V.

Example 4: Suppose we are to insert the view h(e):[1,1] in the following probabilistic deductive database:

pf-idb: $h(X):[1,1] \leftarrow g(X,Y):[1,1], b(Y):[1,1]$
$h(X):[1,1] \leftarrow a(X):[0.5,1]$
$g(X,Y):[1,1] \leftarrow m(X):[1,1], n(X,Z):[1,1], w(Y):[1,1], n(Y,Z):[1,1]$
pf-edb: $m(e):[1,1] \leftarrow$
$n(e,i):[0.5,1] \leftarrow$
update request: insert{h(e):[1,1]}

If we insert the view h(e):[1,1] the insertion procedure generates the following PTQ(Partial Priority Translation Queue):
t_1) {<m(e):[1,1], n(e,Z):[1,1], w(Y):[1,1], n(Y,Z):[1,1], b(Y):[1,1]>, < a(e):[0.5,1]>}
t_2) {<m(e):[1,1], n(e,i):[1,1], w(Y):[1,1], n(Y,i):[1,1], b(Y):[1,1]> }
t_3) {<m(e):[1,1], n(e,i):[1,1], w(u):[1,1], n(u,i):[1,1], b(u):[1,1]> }
t_4) $\emptyset$
FTQ(Full Priority Translation Queue) will contain
t_1) $\emptyset$
t_2) { <a(e):[0.5,1]> }
t_3) { <a(e):[0.5,1]> }
t_4) { <m(e):[1,1], n(e,i):[1,1], w(u):[1,1],n(u,i):[1,1], b(u):[1,1]>, <a(e):[0.5,1]> }

Using our preference criteria for insertion we choose that translation for which the sum of 'our ignorance' is zero. Furthermore, we assume that the value for the variable Y and Z are supplied by the user. □

Let $T \in$ FTQ, then the first-best translation, denoted as T_{fb}, is the translation $T \in$ FTQ s.t. T = *first*(FTQ). Moreover, let $b:[d_1,r_1]$ and $b:[d_2,r_2]$ be annotated ground base predicates. A ground base predicate $b:[d_1,r_1]$ is *preferred* to $b:[d_2,r_2]$ iff $b:[d_1,r_1]$ probabilistically entails $b:[d_2,r_2]$, i.e., $b:[d_1,r_1]$ is preferred to $b:[d_2,r_2]$ iff $[d_1,r_1] \subseteq [d_2,r_2]$.

Procedure For Finding First-Best Minimal Translation For Insertion

Let $(A:[V_1,V_2])\theta$ be a ground basic formula whose annotations are variables, $(A:[k_1,k_2])\theta$ be a strictly ground formula and $INSERT(A:[k_1,k_2])\theta$ be an insert request. Let elements of FTQ and PTQ be sets of the form <p_1,...p_n> where each p_i is a basic formula.

```
STEP1: { View Consistency Checking }
      begin
        construct derivation tree for (A:[V1,V2])θ
        INC_VIEWS := ∅
        IF (A:[V1,V2])θσ succeeds with annotation instantiation σ THEN
              begin
                FOR each σ s.t. [k1,k2] ⊈ ([V1,V2])σ DO
                    INC_VIEWS := { (A:[V1,V2])θσ } ∪ INC_VIEWS
                IF INC_VIEWS ≠ ∅ THEN
                  begin
                        query the user. Q = (Yes/No). {Proceed to insert ?}
                        IF Q = Yes THEN
                          begin
                            FOR each F ∈ INC_VIEWS DO
                               DELETE(F) {invoke our deletion procedure }
                          end
                        ELSE terminate { maintain current view }
                  end
                ELSE
                   INSERT(A:[k1,k2])θ { STEP2 executes this }
        ELSE { no inconsistency }
              INSERT(A:[k1,k2])θ { STEP2 executes this }
      end
STEP2: { Insertion of the View }
      PTQ := { <A:[k1,k2]θ> }
      FTQ:= ∅
      WHILE PTQ ≠ ∅ DO
        begin
          choose first(PTQ)
          { a condition for user-satisfiable threshold values can be placed here }
          Let <p1,...,pi,...,pn> ∈ PTQ
          FOR each pf-clause (a:[l,r] ← D) s.t. max-gu(a,pi)=θ DO
              begin
               PTQ := (<p1,...,pi-1,D,pi+1...,pn>)θ ∪ PTQ
               let t,t' be candidate translations
              CASE1: IF t is already the set of strictly ground pf-edb predicates
              and ∄t' s.t. t |=p t' THEN FTQ := t ∪ FTQ
              CASE2: IF t is already the set of strictly ground pf-edb predicates
              and ∃ t' s.t. t' |=p t THEN FTQ := t ∪ {FTQ\ t'}
              order(FTQ)
              FLAG := true;
              WHILE (Flag and FTQ ≠ ∅) DO
```

```
                    begin
                     T_temp := first(FTQ)
                     IF good(T_temp) THEN
                           begin
                            T_fb := T_temp
                            FLAG:= false
                           end
                     ELSE FTQ := { FTQ\T_temp }*
                    end
            end
        order(PTQ)
       end
```

STEP3: Upon inserting each element in the pf-edb insert the preferred element only

*To force T_{temp} to be a solution we must delete all pf- edb elements that would cause inconsistency when T_{temp} is inserted.

Setting PTQ to empty in the WHILE-DO loop above generates all possible translations. This however can be set to finding only the first translation. The predicate good(T_{temp}) is true iff for all elements e:[l,r] T_{temp}, $\nexists$e':[l',r'] $\in$ pf-edb s.t. $[l,r] \cap [l',r'] = \emptyset$. STEP1 is necessary because the insert update request may cause probabilistic inconsistency in the database w.r.t. other views held by the current pf-ddb. Let R be an insert request, D be a pf-ddb and I be a translation set for R. I is said to be a *valid insertion set* iff $D \cup I \models_p R$.

Lemma 4: Let INC_VIEWS be a set of probabilistically inconsistent views wrt to an insert request INSERT($A:[k_1,k_2])\theta$. If $\exists$ a view $(A:[V_1,V_2])\theta\sigma$ s.t. $[V_1,V_2]\sigma \cap [k_1,k_2] = \emptyset$ then $(A:[V_1,V_2])\theta\sigma \in$ INC_VIEWS.

Theorem 3:(*Correctness Theorem For Insertion*) Let INSERT($A:[k_1,k_2])\theta$ be an insert request and D be a compact pf-ddb. Then the updated probabilistic database U(pf-ddb) $\models_p (A:[k_1,k_2])\theta$.

Theorem 4:(*Completeness Theorem For Insertion*) Let INSERT($A:[k_1,k_2])\theta$ be an insert request and D be a compact pf-ddb. Then there exist a minimal translation for insertion such that U(pf-ddb) $\models_p (A:[k_1,k_2])\theta$.

7. Conclusion

A sound and complete probabilistic view updating procedure is proposed. We have provided a method to choose base predicates such that less views will be affected, using the *Δ-factor*. Our preference criteria have proposed a method to exploit the probabilistic information inherent in the framework to cut down the number of minimal translations.

Acknowledgments. The author wishes to thank Phan Minh Dung and Kanchana Kanchanasut for valuable comments and encouragement. The communications with Raymond Ng and V.S. Subrahmanian have been of benefit to this work.

8. References

[1] Tom Bylander, Dean Allemang, Michael C. Tanner and John R. Josephson: The computational complexity of abduction, *Artificial Intelligence*, Vol. 49, 1991.

[2] Hendrik Decker: Drawing Updates From Derivations, in *Proceedings of the International Conference on Database Theory*, 1990.

[3] M. H. van Emden: Quantitative Deduction and its Fixpoint Theory, *Journal of Logic Programming*, Elsevier Science Publishing Co., 1986.

[4] R. Fagin, G.M. Kuper, J.D. Ullman, M.Y. Vardi: Updating Logical Databases, *Advances in Computing Research*, Vol. 3, JAI Press, 1986.

[5] A. Guessoum and J. W. Lloyd: Updating Knowledge Bases II, TR-90-13, Univ. Bristol, Comp. Sc., 1990.

[6] Michael Kifer and V.S. Subrahmanian: Theory of Generalized Annotated Logic Programming and its Applications, *Journal of Logic Programming*, 1992.

[7] T. Kakas and P. Mancarella: Database Updates through Abduction, Research Report, Dept. of Computing, Imperial College of Science and Technology, London, 1990.

[8] Hector J. Levesque: A Knowledge-level Account of Abduction, in *Proceedings of 11th International Joint Conference in Artificial Intelligence*, Detroit, 1989.

[9] Raymond T. Ng and V.S. Subrahmanian: A Semantical Framework for Supporting Subjective and Conditional Probabilities in Deductive Databases, in *Proceedings of the 8th International Conference in Logic Programming*, 1991.

[10] N. Nilsson: Probabilistic Logic, *AI Journal 28*, pp. 71-87.

[11] Raymond Reiter: Nonmonotonic Reasoning, *Annual Review of Computer Science*, Vol. 2, Annual Reviews Inc., 1987.

[12] E. Shapiro: Logic Programs with Uncertainties: A Tool for Implementing Expert Systems, in *Proceedings of the International Joint Conference in Artificial Intelligence*, William Kauffman, 1983.

[13] Anthony Tomasic: A View Update Translation via Deduction and Annotation, in *Proceedings of the 2nd International Conference on Database Theory*, August 31 - September 2, 1988.

A Framework for Reasoning About Requirements Evolution

Didar Zowghi[1], Aditya K. Ghose[2], and Pavlos Peppas[3]

Abstract. We present a logical framework for modelling and reasoning about requirements evolution in the construction of information systems. Our framework represents a requirements model as a theory of some nonmonotonic logic, while requirements evolution is modelled as a mapping between such theories, based on the AGM logic of belief change [1]. We demonstrate our ideas by using the THEORIST system for nonmonotonic reasoning. Moreover we examine the *Telos* system for requirements modelling in terms of our framework, and we identify some obvious shortcomings and propose possible solutions. We argue that our framework provides a powerful tool both for analysing and comparing existing systems and for developing automated systems to support requirements evolution.

Keywords: AI applications in software engineering, default reasoning, belief revision.

1 Introduction

If we regard a theory as the deductive closure of a given set of axioms, then in essence software engineering is nothing more than the building and managing of large theories. This theory construction typically commences with a collection of activities referred to as Requirements Engineering. The major objective of requirements engineering is defining the purpose of a proposed system and capturing its external behaviour.

Every phase of software development is characterised by continued evolution. Requirements evolve because requirements engineers and users cannot possibly envision all the ways in which the system can be utilised. The environment where the software is situated also changes and so do the software boundaries and business rules governing the utilisation of that software. Implementation has to be changed because designs evolve and defects have to be fixed [16]. Clearly, support for evolutionary processes is needed at all stages of software construction but especially in requirements engineering since it is the requirements modifications that usually initiates this cycle of change throughout software development.

[1] CSIRO-Macquarie University Joint Research Centre for Advanced Systems Engineering, Macquarie University, NSW 2109, Australia. didar@mpce.mq.edu.au

[2] Knowledge Systems Group, Basser Dept. of Computer Science, University of Sydney, NSW 2006, Australia. aditya@cs.su.oz.au

[3] Knowledge Systems Group, Dept. of Computing, School of Mathematics, Physics, Computing and Electronics, Macquarie University, NSW 2109, Australia. pavlos@mpce.mq.edu.au

This paper focusses on the problem of managing requirements evolution. This involves handling constant changes in requirements and maintaining the consistency and completeness of the requirements model. We suggest that the management of requirements evolution is most effective when it is based on a formal underlying framework. The major contributions of this paper are twofold. First, we present a formal framework that can serve as a basis for reasoning with and about requirements. Second, we provide a formal basis for requirements evolution via operations defined in this formal framework. It is assumed that the requirements model is represented in some formal language with a well-defined semantics (an example of such a language is *Telos* [11]). At a meta-level, we view the requirements model as a nonmonotonic theory, specifically a default theory as formalised in [14] [13]. This enables us to obtain complete requirements models by taking initial incomplete requirements specifications and applying relevant defaults from the domain. As well, the formal machinery of generating default extensions is available to resolve contradictions and analyse and select from amongst multiple possible views of a requirements model (corresponding to multiple possible extensions of the corresponding default theory). We then analyse operators for requirements evolution in the *Telos* requirements modelling language using our default-based framework and point out some obvious shortcomings of these operators. This serves to motivate the development of a new set of operators which may serve as the formal basis for requirements evolution. We apply belief revision techniques, as formalised in the so-called AGM theory [1] [4], to define operations through which new requirements may be added or existing requirements may be retracted from a default-based representation of a requirements model. We show how this new approach avoids the problems we identify with the operators in the *Telos* framework. This work thus presents a principled approach to reasoning about requirements evolution which can serve as the basis for analysing existing requirements engineering techniques and, at the same time, provide a useful starting point for defining semantically well-founded systems for managing requirements representation and evolution.

2 A Formal Basis for Reasoning about Requirements

Consider the requirements engineering process involved in developing a word-processor.The initial problem statement only specifies that this word-processor is intended to be used by children. Two assumptions may be made immediately that are related to the domain knowledge and usability. Firstly, since all word processors by default have a spell check functionality, we may specify a requirement for existence of a spelling check function. Secondly, since it is intended for use by children, we may add a set of requirements for the ability to change the colour of screen and text etc. These assumptions are added to the initial statement to represent our current state of belief about the software we are to develop and are then presented to the problem owners for validation. They, in turn, confirm that spell check is indeed a requirement but since they will only have monochrome terminals available there is no need for colour change. So we need to revise our set of beliefs to contract those requirements related to colour.

Requirements engineering is typically initiated by the identification of a problem and the expression of a need for a possibly computerised solution. Requirements engineers normally examine this brief problem statement and based on past experience and possibly limited knowledge of the application domain make *assumptions* and use *defaults* to expand it into a more complete expression of the requirements. This expanded version of requirements is then presented to users for validation and correction. Requirements are normally elicited in natural language, during iterative interactions between the users and requirements engineers. Consequently, the expression of requirements are typically ambiguous, inconsistent, and incomplete. During requirements analysis and modelling, alternative models for the system are elaborated and a conceptual model of the enterprise as seen by the system's eventual users is produced. The specifications are validated and analysed against correctness properties (such as completeness and consistency), and feasibility properties (such as cost and resources needed). Although the final product of requirements engineering is typically a document written almost entirely in natural language, called the Requirements Specification, we shall focus our attention on the requirements model, from which the requirements specification is generated. Our account of the requirements engineering process this far suggests that any formal framework for reasoning about requirements must satisfy the following three properties. Firstly, it must include an explicit notion of defaults so that tentative assumptions and default knowledge about the domain can be brought to bear on an incompletely specified initial set of assumptions to obtain a more complete requirements model. Secondly, it must permit the identification of consistent alternative models which resolve any contradictions arising in an initial set of potentially contradictory and incompletely specified requirements. Thirdly, it must provide an adequate account of how a requirements model evolves as a consequence of new requirements being added or existing requirements being retracted.

The model we present in Figure 1 achieves precisely these three objectives. Fundamentally, a requirements model is viewed as a theory in some nonmonotonic logic. Requirements evolution maps one such theory to another through a process of rational belief revision. The two operators $\mid\sim$ and $*$ encode the two basic, orthogonal processes in our framework. In particular, the operator $\mid\sim$ encodes the process of nonmonotonic inference. We start with an initial incomplete set of requirements and apply relevant defaults or tentative assumptions about the problem domain to complete the requirements model. By applying the $\mid\sim$ operator, we obtain the set of nonmonotonic consequences sanctioned by the requirements model represented as a nonmonotonic theory. There can be possibly multiple, mutually contradictory sets of nonmonotonic consequences (also called extensions). A choice is made from amongst these extensions through a process of iterative interaction between users and requirements engineers. For the purpose of exposition in this paper, we shall commit to a specific nonmonotonic formalism, namely the THEORIST system [14] [13], which we shall describe in the next section. The operator $*$ on the other hand, encodes the process of belief revision. The AGM theory of belief change [1] [4], which we describe in the next section, provides a semantic basis for *rational* belief revision. We maintain that any account of requirements evolution should be based on this semantically well-founded theory.

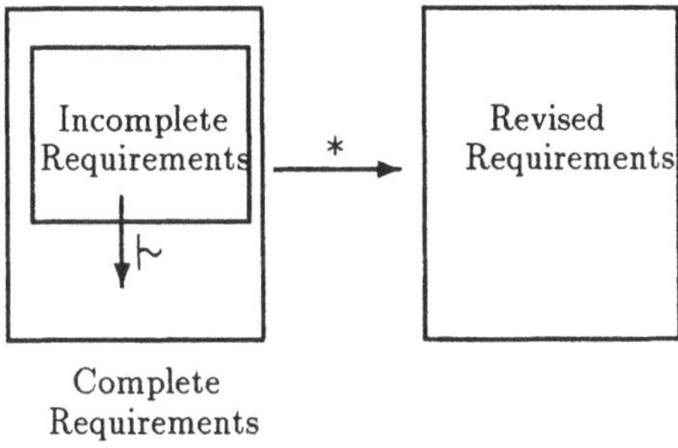

Fig. 1. Modelling Requirements Evolution

3 Formal Preliminaries

3.1 Belief Change: Preliminaries

Belief change is the area of research that studies the process by which a rational agent changes her beliefs about the world in the light of new information (possibly contradicting her current belief state). Much of the research in the area is based on the work of Alchourron, Gardenfors and Makinson [1] who have developed a framework (widely known as the *AGM framework*) for studying the process of belief revision. In the AGM framework, the new information is represented by a sentence of the logical language $\mathcal{L}$, belief states are represented as theories of a $\mathcal{L}$, and the process of belief revision is modelled as a function * over theories, called a *revision function*, satisfying certain postulates (known as the *AGM postulates*) that intend to capture the essence of rational belief revision. The guiding idea used in formulating these postulates was that the new belief state ought to differ *as little as possible* from the old belief state in order to accommodate the new information. This is known as the *Principle of Minimal Change*.

Let $Cn(\Gamma)$, for any set of sentences Γ of $\mathcal{L}$, denote the logical closure of Γ in $\mathcal{L}$. A theory K of $\mathcal{L}$ is any set of sentences of $\mathcal{L}$ closed under logical implication, i.e. $K = Cn(K)$. We shall denote the set of all consistent theories of $\mathcal{L}$ by $\mathcal{K}_{\mathcal{L}}$. Then, a revision function * is any function from $\mathcal{K}_{\mathcal{L}} \times \mathcal{L}$ to $\mathcal{K}_{\mathcal{L}}$, mapping $\langle K, \varphi \rangle$ to K^*_{φ}, which satisfies a set of eight postulates. We shall not present these postulates here for brevity. The AGM framework defines, in a similar way, the operations of *contraction*, in which some sentence ϕ is retracted from K to obtain K^-_{ϕ}, and *expansion*, in which some sentence ϕ is added to K to obtain

K_ϕ^+, given a guarantee that ϕ is consistent with K. The operations of revision, contraction and expansion may be related via the so-called Levi identity [10]: $K_\phi^* = (K_{\neg\phi}^-)_\phi^+$.

Given a theory K and a sentence φ (representing the current belief state and the new information respectively) the revision postulates confine, but do not *uniquely* determine the result K_φ^* of revising K by φ. This is mainly due to the fact that the exact outcome of the revision process depends on certain *extra-logical* factors that are domain-dependent. It turns out that these domain-dependent factors can be encoded with an ordering $\leq$ on the sentences of K, called an *epistemic entrenchment*, that represents the relative epistemic importance of the agent's beliefs. The epistemic importance of a belief in K determines its fate when K is revised. Loosely speaking, for any two formulas φ and ψ such that $\varphi \leq \psi$, whenever a choice exists between giving up φ and giving up ψ the former will be surrendered in order to minimise the epistemic loss. With this revision policy, an epistemic entrenchment conveys all the necessary information to uniquely determine the outcome of revising K by any sentence φ [5].

While the AGM framework provides a useful abstraction for the belief change process, it does not lend itself to implementation in a straightforward way. Several studies (such as [12]) have therefore focussed on *belief bases*, which are finite sets of sentences, instead of logically closed theories, as representations of belief states. Belief base approaches consider priority relations on the belief base, instead of entrenchment relations defined on the entire language, in determining the outcome of a belief change step. In the rest of this paper, we shall only consider AGM-rational operators (i.e., operators which satisfy the relevant AGM postulates) for belief bases.

3.2 Nonmonotonic Inference: Preliminaries

The model we have presented in the previous section commits to a nonmonotonic logic as a meta-level representation language for requirements. Any default-based formalism (such as default logic [15]) becomes an obvious candidate for such a representation language. A default theory includes explicit language constructs for asserting tentative or default knowledge. The accompanying machinery for generating extensions resolves potential contradictions amongst defaults and provides consistent views of the world sanctioned by the default theory.

Our choice of the THEORIST nonmonotonic reasoning system for the purposes of this work is not entirely arbitrary. The THEORIST framework provides the features necessary for this reconstruction and is, at the same time, simple enough to facilitate ease of exposition. Additionally, it provides several advantages over Reiter's default logic, such as avoiding situations where Reiter's default logic is too strong or too weak, guaranteeing the existence of extensions, semi-monotonicity and a constructive definition for extensions.

The THEORIST framework envisages a knowledge base comprising of a set of closed formulas that are necessarily true, called *facts*, and a set of possibly open formulas that are tentatively true, called *hypotheses*. Default reasoning in this framework involves identifying *maximal scenarios* (i.e., extensions), where a scenario consists of the set of facts together with some subset of the set of ground instances of the hypotheses which is consistent with the set of facts. The framework can be augmented with *constraints*, which are closed formulas such that every THEORIST scenario is required to be consistent with the set of constraints. Following [13], we can present the following definition of a maximal scenario.

Definition 3.1 *For a THEORIST specification (F, H, C) where F is the set of facts, H is the set of hypotheses and C is the set of constraints, such that $F \cup C$ is satisfiable, a* maximal scenario *is a set $F \cup h$ such that $h \subseteq H$ and $F \cup h \cup C$ is satisfiable and there exists no h' such that $h \subset h'$ and $F \cup h' \cup C$ is satisfiable.*

In viewing requirements models as default theories, specifically THEORIST knowledge bases, requirements that are known to be true of the domain, together with domain knowledge are treated as *facts* (i.e., elements of F) while defaults or tentative requirements are treated as elements of H. We shall not discuss the role of the set C now, but shall point out that it plays a crucial role when requirements are retracted.

4 A Logical Reconstruction of Belief Change in *Telos*

The *Telos* system [11] is a powerful requirements modelling language with a formally specified syntax and semantics. In this section, we shall demonstrate the utility of our framework by showing how a reformulation of *Telos* in this framework brings out some obvious shortcomings in the *Telos* knowledge base update operators. To do this, we shall consider an abstract *Telos*-like language. We shall assume that a *Telos* knowledge base consists of a set of assertions in a first-order language augmented with a temporal argument. The underlying notion of time is that of Allen's interval-based framework [2]. Every atom in this language is thus of the form $p(\mathbf{x}, t)$, where $\mathbf{x}$ is a vector of terms and t denotes a time interval. The assertion $p(\mathbf{s}, t)$ thus states that the property p is true for the vector of ground terms $\mathbf{s}$ over the interval given by t. The *Telos* framework provides a set of three operations for updating a knowledge base: (i) The TELL command is used to introduce a new object in the knowledge base or to attach attributes to an already defined one. (ii) The UNTELL command is used to assert that a specific relationship of an object that has been explicitly defined does not hold for a certain period of time. (iii) The RETELL command is used to assert that a specific relationship that has been explicitly created for a certain object does not hold for certain time period and some other relationship holds. Superficially, TELL, UNTELL and RETELL appear to be implementations of the three basic belief change operators, expansion, contraction and revision, respectively. Like expansion, TELL adds new beliefs to a belief state with no provision for inconsistency handling. Like contraction, UNTELL retracts beliefs. RETELL, like revision, involves the addition of new beliefs with a concomitant removal of prior beliefs which are inconsistent with the new one. As well, RETELL is defined in a manner analogous to the Levi identity [10], as a contraction (UNTELL) followed by an expansion (TELL). Despite these superficial similarities, there are two crucial differences between these operators and the basic belief change operators. Firstly, RETELL and UNTELL operations do not consider possible violations of integrity constraints. Thus only explicit contradictions need to be considered. This makes the problem of revising the knowledge base almost trivial, but ignores the possibility of integrity constraint violations in real-life situations. Secondly, unlike expansion, the TELL operation results in the addition of a default. Thus $TELL\, p(\mathbf{x}, t)$ results in the addition of a default rule in Reiter's default logic [15] of the form: $\frac{p(\mathbf{x},t):M(t\ meets+\infty)}{(t\ meets+\infty)}$. This states that the time interval associated with the TELL assertion is right infinite as long as it is consistent to assume so. It may be inconsistent to assume so in case there is an explicit UNTELL operation of the form $UNTELL\ p(\mathbf{x}, t')$ such that the intervals t and t' intersect (in which case the default is blocked for an interval corresponding to the intersection of t and t') or if there is a RETELL operation of the form $RETELL$ $p(\mathbf{y}, t'), q(\mathbf{z}, t'')$ (where p is the relation being retracted and q is the new relation being asserted in its place) such that $\mathbf{x} \neq \mathbf{z}$ and t and t'' intersect (in which case the default is blocked for an interval corresponding to the intersection of t and t'').

Clearly, a *Telos* knowledge base is a default theory, and any account of the dynamics of such a knowledge base must be formulated in terms of the dynamics of a default theory. Since the literature on *Telos* provides no such account, we shall attempt to provide one in this section, to set the stage for defining a model of requirements evolution through belief change.

In our logical reconstruction of the dynamics of a *Telos* knowledge base, we shall view a *Telos* knowledge base as a THEORIST specification (F, H, C). The TELL, UNTELL and RETELL operations can then be viewed as operations on a THEORIST specification (F, H, C). We shall focus on logical contradictions that arise between assertions over the same time interval and shall ignore the temporal argument for the rest of the discussion. We shall assume that the set of *Telos* integrity constraints IC is included in F. Following well-established conventions in the literature on belief change, let $(F, H, C)_{\phi}^{TELL}$ denote the outcome of performing a $TELL\ \phi$ operation on a *Telos* knowledge base (F, H, C) and $(F, H, C)_{\phi}^{UNTELL}$ denote the outcome of an $UNTELL\ \phi$ operation on a *Telos* knowledge base (F, H, C). $(F, H, C)_{\phi_1,\phi_2}^{RETELL}$ denotes the outcome of a RETELL operation in which ϕ_1 is retracted and ϕ_2 is asserted in its place. The three operations can be defined as follows: (i) $(F, H, C)_{\phi}^{TELL} = (F, H \cup \phi, C)$, (ii) $(F, H, C)_{\phi}^{UNTELL} = (F, H, C \cup \neg\phi)$, and (iii) $(F, H, C)_{\phi_1,\phi_2}^{RETELL} = (F \cup \phi_2, H - \phi_1, C)$.

For the THEORIST specification (F, H, C) to be a *Telos* knowledge base, it must have a single maximal scenario. Furthermore, *Telos* appears to include an implicit assumption that the set of TELLed propositions is consistent, i.e., the set H is satisfiable. Clearly, such an assumption is unrealistic, since in real-life there are no guarantees that inputs to the knowledge base will not contradict each other. The following results provide a formal specification of the correctness of the UNTELL and RETELL operations as formulated above.

Theorem 1. *If* (F, H, C) *is a* Telos *knowledge base, and* $C \cup \neg\phi \cup F$ *is satisfiable, then* $(F, H, C)_{\phi}^{UNTELL}$ *is a* Telos *knowledge base with a unique maximal scenario which does not contain* ϕ.

Theorem 2. *If* (F, H, C) *is a* Telos *knowledge base, and* $F \cup \phi_2 \cup C$ *is satisfiable, then* $(F, H, C)_{\phi_1,\phi_2}^{RETELL}$ *is a* Telos *knowledge base with a unique maximal scenario which contains* ϕ.

As we have noted earlier, the UNTELL operation ignores the possibility of violating the integrity constraints and is thus guaranteed to be correct only in the case that $C \cup \neg\phi \cup F$ is satisfiable, where ϕ is the relation being UNTELLed. The same holds for the RETELL operation, which is guaranteed to be correct only in the case that $F \cup \phi \cup C$ is satisfiable, where ϕ is the relation being RETELLed.

Example 1. Consider an example which continues on the theme of building a requirements model for a word-processor. Let *colour* denote the requirement that the monitor screen be colour, and *mono* denote the requirement that the monitor screen be monochrome. Let *t_adults* denote that the target market for the word-processor is adults while *t_children* denote that the target market for the word-processor is school-going children. Let the initial set of integrity constraints be given by: $IC = \{colour \leftrightarrow \neg mono, t\_children \rightarrow colour\}$. Consider the following sequence of *Telos* knowledge base updates: (i) TELL *wordproc*, (ii) TELL *colour* (iii) TELL *t_adults*. At this point the *Telos* knowledge base is given (F_0, H_0, C_0) where $F_0 = IC$, $H_0 = \{wordproc, colour, t\_adults\}$, and $C_0 = \{\}$. Let the next update be *RETELL colour, mono*. The new *Telos* knowledge base is (F_1, H_1, C_1) where $F_1 = IC \cup \{mono\}$, $H_1 = \{wordproc, t\_adults\}$, and $C_1 = \{\}$. Let the final operation be *RETELL t_adults, t_children*. At this point, *Telos* fails since the outcome (F_2, H_2, C_2) where $F_2 = F_1 \cup \{t\_children\}$, $H_2 = \{wordproc\}$, and $C_2 = \{\}$, is an inconsistent THEORIST specification (F_2 contains *mono*, which, together with the integrity constraint $colour \leftrightarrow \neg mono$, implies $\neg colour$ as well as *t_children*, which, together with the integrity constraint $t\_children \rightarrow colour$ implies *colour* - F_2 is therefore unsatisfiable). □

5 A Default-Based Requirements Evolution Model

We have seen in Section 2 how a default-based formalism is useful as a requirements modelling language. The previous section demonstrates how the well-known requirements modelling language *Telos* also uses a default-based formalism, although in a restricted sense. In this section, we shall provide a model for requirements evolution based on a revision scheme for default theories. This model can be viewed as a specific instance of the general framework presented in Section 2 and we shall use it to demonstrate that it is possible to define operators for mapping between requirements models which are well-founded in the semantics of rational belief change. Following the approach in the previous section, we shall view a requirements model abstractly as a THEORIST specification (F, H, C). Thus, the basis for our model will be a set of operators for mapping between default theories. In general, a default theory may have several extensions (or maximal scenarios). Thus, in general, a mapping between default theories translates to a mapping between sets of theories (each theory corresponding to a potential default extension). The operators we present in this section are loosely based on similar operators defined for a belief revision scheme for default theories in [7] [8] and [6], which in turn are closely related to operators defined in [3]. We shall consider only operations which revise a requirements model with a new requirement, or retract an existing requirement from a requirements model. In other words, we shall not consider expansion (TELL) operations, given that there are rarely any guarantees that the new requirement being added will not conflict with some existing requirement.

We shall establish some notational conventions first. Following the literature on belief change, we shall denote the revision operation with the symbol $*$ and the contraction operation with the symbol $-$. Thus $(F,H,C)^*_\phi$ and $(F,H,C)^-_\phi$ denote the outcome of a revision with ϕ and a contraction of ϕ, respectively, starting with a THEORIST specification (F,H,C). As well, let $E(\Delta)$ denote the set of maximal scenarios of a THEORIST specification Δ.

Following the spirit of the AGM postulates for belief change, we shall motivate our definition of revision/contraction operators by noting the following four requirements for these operations. Firstly, the outcome should be a consistent default theory. In the context of a THEORIST specification (F,H,C), this implies that $F \cup C$ should be satisfiable. Secondly, the operation should be successful. Thus, every maximal scenario of $(F,H,C)^-_\phi$ must not include ϕ, while every maximal scenario of $(F,H,C)^*_\phi$ must include ϕ. Thirdly, the outcome should be independent of the syntax of the input. If $\phi \equiv \phi'$, then $E((F,H,C)^-_\phi) = E((F,H,C)^-_{\phi'})$ and $E((F,H,C)^*_\phi) = E((F,H,C)^*_{\phi'})$. Finally, the operation should involve minimal change to the default theory. For classical theories, minimal change is ensured by establishing conformance with the AGM postulates. For default theories, this is not very straightforward, as we shall see later.

Based on these requirements, we define the revision operator as follows, $(F,H,C)^*_\phi = (F^{*'}_\phi, H \cup (F - F'), C^{-'}_{\neg F'})$, where $*'$ and $-'$ are AGM-rational revision and contraction operators respectively for classical theories.

Theorem 3. *Let $(F,H,C)^*_\phi = (F',H',C')$. Then, (i) $F' \cup C'$ is satisfiable, (ii) $\forall e : e \in E((F',H',C')) \rightarrow e \models \phi$, and (iii) if $\phi' \equiv \phi$, then $E((F',H',C')) = E((F,H,C)^*_{\phi'})$.*

In the result above, the first condition guarantees that the outcome is a consistent default theory. The second condition guarantees that the revision operation succeeds, i.e., every extension of the resulting default theory contains the new input. The third condition ensures that the operation is independent of the syntax of the input.

Next we define the contraction operator as follows, $(F,H,C)^-_\phi = (F^{-'}_{\neg C^{*'}_{\neg\phi}}, H \cup (F - F'), C^{*'}_{\neg\phi})$, where $*'$ and $-'$ are AGM-rational revision and contraction operators, respectively, for classical theories. We can establish a set of properties for the contraction operation similar to those for the revision operation.

Theorem 4. *Let $(F, H, C)^-_\phi = (F', H', C')$. Then, (i) $F' \cup C'$ is satisfiable, (ii) $\forall e : e \in E((F', H', C')) \rightarrow e \not\models \phi$, and (iii) if $\phi' \equiv \phi$, then $E((F', H', C')) = E((F, H, C)^-_{\phi'})$.*

Example 2. We shall reformulate Example 1 using the new operators $*$ and $-$ we have defined above. Unlike Example 1, both TELL and RETELL operations will be uniformly treated as revision ($*$) operations (thus, in the RETELL operation, the argument denoting the relation being retracted is dropped). We start with the same set of initial integrity constraints *IC*. After the first two revisions with *wordproc* and *t_adults* respectively (we skip the revision with *colour* included in Example 1 to simplify the presentation - the same inconsistency will emerge in the final step in any case), the requirements model (F_0, H_0, C_0) is given by, $F_0 = IC \cup \{wordproc, t\_adults\}$, $H_0 = \{\}$, and $C_0 = \{\}$. Revision with *mono* generates a requirements model (F_1, H_1, C_1) where $F_1 = F_0 \cup \{mono\}$, $H_1 = \{\}$, and $C_1 = \{\}$. Finally, revision with *t_children* will generate a requirements model (F_2, H_2, C_2) where $F_2 = (F_1)^{*'}_{t\_children}$, $H_2 = F_1 - (F_1)^*_{t\_children}$, and $C_2 = \{\}$. At this point, we generate a requirement *colour* because of the integrity constraint $t\_children \rightarrow colour$, which contradicts the *mono* requirement on account of the other integrity constraint $colour \leftrightarrow mono$. The revision process resolves this contradiction and the precise outcome is determined by the priority relation used by the $*'$ operator. One possible outcome is given by $F_2 = IC \cup \{wordproc, t\_adults, t\_children\}$, $H_2 = \{mono\}$, and $C_2 = \{\}$. The point to be noted is that our framework provides support for handling contradictions, unlike *Telos*. □

A crucial question is the extent to which these operators satisfy the requirement that belief revision involve minimal change. For classical theories, conformance with the AGM postulates ensures that the minimal change requirement is satisfied. However, the AGM postulates cease to be useful in the case of default theories since they do not apply to situations where the belief change operators map between sets of classical theories (default extensions). One obvious feature of the operators we define is that the belief change operations on the F and C components of a THEORIST specification are guaranteed to be rational with respect to the AGM postulates. It has been shown in [6] that a closely related set of operators satisfy a reformulated version of the AGM postulates, under a set of reasonable conditions. Briefly, the reformulation involves replacing every statement of the form *"belief set K is a subset of belief set K'"* to a sentence of the form *"for every extension e of a default theory Δ there exists an extension e' of the default theory Δ' such that e is a subset of e'"*. This specific instance of the general framework presented in Section 2 is thus well-founded with respect to the semantics of rational belief change (as formulated in the AGM framework).

In addition to guaranteeing a consistent and rational mapping between requirements models, the revision and contraction operators defined above offer several additional benefits which assume special importance in the context of requirements engineering. Firstly, the explicit representation of contractions in the set of THEORIST constraints C ensures that revisions and contractions are treated in a symmetric manner. In the AGM framework, as well in approaches inspired by it (including Nebel's operators for belief bases [12]), contractions are never represented explicitly, while revisions are. Consequently, the effects of a contraction operation are not guaranteed to persist beyond a single step. Requirements evolution operations such as the *Telos* UNTELL operation must persist over iterated evolution steps, which is only possible given an explicit representation for contractions, such as in our approach. Secondly, our model ensures that requirements are never discarded. A requirement, once added via a revision operation, is contained in either F or H at all future times. Thus, if a new requirement $r2$ contradicts an existing requirement $r1$ contained in F, then $r1$ is demoted to the status of a default (i.e., it becomes an element of H). As well, no maximal scenario of the THEORIST specification will contain $r1$. If, however, $r2$ is later retracted, $r1$ can reappear in a maximal scenario of the resulting THEORIST specification. Thirdly, our models can be extended to generate the priorities over facts and constraints that are needed during requirements evolution. More precisely, one may view every element of F and C as representing a prior requirements evolution step. Every element of F represents a prior revision, while every element of C represents a prior contraction. Thus, priority relations on F and C, which are the only two prerequisites necessary for generating a consistent outcome of a requirements evolution step, can be obtained by merely requiring an ordering on the belief change steps. Results from [8], [7] and [6] show that such an approach provides an elegant and easily implementable solution to a well-known problem with the AGM framework and related systems, namely, the absence of a definition of belief change operations beyond a single step (often referred to as the problem of iterated belief change). Finally, using results from [9], we can show that for requirements models represented as ground theories in THEORIST, the outcome of a requirements evolution step can be computed in linear time (in the cardinality of $F \cup C$) if every step involves a single literal and in polynomial time if every step involves a Horn clause. Our approach thus lends itself to efficient implementation.

6 Conclusion

This paper has presented a logical framework for modelling and reasoning about requirements evolution. The focus of this presentation has been on the problem of effective management of changes to requirements models, while maintaining consistency and completeness. We have demonstrated the strength of this framework by analyzing operators in the TELOS requirements modelling language and pointed out some of their shortcomings. We have then presented a new set of default based operators which serve as the formal basis for the evolution of requirements models. This work has offered a principled approach to reasoning about requirements evolution which acts as the basis for analyzing current techniques in requirements modelling. Furthermore, it provided a starting point for defining semantically well-founded systems for managing requirements models and their subsequent evolution. This framework thus provides a formal account for the requirements engineering process.

7 Acknowledgements

We are grateful to Ray Offen and Norman Foo for many useful comments on this article.

References

1. C. Alchourrón, P. Gärdenfors, and D. Makinson. On the logic of theory change: partial meet contraction and revision functions. *J. of Symbolic Logic*, 50:510–530, 1985.
2. J. Allen. Towards a general model of action and time. *Artificial Intelligence*, 23(2), 1984.
3. G. Brewka. Belief revision in a framework for default reasoning. In *Proc. of the Konstanz Workshop on Belief Revision*, 1989.
4. P. Gärdenfors. *Knowledge in Flux: Modeling the Dynamics of Epistemic States.* MIT Press, Cambridge, MA, 1988.
5. P. Gärdenfors and D. Makinson. Revisions of knowledge systems using epistemic entrenchment. In *Proc. of TARK'88*, 1988.
6. A. Ghose. *Practical belief change.* PhD thesis, Dept of Computing Science, University of Alberta, 1995.
7. A. Ghose, P. Hadjinian, A. Sattar, J.-H. You, and R. Goebel. Iterated belief change. Technical Report TR93-05, University of Alberta, Dept. of Computing Science, 1993.
8. A. Ghose, P. Hadjinian, A. Sattar, J.-H. You, and R. Goebel. Iterated belief change: A preliminary report. In *Proc. of AI'93*, 1993.
9. A. Ghose, A. Sattar, and R. Goebel. Pragmatic belief change: Computational efficiency and approximability. In *Proc. of the Workshop on Belief Revision*, 1993. Held in conjunction with *AI'93*.
10. Isaac Levi. Subjunctives, dispositions and chances. *Synthese*, 34:423–455, 1977.
11. J. Mylopoulos, A. Borgida, M. Jarke, and M. Koubarakis. Telos: Representing knowledge about information systems. *ACM Transactions on Information Systems*, 8(4), 1990.
12. B. Nebel. Belief revision and default reasoning: Syntax-based approaches. In *Proc. of KR'91*, 1991.
13. D. Poole. A logical framework for default reasoning. *Artificial Intelligence*, 36:27–47, 1988.
14. D. Poole, R. Goebel, and R. Aleliunas. Theorist: a logical reasoning system for defaults and diagnosis. In *The Knowledge Frontier: Essays in the Representation of Knowledge*, Springer Verlag, 1987.
15. R. Reiter. A logic for default reasoning. *Artificial Intelligence*, 13, 1980.
16. C. Rich and Y. Feldman. Seven layers of knowledge representation and reasoning in support of software development. In *IEEE Trans. on Software Engg.*, 18, 1992.

An Application of Hierarchical Knowledge Integration in Hand-Written Form Processing

Fon-Lin Lai, Joo-Hwee Lim, Liya Ding, Ah-Hwee Tan & Ho-Chung Lui

Real World Computing Partnership (RWCP), Neuro ISS Laboratory,
Institute of Systems Science, National University of Singapore,
Heng Mui Keng Terrace, Kent Ridge, Singapore 119597

Abstract. In this paper, we present a Hierarchical Interactive Reasoning approach for hand-written form processing, and describe an application of this approach to a prototype form processing system. A priori domain knowledge is closely bound to all levels of a hierarchical structure in which bi-directional inferencing is possible. This approach has significantly improved recognition performance in the prototype system. We also touch on possible future extensions to the approach.

1 Introduction

Information Integration represents a central concept of Theory & Novel Function research in the Real World Computing Program. Basically, the concept behind information integration is to use different sources of knowledge (i.e. information) to achieve a human-like robustness in the task of pattern recognition. There are 2 major ways [1] in which integration of information can be carried out: vertically and horizontally.

In vertical information integration, understanding is achieved through the use of knowledge derived from different levels of abstraction of the same set of information. For example, the printed page of a book could be recognised in the following increasing levels of abstraction:

$$\textit{Printed pixels} \rightarrow \textit{Characters} \rightarrow \textit{Words} \rightarrow \textit{Sentences} \rightarrow \textit{Paragraphs} \rightarrow \textit{Document} \quad (1)$$

In other words, vertical information integration involves the hierarchical linking of a pattern with its symbolic meaning. We include the 'hierarchical' qualifier because each level of abstraction can be considered as a kind of pattern by the higher levels.

In horizontal information integration, understanding is achieved through the use of knowledge derived from different sets or sources of information (or experts), at the same level of abstraction. In this case, a recognition system makes use of multi-modal information to enhance it's performance.

The idea of using contextual knowledge to improve recognition is certainly not a new one [2]. However the existing methods have their limitations: they only provide an ad-hoc way of representing one or two knowledge sources, with no systematic approach towards representing many different knowledge sources in one unified architecture. Learning is also not considered.

In this paper, we propose a systematic approach for representing multiple knowledge sources in a unified architecture, which will provide the basis for an intelligent pattern recognition system. We shall call this approach Hierarchical Interactive Reasoning fOr Information-Integration (HIROI). Our proposed structure will feature a hierarchical structure for Knowledge Representation (KR) and an Inference Engine (IE) with learning capabilities. We will first describe the main features of the HIROI approach (Section 2). We then apply HIROI to a specific form processing prototype system (Section 3) to demonstrate the features described. Finally, we will discuss research issues which will need to be pursued in future work (Section 4).

2 Hierarchical Knowledge Integration

2.1 Features

The foundation for HIROI comes from the area of multi-expert integration and flexible knowledge representation and reasoning. The main features of the system are given below:

A Multi-Level Knowledge Representation Hierarchy. With the use of such a hierarchy, the decision of what an image is, is not taken immediately. Rather, the raw confidence vectors (see Section 3.3) are allowed to propagate upwards so that they may be used by higher level experts to reach independent (or semi-independent) conclusions of their own. As the pattern values are passed up a level of the hierarchy, they are combined into more abstract patterns. The corresponding confidence values are also combined to give the overall confidence of each higher level data. Only those combinations of lower level data which are recognised as valid by the current level's expert are passed on to the next level. In this way, a kind of 'filtering' is carried out where the more unlikely abstractions are not passed on to the next level and resources are conserved during inferencing.

The hierarchical structure also allows for a more structured approach to the representation of data. Without a hierarchy, there would be much duplication of effort when the knowledge base contains data with repeated characteristics. In a non-hierarchical system, as the top-level expert compares the current pattern with its knowledge base, the activation value of certain parts of the pattern will be computed repeatedly, due to identical sub-sets of top-level data. By having a hierarchy in which the sub-components of an image are analysed first (starting from the smallest sub-component), duplication of effort is reduced.

Extended Logic Operations with Soft or Hard Constraints. Logical operations are used to apply the constraints represented by the higher level knowledge sources (i.e. experts) onto the lower level information being fed up the hierarchy.

General Description:

$$H(y) \leftarrow \Phi[L_1(x_1), L_2(x_2), ..., L_n(x_n)], K(y, x_1, x_2, ..., x_n) \quad (2)$$

where L = lower level expert
H = higher level expert
Φ = operation in extended logic
K = knowledge (hard/soft constraint on y, x_1, x_2, ..., x_n)

Constraints may be expressed in the form of rules, relations, dictionaries etc. The constraints applied may be either hard or soft, depending on how complete the expert's domain of knowledge is.

For example, a rule expert for date values may be considered to apply a hard constraint on a date value, because it can give a definite true or false decision on whether a particular date value is valid. A relational expert for telephone numbers and postal codes may be able to determine a trend whereby the combination of digits in a telephone number reflect the postal district. However, because there is no strict rule which relates telephone numbers to postal district, the relational expert can at best only give a soft decision (i.e. probably true or probably false) on whether a particular telephone number and postal code pair is valid. A database of customer names paired with their unique identity card numbers can represent a hard or soft constraint depending on how complete the database is. Obviously, only a complete database can provide a hard constraint.

Multi-Channel Information Integration. This is basically a clustering approach [3] extended to multiple feature sets. Winner/cluster selection is done by checking the matching degree of each feature of each cluster. The winner is selected from only those clusters in which the threshold is satisfied for each feature. If the vigilance of each feature is satisfied for the winner, then a match with an existing cluster has been found and the expectation is read out. Otherwise, the procedure is repeated for the next best winner. If no winner is found which satisfies all the vigilance criteria, then a new node/cluster is formed.

Multi-Expert Knowledge Integration. The horizontal information integration provided by the hierarchical structure allows the decisions of different experts working on overlapping fields to be collated into the most agreeable decision(s). Integration of expert knowledge can be carried out using various techniques such as majority win, weighted voting or dynamic weighted voting [4].

Interactive Bi-Directional Inferencing in Knowledge Hierarchy. Inferencing can be carried out either up (recognition) or down (recall) the hierarchy, and can be in a single pass or multiple passes (Sect 2.3).

2.2 Knowledge Hierarchy

The combination of vertical and horizontal information-integration results in a general hierarchical structure for HIROI, as shown if Figure 1.

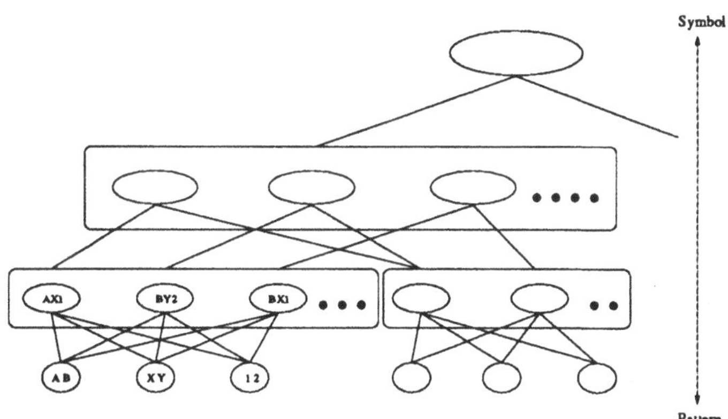

Fig. 1. Multi-level knowledge representation hierarchy.

Nodes along the same level and which lead to the same upper-level node, represent different (but possibly overlapping) sets or sources of information for the higher level, which represents a more abstract level of knowledge.

2.3 Inference Strategy

The hierarchical structure of HIROI allows for a bi-directional inferencing mechanism. With this, two main inference strategies can be used:

Single Pass. With this method, the confidence values of the lowest level experts (e.g. OCR results) are propagated up the hierarchy, with no decision made until the top of the hierarchy has been reached. Here a winner is selected and the expectation is propagated back down the hierarchy.

Multi-Pass. With this method, a winner is selected by each expert at each level as bottom-up propagation of confidence values proceeds. Whenever any expert detects an inconsistency in the set of lower level results, it determines which lower level expert is the most likely one to have made a wrong decision and signals that expert to make a new decision. The lower level expert then provides its "second best" result. In this way, the inference process may involve backtracking, with a final decision being made when all experts (in all levels) are stabilised.

The important difference between the two inference strategies is that the multi-pass strategy may involve backtracking, and so is more complicated than the single pass strategy.

3 Application in Form Processing

Forms are used extensively in everyday life. We use forms to make various types of applications, from jobs to bank loans. Basically, forms are used whenever there is a need to provide structured information required by people from whom a service is being requested. Such information usually has to be extracted from the form by the service providers and stored in electronic form. There is clearly a great potential for manpower savings by automating this transfer of information from form to database, especially when the number of forms is large.

Current OCR technology allows for obtaining very high accuracies in character recognition. However, such performance is still not high enough for real-world usage. Except for the simplest of forms, a form processing system using conventional OCR methods will invariably make errors in a large percentage of forms. This situation thus presents us with our motivation for implementing our HIROI approach in the area of form processing. Through integrating real-world knowledge with conventional OCR techniques in a structured manner, we aim to achieve a more robust form processing system.

3.1 Problem Domain

The problem domain used to demonstrate the HIROI approach is a prototype fax form processing system for a security pass application form (see Figure 2). The application form is used to apply for a security pass to enter a cargo complex. The usual method of application is for a company to fax the particulars of its representative who will be visiting the complex at the stated date and time. The security pass can then be prepared in advance of the visit, using the particulars extracted manually from the faxed form. The task of extracting the data from the faxed form will be transferred to an intelligent recognition system using HIROI.

The specifics of the problem domain are:

- the recognition and interpretation of 200 fax images of hand-written application forms.
- recognition of numeric, upper-case alphabet and alphanumeric characters.
- input to the system is a matrix of confidence values (for the character class of each character position) produced by a conventional multi-layer neural-network-based recogniser, trained by the standard back-propagation learning algorithm.

The knowledge representation and inference hierarchy are as shown in Figure 3.

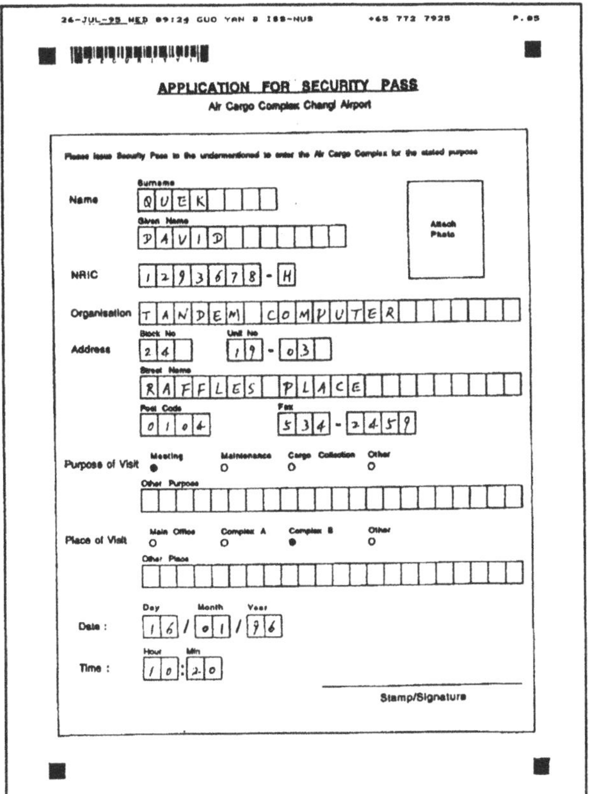

26-JUL-95 WED 09:24 GUO YAN S ISS-NUS +65 772 7925 P.05

APPLICATION FOR SECURITY PASS

Air Cargo Complex Changi Airport

Please issue Security Pass to the undermentioned to enter the Air Cargo Complex for the stated purpose

Name — Surname: QUEK — Given Name: DAVID

Attach Photo

NRIC: 1293678 - H

Organisation: TANDEM COMPUTER

Address — Block No: 24 — Unit No: 19 - 03

Street Name: RAFFLES PLACE

Post Code: 0104 — Fax: 534 - 2459

Purpose of Visit: Meeting ● Maintenance ○ Cargo Collection ○ Other ○

Other Purpose:

Place of Visit: Main Office ○ Complex A ○ Complex B ● Other ○

Other Place:

Date : Day 16 / Month 01 / Year 96

Time : Hour 10 : Min 20

Stamp/Signature

Fig. 2. Sample fax form.

3.2 Knowledge Sources

There are five main types of knowledge sources used in the intelligent form processing system (IFPS) for this prototype application. These are:

Dictionaries. These contain the individual 'words' of valid field entries. IFPS uses one dictionary for the street name field, which was constructed by extracting the individual words from a complete list of Singapore street names.

Lists. These are similar to dictionaries, except that each unit represents a complete field entry, which can be made up of multiple words. Lists of surnames, given names and street names were used by IFPS. The lists of surnames and given names were obtained from real world samples.

Relations. This knowledge source represents the learnt relationship between different fields of the form. The IFPS uses a relational expert to learn any possible

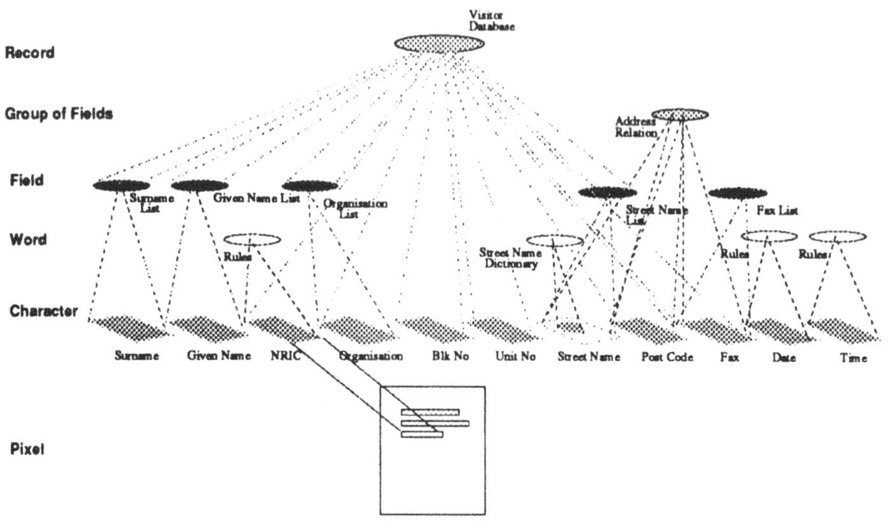

Fig. 3. Knowledge hierarchy of form processing system.

relationships between the street name, fax number and post code fields. The learning is performed using a standard clustering algorithm extended from a single feature to a group of three features. This acquired knowledge then becomes the knowledge source against which a new 3-tuple of fields can be compared. The relation expert is implemented using a neural network.

Databases. These contain verified records based on old forms which have already been processed by the system. The IFPS uses a single database knowledge source, which comprises a list of unique records. Each record contains all the permanent (e.g. identity card number) and semi-permanent (e.g. organisation name) field values extracted from a form. Temporary field values such as time and date of visit are not stored as they are always changing. The database expert is implemented as a neural network, with each record being represented by one node in the network.

Special Rules. These are used to represent definite knowledge about the structure of a field, where some parts of the fields have some range/value constraint due possibly to some other part(s) of the field. In the IFPS, rules were used as knowledge sources for the date, time and identity card (NRIC) number fields. The use of rules requires the construction of a simple function for each rule, which takes a specific combination of characters/ digits for a field and returns a true or false value depending on whether the combination satisfies the rule of not.

The rules used were as follows:

Date:

$$day \in \begin{cases} [1,31], \text{ if month} \in \{1,3,5,7,8,10,12\}, \\ [1,30], \text{ if month} \in \{4,6,9,11\}, \\ [1,29], \text{ if month} \in \{2\} \wedge \text{year divisible by 4 and not by 100}, \\ [1,28], \text{ otherwise.} \end{cases}$$

Time:

$$hour \in [0,23]$$
$$min \in [0,59]$$

NRIC:

$$checksum_i \in \mathrm{C}$$

where: C is the ordered set {J,Z,I,H,G,F,E,D,C,B,A}
$i = (2 \times d_1 + 7 \times d_2 + 6 \times d_3 + 5 \times d_4 + 4 \times d_5 + 3 \times d_6 + 2 \times d_7) \bmod 11$

In addition to the actual rules, the user can also include range constraints to the overall field. For example in this prototype application, it is assumed that people are allowed to apply for the security pass up to only 6 months in advance. Thus, the date field has an additional constraint imposed on it whereby a valid date value is only accepted if it occurs between a 6 month range starting from the current date. In the case of the time field, an assumption that visiting hours are limited to between 0800 and 1800 hrs also imposes an additional constraint on the time field.

It should be noted that because these additional range constraints on the date and time fields are specific to the requirements of the form-issuer, the issuer should make sure that applicants are notified of the constraints when filling in the form. Otherwise, the result would be akin to applying the wrong knowledge base to a field.

3.3 Inference Process

Based on the hierarchical structure of the prototype system (Figure 3), it can be seen that there are 4 separate types of hierarchies (database, relation, rule, dictionary) which act as experts on different (but possibly overlapping) sets of fields in the form. The decision of these experts are voted upon once the same set of OCR confidence vectors has been propagated up each hierarchy, and a decision returned from each. Of the 4 expert types present, only the database expert has a multi-layered hierarchy, with the database expert being supported by the lower-level list experts.

One main feature of HIROI approach is that no definite decision is made until the inferencing reaches the top level of the hierarchy. As a result, the recogniser does not only provide a single character with the highest confidence value for each character position. Instead, it provides a vector of confidence values for the character class of each character position. The length of the vector will depend on the type of recogniser (i.e. character expert) being used. Numeric, alphabet and alphanumeric recognisers are used in the prototype application, providing confidence vectors of length 11, 27 and 37 respectively (i.e. 10, 26 or 36 + 1 for space character).

From the character level, the set of confidence vectors associated with each character position in the form is passed on to the next level. When an intermediate-level expert receives these vectors, it uses them to calculate the word or field level activation (i.e. overall confidence) of all valid combinations of characters. The validity of a combination of characters is determined through the use of the expert's knowledge base. For example, for a list-expert, a combination is valid if it appears in the list of known field values; for a rule-expert, a valid combination is one which satisfies the constraints imposed by the specified rule.

The intermediate-level expert only passes on those words or lists (i.e. fixed combination of characters or words) which are known to it. These higher level data, together with their calculated activation values, are passed on to the next higher level expert, where the process of 'sieving' the data is repeated.

At the top-most level of a hierarchy, the highest level of abstraction of the data (for that hierarchy) is determined in the same way as with the preceding lower levels. But instead of propagating the new abstraction of lower level data to a higher level, the expert makes a decision by selecting the abstraction with the highest current-level activation. If the winner at the top-level expert is above the confidence threshold of the expert, then a match is declared and the set of characters making up the data record is propagated back down the hierarchy.

For example, the database expert receives field level activations for surname, given name, organisation and street name from the corresponding list experts, and character level activations for NRIC, block & unit number, postal code and fax from the recogniser. If a close match is found for a record, and the activation value of the record is higher than any other matches and satisfies the database threshold, then that record is propagated back down the hierarchy to the character level. Thus one hierarchical expert provides one opinion of the true value of the characters identified by the recogniser.

Other hierarchical experts such as the address relation expert or the date and time experts, may provide other opinions on specific fields which may overlap those under the database expert's domain. In this case, a weighted voting is carried out between the opinions of the different experts to find a winner. The optimal values for degree of matching and confidence threshold in the various levels of the hierarchies, as well as the weights assigned to the different expert opinions, are determined heuristically.

If at the top-most level of a hierarchy, the best match is unable to meet the threshold requirements, then the higher level expert does not offer any decision on the values of the characters. Instead the inferencing proceeds back down to the lower level experts which are then asked to make a decision on the character sets related to their respective sub-domains. This backward inference down the hierarchy is recursively carried out for any lower level experts unable to satisfy their confidence threshold for their best match.

Finally, if inferencing returns to the character level without any decision being reached for some sets of characters, then this is equivalent to there being no opinion about the true value of those characters.

3.4 Experimental Results

The following experimental results were obtained based on tests carried out on the form processing system using 200 sample forms. Of the 200 forms, 100 were used as previous records for the database expert. The recognition rates achieved, with zero rejection, were 98.1%, 93.6% and 84.2% for numerals, alphabets and alphanumerals respectively. Table 1 shows the performance of the system at different levels, with and without using HIROI. Table 2 shows the performance for individual fields. The results clearly demonstrate the usefulness of HIROI.

	Char. Level	Field Level	Form Level
Without HIROI	93.7 %	80.9 %	3.5 %
With HIROI	99.3 %	97.8 %	78.5 %

Table 1. Recognition performance summary.

Field Name	Recog. % w/o HIROI	Recog. % with HIROI
surname	78.5	96.0
given-name	74.0	98.5
nric-number	80.5	97.0
organisation	53.5	97.5
block-number	48.5	92.0
unit-number	97.5	99.0
street-name	22.0	99.0
postal-code	89.5	99.0
fax-number	85.0	94.5
date	91.5	98.5
time	93.0	97.0

Table 2. Field-level improvement by HIROI.

Because the domain knowledge forms a important part of the HIROI approach, experiments were also carried out to investigate the effects of knowledge base size as well as confidence threshold on the performance of the system. It was found that the performance of HIROI is directly proportional to the extent of coverage of its knowledge base, while an optimal confidence threshold value (0.7 at form level) can be found where both false positive and false negative results are kept to a minimum.

4 Future Work

We have described a new approach known as Hierarchical Interactive Reasoning fOr Interactive-Integration (HIROI), which provides a systematic way of representing multiple knowledge sources in a unified architecture. To demonstrate the feasibility of this approach, we have applied it to a form processing prototype system and obtained very encouraging results.

Possible future work in the HIROI approach could include addressing the following issues:

- tackling the scale-up problem
  The prototype application demonstrated uses only a very small knowledge base. A real-world system would require a much bigger knowledge base. Thus it would need to have a more efficient method of searching its knowledge base so that it can arrive at a solution within a reasonable length of time.
- elastic matching
  The current approach uses a simple one-to-one matching of new input data with knowledge base data. A more flexible matching mechanism, which can cope with inserted spurious data or missing real data, would make HIROI much more robust.
- non-heuristic method of determining the optimal confidence threshold for incomplete knowledge bases
  This would provide a theoretically sound way of setting threshold values.
- multi-pass inferencing (i.e. intelligent backtracking)
  By incorporating this ability in HIROI, more specialised (and possibly more computationally demanding) experts or recognisers could be called at a lower level of the hierarchy to help resolve ambiguities encountered at a higher level (e.g. finding a match from two records in a database which have many identical fields).

In conclusion, we believe that the HIROI approach provides an effective way of solving practical form processing problems, through the use of real-world knowledge. The structure of HIROI provides a uniform way of representing a priori knowledge and allows for that knowledge to be used in a systematic way.

Acknowledgement

The authors would like to thank the form processing team of Dr. Yan Guo, Mr. Patrick Chan and Mr. Ai-Yuan Guo for developing the form reading and character recognition modules.

References

1. Otsu, N. (1995). RWC program, current situation and perspectives. In *RWC News*, 7-11. Real World Computing Partnership.

2. Srihari, S.N., Y.C. Shin, V. Ramanaprasad, V., and D.S. Lee (1995). Name and address block reader system for tax form processing. In *Proc. of Intl. Conf. on Document Analysis and Recognition, Montreal, Canada*, 5-10. IEEE Computer Society Press.
3. Tan, A.H. and L.N. Teow. (1995) Learning by supervised clustering and matching. In *Proceedings, 1995 IEEE International Conference on Neural Networks, Perth*, volume I, 242-246.
4. Teow L.N. and A.H. Tan. (1995) Adaptive integration of multiple experts. In *Proceedings, 1995 IEEE International Conference on Neural Networks, Perth*, volume III, 1215-1220. IEEE Publisher.

AMI: A Model of Intelligence

D. B. Hoang and M.R James
Basser Department of Computer Science
University of Sydney, NSW 2006, AUSTRALIA
doan@cs.usyd.edu.au, mrj@cs.usyd.edu.au

Abstract

It is reasonable to say that so far neural networks have performed very well on many specific tasks of reasonable size, but their performance is far from satisfactory when applied to realistic but complex tasks such speech recognition and language processing. Yet the brain can perform these tasks efficiently and effortlessly (seemingly) using its optimized mechanisms. It is believed crucial to discover these mechanisms. In this paper, a neural network model of the isocortex as basic building block of intelligent systems is consolidated. The model incorporates mechanisms extracted from cortical circuit as suggested from the study of neuroanatomy. The learning rule compatible with what is known about synaptic adaptation in the neocortex is introduced. Simulations results, which verify the mathematical proof of the model stability and robustness, are presented.

Keywords: *Intelligent systems, neural networks, learning algorithms, neocortex*

1. Introduction

Most Artificial Neural Networks employs an extremely simplified model of a biological neuron as the fundamental building block. We believe that it is difficult to construct highly complex system based on such a low level element or abstraction. Imagine the task of constructing a supercomputer from the base level of transistors, there would be too much interference between components, and it would be impossible to control the interactions. A higher level of component abstraction would be much easier to deal with.

Structures as well as learning paradigms in most current ANNs are deficient in one aspect or another. Deficiencies include forgetfulness, over-training, poor generalization, implausibility, computational complexity, weight saturation, instability, scaling to real-complex problems. Performance of current ANNs is far from satisfactory. Fruitful directions for research in ANN would be to turn to biological examples and discover mechanisms used by the brain, or to investigate more complex nonlinear model with mathematics, or both.

It is acknowledged that computational and mathematical methods are essential in neural network modelling, however, they might also hinder the creative process of modelling. If models are introduced which have to firstly satisfy all the computational and mathematical constraints, then these models do not usually possess high degree of novelty we desperately seek, mainly because the mathematical tools are limited in themselves. We believe that a rich network model which is supported by neurological evidences (or by any other evidences) should be considered first, computational and mathematical considerations should come after the modelling process to provide explanations, guidance, and basis for further understanding and exploration.

In an outline of a theory of isocortex [1], we have extracted some mechanisms from cortical circuits as suggested from the study of neuroanatomy. In 1994 we proposed a neural model of the isocortex [2] as basic building block of intelligent systems. The model is empirical in terms of its properties, yet anatomically and physiologically plausible due to biological consideration. In 1995, we mathematically proved the stability of the fundamental cortical circuit employed in the model [3]. In this paper, a neural network model of the isocortex as basic building block of intelligent systems is consolidated. The model incorporates mechanisms extracted from biological cortical. The learning rule compatible with what is known about synaptic adaptation in the neocortex is introduced. Simulation results, which verify the mathematical proof of the model stability and robustness, are presented.

The paper is organized as follows. Section 2 discusses the approach taken in our ANN modelling. Section 3 introduces the AMI model and its rationales. Section 4 demonstrates the robustness of the model. Section 5 concludes with discussions on future research directions.

2. Our Approach

Our aim is to come up with a model of intelligence, or more specifically a system which can perform intelligent tasks comparable to some functions of the brain. Our research approach comes from two directions. From system abstraction direction, we propose an empirical modular model of an atomic intelligent system which possesses desirable properties. From biological plausibility direction, we look closely into real systems (through the work of neuroanatomists) for mechanisms that supports the properties of the atomic model. Through careful considerations, a resultant model of intelligence is proposed, that is plausible in the sense that it models the selective functionality of the selective part of the brain. The approach is illustrated in Fig. 1.

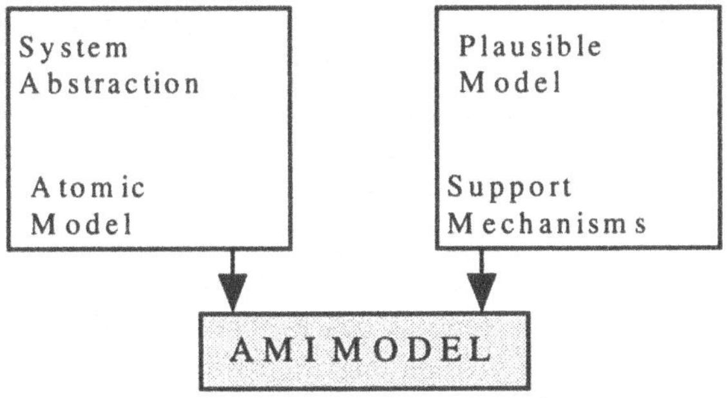

Fig. 1. Approach in modelling

3. The AMI model

3.1 The Architecture

We believe that any complex system can be reduced to its basic atomic components. An atomic component is at an abstraction level which captures some essential ingredients of intelligence as suggested below. The component model is defined in terms of its general properties.

The artificial neural network we propose basically consists of a discriminative compartment, an associative compartment, and feedback connections as shown in Fig. 2.

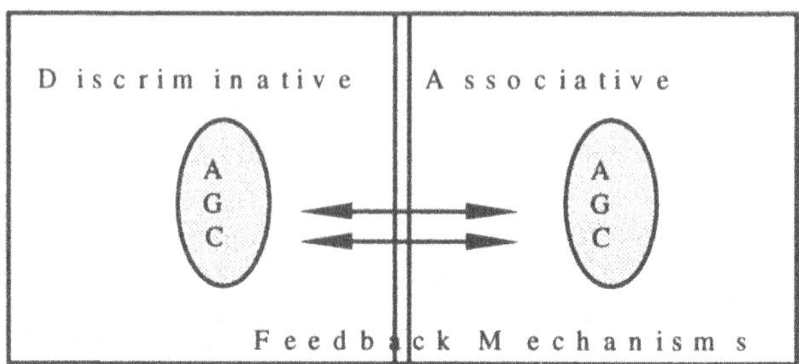

Fig. 2. The basic structure of the AMI model

A complete AMI module should have the following ascribed properties:

- *Discrimination (Differentiation, Analysis, Bottom Up, Competition)* The ability to analyze, to discriminate, and to cluster patterns.
- *Association (Integration, Generalization, Top Down, Pattern Completion, Content addressable memory)* The ability to associate, to correlate and to make generalized decisions
- *Learning*: The ability to adapt and to acquire further intelligence
- *Stability*: Stable microscopically and macroscopically. An essential property of any dynamical system. Microscopically, the module's internal components must settle down to a stable configuration. Macroscopically stable means that once the solution to a problem has been learned, the module should be able to solve that problem thereafter, the acquisition of new knowledge should not significantly impair the module's ability to solve the earlier problem.
- *Sequential Recognition*: The ability to store temporal information and to make decisions in context dependent situations
- *Modularity*: The module can be used for constructing complex systems.

It should be noted that the desirable properties of the model listed above are in no way mutually exclusive. For example, learning obviously occurs in discrimination, in association, as well as in the feedback connections between them. Generalization occurs in the form of clustering within discrimination, as well as in the top-down connections from association to discrimination.

From the biological plausibility direction, we are seeking evidence of the existence of mechanisms which support the essential properties of our atomic model. These mechanisms are found from the work of neuroanatomists.

We put forwards a *model of connections* between cortical modules: The cortex is a convoluted sheet of brain tissue about $2mm$ thick and $1.5m^2$ area, and its structure is reasonably uniform (hence isocortex). It is generally agreed that the cortex consists of 6 main layers running parallel to the surface of the sheet. The cortex may be viewed as a 3-D array of interacting modules, each the diameter (~100μm) of a minicolumn, and depth of a cortical layer. Each minicolumn runs perpendicular to the plane of the sheet and contains neurons from each of the 6 layers. The pattern of intraconnection and interconnections between minicolumns is depicted in Fig. 3. The model has been distilled from the work of neuroanatomists such as Lund, Burkhalter, Wiesel and Gilbert [5].

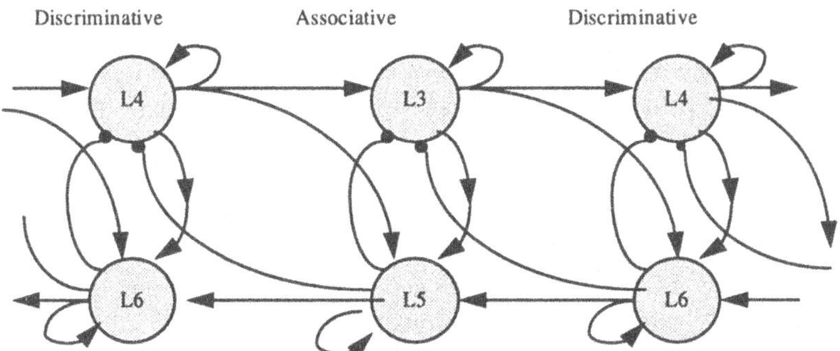

Fig. 3. Model of Cortical Layers Interactions

It should be noted that the pattern of connectivity in Fig. 3 is a result of our selective extraction. It represents only a selection of connectivity rich enough for our model. Only those connections which are perceived to constitute mechanisms that support properties of the model are included. Interpretations of the mechanisms in part are provided by the neurology experts, in part are promoted by us in supporting our model. The full pattern of connectivity is certainly much more complex and is generally not fully understood.

From the outline of a theory of Isocortex, we partition the pattern of connections into compartments as follows. The L4-L6 layer of neurons form a discriminative compartment, the L3-L5 layer of neurons form the associative compartment, and other connections form feedback mechanisms between the two compartments.

The Discriminative Compartment

Afferents entering a cortical area form excitatory synapses with layer 4 (L4) and layer 6 (L6) neurons. L4 neurons send excitatory projections to L6 neurons in the *same* minicolumn. L6 neurons send bowl-shaped inhibitory projections to L4 neurons, undermine other L4's not in the minicolumn. The interactions in this compartment produce a level of competition between L4 neurons, with different L4 neurons tuned to different patterns of afferents. The compartment can be considered as performing bottom up processing, with ability to discriminate patterns based on just the input signals.

The Associative Compartment

Similar pattern of L4-L6 connectivity occurs in the associative compartment, except that L3 neurons form excitatory synapses with each other to implement short term memory. The feedback connection from L5 to L4 is disinhibitory rather than excitatory so that L4 activity is only modulated rather than created. This input can help form topographic maps in L4. This stage performs a form of information association or pattern completion.

The Feedback Connections

There are two main feedback loops: intracompartment feedback loop and intercompartment feedback loop. The intracompartment Automatic Gain Control (AGC) loops (L4-L6, L3-L5) are essential for providing adaptive stability of the model, improve the dynamic range, and prevent saturation of outputs and synaptic weights. The intracompartment or top-down feedback mechanisms (L5->L4/L6, L6->L3/L5) provide gain control of inputs to each compartment. The feedback connections are also used for sequence learning and recall.

In summary, the atomic intelligent module we propose so far consists of two compartments: a discriminative compartment that is formed by multiple pairwise L4/L6 columns of neurons and an associative compartment that is formed by multiple pairwise L3/L5 columns of neurons. L4/L6 columns perform the categorizing and learning function through competition, and L3/L5 columns perform associative function by implementing short term memory.

3.2 Learning Algorithm

Learning in neural network is normally accomplished through an adaptive procedure known as learning rule or algorithm, whereby the weights of the network are incrementally adjusted so as to improve a predefined performance measure over time. For the model described here, unsupervised learning type is of special interest.

The objective of unsupervised learning is to categorise, to discover features or regularities in the training data. The success hinges on some appropriately designed network that encompasses a task-independent criterion of the quality of representation the network is required to learn.

It appears that for biological neurons, changes in the synaptic weight are dependent on the degree of correlation between the level of activity of the incoming axon and the activity of the postsynaptic neuron over short periods of time: the Hebbian learning law.

Models of unsupervised, Hebbian synaptic modification are, however, typically unstable: Synapses are allowed only to increase, hence either all synapses grow until each reaches the maximum allowed strength, or all synapses decay to zero strength, no information will be stored and no selectivity will develop.

To actually use Hebb's principle, that is to prevent the divergence of the Hebbian learning rule, one often has to apply constraints or limits to the learning equations. For example, to achieve the results found biologically, Von der Malsburg [6] proposed the use of constraints conserving the total synaptic strength supported by each input or output neuron to achieve selectivity. Competitive learning rule forces synaptic efficacies to be proportional to the average presynaptic activities [7], [8]. In the CALM model [9], weights are restricted to values between a certain minimum and maximum, and approach the maximum value asymptotically. There is no experimental evidence for the availability of any of these mechanisms in neocortex.

It is clear that in order to use Hebb's learning rule, one has to state conditions for synaptic decrease as specific as those for synaptic increase. Evidence suggests that efficacies of excitatory neocortical synapses are increased (potentiated) if the potential in the postsynaptic neuron is above some threshold (θ) when a presynaptic spike activates the synapse, and decreased (depressed) if the postsynaptic potential is below this threshold.

However, on its own, this learning rule has the same adaptive instability as simple Hebbian learning. Neuron potentials evolve away from the equilibrium potential (θ), and synapses can become maximally potentiated. The Bienenstock, Cooper and Munro (BCM) introduced a learning rule [10] that is stable without having to impose external constraints on the synapses. It allows θ to vary as a nonlinear function of average output of the postsynaptic neuron. The BCM learning rule is as follows:

- A change in a synapse is based on the multiplication of the *pre* and *post* synaptic activities
- Responses above the modification threshold (θ) lead to strengthening of the active synapses, responses below the threshold lead to weakening of the active synapses.
- The threshold varies as a nonlinear function of the average output of the *post* synaptic neuron

The synaptic weights (or efficacies) are adapted according to the following equation.

$$\Delta w = K.pre.b(v)$$

where b(v) is the BCM-type synaptic adaptation function shown in figure 4., v is the postsynaptic membrane voltage, and K is a learning constant.

It was demonstrated in [11] that the modification of excitatory geniculo-cortical synapses according to rules derived from the BCM theory can account for both the outcome and kinetics of experience-dependent synaptic plasticity in kitten striate cortex. However, strong evidence of the "sliding-threshold" mechanism required for stability of the BCM rule has not been found. Moreover the time dependence nature of the threshold means that synapses on a neuron can still be maximally potentiated if the neuron is infrequently stimulated.

In the model described here, the learning threshold remains fixed, while the necessary feedback term (responsible for stability) is generated by the dynamics of the cortical circuit, and stored in a non time-sensitive way as a component of the adaptive synaptic efficacies. In other words, the structure of the model provides the mechanism for stability rather than the sliding threshold. In fact, our learning rule with fixed learning threshold is compatible with what is known about synaptic adaptation in the neocortex, and, unlike the BCM learning theory, does not rely on the availability of a mechanism for time-dependent changes in adaptive equilibrium potentials.

Evidence can be found to support that the optimum value of θ relates to the maximum slope of the NMDA calcium influx.

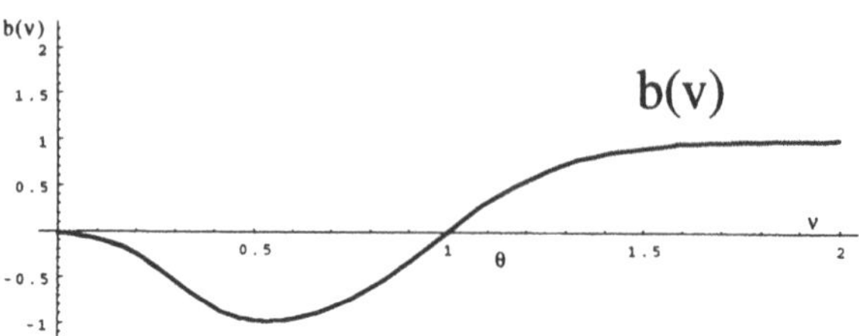

Fig. 4. The BCM-type synaptic adaptation function *b(v)*

4. A Single Column AMI Module

4.1 Description

The module discussed here is a simplified version, consisting of two layers - layer 4 (L4) and layer 6 (L6). These layers constitute the "discriminative" component of the module, providing the ability to discriminate patterns. Neurons within a module are connected by synapses of fixed weight. External input is connected to the module neurons by synapses of variable weight. The weights of the input synapses vary according to the modified BCM learning law as described above. Synapses can excite or inhibit a neuron. An excitatory synapse increases the neuron's membrane voltage, while an inhibitory synapse decreases it. Figure 5 shows a single column module, where y and z are the membrane voltages of the L4 and L6 neurons respectively, g and r are the fixed weights of the excitatory synapses, s is the fixed weight of the inhibitory synapse, x is the input to the module, and w and u are the variable weights of the projection synapses from the input to the neurons.

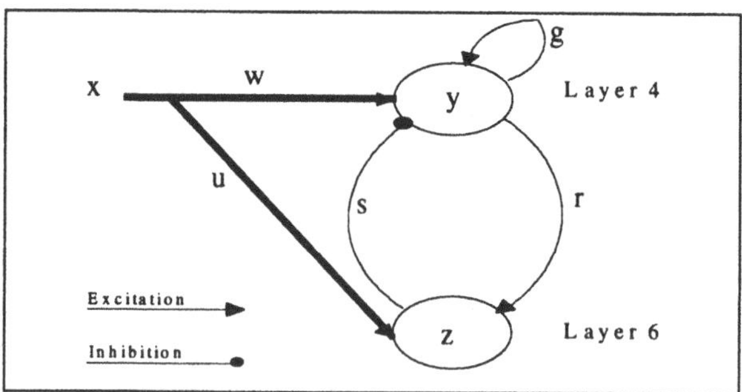

Fig. 5: Diagram of a simple single column AMI module

The behaviour of the module depicted in figure 5 is described by the following system of differential equations:

$$\tau_y \frac{dy}{dt} = -y + wx + gy - sz, \quad (1)$$

$$\tau_z \frac{dz}{dt} = -z + ux + ry, \quad (2)$$

$$\frac{dw}{dt} = K_w x \cdot f(y,\theta_y), \qquad (3)$$

$$\frac{du}{dt} = K_u x \cdot f(z,\theta_z), \qquad (4)$$

where τ_y and τ_z are the time constants of the y and z neurons respectively, K_w and K_u are the adaptation rates of the modifiable synapse weights w and u respectively, and θ_y and θ_z are the neuron learning thresholds used by the BCM-type learning function b. The BCM-type synaptic adaptation function used here is (any function which has the general shape as b(v))

$$b(v,\theta) = \begin{cases} 0 & \text{for } v < 0, \\ \dfrac{27}{4\theta^3} \cdot v^2 \cdot (v-\theta) & \text{for } 0 < v < \theta, \\ 1 - \dfrac{1}{v-\theta+1} & \text{for } v > \theta, \end{cases}$$

where v is the membrane voltage of the post-synaptic neuron, and θ is that neuron's threshold.

Hoang and James [3] show that the conditions for stability of a slightly simplified version of this system are:

$$\frac{K_w}{K_u} < g-1 < \frac{\tau_y}{\tau_z}, \quad (5) \quad \text{and} \quad g-1 < sr \quad (6).$$

It is interesting to note that the adaptive loop is stable under very simple and reasonable conditions relating all intuitive parameters of the circuit. These stability conditions are verified in section 4.3 below.

4.2 Implementation

The simulation simply approximates solution of the above system of differential equations. It does this by calculating the change in each of the quantities y, z, w, and u over a short period of time, Δt, then updating the values and repeating. The smaller the value of Δt, the better (and more time-consuming) the approximation. A typical value of the Δt used here is 0.01

4.3 Robustness

In the section below we verify the stability conditions by simulation, and demonstrate the robustness of a single column module by varying the system's parameters and initial conditions. *Initial conditions* refers to the initial values of w and u.

Effects of the Internal Fixed Synapse Weights s and r

Stability condition (6) relates the fixed self-gain weight g to the product of fixed weights s and r. The simulations performed in this experiment had parameters $\Delta t = 0.01$, $g = 3$, $K_w = K_u = 0.2$, $\tau_y = 2.5$, $\tau_z = 1.0$, $\theta_y = \theta_z = 10$, and $x = 1$. Fig. 6 contains graphs showing the initial values of input synapse weights w and u for which the module converged. Each point on each graph in figure 6 represents a different simulation, with s and r determined by the particular graph, the initial value of w determined by the point on the horizontal axis of that graph and the initial value of u by point on the vertical axis. The system was typically taken to have converged when $\Delta w/\Delta t < 0.01$ and $\Delta u/\Delta t < 0.01$. The point of convergence of the module was checked to ensure that the convergence detected was true. Simulations where $s{\cdot}r \leq 2$ did not converge, as predicted by stability condition (6), and so are not shown in Fig. 6.

The "loop gain" of a module was defined by Hoang and James [3] as $1{+}s{\cdot}r$. It appears that as the loop gain increases, the module is better able to cope with initial weights farther away from the point of convergence. More specifically, figure 6 shows that an increase in s allows a greater range of initial values of w. This trend is not surprising considering the configuration of the module (see figure 5 above). Synapse w excites neuron y, and synapse s inhibits neuron y. Increased inhibition of neuron y by synapse s allows the input to that neuron to increase without the membrane voltage becoming too strong to allow convergence of the system. Figure 6 also shows that an increase in r allows a greater range of initial values of u.

It is clear in Fig. 6 that the region (hashed) of convergence is large measured relative to the point of convergence of the system near the centre of the region. The system is thus robust in the sense that it always achieves the stability for a wide range of initial conditions.

Effects of the Input Synapses Learning Rates

Stability condition (5) above relates the ratio of the input synapse learning (adaption) rates, K_w and K_u to the self gain g. Figures 7 and 8 show the effect of varying the learning rates on convergence of the system.

They show the amount that w and u are still changing after the system converges, in simulations where $s = 5$, $r = 2$, $g = 3$, $\Delta t = 0.01$, $\theta_y = \theta_z = 10$, $\tau_y = 2.5$, $\tau_z = 1.0$, and $x = 1$. The entries in the tables are the values ($\Delta w/\Delta t$, $\Delta u/\Delta t$) after the simulation has been running for 200000 cycles, which is ample time to reach the final state of the system. These values give an indication of how "tight" the convergence is, i.e. how small the oscillation around the point of convergence. The blank entries indicate that the simulation did not converge by any definition. It is clear that the system does not converge for $K_w / K_u \geq g\text{-}1$, as predicted by stability condition (5). The system also does not converge when K_w and K_u are large, irrespective of their ratio. This result, however, does not contradict the stability condition since the condition assumes that τ_w and τ_u are large compared to τ_y and τ_z, in its derivation (in effect, K_w and K_u are small as they are inversely proportional to τ_w and τ_u [3]).

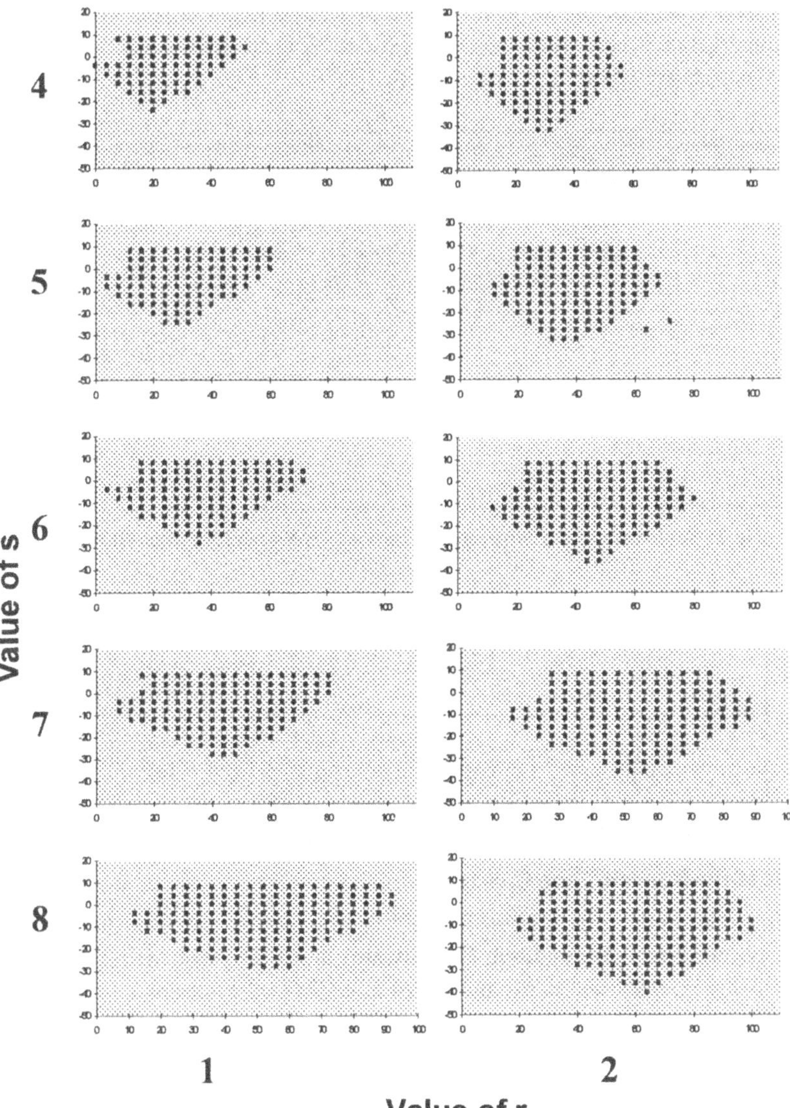

Fig. 6: Area of convergence for various values of fixed synapse weights *s* and *r*. Initial input synapse weight *w* plotted on horizontal axes and *u* on vertical axes.

Fig. 8 shows more detail for small values of K_w and K_u. It appears from this table that convergence is best when the ratio of K_w to K_u is approximately 1, i.e. when the input synapses are changing at similar rates.

K_u

K_w	0.5	1	1.5	2	2.5	3	3.5	4	4.5	5	5.5	6
0.5	(0.00, 0.00)	(0.15, 0.14)	(0.42, 0.58)	(0.44, 1.93)	(0.38, 1.99)	(0.24, 2.92)				(0.43, 3.31)		
1	(0.35, 0.25)	(0.00, 0.00)	(0.62, 0.41)	(0.74, 1.49)	(0.94, 1.66)	(0.86, 0.34)	(0.57, 3.01)		(0.82, 3.23)	(0.53, 4.40)		
1.5		(0.00, 0.00)	(0.66, 0.29)	(1.07, 1.05)	(1.50, 2.23)	(0.72, 2.42)	(0.35, 2.98)	(0.17, 3.42)	(1.19, 0.91)	(0.91, 4.32)		
2		(1.08, 0.50)	(0.73, 0.49)	(0.98, 1.37)	(1.48, 1.97)	(1.30, 2.51)	(1.50, 3.50)	(1.56, 3.41)				
2.5			(0.91, 0.40)	(1.92, 0.57)	(2.10, 1.34)	(1.95, 1.79)	(2.16, 2.50)	(2.10, 1.20)		(1.68, 3.65)		
3			(2.23, 1.17)	(2.02, 0.91)	(1.70, 1.86)	(2.26, 2.99)	(2.95, 1.98)	(2.69, 3.01)				
3.5				(1.17, 1.66)	(2.24, 1.13)	(2.07, 2.40)	(3.38, 0.41)		(2.22, 3.20)	(2.92, 3.05)		
4				(2.04, 1.54)	(2.79, 1.74)	(3.42, 1.68)	(2.70, 3.28)	(3.83, 3.11)	(3.38, 1.20)		(2.87, 4.92)	
4.5					(1.30, 1.30)	(3.56, 2.23)	(2.50, 3.36)	(3.62, 2.83)	(3.96, 0.42)	(2.15, 4.10)		
5					(3.21, 1.83)	(4.95, 2.10)	(2.00, 2.82)	(3.90, 3.87)	(4.13, 3.88)			
5.5						(4.31, 2.11)	(5.28, 0.77)	(4.46, 1.98)	(5.46, 3.48)	(1.73, 3.59)		
6						(4.64, 2.12)	(2.61, 2.45)	(3.49, 3.87)	(5.11, 1.39)	(2.79, 4.60)		
6.5							(5.32, 2.95)	(2.08, 2.63)	(5.66, 3.53)			
7								(6.97, 1.82)	(6.06, 4.49)		(6.97, 4.91)	
7.5								(6.02, 3.00)	(6.01, 3.10)	(3.02, 4.04)	(7.17, 4.60)	
8								(7.17, 3.37)		(6.19, 4.38)		
8.5										(8.38, 4.22)		
9											(7.24, 4.78)	
9.5												
10												

Fig 7: Table showing (Δw/Δt, Δu/Δt) for various Kw and Ku after 20000 cycle

K_u

K_w	0.2	0.4	0.6	0.8	1
0.2	(0.00, 0.00)	(0.00, 0.00)	(0.00, 0.00)	(0.00, 0.05)	(0.09, 0.11)
0.4	(0.36, 0.11)	(0.00, 0.00)	(0.00, 0.00)	(0.00, 0.00)	(0.02, 0.28)
0.6		(0.00, 0.00)	(0.00, 0.00)	(0.00, 0.00)	(0.04, 0.16)
0.8		(0.45, 0.02)	(0.00, 0.00)	(0.00, 0.00)	(0.04, 0.08)
1			(0.00, 0.00)	(0.00, 0.00)	(0.00, 0.00)
1.2			(0.11, 0.29)	(0.00, 0.00)	(0.00, 0.00)
1.4				(0.00, 0.00)	(0.00, 0.00)
1.6				(0.75, 0.31)	(0.00, 0.00)
1.8					(0.16, 0.05)
2					(0.41, 0.54)

Fig 8: Table showing (Δw/Δt, Δu/Δt) for smaller values of K_u and K_w after 200000 cycles

Effects of the Neuron Time Constants

The time constants of the neurons, τ_y and τ_z, are another factor in the convergence of the system. Stability condition (5) indicates that the system will converge when $\tau_y/\tau_z > g-1$. Fig. 9 shows Δw/Δt and Δu/Δt after 200000 cycles of a simulation as τ_y and τ_z change. The simulation parameters used were $s = 5$, $r = 2$, $g = 3$, $\Delta t = 0.01$, $\theta_y = \theta_z = 10$, and $x = 1$. The figure clearly supports the prediction of the stability condition, as simulations where $\tau_y/\tau_z \leq 2$ very rarely converged.

5. Conclusion

We have proposed a biologically plausible neural network model as a building block for intelligent systems. The structure and the learning rule for the model are described in detail. We have verified the conditions for stability of a biologically plausible neural circuit employed in the network model. The mathematically predicted stability conditions are necessary for convergence of a single column module. Provided they are satisfied, the AMI module seems robust and stable for reasonable parameters and initial conditions.

τ_v	0.5	1	1.5	2	2.5	3
0.5						
1						
1.5	(0.00 0.00)					
2	(0.00 0.00)					
2.5	(0.00 0.00)	(0.00 0.00)				
3	(0.00 0.00)	(0.00 0.00)				
3.5	(0.00 0.00)	(0.00 0.00)	(0.00 0.00)			
4	(0.00 0.00)	(0.00 0.00)	(0.00 0.00)			
4.5	(0.00 0.00)	(0.00 0.00)	(0.00 0.00)	(0.17 0.24)	(0.31 0.50)	
5	(0.00 0.00)	(0.00 0.00)	(0.00 0.00)	(0.00 0.00)		

Fig. 9: Table showing ($\Delta w/\Delta t$, $\Delta u/\Delta t$) as τ_y and τ_z change, where $K_u = K_w = 0.5$

6. Acknowledgments

The authors would like to thank Kevin Irwig for running the simulations.

7. References

1. James, M., and Hoang, D. B., "Outline of a theory of Isocortex," Chapter 69, *Computation and Neural Systems*, Eeckman and Bower (Eds), Kluwer Academic Publishers, 1993.
2. Hoang D B, James M, "A Neural Network Model of Isocortex", *Proceedings of the fifth Australian conference on Neural Networks, ACNN'94*, Brisbane, Feb. 1994, pp. 173-176.
3. Hoang, D. B., and James. M., "Stability of a basic biological neural circuit", *Proceedings of the IEEE International Conference on Neural Networks, ICNN'95*, Perth, Nov. 1995, pp.1981-1985.
4. James, M., and Hoang, D.B.,"Pattern learning in a cortical circuit", *Proceedings of the Fourth Annual Computation Neuroscience Meeting CNS*95*, July 1995, California. (in press)
5. Burkhalter, A.,"Intrinsic Connections of Rat Primary Visual Cortex: Laminar Organization of Axional Projections," *Journal of Comparative Neurology*, Vol. 279, 1989, pp. 171-186.
6. Von der Malsburg, C., "Self-organization of orientation sensitive cells in the striate cortex," *Kybernetik*, Vol.14, 1973, pp.85-100.
7. Kohonen, T., *Self-organization and Associative Memory*, Second Edition, Berlin, Springer-Verlag, 1988.
8. Carpenter, G. A., and Grossberg, S., "ART2: Self-organization of stable category recognition codes for analog input patterns", *Applied Optics*, Vol.26, 1987, pp.4919-4930.
9. Murre, J. M. J., Phaf, H., and Wolters, G., "CALM: Categorizing and Learning Module." Neural Networks, Vol. 5, 1992, pp. 55-82.
10. Bienenstock, E. L., Cooper, L. N., and Munro, P. W., "Theory for the development of neural selectivity: Orientation specificity and binocular interaction in visual cortex." *Journal Neuroscience*, Vol. 2, 1982, pp. 32-48.
11. Clothiaux, B., Bear, M. F., and Cooper, L. N., "Synaptic plasticity in visual cortex: Comparison of theory with experiment." *Journal of Neurophysiology*, Vol. 66, No. 5, 1991, pp. 1785-1804.
12. James, M., and Hoang, D.B.,"An Adaptive Model of the Cortical Circuit", *Proceedings of the seventh Australian conference on Neural Networks, ACNN'96*, Canberra, 1996, pp.206-211.

Symbol Processing by Non-Symbol Processor

Setsuo Ohsuga
Department of Information and Computer Science,
School of Science and Engineering,
Waseda University
3-4-1 Ohkubo Shinjyuku-ku Tokyo 169, JAPAN

ABSTRACT

A way of processing symbolic information by non-symbol processor is discussed. Current computer is designed to process only symbolic information. The first objective of this paper is to discuss that some information is lost by the use of symbolic expression in compensation of its simplicity and this lost part of information often plays an important role in the real world. Some concepts, the detail of which could not be described well in symbolic language, have been identified and given names such as intuition, emotion, etc. But these concepts have been left out of scientific research because of the lack of scientific method to study them. For most of the existing scientific areas have been developed depending upon symbolic knowledge. The second objective of this paper is therefore to find a cue for enabling this study by developing a method to process non-symbolic information together with symbolic information in the same system.

1. Introduction

Current computer is designed to process only symbolic information. The scope of its information processing is limited from the simple logic level at the bottom to the program level in a procedural form at the top. Comparing with the human information processing, it is very narrow. At the upper level, it is difficult to do such a high level processing as hypothesis generation and testing which are the basis of creative activity by human being and, at the lower level, it is inconvenient to represent activities including non-symbolic processing such as pattern recognition and intuitive decision making. Researches for expanding this scope are necessary both upward and downward. The author discussed a way of expanding it upward in [OHS95]. This paper discusses a way to expand it downward.

In human being, neural network is the lowest level information processing component to process continuous information. It works on the basis of very simple rule but is assumed that multi-level structures of networks are made to realize the more complex processing. It is also assumed that at some level of this structure, signal is quantized and a symbol manipulation is realized over this level. Within this structure symbol processing and non-symbol processing can be amalgamated. It enables human being to acquire intelligence.

It is natural to assume that this structure may have been emerged by evolution and also that abrupt change in the concept cannot happen by this evolution because evolution is based on very simple biological rule. There is however a conceptual gap between symbolic and non-symbolic information. Such a conceptual gap might not be gotten over by the simple evolution process and there must be an intermediate step to connect them.

Currently in computers, on the other hand, the symbolic processing algorithm is defined substantially differently from the one for non-symbolic processing. This difference came from the difference in the technical approaches to symbolic and non-symbolic information processing so far because of the conceptual gap between symbolic and non-symbolic information. If there is a new concept to connect them, then it is possible to develop computers which can deal with both symbol and non-symbol information.

The author proposes in this paper an intermediate stage in which symbolic processing is achieved by the same algorithm as non-symbolic processing and therefore the same mechanism can be used for both processings. Once simple symbol processing becomes possible and a set of symbols are defined, then the more complex structure of symbolic expressions such as phrase and sentence can be defined as the combination of the primitive symbols.

It means also that the result of non-symbolic processing can be accepted easily by the symbolic processing part. It is expected that different type of intelligence can be achieved with this scheme from those which are achieved on the basis only of symbolic processing. Intuition and sudden cognition of things which we occasionally experience are this kind of intelligence of which the way or even the reason of coming to the conclusions cannot be explained by words. Nevertheless people know that these kinds of activities often lead us to very new ideas. Emotional information is also created mostly in the non-symbolic processing part. It is accepted in the symbolic processing part to generate artistic information. For example, musical concept created in the non-symbolic part is accepted by the symbolic processing part, formalized on the basis of musical theory and represented as a music score [ZAN93]. Knowledge discovery in data (KDD)[PSH91, ZHO94] is also thought as a conversion process of continuous data observed by sensors to symbolic expressions. Robotics can be the first application because these need to fuse continuous signal with logic.

This information processing is different from that of conventional computers which is designed to use and process symbolic information from the beginning. The non-symbolic information processing as mentioned above must be performed on symbol manipulation mechanism in current computers. But it does not always successful. To integrate symbolic and non-symbolic processing is expected to produce fruitful results.

In this paper the author shows that logical inference as a basis of symbol processing is a special case of non-symbol processing. The objective of this paper is thus to show that there is no difference in the basic part between symbol and non-symbol processing mechanisms and find such a non-symbolic processing algorithm. Number of new problems must be solved before the goal of this research is reached. These are:

(1) How can symbol be generated in non-symbol processing mechanism.

(2) How to realize symbol processing by non-symbol processing algorithm.

(3) How to define the different layers of non-symbol processing mechanism which is considered mandatory to realize symbol processing.

(4) How to use this integrated system.

This paper discusses mainly the second issue among them in this paper. Some views for the remaining issues can be obtained though this research but are discussed briefly because of lack of space.

2. Similarity Between Logical Inference And Stochastic Process

Predicate logic is the basis of all symbolic languages. First order logic (FOL) is considered in this paper. The primary objective is to represent logical inference by non-symbolic processing algorithm. There is a close relation between logical deduction and stochastic process [WAT69]. An attention is paid in this relation and representation of stochastic process is used as an intermediate between symbol and non-symbol processing.

2.1 Logical Deduction

The simple deduction is represented as (F, F -> G) / G. This means that G is deduced from predicates F and F -> G. Both F and G includes any number of terms but for the sake of simplicity the discussion is made for the single term predicates, i.e. F(x) and G(x) where x is a variable. In ordinary FOL, universe of discourse is the domain of the variable x. In this paper however many sorted logic (MSL) is used. The difference is that an expression (Qx) [D(x) -> F(x)] in the ordinary logic can be represented as (Qx/d) F(x) in MSL where D(x) is a predicate to define a sort of the variable x and d is a set (an extension) in the universe which is characterized by D(x) (an intension). Q in the prefix denotes a quantifier and is either A (universal quantifier) or E (existential quantifier). For example (Ax)[Man(x) -> Mortal(x)] in the ordinary FOL can be represented (Ax/man) Mortal(x) in MSL where Man(x) is a characteristic 'manhood' of x while 'man' is a set of entities having this characteristic. In the ordinary FOL, the expression (Ex) [F(x) -> G(x)] means that if there is at least one entity e in the universe which does not meet F(e), then this expression is true. This is almost meaningless or carries very few information because in most non-trivial problems universe is very large and includes various entities some of which does not meet F(e). Contrarily, (Ex/d)[F(x) -> G(x)] in corresponding MSL expression carries some information because the domain set d can be small even if the universe is very large, and information 'there is no such element in d that does not meet F(x)', or equivalently, 'all elements in d satisfy F(x)' is meaningful. In this case (Ex/d)G(x) is deduced. MSL is considered here because in the most real applications a finite set of entities in the universe is considered as objects.
The logical deduction above is interpreted as a rule to transform a given expression (Q'x/d)F(x) to (Q"x/d)G(x) by means of (Qx/d) [F(x) -> G(x)]. Both Q' and Q" are quantifiers and Q" is decided by the relation between Q and Q' as follows [OHY85].

(a) If Q:A and Q':A, then Q":A. (b) If Q:A and Q':E, then Q":E.
(c) If Q:E and Q':A, then Q":E. (d) If Q:E and Q':E, then nothing can be said.

With this convention and representing (Qx/d) [F(x) -> G(x)] as I^{FG} to denote inference as a transformer, the deductive inference can be written as, $G = F \cdot I^{FG}$ to mean that G is obtained as a transformation of F by I^{FG}.

2.2 Stochastic Process

Stochastic process represents a changing process of probability distribution of variables. Let us think of a N-state machine and P be a row vector to represent a distribution of probabilities of occurrence of the states. Then a stochastic process can be represented as follows,

$P^{M+1} = (p_1, p_2, \cdots, p_N)^{M+1} = (p_1, p_2, \cdots, p_N)^M \cdot T = P^M \cdot T$
where T denotes a N x N transition matrix, $T = [t_{ij}]$. An element t_{ij} denotes a transition probability from the state i to j. This expression means that the probability distribution of the states at (M+1)-th step in this process can be obtained by multiplying the transition matrix with the probability distribution at M-th step. The transition matrix decides all the behavior of this process.

2.3 Interpretation of Logical Deduction as Stochastic Process

There is a similarity between the deductive process and stochastic process. Let $d=\{a_1, a_2, \cdots, a_n\}$ be a domain of the variable x, and define a state S of a system in respect to F and d as follows. At every instance of knowledge the state $F(a_i)$ (i=1,2 --,n) is either true or false. A vector $(u_1, u_2, \cdots, u_n)^F$ is a state s_k in respect to F of which u_i is either 1 or 0 corresponding to either $F(a_i)$ is true of false. The suffix k represents the order corresponding to the binary number $u_1u_2 \cdots u_n$. Note that this is not the state of each component a_i but of the set d. Thus a state vector $S^F = (s_1, s_2, \cdots, s_N)^F$ is defined as the ordered set of all possible states of d. This is a mutually disjoint and exhaustive set. To each of the N ($=2^n$) states a probability p_k (k=1,2,---,N) is assigned. A probability vector $P^F = (p_1, p_2, \cdots, p_N)^F$ is thus defined. The superfix ^{F} denotes that this vector is with respect to the predicate F. Using this vector P^F and P^G for G and also defining a transition matrix T^{FG} as shown in the next section, a process $P^G = P^F \cdot T^{FG}$ is obtained in the same form as stochastic process instead of $G = F \cdot I^{FG}$.

2.4 Deductive Process as a Part of Stochastic Process

In stochastic process a transition matrix must keep the the following conditions and each element can take any value within this condition.
Condition of Stochastic Processes:
(1) Every component of the matrix must be non-negative, and
(2) For every row, the row sum of the components must be equal to 1.
In addition, transition matrix of deductive process must meet a strong condition. This is derived in two cases. In the following, the set d is assumed finite.

First Case: (Ax/d) [F(x) -> G(x)]
This is equal to $(\sim F(a_1) \vee G(a_1)) \wedge (\sim F(a_2) \vee G(a_2)) \wedge \cdots \wedge (\sim F(a_n) \vee G(a_n))$. In order for this expression being true, every $(\sim F(a_i) \quad G(a_i))$ must be true. Thus if some $F(a_i)$ is known true, then $G(a_i)$ must be true. Otherwise $G(a_i)$ can be either true or false. In terms of state representation, this means that only the following transitions are possible,
$(*, *, \cdots, *, u_i=1, *, \cdots, *)^F \to (*, *, \cdots, u_i=1, *, *, \cdots, *)^G$
$(*, *, \cdots, *, u_i=0, *, \cdots, *)^F \to (*, *, \cdots, u_i=1, *, *, \cdots, *)^G$
$(*, *, \cdots, *, u_i=0, *, \cdots, *)^F \to (*, *, \cdots, u_i=0, *, *, \cdots, *)^G$
where * denotes either 0 or 1 but its value at the corresponding position in the left-hand and right-hand terms must be the same. It is possible to define t_{ij} in T^{FG} to meet this condition. A matrix made in this way is shown in Figure 2. In this figure * denotes some non-zero value. The value * can be different for every t_{ij} but these must meet the Condition of Stochastic Process as shown in (1) and (2) above. It is not difficult to prove that this representation reveals every property as logical inference. For example, if $F(a_i)$ is given true, then the probability of $G(a_i)$ being true is 1 with this transition matrix. This is shown in the next section. Thus, among all possible matrices meeting the Condition of

Stochastic Process (1) and (2) above, only those which meet this additional condition represent the deductive rule of the first case.

Second Case; (Ex/d) [F(x) -> G(x)]

This is equal to $(\sim F(a_1) \vee G(a_1)) \vee (\sim F(a_2) \vee G(a_2)) \vee$ ----$\vee (\sim F(a_n) \vee G(a_n))$. If some $F(a_i)$ is false, then this expression holds true. In this case, $G(a_i)$ for any a_i can be either true or false and nothing can be said on G any further. All what can be said definitely for this case is that when (Ax/d)F(x) is true, some $G(a_i)$ must be true, or (Ex/d)G(x) holds. In this way, a transition matrix for the second case is obtained. Only condition for a transition matrix to represent this deductive rule is $t_{N0} = 0$.

Let an input to the process with this transition matrix be a probability vector $(0,0,\text{----},0,1)^N$, i.e. (Ax/d)F(x) in logical expression, then $(0, *, *, \text{----}, *)^{N+1}$ is deduced as the output. This is (Ex/d)G(x). For any other input the output with the finite state probabilities for all p_i's including p_1 (for the state (0,0,---,0)) is deduced. That is, nothing can be said on G(x) (the case (d) of 3.1).

Thus in both cases deductive rules are represented by the special case of transition matrix. If an arbitrary transition matrix can be implemented by some non-symbolic information processing mechanism, this mechanism can also represent logical inference. Therefore transition matrix can be an intermediate between symbolic and non-symbolic processing.

2.5 Probability Distribution of Predicates Being True

Let, for some element a_i of $d=\{a_1, a_2, \text{---}, a_n\}$, the probability of $F(a_i)$ being true be 1. Nothing is said for the other elements. In the probability vector, the probabilities corresponding to the states of which i-th idex is u_i is non-zero while the others are zero. Recall that a state s_k in the state vector S^{iF} in respect to F

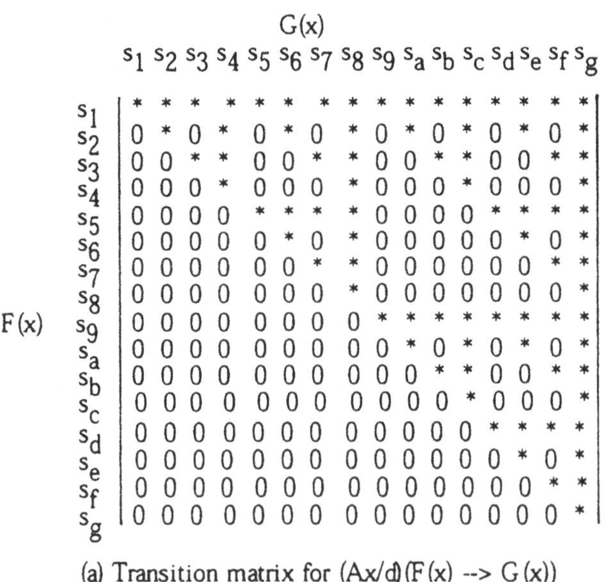

F(x) \ G(x)	s_1	s_2	s_3	s_4	s_5	s_6	s_7	s_8	s_9	s_a	s_b	s_c	s_d	s_e	s_f	s_g
s_1	*	*	*	*	*	*	*	*	*	*	*	*	*	*	*	*
s_2	0	*	0	*	0	*	0	*	0	*	0	*	0	*	0	*
s_3	0	0	*	*	0	0	*	*	0	0	*	*	0	0	*	*
s_4	0	0	0	*	0	0	0	*	0	0	0	*	0	0	0	*
s_5	0	0	0	0	*	*	*	*	0	0	0	0	*	*	*	*
s_6	0	0	0	0	0	*	0	*	0	0	0	0	0	*	0	*
s_7	0	0	0	0	0	0	*	*	0	0	0	0	0	0	*	*
s_8	0	0	0	0	0	0	0	*	0	0	0	0	0	0	0	*
s_9	0	0	0	0	0	0	0	0	*	*	*	*	*	*	*	*
s_a	0	0	0	0	0	0	0	0	0	*	0	*	0	*	0	*
s_b	0	0	0	0	0	0	0	0	0	0	*	*	0	0	*	*
s_c	0	0	0	0	0	0	0	0	0	0	0	*	0	0	0	*
s_d	0	0	0	0	0	0	0	0	0	0	0	0	*	*	*	*
s_e	0	0	0	0	0	0	0	0	0	0	0	0	0	*	0	*
s_f	0	0	0	0	0	0	0	0	0	0	0	0	0	0	*	*
s_g	0	0	0	0	0	0	0	0	0	0	0	0	0	0	0	*

(a) Transition matrix for (Ax/d)(F(x) --> G(x))

Fig. 1 Transition matrix for logical inference ($d = \{a_1, a_2, a_3, a_4\}$)

is the vector $(u_1, u_2, \ldots, u_n)^F$ of which u_i is either 1 or 0 corresponding to either $F(a_i)$ is true of false. Let us assume that these non-zero probabilities are of the same value unless there is special reason to make them different.
Example; Let $d=\{a_1, a_2, a_3\}$ and $F(a_3)$ be true, i.e. $u_3 = 1$. Then,
$S^F = (s_{000}, s_{001}, s_{010}, s_{011}, s_{100}, s_{101}, s_{110}, s_{111})^F$
of which the corresponding probability vector is,
$P^F = (0, \quad 1/4, \quad 0, \quad 1/4, \quad 0, \quad 1/4, \quad 0, \quad 1/4)$
This vector is made an input to the transition matrix. Let the output R^G be,
$R^G = (r_{000}, r_{001}, r_{010}, r_{011}, r_{100}, r_{101}, r_{110}, r_{111})$
Let this probability vector corresponds to the similar state vector S^G as S^F. In S^G an attention is paid on the states of which i-th idex is 1 corresponding to $G(a_i)$ being true. The terms in R^G which correspond to these state are taken out. Their sum is the probability of $G(a_i)$ being true irrespective of the other elements. In the above case, this is $r_{001} + r_{011} + r_{101} + r_{111}$.
The relation between this probability vector and transition matrix is studied. In the case of the matrix being equivalent with logical inference, the terms in R^G which correspond to the states of $G(a_i)$ being false (correspond to zero terms of input vector P^F) are also zero. As the consequence the sum of the remaining terms (corresponding to the states of $G(a_i)$ being true) is1. That is, the probability of $G(a_i)$ being true is 1 if that of $F(a_i)$ being true.
It is proved as follows. k-th element of R^G is obtained as a vector product of input vector and k-th column of the transition matrix, that is, a sum of element wise products. Let this k-th element of R^G corresponds to the state of $G(a_i)$ being false. Let, in the input vector, the m-th element be a non-zero term corresponding to the state of $F(a_i)$ being true. At the cross point of m-th row and k-th column of the transition matrix is a transition provability t_{mk}. This is a transition probability for the case $F(a_i)$ being true and $G(a_i)$ being false. In order for the transition matrix to represent logical inference, such a probability must be zero by definition. Every term in the input vector corresponding to $F(a_i)$ being false is zero. Therefore, every product term included in the vector product and accordingly k-th element of R^G is zero. Since the total sum of the element of R^G is 1, the probability of $G(a_i)$ being true is 1.
Example; The case of $d=\{a_1, a_2, a_3\}$ and $F(a_3)$ being true, as was used in the last example, is considered. The input probability vector is $P^F = (0, 1/4, 0, 1/4, 0, 1/4, 0, 1/4)$ and the transition process is represented as follows.

$$1/4(0,1,0,1,0,1,0,1)\begin{vmatrix} * & * & * & * & * & * & * & * \\ 0 & * & 0 & * & 0 & * & 0 & * \\ 0 & 0 & * & * & 0 & 0 & * & * \\ 0 & 0 & 0 & * & 0 & 0 & 0 & * \\ 0 & 0 & 0 & 0 & * & * & * & * \\ 0 & 0 & 0 & 0 & 0 & * & 0 & * \\ 0 & 0 & 0 & 0 & 0 & 0 & * & * \\ 0 & 0 & 0 & 0 & 0 & 0 & 0 & * \end{vmatrix} = (r_1, r_2, r_3, r_4, r_5, r_6, r_7, r_8)$$

Here $R^G = (r_1, r_2, r_3, r_4, r_5, r_6, r_7, r_8) = (0, r_2, 0, r_4, 0, r_6, 0, r_8)$. The term r_1, r_3, r_5, r_7 are the products of P^F and the first, third, fifth and seventh columns of the matrix respectively resulting in zero. In contrast with them the non-zero terms of P^F, say, second, fourth, sixth andeighth terms are multiplied

to the elements of the corresponding row of the matrix and the non-zero products are summed up in the corresponding terms in R^G , say, r_2, r_4, r_6, r_8. Since every row sum of the matrix is 1, the total sum of r_2, r_4, r_6 and r_8 becomes (number of non-zero terms of P^F) x 1/ (number of non-zero terms of P^F) = 1. This means that the probability of $G(a_j)$ being true is 1. This was the condition of the transition matrix representing the logical inference.
This method of obtaining the output predicate probability is general and can be applied to an arbitrary transition matrix. If this probability is obtained for every element in the set d, then a probability distribution of $G(a_j)$ being true is derived. In case of a general transition matrix, theprobability distribution spreads over all domain. This represents the ambiguity included in the inference rule (ref.6.2).

2.6 From Stochastic Process to Logical Inference by Learning.

Let us assume that there is some real phenomenon which can be described completely by FOL. It is possible to attain a transition matrix to represent this process by learning. Let us assume to begin with a matrix of which all the elements are the same and a series of observations be made. If a pair $(F(a_i), G(a_j))$ is observed, namely $G(a_j)$ could be observed for the occurrence of $F(a_i)$, then all elements of the transition matrix corresponding to the states relating both with $F(a_i)$ and $G(a_j)$ (see Figure 2) are increased by certain amount, say Δ, while the other elements are reduced uniformly by the amount $k\Delta$ / M where k is the number of element to be increased and M is number of remaining non-zero elements in a row. The elements to be increased are those at the cross points of the states of the forms $(*, *, --, *, u_i=1, *, --, *)^F$ and $(*, *, --, u_j=1, *, *, --, *)^G$ respectively where * is either 0 or 1. Conditions of Stochastic Process (3.4) must always be kept. By repeating this process for a series of observation, the matrix approaches gradually to the one representing the logical inference.
Feedback system is indispensable for achieving this learning. This is a higher level system than the inference system. In this sense multi-level system becomes necessary for generating symbolic information processing system based on non-symbolic processing algorithm.

2.7 Reduction of Transition Matrix by Partial Merging

When a set d gets large the transition matrix becomes very large and this method becomes impractical. It is possible to reduce it by partitioning a set d into a set of subsets and making a state vector of this sets instead of expanding the set d directly into the elements. Let the set be partitioned into a set of the subsets, d = {d1, d2, --, dk}, such that an expression $(A\ x/d_i)F(x)$ can be given to every d_i (i = 1,2,--,k). A probability is given to each state made from them resulting in a probability vector $P^F = (p_1, p_2, ---, p_K)^F$ where $K = 2^k$. This is an intermediate between symbolic and non-symbolic representations. Let it be called a partial symbolization. This is an effective method practically in many cases. In particular it can be used conveniently to deal with a set including some exceptions. For example, a set 'birds' can be classified into two groups; those which can fly and which cannot fly. Within every expression $(A\ x/d_i)F(x)$, (i = 1,2,--,k), the characteristics of symbol expression such as ambiguity appear as is discussed in 6.

3. Execution of Logical Inference by Neural Network

Stochastic process can be implemented by means of neural network. Operation involved in executing stochastic process is to obtain vector products, i.e. summation of all products of prior state probability and transition probability for every corresponding vector component. That is, a posterior state probability p_j^{N+1} is obtained by $\sum_i p_i^N \cdot t_{ij}$. This calculation is executed by a neural network as shown in Figure 3. In this network, an arc from an input node n_i^F to output node n_j^G is given a weight value t_{ij}, a transition probability. For representing logical deduction by a transition matrix, the input nodes and the output nodes correspond to the states of the system in respect to (F and d) and (G and d) respectively. These state vectors are produced by combining the individual state of each element of the given set d. This is the same as decoding. If only the positive (logically true) signal is to be used, these state vectors are produced as shown in the left end and also in the right end of Figure 3. Other than this main circuit, a feedback path is necessary to modify the weights of arcs by learning. Given the observed pair ($F(a_i)$, $G(a_j)$), this circuit augments the weight of arcs which form the paths from the input node n_i^F to output node n_j^G and reduces the weights of the other arcs. Figure 3 shows a case ($F(a_1)$, $G(a_2)$) as an example. This neural network is for representing the relation between the formulas F and G. The similar networks are made and combined with this. For example, if there is a relation between G and H, then the node set { n_j^G } becomes an input vector for the network between G and H. Thus a global transition network is formed using these small networks as building block. In this global network, each building block may or may not be a logical deduction network. A blocks other

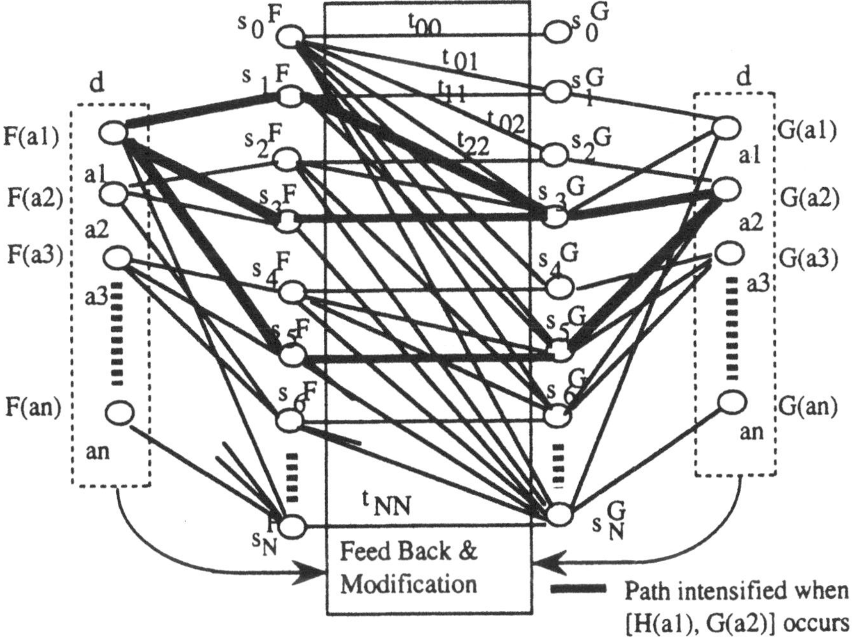

Fig.2 Neural network to represent transition process

than the logical block cannot necessarily be a standard stochastic process block but be any type of network. Every building block in this global network works as a modifier of probability distribution of input vector. Whatever the case may be, the output is a probability distribution. It can be (approximately) represented in a logical form if it is necessary. In this way logical (symbolic) processing and numerical (non-symbolic) processing can be amalgamated. This global network represents a knowledge base.

4. Non-Symbolic and Symbolic Representation Layers and Automatic Conversions Between Them

Even though symbol processing is possible by non-symbolic processor in principle, domain of variable is fixed in advance and complex logical expression is difficult. It is performed better by a symbol processor which however is not suited for non-symbol processing. Therefore a system composed of two separate sub-systems to perform symbol processing and non-symbol processing respectively and arranged in the different layers is considered with a couple of convertors to convert information from symbolic to non-symbolic representation layer and vice versa. The convertors are a coder and a decoder. Since these converters work according to the content of information automatically, these are called automatic coder (auto-coder for short) and automatic decoder respectively. The former generates a set of symbols from non-symbolic information automatically when the transition matrix meet the condition of logical inference while the latter generates the non-symbolic information from symbolic information. Automatic coding is a kind of abstraction and the coder tries to generate a best code from the given non-

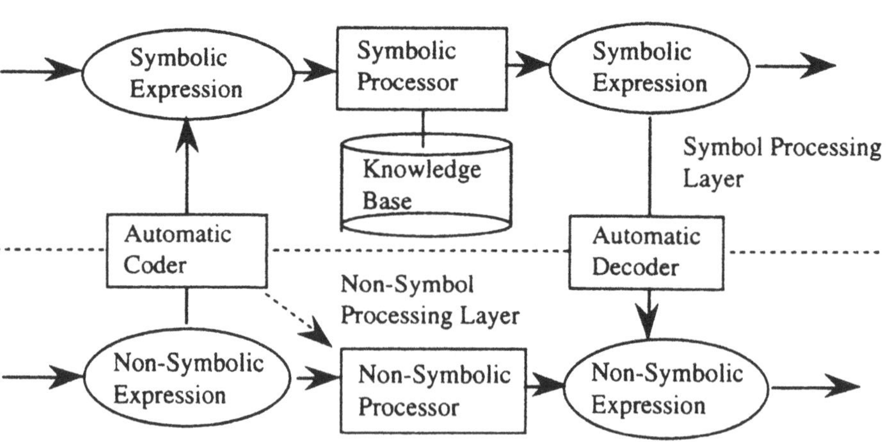

Fig.3 Hybrid system with automatic coder

symbolic information. The decoder is the same as ordinary decoder. The system configuration is shown in Figure 4. This is called a hybrid system hereafter.
The role of auto-coder is to find a set of symbols to which a predicate is introduced and a probability distribution over the set of predicates such that the probability vector produced by the combination of the predicates matches the state probability vector of stochastic process. Exact matching is impossible because in general the number of states is larger than the number of symbols. Therefore an approximate matching within a certain error criterion is looked for. If the transition matrix is already given, then the conversion starts with it. Otherwise learning is necessary as discussed before. Not only the transition matrix but the input probability vector is learnt altogether. Automatic coding is achieved on the basis of the input probability vector. In general the number of states N in an arbitrary transition process is not exactly 2^n. In this case a least n such that $2^n \geq N$ is used. Then some states are selected from the state vector and split each of the state into two (or more) states so that the total number of states becomes N. Correspondingly the state probability p_i of each selected state s_i is split into p_{i1} and p_{i2}. Here is a freedom of deciding p_{i1} (or p_{i2}). Thus the number of free variables increases to $n+2^n-N$. It increases the possibility of approximate matching. If this approximation fails the number of symbols is increased.
The procedure of automatic coding is defined but abbreviated here.

5. Limit and Ambiguity of Symbolic Expression

5.1 Limit of Expressive Power of Symbolic Representation

Transition matrix decide every behavior of a stochastic process. Even a slight variation in the transition matrix can bring the process to the completely different state probability after the long sequence of processes. Every element in the matrix can take any value within the Condition of Stochastic Process. Thus stochastic processes covers the space defined by N x N transition matrix very dense. In contrast with this there is such a stronger structural constraint to a matrix to represent logical inference such that some key elements in the matrix must be zero. The other elements can take any value unless they violate the Condition of Stochastic Process. Thus transition matrix of logical inference is a subset of arbitrary transition matrix and accordingly logical inference is a part of stochastic process. Hence stochastic process is divided into three classes, the first class to represent the first type logical formula, i.e., (Ax/d) [F(x) -> G(x)], the second class to represent the second type logical formula, i.e., (Ex/d) [F(x) -> G(x)], and the third class for the other processes to which no logical formula corresponds.
Any value can appear as transition probability in ordinary stochastic process unless it violate the Condition of Stochastic Process and there can be a real phenomenon which needs to be represented by this process. But if this process violates the condition imposed to the transition matrix to represent logical inference, then it cannot be described as a symbol processing. Additional expression becomes necessary to describe such phenomena in symbolic form.
It is concluded from this fact that predicate logic is a system to describe only a part of all possible cases in a simple form. If it is necessary to describe the other cases, then the more description must be added. Sometimes this added part of description is more difficult for ones to understand correctly. This is a sacrifice of using the simple symbolic expressions. Stochastic process has the larger expressive power but its expression is inconvenient to use in daily life.

5.2 Ambiguity of Symbolic Expression

The fact that very many different processes are included in the same class and are represented by the same logical expression means that logical expression is defined as a framework and any variation in this framework is not taken into account. This is a very rough or ambiguous way of expressing things and it cannot discriminate small difference existing in the objects.

Matrix representation of logical inference as shown in Figure 2 can represent situations the more precisely by given the precise probability distribution to *'s. If one wishes to represent it by symbolic language, then the more words is necessary. For example such an expression is made, "If F then G for all objects in d and G(a) can happen to be more frequently than the other objects". The first half of this statement represents (Ax/d) [F(x) -> G(x)], and the last half adds a comment on the uneven chance of occurrence of objects in this framework. It is clear however that it is inconvenient to represent this fluctuation from the standard expression in words. Other way of representing this ambiguity is necessary.

Ambiguity representation is required to meet the conditions as follows. (1) It must be comprehensive. (2) Ambiguity reduces as data increases. (3) This ambiguity processing must be made as an additional information to the standard expression in a simple theoretical way.

Ambiguity of logical expression is included both in fact / data and inference rule which can change the ambiguity of logical expression as logical operation proceeds. It is assumed here that this kind of ambiguity is included in inference rule and no ambiguity is included in any inference engine.

[Ambiguity of data/fact]; Ambiguity included in a predicate (Ax/d)F(x) is represented by a probability distribution $Q = (q_1, q_2, --, -q_n)$ where q_i denotes a probability of $F(a_i)$ being true. Fact representation including ambiguity is then a couple [(Ax/d)F(x), Q].

[Ambiguity of inference rule]; Ambiguity included in inference rule is defined as 'ambiguity of conclusion derived from the inference rule when premise is free from ambiguity '.

A probability distribution of the output predicates over the domain set was defined in 3.5. This concept is applied in the case of general transition matrix. In this case, transition matrix t_{mk} at the cross point of the non-zero (m-th) term of the input vector and k-th column corresponding to the state of $G(a_i)$ being false is not always zero. Accordingly the element of R^G corresponding to $G(a_i)$ being false is not zero. In the example above, r_1, r_3, r_5 and r_7 may have non-zero values and the sum of r2, r4, r6 and r8 reduces by the sum of r_1, r_3, r_5 and r_7. That is, even if $F(a_i)$ is true, the probability r^* $(= r_2+r_4+r_6+r_8)$ of $G(a_i)$ being true is less than 1. This is ambiguity or uncertainty of inference.

When sum of r_1, r_3, r_5 and r_7 remains small, namely t_{mk} is not large, this transition matrix may still be used as the inference with ambiguity. In this case the probability of the consequence of inference being true must be evaluated in parallel with the inference.

The discussion so far assumed that the probability of $F(a_i)$ being true is 1. By multiplying the probability of $F(a_i)$ being true with r^*, the real probability of $G(a_i)$ being true is derived. Inference engine calculates the probability distribution of the consequence from the ambiguities of input and of inference rule in parallel

with logical inference on the basis of symbolic expression. The former is to obtain the probability distribution of the consequent predicates over the domain set d by multiplying component by component the probability distributions of input and inference rule. It is summarized as follows.
Let the input (premise or question) be represented by a pair [(Ax/d)F(x), Q] where $Q = (q_1, q_2, \text{---} q_n)$ is the probability of $F(a_i)$ being true for each element of d. Similarly the inference rule is represented by a pair [(Ax/d)(F(x) --> G(x)), R] of the logical inference rule on the basis of d and a probability distribution R = (r1,r2, --, rn) to represent the ambiguity of the inference rule. Then the consequence of the inference is again a pair [(Ax/d)G(x), S] of which $S = (p_1 r_1, p_2 r_2, \text{---}, p_n r_n)$.
Here it is assumed that the set d is common to the input and the inference rule. In general these are the different. In this case a new domain set of the consequence must be made from those of the input and the inference rule. However this discussion is abbreviated here. Refer to [OHY85].
Ambiguity evaluation can be used for knowledge discovery and refinement as is discussed in the next section. It can also be used for control of search operation. For example, it is possible to stop operation in a exploratory inference when the probability for every element becomes below a certain level.

6. Knowledge Discovery and Knowledge Refinement

Hybrid systems can be used for knowledge discovery. Let us assume that some causal relation seems to exist between observation. Let the observations be classified into finite classes and represented by a states set. Clustering and the other methods may be used here. A scheme of transition process is introduced as the framework to represent the causal relation. Through learning in this framework a tendency of the transition between input and output is learnt. If it succeeds in having a near stationary transition process, an auto-coder gives names to the input (F) and output (G) depending on their characteristics. If there is some similar concept in the system its name should be used because then discovered knowledge can be used together with existing knowledge in knowledge base. Human intervention may be necessary here. The coder symbolizes the input and the transition matrix. Even if this matrix does not reveals the complete equivalence with logical inference, the symbolization can be done if the probability of the logical consequence being true is over a certain level. A probability distribution over the set d must be accompanied with the logical expression. The discovered knowledge is saved in the knowledge base. Once symbolized the process can be refined in the various ways afterward.
When probability of predicate for some element of the domain becomes below a certain threshold level, then the element is deleted from the set. This ensures the credibility of the logical consequence. This is a knowledge refinement. It is also possible to add new elements to d or to merge two sets into one. It give us a chance to restructure the knowledge representation by learning more easily than to do everything on the basis of symbolic representation. For refining knowledge a high level system besides the learning system is necessary.

7. Conclusion

A way of processing symbolic information by non-symbolic processor has been discussed. Strictly speaking what has been discussed in this paper is not the symbol processing as is defined. Formally symbol processing is to give a symbolic name to an object (entity or phenomenon) as the representative of this real object and process everything afterward by this name without looking into the detail anymore. It requires that every necessary knowledge for processing the object is also represented in symbolic language.
What is intended in this paper however is first to clarify the fact that some information has been lost in compensation of the simplicity acquired by this symbolic representation and processing, and this lost part of information often plays an important role in the real world.
To use symbolic language, i.e. to confine the scope of information to the world describable by symbolic language may have been unavoidable because real object is often very complex and it is difficult for people to represent it precisely. People could identify some concepts which could not be described in language precisely and give them names such as intuition, emotion, etc. However these concepts have been left out of science because of the lack of scientific method to study them. For most of the existing scientific areas have been developed based on symbolic knowledge.
Today we can have a method to amalgamate non-symbolic information processing with symbolic processing. It is expected that by combining the non-symbolic information processing with existing symbolic knowledge processing the scope of studies expand in many research areas. The second objective of this paper is to find a cue for this study. As the matter of course this is a very difficult task and what has been discussed here is only the first step. The author believe however that this research extends further and can be a new paradigm of information processing.

REFERENCE

[NON95] Nonaka, I. and Takeuchi, H.; The Knowledge Creating Company, Oxford Univ. Press, 1995

[ZAN93] Zannos, I.; Minimus: A Musical Programming Language Based on Music Space and Concurrency, Ph.D. Dissertation, The University of Tokyo, 1993

[OHY85] Ohsuga, S. and Yamauchi, H. Multi-Layer Logic - A Predicate Logic Including Data Structure As Knowledge Representation Language, New Generation Computing, 1985;

[OHS95] Ohsuga, S.; A Way of Designing Knowledge Based Systems, Knowledge Based Systems, Vol.6, No.1, 1995,

[PSH91] Piatestsky-Shapiro, G. and Frawly, W.J. (eds.); Knowledge Discovery in Databases, AAAI Press and The MIT Press, 1991

[WAT69] Watanabe, S.; Knowing and Guessing- A Formal and Quantitative Study, John-Wiley, 1969

[ZON94] Zhong, N. and Ohsuga, S.; Discovering Concept Clusters by Decomposing Databases, Data & Knowledge Engineering, Vol.12, N0.2, 1994, 223-24

Fall Diagnosis Using Dynamic Belief Networks

A. E. Nicholson

Department of Computer Science, Monash University,
Clayton, VIC 3168, Australia,
annn@cs.monash.edu.au.

Abstract. The task is to monitor walking patterns and give early warning of falls using foot switch and mercury trigger sensors. We describe a dynamic belief network model for fall diagnosis which, given evidence from sensor observations, outputs beliefs about the current walking status and makes predictions regarding future falls. The model represents possible sensor error and is parametrised to allow customisation to the individual being monitored.

1 Introduction

The task is to monitor the stepping patterns of elderly people, or recovering patients. Not only are actual falls to be detected causing an alarm to be raised, but irregular walking patterns, stumbles and near falls are to be monitored, and early warning of possible falls made in time for giving assistance. The monitoring is performed using two kinds of sensors: foot-switches which provide information about a foot step; and a mercury sensor which is triggered by a change in height such as going from standing upright to lying horizontal, and hence indicates a fall has occurred. Timing data for the observations is also given.

Previous work in this domain performed fall diagnosis with a simple state machine [3], however this does not allow representation of either degrees of belief as to the person's ambulatory status, or of the uncertainty in the sensor readings. *Dynamic belief networks* integrate a mechanism for inference under uncertainty with a secure Bayesian foundation, and are suitable for domains, such as the fall diagnosis problem, where the world changes and the focus is reasoning over time. In this paper we present a dynamic belief network model for the fall diagnosis problem, an interesting practical application of an AI approach to the real world problem of medical monitoring.

The organisation of this paper is as follows. The fall diagnosis problem is described in detail in Sect. 2. Sect. 3 gives an introduction to dynamic belief networks. In Sect. 4 we develop a complete belief network model for the fall diagnosis problem, with results given in Sect. 5. Extensions to the basic network are described in Sect. 6.

2 The Fall Diagnosis Problem

Davies [3] describes a project with Prof. Ian Brown at Monash University, Dept. of Electrical Engineering, for monitoring the stepping pattern of elderly people

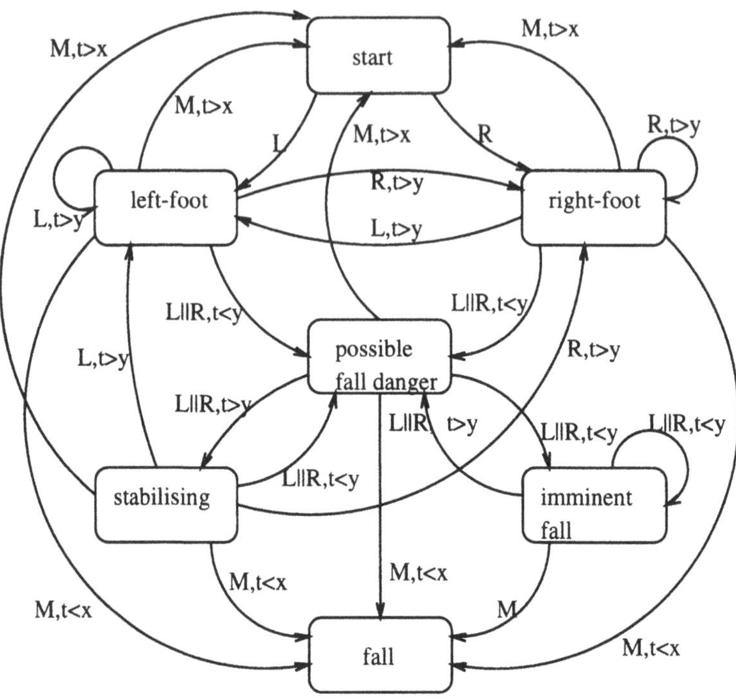

Fig. 1. Davies' State Machine for the fall diagnosis problem [3]

and patients. Step data is obtained using foot-switches and sent via a mobile data network to a remote monitoring station, which attempts to detect falls and near falls by using a state transition diagram, shown in Fig. 1. This model was developed by Davies in conjunction with expert medical practitioners.

The sensor observations are as follows: **L:** data from the left foot switch; **R:** data from the right foot switch; **M:** data from a mercury switch indicates a change in height. Each sensor observation is accompanied by a time, which is the time duration of the sensor observation. This timing information is crucial in performing fall diagnosis: y is the threshold time below which a foot switch reading is considered a stumble; x is the threshold time below which the mercury trigger is taken to indicate a fall (a slow change in height would be consistent with intended sitting or lying down). [1]

The states of the state machine are as follows. **start** is a state of ignorance, entered when a slow mercury trigger is recorded, or when the machine is restarted after a fall alarm. **left-foot, right** are walking states, indicating which foot is currently forward in the process of walking. Normal stepping patterns, indicated by an observation time interval of $> y$, should see the state machine alternate between these two states. **possible-fall-danger** is an intermediate waiting state, entered after any abnormally fast step which may have been a

[1] Davies used the threshold times of $x = 2s$, $y = 0.8s$.

stumble, as the next input will determine if the patient is really stumbling or if the reading was a lone occurrence. The **stabilising** state will be reached after **possible-fall-danger** if a slow-controlled step is observed. The **imminent-fall** state will be reached after **possible-fall-danger** if another quick step is observed. The system currently increments a counter storing the number of near falls detected in the day. The **fall** state will be reached from **imminent-fall** with any triggering of the mercury switch, in which case the system sounds a local alarm and places an emergency call to the base station. This fall state is also reached from states other than **imminent-fall**, however in these cases the time data for the mercury switch must be $< x$ seconds.

This state machine model has a number of limitations. First, there is no representation of degrees of belief in the current state of the person's ambulation. Second there is no distinction between actual states of the world and observations of that state, for example, the fall state is really a **fall-alarm** state. That is, there is no explicit representation of the uncertainty in the sensor observation [8]. Possible sensor errors include: false positives, where the sensor wrongly indicates that an action (left, right, lowering action) has occurred (also called clutter, noise or false alarms); false negatives, where an action occurred but the sensor was not triggered and no observation was made (also called missed detection); wrong timing data. Also, there is no difference between a sequence of alternate foot steps, and a sequence of same foot steps (hopping).

3 Dynamic Belief Networks

Belief networks are directed acyclic graphs, where nodes correspond to random variables, which we assume to take discrete values (although in general they need not be discrete). In this paper the variables pertain to the world state or the sensor observations. The relationship between any set of state variables can be specified by a joint probability distribution. The nodes in the network are connected by directed arcs, which may be thought of as causal or influence links. The connections also specify the independence assumptions between nodes. Each node has associated with it a *probability distribution*, which, for each combination of the variables of the parent nodes (called a *conditioning case*), gives a probability of each value of the node variable. The probability distribution for a node with no predecessors is the prior distribution. Evidence can be specified about the state of *any* of the nodes in the network — root nodes, leaf nodes or intermediate nodes. This evidence is propagated through the network affecting the overall joint distribution (as represented by the conditional probabilities). There are a number of exact and approximate inference algorithms available for performing belief updating [11]; in this paper we are not concerned with the particular algorithm.

Belief networks have been been used in various applications, such as medical diagnosis and model-based vision which initially were more static, i.e. essentially the nodes and links do not change over time. Such approaches involve determining the structure of the network; supplying the prior probabilities for root nodes and conditional probabilities for other nodes; adding or retracting evidence about nodes; repeating the inference algorithm for each change in evidence.

More recently researchers have used belief networks in *dynamic* domains such as the fall diagnosis problem, where the world changes and the focus is reasoning over time [4, 6, 9]. Such dynamic applications include robot navigation and map learning based on *temporal* belief networks [4], monitoring robot vehicles [7], oil forecasting [2], [12], forecasting sleep apnea [1], automated vehicle control [5] and traffic plan recognition [13]. For such applications the network grows over time, as the state of each domain variable at different times is represented by a *series* of nodes. These dynamic networks are Markovian, which constrains the state space to some extent, however it is also crucial to limit the history being maintained in the network.

A generic dynamic belief network structure for monitoring application is shown in Fig. 2 [9]. The types of nodes are: **World** nodes, which describe the central domain variables (for example, position, heading, velocity) variables; **Event** nodes, which represent a change in the state of a world node; **Observation** nodes, which represent direct observations of world nodes, or the observable effects of an event. Time is discretised at irregular intervals, usually divided by the occurrence of discrete events. Each time slice within the network represents the static environment during that time interval. The structure within time slices is often regular. These networks are typically highly connected, particularly between adjacent time slices. The conditional probability distributions (CPDs) are shown in rectangular boxes. The CPDs of nodes with parents in the previous time slice are usually a function of the time interval. After addition of sensor observations as evidence to the DBN (indicated by dark shading), belief updating is performed, providing prediction for the values of the world nodes at time slice $T+1$.

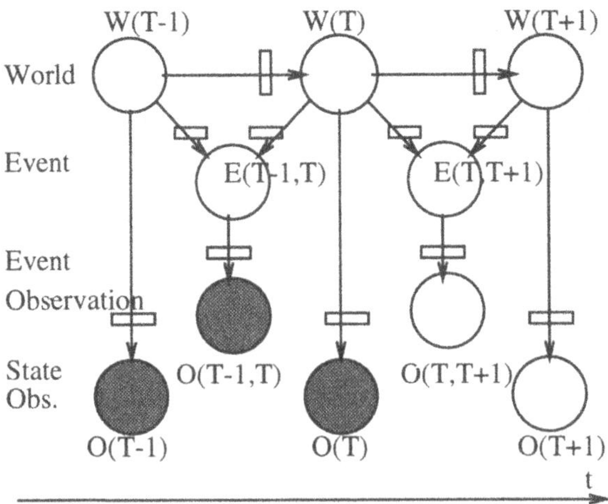

Fig. 2. Generic structure for a dynamic belief network

4 Basic DBN Model for Fall Diagnosis

Davies' state machine essentially defines the fall diagnosis problem as a set of *if-then-else* rules. When developing the DBN model, a key difference is that we focus on the causal relationships between domain variables, and make a clear distinction between observations and actual states of the world. A DBN for the fall diagnosis problem is given in Fig. 3. In the rest of this section, we describe the various features of this network in such a way as provide an insight into the network development process.

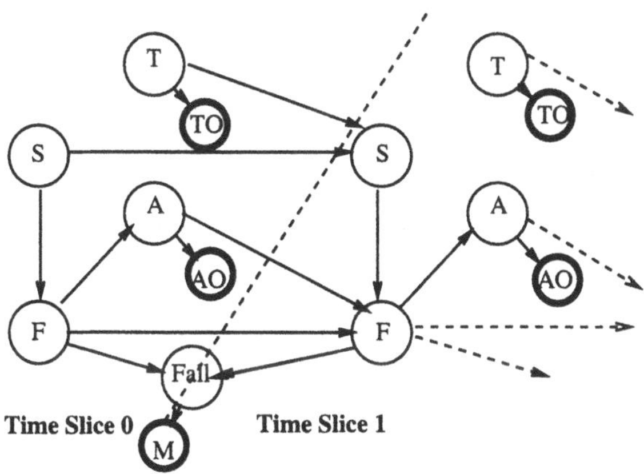

Fig. 3. Dynamic Belief Network for fall diagnosis problem including interslice arcs. The smaller nodes with thicker outlines are the sensor observations.

Nodes

When considering how to represent a person's walking situation, possibilities include whether the person is stationary on both feet, on a step with either the left or right foot forward, or has fallen and hence is no longer on their feet. We call the main world node representing this `F`, which may take 4 possible values: **both**, **left**, **right**, **off**. The event node `Fall`, which is a boolean, indicates whether a fall has taken place between time slices.

Fall warning and detection relies on an assessment of the person's walking pattern. The node `S` maintains the person's status, and may take the possible values **ok** and **stumbling**.

The action variable, `A`, may take the possible values **left**, **right**, or **none**. The last value is necessary for the situation where a time slice is added because the mercury sensor has triggered (i.e. the person has fallen) but no step was taken, or a foot switch false positive observation was registered. [2]

[2] Note that we can easily extend the model to handle a person jumping, by adding an additional possible value for `A`, say `jump`.

There is an observation node for each of the two sensors. The foot switch observations are essentially observations on the step actions, and are represented by the `AO` node which contains the same values as the action node. The mercury sensor trigger is represented by the node `M`, which represents a boolean variable.

The time between sensor observations is given by the node `T`. Given the problems with combining continuous and discrete variables [14, p.465] and the limitations of the sensor, node `T` has discrete values representing tenths of seconds. In order to represent the uncertainty in the sensor data, we say it can take values within an interval around the sensor time reading that generates the addition of a new time slice to the DBN. If there is some knowledge of the patients expected walking speed, values in this range can be added also. The time observation node, `TO`, has the same state space as `T`.

There is a new copy of each node added for each time slice; we will indicate the time slice by the subscript. The possibility of adding more time slices is shown by the dashed arcs to the right.

Note that there is no need to explicitly include **imminent-fall** or **fall** in the status node. The belief of a fall in the current time slice i is given by the posterior obtaining after adding evidence and running the inference algorithm, that is, $\mathtt{bel(Fall}_i\mathtt{=T)}$, [3], and a warning about an imminent fall can be based on the predictions for the next time slice, that is whether $\mathtt{bel(Fall}_{i+1}\mathtt{)}$ is greater than some warning threshold.

Structure and Conditional Probability Distributions

The CPDs for the nodes `A`, `F`, `Fall` and `S` are given in Table 1. The model for walking is represented by the arcs from $\mathtt{F}_i$ to $\mathtt{A}_i$, and $\mathtt{F}_i$, $\mathtt{A}_i$ and $\mathtt{S}_i$ to $\mathtt{F}_{i+1}$.

We assume that normal walking involves alternating left and right steps. Where the left and right are symmetric, only one combination is included in the table. We have priors for starting on both feet (r) or already being off the ground (s). Because we have restricted the possible actions to moving either feet or neither, there is no way for this model to reflect a person getting to their feet; we are assuming use of the model will begin with the person upright, and if not, they stay off their feet. Looking at the CPD for $\mathtt{F}_{i+1}$, we can see that a left step can have the walker finish on one foot or both feet, depending on whether it is a half or full step. By definition, if a person finishes on a particular foot, it rules out some actions; for example, if $\mathtt{F}_{i+1} = \mathtt{left}$, the action could not have been **`right`**. These zero conditional probability are omitted from the table.

The CPD for $\mathtt{F}_{i+1}$ for the conditioning cases where $\mathtt{S}_{i+1} = \mathtt{stumbling}$ is exactly the same as for `ok` except the p and q probability parameters will have lower values, representing the higher expectation of a fall; that is, $p_i' < p_i$, $q_i' < q_i$, for all relevant i.

If there are any variations on walking patterns for an individual patient, for example if one leg was injured, the DBN can be customised by varying the

[3] Also given by $\mathtt{bel(F}_i\mathtt{=off)}$; the redundancy is useful for describing the problem, but could be removed to improve computational efficiency.

Table 1. CPDs for step action node A, the foot node F, the Fall node and the walking status node S

P(F_0=left‖right‖)	= (1-r-s)/2	
P(F_0=both‖)	= r	
P(F_0=off‖)	= s	
P(A=left|F=right)	= u	alternate feet
P(A=right|F=right)	= v	hopping
P(A=none|F=right)	= 1-u-v	stationary
P(A={left‖right}|F=both)	= w/2	start with left or right
P(A=none|F=both)	= 1-w	stationary
P(A=none|F=off)	= 1	can't walk when off feet
P(F_{i+1}=left|F_i=right,A_i=left,S_{i+1}=ok)	= p_1	succ. alternate step
P(F_{i+1}=both|F_i=right,A_i=left,S_{i+1}=ok)	= q_1	half-step
P(F_{i+1}=off|F_i=right,A_i=left,S_{i+1}=ok)	= 1-p_1-q_1	fall prob
P(F_{i+1}=left|F_i=left,A_i=left,S_{i+1}=ok)	= p_2	succ. hop
P(F_{i+1}=both|F_i=left,A_i=left,S_{i+1}=ok)	= q_2	half-hop
P(F_{i+1}=off|F_i=left,A_i=left,S_{i+1}=ok)	= 1-p_2-q_2	fall prob
P(F_{i+1}=left|F_i=both,A_i=left,S_{i+1}=ok)	= p_3	succ. first step
P(F_{i+1}=both|F_i=both,A_i=left,S_{i+1}=ok)	= q_3	unsucc. first step
P(F_{i+1}=off|F_i=both,A_i=left,S_{i+1}=ok)	= 1-p_3-q_3	fall prob
P(F_{i+1}=left|F_i=left,A_i=none,S_{i+1}=ok)	= p_4	
P(F_{i+1}=off|F_i=left,A_i=none,S_{i+1}=ok)	= 1-p_4	fall when on left foot
P(F_{i+1}=right|F_i=right,A_i=none,S_{i+1}=ok)	= p_5	
P(F_{i+1}=off|F_i=right,A_i=none,S_{i+1}=ok)	= 1-p_5	fall when on right foot
P(F_{i+1}=both|F_i=both,A_i=none,S_{i+1}=ok)	= p_6	
P(F_{i+1}=off|F_i=both,A_i=none,S_{i+1}=ok)	= 1-p_6	fall when on both feet
P(F_{i+1}=off|F_i=off,A_i=left,S_{i+1}=any)	= 1	no "get up" action
P(Fall=T | F_{i+1}=off,F_i={left‖right‖both})	= 1	from upright to ground
P(Fall=F | F_{i+1}=any,F_i=off)	= 1	can't fall if on ground
P(S_{i+1}=ok|T_i=t)	= 1	if t $\geq$ y
P(S_{i+1}=stumbling|T_i=t)	= 1	if t $<$ y

probability parameters, s, r, p_i, q_i, u, v and w, and removing the assumption that left and right are completely symmetric. For example, we can relax the assumption that the person is equally likely to start on the left foot as the right. Note that having different p parameters indicates different expectations of a fall when the person is walking compared to hopping. Also, a person can end up off their feet even if the status node S is indicating **ok**.

The fall event node **Fall** has F_i and F_{i+1} as predecessors; a fall only occurs when the subject was on his or her feet to start with ($F_i \neq$ **off**), and finishes off their feet (F_{i+1} = **off**). [4]

The value of walking status node **S** is determined solely by the time between sensor readings (see next section for an extension which takes into account status history). In this DBN model, the **T** node has no predecessors. One possible model is to have uniform priors, or the prior can also be modified, based on sensor observations over time, to reflect an individual's ordinary walking speed.

When constructing the conditional probability distributions for the various observation nodes, the confidence in the observation is given by some value based on a model of the sensor's performance and is empirically obtainable; *pos* is the sensitivity of the positive sensor data, *neg* is the specificity of the negative sensor data (or, 1-*neg* is the probability of ghost data). We make the default assumption that missing or wrong data are equally likely — this need not be the case and can be replaced by any alternative plausible values.

Each observation node has a single predecessor: the mercury trigger observation node **M** has predecessor **F**; the foot-step action observation node **AO** has predecessor **A**; the time observation node **TO** has predecessor **T**. The conditional probability distributions for **M**, **AO** and **TO** are shown in Table 2. Note that the CPD for the case where the sensor is defective is uniform over the other time values; this could easily be changed to cluster around the true time interval. If the timing sensor fails and no data is obtained, fall diagnosis becomes impossible, so we do not handle the case of missing time data.

Note that when the monitoring begins, we do not need to have a known start state; we need only have a prior over the possible starting positions. Because the standard left foot, right foot, walking model, is represented by the conditional probability distribution between F_i and F_{i+1}, if the first data received is a **left** S_i, then after belief updating, the belief vector will include **bel**(F_i=**off**) = 0, **bel**(F_i=**left**) < 0.25, **bel**(F_i=**left**) > 0.25 and **bel**(F_i=**left**) > 0.25. The DBN presented is one possible model for the fall diagnosis problem; many other variations are possible. For example, the DBN does not handle the case where both foot switches provide data at the same time. See [10] for a comparison of the use of action nodes in this model with other monitoring and planning applications.

5 Results

The results described in this section were obtained using the Lisp-based IDEAL belief network development environment [15] on a GNU Common Lisp platform. We present results of a Fall Diagnosis network modelled for a given set of parameters: $s = 0.0$, $r = 0.9$, $u = 0.7$, $v = 0.2$, $w = 0.1$, $p_1 = 0.6$, $q_1 = 0.3$, $p'_1 =$

[4] We do not model the situation Davies described where the mercury trigger data is ignored if the time is ≥ x; this would be more correctly modelled by: adding an additional value, **sitting** to the state **F**; adding an additional value, **sit**, to the action **A**; adding another alternative, **sat**, to the fall event **fall**; adding a connection from T_i to A_i; changing the CPD for A_i to say that if the time is above the threshold, then the **sit** action is possible.

Table 2. CPDs for observation nodes **M** (mercury trigger), **AO** (foot switch), **TO** (time data)

P(M=T|Fall=T)	$= pos_1$	ok
P(M=F|Fall=T)	$= 1\text{-}pos_1$	missing
P(M=F|Fall=F)	$= neg_1$	ok
P(M=T|Fall=F)	$= 1\text{-}neg_1$	false alarm
P(AO=left|A=left)	$= pos_2$	ok
P(AO=right|A=right)	$= pos_2$	ok
P(AO=right|A=left)	$= (1\text{-}pos_2)/2$	wrong
P(AO=left|A=right)	$= (1\text{-}pos_2)/2$	wrong
P(AO=none|A=left)	$= (1\text{-}pos_2)/2$	missing
P(AO=none|A=right)	$= (1\text{-}pos_2)/2$	missing
P(AO=none|A=none)	$= neg_2$	ok
P(AO=left|A=none)	$= (1\text{-}neg_2)/2$	false alarm
P(AO=right|A=none)	$= (1\text{-}neg_2)/2$	false alarm
P(TO=x|T=x)	$= pos_3$	ok, $\mathbf{y} \neq \mathbf{x}$, T and TO have m values.
P(TO=y|T=x)	$= 1 - pos_3/m\text{-}1$,	ok, $\mathbf{y} \neq \mathbf{x}$, T and TO have m values.

0.5, $q_1' = 0.4$ $p_2 = 0.6$, $q_2 = 0.3$, $p_2' = 0.5$, $q_2' = 0.4$, $p_3 = 0.6$, $q_3 = 0.3$, $p_3' = 0.5$, $q_3' = 0.4$, $p_4 = 0.95$, $p_4' = 0.85$, $p_5 = 0.95$, $p_5' = 0.85$, $p_6 = 0.9$, $p_6' = 0.8$, $pos_1 = 0.9$, $pos_2 = 0.9$, $pos_3 = 0.9$, $neg_1 = 0.95$, $neg_2 = 0.95$. The **T** and **TO** time nodes had 4 possible values, $\mathtt{t}_1$, $\mathtt{t}_2$, $\mathtt{t}_3$, and $\mathtt{t}_4$; the lowest, $\mathtt{t}_1$ was below the threshold **y** and meant the subject was considered to be stumbling.

After constructing the DBN, we entered a sequence of evidence, that is simulated observations from the sensors, and performed belief updating after every new piece of evidence was added. Table 3 shows the posterior probabilities, or beliefs, of the values of nodes in the network across this sequence of data. For reasons of space, we left out the initial $\mathtt{S}_0$ node and the $\mathtt{T}_2$ and $\mathtt{TO}_2$ nodes from the model, and do not give all the beliefs, especially if they are uniform or otherwise obvious. Probabilities have been rounded to 4 decimal places. Evidence added results in a 1.0 belief for that value, shown in bold in the table; also bolded are the beliefs described below in the text. The evidence sequence added, and the effect on the beliefs, was as follows.

No evidence added: All beliefs are based on the parameters. Belief in an immediate fall is small, bel($\mathtt{Fall}_0$ = T)=0.1194, but chance of being off feet in 2 steps is higher, bel($\mathtt{F}_0$=T)=0.2238.

$\mathtt{TO}_0$ set to $\mathtt{t}_1$: This increases the probability that the person is stumbling, that is, bel($\mathtt{S}_1$ = **stumbling**)=0.9, which in turn slightly increases the belief in a fall, bel($\mathtt{Fall}_0$ = T) = 0.1828.

$\mathtt{AO}_0$ set to left: Foot switch information leads to a change in the belief in the initial starting state; bel($\mathtt{F}_0$=**right**) has increased from 0.05 to 0.2550, reflecting the model of alternate foot steps.

$\mathtt{M}_0$ **set to false:** The negative mercury trigger data makes it very unlikely that a fall occurred, bel($\mathtt{Fall}_0$=T)=0.0203.

$\mathtt{TO}_0$ **set to** $\mathtt{t}_2$**:** "Resetting" of the original timing data makes it less likely the person was stumbling, reducing the belief in a fall, bel($\mathtt{Fall}_0$=T) = 0.0098.

$\mathtt{M}_0$ **set to true:** However, resetting the mercury trigger data makes a fall most probable, bel($\mathtt{Fall}_0$=T)=0.6285, although there is still the chance that the sensor has given a wrong reading.

$\mathtt{M}_1$ **set to false,** $\mathtt{TO}_1$ **set to** $\mathtt{t}_4$**,** $\mathtt{AO}_1$ **set to none:** No action, and no mercury trigger data confirms the earlier fall, bel($\mathtt{Fall}_0$=T)=0.7903, since if the person is already on the ground they won't take a left or right step.

6 Extensions to the DBN

The states **imminent-fall**, **possible-fall**, and **stabilising** in the original state machine are an attempt to capture the idea that the history beyond the current time interval gives information about the likelihood of a fall soon. This is represented in a DBN by the use of a history node [9], which maintains a count of how long the agent has been exhibiting one type of behaviour. For our domain, this would be a status history node, $\mathtt{H}_i$, for each time slice; its predecessors are the previous and current walking status nodes, $\mathtt{S}_{i-1}$ and $\mathtt{S}_i$. H then becomes a predecessor of $\mathtt{F}_{i+1}$, and the CPD entries are changed so that the probability of falling is a function of the stumble count.

We can also improve the model of what a person's ordinary walking pace is by adding an arc from $\mathtt{T}_i$ to $\mathtt{T}_{i+1}$, which would allow a representation of the expectation that the walking pace should remain fairly constant.

The DBN described in the previous section provides a mechanism for handling (by implicitly rejecting) certain inconsistent data. It represents adequately the underlying assumptions about the data uncertainty, however it does not provide an explanation of *why* the observed sensor data might be incorrect. We can represent the most usual source of incorrect data, namely a defective sensor, by the addition of a sensor status node SS [8] for each sensor. Each sensor status node becomes a predecessor of the corresponding observation node, and there is a connection between sensor status nodes across time slices. See [10] for details of the extensions described in this section.

7 Conclusions

We have shown the development of a dynamic belief network model for fall diagnosis which overcomes the limitations of early work. Given evidence from sensor observations, the model outputs beliefs about the current walking status and makes predictions regarding future falls. The model represents possible sensor error, and is parametrised to allow customisation to the individual being monitored.

Table 3. Changing beliefs as evidence is added or changed.

Node	Val	None	$TO_0=t_1$	AO_0=left	M_0=F	$TO_0=t_2$	M_0=T	SET
T_0	t_1	0.25	0.9000	0.9000	0.8914	0.0305	0.0535	0.0616
	t_2	0.25	0.0333	0.0333	0.0361	0.9026	0.8812	0.8736
	t_3	0.25	0.0333	0.0333	0.0361	0.0334	0.0326	0.0323
	t_4	0.25	0.0333	0.0333	0.0361	0.0334	0.0326	0.0323
TO_0	t_1	0.25	**1.0**	**1.0**	**1.0**	0.0	0.0	0.0
	t_2	0.25	0.0	0.0	0.0	**1.0**	**1.0**	**1.0**
F_0	left	0.05	0.05	0.0870	0.0860	0.0856	0.0964	0.0911
	right	0.05	0.05	**0.2550**	0.2717	0.2515	0.2792	0.2767
	both	0.90	0.90	0.6581	0.6422	0.6628	0.6244	0.6322
	off	0.0	0.0	0.0	0.0	0.0	0.0	0.0
A_0	left	0.09	0.09	0.6403	0.6483	0.6453	0.6047	0.5427
	right	0.09	0.09	0.0356	0.0360	0.0359	0.0336	0.0302
	none	0.82	0.82	0.3241	0.3156	0.3188	0.3617	0.4271
AO_0	left	0.1265	0.1265	**1.0**	**1.0**	**1.0**	**1.0**	**1.0**
	right	0.1265	0.1265	0.0	0.0	0.0	0.0	0.0
	none	0.7470	0.7470	0.0	0.0	0.0	0.0	0.0
$Fall_0$	True	**0.1194**	**0.1828**	0.1645	**0.0203**	**0.0098**	**0.6285**	**0.7903**
	False	0.8806	0.8173	0.8355	0.9797	0.9902	0.3715	0.2096
M_0	True	0.1515	0.2053	0.1898	0.0	0.0	**1.0**	**1.0**
	False	0.8485	0.7947	0.8102	**1.0**	**1.0**	0.0	0.0
S_1	ok	0.75	0.1	0.1	0.1086	0.9695	0.9465	0.9383
	stum'g	0.25	**0.9**	0.9	0.8914	0.0305	0.0535	0.0617
F_1	left	0.0638	0.0425	0.2737	0.3208	0.5120	0.1921	0.0340
	right	0.0638	0.0425	0.0168	0.0197	0.0303	0.0114	0.0020
	both	0.7530	0.7322	0.5451	0.6391	0.4478	0.1680	0.1736
	off	0.1194	**0.1828**	0.1645	0.0203	0.0098	0.6285	0.7903
T_1	t_1	0.25	0.25	0.25	0.25	0.25	0.25	0.0326
	t_4	0.25	0.25	0.25	0.25	0.25	0.25	0.9006
TO_1	t_4	0.25	0.25	0.25	0.25	0.25	0.25	**1.0**
A_1	left	0.0950	0.0749	0.0938	0.1099	0.1461	0.0548	0.0035
	right	0.0950	0.0749	0.2222	0.2605	0.3869	0.1451	0.0092
	none	0.8090	0.8502	0.6841	0.6296	0.4670	0.8001	0.9872
AO_1	left	0.1308	0.1137	0.1297	0.1434	0.1741	0.0966	0.0
	right	0.1308	0.1137	0.2389	0.2714	0.3788	0.1734	0.0
	none	0.7383	0.7730	0.6315	0.5851	0.4671	0.7301	**1.0**
$Fall_1$	True	0.1044	0.0975	0.0959	0.1124	0.1099	0.0412	0.0024
	False	0.8956	0.9025	0.9041	0.8876	0.8901	0.9588	0.9976
M_1	True	0.1387	0.1329	0.1315	0.1455	0.1434	0.0850	0.0
	False	0.8612	0.8671	0.8685	0.8545	0.8566	0.9150	**1.0**
S_2	ok	0.75	0.75	0.75	0.75	0.75	0.75	0.9673
	stum'g	0.25	0.25	0.25	0.25	0.25	0.25	0.0327
F_2	left	0.0673	0.0531	0.0898	0.1053	0.1472	0.0552	0.0258
	right	0.0673	0.0531	0.1335	0.1565	0.2291	0.08594	0.0076
	both	0.6415	0.6136	0.5164	0.6055	0.5040	0.1891	0.1740
	off	**0.2238**	0.2802	0.2603	0.1327	0.1197	0.6698	0.7927

Acknowledgements We wish to thank Dr. Jon Oliver for suggesting this fall diagnosis problem as an application for dynamic belief networks.

References

1. P. Dagum and A. Galper. Forecasting sleep apnea with dynamic network models. In *Proceedings of the Ninth Conference on Uncertainty in AI*, pages 64–71, 1993.
2. P. Dagum, A. Galper, and E. Horvitz. Dynamic network models for forecasting. In *Proceedings of the 8th Conference on Uncertainty in Artificial Intelligence*, pages 41–48, 1992.
3. James Davies. Fall diagnosis with a mobile data network. Unpublished BCSE Honours Report, Dept. of Electrical Engineering, Monash University, 1995.
4. Thomas Dean and Michael P. Wellman. *Planning and control.* Morgan Kaufman Publishers, San Mateo, Ca., 1991.
5. Jeff Forbes, Tim Huang, Keiji Kanazawa, and Stuart Russell. The BATMobile: Towards a bayesian automated taxi. In *Proceedings of the 14th Int. Joint Conf. on Artificial Intelligence (IJCAI'95)*, pages 1878-1885, 1995.
6. U. Kjærulff. A computational scheme for reasoning in dynamic probabilistic networks. In *Proceedings of the 8th Conference on Uncertainty in Artificial Intelligence*, pages 121–129, 1992.
7. A. E. Nicholson and J. M. Brady. The data association problem when monitoring robot vehicles using dynamic belief networks. In *Proc. of the 10th European Conf. on Artificial Intelligence (ECAI-92)*, pages 689–693, 1992.
8. A. E. Nicholson and J. M. Brady. Sensor validation using dynamic belief networks. In *Proceedings of the 8th Conference on Uncertainty in Artificial Intelligence*, pages 207–214, 1992.
9. A. E. Nicholson and J. M. Brady. Dynamic belief networks for discrete monitoring. *IEEE Systems, Man and Cybernetics*, 24(11), 1994.
10. A.E. Nicholson. A case study in dynamic belief networks: monitoring walking, fall prediction and detection. Technical Report Technical Report 96/251, Department of Computer Science, Monash University, 1996.
11. Judea Pearl. *Probabilistic Reasoning in Intelligent Systems.* Morgan Kaufmann, San Mateo, Ca., 1988.
12. Gregory M. Provan. Tradeoffs in constructing and evaluating temporal influence diagrams. In *Proceedings of the 9th Conference on Uncertainty in Artificial Intelligence*, pages 40–47, 1993.
13. David Pynadeth and Michael P. Wellman. Accounting for context in plan recogniition, with application too traffic monitoring. In *Proceedings of the 11th Conference on Uncertainty in Artificial Intelligence*, pages 472–481, 1995.
14. Stuart Russell and Peter Norvig. *Artificial Intelligence: A Modern Approach.* Prentice-Hall, 1994.
15. Sampath Srinivas and Jack Breese. Ideal: Influence diagram evaluation and analysis in lisp. Technical Report Technical Memorandum No. 23, Rockwell International Science Center, 1989.

Remembrance of Discourse Based on Textual Continuity: A Spreading Activation Network

Samuel W.K. Chan and James Franklin
School of Computer Science & Engineering
The University of New South Wales
Sydney NSW 2052 Australia

Abstract. In this paper, we present a computational model for transforming discourses into Quasi-Mental Clusters (QMCs) through a convergence process. The process is interpreted as a particular transformation of a given set of discourse segments and concepts by examining the textual continuity. Examinations include testing the *local cohesion* in a cohesion parsing as well as the *global coherence* in semantic decomposition. In the convergence process, sentences in a discourse are represented as nodes in a spreading activation network. Competing coalitions of the nodes drive the network into a stable equilibrium. We argue the resulting QMCs are useful data structures in remembrance, summarization and knowledge discovery in discourses.

1 Introduction

Understanding a discourse is considered to involve a series of specific processing phases whose final result is a complete semantic, mental representation [13,14]. This result is not only a representation of the text, but rather of what the text is about. It has been shown that when a reader is asked to recall a discourse, vast amounts of information within the discourse are found to be reduced to essentials [2,7]. Details are selectively ignored in order to produce a distilled version of the original text. This process emphasizes central elements of the discourse while the peripheral details are neglected. It is further demonstrated that discourse can be represented as a skeleton, or a summary, in which the relationships among the clauses can be chunked in a way that replicates the semantic structure of the original discourse [11]. Textual continuity, which differentiates a text from a random sequence of sentences, is a prime factor in discourse summarization [6].

Any process model for summarization and recall must confront a number of difficult questions: Exactly what kinds of semantic relations are crucial in building the discourse structure? What processes are used to distil the discourse into essentials for recall? In this paper, we will propose a method for discourse analysis that addresses each of these issues. The most fundamental objective is to construct a computational model which generates the Quasi-Mental Clusters (QMCs) from discourse. These clusters represent the narrative prose and the relations among the ideas in discourse. In this paper, first, we give an overview of our discourse representation and the system architecture. In Section 3, we describe a *cohesion parsing* based on constraint propagation, followed by a brief discussion on semantic decomposition. Section 5 shows how the QMCs are formed with a detailed example. Experimental results are shown in Section 6, followed by a discussion.

2 Discourse Representation and Architecture

It is generally agreed that discourse is divided into constituent *discourse segments* and comprises intentions and relations among them. The intentions provide the basic rationale for the discourse, and the relations represent the connections among the segments [9]. In our consideration of how text-content is represented, a *discourse network D* is employed to represent the semantic relationships existing among the segments as shown in Figure 1.

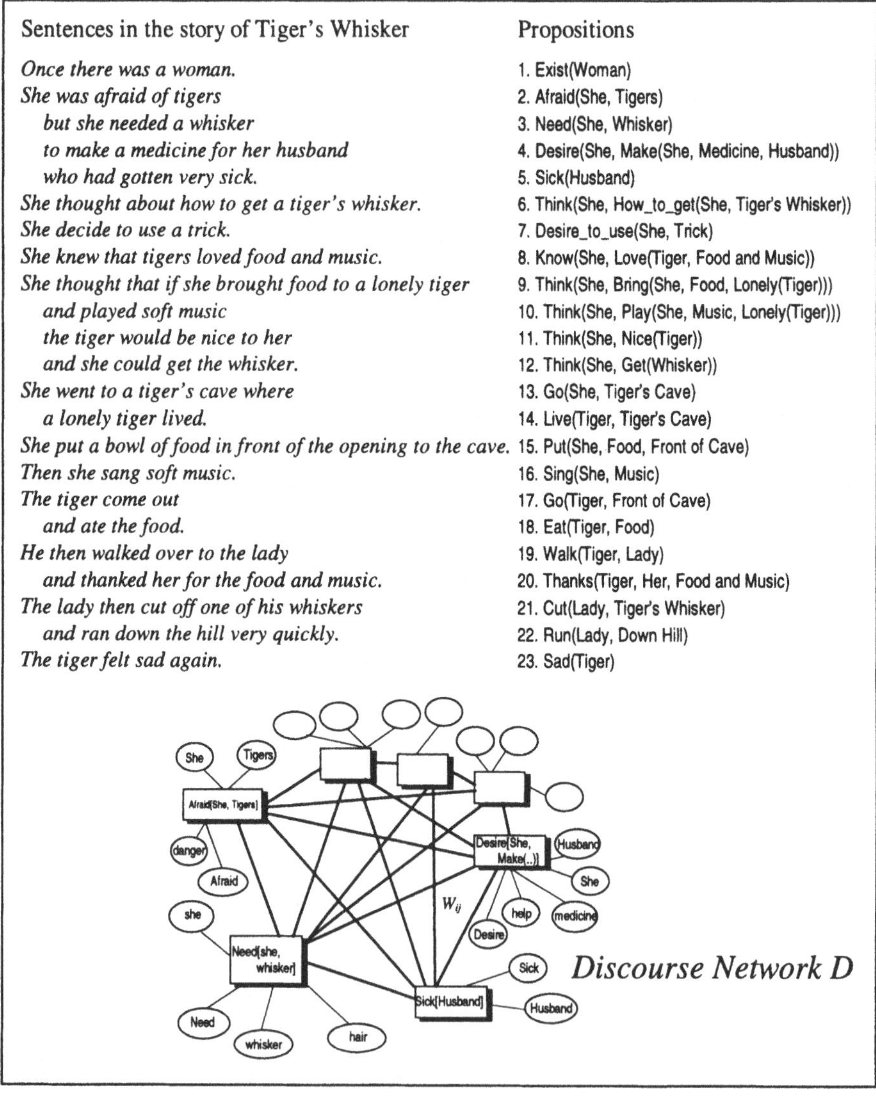

Sentences in the story of Tiger's Whisker	Propositions
Once there was a woman.	1. Exist(Woman)
She was afraid of tigers	2. Afraid(She, Tigers)
but she needed a whisker	3. Need(She, Whisker)
to make a medicine for her husband	4. Desire(She, Make(She, Medicine, Husband))
who had gotten very sick.	5. Sick(Husband)
She thought about how to get a tiger's whisker.	6. Think(She, How_to_get(She, Tiger's Whisker))
She decide to use a trick.	7. Desire_to_use(She, Trick)
She knew that tigers loved food and music.	8. Know(She, Love(Tiger, Food and Music))
She thought that if she brought food to a lonely tiger	9. Think(She, Bring(She, Food, Lonely(Tiger)))
and played soft music	10. Think(She, Play(She, Music, Lonely(Tiger)))
the tiger would be nice to her	11. Think(She, Nice(Tiger))
and she could get the whisker.	12. Think(She, Get(Whisker))
She went to a tiger's cave where	13. Go(She, Tiger's Cave)
a lonely tiger lived.	14. Live(Tiger, Tiger's Cave)
She put a bowl of food in front of the opening to the cave.	15. Put(She, Food, Front of Cave)
Then she sang soft music.	16. Sing(She, Music)
The tiger come out	17. Go(Tiger, Front of Cave)
and ate the food.	18. Eat(Tiger, Food)
He then walked over to the lady	19. Walk(Tiger, Lady)
and thanked her for the food and music.	20. Thanks(Tiger, Her, Food and Music)
The lady then cut off one of his whiskers	21. Cut(Lady, Tiger's Whisker)
and ran down the hill very quickly.	22. Run(Lady, Down Hill)
The tiger felt sad again.	23. Sad(Tiger)

Figure 1: A modified version of *Tiger's Whisker* story and its corresponding propositions are shown above. A fragment discourse network *D* representing the story is displayed below. The rectangle boxes represent the propositions while the ellipses are the corresponding context nodes.

The processing operation which we put forward is not a direct translation of encountered discourse into the structure, but rather a procedural model which establishes a network of relations between segments in the discourse. We begin by defining a discourse network *D*, as a set of propositions, which stands in functional relations to each other and is represented as a graph characterized by a 5-tuple
$D = <V, C, A, E, W>$ where

- *V* is a finite set of propositions composing the discourse.
- *C* is a finite set of context nodes composing the propositions.
- *A* is a set of arcs representing the semantic relations amongst the propositions.
- *E* is a set of weights of the arcs.
- *W* is a function $W: A \rightarrow E$ which assigns weights to arcs.

As interest has extended generally from what happens within sentences to what happens between or beyond them, the main factors in textual continuity, *local cohesion* and *global coherence*, have become popular issues in discourse analysis. Local cohesion is the coherence among the sentences in the nearby segments. In Halliday's terminology, sentences are cohesive to the extent that there are many expressions whose interpretations depend in some way on the analysis of the preceding expressions in the discourse [12]. In addition, it has been observed that not every sequence of sentences makes up a text. In a coherent text, sentences are perceived as working together to build up a unified whole through global coherence [19]. In order to reflect a complete account of how readers interpret sentences as part of a larger discourse, in the next sections, we shall develop a means whereby textual continuity can be formally modelled and quantitative coefficients are devised to assess the degree of continuity of a discourse.

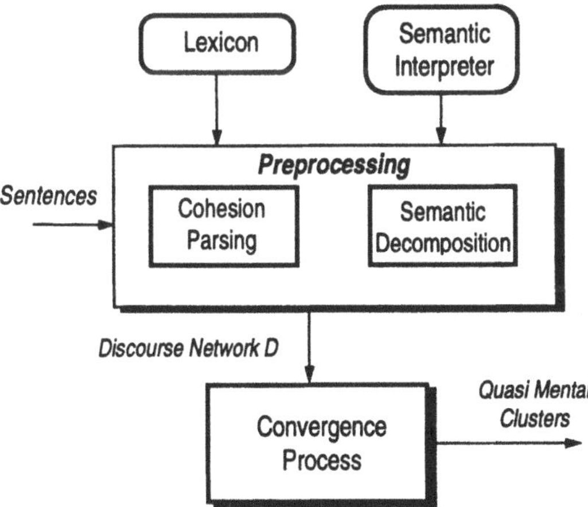

Figure 2: The System Architecture

The architecture that we present in this paper is outlined in Figure 2. Sentences, in terms of propositions, are input into the system. In the preprocessing, cohesion parsing is first deployed and constraints are efficiently propagated in the parsing in order to resolve semantic ambiguity as well as filter out any incohesive propositions. Global coherence is analyzed in the semantic decomposition. As a result, a discourse network D, as shown in Figure 1, is formed. QMCs are encapsulated in the convergence process. We shall describe the details in the following sections.

3 Cohesion Parsing

Cohesion parsing, for each incoming proposition, is achieved in a constraint net which is formulated as a constraint satisfaction problem over a set of finite elements [18]. The elements in the net may represent words, phrases, and more importantly, the buffers. Buffers are designed to carry each prior analyzed proposition over into the current processing cycle, in the hope that they will serve as common bridging elements between the propositions. An efficient *filtering algorithm* is employed to reduce the incohesive ones.

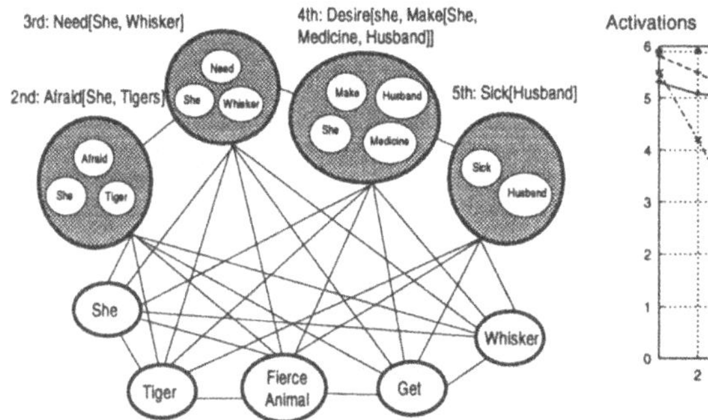

Figure 3: It shows a constraint net with the proposition buffers while the sixth proposition is under analysis in the cohesion parsing.

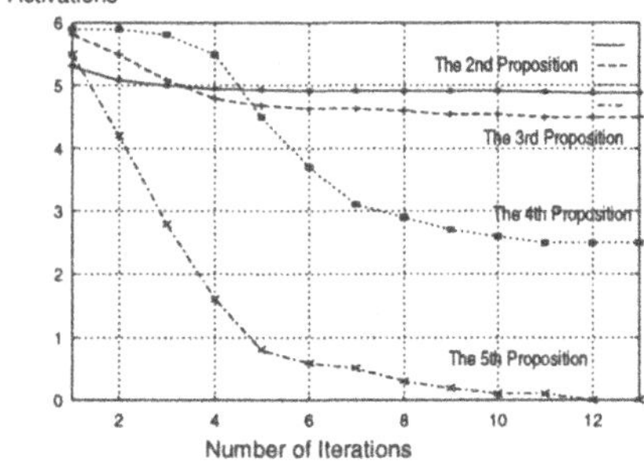

Figure 4: The activations change in the buffers during the cohesion parsing (All the propositions are shown in Figure 1.)

3.1 Formation of Initial Constraint Net

Whenever a proposition is processed, both textual information and sentential knowledge are extracted from a lexicon. As a result, not only a list of linguistic elements is activated, but also a fully interconnected constraint net is constructed. Figure 3 shows an initial constraint net while the sixth proposition, as shown in Figure 1, is under analysis. Connections among elements have strength values which are calculated through a knowledge extraction process. The process makes use of logical inferences in a subsymbolic lexicon. Details of the extraction process are omitted due to the limited scope of this paper; however, the interested readers may refer to the authors' publications [3-5]. A brief summary is as follows:

- Links between elements may be deduced from some knowledge rules. For example, the rule "*tiger→danger→afraid*" may give positive links between *tiger*, *danger* and *afraid.*
- Elements have positive links if they have high similarity measures, for example, *tiger↔fierce animal*.
- Links will be set to positive if the elements are the overlapping arguments [17], for instance, the elements, *she*, *tiger*, *whisker* in Figure 3.
- Strong negative links may arise when elements, with both alternative meanings of a homonym, are constructed.
- Others may be set to small negatives.

This rough, piecemeal, and approximate representations of the proposition is then subjected to the cohesion parsing using a filtering algorithm. The algorithm is to reduce the dimensionality of the net, as well as to analyze the influence of each proposition buffer with respect to the current one, so that a very complicated net could act as if only a small number of independent elements or buffers are involved.

3.2 The Filtering Algorithm

The algorithm is used to integrate the meanings into a coherent whole, or more importantly, it is used to identify the incohesive buffers and remove them from the context.

```
The knowledge matrix K is derived from the knowledge extraction process as
shown in Section 3.1
Filtering–Algorithm
for each proposition I do
begin
    allocate a buffer for each prior analyzed proposition in the net
    for each linguistic element i in I do
    begin
          allocate a node for the element i in the constraint net
          allocate some associated nodes for element i from the lexicon
          assign the initial activation values, U_0(i) for all the nodes
    end
    derive a matrix K, which contains connection strengths between the nodes
    while tolerance ≥ threshold do
    begin
          U_{t+1} ← T[U_t K], where T is a vector normalization operation
          calculate the new tolerance by comparing U_t with U_{t+1}
    end
    evaluate the activation of I, a_I(0)=ΣU_f, where U_f is the final activation of
    the linguistic element f in I
end
```

The parsing depends on reactivating the prior analyzed propositions. The linguistic elements, both in the proposition and the buffers, strengthen or inhibit each other until a stable state is reached. Figure 4 shows the activation changes in the corresponding buffers. Activations of the buffers, with little cohesion, will readily decay to zero. On the contrary, the highly cohesive propositions have steady activations throughout the parsing. As a result, the activation change in each buffer indicates the degree of cohesion of each previous proposition with respect to the current one. Let $LC = (LC)_{ij}$ be a square matrix representing the weights defined only by the effect of local cohesion,

$$LC_{ij} = \exp(-\varepsilon \,|\, \mu_{ij} \,|) \qquad \text{where}$$

$$\mu_{ij} = \left.\left(\frac{\text{change of activation of buffer } i}{\text{activation of buffer } i}\right)\right|_{\text{proposition } j} \tag{1}$$

4 Semantic Decomposition

Local cohesion goes a long way towards explaining how the sentences of a discourse hang together, but it does not tell the whole story. A discourse plainly has to be coherent as well as cohesive, in that the concepts and relationships expressed should be relevant to each other, thus enabling readers to make plausible inference about the underlying meaning. For example, the following excerpt, ".. *A week has seven days. Every day I feed my cat. It has four legs. It is on the mat which has three letters. ..*" is highly cohesive but nonetheless incoherent. Although temporality, spatiality, and causality are the intertwining links in global coherence when behavioral episodes are unfolded in discourse [19], we limit our scope in this article to the discussion of causal continuity, simply because it is ascertained that readers attempt to tie each event or fact encountered to the prior text and relevant background knowledge [8]. To capture the causal continuity, although there has been much discussion in handling inferences at the sentential and inter-sentential levels, in this empirical study, each of the subsequent propositions is read in terms of whether it instantiates some expectation of the previous statements. When an instantiation is found for a prior event, an arrow is assigned manually to the instantiating event from the event that is causally prior to it. Although the assignment is hand-crafted in this empirical study, it needn't be very precise or sophisticated. It is to be just powerful enough so that the right connections are likely to be among those generated, even though irrelevant or even outright inappropriate connections will also be deduced. In our simulations, let $GC = (GC)_{ij}$ be a square matrix representing connections defined only by the effect of causal continuity. The proposition pairs that are involved in the causal continuity are given mutually excitatory connections, where

$$GC_{ij} = \begin{cases} \xi > 0, & \text{if units } i, j \text{ are coherent related} \\ 0, & \text{otherwise} \end{cases} \tag{2}$$

5 The Convergence Process

An overall weight matrix W in the discourse network D is constructed by a combination of each effect as discussed above and shown in (3).

$$W_{ij} = \begin{cases} \omega_1 LC_{ij} + \omega_2 GC_{ij}, & \text{if } LC_{ij} \text{ or } GC_{ij} \neq 0 \\ -\eta, & \text{or otherwise} \end{cases} \tag{3}$$

Each entry W_{ij} in W is a numerical value that represents the degree of continuity between the propositions. It is apparent that positive excitatory links, with values $\omega_1 LC_{ij}+\omega_2 GC_{ij}$, are between all the linguistic related nodes while negative inhibitory links, $-\eta$, are among the unrelated ones. ω_1, ω_2 are constants specifying the relative importance of each effect.

5.1 The Convergence Algorithm

When the matrix W has been constructed, one can start the convergence process to encapsulate the Quasi-Mental Clusters (QMCs) from the discourse network D. The clusters are extracted via the interactive activation and competition mechanisms. The convergence algorithm is summarized as follow:

Step 1: Construct the overall weight matrix, W, as shown above. Initialize a state vector for the propositions, $A(0) = (a_1(0), a_2(0), \ldots, a_M(0))$ where $a_i(0)$ is the activation of the proposition i as shown in the filtering algorithm. M is the number of the propositions in the discourse.

Step 2: At each discrete time, t, activations spread among the nodes of propositions and are updated by the following function:

$A(t+1) = \beta A(0) + \gamma A(t) + \alpha WA(t)$

Step 3: Vector $A(t+1)$ is normalized according to the saturation and habituation functions.

$A(t+1) = [SAT\,(A(t+1))]\,\sigma(t)$ where

$$SAT(x) = \begin{cases} 1, & 1 < x \\ x, & -1 \leq x \leq 1 \\ -1, & x < -1 \end{cases}$$

Step 4: Reinforcement of W_{ij}, is given by the modified Hebbian learning, where $\delta W_{ij}(t) = \varphi\{[a_i(t+1) - a_i(t)]a_j(t) + [a_j(t+1) - a_j(t)]a_i(t)\}$ where φ is the learning rate.

Step 5: Apply steps 2 to 4 for a number of iterations.

Step 6: The final strength between each pair of node i, j in discourse network is $W_{ij}^* = \Psi(W_{ij})$,

$\Psi(x) = \dfrac{1}{1+e^{-\lambda(x-\theta\bar{x})}}$ where λ is the gain, θ is the linkage constant, and $\bar{x}$ is the mean of x.

The algorithm is a modified version of Brain-State-in-a-Box network with M nodes which are highly interconnected and feedback upon themselves. It is proved to be capable of capturing the main properties of the human conceptual systems and has been used in various psychological models [1]. Information in this system is represented by an M-dimensional vector. The system operates by accepting a pattern of activations and amplifying that pattern through the feedback loop. In step 2, the system receives a constant input, $\beta A(0)$, in which the initial activation of each proposition is constantly present. The second term, $\gamma A(t)$, causes the current state to decay slightly. This term has the qualitative effect of causing error to eventually decay to zero as long as γ is less than 1. The third term, $\alpha WA(t)$, passes the current state through the matrix and adds more information reconstructed from the cross connections. In step 3, the saturation function $SAT(x)$ is the nonlinearity in the system. This confines the states to the hypercube $[-1, 1]^M$. When released from the initial state, the discourse network converges to one of the stable vertices of the hypercube. In addition, $\sigma(t)$ is introduced as a habituation variable into the system. It provides a mechanism to get the node state out of a corner it has gotten into. Once a node has reached its maximum firing rate, this process becomes effective over a fixed period of time and lowers the input sensitivity of the node. The formation and the reinforcement of the weights are represented in step 4. It is apparent that the strongest connections will tend to form between pairs of nodes that maintain high levels of activation for a prolonged period of time. Finally, the function Ψ, in step 6, serves to eliminate the weaker connections which result from weak associations.

5.2 An Example

In order to illustrate the above ideas clearly, the children's story, as shown in Figure 1, is demonstrated in a series of simulations. Figure 5 illustrates the discourse network so formed with 23 nodes, each representing a proposition, with context nodes being suppressed, and about 60 semantic connections amongst them. The dotted lines represent the links of local cohesion and the causal continuities between propositions are in solid arrows while the inhibitory connections are not shown. The strength of each connection is defined in (3) and is then subjected to the convergence process.

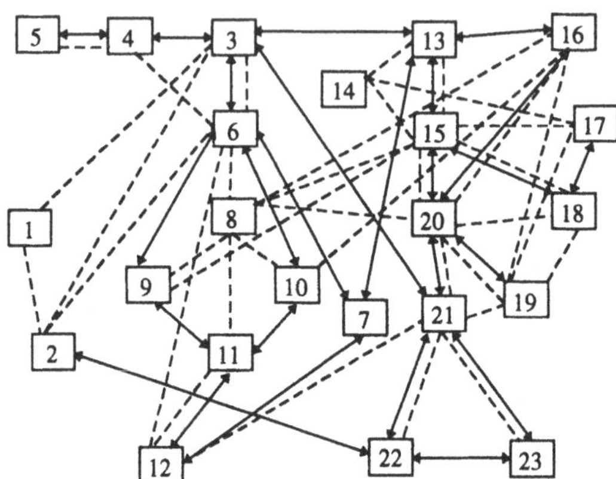

Figure 5: The Story of *Tiger's Whisker* in the form of discourse network

In the convergence process, activations of the propositions are changed and a re-arranged pattern of activations is shown in Figure 6. The three-dimensional mesh plot is interpreted by noting that the height of each point in the mesh plot corresponds to the activation of a proposition in the discourse network. All points lying on the same horizontal line correspond to the same proposition (e.g. 8. *KNOW* (*She, LOVE* (*Tiger, Food and Music*))) at different points in time. All points lying on the same vertical line correspond to the activations of all propositions associated with a situation at a particular instant of time where time is ordered from the left-hand side of the graph to the right-hand side.

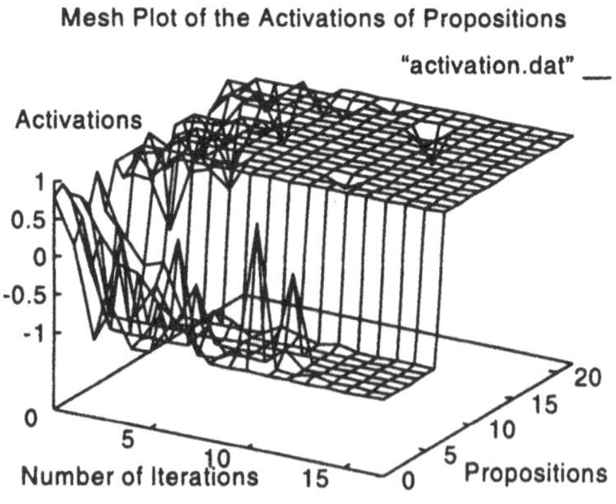

Figure 6: The activation change in the story

In Figure 6, it is apparent, after 15 iterations, all propositions become saturated with activations either -1 or 1. Figure 7 shows the resultant QMCs in the example.

The gray lines and solid lines represent the clusters formed with final strengths equal to 0.8 and 1.0 respectively.

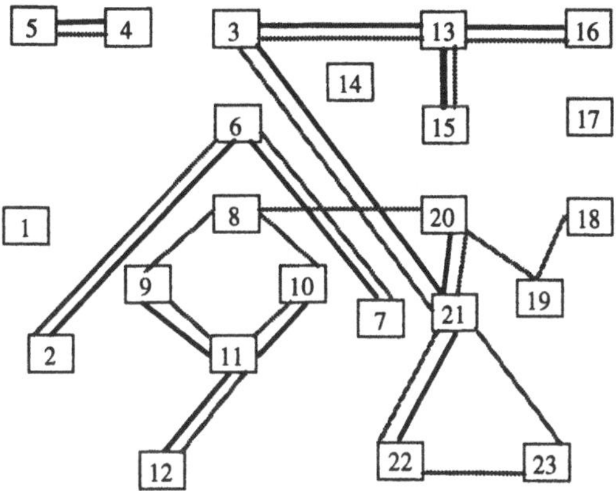

Figure 7: The Final Quasi-Mental Clusters (QMCs)

Obviously, the likelihood of extracting the QMCs from the discourse during the convergence process depends on the textual continuity and the activations that the propositions have in the circumstances. These clusters are expected to be better retained over time because they are consolidated into a more coherent representation. These clusters can be regarded as the chunks of knowledge extracted from the discourse. For instance, the cluster 3-13-15-16 may suggest the fact *"Fawning is one of the ways of getting what you want."* The singletons, the ones without any connections, such as the 1st, 14th & 17th propositions, are less likely to be recalled.

6 Results

The prototype of the system is developed in C and implemented on a DEC Alpha 2000 5/250 under the UNIX environment. Simulation experiments, with ten proposition buffers, were conducted to illustrate the effectiveness of our method. We restrict ourselves, in this article, to stories describing sequences of events which follow one another in approximately linear temporal sequences. However, the ideas suggested here are certainly not only applicable to this restricted class of stories. In our experiments, four children's stories by Stein & Glenn [15] are analyzed in a series of simulations as shown in above. We compare our resultant QMCs with the psychological model, proposed by Trabasso & Sperry [16], in which only causal linkage is used to recall from memory and their experiments are done with two groups of 12 fifth-grade children. Text information is recalled after a long period of time. Some statistical data, including the correlation coefficients for each of the four stories, are shown in Table 1. In the Table, each correlation coefficient compares the number of connections a story clause possessed with respect to Trabasso's representation to the number of connections a story clause possessed with respect to our QMCs. Although the correlation coefficients are not significantly high, they suggest the QMCs preserves some of the functional properties of the psychological findings. In particular, nodes with more connections in their findings also have higher connectivity in our QMCs.

Story	Story 1	Story 2	Story 3	Story 4
Number of words	163	173	178	160
Number of sentences	13	17	10	13
Number of propositions	23	25	23	25
% of QMCs formed*	0.31	0.38	0.34	0.42
Correlation coeff.*	0.62	0.56	0.53	0.57
% of QMCs formed**	0.20	0.26	0.23	0.29
Correlation coeff.**	0.51	0.42	0.65	0.45

Table 1: Comparison of the QMCs with Trabasso's model for strength = 0.8*, 1.0**. *Tiger's Whisker, Judy's Birthday, Epaminondas, The Fox & the Bear* are the four stories under analysis respectively.

7 General Discussion

The structure of discourse has been studied from many perspectives using a variety of terms. For example, Halliday and Hasan distinguish between cohesion, which arises from nonstructural semantic ties in text, and coherence, which arises from the structural relations of syntax, morphology, and phonology [12]. Trabasso and Sperry advocate causal coherence as the major textual continuity in building up a discourse [16]. The importance of a discourse segment in a text depends directly upon the number and the quality of the relations that the segment has to others. van Dijk and Kintsch choose not to distinguish between cohesion and coherence, and focus their efforts on semantic coherence [17]. Centering theory concurs with these approaches in the view that the essential issue in discourse analysis is the semantic integration of a text [10,11]. However, it does not distinguish among different kinds of coherence, instead concentrating on specifying how a coherent interpretation can be achieved via a variety of linguistic cues. In this paper, we have identified the general "thread" of discourse as well as the way that individual sentences fit together to achieve understanding. We have discussed a model of discourse summarization and recall, based on textual continuity, in a spreading activation network. It is not our intention to imply that the model presented here fully captures the various types of continuity which a discourse might exhibit. Rather, the purpose has been to focus on the organization and the semantic chunking of discourse. A distinctive property of our model is it incorporates the discourse analysis on the basis of the local cohesion and global coherence. Experiments show our model captures some important aspects of the remembrance of discourse.

One of the components that is not developed in our model is linguistic parsing. This model bypasses this stage and starts out with a non-proper text, i.e., a sequence of propositions. Our process only takes place after the discourse has already been divided into propositions. Despite of this issue, our model provides a promising approach in sentence processing research.

Acknowledgements

The authors would like to thank two of the anonymous reviewers for their encouraging comments and suggestions. The first author is also grateful to the financial support from Australian Postgraduate Award, University of New South Wales postgraduate scholarship, and Ansett Australia award.

References

[1] Anderson, J.A., & Murphy, G.L. (1986). Psychological concepts in a parallel system. *Physica D*, **22**, 318-336.

[2] Brainerd, C.J., & Reyna, V.F. (1990). Gist is the grist: Fuzzy-trace theory and the new intuitionism. *Development Review*, **10**, 1, 3-47.

[3] Chan, S.W.K. (1995). Inferences in natural language understanding. *Proceedings of the Fourth IEEE International Conference on Fuzzy Systems*, Yokohama, Japan, 935-940.

[4] Chan, S.W.K., & Franklin, J. (1994). Symbolic connectionism in tiers: A strategy of discourse comprehension. In C. Zhang, J. Debenham, & D. Lukose (Eds.), *Artificial Intelligence: Sowing the Seeds for the Future*, World Scientific, 434-441.

[5] Chan, S.W.K., & Franklin, J. (1995). A neurosymbolic integrated model for semantic ambiguation resolution. *Proceedings of the IEEE International Conference on Neural Networks*, Perth, Australia, 2965-2970.

[6] Ehrlich, M.-F., & Charolles, M. (1991). Aspects of textual continuity: Psycholinguistic approaches. In G. Denhiere & J.-P. Rossi (Eds.), *Text & Text Processing*, North-Holland, 269-285.

[7] Ellis, H.C., & Hunt, R.R. (1989). *Fundamentals of Human Memory and Cognition*. Dubuque: Brown.

[8] Fletcher, C.R., Hummel, J.E., & Marsolek, C.J. (1990). Causality and the allocation of attention during comprehension. *Journal of Experimental Psychology: Learning, Meaning, and Cognition*, **16**, 2, 233-240.

[9] Grosz, B.J. (1974). The structure of task oriented dialogs. *IEEE Symposium on Speech Recognition,* Pittsburgh, 250-253.

[10] Grosz, B.J., Joshi, A.K., & Weinstein, S. (1995). Centering: A framework for modeling the local coherence of discourse. *Computational Linguistics*, **21**, 203-225.

[11] Grosz, B.J., & Sidner, C.L. (1986). Attention, intention, and the structure of discourse. *Computational Linguistics*, **12**, 175-204.

[12] Halliday, M.A.K., & Hasan, R. (1976). *Cohesion in English*. London: Longman.

[13] Johnson-Laird, P.N. (1983). *Mental Models*. Cambridge, MA: Harvard University Press.

[14] Kintsch, W., & van Dijk, T.A. (1978). Toward a model of text comprehension and production. *Psychological Review*, **85**, 5, 363-394.

[15] Stein, N.L., & Glenn, C.G. (1979). An analysis of story comprehension in elementary school children. In R.O. Freedle (Ed.), *New Directions in Discourse Processing*. Hillsdale, NJ: Erlbaum, 53-120.

[16] Trabasso, T., & Sperry, L.L. (1984). Causal cohesion and story coherence. In H. Mandl, N.L. Stein, & T. Trabasso (Eds.), *Learning and Comprehension of Text*, NJ: Erlbaum, 83-111.

[17] van Dijk, T.A., & Kintsch, W. (1983). *Strategies of Discourse Comprehension*. NY: Academic.

[18] Waltz, D.L., & Pollack, J.B. (1985). Massively parallel parsing: A strongly interactive model of natural language interpretation. *Cognitive Science*, **9**, 51-74.

[19] Zwaan, R.A., Magliano, J.P., & Graesser, A.C. (1995). Dimensions of situation model construction in narrative comprehension. *Journal of Experimental Psychology: Learning, Memory, and Cognition*, **21**, 2, 386-397.

Lexical Access Using Minimum Message Length Encoding

Ian Thomas, Ingrid Zukerman, Jonathan Oliver[1] and Bhavani Raskutti[2]

[1] Department of Computer Science, Monash University, Clayton, VICTORIA 3168, AUSTRALIA
[2] Artificial Intelligence Section, Telstra Research Laboratories, Clayton, VICTORIA 3168, AUSTRALIA

Abstract. A method for deriving equivalence classes for lexical access in speech recognition is considered, which automatically derives equivalence classes from training data using unsupervised learning and the Minimum Message Length Criterion. These classes model insertions, deletions and substitutions in an input phoneme string due to mis-recognition and mis-pronunciation, and allow unlikely word candidates to be eliminated quickly. This in turn allows a more detailed examination of the remaining candidates to be carried out efficiently.

1 Introduction

In the process of speech recognition, we compare the signal parameters that represent an input word (or utterance) with a set of signal parameters that represents in some form the training words (or utterances). Regardless of the form of the signal parameters, if we are able to quickly and reliably eliminate a significant portion of the candidates from further consideration, we can then use an exhaustive matching method for the remaining candidates.

The *Lexical Access Problem* consists of deciding which word from a lexicon corresponds to an input sequence of phonemes (coming from some underlying speech recognition process). The lexicon is typically a large collection of words, along with their corresponding phoneme sequences, as seen in a training corpus.

Lexical access is more difficult than simple table lookup, as a phoneme sequence may have extra or missing phonemes, and some existing phonemes may have been transcribed incorrectly. These insertions, deletions and substitutions may be due to (1) mis-recognition, through poor equipment, bad recording conditions, or poorly trained phoneme models; or (2) mis-pronunciation, where a speaker has said a word in a different way to lexicon versions of that word. Mis-pronunciation is caused primarily by different dialects and accents. For example, the word "another" may been pronounced as several different sequences of phonemes:

Lexicon entry[1]:	another	ax n ah dh axr
Data:	another	er n ah dh axr
	another	en ah dh axr
	another	ax n ah dh er

This paper considers an unsupervised learning method which eliminates large numbers of the candidates from consideration during lexical access, so that a more detailed examination of the remaining candidates can be carried out.

1.1 Cohort Theory

A standard way to quickly eliminate candidates is variously called the *Phonetic Refinement Algorithm* or *Cohort Theory* [7]. In this method, a set of *equivalence classes* is found, such that each class is a set of words from the lexicon that are the same under some sort of filter or encoding of their characteristics [1]. Knowing the equivalence class that an input word goes into eliminates from consideration candidates from other classes.

A common approach for using equivalence classes consists of segmenting lexicon words into sequences of *Broad Sound Groups (BSGs)*, such as vowels, fricatives and stops, and classifying these sequences into equivalence classes. The input speech signals are then segmented into BSG sequences and matched against the equivalence classes. The use of BSGs supports a more reliable recognition process than that supported by individual phonemes, since an error in a phoneme in an input string is most likely to occur within the same BSG [10]. Hence, a word with an erroneous phoneme is likely to end up in the same equivalence class as the correct word. A more complicated second stage of verification may then be used to uncover the intended word corresponding to the input phoneme string.

Insertions and deletions in a phoneme string can be handled in a variety of different ways. In practical systems, the classification of an input word into equivalence classes is often done by a Dynamic Programming matching algorithm applied to a common-initial-subsequence tree that is built up from the BSG sequences. The costs of individual phoneme insertions and deletions vary to reflect known acoustic effects and constrain the final equivalence classes produced [2, 4]. Another way of handling insertions and deletions is to store a representation of each word in the lexicon, and produce alternatives using a set of hand-crafted phonological rules that account for the insertion and deletion of phonemes in various contexts [8, 9]. Huttenlocher and Zue [5] use two methods for handling insertions and deletions. They use multiple versions of each word to account for likely insertions and deletions, and restrict analysis to parts of words that are most invariant (e.g., stressed syllables).

[1] Phonemes are described using ARPAbet symbols, which are used in the TIMIT corpus [3]. ARPAbet is a typewritten version of the standard International Phonetic Alphabet.

The method presented in this paper automatically derives equivalence classes which contain words that differ from each other due to the substitution, insertion and/or deletion of phonemes. This obviates the need to apply a separate process which considers phoneme insertions and deletions during the initial hypothesis-constraining phase of the word recognition process.

2 Method

In cohort theory, the words in an equivalence class must be similar acoustically. We use a form of unsupervised learning to determine the "best" set of equivalence classes which represents a corpus of training words. We then place a test phoneme string into the class which has training items that are most similar to it.

2.1 Unsupervised Learning using Snob

The Snob system [6, 11, 12] classifies objects into classes that are characterised by "similar" values for attribute measurements of its member objects. The system uses a number of heuristics to search for likely classes, and then measures the quality of the classes chosen. This quality measure is used to guide the search for the "best" classes.

The quality of a class distribution is evaluated by means of the *Minimum Message Length (MML)* criterion [13]. A set of classes is represented as a message made up of two parts: (1) a *class description segment* that describes the number of classes and the distribution of attribute values of the objects within each class; and (2) an *object description segment* that describes for each object the class to which it belongs and the deviation of the object's attribute values from the distribution of attribute values in the class.

The Minimum Message Length criterion is derived from Bayes Theorem:

$$P(H|D) = \frac{P(H) \times P(D|H)}{P(D)}$$

where H is the hypothesis and D is the data.

An optimal code for an event E with probability $P(E)$ has message length $ML(E) = -\log_2(P(E))$. Hence, the message length for a hypothesis given the data is:

$$ML(H|D) = ML(H) + ML(D|H)$$

which corresponds to the two parts of the message. The $P(D)$ can be eliminated, since we are trying to compare different models of the same data and therefore $P(D)$ is constant. The minimisation of $ML(H|D)$ is the criterion for model selection.

The message can be thought of as an explanation of the data. The first segment is a theory about the best class distribution, and the second a description of the data in terms of that theory. If the theory explains the data well, then the data description will be short, and the whole message will be short. If the theory is poor, then the data description will be longer, causing a longer message length. The "best" theory is the one with the shortest total message length. A complicated theory segment will not necessarily cause a long total message length, nor will a short theory automatically cause a short message length. The final length of a message depends both on the length of the theory and on how well the theory describes the data.

2.2 Recognition Using a Snob Distribution

Discrimination of the training words is performed using Snob to generate equivalence classes such that the class distribution has the lowest message length. Then, given a test word t encoded as an object O (which is a collection of attribute values), we use the distribution of attribute values of the objects in each class generated by Snob in order to decide to which class the object O is most likely to belong. This similarity calculation is described below. The class c with the maximum value of $Pr(O$ belongs in $c)$ over all the classes C is the best class for O.

$$Pr(O \text{ belongs in } c) = \frac{f_c(O)}{\sum_{i=0}^{C} f_i(O)},$$

where

$$f_c(O) = \left(\prod_{i=0}^{N} attrprob_c(i)\right) \times relfreq(c),$$

N is the number of attributes of an object O, C is the number of classes, $attrprob_c(i)$ is the probability of the value of attribute i in class c, and $relfreq(c)$ is the relative frequency of class c.

2.3 Encoding for Phonetic Similarity

The choice of representation of a test word t as an object O is crucial, since we want an encoding where two items that are acoustically similar are encoded as a set of similar attributes.

As indicated in Section 1.1, a common encoding is one where a phoneme sequence is encoded as a BSG sequence. However, such an encoding requires additional processing to account for insertions and deletions [2, 4, 5, 9]. Specifically, in the case of Snob, insertions and deletions cause surrounding phonemes to be mis-aligned with equivalent phonemes in other words. In this research we investigated three different encoding methods which maintain the alignment of the information pertaining to different attributes (a sample encoding using each method is given in Fig. 1):

Broad Sound Group Frequency. The attributes are the frequencies of the eight different BSG sounds. If two words differ only by one vowel, then the vowel frequency count will differ by one, but other attribute values will stay the same.

neoclassic
n iy ix k l ae s ix kcl

BSG sequence
nasal vowel vowel stopRelease glide vowel fricative vowel stopClosure

BSG frequency
1 stopClosures, 1 stopReleases, 0 affricate, 1 fricative,
1 nasal, 1 glide, 4 vowels, 0 pauses

BSG frequency + length
1 stopClosures, 1 stopReleases, 0 affricate, 1 fricative,
1 nasal, 1 glide, 4 vowels, 0 pauses, length 9

Bigram frequency
1 nasal/vowel
1 vowel/vowel
1 vowel/stopRelease
1 stopRelease/glide
1 glide/vowel
1 vowel/fricative
1 fricative/vowel
1 vowel/stopClosure
1 stopClosure/endWord
0 all other bigrams

Fig. 1. Sample word under four different encodings

Broad Sound Group Frequency plus Length. An extra attribute that represents the length of the word is added to BSG frequency attributes.

Broad Sound Group Bigram Frequency. Every combination of two BSGs is an attribute, and the attribute value is the frequency of that bigram. So each object is represented by 81 attributes (there are 8 BSG symbols plus an end-of-word marker). This allows some positional context of phonemes to be taken into consideration during classification.

3 Results

A study was done on the TIMIT corpus [3], which is a collection of American-English read sentences with correct time-aligned acoustic-phonetic and orthographic (word-aligned) transcriptions. The data set contains 3696 sentences spoken by 462 speakers from 8 different dialect divisions across the United States. Each speaker says five phonetically-compact sentences and three phonetically-diverse sentences to give a good coverage of the phonemes in the language. The sentences were recorded using a high-quality, headset-mounted microphone in a

```
The Mayan neoclassic scholar disappeared while surveying ancient ruins.

the         |mayan              |
DH    AX    |M    AY    ax   N  |
DH    AX    |M    AY    eh   N  |


neoclassic                                  |
N     IY    ow    K     L     AE    S     ih    k     |
N     IY    ix    K     L     AE    S     ix    kcl   |


scholar                     |disappeared                                    |
S     K     AA    L    AXR  |D    ih    S     ax    P     iy    r     d     |
S     K     AA    L    AXR  |D    ix    S     ix    P     ih    axr   dx    |

while                  |surveying                   |
hh    W     ay    L    |S    axr   V     EY    ix    NG  |
ax    W     aa    L    |S    er    V     EY    -     NG  |

ancient                                |ruins                  |
-     EY    N     SH    ix    n     t  |R     uw    ih    N    Z   |
q     EY    N     SH    -     en    tcl|R     ux    ix    N    Z   |
```

Fig. 2. A typical TIMIT sentence aligned with expected phonemes from a lexicon

Table 1. Class sizes for three different encodings

Encoding method	Number of classes	Average class size	Standard deviation of class size
BSG frequency	7	2693.43	1625.78
BSG frequency + length	31	608.19	353.63
Bigram frequency	38	496.16	336.74

noise-isolated room, and speakers were instructed to read prompts in a "natural" voice. An example of a TIMIT sentence aligned with expected phonemes from a lexicon is given in Fig. 2. The first row shows the words of the utterance, the second row the expected phonemes from a lexicon, and the third row the actual TIMIT phonemes. This training set generated 18854 training words.

The test set contained 4707 words represented as phoneme strings which were collected from 26% of the speakers. No speaker was in the test and training sets. The exact boundaries of a word are assumed to be known.[3]

Table 1 shows the number of training words that went into each class for the three encoding methods. The second and third methods produce more classes of smaller size than the first method. This means that if we classify (using Snob) an input word accurately, the second and third methods will eliminate

[3] We are currently investigating removing this assumption and allowing connected-word recognition on entire sentences.

Table 2. Sample words in equivalence classes for bigram frequency encoding

Class 1	Class 2	Class 3	Class 4 ...
me	odds	emerge	of
more	apple	image	odd
my	eggs	enough	had
now	echo	amaze	said
knee	certain	advance	set
the	upper	unless	that
to	occur	enamel	at
not	outer	agenda	egg
know	atoms	engulfed	step
meet	aloud	efficient	sought
mind	again	inaugural	ought
mine	effect	attendants	act
nine	awkward	equipment	urged
memo	obtain	accordingly	food
number	earthquake	remembered	aid
instead	advance	eyestrain	eight
moment	overweight	amounts	out
mechanism	occupied	unpleasant	it
experiment	eruption	interesting	oak
extraordinary	unbeatable	underwriting	or

a larger proportion of the candidates than the first method. The addition of a length attribute to the BSG frequency attributes produces a large increase in the number of classes. Unfortunately, this method also shows a great reliance on the length attribute, which is likely to change for insertions and deletions in the input string. The other eight attributes become less relevant in this encoding, and the classification basically becomes a classification by length of input word. Table 2 shows examples of words placed in equivalence classes using the bigram frequency encoding. Words in the same class appear different, as Snob uses significant sections of the phoneme string to make classifications based on the occurrence of words in the training corpus, and not on the lexicon words themselves.

A comparison of the performance of the equivalence classes with the different encoding methods is shown in Table 3. A class is "correct" if at least one instance of the test word was found in that class as a result of training. When a test word is put into the correct class, a second stage intra-class process has a chance to uncover the correct candidate.

The overall probability of recognising the correct word for a test item t can be described as:

$$Pr(t \text{ correctly recognised}) = \sum_{c \in C} Pr(t \text{ matches class } c) \times Pr(select(t, c)),$$

where

Table 3. Percentage of correctly classified test items

Encoding method	Percentage of test items classified correctly in the highest probability class	Percentage of test items classified correctly in the two highest probability classes
BSG frequency	96%	98%
BSG frequency + length	93%	95%
Bigram frequency	94%	96%

C is the set of classes containing the correct word, and
$Pr(select(t, c))$ is the probability that t is correctly chosen in class c.

The first factor is obtained from Snob's classification. However, in order to compute the second factor we need some information about how the second stage of the word recognition process is performed.

If we assume that the second stage recognition is just a random choice, the second stage probability becomes the fraction of the instances in the class that represent the correct word:

$$Pr(select(t, c)) = \frac{\text{number of instances of } t \text{ in class } c}{\text{total number of instances in class } c}$$

Table 4 shows recognition probabilities of 4707 test words with this worst-case random second stage. The last column contains the number of bits required to transmit the objects corresponding to these words, where the class description segment of the message encodes the class distribution generated by Snob, and the object description segment encodes information about each test object (Section 2.1). While the recognition probabilities are unrealistically low, their comparison indicates that the bigram encoding has the best recognition probability. At first glance, this may appear to be related to the low number of instances in the equivalence classes obtained with the bigram encoding, and thus the increased $Pr(select(t, c))$. However, it is important to note that the probability that a test item will be put into the correct equivalence class with the bigram method is not substantially different from the probabilities obtained with the other encodings (Table 3). That is, although the bigram method has produced more classes than the other methods, the probability of classification into the correct class remains high.

In order to get more realistic results, we built a recogniser that compares the sequence of phonemes in a test word with the training candidates in the highest probability class returned by Snob for this test word. The test phoneme strings were compared with these candidates using either the BSG or bigram frequency difference, a phoneme frequency difference, and the number of matches found with an edit distance algorithm. Candidates that were different from the test item by more than a threshold were eliminated. These comparisons, which were

Table 4. Probability of picking a correct word using a random second stage

Encoding method	Number of classes	Average recognition probability	Number of zero probabilities in the test set[4]	Number of bits
BSG frequency	7	0.0164336	0	40421.9
BSG frequency+length	31	0.0703322	5	32457.5
Bigram frequency	38	0.0738991	10	32057.6

Table 5. Position of the correct word in the final candidate list

Encoding method	Frequency count for the position of the correct word in the final candidate list								Number of test words found in final list	Average position of correct word in final candidate list
	1	2	3	4	5	6	7-11	12+		
BSG freq	1062	494	342	261	156	252	621	1307	4495	10.4452
BSG freq+length	992	444	347	249	145	239	627	1313	4356	10.4740
Bigram freq	1483	579	322	267	125	232	558	802	4368	6.0236
Bigram freq (no Snob)	1495	590	329	272	137	235	571	851	4480	6.5176

run on the test set with each of the three encoding methods, yielded a final list of candidate words, which were ranked according to the goodness of the match.

Table 5 shows the positions of the 4707 test words in the final lists of candidate words generated by this process for the three encoding methods. For example, with the BSG frequency encoding, out of 4495 test words found in the final list, 1062 had the correct word at the top of the candidate list. It also shows the position of the correct word using the bigram frequency encoding without the Snob classification (that is, we have one class containing all the possible candidates). The average position of the correct word in the candidate list generated without the Snob classification is only slightly worse than in the candidate list generated with it. However, the number of comparisons required to produce these lists for an input word is much higher without the Snob classification than with it (Fig. 3).

[4] Some test items had a zero chance of being recognized correctly, as there were no instances of the correct word in any of the classes which had a non-zero probability of being selected. This happens when the training instances of the correct word are too different from the test items for any connection to be made.

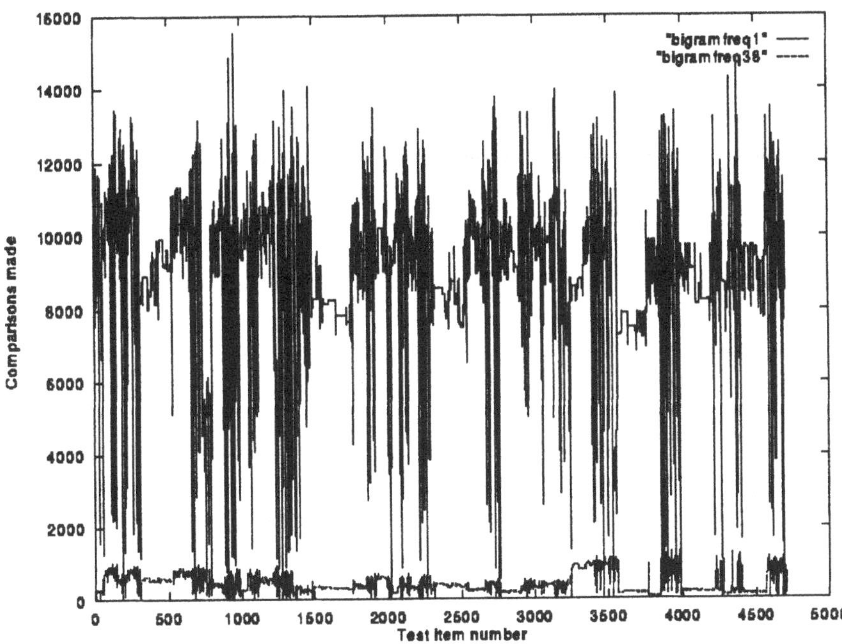

Fig. 3. Number of comparisons to produce a final candidate list for 1 class or 38 classes

4 Conclusion

As the size of vocabularies used in modern speech systems increases, so does the need to eliminate quickly unlikely candidates. If this can be done reliably, more rigorous techniques, such as Hidden Markov Models, can be used to examine the remaining candidates, and still produce results in good time.

In this paper, we have presented a method for deriving equivalence classes that account for a large number of training words. Our method uses the MML principle to evaluate the goodness of the resulting class distribution, yielding classes that have simple and tight distributions of the attribute values of its members. Slight alterations of phonemes (obtained through mis-recognition and mis-pronunciation) maintain the class membership of a word, while relatively gross changes cause the classification of a word into another class.

This dissimilarity between the items in different classes allows the classification of a test word into the class most likely to have had an instance of this word during training, using what amounts to no more than a similarity measure. This avoids a dynamic programming search of a full tree of BSG sequences, and allows second and third best choices of class membership to be explored. Our approach allows insertion and deletion behaviour to be expressed automatically through the selection of equivalence classes which take insertion and deletion patterns into account from actual training data. This is in contrast to using any standard set of phonological rules [8, 14]. Such rules may exploit precise phonological knowledge (such as pre-boundary lengthening of phones), but there is the price of the effort of building them.

Careful choice of encoding methods allows the features of the training words to be expressed so that phonetically similar words are grouped together. Although the results with bigrams alone are encouraging, more complicated encodings that represent more features of the training words (such as stressed and unstressed phonemes) are possible, allowing Snob to make more accurate decisions when building the class distribution. The addition of such information is currently under investigation.

The context of this work has been isolated word recognition, where word boundaries are known, and accurate BSG frequency counts can be made. Our technique is currently being extended to connected-word speech, where word boundaries are being postulated on the basis of a language model.

References

1. Altman, G. and Carter, D., Lexical stress and lexical discriminability: Stressed syllables are more informative, but why? *Computer Speech and Language* **3**, 265–275, 1989.
2. Chen, F.R., Lexical access and verification in a broad phonetic approach to continuous digit recognition. In *Proceedings of the IEEE International Conference on Acoustics, Speech and Signal Processing*, 21.7.1–21.7.4, 1986.
3. Fisher, W.M., Doddington, M., George, R., and Goudie-Marshall, K.M., The DARPA speech recognition database: Specifications and status. In *Proceedings of the DARPA Speech Recognition Workshop*, Report No. SAIC-86/1546, February 1986.
4. Fissore, L., Micca, G., and Pieraccini, R., Strategies for lexical access to very large vocabularies. *Speech Communication* **7**, 355–366, 1988.
5. Huttenlocher, D.P. and Zue, V.W., A model for lexical access from partial phonetic information. In *Proceedings of the IEEE International Conference on Acoustics, Speech and Signal Processing*, 26.4.1 - 26.4.4, 1984.
6. Patrick, J.D., Snob: A program for discriminating between classes. Technical Report 91/151, Monash University, March 1991.
7. Pisoni, D.B., Nusbaum, H.C., Luce, P.A., and Slowiaczek, L.M., Speech perception, word recognition and the structure of the lexicon. *Speech Communication* **4**, 75–95, 1985.
8. Rudnicky, A.I., An unanchored matching algorithm for lexical access. In *Proceedings of the IEEE International Conference on Acoustics, Speech and Signal Processing*, 469–472, 1988.
9. Rudnicky, A.I., Baumeister, L.K., DeGraaf, K.H., and Lehmann, E., The lexical access component of the CMU continuous speech recognition system. In *Proceedings of the IEEE International Conference on Acoustics, Speech and Signal Processing*, 10.5.1–10.5.4, 1987.

10. Thomas, I.E., Zukerman, I., and Raskutti, B., Accounting for pronunciation of phonemes in corpora. In *Proceedings of the Second Conference of the Pacific Association of Computational Linguistics*, forthcoming.
11. Wallace, C.S. and Boulton, D.M., An information measure for classification. *Computer Journal* **11**, 185–194, 1968.
12. Wallace, C.S. and Dowe, D.L., Intrinsic classification by MML – the Snob program. In Zhang, C., Debenham, J., and Lukose, D. (Eds.), *Proceedings of the 7th Australian Joint Conference on Artificial Intelligence*, 37–44, World Scientific, Singapore, 1994.
13. Wallace, C.S. and Freeman, P.R., Estimation and inference by compact coding. *Journal of the Royal Statistical Society (Series B)* **49**, 240–252, 1987.
14. Withgott, M.M. and Chen, F.R., *Computational Models of American Speech*. Center for the Study of Language and Information, 1993.

Using Neural Nets to Investigate Lexical Analysis

Malti Patel

Abstract. The use of neural networks in the investigation of psychological theories is fairly recent. In this paper, we will show how the implementation of a particular reading model using neural nets has lead to interesting insights into how the meanings of a word may be accessed. Theories already exist as to how humans do this. The results from the neural net implementation give results which differ from these theories and as such give new insights into this area.

1 Introduction

Many experiments have been performed to determine how people store the spelling, pronunciations and meanings of words, and how these representations are used by the processes involved in reading, determining whether something is a word, and so on. Data from these experiments have previously been used to hypothesise exactly what is happening in the brain. There is no concrete evidence to support these hypotheses. With the advent of neural networks, we can at last start to test these theories.

In this paper, we will be using a neural net to examine how the meanings (senses) of a word are accessed when a word is read. For example, when you see the word BALL, do you just think of something that is round and bounces, or do you also, at some level, think of the meaning associated with dancing, i.e. "going to a BALL".

2 Theories of Lexical Access

Lexical access simply means accessing words stored in the brain. There are three main theories as to how the meaning(s) of a word is accessed. We will look at these briefly. There is evidence to support all theories (see [2] for a review).

- **Exhaustive Access Theory**
  This states that all the meanings of a word are accessed when we see a word. A choice is then made according to the context.
- **Ordered Access Theory**
  This states that meanings are accessed serially in order of their frequency. Each meaning is matched against the context until the correct meaning is found. This means that when the most frequent meaning of a word is encountered, the word is effectively acting like an unambiguous word.

- **Context-Guided Access**
  This states that only the meaning associated with the relevant context is accessed.

From the outside, the first theory seems implausible since most people would say that other meanings of the same word were not noticed. For example, seeing the word BALL, most people would say that they never thought of the meaning associated with dancing. Theory 3 seems the most plausible since most people would think that they only associate one meaning whenever a word is encountered.

3 The Dual-Route Cascaded Reading Model (DRC)

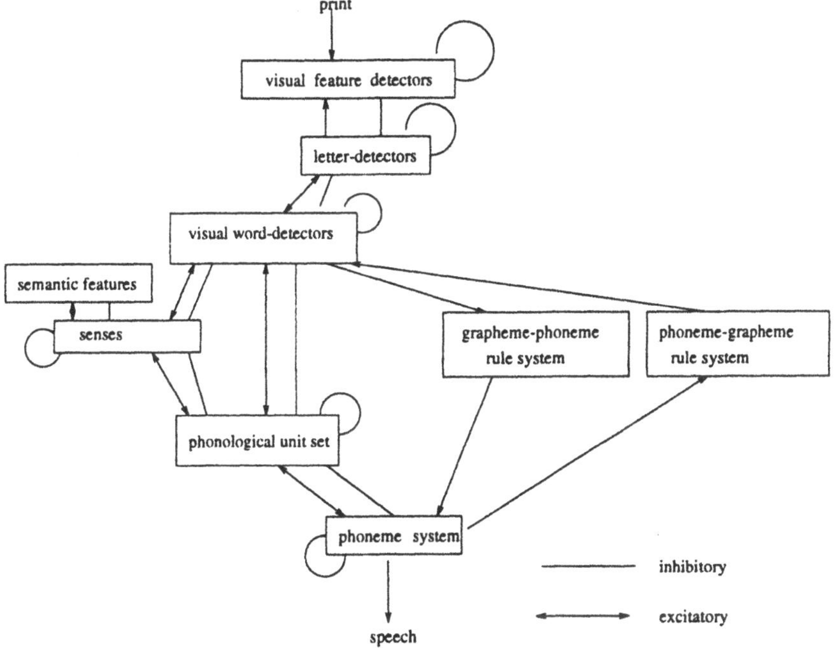

Fig. 1. The Dual-Route Cascaded Reading Model

The DRC [1] [1] is a theory of reading aloud which has been implemented using a localist neural network. It currently pronounces about 8000 words. Figure 1 shows the structure of this model with the various excitatory and inhibitory links. The spelling of a word is input in terms of its letter features. The model has to pronounce the word using the two routes shown.

---

[1] I would like to thank Max Coltheart for his invaluable help during the implementation of the semantic component of the DRC and also Michael Haller for help with the code.

The grapheme-phoneme rule route relies on rules to pronounce a word. For example, one rule would say that when the letters "oo" are encountered, they should be pronounced as in "mood" not as in "flood".

Sense 2 hired hand, hand, hired man – (a hired laborer on a farm or ranch)
: laborer, manual laborer, labourer – (works with hands)
: workman, working man, working person
: employee – (a worker who is hired to perform a job)
: worker – (a person who has employment)
: person, individual, someone, man, mortal, human, soul – (a human being)

: life form, organism, being, living thing – (any living entity)
: entity – (something having concrete existence; living or nonliving)
: causal agent, cause, causal agency – (any entity that causes events to happen)
: entity – (something having concrete existence; living or nonliving)

Sense 8 hand, manus, hook, mauler, mitt, paw – (the (prehensile) distal extremity of the superior limb)
: extremity, appendage – (a bodily appendage or appendagelike part)
: external body part
: body part, member
: part – (any part of an animal or plant such as an organ or extremity)
: natural object – (an object occurring naturally; not made by man)
: object, inanimate object, physical object – (a nonliving entity)
: entity – (something having concrete existence; living or nonliving)

Fig. 2. WordNet Definitions for some Senses of HAND

One WordNet Definition of HEAD

head – (the upper or front part of the body in animals (including man) that contains the face and brains)
: external body part
: body part, member
: part – (any part of an animal or plant such as an organ or extremity)
: natural object – (an object occurring naturally; not made by man)
: object, inanimate object, physical object – (a nonliving entity)
: entity – (something having concrete existence; living or nonliving)

One WordNet Definition of HAND

hand, manus, hook, mauler, mitt, paw – (the (prehensile) distal extremity of the superior limb)
: extremity, appendage – (a bodily appendage or appendagelike part)
: external body part
: body part, member
: part – (any part of an animal or plant such as an organ or extremity)
: natural object – (an object occurring naturally; not made by man)
: object, inanimate object, physical object – (a nonliving entity)
: entity – (something having concrete existence; living or nonliving)

Fig. 3. Comparison of WordNet Definitions for HEAD and HAND

The other route has a specific entry for each word recognized by the model and uses both the spelling and meaning(s) of a word to pronounce it. For example, the spelling of BALL would be represented by one unit in the *visual word-detectors* component, its pronounciation would be represented by one unit in the *phonological unit set*. One unit is used to represent each sense (meaning) of BALL in the *senses* component. The features used to define each sense (e.g. round, bounces) are stored in the *semantic features* component. There are connections between the sense of a word and the semantic features used to define it. The semantic features were obtained from a psycholinguistic on-line dictionary called WordNet (see [3]). Figure 2 shows some of the WordNet definitions of HAND. WordNet is consistent in that all word meanings are represented using the same large set of semantic features. This means that semantically related words will have similar meanings as shown in Figure 3 which shows how HAND and HEAD share some of the same semantic features in WordNet.

Sense 1 kind, sort, type, form – ("sculpture is a form of art" or "what kind of man is this?")

S1 : category, class
S2 : concept, conception
S3 : idea, thought – (the content of cognition; "it was not a good idea")
S4 : content, cognitive content, mental object – (the sum or range of what has been perceived, discovered, or learned)
S5 : cognition, knowledge – (the psychological result of perception and learning and reasoning)
S6 : psychological feature – (a feature of the mental life of a living organism)

kind (vs. unkind) – (having or showing a tender, considerate, and helpful nature)

S7 : benignant, gracious – (characterized by kindness and warm courtesy esp. of a superior: "a kind master"; or of a king to his subjects: "a benignant king")
S8 : benign, gentle, kindly – (of disposition or manner: "the benign ruler of millions"; "a gentle, kindly soul")
S9 : kindhearted, tender – (of an innately kind dispositioin: "a generous and kindhearted teacher")

Fig. 4. WordNet Definitions for some Senses of KIND

Each word is represented by an orthographic unit in the visual word-detectors component. For the semantic component, we require connections from a word to its meaning(s). Since many words are ambiguous, we have a senses component where one unit is used to represent one sense of a word. For example, say KIND has two senses, then the orthographic unit for KIND will have one excitatory connection to the unit which represents sense one and another excitatory connection to the unit which represents sense two in the senses component. Each sense has excitatory connections to the semantic features used to define it. In this way, the three components representing words, senses and semantic features are connected together.

Figure 4 shows the semantic features used to define the senses of KIND by WordNet. Each of these semantic features will be represented by one unit in the semantic features component. Figure 5 illustrates the connections between the word KIND, its senses and the semantic features used to define the senses. The semantic features S1-S6 represent the WordNet definitions for sense one of KIND, i.e. S1 = " category class", S2 = "concept definition" and so on. Similarly the second sense is defined by semantic features S7-S9.

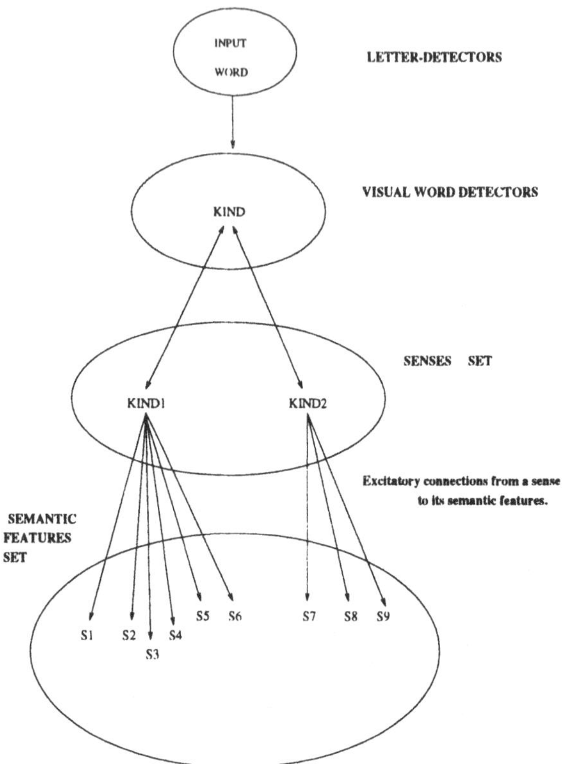

Fig. 5. Representation of the Senses of KIND

Most words have more than one sense, hence we have a situation where the senses of the input word must compete against each other in order to win. Because of this, we have lateral inhibition between the senses. This allows the senses with a high frequency to decrease the activations of the lower frequency senses of the word. Lateral inhibition only occurs between senses of the same word, thus, a sense of SIGN does not inhibit a sense of GROUND, only the other senses of SIGN.

A sense has excitatory connections to the semantic features used to define it, and inhibitory connections to all other semantic features. Similarly, a semantic feature has excitatory connections to all the senses in which it is used (a semantic feature can appear in many senses, therefore in many words), and inhibitory connections to all senses in which it does not appear.

The connections between the words, senses and semantic features mean that when a word is input, it will highly activate its senses and their semantic features. They, in turn, will also inhibit non-related senses and semantic features. Thus, eventually, not only will the system pronounce the word input, but it will also output the correct meaning of the word input, i.e. the one with the highest frequency value.

When adding the semantic component, the aim was that the system output the sense with the highest frequency of the input word. For the highest frequency sense to win, there must obviously be information about the frequency values of the various senses of a word. Such data is fairly difficult to obtain since frequency values are usually given for a whole word and not its separate meanings. However, we were able to obtain data for the senses of 450 words (see [4]). Thus, currently we have the system running on 450 words when incorporating the semantic component.

The sense with the highest activation wins. The frequency factor determines how much activation a sense receives, i.e. a high frequency value leads to more activation being received by a sense. Since we want a winner take all situation, the senses of a word compete against each other by means of lateral inhibition. Hence, for a word, the sense with the most activation can send more inhibition to the other senses of that word.

4 Results from the Model

From the 450 words pronounced by the model, we chose three groups consisting of 25 words each. The first group represented words with equiprobable senses, i.e. their frequency values are fairly close together. The second group consisted of words with polarized senses, i.e. their frequency values are fairly wide apart. The third group consisted of words which have three senses. The aim was to look at the activation values of the senses in order to see if there was a significant difference between the three groups.

There is a notable difference between the activation values of the senses depending upon which group they are in. For example, if a word has equiprobable senses, then there is a great likelihood that the low frequency (LF) sense will have a fairly high activation value. On the other hand, if a word has polarized senses, then its LF sense receives much less activation.

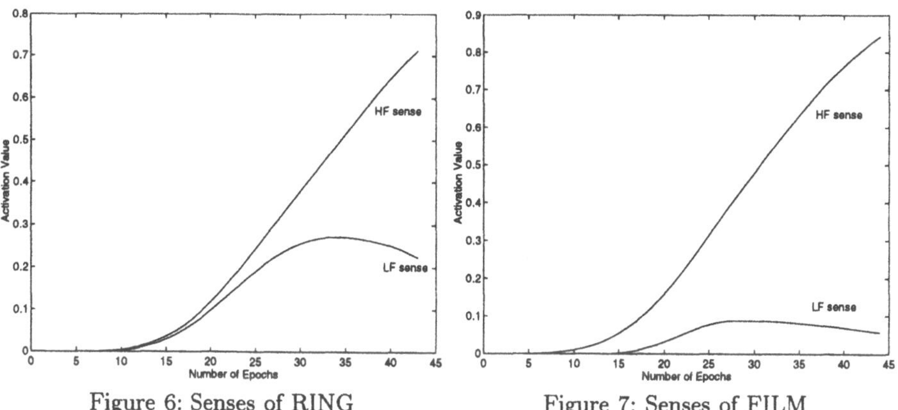

Figure 6: Senses of RING

Figure 7: Senses of FILM

Figure 6 shows the activation values for the equiprobable senses of RING.

The LF sense peaks at an activation value of 0.271. Figure 7 shows the activation values for the polarized senses of FILM. As seen, the LF sense receives much less activation, peaking at a value of 0.088. Figure 8 superimposes the information from the previous two figures. The high frequency sense (HF) of FILM receives much more activation than the HF sense of RING. The lateral inhibition between senses may lead to this effect. Since the LF sense of RING has a fairly high activation, it can inhibit and therefore lower the activation value of the HF sense of RING. The LF sense of FILM cannot do this since its activation value is too low to inhibit the HF sense of FILM by much.

For all groups, in the majority of cases, the LF sense received activation which eventually decreased. Psychologically, this is something which we would expect, i.e. a person sees an ambiguous word and only one sense "comes to mind". The simulations show this by the activation of the LF sense decreasing and therefore this sense is "forgotton". If the activations of both senses continued to increase, then the model would be giving psychologically implausible results since people don't usually think of all senses of an ambiguous word simultaneously. This did happen in some cases but was not due to the model and is discussed below.

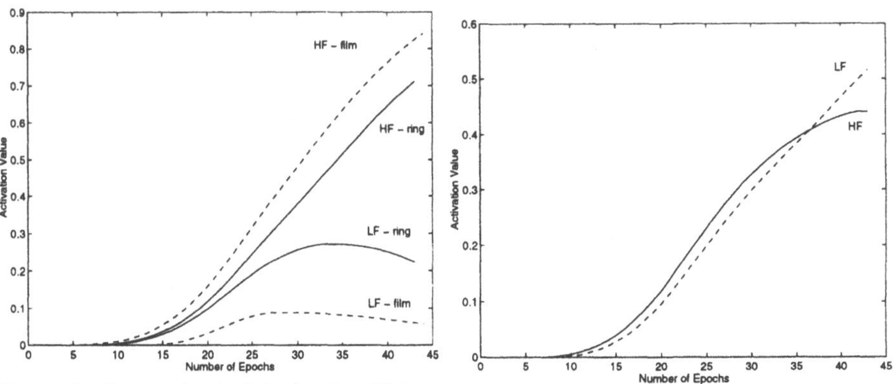

Figure 8: Comparison of Activation Values for Senses of RING and FILM

Figure 9: Senses of COUNT

One problem with the group of equiprobable senses was that occasionally the LF sense would win, i.e. receive more activation than the HF sense. Looking at these cases, it is fairly obvious that this problem is due to the way in which WordNet defines senses. In all these cases, the LF sense was defined by more semantic features than the HF sense. This meant that the LF sense was receiving more support and therefore more activation from its semantic features. Figure 9 shows such a case with the word COUNT. As seen, the activation of the LF sense eventually catches up and overtakes activation of the HF sense.

Usually, the LF sense had about four more semantic features used to define it than the HF sense. Thus, for equiprobable senses, the number of semantic features used to define them makes a big difference to the amount of activation which they receive. This is clearly a problem with using WordNet to define the senses of a word and not with the model itself. Future work may involve looking at other means of semantic representation where the number of semantic features is not such a problem.

For polarized senses, the number of semantic features used to define a sense made no difference in that the HF sense always won. This seems to imply that the semantic features only had a bad effect when the frequency values of two senses were close together. As such, we believe that the conclusions to be drawn from these results (see next section) are valid and not dependent upon the WordNet definitions. The results are due to the structure of the DRC. Since this is based on sound psychological principles we feel that the results are psychologically plausible.

Results from the group of words with three senses were similar to the other two groups. Typically, the activation value of a sense depended on its frequency value. This is shown by Figure 10 which shows the activations of the senses of GRAFT. As expected, activation of a sense increases as its frequency value increases. Also, activation of the medium frequency (MF) and LF senses diminish eventually.

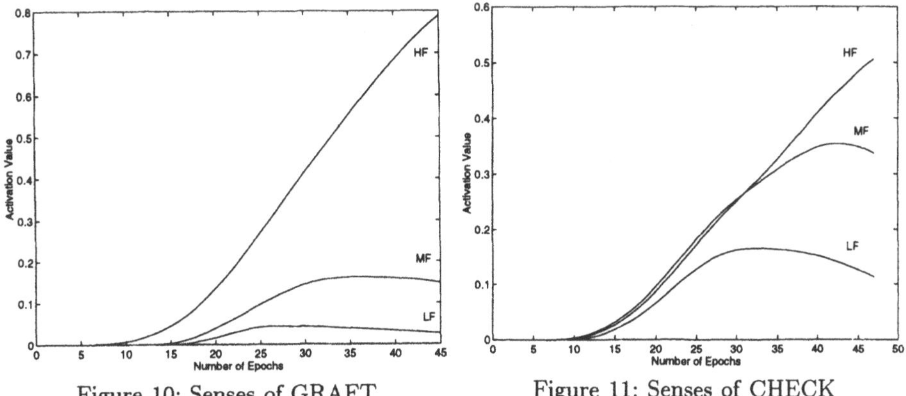

Figure 10: Senses of GRAFT

Figure 11: Senses of CHECK

There were some senses in this group whose frequency values were close together whereas others were quite wide apart. Thus, we have an effect where some of these senses can be deemed to be equiprobable and others polarized. To see the effect of three equiprobable senses competiting against each other, we took a word with three senses whose frequency values were close together and studied what occurred if we ran the model using just:

a) the HF and MF senses

b) the HF and LF senses

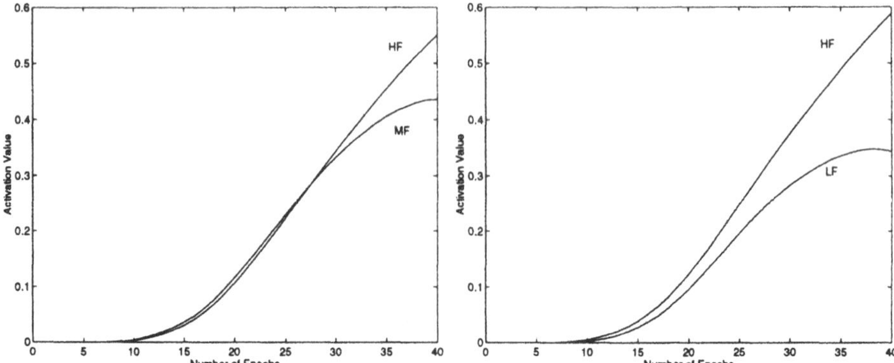

Figure 12: Comparing Activations of the HF and MF Senses of CHECK

Figure 13: Comparing Activations of the HF and LF Senses of CHECK

In effect we were now treating the word as having two equiprobable senses. The word we studied was CHECK - Figure 11 shows the activations of its three senses. Senses one and two of CHECK have the same frequency value. Since sense one is defined using three semantic features and sense two is defined using six semantic features, the latter wins due to having more semantic features. Sense one will now be known as the MF sense of CHECK. The LF sense of CHECK is defined using six semantic features. As seen from Figure 11, activation of the MF and LF senses decreases. The MF sense reached an activation of 0.254 before decreasing. Similarly, the LF sense reached an activation of 0.165.

We ran the model using cases a) and b) above, i.e. running the model using just the HF and MF senses and then running it with just the HF and LF senses. Figure 12 illustrates the result of case a) and shows that the activation of the MF sense continued to increase. This indicates that the HF sense by itself is unable to inhibit the LF sense enough to decrease its activation. The MF sense had an activation value of 0.436 at the end which is much larger than when the three senses were competing against each other.

Figure 13 illustrates the result of case b) and shows that the activation of the LF sense did decrease but it reached a much higher activation value of 0.348.

The results from cases a) and b) which omit one of the senses and hence treat the remaining two as equiprobable senses, show that it is fairly difficult for the HF sense to inhibit the activation of the other sense. In both cases, the activation of the lower frequency sense was much higher than when all three senses are active. The effect of the three senses competiting against each other is to lower the activation of the MF and LF senses quite significantly. Thus, the activation of a third sense obviously has a large effect on the activation of the two other senses for cases where the frequency values of all three senses are fairly close.

In summary, the LF senses in the equiprobable group received much more activation than the LF senses in the polarized group. For equiprobable senses the frequency values are close together and hence it is plausible that the LF sense would receive significant activation. This is not the case for polarized senses where the LF sense has a small frequency value which will not be sufficient for it to receive much activation. For words with three senses, activation of the MF and LF senses is fairly low due to the fact that a sense receives inhibition from two senses. Also, the amount of activation received by a sense depends upon the difference between its frequency value and those of the other two senses. Overall, it seems as if the *difference* in the frequency values of the senses of a word has a great effect as to how much activation each sense receives.

5 Relating Results to the Theories of Lexical Access

Comparing the theories of lexical access against the results we can offer new insights as to what may be occurring. It may be that the different theories arise because of the types of senses, i.e. polarized or equiprobable, as opposed to there actually being different ways of accessing meanings.

The exhaustive access theory states that all meanings are accessed. As seen, in the case of equiprobable senses, this may well be the case. The activation of the meanings are all highly active and therefore it could be said that all meanings are accessed.

The ordered access theory states that meanings are accessed in order of frequency. This could well be true of polarized senses where the activation of the LF sense is so far from the HF sense that it could well be viewed that the HF sense came to mind first followed later by the LF sense if the former was incorrect.

Contextually-guided access is plausible when reading a sentence or text if we view words as being connected according to their semantics. This means, that seeing a word like NURSE would automatically send activation to semantically associated words such as DOCTOR. In our model, we have implemented this via the WordNet definitions of words which are stored in the semantic features component. For example, in WordNet, the related meanings of HEAD and HAND share some of the same semantic features. Thus, we have an associative semantic representation such that if HEAD is input, it will also activate the related sense of HAND. This means, that if related words are input, the activation of the semantic features will lead to semantically related meanings being activated.

The three theories of lexical access may be incorrect in that they do no actual indicate how people access meanings. Rather, the theories are describing accessing different types of meanings - the exhaustive access theory decribes accessing equiprobable meanings and the ordered access theory describes accessing polarized meanings. Ultimately, it is the difference in the frequency values of the meanings of a word which determine how those meanings are accessed, not that all meanings are accessed in the same way. If the difference between the senses is very large, then the LF sense may receive very little activation. As the difference between the frequency values of two senses decrease, so the activation of the LF sense becomes higher. Hence, we have a continuum whereby the activation of the LF sense reflects how likely it is to be brought to the "attention" or "consciousness" of a person reading the word.

When reading a sentence or some text, it is easy to imagine that activation is being sent to semantically related words. For example, say that word X is semantically related to the LF sense of word Y. Say word X appears on the screen. Activation would automatically be sent to the LF sense of word Y. Now when word Y appears on the screen, there is a greater probability that its LF sense would be more active than the HF sense. Hence, we get evidence for contexually-guided access since in this case it is not the frequency of a sense which matters but how much activation semantically related senses have received.

Overall, it seems that it is the difference between the frequencies of senses which determines how they are accessed and not that all senses are accessed in the same manner as stated by the different access theories. It may be that people are "conscious" of all meanings which are equiprobable and of the HF meanings of polarized meanings. In the latter case, the LF meaning may only come to mind if the HF sense is incorrect for the current context. This would explain how the exhaustive and ordered access theories arise. As shown above, all three theories are plausible if we examine the frequencies and activation values of the senses of a word.

6 Conclusion

We have shown how a neural net implementation of a psychological theory of reading can be used to examine different theories of lexical access. The neural net is modelled on a theory which has much well-established data to supprt it, therefore, it is a plausible model of what occurs in the brain when people read.

The neural net has shown at a very low level how the meanings of a word may be accessed when we read. This is not possible when devising experiments to test how people access meanings. The former lead to theories which our results have shown may be based on the wrong assumption - namely, people do not access meanings in a certain way, but that the difference in the frequencies of the meanings of a word determines whether or not they will be accessed. If the difference is large, then the LF meaning will not receive much activation and will appear not to have been accessed unless necessary. If the difference is small, then the meanings will receive a similar amount of activation and all meanings may appear to have been accessed.. Thus, the difference indicates how much activation a meaning will receive and hence if it will be "noticed" by the person reading.

Neural nets can be used in cognitive modelling to test psychological theories at a practical level. As such, they have a large role to play since there are many theories which can be tested. As seen, they can lead to interesting new insights into how language is stored and accessed by the brain.

References

1. M. Coltheart, B. Curtis, P. Atkins, and M. Haller. Models of reading aloud: Dual-route and parallel-distributed-processing approaches. *Psychological Review*, 100:589–608, 1993.
2. Alan Garnham. *Psycholingustics: Central Topics*. Methuen and Co, 1985.
3. G.A. Miller, R. Beckwith, R. Fellbaume abd C. Gross, D. Miller, and R. Tengi. Five papers on wordnet. Csl report, Princeton University, 1990.
4. L.C. Twilley, D. Dixon, D. Taylor, and K. Clark. University of norms of relative meaning frequency for 566 homographs. *Memory and Cognition*, 22:111–126, 1994.

Validity of Normality Assumption in CSP Research

Alvin C. M. Kwan

Department of Computer Science, University of Essex, Essex CO4 3SQ, U.K.
email: alvin@essex.ac.uk

Abstract. There are many new methods for solving constraint satisfaction problems proposed in recent years. Due to their complexity, a theoretical analysis on their average-case behaviours seems to be very difficult. Researchers tend to adopt an empirical approach to evaluate constraint satisfaction techniques. When empirical results are ready, statistical techniques are often employed for analysis. The question is which statistics to use. Some recent research uses parametric tests such as *t*-test and ANOVA. However those tests assume that the characteristic of the normal curve can be applied. In this paper, we provide evidence that the normality assumption is often not valid in the results produced by a range of constraint satisfaction algorithm-heuristic combinations on random binary constraint satisfaction problems and 3-colouring problems, particularly when a problem is within the "mushy region", which are popular benchmark problems for evaluating CSP methods. The failure of normality assumption highlights the need for some statistics which do not rely on the normality assumption to analyse empirical results from CSP research. We believe that non-parametric techniques could be the right tools for that purpose.

1 Introduction

A constraint satisfaction problem (CSP) can be informally defined as a set of variables, each of them associated with a set of feasible domain values which the variable can be instantiated to, and a set of constraints, each of them imposes some restrictions on the values of its constrained variables can take. The aim is to find a solution to the problem such that every variable is assigned a value without violating any constraints [18].

Many new CSP methods, notably new algorithms and heuristics, have been proposed in recent years. Since analysing the average-case behaviour of those techniques is very difficult, most evaluations are done in an empirical way. The most frequently adopted performance indicators for evaluating CSP methods appear to be the number of compatibility checks and the cpu time that they need to solve a problem. In a typical CSP method evaluation exercise, sets of problems with each set usually contains a few dozen to several thousand problem instances which are characterised by some parameterised value are generated and each CSP method under investigation is applied to solve them.

After collecting the required data from an experiment, the immediate question is how to analyse them. The most frequently used statistics are simple measures such as mean or median. The mean is vulnerable to outliers whereas median totally ignores them. Parametric tests such as ANOVA and *t*-test are used in some research [5, 6]. However such parametric tests often rely on the fact that the data has characteristics of the normal curve. The validity of this assumption in CSP research is in doubt. The problem of non-normality of data in a *NP*-complete problem is observed and reported in [12]. In that research, the Davis-Putnum algorithm was applied to test the satisfiability of randomly generated 3-SAT problems. The number of steps that the algorithm took in each run was recorded. Sample means for different sample sizes were then calculated. Mitchell found that the sample means varied significantly as the sample size was increased. This suggested that the central limit theorem did not hold unless a very large sample size was used. As a result, the normality assumption was undermined.

According to our previous computational experience, the number of compatibility checks or the cpu time needed for a CSP algorithm-heuristic combination to solve CSPs may have a great variation even for CSPs which share very similar characteristics.[1] We conjecture that the normality assumption could be violated in some occasions. If this is true, the implication is twofold. Firstly, previous reported research results based on parametric statistics could be prone to error. Secondly, the CSP research community has to consider some statistical tools which do not rely on normality assumption for analysing experimental results.

The aim of this paper is to provide evidence that the normality of data should not be taken for granted when evaluating CSP methods. Our procedures for verifying normality of data are presented in the next section. The design and results of experiments on random binary CSPs and 3-colouring problems, two popular problems for benchmarking CSP methods, will be described in section 3 and section 4 respectively. We discuss our conclusions in the final section.

2 Procedures for Verifying Normality of Data[2]

A normal distribution can be represented by a normal curve when scores are plotted against frequency on a graph. A normal curve has three important characteristics. Firstly, the mean, the median and the mode are all located in the middle of the curve. Secondly, the frequency of scores declines in a predictable way as the scores deviate farther and farther away from the centre of the curve. Thirdly, normal curves are bilaterally symmetrical and usually have a bell shape, but not all symmetrical curves are normal [19].

---

[1] For simplicity, we only consider the number of compatibility checks as the performance indicator for comparing algorithm-heuristic combinations in this paper. However, we believe that the observations presented in this paper should be equally valid if cpu time is used as a performance indicator instead.

[2] There are two reasons for us to include the details of this "standard" statistic rather than only making a reference in this paper. Firstly, it appears that the procedures of testing normality of data are not widely available in books on statistics. Secondly, we found different descriptions on the computation of those statistics in different sources. In order to avoid possible confusion and to make this paper more self-contained, we present full details of the procedures that we used in this research. However it is important to emphasise that most of the material presented in this section are adopted from [17].

The deviation of data from normality can be measured in terms of *skewness* and *kurtosis*. Skewness is a measure of the central tendency of the peak of the curve of the data whereas kurtosis is a measure of the relative peakedness of the curve of the data. We shall refer to skewness and kurtosis as g_1 and g_2 respectively, statistics based on the sum of the third and the fourth moments of deviations from mean, as used in [17]. The basic idea behind these measures is to accentuate the extreme values of the scores. Figures 1 and 2 show the curves of different skewness and different kurtosis respectively.

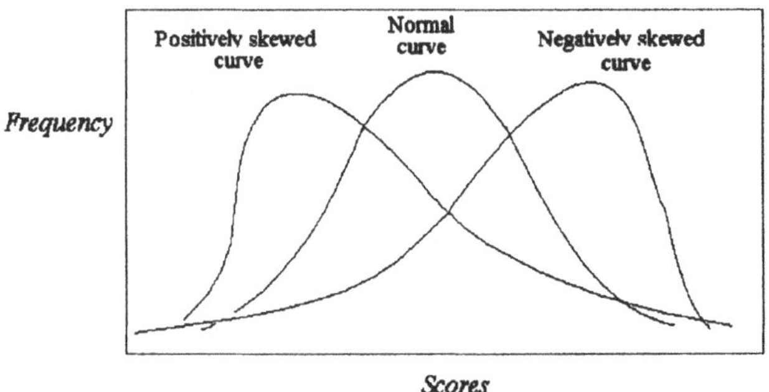

Figure 1. Frequency curves of different skewness

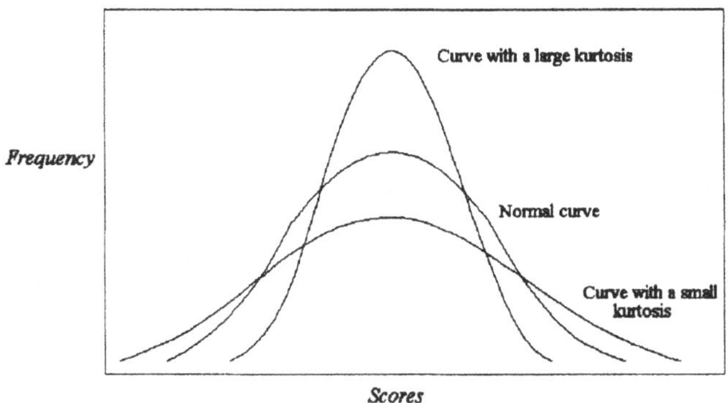

Figure 2. Frequency curves of different kurtosis

Suppose X_i is the value of i-th element of sample X and $\overline{X}$ is the sample mean. S_j denotes the sum of the j-th powers of deviations from the sample mean, *i.e.*,

$$S_j = \sum_{i=1}^{N} \left(X_i - \overline{X}\right)^j$$

where N is the sample size. g_1 and g_2 are defined as follows as given in [17]:

$$g_1 = k_3 / (k_2 \sqrt{k_2}) \quad \text{and} \quad g_2 = k_4 / k_2^2$$

where

$$k_2 = S_2/(N-1);$$
$$k_3 = N S_3/(N-1)(N-2);$$
$$k_4 = \left[N(N+1)S_4 - 3(N-1)S_2^2\right] / (N-1)(N-2)(N-3)$$

If g_1 and g_2 are equal to zero, there is no departure from normality as far as these measures are concerned. g_1 is positive when data are skewed positive and negative when data are negatively skewed.[3] g_2 is positive when the curve is more peaked than normal, *i.e.*, there is an excess of items near the mean, and negative when the distribution curve is flat-topped. Z scores of skewness and kurtosis, denoted by $Zg1$ and $Zg2$ respectively are defined as follows:

$$Zg1 = g_1 / \sqrt{6N(N-1)/(N-2)(N+1)(N+3)}$$
$$Zg2 = g_2 / \sqrt{24N(N-1)^2/(N-3)(N-2)(N+3)(N+5)}$$

Thus if $Zg1$ or $Zg2$ is greater than 1.96 or less than -1.96, the distribution is considered to be non-normal with $p \leq 0.5$.

3 Experiments on Random Binary CSPs

3.1 Experimental Design

In order to investigating whether the normality assumption holds in general, we decided to conduct our experiments on randomly generated binary CSPs which have been widely used as benchmark problems for evaluating CSP techniques.

The binary CSPs are characterised by a 4-tuple <*n*, *m*, *p*1, *p*2> such that *n* is the number of variables, *m* is the uniform domain size for each variable, constraint density, denoted by *p*1, is the proportion of pairs of variable that a constraint exists between them and constraint tightness, denoted by *p*2, is the proportion of incompatible pairs of values for each pair of variables if there exists a constraint between them. No universal constraints (that allows any pair of values) or null constraints (that do not allow any pair of values) were allowed. At each data point, 50 samples were generated. All the generated problems have connected constraint graphs. Since we are interested in how often that the normality assumption is violated, CSPs with different characteristics were used for testing.

Given a set of CSPs, different algorithm-heuristic combinations might produce results with very different distributions. To counter this, several algorithm-heuristic

[3] Note that a positively skewed distribution implies that the median is smaller than the mean and a negatively skewed distribution has its mean smaller than the median.

combinations were used on each problem to find the first solution or exhaust the search space otherwise. These included backmarking and conflict-directed backjumping (BM-CBJ) [14] with minimal width heuristic (MWO) [4], forward checking with backmarking and conflict-directed backjumping (FC-BM-CBJ) [13] with a heuristic called BZ which is derived from Brélaz heuristic [1][4], minimal forward checking with backmarking and conflict-directed backjumping (MFC-BM-CBJ) [11] with either BZ or MWO. The backmarking element in all these algorithms employed a 2-dimensional data structure for storing minimal backup level as described in [10]. These algorithms were chosen because they represent a spectrum of CSP techniques which perform different degree of constraint propagation during search. The purpose of employing backmarking and conflict-directed backjumping in all the chosen algorithms was to reduce the possibility of thrashing during search. We hoped that this allowed us to alleviate the possibility of encountering exceptionally hard problems [9, 7] which usually result in producing non-normal distributions, particularly when a small sample size is adopted.

3.2 Results

In the first series of experiments, we ran the selected algorithm-heuristic combinations on CSPs with the following characteristics.

$n = 10; m = 5;\ p1 = 0.2, 0.3, ..., 1;\ n = 10; m = 10; p1 = 0.2, 0.3, ..., 1$
$n = 10; m = 20; p1 = 0.2, 0.3, ..., 1;\ n = 20; m = 5;\ p1 = 0.1, 0.2, ..., 1$
$n = 20; m = 10; p1 = 0.1, 0.2, ..., 1;\ n = 20; m = 20; p1 = 0.1, 0.2, ..., 1$
$n = 30; m = 5;\ p1 = 0.1, 0.2, ..., 1;\ n = 30; m = 10; p1 = 0.1, 0.2, ..., 1$
$n = 40; m = 5;\ p1 = 0.1, 0.2, ..., 1$

For all the above settings, $p2$ was varied from 0.04 to 0.96 with an increment of 0.04. For each of the data points, we computed Z_{g1} and Z_{g2} of the distribution produced by each of the algorithm-heuristic combinations on the 50 samples at that data point. The number of distributions which were found non-normal for the chosen algorithm-heuristic combinations for different n and m is given in Table 3. Note that we regard a distribution as non-normal if either its skewness or its kurtosis is beyond normality with a confident level of 95%.

Each entry of Table 3 has two numbers. The first is the number of non-normal distributions found whereas the second is the number of total data points examined. For example, the top leftmost entry in the table means that when FC-BM-CBJ with BZ is used to tackle the CSPs, which have 10-variable and a uniform domain size of 5, from 216 data points, 107 of them have a non-normal distribution.

From Table 3, it is clear that FC-BM-CBJ with BZ quite often produces results with a non-normal distribution. The other three algorithm-heuristic combinations produce significantly more non-normal results for problems with $m = 5$ than with m

---

[4] BZ is a variant of the fail-first heuristic [8]. The difference between them is that BZ breaks ties by selecting the future variable connected to the most other future variables whereas the fail-first heuristic selects one arbitrarily.

= 10 or 20. It appears that the normality assumption is often violated when m is small, say $m = 5$, in all the selected combinations.

	FC-BM-CBJ + BZ[5]	MFC-BM-CBJ + BZ	MFC-BM-CBJ + MWO	BM-CBJ + MWO
$n = 10; m = 5$	107 (216)	117 (216)	122 (216)	108 (216)
$n = 10; m = 10$	100 (216)	11 (216)	16 (216)	14 (216)
$n = 10; m = 20$	95 (216)	10 (216)	14 (216)	12 (216)
$n = 20; m = 5$	104 (240)	121 (240)	122 (240)	122 (240)
$n = 20; m = 10$	91 (240)	27 (240)	23 (240)	26 (240)
$n = 20; m = 20$	80 (240)	23 (240)	29 (240)	27 (240)
$n = 30; m = 5$	102 (240)	112 (240)	113 (240)	111 (240)
$n = 30; m = 10$	79 (240)	24 (240)	26 (240)	28 (240)
$n = 40; m = 5$	90 (240)	108 (240)	125 (240)	119 (240)

Table 3. Number of data points which have a non-normal distribution ($p < 0.05$) for random binary CSPs (sample size at each data point = 50)

When we examined the raw results, two trends were observed. First, almost all non-normal distributions that we found are heavily positively skewed, with many of them also associated with a large kurtosis. Second, all the adopted combinations produced non-normal distributions across the "mushy region"[6] [16] when $p1$ was set to 0.1.[7] In particular, most of the distributions associated with the data points across the "mushy region" produced by FC-BM-CBJ with BZ for small $p1$ (0.1 - 0.3) were found to be non-normal.

The second observation is particularly interesting. CSPs near to the 50% satisfiable point, also known as the crossover point [3], have been used in a number of recent research in evaluating CSP methods. In particular, many of those benchmark problems have a rather small $p1$. However, our finding appears to suggest that when m or $p1$ is small, the normality assumption is very often violated near the crossover point. We conjectured that when both m and $p1$ have small values, the chance of having the normality assumption valid would be very slim for problems close to the crossover point. In order to verify this conjecture, the same algorithm-heuristic combinations were run on larger CSPs with $n = 60$, $m = 5$ and $p1$ = 0.1, 0.2 and 0.3. Again $p2$ was varied from 0.04 to 0.96 with a step of 0.04 and 50 samples were generated at each data point. For each chosen $p1$, we recorded the largest range of $p2$ in which the distribution associated with each of our sampled $p2$

[5] The plus sign "+" stands for "combined with". For example "FC-BM-CBJ+BZ" means FC-BM-CBJ combined with BZ.

[6] The "mushy region" denotes the range of values of the order parameter over which the phase transition from solubility to insolubility takes place [16]. In our case, $p2$ was the order parameter since n, m and $p1$ were fixed in the experiments.

[7] Note that this excludes the 10-variable CSPs as the smallest $p1$ which allows a connected constraint graph is 0.2.

within the range is non-normal. The results are summarised in Table 4. For ease of reference, the crude boundaries of the mushy regions are also given. Note that the mushy regions are often very narrow for the 60-variable CSPs. Phase transition [2] happened "instantaneously" in several occasions because a coarse $p2$ increment was used. To overcome this problem, we define the $p2$'s range associated with a "crude" mushy region starting from the largest $p2$ which has all its 50 CSPs soluble and ending at the smallest $p2$ which has all its 50 CSPs insoluble in our samples.

		FC-BM-CBJ + BZ	MFC-BM-CBJ + BZ	MFC-BM-CBJ + MWO	BM-CBJ + MWO
$p1 = 0.1$	"crude" mushy region	0.32 - 0.40	0.32 - 0.40	0.32 - 0.40	0.32 - 0.40
	non-normal $p2$'s range	0.20 - 0.52	0.20 - 0.68	0.20 - 0.84	0.16 - 0.72
$p1 = 0.2$	"crude" mushy region	0.20 - 0.24	0.20 - 0.24	0.20 -0.24	0.20 -0.24
	non-normal $p2$'s range	0.16 - 0.32	0.04 - 0.32	0.12 - 0.36	0.08 - 0.76
$p1 = 0.3$	"crude" mushy region	0.12 - 0.20	0.12 - 0.20	0.12 - 0.20	0.12 - 0.20
	non-normal $p2$'s range	0.12 - 0.24	0.08 - 0.20	0.08 - 0.36	0.08 - 0.52

Table 4. Range of $p2$ with a non-normal distribution ($p < 0.05$) for 60-variable random binary CSPs (sample size at each data point = 50)

It is clear from Table 4 that all the data points within the "crude" mushy regions of the 60-variable CSPs have a non-normal distribution when $p1 = 0.1$, 0.2 and 0.3. It can also be observed from the table that the lower the $p1$, the greater the $p2$'s range associated with a non-normal distribution. These results suggest that we have to be careful in interpreting the inference drawn from parametric statistics based on the results of running a CSP method on problems close to the crossover point which have small m and $p1$.

4 Experiments on 3-Colouring Problems

4.1 Experimental Design

It has been shown in §3.2 that we should not assume normality of distribution when analysing results based on experimenting random binary CSPs which have small m and $p1$ within or close to mushy regions. In order to see whether the same observation can be drawn from other types of CSPs, experiments on 3-colouring problems were performed. The reason for choosing 3-colouring problems was that they have a small domain size. In addition, the approximate location of phase transition for 3-colouring problems has been reported to occur when the average node degree of a graph, denoted by d, is about 4.6 in the literature [9]. For graphs with reasonably large number of nodes, denoted by n, it is expected that phase transition happens at a rather small $p1$ because the relationship between d and $p1$ are dictated by the following equation:

$$d = (n\text{-}1) * p1$$

In our experiments, connected graphs of different sizes (n = 20, 30, ..., 110 and 200) were randomly generated. For each value of n, 100 graphs were generated for each value of d starting from 2.0 to 7.0 with an increment of 0.1. 56,100 graphs were used in total. The four algorithm-heuristic combinations mentioned in §3.1 were used to colour each graph except that MFC-BM-CBJ with BZ was not used for colouring the 200-node graphs as this combination was found much less efficient than the other combinations when colouring the other graphs ($n \leq 100$).

4.2 Results

The empirical results were analysed as what we did for the random binary CSPs. Table 5 displays the number of data points which are associated with a non-normal distribution ($p < 0.05$). The interpretation of Table 5 is the same as Table 3.

	FC-BM-CBJ + BZ	MFC-BM-CBJ + BZ	MFC-BM-CBJ + MWO	BM-CBJ + MWO
$n = 20$	44 (51)	43 (51)	44 (51)	43 (51)
$n = 30$	47 (51)	45 (51)	43 (51)	43 (51)
$n = 40$	44 (51)	46 (51)	39 (51)	39 (51)
$n = 50$	43 (51)	48 (51)	39 (51)	38 (51)
$n = 60$	43 (51)	48 (51)	40 (51)	40 (51)
$n = 70$	43 (51)	48 (51)	40 (51)	39 (51)
$n = 80$	45 (51)	48 (51)	40 (51)	40 (51)
$n = 90$	44 (51)	48 (51)	40 (51)	38 (51)
$n = 100$	44 (51)	49 (51)	40 (51)	39 (51)
$n = 110$	46(51)	48 (51)	44 (51)	44 (51)
$n = 200$	45(51)	N/A	38 (51)	38 (51)

Table 5. Number of data points which have a non-normal distribution ($p < 0.05$) for 3-colouring problems (sample size at each data point = 100)

From Table 5, it is clear that for all the three algorithm-heuristic combinations that we used, most of the results (on average, over 80%) produce a non-normal distribution. When examining the raw results, we found that almost all the non-normal distributions have a large skewness as well as a large kurtosis. In addition, all the data points across the "mushy region", no matter which algorithm-heuristic combination was used, are associated with a non-normal distribution (see Table 6). These findings are consistent with the results we have found earlier when experimenting random binary CSPs. Note that Table 6 is interpreted in a similar way as in Table 6. The main differences are that mushy regions are used instead of "crude" mushy regions and the non-normal d's range is identified instead of the $p2$'s range.

Table 6 provides more evidence to our conjecture that the normality assumption should not be taken for granted when analysing CSP research results when the problems have low constraint density and domain size which are near to the crossover point.

		FC-BM-CBJ + BZ	MFC-BM-CBJ + BZ	MFC-BM-CBJ + MWO	BM-CBJ + MWO
$n = 20$	mushy region	2.8 - 5.8	2.8 - 5.8	2.8 - 5.8	2.8 - 5.8
	non-normal *d*'s range	2.7 - 7.0	2.7 - 6.8	2.8 - 7.0	2.9 - 7.0
$n = 30$	mushy region	3.1 - 5.0	3.1 - 5.0	3.1 - 5.0	3.1 - 5.0
	non-normal *d*'s range	2.4 - 7.0	2.6 - 7.0	3.0 - 7.0	3.0 - 7.0
$n = 40$	mushy region	3.2 - 5.1	3.2 - 5.1	3.2 - 5.1	3.2 - 5.1
	non-normal *d*'s range	2.7 - 7.0	2.5 - 7.0	3.2 - 7.0	3.2 - 7.0
$n = 50$	mushy region	3.4 - 5.1	3.4 - 5.1	3.4 - 5.1	3.4 - 5.1
	non-normal *d*'s range	2.9 - 7.0	2.3 - 7.0	3.2 - 7.0	3.3 - 7.0
$n = 60$	mushy region	3.8 - 4.9	3.8 - 4.9	3.8 - 4.9	3.8 - 4.9
	non-normal *d*'s range	3.1 - 7.0	2.3 - 7.0	2.8 - 7.0	3.1 - 7.0
$n = 70$	mushy region	3.2 - 5.1	3.2 - 5.1	3.2 - 5.1	3.2 - 5.1
	non-normal *d*'s range	2.8 - 7.0	2.3 - 7.0	3.2 - 7.0	3.3 - 7.0
$n = 80$	mushy region	3.1 - 4.9	3.1 - 4.9	3.1 - 4.9	3.1 - 4.9
	non-normal *d*'s range	2.7 - 7.0	2.3 - 7.0	3.1 - 7.0	3.1 - 7.0
$n = 90$	mushy region	4.0 - 4.9	4.0 - 4.9	4.0 - 4.9	4.0 - 4.9
	non-normal *d*'s range	3.1 - 7.0	2.3 - 7.0	3.2 - 7.0	3.4 - 7.0
$n = 100$	mushy region	3.8 - 4.8	3.8 - 4.8	3.8 - 4.8	3.8 - 4.8
	non-normal *d*'s range	2.7 - 7.0	2.3 - 7.0	3.1 - 7.0	3.4 - 7.0
$n = 110$	mushy region	3.1 - 5.0	3.1 - 5.0	3.1 - 5.0	3.1 - 5.0
	non-normal *d*'s range	2.6 - 7.0	2.3 - 7.0	2.9 - 7.0	2.9 - 7.0
$n = 200$	mushy region	4.2 -4.8	4.2 -4.8	4.2 -4.8	4.2 -4.8
	non-normal *d*'s range	2.7 - 7.0	N/A	3.4 - 7.0	3.4 - 7.0

Table 6. Range of *d* with a non-normal distribution ($p < 0.05$) for 3-colouring problems (sample size at each data point = 100)

5 Conclusions

The success of an empirical approach relies on a rigorous experimental design and statistical analysis of the results. Interpreting the results using an inappropriate statistical tool could lead to an inaccurate or even misleading conclusion. Many statistical tools require the fulfilment of certain assumptions, notably the normality assumption, for their application. We have provided evidence in this paper that the normality assumption should not be taken for granted in CSP research.

According to our research results based on random binary CSPs and 3-colouring problems, the normality assumption is often violated for a number of algorithm-heuristic combinations when applied to CSPs which have a low constraint density or small domain sizes within or close to mushy regions. This point deserves extra attention as many studies of CSP methods have used this type of problems, particularly those near to the crossover points, as benchmark problems. Although some parametric tests like *t*-test and ANOVA are quite robust, they could still result in making error-prone inference when normality assumption is seriously violated. One way to alleviate the problem is to adopt a more conservative level of confidence to avoid errors. However we believe that non-parametric statistics such as Wilcoxon's signed rank test [15] are in general more appropriate for analysing CSP research results as they do not assume a normal distribution of data.

Acknowledgements

Thanks are given to James Borrett who helped to implement the Brélaz heuristic and commented on an early draft of this paper and to Edward Tsang for suggesting improvements to this paper. This research was supported by the University of Essex research promotion fund ref. R7207 and by the EPSRC research grant ref. GR/J/42878.

References

[1] Brélaz, D. New Methods to Color the Vertices of a Graph. *Communications of the ACM* 22(4), 251-256, 1979.

[2] Cheeseman, P., Kanefsky, B. & Taylor, W.M. Where the Really Hard Problems Are. In *Proceedings IJCAI-91*, 331-337, 1991.

[3] Crawford, J.M. & Auton, L.D. Experimental Results on the Crossover Point in Satisfiability Problems. In *Proceedings AAAI-93*, 21-27, 1993.

[4] Freuder, E. A Sufficient Condition for Backtrack-Free Search. *J. ACM* 29, 24-32, 1982.

[5] Freuder, E.C. & Wallace, R.J. Selective Relaxation for Constraint Satisfaction Problems. In *Proceedings 1991 IEEE International Conference on Tools for Artificial Intelligence*, 332-339, 1991.

[6] Frost, D. & Dechter, R. Look-ahead Value Ordering for Constraint Satisfaction Problems. In *Proceeding IJCAI-95*, 572-578, 1995.

[7] Gent, I.P. & Walsh, T. Easy Problems are Sometimes Hard. *Artificial Intelligence* 70, 335-345, 1994.

[8] Haralick, R.M. & Elliott, G.L. Increasing Tree Search Efficiency for Constraint Satisfaction Problems. *Artificial Intelligence* 14, 263-314, 1980.

[9] Hogg, T. & Williams, C.P. The Hardest Constraint Problems: A Double Phase Transition. *Artificial Intelligence* 69, 359 - 377, 1994.

[10] Kondrak, G. & van Beek, P. *A Theoretical Evaluation of Selected Backtracking Algorithms*. In *Proceedings IJCAI-95*, 541-547, 1995.

[11] Kwan, A.C.M. & Tsang, E.P.K. Minimal Forward Checking with Backmarking. Technical Report CSM-260, Department of Computer Science, University of Essex, U.K., 1996.

[12] Mitchell, D.G. Respecting Your Data. In *Proceedings AAAI-94 Workshop on Experimental Evaluation of Reasoning and Search Methods*, 28-31, 1994.

[13] Prosser, P. Forward Checking with Backmarking. In Meyer (ed.): *Constraint Processing*, LNCS 923, Springer-Verlag, 185-204, 1995.

[14] Prosser, P. Hybrid Algorithms for the Constraint Satisfaction Problem. *Computational Intelligence* 9(3), 268-299, 1993

[15] Scheaffer, R.L. & McClave, J.T. *Probability and Statistics for Engineers, 3rd edition*, Pws-Kent, 1990.

[16] Smith, B.M. Phase Transition and the Mushy Region in Constraint Satisfaction Problems. In *Proceedings ECAI-94*, 100-104, 1994.

[17] Snedecor, G.W. *Statistical Methods* (5th edition). Iowa State University Press, 1956.

[18] Tsang, E. *Foundations of Constraint Satisfaction.* Academic Press, London, 1993.

[19] Vincent, W.J. *Statistics in Kinesiology*. Human Kinetics, USA, 1995.

An Improved Generic Arc Consistency Algorithm and Its Specializations

Bing Liu

Department of Information Systems and Computer Science
National University of Singapore
Lower Kent Ridge Road, Singapore 119260
liub@iscs.nus.sg

Abstract

Many general and specific arc consistency algorithms have been produced in the past for solving Constraint Satisfaction Problems (CSP). The important general algorithms are AC-3, AC-4, AC-5 and AC-6. AC-5 is also a generic algorithm. It can be reduced to AC-3, AC-4 and AC-6. Specific algorithms are efficient specializations of the general ones for specific constraints. Functional, anti-functional and monotonic constraints are three important classes of specific constraints. AC-5 has been specialized to produce an O(*ed*) algorithm (in time) for these classes of constraints. However, this specialization does not reduce the space requirement. In practical applications, both time and space requirements are important. This paper makes two contributions. First, it proposes an improved generic arc consistency algorithm, called AC-5*, which can be specialized to reduce both time and space complexities. Second, it presents a more efficient technique for handling an important subclass of functional constraints, namely *increasing functional constraints* (IFC).

1. Introduction

Arc consistency techniques are the key techniques for solving CSPs. Past research has produced many general and specific arc consistency algorithms. The most important general algorithms are AC-3 [6], AC-4 [8], AC-5 [10] and AC-6 [1]. AC-5 is also a generic algorithm, and it can be reduced to AC-3, AC-4 and AC-6. Among these algorithms, AC-3 has the optimal space complexity of $O(e + nd)$ [8], while AC-4 and AC-6 have the optimal time complexity of $O(ed^2)$ [8, 1], where n is the number of variables, e is the number of arcs, and d is the size of the domain.

Specific algorithms are efficient specializations of the general ones for specific constraints [9, 10]. These algorithms typically exploit the semantics of individual constraints in consistency check, and they are more widely used in practical applications than the general ones. Functional (FC), anti-functional (ATFC) and monotonic constraints (MC) are three important classes of specific constraints.

In recent years, the CSP model has been implemented in constraint programming languages, such as CHIP [9] and Ilog Solver [3], for solving practical combinatorial search problems, such as scheduling and resource allocations [3, 10]. The basic constraints used in these languages are special cases of FC, ATFC and MC.

In [10], AC-5 is specialized to produce an algorithm running in $O(ed)$ (the optimal time complexity [10]) for these three classes of constraints. However, due to its fixed queue element representation, it cannot be specialized to reduce the space complexity. It still requires $O(ed + nd)$ space, which is worse than that of AC-3.

In practical applications, both time and space requirements are important in selecting an algorithm. Then, the question is: can we have a generic algorithm that can be specialized for these classes of constraints to achieve both the optimal time complexity of $O(ed)$ and the optimal space complexity of $O(e + nd)$ (at the same time)? The answer is almost yes.

This paper makes two contributions. First, we propose an improved (over AC-5) generic arc consistency algorithm, called AC-5*. It is parametrized on two procedures and a queue element representation. Its key feature is that it can be specialized to produce efficient specific algorithms in terms of both time complexity and space complexity. It can also be reduced to AC-3, AC-4, AC-5 and AC-6 by proper implementation of the two procedures and the queue element.

Second, we introduce a more efficient technique to check an important sub-class of functional constraints, namely, *increasing function constraints* (IFCs). In this method, IFCs need to be checked only once, rather than many times as in a typical consistency check process. The main idea of this technique was first introduced in [5]. This paper enhances the technique and presents two implications of it.

1. Although the new technique is still $O(ed)$ (in time) for IFCs, the same as that of AC-5, experiments show that it outperforms the existing techniques substantially.
2. Together with AC-5*, we can produce an arc consistency algorithm for IFCs, ATFCs and MCs that has both the optimal time and the optimal space complexities. This cannot be achieved with existing techniques.

These results are significant in practice because the basic functional constraint used in the current constraint programming languages [9, 3] is actually an IFC.

2. Preliminaries

A CSP is defined as follows: (1) variables – a finite set of n variables $\{1, 2, ..., n\}$, and (2) domains – each variable i takes its values from an associated finite domain D_i, and (3) constraints – a set of binary constraints C among variables. We assume, for simplicity, that there is only one constraint, denoted as C_{ij}, between a pair of variables i and j.

A graph G can be associated with a CSP, where each node represents a variable i, and each edge between two variables i and j represents a constraint, which is expressed as two directed arcs, (i, j) and (j, i). We denote by e the number of arcs in G, by d the size of the largest domain, and by $arc(G)$ the set of arcs in G.

In this paper, we assume the standard definitions of arc consistency [7, 10]. We now define functional (FC) and increasing functional (IFC) constraints. We will not define anti-functional and monotonic constraints as they can be found in [10]. Since our techniques require a total ordering on the domain, let us define it here first.

Definition 1. A domain $D_i = \{v_1, ..., v_a\}$ is totally ordered iff $v_k < v_{k+1}$.

Definition 2. Given two variables i and j, we denote $i \rightarrow j$ iff for all $v \in D_i$ there exists at most one $w \in D_j$ such that $C_{ij}(v, w)$ holds. If it exists, then $w = f_{ij}(v)$.
A constraint is functional iff $i \rightarrow j$ and $j \rightarrow i$.

Definition 3. Given two variables, we denote $i \uparrow j$ iff (1) $i \rightarrow j$, and (2) for all $u, v \in D_i$ such that both $f_{ij}(u)$ and $f_{ij}(v)$ exist in D_j then $u < v$ implies $f_{ij}(u) < f_{ij}(v)$.

Observe that if $i \uparrow j$ (or equivalently $j \uparrow i$) then the constraint C_{ij} must be functional, and we call such a constraint *increasing functional constraint*.

An example of an IFC is $x = y + 5$. An example of an ATFC is $x \neq y$, and an example of a MC is $x \leq y + 1$.

The basic constraints in the current constraint languages are special cases of FC, ATFC and MC [10, 3]. In fact, they are equations ($aX = bY + c$), inequalities ($aX \leq bY + c$) and disequations ($aX \neq bY$), where a, b and c are constants and $a, b \geq 0$. Domain values are natural numbers. According to Definition 3, the equation $aX = bY + c$, which is a special case of FC, is also a special case of IFC.

Most of the earlier algorithms do not use the semantics of constraints to achieve better efficiency. AC-5 is different as the implementation of its two procedures ArcCons and LocalArcCons are left open. This means that for different constraints different procedures can be used. ArcCons checks an arc when it is first encountered, and LocalArcCons rechecks it if its consistency is broken. [10] provides the special ArcCons and LocalArcCons procedures for checking FCs, ATFCs and MCs in time O(ed). In this paper, we call these two procedures the *initial check* procedure and the *recheck* procedure respectively for intuitive reasons. This separation is important because of efficiency reasons [4].

3. AC-5* Algorithm

Since AC-5* is intended to improve AC-5, before presenting AC-5*, we make some observations about AC-5. Take note that all arc consistency algorithms work with a queue Q containing elements to be rechecked.

- The key feature of AC-5 is that its Q contains elements $((i, j), w)$, where (i, j) is an arc and w is a value that has been removed from D_j.
- Due to this queue element representation, AC-5 achieves the time complexity of O(ed), and the space complexity of O($ed + nd$) for FCs, ATFCs and MCs. The space complexity is worse than that of AC-3, which is O($e + nd$).
- From AC-5, it can be observed that for ATFCs and MCs, value w is not used in its LocalArcCons implementations. Only the minimum and maximum domain values and the domain size are employed. Using w for these constraints is a waste of space. However, for FCs, using w is important. If we know a value w that has been removed from j, we can remove its corresponding value in i in constant time. This results in an O(ed) algorithm. If w is not known, only an O(ed^2) algorithm (in time) can be achieved for FCs.

We now present AC-5* (Figure 1). Like AC-5, AC-5* also has two steps, the initial check step (line 2-3), and the recheck step (line 4-8). In initial check, each arc in $arc(G)$ is checked once to enforce arc consistency. In recheck, *ReCheck* is applied to each element of the queue Q, possibly generating new elements in Q.

The algorithm is parametrized on two procedures, *InitialCheck* and *ReCheck*, and the representation of the queue element *ELT*. Their implementations are left open. Since different queue elements can have different representations in the same algorithm, it allows AC-5* to be specialized to save space in addition to time. This is the key difference between AC-5* and AC-5.

Algorithm AC-5*
  begin
    $Q \leftarrow \varnothing$;
    for each $(i, j) \in \text{arc}(G)$ **do**
      InitialCheck((i, j), Q);
    while Q not empty **do**
      begin
        delete an element *ELT* from Q;
        ReCheck(*ELT*, Q)
      end
  end

Figure 1. AC-5* algorithm

In AC-5*, we classify arcs (or constraints) into two classes:

1. Arcs that require w to produce an efficient algorithm, e.g., FC arcs. We call this set of arcs *W_arcs*.
2. Arcs that do not require w to produce an efficient algorithm, e.g., ATFC and MC arcs. We call this set of arcs *NW_arcs*.

We now present the specifications for the two abstract procedures *InitialCheck* and *ReCheck*, and the queue element *ELT*. In AC-5*, a queue element could either be (i, j) or $((i, j), w)$. If arc (i, j) is a *W_arc*, $((i, j), w)$ is used. If arc (i, j) is a *NW_arc*, (i, j) is used. Figure 2 shows *InitialCheck* and *ReCheck*. Notice that there are two *ReCheck* procedures (I and II) because of the two queue element representations. *Enqueue* is given in Figure 3. *Remove* removes the values in Δ from D_i.

Procedure InitialCheck (**in** (i, j), **inout** Q)
  $\Delta \leftarrow \{v \in D_i \mid \forall w \in D_j: \neg C_{ij}(v, w)\}$;
  Remove(Δ, i);
  Enqueue(i, Δ, Q)

I **Procedure** ReCheck (**in** (i, j), **inout** Q)
  $\Delta \leftarrow \{v \in D_i \mid \forall w \in D_j: \neg C_{ij}(v, w)\}$;
  Remove(Δ, i);
  Enqueue(i, Δ, Q)

II **Procedure** ReCheck(**in** $((i, j), w)$, **inout** Q)
  $\Delta_1 \subseteq \Delta \subseteq \Delta_2$ with $\Delta_1 \leftarrow \{v \in D_i \mid C_{ij}(v, w) \text{ and } \forall w' \in D_j: \neg C_{ij}(v, w')\}$
  $\Delta_2 \leftarrow \{v \in D_i \mid \forall w' \in D_j: \neg C_{ij}(v, w')\}$
  Remove(Δ, i);
  Enqueue(i, Δ, Q)

Figure 2. *InitialCheck* and *ReCheck* procedures

Procedure Enqueue (**in** i, Δ, **inout** Q}
  if $\Delta \neq \varnothing$ **then** **begin**
    $Q \leftarrow Q \cup \{((k, i), v) \mid (k, i) \in W\_arc(G) \text{ and } v \in \Delta\}$;
    $Q \leftarrow Q \cup \{(m, i) \mid (m, i) \in NW\_arc(G)\}$
  end

Figure 3. *Enqueue* procedure

AC-5* may be seen as an integration of AC-3 and AC-5 because of its two *ELT* representations. Its correctness follows directly from that of AC-5 and AC-3. All the general properties of AC-5 still apply. With proper implementation of the three items, AC-5* can be reduced to AC-3, AC-4, AC-5, and AC-6.

- AC-3 is clearly a particular case of AC-5* where the implementations of *InitialCheck* and *ReCheck* are the same. The queue element *ELT* is simply (i, j).
- AC-4 is also a particular case of AC-5* where *ELT* is $((i, j), w)$, but *ReCheck*'s implementation does not use i.[3] *ReCheck* prunes inconsistent values by maintaining a data structure S of size $O(ed^2)$. *InitialCheck* initializes S.
- AC-5 is also a special case of AC-5* where *ELT* is $((i, j), w)$. Note that AC-5* puts *Enqueue* and *Remove* in *InitialCheck* and *ReCheck*. This gives more flexibility in specializing the two procedures.
- Like AC-4, AC-6 is again a special case of AC-5*. Unlike AC-4, *ReCheck* prunes inconsistent values by finding successive value supports and maintaining this information in a data structure S of size $O(ed)$. *InitialCheck* initializes S.

Like AC-5, AC-5* can also be specialized to produce an $O(ed)$ algorithm (in time) for FCs, ATFCs and MCs. The space complexity is, however, reduced.

- For ATFCs and MCs, the space complexity is $O(e + nd)$ since we can use (i, j) as *ELT*, instead of $O(ed + nd)$ as AC-5.
- For FCs, the space complexity is still $O(ed + nd)$, which is the same as AC-5, since we use $((i, j)\ w)$ as *ELT*.

The key advantage of AC-5* is that it achieves the space complexity of $O(e + nd)$ for ATFCs and MCs. We will not present all the specific procedures for *InitialCheck* and *ReCheck* here as they can be easily obtained by modifying those in AC-5. In Section 4, we present a technique for IFCs that does not need w to produce an $O(ed)$ algorithm in time. This results in the space complexity of $O(e + nd)$ for IFCs.

4. An Implementation of AC-5*

We may view AC-3, AC-4, AC-5, and AC-6 as special implementations of AC-5*. In this section, we present another implementation with its specializations. For easy reference, we call this implementation, AC-5*$_3$, as it is similar to AC-3. The main difference is that AC-3 does not distinguish initial check and recheck.

Here, we will also describe our new technique for checking IFCs, which is an improvement over that in [5]. The main improvement is in the handling of cycles of IFCs, which were not handled satisfactorily [5]. With this technique, we can achieve the optimal space complexity of $O(e + nd)$ and the optimal time complexity of $O(ed)$ for IFCs, ATFCs, and MCs. Although the time complexity for IFCs is still the same as that in AC-5, test results show that the new technique runs substantially faster than the existing ones. We will not describe the specialized procedures for ATFCs and MCs as they are almost the same as those in AC-5.

In AC-5*$_3$, the queue element *ELT* is only (i, j). $((i, j), w)$ is not used because for these three classes of constraints, having w does not help. Thus, all the arcs are *NW_arcs*. Hence, the space complexity is $O(e + nd)$ as AC-3. Due to the new method for IFCs, in line 2 of AC-5*, each IFC is expressed as one arc (or edge), either (i, j) or (j, i), rather than two arcs. This simplifies the technique.

4.1 Domain representation

The domain data structures for AC-5*$_3$ are shown in Figure 4. This representation is similar to that in AC-5. However, there are some key differences, which will be made clear from the description below. Like AC-5 and AC-6, we assume a total ordering on the domain.

Figure 4(A) shows the top level structure. The field *merge* tells whether this domain has merged with another domain. Its meaning will become clear later. The field *element* is a set of pairs (v, *loc*) organized as a hash table on key v, where $v \in V$, and *loc* is a structure (Figure 4(B)) with its field *index* holding the array index of v in D_i.*values* (when a value is not even in the original D_i, D_i.*element*(v) will give 0). This field is different from that in AC-5, where v directly points to the index rather than a structure *loc* that indirectly points to the same index. This change is important for the new technique for IFCs. The field *values* contains the real values of the domain. The *info* field contains all the information about the current domain. Its data structure is shown in Figure 4(C). This is also different from AC-5 as AC-5 keeps all the information in the domain data structure in Figure 4(A). This modification is crucial to our new technique for IFCs.

Regarding the *info* structure, the field *size* gives the domain size. The fields *min* and *max* are used to access the minimum and maximum values in the domain. The fields *pred* and *succ* allow accessing in constant time the successor and predecessor of a value in the domain. This representation allows the algorithm to reason about array indices rather than values. The field *arcs* stores the arcs (which are kept elsewhere in AC-5) related to the variable except those IFC arcs because our new technique checks them only once. Then, there is no need to store them.

4.2 Check IFCs

This subsection presents the technique for checking IFCs in AC-5*$_3$. In a normal process, a constraint needs to be checked many times to maintain consistency. Recheck is necessary when its previously established consistency is broken by other constraints. In the new method, IFCs only need to be checked once. The main idea is to exploit the fact that consistent values in the domains of an IFC are one-to-one correspondent and in an increasing order. So, in initial check, we can merge the two domains by making them share some key information. Later on, domain change of one variable will be felt automatically by the other. In this way, rechecks of the constraint can be avoided.

Before presenting the detailed technique, we distinguish two types of CSPs, static CSPs and incremental CSPs. A static CSP refers to a CSP whose constraint network is completely available before arc consistency is enforced. An incremental CSP refers to a CSP whose variables and constraints may coming incrementally during the problem solving process. Most real-life CSPs are incremental ones.

The new technique has different properties for the two types of CSPs. For a static CSP, we can arrange the sequence of the arcs so that all the IFCs can be merged in initial check. Then, recheck will not be needed. However, for an incremental CSP, such ordering may not be possible. Then, the new technique does not guarantee that every IFC will need only one check. We shall discuss this further in Section 4.2.2.

Let $V = \{v_1, ..., v_a\}$ with $v_k < v_{k+1}$ be the original domain of i;

$D_i = \{v_{p_1}, ..., v_{p_m}\} \subseteq V$ with $p_k < p_{k+1}$ and m > 0

Syntax

D_i.*merge*: integer $\in \{0, ..., n\}$, where n is the number of variables in the CSP

D_i.*element*: set of pairs (v, *loc*) with $v \in V$ and *loc* is a structure, organized as a hash table on key v.

D_i.*values*: array [1..a] of elements $\in V$

D_i.*info*: an *info* structure

Semantics

D_i.*merge* $\neq 0$, if this domain has been merged with another domain
$= 0$, otherwise

loc.index(D_i.*element*(v)) $= p$ (with $v = v_p$), if $v \in D_i$
$= 0$, otherwise

D_i.*values*[p] $= v_p$

D_i.*info* points to an *info* structure (see below)

(A). Domain data structure

Syntax

loc.index: integer

Semantics

loc.index $= p \in \{0, ..., a\}$

(B). *loc* data structure

Syntax

info.size: integer

info.min: integer $\in \{1, ..., a\}$

info.max: integer $\in \{1, ..., a\}$

info.succ: array [1..a] of integers $\in \{1, ..., a\}$

info.pred: array [1..a] of integers $\in \{1, ..., a\}$

info.arcs: a set of relevant arcs.

Semantics

info.size $= m$

info.min $= p_1$

info.max $= p_m$

info.succ[p_k] $= p_{k+1}$ $(1 \le k < m)$, *info.succ*[p_m] $= +\infty$

info.pred[p_{k+1}] $= p_k$ $(1 \le k < m)$, *info.pred*[p_1] $= -\infty$

info.arcs $= \{(l, i) \mid (l, i) \in arc(G)$ and (l, i) is not an IFC$\}$

(C). *info* data structure

Figure 4. Domain data structures

4.2.1 Procedure *InitialCheck* for IFCs

We now present *InitialCheck* for IFCs (Figure 5). Two sub-procedures are used. The first one is *MergeCheck* (Figure 6), which merges the two variables. The second one is *NonMergeCheck* (Figure 7), which does not merge the two variables.

Procedure InitialCheck(**in** (i, j), **inout** Q)
if D_j.*merge* = 0 **then** *MergeCheck*((i, j), Q)
elseif D_i.*merge* = 0 **then** *MergeCheck*((j, i), Q)
else *NonMergeCheck*((i, j), Q)

Figure 5. *InitialCheck* for IFCs

```
Procedure MergeCheck(in (i, j), inout Q)
    DELETE_i ← false; DELETE_j ← false;
    newValues ← make an array of the same size as D_i.values;
    for each v (= D_i.values[index_i]) ∈ D_i do
        if f_ij(v) ∉ D_j then     begin
                                        delete v from D_i;
                                        DELETE_i ← true
                                  end
        else     begin
                       newValues[index_i] ← f_ij(v);
                       D_j.element(f_ij(v)) ← D_i.element(v);
                       delete f_ij(v) from D_j without modifying D_j.element
                 end;
    if DELETE_i then Q ← Q ∪ {arc | arc ∈ D_i.info.arcs};
    for each w ∈ D_j do     begin
                                 loc.index(D_j.element(w)) ← 0;
                                 DELETE_j ← true
                            end
    if DELETE_j then Q ← Q ∪ {arc | arc ∈ D_j.info.arcs};
    if D_i.merge = 0 then D_i.merge ← i;
    D_j.merge ← D_i.merge;
    D_i.info.arcs ← D_i.info.arcs ∪ D_j.info.arcs;
    D_j.values ← newValues;
    D_j.info ← D_i.info
```

Figure 6. Procedure *MergeCheck* for IFCs

MergeCheck merges D_i and D_j by making them share the same *info* and some information in their *element* fields. See [5] for an example and the proof of its correctness. *NonMergeCheck* given in Figure 7 consists of two parts, the first part (line 2-16) is used when $D_i.merge = D_j.merge$, and the second part (line 17-22) is used otherwise. Procedure *ReCheck* is obvious and omitted.

4.2.2 Time complexity

Due to the use of hash table, each value in D_i (or D_j) needs to be checked only once in *MergeCheck* or *NonMergeCheck*. Thus, *InitialCheck* is O(d). Now, the question is: can we avoid going to the second part (line 17-22) of *NonMergeCheck*? If we can, then every IFC can be merged, and no recheck is needed. Hence, AC-5*$_3$ is O(ed) for IFCs, which is the same as that in AC-5. But AC-5*$_3$ eliminates the rechecks needed in AC-5, not to mention AC-5*$_3$'s superior space complexity. However, if we cannot avoid going there, those not merged IFCs still need rechecks, and the consistency check in *ReCheck* is O(d), which is not as good as that in AC-5.

From the above discussion, we can derive a condition for checking all the IFCs in a CSP only once. Take note that every IFC is expressed as one edge (or arc).

Single Check Condition: For each IFC (i, j), when (i, j) is checked, it satisfies

(a) $D_i.merge = 0$ or $D_j.merge = 0$, or;

(b) $D_i.merge = D_j.merge$, with $D_i.merge \neq 0$.

It turns out that whether the condition is guaranteed to be satisfied depends on if the CSP is a static one or an incremental one.

```
Procedure NonMergeCheck(in (i, j), inout Q)
    if Di.merge = Dj.merge then
        begin
            DELETE ← false;
            for each v ∈ Di do
                if fij(v) ∉ Dj then  begin
                                          delete v from Di;
                                          DELETE ← true;
                                      end
                elseif Dj.element(fij(v)) and Di.element(v) have different locs then
                        begin
                            delete v from Di;
                            delete fij(v) from Dj;
                            DELETE ← true;
                        end
            if DELETE then Q ← Q ∪ {arc | arc ∈ Di.info.arcs};
        end
    else  begin
            if Check((i, j)) then Q ← Q ∪ {arc | arc ∈ Di.info.arcs};
            if Check((j, i)) then Q ← Q ∪ {arc | arc ∈ Dj.info.arcs};
            Di.info.arcs ← Di.info.arcs ∪ {(j, i)};
            Dj.info.arcs ← Dj.info.arcs ∪ {(i, j)};
          end
  Procedure Check(in (i, j))
      DELETE ← false;
      for each v ∈ Di do  if fij(v) ∉ Di then  begin
                                                   delete v from Di;
                                                   DELETE ← true;
                                               end;
      return DELETE;
```

Figure 7. Procedure *NonMergeCheck* for IFCs

Theorem: For a static CSP, we can always fix an order of arcs to be checked initially so that the above condition is satisfied.

The theorem can be proven quite easily. Interested readers, please refer to [4].

For an incremental CSP, we no longer have the freedom to order the constraints to satisfy the above condition. However, it can be partially satisfied. Thus, those IFCs that do not satisfy the condition still need recheck. Fortunately, our experiences of building practical systems show that there are normally many clusters of IFCs in a real-life CSP, and each cluster typically has only 2 to 3 variables. Then, the above condition is always satisfied. Then the $O(ed)$ result still stands.

5. Experimental Results

In this section, we compare the performances of the specializations of AC-3, AC-5 and AC-5*. The focus is on showing how the new technique for IFCs performs compared to the existing techniques. The constraints involved in the comparison are equations, inequalities and disequations, which are the basic constraints of the current constraint languages [10]. Equations are special cases of IFC (see Section 2). All the algorithms are implemented in CMU Common Lisp on SPARC-2.

We implemented AC-3, AC-5, AC-5*$_{IFC}$, and AC-5*$_3$ with specialized techniques for checking those classes of constraints. AC-3 uses the specialized techniques in [9], and AC-5 uses the specialized techniques in [10]. They both use the same domain data structure in [10] (in [5], AC-3 uses the data structure in [9]). AC-5*$_{IFC}$ uses the new technique for merging IFCs, and the techniques in [10] for the other constraints and also for those not merged IFCs. AC-5*$_3$ uses the techniques (initial check and recheck) described in Section 4 for IFCs and similar techniques to those in [10] for other constraints.

We report two sets of tests. One set uses CSPs with only IFCs, in particular, equations as discussed in Section 2. The other set uses typical scheduling problems. Scheduling problems are used here because most applications of constraint programming are in scheduling, sequencing and other similar domains.

For the first set of tests, variables, domains and constraints are randomly generated. The constraints are also randomly ordered, which is to reflect the incremental nature of the practical CSPs. The number of variables ranges from 40 to 80, the domain sizes range from 10 to 100, and the number of constraints ranges from 45 to 90. Figure 8 shows the time comparison of AC-3 and AC-5*$_3$ in percentage terms over 30 problems. The performance of AC-3 is taken as 100% (shown as the dash line). AC-5*$_3$ takes only 55% to 80% of the time for AC-3 for arc consistency.

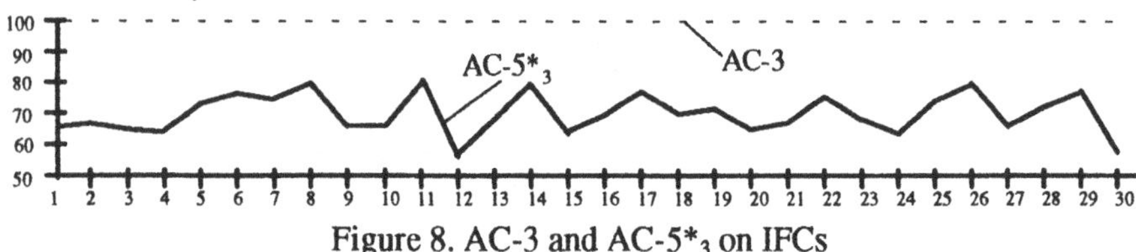

Figure 8. AC-3 and AC-5*$_3$ on IFCs

Figure 9 shows the comparison of AC-5 and AC-5*$_{IFC}$ on the same set of IFC CSPs. AC-5*$_{IFC}$ only uses 60% to 82% of the time taken by AC-5.

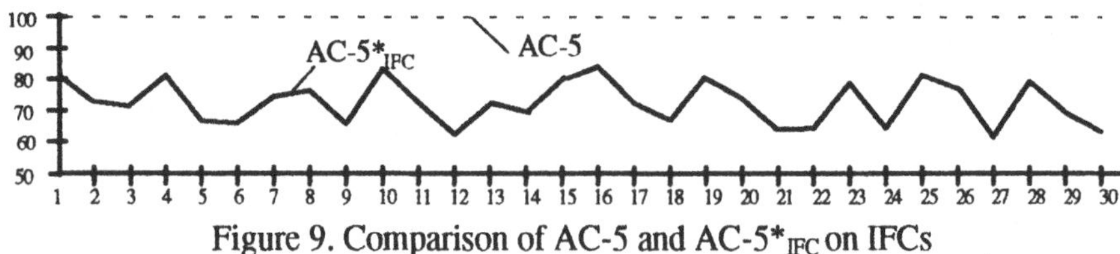

Figure 9. Comparison of AC-5 and AC-5*$_{IFC}$ on IFCs

Our second set of tests is intended to show what we may see when the new technique is used in real applications. The test problems are typical job scheduling problems. In the scheduling domain, we need to schedule a number of jobs $J = \{J_1, J_2, ..., J_n\}$, and each job consists of a number of operations $J_i = \{Op_{i_1}, Op_{i_2}, ... Op_{i_m}\}$. The operations in each job have to be performed in a fixed sequence. So the start time S_{i_k} of one operation and the end time $E_{i_{k-1}}$ of its previous operation must satisfy $S_{i_k} \geq E_{i_{k-1}}$. Each operation also has a duration Du_{i_k}. Then, we have the constraint $E_{i_k} = S_{i_k} + Du_{i_k}$ (which is an IFC). Each job has a due time Dt_i, by which it must be finished, i.e., $E_{i_m} \leq Dt_i$. There are also some other constraints not listed here. These by no means describe a full scheduling problem. A real problem also needs to consider resources, and requires a good solution. However, they are more to do with heuristic search strategies rather than consistency check, and they are out of the scope of this paper. The results reported here are only for achieving consistency.

For this set of tests, we fix the number of operations to be 5 for each job, which means 10 variables per job. Each domain has 100 values. However, the number of jobs is randomly generated for each problem, ranging from 4 to 8. The constraints are also randomly sequenced. In each problem, around half of the constraints are IFCs. Figure 10 and 11 show the performance comparisons of AC-3 and AC-5*$_3$, and AC-5 and AC-5*$_{IFC}$ respectively (over 30 problems). It can be seen that the new technique produces substantial saving. AC-5*$_3$ takes 55% to 70% of the time for AC-3. AC-5*$_{IFC}$ only takes 54% to 71% of the time for AC-5.

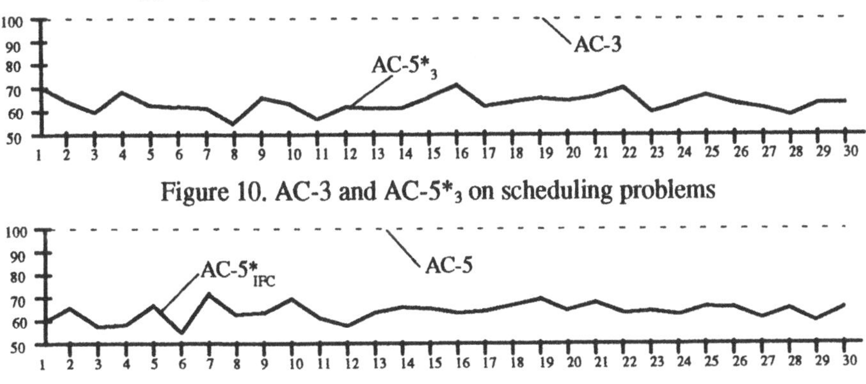

Figure 10. AC-3 and AC-5*$_3$ on scheduling problems

Figure 11. Comparison of AC-5 and AC-5*$_{IFC}$ on scheduling problems.

These comparisons show that the new technique consistently produces considerable saving.

6. Related Work

Many general arc consistency algorithms have been developed in the past. AC-3 has the optimal space complexity of O(e + nd) [7, 8], but its time complexity is O(ed^3) [7]. AC-4 has the optimal time complexity of O(ed^2) [8], but its space complexity is O(ed^2) [8]. AC-6 reduces the space complexity of AC-4 to O(ed) from O(ed^2) [1].

AC-5 provides an generic algorithm that can exploit the structure of the domain and the structure of the constraint to produce more efficient algorithms for specific constraints. The most commonly used specific constraints are FCs, ATFCs and MCs. Their subclasses (i.e., equations, disequations and inequalities) form the core of the current constraint languages, e.g., CHIP [9], Ilog Solver [3], etc. In [10], AC-5 is specialized to achieve an O(ed) algorithm in time for these constraint classes. However, AC-5 cannot be specialized to reduce the space complexity.

AC-5* is an improvement over AC-5. It is also a generic algorithm. But because of its two queue element representations, it can be specialized to produce efficient algorithms for specific constraints both in time and in space.

Although the new technique for IFCs is still O(*ed*) in time, experiment results have shown that it is more efficient than that in AC-5. More importantly, it is now possible to have an arc consistency algorithm for IFCs, ATFCs and MCs, which is both optimal in time and also optimal in space.

Recently, [2] proposed another general arc consistency algorithm AC-7. The main idea of AC-7 is to take advantage of the bidirectionality of constraints to reduce the number of consistency checks. Its space requirement is still O(*ed*) like AC-6 [1]. [2] did mention that the semantics of constraints can be used to infer or reduce constraint checks. However, it is not clear how AC-7 could be specialized to reduce both the time and space complexities for IFCs, ATFCs and MCs.

7. Conclusion

This paper proposed an improved generic arc consistency algorithm AC-5*. It can be specialized to produce efficient algorithms for specific constraints not only in time but also in space. This is significant because for practical applications, both time and space complexities are important. Furthermore, the paper presented a new consistency technique for IFCs. It checks almost all IFCs only once rather than many times. With this technique and AC-5*, we can have an arc consistency algorithm that is both optimal in time and optimal in space for IFCs, ATFCs and MCs. The main application of these techniques will be in constraint programming.

Acknowledgments: I thank Kim-Heng Teo for his valuable comments on various parts of this paper.

References

[1] C. Bessiere and M. Cordier, "Arc-consistency and arc-consistency again," *Artificial Intelligence*, 65:179-190, 1994.

[2] C. Bessiere, E. Freuder and J-C. Regin, "Using inference to reduce arc consistency computation," *IJCAI-95*, 592-598, 1995.

[3] Ilog Solver Reference Manual, ILOG, 1993.

[4] B. Liu, *AC-5*: an improved AC-5 and its specializations*, 1996. DISCS Technical Report. 1996.

[5] B. Liu, "Increasing functional constraints need to be checked only once," *IJCAI-95*, Montreal, Canada, August 19-25, 1995.

[6] A. K. Mackworth, "Consistency in networks of relations," *Artificial Intelligence*, 8:99-118, 1977.

[7] A. K. Mackworth, and E. C. Freuder, "The complexity of some polynomial network consistency algorithms for constraint satisfaction problems," *Artificial Intelligence*, 25:65-74, 1985.

[8] R. Mohr and T.C. Henderson, "Arc and path consistency revisited," *Artificial Intelligence*, 28:225-233, 1986.

[9] P. van Hentenryck, *Constraint satisfaction in logic programming*, 1989.

[10] P. van Hentenryck, Y. Deville and C-M. Teng, "A generic arc-consistency algorithm and its specifications," *Artificial Intelligence*, 27:291-322, 1992.

High-Level Synthesis Optimisation with Genetic Algorithms

Jem Daalder[1], Peter W. Eklund[1], Kenji Ohmori[2]

[1] Department of Computer Science
University of Adelaide
Adelaide 5005
South Australia
[2] Department of Industrial and Systems Engineering
Hosei University
Koganei-shi, Tokyo

Abstract. *The results of a genetic algorithm optimisation of the scheduling and allocation phases of high-level synthesis are reported. Scheduling and allocation are NP complete, multi-objective phases of high-level synthesis. A high-level synthesis system must combine the two problems to produce optimal results. The genetic algorithm described provides a robust and efficient method of search capable of combining scheduling and allocation phases, and responding to the multiple and changing objectives of high-level synthesis. The results show the genetic algorithm succeeds in finding optimal or near optimal results to classic benchmarks in small computational time spans.*

1 Introduction

High-level synthesis (HLS) is the automated synthesis of a register transfer level circuit from a behavioural description, summarised in [W94]. A behavioural circuit description specifies the ultimate goals of the circuit in terms of its logical function, timing and chip area constraints. High-level synthesis systems use the behavioural description to generate a structural design implementing a specified behaviour. The structural design consists of functional units such as arithmetic logic units (ALUs), multipliers, registers and buses.

High-Level Synthesis involves two NP Complete optimisations. The first is a problem of scheduling in which the operations given by the behavioural description are assigned a control step. The second, which may be performed before, after or simultaneously to scheduling, is allocation, which assigns functional units to operations given in the behavioural description. These two optimisation phases have multiple minimisation objectives; i.e. to minimise functional units, control steps needed by the circuit, registers needed to store values, and the number of buses to inter-connect the circuit. It is not possible to minimise all objectives; the desired goals for the circuit must be considered by the optimisation process for the optimisation of all objectives. Previous solutions to the problem have failed to adapt well to changing objectives.

The paper is structured by providing a brief discussion of the phases of high-level synthesis. A classic benchmark problem and its encoding is discussed. The paper examines random population generation, objective functions, genetic operators and the GA's results for the benchmark problem. The status of high-level synthesis research is well summarised in [W94], and a well maintained bibliography of genetic algorithm application to electronics and VLSI design and testing has been compiled by Jarmo T. Alander[A94].

2 High-Level Synthesis

The first stage in the automated generation of ASICs is specification of circuit function at a behavioural level in terms of logical function, circuit area and circuit timing. The design is typically specified algorithmically, often in high level languages such as Pascal and C, but more typically in a hardware description language such as VHDL[I93]. Figure 1 shows a C language description of a circuit function to solve a differential equation. High-level synthesis systems convert the

```
{ int x=0,y=0,u=0,dx=1,done,a,x1,y1,u1;
     do {
       x1 = x+dx;
       u1 = u - (3*x*u*dx) - (3*y*dx);
       y1 = y+u*dx;     x = x1; y = y1; u = u1;
     } while (done = x +dx < a);
}
```

Fig. 1. Sample C behavioural description for a simple differential equation.

algorithmic description into an internal representation. Dataflow graphs are most often chosen for this representation, as they allow the dependency relationships between data, functional units and read and write operations to be naturally specified.

A dataflow graph representation consists of a set of nodes, each node representing a single operation of the original behavioural description. Two nodes o_i and o_j are connected with an arc if a data dependency exists between them, i.e. the output of node o_i is an input to node o_j. This arc indicates the execution of the operation represented by node o_j cannot be executed before the output result of node o_i is available. As the dataflow graph describes only data dependencies, it is an excellent representation of the potential parallelism in a behavioural description, i.e it shows the operations that may be executed concurrently as no dependency exists between them.

Data flow graphs are unable, without augmentation, to describe external conditions affecting reactive or embedded systems. Some control flow information such as loop and conditional constructs are added to the standard graph to create a control dataflow graph. Figure 2 shows the control dataflow graph (CDFG) for the behavioural example given in figure 1 [O95]. The graph has eleven nodes, six requiring multiplication operations, and 5 requiring ALU operations. The final

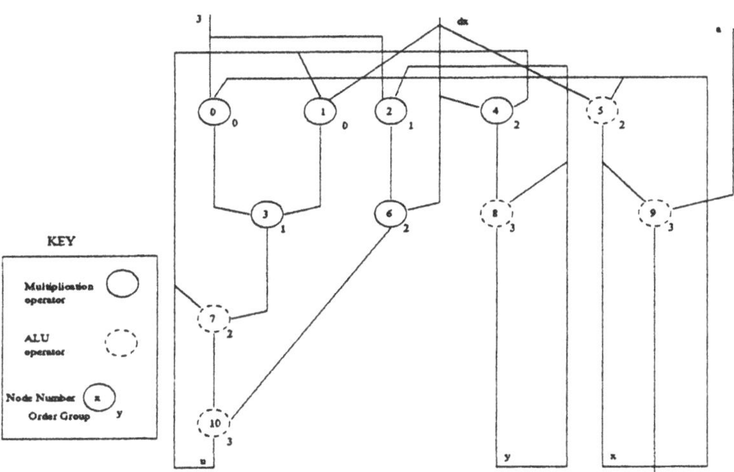

Fig. 2. Control dataflow graph.

output leaves the graph from node eight, and there are three external inputs; **3,dx** and **a**. There are also three initialised inputs within the graph; **u,y** and **x**.

The dataflow graph representation allows the minimum number of slots for a cycle of execution of the dataflow graph to be determined by examining the critical path length of the graph. In figure 2, the critical path length is four.

The next task in HLS is scheduling of operation nodes and memory access into slots. Operations are assigned a propagation delay value and partitioned into specific control steps. This step can be proceeded by, followed by, or performed simultaneously with allocation of hardware structures and datapath synthesis. Allocation sets aside the required number of functional units (ALUs and multipliers), registers, buses and interconnections. Although scheduling and allocation can be performed separately, it is impossible to find optimal solutions in many cases as decisions made in the first phase may well prevent an optimal solution being found for the problem considered as a whole.

Realisation of the circuit datapath is done either by assigning the high level modules to predesigned gate array templates, or synthesising the circuit datapath directly with module generators.

The classic high-level synthesis benchmark problem, from [PKG86], is to realise a register transfer level circuit that solves a differential equation (1). The C code behavioural description is given in figure 1, and the control dataflow graph representation given in figure 2.

$$y'' = -3xy' - 3y \qquad (1)$$

3 The GA for High-Level Synthesis

3.1 Block Scheduling

Within the dataflow graph ordering information must be respected. Any node a in the dataflow graph must have resources allocated earlier than a node b if the latest allowable slot of node a precedes the earliest allowable slot of node b. This allocation strategy is necessary to prevent deadlock arising; i.e the allocation of resources to later nodes preventing the allocation of resources to earlier nodes. Nodes in the graph are therefore divided into scheduling blocks by sorting the nodes using their latest output slot as the key. Each node having the same latest output slot is assigned an order group number that defines the group of the node. Each group must be allocated resources before members of the next group. Freedom to order resource allocation remains within each group. The *followers* of a node are those nodes that may not execute until after the original node. Figure 2 shows the sorted order for the nodes in the graph, and lists the order group for each node.

3.2 The Encoding

In developing a terse, scalable encoding for the high-level synthesis problem a number of factors were considered; the allocation and scheduling problems must be combined to reach optimal or near optimal solutions, the problem has a large number of constraints that must be both reflected and respected by the method of encoding, the minimum possible alphabet must be used to reduce the search space size and the chance of generating individuals that violate the constraints, and the encoding method must have some ability to scale to large problems.

The chromosome must encode three things; a hierarchical list of operations (nodes) and the inter-dependencies between them (including scheduling constraints for each node), the operational units to execute the above operations in the required order, and the storage required to store the values between the above operations .

A node by node encoding is capable of expressing the variability within the problem, in an extremely compact manner. The following aspects are variable for each node: the slot where a node is scheduled (limited by the earliest and latest allowable slots of the node, and the scheduling of the nodes of which this node is a follower), the actual device (ALU or multiplier) allocated to the node, the register that receives output from the device allocated to the node (limited by the maximum number of available registers and those already allocated), and the input connections of the node's input ports; i.e. as each node has two input ports, the inputs can be connected in two ways.

As an example, consider the encoding of a complete solution to the eleven node problem. Each node will be represented by a gene. Each gene requires an integer in the range $[0, number\_of\_slots]$ to represent the slot allocated to the node. As the type of a nodes operation does not change, we do not need to represent the type of device in the chromosome. We therefore require only one integer $[0, number\_of\_devices\_of\_that\_type]$ to represent the number of the device allocated. An integer with range $[0, number\_of\_registers]$ can be used to specify the output register for the node, and a final integer with range $[0, 1]$ can be used to discriminate the input line configuration. The final chromosome therefore requires 11 genes of 4 integers, or just 44 integers to represent a solution to the HLS problem.

3.3 Random Population Generation

The goal of random population generation in the genetic algorithm is to produce a population of individuals that are valid solutions to the problem, containing sufficient variety of information for evolution to occur.

From each order group nodes are chosen randomly for resource allocation. Each node is first allocated a slot. This slot is chosen at random from the node's range of allowable slots. The allowable slots for all follower nodes of this node are adjusted to be later than the slot allocated to the current node. As an example, node 3 in figure 2 has earliest allowable slot 0, and latest allowable slot 2. If node 3 is scheduled for slot 2, then the earliest allowable slot for all following nodes is set to slot 3. Node 8's slot range, previously $[1, 3]$, becomes limited to $[3, 3]$.

To determine the maximum number of devices required one schedules as many as possible nodes of a particular type on to the one slot as is possible given slot limitations.

Following the allocation slots to nodes, the operation type of each node is checked. A device (ALU or multiplier) as appropriate is allocated if it is free from the allocated slot to the slot at which the device is no longer needed. The process of slot and device allocation continues until all nodes from all order groups have been allocated a slot and a functional unit. Each node also receives a random value indicating the input line configuration. Registers cannot be allocated simultaneously; it is impossible to allocate registers before all nodes have been scheduled, as the outputs from nodes may need to be stored for multiple slots until the node receiving the output as input is scheduled for execution.

As the slot for all nodes has been allocated, register allocation can now be performed. The input registers of any node are determined by the output registers of each node, so we need only allocate output registers to each node. Again, members of each group are chosen at random in the order defined by the order groups, and allocated available registers at random from a pool of available registers.

Register allocation is complicated by initialisation values. To reduce the size of the dataflow description of the behavioural description, the outputs of certain nodes are initialised to initial input values for nodes receiving those outputs. This reduces the number of nodes needed to represent a behavioural description. For example, node eight in figure 2 has an output initialised to the value given by variable y. The register must also be allocated for the slots required until its other output nodes make use of the later generated (not initialised) output value. Once a register that is free for all of the required slots is chosen at random, the register number is used as the allele value for the locus of each gene in the chromosome. The chromosome is now complete, and is a randomly generated, legal solution to the problem of high-level synthesis. Figure 3 shows a fragment of an example chromosome that is a randomly generated solution to the eleven node problem.

```
Node 1   Node 2   Node 3   Node 4   Node 5   ..... Node 11
0 2 6 0  0 0 5 0  1 5 8 0  1 1 2 0  0 4 1 1  ..... 3 0 3 1
(eg Node 5 has slot 0, ALU 4, register 1 and input configuration 1)
```

Fig. 3. Example random chromosome.

3.4 Objective Functions

The objective function used for this problem is divided into six sub-functions. Each sub-function evaluates the success of the solution in the minimisation of one of the six objectives of the high-level synthesis problem. The individual fitness scores for each evaluation function are combined in a weighted function that reflects the required objectives of the optimisation process. To adapt the genetic algorithm solution to the possible objectives of the scheduling and allocation problems requires only changing the weights assigned to each evaluation function.

The objective function for slots, registers and devices examines the chromosome and returns the number of slots used by the solution, for one cycle of the graph. The lower bound on this number is the critical path length of the dataflow graph. The devices evaluation function returns the combined score for ALU and multiplier usage. Each of these scores is a count of the number of devices of that type used by the solution encoded in the chromosome. The registers evaluation function also returns the number of unique registers used by the encoded solution in the chromosome.

If the input port of a device[3] receives input from multiple output lines of multiple registers at different slots, as is typically the case in circuits which re-use devices to minimise circuit area, a bus is needed to prevent the electrical signals from each register being mixed[4]. The number of registers connected to any one bus is known as the fan in of a bus. The number of buses required is determined by the allocation of devices and registers in any given circuit. They are therefore not encoded in the chromosome, but they form part of the evaluation function, as they have an effect on the quality of the solution encoded within the chromosome with respect to the objectives of the problem. The sixth objective function returns the number of fan outs in the circuit.

3.5 Selection

A prime reason for premature convergence in the GA is the selection mechanism. In randomly generated populations there are a large number of average fitness

[3] Each functional unit has two input ports.

[4] In this paper, a multiplexor is considered to be a special case of a bus.

individuals and a few exceptionally fit individuals. Standard roulette wheel selection allocates chunks of the roulette wheel to these exceptional individuals that are too large, and these few individuals are selected too often for reproduction. These individuals come to saturate the population in very little time, and therefore little of the information present in the original population survives into later generations. To overcome this, individuals are selected for breeding using a linear selection algorithm[G89] that uses a variable bias to determine the probabilities of selection.

4 Operators and Results

A population of 1000, 44 integer, 11 gene chromosomes was used. The probability of crossover was 0.8 and the probability of mutation was 0.1. A selection bias of 2.0 was used, and the maximum number of generations limited to 100. Although tuning of the parameters often improves results, the parameters were kept constant so that the results for each of the operators are easily visible.

Single point crossover and single point mutation: the results using only traditional single point crossover are given in figure 4. On the y axis is the time taken for the genetic algorithm to converge on a point in the solution space on which it did not improve in the rest of the one hundred available generations. Results for near optimal solutions and optimal solutions are both presented, a near optimal solution being defined as one which has the optimal results for three of the possible objectives, and results within 75% of the optimal for the remaining three objectives. The number of trials in which the GA found these solutions is given on the z axis. This percentage is calculated from 40 trials, each with a different random population.

The GA very quickly converges on a solution (in an average of about 30 generations), and only finds a near optimal solution on 45% of occasions. The optimal solution was found in only 10% of the trials. The poor results are caused by premature convergence of the genetic algorithm. The genetic algorithm is too eagerly exploiting and propagating large building blocks, saturating the population with them. To overcome premature convergence, mutation is used to regain information lost from the population by the genetic algorithm (or to add information the population never had). Figure 4 right shows the results for single point mutation and single point crossover.

Multiple point crossover and single point mutation: a multi-point crossover operator was implemented which retained more, smaller building blocks. This operator reduced the size of the schemata (building blocks) being recombined by crossover. The reduction of building block saturation improves the performance of the genetic algorithm by increasing the amount of recombination that occurs. Figure 5 gives the results for multi-point crossover with single point mutation. Convergence has slowed significantly, the GA on average converging on its final

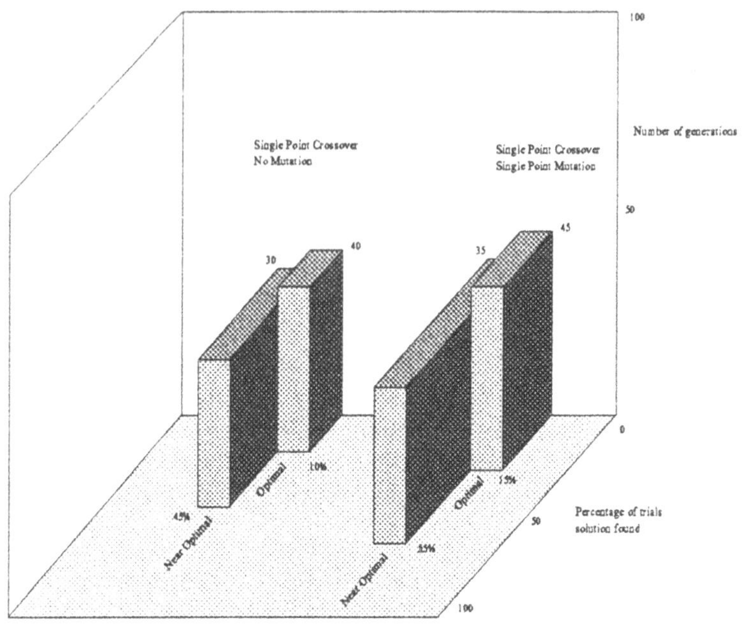

Fig. 4. Results of the single point operators.

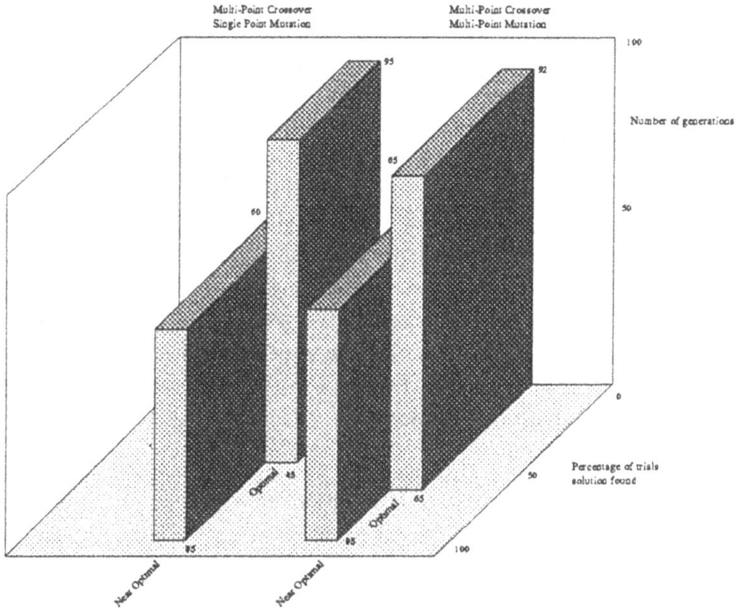

Fig. 5. Results of the multiple point operators.

solution in 60 generations. The number of trials in which near optimal solutions were found increased to 95%. This result is much more satisfying. The number of trials in which the optimal solution was found is still only 45%, and the average time taken to find the optimal solution once a near optimal solution has been found is significant.

Multiple point crossover and multiple point mutation: to increase the number of optimal solutions found, we must overcome the information loss that occurs when the GA converges on a solution. Single point mutation was unable to recover significant amounts of the information lost by the eager reproduction and crossover operators. To this end, we implement a multi-point mutation operator that increases the amount of information added back to the population by the mutation operator. The results, in figure 5, show that this was effective, and increased the percentage of trials in which an optimal solutions was found to 65%. The extra time needed to find the optimal solution (past a near optimal solution) was reduced.

Multiple point crossover and double mutation: we are not satisfied with the percentage of trials in which optimal solutions were found. Certain types of building blocks are often lost, but never recovered by the mutation operator. We add a mutation operator which allows resources to be swapped between nodes, and this allows these building blocks to be recovered. This improves the results noticeably, with 75% of the trials resulting in the optimal solution being found. These results are good, however, the time taken for the optimal solution to be found after convergence on a near optimal solution is significant. The reason for this extra time is mutation occurs with low frequency, and the missing building blocks are only slowly added back into the population.

Multiple point crossover and adaptive triple mutation: the final GA uses a multi-point crossover, and an adaptive multi-point mutation operator, which uses three different types of mutation; multi-point random mutation, swapping mutation and a further type of mutation, knowledge guided mutation. Refusal to use problem domain knowledge provides the genetic algorithm with a great deal of its generality, but in some ways limits the search abilities. The high-level synthesis problem is essentially a problem of minimisation, only the importance of various objectives changes; i.e. we always want to minimise some resource usage. It is only variable in so much as we may wish to minimise some resource more than others.

It is sensible to bias the information in our population, and the direction of our search, towards minimal resource usage, be it slots, devices, registers or inter-connections. However, previous solutions to the problem limit their adaptability by requiring certain objectives to be minimised before other objectives are considered. The goal becomes to bias the search with the knowledge of the minimisation goals, but not to lose generality and adaptability.

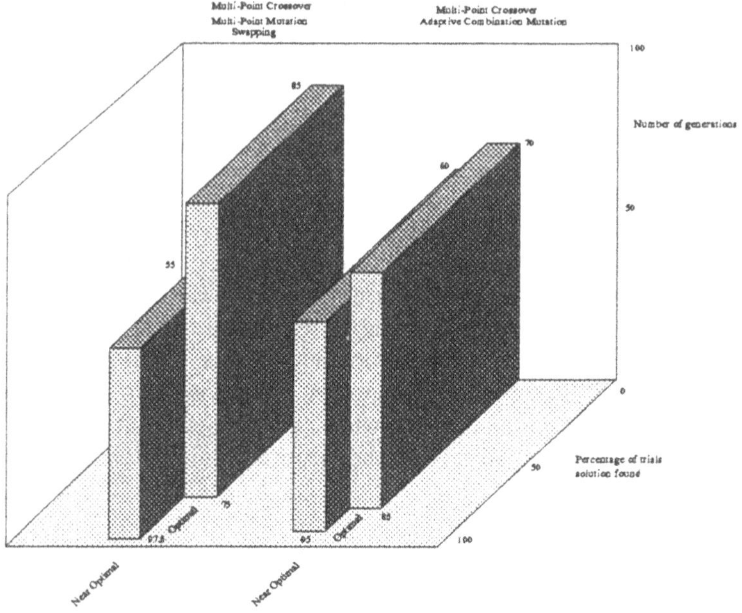

Fig. 6. Results of the multiple point operators with adaptation.

Multi-point knowledge guided mutation is an attempt to do this. The operator continues to change allele values at loci within the gene, but does this with a generalised minimisation strategy. Regardless of the resource to be optimised, the knowledge guided mutation operator biases the mutation towards minimising resource usage. It does this by examining the chromosome and building a resource usage table that describes which resources are currently in use by the solution encoded by the chromosome. Following the building of the resource usage table, it chooses already used resources at random from the pool of *used* resources, and attempts to allocate the resource to the node being mutated. If none of the currently used resources are allocatable to the node being mutated, it proceeds as per normal mutation and allocates a resource from the pool of *unused* resources. In this way, the knowledge guided multi-point mutation operator biases the search in favour of resource usage minimisation (through resource re-use).

In an effort to adapt to loss of diversity within a population, the adaptive mutation operator adjusts the amount of mutation (i.e. the number of points mutated), and the probability of mutation in a fashion related to the assessed level of diversity remaining in a population.

The level of population diversity is measured by taking a random sample of individuals from the population, and measuring the amount of difference in the sample. Although this is only a statistical level of population diversity, a sample size of 10% of the population size provides an accurate measure of the level of diversity with a low statistical variance.

If the level of assessed diversity remaining in a population falls below a specifiable 'bumper point', the probability of mutation is increased exponentially toward 1.0, and the number of mutation points increased exponentially towards a definable maximum number of mutation points to be mutated by the multipoint mutation operator. In this way, a simple feedback system is implemented to balance the amount of diversity in a population.

The final results are given in figure 6. These results are extremely good; in an average of 60 generations, near optimal solutions are found with a frequency of 95%, and the GA successfully continues the evolution process to allow the optimal solution to be found in 85% of trials in just 70 generations. Linear reproduction and multi-point crossover have successfully prevented premature convergence on sub-optimal solutions, and the adaptive triple mutation has dramatically increased the number of trials in which the optimal solution has been found, and significantly decreased the time taken to find the optimal solutions. On occasions when even a near optimal solution is not found, the solution generated is almost always extremely close to a near optimal solution. These results are generated using no special tuning. Better results can be obtained by tuning the initial random population, probabilities of the genetic operators and the population size.

5 Conclusions

Simultaneous optimisation of scheduling and allocation in high-level synthesis is an NP-complete problem. Previous solutions have been short-sighted in their approach, and limited in their ability to adapt to changing objectives and technology.

The genetic algorithm solution to the optimisation of scheduling and allocation is inevitably complex, with considerable thought and tuning required to obtain good results. To express the combined problem of scheduling and allocation in a fixed length chromosome is difficult, and to do so in a way that is scalable to problems of larger size is a problem of significant complexity. A node by node method of encoding provides a reasonable means of doing this for graphs of small size, however the chromosome is inevitably large.

Large chromosomes cause significant problems in the action of the typical genetic algorithm with one point mutation and crossover. These problems of convergence can be overcome with better selection mechanisms and multipoint operators which reduce the information lost, or increase the building blocks considered by the genetic algorithm. This greatly improves the genetic algorithm's performance.

For a relatively small problem such as the eleven node benchmark, any solution should have significant success in finding the optimal solution in extremely short time. To make use of problem domain knowledge, without losing generality, is the key to excellent results. The genetic algorithm requires only a simple change in the weightings of the objective function to adapt to changing objectives, and can make use of the general principal of minimisation to greatly improve the potential of the GA in finding optimal solutions.

The results for traditional benchmarks are excellent, with near optimal results found in excellent time, and optimal results found with high frequency. The potential of the genetic algorithm for the flexible and efficient optimisation of high-level synthesis has been shown.

References

[A94] Alander, Jarmo T.: An Indexed Bibliography of Genetic Algorithms in Electronics and VLSI Design and Testing. Tech Report, Department of Information Technology and Production Economics, University of Vaasa. 1994

[G89] Goldberg, D.E.: Genetic Algorithms in Search, Optimisation, and Machine Learning. Addison-Wesley 1989

[I93] IEEE: IEEE Standard VHDL Language Reference Manual. **ANSI/IEEE Standard 1076-1993**

[O95] Ohmori, K.: High-Level Synthesis using Genetic Algorithms. Proceedings on the IEEE Conference on Evolutionary Computing. 1995

[PKG86] Paulin, P.G and Knight, J.P and Girczyc, E.F.: HAL : A multi-paradigm approach to automatic data-path synthesis. Proceedings of the 23rd Design Automation Conference. 1986 236-270

[W94] Walker, R.A.: The status of high-level synthesis. IEEE Design and Test of computers. **Winter** (1994) 42-54

A Qualitative Reasoning Based on an Ontology of Fluid Systems and Its Evaluation

Yoshinobu KITAMURA, Mitsuru IKEDA and Riichiro MIZOGUCHI

I.S.I.R., Osaka Univ.
8-1 Mihogaoka, Ibaraki, Osaka 567, Japan
{kita,ikeda,miz}@ei.sanken.osaka-u.ac.jp

Abstract. This research is concerned with causal understanding and qualitative reasoning of behavior of physical systems, which are crucial issues of model-based problem solving. In this paper, a new method of qualitative reasoning and causal ordering is proposed and its application to a power plant is presented. The method is based on our kernel ontologies of causality and time-resolution and a domain ontology of fluid systems. These ontologies help make the design rationales of our method explicit and facilitate reusability of our models. The whole of the target system is represented by combining a set of local component models and global constraints. The component models include local and causal characteristics of each component which are independent of context for their reuse on the basis of the ontology of causality. Global constraints with time-scales are derived according to the general properties of the physical entity which are prepared beforehand as a part of the domain ontology. They contribute to providing intuitive causal ordering of complex behavior originated in various configurations of components, including inter-component negative feedback. Furthermore, the method has been successfully applied to a power plant. All the reasoning results matched those obtained by a domain expert including their ambiguities.

1 Introduction

Causal understanding and qualitative reasoning of behavior of physical systems are crucial issues of model-based problem solving. In this article, a new method of qualitative reasoning and causal ordering is proposed and its application to a power plant is presented. The main issue we discuss is to identify constituents of models and causality suitable to reasoning about behavior of a target system satisfying composability and reusability of the models. *Ontologies* are explicit descriptions of *design rationales* of model-based systems and help to exhibit necessity and sufficiency of the constituents of models for the necessary performance[8]. The method is based on our kernel ontologies of causality and time-resolution and a domain ontology of fluid systems. In section 2, we describe our design rationales referring to these ontologies. Firstly, the performance necessary for reasoning methods with respect to causal time-resolution is discussed. Next, we show conventional methods cannot satisfy the requirements. Lastly, our approach satisfying the required performance is outlined. In section 3, we describe the model representation and discuss categories of causal relations to capture context-independent causal properties of components. In section 4, the details of the reasoning method is described. Moreover, an application of the method to a power plant is presented in section 5. Related work is discussed in section 6.

Table 1. Units of time resolution for causal ordering

T1: Intra-Component Time Unit: Time intervals between two changes of parameters within *a component.*

T2: Inter-(Neighboring)Components Time Unit: Time intervals between two changes of parameters in *neighboring components.*

T3: Global Time Unit: Time intervals between two (not simultaneous) changes of parameters in *non-neighboring* components.

T4: Globally Simultaneous Time Unit: Time intervals between two *simultaneous* changes of parameters in non-neighboring components.

T5: Completely-Satisfied-State Time Unit: Time intervals between two consecutive completely-satisfied-states in which every parameter has a unique value which satisfies all constraints in the system. If not, states are called as partially-satisfied-states.

T6: Partial-Equilibrium-State Time Unit: Time intervals between two consecutive partial-equilibrium-states in which a part of the system reaches equilibrium states.

T7: Complete-Equilibrium-State Time Unit: Time intervals until the whole of the system reaches equilibrium states.

2 The Design Rationales

Among a number of requirements for qualitative reasoning methods we concentrated on the following three: (1)capability in causal explanations in terms of components, (2)reusability of component models and (3)disambiguation of reasoning results, adopting the device ontology[1]. The reasoning engine is designed to reason qualitative behavior of target systems subjected to a perturbation caused by factors external to the system. Such reasoning is a part of diagnostic task, i.e., fault-hypotheses verification, which reasons abnormal behavior of the system with a fault and generates symptoms caused by it. Given an initial (anomalous) value of a parameter, the reasoning engine generates changes of values of parameters over time together with causal relations among the changes for explanations.

2.1 Causal Time-Resolution

Since human recognition of causal relations is based on recognition of time delay(i.e. time interval) between the cause and the effect, the performance of a reasoning engine with respect to causal ordering depends on *time-resolution* of the engine. In order to realize such an inference engine that can recognize a fine-grained causality, we have identified the seven units of time-resolution shown in Table 1. Time intervals between two causal changes of parameters are categorized. They represent the performance necessary for reasoning systems with respect to causal ordering.

The necessity to distinguish among these time units is justified by human recognition of causality. Firstly, in order to recognize the behavior in terms of components on the basis of the device ontology, humans assume time delay for interactions between neighboring components due to cognitive distance between them. Thus, humans distinguish time intervals of interactions between components from those of intra-component phenomena, i.e. distinguish T2 from T1. Next, since there are global phenomena such as changes in temperatures caused by global heat balances, discrimination of global phenomena(T3) from neighboring propagations(T2) is necessary. The length of the time interval of T3 is longer than that of T2 because of the structural distance between the cause and the effect. There are, however, cases where changes in non-neighboring components are simultaneous, called *globally simultaneous phenomena*. For example, on the assumption that fluid is incompressible, flow rate of such fluid at each component changes at the same time. Thus, T4 is needed. The length of the time interval of T4 is longer than that of T1 because of the concept of components and shorter than that of T2 because of its simultaneity. T5 represents the time intervals between two consecutive *completely-satisfied-states* in which every parameter value satisfies all constraints in the system. T1-T4 represent, on the other hand, the time intervals between *partially-satisfied-states* in which values of parameters satisfy only a set of constraints. (In the case of T2, for example, the values satisfy a set of constraints in a component.) Such causal orders in T1-T4 are cognitive in a sense that they are not justified by mathematical representations of the models. Therefore, the following inequalities concerning relative lengths of time intervals represented by the units hold.

$$T1 < T4 < T2 < T3 < T5 < T6 < T7$$

2.2 Conventional Methods

A main issue to discuss is what contents of domain models we have to represent for distinguishing these time intervals from one another. QSIM[6] uses only qualitative differential equations and adopts a generate-and-test method for constraint satisfaction. Thus, no causal relation among partially-satisfied-states in T1-T4 is identified. The time of QSIM corresponds to T5, and thus QSIM can distinguish only among T5-T7. Although Iwasaki's causal ordering theory[4] can derive a part of causal relations in T1-T4, the theory does not try to derive causal relations among changes caused by *inherently simultaneous equations*[1]. Moreover, it cannot distinguish among T1-T4 due to the lack of the concept of components. The most influential reasoning method based on components has been proposed by de Kleer and Brown in [1]. Our method inherits the device ontology from it. Their reasoning method can generate causal relations in terms of components in *mythical time* corresponding to our T2 according to their general heuristics. Causal relations generated by them, however, are ambiguous due to the arbitrariness of heuristics application. Moreover, since there are no concept of global phenomena, the method cannot distinguish among T2-T4 and may generate ambiguous results for the case of complex topology or feedbacks as mentioned in [10]. The performance of other conventional methods will be mentioned in section 6. In summary, there are no methods of adequate performance.

2.3 Our Approach

Our approach to satisfy the necessary causal time-resolution is to take a positive attitude towards incorporating such knowledge that cannot be represented in terms of mathematical equations, satisfying context-independence of the models. Causal characteristics of

[1] This term represents such simultaneous equations which cannot be solved by substitution alone, borrowed from [1]. In terms of [4], minimal complete subsets.

components are explicitly described, called *causal specifications*. The classification of causal relations shown in the next section helps capture causal properties independent of context. Moreover, we employ *global constraints* derived from general properties of the physical entity such as heat and fluid. Time-scales of phenomena are also described. According to such models, our reasoning engine can distinguish among all the units of the causal time-resolution and derive appropriate causal relations without ambiguity.

The following assumptions contribute to efficiency of the reasoning process. Firstly, we assume that the target system has a normal equilibrium state without any perturbation. This assumption is based on the fact that the intended continuous behavior of mechanical artifacts can be represented by the equilibrium state model by selecting appropriate parameters[2]. Next, we assume that effects of inter-component negative feedbacks do not override instantaneously the original values. The heuristics on this assumption allow the reasoner to determine the values in a feedback loop, as we will see in section 4. Next, although the reasoner copes with mainly transitional behavior from a normal complete-equilibrium state to a final abnormal one, the reasoner generates values only in equilibrium states of T6 and/or T7 for disambiguation of reasoning result in the case of specific parameters. Lastly, we assume that all constraints are continuous, and thus the reasoner cannot treat discrete changes.

3 The Model Representation

The overall structure of the system is represented by a combination of component models and connections on the basis of the device ontology[1]. A component model consists of (1)a set of parameters, (2)constraints over parameters, (3)ports for connections, (4)*causal specifications* representing causal properties of the component, and (5)*time scale* of phenomena.

3.1 Parameters, Constraints, and Ports

A parameter takes one of the three qualitative values related to the deviation from a normal value. [+]([-]) represents a quantity greater(less) than the normal value, i.e. abnormal values. [0] represents a quantity equal to the normal value. The normal value of a parameter is defined as a permitted range of the parameter when the overall system is in a normal equilibrium state without any perturbation. In the normal equilibrium state, all derivatives of parameters with respect to time equal to zero.

Constraints are described in terms of qualitative operators and parameters. $D(p)$ represents a derivative of a parameter p with respect to time. It takes one of the three qualitative values [+],[-],[0] which correspond to the sign of derivatives. The integral equation: $p_{(t+1)} = p_{(t)} + D(p)_{(t)}$ holds. Constraints "$\exists t,\ D(p)_{(t)} = [0]$" mean that the parameter converges to the equilibrium state.

A parameter can belong to some ports for connections among components. The connection information is represented by relations between the ports. There are global constraints which have connections to local components, as we will see in section 3.3.

[2] For example, stable oscillation is represented by the equilibrium state modeled in terms of the frequency and amplitude parameters.

Table 2. Categories of causal relations

	Focused scope	Causal chains
Isolated internal causality	inside of the component	within the component
External causality	between components	other components
Combined internal causality	inside of the component	other components

3.2 Causal Specifications

The causal specifications represent causal characteristics of the components in order for the reasoner to enable to identify complex causal relations. Such properties prone to dependent on context as discussed in [1][3] and [11]. It motivated us to classify causality of components. We have identified three categories of causal relations shown in Table 2. Causal relations between two changes of values of parameters within a component are categorized with respect to structural scopes focused and locations of parameters of causal chains between the cause and the effect. The classification provides viewpoints for capturing causal properties of components. Causal properties captured from the viewpoint of *the isolated internal causality* are local and independent of the context specified by the whole of the target system. A *causal specification* is an attribute of a parameter, which is denoted by the following two flags representing causal conditions captured from the viewpoint of the isolated internal causality.

Cause,C: Changes of the value of the parameter can cause those of values of other parameters in the component through events within the component.
Effect,E: Changes of the value of the parameter can be caused by those of values of other parameters in the component through evetns within the component.

A causal specification takes one of the three values, $C\tilde{E}$, $\tilde{C}E$ and CE, where "~ " is a negation symbol. If there can be a parameter whose change affects the value of the parameter under consideration, then the flag E is associated with the parameter under consideration. And, if there can be a parameter whose value is afffected by that of the parameter under consideration, then the flag C is associated with the parameter under consideration. If there is no such parameter, $\tilde{C}$ ($\tilde{E}$) is associated. Parameters with a constant value, for example, a resistance R in an electric circuit[4], have $C\tilde{E}$ as causal specification. The values of such parameters are changed only by influences of other components and/or factors external to the model of the system such as faults. Thus, a parameter is *exogenous*[4] to the model of the target system if and only if it has $C\tilde{E}$ as causal specification and has no connection with other components. The exogenous parameters are candidates of the faults in the diagnostic tasks.

[3] As mentioned in No-Function-In-Structure principle[1], function of components is context-dependent. While we discuss a functional model in another paper[9], we concentrate on the modeling at the behavior level in this paper.

[4] On the assumption that the resistance R is not changed by heat.

3.3 Global Constraints and Time-Scales

In order to cope with global phenomena discussed in section 2.1, global constraints over local components are described. Such global constraints are justified by general properties of the physical entity such as heat and fluid. Since such properties are specified by the physical laws and the generic topologies of connections among components such as loop, they can be prepared beforehand for each generic topology as a part of the domain ontology. For example, such a general property for the generic loop topology holds in which changes of the temperatures in a loop are caused by the difference between the inflow and the outflow of thermal energy according to heat conservation law. Global constraints are instantiated according to concrete configurations.

Time-scales of phenomena enable the reasoning engine to distinguish *globally simultaneous* phenomena such as changes of flow-rate of incompressible fluid as T4. The global constraints representing such phenomena are called *globally simultaneous constraints* and marked with "simultaneous". Other constraints and local component models are marked with "not-simultaneous".

4 The Reasoning Method

The reasoning engine is designed to generate sequences of states representing changes of parameter values over time. A state consists of states of parameters, each of which consists of a qualitative value, a flag representing assignment of the value, three time counters: T_f,T_s,T_v. These time counters correspond to T4, T2 and T5 mentioned in section 2.1, respectively. The T_f and T_s counters increase when the values are propagated to other components. The T_v counter increases when a value is changed by its derivative through the integral equation mentioned in section 3.1. The orders of states in the sequences mean causal orders among changes. A difference of the time counters between two states represents the cognitive length of the time interval of the two changes and the category of the causal relations. In the initial state, an abnormal value of an exogenous parameter must be specified. Other parameters are assumed to take normal values.

The reasoning engine has two processes, that is, intra-component reasoning and inter-component reasoning. Given abnormal values propagated from other components, the intra-component reasoning process determines values of other parameters in the component. According to constraints and causal specifications, abnormal values are propagated from parameters marked with "C" to those with "E". If a value of a parameter marked with "C$\tilde{\text{E}}$" is not determined by other components, it can be assumed to remain an old value in the precedent state. Such assumptions enable to solve inherently simultaneous equations. In the inter-component reasoning process, on the other hand, abnormal values are propagated to parameters of neighboring components according to connections between ports. If values are propagated to *globally simultaneous constraints*, the T_f time counter increases. If not, the T_s time counter increases. The reasoning orders are according to the topology of connections among components and the time counters.

When a loop exists in the propagation path, a value of a parameter may cause a change of the parameter itself after propagating the loop around, so called feedback.

The new value of the parameter after the feedback may become ambiguous[4]. If the difference of the time counters between the new value and the original value is only T_f representing instantaneous changes in T4, the reasoning engine determines the value the same as the original value, since there is no instantaneous feedback, according to the heuristics mentioned in section 2.3. If the difference of the time counters is greater than T_f, that is the time intervals of phenomena are grater than T4, the value remains ambiguous. We will see an example of a feedback in the next section.

5 Application to a Power Plant

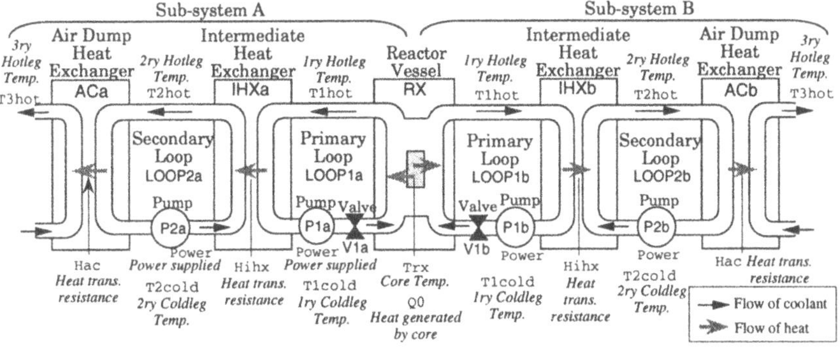

Fig. 1. Outline of the heat transportation system

This section describes the application of our method to a nuclear power plant. To concentrate on the behavior of the flow of thermal energy and the fluid, we built a model of the heat transportation system of the power plant. Figure 1 shows the outline of the system. The plant transports thermal energy generated in the reactor vessel(RX) into the open air[5] through two heat exchangers(IHX and AC). The system has two subsystems(called A and B) each of which has two loops(called primary and secondary) in which the coolant circulates.

The model of the whole system consists of 27 components, 143 parameters and 102 constraints. Major components and parameters[6] are shown in Figure 1. A component model is an instance of a component class, such as heat exchangers and pumps. The component class models are based on our domain ontology of fluid systems. Figure 2 shows the qualitative model of the heat exchanger in the primary loop in the subsystem A (called IHXa). Figure 3 shows that of the pump (called P1a). According to the ontology, the pump changes the flow-rate reacting to changes in the power supplied to the pump

[5] Because this is a test plant, it has no power generator.

[6] The parameter name should be unique in each component. Thus, in Fig. 1, different parameters are shown as the same name.

and the total pressure-drop along the loop. We have identified four global properties of heat and fluid as a part of the domain ontology of fluid systems. In the case of the target system, 16 global constraints are derived according to them. Figure 4 shows a heat conservation law in the primary loop of the subsystem A.

Name: IHXa
Time-Scale: not-simultaneous
Ports:

symbol	*connected comp.*	*connected port*
in1	RX	out1a
out1	P1a	in
in2	P2a	out
out2	ACa	in1
heat1	LOOP1a_HEAT	out
heat2	LOOP2a_HEAT	in
flow1	LOOP1a_FLOW	rst2
flow2	LOOP2a_FLOW	rst1
dp1	LOOP1a_DP	rst2
dp2	LOOP2a_DP	rst1

Parameters:

symbol	*description*	*causal spec.*	*port*
T1hot	1ry Coolant inlet Temp.	CẼ	in1,heat1
T1cold	1ry Coolant outlet Temp.	C̃E	out1,heat1
T2cold	2ry Coolant inlet Temp.	CẼ	in2,heat2
T2hot	2ry Coolant outlet Temp.	C̃E	out2,heat2
Q12	Heat transported to 2ry coolant	CE	heat1, heat2
Hihx	Heat trans. resistance.	CẼ	
Flow1	Flow rate of 1ry coolant	CẼ	flow1
Flow2	Flow rate of 2ry coolant	CẼ	flow2
P1io	Pressure drop of 1ry coolant	C̃E	dp1
P2io	Pressure drop of 2ry coolant	C̃E	dp2

Constraints:

```
Q12 = Hihx * ((T1hot + T1cold)/2 - (T2hot + T2cold)/2)
Q12 = Flow1 * (T1hot - T1cold)
Q12 = Flow2 * (T2hot - T2cold)
P1io = Flow1
P2io = Flow2
```

Fig. 2. The qualitative model of IHXa

Name: P1a
Time-Scale: not-simultaneous
Port:

symbol	*connected comp.*	*connected port*
in	IHXa	out1
out	V1a	in
flow	LOOP1a_FLOW	driver
dp	LOOP1a_DP	driver

Parameters:

symbol	*description*	*causal spec.*	*port*
Power	Power supplied	CE	
Flow	Flow rate	C̃E	flow
Pio	Difference of pressure between inlet and outlet	CẼ	dp
Tin	Coolant Temp.(inlet)	CẼ	in
Tout	Coolant Temp.(outlet)	C̃E	out

Constraints:

```
Power = Flow * Pio
Tin = Tout
```

Fig. 3. The model of the Pump in LOOP1a

Name: LOOP1a_HEAT
Time-Scale: not-simultaneous
Port:

symbol	*connected comp.*	*connected port*
in	RX	heata
out	IHXa	heat1

Parameters:

symbol	*description*	*causal spec.*	*port*
Q01	Heat transported from RX	$C\tilde{E}$	in
Q12	Heat transported to IHX	$C\tilde{E}$	out
T1hot	Coolant Temp.(hotleg)	$\tilde{C}E$	in,out
T1cold	Coolant Temp.(coldleg)	$\tilde{C}E$	in,out

Constraints:

```
D(T1hot) = Q01 - Q12
D(T1cold) = Q01 - Q12
```

$\exists t,\ D(T1hot)_{(t)} = [0]$
$\exists t,\ D(T1cold)_{(t)} = [0]$

Fig. 4. The model of LOOP1a concerning heat conservation law

Table 3. Results of qualitative simulation

	RX Q0 [+]	IHXa Hihx [-]	ACb Hac [-]	P1a Power [-]	P2b Power [-]
Trx	(1)+	(2)+	(3)+	(1)+	(2)+
A T1hot	(1)+	(2)+	(3)+	(1)+	(2)+
T1cold	(2)+	(1)+	(4)+	(1)-	(3)+, (4)?
T2hot	(2)+	(1)-	(4)+	(1)-	(3)+, (5)?
T2cold	(3)+	(2)-	(5)+	(2)-	(4)+, (6)?
T3hot	(3)+	(2)-	(5)+	(2)-	(4)+. (6)?
B T1hot	(1)+	(2)+	(3)+	(1)+	(2)+
T1cold	(2)+	(3)+	(2)+	(2)+	(1)+, (4)?
T2hot	(2)+	(3)+	(2)+	(2)+	(1)+, (5)?
T2cold	(3)+	(4)+	(1)+	(3)+	(1)-, (6)?
T3hot	(3)+	(4)+	(1)-	(3)+	(1)-, (6)?

Table 3 shows the simulation results. Given one of the five anomalous perturbations in the top-most raw, the reasoning engine determines values of the other parameters when the system eventually reaches the heat balanced state. The numbers associated with the qualitative values[7] represent causal orders. All results in the table correspond to those of a domain expert. Although results when the system is subjected to decrease of the power suppied to pump2b are ambiguous, domain experts cannot determine the value without *quantitative* values of the flow-rate either.

Figure 5 shows a part of the causal relations generated by the reasoning engine in the case of decreasing the power supplied to P1a. When the power supply `Power` takes `[-]`, the reasoning engine derives the flow-rate `Flow` = `[-]` in T1 (see the sequence No.2 in Figure 5) by introducing an assumption that the difference of the pressure of the pump `Pio` specified as $C\tilde{E}$ is `[0]`. The change of `Flow` is propagated to the all

[7] The value "?" represents ambiguous values.

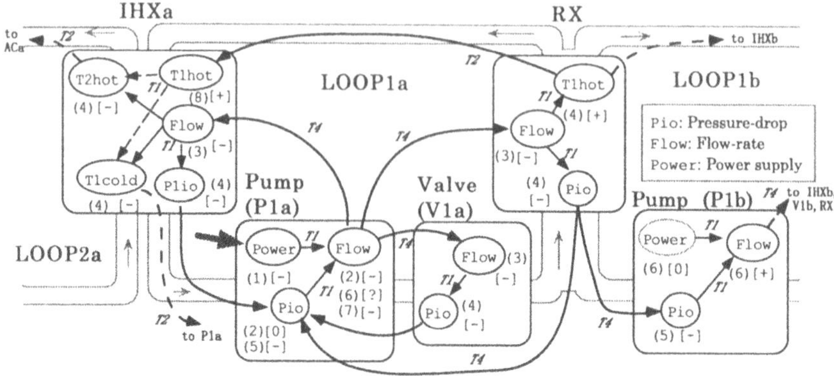

Fig. 5. A part of causal relations in the case of decreasing the power supplied to the P1a

components in LOOP1a, i.e. IHXa, RX and V1a, simultaneously in T4 by the globally simultaneous constraint concerning flow-rate. In each component, each pressure-drop decreases (No.4) because pressure-drop is proportional to flow-rate. Then, the total pressure-drop along LOOP1a changes to `[-]` by the globally simultaneous constraint concerning pressure-drop. Since the `Pio` of the pump equals to the total pressure-drop, `Pio` = `[-]` is derived (No.5) and then the assumed value is dismissed, so-called feedback. Then, value of `Flow` becomes ambiguous (No.6) because of `Power` = `[-]` and `Pio` = `[-]`[8]. Since the time delay along the feedback loop is T4+T1+T4+T1 representing instantaneous phenomena, according to the heuristics, that is, there is no instantaneous feedback, the system obtains `Flow` = `[-]` which matches reality (No.7). The decrease of the pressure-drop in RX, on the other hand, is propagated to the other pump P1b (No.5). It causes increase of the flow-rate in LOOP1b. Moreover, in RX and IHXa, the decrease of the flow-rate of LOOP1a also causes the changes in the temperatures of the coolant (No.4). Since these changes are not simultaneous, i.e. in T2, these are propagated to the other components after the simultaneous phenomena (No.8).

Figure 6 shows the causal relations when the heat transfer resistance `Hihx` of IHXa decreases[9]. Firstly, in IHXa, the reasoning engine derives `T1cold` = `[+]` and `Q12` = `[-]` (the sequence No. 2 in Fig. 6). The value of `T1cold` is propagated to RX through P1a and V1a, then `T1hot` = `[+]` and `Q01` = `[0]` (No.8) are derived in RX. When `Q01` = `[0]` and `Q12` = `[-]` are propagated to LOOP1a_HEAT (No.9), `D(T1hot) = [+]` and `D(T1cold) = [+]` are derived (No.10). These mean the temperatures in the loop are increasing in T3, caused by the difference between the inflow (`Q01`) and outflow (`Q12`) of thermal energy. Long enough time in T6 after the occurrence of anomaly, the loop achieves an equilibrium state, and hence the temperatures are stable. Thus, although `Q12` becomes ambiguous (No.12), the reasoning engine obtains `Q12 = [0]` in the equilibrium state in T6 (No.14). This reasoning result shows the increase of the

[8] Note that multiplication has the same effect as addition because the qualitative values represent not sign but deviation from a normal value.

[9] In contrast with the result shown in Table 3, Figure 6 shows the result in the case where the system has only the subsystem A without the subsystem B.

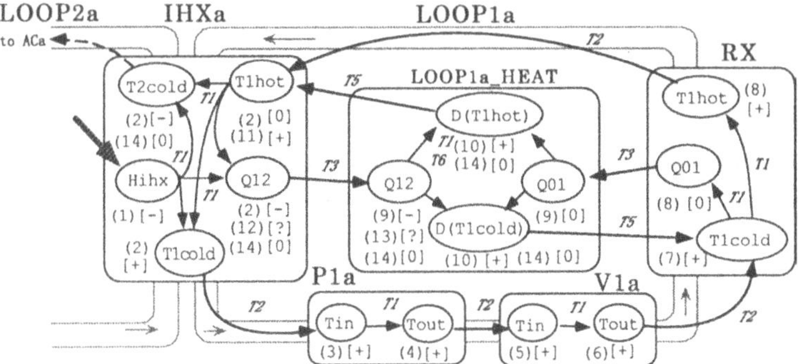

Fig. 6. A part of causal relations in the case where the heat transfter resistance of IHXa decreases (without the subsystem B)

temperatures of LOOP1a compensates the decrease of the heat transfer resistance of IHXa, and then the temperatures of LOOP2a become equal to the normal values[10].

The reasoning system has been implemented in Common ESP, an object-oriented Prolog, on a UNIX workstation.

6 Related Work

A lot of research has been carried out on qualitative reasoning for causal understanding [1, 2, 4, 6, 10, 11, 12, 13, 14]. In [1] and [12], although general causal properties of devices have been identified, causal relations generated by their methods are ambiguous in the case of inherently simultaneous equations. The TQ analysis[14] provides heuristics to analyze limited kinds of feedback involving integration. A part of our causal specification corresponds to the descriptions of "exogenous parameters"[4] of each component. Skorstad discusses context-dependence ("instability") of such descriptions[11]. In [2] and [13], causal properties of physical processes are described.

The concept of time-scale itself is not new and has been proposed in other papers such as [5] and [7]. The global constraint about heat presented in section 5 corresponds to an energy constraint[3] (a global filter) for QSIM.

7 Summary

A new method of qualitative reasoning and causal ordering is proposed. The method is based on ontologies of causality and time-resolution and a domain ontology of fluid systems. The reasoning engine generates complex causal relations originated in various configurations of components according to causal specifications independent of the context. The generated causal relations include those among the transitional states between

[10] In the case where the system also has the subsystem B, these phenomena do not happen as shown in Table 3

completely-satisfied-states constrained by the inherently simultaneous equations. Moreover, its performance evaluation through application to the power plant is described. The reasoning result matches exactly those of a domain expert.

The assumptions underlying the model and the reasoning engine are explicitly discussed in section 2.3. The experiment suggests appropriateness of the assumptions. Understanding the limitation of the method remains as future work. In the application mentioned in section 5, global constraints are manually described as global components. Currently, investigation on mechanism which automatically generates global constraints from general properties is in progress.

Acknowledgments

The authors would like to thank Shinji Yoshikawa and Kenji Ozawa from Power Reacter and Nuclear Fuel Development Corp. and Munehiko Sasajima from I.S.I.R., Osaka Univ. for their help and comments on building the model of the power plant.

References

1. de Kleer, J., Brown, J. S.: A Qualitative Physics Based on Confluences. Artificial Intelligence, Vol.24, pp.7-83 (1984).
2. Forbus, K. D.: Qualitative Process Theory, Artificial Intelligence, Vol.24, pp.85-168 (1984).
3. Fouché, P., Kuipers, B. J.: Reasoning about Energy in Qualitative Simulation, IEEE Trans. on Systems, Man, and Cybernetics, Vol.22, No.1, pp.47-63 (1992).
4. Iwasaki, Y., Simon, H. A.: Causality in Device Behavior, Artificial Intelligence, Vol.29, pp.3-32 (1986).
5. Iwasaki, Y., Simon, H. A.: Causality and Model Abstraction, Artificial Intelligence, Vol.67, pp.143-194 (1994).
6. Kuipers, B. J.: Qualitative Simulation, Artificial Intelligence, Vol.29, pp.289-338 (1986).
7. Kuipers, B. J.: Qualitative Reasoning, MIT Press (1994)
8. Mizoguchi, R., Ikeda, M.: Towards Ontology Engineering, Technical Report AI-TR-96-1, I.S.I.R., Osaka Univ. (1996).
9. Sasajima, M., Kitamura, Y., Ikeda, M., Mizoguchi, R.: FBRL: A Function and Behavior Representation Language, Proc. of the IJCAI'95, pp.1830-1836 (1995).
10. Schryver, J. C.: Object-Oriented Qualitative Simulation of Human Mental Models of Complex Systems, IEEE Trans. on Systems, Man, and Cybernetics, Vol.22, No.3, pp.526-541(1992).
11. Skorstad, G. : Finding Stable Causal Interpretations of Equations. Recent advances in Qualitative Physics, Faltings and Struss(Ed.), pp.399-413, MIT Press(1992).
12. Top, J., Akkermans, H.: Computational and Physical Causality, Proc. of the IJCAI'91, pp.1171-1176 (1991).
13. Washio, T.: Causal Ordering Methods based on Physical Laws of Plant Systems, MITNRL-033, MIT Nuclear Reactor Laboratory (1989)
14. Williams, B. C.: Qualitative Analysis of MOS Circuits. Artificial Intelligence, Vol.24, pp.281-346 (1984).

Parallel Cost-Based Abductive Reasoning for Distributed Memory Systems

Shohei Kato, Hirohisa Seki, and Hidenori Itoh

Department of AI and Computer Science
Nagoya Institute of Technology

Gokiso, Showa-ku, Nagoya 466, Japan
E-mail:{ shohei@juno.ics, seki@ics, itoh@ics}.nitech.ac.jp

Abstract. This paper describes efficient parallel first-order cost-based abductive reasoning for distributed memory systems. A search control technique of parallel best-first search is introduced into abductive reasoning mechanism, thereby finding much more efficiently a minimal-cost explanation of a given observation. We propose a PARallel Cost-based Abductive Reasoning system, PARCAR, and give an informal analysis of PARCAR. We also implement PARCAR on an MIMD distributed memory parallel computer, Fujitsu AP1000, and show some performance results.

1 Introduction

The demands of AI for industrial and engineering applications become stronger and stronger in recent years. The research for expert systems and knowledge-base systems is indispensable for practical AI applications. The reasoning mechanisms in the systems, complying with the demand for more intelligent inferences, come to shift from deductive to non-deductive, such as default, abductive, and inductive reasoning and reasoning under uncertainty. In the field of deductive reasoning, research for exploitation of parallelism in logic programming has been reported significantly (e.g. [CWY91], [LWH+90], [AK90]). We are taking our stand on that non-deductive reasoning mechanisms should be also parallelized so as to deal with large scale knowledge-bases within realistic time. We, therefore, adopt abductive reasoning as a reasoning mechanism of the systems and aim to propose an efficient abductive reasoning system by means of its parallelization.

Abductive reasoning, a form of non-deductive inference which can reason suitably under the incomplete knowledge (e.g., [Poo88]), has attracted much attention in AI and also has many interesting application areas such as diagnosis, scheduling and design. In general, abductive reasoning might find more than one solution. We, however, do not always require all the solutions. We often need the most preferable solution instead. Some work has been reported to solve such problem, by giving costs to hypotheses as the criterion judging which hypothesis to be selected preferably (e.g.,[Poo93],[CS94]). Then, we [KSI94] have proposed an abductive reasoning system which can find efficiently the most preferable solution of a given query, by introducing a search control technique of A* [Nil80] into abductive reasoning mechanism.

In addition to the search control technique in [KSI94], we propose a method for distributing the search space to multiple processors and exploring each distributed search space with synchronizations and communications. We introduce a search control technique of distributed best-first heuristic search into abductive reasoning mechanism, thereby obtaining much more efficiently the most preferable explanation of a given observation. We then implemented parallel cost-based abductive reasoning system, PARCAR on an MIMD distributed memory parallel computer, Fujitsu AP1000. The performance results of PARCAR on AP1000 are also shown.

The organization of the paper is as follows. In Section 2, we give a brief description of our framework of abductive reasoning. Section 3 describes PARCAR algorithm. In section 4 we discuss related work. Section 5 give an informal analysis of PARCAR and related work. Section 6 shows some performance results of PARCAR on AP1000.

2 Problem Definition

This section describes our framework of abductive reasoning, *cost-based abduction.* we consider abductive reasoning to find the most preferable explanation of an observation, by giving each hypothesis a non-negative real number as its cost for the criterion of selection of preferable hypotheses.

Definition 1. Suppose that a set of first-order Horn clauses F, called *facts*, and a set of atoms (unit clauses) H, called the set of *hypotheses*, are given. Suppose further that an existentially quantified conjunction O of atoms, called *an observation* or simply a *goal*, is given. Then, *the most preferable* (or *an optimal*) *explanation* E of O from $F \cup H$ is a set D of instances of elements of H such that

$F \cup E \vdash O$ (O can be proved from $F \cup E$) (AR1)

$F \cup E \nvdash \mathit{false}$ ($F \cup E$ is consistent) (AR2)

$\mathit{cost}(E) \leq \mathit{cost}(D)$ for all $D:\ F \cup D \vdash O, F \cup D \nvdash \mathit{false}$
($\mathit{cost}(D)$ is minimum among all sets of hypotheses which satisfy AR1 and AR2), (AR3)

where $\mathit{cost}(H)$ is the sum of costs of hypotheses in H[1]. Abductive reasoning is now defined to be a task of finding an optimal explanation E of O from $F \cup H$. In this framework, F is assumed to be consistent and treated as always true. □

Definition 2. A headless clause in F is called a *consistency condition*. A consistency condition is denoted by "$\mathit{false} \leftarrow A_1, \cdots, A_n$", where A_i $(1 \leq i \leq n;\ n \geq 1)$ is an atom and false designates falsity. □

Example 1. Figure 1 shows a simple example P_{ex}. Suppose that an observation "p(X,Y)" is given. Knowledge-base P_{ex} and goal "$\leftarrow p(X,Y)$" correspond to $F \cup H$ and O respectively. □

[1] We suppose that $\mathit{cost}(D) = 0$ if $D = \phi$.

Facts	Hypotheses : Costs
p(X,Y) ← a(X),c(Y).	c(1). : 5 c(2). : 6
p(X,Y) ← b(X),d(Y).	c(3). : 7
a(X) ← e(X).	b(1). : 2 b(2). : 3
e(1).	b(3). : 2
false ← b(X),d(X).	d(1). : 2 d(2). : 4

Fig. 1. An Example P_{ex}

Any first-order proof procedure works as an abductive reasoning system if it distinguishes hypotheses from facts, satisfying the conditions given in Definition 1.

Example 2. Figure 2 shows SLD-trees [Llo84] for $P_{ex} \cup \{\leftarrow p(X,Y)\}$ and $P_{ex} \cup \{\leftarrow false\}$.
In the trees, an atom L in the form of ML means that L is assumed to be true. It is called *assumed atom* [KSI93].

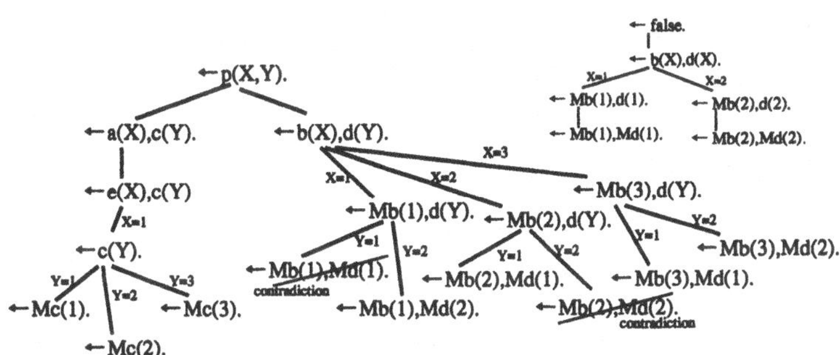

Fig. 2. An Example of Abductive Reasoning for P_{ex}

It follows from SLD-tree for $P_{ex} \cup \{\leftarrow false\}$ that it causes inconsistency to assume that any of $\{b(1), d(1)\}$ or $\{b(2), d(2)\}$ is true (we call each set of hypotheses *set of incompatible hypotheses*). We also know that $p(3,1)$, for example, has the most preferable explanation $\{b(3), d(1)\}$, since the cost of the set of hypotheses is a minimum among all sets of hypotheses obtained from all successful leaves in the SLD-tree for $P_{ex} \cup \{\leftarrow p(X,Y)\}$, while maintaining the consistency. □

In this paper, if some consistency conditions exist in a given knowledge-base, we suppose that all sets of incompatible hypotheses are derived in advance, by constructing SLD-derivation for $\leftarrow false$.

The above SLD-tree for $P_{ex} \cup \{\leftarrow p(X,Y)\}$, however, shows that the unnecessary search to finding an optimal explanation is very large. We therefore apply a distributed heuristic search technique to our abductive reasoning. Preliminary to our reasoning system, we define a following function to evaluate search spaces explored by the system.

Definition 3. Let P be given facts and hypotheses (knowledge-base), and O be an observation. To each goal g, "$\leftarrow \mathsf{M}L_1, \cdots, \mathsf{M}L_i, A_{i+1}, \cdots, A_n$", in SLD-tree for $P \cup \{\leftarrow O\}$, the evaluation function $f(g)$ is defined as follows:

$f(g) = cost(\{L_1, \cdots, L_i\}) + \hat{h}(g)$,
where $\hat{h}(g)$ is an estimated cost satisfying the following conditions.
$0 \leq \hat{h}(g) \leq h(g)$
$h(g) = cost(\bigcup_{j=i+1}^{n} \text{an optimal explanation of } A_j)$.

$cost(\{L_1, \cdots, L_i\})$ means the cost of the derivation from $\leftarrow O$ to g. $h(g)$ also means an actual cost of an optimal derivation from g to any successful leaf. We assume that A_j has a makeshift explanation whose cost is ∞ if there is no explanation of A_j. □

The evaluation function defined as above enables heuristic search to be applied to finding an optimal explanation of given observation. In [KSI94], we have actually implemented an efficient abductive reasoning system, by introducing a search control technique of A* into abductive reasoning mechanism. This paper proposes a parallelization of the abductive reasoning system. In addition to the search control technique in [KSI94], we propose a method for distributing the search space to multiple processors and exploring each distributed search space with synchronization and communication.

3 PARCAR algorithm

The section describes our PARallel Abductive Reasoning system, PARCAR. It incorporates a distributed heuristic search algorithm into the reasoning mechanism. Abductive reasoning imposes much computation on expanding nodes in search space. The computational cost largely depends upon the number of successor nodes generated by node expansion. Then, PARCAR performs the load balancing based on the number of successor nodes. The Complexity of data structure of goals labeled nodes enlarges communication overhead for node distribution. PARCAR is designed so that it can keep the communication overhead down, by giving adequate independence from communications to each processor.

PARCAR proceeds iteratively. Figure 3 shows the algorithm. In the figure, n is the number of processors, and $OPEN_i^j, CLOSED_i^j, Gmin^j, SG^j, RS^j$, and ANS^j are sets of goals dealt to processor $j (1 \leq j \leq n)$ at i-th iteration. $OPEN_i^j$ and $CLOSED_i^j$ contain goals which are not expanded yet and were already expanded by processor j at i-th iteration, respectively. SG^j contains goals labeled leaves in sub tree constructed by j. ANS_j contains goals labeled successful leaves obtained by j. These sets are implemented as ordered sets where each goal g is in order of a value of its evaluation function $f(g)$.

The algorithm consists of iterations of series of three procedures, "goal expansion", "sub-goal distribution", and "sub-goal reception". Let $T_{i,l(l \geq 1)}^j$ be a sub-SLD-tree constructed by processor j at i-th iteration, and $|T_{i,l}^j|$ be number of goals in $T_{i,l}^j$. In each processor j, these procedures at i-th iteration behave intuitively as follows:

PARCAR: PARallel Abductive Reasoning system

```
Input: a program: P, an observation: O
Output: a solution: (answer, an optimal explanation) (with success) or false (with failure)
begin
  OPEN^1_0 := {←O}; i := 0; phase^j := progress; t := ∞;
  OPEN^{j(1<j≤n)}_0 := φ; CLOSED^{j(1≤j≤n)}_0 := φ; ANS^{j(1≤j≤n)} := φ;
  repeat
    OPEN' := OPEN^j_i; SG^j := φ; escape := false; shifted := false;
    repeat                                              % Goal Expansion Procedure
      Gmin^j := {∀g ∈ OPEN' ∪ SG^j | for all g' ∈ OPEN' ∪ SG^j : f(g)≤f(g')};
      Generate all resolvents (called subgoals) of ∀g_min ∈ Gmin^j and ∃C ∈ P
      (the set of the subgoals is denoted by RS^j). ;
      Check the consistency of goals in RS^j, and remove the inconsistent goals from RS^j †. ;
      ANS^j := {∀g∈RS | g is a successful leaf, and f(g) is less than any other successful leaves};
      SG^j := SG^j ∪ RS^j ;
      CLOSED^j_{i+1} := CLOSED^j_{i+1} ∪ {g} ;
      OPEN' := OPEN' \ Gmin^j ; SG^j := SG^j \ Gmin^j ;
      if (ANS^j ≠ φ)                                   then escape := true ;
      if ( phase^j = progress and (|SG^j| + |CLOSED'|≥K or OPEN' ∪ SG^j = φ) )
                                                       then escape := true ;
      if ( phase^j = confirmation and (∀g ∈ OPEN' ∪ SG^j | f(g) > t or ∃g ∈ ANS^j | f(g) < t )
                                                       then escape := true ;
    until (escape)
    OPEN^j_{i+1} := OPEN' ;
    if (phase^j = progress) then
      begin
        distribution_goals(ANS^j, SG^j);               % Subgoal Distribution Procedure
        reception_goals(OPEN^j_{i+1}, phase^j, shifted); % Subgoal Reception Procedure
      end
    i := i + 1;
  until ( (phase^j = confirmation and not shifted) or (OPEN^{j(1≤j≤n)}_i = φ) )
  ANS := {∀g∈ANS ∪ ANS^{j(1≤j≤n)} | for all g'∈ANS ∪ ANS^{j(1≤j≤n)} : f(g)≤f(g')}
  if (∃←ML_1 ··· ML_m ∈ ANS) then return (answer,{L_1···L_m})
  else return false
end.
```

† A goal $\leftarrow ML_1, \cdots, ML_i, A_{i+1}, \cdots, A_n$ is inconsistent if any set of incompatible hypotheses is a subset of $\{L_1, \cdots, L_i\}$.

Fig. 3. The PARCAR Algorithm

goal expansion procedure goes on in either of following 2 ways according to its phase:

in *progress phase*,

by best-first expanding goals gs in order of $f(g)$s, the procedure constructs $T^j_{i,l}$s whose roots are labeled goals in $OPEN^j_i$ until $\sum_l |T^j_{i,l}| \geq K$, where K is a parameter given by user. The procedure, however, halts immediately when it finds a successful leaf (i.e., an answer), or has no goal to expand.

in *confirmation phase*,

by best-first expanding goals gs in order of $f(g)$s, the procedure constructs $T^j_{i,l}$s whose roots are labeled goals in $OPEN^j_i$ until $f(g)s \geq t$ for all leaves gs in $\bigcup_l T^j_{i,l}$ or it finds a new answer whose cost is less than t, where $t =$

$min\{f(g_{ans}) \mid g_{ans}$ is labeled a successful leaf obtained in *progress* phase$\}$. Then, PARCAR terminates in success.

Figure 4 shows a model of a sub-SLD-tree constructed by processor j at i-th iteration.

subgoal distribution procedure checks whether an answer has been found by *goal expansion procedure.* If so, it broadcasts the request for shifting to *confirmation* phase with the cost of the answer. Then, it distributes the goals gls labeled leaves in $\bigcup_l T^j_{i,l}$ in order of $f(gl)$s. The goal g, such that $f(g)$ is m-th least among the leaves, is put to processor $((j+m)\, mod\, n)$.

subgoal reception procedure shifts to *confirmation* phase and assigns $shifted$ "true" and gives t the cost as a threshold for termination in *confirmation* phase, if the procedure receives a request and a cost from any processors. Then, it merges goals distributed from all processors into $OPEN^j_{i+1}$.

The algorithm is admissible[2] for all finite SLD-trees, if $\hat{h}(g) \geq h(g)$ for all goals g in the SLD-trees. The method of discovering effective heuristic $\hat{h}(g)$ efficiently while maintaining the admissibility is shown in [KSI94].

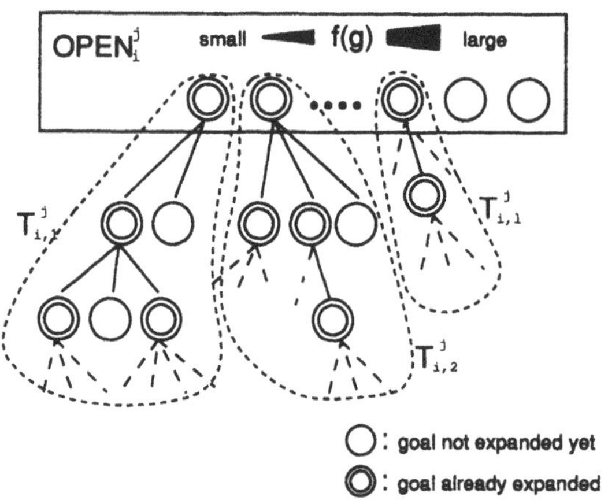

Fig. 4. A Model of a Sub-SLD-tree Constructed by Processor j at i-th iteration

4 Related Work

The most known or-parallel Prolog models are Aurora Prolog system [LWH+90] on shared memory multiprocessors and Muse Prolog system [AK90] on a multiprocessor machine with distributed and shared memory. The depth-first constructing an SLD-tree in Prolog complicates or-parallelization. On the other

[2] Let us say that a search algorithm is admissible for an SLD-tree if it always terminates in an optimal path from root node to any successful leaf whenever a path from root node to a successful leaf exists in the tree.

hand, Our cost-based abduction constructs an SLD-tree in a breadth-first manner because of necessity for obtaining a minimum-cost explanation. The breath-first manner promotes more parallelism and simplifies the division of search space into processors. Each processor carries out best-first search in a part of the space.

Huang and Davis [HD89] have proposed parallel iterative A* search (PIA*). In PIA* , each processor j at i-th iteration usually expands one node g in a priority queue WL_i^j (it corresponds to $OPEN_i^j$ in PARCAR) such that $f(g) \leq t$, where $t = min\{f(g)$ for all $g \in \bigcup_{j=1}^{n} WL_i^j\}$. So, PIA* is a simple parallelization of A* . Some properties of PIA* , however, are unsuited for cost-based abduction. PIA* performs the load balancing in goal expansion procedure based on the number of goals expanded by processor j at a single iteration. We think that it depends upon the assumption that the number of subgoals generated by expanding a goal is nearly constant. The number of them, however, is not constant in general. For example, in the SLD-tree in figure 1, PIA* makes processor PE1 expand $\leftarrow a(X), c(Y)$ and processor PE2 expand $\leftarrow b(X), d(Y)$ (see the branches from depth 2 to 3 in figure 1). PE1 generates 1 subgoal while PE2 generates 3 subgoals. Cost-based abduction imposes several tasks on the generation of subgoal: unification, propagation of binding for variables, and so on. The computational costs of these tasks cannot be negligible. Therefore, the difference of the number of subgoals generated by each processor may become an obstacle to the load balancing in PIA* . PARCAR performs the load balancing in goal expansion procedure based on the number of subgoals generated by processor j at a single iteration. We will investigate performances of the load balancing in section 6.

The total number of goals expanded for finding an optimal solution is nearly same between PIA* and PARCAR. Let G_i^j be a quantity of task in processor j at i-th iteration, and suppose that G_i^j is approximated as the number of goals generated by j at i-th iteration. In PIA* , G_i^j is nearly equal to the average number of subgoals generated by expanding a goal. This means that PIA* imposes a large amount of iterations on j. As a result, each processor needs to communicate with other processors for many times. The communication cost may become a bottleneck with the number of processors increasing. In PARCAR, G_i^j can be adjusted by changing the parameter K to keep the communication cost down. This will be argued in section 5 and 6.

5 Analysis

We will give an informal analysis of computational cost and speedup of PARCAR on a parallel computer and a knowledge-base which meet the following assumptions.

Assumption 5.1 assumption concerned with SLD-derivation

- Constant cost C_{unify} for unification is imposed on a processor.
- A processor takes constant cost C_{res} to generate a resolvent (a subgoal) of a goal and an input clause.

– The number C_{match} of subgoals generated from a goal is constant. □

Let R be the number of rules in the knowledge-base. Then, computational time $T_{sld}(1)$ for generating all subgoals from a goal (doing one-step SLD-derivation) is approximated as: $T_{sld}(1) = R \cdot C_{unify} + C_{match} \cdot C_{res}$.

Assumption 5.2 assumption concerned with consistency checking

– Constant cost C_{cc} for consistency checking on a pair of a goal and a consistency condition is imposed on each processor. □

Let R_{cc} be the number of consistency conditions in the knowledge-base. Then, computational time to check consistency of C_{match} goals is approximated as:

$$T_{cc}(C_{match}) = C_{match} \cdot C_{cc} \cdot R_{cc}.$$

Assumption 5.3 assumption concerned with processor communication

– A processor takes constant communication cost C_{comm} to communicate a message with any other processor, irrespective of both the size of the message and the distance between the two processors. □

Assumption 5.4 assumption concerned with set operations

– A processor takes constant cost C_{mo}, C_{mc}, and C_{ms} to insert a goal into *OPEN* , *CLOSED* , and *SG* , respectively. □

For example, computational time to insert K goals into *OPEN* is approximated as:

$$T_{merges}(OPEN, K) = K \cdot C_{mo}.$$

Let T_{exp} be computational time for goal expansion procedure, and T_{comm} be computational time for 2 procedures, subgoal distribution and subgoal reception. Then, computational time for each processor to proceed with a single iteration is:

$$T^1_{\text{PARCAR}} = T_{exp} + T_{comm}.$$

In PARCAR, each processor generates K subgoals in a single iteration. So, one-step SLD-derivation is done K/C_{match} times in goal expansion procedure. Then, T_{exp} is expressed as:

$$\begin{aligned} T_{exp} = {} & K/C_{match} \cdot (T_{sld}(1) + T_{cc}(C_{match})) \\ & + T_{merges}(CLOSED, K/C_{match}) + T_{merges}(SG, K). \end{aligned}$$

Each processor also send and receive K subgoals in subgoal distribution and subgoal reception procedure, respectively. Then, T_{comm} is expressed as:

$$T_{comm} = C_{comm} \cdot n + K \cdot C_{mo}.$$

Thus,

$$T^1_{\text{PARCAR}} = K/C_{match} \cdot (T_{sld}(1) + T_{cc}(C_{match}) + C_{mc}) + K \cdot C_{ms} + C_{comm} \cdot n + K \cdot C_{mo}.$$

In PIA* , each processor expands one goal, and C_{match} subgoals are generated in a single iteration. Then, the computational time $T^1_{\text{PIA}^*}$ is:

$$T^1_{\text{PIA}^*} = T_{sld}(1) + T_{cc}(C_{match}) + C_{mc} + C_{match} \cdot C_{ms} + C_{comm} \cdot n + C_{match} \cdot C_{mo}.$$

Now, let Gs be total amount of goals which are expanded by all processors so as to obtain an optimal solution, and n be the number of processors. Then, PARCAR imposes $(Gs \cdot C_{match})/(n \cdot K)$ iterations on each processor. Runtime of PARCAR with n processors is estimated at:

$$T_{\text{PARCAR}}(Gs,n) = \sum^{(Gs\cdot C_{match})/(n\cdot K)} T^1_{\text{PARCAR}}$$
$$= Gs/n(T_{sld}(1) + T_{cc}(C_{match}) + C_{match}(C_{mo} + C_{ms}) + C_{mc} + C_{match}/K \cdot C_{comm} \cdot n).$$

On the other hand, PIA* imposes Gs/n iterations on each processor, and its runtime is estimated at:

$$T_{\text{PIA}^*}(Gs,n) = \sum^{(Gs/n)} T^i_{pia^*}$$
$$= Gs/n(T_{sld}(1) + T_{cc}(C_{match}) + C_{match}(C_{mo} + C_{ms}) + C_{mc} + C_{comm} \cdot n).$$

The ratio is:

$$\frac{T_{\text{PIA}^*}(Gs,n)}{T_{\text{PARCAR}}(Gs,n)} = \frac{K(A + C_{comm} \cdot n)}{K \cdot A + C_{match} \cdot C_{comm} \cdot n},$$

where $A = T_{sld}(1) + T_{cc}(C_{match}) + C_{match} \cdot (C_{mo} + C_{ms}) + C_{mc}$.

This means that PARCAR becomes more efficient than PIA* when $K \geq C_{match}$[3].

$T_{\text{PIA}^*}(Gs,n)$ and $T_{\text{PARCAR}}(Gs,n)$ are also expressed in the form of the sum of parallel factor (1st term) and serial factor (second term) as follows:

$$T_{\text{PARCAR}}(Gs,n) = Gs \cdot A/n + Gs \cdot C_{comm} \cdot C_{match}/K.$$
$$T_{\text{PIA}^*}(Gs,n) = Gs \cdot A/n + Gs \cdot C_{comm}.$$

In the both algorithm, goal expansion procedure can be parallelized, while processor communication becomes an obstacle to parallelization. The above equations show that PARCAR is superior to PIA* , in respect to speedup, when $K \geq C_{match}$.

In this section, we have assumed that C_{match} is constant, with the aim of investigating communication overhead. On practical applications, C_{match} is variable depending on goals and the knowledge-base[4]. In this case, the variation of C_{match} may become an obstacle to the load balancing in PIA* , since each processor generates C_{match} subgoals and communicates them with other processors. On the other hand, PARCAR prevents the obstacle by keeping the number of subgoals constant K.

6 Experimental Results

We have made some experiments on an MIMD distributed memory parallel computer Fujitsu AP1000. We have considered a diagnostic problem to diagnose an m-bit ripple carry adder circuit. We have represented each hypothesis as a state in which a gate x is, (i.e., $ok(x)$, $stuck0(x)$, or $stuck1(x)$), and have given each hypothesis $|log_e \mathcal{P}(state(x))|$ as its cost, where $\mathcal{P}(state(x))$ is a probability of x being in $state$[5]. Figure 5 shows the experimental results on the problem, by changing the size m of the circuit[6]. Our experimental system is written in C. In the experiments, a parameter for PARCAR, $K = 50$ and for all goals

[3] PARCAR gets K adjusted to $K \gg C_{match}$.

[4] On example problem in section 6, for example, $0 < C_{match} < 6$.

[5] It follows from $0 \leq \mathcal{P}_i \leq 1$ and $\prod_i \mathcal{P}_i = exp(\sum_i |log_e \mathcal{P}_i|)$ that $\prod_i \mathcal{P}_i$ is maximum if $\sum_i |log_e \mathcal{P}_i|$ is minimum.

[6] The scale of knowledge-base which represents the problem is in proportion to m: facts consist of $17m + 24$ first-order Horn clauses and set of Hypotheses contains $15m + 3$ unit clauses.

gs, $\hat{h}(g)$s= 0. In this particular example, the results indicate that PARCAR is about 2.5 ∼ 5.8 times faster than PIA* as the problem becomes larger. Figure 6 shows the speedups. The speedup of PARCAR comes nearer to linear when the problem size becomes larger, while the speedup of PIA* falls below linear.

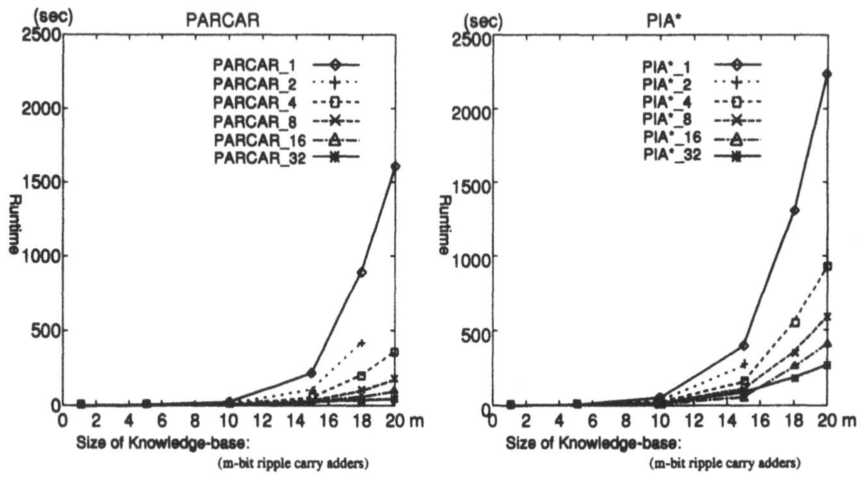

Fig. 5. Experimental Results

For more precisely, table 1 shows the detail of the results on the problem with its size $m = 20$. In the table, T_{exp} and T_{comm} are the execution time of goal expansion and of message communication[7], for a processor at a single iteration, respectively. $|CLOSED|$ means total amount of goals expanded until an optimal solution is obtained (corresponding to Gs in section 5), that is, the amount of the search. $\overline{Aber}(T_{exp})$ is the average of $Aber(T_{exp})$ for iterations, where $Aber(T_{exp}) = Dev(T_{exp}) / \overline{T}_{exp} \times 100$, $\overline{T}_{exp}$ is an average of T_{exp}s for all processors, and $Dev(T_{exp})$ is standard deviation of T_{exp}s. $\overline{Aber}(T_{exp})$ indicates how many percents T_{exp} taken by a processor becomes different from its average. $\overline{T}_{comm}$ is the average of T_{comm}s for all processors. The values of $|CLOSED|$ show that there is little difference between PARCAR and PIA* in respect to the amount of search. This means that the efficiency of algorithm causes the runtime difference between PARCAR and PIA* . Then, we have firstly investigated the communication overhead and the amount of iterations. The results indicate that PARCAR takes about 1.9 ∼ 2.3 times overhead to execute message communication; it takes about 1/38 ∼ 1/10 iterations instead, in comparison with PIA* . This means that PARCAR reduce the communication overhead by adequate increasing the quantity of task at a single iteration and keeping the amount of iterations down, because the communication cost is approximately $\overline{T}_{comm} \times iterations$.

[7] T_{comm} is the sum of the execution times for subgoal distribution and for subgoal reception procedure.

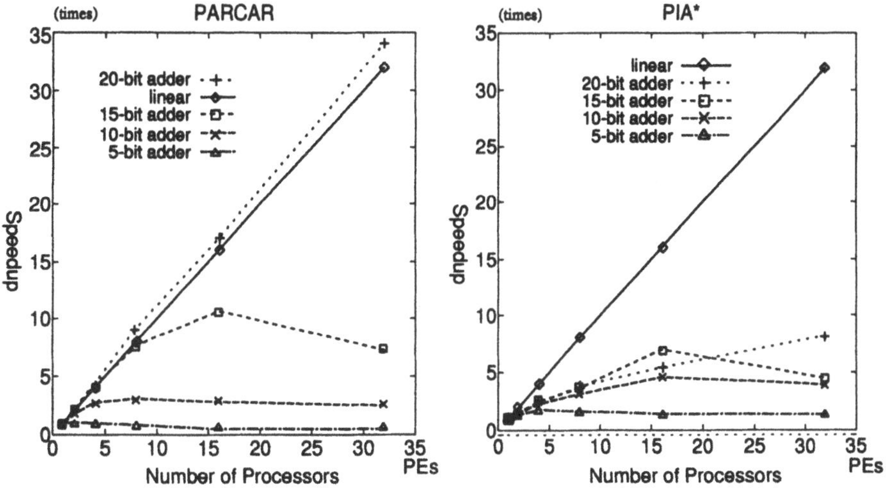

Fig. 6. Speedups

The variance of computational costs of the goal expansion procedure among processors should be restrained in order to promote the parallelism of the algorithm. As its index, We have secondly measured $\overline{Aber}(T_{exp})$ for iterations after all processors have more than one goal in $OPEN_i^j$. For example, the values of $\overline{Aber}(T_{exp})$ on 8 processors shows that PARCAR keeps T_{exp} within $\overline{T}_{exp} \pm 7.7\%$ for all processors, while PIA* may make T_{exp} more than $\overline{T}_{exp} \times 1.45$. The results show that PARCAR is superior to PIA* with respect to the load balancing.

Table 1. The Detail of the Results on the Problem with Its Size $m = 20$

	PARCAR				PIA*			
Processors	32	16	8	4	32	16	8	4
Runtime (sec)	47	94	174	366	275	416	593	931
Iterations	15	40	62	120	571	733	925	1137
$\|CLOSED\|$	24508	23653	23275	23437	22473	22978	23046	23121
$\overline{Aber}(T_{exp})$ (%)	55.8	12.6	7.7	8.3	71.4	57.3	48.5	45.5
$\overline{T}_{comm}$ (sec)	1.089	1.241	1.457	1.740	0.588	0.552	0.592	0.774

7 Concluding Remarks

We proposed a parallelization of cost-based Horn abduction for distributed memory systems. A search control technique of parallel best-first search was introduced into abductive reasoning mechanism, thereby obtaining much more efficiently an optimal explanation of the given observation. We proposed a PARallel Cost-based Abductive Reasoning system, PARCAR, and gave an informal analysis of PARCAR. We then implemented PARCAR on an MIMD distributed memory parallel computer, Fujitsu AP1000. The good performance results were given by some experiments on AP1000. In the experiments, we supposed that $\hat{h}(g) = 0$ for all goals g (see definition 3), because the experiments were to evaluate the parallelism of the algorithms. We have proposed the pre-analysis to discover effective admissible heuristic function $\hat{h}(g)$ in [KSI94]. It can also make PARCAR more efficient, by pruning the search space.

In this paper, we mainly describe the method for dividing the search space to processors and constructing the search-tree by each processor. We have also performed loop-check function, which is required in case knowledge-base is recursively defined, by pipelining. In the case, we have promoted the parallelism of pipelining, by equalizing the number of leaves in a search tree constructed by each processor.

References

[AK90] Khayri A. M. Ali and Roland Karlsson. The Muse Or-Parallel Prolog Model and its Performance. In *Proc. of the North American Conf. on Logic Programming*, pages 757–776. The MIT Press, 1990.

[CS94] E. Charniak and S. E. Shimony. Cost-based abduction and MAP explanation. *Artificial Intelligence*, 66:345–374, 1994.

[CWY91] Vitor S. Costa, David H. D. Warren, and Rong Yang. The Andorra-I Engine: A Parallel Implementation of the Basic Andorra Model. In *Proc. of the Eighth Intl. Conf. on Logic Programming*, pages 825–839. The MIT Press, 1991.

[HD89] S. Huang and L. S. Davis. Parallel Iterative A^* Search: An Admissible Distributed Heuristic Search Algorithm. In *Proc. of the IJCAI-89*, pages 23–29, 1989.

[KSI93] S. Kato, H. Seki, and H. Itoh. An Efficient Abductive Reasoning System Based on Program Analysis. In *Static Analysis, Proc. of the 3rd Intl. Workshop, LNCS-724*, pages 230–241, Padova, 1993. Springer-Verlag.

[KSI94] S. Kato, H. Seki, and H. Itoh. Cost-based Horn Abduction and its Optimal Search. In *Proc. of the 3rd Intl. Conf. on Automation, Robotics and Computer Vision*, pages 831–835, Singapore, November 1994.

[Llo84] J. W. Lloyd. *Foundations of Logic Programming.* Springer, 1984. Second, extended edition, 1987.

[LWH+90] E. Lusk, David H. D. Warren, S. Haridi, et al. The Aurora or-parallel Prolog system. *New Generation Computing*, 7(2,3):243–271, 1990.

[Nil80] N. J. Nilsson. *Principles of Artificial Intelligence.* Tioga, Palo Alto, CA, 1980.

[Poo88] D. Poole. A Logical Framework for Default Reasoning. *Artificial Intelligence*, 36:27–47, 1988.

[Poo93] D. Poole. Probabilistic Horn abduction and Bayesian networks. *Artificial Intelligence*, 64:81–129, 1993.

A History-Oriented Envisioning Method

Takashi Washio and Hiroshi Motoda
Division of Intelligent Systems Science,
The Institute of Scientific and Industrial Research, Osaka University
8-1 Mihogaoka, Ibaraki, Osaka 567, Japan
E-mail {washio,motoda}@sanken.osaka-u.ac.jp
Phone: 81-6-879-8540, Fax : 81-6-879-8544

Abstract
A novel and generic approach named as "history-oriented envisioning" is proposed to qualitatively envision all the possible and the sound situations focusing on our intended partial behaviors and actions of an objective system. Some basic notations called a "partial history" and a "partial situation" are introduced as the extensions of the conventional history and its situations representing qualitative, temporal behaviors and actions of the system. They provide the basic information of the intended partial behaviors and actions to the history-oriented envisioning. A major characteristic of the envisioning proposed here is its low complexity attained by the specified history of behaviors and actions in addition to the conventional scenario. Another important characteristic is its incremental structure enabling the iterative import of the predicted and/or observed information of the objective system. The feasibility of the proposed method is demonstrated by an example of controlling a steam generator of a plant. This method provides a basic measure to qualitatively estimate and plan system behaviors, and is considered to be applicable to wide engineering areas such as simulation, planning, design and diagnosis.

1 Introduction

One of the primary tasks of qualitative reasoning is the envisioning of system "behaviors" [de Kleer and Brown 1984; Forbus 1984, 1988; Kuipers 1984, 1986]. The "behaviors" are collection of possible situation transitions that result by system operations. The conventional framework of the envisioning consists of "attainable envisioning" and "total envisioning". The former derives the qualitatively possible situation transitions achievable from a specified initial state of a system. The latter derives all the possible situation transitions that may occur in the operations. The basic idea of these methods is to evaluate possible and sound behaviors of a system while maintaining a set of initially given background assumptions associated with the exogenous quantity states, views and processes of the system without imposing intentional changes of the assumptions.

In contrast with this standard methodology, the authors are interested in the envisioning in case that some portions of the evolutional system behaviors are specified in advance by our intention. Some work to introduce exogenously specified quantity, view and process transitions into the envisioning has been conducted [Forbus 1989; Drabble 1993; Iwasaki et al. 1993; Vescovi et al. 1993]. Forbus defined an "action" as an exogenous replacement of some background assumptions in a system scenario, and established "action-augmented envisioning" that enumerates all the possible transitions among combinations of quantity states, views, processes and actions. Drabble extended the notion of the actions to involve the exogenous specification of quantity states and to have qualitative time intervals. He also introduced a hierarchical sequence of actions to represent complex influences that are exogenously driven. Iwasaki and Vescovi proposed a language to specify intended functional behaviors in terms of causal transition rules. The latter two studies utilize in principle the repetitions of the attainable envisioning to search for their intended system behaviors. However, the difficulty of combinatorial explosion of the derived situations has been reported in the aforementioned envisioning methods, especially for the total and action-augmented envisioning, when the methods were adopted to practical scale applications [Caloud 1987; Forbus 1989; Forbus and Falkenhainer 1990, 1992; Amador et al. 1993]. For example, a self-explanatory simulation system "SimGen Mk2" to envision only local states of a system requires 4 hours to compile a simulator for a model of 9 containers and 12 pipes [Forbus and Falkenhainer 1992]. The main cause of this difficulty arises from the vast number of possible states envisioned, e.g. almost 1012 states, even for such a simple system.

An efficient remedy to this difficulty is to restrict the scope of the envisioning within the partial behaviors and actions intentionally specified following our interests, observations or the objectives of application tasks. For example, consider to control a steam generator in a power plant depicted in Fig.1. It has a primary water tube (p-tube) passing through a secondary boiler tank (s-tank). Highly pressurized hot water is supplied from a primary heat source by a pump. When the temperature of the primary water (p-water) is higher than the boiling point of the secondary water (s-water) in the low pressure tank, the heat flow from the primary to the secondary side can boil the secondary water. To compensate for the decrease of amount of the secondary water due to the escape of the steam (s-steam) to a turbine generator, the extra water feed (f-water) to the tank through a feed pipe (f-pipe) is required. An appropriate flow control of f-water is crucial for an efficien and safe operation of the power plant. If we apply the conventional envisioning methods to plan the control strategies, the envisioning system must address all the internal states of this component together with all the combinations of states of boundary quantites such as inlet temperatures of p-water, f-water and flow rate of p-water. This induces large ambiguity and complexity of the solution. On the other hand, by allowing only the state trajectories satisfying our observation that "the temperature of p-water is increasing." and our control objectives that "boiling of s-water should occurre." for instance, the ambiguity and the complexity of the resultatnt envisionment become considerably reduced without loss of utility for our planned task to figure out any strategies to start up the steam generation. As the information on task objectives and system boundaries is available in many engineering applications, this approach can be widely used to enhance the applicability of envisioning methods. Many work on simulation, planning, diagnosis and design in the field of qualitative reasoning utilizes the envisioning to obtain the information associated with specific system behaviors [DeCoste 1990, 1993; Drabble 1993; Forbus 1986; Forbus and Falkenhainer 1990, 1992; Ishida and Eshelman 1988; Iwasaki 1993; Pearce 1988; Umeda et al. 1991; Yannou 1993]. Their efficiency may also be increased by this approach.

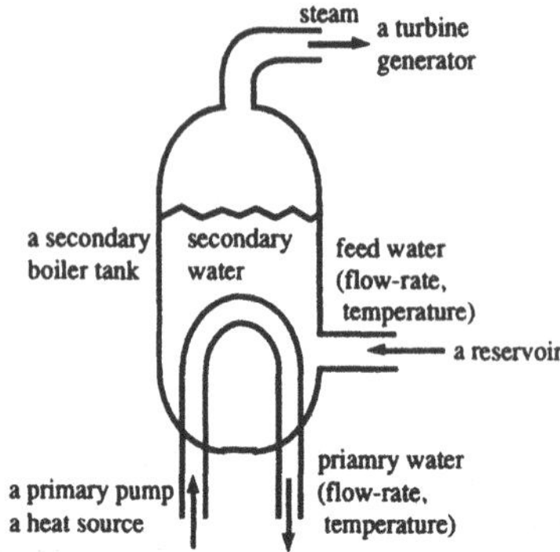

Fig. 1. A steam generator in a power plant for electricity generation.

The work presented here is to propose a novel and generic envisioning method focused on specific partial behaviors and actions of a system, called "history-oriented envisioning". The feasibility of the proposed method is demonstrated by an example of controlling a steam generator in the latter half of this paper.

2 Partial Situation and Partial History

We define first an efficient representation of the partial behaviors and actions that we intentionally specify. The fundamental structure of temporal behaviors and actions has been discussed in detail in the past work [Hayes 1979; Forbus 1984, 1989; Williams 1984; Dean and McDermott 1987]. Hayes and Forbus defined a sequence of changes of objects in a scenario as a "history" consisting of "situations". A situation of a history denotes a piece of a history at a particular time, and is either of "episodes" or "events". Events always last only for an instant, while episodes usually occur over a time interval. Each episode has a start and an end which are events that serve as its boundaries. Both of an event and an episode can involve the descriptions of quantity states, views, processes, actions, their relations and their transitions at some time (or a time interval). An assertion representing one of such descriptions is called a "token" [Dean and McDermott 1987]. Each token states a primitive fact in an event or an episode such as "amount of water in a pot is 1kg." or "boiling of water occurred."

Based on these definitions, some novel ideas on the history are introduced as follows.

Definition 1: A "partial event" is a set of some tokens involved in an event of a history.
A "partial episode" is a set of some tokens involved in an episode of a history.
Definition 2: A "partial situation" of a history is either of a partial event and a partial episode.

The notation of a partial situation consists of a list of individuals that must exist, a list of quantity values and relations indicating the objects' states, a list of views, a list of processes and a list of actions. The detailed descriptions of the contents in each list follow the notations in QP-theory [Forbus 1984]. T-operators are used to say that a particular token is true at some time, and M-operators represent the measured value of a quantity at some time. An extra notation represented as a predicate "Status(x, y)" has been newly introduced in our description. The symbol x is one of a view, a process and an action. The symbol y is one of "active", "inactive", "activated" and "inactivated". For instance, Status(Process_A, active) means that Process_A keeps its active status during a partial situation. Status(Action_B, inactivated) says Action_B is finished during a partial situation.

Two of the partial situations for an example of catching a ball falling through a flame depicted in fig.2 are as follows.

```
Partial Situation Heat-Flow-to-Ball-Active(?time)
  Individuals:  ball a ball
                flame a flame
  Quantities:   (T A[temperature-of(ball)]<A[temperature-of(flame)] ?time)    (1)
                (M A[temperature-of(ball)] ?time) = Tl
                (M Ds[temperature-of(ball)] ?time) = 1
  Views:
  Processes:    (T Status(Heat-Flow(flame, ball, flame-ball),
                 Active) ?time)
  Actions:

Partial Situation Catching-Ball-under-Flame(?time)
  Individuals:  ball a ball
                flame a flame                        (2)
                basket a basket
  Quantities:   (M A[position-of(ball)] ?time) = (-∞,H1)
                (M Ds[position-of(ball)] ?time) = -1
  Views:        (T Status(Contained-Stuff(ball, basket),
                 Activated) ?time)
  Processes:
  Actions:      (T Status(Catch-In(ball, basket),
                 Activated) ?time)
```

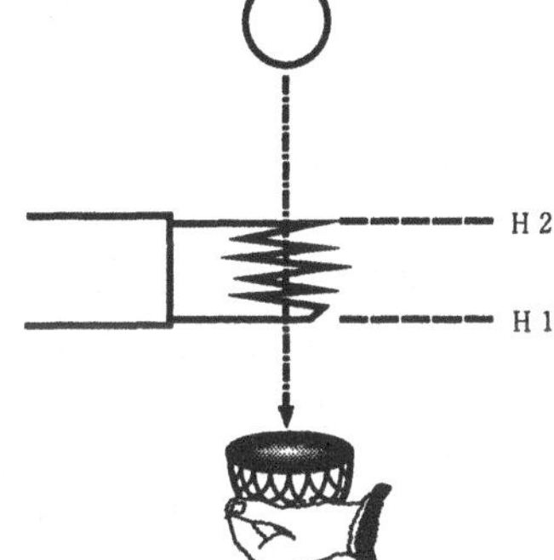

Fig.2. Catching a ball falling through a flame.

The term "?time" of the T-operator and M-operator represents the temporal specification of the partial situation, and its value is specified by the description of partial history as explained later. The former partial situation represents that the objects; a ball and a flame exist at a particular time. The tempetature of the ball and the sign of its derivative are Tl and positive respectively. The temperature of the ball is lower than that of the flame. The process of heat flow is taking place at the same time. The latter means that the objects; a ball, a flame and a basket exist, and the ball falling thorugh the flame is caught and settled in the basket at some time. Some lists and their contents can be left unspecified in a partial situation. For instance, the position of the ball are not given in the former partial situation, but the quantity must be given to specify a unique state of the ball. A distinct partial situation is "No-Specification(?time)" in which all lists are empty. This partial situation is used to represent that any behaviors and actions are unspecified at some time.

The contents in the lists of individuals and quantities of a partial situation are used as the assumptions for the history-oriented envisioning. For instance, the assertion of "ball a ball" in the individual lists is an assumption specified by the partial situations in the above examples. On the other hand, the views, the processes and the actions in their lists do not represent their assumptions directly. The views and the processes in the scenario and the domain model of the QP-theory have the information of "Individuals", "Preconditions" and "Quantity Conditions" [Forbus 1984]. Also, the actions have the part of "Individuals" [Forbus 1989]. These are their assumptions for them to be active. Accordingly, the unifications of the contents in the view, the process and the action lists to the scenario and the domain model in the envisioning system provide their assumptions for the partial situation. For instance, the unification of "Heat-Flow(flame, ball, flame-ball)" in the process lists of the partial situation (1) to the following domain model (3) of the heat-flow process instantiates the contents in the "Individuals", "Preconditions" and "Quantity Conditions" of the process as the corresponding assumptions.

```
Process Heat-Flow(?src, ?dst, ?path)
  Individuals:           ?src an object, Has-Quantity(?src, heat)
                         ?dst an object, Has-Quantity(?dst, heat)
                         ?path a Heat-Path, Heat-Connection(?path, ?src, ?dst)
  Preconditions:         Heat-Aligned(?path)                                    (3)
  Quantity Conditions:   A[temperature(?src)]>A[temperature(?dst)]
  Relations:             Quantity(flow-rate)
                         flow-rate = (temperature(?src)-temperarture(?dst))
  Influences:            I-(heat(?dst), A[flow-rate])
                         I+(heat(?src), A[flow-rate])
```

Another important assumption in a partial situation is the duration of ?time. Its specification controls the generation of the limit hypotheses in the envisioning process as explained later. The history-oriented envisioning utilizes all of the assumptions described here for a scenario involving the partial situation.

The definition of a "partial history" is given based on the partial situations.

Definition 3: A "partial history" of a history is a set of partial situations of the history which time intervals and instants are totally ordered in time domain.

A partial history has a list of the T-operators to say that a particular partial situation is true at some time. It also has a list of time constraints. An example of a partial history for the ball is shown here.

```
Partial History  Initial-and-Final-Ball
  Partial Situations:   (T Initial-Position-of-Ball(I0) I0)
                        (T Position-Decreasing-of-Ball-above-Flame(I1) I1)
                        (T Heat-Flow-to-Ball-Active(I2) I2)
                        (T No-Specification(I3) I3)
                        (T Position-Decreasing-of-Ball-under-Flame(I4) I4)
                        (T Catching-Ball-under-Flame(I5) I5)                   (4)
  Time Constraints:     (start(I0)=end(I0)), (end(I0)=start(I1)), (start(I1)<end(I1)),
                        (end(I1)=start(I2)),(start(I2)≦end(I2)), (end(I2)=start(I3)),
                        (start(I3)<end(I3)), (end(I3)=start(I4)), (start(I4)<end(I4)),
                        (end(I4)=start(I5)), (start(I5)=end(I5))
```

The partial situations before No-Specification(I3) specifies the partial behaviors of a ball beginning with its initial position until it touches the flame, while those after No-Specification(I3) describes the partial behaviors and actions associated with the ball under the flame until it is caught in a basket. Hence, this partial history specifies two clusters of partial situations mutually apart in time domain.

The list of time constraints specifies the temporal characteristic of each partial situations, and follows the conditions indicated below with respect to its duration.

start(?time)=end(?time) ⇔ ?time is an instant.,
start(?time)<end(?time) ⇔ ?time is an interval., (5)
start(?time)≦end(?time) ⇔ The duration of ?time is unspecified.

For example, (T Initial-Position-of-Ball(I0) I0) and (T Catching-Ball-under-Flame(I5) I5) hold only at an instant. Thus they have the identical starting and ending times, and must be partial events. The partial situation, (T Heat-Flow-to-Ball-Active(I2) I2), is specified as either of a partial event and a partial episode, because its duration is not given in this example.

The value of ?time of each partial situation specified in the partial history is substituted to the variable ?time in the representation of the respective partial situation. For example, the values of I2 and I5 are substituted to the variables of partial situation (1) and (2), respectively. Then, the value is used to check the temporal characteristic of the partial situation and control the envisioning process explained later by following the rules indicated bellow.

Condition on Limit Hypotheses:
A partial situation involves some limit hypotheses.
⇒ ?time is an instant, i.e. the partial situation is a partial event. (6)
?time is an interval, i.e. the partial situation is a partial episode.
⇒ A partial situation does not involve any limit hypotheses.

These conditions states that any partial situation involving some limit hypotheses should be a partial event. However, a partial event does not necessarily involve limit hypothesis, because some tokens not belonging to the partial event within the event may be some limit hypotheses. On the other hand, any partial episode should not involve any limit hypothesis by definition.

A partial history given to the history-oriented envisioning is part of the scenario for the envisioning. Some partial histories may not be realized in the possible histories of the scenario. For example, the heat flow from the flame to the ball does not take place before the ball touches the flame . When such a partial history is specified, the history-oriented envisioning halts at its intermediate step, and does not generate any envisionment consistent with the partial history.

3 History-oriented Envisioning

3.1 Overview of History-oriented Envisioning

The outline of the history-oriented envisioning is depicted in Fig.3. The vertical direction from the top to the bottom of the box stands for the time evolution of the behaviors and actions of an objective system. The horizontal axis represents the spectrum of the assumptions in the envisioning process. The shadowed area is the input information to the history-oriented envisioning, while the white part is its output. The domain model and a part of the scenario for the objective system are fixed over the entire time evolution in the envisioning. The conventional envisioning enumerates the situation nodes grounded on all the possible and sound combinations of the open assumptions associated with the system. On the other hand, the history-oriented envisioning imports the given specifications on some part of the assumptions for each time interval and instant in the form of the partial situation. It derives situation nodes that are allowed within all the possible and sound combinations of the remaining open assumptions following the

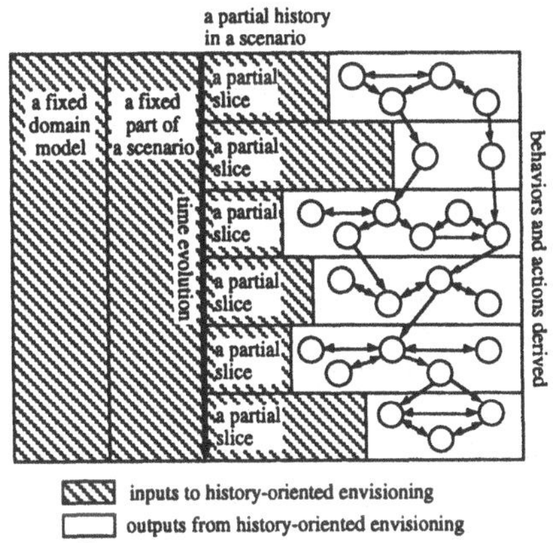

Fig.3. The outline of history-oriented envisioning.

order of the specified time interval or instant. Accordingly, the history-oriented envisioning focuses on only the situations of the objective system that match the specified partial behaviors and actions. The number of the derived situation nodes and the computation time are significantly reduced due to the low ambiguity of the conditions that are exponential to the number of the open assumptions.

3.2 Algorithm

A partial history for the history-oriented envisioning must be compiled in advance to derive all the assumptions associated with its partial situations. The algorithm to compile the partial histories is depicted in Fig.4. This derives the set of assumptions, Psi, for every partial situation, PS(i) (i=1,---,n), and its time constraints, TC(i), in the partial history by unifying their views, processes and actions to the scenario and the domain model in the envisioning system. The series of the partial situations and their time constraints in a partial history is sequentially compiled. (Step 3) and (step 4) collect the assumptions of a partial situation. (Step 3) obtains the assumptions explicitly represented in the individuals lists, the quantities lists and the time constraints of the partial situation, while (step 4) derives implicit ones of the views, processes and actions not directly represented in the partial situation. (Step 2) and (step 5) check the violation of Condition on Limit Hypotheses in the given partial situations, and quit the compiling if any violations are detected. (Step 2) checks any explicit limit hypotheses appearing in a partial episode, e.g., (T Status(Catch-In(ball, basket), Activated) Interval). On the other hand, (step 5) checks any implicit limit hypotheses appearing in the assumptions of a partial episode unified in (step 4),e.g., (A[temperature(ball)]=

(step 1) i←1.
(step 2) Choose the ith partial slice PS(i) and the time constraints TC(i) on PS(i).
If any explicit limit hypotheses appear in any lists of the individuals, the quantities, the views, the processes and the actions in PS(i), check Condition on Limit Hypotheses. If it is violated, then stop.
(step 3) Let Psi be a set of the contents in TC(i), the individuals lists and the quantities lists of PS(i).
(step 4) Unifiy the views, the processes and the actions in their lists to the scenario and the domain model in the envisioning system, and let Psu be a set of the contents in the individuals, the preconditions and the quantity conditions of the unified predicates.
Psi←Psi ∪ Psu.
(step 5) If any implicit limit hypotheses appear in Psi, check Condition on Limit Hypotheses. If it is violated, then stop. If i<n, then go to (step 2), else end.

Fig.4. An algorithm of compiling a partial history.

(step 1) i←1. Let the set of assumptions Pi be Pf ∪ Psi.
Perform a total (or action-augmented) envisioning under Pi, and let Q be a set {q(i,j) | q(i,j) is jth situation node generated in the envisioning, and j=1,---,mi.}. If Q is null, then stop.
(step 2) R←{}.
For j=1 to mi {
(step 2.1) Let the set of assumptions P'i,j be Pf ∪ Initial(q(i,j)). Perform one step attainable (or attainable action-augmented) envisioning under P'i,j.
(step 2.2) Filter only the situation nodes which satisfies all conditions specified in Psi+1.
Let Rf be a set of the filtered situation nodes, and R←R ∪ Rf. }
If R is null, then stop.
(step 3) Remove every situation node from Q which is not reachable to any r(j) ∈ R (j=1,---,mr).
(step 4) i←i+1. S←{}.
For j=1 to mr {
Let the set of assumptions Pi,j be Pf ∪ Psi ∪ Initial(r(j)). Perform an attainable (or attainable action-augmented) envisioning under Pi,j.
Let Sf be a set of the situation nodes generated in the envisioning, and S←S ∪ Sf. }
(step 5) S is represented as {q(i,j) | j=1,---,mi.}. Q←Q ∪ S.
If i<n, then go to (step 2), else end.

Fig. 5. An algorithm of history-oriented envisioning.

100)&(Ds[temperature(ball)]=1) in the quantity conditions of a process.

Once, all the assumptions are obtained, they are applied to the algorithm of the history-oriented envisioning represented in Fig.5. It is noted that this incrementally accepts the assumption sets of partial situations in a partial history in accordance with their total order described in the time constraints of the history. Pf is the fixed portion of the background assumptions for a scenario over the envisioning. Pf corresponds to the conventional scenario excluding the partial history.

(Step 1) is to enumerate all the possible situations for the first partial situation. The total envisioning (or action-augmented envisioning, if possible actions must be taken into account.) under the conditions of Pf and Ps1 is required at this step because any preceding situations have not been specified. If the first partial situation is not consistent with the Pf, then no solutions are obtained, and the process halts.

(Step 2) is to identify all the situations for the next partial situation which are directly caused by the current situations. In (step 2.1), all the possible one step transitions from a current situation to the next are figured out. The one step attainable (or attainable action-augmented) envisioning is an ordinal attainable (or attainable action-augmented) envisioning under a given initial condition, q(i,j), but it is limited to one situation transition. The notation, Initial(q(i,j)), expresses that q(i,j) is a given initial condition for the envisioning. (Step 2.2) filters out any inconsistent situations with the next partial situation. When the next partial situation is the No-Specification(?time), all the situations obtained in (step 2.1) is passed. On the contrary, when any current situations can not transit to any consistent situations with the specifications of the next partial situation, the process halts.

(Step 3) is a sort of retrospective reasoning, while the other steps are perspective. Q contains all the possible histories from the first to the current partial situation. Because the results of the filtering in (step 2) limits the possible transitions from the given partial situations, some histories in Q may not be causatively connected to the next partial situation. This step eliminates such dead end histories in Q.

(step 4) enumerates all possible situations in the new partial situation causatively occured from the previous partial situation based on the attainable (or attainable action-augmented) envisioning. Each envisioning starts from a situation figured out in (step 2), and a list of all possible situations evolved for this partial situation is obtained.

(step 5) simply accumulates the situations for the new partial situation in Q. An envisionment following the given partial history is rested in Q, when all partial situations in the partial history have been processed.

The heaviest computational load in this algorithm is at (step 4). The load strongly depends on the number of its initial states R generated in (step 2), and the number mostly depends on the efficiency of the situation filtering in (step 2.2) associated with the preceeding partial situations. Hence, the computational load will be substantially reduced when many specifications are included in each partial situations. The loads of the other steps are not very significant. The total (or action-augmented) envisioning in (step 1), whose algorithm is essentially efficient, is performed only once, and its processing speed is accelerated by specifying the first partialsituation. (Step 2) that performs only one step reasoning for each situation transition is quite efficient. (Step 3) is merely a network search for which various efficient algorithms are available. The simplicity of (step 5) is trivial.

An advantage of this algorithm is that the conventional total and attainable envisioning [Forbus 1984, 1988, 1989] can be utilized as parts of its process while reducing the solutions and processing time based on the information in a partial history. A unique difference of the envisioning utilized here from the conventional one is the imposition of the following rules on the generation of situation nodes that are associated with Condition of Limit Hypotheses on the assumption of TC(i). They reject the situation nodes involving any limit hypotheses in a finite time interval.

(start(Ii)=end(Ii))&(The assumptions of PS(i) do not involve any limit hypotheses.)
$\Rightarrow$ (The assumptions generated for the situation node in the envisioning
must involve some limit hypotheses.),
(start(Ii)<end(Ii)) (7)
$\Rightarrow$ (The assumptions generated for the situation node in the envisioning
must not involve any limit hypotheses.),
where Ii is an instant or an interval for PS(i).

Another advantage is its incremental structure to process a partial history. This enables on-line application where new partial situation information is imported step by step. Especially, when each partial situation is well specified in on-line use, real time processing will be possible. These features of the algorithm are expected to be highly profitable for the real time applications of control, planning, measurement interpretation and diagnosis.

3.3 Soundness and Complexity

The standard total (or action-augmented) envisioning is sound for all the possible system behaviors and actions under closed world assumptions the members of which are the only possible assumptions for the scenario [Forbus 1988]. The standard attainable (or attainable action-augmented) envisioning is also sound for its possible initial conditions under the closed world assumptions. Hence, each standard envisionment generated in (step 1), (step 2.1) and (step 4) in the algorithm depicted in fig.5 is sound for the given assumptions. The other steps; (step 2.2) and (step 3) reduce the generated nodes. (Step 2.2) is clearly sound because it just filters situation nodes that are consistent with the constraints required for the transitions from the current situation to the next just like the standard envisioning internally does. (Step 3) is also sound since it keeps track of all the histories which do not contradict the assumptions of any partial situations and the scenario's fixed part in the context of a given partial history. These observations support the soundness of the history-oriented envisioning conducted by the algorithm of Fig.5 under the closed world assumptions.

The complexity of an envisioning process sensitively depends on the number of unspecified assumptions for an envisionment [Forbus 1988, 1989]. Let P be the set of assumptions for a scenario, where its fixed portion is $Pf \subseteq P$. The set of unspecified assumptions for the standard envisioning is Pu=P-Pf, because it does not utilize any information of a partial history. If Pu consists of pairs of in and out of assumptions, i.e., p and $\neg$p, the number of states could increase by $O(2^{|Pu|-1})$. On the contrary, each partial situation specifies some portion of P-Pf in the history-oriented envisioning. The part of unspecified assumptions in P with respect to the first partial situation is $Pu1=P-Pf \cup Ps1$. Hence, the complexity of the total envisioning in (step 1) of fig.5 is proportional to $O(2^{|Pu1|-1})$. The attainable envisioning through (step 2) to (step 4) is performed for the unspecified assumptions of $Pui=P-Pf \cup Psi$, and its initial situations are limited to the preceding envisionment. Accordingly, its initial complexity could be less than $O(2^{|Pui|-1})$. These lead to the maximum complexity of $O(2^{|Pu1|-1})+O(\sum_{i=2} 2^{|Pui|-1})$ for the history-oriented envisioning. Since the number of partial situations in a partial history, n, is independent of the assumptions, and also each, |Pui| is equal or less than |Pu|, the complexity of the history-oriented envisioning can be quite small comparing with the standard.

4 An Example

The proposed history-oriented envisioning has been applied to the control of a steam generator depicted in Fig.1 commonly used in power plants for electricity generation, and its performance evaluated. At the beginning of its operation, the secondary water has not started boiling yet. We could qualitatively determine the future change of the primary water flow rate and its temperature based on the operational conditions of the heat source and the primary pump in the upper stream. The future change of the temperature of the secondary feed water is also qualitatively assumed based on the information of its reservoir. The temperatures of p-water and f-water are assumed to increase monotonically, while the flow rate of p-water is assumed to decrease monotonically in the mean time, and three of them are assumed to reach an equilibrium at certain levels after some time. Our task is to plan all the sound control strategies of the secondary water that is fed to the tank to start boiling after the transient of the three boundary quantities is over.

```
Partial History  Boiling-Control
  Partial Slices:       (T Initial-State(I0) I0)
                        (T Start-of-Transient(I1) I1)
                        (T Monotonic-Transient(I2) I2)
                        (T End-of-Transient-and-
                         Start-of-Boiling(I3) I3)
                        (T Final-State(I4) I4)
  Time Constraints:     (start(I0)=end(I0)), (end(I0)=start(I1)),
                        (start(I1)=end(I1)), (end(I1)=start(I2)),
                        (start(I2)<end(I2)), (end(I2)=start(I3)),
                        (start(I3)=end(I3)), (end(I3)=start(I4)),
                        (start(I4)=end(I4))
```

Fig. 6. A partial history to control the boiling of secondary water.

A possible partial history corresponding to our mission can be written as shown in Fig.6. It specifies the intended behaviors of the steam generator together with the assumed changes of the boundary quantities such as the temperatures of p-water and f-water. The occurrence of boiling of the secondary water is intended at the final stage of the transients. Figure 7 represents two partial situations in the partial history. The former specifies the initial situation associated with the three boundary quantities, an endogenous quantity, i.e. temperature-of(s-water), and the intended processes. The latter specifies that the endogenous temperature-of(s-water) reaches its boiling point, and simultaneously the boiling process is activated when the three boundary quantities reach their goal levels maintaining the amount-of(s-water), the heat-flow and the fluid-flow.

The fixed portion of the scenario for this system and its partial history in Fig.6 has been compiled to the assumptions and applied to the algorithm of history-oriented envisioning. The algorithm has been implemented and a program specific to this type of examples has been developed and tested out on a SPRAC-10 machine. A more generic program is currently under development. Figure 8 depicts the resultant envisionment indicating all the possible and sound strategies to control the boiling under the given partial history. A total of 29 situations were found. The author have tried to derive the total envisionment of this steam generator without specifying any partial history for comparison. However, the solution was not obtained due to the limitation of the memory capacity of the current program. The possible situations in the total envisionment can be at least more than 6000 even for this simple system since it has 4 free boundary quantities. The planning of control strategies for process systems such as this example is highly expensive unless appropriate constraints are introduced.

5 Discussions and Related Works

One of the major characteristics of the history-oriented envisioning is the direct specifications of behaviors and actions to the envisioning process in addition to the conventional scenario. The envisioning focuses only on the specified situations and their histories, and derives situations including those with small computational load. Iwasaki and Vescovi introduced a language, CFRL, to specify intended functional behaviors [Iwasaki et al. 1993; Vescovi et al. 1993]. However, the CFRL just filters intended behaviors from the possible behaviors that result in the envisioning, and hence does not control the envisioning process directly. In contrast, the efficient behavior focusing capability of the history-oriented envisioning enhances the applicability of the envisioning theory to the problems of practical scale.

Another major characteristic is the explicit use of not only our intentional actions to eliminate unrequired or useless solutions for our reasoning tasks but also the information on the behaviors' history we intend on the objective system. Drabble developed a system, EXCALIBUR, for planning and reasoning with process systems [Drabble 1993]. It utilizes some attainable envisioning processes, and can manage the actions changing continuous process quantities not only the ones causing discontinuous change of views and processes. It can also take a tree and hierarchical structure of action sequences, but the behavior that evolves in the process cannot be explicitly specified in the envisioning. As many applications such as planning, simulation and design in practical fields are usually seeking objective processes or intended behavior sequences that can be specfied in advance, the history-oriented envisioning provides an efficient approach to the synthetic tasks.

The third important characteristic is the incremental structure of the history-oriented envisioning. Work on the measurement interpretation utilizes the total envisionments of the objective system to interpret the situation transition [Forbus 1986; DeCoste 1990, 1993]. However, the total envisioning is quite expensive for processes of practical scale. In contrast, the incremental feature of the history-oriented envisioning enables to take a sequence of behaviors and actions one by one in the on-line monitoring process. If there is a reasonable amount of information taken, its

```
Partial Slice  Initial-State(?time)
  Individuals:  p-tube   a pipe
                f-pipe   a pipe
                s-tank   a container
                p-water  a contained liquid
                s-water  a contained liquid
                f-water  a contained liquid
  Quantities:   (T A[temperature-of(p-water)]
                  >A[temperature-of(f-water)] ?time)
                (M A[temperature-of(p-water)] ?time) = Tpmin
                (M Ds[temperature-of(p-water)] ?time) = 0
                (M A[temperature-of(f-water)] ?time)= Tfmin
                (M Ds[temperature-of(f-water)] ?time) = 0
                (T A[temperature-of(s-water)] ?time)
                  <A[t-boil(s-water)] ?time)
                (M Ds[temperature-of(s-water)] ?time) = 0
                (M A[flow-rate-of(p-water)] ?time) = Fpmax
                (M Ds[flow-rate-of(p-water)] ?time) = 0
  Views:
  Processes:    (T Status(Heat-flow(p-water, s-water,
                  p-tube), Active) ?time)
                (T Status(Fluid-flow(f-water, s-water,
                  f-pipe), Active) ?time)
                (T Status(Boiling(s-water, Heat-flow),
                  Inactive) ?time)
  Actions:

Partial Slice  End-of-Transient-and-Start-of-Boiling(?time)
  Individuals:  p-tube   a pipe
                f-pipe   a pipe
                s-tank   a container
                p-water  a contained liquid
                s-water  a contained liquid
                f-water  a contained liquid
  Quantities:   (T A[temperature-of(p-water)]
                  >A[temperature-of(f-water)] ?time)
                (M A[temperature-of(p-water)] ?time) = Tpmax
                (M Ds[temperature-of(p-water)] ?time) = 1
                (M A[temperature-of(f-water)] ?time) = Tfmax
                (M Ds[temperature-of(f-water)] ?time) = 1
                (T A[temperature-of(s-water)] ?time)
                  =A[t-boil(s-water)] ?time)
                (M Ds[temperature-of(s-water)] ?time) = 0
                (M A[flow-rate-of(p-water)] ?time) = Fpmin
                (M Ds[flow-rate-of(p-water)] ?time) = -1
                (M A[amount-of(s-water)] ?time) = (0,Msmax)
  Views:
  Processes:  (T Status(Heat-flow(p-water, s-water,
                  p-tube), Active) ?time)
                (T Status(Fluid-flow(f-water, s-water,
                  f-pipe), Active) ?time)
                (T Status(Boiling(s-water, Heat-flow),
                  Activated) ?time)
  Actions:
```

Fig. 7. An example of a partial slice for the control of the secondary water boiling.

attainable envisioning in each step will be quite cheap, thus making its real time use possible. This characteristic meets the practical needs of analytic tasks such as measurements interpretation, control and diagnosis.

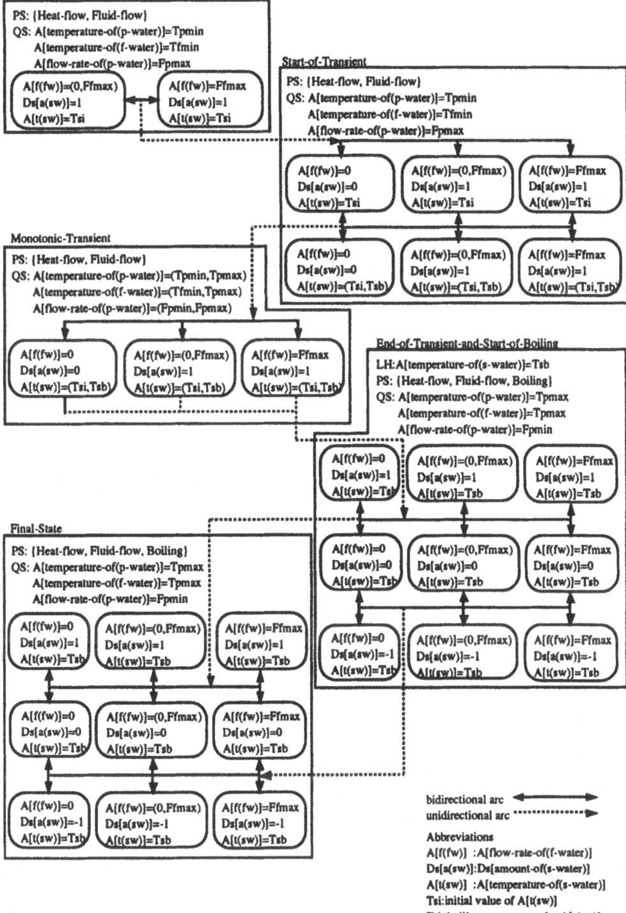

Fig.8. A situation transition diagram of a steam generator for a partial history.

6 Conclusion

A history-oriented envisioning method has been proposed. It is characterized by its capability of receiving some intended behaviors of a system from outside. These behaviors are called "partial situations and a partial history". The method has been applied to an example of control strategy planning for a steam generator and its eficeincy confirmed. The major characteristic of the history-oriented envisioning are summarized as follows.

(1) The envisioning is sound. Its computational complexity is low and it is much more efficient than the conventional envisioning.
(2) Envisioning is focused on a sequence of intended partial behaviors and actions.
(3) Envisioning can be incremental to import the assumptions in an iterative manner.

The ideas presented here will promote a new progress of qualitative envisioning theory toward its application to more practical tasks of simulation, planning, design, measurements interpretation, control and diagnosis.

The future work that remains to be explored includes:

(1) Extension of a partial history: At present the structure of a partial history is a sequence of partial situations although the sequence can be fragmented by the "No-Specification" partial situation. Its extension to a tree, graph and hierarchical structures or transition rules from a history as in the EXCALIBUR and the CFRL will enhance the usability of the history-oriented envisioning.
(2) Seeking for a better algorithm: The current algorithm for the history-oriented envisioning is a first step to evaluate the basic performance. More efficient algorithm might be developed.

(3) Development of a computer program for general use: The domains of process systems that can be envisioned in the current program is quite limited. The authors are currently working on a more general program for history-oriented envisioning.

Acknowledgments
The authors wishes to express our thanks to Prof. Masaharu Kitamura in the Nuclear Engineering Department of Tohoku University for the useful discussions.

References

[Amador et al. 1993] Franz G. Amador, Adam Finkelstein and Daniel S. Weld. Real-Time Self-Explanatory Simulation. In proceedings AAAI-93, pp.562-567, 1993.

[Caloud 1987] Philipe Caloud. Toward Continuous Process Supervision. In proceedings IJICAI-87, pp. 1086-1089, 1987.

[Dean and McDermott 1987] Thomas Dean and Drew V. McDermott. Temporal Database Management. Artificial Intelligence, 36(3):375-399, 1988.

[DeCoste 1990] Dennis DeCoste. Dynamic Across-Time Measurement Interpretation. In proceeding AAAI-90, pp.373-379, 1990.

[DeCoste 1993] Dennis DeCoste. Dynamic Across-Time Measurement Interpretation. Artificial Intelligence, 51(1-3):273-341, 1993.

[de Kleer and Brown 1984] Johan de Kleer and John Seely Brown. A Qualitative Physics Based on Confluence. Aritificial Intelligence, 24:7-83, 1984.

[Drabble 1993] Brain Drabble. EXCALIBUR: A Program for Planning and Reasoning with Process. Aritificial Intelligence, 62:1-40, 1993.

[Forbus 1984] Kenneth D. Forbus. Qualitative Process Theory. Aritificial Intelligence, 24:85-168, 1984.

[Forbus 1986] Kenneth D. Forbus. Interpreting Measurement of Physical Systems. In proceeding AAAI-86, pp.113-117, 1986.

[Forbus 1988] Kenneth D. Forbus. QPE: Using Assumption-based Truth Maintenance for Qualitative Simulation. Artificial Intelligence in Engineering, 3(4):200-215, 1988.

[Forbus 1989] Kenneth D. Forbus. Introducing Actions into Qualitative Simulation. In proceedings IJCAI-87, pp.1273-1278, 1989.

[Forbus and Falkenhainer 1990] Kenneth D. Forbus and Brain Falkenhainer. Self-explanatory Simulations: An Integration of Qualitative and Quantitative Knowledge. In proceedings AAAI-90, pp. 380-387 1990.

[Forbus and Falkenhainer 1992] Kenneth D. Forbus and Brain Falkenhainer. Self-explanatory Simulations: Scaling Up to Large Models. In proceedings AAAI-92, pages 685-690, 1992.

[Kuipers 1984] Benjamin Kuipers. Commonsense Reasoning about Causality: Deriving Behavior from Structure. Aritificial Intelligence, 24:169-203, 1984.

[Kuipers 1986] Benjamin Kuipers. Qualitative Simulation. Aritificial Intelligence, 29:289-338, 1986.

[Hayes 1979] P. J. Hayes. The naive physics manifesto, in: D. Michie (Ed.), Expert Systems in the Electric Age (Edinburgh University Press, Edinburgh, 1979).

[Ishida and Eshelman 1988] Y. Ishida and L. Eshelman. AQUA: Integrating Model-Based Diagnosis and Syndrome-Based Diagnosis, cmu-cs-87-111, 1987.

[Iwasaki et al. 1993] Yumi Iwasaki, Richard Fikes, Marcos Vescovi, and B. Chandrasekaran. How Things Are Intended to Work: Capturing Functional Knowledge in Device Design. In proceedings IJICAI-93, pp.1516-1522, 1993.

[Pearce 1988] D. A. Pearce. The Induction of Fault Diagnosis Systems from Qualitative Models. In proceedings AAAI-88, pp. 353-357, 1988.

[Umeda et al. 1991] Yasushi Umeda, Tetsuo Tomiyama, and Hiroyuki Yoshikawa. A Design Methodology for a Self-maintenance Machine. DE-Vol.31, Design Theory and Methodology - DTM'91 - edited by L.A. Stauffer, Book No. G00641, 1991.

[Vescovi et al. 1993] Marcos Vescovi, Yumi Iwasaki, Richard Fikes, and B. Chandrasekaran. CFRL: A Language for Specifying the Causal Functionality of Engineered Devices. In proceedings AAAI-93, pp.626-633, 1993.

[Williams 1984] Brian C. Williams. Qualitative Analysis of MOS Circuits. Aritificial Intelligence, 24:281-346, 1984.

[Williams 1986] Brian C. Williams. Doing time: putting qualitative reasoning on firmer ground, In proceedings AAAI-86, 1986.

[Yannou 1993] Bernard Yannou. Qualitative Design with Envisionment. In working papers QR'93, pp.250-259. 1993.

Team Learning of Recursive Languages

Sanjay Jain[1] and Arun Sharma[2]

[1] Dept. of Info. Systems & Computer Science, National University of Singapore, Singapore 119260, Republic of Singapore, Email: sanjay@iscs.nus.sg
[2] School of Computer Science and Engineering, The University of New South Wales, Sydney, NSW 2052, Australia, Email: arun@cse.unsw.edu.au

Abstract. A team of learning machines is a multiset of learning machines. A team is said to successfully learn a concept just in case each member of some nonempty subset, of predetermined size, of the team learns the concept. Team learning of languages turns out to be a suitable theoretical model for studying computational limits on multi-agent machine learning. Team learning of recursively enumerable languages has been extensively studied. However, it may be argued that from a practical point of view all languages of interest are recursive.
This paper gives theoretical results about team learnability of recursive languages. These results are mainly about two issues: redundancy and aggregation. The issue of redundancy deals with the impact of increasing the size of a team and increasing the number of machines required to be successful. The issue of aggregation deals with conditions under which a team may be replaced by a single machine without any loss in learning ability. The learning scenarios considered are:
(a) Identification in the limit of accepting grammars for recursive languages.
(b) Identification in the limit of decision procedures for recursive languages.
(c) Identification in the limit of accepting grammars for indexed families of recursive languages.
(d) Identification in the limit of accepting grammars for indexed families with enumerable class of grammars for the family as the hypothesis space.
Scenarios which can be modeled by team learning are also presented.

1 Introduction

Algorithmic identification in the limit of two concept classes, computable functions and recursively enumerable languages, have been studied extensively in the computational learning theory literature.

We first describe the learning of a computable function. A learning machine is fed the graph of a computable function one ordered pair at a time, and the machine, from time to time, conjectures a sequence of computer programs. The machine is said to learn the function just in case its conjectures converge to a program for the function. Recently, learning of functions by teams of learning machines has become a very active area of research and has been suggested as a theoretical model for multi-agent learning (for example, see [19, 18, 7, 4, 3, 12]).

However, the utility of function learning as a model for machine learning is somewhat limited. Data available to most learning systems are of two kinds: positive data and complete (both positive and negative) data. In learning from only positive data a learner is only guaranteed that it will eventually see all the positive data, whereas in learning from complete data a learner will eventually be presented with all the positive and all the negative data. It turns out that function learning models only learning from complete data. The negative data is implicitly available to a learning machine because the input to a function learning machine is the graph of the function, To see this: if the ordered pair $(2,5)$ is encountered in the graph, then a learning machine can safely assume that any pair of the form $(2,x)$, $x \neq 5$, does not belong to the function. The point is that a learner can deduce the negative data based on the positive data.[3]

However, this problem does not arise in the case of identification in the limit of languages (described in the next section), as both learning from positive data and complete data can be modeled. For this reason, team learning of languages is a more suitable model of multi-agent learning.

Team learning of recursively enumerable (r.e.) languages has been extensively studied (see [8, 10, 11].) Since it can be argued that most AI applications deal with computable concepts, team learning of recursive languages (languages that have algorithmic decision procedures) would be a more appropriate model for multi-agent learning. The present paper begins such a study.

In what follows, we proceed formally. In Section 2, we introduce the preliminary notions about identification in the limit of languages by single machines. In Section 3, we motivate and describe identification of languages by teams of machines. Section 4 contains a discussion of the fundamental results about team learning of r.e. languages. In Section 5, we present results about team learning of recursive languages and in Section 6, we present results about team learning of indexed families of recursive languages. Finally, in an appendix, we sketch one of the proof techniques.

2 Learning by a single machine

Let N denote the set of natural numbers, $\{0, 1, 2, \ldots\}$. As already noted our domain is the collection of recursively enumerable languages over N. A grammar for a recursively enumerable language L is a computer program that accepts L (or, equivalently, generates L [6]). For any recursively enumerable language L, the elements of L constitute its positive data and the elements of the complement, $N - L$, constitute its negative data. We next describe notions that capture the presentation of positive data and presentation of both positive and negative data.

Definition 1. A *text* for the language L is an infinite sequence (repetitions allowed) consisting of all and only the elements of L. T denotes a typical variable for texts.

So, a text for L represents an instance of positive data presentation for L. The next definition introduces a notion that represents an instance of both positive and negative data presentation for L.

Definition 2. An informant for L is an infinite sequence (repetitions allowed) of ordered pairs such that for each $n \in N$ either $(n, 1)$ or $(n, 0)$ (but not both) appear in the sequence and $(n, 1)$ appears only if $n \in L$ and $(n, 0)$ appears only if $n \notin L$.

[3] Of course this discussion does not hold for identification of partial functions, but the present paper is about identification of total computable functions.

A learning machine may be thought of as an algorithmic device that takes as input finite initial sequences of texts and informants and that from time to time conjectures computer programs as hypotheses. **M** denotes a typical variable for learning machines. We now consider what it means for a learning machine to successfully learn languages. The criterion of success considered in the present paper is Gold's [5] *identification in the limit*. We first introduce it for learning from positive data.

Definition 3. [5]

(a) **M TxtEx**-*identifies* an r.e. language L just in case **M**, fed any text for L, converges to a grammar for L. In this case we say that $L \in \mathbf{TxtEx}(\mathbf{M})$.

(b) **M TxtEx**-*identifies* a collection of languages, $\mathcal{L}$, just in case **M TxtEx**-identifies each language in $\mathcal{L}$.

(c) **TxtEx** denotes all such collections $\mathcal{L}$ of r.e. languages such that some machine **TxtEx**-identifies $\mathcal{L}$.

The class **TxtEx** is a set theoretic summary of the capability of machines to **TxtEx**-identify collections of r.e. languages. Intuitively, if a collection $\mathcal{L} \in \mathbf{TxtEx}$, then there exists a machine that **TxtEx**-identifies each language in the collection $\mathcal{L}$.

It is easy to see that any class consisting of just one language is identifiable because a "dumb" machine that ignores its input and keeps on emitting a grammar for the only language in the class is successful on that language; however, such a machine is unsuccessful on every other language. It is precisely for this reason, that we introduced Part (b) in the above definition because machines that learn only one language are not very interesting. Also, **FIN**, the collection of finite languages, belongs to **TxtEx** because a machine employing the heuristic of emitting a grammar for all the elements it has seen at any given time will suffice because eventually it will see all the elements in the finite language.

We now define identification from both positive and negative data.

Definition 4. [5]

(a) **M InfEx**-*identifies* an r.e. language L just in case **M**, fed any informant for L, converges to a grammar for L. In this case we say that $L \in \mathbf{InfEx}(\mathbf{M})$.

(b) **M InfEx**-*identifies* a collection of languages, $\mathcal{L}$, just in case **M InfEx**-identifies each language in $\mathcal{L}$.

(c) **InfEx** denotes all such collections $\mathcal{L}$ of r.e. languages such that some machine **InfEx**-identifies $\mathcal{L}$.

3 Learning by a team

A team of learning machines is a multiset[4] of learning machines. Before we formally define learning by a team, it is worth considering the origins of team learning. Consider the following theorem for **TxtEx**-identification.

Theorem 5. [2] *There are collections of languages* $\mathcal{L}_1$ *and* $\mathcal{L}_2$ *such that*

(a) $\mathcal{L}_1 \in \mathbf{TxtEx}$,

[4] A *multiset* is like a set, but elements need not be distinct. For example, the cardinality of set $\{2, 2, 3\}$ is 2, but the cardinality of the multiset $\{2, 2, 3\}$ is 3.

(b) $\mathcal{L}_2 \in$ **TxtEx**, *but*
(c) $(\mathcal{L}_1 \cup \mathcal{L}_2) \notin$ **TxtEx**.

The above result[5], popularly referred to as the "non-union theorem," says that the class **TxtEx** is not closed under union. In other words, there are collections of languages that are identifiable, but the union of these collections is not identifiable. This result may be viewed as a fundamental limitation on building a general purpose device for machine learning, and, to an extent, justifies the use of heuristic methods in Artificial Intelligence. However, this result also suggests a more general criterion of identification in which a team of learning machines is employed and success of the team is the success of any member in the team. We illustrate this idea next.

Consider the collections of languages $\mathcal{L}_1$ and $\mathcal{L}_2$ in Theorem 5. Let $\mathbf{M}_1$ **TxtEx**-identify $\mathcal{L}_1$ and $\mathbf{M}_2$ **TxtEx**-identify $\mathcal{L}_2$. Now, if we employed a team of $\mathbf{M}_1$ and $\mathbf{M}_2$ to identify $\mathcal{L}_1 \cup \mathcal{L}_2$ and weakened the criterion of success to the requirement that success is achieved just in case any one member in the team is successful, then the collection $\mathcal{L}_1 \cup \mathcal{L}_2$ becomes identifiable by the team consisting of $\mathbf{M}_1$ and $\mathbf{M}_2$ under this new criterion of success. This idea can be extended to teams of n machines out of which at least m ($m \leq n$) are required to be successful. The formal definitions for team identification of languages are presented next. J. Case first suggested the notion of team identification for functions based on the non-union theorem of the Blums [2], and it was extensively investigated by C. Smith [19]. The general case of m out of n teams is due to Osherson, Stob, and Weinstein [15]. Jain and Sharma [8] first investigated team learning for recursively enumerable languages.

Definition 6. Let $m, n \in N$ and $0 < m \leq n$.

(a) A team of n machines $\{\mathbf{M}_1, \mathbf{M}_2, \ldots, \mathbf{M}_n\}$ is said to $\mathbf{Team}_n^m\mathbf{TxtEx}$-identify a language L just in case at least m members in the team **TxtEx**-identify L. In this case we write $L \in \mathbf{Team}_n^m\mathbf{TxtEx}(\{\mathbf{M}_1, \mathbf{M}_2, \ldots, \mathbf{M}_n\})$.

(b) A team of n machines $\{\mathbf{M}_1, \mathbf{M}_2, \ldots, \mathbf{M}_n\}$ is said to $\mathbf{Team}_n^m\mathbf{TxtEx}$-identify a collection of languages $\mathcal{L}$ just in case the team $\mathbf{Team}_n^m\mathbf{TxtEx}$-identifies each language in $\mathcal{L}$.

(c) $\mathbf{Team}_n^m\mathbf{TxtEx}$ is defined to be the class of sets $\mathcal{L}$ of r.e. languages such that some team of n machines $\mathbf{Team}_n^m\mathbf{TxtEx}$-identifies $\mathcal{L}$.

We can similarly define the class $\mathbf{Team}_n^m\mathbf{InfEx}$ for team learning from both positive and negative data.

4 Previous Results: Team learning of r.e. languages

We now survey some of the results about team learning of r.e. languages. The results that we present here are about redundancy and aggregation. We direct the reader to [8, 10, 9, 11] for additional results.

First, it is easy to show the following proposition.

[5] Taking $\mathcal{L}_1 = \{N\}$ and $\mathcal{L}_2 = \mathbf{FIN}$ yields a proof because of Gold's [5] result that no collection of languages that contains all the finite languages and an infinite language can be identified in the limit from only positive data.

Proposition 7. *Let $k, m, n \in N$ such that $0 < m \leq n$ and $k \geq 1$.*
(a) $\mathbf{Team}_n^m\mathbf{TxtEx} \subseteq \mathbf{Team}_{n \cdot k}^{m \cdot k}\mathbf{TxtEx}$.
(b) $\mathbf{Team}_n^m\mathbf{InfEx} \subseteq \mathbf{Team}_{n \cdot k}^{m \cdot k}\mathbf{InfEx}$.

The above proposition says that for both texts and informants, all the collections of languages that can be learned by a given team can also be learned if we multiply the size of the team and the number of machines required to be successful by the same factor. In other words, introducing redundancy does not hurt. The question is: Does it help ? We consider team learning from informants first, followed by team learning from texts.

4.1 Team learning from informants

For identification from both positive and negative data, introducing redundancy in the team does not yield any extra learning ability.

Theorem 8. *Let $k, m, n \in N$ such that $0 < m \leq n$ and $k \geq 1$. Then* $\mathbf{Team}_n^m\mathbf{InfEx} = \mathbf{Team}_{n \cdot k}^{m \cdot k}\mathbf{InfEx}$.

The above result says that the collections of languages that can be identified by teams employing n machines and requiring at least m to be successful are exactly the same as those collections which can be identified by teams employing $n \cdot k$ machines and requiring at least $m \cdot k$ to be successful.

We next consider the question of aggregation, that is, under what conditions can a team be replaced by a single machine without any loss in learning ability. Part (a) of the next result says that if a majority of the members in the team are required to be successful, then employing a team does not yield any extra learning ability. Part (b) of the result says that $\frac{1}{2}$ is indeed the cutoff. In the sequel, we refer to such cutoff points as *aggregation ratios*.

Theorem 9. *(a)* $(\forall m, n \mid \frac{m}{n} > \frac{1}{2})[\mathbf{Team}_n^m\mathbf{InfEx} = \mathbf{InfEx}]$.
(b) $\mathbf{InfEx} \subset \mathbf{Team}_2^1\mathbf{InfEx}$.

A proof of the above result can be worked out using techniques from Pitt [17].

4.2 Team learning from texts

Surprisingly, introducing redundancy in the team does help sometimes in the context of learning from only positive data. The following result says that there are collections of languages that can be **TxtEx**-identified by teams employing 4 machines and requiring at least 2 to be successful, but cannot be **TxtEx**-identified by any team employing 2 machines and requiring at least 1 to be successful. $\supset$ denotes proper superset.

Theorem 10. $\mathbf{Team}_4^2\mathbf{TxtEx} \supset \mathbf{Team}_2^1\mathbf{TxtEx}$.

Even more surprising is the next theorem which implies that the collections of languages that can be **TxtEx**-identified by teams employing 6 machines and requiring at least 3 to be successful are exactly the same as those collections that that can be **TxtEx**-identified by teams employing 2 machines and requiring at least 1 to be successful.

Theorem 11. $(\forall j)[\mathbf{Team}^{2j+1}_{4j+2}\mathbf{TxtEx} = \mathbf{Team}^{1}_{2}\mathbf{TxtEx}]$.

The complete picture is actually quite complicated. The status of teams with success ratio $\frac{1}{2}$ is completely known, but only partial results are known for other team ratios $(\frac{1}{k}, k > 2)$; we direct the reader to [9].

The next result sheds light on when a team learning languages from texts can be aggregated into a single machine without loss in learning ability. Part (a) of the result says that if *more than two-thirds* of the members in the team are required to be successful, then employing a team for learning languages from texts does not yield any extra learning ability. Part (b) of the result says that $\frac{2}{3}$ is indeed the cutoff.

Theorem 12.
(a) $(\forall m, n \mid \frac{m}{n} > \frac{2}{3})[\mathbf{Team}^{m}_{n}\mathbf{TxtEx} = \mathbf{TxtEx}]$.
(b) $\mathbf{TxtEx} \subset \mathbf{Team}^{2}_{3}\mathbf{TxtEx}$.

5 Results: Team learning of recursive languages

It may justifiably be argued that recursively enumerable languages are too general to usefully model concepts of practical interest. For this reason, it is worth considering the effects of team learning on restricted collections of languages. In this section, we present results about redundancy and aggregation for recursive languages. We denote the class of recursive languages by **REC**.

It turns out that even for recursive languages, redundancy does help sometimes. Our proof of Theorem 10 is actually a proof of the following theorem (because the language class constructed as the witness for $\mathbf{Team}^{2}_{4}\mathbf{TxtEx}$ being a strict super set of $\mathbf{Team}^{1}_{2}\mathbf{TxtEx}$ consist only of recursive languages). (*Notation*: The power set of a set A is denoted 2^A.)

Theorem 13. $(\mathbf{Team}^{2}_{4}\mathbf{TxtEx} \cap 2^{\mathbf{REC}}) \supset (\mathbf{Team}^{1}_{2}\mathbf{TxtEx} \cap 2^{\mathbf{REC}})$.

For similar reasons, the aggregation ratio for team identification of recursive languages turns out to be $\frac{2}{3}$, as recorded in the following theorem.

Theorem 14.
(a) $(\forall m, n \mid \frac{m}{n} > \frac{2}{3})\ [(\mathbf{Team}^{m}_{n}\mathbf{TxtEx} \cap 2^{\mathbf{REC}}) = (\mathbf{TxtEx} \cap 2^{\mathbf{REC}})]$.
(b) $(\mathbf{TxtEx} \cap 2^{\mathbf{REC}}) \subset (\mathbf{Team}^{2}_{3}\mathbf{TxtEx} \cap 2^{\mathbf{REC}})$.

It may be argued that if we are restricting ourselves to learning of recursive languages then we should consider identifying decision procedures instead of grammars (accepting procedures). The following definition formalizes this notion. (*Notation*: A *characteristic function* of a language A is the function which is 1 on elements of A and 0 on non-elements of A.)

Definition 15. [5]
(a) **M** **TxtExCI**-*identifies* a recursive language L just in case **M**, fed any text for L, converges to a program that computes the characteristic function of L. In this case we say that $L \in \mathbf{TxtExCI}(\mathbf{M})$.

(b) **M** **TxtExCI**-*identifies* a collection of languages, $\mathcal{L}$, just in case **M** **TxtExCI**-identifies each language in $\mathcal{L}$.

(c) **TxtExCI** denotes all such collections $\mathcal{L}$ of recursive languages such that some machine **TxtExCI**-identifies $\mathcal{L}$.

It should be noted that the hypothesis space of the learner in the above definition is still the set of all programs; it is only required that the final converged program compute the characteristic function of the language being learned. Osherson and Weinstein [16] observed the following fact which implies that there are collections of recursive languages for which a grammar can be identified from texts, but for which a decision procedure cannot be identified from texts.

Theorem 16. [16] $\mathbf{TxtExCI} \subset (\mathbf{TxtEx} \cap 2^{\mathbf{REC}})$.

We next consider team identification of decision procedures for recursive languages from texts. Clearly, the class $\mathbf{Team}_n^m\mathbf{TxtExCI}$ can be defined. Until now, we have seen that in the case of learning from only positive data (texts), redundancy sometimes results in increased learning ability. Surprisingly, the following theorem shows that redundancy does not pay when the team is learning decision procedures.

Theorem 17. *Let* $k, m, n \in N$ *such that* $0 < m \leq n$ *and* $k \geq 1$. *Then* $\mathbf{Team}_n^m\mathbf{TxtExCI} = \mathbf{Team}_{n \cdot k}^{m \cdot k}\mathbf{TxtExCI}$.

We sketch a proof of the above result in the Appendix. The aggregation ratio for **TxtExCI** turns out to be $\frac{1}{2}$ as shown by the following theorem.

Theorem 18. *(a)* $(\forall m, n \mid \frac{m}{n} > \frac{1}{2})[\mathbf{Team}_n^m\mathbf{TxtExCI} = \mathbf{TxtExCI}]$.

(b) $\mathbf{TxtExCI} \subset \mathbf{Team}_2^1\mathbf{TxtExCI}$.

6 Results: Indexed families of recursive languages

We next consider identification of indexed families of recursive languages.

A sequence of nonempty languages $L_0, L_1, \ldots$ is an indexed family just in case there exists a computable function f such that for each $i \in N$ and for each $x \in N$,

$$f(i, x) = \begin{cases} 1 & \text{if } x \in L_i, \\ 0 & \text{otherwise.} \end{cases}$$

In other words, there is a uniform decision procedure for languages in the class. Angluin [1] was the first researcher to restrict investigations to indexed families of recursive languages; she was motivated by the fact that most language families of practical interest are indexed families (e.g., the collection of pattern languages). We denote by **INDEX** the collection of all indexed families of recursive languages. Again, we restrict ourselves to texts, as informants do not yield any new insight.

Since we are considering indexed families, it makes sense to consider scenarios where the hypothesis space available to the learning machine is an enumerable class of grammars. We first introduce some notation.

Let Σ be a fixed terminal alphabet. A grammar G over Σ defines an accepting grammar. $\mathbf{Lang}(G)$ is the language accepted by G.

$\mathcal{G} = G_0, G_1, G_2, \ldots$ is a hypothesis space just in case $\mathcal{G}$ is an enumerable family of grammars over Σ such that membership in $\mathbf{Lang}(G_i)$ is uniformly decidable for all $i \in N$ and all strings $s \in \Sigma^*$. When a learning machine emits i, we interpret it to mean that it is conjecturing the grammar G_i. We say that the class of languages $\{\mathbf{Lang}(G_i) \mid i \in N\}$ is defined by the hypothesis space $\mathcal{G}$. We also refer to the collection $\{\mathbf{Lang}(G_i) \mid i \in N\}$ as range($\mathcal{G}$); it is easy to see that range($\mathcal{G}$) is an indexed family.

Below we adapt Gold's criterion of identification in the limit to the identification of indexed families with respect to a given hypothesis.

Definition 19. Let $\mathcal{L}$ be an indexed family and let $\mathcal{G}$ be a hypothesis space.

(a) Let $L \in \mathcal{L}$. A machine **M** **TxtEx**-*identifies* L with respect to $\mathcal{G}$ just in case **M**, fed any text for L, converges to j and $L = \mathbf{Lang}(G_j)$.

(b) A machine **M** **TxtEx**-*identifies* $\mathcal{L}$ with respect to $\mathcal{G}$ just in case for each $L \in \mathcal{L}$, **M** **TxtEx**-identifies L with respect to $\mathcal{G}$.

There are three kinds of identifiable classes of interest that have been studied in the literature. (a) class comprising; (b) class preserving; and (c) exact.

If the indexed family $\mathcal{L}$ is identified with respect to a hypothesis space $\mathcal{G}$ such that $\mathcal{L} \subseteq$ range($\mathcal{G}$) then the identification is referred to as class comprising. However, if it is required that the indexed family be identifiable with respect to a hypothesis space $\mathcal{G}$ such that $\mathcal{L} =$ range($\mathcal{G}$) then the identification is referred to as class preserving. Finally, if the identification of the indexed family $\mathcal{L}$ defined by the hypothesis space $\mathcal{G}$ is required to be with respect to $\mathcal{G}$ itself, then the identification is referred to as exact. More formally:

Definition 20. (a) $[\mathbf{TxtEx}]_{\mathbf{Index}}$ denotes the collection of all indexed families $\mathcal{L}$ for which there is a machine **M** and a hypothesis space $\mathcal{G}$ such that **M** **TxtEx**-identifies $\mathcal{L}$ with respect to $\mathcal{G}$.

(b) $[\mathbf{TxtEx}]_{\mathbf{CIndex}}$ denotes the collections of all indexed families $\mathcal{L}$ for which there is a machine **M** and a hypothesis space $\mathcal{G}$ such that **M** **TxtEx**-identifies $\mathcal{L}$ with respect to $\mathcal{G}$ and $\mathcal{L} =$ range($\mathcal{G}$).

(c) $[\mathbf{TxtEx}]_{\mathbf{EIndex}}$ denotes the collections of all indexed families $\mathcal{L}$ defined by a hypothesis space $\mathcal{G}$ for which there is machine **M** such that **M** **TxtEx**-identifies $\mathcal{L}$ with respect to $\mathcal{G}$.

So, $[\mathbf{TxtEx}]_{\mathbf{Index}}$ denotes the collections of indexed families identifiable in the class comprising mode, $[\mathbf{TxtEx}]_{\mathbf{CIndex}}$ denotes the collections identifiable in the class preserving mode, and $[\mathbf{TxtEx}]_{\mathbf{EIndex}}$ denotes the collections identifiable in the exact mode. Lange and Zeugmann [13] have shown that

$$[\mathbf{TxtEx}]_{\mathbf{Index}} = [\mathbf{TxtEx}]_{\mathbf{CIndex}} = [\mathbf{TxtEx}]_{\mathbf{EIndex}}.$$

We refer the reader to [20] for a discussion of these classes when restricted to certain monotonic constraints. Meyer [14] is a study of identification of indexed families by probabilistic machines under monotonic constraints.

Similar to the above classes, we can define a hypothesis space of decision procedures and define the class $[\mathbf{TxtExCI}]_{\mathbf{Index}}$ for the class comprising case. It turns out that for indexed families of recursive languages, learning grammars and decision procedures are equivalent.

Proposition 21. $[\mathbf{TxtEx}]_{\mathbf{Index}} = [\mathbf{TxtExCI}]_{\mathbf{Index}}$.

Hence we only consider grammar identification in our investigation of team learning for indexed families. One can then define the classes:

$$[\mathbf{Team}_n^m\mathbf{TxtEx}]_{\mathbf{Index}},\ [\mathbf{Team}_n^m\mathbf{TxtEx}]_{\mathbf{CIndex}},\ \text{and}\ [\mathbf{Team}_n^m\mathbf{TxtEx}]_{\mathbf{EIndex}}.$$

The following two theorems summarize that in the case of learning indexed families of recursive languages from texts, redundancy does not pay and the aggregation ratio is $\frac{1}{2}$ for each of the three modes of identification, namely, class comprising, class preserving, and exact. Hence, having a more structured hypothesis space makes a difference.

Theorem 22. *Let* $k, m, n \in N$ *such that* $0 < m \leq n$ *and* $k \geq 1$.
Let $\mathbf{I} \in \{\mathbf{Index}, \mathbf{CIndex}, \mathbf{EIndex}\}$. *Then* $[\mathbf{Team}_n^m\mathbf{TxtEx}]_{\mathbf{I}} = [\mathbf{Team}_{n\cdot k}^{m\cdot k}\mathbf{TxtEx}]_{\mathbf{I}}$.

Theorem 23. *Let* $\mathbf{I} \in \{\mathbf{Index}, \mathbf{CIndex}, \mathbf{EIndex}\}$.
(a) $(\forall m, n \mid \frac{m}{n} > \frac{1}{2})[[\mathbf{Team}_n^m\mathbf{TxtEx}]_{\mathbf{I}} = [\mathbf{TxtEx}]_{\mathbf{I}}]$.
(b) $[\mathbf{TxtEx}]_{\mathbf{I}} \subset [\mathbf{Team}_2^1\mathbf{TxtEx}]_{\mathbf{I}}$.

Finally we consider team identification of indexed families where the learning machines are allowed to conjecture any r.e. index, that is, the hypothesis space is not restricted to an enumerable family of grammars. In this case it turns out that redundancy pays in some cases, and the aggregation ratio is $\frac{2}{3}$. The next two theorems summarize this result.

Theorem 24. $(\mathbf{Team}_4^2\mathbf{TxtEx} \cap \mathbf{INDEX}) \supset (\mathbf{Team}_2^1\mathbf{TxtEx} \cap \mathbf{INDEX})$.

Theorem 25. *(a)* $(\forall m, n \mid \frac{m}{n} > \frac{2}{3})\ [(\mathbf{Team}_n^m\mathbf{TxtEx} \cap \mathbf{INDEX}) = (\mathbf{TxtEx} \cap \mathbf{INDEX})]$.
(b) $(\mathbf{TxtEx} \cap \mathbf{INDEX}) \subset (\mathbf{Team}_3^2\mathbf{TxtEx} \cap \mathbf{INDEX})$.

Acknowledgements We would like to thank the referees for several valuable suggestions. Some of the results in this paper were discussed at the ML95 Workshop on Agents that Learn from Other Agents in Lake Tahoe. Research of Arun Sharma has been partially supported by a grant from the Australian Research Council.

APPENDIX

Due to space restrictions, it is not possible to give all the proofs. We sketch a proof technique that is crucial in showing several of the results in the present paper. This technique originating in the work of Pitt [17] allows us to determine when a team of machines can be aggregated into a single machine. To facilitate the description, we first introduce some notation.

Notation: We let φ denote an acceptable programming system. Since there are countably infinite number of programs in the programming system φ, we refer to each program with its index (or, its number). We let φ_i stand for the partial computable function computed by the program with index i in the φ-system. We denote $\varphi_i(x)\downarrow$

to mean that the program with index i in the φ-system on input x is defined. We write $\varphi_i(x)\downarrow = y$, or simply $\varphi_i(x) = y$, to mean that the program with index i in the φ-system outputs y. We write $\varphi_i(x)\uparrow$ to denote that the program with index i in the φ-system on input x does not halt.

We refer to i as a grammar (acceptor) for L just in case L is the domain of φ_i. That is, L is the recursively enumerable language accepted by the φ-program with index i. A recursive language has a computable decision procedure. We refer to i as a decision procedure (or, the characteristic index) for a recursive language L just in case $\varphi_i(x) = 1$ if $x \in L$ and $\varphi_i(x) = 0$ if $x \notin L$. Suppose i is not a decision procedure for L, then we consider two kinds of errors that i can make in deciding if a element belongs to L. Suppose $\varphi_i(x)\downarrow$ and either $\varphi_i(x) \neq 1$ when $x \in L$ or $\varphi_i(x) \neq 0$ when $x \notin L$, then we say that i makes an *error of commission* at x. On the other hand if $\varphi_i(x)\uparrow$, then we say that i makes an *error of omission* at x.

Finally, for a finite set S of programs, let unify(S) be a program defined as follows:

$\varphi_{\text{unify}(S)}(x)$

Search for $i \in S$ such that $\varphi_i(x)\downarrow$.

If and when such an i is found, let $\varphi_{\text{unify}(S)}(x) = \varphi_i(x)$.

End

Intuitively, unify(S) just computes the union of functions computed by programs in S (on inputs where more than one program in S converge but to different values, unify(S) can arbitrarily choose one of the converging programs). It is easy to observe that if S contains at least one decision procedure for L and only programs that make only errors of omission in deciding membership in L, then unify(S) is a decision procedure for L. This observation will be useful in extracting (in the limit) a decision procedure for a recursive language L from a set of programs F, at least one of which is a decision procedure for L, and a text for L. This is the subject of the next claim.

Claim 1 *Given a finite set of programs, F, and a text T for L, such that at least one of the programs in F is a decision procedure for L, one can find, in the limit, on F and T a decision procedure for L.*

Proof. (Sketch) Suppose F, and a text T for L be given. We show how to construct a decision procedure for L in the limit.

Let $S_1 = \{i \in F \mid (\exists x \in L)[\varphi_i(x)\downarrow = 0]\}$.

So, programs in S_1 are not decision procedures for L. S_2 below tries to search for programs which accept elements in the complement of L.

Let $S_2 = \{i \in F - S_1 \mid (\exists j \in F - S_1)(\exists x)[\varphi_i(x)\downarrow \neq 0 \wedge \varphi_j(x)\downarrow = 0]\}$. Note that if $i \in F - S_1$ as witnessed by x and j, then $x \notin L$ (since otherwise j would be in S_1).

It should be noted that both S_1 and S_2 can be constructed from F and T in the limit.

We now claim that unify($F - (S_1 \cup S_2)$) is a decision procedure for L. To see this first note that all programs in F which reject an element of L are in S_1. Thus all elements in $F - S_1$ either accept each element of L or diverge on elements of L. Also since there is a decision procedure for L in F (there exists one such by the assumption), it follows that there is a decision procedure for L in $F-S_1$. Now for any element i in $F-S_1$ such that for some $x \notin L$, $\varphi_i(x)\downarrow = 1$, we have that $i \in S_2$. This follows by the definition of S_2 and the fact that there exists a decision procedure for L in $F-S_1$. Now it is straightforward to see that for each $j \in F-(S_1 \cup S_2)$, for each x, either $\varphi_j(x)\uparrow$ or $\varphi_j(x)$ correctly determines the membership of x in L; that is, j is either a decision procedure for L or only makes errors of omission. It follows that unify$(F-(S_1 \cup S_2))$ is a decision procedure for L. □

We now sketch how the above claim can be used to establish Theorem 17. We will first show that for arbitrary m and n, $\mathbf{Team}_n^m\mathbf{TxtExCI} \subseteq \mathbf{Team}_{\lfloor n/m \rfloor}^1\mathbf{TxtExCI}$. From this it follows that, $\mathbf{Team}_{k \cdot n}^{k \cdot m}\mathbf{TxtExCI} \subseteq \mathbf{Team}_{\lfloor n/m \rfloor}^1\mathbf{TxtExCI}$. It is also easy to see that $\mathbf{Team}_{\lfloor n/m \rfloor}^1\mathbf{TxtExCI} \subseteq \mathbf{Team}_n^m\mathbf{TxtExCI}$. The theorem follows.

We now show that

$$\mathbf{Team}_n^m\mathbf{TxtExCI} \subseteq \mathbf{Team}_{\lfloor n/m \rfloor}^1\mathbf{TxtExCI}.$$

Suppose $\mathbf{M}_1, \mathbf{M}_2, \ldots., \mathbf{M}_n$ are given. Suppose further that T is a text for L and these machines $\mathbf{Team}_n^m\mathbf{TxtExCI}$ identify L. We observe the following:

(a) The number of machines converging to a program (perhaps an incorrect one) among $\mathbf{M}_1, \mathbf{M}_2, \ldots., \mathbf{M}_n$ on text T lies in one of the intervals, $[i \cdot m, (i+1) \cdot m)$ where $1 \leq i \leq \lfloor n/m \rfloor$ and

(b) if the number of converging machines lies in the interval $[i \cdot m, (i+1) \cdot m)$, then at least one of the first $i \cdot m$ converging machines on T converges to a decision procedure for L. This is because at least m machines are guaranteed to converge to a correct decision procedure and the cardinality of the interval $(i \cdot m, (i+1) \cdot m)$ is $m-1$.

We now construct $\lfloor n/m \rfloor$ machines as follows: machine $\mathbf{M}'_i$ where $1 \leq i \leq \lfloor n/m \rfloor$, on text T, searches for the first $i \cdot m$ machines converging on T. Let F_i be the set of programs to which these machines converge to. $\mathbf{M}'_i$ then, assuming that F_i contains a decision procedure for L, using the above claim tries to find a decision procedure for L.

Note that the assumption — F_i contains a decision procedure for L — is true for at least one i, and thus at least one of the $\lfloor n/m \rfloor$ machines succeeds in **TxtExCI**-identifying L.

The above technique can easily be adapted to yield proofs for Theorems 8, 9(a), 17, and 18(a). A modification of the technique can also be used to prove Proposition 21 and Theorems 22 and 23(a). Proof of Theorems 24 and 25 requires somewhat involved adaptation of techniques from [9]. Due to lack of space, we omit details.

References

1. D. Angluin. Finding patterns common to a set of strings. *Journal of Computer and System Sciences*, 21:46–62, 1980.
2. L. Blum and M. Blum. Toward a mathematical theory of inductive inference. *Information and Control*, 28:125–155, 1975.
3. R. P. Daley, B. Kalyanasundaram, and M. Velauthapillai. Breaking the probability 1/2 barrier in fin-type learning. In *Proceedings of the Fifth Annual Workshop on Computational Learning Theory, Pittsburgh, Pennsylvania*, pages 203–217. A. C. M. Press, 1992.

4. R. P. Daley, L. Pitt, M. Velauthapillai, and T. Will. Relations between probabilistic and team one-shot learners. In L. Valiant and M. Warmuth, editors, *Proceedings of the Workshop on Computational Learning Theory*, pages 228–239. Morgan Kaufmann Publishers, Inc., 1991.
5. E. M. Gold. Language identification in the limit. *Information and Control*, 10:447–474, 1967.
6. J. Hopcroft and J. Ullman. *Introduction to Automata Theory, Languages, and Computation.* Addison-Wesley Publishing Company, 1979.
7. S. Jain and A. Sharma. Finite learning by a team. In M. Fulk and J. Case, editors, *Proceedings of the Third Annual Workshop on Computational Learning Theory, Rochester, New York*, pages 163–177. Morgan Kaufmann Publishers, Inc., August 1990.
8. S. Jain and A. Sharma. Language learning by a team. In M. S. Paterson, editor, *Proceedings of the 17th International Colloquium on Automata, Languages and Programming*, pages 153–166. Springer-Verlag, July 1990. Lecture Notes in Computer Science, 443.
9. S. Jain and A. Sharma. Computational limits on team identification of languages. Technical Report 9301, School of Computer Science and Engineering; University of New South Wales, 1993.
10. S. Jain and A. Sharma. Probability is more powerful than team for language identification. In *Proceedings of the Sixth Annual Conference on Computational Learning Theory, Santa Cruz, California*, pages 192–198. ACM Press, July 1993.
11. S. Jain and A. Sharma. On aggregating teams of learning machines. *Theoretical Computer Science A*, 137(1):85–108, January 1995.
12. S. Jain, A. Sharma, and M. Velauthapillai. Finite identification of function by teams with success ratio 1/2 and above. *Information and Computation*, 121(2):201–213, September 1995. To Appear.
13. S. Lange and T. Zeugmann. Learning recursive languages with a bounded number of mind changes. *International Journal of Foundations of Computer Science*, 4(2):157–178, 1993.
14. L. Meyer. Probabilistic language learning under monotonicity constraints. In *Algorithmic Learning Theory, 6th International Workshop, ALT'95, Fukuoka, Japan*, pages 169–184. Springer-Verlag, October 1995. Lecture Notes in Artificial Intelligence 997.
15. D. Osherson, M. Stob, and S. Weinstein. Aggregating inductive expertise. *Information and Control*, 70:69–95, 1986.
16. D. Osherson, M. Stob, and S. Weinstein. *Systems that Learn, An Introduction to Learning Theory for Cognitive and Computer Scientists.* MIT Press, Cambridge, Mass., 1986.
17. L. Pitt. Probabilistic inductive inference. *Journal of the ACM*, 36:383–433, 1989.
18. L. Pitt and C. Smith. Probability and plurality for aggregations of learning machines. *Information and Computation*, 77:77–92, 1988.
19. C. Smith. The power of pluralism for automatic program synthesis. *Journal of the ACM*, 29:1144–1165, 1982.
20. T. Zeugmann and S. Lange. A guided tour across the boundaries of learning recursive languages. In K.P. Jantke and S. Lange, editors, *Algorithmic Learning for Knowledge-Based Systems*, pages 190–258. Lecture Notes in Artificial Intelligence No. 961, Springer-Verlag, 1995.

Combining Views on Concepts in Unsupervised Concept Learning

TuBao Ho*

Japan Advanced Institute of Science and Technology – Hokuriku
Tatsunokuchi, Ishikawa, 923-12 JAPAN

Abstract. Classical, prototype and exemplar views on concepts are combined in an unsupervised concept learning system. A flexible matching procedure, which interprets the concept hierarchy in using additional probabilistic and instance-based recognition constraints, allows the system to improve its inference performance. This paper describes the system and evaluates experimentally its performance.

1 Introduction

There are two situations occurred in inductive concept learning depending on the degree of supervision. Early work in concept learning focused on the simpler *supervised* task in which the learner is asked to characterize concepts from a given set of their labelled instances. Though much less mature than supervised learning, *unsupervised* task can arise as often as supervised task in real-world problems, and there has been also a considerable interest in this task where the learner is asked to determine concepts and knowledge structures from a given set of unlabelled objects. This task essentially relates to two mutual problems: (1) *hierarchical clustering* (i.e., finding a hierarchical clustering that determines useful subsets of an unlabelled object set), and (2) *characterization* (i.e., finding an intensional definition for each of these subsets of objects).

The design and development of an unsupervised concept learning system requires mainly three choices: a representation formalism, a procedure for extracting the concept hierarchy, and an interpreter that decides to which concept an unknown instance belongs. These choices relate to human understanding of concepts and their formation. Main *properties* of concepts studied in psychology, which has a strong influence on these choices for computer models of concept formation, can be summarized as in [1].

Essentially, unsupervised concept learning methods differ from each other in two main factors: views on concepts and constraints on categorization. Among *views on concepts* in cognitive science which have affected views in concept learning, the classical, prototype and exemplar ones are widely known and used. Main strengths and limitations of these views can be summarized as in [Kangassalo 93]. Moreover, unsupervised concept learning systems compose solutions to the problem by employing one or another of three main *constraints on categorization*

* Also with the Institute of Information Technology, Hanoi, Vietnam

based on similarity (categories consist of similar objects), feature correlation (maximize intra-correlations and minimize inter-correlations), and syntactical structure of the concept hierarchy.

CLUSTER/2 [Michalski 83] is one conceptual clustering method that forms categories with 'good' conjunctions of common features to all category members. COBWEB [Fisher 87] is often referred to as having many positive characteristics. It employs a probabilistic representation for concepts and a heuristic measure called category utility. Like COBWEB, ARACHNE [McKusick 91] represents knowledge as a hierarchy of probabilistic concepts, and focuses on the structural quality of the hierarchy while maintaining a high predictive accuracy. AUTOCLASS [Cheeseman 95] employs a probabilistic representation for each cluster and a Bayesian method for extracting the concept hierarchy. Its bias is defined by a collection of prior probability distribution over the space of clusters including priors on the number of true clusters and priors on their attributes. However each system based on one view on concepts is often limited in capturing the rich variety of conceptual knowledge.

This paper presents an attempt to combine the advantages and overcome some of the disadvantages of used views on concepts. We extended the unsupervised concept learning system OSHAM (standing for Making Automatically a Hierarchical Structure of Objects) [Ho 95] that based on FCA, a variant of classical view on concepts, to a hybrid system.

2 Hybrid system OSHAM

According to three main choices for unsupervised concept learning systems, this section presents the hybrid OSHAM in aspects of representing concepts, building concept hierarchies, and matching unknown instances.

2.1 Representation of concepts

Denote by $\mathcal{O}$ the given set of objects, $\mathcal{A}$ the set of all possible attributes describing objects, and $\mathcal{H}$ the concept hierarchy to be learned. There exists a binary relation $\mathcal{R}$ between $\mathcal{O}$ and $\mathcal{A}$, i.e., $\mathcal{R} \subseteq \mathcal{O} \times \mathcal{A}$. In the case of binary attributes, $(o, a) \in \mathcal{R}$ is understood as the fact that object o has attribute a. In the case of multi-valued symbolic or numeric attributes, $(o, a) \in \mathcal{R}$ is understood as the fact that object o has value v of attribute a.

Basis of the most widely understanding of a concept is the function of collecting individuals into a group with certain common properties. One distinguishes these common properties as the *intension* of the concept that determines its *extension* which are objects accepted as members of the concept. The relationship between intension and extension of concepts is popularized in the machine learning community by the description of the space of instances and the space of hypotheses [Mitchell 82]. Similarly, this relationship was mathematically formulated in the theory of formal concept analysis (FCA) [Wille 82], [Wille 92]. The starting point in FCA is two *derivation operators* ρ and λ between the power sets of $\mathcal{A}$ and $\mathcal{O}$, determined by $\rho(S) = \{o \in \mathcal{O} \mid \forall a \in S, (o,a) \in \mathcal{R}\}$ for $S \subseteq \mathcal{A}$, and $\lambda(X) = \{a \in \mathcal{A} \mid \forall o \in X, (o,a) \in \mathcal{R}\}$ for $X \subseteq \mathcal{O}$.

An attribute subset S of $\mathcal{A}$ is called *closed* if $\lambda\rho(S) = S$ (X of $\mathcal{O}$ is closed if $\rho\lambda(X) = X$). A *formal concept* C in FCA is a pair (X, S) with $X \subseteq \mathcal{O}$, $S \subseteq \mathcal{A}$ satisfying $\rho(S) = X$ and $\lambda(X) = S$ (i.e., X and S are closed). X and S are called the *extension* and the *intension* (defining features) of C, respectively. Concept (X_1, S_1) is a *subconcept* of concept (X_2, S_2) if $X_1 \subseteq X_2$ which is equivalent to $S_1 \supseteq S_2$, and (X_2, S_2) is then a *superconcept* of (X_1, S_1). The fundamental theorem of FCA states that the set of all formal concepts associated with the superconcept-subconcept relation is a *complete lattice* (Galois lattice).

Recently, several concept learning systems have been developed in the framework of Galois lattices. In [Carpineto 93], [Godin 94] the authors generated incrementally all possible formal concepts. In other work, i.e. [Mephu Nguifo 94], [Ho 95], a part of the concept lattice is extracted as a concept hierarchy by some heuristics. Although Galois lattices provide a powerful tool for learning concepts, the notion of formal concepts is a variant of the classical view on concepts with its limitations. Otherwise, to find all possible formal concepts is perhaps intractable in the worse case, and moreover human behavior in most cases seems not relate to all possible formal concepts.

OSHAM employs formal concepts in FCA as basis for representing its concepts with complementary components. It also employs the Galois lattice as the generalization space to carry out its search for the concept hierarchy. Concepts are formed in $\mathcal{H}$ at different levels of generality, from the most general (root concept) to the most specific in each branch (leaf concept). Each concept C_k is associated with its *level* $l(C_k)$, two lists of its *superconcepts* $f(C_k)$ and *subconcepts* $s(C_k)$. The *intension* of C_k, denoted by $i(C_k)$, is inherited by all of its subconcepts. Thus, the intension of each subconcept of C_k has all features in $i(C_k)$ plus its own special features. The *extension* of C_k, denoted by $e(C_k)$, is classified into extensions of its subconcepts C_{k_i} in next levels in the splitting process of C_k into subconcepts. In fact, this is a process of looking for regularities in instances of a more general concept C_k as good nonnecessary features that correspond to more specific subconcepts of C_k. In this process it may happen that some instances of C_k do not have special features of any subconcept C_{k_i}, and will not be classified as instances of any subconcepts C_{k_i}. Denote this set by $C_k^r = e(C_k) \setminus \bigcup_{i=1}^{n} e(C_{k_i})$. We are interested in the *probability of occurrence* of C_k as well as the *conditional probability* of its unclassified objects, denoted by $p(C_k)$ and $p(C_k^r|C_k)$ respectively.

Several complementary components for the concept representation are measured by using a similarity distance between each pair of instances. We define the *distance* $\delta(o_p, o_q)$ between two instances o_p, o_q as an extension of the Jaccard distance

$$\delta(o_p, o_q) = 1 - \frac{\sum_{a \in \lambda(\{o_p, o_q\})} \gamma(a)}{\sum_{a \in \lambda(\{o_p\}) \cup \lambda(\{o_q\})} \gamma(a)} \tag{1}$$

where $\gamma(a) \in \mathbb{Z}^+$ are positive integer weights of attributes a (with value 1 by default). The attribute weights $\gamma(a)$ embody background knowledge about the environment and concepts (importance of attributes, attribute rank by potential relevancy, etc.). The *dispersion* of instances in the extension of C_k, denoted by $d(C_k)$, is defined as the average distance between all pairs of instances in its extension $e(C_k)$

$$d(C_k) = \frac{2 \times \sum_{o_p, o_q \in e(C_k)} \delta(o_p, o_q)}{card(e(C_k))(card(e(C_k)) - 1)} \tag{2}$$

In the case when $d(C_k^r)$ is high enough we may consider that these unclassified instances in C_k^r are *exceptional* instances of C_k. Broadly speaking, exceptional instances of a concept are those which are very different from most concept's instances. Exceptional instances and the homogeneity of concepts provide useful information to improve the system inference performance as mentioned in the next subsection.

Extensions of all subconcepts C_{k_i} of C_k and the set of unclassified C_k^r forms a partition P of the extension of C_k. Denote by $W(C_k)$ the average of all $d(C_{k_i})$ and $d(C_k^r)$. The dissimilarity between subconcepts of C_k, denoted by $B(C_k)$, is defined as the average of distances $\Delta(c(C_{k_i}), c(C_{k_j}))$ between all pairs of subconcepts C_{k_i}, C_{k_j}, where the distance $\Delta(c(C_{k_i}), c(C_{k_j}))$ is determined as the smallest distance among the distances of all pairs of instances $o_p \in C_{k_i}$ and $o_q \in C_{k_j}$

$$\Delta(c(C_{k_i}), c(C_{k_j})) = Min_{o_p \in C_{k_i}, o_q \in C_{k_j}} \{\delta(o_p, o_q)\} \tag{3}$$

The *quality* of splitting a concept C_k into subconcepts in a next level, denoted by $q(C_k)$, is measured by

$$q(C_k) = B(C_k)/W(C_k) \tag{4}$$

Summarily, OSHAM represents each concept C_k in $\mathcal{H}$ by a 10-tuple

$$< l(C_k), f(C_k), s(C_k), e(C_k), i(C_k), p(C_k), d(C_k), p(C_k^r|C_k), d(C_k^r), q(C_k) > \tag{5}$$

2.2 Building concept hierarchies

The construction of a concept hierarchy in OSHAM is a recursive process of splitting each existing concept into subconcepts at lower levels without knowing *a priori* the number of subconcepts. There are many possible combinations of a concept's features that allow us to form its subconcepts but they characterize the concept differently. OSHAM tends to find sufficiently general and discriminant subconcepts while determining typical instances of the superconcept. The idea of forming sufficiently general and discriminant subconcepts lies in a trade-off between the coverage and the length of intensions of subconcepts that maximizing (4). The OSHAM algorithm given in Table 1 forms gradually and recursively the concept hierarchy $\mathcal{H}$, initially with the root concept whose extension is the set of all instances of $\mathcal{O}$ and its intension is $\lambda(\mathcal{O})$ which is often empty. In each application of OSHAM to an existing splittable concept C_k, OSHAM will split sequently this concept into subconcepts C_{k_i} one by one, until an unsplittable condition holds.

When finding subconcepts of C_k, to avoid an impractical exhaustive search in the concept lattice, OSHAM generates and tests only a certain number of the most promising hypotheses in the search space and chooses the best one. Conditions 2(a)-(c) determine whether concept C_k is possible or worth to split further. In particular, 2(a) ensures that there exists at least one formal subconcept of C_k, 2(b) guarantees a consideration on concepts that cover at least some minimum number α of instances, and 2(c) prevents splitting C_k when its unclassified instances are homogeneous enough.

Parameters α, β, η allow the user to form concept hierarchies with flexible size and homogeneity. In principle the smaller α and/or β the larger size of $\mathcal{H}$, and the larger η the higher quality of generated concepts on $\mathcal{H}$. We consider that the unclassified instances of a concept C_k in C_k^r are less typical and representative than its instances classified into subconcepts C_{k_i}.

Input concept hierarchy $\mathcal{H}$ and an existing splittable concept C_k.
Result $\mathcal{H}$ formed recursively.
Top-level call OSHAM(root concept, $\emptyset$).
Variables α, β, η are given thresholds.

1. Suppose that $C_{k_1}, ..., C_{k_n}$ are subconcepts of C_k found so far. While C_k is still splittable, find a new subconcept $C_{k_{n+1}}$ of C_k that corresponds to the hypothesis with maximal $q(C_k)$ among η hypotheses $C_{k^1_{n+1}}, ..., C_{k^\eta_{n+1}}$. Each hypothesis $C_{k^t_{n+1}}$ is generated by doing the following steps (a)–(d)
   (a) Find an attribute a^* so that $\bigcup_{i=1}^{n} e(C_{k_i}) \cup \rho(\{a^*\})$ is the largest cover of $e(C_k)$
   (b) Find a maximum closed attribute subset S containing a^*
   (c) Form subconcept $C_{k^t_{n+1}}$ with $i(C_{k^t_{n+1}}) = S$ and $e(C_{k^t_{n+1}}) = \rho(S)$
   (d) Evaluate $q(C_k)$ with the new $C_{k^t_{n+1}}$
2. Update $C_k^r = e(C_k) \setminus \bigcup_{i=1}^{n+1} e(C_{k_i})$. If one of the following conditions holds then C_k is considered unsplittable
   (a) there exist not any closed proper subset of attributes on C_k^r
   (b) $card(C_k^r) \leq \alpha$
   (c) $d(C_k^r) \leq \beta$
3. Apply OSHAM$(C_{k_i}, \mathcal{H})$ to each C_{k_i} formed in step 1.

Table 1. The OSHAM algorithm

OSHAM is refined by several auxiliary procedures: 1(a) by MaxCoverage $(a^*, C_k, \mathcal{H})$, 1(b) by MaxClosedAttSet $(a^*, C_k, \mathcal{H})$, and 2(a) by ClosedProperAttSet $(C_k, \mathcal{H})$. In these procedures, denote by A_{C_k} the set of attribute-value pairs which are different from those used in the branch from the root concept to the concept C_k being considered, and by $\varphi(S) = card(\rho(S))/card(\mathcal{O})$ for $S \subseteq \mathcal{A}$.

MaxCoverage($a^*, C_k, \mathcal{H}$)
Find $a^* \in A_{C_k}$ satisfying
$card(\bigcup_{i=1}^{n} e(C_{k_i}) \cup \rho(\{a^*\})) = max_{a \in A_{C_k}} card(\bigcup_{i=1}^{n} e(C_{k_i}) \cup \rho(\{a\}))$
if this maximum holds at several a^* **then** choose arbitrary one a^* arbitrary that minimizes (the minimum intersection condition).
$card(\bigcup_{i=1}^{n} e(C_{k_i}) \cap \rho(\{a^*\}))$ (the minimum intersection condition).

MaxClosedAttSet($a^*, C_k, \mathcal{H}$)
(Find the closed attribute subset containing a given attribute a^*)

Let $S = \{a^*\}$.
for every $a \in A_{C_k} \setminus a^*$ **do if** $\rho(\{a\}) = \rho(\{a^*\})$ **then** $S = S \cup \{a\}$.

ClosedProperAttSet($C_k, \mathcal{H}$)
(Verify whether there exists a closed proper subset of A_{C_k} in C_k^r)

1. Determine a^* as the attribute that satisfies $\varphi(\{a^*\}) = max_{a \in A_{C_k}} \varphi(\{a\})$.
2. Determine the subset of attributes $S = \{a \in A_{C_k} | \rho(\{a\}) = \rho(\{a^*\})\}$.
3. **if** $\varphi(\{a^*\}) < 1$ **then** *success* with S is a closed subset of A_{C_k} **else** *failure*.

Table 2. Auxiliary OSHAM procedures

2.3 Matching unknown instances

The objective of matching process is to give a decision about to what concept on the generated concept hierarchy an unknown instance e belongs. In OSHAM this process consists of two stages: (1) to find all concepts on $\mathcal{H}$ so that e matches their intensions, and (2) to decide among these concepts which one is the concept that matches e best. This process is inspired from the system POSEIDON [Michalski 90] but in another way.

The first stage is simple. OSHAM checks every branch of $\mathcal{H}$ to find concepts that match e intensionally. By the generality on $\mathcal{H}$, we call a *matched* concept of e the most specific concept on a branch from the root (with the highest level in the branch) that matches e intensionally. Naturally, there are three types of outcomes from this stage: only one concept on $\mathcal{H}$ that matches e (*single-match*), many concepts on $\mathcal{H}$ that match e (*multiple-match*), and no concept on $\mathcal{H}$ that matches e (*no-match*). As a result of this stage, OSHAM lists all matched concepts associated with their available information. The second stage occurs in real-world problems when the user needs to conclude the best matched concept of e, or better to conclude the best match with some degree of match. A flexible matching procedure that exploits available information of matched concepts has been proposed to reach a final conclusion by combining constraints of defining features, conditional probability and the nearest neighbor instances. For each matched concept C_k of e we are interested in on what level C_k is; is C_k an intermediate or leaf concept; how good C_k is, e.g., $d(C_k), p(C_k), d(C_k^r)$, etc. Concerning the unknown instance e we are also interested in how large the distance between e and its nearest neighbor from the training set, denoted by $NN(e)$, and what is the concept that matches the nearest neighbor of e.

Denote by $c[e]$ the concept that matches e best, by $c[NN(e)]$ the concept that matches $NN(e)$, and for each concept C_k denote by $F(e, C_k) = 1$ if C_k is a matched concept of e, otherwise $F(e, c_k) = 0$. Table 3 presents the flexible matching procedure proposed in OSHAM for the second stage, derived from our experiments on various data sets. In this procedure, σ is a given threshold, max indicates the highest level when comparing those of several concepts, and saying that C_k *qualified* means that at least one of the following conditions holds: $l(C_k)$ is high; C_k is a leaf concept on $\mathcal{H}$; $d(C_k)$ and/or $p(C_k)$ is low. This statement is somewhat subjective and may be given by the domain experts or by OSHAM based on its evaluation of sizes of $\mathcal{O}$, $\mathcal{A}$, and $\mathcal{H}$.

---

if $\exists! C_k$: $F(e, C_k) = 1$ (*single-match*)

> **if** $c[NN(e)] = C_k$ **then** $c[e] = C_k$;
> **else if** $c[NN(e)] \neq C_k$, C_k qualified **then** $c[e] = C_k$;
> **else if** $c[NN(e)] \neq C_k$, C_k not qualified **then** $c[e] = c[NN(e)]$;

if $\exists C_1, ..., C_K, K > 1$: $F(e, C_k) = 1, \forall k \in \{1, ..., K\}$ (*multi-match*)

> **if** $\exists! k : l(C_k) = max$ **then**
>   **if** $c[NN(e)] = C_k$ **then** $c[e] = C_k$;
>   **else if** $C_k = leaf$ **then** $c[e] = C_k$;
>   **else if** $C_k \neq leaf$, $c[NN(e)] = leaf$ **then** $c[e] = c[NN(e)]$;
>   **else if** $p(C_k) \times p(C_k^\tau | C_k) \geq p(c[NN(e)]) \times p(c^\tau[NN(e)] | c[NN(e)])$
>   **then** $c[e] = C_k$ **else** $c[e] = c[NN(e)]$;
>
> **if** $\exists k, h : l(C_k) = l(C_h) = max$ **then**
>   **if** $c[NN(e)] = C_k$ **then** $c[e] = C_k$;
>   **else if** $l(c[NN(e)]) \geq l(C_k)$ **then** $c[e] = c[NN(e)]$;
>   **else if** $p(C_k) \times p(C_k^\tau | C_k) \geq p(C_h) \times p(C_h^\tau | C_h)$ **then** $c[e] = C_k$;

if $\neg \exists C_k$: $F(e, C_k) = 1$ (*no-match*)

> **if** $\delta(NN(e), e) \leq \sigma$ **then** $c[e] = c[NN(e)]$ **else** $c[e] = \emptyset$ (no match).

Table 3. Procedure for matching an unknown instance

3 Evaluation of OSHAM

The most important distinction in evaluating the performance of a concept learning system concerns how it uses the learned knowledge for classification and prediction [Langley 96]. In supervised concept learning the most widely used criterion is the error rate which can be obtained as the ratio of the number of misclassifying cases to the number of cases examined. However, there is less agreement on the evaluation of unsupervised concept learning as the class name (label of instances) is not available in the provided data and this error rate can not be estimated directly. Most unsupervised learning systems are evaluated on three elements of knowledge, learning and performance. However, as pointed out and used in some works, e.g. [McKusick 91], a good way is to employ supervised data sets in evaluating the performance of unsupervised learning systems straightforwardly. It means that we run an unsupervised learning system with a known supervised data set but hide the class name in forming and matching the concept hierarchy with unknown instances, and after these phases we use the class name only to estimate the predictive accuracy of the system. We may also use the class name of supervised training instances to predict the name of a concept C_k as the most frequently occurring name of instances in $e(C_k)$.

We used popular data sets from the UCI Repository of machine learning databases, included Wisconsin Breast Cancer, Congressional Votes, Hayes-Roth, Mushroom, Soybean Disease, Tic-Tac-Toe endgame and monks. Although OSHAM's parameters can be adjusted to obtain more suitable concept hierarchies, in order to have a fair evaluation of OSHAM, its parameters are fixed for all experiments with $\alpha = 1\%$ of the size of the training set and $\beta = 15\%$ of the number of attributes.

3.1 About the concept hierarchy

Fig. 1 presents the first four levels of the concept hierarchy obtained by OSHAM from the Wisconsin Breast Cancer data.

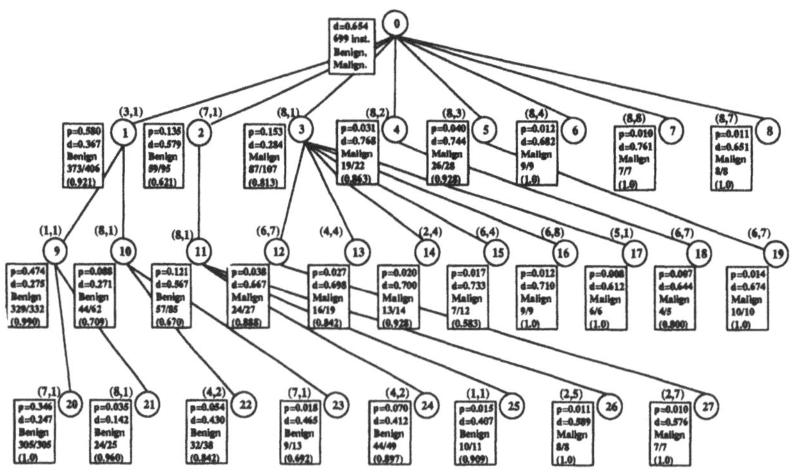

Fig. 1. Part of the concept hierarchy from Wisconsin breast cancer data

This data set consists of 699 observations of two classes of Benign and Malignant on 9 symbolic symptoms: Clump Thickness, Uniformity of Cell Size, Uniformity of Cell Shape, Marginal Adhesion, Single Epithelial Cell Size, Bare Nuclei, Bland Chromatin, Normal Nucleoli, Mitoses, each has 10 possible values. In Fig. 1 these attributes and their values are denoted by 1, 2, ..., 10 and each attribute-value pair is written between two parentheses. The intension of each concept is obtained by aggregating defining features along the branch from the root to the concept, for example, $i(C_{27}) = (8,1) \wedge (6,7) \wedge (2,7)$.

Associated to each concept in Fig. 1 is only some available information extracted from the concept representation. Two first lines are the concept occurrence probability p and the dispersion d of concept's instances. These two values p and d are obtained from unsupervised data. Two next lines indicate the predicted name of the concept (Benign or Malignant) and the ratio of the number of instances with this predicted name to the total number of the concept instances. The decimal value of this ratio, as a measure for the predictive accuracy of the concept, is shown between parentheses in the last line. Information in the three last lines, which supports the evaluation of the system, are obtained by using the class name. Information about concepts, for example C_{11}, is fully represented as follows

CONCEPT 11
Level = 2
Super_Concepts = { 2 }, Sub_Concepts = { 24 25 26 }
Features = (Mitoses, 1) ∧ (Normal Nucleoli, 1)
Unclassified/Total_instances = 17/85
Unclassified_instances = { 32 50 67 98 128 201 ... 575 611 636 }
Concept_probability = 0.121602
Unclassified_instance_conditional_probability = 0.20
Concept_dispersion = 0.567135
Unclassified_instance_dispersion = 0.645425
Subconcept_partition_quality = 3.263966
Concept_name = Benign (57/85, predictive_accuracy = 0.670588)

Though concept hierarchies produced by OSHAM look like those produced by some supervised concept learning systems, such as C4.5, the ways these systems function are quite different. Essentially, C4.5 uses the class information to select an attribute at each node then splits this node by values of the chosen attribute, while OSHAM splits each node by detecting regularities according to its representation of concepts without using the class information.

3.2 Making inference

A single train-and-test experiment is often used in machine learning for estimating performance of learning systems. Although resampling techniques (multiple train-and-test experiments) are much more computationally expensive, they can give a more precise evaluation than a single train-and-test experiment. Recent works in machine learning showed that the cross validation is a suitable resampling technique for the accuracy estimation. To obtain a more reliable estimation of the performance of OSHAM, we carried out a 10-fold cross validation in our experiments. Each data set $\mathcal{O}$ is randomly divided into 10 mutually exclusive subsets $\mathcal{O}_1, \mathcal{O}_2, ..., \mathcal{O}_{10}$ of approximately equal size. OSHAM is tested 10 times on each data set, each time for $k \in \{1, 2, ..., 10\}$ a concept hierarchy is generated on $\mathcal{O} \setminus \mathcal{O}_k$ and tested on $\mathcal{O}_k$. The error rate on each data set is the average of its error rates after 10 running times. It is also necessary to note that the error rates obtained by a cross-validation experiment is more reliable but often higher than those obtained by a single train-and-test experiment.

	C4.5	CART	COBWEB	OSHAM
Breast Cancer	93.3	94.1		92.3
US Voting	94.5	93.8	90.0	93.0
Hayes-Roth	75.0	75.0		63.2
Mushroom	100.0	100.0		94.5
Soybean Disease	97.8	97.8	100.0	100.0
Tic-Tac-Toe	88.0	86.2		91.1
Monks1	76.6	76.6	71.8	77.3
Monks2	65.3	65.3	67.4	72.4
Monks3	92.6	96.3	69.1	76.6

Table 4. Comparison of OSHAM with some inductive learning methods

Results of OSHAM on these data sets are compared with those of two supervised concept learning systems C4.5 [Quinlan 93] and CART [Breiman 84] which are experimented carefully in the same condition of OSHAM with a 10-fold cross validation. These results are also compared with those of the unsupervised concept learning system COBWEB in several cases. Results of COBWEB on Congressional Votes data are taken from [McKusick 91], on Soybean Disease data from [Fisher 87], and on monks data from [Thrun 91]. As shown in Table 4, in these experiments, OSHAM attained a prediction accuracy which is lightly lower than those of C4.5 and CART and is often lightly higher than those of COBWEB.

4 Conclusion

We have described how we combine different views on concepts in the unsupervised concept learning system OSHAM in order to improve its performance. OSHAM enriches the FCA-based representation of concepts by complementary components associated with probabilistic values, typical instances, and a quality criterion for the concept hierarchy. The proposed matching strategy which combines logical, threshold and nearest neighbour conditions, allows OSHAM to predict flexibly unknown instances.

Experiments show the high prediction accuracy of OSHAM with different data sets. Main advantages of OSHAM are the following

- OSHAM conserves the strengths and reduces the limitations of the classical view on concepts. It is able to specify concepts with clear semantics from contexts with the attribute-value representation. Moreover, it is able to specify unclear instances with additional information (occurrence probability, dispersion, etc.).

- Extracted at different levels of generality and with necessary information for the matching process, concepts are flexible and sensitive with the context. Moreover, the coherence between concepts is clearly explained.
- As noticed in [Langley 96] that the interpretive process is a central issue in machine learning, the most important feature of OSHAM is that it allows interpreting learned knowledge by combining logical, threshold, and competitive matching approaches. By experimental studies, OSHAM concepts are often expressive and with high predictiveness.

OSHAM has been implemented in the X Window and used as a knowledge acquisition system [Ho 96]. It is being improved to deal better with uncertain data.

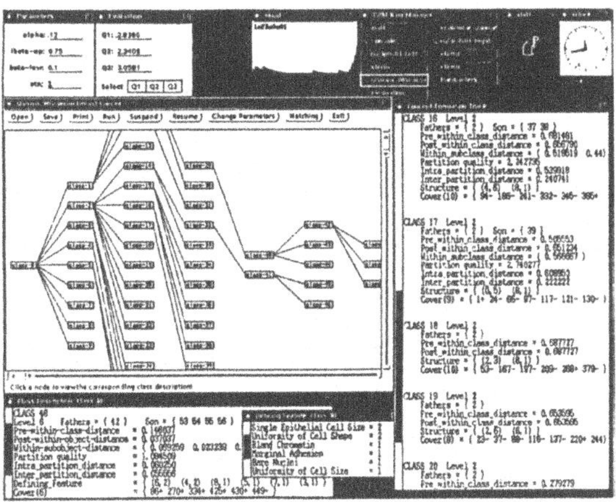

Figure 2. Screen of OSHAM in the X Window

References

[Breiman 84] Breiman, L., Friedman, J., Olshen, R. and Stone, C.: *Classification and regression trees*, Belmont, CA: Wadsworth (1984).

[Carpineto 93] Carpineto, C. and Romano G.: GALOIS: An order-theoretic approach to conceptual clustering. *Proc. 10th Int. Conf. on Machine Learning*, Amherst, pp. 33–40 (1993).

[Cheeseman 95] Cheeseman, P. and Stutz, J.: Bayesian Classification (AutoClass): Theory and Results. *Advances in Knowledge Discovery and Data Mining* , U.M. Fayyad, G. Piatetsky-Shapiro, P. Smyth, R. Uthurusamy (Eds). The AAAI Press, pp. 61–83 (1995).

[Fisher 87] Fisher, D.: Knowledge acquisition via incremental conceptual clustering., *Machine Learning*, Vol. 2, pp. 139–172 (1987).

[Godin 94] Godin, R. and Missaoui, R.: An incremental concept formation approach for learning from databases. *Theoretical Computer Science*, 133, pp. 387–419 (1994).

[Ho 95] Ho, T.B.: An approach to concept formation based on formal concept analysis. *IEICE Trans. Information and Systems*, Vol. E78-D, No. 5, 553–559 (1995).

[Ho 96] Ho, T.B.: Integrating inductive learning and knowledge acquisition in the expert system generator TESOR. *Proc. 3rd World Congress on Expert Systems*, Seoul, pp. 925–932 (1996).

[Kangassalo 93] Kangassalo, H.: "On the concept of concept for conceptual modelling and concept detection", in *Information Modelling and Knowledge Bases III*, S. Ohsuga et al. (Eds.), IOS press, pp. 17–58 (1992).

[Langley 96] Langley, P.: *Elements of Machine Learning*, Morgan Kaufmann (1996).

[McKusick 91] McKusick, K.B. and Langley, P.: Constraint on tree structure in concept formation. *Proc. Int. Joint Conf. on Artificial Intelligence*, IJCAI'91, pp. 810–816 (1991).

[Mephu Nguifo 94] Mephu Nguifo, E.: Galois lattice: A framework for concept learning. *Proc. 6th IEEE Int. Conf. Tools with Artificial Intelligence TAI'94* , New Orleans, pp. 461–467 (1994).

[Michalski 83] Michalski R. S. and Stepp R. E.: Learning from observation: conceptual learning. *Machine Learning: An Artificial Intelligence Approach*, Vol. 1, R. S. Michalski, J. G. Carbonelle, T. M. Michell (Eds.), Morgan Kaufmann, pp. 331–363 (1983).

[Michalski 90] Michalski, R.S.: "Learning flexible concepts: Fundamental ideas and a method based on two-tiered representation", in R. S. Michalski and Y. Kodratoff (Eds.), *Machine Learning: An Artificial Intelligence Approach, Vol. III*, Morgan Kaufmann (1990).

[Mitchell 82] Mitchell, T.: Generalization as search. *Artificial Intelligence*, 18, pp. 203–226 (1982).

[Quinlan 93] Quinlan, J. R.: *C4.5: Programs for Machine Learning*, Morgan Kaufmann (1993).

[Thrun 91] Thrun, S.B., Bala, J., Bloedorn, E., Bratko, I., Cestnik, B., Cheng, J., DeJong, K., Dzeroski, S., Fahlman, S.E., Fisher, D., Hamann, R., Kaufman, K., Keller, S., Kononenko, I., Kreuziger, J., Michalski, R.S., Mitchell, T., Pachowicz, P., Reich, Y., Vafaie, H., Van de Welde, W., Wenzel, W., Wnek, J., Zhang, J.: The monks problems: a performance comparison of different learning algorithms. *Technical report CMU-CS-91-197*, Carnegie Mellon University (1991).

[Wille 82] Wille, R.: Restructuring lattice theory: an approach based on hierarchies of concepts. *Ordered Sets*, I. Rival (Ed.), Reidel, pp. 445–470 (1982).

[Wille 92] Wille, R.: Concept lattice and conceptual knowledge systems. *Computers and Mathematics with Applications*, Vol. 23, pp. 493–515 (1992).

[Wrobel 92] Wrobel, S., *Concept Formation and Knowledge Revision*, Kluwer Academic Publishers (1994).

The Complexity of Batch Approaches to Reduced Error Rule Set Induction

Mike Cameron-Jones

Department of Applied Computing and Mathematics,
University of Tasmania, Launceston,
Tasmania, Australia.
(Michael.CameronJones@appcomp.utas.edu.au)

Abstract. Cohen [3] introduced a rule set improvement method, Grow, that is used in classifier learning in a similar way to standard reduced error pruning methods, but is based on "reduced error rule set re-growth". Here we follow Cohen's suggestion that order of magnitude analysis of the time complexity of such reduced error methods on random data provides insight into their behaviour on real data sets that are noisy. We consider the growth of rule sets produced for such data by these methods, and suggest that the size of the final rule set is roughly of order n, for n training items, whereas Cohen assumed it was roughly constant. This leads to increased estimates of the relevant time complexities. We propose a simple improvement to the implementation to reduce the order of the time complexities by about n. We give experimental results in support of our rough order of magnitude claims.

1 Introduction

This paper examines the growth of rule sets and consequent growth of learning time with increase in (random) training set size when using what we term "batch" approaches to reduced error rule set induction. These methods first fit an initial rule set to part of the training data, then form a final rule set, consisting of some (simplifications of) rules from the initial rule set, chosen by attempting to minimise the final rule set error on the remainder of the training data. Reduced Error Pruning (REP) is a well known method of this type, which has been applied to decision trees [8], and to rule sets [1].

The work described here is inspired by Cohen's paper [3], in which he introduced the Grow method of rule set improvement, and compared it with an REP method. The reader is referred to the original paper for Cohen's experimental results on real data sets which demonstrate the comparative practical utility of Grow. Here we follow up Cohen's suggestion that analysis should be conducted of the time complexity of such methods on random data, as this provides a guide to the time complexity on noisy data sets, a part of which are similar to random data. Cohen [4] provides some empirical support for this view, showing the time taken by some rule set induction methods on artificial data corrupted by noise, similar to the circumstance that might be encountered with real data. Cohen's time complexity analysis [3] for n training items of random binary data, suggests that Grow is $O(n^2 \log n)$, which is no worse than learning the initial rule set ($\Omega(n^2 \log n)$) and much faster than REP ($\Omega(n^4 \log n)$). (Recall that $O()$ concerns an asymptotic upper bound, $\Omega()$ an asymptotic lower bound, and $\Theta()$ an asymptotic upper and lower bound – see e.g. [5] for formal definitions.)

However, our analysis, contrary to Cohen's, suggests that on random binary data the time complexities for Grow and his version of REP are of roughly similar order of magnitude. Our analysis diverges from that of Cohen in respect of the assumptions about the size of the final rule set, which increases in our analysis, but remains constant in Cohen's. We provide empirical evidence in support of our analysis, and also suggest how these complexities of Grow and REP can be reduced in order by about a factor of n.

The rest of the paper consists of four parts. There is a description of the learning methods together with relevant bounds on time complexity. This is followed by estimates of the order of the size of rule sets formed from random data (including random binary data as considered by Cohen) and the resulting estimates of the time complexities for such data. The experimental results on such data precede the conclusions.

2 Learning Methods

The general problem considered by Cohen is that of learning a rule set for classification using attribute-value data. Each rule is of the general form: if conditions are true, then predict class whatever. (Each condition is a test on a single attribute.) If an item to be classified matches more than one rule, the conflict is resolved in favour of the rule that was more (/most) accurate on the training data, where accuracy is defined in terms of items correctly matched as a proportion of all items matched. There is also a default rule which is used to classify any item which fails to match any rule with conditions.

As stated above, Cohen's REP and Grow approaches split the training data into two parts and learn the initial rule set from one part. This part, containing 70% of the n items of training data will be referred to here as the *primary training set*, and the second part will be referred to as the *secondary training set*.

2.1 Fitting the Initial Rule Set

The initial rule set is found by learning a separate rule set for each class. These rule sets are then combined. Each such rule set is learned by applying pFOIL, (a propositional version of FOIL, [2]) to the (two-class) problem of discriminating the (positive) items of the one class from the (negative) items of all other classes. The method builds a rule set by repeatedly adding rules, one at a time, which cover at least one positive item not covered by a previous rule, while covering no negative items (assuming no items with duplicate attributes and different classes). Rule addition ceases when all positive items are covered. Each rule is grown by repeatedly adding conditions, one at a time, until no negative items are covered. The choice of condition is made by an information-based heuristic, which requires evaluation of how many positive and negative items, covered by the rule so far, would be covered if the condition were added.

Restricting the analysis to two-class problems, with an equal number of items of each class, and stratifying the training data split to retain the class balance, a lower bound can be found for the complexity of the process of learning the initial rule set. As per Cohen, let the number of rules in the initial rule set be r, and the total number of conditions be c. The time complexity of the rule fitting process, $Time(Fit(r, c, n))$, is then $\Omega(rn)$, and if the cost of evaluating conditions is independent (not true of threshold conditions in FOIL), this increases to Cohen's bound of $\Omega(cn)$. (For space reasons we omit our detailed justifications of such bounds – those that differ from Cohen's do not affect our rough average case analysis on random data, and can be found in an early draft version of this paper available by anonymous ftp, as growdraft.ps in pub/mcameron at ftp.appcomp.utas.edu.au .)

2.2 Reduced Error Pruning

Cohen put forward an REP method as the "strawman" against which Grow was compared. His REP method takes the initial rule set and repeatedly makes the best simplification, until only the default rule remains. The best of the resulting series of rule sets is chosen as the final rule set. At each stage the simplifications considered are deleting one or more conditions from the end of a rule, or deleting a rule. "Best" is defined as the rule set that makes fewest errors on the secondary training set, after adjusting the default class to minimise these errors. (The choice of default class may vary among different simplifications.) Note that when evaluating a potential simplification, the number of errors is determined straightforwardly, using the *whole* classifier – an inefficient approach which can be improved as explained later.

Bounds on the complexity of REP depend upon the time cost of determining the number of errors made by a classifier (of r rules and c conditions when applied to n items), $Time(Eval(r, c, n))$, which is $\Omega(rn)$ and $O(cn)$, using a naive evaluation method as per Cohen. The complexity of REP, $Time(REP(r, c, n))$, is then $\Omega(r^3 n)$ and $O(c^3 n)$.

2.3 Grow

Cohen proposed the Grow algorithm which is based on the Grove system [7]. The algorithm produces the final rule set from the initial rule set in two phases.

First the individual rules in the initial rule set are simplified using the primary training set again to produce an intermediate rule set, consisting of the initial rule set, and simplifications of the initial rules. This process takes each individual rule, makes the best simplification, then the best simplification of the simplified rule, ...Simplifications are the same as considered for a rule in REP. "Best" means that the rule makes fewest errors, (false positives and false negatives), on the primary training set.

The final rule set is then produced from the intermediate rule set by repeatedly adding the best rule to the rule set so far, starting from the default rule, and terminating when there is no single rule the addition of which will improve the rule set. "Best" is determined in terms of fewest errors on the secondary training set for the rule set, having chosen the default to minimise the errors. Ties among potential additions are broken by choosing the rule with highest accuracy on the primary training set, and if still tied, in favour of the rule with fewer conditions.

There are some interesting differences between Grow and Cohen's REP. Firstly Grow can form a rule set containing different simplifications of the same rule; thus it is searching a potentially bigger space of final rule sets than REP. Secondly, disregarding the former, one would expect it to be faster because it stops when no single change can improve the rule set, whereas the REP method continues simplifying until the rule set is reduced to nothing. (Other REP methods stop when no single change improves the rule set, and such methods could be faster than Grow in the event that the initial rule set is close to the final one.) Finally, Grow's approach of adding to an empty theory, stopping when no single addition is favourable, yields a bias towards simplicity.

The time complexity of the Grow procedure, unlike that of Cohen's REP procedure depends upon the number of rules in the final rule set, s, and the number of conditions, d. The time complexity, $Time(Grow(r, c, n))$, is $\Omega(s^2rn)$ and $O(scdn)$. Note that in the case where the original rule set is rebuilt ($s = r$) our lower bound for Grow is equal to that of REP. Next we consider the size of the rule sets for random data.

3 Random Data

As has already been mentioned, the interest in random data comes from the relation in terms of time complexity, to learning on noisy data, a part of which may be regarded as similar to random data. The type of random data chosen by Cohen had random binary attributes. We will also consider another kind of random data: that with a single continuous attribute. In both cases we consider data with only two classes.

For the binary attribute data, we will focus on the case where we have a truth table with m attributes, and the training data consists of all 2^m entries. There is no unseen test data to check the accuracy of our concept, as we know there is no value in checking it. In order to maintain the assumptions of the previous analysis re the class distribution, half the entries are randomly selected to correspond to one class, the rest to the other class. The presumption of such a complete truth table is more specific than Cohen's assumption, and we will also comment on the more usual case, where the training data consists of only a sample, not the complete data set.

The continuous attribute data consists of instances with a random continuous attribute uniformly distributed between 0 and 1 . The class is randomly chosen so as to give a balanced class distribution. FOIL uses threshold tests as conditions, thus forming rules which correspond to intervals (except at the ends).

Note that we are interested here in the order of *average* rule set sizes, not in absolute upper or lower bounds. An absolute bound on random binary data would just be the corresponding bound on binary data, and there would be no value in thinking of the data as random, similarly for the continuous data.

Further, the crude nature of the analysis is such that we will estimate that bounds are "roughly of" a specified order. A rough order here means that we will ignore factors that grow more slowly asymptotically than a power of n. Thus for example, $n \log n$ and $\frac{n}{\log n}$ are both roughly of order n. A subscript r will be used for a rough order, eg $\Theta_r(n)$.

3.1 The Initial Rule Set

The bounds on time complexity in section 2 depend on the number of rules and conditions in the initial rule set. Here we examine the growth of the initial rule set.

First we consider the continuous attribute data. If we consider ordering the $0.7n$ primary training data items by the value of the continuous attribute, and associate the values 0 and 1 with the two classes, then we can consider the string of class values. If the initial rule set fits the data exactly, there will be as many rules as there are runs of 0 and runs of 1. If the string were a long random binary string obtained by fair coin tosses, the average number of such runs would be $0.35n$, which is $\Theta_r(n)$. (Our string does not have these exact properties as the class distribution is perfectly balanced, but it is a good approximation for large n.)

For the binary data Cohen informally argues that the incompressibility of noise implies that there will be order n rules each with order $\log n$ conditions. Here we present a more formal argument that the number of rules is roughly of order n.

An absolute upper bound can be found by considering the problem of fitting an m attribute parity function with all $n = 2^m$ items. This requires n rules, each with m conditions. Everything else (even random noise on average!) is simpler in this respect, requiring fewer rules.

Now by considering the $0.7n$ bits indicating truth or falsity, and considering transmitting them as a DNF, a lower bound on the average number of rules can be found. There are 3^m possible disjuncts, which could thus be transmitted at a cost of $m \log 3$ bits each, permitting fractional bits. (Assume we use the null disjunct to mark the end of the sequence.) If the average number of disjuncts (less one) were less than $\frac{0.7n}{m \log 3}$, the average cost of transmitting the DNF would be less than that of the average cost of transmitting the raw string. Hence if the strings are on average incompressible, being purely random strings, the average number of rules must be at least of order $\frac{n}{m}$. If we have a complete truth table this is of order $\frac{n}{\log n}$, and if we sample from a truth table with fixed m the bound is of order n. Thus we estimate that the average number of rules is $\Theta_r(n)$.

If one is more precise, one considers the point that the string is marginally compressible, as we know that the number of trues exactly equals the number of falses, but this does not change the order result. Note also that for sufficiently small samples of large truth tables, an attribute will correspond to the class value and rule set size will be independent of n, so our bounds (like Cohen's) are not applicable in such cases.

3.2 The Final Rule Set

The time complexity of Grow depends upon the size of the final rule set, hence we attempt to estimate the order of this. As this is done by considering a set of rules selected from the initial rule set so as to minimise secondary training set error, our order result does not depend upon the details of the Grow algorithm, and is applicable to other batch reduced error methods such as REP. However, algorithm details do affect the exact size of the rule set, and Grow's bias to simplicity tends to yield a smaller rule set than REP.

The key idea that we wish to propose in the estimation of the final rule set size is that the random nature of the data means that when a rule is derived from the primary training set, it may be regarded as similar to a randomly constructed rule when applied to the secondary training set, as it reflects no regularity in the secondary training set. This view must be treated with some caution, as, for example, we know in the binary case that a rule with all m conditions cannot match a secondary training set item, if it has been derived from the primary training set, whereas a randomly constructed rule of m conditions would have a chance of such a match. However, this view forms a useful approximation.

Cohen argues (for Grow) that "the algorithm should only generate a small set of rules; ie s should be of constant size". Although it is true that the final rule set that one might wish to derive from such random data, would be of constant size, in fact empty, we suggest that this is not what occurs. We expect the average size of the final rule set to increase when n does. However, we lack a rigorous argument about the precise nature of this increase, and describe a chain of approximate reasoning that leads to a conjecture.

We first consider a variant of the continuous attribute case, in which the initial rules cannot be simplified, but are treated as though each rule is a single interval condition ($a < x \leq b$). In this case no rules overlap in their coverage, hence if performance is optimised on the secondary training set, the final rule set will contain all rules for one class that are correct on more items than they are wrong, with the other class as the default.

With such data, doubling the number of items should be equivalent, in terms of average properties, to adding another data set of the original size distributed from 1 to 2, and halving the values of all attributes. Thus if we disregard end effects, there will now be on average twice as many rules in the initial rule set covering one secondary training set item of the class predicted by the rule and none of the other class, twice as many covering two secondary training set items of the class predicted by the rule and none or one of the other class, ... Hence, on average twice as many rules should be selected to minimise secondary training set error. The true situation is not so straightforward, as rules can be simplified.

Now in the binary attribute data, consider the issue of whether a rule from the initial rule set might be selected for the final rule set. Assume n is a power of 2 and let the rule have $\log n - k$ conditions. (That is k fewer conditions than the number of attributes.) If this were a randomly formed rule, we would expect it to cover $0.3 \cdot 2^k$ secondary training set items on average. The probability that a randomly formed rule which covers that many items is correct on those items is:

$$P(correct) = (\frac{1}{2})^{0.3 \cdot 2^k}$$

(This argument, due to Ross Quinlan, is simpler than the original argument used to obtain such a probability independent of n.)

Thus for initial rules with a fixed k, a fixed fraction would be correct on the secondary training set. If the final rule set consisted of a fixed fraction of these, for example all those for one class (with the other as the default class), then the number of such rules in the final rule set would be of the same order as those in the initial rule set. The situation is much more complex than this, eg rules which cover many examples of the correct class and few of the wrong class may be selected. However, this simple line of reasoning suggests the following conjecture on final rule set growth:

Conjecture 1. *When a batch reduced error method, such as Grow or REP, is applied to random data (of the forms specified above), the average number of rules in the final rule set is* $\Theta_r(n)$.

3.3 Time Complexities

Given the above results (and conjecture) regarding the rough order of the average number of rules, we can follow a crude approach and substitute into the previous expressions for bounds on time complexities. We further assume that the number of conditions per rule is growing no faster than order $\log n$, as per the complete truth table case and threshold tests halving coverage.

$Time(FitRand(n))$, the time complexity of fitting n random data items of the types considered, is then $\Theta_r(n^2)$, where the assumption on conditions contributes to the upper bound. This result is compatible in rough order terms with Cohen's lower bound of $\Omega(n^2 \log n)$

$Time(REPRand(n))$, the average time complexity for reduced error pruning a rule set formed from n items of random data, is $\Theta_r(n^4)$, which is compatible in rough order terms with Cohen's lower bound of $\Omega(n^4 \log n)$.

However, the corollary of Conjecture 1 is that $Time(GrowRand(n))$, the average time complexity for growing a rule set formed from n items of random data, is closer to that of REP than that of finding the initial rule set. Straightforward substitution for s as order n would lead to a time complexity for Grow of

$\Theta_r(n^4)$. This is not compatible in rough order terms with Cohen's upper bound of $O(n^2 \log n)$.

The growth of the rule sets is such that Grow's $\Theta_r(n^4)$ time complexity applies to a range of possible similar batch reduced error rule set growing methods, which grow the final rule set a rule at a time, naively evaluating all potential rule additions at each step. Similarly REP's time complexity applies to a range of possible similar batch reduced error pruning methods.

3.4 FastGrow

All the time complexities considered above follow the approach of Cohen in always determining the errors on the secondary training set by using an entire classifier. However, the implementation of Grow (and REP) can be improved by avoiding the redundant re-matching of unchanged rules in the classifier, when working out which rule should be added (or pruned) next. The resulting implementation of Grow, described here, will be referred to as *FastGrow*.

After a rule has been added to the classifier, this method records for each secondary training item which classifier rule is the one classifying it. Thus, when assessing the addition of a new rule, the effect of adding the new rule can be determined by trying at most the new rule on each item, as the conflict resolution procedure is based on using the single most accurate rule. (It is "at most" the new rule, as when the new rule is less accurate than the currently classifying rule, it does not matter whether the new rule matches.) There is no need to re-match any of the rules already in the classifier.

This procedure could be applied with other simple conflict resolution procedures, and a similar approach can be used for REP. The latter is slightly more difficult, as one must record not just the currently classifying rule, but also the rule which would have classified the item, had the currently classifying rule been removed.

When the rough orders of the average time complexities on random data of FastGrow (and a similarly improved REP) are found, this improves them to $\Theta_r(n^3)$.

4 Experimental Results

In this section we present some experimental results in support of our conjectures re the average size of the final rule set and the consequent average time complexity of Grow, using random data of the types specified in the previous section.

The initial rule sets are grown using a version of FOIL, which has had various features removed to attempt to accord with the form of rule learning system intended by Cohen. The most significant change is the deletion of FOIL's Minimum Description Length (MDL) approach to avoiding overfitting noisy data. As one would expect, and in accordance with Cohen's results using his MDL approach, experiments (not reported here) show that times are reduced by using this approach to avoiding overfitting. (Note that REP's time is also reduced by using these simpler initial rule sets.) REP, Grow and FastGrow have been implemented to handle the type of data considered here - not the full range of relational theories that FOIL can produce.

The experiments were conducted for different values, of n, $\{32, 64, 128, 256, 512, 1024\}$, for three types of data. The first was the complete binary truth table data, which has 5 to 10 attributes correspondingly. The second was sampled binary data with 30 binary attributes - this was done by random resampling, but even the largest sample constitutes only a small part of the instance space. The third type of data was that with the single continuous attribute.

For each trial the following were recorded: the number of rules in the initial rule set and the number of rules in the final rule set produced by Grow; the time taken to fit the initial rule set, the time taken by Grow, the time taken by FastGrow. Times and final rule set sizes are also reported for REP, but these are over a more limited range of n. Times were measured in CPU seconds on a DECstation 5000/240. The reported results are the average over 50 trials.

The range of values of the quantities, and the form of our conjectures are such that $\log - \log$ plots are appropriate. The asymptotic slope of a $\log - \log$ plot of a polynomial function (with positive terms) is equal to the degree of the highest order term. Here the slope (between the two largest values of n) will be interpreted in terms of the corresponding degree - for example, a slope of two corresponds to a function of order n^2.

This slope information is presented in Table 1, for the different methods and all three types of data. Each slope represents the result of taking the difference between two values, each of which is the log of a mean which has an associated standard error. This variability is represented by giving the larger fractional standard error to the nearest percent (or fraction thereof) in parentheses after the slope value.

Table 1. Table of estimated orders

Item	Complete Truth Table	Incomplete Truth Table	Continuous Data
Initial Rules	1.0 (1%)	0.9 (0.5%)	1.0 (1%)
Final Rules (Grow)	1.0 (2%)	1.0 (3%)	1.1 (3%)
Final Rules (REP)	1.0 (4%)	0.9 (3%)	1.0 (5%)
Fit	2.0 (1%)	1.9 (0.5%)	2.0 (1%)
REP	4.1 (3%)	4.0 (2%)	4.0 (8%)
Grow	4.0 (4%)	3.6 (6%)	3.8 (6%)
FastGrow	2.7 (2%)	2.7 (2%)	2.8 (3%)

Figures 1 and 2 are the graphs for the number of rules and the times for the complete truth table data.

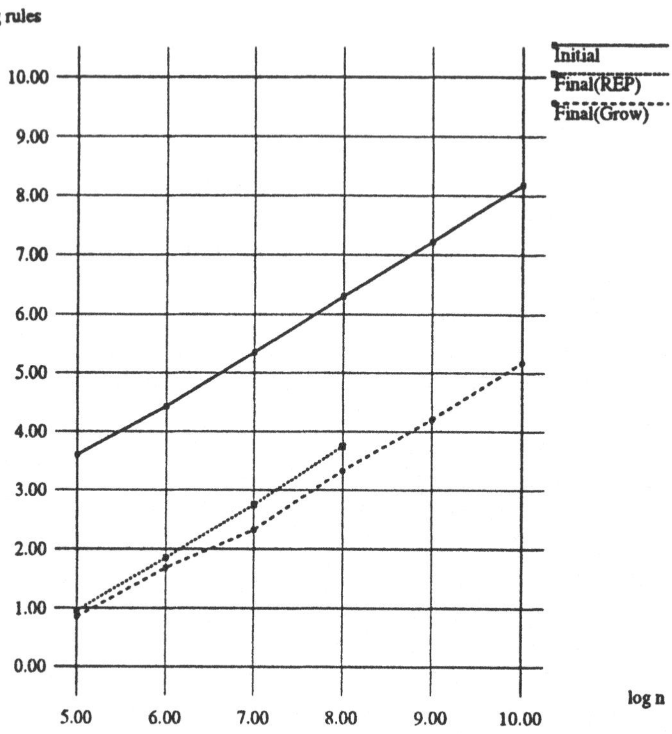

Fig. 1. log of number of rules versus log of number of instances – Complete truth table

The results provide support for the aspects of Cohen's analysis and ours that are compatible – the size of the initial rule set is about order n, the time to find the initial rule set is about order n^2 and the time for REP is about order n^4.

The results provide support for our claim that the number of rules in the final rule set output by the Grow procedure is roughly of order n, not constant as assumed by Cohen. The number of rules in the final rule set from REP is of similar order, though larger – as previously mentioned the Grow approach yields a greater bias to simplicity.

The results also provide support for our claim that Grow is of much higher order than fitting the initial rule set, and is closer in order to REP, contrary to Cohen's claim. Finally FastGrow can be seen to improve the order by a factor of about n in accordance with our claim.

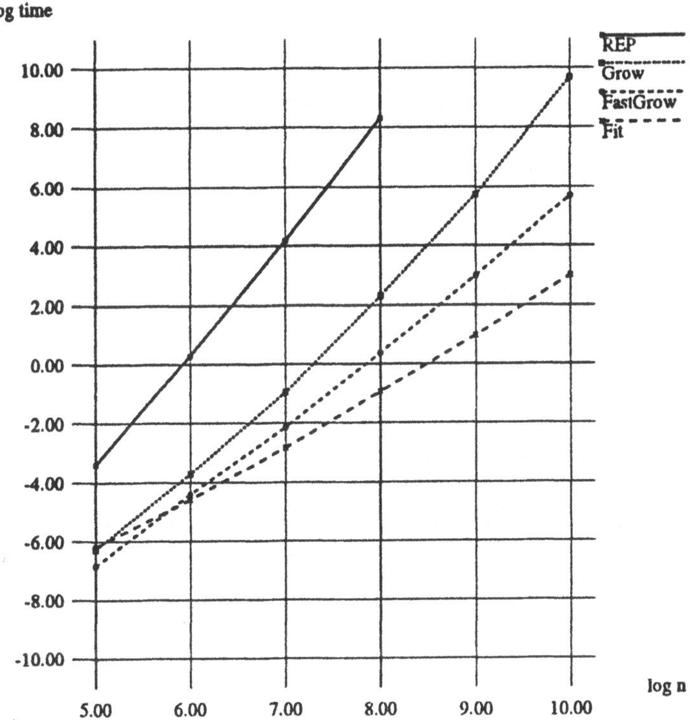

Fig. 2. log of times in CPU seconds versus log of number of instances – Complete truth table

5 Conclusions

This paper has examined the growth of rule sets formed by batch reduced error methods applied to random data sets, providing arguments and empirical evidence to suggest that the rule sets increase in size as the training data does. The implications of this for the time complexity of the two batch reduced error methods examined by Cohen have been demonstrated. In this respect (and hence when applied to noisy data sets with a proportion of data similar to random data) Cohen's Grow method is not a substantial improvement in order of magnitude terms over the REP approach.

We have suggested a simple improvement to Grow, which can also be applied to REP, and shown that this appears to reduce the order of Grow's time complexity by a factor of about n on this type of data.

Recent work [6] (augmented in [4] which cites a draft version of this paper), has pursued an incremental reduced error approach (IREP), in which individual rules are fitted then pruned, rather than the whole rule set being fitted then pruned or regrown. The central idea in our analysis of final rule set growth in the batch methods – a rule formed on random primary training data can be regarded as a random rule when applied to the secondary training data – also applies in the IREP case. There it provides support for the view that the stopping condition, which determines when to stop learning further rules, is pivotal to the success of IREP. If IREP correctly identifies the point at which it is finding such random rules, it prevents the rule set growth identified here, with consequent benefits for efficiency.

Acknowledgements

The research reported was made possible by grants from the Australian Research Council (J.R.Quinlan, Principal Investigator) and assisted by research agreements with Digital Equipment Corporation.

I would especially like to thank William Cohen for generously responding to requests for further information regarding Grow and for commenting on the work described in this paper.

Finally thanks are due to Jacky Hartnett for comments on the paper.

References

1. Brunk, C.A., Pazzani, M.J.: An investigation of noise-tolerant relational concept learning algorithms. Proceedings of the Eighth International Workshop of Machine Learning (1991) 389–393
2. Cameron-Jones, R.M., Quinlan, J.R.: Efficient top-down induction of logic programs. SIGART **5** (1994) 33–42
3. Cohen, W.W.: Efficient pruning methods for separate-and-conquer rule learning systems. Proceedings of the Thirteenth International Joint Conference on Artificial Intelligence (1993) 988–994
4. Cohen, W.W.: Fast effective rule induction. Proceedings of the Twelfth International Conference on Machine Learning (ML95) (1995) 115–123
5. Cormen, T.H., Leiserson, C.E., Rivest, R.L.: Introduction to Algorithms. MIT Press (1990)
6. Fürnkranz, J., Widmer, G.: Incremental reduced error pruning. Proceedings of the Eleventh International Conference on Machine Learning (ML94) (1994) 70–77
7. Pagallo, G., Haussler, D.: Boolean feature discovery in empirical learning. Machine Learning **5** (1990) 71–99
8. Quinlan, J.R.: Simplifying decision trees. International Journal of Man-Machine Studies **27** (1987) 221–234

Learning Simple Recursive Concepts by Discovering Missing Examples

Chowdhury Rahman Mofizur and Masayuki Numao

Dept. of Computer Science, Tokyo Institute of Technology
2-12-1 Oh-Okayama, Meguro-ku, Tokyo 152
Email: {rahman,numao}@cs.titech.ac.jp

Abstract. In this paper we introduce a system, SmartPlus, which learns recursive concepts from a small incomplete training set the members of which all lie on non-intersecting resolution path with respect to the target recursive theory and involve different constants. Unlike recent approaches to this learning problem, our method is based upon discovering the missing examples from the training set. Here missing examples mean the ground facts corresponding to the first recursive call of the given positive examples. After finding the missing examples SmartPlus perform a heuristic (independent of training set size) based top-down search through the hypothesis space in order to learn the recursive clauses. We provide some experimental results which verifies SmartPlus's capacity to learn recursive concepts from a small number of examples (4 to 5 positive examples and negative examples of the same order) all lying on non-intersecting resolution path involving different constants.

1 Target Learning Problem and Existing Approaches

There has been a rising interest in learning recursive concepts from a small incomplete training set. Inductive algorithms (e.g., GOLEM [9], FOIL [10]) based on generalization under θ-subsumption require a complete training set for the successful learning of recursive concepts. In order to be a training set complete, every positive example in it should be backed by a second example the resolution distance of which from the former is one. For example, existence of the training example `append([1,2],[3],[1,2,3])` necessarily demands the presence of `append([2],[3],[2,3])` in the training set in order to ensure the extensional proof of the former using the latter by the target recursive clause. Attempts have been made to overcome this restriction using a generalization technique based on inverse implication. Most of these approaches (e.g., LOPSTER [7], CILP [6]) use sub-unification, a technique which, from the structural differences between the arguments of a pair of example, discovers the reduction pattern involved in recursion as well as the depth of recursion. However sub-unification between two examples is only possible if they lie on the same resolution path with respect to the target recursive theory, although the resolution distance between them might be more than one.

To provide either a complete training set (for the successful learning based on θ-subsumption) or training examples lying on the same resolution path (for the successful learning based on inverse implication), one must possess some prior knowledge about the target recursive theory. However, when attempt is made to learn from a small number of random examples (i.e., assuming no prior knowledge), both learning strategies fail because the training set might be neither complete nor it might contain examples lying on the same resolution chain. Hence it is required to devise some techniques to learn recursive concepts from a small training set the members of which all lie on non-intersecting resolution path and involve different constants. There has been considerable efforts in this direction in recent years. We highlight some of them below.

CRUSTACEAN [1], by observing the regularities in the decompositions of a set of randomly chosen training examples, learns one base clause and one two-literal recursive (purely recursive) clause. FORCE2 [2] learns a more general definition consisting of one base clause and one tail recursive clause from a randomly chosen sample. However, it needs an input oracle function which determines whether an example from the random sample is an instance of the base clause or it is an instance of the recursive clause. TIM [3] learns the same kind of recursive definitions as FORCE2, however it does not require any additional oracle function. Rather it is based on a search for common structural regularities of saturations of the given positive examples. SMART [8] adopts a completely different approach to learn recursive definitions consisting of one base clause and one recursive clause of arbitrary complexity. It first combinatorially decomposes the random sample to discover the base clause and then employs an efficient top-down breadth-first iterative broadening search to induce the recursive clause. In SKILit [4], recursive definitions are induced by the method of iterative bootstrap induction. SKILit performs a restricted breadth-first search by employing a kind of relational pathfinding and program structure schemata.

2 SmartPlus: A Different Learning Approach

Learning from a small incomplete training set is particularly hard because the training set lacks some important examples. These missing examples are the collection of true ground facts corresponding to the first recursive call of the given positive examples and are essential for inducing the recursive clauses using a generalization technique based on θ-subsumption. In this paper, we describe an implementation, SmartPlus, which seeks to find the missing examples from the incomplete training set. Once it discovers the missing examples, it employs a top-down beam search based on likelihood heuristic in order to induce the recursive clauses one after another. Likelihood heuristic utilizes the goal directed usefulness of a literal in a clause and its indifference to training set size makes its suitable for learning from a small training set. We will show SmartPlus's learnability in the following two categories of recursive concepts although the procedure is not strictly limited to these categories only:
(i) Recursive concepts consisting of one base clause and one tail recursive clause (analogous to FORCE2 [2] and TIM [3]). For example:

```
append([],X,X).                                        (pgm1)
```

```
append(X,Y,Z):- split(X,H,T),split(Z,H,Q),append(T,Y,Q).
```

(ii) Recursive concepts consisting of one base clause and multiple tail recursive clauses containing mutually exclusive conditional literals. For example:

```
rdup([],[]).                                                    (pgm2)
rdup(X,Y):- split(X,H,T),member(H,T),rdup(T,Y).
rdup(X,Y):- split(X,H,T),notmember(H,T),split(Y,H,Q),rdup(T,Q).
```

(pgm2) is intended for removing duplicate elements from a list (please see the ground examples in Table 1) the constituent recursive clauses of which contain mutually exclusive conditional literals `member(H,T)` and `notmember(H,T)` respectively.

The input to SmartPlus is a small number of positive and negative ground examples of the target concept and intensional background predicates with appropriate input/output mode and type declaration. Table 1 shows a sample input for learning (pgm2). It may be noticed that every positive example is composed of different constants so that the resolution paths do not intersect with each other and that the training set does not contain any base example of the recursive concept. We force SmartPlus to learn from such a training set in all our experiments because in the worst case a random sample might contain examples with these characteristics.

Table 1. Input to the SmartPlus system

Positive examples	Negative examples	Background predicates
rdup([2,9,2,4],[9,2,4])	rdup([2,1,3],[1,3])	split([X|Y],X,Y).
rdup([5,7],[5,7])	rdup([2,1,1],[2,1,1])	join(X,Y,[X|Y]).
rdup([a,c,c,b],[a,c,b])	rdup([1,1,3],[1,1,3])	mem(X,[X|Y]).
rdup([1,1,3],[1,3])	rdup([1,1,1,3],[1,1,3])	mem(X,[Y|Z]):- mem(X,Z).
	rdup([9,2,4],[3,2,4])	notmem(X,Y):- \+ mem(X,Y).

SmartPlus consists of three distinguishable modules:

Module 1: This module discovers the base cases corresponding to each positive training example and subsequently the base clause of the target definition. This procedure is an adaptation of the technique used in our earlier SMART [8] system. To derive the base cases, SmartPlus reduces each positive example in a combinatorial way with the help of some reduction functions. These reduction functions are functionally equivalent to some input background predicates.

Module 2: The reduction functions and their application depths in deriving the base examples (in module 1) are analyzed to infer the ground facts corresponding to the first recursive call of the given positive examples. These missing facts are asserted as background information for subsequent use by module 3.

Module 3: Module 3 induces the recursive clauses one by one by performing a top-down heuristic based beam search through the hypothesis space. During top-down search the missing facts found in module 2 are used in the extensional proof of the training examples by the proposed recursive clauses.

3 Module 1: Base Clause Generation

A non-base training example suffers repetitive reduction in one or more recursive clauses until it finally resolves with the base clause. Therefore, every non-base training example has a corresponding ground instantiation of the base clause. SmartPlus infers the base example (ground instantiation of the base clause) corresponding to each positive training example and takes the least general generalization (lgg) of the base examples as the target base clause. With the help of some reduction functions, SmartPlus reduces each training example to generate the probable base cases. Let us elaborate the procedure using the training set introduced in Table 1. To generate the probable base cases for the training example `rdup([2,9,2,4],[9,2,4])`, each argument of this example is reduced in every sensible ways. The first argument `[2,9,2,4]`, after the application of reduction functions at different depths, reduces to the following terms:

```
([2,9,2,4],[none,0]), ([9,2,4],[pair(2),1]), ([2,4],[pair(2),2]),
([4],[pair(2),3]), ([],[pair(2),4])
```

The reduction functions and their application depths have been shown inside square brackets along with the reduced terms. For example, the reduction function `[none,0]` means no reduction. Each single application of the reduction function `pair(2)` removes one element from a list. For example, the application of `pair(2)` twice upon the original argument `[2,9,2,4]` has produced the reduced term `[2,4]`. Note that `pair(2)` is functionally equivalent to the background predicate `split` and `join` in Table 1. In the same way as for the first argument, the second argument is reduced to the following terms:

```
([9,2,4],[none,0]), ([2,4],[pair(2),1]), ([4],[pair(2),2]),
([],[pair(2),3])
```

In the second step, the system combines these two sets of reduced terms in order to generate the probable base cases corresponding to `rdup([2,9,2,4],[9,2,4])`. Following is a partial listing of the probable base cases (due to the lack of space, we have omitted the predicate name and shown only the arguments) of the training example `rdup([2,9,2,4], [9,2,4])` along with the reduction functions and application depths:

([2,9,2,4],[9,2,4])	[none,0][none,0]	([2,9,2,4],[2,4])	[none,0][pair(2),1]
([2,9,2,4],[4])	[none,0][pair(2),2]	([9,2,4],[9,2,4])	[pair(2),1][none,0]
([9,2,4],[2,4])	[pair(2),1][pair(2),1]	([2,4],[9,2,4])	[pair(2),2][none,0]
([2,4],[4])	[pair(2),2][pair(2),2]	([4],[])	[pair(2),3][pair(2),3]
....	....	....	....

Let this reduced example set be $\mathcal{R}_{ex1}$. SmartPlus generates the probable base cases for each of the other three training examples. Let us denote these sets $\mathcal{R}_{ex2}$, $\mathcal{R}_{ex3}$ and $\mathcal{R}_{ex4}$ for the 2nd, 3rd and 4th training example respectively.

The next task is to combine the $\mathcal{R}_{exi}$ sets by taking one element from each of them in order to generate the probable base cases for the entire training set.

To illustrate, let us combine the sets $\{a,b,c\}$ and $\{d,e\}$. The result is the sets $\{a,d\}$, $\{a,e\}$, $\{b,d\}$, $\{b,e\}$, $\{c,d\}$ and $\{c,e\}$. Let the result of the combination operation be the sets bg_1, bg_2, bg_3, ..., bg_n each consisting of one member from each of the $\mathcal{R}_{exi}$ sets. The following is the enumeration of some of them:

```
{rdup([9,2,4],[2,4]), rdup([7],[]), rdup([c],[]), rdup([1,3],[3])}
{rdup([2,4],[4]), rdup([],[]), rdup([c,c],[c]), rdup([3],[3])}
{rdup([4],[]), rdup([7],[7]), rdup([],[]), rdup([1,3],[])}
..................
```

Since the system does not know which bg_i $(1 \le i \le n)$ conforms to the true base examples for the training set, SmartPlus takes their lgg one by one until a consistent clause is found. The bg_is are sorted according to the reduction depths. The lgg of bg_k having higher reduction depth is taken prior to taking the lgg of other bg_is having smaller reduction depths. While taking the lgg of each bg_i one by one, an unintended base clause is detected if it resolves with some negative examples. The base clause which is consistent with the available negative examples is taken as the target one. But this procedure requires an extensive set of user provided negative training examples in order to wipe out all the incorrect base clauses. Now the problem turns out to be how to come up with the correct base clause specially when the training set includes a small number of negative examples. We solve this problem in the following way:

Assuming only one recursive call in the target recursive clauses, only one member in $\mathcal{R}_{exi}$ corresponds to the true base case for each individual training example. If, e.g., bg_m happens to be the true base cases for the training set, other bg_i $(i \ne m)$ cannot be the same for the following reasons. Let us suppose that bg_k $(m \ne k)$ also corresponds to the true base cases for the training set. Then it implies that two different base cases exist for some training example which is impossible. Hence while we take the lgg of a particular bg_i, e.g., bg_m, the members of other bg_is, i.e., bg_1, bg_2, ..., bg_n excluding any from bg_m are provided as negative base examples. Note that these examples are not necessarily the negative examples of the target concept, rather these act as the negative base cases. After taking the lgg of bg_m, its consistency is tested against the following negative examples in addition to the user provided negative examples:

$$\{\forall X \mid (X \in bg_i, 1 \le i \le n) \wedge (X \notin bg_m)\}$$

If the lgg is consistent with the negative examples, it is taken as the target base clause. If not, next group is tried and so on. Since system generated negative examples are considerably large in number, dependency on user provided negative examples for correct base clause induction is reduced by the same amount.

Let N_t be the size of the training set, N_a be the arity of the target predicate and d_{avg} be the average maximum number of reductions each argument of the training examples suffers. In this case, on the average, $(d_{avg})^{N_a}$ probable base cases are generated from each training example. The combination operation between the generated base cases creates $\left((d_{avg})^{N_a}\right)^{N_t}$ candidates for the lgg computation. Module 1 thus needs to compute in the worst case $(d_{avg})^{N_a N_t}$ lggs in order to induce the correct base clause.

4 Module 2: Inferring Missing Examples

The reduction functions along with their application depths in deriving the base examples are used to infer the missing examples. For the training set in Table 1, module 1 finds the following base examples (pointed at by arrows):

```
rdup([],[]) <--  rdup([2,9,2,4],[9,2,4])   [pair(2),4][pair(2),3]
rdup([],[]) <--  rdup([5,7],[5,7])         [pair(2),2][pair(2),2]
rdup([],[]) <--  rdup([a,c,c,b],[a,c,b])   [pair(2),4][pair(2),3]
rdup([],[]) <--  rdup([1,1,3,1],[3,1])     [pair(2),4][pair(2),2]
```

Except for the 2nd training example, the application depths of the reduction functions to individual arguments differ from each other. For example, the application depths of the reduction functions to the 1st and 2nd arguments of the training example **rdup([a,c,c,b],[a,c,b])** are 4 and 3 respectively. Different reduction depths imply the example in question resolves with multiple recursive clauses before it finally unifies with the base clause. For example, **rdup([a,c,c,b],[a,c,b])** at first reduces to **rdup([c,c,b],[c,b])** by resolving with the 2nd recursive clause of (pgm2). In this clause both arguments of the example suffer reduction. **rdup([c,c,b],[c,b])** then resolves with the 1st clause and reduces to **rdup([c,b],[c,b])**. Note that in this clause only the first argument suffers reduction while the second remains the same. **rdup([c,b],[c,b])** then successively reduces to **rdup([b],[b])** and **rdup([],[])** by resolving with the 2nd clause twice before being unified with the base clause. Let us now consider the 2nd training example. It resolves with the 2nd clause of (pgm2) twice before it finally resolves with the base clause. Because of resolving with the same clause, its arguments suffer equal number of reductions.

Module 2 separates the training examples into two classes. Training examples the arguments of which suffer different depths of reductions are separated into one class called *mult_recursion* class. The rest constitutes the *single_recursion* class. In our example training set, the mult_recursion class consists of the training examples **rdup([2,9,2,4],[9,2,4])**, **rdup([a,c,c,b],[a,c,b])**, and **rdup([1,1,3,1],[3,1])** and the single_recursion class consists of the single example **rdup([5,7],[5,7])** respectively. SmartPlus works differently for each class in order to discover the missing examples.

For each training example of the single_recursion class, the missing example is found by applying the same reduction functions as used in deriving the base case to the original arguments, but this time with a minimum reduction depth. For example, the application of the reduction function **pair(2)** with a minimum reduction depth (here one) to the arguments **[5,7]** and **[5,7]** of the training example **rdup([5,7],[5,7])** generates the arguments **[7]** and **[7]** respectively for the missing example. Hence the missing example discovered becomes **rdup([7],[7])** and is asserted as a background knowledge (not as an example) for subsequent use in inducing the recursive clauses.

Let us now find the missing fact for the example **rdup([a,c,c,b],[a,c,b])** which belongs to the mult_recursion class. SmartPlus at first applies the same reduction functions as used in deriving the base case to the original arguments, but with a minimum application depth. The generated terms become `[c,c,b]` and `[c,b]` for the arguments `[a,c,c,b]` and `[a,c,b]` respectively. SmartPlus now creates new examples of which the first argument is chosen from the terms `[a,c,c,b]` (original) and `[c,c,b]` (reduced) and the second argument is chosen from the terms `[a,c,b]` and `[c,b]` respectively. After removing the original training example `rdup([a,c,c,b],[a,c,b])`, the newly created examples look as follows:

```
rdup([a,c,c,b],[c,b])  rdup([c,c,b],[c,b])  rdup([c,c,b],[a,c,b])
```

SmartPlus now presents these examples one by one to the user and asks whether they are the members of the target concept or not. If the user replies with a negative answer, the example in question is asserted as a negative training example. For example, the first example above is asserted as a negative training example after the user confirms that it is a false instance of the target concept. The true missing example is found as soon as the user feeds the system with a positive reply. This happens for the second example. Having been discovered the missing example, the remaining examples (here `rdup([c,c,b],[a,c,b])`) which have not yet been presented to the user are asserted as negative training examples. Note that SmartPlus does not need any query if it is provided with a sufficiently large number of negative examples. For example, if the negative training examples in Table 1 include the 1st and 3rd examples above, SmartPlus does not need any query at all. However, in practice it is sometimes impractical to supply an extensive set of negative examples. That is why SmartPlus prefers some user interaction instead of burdening the user from supplying an extensive set of negative training examples. Note also that the procedure for finding the missing examples not only discovers the missing examples, but creates some new negative examples (near misses) which are useful for inducing the recursive clauses in a top-down fashion.

If all the examples in the training set fall in the single_recursion class, it implies that the training examples repeatedly resolve with a single recursive clause before they finally unify with the base clause. This, on the other hand, means that the target recursive concept consists of a single recursive clause. Thus soon after the base clause is discovered by module 1, SmartPlus becomes able to predict the nature of the target recursive concept (whether containing single or multiple recursive clauses). Note that the procedure for discovering the missing facts corresponding to the members of the single_recursion class does not need any user interaction. Consequently SmartPlus learns recursive concepts consisting of a single recursive clause without requiring any user involvement.

5 Module 3: Induction of Recursive Clauses

SmartPlus learns the recursive clauses in a general to specific manner by performing a beam search based on likelihood heuristic. It randomly selects a positive seed example and begins to specialize the most general term of this seed example. Clause specialization is carried out by (i) unifying variables and (ii) adding background predicates to the clause body which means that SmartPlus uses function-free Horn clause expression as its hypothesis language. After each specialization step, SmartPlus performs the following tasks: It first checks the generated specializations for consistency. If one found, it removes the positive examples covered by the clause and starts afresh from another seed example if there remains any positive examples to be covered. However if no consistent clause is found, SmartPlus selects the best N (beam width) clauses evaluated on likelihood heuristic and repeats the whole process. The coverage of examples by a proposed clause is checked extensionally, i.e., by unifying the recursive call in the body of the clause with the already discovered missing facts.

Likelihood is extracted from the Merit Heuristic employed in CHAM [5]. Merit heuristic is the sum of two components: the information gain [10] measuring the discriminating ability of a clause and the likelihood evaluating the goal directed usefulness of a clause. Since information gain is only suitable when a large collection of training examples are available at hand, therefore this cannot be used effectively to measure the usefulness of a clause when the training set is very small. We have only extracted the likelihood component from the Merit heuristic which is indifferent to training set size and thus particularly suitable for learning from a small training set.

Likelihood measures the goal directed closeness of a partially generated clause from the goal clause. A logic program transforms the initial state of the input variables of the head of a clause to the goal state of the output variables through intermediate states. The existentially quantified variables in the antecedents of a clause represent these intermediate states. The closeness between a partially generated clause and the goal clause is measured by computing the closeness distance from the input and existentially quantified variables from the output ones. It is easy to visualize that the appropriate selection of antecedent which is closer to the goal state at each induction step is expected to eventually converge to the desired clause. To measure the likelihood of a partially generated clause, the seed example is used to instantiate the variables in the body of the clause. The likelihood of a clause:

$$\mathit{\Gamma}(\text{Clause}) = \frac{\sum_{i=1}^{m}\sum_{j=1}^{n}\gamma(VIn_i, VOut_j)}{\sum_{i=1}^{m}\sum_{j=1}^{n}\sigma(VIn_i, VOut_j)}$$

where m is the number of input and existentially quantified variables in the clause, and n is that of output variables. $\gamma(v_1, v_2)$ and $\sigma(v_1, v_2)$ define closeness between the ground instantiation of the variables v_1 and v_2 as follows:

- Closeness between two atoms:
  $\gamma(atom1, atom2) = 1$ if $atom1 = atom2$; 0 otherwise
  and $\sigma(atom1, atom2) = 1$.
- Closeness between two lists:

$$\gamma(list1, list2) = \frac{\max(\text{length of matched sublists})}{\max(\text{length of } list1,\ \text{length of } list2)}$$

  and $\sigma(list1, list2) = 1$.
- $\gamma(v_1, v_2) = \sigma(v_1, v_2) = 0$ if v_1 and v_2 have different types.

6 Experimental Results and Discussions

SmartPlus has been implemented in SICStus prolog 2.1 and run on SUN Sparc Station 20/61. Table 2 and 3 summarize some initial experimental results. It is seen from Table 3 (which is an extension of Table 2) that target definitions consisting of a single recursive clause require no user intervention, however, definitions consisting of multiple recursive clauses do need some user interaction in the form of concept membership queries. If the newly created negative examples in module 2 (see Table 3) were included in the training set of Table 2, no user intervention would have been required at all. Table 3 also shows the average number of negative base examples created by the system (in module 1) in inducing the base clauses.

The procedure for inducing the base clause can potentially generate overly specific or overly general base clauses which are removed by checking their consistency with the negative examples. However, if the user entirely depends on the system, system generated negative examples may not be sufficient enough to prevent the occurrence of an unintended base clause. Therefore, the accuracy of SmartPlus in base clause induction will increase as the user provides more negative examples to the system. Since SmartPlus discovers the ground facts corresponding to the first recursive call of the given positive examples, any other generalization technique based on θ-subsumption (e.g., RLGG [9]) can be used besides the heuristic-based approach applied in SmartPlus. One of the effects of using likelihood heuristic is that most of the learned concepts in Table 2 are different in syntax from tail recursions. This is because of the fact that likelihood heuristic prefers those literals to add to the body of a clause which include existentially quantified variables very close to the final output variables.

SmartPlus is basically suitable for learning recursive concepts involving structured data types, e.g., list, peano integers (i.e., $s(0), s(s(0))$ etc.). For non-structured data types, the terms in the examples should first be converted to structured types before SmartPlus can be used to learn the target concepts. However there are terms which cannot be converted to structured types and consequently recursive concepts involving these terms are not learnable by SmartPlus.

We carried out an experiment to see how SmartPlus reacts when it is provided with more complex reduction functions. In addition to `pair(2)`, we provided the system `conc(2)` which is functionally equivalent to the following predicate:

```
concat(X,[],[X]).
concat(X,[Y|V],[Y|Z]):- concat(X,V,Z).
```

For example, the single application of `conc(2)` to the term `[1,2,3]` generates `[1,2]`, applying it twice generates `[1]` and so on. We provided the system the following positive and negative examples of a predicate the task of which is to reverse a list:

```
Positive examples                      Negative examples
------------------                     ------------------
rev([4,5,2],[2,5,4])                   rev([3,2,1],[3,1,2])
```

```
rev([a,b,c],[c,b,a])
rev([6,7,8],[8,7,6])
rev([3,1],[1,3])
```

```
rev([3,2,1],[3,1,2])
rev([3,2,1],[1,3,2])
rev([3,2,1],[2,3,1])
```

Table 2. Experiments with SmartPlus

Positive examples	Negative examples	Concept learned
last(1,[0,1]) last(2,[2,4,2]) last(5,[6,3,5]) last(a,[b,a,a])	last(2,[1,3,3]) last(2,[2,3]) last(2,[])	/*Last element of a list*/ last(X,[X]). last(X,Z):- split(Z,Y,W),last(X,W).
mem(1,[3,1,2]) mem(4,[5,6,4]) mem(a,[b,a,c]) mem(7,[8,9,7])	mem(1,[3,5]) mem(2,[3,3]) mem(3,[]) mem(1,[3])	/*Member of a list*/ mem(X,[X|Y]). mem(X,Y):- split(Y,W,Z),mem(X,Z).
app([1,2],[3,4],[1,2,3,4]) app([5,6],[7,8],[5,6,7,8]) app([a,b,c],[d],[a,b,c,d]) app([f],[],[f])	app([1],[3,4],[1,4,3]) app([],[3,4],[]) app([1,2],[3],[2,1,3] app([],[4,5],[5])	/*Appending two lists*/ app([],X,X). app(X,Y,Z):- split(X,P,Q), app(Q,Y,W),join(P,W,Z).
dl(1,[2,3,1],[2,3]) dl(4,[5,4,4],[5,4]) dl(a,[b,a,c],[b,c]) dl(6,[7,6],[7])	dl(2,[2,1,3],[2,1,3]) dl(1,[],[]) dl(1,[4],[]) dl(1,[],[3]) dl(4,[4,0],[])	/*deleting the first occurrence of an atom in a list*/ dl(X,[X|Z],Z). dl(X,Y,Z):- split(Y,V,W),dl(X,W,Q), join(V,Q,Z).
sub([1,5],[1,5,3],[3]) sub([6],[6,4,2],[4,2]) sub(a,b],[a,b,c,d],[c,d]) sub([7],[7,8],[8])	sub([2,5],[1,5,3],[3]) sub(1,5],[1,5,3],[1,5,3])	/*Finding the rear end of a list*/ sub([],[X|Y],[X|Y]). sub(X,Y,Z):- split(Y,V,W),dl(V,X,Q), sub(Q,W,Z).
del(2,[3,2,4],[3,4]) del(1,[1,5,1,6],[5,6]) del(7,[8,0,7],[8,0]) del(a,[b,c],[b,c])	del(2,[2,2,4],[2,4]) del(a,[d,b,c],[b,c]) del(7,[3,8,0,7],[8,0]) del(2,[1,1,5,1,6],[5,6])	/*Deleting all the occurrences of an atom in a list*/ del(X,[],[]). del(X,Y,Z):- split(Y,P,Q),del(X,Q,W), join(P,W,Z),noteq(X,P). del(X,Y,Z):- split(Y,P,Q),del(X,Q,Z), eq(P,X).
rdup([2,9,2,4],[9,2,4]) rdup([5,7],[5,7]) rdup([a,c,c,b],[a,c,b]) rdup([1,1,3],[1,3])	rdup([2,1,3],[1,3]) rdup([2,1,1],[2,1,1]) rdup([1,1,3],[1,1,3]) rdup([1,1,1,3],[1,1,3]) rdup([9,2,4],[3,2,4])	/*Remove duplicates from a list*/ rdup([],[]). rdup(X,Z):- split(X,P,Q),rdup(Q,W), join(P,W,Z),notmem(P,Q). rdup(X,Z):- split(X,P,Q),rdup(Q,Z), mem(P,Q).
uni([a,b,c],[a],[b,c,a]) uni([e,f],[g],[e,f,g]) uni([1,3],[1,2],[3,1,2]) uni([6,4],[5],[6,4,5])	uni([b,c],[b,a],[b,a]) uni([g,e,f],[g],[g,e,f,g]) uni([a,b],[b],[b]) uni([],[b,a],[]) uni([],[b,a],[a]) uni([3,1],[1,2],[1,2])	/*Union of two lists*/ uni([],[X|Y],[X|Y]). uni(X,Y,Z):- split(X,P,Q),uni(Q,Y,W), join(P,W,Z),notmem(P,Y). uni(X,Y,Z):- split(X,P,Q),uni(Q,Y,Z), mem(P,Y).

Table 3. Experiments with SmartPlus (continued)

No. of system generated negative base examples	Newly created negative examples (in module 2)		No. of user interaction	Time (sec)
14	Nil		Nil	0.4
16	Nil		Nil	0.7
84	Nil		Nil	119
28	Nil		Nil	23
61	Nil		Nil	41
36	del([7,[8,0,7],[0]) del(1,[5,1,6],[6]) del([2,[3,2,4],[4])	del(7,[0,7],[8,0]) del([1,[1,5,1,6],[6]) del(2,[2,4],[3,4])	4	18
58	rdup([1,1,3],[3]) rdup([a,c,c,b],[c,b]) rdup([2,9,2,4],[2,4])	rdup([1,3],[3]) rdup([c,c,b],[a,c,b]) rdup([9,2,4],[2,4])	5	45
76	uni([1,3],[1,2],[1,2]) uni([a,b,c],[a],[c,a])	uni([3],[1,2],[1,2]) uni([b,c],[a],[c,a])	4	114

SmartPlus successfully found the base clause by taking the lgg of the following base examples:

```
rev([],[]) <--  rev([4,5,2],[2,5,4])      [pair(2),3][conc(2),3]
rev([],[]) <--  rev([a,b,c],[c,b,a])      [pair(2),3][conc(2),3]
rev([],[]) <--  rev([6,7,8],[8,7,6])      [pair(2),3][conc(2),3]
rev([],[]) <--  rev([3,1],[1,3])          [pair(2),2][conc(2),2]
```

It then discovered the missing examples using module 2 and finally induced the recursive clause using module 3. It required no user interaction and found the following predicate definition in 38 seconds:

```
rev([],[]).
rev(X,Z):- split(X,P,Q),rev(Q,V),concat(P,V,Z).
```

Note that this is not a tail recursive program. Now we repeated this experiment without providing the `conc(2)` function. The system again successfully found the base clause by taking the lgg of the following base examples:

```
rev([],[]) <--  rev([4,5,2],[2,5,4])      [pair(2),3][pair(2),3]
rev([],[]) <--  rev([a,b,c],[c,b,a])      [pair(2),3][pair(2),3]
rev([],[]) <--  rev([6,7,8],[8,7,6])      [pair(2),3][pair(2),3]
rev([],[]) <--  rev([3,1],[1,3])          [pair(2),2][pair(2),2]
```

However it found the following missing examples using module 2:

```
rev([5,2],[5,4])  rev([b,c],[b,a])  rev([7,8],[7,6])  rev([1],[3])
```

All these discovered examples being false instances of the target predicate, SmartPlus failed to learn the target program. This experiment thus shows that the power of SmartPlus in inducing recursive programs (whether tail recursive or not) from incomplete training set depends largely on the availability of the appropriate reduction functions. Without appropriate reduction functions, the system may successfully find the base clause, but it will fail to discover the correct missing examples and consequently it will fail to induce the target program.

7 Conclusion

We have illustrated a detailed procedure for inducing recursive definitions from a very small incomplete training set the members of which all lie on non-intersecting resolution path and involve different constants. The procedure is based upon discovering the missing facts from the training set which are essential for a generalization technique based on θ-subsumption. The most costly operation in the proposed technique is the combinatorial decomposition of the training examples in module 1 which increases sharply with the example size and number of the given positive examples. We are currently investigating suitable heuristics to reduce this cost. We are also trying to automate the process of generating appropriate reduction functions corresponding to the available background predicates.

References

1. D. W. Aha, S. Lapointe, C. X. Ling, and S. Matwin. Inverting implication with small training sets. In *European Conference on Machine Learning*, 1994.
2. W. W. Cohen. Pac-learning a restricted class of recursive logic programs. In *3rd International Workshop on Inductive Logic Programming, J. Stefan Institute, Ljubljana, Slovenia*, 1993.
3. Peter Idestam-Almquist. Efficient induction of recursive definitions by structural analysis of saturations. In *5th International Workshop on Inductive Logic Programming, Leuven, Belgium*, 1995.
4. Alipio Jorge and Pavel Brazdil. Architecture for iterative learning of recursive definitions. In *5th International Workshop on Inductive Logic Programming, Leuven, Belgium*, 1995.
5. B. Kijsirikul, M. Numao, and M. Shimura. Efficient learning of logic programs with non-determinate, non-discriminating literals. In *8th International Workshop on Machine Learning*, 1991.
6. S. Lapointe, C. Ling, and S. Matwin. Constructive inductive logic programming. In *International Joint Conference on Artificial Intelligence*, 1993.
7. S. Lapointe and S. Matwin. Sub-unification: A tool for efficient induction of recursive programs. In *9th International Workshop on Machine Learning*, 1992.
8. Chowdhury Rahman Mofizur and Masayuki Numao. Top-down induction of recursive programs from small number of sparse examples. In Luc De Raedt, editor, *Advances in Inductive Logic Programming*, volume 32 of *Frontiers in Artificial Intelligence and Applications*. IOS Press, 1996.
9. S. Muggleton and C. Feng. Efficient induction of logic programs. In *1st International workshop on Algorithmic Learning Theory*, 1990.
10. J. R. Quinlan. Learning logical definitions from relations. *Machine Learning*, 5:239–266, 1990.

On Semantic Resolution with Lemmaizing and Contraction

Maria Paola Bonacina*[1] **and Jieh Hsiang** **[2]

[1] Department of Computer Science
The University of Iowa, Iowa City, IA 52242-1419, USA
bonacina@cs.uiowa.edu
[2] National Taiwan University, Taipei, Taiwan
hsiang@csie.ntu.edu.tw

Abstract. Reducing redundancy in search has been a major concern for automated deduction. Subgoal-reduction strategies prevent redundant search by using *lemmaizing* and *caching*, whereas contraction-based strategies prevent redundant search by using *contraction* rules, such as *subsumption*. In this work we show that lemmaizing and contraction can coexist in the framework of *semantic resolution*. On the lemmaizing side, we define two meta-level inference rules for lemmaizing in semantic resolution, one for unit and one for non-unit lemmas, and we prove their soundness. Rules for lemmaizing are meta-rules because they use global knowledge about the derivation, e.g. ancestry relations, in order to derive lemmas. On the contraction side, we give contraction rules for semantic strategies, and we define a *purity deletion* rule for first-order clauses that preserves completeness. While lemmaizing generalizes success caching of model elimination, purity deletion echoes failure caching. Thus, our approach integrates features of backward and forward reasoning.

1 Introduction

Some of the most successful theorem-proving programs existing today implement either contraction-based strategies (e.g., [1, 11, 13]) or subgoal-reduction strategies (e.g., [2, 17]). Contraction-based strategies (e.g., [4, 5, 10, 16]) are *forward-reasoning* strategies, that prove the target theorem by deriving consequences from the axioms. (Most forward-reasoning resolution strategies do not differentiate between the target theorem (negated) and the axioms. They treat them as a single set of clauses and try to derive a contradiction from it.) The primary strength of these strategies, is that they apply eagerly contraction inference rules, such as *simplification* and *subsumption*, to delete *redundant* clauses. By effectively reducing redundancy, contraction-based strategies keep the size of the database in check and have been used successfully to prove many problems beyond the reach of other types of strategies (e.g., [1, 11, 13]).

* Supported in part by grant CCR-94-08667 of the National Science Foundation.
** Supported in part by grant 85-2221-E-002-009 of the National Science Council.

The subgoal-reduction strategies are *linear*, *backward-reasoning* strategies. In such a strategy an inference step consists in reducing the current goal to a set of subgoals, starting from the input goal. Typical examples are *model elimination* [12], and the *Prolog technology theorem provers* [17]. A weakness of a pure subgoal-reduction strategy is that by concentrating only on the current goal it has no memory of previously solved goals. Therefore, if the same subgoals, or instances thereof, are generated at different stages, the strategy would solve them independently, repeating the same steps. More sophisticated subgoal-reduction strategies avoid such repetitions by using techniques of *lemmaizing*, that is, saving solved goals as lemmas. Lemmaizing for model elimination was presented already in [12]. However, its first implementation in [9] was less efficient than expected [2], because unrestricted lemmaizing generated too many lemmas. More recently, lemmaizing and *caching* [15] in Horn logic have been reintroduced successfully in the framework of Prolog technology theorem proving [3]. Caching comprises *success caching* and *failure caching*. The former is conceptually very close to lemmaizing: solutions are stored in a *cache* for fast retrieval, rather than being added as lemmas. The latter adds the capability of using the information that a goal has failed before to avoid trying to solve it again. Related techniques, called *memoing* or *tabling*, have been explored independently in logic programming [19]. The experimental work has been followed by the theoretical analysis of [14], which shows that lemmaizing and caching reduce from exponential to linear the amount of duplication in the search spaces of model elimination for problems in propositional Horn logic.

Our intent in this paper is to show that lemmaizing and caching are meta-level inferences that may apply to different types of strategies, including strategies that are not based on subgoal reduction. For this purpose, we consider *semantic resolution* strategies. The reason of this choice is that, among resolution strategies, semantic strategies are those that provide a general notion of "goal", by partitioning the database in a consistent set of "axioms" and a *set of support* of "goals". We define meta-rules for lemmaizing in semantic-resolution strategies and we give inference rules that implement them. Lemmaizing in model elimination then becomes a special case[3]. This generalization of lemmaizing is significant in at least two ways:

1. Semantic strategies require that all their inferences are *supported*, i.e. have a premise in the set of support. We observe that lemmaizing consists in generating lemmas from the complement of the set of support (e.g., from the axioms in model elimination), that is, lemmas are unsupported inferences. Semantic-resolution strategies may do forward or backward reasoning depending on how the set of support is defined. If supported inferences are forward inferences, lemmaizing adds backward reasoning to a forward-reasoning strategy; if supported inferences are backward inferences, lemmaizing adds forward reasoning to a backward-reasoning strategy. Therefore, our

[3] The treatment of model elimination in our approach has been omitted for reasons of space and may be found in [6].

treatment makes lemmaizing a general technique for combining forward and backward reasoning in semantic resolution.

2. We point out that lemmaizing is a *meta-level rule*. A derivation is made of inference steps, each justified by an inference rule. Lemmaizing derives a lemma based on a fragment of the current derivation. Therefore, it is an inference at the meta-level with respect to the basic inferences.

In the second part of the paper, we describe how contraction inference rules can be incorporated into semantic-resolution strategies. Furthermore, we define a generalized notion of *purity deletion*, and show how it provides additional power in reducing redundancy in these strategies. Roughly speaking, purity deletion is similar to failure caching, although in a forward-reasoning setting.

In summary, one can have a semantic-resolution strategy that features both contraction and lemmaizing, that are two strengths of contraction-based and subgoal-reduction strategies respectively. Furthermore, contraction-based strategies, unlike subgoal-reduction strategies, are equipped with tools, such as contraction and indexing, to deal with a database of generated and kept clauses. Therefore, while lemmaizing in semantic resolution will certainly need to be restricted, contraction-based strategies might be less sensitive than subgoal-reduction strategies to the risk of generating too many lemmas.

The rest of the paper is organized in the following way. In Section 2 we give a brief summary of semantic resolution and how it plays a role in terms of forward and backward reasoning methods. Section 3 contains the treatment of lemmaizing as meta-level inference rules for semantic resolution. In Section 4 we define concrete inference rules for lemmaizing in strategies with set of support. In Section 5 we show how to incorporate contraction rules in semantic strategies with lemmaizing, and we present purity deletion. For reasons of space, we have left all the proofs in a longer version of this paper [6].

2 Semantic resolution strategies

In *semantic resolution*[4] the application of resolution to a set of clauses S is controlled by a given interpretation I, in such a way that the consistent subset $T \subset S$ that contains the clauses satisfied by I is not expanded. Only resolution steps with at most one premise from T are allowed: a clause in either T or $S-T$, called *nucleus*, resolves with one or more clauses in $S-T$, called *electrons*, until a resolvent that is false in I, and therefore belongs to $S-T$, is generated. Semantic resolution may also assume an ordering on predicate symbols, and then require that the literal resolved upon in an electron contains the greatest predicate symbol in the electron.

Hyperresolution is semantic resolution where the interpretation I is defined based on sign: in *positive* hyperresolution, I contains all the negative literals, T contains the non-positive clauses, $S - T$ contains the positive clauses, and the electrons are positive clauses (from $S - T$) that resolve with all the negative

[4] References were omitted in this section for brevity. They may be found in [6].

literals in the nucleus (from T) to generate a positive hyperresolvent. *Negative* hyperresolution is defined dually. Hyperresolution is more restrictive than generic semantic resolution, because resolution steps where both nucleus and electron are in $S - T$ may not happen (e.g., two positive clauses do not resolve).

In *resolution with set of support* a *set of support* (SOS) is a subset of S such that $S - SOS$ is consistent. Only resolution steps with at most one premise from $S - SOS$ are allowed and all generated clauses are added to SOS. To keep the notation uniform, we use $T = S - SOS$ for the consistent subset in all strategies. Resolution with set of support fits in the paradigm of semantic resolution, under the interpretation that the clauses in T are true, the clauses in SOS and all their descendants are false. *Positive resolution* and *negative resolution* are sometimes considered supported strategies where SOS contains the positive or negative clauses, respectively. However, they are not semantic strategies in the proper sense, because they do not partition the clauses based on an interpretation, with the provision that the consistent set is not expanded.

The original idea of *set-of-support strategy* was that the axioms of a problem usually form a consistent set and that a strategy should not expand such a set, but rather work on the goals. In this interpretation, T contains the axioms, SOS contains the goal clauses (the clauses obtained from the transformation into clausal form of the negation of the target theorem) and the effect of working with a set of support is that most of the work done by the strategy is done on the goals, yielding *backward-reasoning* strategies. The general definitions of semantic resolution and resolution with set of support, however, imply neither backward reasoning nor forward reasoning. For instance, if the axioms are non-negative clauses and the goals are negative clauses, the positive strategies are forward-reasoning strategies and the negative strategies are backward-reasoning strategies compatible with the set-of-support strategy. This is the case in Horn logic. In general, the partition of S into T and SOS based on the distinction between axioms and goals may not agree with the partition based on sign (e.g., the goals may not be negative clauses), so that hyperresolution and the set-of-support strategy are not always compatible.

Linear resolution can be regarded as a linear refinement of resolution with set of support. Given a set of clauses $S = T \cup \{C_0\}$ with a selected *top clause* C_0, the strategy builds a linear derivation, where at step i clause C_{i+1} is generated by resolving the *center clause* C_i with a *side clause*, either a clause in T (an *input clause*), or a clause C_j such that $j < i$ (an *ancestor clause*). If T is consistent and C_0 is the negation of the target, the center clauses form the set of support, and the only needed resolution steps between clauses in SOS are the resolutions with ancestors. Because the strategy is linear, it makes the backward-reasoning character more pronounced: there is a notion of *current goal*, the most recently generated center clause, and each step consists in reducing the current goal to a subgoal. We call such linear, backward-reasoning strategies *subgoal-reduction strategies*.

Linear resolution, however, requires keeping the ancestors around. *Linear input resolution*, where all side clauses are input clauses, is complete for Horn logic, but not for first-order logic. On the other hand, *model elimination* [12] enjoys the advantage of being a linear input strategy that is complete for first-order logic. Roughly speaking, ancestor-resolution inferences are made unnecessary by saving the literals resolved upon in the goals as *framed literals*, and allowing the latter to resolve away subgoal literals[5]. It follows that each step involves either the current goal and an input clause (analogous to an input resolution step) or the current goal only. Therefore, subgoal-reduction strategies based on model elimination usually work on a stack of goals, rather than on a database of clauses, and at each step focus exclusively on the current goal, on top of the stack. The search plan is depth-first search with backtracking, and iterative deepening (DFID) to ensure refutational completeness. Finally, since the axiom set of a problem is static, these strategies yield fast implementations using the Warren Abstract Machine.

3 Generation of lemmas

In this section we present our treatment of lemmaizing. In Sections 3.1 and 3.2 we give meta-rules for lemma generation in the class of semantic strategies. We assume derivations in the form

$$(T_0; SOS_0) \underset{C}{\vdash} (T_1; SOS_1) \underset{C}{\vdash} \ldots (T_i; SOS_i) \underset{C}{\vdash} \ldots,$$

where C is any strategy in the class, all generated resolvents are added to the SOS component, but the T component is not assumed to be constant, because it may be modified by contraction or lemmaizing. In Section 4 we give inference rules that implement the meta-rules for resolution with set of support.

3.1 Generating unit lemmas

Intuitively speaking, if $T \cup \{\neg L\} \models \Box$, then $T \models L\sigma$ for some substitution σ, and $L\sigma$ can be treated as a lemma of T and be added to T. Generalizing this idea slightly, if a clause $C\sigma$ is deduced from $\neg L \vee C$ using T alone (without using any other clause in SOS), it means that $T \cup \{\neg L \vee C\} \models C\sigma$. Then $L\sigma$ can also be added as a lemma to T.

There is a caveat, however. For this argument to be sound, it is necessary for the C in $\neg L \vee C$ not to take any part in the derivation of $C\sigma$ from $T \cup \{\neg L \vee C\}$. More precisely, the derivation of $C\sigma$ from $T \cup \{\neg L \vee C\}$ does not include any resolution or factoring step with a selected literal[6] in C. This is necessary to make sure that the existence of a derivation of $C\sigma$ from $T \cup \{\neg L \vee C\}$ implies the existence of a derivation of $L\sigma$ from T. If the derivation from $T \cup \{\neg L \vee C\}$ involves literals in C, then the existence of a derivation of $L\sigma$ from T is not

[5] Model elimination may be presented in many ways, e.g. as a refinement of linear resolution or as a tableaux-based method. We refer to [6] for more details.

[6] A selected literal is a literal resolved upon in a resolution step or unified in a factoring step.

ensured, because the steps involving the literals in C may not be reproducible in a derivation from T. The following definitions will capture this requirement.

Definition 3.1 *Let C be a clause and C' be a binary resolvent or a factor of C. The relation $A \mapsto B$ holds if A is a literal in C different from the selected literal(s) in generating C', B is a literal in C' and $B = A\sigma$, where σ is the most general unifier of the inference generating C'.*

The relation $A \mapsto B$ captures the inheritance of literals that are not selected. By using the transitive closure $\mapsto^*$ of $\mapsto$, we can represent inheritance of literals through a sequence of steps:

Definition 3.2 *Given a resolution derivation $S \vdash^* S'$, where S and S' are sets of clauses, a clause $C' \in S'$ is a* strict descendant *of a clause $C \in S$, if for every literal $A' \in C'$ there is a literal $A \in C$, such that $A \mapsto^* A'$.*

Definition 3.3 *Let S be a set of clauses. $C\sigma$ is* linearly derived from $\neg L \vee C$ by using S *if there is a linear resolution derivation with input set of clauses S, top clause $\neg L \vee C$ and last center clause $C\sigma$. We denote such a derivation by $\neg L \vee C \mid\!\leadsto_S C\sigma$.*
If the derivation is a linear input derivation (i.e., all side clauses come from S) and $C\sigma$ is a strict descendant of $\neg L \vee C$, we say that $C\sigma$ is strictly linearly derived from $\neg L \vee C$ by using S *and we write $\neg L \vee C \mid\!\leadsto_S^h C\sigma$.*

Coming back to the SOS strategy, given sets SOS and T, $\neg L \vee C \mid\!\leadsto_T^h C\sigma$ indicates that $C\sigma$ is derived from $\neg L \vee C$ and T, and that in the derivation, no literals in C and no clauses in SOS are involved in any of the inference steps. We have now all the elements to write the first meta-rule for lemma generation:

Definition 3.4 Unit Lemmaizing*: if $\neg L \vee C \mid\!\leadsto_T^h C\sigma$, then add lemma $L\sigma$ to T.*

Then we prove the soundness of Unit Lemmaizing:

Theorem 3.1 *If $\neg L \vee C \mid\!\leadsto_T^h C\sigma$, then $T \models L\sigma$.*

3.2 Generating non-unit lemmas

The derivation $\neg L \vee C \mid\!\leadsto_T^h C\sigma$ in the condition for Unit Lemmaizing satisfies the restrictions that all side clauses of the (linear) derivation come from T and that the literals in C are not selected in the derivation. In Horn logic, since linear input resolution is complete and factoring is not necessary, Unit Lemmaizing is the only form of lemmaizing. In first-order logic, one may have a derivation $\neg L \vee C \mid\!\leadsto_{T \cup SOS} C\sigma$, in which members of the set SOS are also used and $C\sigma$ is not necessarily a strict descendant of C. This condition leads to a more general meta-rule for lemmaizing, that may generate also non-unit lemmas. The general form of a lemma will be $(L \vee F)\sigma$, or $(\neg F \supset L)\sigma$, where $\neg F\sigma$ is the "premise" for $L\sigma$ to hold. Operationally, F contains those subgoals of $\neg L$ that are resolved in the derivation $\neg L \vee C \mid\!\leadsto_{T \cup SOS} C\sigma$ by using SOS or C, but cannot be resolved by using T only. They are formally defined as follows:

Definition 3.5 *Given a derivation* $\neg L_1 \vee \cdots \vee \neg L_k \vee C \vdash\!\!\!\leadsto_{T \cup SOS} C\sigma$, *for all* i, $1 \leq i \leq k$, *the* residue *of* $\neg L_i$ *in* T, *denoted by* $R_T(\neg L_i)$, *is defined as follows: let* $D = L' \vee Q_1 \vee \ldots \vee Q_m$ *be the clause that resolves with* $\neg L_1 \vee \cdots \vee \neg L_k \vee C$ *upon* $\neg L_i$ *and* L'; *then*

$$R_T(\neg L_i) = \begin{cases} \neg L_i & \text{if } D \in SOS, \\ false & \text{if } D \in T \text{ and } m = 0, \\ R_T(Q_1) \vee \ldots R_T(Q_m) & \text{if } D \in T \text{ and } m \geq 1, \\ \neg L_i & \text{if } \neg L_i \text{ is removed by factoring} \\ & \text{with a literal in } C, \\ R_T(\neg L_j) & \text{if } \neg L_i \text{ is removed by factoring} \\ & \text{with } \neg L_j \text{ for } 1 \leq j \neq i \leq k. \end{cases}$$

Example 3.1 *Assume that* $\neg L \vee C \vdash\!\!\!\leadsto_{T \cup SOS} C\sigma$ *is made of the following steps:*

1. $\neg L \vee C$ *resolves with* $L \vee P$ *generating* $P \vee C$,
2. $P \vee C$ *resolves with* $\neg P \vee Q \vee R$, *generating* $Q \vee R \vee C$,
3. $Q \vee R \vee C$ *resolves with* $\neg Q$, *generating* $R \vee C$,
4. $R \vee C$ *resolves with* $\neg R$, *generating* C.

We now analyze the residue $R_T(\neg L)$, *according to different situations. If* $L \vee P \in SOS$, *then* $R_T(\neg L) = \neg L$. *If* $L \vee P \in T$, *then* $R_T(\neg L) = R_T(P)$. *In the latter case, if* $\neg P \vee Q \vee R \in SOS$, *then* $R_T(\neg L) = R_T(P) = P$. *On the other hand, if* $\neg P \vee Q \vee R \in T$, *then* $R_T(\neg L) = R_T(P) = R_T(Q) \vee R_T(R)$. *Since* $R_T(Q) = Q$ *if* $\neg Q \in SOS$ *and* $R_T(Q) = false$ *if* $\neg Q \in T$, *and the same is true for* R, *the value of* $R_T(\neg L)$ *in the last case can be determined by the different combinations of* $R_T(Q)$ *and* $R_T(R)$.

A meta-rule for *Generalized Lemmaizing* can then be formulated:

Definition 3.6 *If* $\neg L \vee C \vdash\!\!\!\leadsto_{T \cup SOS} C\sigma$, *then add lemma* $(L \vee R_T(\neg L))\sigma$ *to* T.

Unit Lemmaizing is the special case of Generalized Lemmaizing where $R_T(\neg L)$ is *false*, and thus $(L \vee R_T(\neg L))\sigma$ reduces to $L\sigma$. If $R_T(\neg L)$ is $\neg L$, it means that $\neg L$ itself cannot be resolved in T and therefore no lemma should be added. Indeed, in such a case $(L \vee R_T(\neg L))\sigma$ is a tautology.

Proposition 3.1 *Given a derivation* $\neg L \vee C \vdash\!\!\!\leadsto_{T \cup SOS} C\sigma$, *if literal* $\neg L$ *can be eliminated only by a resolution step with a side clause from* SOS *or by factoring, then no non-trivial lemma can be generated.*

We conclude with the soundness of Generalized Lemmaizing:

Theorem 3.2 *If* $\neg L \vee C \vdash\!\!\!\leadsto_{T \cup SOS} C\sigma$, *then* $T \models (L \vee R_T(\neg L))\sigma$.

4 Inference rules for Generalized Lemmaizing

In this section we assume that the underlying strategy is resolution with set of support and we give a set of inference rules for resolution and factoring that implement our meta-rules for lemmaizing within such a strategy. In the inference rules the expression $[F]_L$ is used to denote that F, a conjunction of literals, is a potential list of premises for resolving away the literal L completely using only clauses in T. In other words, F is part of the residue of L. When F in $[F]_L$ contains the entire residue of L, the lemma $\neg L \vee F$ can be generated. Some of the inference rules generate a resolvent with literals labelled by a subscript L, such as Q_L. These are subgoals produced while resolving away L, and they themselves need to be resolved away before a lemma concerning L can be generated. We call a literal with subscript L an *L-subgoal.*

The inference rules are separated into three categories, one for resolution, one for factoring, and one for lemmatization.

4.1 The resolution rules

Several different resolution rules are needed since, in a set of support strategy, the sets SOS and T play different roles.

In the first rule for resolution, literal L in $L \vee C$ is resolved with a non-unit clause from T, and a lemma involving $L\sigma$ is initiated:

Resolution with lemma initiation

$$\frac{(T \cup \{\neg L' \vee D\}; SOS \cup \{L \vee C\})}{(T \cup \{\neg L' \vee D\}; SOS \cup \{L \vee C, (D_{L\sigma} \vee [false]_{L\sigma} \vee C)\sigma\})} \quad L\sigma = L'\sigma$$

where L and L' are literals, C and D are disjunctions of literals and σ is the most general unifier of L and L'. $D_{L\sigma}$ has the same literals as D, except that they are labelled by a subscript $L\sigma$. These are the $L\sigma$-subgoals, that need to be resolved away before a lemma concerning $L\sigma$ can be generated. The expression $[false]_{L\sigma}$ means that at this stage the premise of a potential lemma $L\sigma$ is empty. In this inference rule we assume that neither of the clauses involved in the resolution step has any subscripted literals. If the T-clause is a unit clause, no lemma is initiated, and plain unit resolution applies, because lemmaizing would produce an instance of the unit clause in T.

In the second rule for resolution, $\neg L$ is resolved with a clause from SOS:

Plain resolution

$$\frac{(T; SOS \cup \{L' \vee D, \neg L \vee C\})}{(T; SOS \cup \{L' \vee D, \neg L \vee C, (D \vee C)\sigma\})} \quad L\sigma = L'\sigma$$

We assume that neither of the two clauses involved in the resolution step has any subscripted literals. In this case, if one were to produce a residue for L, it would be L itself (by the first case of Definition 3.5), which would result in a lemma that is a tautology (Proposition 3.1) Thus, there is no need to initiate a lemma.

The next two rules have the condition $P\sigma = L'\sigma$:

Residue extension

$$\frac{(T; SOS \cup \{\neg L' \vee Q, P_L \vee D_L \vee C \vee [F]_L\})}{(T; SOS \cup \{\neg L' \vee Q, P_L \vee D_L \vee C \vee [F]_L, (Q_{L\sigma} \vee D_{L\sigma} \vee C \vee [F \vee P]_{L\sigma})\sigma\})}$$

In this rule, F is the lemma for L being constructed, and $P_L \vee D_L$ is the disjunction of the L-subgoals to be solved. Since P, an L-subgoal, is resolved with a clause in SOS, the remaining literals coming from that clause also become part of the set of L-subgoals, and P has to be added to the residue list. We remark that the clause $\neg L' \vee Q$ may also be labelled. For instance, $\neg L' \vee Q$ may have the form $\neg L'_M \vee E_M \vee B \vee [H]_M$. Then, the above rule may generate two resolvents: $(E_{L\sigma} \vee B_{L\sigma} \vee D_{L\sigma} \vee C \vee [F \vee P]_{L\sigma})\sigma$ and $(D_{M\sigma} \vee C_{M\sigma} \vee E_{M\sigma} \vee B \vee [H \vee \neg L']_{M\sigma})\sigma$.

Subgoal elimination

$$\frac{(T \cup \{\neg L' \vee Q\}; SOS \cup \{P_L \vee D_L \vee C \vee [F]_L\})}{(T \cup \{\neg L' \vee Q\}; SOS \cup \{P_L \vee D_L \vee C \vee [F]_L, (Q_{L\sigma} \vee D_{L\sigma} \vee C \vee [F]_{L\sigma})\sigma\})}$$

This rule is similar to *residue extension* except that the resolved literal P is not added to the residue list. This is because the clause which resolves P away is from T.

4.2 The factoring rules

Similar to the resolution rules, the factoring rules need to consider the behaviour of the L-subgoals and residues. All the following rules have the condition $P\sigma = P'\sigma$:

Residue extension factoring

$$\frac{(T; SOS \cup \{P_L \vee D_L \vee [F]_L \vee C \vee P'\})}{(T; SOS \cup \{P_L \vee D_L \vee [F]_L \vee C \vee P', (D_{L\sigma} \vee [F \vee P]_{L\sigma} \vee C \vee P')\sigma\})}$$

This rule says that if an L-subgoal is eliminated by factoring with a "normal" SOS-literal, then it needs to be considered as part of the residue of L.

Subgoal deletion factoring

$$\frac{(T; SOS \cup \{P_L \vee D_L \vee P'_L \vee C\})}{(T; SOS \cup \{P_L \vee D_L \vee P'_L \vee C, (D \vee P'_{L\sigma} \vee C)\sigma\})}$$

This rule says that, when factoring between two L-subgoals, one of them can be eliminated. This rule corresponds to the fifth case in Definition 3.5.

Plain factoring

$$\frac{(T; SOS \cup \{P \vee D_L \vee P' \vee C\})}{(T; SOS \cup \{P \vee D_L \vee P' \vee C, (D_L \vee P' \vee C)\sigma\})}$$

4.3 The lemma generation rule

Lemmaizing

$$\frac{(T; SOS \cup \{[F]_L \vee C\})}{(T \cup \{\neg L \vee F\}; SOS \cup \{C\})} \quad C \textit{ does not contain any } L\textit{-subgoals}$$

In the rule for lemmaizing, all the subgoals of the literal L have been solved, and therefore $\neg L$ with its residue is turned into a lemma.

Example 4.1 *If $T = \{P \vee R, \neg R\}$ and $SOS = \{\neg P \vee \neg Q\}$, the first resolvent is $\neg Q \vee R_{\neg P} \vee [false]_{\neg P}$. The new $(\neg P)$-subgoal in the resolvent resolves with $\neg R$ of T and derives $\neg Q \vee [false]_{\neg P}$. By the Lemmaizing rule, the last resolvent becomes $\neg Q$ and a lemma P can be added to T. Note that since set-of-support forbids resolution among members of T, the same lemma cannot be obtained from T directly.*

Example 4.2 *If T contains $\neg P \vee \neg Q$ and SOS contains $P \vee \neg Q$, then $\neg Q_P \vee [false]_P \vee \neg Q$ is inferred by Resolution with lemma initiation. A factoring step generates the factor $[false \vee \neg Q]_P \vee \neg Q$. Since $\neg Q$ is the residue of P, the lemma $\neg P \vee \neg Q$ is generated. In this case the lemma is already in T so that it is not added.*

5 Eliminating redundancy in contraction-based strategies

Forward-reasoning resolution strategies often adopt contraction inference rules such as *clausal subsumption* and *clausal simplification* to reduce the database of clauses. Since space explosion is usually the critical factor deciding whether a successful derivation is possible, the more power contraction exhibits, the more effective the proof method is. The combination of the set-of-support strategies and contraction strategies seems to have been implemented in some provers including OTTER, but it is rarely studied in the theorem-proving literature. In this section we discuss two results. First we present schemes of inference rules to incorporate contraction in semantic strategies, including strategies with lemmaizing. Then we introduce a notion of *purity* with which one can utilize unresolvable literals to detect and delete redundant clauses. The latter is similar to "failure caching" in the Prolog technology theorem proving framework.

5.1 Incorporating contraction in semantic strategies with lemmaizing

We start with an example which shows that naïve contraction in a semantic strategy may destroy its completeness:

Example 5.1 *Assume a semantic strategy featuring clausal simplification and a contraction-first search plan. Given $T = \{\neg P, P \vee Q\}$ and $SOS = \{\neg Q\}$, the strategy looks for contraction steps first, and it contracts $P \vee Q$ in T to P, by* *clausal simplification by* $\neg Q$*. It follows that* $T = \{\neg P, P\}$ *and* $SOS = \{\neg Q\}$*. The set* T *has become inconsistent and no refutation can be found by a semantic strategy, since resolution between clauses in* T *is not allowed.*

Intuitively, if contraction "moves" the inconsistency of $T \cup SOS$ into T, the semantic strategy becomes incomplete, because a semantic strategy assumes that T is consistent, and therefore is not able to detect an inconsistency in T. Thus, if I is the interpretation controlling the semantic strategy, a clause generated by contraction should be added to T only if the clause is true in I. The following schemes of inference rules for contraction capture this idea:

Contraction of SOS

$$\frac{(T; SOS \cup \{C\})}{(T; SOS \cup \{D\})} \quad C \textit{ is contracted to } D$$

If a clause in SOS is contracted, the resulting clause is also false in I and belongs to SOS.

Contraction of T by T

$$\frac{(T \cup \{C\}; SOS)}{(T \cup \{D\}; SOS)} \quad C \textit{ is contracted to } D \textit{ by clauses in } T$$

If a clause in T is contracted by clauses in T, the resulting clause is also true in I and therefore belongs to T.

Contraction of T by SOS

$$\frac{(T \cup \{C\}; SOS)}{(T; SOS \cup \{D\})} \quad C \textit{ is contracted to } D \textit{ by clauses in } SOS \textit{ and } I \not\models D$$

$$\frac{(T \cup \{C\}; SOS)}{(T \cup \{D\}; SOS)} \quad C \textit{ is contracted to } D \textit{ by clauses in } SOS \textit{ and } I \models D$$

If a clause in T is contracted by clauses in SOS, one needs to resort to the definition of I in order to decide the affiliation of the new clause. Otherwise, incompleteness such as shown in Example 5.1 may occur. For instance, for hyperresolution, D is placed according to the sign of its literals. In resolution with set of support, all clauses descending from SOS clauses are regarded as false clauses and belong to SOS. Thus, the above two rules can be combined into the following simpler scheme:

$$\frac{(T \cup \{C\}; SOS)}{(T; SOS \cup \{D\})} \quad C \textit{ is contracted to } D \textit{ by clauses in } SOS$$

In case of deletion rules such as subsumption, C is simply deleted and no clause D is generated.

Example 5.2 *If the strategy is resolution with set of support and clausal simplification is applied to* $T = \{\neg P, P \vee Q\}$ *and* $SOS = \{\neg Q\}$ *of Example 5.1, according to the above schemes, we get* $T = \{\neg P\}$ *and* $SOS = \{\neg Q, P\}$*. Resolution of* $\neg P \in T$ *and* $P \in SOS$ *completes the proof.*

The following theorem summarizes the compatibility of contraction with semantic strategies:

Theorem 5.1 *Let I_1 denote a resolution inference system, I'_1 a semantic restriction of I_1, and I_2 a set of sound contraction inference rules. If I'_1 is refutationally complete and $I_1 \cup I_2$ is refutationally complete, then $I'_1 \cup I_2$, where the contraction rules in I_2 are applied according to the above schemes, is also refutationally complete.*

For instance, I_2 can contain clausal simplification and clausal subsumption. Results on the completeness of forward-reasoning (ordered) resolution strategies with contraction (i.e., the completeness of $I_1 \cup I_2$) may be found in the literature (e.g., [4, 10]).

The above schemes and theorem remain valid for resolution with set of support and lemmaizing with lemmas generated according to the rules of Section 4.1. One only needs to take care that whenever a contraction inference rule eliminates a subscripted literal in an SOS clause by applying another SOS clause, the residue is updated. We give an inference rule for clausal simplification as an example:

Clausal simplification of SOS by SOS

$$\frac{(T; SOS \cup \{Q, \neg Q'_L \vee C \vee [F]_L\})}{(T; SOS \cup \{Q, C \vee [F \vee \neg Q']_L\})} \quad Q\sigma = Q' \ \textit{for some}\ \sigma$$

where Q is a unit clause which may be either positive or negative. It is presented here as positive just for convenience. If Q' is not subscripted, the inference rule works in the same way but no residue is added. Notice that the difference between this clausal simplification rule and the subgoal elimination rule of Section 4.1 is that clausal simplification replaces a clause by another one, whereas subgoal elimination adds a new clause.

5.2 Purity deletion

One technique used quite effectively in subgoal-reduction strategies that has not been used at all in forward reasoning is the notion of *failure caching*. Failure caching says that if a goal literal fails, then it can be used to fail any similar goals in the future. Since there is usually no notion of a goal in a forward-reasoning strategy, it is little wonder that failure caching has not been used in this context.

A goal literal (in a subgoal-reduction strategy) fails if it does not unify with any literal of opposite sign in the given set of clauses. One can in fact adopt this idea to get the opposite effect of lemmaizing. To be more precise, if a literal cannot be resolved away, then obviously it cannot play a role in any derivation of refutation. Therefore, any clause which contains such a literal can be deleted. In fact, this idea already existed in the Davis-Putnam procedure [8], in which such a literal was called a *pure* literal. We adopt the name and generalize the notion by the following inductive definition:

Definition 5.1 *Let S be a set of clauses and A be a literal occurring in S.*

1. *If for all clause $C \in S$ there is no literal $B \in C$, such that $A\sigma = \neg B\sigma$ for some substitution σ, then A is* pure *in S.*
2. *If for all the clauses $C \in S$ that contains a B such that $A\sigma = \neg B\sigma$ for some σ, C contains an instance of a pure literal, then A is* pure *in S.*

Condition 1 (*basic purity*) is the basis of the definition, and Condition 2 is the inductive case, that represents a sort of *transitive closure* of purity. Its logical justification is that a clause that contains a pure literal is not necessary for the refutation, and therefore a literal that can resolve only with unnecessary clauses is also unnecessary, or pure.

Proposition 5.1 *If a literal A is pure, then any instance of A is also pure.*

Our inference rule states that any clause which contains a pure literal can be deleted:

Purity deletion

$$\frac{S \cup \{C\}}{S} \; \exists A \in C,\ A \textit{ is pure}$$

If clauses that contain pure literals are deleted, more literals may become pure. The inductive case of the definition of purity captures the propagation of basic purity caused by the application of the Purity Deletion rule: if all the clauses that A may resolve with contain a pure literal, all such clauses will be deleted by the Purity Deletion rule and therefore A will become pure according to basic purity. The inductive part of the definition "anticipates" this propagation effect. Therefore, in order to show that clauses containing pure literals can be deleted while preserving refutational completeness, it is sufficient to consider the basis of the definition of purity.

In propositional logic, if S is an unsatisfiable set of clauses and A is pure in S, then $S' = S - \{C | A \in C\}$ is also unsatisfiable. This is because if S' were satisfiable, there would be a Herbrand model I of S'. Since neither A nor $\neg A$ appears in S', neither of them needs to be in I. Then $I \cup \{A\}$ would be a model of S, contradicting the fact that S is unsatisfiable. The same reasoning does not apply in this form to a set of first-order clauses for the following reason: if A is a ground first-order literal, the fact that neither A nor $\neg A$ appears in S' does not imply that neither of them is in I, because A may be in the Herbrand base of S' even if it does not occur in S', and therefore either A or $\neg A$ may be in I. A mapping of ground first-order atoms into propositional variables, however, is sufficient to extend the reasoning to sets of ground first-order clauses:

Lemma 5.1 *Let S be a finite set of ground first-order clauses and $A(\bar{t})$ be a pure literal in S. If S is unsatisfiable, then $S' = S - \{C | A(\bar{t}) \in C\}$ is unsatisfiable.*

By applying the Herbrand theorem, the lemma can then be lifted to a set of general first-order clauses:

Theorem 5.2 *Let S be a finite set of first-order clauses and $A(\bar{t})$ a pure literal in S. If S is unsatisfiable, then $S' = S - \{C | A(\bar{t}) \in C\}$ is unsatisfiable.*

In summary, a pure literal in the forward-reasoning context has some similarity with a failed goal of subgoal-reduction strategies, since both notions are based on the impossibility of unifying the literal. Indeed, instances of pure literals are pure, like instances of failed goals also fail. In this sense, purity deletion echoes failure caching in forward-reasoning strategies.

6 Discussion

Forward-reasoning resolution strategies for first-order logic often suffer from generating too many irrelevant clauses. In order to control the growth of the database of clauses, contraction inference rules are usually employed. Subgoal-reduction strategies, on the other hand, lack the ability of producing useful lemmas which may reduce the search effort. The question of how to combine the best of the two worlds has long been a challenge to the automated deduction community.

In this paper we address this question by showing how the technique of lemmaizing can be extended and used in the general context of semantic strategies. We show how contraction rules can be incorporated in semantic strategies, even with lemmaizing. We also presented a new redundancy deletion method for forward-reasoning strategies which is based on a notion of purity.

Lemmaizing is a concept used in the logic programming community for saving previous execution results for later use. It has been used effectively both in enhancing Prolog [19] and in Prolog technology theorem proving [3]. In this paper we have shown how to generalize lemmaizing to semantic resolution, and how to integrate lemmaizing and contraction in such a strategy. Our approach has a number of advantages. Unlike previous work on lemmatization which is mostly limited to model elimination, it provides a general way of adding lemmas to the complement of the set of support. Therefore, it provides a flexible way of adding some forward-reasoning ability to goal-oriented strategies or, vice versa, some backward-reasoning ability to forward strategies. Our method also works with non-unit lemmas, and it does not have the left-to-right order of evaluation restriction which is common with subgoal-reduction strategies such as model elimination. Lastly, our work on purity highlights an intuitive correspondence between purity deletion and failure caching. This is complementary to the intuitive correspondence between subsumption and success caching suggested in [18], and therefore reinforces the understanding that while contraction eliminates redundancy in contraction-based strategies, caching eliminates redundancy in subgoal-reduction strategies.

Acknowledgements

We would like to thank Mark Stickel for answering our questions on caching in model elimination.

References

1. S. Anantharaman and J. Hsiang, Automated Proofs of the Moufang Identities in Alternative Rings, *Journal of Automated Reasoning*, Vol. 6, No. 1, 76–109, 1990.
2. O. L. Astrachan and D. W. Loveland, METEORs: High performance theorem provers using model elimination, in R.S.Boyer (ed.), *Automated Reasoning: Essays in Honor of Woody Bledsoe*, Kluwer Academic Publisher, Dordrecht, 1991.
3. O. L. Astrachan and M. E. Stickel, Caching and Lemmaizing in Model Elimination Theorem Provers, in D. Kapur (ed.), *Proc. of the 11th CADE*, Springer Verlag, LNAI 607, 224–238, 1992.
4. L. Bachmair and H. Ganzinger, On Restrictions of Ordered Paramodulation with Simplification, in M. E. Stickel (ed.), *Proc. of the 10th CADE*, Springer Verlag, LNAI 449, 427–441, 1990.
5. M. P. Bonacina and J. Hsiang, Towards a foundation of completion procedures as semidecision procedures, *Theoretical Computer Science*, Vol. 146, 199–242, July 1995.
6. M. P. Bonacina and J. Hsiang, On semantic resolution with lemmaizing and contraction, Tech. Rep., Dept. of Computer Science, University of Iowa, Sept. 1995.
7. C. L. Chang and R. C. Lee, *Symbolic Logic and Mechanical Theorem Proving*, Academic Press, New York, 1973.
8. M. Davis and H. Putnam, A computing procedure for quantification theory, *Journal of the ACM*, Vol. 7, 201–215, 1960.
9. S. Fleisig, D. Loveland, A. Smiley and D. Yarmash, An Implementation of the Model Elimination Proof Procedure, *Journal of the ACM*, Vol. 21, 124–139, 1974.
10. J. Hsiang and M. Rusinowitch, Proving Refutational Completeness of Theorem Proving Strategies: the Transfinite Semantic Tree Method, *Journal of the ACM*, Vol. 38, No. 3, 559–587, July 1991.
11. D. Kapur and H. Zhang, RRL: a Rewrite Rule Laboratory, in E. Lusk, R. Overbeek (eds.), *Proc. of the 9th CADE*, Springer Verlag, LNCS 310, 768–770, 1988.
12. D. W. Loveland, A Simplified Format for the Model Elimination Procedure, *Journal of the ACM*, Vol. 16, No. 3, 349–363, July 1969.
13. W. W. McCune, Otter 3.0 Reference Manual and Guide, Tech. Rep. ANL-94/6, Mathematics and Computer Science Division, Argonne Nat. Lab., Jan. 1994.
14. D. A. Plaisted, The Search Efficiency of Theorem Proving Strategies, in A.Bundy (ed.), *Proc. of the 12th CADE*, Springer Verlag, LNAI 814, 57–71, 1994, and Tech. Rep. MPI-I-94-233, Max Planck Institut für Informatik.
15. D. A. Plaisted, Non-Horn Clause Logic Programming Without Contrapositives, *Journal of Automated Reasoning*, Vol. 4, No. 3, 287–325, 1988.
16. M. Rusinowitch, Theorem-proving with Resolution and Superposition, *Journal of Symbolic Computation*, Vol. 11, No. 1 & 2, 21–50, Jan./Feb. 1991.
17. M. E. Stickel, A Prolog Technology Theorem Prover: Implementation by an Extended Prolog Compiler, *Journal of Automated Reasoning*, Vol. 4, 353-380, 1988.
18. M. E. Stickel, PTTP and Linked Inference, in R. S. Boyer (ed.), *Automated Reasoning: Essays in Honor of Woody Bledsoe*, Kluwer Academic Publishers, Dordrecht, 1991.
19. D. S. Warren, Memoing for logic programs, *Communications of the ACM*, Vol. 35, No. 3, 94–111, Mar. 1992.

Tableaux for Expansion and Contraction

Roderic A. GIRLE
Philosophy Department
University of Auckland, Auckland, NEW ZEALAND

e-mail: r.girle@auckland.ac.nz

ABSTRACT

The classical AGM account (Alchourrón, Gärdenfors and Makinson [1985]) of belief revision is an account of the process of changing sets of beliefs by either adding beliefs consistent with a belief set (*expansion*), or giving up beliefs (*contraction*). The AGM account is built on the notion of classically consistent theories which are closed under deductive consequence and include all the theorems of their base logic. We present an account of belief sets and belief change in terms of model-sets (Hintikka [1969]) and tableaux with flagged formulas. The account is four valued rather than two valued, and uses the values *true, not true, false* and *not false*. These are "believed" values. The account allows for paraconsistency. We draw on the semi-classical logics around **RM** (Dunn [1976]). The use of flagged formulas allows for a more subtle approach to both expansion and contraction.

Keywords: belief revision, paraconsistency, tableaux.

1.0 Introduction

The logic of belief revision provides a model for an ideal believer's belief states and their changes. The changes in belief state can, on many accounts, be categorised as of two basic kinds. When a belief is added to a belief state with which it is consistent there is *expansion*. When a belief is removed from a belief state there is *contraction*. *Revision* is a third kind of change which is definable in terms of the other two. When a belief is added to state with which it is inconsistent, first there is a contraction of all the beliefs which cause the inconsistency, and then an expansion with the new belief.

The AGM account (Alchourrón, *et. al.* [1985]), the classical account, begins with standard propositional logic in a deductive form, and builds its model of belief states as closed deductive theories which include all the theorems of the base logic. Belief sets are taken to be these closed theories. Belief changes are described in terms of relationships between the belief set theories. The account is essentially proof theoretic. But there is nothing to prevent the account from being semantic.

Nevertheless, a consideration of what a semantic account would be like opens up some interesting possibilities. It opens up the possibility of using truth-values other than just the set {**t, f**}. It also opens up the possibility of quite different accounts of belief states. The states described in AGM are states which, while not *omniscient* in the way of maximal sets, are omniscient in other problematic ways.

Belief states which contain all the theorems or valid sentences of a base logic make the believer *logically omniscient*, or *Cartesian*. If a believer believes all the consequences of their beliefs, then they are *deductively omniscient*. There is an extensive literature about both these kinds of omniscience. Both logical and deductive omniscience are seen as problematic. (Girle [1989b], Hocutt [1972])

We can avoid both of these forms of omniscience if we use model-set/model-system semantics (Hintikka [1969]), and make model-sets the formal models of belief states. Model-set semantics can be used to develop semantic tableaux. The tableaux are then available for both the expansion and contraction of belief states.

We will also be able to consider some variations on the notions of both expansion and contraction. The notions in the AGM account are essentially to do with "positive" belief. But, it may well be important in some contexts to know that the believer is "positively" undecided. The believer wishes to affirm that they neither believe nor disbelieve some proposition.

In this paper we will take the model-set account of belief states and use model-sets to give an account of belief states and belief state change. The mechanics of the system will be formulated in tableau terms. The tableaux make use of four values rather than two.

2.0 Values and Systems

We begin with a general point. According to Gärdenfors ([1988]) any epistemological theory will have two major features. There will be both an account of epistemic states, and an account of how those states change as a result of epistemic input. Epistemic inputs can be either the addition of belief content to an epistemic state or the derogation of belief content.

In the AGM account of belief revision the epistemic states are modelled in propositional fashion by belief sets. Belief sets are sets of sentences expressing the believed propositions. As Gärdenfors (pg. 22 [1988]) says:

> "Modelling epistemic states by sets of sentences is connected with a typology of epistemic attitudes that for any sentence *A* allows only the following three possibilities:
> *A* is accepted,
> *A* is rejected,
> *A* is indetermined, that is, *A* is neither accepted nor rejected.
> This typology can be reduced to two items by requiring *A* to be rejected iff $-A$ is accepted."

Belief sets contain accepted beliefs. This means that they contain the negations of rejected beliefs.

Given some language, there will be true sentences, false sentences, those which are neither true nor false. The sentences which are neither true nor false express propositions about which the agent has no belief. In Gärdenfors' terminology, they are *indetermined*.

The AGM belief sets are theories which contain all the theorems of the base logic (classical propositional logic), all the beliefs, and are closed under logical consequence. Belief states are modelled in a necessarily infinitistic way. They are definitely Cartesian.

In this paper we take the three assignments of Gärdenfors in a more explicit way, and consider a semantics for belief revision which effectively includes the three values *true, false* and *null*, and adds the value *both true and false* for contradictory belief. We will make some further comment about contradictory belief in section 4.0 below. These values are analogous to the value-sets in Dunn ([1976]) in the semantics for **RM**:

$$\{\{\ \}, \{\mathbf{t}\}, \{\mathbf{f}\}, \{\mathbf{t}, \mathbf{f}\}\}$$

The three non-null sets are used for **RM**.

In the semantics below we represent these in a different way. We use the values: *true, not true, false* and *not false*. These are abbreviated with: **t, nt, f** and **nf** respectively. Each sentence is assigned one of the four value-sets:

$$\{\mathbf{t}, \mathbf{f}\}, \{\mathbf{t}, \mathbf{nf}\}, \{\mathbf{f}, \mathbf{nt}\}, \{\mathbf{nt}, \mathbf{nf}\}$$

These value-sets represent *both true and false, just true, just false*, and *neither true nor false* respectively. We use all four sets. Instead of theories we make use of Hintikka's model-set/model-system semantics (Hintikka [1969]). Model-sets are not necessarily infinite and they include formulas of any of the four values.

The values are represented in the semantics by four truth-value flags. These flags are used in *flagged formulas*. So, **t***P* asserts that *P is at least true*. **f***P* asserts that *P is at least false*. **nt***P* asserts that *P is not true*. **nf***P* asserts that *P is not false*.

The use of these flagged formulas make it possible to add to a belief set the assertion that *P* is not believed true or false by adding **nt***P* and **nf***P* to the believer's belief set. In the case of contraction, when a belief is repudiated then **t***P* will not just be removed, but be replaced by **nt***P*. In this way a more thorough account will be given of the believer's belief state, and the way it grows and changes will be better reflected.

The use of these flagged formulas make it easy to set up tableaux and to implement these as automatic validity and consistency checkers (Girle [1989a]).

3.0 Semi-classical Model-set Semantics

We begin with the semi-classical logics **RM**, **RM-all** (**RM** with **all** values), and **RM-∅** (**RM** with the ∅ value). We can then define the set of valid formulas and semi-classical logical consequence for each logic.

The syntax for the **RM** logics includes propositional formulas constructed with the standard operators: $\sim, \&, \vee, \rightarrow$

The semantics for the **RM** logics is a model-set/model-system semantics. (Hintikka [1969], Girle [1982, 1995])

An **RM**-model-system, Ω, is a set of sets, κ_i $(i \geq 0)$, of flagged formulas, satisfying the conditions below. Members of a model-system are called *model-sets*. The model-system is the field of a binary relation, R. If $\kappa_i R \kappa_j$, then κ_i is said to have *relevant access* to κ_j. In each model-system there is a *base* model-set, designated as κ_0. Given the range of truth values, the semantics sets out separate conditions for true/not-true and for false/not-false. The membership conditions are taken from the following (where the letters $A, B, C, \ldots$ are formula schema):

(*C.*t∅) $\{\mathbf{t}A, \mathbf{nt}A\}$ *is not a sub-set of any model-set.*
(*C.*f∅) $\{\mathbf{f}A, \mathbf{nf}A\}$ *is not a sub-set of any model-set.*
(*C.*∅∅) $\{\mathbf{nt}A, \mathbf{nf}A\}$ *is not a sub-set of any model-set.*
(*C.*tf∅) $\{\mathbf{t}A, \mathbf{f}A\}$ *is not a sub-set of any model-set.*
(*C.*t~) *If* $\mathbf{t}{\sim}A \in \kappa_i$, *then* $\mathbf{f}A \in \kappa_i$.
(*C.*nt~) *If* $\mathbf{nt}{\sim}A \in \kappa_i$, *then* $\mathbf{nf}A \in \kappa_i$.
(*C.*f~) *If* $\mathbf{f}{\sim}A \in \kappa_i$, *then* $\mathbf{t}A \in \kappa_i$.
(*C.*nf~) *If* $\mathbf{nf}{\sim}A \in \kappa_i$, *then* $\mathbf{nt}A \in \kappa_i$.
(*C.*t&) *If* $\mathbf{t}(A \,\&\, B) \in \kappa_i$, *then* $\mathbf{t}A \in \kappa_i$ *and* $\mathbf{t}B \in \kappa_i$.
(*C.*nt&) *If* $\mathbf{nt}(A \,\&\, B) \in \kappa_i$, *then either* $\mathbf{nt}A \in \kappa_i$ *or* $\mathbf{nt}B \in \kappa_i$.
(*C.*f&) *If* $\mathbf{f}(A \,\&\, B) \in \kappa_i$, *then either* $\mathbf{f}A \in \kappa_i$ *or* $\mathbf{f}B \in \kappa_i$.
(*C.*nf&) *If* $\mathbf{nf}(A \,\&\, B) \in \kappa_i$, *then* $\mathbf{nf}A \in \kappa_i$ *and* $\mathbf{nf}B \in \kappa_i$.
(*C.*t∨) *If* $\mathbf{t}(A \vee B) \in \kappa_i$, *then either* $\mathbf{t}A \in \kappa_i$ *or* $\mathbf{t}B \in \kappa_i$.
(*C.*nt∨) *If* $\mathbf{nt}(A \vee B) \in \kappa_i$, *then* $\mathbf{nt}A \in \kappa_i$ *and* $\mathbf{nt}B \in \kappa_i$.
(*C.*f∨) *If* $\mathbf{f}(A \vee B) \in \kappa_i$, *then* $\mathbf{f}A \in \kappa_i$ *and* $\mathbf{f}B \in \kappa_i$.
(*C.*nf∨) *If* $\mathbf{nf}(A \vee B) \in \kappa_i$, *then either* $\mathbf{nf}A \in \kappa_i$ *or* $\mathbf{nf}B \in \kappa_i$.
(*C.*t→) *If* $\mathbf{t}(A \to B) \in \kappa_i$, *then*
either $\mathbf{nt}A \in \kappa_i$ *and* $\mathbf{f}A \in \kappa_i$ *or* $\mathbf{nt}A \in \kappa_i$ *and* $\mathbf{nf}B \in \kappa_i$
or $\mathbf{t}B \in \kappa_i$ *and* $\mathbf{f}A \in \kappa_i$ *or* $\mathbf{t}B \in \kappa_i$ *and* $\mathbf{nf}B \in \kappa_i$.
(*C.*t→) *If* $\mathbf{t}(A \to B) \in \kappa_i$ *and* $\kappa_i R \kappa_j$, *then*
either $\mathbf{nt}A \in \kappa_j$ *and* $\mathbf{f}A \in \kappa_j$ *or* $\mathbf{nt}A \in \kappa_j$ *and* $\mathbf{nf}B \in \kappa_j$
or $\mathbf{t}B \in \kappa_j$ *and* $\mathbf{f}A \in \kappa_j$ *or* $\mathbf{t}B \in \kappa_j$ *and* $\mathbf{nf}B \in \kappa_j$.
(*C.*nt→) *If* $\mathbf{nt}(A \to B) \in \kappa_i$, *then there is some model-set*
in the same model-system, say κ_j, *such that* $\kappa_i R \kappa_j$ *and*
either $\mathbf{t}A \in \kappa_j$ *and* $\mathbf{nt}B \in \kappa_j$ *or* $\mathbf{nf}A \in \kappa_j$ *and* $\mathbf{f}B \in \kappa_j$.
(*C.*f→) *If* $\mathbf{f}(A \to B) \in \kappa_i$, *then* $\mathbf{t}A \in \kappa_i$ *and* $\mathbf{f}B \in \kappa_i$.
(*C.*nf→) *If* $\mathbf{nf}(A \to B) \in \kappa_i$, *then either* $\mathbf{nt}A \in \kappa_i$ *or* $\mathbf{nf}B \in \kappa_i$.
(*C.Hered.* t) *If* $\mathbf{t}A \in \kappa_i$ *and* $\kappa_i R \kappa_j$, *then* $\mathbf{t}A \in \kappa_j$.
(*C.Hered.* f) *If* $\mathbf{f}A \in \kappa_i$ *and* $\kappa_i R \kappa_j$, *then* $\mathbf{f}A \in \kappa_j$.

The conditions for **RM** are all the above except for (*C.*∅∅)
The conditions for **RM-∅** are all the above except for (*C.*tf∅)
The conditions for **RM-all** are all the above except for both (*C.*∅∅) and (*C.*tf∅)

Where S ∈ {**RM, RM-∅, RM-all**} we define Validity

Def 1. S-Valid(A) iff there is no κ_0 such that $\mathbf{nt}A \in \kappa_0$

To define Semantic Consequence in S we need first to define the set $\mathbf{t}\Gamma$, where Γ is a set of unflagged formulas:

$$\mathbf{t}\Gamma = \{\mathbf{t}A : A \in \Gamma\}$$

Def 2. $\Gamma \models B$ iff there is no κ_0 such that both $\mathbf{t}\Gamma \subseteq \kappa_0$ and $\mathbf{nt}B \in \kappa_0$.

4.0 The Logical Character of the RM family

There are four observations. The first three reflect on the logical character of the **RM** family. The fourth concerns the nature of the model-set/model-system semantics.

First we note that even though these logics are non-classical, Double Negation equivalence and DeMorgan's Laws are Valid. One way of describing this is to say that, even though there are separate conditions for truth and falsity, they are quite classical for the operators $\sim$, & and $\vee$.

Second, the conditions for $\rightarrow$ are definitely non-classical. It is for the arrow that the possible world style of semantics is required. Nevertheless, the conditions for the false arrow are the same as for the material conditional. An arrow is false iff it has a straightforward counterexample, a true antecedent and a false consequent. Things are far more complex for the true arrow, as can be seen from the conditions above. Suffice it to say at this point that the true arrow with a true antecedent will have a true consequent, and a true arrow with a false consequent will have a false antecedent. So, in one sense, *modus ponens* holds for truth and *modus tollens* holds for falsehood. We discuss this further below.

Third, two of the logics are paraconsistent. A paraconsistent logic is one in which the following argument form is not valid:

$$\frac{(A \,\&\, \sim A)}{\therefore \quad B}$$

This is the *ex falso quodlibet* argument form. It is valid in classical first-order logic. It is the validity of *ex falso quodlibet* which sends classical logic into a frenzy of inferential idiocy in the face of contradiction.

The semantic fate of *ex falso quodlibet* in **RM** and **RM-all** can be seen by setting out a refutation tableau. We use "*(i)*" for "$\in \kappa_i$":

1.	$\mathbf{t}\,(A \,\&\, \sim A)$	*(0)*	*Premise*
2.	$\mathbf{nt}\,B$	*(0)*	*Not-true Conclusion*
3.	$\mathbf{t}\,A$	*(0)*	*from* 1. *(C.* **t**&*)*
4.	$\mathbf{t}\sim A$	*(0)*	*from* 1. *(C.* **t**&*)*
5.	$\mathbf{f}\,A$	*(0)*	*from* 4. *(C.* **t**$\sim$ *)*

There is no breach of the conditions for **RM** and **RM-all**. The conditions would be breached, and the tree close for **RM-∅**. The counter-example is:

$$\Omega = \{\kappa_0\}$$

$$\kappa_0 = \{\mathbf{nt}\,B, \mathbf{t}\,A, \mathbf{f}\,A\}$$

It is "surprising" that we see:

$$\{\mathbf{t}\,A, \mathbf{f}\,A\} \subseteq \kappa_0$$

Paraconsistent logics enable us to cope with contradictory belief sets. Such sets are non-trivial in paraconsistent logic. The advantages of this are discussed in many places including (Girle [1992] and [1995]). Briefly, two of the advantages are that the model of the ideal agent is more realistic, because real life believers often have inconsistent belief sets without the triviality concomitant upon a classical account of belief sets. The paraconsistent account also avoids the dangers of triviality arising from deeply hidden contradictions in a single agent's beliefs, or in a shared or distributed set of beliefs. This danger is all the more acute in a first-order system because of undecidability. It is inconsistency, especially, for which there is no decision procedure.

Nevertheless, our advocacy of a paraconsistent approach is not to be taken as an advocacy the view that there are no problems with inconsistent belief sets. Of course, there are. In most cases, it is important to have a strategy for getting rid of inconsistency. But in some cases it may be undesirable, for the time being, to remove inconsistency. If the inconsistencies are best not removed, then a paraconsistent logic will allow them to remain with minimum disruptive effect.

Fourth, the semantics for model-sets are *decompositional* rather than *constructional*. Standard semantics builds models by beginning with a truth-value assignment to all the atomic formulas (of a propositional logic), and then gives a recursive account of how values "spread upwards" to more complex formulas by appeal to their syntactic construction. In model-set semantics, the values are given to formulas of any complexity and then "spread downwards" by decomposing the formulas and assigning values to the sub-formulas. Standard semantics is bottom up, model-set semantics is top down.

The top down nature of the semantics means that it can be applied directly in semantic tableau. The conditions for membership of model-sets in model-systems give rules for tableaux (Girle [1982, 1989a]).

5.0 Tableaux for the Logics Near RM

The conditions above readily convert to the tableau schema below:

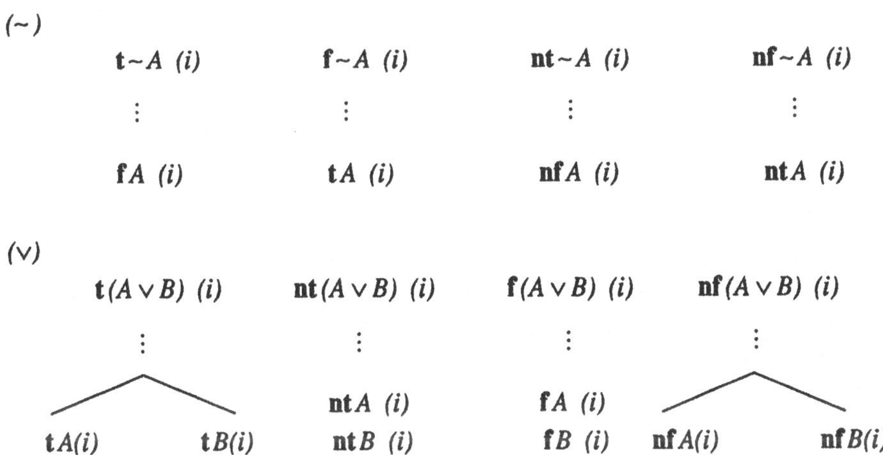

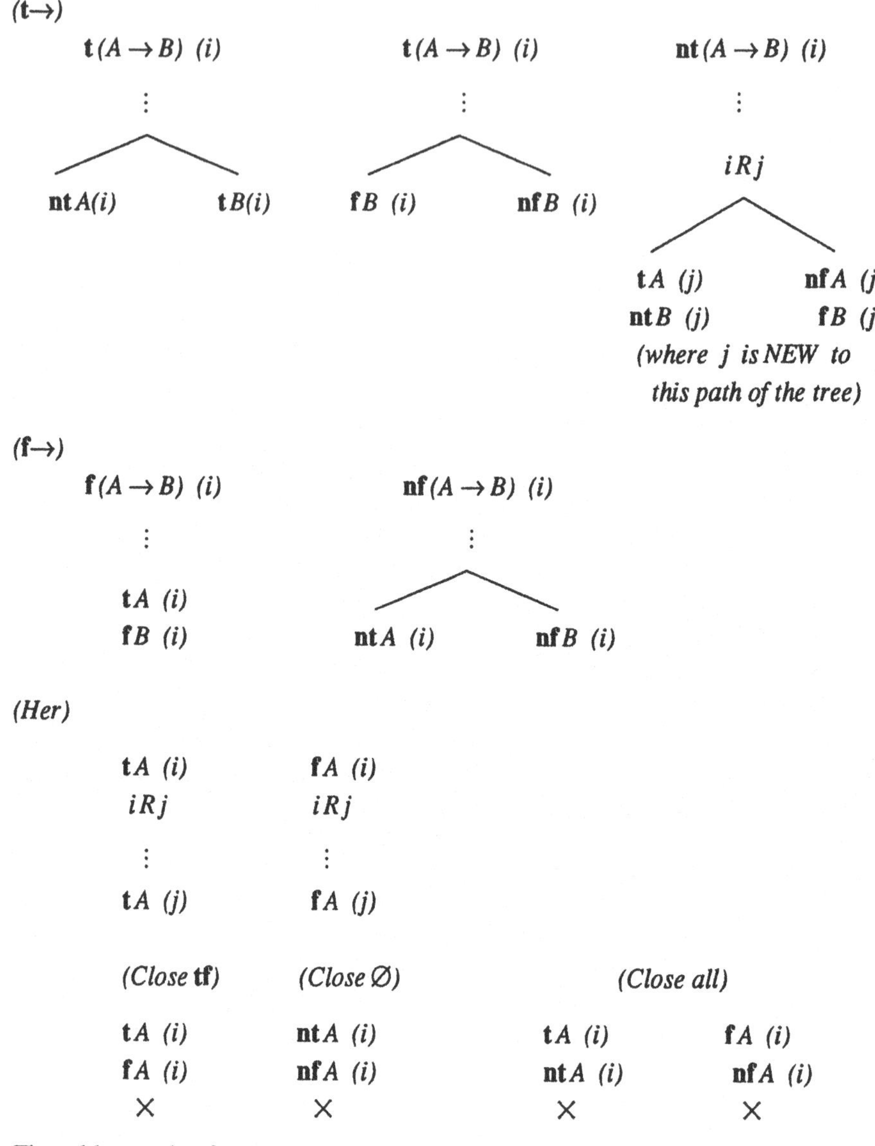

The tableau rules for & can easily be worked out and are "DeMorgan Symmetric" with the rules for $\vee$.

The tableau rules *(Close all)* apply to all the logics around **RM**. If *(Close all)* are the only closure schema, then we have the tableau rules for **RM-all**. If we add just the rule *(Close* $\varnothing$*)* then we have the tableau rules for **RM-**$\varnothing$. If we add just *(Close* **tf***)* then we have the rules for **RM**.

6.0 Base Model-sets and Belief Sets

If we were to make *base* model-sets our belief sets, then we would gain several things from this departure from the use of theories as the models for belief states. First, we would have a *non-Cartesian* account of belief states. Belief states would not contain all the theorems (valid formulas) of the base logic. We would have *partial* sets in the sense of van Bentham (Chapter 8 [1988]) and Jaspers ([1995]). van Bentham uses tableaux as examples of partiality. The belief sets would still behave in a logically well regulated way, relative to the base logic. But this would be the result of the semantic regulation of the model-sets.

Secondly, there would not be full logical consequence closure, or deductive omniscience. There would be some closure. It would be the decompositional closure regulated by the decompositional conditions. This would not be as determinate as the closure in the AGM and analogous accounts. The closure operations could be displayed by semantic tableaux. Each open path of a tableau would give the possible contents of the belief set.

Thirdly, if one were to add to the belief set (base model-set), then a tableau would show whether this could be done by expansion, or whether a revision would be required. In the former case, there would be open paths to show the expansion options. If there were no open paths, then the closed tableau would show how the new belief contradicts the contents of the present belief set. The tableau would then provide the candidates for contraction.

Fourth, expansion and contraction could be more subtle than is presently possible in the AGM account. We consider these possibilities in more detail in the next section.

Fifth, the implementation technology for the tableaux for this approach has been thoroughly explored.

7.0 Expansion and Contraction

Standard AGM theory can be set out in terms of just *expansion* and *contraction*. Expansion is where a belief is added to a set of beliefs to give an expanded belief set. Contraction is where a belief is taken away from a set of beliefs to give a contracted belief set. A *revision* of a belief set with respect to A is where the set is first contracted by the removal of $\sim A$, and then expanded by the addition of A.

In the AGM account the belief sets are closed under logical consequence. So, if we define:

$$Cn(\Gamma) = \{A : \Gamma \vdash A\}$$

then, for any belief set K, we have:

$$K = Cn(K)$$

If K is expanded, by the addition of B, to get K', then:

$$K' = Cn(K \cup \{B\})$$

If K is contracted, by the deletion of B, to get K', then the closure of K' does not contain B:

$$K' = Cn(K - H) \text{ and } B \in H \text{ and } B \notin K'$$

This account of contraction means that when a belief is abandoned, many other beliefs may have to be abandoned also. Enough beliefs will have to be abandoned so that the remaining, contracted, belief set will not include B in its consequence set, and hence in itself. Gärdenfors recommends "minimal change" in contraction ([1988] p.66 ff.). In any case, there may be many ways of determining H. So, there may be many ways of contracting K with respect to B. A major problem in belief revision theory is the problem of deciding just which set of beliefs, H, should be removed from K when it is contracted.

7.1 Expansion

We now turn to a more detailed consideration of expansion. The standard postulates for expansion in the AGM theory are:

Where K is an AGM belief set, the expansion of K by P is: K^+_P

(K^+1) K^+_P is a belief set

(K^+2) $P \in K^+_P$

(K^+3) $K \subseteq K^+_P$

(K^+4) If $P \in K$ then $K^+_P = K$

(K^+5) If $K \subseteq H$ then $K^+_P \subseteq H^+_P$

(K^+6) For all belief sets K and all sentences P, K^+_P is the smallest belief set that satisfies (K^+1)-(K^+5).

It might be thought that all we have to do is generalise these postulates to four flags to get the postulates for model-set expansion and all will be just as it is in the AGM account. At one very high level of abstraction this might be true, but at the direct level of application to particular belief sets this is not so. It has to be remembered that model-sets can contain formulas with any of the four flags – provided, of course, that the membership conditions are satisfied. Consider the following straight forward generalisation of AGM and then a particular belief set:

Where κ is a belief set and ϕ is a flag, the expansion of κ by ϕP is: $\kappa^+{}_{\phi P}$

($K^+\phi 1$) $\kappa^+{}_{\phi P}$ is a belief set

($K^+\phi 2$) $\phi P \in \kappa^+{}_{\phi P}$

($K^+\phi 3$) $\kappa \subseteq \kappa^+{}_{\phi P}$

($K^+\phi 4$) If $\phi P \in \kappa$ then $\kappa^+{}_{\phi P} = \kappa$

($K^+\phi 5$) If $\kappa \subseteq \lambda$ then $\kappa^+{}_{\phi P} \subseteq \lambda^+{}_{\phi P}$

($K^+\phi 6$) For all belief sets κ and all flagged sentences ϕP, $\kappa^+{}_{\phi P}$ is the smallest belief set that satisfies ($K^+\phi 1$)-($K^+\phi 5$).

Now consider the following (model-set) belief set, κ.

$\kappa = \{\mathbf{t}p, \mathbf{t}(p \rightarrow r), \mathbf{nt}\,s, \mathbf{nf}\,s\}$

There are three things about κ. First, let us compare this with an AGM belief set. κ is not an AGM belief set. The AGM belief set, say K, would be the deductive closure of the set union of the set of base logic theorems and the set $\{p, (p \rightarrow r)\}$:

$$\mathrm{K} = Cn(\{p, (p \rightarrow r)\})$$

We could "derive" K from κ:

$$\mathrm{K} = Cn(\{A : \mathbf{t}A \in \kappa \text{ or } \mathbf{f}{\sim}A \in \kappa\})$$

But note that there would be no positive acknowledgment of $\mathbf{nt}\,s$ and $\mathbf{nf}\,s$ in K.

Second, the agent, by means of $\mathbf{nt}\,s$ and $\mathbf{nf}\,s$ in our κ, makes it clear that they have no opinion about s. This is a *positive agnosticism*. There might also be a more equivocal agnosticism. There may be a situation in which an agent wished to deny truth (or falsehood) without being able positively to affirm falsehood (or truth). Such avoidance of the Law of Bivalence is not unknown. This can be made quite explicit in a model-set, but not in an AGM belief set.

Third, it can easily be shown that the κ above is a model-set in all of the **RM** family of logics. It does not breach any of the membership conditions.

Now consider what happens when the agent decides to add $\mathbf{t}(p \rightarrow s)$ to κ. There would be no real problem for such an addition to K in AGM. We would get the expanded set $\mathrm{K}^{+}_{(p \rightarrow s)}$ It would be the set:

$$\mathrm{K}^{+}_{(p \rightarrow s)} = Cn(\{p, (p \rightarrow r), (p \rightarrow s)\})$$

But for our account, the flagged formula *cannot just be added* to κ. If it were, we would have the model-set κ′:

$\kappa' = \{\mathbf{t}(p \rightarrow s), \mathbf{t}p, \mathbf{t}(p \rightarrow r), \mathbf{nt}\,s, \mathbf{nf}\,s\}$

This set is *not* a model-set for any of the **RM** family of logics. The tableau with this set at its root will *close*:

1.	$\mathbf{t}(p \rightarrow r)$	*(0)*	in κ and κ′
2.	$\mathbf{t}p$	*(0)*	in κ and κ′
3.	$\mathbf{nt}\,s$	*(0)*	in κ and κ′
4.	$\mathbf{nf}\,s$	*(0)*	in κ and κ′
5.	$\mathbf{t}(p \rightarrow s)$	*(0)*	in κ′
6.	$\mathbf{nt}p$ *(0)* × / $\mathbf{t}s$ *(0)* ×		from 5.

An inspection of the tableau shows that either $\mathbf{t}p$ or $\mathbf{nt}\,s$ will have to be removed from κ (or somehow dealt with) if the addition of $\mathbf{t}(p \rightarrow s)$ is to succeed. So, the addition of this new belief is not, as it would be in AGM, just an expansion. It is now a revision. First there has to be a contraction, then an expansion.

But there is more. The new fifth postulate becomes problematic. To see why, let us ring the changes and make:

$$\lambda = \{\mathbf{t}p, \mathbf{t}(p \rightarrow r), \mathbf{nt}s, \mathbf{nf}s\}$$

$$\kappa = \{\mathbf{t}p, \mathbf{t}(p \rightarrow r), \mathbf{nf}s\}$$

so that $\kappa \subseteq \lambda$. Now we know that (new) κ can be expanded with $\mathbf{t}(p \rightarrow s)$. But λ cannot. From a formal point of view the expansion of λ to λ' does not exist. In other words, if:

$$\lambda' = \{\mathbf{t}(p \rightarrow s), \mathbf{t}p, \mathbf{t}(p \rightarrow r), \mathbf{nt}s, \mathbf{nf}s\}$$

then λ' is not a model-set. So the fifth postulate fails. Of course, in AGM the derived sets, L and K, would be identical and the case would not be a counter-example to the fifth postulate.

The result is that our account is of non-monotonic expansion. This could be source of great rejoicing to the lovers of non-monotonic logic.

7.2 Contraction

We turn now to contraction. The real problem with contraction in the AGM account is a problem of how to choose what to *remove* from a belief set. If a choice has to be made, then beliefs of lesser importance would be removed before those of greater importance. Various ways of ordering the beliefs in terms of greater and lesser importance are *entrenchment* orderings. Entrenchment ordering is transitive. When deciding on what to remove, the lesser entrenched beliefs are removed first.

Logical considerations also indicate that if $A \vdash B$ then *A is less entrenched than B*. If we remove B then A has to go. But, logical considerations alone cannot provide a complete entrenchment ordering of beliefs in a belief set. Other considerations have to come into play.

In our account it would be best *not* to remove any elements, but to *re-flag* them. Information is not altogether lost. Consider our case above. We have the parenthetical remark, "or somehow dealt with", after the tableau. The tableau shows how the addition of $\mathbf{t}(p \rightarrow s)$ generates two options which both fail. The tableau pinpoints the logical source of the failure in both cases.

We could either re-flag $\mathbf{nt}s$ to $\mathbf{t}s$ or re-flag $\mathbf{t}p$ to $\mathbf{nt}p$. In the first case the revised κ becomes κ':

$$\kappa' = \{\mathbf{t}(p \rightarrow s), \mathbf{t}p, \mathbf{t}(p \rightarrow r), \mathbf{t}s, \mathbf{nf}s\}$$

In the second case the revised κ becomes (let us say) κ'':

$$\kappa'' = \{\mathbf{t}(p \rightarrow s), \mathbf{nt}p, \mathbf{t}(p \rightarrow r), \mathbf{t}s, \mathbf{nf}s\}$$

Both κ' and κ'' are model-sets. (In fact they are subsets of possible model-sets, just as κ is.) They give us the options for contraction. If we also had some entrenchment ordering, even a quite arbitrary one, it would tell us at once what should be re-flagged.

Our approach means that belief sets are always growing. This might raise fears of combinatorial explosion. But, the growth is not the sort of growth that would ensue if the sets grew to encompass all that is entailed by deductive closure.

8.0 Conclusion

The base logics around **RM**, and their model-set/model-system semantics provide us with a way alternative to the AGM account of modelling an ideal agent's belief states and belief changes. The account is multi-valued, semantic, and paraconsistent. It offers a different, more limited and more subtle, and more realistic account of the belief agent's states, powers and belief change options.

We have shown that the tableau mechanisms are most effective in handling expansion and contraction. Tableaux give us a way of managing change for finite belief sets. There is a maximal conservation of information and a more subtle approach to belief change.

9.0 References

Alchourrón, C.E., P. Gärdenfors, and D. Makinson. 1985. "On the logic of Theory Change: Partial meet functions for contraction and revision." *Journal of Symbolic Logic* 50: 510-530

Dunn, J.M. 1976. "A Kripke-Style Semantics for R-Mingle Using a Binary Accessibility Relation", *Studia Logica*, 35, 163-172.

Gärdenfors, P. 1988. *Knowledge in Flux: Modeling the Dynamics of Epistemic States*, The MIT Press, Cambridge, Mass.

Girle, R.A. 1982 "Semantic Tableau for Logics around **RM**", *Australian Logic Teachers' Journal*, 6(3), 1-20.

Girle, R.A. 1989a "Logic Programming with Semi-classical Model-set Semantics", *Ninth International Workshop Expert Systems and their Applications, General Conference, Volume 1*, Avignon, May 29-June 2, 101-114.

Girle, R.A. 1989b. "Computational Models for Knowledge", *Proceedings of the Australian Joint Artificial Intelligence Conference*, Melbourne, Vic, Nov. 14-17, 104-119

Girle, R.A. 1992. "Inconsistent Belief and Logic" in *Advances in Artificial Intelligence Research, Vol 2*, Eds. Fishman, M.B. and J.L. Robards, JAI Press, London, 23-36.

Girle, R.A. 1995. "Tolerating Contradiction in Knowledge Representation", *Proceedings of the Eighth Florida Artificial Intelligence Research Symposium*, Melbourne, Florida, April 27-29, 1-5.

Hintikka, J.K. 1969. *Models for Modalities*, Reidel, Dordrecht.

Hocutt, M.O. 1972. "Is Epistemic Logic possible?", *Notre Dame Journal of Formal Logic* 13 (4), 433-453

Jaspars, Jan. O. M. 1995. "Partial Up and Down Logic", *Notre Dame Journal of Formal Logic*, 36 (1), 134-157

van Bentham, J. 1988. *A Manual of Intensional Logic* 2nd Ed. Revised and Expanded, CSLI, Stanford.

Translating Machine-Generated Resolution Proofs into ND-Proofs at the Assertion Level

Xiaorong Huang

Fachbereich Informatik, Universität des Saarlandes
Postfach 15 11 50, D-66041 Saarbrücken, Germany
e-mail: huang@cs.uni-sb.de

Abstract. Most automated theorem provers suffer from the problem that the resulting proofs are difficult to understand even for experienced mathematicians. Therefore, efforts have been made to transform machine generated proofs (e.g. resolution proofs) into natural deduction (ND) proofs. The state-of-the-art procedure of proof transformation follows basically its completeness proof: the premises and the conclusion are decomposed into unit literals, then the theorem is derived by multiple levels of proofs by contradiction. Indeterminism is introduced by heuristics that aim at the production of more elegant results. This indeterministic character entails not only a complex search, but also leads to unpredictable results.

In this paper we first study resolution proofs in terms of meaningful operations employed by human mathematicians, and thereby establish a correspondence between resolution proofs and ND proofs at a more abstract level. Concretely, we show that if its unit initial clauses are CNFs of literal premises of a problem, a unit resolution corresponds directly to a well-structured ND proof segment that mathematicians intuitively understand as the application of a definition or a theorem. The consequence is twofold: First it enhances our intuitive understanding of resolution proofs in terms of the vocabulary with which mathematicians talk about proofs. Second, the transformation process is now largely deterministic and therefore efficient. This determinism also guarantees the quality of resulting proofs.

1 Introduction

Most automated theorem provers suffer from the problem that they can produce proofs only in formalisms difficult to understand even for experienced mathematicians. In many applications, in particular if it is used as a mathematical assistant, it is crucial that the system and a user can communicate in an effective way. Only if a system also talks his language, a user will be convinced by machine-found proofs and feel his understanding of the topic improved. Since no current system can solve a wide range of challenging problems efficiently and the situation will not change in the near future, a user has to understand intermediate results in order to provide further guidance. Therefore, various efforts have been made to *reconstruct* natural deduction (ND) proofs [Gen35] from such machine-generated proofs [And80, Mil83, Pfe87, Lin90, SK95].

Current procedures that transforms resolution proofs follow basically their completeness proof. Starting from a problem in a ND framework that contains the hypotheses and the conclusion, it first recursively decomposes the premises and the conclusion until literals are reached. Then the conclusion is proved by multiple levels of proofs by contradiction. To come up with more elegant proofs, this basic procedure was enriched with heuristics. Up to now there are only isolated heuristics that cover some specific proof structures, and they are often formulated as vague guide lines [Lin90, PN90]. When no heuristics are applicable, ND proofs thus constructed tend to be very awkward. Below is an artificial example to illustrate the worst case. The proof is encoded in the linearized version of natural deduction first used in [And80], which we will use throughout this paper. The numbers after the line number represent the logical hypotheses a line depends on. The inference rule that justifies a line is given after the conclusion formula, followed by the premise lines. Considering that this problem can be proved with one step of modus-ponens, the proof below is indeed awkward enough.

No	Hyp		Formula	Reason
1.	1	$\vdash$	A	(Hyp)
2.	2	$\vdash$	$A \Rightarrow B$	(Hyp)
3.	3	$\vdash$	$\neg B$	(Hyp)
4.	2	$\vdash$	$\neg A \vee B$	(Tau 2)
5.	5	$\vdash$	$\neg A$	(Hyp)
6.	1,5	$\vdash$	$\bot$	(¬E 1 5)
7.	7	$\vdash$	B	(Hyp)
8.	3,7	$\vdash$	$\bot$	(¬E 3 7)
9.	1,2,3	$\vdash$	$\bot$	(Case 4 6 8)
10.	1,2	$\vdash$	B	(Ind 9)

Not only the quality is not predicable, such heuristics introduces a complex search space. Take the proof above again as an example, the system must choose between modus-ponens and case analysis. In some sense, the previous transformation procedures involve a search anew for a proof in the ND framework, utilizing some information of a proof found in another formalism. It is therefore not very surprising that the transform is sometimes more expensive than the original problem solving.

Another problem with the current approach is its target representation itself. Although each single step in an ND proof is easy to understand, the entire proof is usually at the level of a logic calculus and contain too many tedious steps. In contrast, informal proofs found in standard mathematical textbooks are primarily justified by applications of definitions or theorems. For instance, the derivation of $a \in F$ from $U \subset F$ and $a \in U$ is usually justified by applying the definition of a subset encoded as

$$\forall S_1, S_2 . S_1 \subset S_2 \Leftrightarrow \forall x . x \in S_1 \Rightarrow x \in S_2 \tag{1}$$

In [Hua94b], the author formalized the intuitive notion of the application of a definition or a theorem (collectively called *assertions*), as well as a procedure that substantially shortens ND proofs by abstracting them to the assertion level.

This paper attempts to show certain resolution proofs can be understood intuitively in the same way. Concretely, we will consider unit resolution proofs where the initial unit clauses are produced from literal hypotheses lines of the problem formulated in ND. We call them *SSPU*-resolutions (unit resolutions for simple-structured problems). Let us first examine the resolution proof below, obtained by restructuring a machine-found proof (compare Section 3.3). The numbering of the clauses are quite unnatural, but their meaning will become clear, once we show how they are derived from the original ones.

Example 1

The set of initial clauses:

$C1 = \{+(a * a^{-1} = e)\}$ $\qquad$ $C2 = \{+(e * a^{-1} = a^{-1})\}$

$C3 = \{-(x \in S), -(y \in S), -(x * y^{-1} = z), +(z \in S)\}$

$C4 = \{+(a \in S)\}$ $\qquad$ $C5 = \{-(a^{-1} \in S)\}$

The resolution steps:

C3,1 & C4,1 : add R2': $\{-(y \in S), -(a * y^{-1} = z), +(z \in S)\}$
R2',1 & C4,1 : add R3': $\{-(a * a^{-1} = z), +(z \in S)\}$
C3,2 & C4,1 : add R4': $\{-(x \in S), -(x * a^{-1} = z), +(z \in S)\}$
R3',1 & C1,1 : add R5': $\{+(e \in S)\}$
R4',2 & C2,1 : add R6': $\{-(e \in S), +(a^{-1} \in S)\}$
R5',1& R6',1 : add R1': $\{+(a^{-1} \in S)\}$
R1',1& C5,1 : add R7: $\square$

Fig. 1. An *SSPU*-resolution Proof

Note that $C3$ is the CNF the subgroup criterion given below:

$$\forall x. \forall y. x \in S \land y \in S \Rightarrow y * x^{-1} \in S \tag{2}$$

This resolution proof basically consists of two applications of (2). The first one is the subproof rooted at $R5'$ that derives $e \in S$ from $a \in S$ and $a * a^{-1} \in S$. The second one is the subproof rooted at $R1$', which derives $a^{-1} \in S$ from $e \in S$, $a \in S$ and $e * a^{-1} \in S$.

Section 2 characterizes *SSPU*-resolutions, which can be understood as a sequence of applications of assertions. Based on this correlation Section 3 specifies a deterministic procedure that transforms *SSPU*-resolutions into neatly structured ND proofs with assertion level justifications. This section also describes how *SSPU-refutable* proofs can be restructured into *SSPU*-resolution proofs. Section 4 contains techniques that split an arbitrary resolution into interrelated *SSPU*-resolution segments. The transformation process as a whole is largely deterministic and therefore efficient, reducing heuristic search only to the strategies that split nonunit-refutable proofs to unit-refutable proofs. This determinism also guarantees the quality of resulting proofs. Finally, we conclude this paper with a discussion of future improvements.

2 Application of an Assertion

To obtain proofs similar to those found in mathematical textbooks, the author has proposed a more abstract level of justifications for ND-style proofs, called *assertion level* [Hua92, Hua94b], where derivations are justified by the application of definitions or theorems (collectively called *assertions*).

Example 2 The application of the definition of subset (1) discussed in the introduction is logically equivalent to the compound proof segment below[1]:

$$\dfrac{\dfrac{\dfrac{\dfrac{\dfrac{\mathcal{A}:\ \forall S_1, S_2.\, S_1 \subset S_2 \Leftrightarrow (\forall x.\, x \in S_1 \Rightarrow x \in S_2)}{U \subset F \Leftrightarrow (\forall x.\, x \in U \Rightarrow x \in F)}\forall E}{U \subset F \Rightarrow (\forall x.\, x \in U \Rightarrow x \in F)}\Leftrightarrow E \qquad U \subset F}{\forall x.\, x \in U \Rightarrow x \in F}\Rightarrow E}{a \in U \Rightarrow a \in F}\forall E \qquad a \in U}{a \in F}\Rightarrow E$$

Actually, the notion of the application of an assertion is specified in terms of a so-called *decomposition-composition* constraint imposed on such proof segments [Hua92, Hua94b]. The following two definitions are necessary for the discussion of this constraint.

Definition (Decomposition Rule) An inference rule of the form $\frac{\Delta\vdash F, \Delta\vdash P_1,\ldots,\Delta\vdash P_n}{\Delta\vdash Q}$ is a *decomposition* rule with respect to the formula schema F, if all applications of it, written as $\frac{\Delta\vdash F', \Delta\vdash P'_1,\ldots,\Delta\vdash P'_n}{\Delta\vdash Q'}$, satisfy the following condition: each $P'_1, \ldots, P'_n$ and Q' is

- (the negation of) a proper subformula of F', or
- (the negation of) a specialization of F' or of one of its proper subformulas.

Intuitively, a decomposition rule derives a conclusion that is part of one of its premises. Furthermore, other premises are also part of this special premise. Under this definition, $\frac{\Delta\vdash A\wedge B}{\Delta\vdash A}\wedge\mathrm{E}$ and its dual, $\frac{\Delta\vdash A\Rightarrow B, \Delta\vdash A}{\Delta\vdash B}\Rightarrow\mathrm{E}$, as well as $\frac{\Delta\vdash\forall x.\, P[x]}{\Delta\vdash P[a]}\forall\mathrm{E}$ are the only decomposition rules in the natural deduction calculus $\mathcal{NK}$ [Gen35]. To emphasize that the variable x occurs in P, we represent P by $P[x]$. Furthermore, we added the rule $\frac{\Delta\vdash A\vee B, \Delta\vdash\neg B}{\Delta\vdash A}\vee\mathrm{E}$ and its dual to decompose disjunctions. The definition of composition rule is similar, but omitted due to space restrictions.

The decomposition-composition constraint can now be stated in a fairly simple way with the help of proof tree above. It requires that derivation along the branch from the assertion $\mathcal{A}$, which is always a leaf, to the root are all justified by a decomposition rule. This branch is called the *main branch*, which consists exclusively of a sequence of decompositions. Other premises needed in the series of decompositions along the main branch (the leaves $U \subset F$ and $a \in U$ in the proof above) can be obtained by compositions. This actually guarantees that all intermediate nodes in such a proof tree is (the negation of) a subformula of the assertion applied, which explains why we call it an application of an assertion [Hua92, Hua94b].

2.1 *SSPU*-Resolution

This section characterizes a class of resolution proof segments that can be seen as a sequence of applications of certain assertions. Since this concept is first

[1] Only in this example, we present an ND proof as a tree to discuss the constraints.

defined in terms of ND proofs, we thereby establish a correspondence between these seemingly very different formalisms at a more abstract level. We begin with the characterization of one step of application of an assertion in terms of resolution.

Theorem 1 (R-Application of an assertion)

Let π be a resolution proof with one non-unit initial clause A, n unit initial clauses $P_1, P_2, \ldots, P_n$, and a unit final resolvent Q. $\frac{P_1, P_2, \ldots, P_n}{Q}$ can be justified as an application of A', if $P_1, P_2, \ldots, P_n$ and Q are ground and contain no skolem constant, and A is the the CNF of A'.

We call such a resolution proof segment an *R-application*. Instead of a formal inductive proof (see [HM96]), we provide an intuitive explanation. To do so, let us reexamine the decomposition-composition constraint. Basically it says, if an assertion is universally quantified, instantiate it only with one constant; if it is a conjunction, use only one branch of it; if it is a disjunction, try to negate the other branches and then use the remaining branch. ND inference rules handling hypotheses and thereby causing branching of a proof, like the case analysis and choice rule, are forbidden. Translated into resolution, this constraint means that only one clause normalized from an assertion is involved (hence only one non-unit clause, actually a condition stronger than necessary), and variables can be instantiated only once (hence ground premises). The unit premises and the unit conclusion condition can be understood in light of the $\vee$E rule. The restriction on skolem constants is due to the lack of decomposition rules for instantiating existentially quantified formulas.

Example 2 (Continued)

Let us return to the example used in the last section, and examine the corresponding *R-application* illustrated below:

The set of initial clauses:

$C1 = \{+(a \in U)\}$ $\quad\quad$ $C2 = \{+(U \subset V)\}$

$C3 = \{-(S_1 \subset S_2), -(x \in S_1), +(x \in S_2)\}$

The resolution steps:

C2,1 & C3,1: add R1: $\{-(x \in U), +(x \in V)\}$

R1,1 & C1,1: add R2: $+(a \in V)$

Apparently different formulations of the same problem may lead to the same clause form. Since the transformation of a resolution proof starts with a original problem formulation, it is sensitive to the structure of such formulations. Below we first consider an R-application with a simple problem structure.

Definition (Simple-Structured Problem)

A simple-structured problem (*SSP*) is of the following structure:

$$(A_1 \wedge \cdots \wedge A_m) \wedge (P_1 \wedge \ldots \wedge P_n) \Rightarrow Q$$

where $(A_1 \wedge \ldots \wedge A_m)$ is a conjunction of definitions or theorems, $(P_1 \wedge \ldots \wedge P_n)$ is a conjunction of (quantified) literals serving as the premises of the current problem, and the (quantified) literal Q is the conclusion.

Definition (*SSPU*-resolution)

A unit resolution is called an *SSPU*-resolution (unit resolution for simple-structured problems), if the initial unit clauses are produced from the premises and the conclusion of a *SSP* problem.

An *SSPU*-resolution is called *ground*, if all its unit clauses are ground and contain no skolem constants. This implies that the premises and the conclusion are all ground literals. An *SSPU*-resolution is called *degenerated* if it contains the empty clause □ as its only resolvent. This is the case when two initial unit clauses are contradictory.

3 From *SSPU*-Resolution to Assertion Level ND-Proofs

3.1 The Basic Procedure for Ground *SSPU*-Resolution

This subsection first presents a deterministic algorithm that transforms *SSPU*-resolution proofs into ND proofs at the assertion level. We start with a procedure for ground *SSPU*-resolutions. It is based on the observation that a ground *SSPU*-resolution is a sequence of *R-applications* according to theorem 1. Apart from the resolution proof and the ND proof under construction, our algorithm maintains a relation δ that associates every unit initial clause and unit resolvent r with an ND proof line l, where r is the CNF of the formula in line l. This is denoted by $\langle r, l\rangle \in \delta$, and is an extension to the δ relation used in [Lin89].

Basic Procedure:

1. Initialization: Introduce the assertions, the premises and the negation of the conclusion as hypothesis lines, and initialize the δ relation to establish the correspondence between the initial clauses and the initial ND lines.
2. Translation: For every unit resolvent r do the following (suppose the subtree in the resolution proof rooted by r has leaves $(r_1, \ldots, r_n)$, $\langle r_i, l_i\rangle \in \delta$. C is the unique non-unit initial clause in this subtree, being the CNF of an ND line L): add a line l to the ND proof, which derives r from lines $l_1, \ldots, l_n$ by applying the assertion L, add $\langle r, l\rangle$ to δ.
3. Derive the conclusion by contradiction.

We will illustrate algorithm using example 1 throughout the paper. The development of the example is reverse to the order of actual processing: each time the input proof is produced by the operation described in the next session. The original proof found by the MKRP system [EO86] will be given in section 4.

Example 1(Continued)

The input resolution proof for this session can be found in Fig. 1. Together with the problem formulation below, it forms an *SSPU*-resolution proof:

- Premises: $a \in S \wedge a * a^{-1} = e \wedge e * a^{-1} = a^{-1}$
- Assertion: $\forall x. \forall y. x \in S \wedge y \in S \Rightarrow y * x^{-1} \in S$
- Conclusion: $a^{-1} \in S$

Both unit resolvents R5' and R1' in the proof in Fig. 1 are derived by an application of $C3$. First the sequence (a subtree) R2', R3', R5' derives $e \in S$ from the premises $a \in S$ and $a * a^{-1} = e$. Second the sequence R4', R6', R1' derives $a^{-1} \in S$ using as premises $a \in S$ and $e * a^{-1} = a^{-1}$. Finally, R1' is used to derive □. This is a ground *SSPU*-resolution proof that can be transformed into an assertion level ND-proof by our basic procedure, see next page.

No	Hyp		Formula	Reason
			Initialization	
1.	1	$\vdash$	$\forall x, y, z. x \in S \wedge y \in S \wedge x * y^{-1} = z \Rightarrow z \in S$	(Asser1)
2.	2	$\vdash$	$a * a^{-1} = e$	(Hyp)
3.	3	$\vdash$	$e * a^{-1} = a^{-1}$	(Hyp)
4.	4	$\vdash$	$a \in S$	(Hyp)
5.	5	$\vdash$	$\neg(a^{-1} \in S)$	(Hyp)
			Translation	
6.	2,1,4	$\vdash$	$e \in S$	(Asser1 4 4 2)
7.	2,3,1,4	$\vdash$	$a^{-1} \in S$	(Asser1 6 4 3)
8.	2,3,1,4,5	$\vdash$	$\bot$	($\neg$E 5 7)
			Contradiction	
9.	2,3,1,4	$\vdash$	$a^{-1} \in S$	(Ind 8)

Note that the conclusion has already been derived in line 7 and that the last two lines are superfluous. This always happens when the conclusion clause is used only in the last step. Actually, we employ a refined version that avoids such indirect proofs. In this example, it skips line 5, 8 and 9.

Theorem 2 (Transformation Theorem)
Let $R_1, R_2, \ldots, R_n$ be the sequence of unit resolvents of a ground SSPU-*resolution proof π. Our basic procedure above produces from π an ND-style proof at the assertion level with $R_1, R_2, \ldots, R_n$ as its intermediate results.*
This theorem follows direct from theorem 1 by induction.

3.2 Decomposing Leaves of *SSPU*-resolution

Viewing proofs as trees, a unit resolution is a sequence of subtrees rooted at a unit resolvent. The basic procedure subsequently transforms such subtrees into an assertion level step in an ND proof, if the premises (the leaves) and the conclusion (the root) are ground literals. Otherwise, additional transformations are needed in order either to instantiate an *SSPU*-resolution, or to decompose the ND proof lines associated with the leaves of a resolution proof into literals.

Rule I$\forall$ below instantiates universal quantifiers which appear in a premise line. See [HM96] for a complete set of rules, these rules are adapted from [And80, Lin90].

I$\forall$ Rule

$$\begin{array}{llll} l_1 & \mathcal{A} & \vdash \forall x. F[x] & \text{Rule } \mathcal{R} \\ l_3 & \mathcal{A} & \vdash G & \pi \end{array} \quad \rightsquigarrow \quad \left\{ \begin{array}{llll} l_1 & \mathcal{A} & \vdash \forall x. F[x] & \text{Rule } \mathcal{R} \\ l_2 & \mathcal{A} & \vdash F[a] & \forall E\ l_1 \\ l_3 & \mathcal{A} & \vdash G & \pi' \end{array} \right.$$

Note that the resolution proof π that justifies l_3 must be instantiated to π'. The δ relation must be updated so that the literals connected with l_1 are connected with l_2 afterwards.

3.3 Constructing *SSPU*-Resolutions by Permutation

Unit-refutable resolutions can be restructured into unit resolutions. If they are associated with a *SSP*, we call them *SSPU-refutable*. This property can be easily tested using the following property, which can be proven by induction.

Property ($SSPU$-refutable)

Let C, L, U be the number of non-unit initial clauses, the number of literals in non-unit initial clauses, and the number of unit initial clause in a ground version of a resolution proof π, π is SSPU-refutable *iff* $2(C-1)+U=L$.

Algorithm Permuting $SSPU$-Resolution Proofs

- subsequently do for every resolvent r:
  - If r does not results from a unit resolution step, then postpone r by removing r and connecting other resolvents using r as a parent clause to a proper parent clause of r.
  - If r results from a unit resolution step, keep r.
  - If a postponed resolution can be carried out as a unit resolution step, carry it out.
- If the empty clause is derived, report success, otherwise failure.

Example 1 (Continued)

The resolution proof below is an instantiation of a proof found by the theorem prover MKRP for the theorem stated previously. Note that the unit initial clauses are all ground. The resolution proof used in Fig. 1 can be obtained by the algorithm above.

The set of initial clauses:

$C1=\{+(a*a^{-1}=e)\}$ $\quad C2=\{+(e*a^{-1}=a^{-1})\}$

$C3=\{-(x\in S),-(y\in S),-(x*y^{-1}=z),+(z\in S)\}$

$C4=\{+(a\in S)\}$ $\quad C5=\{-(a^{-1}\in S)\}$

The resolution steps:

C3,4 & C3,1: add R1: $\{-(x\in S),-(y\in S),-(x*y^{-1}=z),-(y'\in S),$
$-(z*y'^{-1}=z'),+(z'\in S)\}$

R1,1 & C4,1: add R2: $\{-(y\in S),-(a*y^{-1}=z),-(y'\in S),$
$-(z*y'^{-1}=z',+(z'\in S)\}$

R2,1 & C4,1: add R3: $\{-(a*a^{-1}=z),-(y'\in S),-(z*y'^{-1}=z'),+(z'\in S)\}$

R3,2 & C4,1: add R4: $\{-(a*a^{-1}=z),-(z*a^{-1}=z'),+(z'\in S)\}$

R4,1 & C1,1: add R5: $\{-(e*a^{-1}=z'),+(z'\in S)\}$

R5,1 & C2,1: add R6: $\{+(a^{-1}\in S)\}$

R6,1 & C5,1: add R7: $\Box$

Fig. 2. Instantiated MKRP-Resolution Proof

Notice, clauses R2' to R6' in Fig. 1 are transformed from R2 to R6. R1' corresponds to R1, which is postponed. The difference between the two proofs can be intuitively described as follows: since R1 in Fig. 2 can be viewed as an application of C3 on itself, the two natural sequences in Fig. 1 are mixed up here. A refinement is also made to even produce *direct* $SSPU$-resolution proofs, where the conclusion clause is postponed until the last step.

3.4 The Basic Procedure Enriched

Based on the discussion above, now we can present the complete basic procedure that transforms all *SSPU-refutable* resolutions into an ND proof at the assertion level.

Basic Procedure (Enriched):

2. Translation:
   (a) For each unit leaf r in the resolution proof such that $(r,l) \in \delta$, decompose l until it is a ground literal (see section 3.2),.
   (b) Create an $SSPU$-resolution proof from a *SSPU-refutable* proof by permutation(see section 3.3).
   (c) If degenerated $SSPU$-resolution, apply rule I$\perp$ (see below).
   (d) for every unit resolvent r do the following (suppose the subtree in the resolution proof rooted by r has leaves $r_1, \ldots, r_n$, and $(r_i, l_i) \in \delta$. C is the unique non-unit initial clause in this subtree, being the CNF of an ND line L): add a line l to the ND proof, which derives r from lines $l_1, \ldots, l_n$ by applying the assertion L, add $\langle r, l\rangle$ to δ.

I$\perp$ Rule

$$\begin{array}{llll} l_1 & \mathcal{A} & \vdash F & \text{Rule } \mathcal{R} \\ l_2 & \mathcal{A} & \vdash \neg F & \text{Rule } \mathcal{R}' \end{array} \quad \leadsto \quad \left\{\begin{array}{llll} l_1 & \mathcal{A} & \vdash F & \text{Rule } \mathcal{R} \\ l_2 & \mathcal{A} & \vdash \neg F & \text{Rule } \mathcal{R}' \\ l_3 & \mathcal{A} & \vdash \perp & (\neg E l_1, l_2) \end{array}\right.$$

To summarize, the algorithm above creates an indirect ND-style proof at the assertion level for every *SSPU-refutable* proof. The resulting proof is basically a sequence of applications of assertions involved, interleaved with some instantiations and decompositions. If the conclusion clause is used only in the last step, it even produces a direct proof.

4 Splitting an Arbitrary resolution into SSPU-Refutable Proof Segments

To become a $SSPU$-resolution, however, a proof needs enough unit clauses. In this section, we introduce transformation rules which split an arbitrary resolution proof into a set of interrelated $SSPU$-resolution proofs. Since non-unit clauses are CNFs of disjunctive premises (including negated conjunctions) or a conjunctive conclusion, we need two dual rules to handle them. The M-Case rule below is one of them. It splits the original resolution proof π into π_1 and π_2 [HM96].

M-Case Rule

$$\begin{array}{llll} l_1 & \mathcal{A} & \vdash F \vee G & \text{Rule } \mathcal{R} \\ l_4 & \mathcal{A} & \vdash H & \pi \end{array} \quad \leadsto \quad \left\{\begin{array}{llll} l_1 & \mathcal{A} & \vdash F \vee G & \text{Rule } \mathcal{R} \\ l_2 & F & \vdash F & \text{Hyp} \\ l_3 & \mathcal{A}, F & \vdash H & \pi_1 \\ l_4 & G & \vdash G & \text{Hyp} \\ l_5 & \mathcal{A}, G & \vdash H & \pi_2 \\ l_6 & \mathcal{A} & \vdash H & \text{Case}(l_1, l_3, l_5) \end{array}\right.$$

Summarizing the discussion up to now, our procedure first splits an arbitrary resolution proof into *SSPU-refutable* subproofs, and then proceeds according to the relation between $SSPU$-resolution and the application of assertions. The slitting is basically the same as the traditional procedure, only it is carried out in a controlled way: We distinguish between premises to be decomposed to literals, and definitions and theorems that should act as the assertions in *SSPU*-resolutions. For the split of resolution proofs and for the decomposition of ND lines connected to the leaves of *SSPU-refutable* proofs, we have adapted a complete subset of the transformation rules described in [Lin90]. Below is the integrated algorithm that transforms an arbitrary resolution proof into an ND proof with assertion level justifications. Note that since steps justified by the application of an assertion is defined in terms of a compound ND proof segment, they can be expanded correspondingly if required by a user.

An Integrated Algorithm:

1. If the input resolution is *SSPU*-refutable, then call the basic procedure.
2. Otherwise partition the premises into premises and assertions if not already specified and split one non-unit clause which is the CNF of a premise. Recursively call this algorithm with all subproofs created by splitting.

The completeness of the algorithm is obvious. If a resolution proof has enough unit clause, we can always decompose (if necessary) the corresponding ND lines to make it a *SSPU*-resolution. Otherwise, we can alway split it to increase the number of unit clauses. The basic procedure is very efficient, since the transformation of *SSPU*-resolution and the permutation are both linear. Since the heuristic search used in previous systems is restricted to the strategies concerning the split of resolution proofs, which is seldom used more than one or two times in most tasks, our transformation is usually much cheaper than the original search process. Actually, a high percentage of real-world mathematical problems we have encountered are *SSPU*-resolution, including all examples handled by Lingenfelder [Lin89, Lin90], although this is a question of statistics.

Example 1 (Continued)

Finally, we examine the entire transformation process of example 1 already discussed in section 3.1 and 3.3. The original proof produced by the theorem prover MKRP is given below (edited for layout and renaming):

The set of initial clauses:

$C1 = \{+(u * u^{-1} = e)\}$ $\qquad C2 = \{+(e * w = w)\}$

$C3 = \{-(x \in S), -(y \in S), -(x * y^{-1} = z), +(z \in S)\}$

$C4 = \{+(v \in S)\}$ $\qquad C5 = \{-(q^{-1} \in S)\}$

The resolution steps:

C3,4 & C3,1:	add R1:	$\{-(x \in S), -(y \in S), -(x * y^{-1} = z), -(y' \in S),$ $-(z * y'^{-1} = z'), +(z' \in S)\}$
R1,1 &C4,1:	add R2:	$\{-(y \in S), -(v * y^{-1} = z), -(y' \in S),$ $-(z * y'^{-1} = z', +(z' \in S)\}$
R2,1 &C4,1:	add R3:	$\{-(v * v^{-1} = z), -(y' \in S), -(z * y'^{-1} = z', +(z' \in S)\}$
R3,2 &C4,1:	add R4:	$\{-(v * v^{-1} = z), -(z * v^{-1} = z'), +(z' \in S)\}$
R4,1 &C1,1:	add R5:	$\{-(e * v^{-1} = z'), +(z' \in S)\}$
R5,1 &C2,1:	add R6:	$\{+(v^{-1} \in S)\}$
R6,1 &C5,1:	add R7:	$\square$

This proof can be transformed into an assertion level ND proof by the following steps. The initialization creates line 1, line 2, line 3, and line 10. Decomposition of the conclusion line 10 then adds line 9 and line 4. Simultaneously, all variables in the unit initial clauses, namely u, w, v, q are instantiated to a, a^{-1}, a, a, as given in Fig. 2, producing line 5 and line 6. The instantiated resolution proof is then permuted as described in section 3.3. Finally, the basic procedure translates two *R-applications* as described in section 3.1, and adds line 7 and line 8. Note that the two assertion level steps in line 7 and line 8 can be expanded into calculus level ND proof segments in a schematic way.

NNo	Hyp		Formula	Reason
1.	1	$\vdash$	$\forall x, y, z.\, x \in S \wedge y \in S \wedge x * y^{-1} = z \Rightarrow z \in S$	(Asser1)
2.	2	$\vdash$	$\forall u.\; u * u^{-1} = e$	(Def-Inverse)
3.	3	$\vdash$	$\forall u.\; e * u = u$	(Def-Unit)
4.	4	$\vdash$	$a \in S$	(Hyp)
5.	2	$\vdash$	$a * a^{-1} = e$	(Def-Inverse)
6.	3	$\vdash$	$e * a^{-1} = a^{-1}$	(Def-Unit)
7.	2,1,4	$\vdash$	$e \in S$	(Asser1 4 4 5)
8.	2,3,1,4	$\vdash$	$a^{-1} \in S$	(Asser1 7 4 6)
9.	2,3,1	$\vdash$	$a \in S \Rightarrow a^{-1} \in S$	($\Rightarrow$I 8)
10.	2,3,1	$\vdash$	$\forall x.\, x \in S \Rightarrow x^{-1} \in S$	($\forall$I 9)

This work is implemented as part of a system called *PROVERB*, which transforms and verbalizes machine-found proofs [Hua94a]. The final proof above can be verbalized by the system *PROVERB* as following:

> "Let a be in S. According to the definition of inverse element, $a * a^{-1} = e$. According to our hypothesis, e is in S. $e * a^{-1} = a^{-1}$ according to the definition of unit. Again according to our hypothesis, a^{-1} is in S."

5 Discussion

Instead of formulating transformation strategies at the level of ND inference rules as in earlier works, we try to understand resolution proofs directly in terms of the vocabularies human mathematicians use to talk about proofs. We have shown, that an *SSPU*-resolution corresponds directly to ND proof segments that mathematicians intuitively understand as the application of an assertion. The significance of this result is mainly twofold. First, contrary to the intuition of many, some resolution proofs, after some restructuring, become quite readable themselves. This leads to a natural correspondence between resolution proofs and ND proofs at a more abstract level. Second, since variations at the calculus level are abstracted away, the main part of our algorithm is deterministic. Better resulting proofs can now be obtained for all examples involving interesting definitions and theorems, as it is usually the case in mathematical problems. For these problems the cost of transformation is linear. Nevertheless, there are limitations to our approach. The performance does not improve much for typical logical exercises concerning primarily manipulations of nested quantifications. A simple example is the theorem $\exists x.\, \forall y.\, [P(x) \Rightarrow P(y)]$.

The system *PROVERB* as it stands is already used in various ways. Assertion level proofs that are transformed from resolution proofs or that are abstracted from ND proofs are used to facilitate user's understanding, to serve as the basis to formulate methods of proof planning, and to produce natural language proofs.

Although we replaced the basic transformation procedure used [Lin90], It is reasonable to investigate how certain global strategies experimented there can be incorporated into our procedure, in particular those concerning the split of resolution proofs and concerning the insertion of a lemma [PN90, Lin90]. We are also working to extend the notion of $SSPU$-resolution to deal with factorizations and paramodulations. Another interesting future development is the adaptation of this technique for other proof formalisms, for instance expansion trees and connection proofs [SK95].

References

[And80] P. Andrews. Transforming matings into natural deduction proofs. In *Proc. of the 5th International Conference on Automated Deduction*, 1980.

[EO86] N. Eisinger and H. J. Ohlbach. The Markgraf Karl Refutation Procedure. In *Proc. of 8th International Conference on Automated Deduction*, 1986.

[Gen35] G. Gentzen. Untersuchungen über das logische Schließen I. *Math. Zeitschrift*, 39:176–210, 1935.

[HM96] X. Huang and A. Maier. Natual deduction proofs can be short as resolution proofs. Seki-report, Universität des Saarlandes, 1996. forthcoming.

[Hua92] X. Huang. Applications of assertions as elementary tactics in proof planning. In V. Sgurev and B. du Boulay, editors, *Artificial Intelligence V - Methodology, Systems, Applications*, pages 25–34. Elsevier Science, 1992.

[Hua94a] X. Huang. *PROVERB*: A system explaining machine-found proofs. In *Proc. of 16th Annual Conference of the Cognitive Science Society*, 1994.

[Hua94b] X. Huang. Reconstructing proofs at the assertion level. In *Proc. of 12th International Conference on Automated Deduction*, Springer, 1994.

[Lin89] C. Lingenfelder. Structuring computer generated proofs. In *Proc. of IJCAI-89*, 1989.

[Lin90] Christoph Lingenfelder. *Transformation and Structuring of Computer Generated Proofs*. PhD thesis, Universität Kaiserslautern, 1990.

[Mil83] D. Miller. *Proofs in Higher-Order Logic*. PhD thesis, CMU, 1983.

[Pfe87] F. Pfenning. *Proof Transformation in Higher-Order Logic*. PhD thesis, CMU, 1987.

[PN90] F. Pfenning and D. Nesmith. Presenting intuitive deductions via symmetric simplification. In *Proc. of 10th International Conference on Automated Deduction*, 1990.

[SK95] S. Schmitt and C. Kreitz. On transforming intuitionistic matrix proofs into standard-sequent proofs. In *Proc. of the 4th Workshop on Theorem Proving with Analytic Tableaux and Related Methods*, 1995.

Evidential Temporal Representations and Reasoning

Bingning Dai David A. Bell John G. Hughes
School of Information and Software Engineering Faculty of Informatics
University of Ulster at Jordanstown
Newtownabbey
Co. Antrim, BT37 0QB
Northern Ireland, UK.
E-mail: B.Dai, DA.Bell, JG.Hughes@ulst.ac.uk

Abstract. The work described in this paper is part of the theoretical foundation for an expressive Temporal Evidential Database model, which has many applications in areas that recognise *the changing and uncertain world*, such as robotics, diagnosis, and natural language understanding. In this paper, based on Allen's interval algebra, (1) a modified interval algebra is proposed, which incorporates the concept of *chronon* from temporal databases to avoid the point-or-interval dilemma in temporal reasoning formalisms; (2) *constant-time-stamps* are introduced into temporal relationship networks to model absolute time; (3) indefinite temporal information is modelled using *evidential intervals*. Through reasoning in the resulting Evidential Temporal Constraint Networks, not only all possible temporal relationships between two given events can be found, but also the credibility of these relationships can be deduced in a tractable way. The latter has been neglected in past temporal reasoning research while is necessary in querying temporal databases where indefinite information is about when an event occurs or occurred rather than whether the event occurs or occurred or not.

1 Introduction

Most of the present temporal reasoning formalisms have been focused on reasoning about qualitative and quantitative temporal relationships (note that *temporal relationships*, *relative temporal information* and *temporal constraints* are loosely of the same meaning), regardless of whether they are based on points, intervals, or points and intervals (see [17] for a more detailed introduction). Allen's interval algebra [1] is most influential, and there has been much work focusing mainly on the tractability of the algebra (e.g., [18], [21] and [22]). Relatively little effort has been put on considering issues of absolute time, indefinite time and the credibility of temporal relationships. Among the exceptions are [12] introducing absolute time into temporal relationship graphs, [5], [6] and [3] using fuzzy representations for time.

In temporal databases, although relative temporal information and indefinite temporal information have received some attention ([4], [13] and [14]), only [7] has considered the evaluations of the credibility of temporal relationships in queries. These evaluations are necessary just as in non-temporal indefinite databases (e.g., [15]). Note that in these temporal databases, indefinite information is about when an event occurs or occurred rather than whether the event occurs or occurred or not [7].

Based on the above observations, this paper is trying to lay a theoretical foundation to tackle these unsolved problems. The temporal ontology introduced in this paper incorporates Allen's interval temporal algebra with the *chronon* concept in temporal databases [11]. Absolute times are modelled using *constant-time-stamps*. Viewing mass functions as generalised probability distributions, Dempster-Shafer (D-S) theory is applied to representing indefinite time and indefinite temporal relationships in an Evidential Temporal Constraint Network (ETCN). The credibility degree of a temporal relationship in the network can be computed and then represented by evidential functions (e.g., belief functions *bel* and plausibility functions *pls*).

The evidential temporal model based on this ontology allows the representations of both valid time and transaction time using bi-temporal elements [10] managed in an ETCN. The model is part of the Temporal Evidential Database System (TEDS). Using D-S theory and its extensions to represent the credibility of information is a distinctive feature of the TEDS. The application example of the TEDS at present is a medical record database system, while the TEDS can have many other applications in areas that recognise *the changing and uncertain world*, such as robotics, diagnosis, and natural language understanding.

The rest of this paper is organised as follows. Section 2 presents the temporal ontology without indefinite information. It will be shown how the chronon view is incorporated into an interval algebra and thus to avoid the point-or-interval dilemma (e.g., [2] and [12]). Section 3 is a brief introduction to the basics of D-S theory. In Section 4, evidential representations of indefinite time and temporal relationships in ETCNs are illustrated. Conclusions and future work are presented in Section 5.

2 Temporal Ontology

2.1 Points and Intervals

In our model, the time primitives are intervals derived from points. The concept of *point* is different from that in AI. A point here is a time unit with a given granularity, which is in accordance with the *chronon* concept defined in temporal databases [11].

Let P be a finite set of such discrete time points. By defining a complete order "$\prec$" and "=" in the usual sense on P, P is bounded by p_{start} (the lower bound) and p_{end} (the upper bound). Functions *prec* and *succ* get the precedence and the successor of a given point respectively. There are different such P's according to different granularity and bounds. For example, {*1Jan95, 2Jan95, ..., 31Dec95*} is a P with the granularity *day* and bounded by *1Jan95* and *31Dec95*. In the TEDS, such P's are managed in a system dictionary and p_{start} and p_{end} are unified in the sense that all the p_{start}'s begin at the same p_{start} that has the finest granularity and all the p_{end}'s end at the same p_{end} that has the finest granularity. For example, another P which can appear in the TEDS with the previous example is {*Jan95, Feb95, ..., Dec95*} with the granularity *month* and bounded by *Jan95* and *Dec95*.

A time interval is defined as a pair of points $\langle i_s, i_e \rangle$, where $i_s, i_e \in P$, $i_s \prec i_e$ or $i_s = i_e$. All of these intervals are closed at both ends. If $i_s = i_e$, the interval represents a point. The finite set of these intervals is I.

When necessary, a time point can be transformed into an interval with a finer granularity, or another point containing it with a coarser granularity. Similarly, an interval may be transformed by transforming its end points first. When the transformed end points are two intervals, take the starting point of the original starting point as the new starting point and the end point of the original end point as the new end point. Table 1 shows two examples of such transformations.

Table 1. Transforming intervals with different granularities

day(finer granularity)	*month*(original granularity)	*year*(coarser granularity)
⟨*1Feb1995,28Feb1995*⟩	*Feb1995*	*1995*
⟨*1Mar1995,31May1995*⟩	⟨*Mar1995,May1995*⟩	*1995*

2.2 Facts and Events

In AI, a basic distinction between facts and events is that whether they are instantaneous or have duration. Since there are only intervals in our model, a physical time point is the time that starts some chronons and ends some chronons. The physical time point that ends p and the physical time point that starts *succ*(p) are the same. So are the physical time points that ends *prec*(p) and that starts p. The assumptions are: a fact that holds during $\langle i_s, i_e \rangle$ is true from the physical time point that starts i_s to the physical time point that ends i_e; an event that happens during $\langle i_s, i_e \rangle$ takes place at the physical time point that starts i_s or the physical time point that ends i_e. Thus, the arguments over points and intervals in AI are avoided by not discussing physical time points directly.

2.3 Interval Temporal Relationships

In Allen's interval algebra, there are thirteen possible relationships between two time intervals. They are: *before*, *after*, *equal*, *meets*, *met-by*, *overlaps*, *overlapped-by*, *during*, *contains*, *starts*, *started-by*, *finishes* and *finished-by*. As the result of the discussions in the previous two subsections, *meets* and *met-by* are not needed in our model, which were intended to represent physical time points in the logic[1]. Thus, given two intervals i and i' with the same granularity, there are basically six relationships from i to i' in our model. The other five relationships can be defined by these relationships from i' to i. All these relationships can be mapped into the relationships among their end points. The mapping is shown in the following table:

Table 2. The relationships between two time intervals: $i = \langle i_s, i_e \rangle$ and $i' = \langle i'_s, i'_e \rangle$, and the relationships among their end points[2]

from i to i'	from i' to i	among end points
before (<)	after (>)	$i_e \prec i'_s$
equal (=)	equal (=)	$i_s = i'_s$, $i_e = i'_e$
overlaps (*o*)	overlapped-by (*oi*)	$i_s \prec i'_s$, $i_e \prec i'_e$, $i'_s \prec i_e$
during (*d*)	contains (*di*)	$i'_s \prec i_s$, $i_e \prec i'_e$
starts (*s*)	started-by (*si*)	$i'_s = i_s$, $i_e \prec i'_e$
finishes (*f*)	finished-by (*fi*)	$i'_s \prec i_s$, $i_e = i'_e$

The pair of relationships in each row in Table 2 are the *inverse* of each other. Let

$$R = \{<, >, =, o, oi, d, di, s, si, f, fi\},$$

two subsets $R_1, R_2 \subseteq R$ are called *inverse* of each other if there is a one-one mapping between them, where every two matched relationships are the inverse of each other. For example, $\{d, si, =\}$ and $\{di, s, =\}$ are the inverse of each other.

Note that explicit definitions for point-point, point-interval, and interval-point temporal relationships are not necessary in our model, because points are represented as intervals with identical end points. For example, if $i_s = i_e$ and $i'_s = i'_e$ in Table 2 meaning that i and i' are two points, the temporal relationships between i and i' can only be $\{<, =, >\}$, which is just the case.

2.4 Temporal Constraint Networks Representing Absolute and Relative Time

The temporal constraint networks (TCNs) representing absolute and relative time are similar to Allen's temporal relationship networks [1], where the nodes represent individual intervals and each arc is labelled to indicate the possible relationships between the two intervals represented by its nodes. The transitivity table for the temporal relationships, which is omitted here due to the limited space, is similar to the temporal relationship transitivity table in [1], excluding the *m*, *mi* rows and columns, and all the *m*, *mi* in other items. See Fig. 1.a and 1.b for examples.

---

1 *meets* was even further axiomatised to represent both points and intervals in [16].

2 The notations of temporal relationships are the same as in [1].

Intervals which are absolutely known are stamped by constant time, called *constant-time-stamps*. For example, given "Patient A was under treatment T in May" and i_1 standing for the interval when "Patient A was under treatment T" happened, i_1 is stamped by *May* in the TCN (See Fig. 1.c for a similar example). The temporal constraints among such constant-time-stamped intervals can be completely computed. Thus, these intervals form a reference sub-network. This sub-network improves the tractability of the relationship transitivity or the constraint propagation ([1] and [12]).

Informally, to represent disjunctive temporal information[3] in TCNs such as

$$i_1\ r_1\ i_2 \vee i_1\ r_2\ i_3,$$

two nodes are created for i_1 connected by an arc labelled specially as "or". One of such nodes is connected to i_2 labelled r_1 and the other is connected to i_3 labelled r_2. The number of repetitions of the interval in question is equal to the number of the disjuncts (Fig. 1.d).

i1 {o,s} → i2 {<} → i3

a. Basic

i1 {o,s} → i2 {<} → i3; i1 {<} → i3

b. After transitivity

i1 {>, oi} → i2
or
i1 {>, oi} → i3

d. With disjunctive information

i1 {o,s} → i2(<1May1995,20May1995>) {<} → i3(<28May1995,3July1995>); i1 {<} → i3

c. With constant-time-stamped intervals

Fig. 1. Examples of temporal constraint networks

3 Dempster-Shafer (D-S) Theory[4] Basics

In D-S theory, a *frame of discernment* Θ is the set of propositions about the mutually exclusive and exhaustive possibilities in a domain, which is a finite non-empty set.

Definition 1. *A mass function m is:* $m: 2^{\Theta} \to [0,1]$, *where*

$$m(\emptyset) = 0, \sum_{X \subseteq \Theta} m(X) = 1.$$

An $X(\subseteq \Theta)$ *is called a focal element of m when* $m(X) > 0$. ◊

---

3 This will not be elaborated further due to the limited space and its less relevance to the main points of this paper.

4 Please refer to [8], [9] and [19] for elaboration of this theory.

In the rest of this paper, a mass function will be denoted by $\{S_1/m(S_1), ..., S_n/m(S_n)\}$, where $S_i(1 \le i \le n)$ are the focal elements, i.e. $m(S_i) > 0$. And the following notations will be used hence forth while not causing ambiguity: (1) since when there is only one focal element S, its mass must be 1, the mass function will be denoted by S; (2) a set will be denoted by its member directly omitting the braces if it is a singleton.

Definition 2 (Evidential functions *bel* and *pls*). *Given a mass function m, a belief function bel is defined on* 2^Θ, *for all* $A \subseteq \Theta$: $bel(A) = \sum_{X \subseteq A} m(X)$. *Then a plausibility function pls is defined as* $pls(A) = \sum_{X \cap A \neq \varnothing} m(X) = 1 - bel(\overline{A})$, *for all* $A \subseteq \Theta$. ◊

Theorem 1 (Combination of mass functions). *Let* m_1, m_2 *be mass functions on the same frame* Θ. *Suppose* $E = \sum_{X \cap Y = \varnothing} m_1(X) m_2(Y) < 1$. *Denote* $N = \sum_{X \cap Y \neq \varnothing} m_1(X) m_2(Y)$. *Then the function* m: $2^\Theta \to [0,1]$ *defined by*

$$1)\ m(\varnothing) = 0, \qquad 2)\ m(A) = \frac{1}{N} \sum_{X \cap Y = A} m_1(X) m_2(Y) \text{ for all subsets } A \neq \varnothing \text{ of } \Theta$$

is a mass function, called the orthogonal sum of m_1 *and* m_2, *and denoted* $m_1 \oplus m_2$. ◊

If $N = \sum_{X \cap Y \neq \varnothing} m_1(X) m_2(Y) = 0$, the orthogonal sum $m_1 \oplus m_2$ does not exist and m_1 and m_2 are said to be *totally contradictory*.

4 Evidential Temporal Representations

4.1 Evidential Representations of Indefinite Time and Temporal Relationships

Indefinite time in our model is represented by a mass function (as defined in D-S theory) on the power set of the set of intervals (i.e. 2^I). An interval represented by such a mass function is called an *evidential interval*. The evidential representations of temporal relationships are mass functions on $R = \{<, >, =, o, oi, d, di, s, si, f, fi\}$. A temporal relationship represented by such a mass function is called an *evidential temporal relationship*. Totally ignorance (*no info* in the transitivity table) now has the evidential form $\{\{R\} / 1\}$.

In [20], some examples of situations where time may be indefinite were given. Further thinking indicates that the reasons for indefinite temporal information can be classified into imperfect/uncertain knowledge of time and granularity-related categories. The former requires evidential representations when temporal information is recorded and is much related to philosophical considerations. The latter may arise in both recording and the retrieval of temporal information when comparisons of time are needed.

At the time of information input, a piece of temporal information with a finer granularity is transformed to a required granularity in the system. The mass on an evidential interval may be summed up to obtain the new evidential interval. However, this may cause an information loss. It is the task of system design to prevent the information loss. It is assumed this will never happen in a proper system. If the temporal information is with a coarser granularity, it is transformed directly as mentioned in Section 2.1. If there is an explicit assumption for the transformation, this assumption will take effect. For example, if it is assumed a month always means a uniform probability distribution on the days in that month, $\langle May, May \rangle$ will be transformed to $\{\langle 1May, 1May \rangle/\frac{1}{31}, \langle 2May, 2May \rangle/\frac{1}{31}, ..., \langle 31May, 31May \rangle/\frac{1}{31}\}$. Otherwise, it is transformed to $\langle 1May, 31May \rangle$. This is more flexible for real world applications.

At the time of comparing two intervals, the temporal variable with a coarser granularity will be transformed to the finer granularity. The same principle applies as in handling input information.

4.2 Evidential Temporal Constraint Networks

The constant time introduced in Section 2.3 is extended to evidential intervals. A constant time there can be represented by an evidential interval with one singleton focal element. For example, the evidential interval for the constant time $\langle May, May \rangle$ is $\{\{\langle May, May \rangle\}/1\}$ which will still be denoted as $\langle May, May \rangle$ as assumed in Section 3 that actually has been followed in Section 4.1.

Now intervals in an ETCN may be stamped with evidential intervals, it is necessary to derive the evidential temporal relationships among these evidential-interval-stamped intervals. Then while evidential temporal relationships present in the ETCN, their transitivity also need to be supported. In the following subsection, the derivations of evidential temporal relationships are introduced for these two situations.

4.3 Derivations of Evidential Temporal Relationships

Given two evidential intervals derived from a same P,

$$i_1 = \{I_{11} / m_1(I_{11}), I_{12} / m_1(I_{12}), ..., I_{1k_1} / m_1(I_{1k_1})\},$$
$$i_2 = \{I_{21} / m_2(I_{21}), I_{22} / m_2(I_{22}), ..., I_{2k_2} / m_2(I_{2k_2})\},$$

where $I_{ij_i}(j_i = 1, 2, ...k_i, i = 1, 2) \in 2^I$ are the focal elements for $m_i(i = 1, 2)$, following is the algorithm to derive the evidential relationship between them:

Algorithm 1 (Derive the evidential relationship between two evidential intervals).

1. *Construct the set S as* $\{I_{1l_1} \times I_{2l_2} / m(I_{1l_1} \times I_{2l_2}) | m(I_{1l_1} \times I_{2l_2}) = m_1(I_{1l_1}) * m_2(I_{2l_2}),\ l_1=1, \ldots, k_1,\ l_2=1, \ldots, k_2\}$;
2. ***For each*** $I_{1l_1} \times I_{2l_2}$ *in S,*
   2.1. ***For each*** *(definite) interval pair in the* $I_{1l_1} \times I_{2l_2}$, *find the corresponding temporal relationship according to Table 2;*
   2.2. *Replace the* $I_{1l_1} \times I_{2l_2}$ *in S with the set* R_l *(without repetition) of such relationships;*
3. *Merge identical* R_l*'s in S into one set and assign the sum of their masses to the set;*
4. ***Return*** *S.* ◊

Theorem 2. *The set S constructed by Algorithm 1 is a mass function on R, i.e. an evidential temporal relationship.*

Proof. In Step 1, the original set $S = \{I_{1l_1} \times I_{2l_2} / m(I_{1l_1} \times I_{2l_2}) | m(I_{1l_1} \times I_{2l_2}) = m_1(I_{1l_1}) * m_2(I_{2l_2}),\ l_1 = 1, \ldots, k_1,\ l_2 = 1, \ldots, k_2\}$ represents another mass function on $I \times I$ because $I_{1l_1} \times I_{2l_2} \subseteq I \times I$,

$$\sum_{l_1=1}^{k_1}\sum_{l_2=1}^{k_2} m(I_{1l_1} \times I_{2l_2}) = \sum_{l_1=1}^{k_1}\sum_{l_2=1}^{k_2} m_1(I_{1l_1}) * m_2(I_{2l_2}) = \sum_{l_1=1}^{k_1} m_1(I_{1l_1}) = 1, \text{ and } m(\varnothing) = 0.$$

Since all the temporal relationships in R is defined between two intervals, for each member in $I \times I$, one and only one corresponding member in R can be found. While for each member in R, at least one corresponding member in $I \times I$ can be found. In Step 2, therefore, for each $I_{1l_1} \times I_{2l_2} \subseteq I \times I$, an $(\varnothing \subset) R_l \subseteq R$ can be found. Although there are possibly more than one $I_{1l_1} \times I_{2l_2} \subseteq I \times I$ that are mapped to a same R_l, Step 3

ensures $m_R(R_l) = \sum_{\text{for all } I_{1l_1} \times I_{2l_2} \text{ mapped to } R_l} m(I_{1l_1} \times I_{2l_2})$, and all R_l's ($1 \le l \le k$, $k \le k_1 * k_2$) in S are different in the result of Algorithm 1. Finally, because

$$\sum_l m_R(R_l) = \sum_l \sum_{\text{for all } I_{1l_1} \times I_{2l_2} \text{ mapped to } R_l} m(I_{1l_1} \times I_{2l_2}) = \sum_{l_1}\sum_{l_2} m(I_{1l_1} \times I_{2l_2}) = 1$$

and $m_R(\varnothing)=0$, the set S constructed by Algorithm 1 is a mass function on R (see Definition 1). It is the evidential relationship between the two evidential intervals. ◊

Theorem 3. *Given two evidential intervals* i_1 *and* i_2, *there is a one-one mapping between the focal elements of the Algorithm 1-derived evidential temporal relationship from* i_1 *to* i_2 *and the one from* i_2 *to* i_1. *Each matching pair is a pair of inverses.* ◊

Theorem 3 is a direct conclusion from Theorem 2. It will play an important role in the efficient implementation of an ETCN.

Example 1. *Given* i_1=⟨2,7⟩ *and* i_2={{⟨3,4⟩, ⟨3,5⟩}/0.5, ⟨3,6⟩/0.2, {⟨3,7⟩, ⟨3,8⟩}/0.3}, *derive the evidential temporal relationship from* i_1 *to* i_2 *using Algorithm* 1. *The intermediate result* (*after Step* 2) *is* {*di*/0.5, *di*/0.2, {*fi*, *o*}/0.3} *and the final result is* {*di*/0.7, {*fi*, *o*}/0.3}. *According to Theorem* 3, *the evidential temporal relationship from* i_2 *to* i_1 *is* {*d*/0.7, {*f*, *oi*}/0.3}. ◊

In previous discussions (notably in the Step 1 of Algorithm 1), mass functions have been viewed as generalised probability distributions, which are assumed to be independent. Note that in D-S theory, a mass function is equivalent to a probability distribution when it has only singleton focal elements. Thus, the evidential temporal relationship between two evidential intervals that have only singleton focal elements has only singleton focal elements too. This is informally explained in Example 2.

Example 2. (*Taken from* [7], *p.*336, *Figure* 1, e_2 *and* e_3.)

{⟨30*May*,30*May*⟩/0.05, ..., ⟨18*June*,18*June*⟩/0.05}

↓{</0.835, =/0.0275, >/0.1375}

{⟨8*June*,8*June*⟩/0.05, ..., ⟨27*June*,27*June*⟩/0.05}

The mass of < *is the same as derived in* [7] *using probabilistic functions.* ◊

Similarly, given the evidential relationships between i_1 and i_2, i_2 and i_3 respectively,

$r_1 = \{R_{11} / m_{R1}(R_{11}), R_{12} / m_{R1}(R_{12}), ..., R_{1k_1} / m_{R1}(R_{1k_1})\}$,

$r_2 = \{R_{21} / m_{R2}(R_{21}), R_{22} / m_{R2}(R_{22}), ..., R_{2k_2} / m_{R2}(R_{2k_2})\}$,

to derive the evidential relationship from i_1 to i_3, there is:

Algorithm 2 (Derive the evidential relationship between two intervals given their relationships to a third interval).

1. *Construct the set S as* $\{R_{1l_1}{\times}R_{2l_2}/m_R(R_{1l_1}{\times}R_{2l_2}) | m_R(R_{1l_1}{\times}R_{2l_2}){=}m_{R1}(R_{1l_1}){*}m_{R2}(R_{2l_2}), l_1{=}1,...,k_1, l_2{=}1,...,k_2\}$;
2. ***For each*** $R_{1l_1}{\times}R_{2l_2}$ *in S*,
   - 2.1. ***For each*** (*definite*) *relationship pair in the* $R_{1l_1}{\times}R_{2l_2}$, *find the corresponding set of temporal relationships using the transitivity table in Section* 2.4;
   - 2.2. *Replace the* $R_{1l_1}{\times}R_{2l_2}$ *in S with the set* R_l *that is the union of such sets*;
3. *Merge identical* R_l*'s in S into one set and assign the sum of their masses to the set*;
4. ***Return*** *S*. ◊

Theorem 4. *The set S constructed by Algorithm 2 is a mass function on R, i.e. an evidential temporal relationship.*

Proof. The proof is similar to Theorem 2. Note that the only difference is the construction of the substitutions (R_i's) for the focal elements in the original S (Step 2). In fact, if the temporal relationships between definite intervals in Algorithm 1 are viewed as singleton sets, the R_i's in it are the unions of such singleton sets. ◊

The inversion theorem also holds for Algorithm 2.

Theorem 5. *Given three intervals i_1, i_2 and i_3, and the evidential temporal relationships between i_1 and i_2, i_2 and i_3, there is a one-one mapping between the focal elements of the Algorithm 2-derived evidential representations of the temporal relationship from i_1 to i_3 and the one from i_3 to i_1. Each matching pair is a pair of inverses.* ◊

Example 3. *This example shows how Algorithm 2 works.*

Given $i_1 \xrightarrow{\{\{<,=\}/0.3,\{>,=\}/0.7\}} i_2 \xrightarrow{>} i_3$, $\{\{\{<,>\},\{=,>\}\}/0.3,\ \{\{>,>\},\{=,>\}\}/0.7\}$ *is constructed first. Obtain R for* $\{<, >\}$, $>$ *for* $\{=, >\}$, *and* $>$ *for* $\{>, >\}$ *from the transitivity table. Because* $R \cup \{>\} = R$ *and* $\{>\} \cup \{>\} = \{>\}$, *the result is*

$i_1 \xrightarrow{\{R/0.3,>/0.7\}} i_3$. ◊

4.4 Reasoning in ETCN

The distinctive function of reasoning in an ETCN is to answer a question concerning the credibility of a temporal relationship, such as "Is patient A likely to have been infected with Virus A earlier than patient B?", while it is known both patients have been infected but exactly when is unknown.

Algorithm 3 (Compute the *bel* and *pls* of the temporal relationship of two intervals in an ETCN).

1. *Look for all the paths between the two components being compared;*
2. ***If** no path is found, **return** unknown; **otherwise***
3. ***For each** path found, perform relationship transitivity along the path using Algorithms* 1 *and* 2;
4. *Compute the orthogonal sum of all the resulting mass functions according to Theorem* 1;
5. *Compute the bel and pls based on the final mass function (i.e. the orthogonal sum) using Definition* 2;
6. ***Return** the bel and pls.* ◊

Definition 3 (Inconsistent ETCN). *Compute the bel and pls of each pair of nodes in an ETCN using Algorithm* 3. *If totally contradictory mass functions are obtained from any pair, the ETCN is inconsistent.* ◊

To determine whether a piece of temporal information is consistent with an ETCN, add the information into the ETCN. If the ETCN becomes inconsistent, the information is inconsistent with the network. Otherwise, it is consistent with the network and the network is updated after its entry. The inconsistency definition in ordinary TCNs is a special case of this one. A simple example is depicted in Fig. 2.

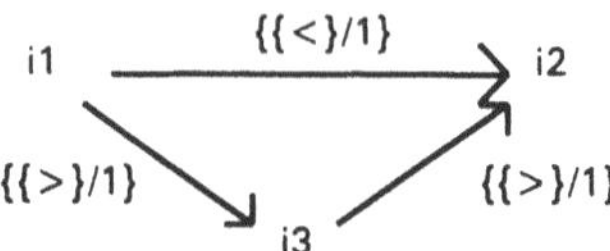

For i1 and i2, the path i1-i3-i2 results in {{>}/1}, which is totally contradictory with {{<}/1} along i1,i2.

Fig. 2. An inconsistent ETCN

5 Conclusion

The major points of our work described in this paper are: (1) introducing constant-time-stamps into a modified algebra of Allen's interval algebra to represent absolute and relative time; (2) using ETCNs to represent definite and indefinite time and obtaining the credibility of temporal relationships in it. The former is inspired by [12], where absolute-time-stamped database is introduced as a practical solution to the problem of computational complexity of retrieval. As to the latter, the three algorithms reported in this paper can fully exploit extant techniques in TCNs. The computations of evidential functions do not increase the computational complexity of these techniques. All these lay a sound theoretical foundation for the evidential temporal model based on this ontology in the TEDS which has a wide range of applications.

Future work will be biased towards database consideration in the TEDS. Another important theoretical issue is database update/belief revision when indefinite non-temporal information and temporal information present themselves at the same time in the TEDS, where both valid time and transaction time are modelled.

References

[1] J. F. Allen: Maintaining Knowledge about Temporal Intervals. *Communications of the ACM*, 26(11):832-843, November 1983.

[2] J. F. Allen and P. J. Hayes: Moments and Points in an Interval-based Temporal-based Logic. *Comput. Intell. (Canada)*, 5:225-238, 1989.

[3] S. Barro, R. Marin, J. Mira, and A. R. Paton: A Model and a Language for the Fuzzy Representation and Handling of Time. *Fuzzy Sets and Systems*, 61(2):153-175, 1994.

[4] S. Chaudhuri: Temporal Relationships in Databases. *Proc. of the 14th VLDB Conf.*, pp. 160-170, 1988.

[5] Z. Chen and F. Terrier: About Temporal Uncertainty. *Proc. of IEEE/ACM Int'l Conf. on Developing and Managing ES Programs*, pp. 223-230, October 1991.

[6] Z. Chen: Fuzzy Temporal Reasoning for Process Supervision. *Expert Systems*, 12(2):123-137, 1995.

[7] C. E. Dyreson and R. T. Snodgrass: Valid-time Indeterminacy. *Proc. of IEEE 9th Int'l. Conf. on Data Engineering*, pp. 335-343, 1993.

[8] J. Guan and D. A. Bell: *Evidence Theory and its Applications, Vol. 1*, North-Holland, 1991.

[9] J. Guan and D. A. Bell: *Evidence Theory and its Applications, Vol. 2*, North-Holland, 1991.

[10] C. S. Jensen, M. D. Soo, and R. T. Snodgrass: Unification of Temporal Data Models. *Proc. of IEEE 9th Int'l. Conf. on Data Engineering*, pp. 262-271, 1993.

[11] C. S. Jensen, J. Clifford, R. Elmasri, et al.: A Consensus Glossary of Temporal Database Concepts. *SIGMOD RECORD*, 23(1):52-64, March 1994.

[12] B. Knight and J. Ma: A Temporal Database Model Supporting Relative and Absolute Time. *The Computer Journal*, 37(7):588-597, 1994.

[13] M. Koubarakis: Representation and Querying in Temporal Databases: the Power of Temporal Constraints. *Proc. of IEEE 9th Int'l. Conf. on Data Engineering*, pp. 327-334, 1993.

[14] M. Koubarakis: Database Models for Infinite and Indefinite Temporal Information. *Information Systems*, 19(2):141-173, 1994.

[15] S. K. Lee: Imprecise and Uncertain Information in Databases: an Evidential Approach. *Proc. of IEEE 8th Int'l Conf. on Data Engineering*, pp. 614-621, 1992.

[16] J. Ma and B. Knight: A General Temporal Theory. *Comp. J.*, 37:114-123, 1994.

[17] A. Montanari and B. Pernici: Temporal Reasoning. *Temporal Databases: Theory, Design & Implementation*, Chapter 12, pp. 534-562, A. U. Tansel, et al. (eds.), Benjamin/Cumming Publishing Company, Inc., 1993.

[18] B. Nebel and H. J. Burckert: Reasoning about Temporal Relations - A Maximal Tractable Subclass of Allen's Interval Algebra. *Journal of the ACM*, 42(1):43-66, 1995.

[19] G. Shafer: *A Mathematical Theory of Evidence*, Princeton, N.J., Princeton University Press, 1976.

[20] R. T. Snodgrass: Temporal Databases. *Theories and Methods of Spatio-Temporal Reasoning in Geographic Space*, LNCS 639:22-64, Springer-Verlag, 1992.

[21] P. van Beek: Approximation Algorithms for Temporal Reasoning. *Proc. of the 11th IJCAI*, pp. 1291-1296, Detroit, MI, 1989.

[22] P. van Beek: Reasoning about Qualitative Temporal Information. *Proc. of AAAI-90*, pp. 728-734, Boston, MA, 1990.

Using Artificial Neural Networks for Meteor-Burst Communications Trail Prediction

Stuart Melville	Geoff Sutcliffe	David Fraser
Dep't of Computer Studies	Dep't of Computer Science	Dep't of Electronic Engineering
ML Sultan Technikon	James Cook University	University of Natal
Durban, South Africa	Townsville, Australia	Durban, South Africa
stuart@wpogate.mlsultan.ac.za	geoff@cs.jcu.edu.au	dfrase@elaine.ee.und.ac.za

Abstract

The use of meteor ionisation trails as 'cheap satellites' to reflect radio waves between two points on the earth's surface is an established technique, called Meteor Burst Communications (MBC). For MBC systems to take advantage of the different amplitude and duration patterns of different trail types it is necessary to predict these patterns from features of initial signals reflected from the trails. The work described in this paper attempts to predict trail amplitude, duration, and trail type using neural networks. Results include a picture of what features of the beginning of the trail are most and least important for recognising various characteristics of the rest of the trail, some significant results as regards trail type prediction, and high correlations between actual and predicted peak amplitudes of trails. The latter is an important result.

Keywords: Neural networks, Applications to telecommunications.

1. Introduction

Billions of meteors[1] enter the earth's atmosphere every day.There is an inverse relationship between meteor size and meteor frequency [LM+90]. Although the vast majority of the meteors are small (around the size of a grain of sand), their solar orbital velocity is high enough that on entering the upper atmosphere (between 80 and 120km from the earth's surface) and burning up, they leave ionisation trails tens of kilometres long.

While Nagaoka [Nag29] was the first to postulate a connection between meteors and radio reflections, his initial hypothesis that the meteors would be impediments to radio communication was soon discovered to be incorrect. Picard [Pic31] and Skellet [Ske32] independently determined that meteors, or more specifically the trails of ionisation that they leave in their wake, could enhance radio reflection. The use of meteor ionisation trails as 'cheap satellites' to reflect radio waves between two points on the earth's surface (limited by the earth's curvature to about 2000km apart) has since become an established technique. This form of communication is called Meteor-Burst Communications (MBC).

The advantages of MBC include:

- Low price. Ionised trails are free and the communication hardware is relatively cheap [Whi88, CR87].
- Robustness. The ground stations are simple and reliable [BB77, Cro77, Day82]. Meteor trails 'cannot be shot down', which makes MBC attractive for military applications [Hel87, Oet80, Boy88]. The transmission is largely impervious to electrical interference, such as polar and auroral disturbances [Hel87, DG+57].

[1]Strictly speaking, they are meteoroids immediately prior to entering the atmosphere, and meteors thereafter

- Suitability for remote use. MBC systems have a range of up to 2000km, and due to their robustness and low power consumption the ground stations have low maintenance requirements [Mor88].
- Resistance to ground interception and jamming. The small footprint of the reflection means that to intercept or jam the signal requires being close to the receiving ground station [Hel87].

A number of large-scale MBC systems are in place. Important systems include:

- The United States Department of Agriculture's SnoTel telemettry system [BB77, Cro77, Day82], which comprises some 500 stations in the American West.
- The Alaska Air Command system of the US Air Force [KR86, Hof88, Sch90].
- The Chinese MBC network used by the Chinese military for communications from base stations in Beijing, Lanzhou and Urumqi to remote army camps, operating as the standard link for low priority traffic and the backup link for high priority traffic [Sch90].

A detailed review of MBC systems appears in [MF93].

The major difficulty with MBC is that an ionisation trail must be correctly orientated in the correct area of the sky between stations for communication to take place. The average time between usable trails varies according to known daily and seasonal cycles in meteor arrival rates, as well as being dependent on the transmitter power and the antennas used. Current state-of-the-art systems have delays of less than a second between usable trails. The channel is still sporadic however, and this means that MBC is most suited to data transmission, as opposed to real-time voice or video.

This paper first describes the different types of meteor trails, and the effect of the differnet types on the communications capacity of the MBC channel. The advantages of being able to accurately predict future trail amplitude and duration characteristics on the basis of signal reception in the early part of a trail are explained. After this various neural net approaches to the prediction of trail type, duration, and peak amplitude are discussed. and important results highlighted.

2. The Problem

It has long being established that there are different types of meteor trails with different duration and amplitude characteristics [Sug64, HB67, Ost85, Wei87]. Figure 1 and Figure 2 below show examples of trails recorded over an 1100km link between Arniston and Pretoria in South Africa [ML+89]. The recording starts when a signal received from the transmitter achieves a certain signal-to-noise ratio (10dB), for at least 20ms. Thereafter samples of the signal amplitude in dBm are taken every 5ms until the signal dips below a turn-off threshhold. (Actually the system monitors for a period of 400ms after this to ensure that the turn-off has not been premature. For example, the situation where one trail with a noise spike in the middle is recorded as two distinct trails is avoided.)

Theory suggests two basic trail types, underdense and overdense [WBG84], recorded examples of these are shown in Figure 1 and Figure 2 respectively. In practise a number of other features interfere with the classic fast-rising, slow-dropping, short-duration (400ms or so) triangle of an underdense trail, and the high-amplitude, longer-duration (seconds) smooth parabola of an overdense trail. In particular, upper atmosphere winds tend to distort these patterns considerably, as in the case in Figure 2. The TrailStar expert system [ML+89] distinguishes 29 distinct trail types, based on trail features (see Section 2.1 for a description of some trail features). While some of these 29 types are clearly subtypes of the two classic shapes, other cases are not clearly recognisable as being either underdense or overdense.

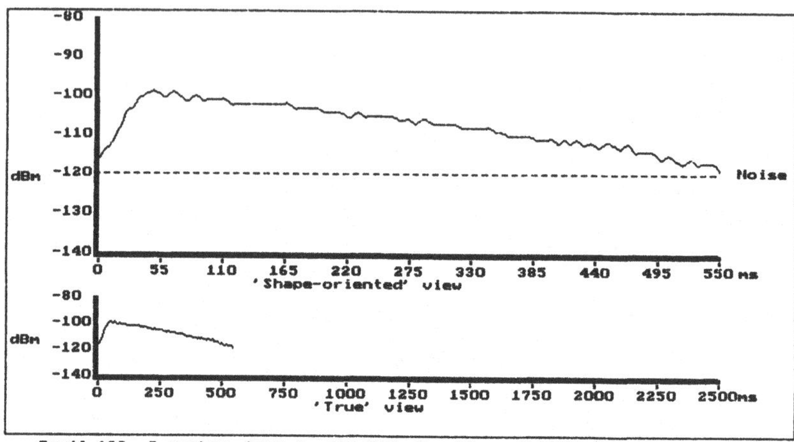

Figure 1: Underdense trail

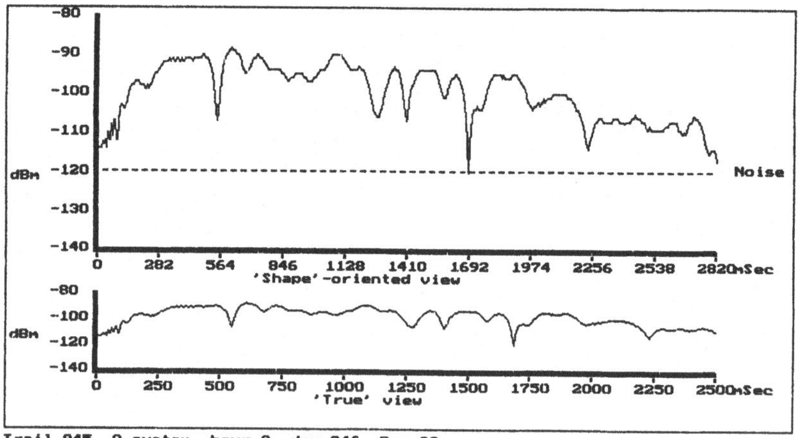

Figure 2: Overdense trail

Note on figures: Each figure shows two views of the same trail. The lower axes give a 'real' view of the trail, with one pixel plotted for each sample (samples taken every 5ms), while the upper axes give a 'shape' view, where the trail is scaled to fill the entire X-axis. The 'shape' view is useful in studying individual trails, while the 'real' view is used for comparing trails.

The different trail shapes have major implications for MBC. Knowing the future shape of a trail would allow for more effective utilisation of channel capacity: longer duration trails provide more opportunity for data transmission, and higher-amplitude trails can support higher data rates. Importantly, the long durations and high amplitudes of the overdense subtypes means that they contribute the bulk of throughput, despite being the least-commonly occurring trails [LMM90]. At the same time, if wait time for short messages (which don't require a great deal of bandwidth) is at issue then MBC systems need to make optimal use of the far more commonly occurring underdense subtypes [ML92].

For communication systems to take advantage of different trail shapes it is necessary to predict the trail shape from the features of the initial part of the trail. The "initial part" of a trail is limited here to the first 50ms to 100ms, as many entire trails in the underdense subtypes are as short as 300ms. The TrailStar system is inadequate for this task, as it only classifies the trails based on features of the entire trail. The TrailStar system cannot identify many of the 29 types from only this initial data, and does not consider trail amplitude and duration *within* types. For example, it might be known that a trail is of the sinusoidal overdense type, and thus would typically have a duration of between 2 seconds and 5 seconds, and have a peak amplitude of 15 dBm to 20 dBm above the background noise. However, the precise peak amplitude (and hence maximum data rate attainable) and duration (and hence usable time) would not be known, and this information could be more useful than the trail type. The work described in this paper attempts to predict trail amplitude, trail duration, and trail type as three distinct tasks, using neural networks.

2.1 Trail Features and Types

The TrailStar system uses over 100 features to classify trails. However, many of the features are based on trail reflection information which is not available in the first 50ms to 100ms of a trail. Twenty six features have been determined to be calculable from the early period of a trail together with the background noise level and the time since the previous trail was recorded. The 26 feature descriptors are:

- F1: The offset of the best straight line fit.
- F2: The slope of the best straight line fit.
- F3: The variance of the samples from the best straight line fit.
- F4: The minimum amplitude found.
- F5: The maximum amplitude found.
- F6: The number of samples found at the peak amplitude (possible plateaus).
- F7 The position at which the peak amplitude is first encountered.
- F8: The number of local minima.
- F9: The number of local maxima.
- F10: The number of extrema.
- F11: The offset of the best straight line fit up to the peak amplitude.
- F12: The slope of the best straight line fit up to the peak amplitude.
- F13: The variance of the samples from the best straight line fit up to the peak amplitude.
- F14: The offset of the best straight line fit from the peak amplitude onwards.
- F15: The slope of the best straight line fit from the peak amplitude onwards.
- F16: The variance of the samples from the best straight line fit from the peak amplitude onwards.
- F17: The position where the initial amplitude rise ends.

F18: The position where the fall from the peak amplitude begins (not the same as F7 when upper plateaus at peak amplitude are encountered).

F19: The position where the greatest dBm difference from the best straight line fit is found.

F20: The τ value of the slope from the peak amplitude to the end.

F21: The x^2 coefficient of the best parabola fit.

F22: The x coefficient of the best parabola fit.

F23: The constant of the best parabola fit.

F24: The variance of the samples from the best parabola fit.

F25: The background noise level.

F26: The time since the previous trail.

Note that the features in this list are with respect to only the first 50 or 100ms of a trail, i.e., the first 10 or 20 samples.

3. The Neural Network Solution

The availability of a large database of trail recordings with known type, duration and amplitude, suggested a neural network approach to predicting these values from initial trail data. For the neural network classification the 29 trail subtypes were grouped into three generic classes: the underdense class, the overdense class, and a 'non-classic' class comprising those subtypes which are not overtly underdense or overdense, or had features of both (see Figure 3 for an example). This was necessary as many of the 29 subtypes determined in [ML+89] are not distinguishable from the early part of the trail. In terms of the categorization done by TrailStar, the underdense class contains trail types 5, 9, 10, 11, 12, 13, 14, 16, 17, 18, 24 and 29; the overdense class contains trail types 19, 20, 21, 26, 27, and 28; and the non-classic class contains trail types 2, 3, 4, 6, 7, 8, 15, 22, 23 and 25. Trail type 1 (erroneous data) is excluded from consideration.

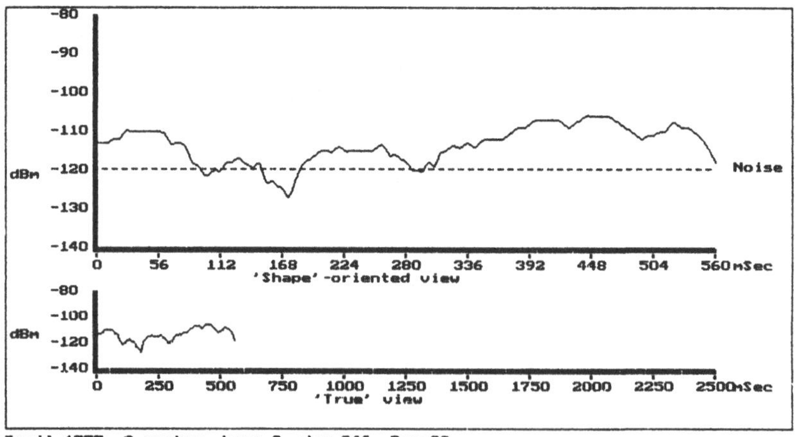

Figure 3: A sample 'non-classic' class trail

Trail recordings of 100000 trails were selected at random from the database of trail recordings. From the trail data the 26 features were calculated from the initial trail samples, as inputs to the neural network. These features were calculated for the first 20 samples (100ms), and also for the first 10 samples (50ms) to see if faster prediction is possible. The trails were also classified by TrailStar into one of the 29 TrailStar types using the entire trail data, and then put into one of the three classes. The trail class, duration, and peak amplitude formed the expected output for neural network training.

The input/output combinations were divided into two groups; a training group of 96000 examples, and a test group of just over 4000 examples. Supervised learning was then used to train the network to predict trail class, duration, and amplitude, from the 26 trail features. Neuralware's Neuralworks version 2.0 [Neu93] was used to build the required neural networks.

3.1 Trail Type Nets and Results

Trail classification proved to be a particularly vexing problem. Initially a backpropagation network was used with 26 input Processing Elements (one for each input feature descriptor), 58 PEs in a hidden layer, and one output PE (the trail class). Training this network gave either convergence without generalisation (low RMS error but low correlation of actual/predicted too) or did not converge at all. The next attempt was to use an LVQ network, as LVQ networks are supposedly well suited to classification type problems [Neu93]. In this network three output fields were used, allowing three different 'bit patterns' (000, 010, 111) to represent the three trail classes. This approach also failed, with the network converging on the most common trail types, non-classic and underdense.

Neither the backpropagation nor the LVQ network was predicting overdense trails at all, and it seemed likely that this was due to the relatively low number of overdense trails in the training data (as one would expect; they only form a small proportion of trails). To counter this perceived swamping of the overdense trails, 5000 trails of each of the three classes were extracted from the 96000, based on the fact that there were just over 5000 overdense trails available. This formed a new training set of 15000 examples with equal representation of each trail class. The 4000 test trails were left unaltered. While this step did lead to some predictions of overdense trails, correlations were still poor. Guessing that this might be due to the network being overexposed to 'happenstance' features (and so failing), a subset of the input features was used. The features were selected according to their relative importance in the TrailStar typing scheme. The subset contained just nine features, these being F2, F3, F4, F5, F7, F10, F22, F23, and F24. This improved performance somewhat, giving predicted/actual correlations of approximately 0.4. It was felt that better could be achieved, and at this stage it was decided to add an additional hidden layer to the network to aid in the recognition of more complex patterns. This layer consisted of five PEs, making the network configuration 9 input layer PEs, 58 first hidden layer PEs, 5 second hidden layer PEs, and 1 output layer PE. It is from this configuration that the final results were obtained.

The eventual weights on the inputs (for the case where the features were derived from 20 trail samples) were as follows :

F2:0.259
F3:-0.946 (The variance of the samples from the best straight line fit)
F4:-0.268
F5:-0.261
F7:1.000 (The position at which the peak amplitude is first encountered)
F10:-0.667
F22:0.048 (The x coefficient of the best parabola fit)
F23:-0.523
F24:-0.975 (The variance of the samples from the best parabola fit)

Only the x coefficient of the best parabola fit seemed to have negligible effect (weighted less than 0.1). It is interesting that the parabola and line variance measures had high weights (greater than 0.9 in magnitude) after training; such measures seem to be important descriptors. The strong role played by the peak amplitude position (weight of 1) was less expected and constitutes an important finding.

Trail class	Predictions				
	Total	Ud	Od	Non-C	Correct
Underdense	1942	881	76	985	45%
Overdense	286	11	109	166	38%
Non-classic	1791	188	471	1132	63%
Total	4019	1080	656	2283	53%

Table 1: Results of class prediction; 20 samples

Trail class	Predictions				
	Total	Ud	Od	Non-C	Correct
Underdense	1966	701	83	1182	36%
Overdense	278	12	103	163	37%
Non-classic	1776	129	558	1089	61%
Total	4020	842	744	2434	47%

Table 2: Results of class prediction; 10 samples

It is clear from the data in Table 1 and Table 2 that the network is fairly proficient at distinguishing between underdense and overdense trails, with only a very small number of underdense trails being predicted as overdense, and vice versa. The problem remaining is that the network easily confuses underdense and overdense with non-classic. Of course this should be expected, as the non-classic class contains precisely those trails that have both overdense and underdense features.

The fact that around 50% of predictions are correct, together with the above described underdense/overdense discrimination, is particularly encouraging. The correlations look worse due to the effect of the non-classic group. Notwithstanding that, the correlations of 0.534 (prediction based on 20 samples) and 0.428 (prediction based on 10 samples) are encouraging.

3.2 Duration Nets and Results

A good prediction of trail duration is highly unlikely. Some types of trails, such as rectified sines (see Figure 4), repeat a basic pattern n times. There is no way to detect, on the basis of the first 50ms or 100ms, just what n is going to be. However an attempt at neural network prediction was made.

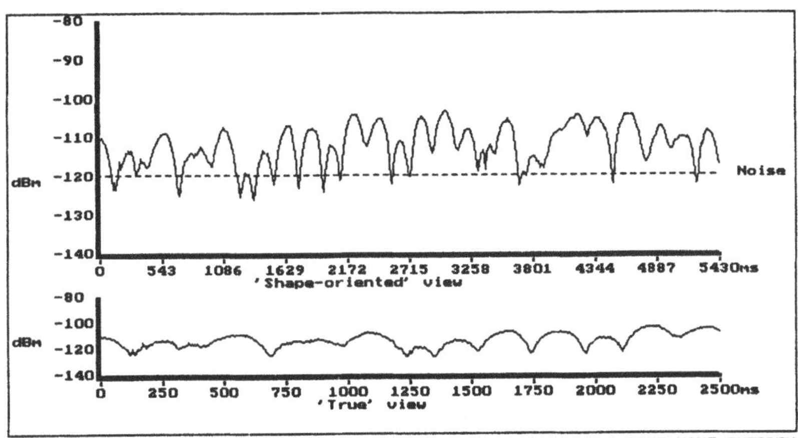

Figure 4: Rectified sine trail

The backpropagation network used here had 26 input PEs, 58 PEs in a hidden layer, and one output PE (the duration). After extensive training (several million epochs) no further convergence seemed to be occurring, and the weights were fairly evenly distributed amongst inputs, indicating that most of the inputs were having a significant effect on the network. Input weights were as follows after training:

F1:-0.470	F2:0.585	F3:-0.948	F4:-0.244	F5:0.167
F6:-0.579	F7:0.789	F8:-0.677	F9:-0.818	F10:-0.712
F11:-0.712	F12:0.813	F13:-0.998	F14:-0.239	F15:-0.856
F16:-0.952	F17:0.789	F18:0.789	F19:0.867	F20:0.552
F21:0.052	F22:0.138	F23:-0.517	F24:-0.934	F25:-0.999
F26:0.000				

(Values shown are for the 20 sample case, the 10 sample results are similar.)

The features with weights of particular interest are:

F3:-0.948	(The variance of the samples from the best straight line fit)
F13:-0.998	(Variance from the best straight line fit up to the peak amplitude)
F16:-0.952	(The variance from the best straight line fit from the peak amplitude onwards)
F21:0.052	(The x2 coefficient of the best parabola fit)
F24:-0.934	(The variance of the samples from the best parabola fit)
F25:-0.999	(The background noise level)
F26:0.000	(The time since the previous trail was encountered)

After the classification results it came as no surprise that the variance measures were of great importance (weighted greater than 0.9 in magnitude). The high weight assigned to background noise is somewhat puzzling, and merits further investigation. As regards low (less than 0.1 in magnitude) weights only F21 and F26 seem to have minimal effect.

Scatter graphs of the actual vs predicted trail durations for the 20 sample case are shown in Figure 5 below. The right-hand graph shows the more common duration trails (up to 1000ms) at higher resolution.

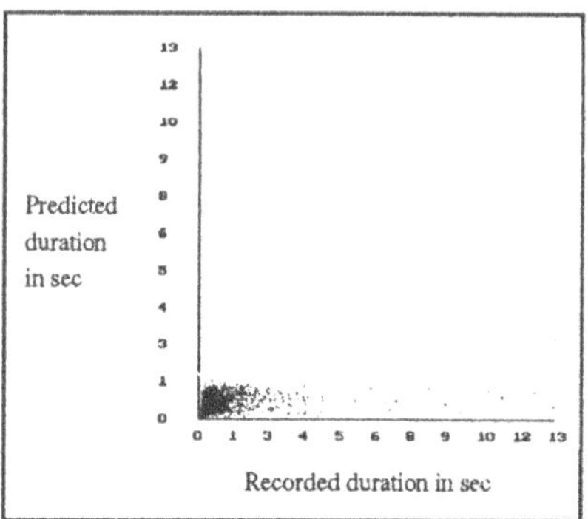

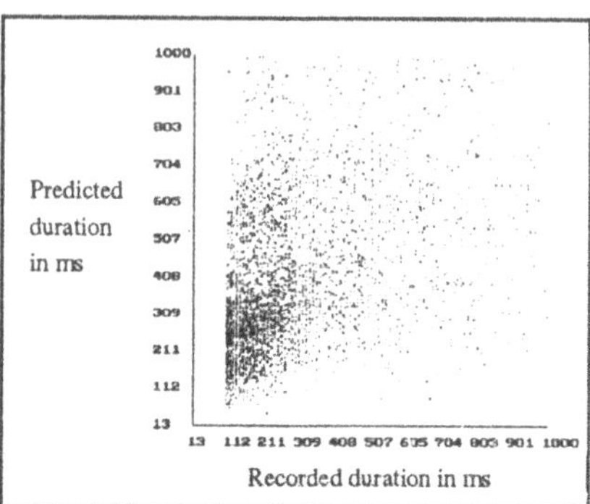

Figure 5: Duration prediction, 20 samples

It is apparent that the prediction is not particularly accurate, as was expected. The Pearson coefficients of correlation are 0.303 for the 20 sample case and 0.206 for the 10 sample case. Although these coefficients are statistically significant due to the large sample size, they indicate only a weak positive correlation between actual and predicted results. Such results are better than nothing, but work on finding more effective discriminators must continue.

3.3 Amplitude Nets and Results

For the amplitude prediction a backpropagation network using 26 input PEs, a hidden layer of 80 PEs, and a single output PE, was used. The network was trained on the 96000 training examples for both the 10 and 20 sample cases. Input weights were as follows after training:

F1:-0.182	F2:0.308	F3:-0.887	F4:-0.111	F5:0.042
F6:-0.263	F7:0.263	F8:-0.667	F9:-1.000	F10:-0.818
F11:-0.744	F12:0.813	F13:-0.998	F14:-0.118	F15:-0.847
F16:-0.998	F17:0.789	F18:-0.158	F19:0.867	F20:0.552
F21:-0.292	F22:0.370	F23:-0.470	F24:-0.990	F25:-0.999
F26:0.000				

(Values shown are for the 20 sample case, the 10 sample results are similar)

The features with weights of particular interest are:

F3:-0.887 (The variance of the samples from the best straight line fit)
F5:0.042 (The maximum amplitude found)
F9:-1.000 (The number of local maxima)
F13:-0.998 (Variance from the best straight line fit up to the peak amplitude)
F16:-0.998 (The variance from the best straight line fit from the peak amplitude onwards)
F24:-0.990 (The variance of the samples from the best parabola fit)
F25:-0.999 (The background noise level)
F26:0.000 (The time since the previous trail was encountered)

The above makes fascinating reading. It is particularly startling that the peak amplitude found in the early part of a trail seems to be of virtually no significance in predicting the peak amplitude of the entire trail. This merits further investigation. The only other feature that has little effect (weighted less than 0.1 in magnitude) is the wait time since the previous trail, a result in keeping with the duration findings.

As regards important (weight greater than 0.9 in magnitude) features, once again the variances stand out, with F13, F16 and F26 all exceeding 0.9 in absolute value. F3 is only slightly less important (magnitude of 0.887). Background noise again has a high weight, in keeping with the duration results, and this deserves further study. Of particular interest is that the number of local maxima found has the greatest magnitude weight of any input (1.0 in magnitude). A more detailed analysis of this important result is necessary.

Results from these networks were most impressive, as can be seen from Figure 6 below, which shows the 10 sample case. The correlation is even stronger in the 20 sample case. (The vertical striation in the Figure is because amplitude is measured discretely).

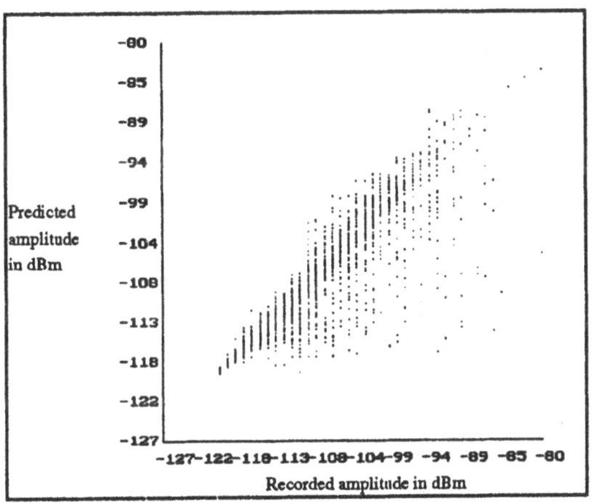

Figure 6: Amplitude prediction, 10 samples

The correlation coefficients produced were 0.911 for the 20 sample case, and 0.823 for the 10 sample case. These are high positive correlations. Having such a reliable predictor of the eventual peak amplitude from sampling just the first 50ms of the trail has tremendous and obvious implications for vast improvements in MBC throughput.

4. Conclusion

This paper has describes an emperical study into the use of neural nets to predict future characteristics of meteor trails. Being able to predict in real-time what communication capacity the upcoming trail will have, enables greater utilisation of the trail than is currently possible. Results include:

- A most necessary (for future work) picture of what features at the beginning of the trail are most and least important for recognising various characteristics of the rest of the trail.

- Some expected, though still disappointing, poor correlations between predicted and actual durations.
- Some significant results as regards trail type prediction.
- High correlations between actual and predicted peak amplitudes of trails, even on the basis of data from just 50 ms at the beginning of trails. This is an important result with immediate implications for the design of MBC systems. This result justifies the entire research effort.

MBC systems have the potential to provide cheap and reliable communications in remote and developing areas. This is particularly relevant to the Pacific Rim, where large distances and inaccesiblity make the cost of installing traditional communication systems prohibitive. The Chinese MBC system [Sch90] is a working example of this. The improved performance that can be realised from real-time prediction of trail patterns will considerably enhance such systems.

Acknowledgement: This research was financed by Salbu (Pty) Ltd.

5. References

[BB77] Barton, M., Burke, M., SNOTEL - An Operational Data Acquisition System using Meteor-Burst Technology, paper presented at the Western Show Conference, (1977).

[Boy88] Boyle, D., Long Distance Communications - Back to Ionization, *International Defence Review* 21, 491-493, (1988).

[Cro77] Crook, A.G., SNOTEL : Monitoring Climatic Factors to Predice Water Supplies, *Journal of Soil and Water Conservation* 32, 294-295, (1977).

[CR87] Cannon, P.S., and Reed, A.P.C., The Evolution of Meteor-Burst Communication Systems, *Journal of the Institution of Electronic and Radio Engineers* 57, 101-112, (1987).

[Day82] Day, W.E., Meteor-Burst Communications Bounce Signals Between Remote Sites, *Electron* 55, 71-75, (1982).

[DG+57] Davis, G.W.L., Gladys, S.J., Lang, G.R., Luke, L.M., Taylor, M.K., The Canadian JANET System, *Proceedings of the IRE* 45, 1666-1678, (1957).

[HB67] Hawkins, G.S., and Brown, J.C., A Comprehensive Study of the Characteristics of Meteor Echoes - I, Smithsonian Astrophysical Observatory, Report # NASA-CR-92667 (1967).

[Hel87] Hellweg, G.A., *Meteor-Burst Communications : Is This What the Navy Needs?*, Master's Thesis, Naval Postgraduate School, Monterey, U.S.A., (1987).

[Hof88] Hoff, J. A., The Utility of Meteor Burst Communications, Conference Record of the 1988 IEEE Conference on Military Communications, (1988).

[KR86] Kokjer, K.J., Roberts, T.D., Networked Meteor-Burst Data Communications, *IEEE Communications Magazine* 24, 23-29, (1986).

[LMM90] Larsen, J.D., Melville, S.W., and Mawrey,R.S.M., Adaptive Data Rate Capacity of Meteor-Burst Communications, *Conference Record of the 1990 IEEE Conference on Military Communications*, Vol 2, 40.1.1 - 40.1.5, (1990).

[LM+90] Larsen, J.D., Melville, S.W., Mawrey, R.S., Letschert, R.Y., and Goddard, W.D. Throughput Capacity of Meteor Burst Communications, *Transactions of the SAIEE* 81 (1), 20 - 30, (1990).

[Mor88] Morgan, E.J., Meteor Burst Communications : An Update, *Signal* 42, 55-61, (1988).

[MF93] Melville, S.W., and Fraser, D.D., Meteor-burst Communication: A Review, *Transactions of the SAIEE* 84 (2), 60 - 68, (1993).

[ML+89] Melville, S.W., Larsen, J.D., Letschert, R.Y., and Goddard, W.D., The Classification of Meteor Trail Reflections by a Rule-Based System, *Transactions of the SAIEE* 80 (1), 104 - 116, (1989).

[ML92] Melville, S.W. and Larsen, J.D., Wait Time in Meteor-Burst Communications, *Transactions of the SAIEE* 83 (1), 32 - 37, (1992).

[Nag29] Nagaoka, H., Possibility of Disturbance of Radio Transmission by Meteor Showers, *Proceedings of the Imperial Academy of Tokyo* 5, p 632, (1929).

[Neu93] Neuralware, Inc. *Neural Computing*. Technical Publications Group: Pittsburgh, (1993).

[Oet80] Oetting, J.D., An Analysis of Meteor-Burst Communications for Military Applications, *IEEE Transactions on Communications* 38, 1591 - 1601, (1980).

[Ost85] Ostergaard, J.C., Characteristics of High-Latitude Meteor Scatter Propagation Parameters over the 45 to 104 Mhz Band, *AGARD Conference Proceedings* 382, (1985).

[Pic31] Pickard, G.W., A Note on the Relation of Meteor Showers and Radio Reception, *Proceedings of the IRE* 19,1166-1170, (1931).

[Sch90] Schanker, J. Z., *Meteor Burst Communications*. Artech House, Inc., Norwood, MA, (1990).

[Ske32] Skellet, A.M., The Ionizing Effect of Meteors in Relation to Radio Propagation, *Proceedings of the IRE* 20, 1933-1940, (1932).

[Sug64] Sugar, G.R., Radio Propagation by Reflection from Meteor Trails, *Proceedings of the IEEE* 52, pp 11 - 136, (1964).

[WBG84] Weitzen, J.A., Birkemeier, W.P., and Grossi, M.D., An Estimate of the Capacity of the Meteor-Burst Channel, *IEEE Transactions on Communications* 32, 972-974, (1984).

[Wei87] Weitzen, J.A., A Data Base Approach to the Analysis of Meteor Burst Data, *Radio Science* 22, 133 - 140, (1987).

[Whi88] Whittaker, C.J., Meteor Burst Communication, *Journal of Research of the Signals Institute* 18, 185-190, (1988).

Modeling Commonsense Rules in an Inference Network

Boon Toh LOW*

Department of Systems Engineering and Engineering Management
The Chinese University of Hong Kong
Shatin, N.T., Hong Kong

Abstract. In commonsense reasoning, conditional statements of the form "IF condition(s) THEN conclusion(s)" are the most common and important constructions. While material implication is generally used in classical logic based belief representation systems, its dual implication could be semantically too strong for expressing commonsense IF-THEN rules because not all contributing conditions of a rule can be expressed (the Qualification Problem [18]) and the negation of conclusions do not always imply the negation of the conditions. This paper studies a hybrid neural-symbolic belief representation system called *Neural-Logic Belief Network* (NLBN) [14] where IF-THEN rules can be more realistically captured for commonsense reasoning. Deduction of an IF-THEN rule in this formalism is considered as information flow from the condition(s) to the conclusion(s). In this system, the strength of conclusions can be modeled by using individual rule mapping functions.

Areas: inference network, belief systems, conditionals, commonsense reasoning.

1 Fundamental Commonsense Rules

Conditional statements in the form "IF condition(s) THEN conclusion(s)" are the most important constructions in reasoning systems. This can be endorsed by many human activities either directly or indirectly. For example, expert systems are largely rule-based [20]; diagnostic knowledge is generally expressed as a set of rules such as the MYCIN project [5] which relates medical symptoms to possible causes via IF-THEN rules; scientific and mathematical proofs are based largely on conditional constructions [3]; computer programs are a series of rules of the form: "IF the condition is matched THEN execute the conclusion" [10]; and so on.

In belief representation and cognitive science communities, there are many studies on conditional rules (e.g. [1], [22]). The large quantity of publications holding different views about representing and reasoning human conditional beliefs supports this observation. What then are the main characteristics of a commonsense IF-THEN rule? From the view point of modeling the belief states of

* btlow@se.cuhk.edu.hk

a human-like agent in Artificial Intelligence, rules can be part of the inherited beliefs (genetically, culturally, etc.), or, they can be considered as the descriptive structure for generalization of inputs if they are learned by the agent from his/her observations [25]. Since any human-like agent cannot possess every piece of knowledge in the universe, the conditional beliefs that he/she acquired are just approximations to the best of his/her knowledge. He/she will not be able to list all possible conditions for a given conclusion. This characterizes the first element of a commonsense conditional belief: **(i) rules are incomplete conditional descriptions of the world perceived by an agent**.

A commonsense rule usually conveys its meanings in a simple structure: "if condition is valid then conclusion is followed" and no additional semantics are implied. Take a simple example: "*if I work hard then I shall succeed.*" It can be easily verified that additional meaning such as a backward implication "*if I do not succeed means I did not work hard*" does not hold in the intended declarative semantics of a commonsense rule. This simple and direct semantic encapsulation highlights the second characteristic of a commonsense rule: **(ii) rules are unidirectional**.

For a human-like agent, as different conclusions may be derived from different rules acquired separately, there is no guarantee that all rules possessed are accurate. In other words, commonsense IF-THEN rules may not represent the ultimate truth in the state of mind. The agent may believe more firmly in some of them because they happen to be the inherited core beliefs, or, the conditional relations can be easily verified and observed. The agent may be more cautious with other conditional beliefs because they are derived from limited observations or unreliable/contradictory information such as the general rule-of-thumb. Hence we conclude that rules have different degrees of reliabilities. Given a conditional belief, we expect the degree of the conclusion to vary proportionally according to different degrees of belief of its condition. This suggests that there are mapping functions to transform reliabilities of conditions to their corresponding conclusions. Note that commonsense beliefs are very individualized so mapping functions from the degree of condition to the conclusion degree for any IF-THEN rule can be very different from one rule to another, and also from a belief agent to another agent. For example, you may believe very strongly that "*if the sky is covered with thick dark cloud then it will rain*" but someone else may only believe that "*it will probably rain*". Since human beings are able to cater for these possible variations in their commonsense conditional beliefs, we assert that: **(iii) rules have individual flexible mapping functions which indicate their deductive reliabilities**.

As information can be gathered from different sources, different rules may give rise to conflicting conclusions and preferences must be sought to arrive at certain conclusions such that some of the rules are not obeyed, or, in other words, defeated by others. In human-like reasoning, however, these rules are just being defeated and suppressed. They are not immediately removed from the beliefs. This brings us to the fourth major element of commonsense rules: **(iv) rules are defeasible**.

In the belief representation and reasoning community, there is strong emphasis on declaring knowledge in the form of conditional rules for deductive reasoning [4] (also inductive and abductive reasoning). All classical logic-based knowledge systems such as [2] and [17], which dominate the major trends of current research, represent rules as logical material implication relations from conditions to conclusions. This standard interpretation of commonsense rules can be both semantically and syntactically too restrictive if it is to be judged by the four characteristics of commonsense rules. For any given conditional knowledge expressed by a material implication such as $a \rightarrow b$, its equivalent backward implication $\neg b \rightarrow \neg a$ is always in the knowledge base. If this is the desired property of the IF-THEN rules from the domain knowledge modeled, this translation is perfectly acceptable. Unfortunately not all real-world conditional knowledge agrees with the dual-implication inherited from classical logic. For instance, a rule "*if the switch is turned on then the heater generates heat*" does not imply "*if the heater does not generate heat then the switch is not turned on*" as the latter could be due to other reasons such as faulty parts, no electricity supply, ..., etc. This incompleteness characteristic of commonsense rules is closely related to the *qualification problem* of the *frame problem* [19] where it is impossible to declare all conditions for a rule. So when the conclusion fails, since not all conditions are specified, the negation of them may not be implied.

To avoid the limitations of monotonicity, most current commonsense belief representation and reasoning systems are nonmonotonic [9]. Nonmonotonicity is derived from defeating conclusions of some beliefs in view of new information. In any classical logic-based knowledge system, the defeasibility characteristic of rules can be difficult to model as any defeated rule found to be inconsistent with the logical knowledge base has to be expelled from it (e.g. [8]). Although Hypothetical Reasoning [24] tries to retain inconsistent knowledge by dividing knowledge into facts and assumptions, it continues to suffer from the restrictive semantics associated with two-valued material implications. Defaults in Reiter's default logic [23] are a better formalism than material implication for representing IF-THEN rules. They capture the defeasible aspect of commonsense rules but not all commonsense rules can be represented as defaults and sometimes there may be no extension or multiple extensions for a given set of beliefs [16]. Conditional logics and counterfactuals [11] are further alternatives, but they are not only controversial but also rather elaborate. A more natural way for representing IF-THEN rules is the Truth Maintenance Systems [6]. They use justification links between propositional nodes to model unidirectional and defeasible rules. But the setback is knowledge with different degrees has not been considered and mapping functions cannot be expressed.

To model the four characteristics above, we study the representation of IF-THEN rules in an inference network called NLBN. The next section outlines the fundamentals of the belief system and introduces the basic representation of commonsense rule. Section 3 proposes a way to incorporate different mapping functions to rules and section 4 conclude this paper with a pointer to future studies.

2 A Brief Description of the Hybrid Network

A *Neural-Logic Belief Network* (NLBN) is a general belief revision system with a set of well-defined belief update operators [14]. It is a finite acyclic directed graph consists of *nodes* representing propositions and directed *links* representing relations with a neural network computation model. There are two types of nodes:

- *Input nodes* are nodes without any incoming link to represent external input propositions.
- *Base nodes* are other nodes in the network to denote the current propositions in the knowledge system.

Each node represents a *proposition* and has a *node value* to indicate its current belief state. Input nodes receive external input beliefs and propagate them via directed *input links* to the relevant base nodes. As incompleteness and inconsistency are part of real-world knowledge, input nodes can represent different beliefs of the same proposition from different sources. For base nodes, each proposition is uniquely represented by a single node and the collection of all base nodes represents the belief state, usually denoted as S.

A node value is an ordered pair: (*proposition-value, degree-of-belief value*). As there is no bias towards either positive or negative beliefs, an ordered-pair (t, f) is used to denote the proposition-value, where t denotes the positive support (excitatory) and f represents the negative (inhibitory) aspect of beliefs. Let "1" represents there is information and "0" represents no information, $(t, f) =$ (1, 0) means that the proposition associated with the node is believed, (t, f) = (0, 1) means the negation of the proposition is believed, and $(t, f) =$ (0, 0) that it is neither believed nor not-believed. ((0, 0), 0) is the default node value including beliefs (propositions) that are currently not represented by the belief network (i.e. unknown beliefs). The degree-of-belief values (written as deg[(proposition)]) induce a total asymmetric order (TAO) on the strength or certainty of the propositions. For example, we may have a total order for beliefs such as:

0 <possibly<weakly<probably<usually<normally<mostly<strongly<surely<definitely<true

Given a Neural-Logic Belief Network, a base node a having a node value ((1, 0), deg[a]) means that a is in the belief state S, i.e. $a \in S$ and $\neg a \notin S$, with a degree-of-belief deg[a]; a node value of ((0, 1), deg[a]) means $\neg a \in S$ and $a \notin S$. A base node a ((0, 0), 0) denotes both $a \notin S$ and $\neg a \notin S$ and a ((0, 0), deg[a]>0) means a currently has contradictory beliefs at deg[a], i.e. $a \in S$ and $\neg a \in S$. Node values of ((1, 0), 0) and ((0, 1), 0) have no meaningful semantics and they are not valid node values. There are three types of directed links:

- *Combinative-links* are the most basic links in the network to make all kinds of relations among base nodes.
- *Rule-links* are used to represent IF-THEN relations from condition nodes to the conclusion nodes.

- *Input-links* are used to propagate input values from input nodes to base nodes.

These directed links serve as signal transmission channels from one node to another. The strength of information passing through any link is controlled (reduced or amplified) by an ordered pair of link weights (u, v) associated with each directed link where $u, v \in$ {Real Numbers}. Analogous to the proposition-values, u is an excitatory value and v is an inhibitory value.

The computation functions for propositional belief networks are similar to that of a neural-net where at each base node, a summation function totals the inputs from incoming combinative-links, i.e. the products of the link-weights and the incoming node's proposition-value. This value then goes through a thresholding function which decides the node value for the node. For input-links and rule-links, instead of summing all inputs, each incoming link is considered as alternative input and computed accordingly. A selection function is then used to pick up the strongest input among the computed alternative values.

Computation of node values (proposition-values and degree-of-belief values) depends on the type of incoming links to the node concerned [14]. For input-nodes, where there is no incoming links directed at them, their node values are the direct external inputs. The computation function for a base node $o((t_o, f_o), deg[o])$ with n incoming combinative-links are similar to that of a neural-net where a *summation function* totals the inputs from n incoming combinative-links, i.e. the products of incoming node's proposition-value and its corresponding link-weights:

$$NET{=}\sum\{(t_i \times u_i) - (f_i \times v_i)\} \text{ where } 0 < i < n.$$

This value then goes through the following *thresholding function* which decides the proposition-value for node o:

$$(t_o, f_o) = \begin{cases} (1,0) \text{ if } NET \geq 1 \\ (0,1) \text{ if } NET \leq -1 \\ (0,0) \text{ otherwise} \end{cases}$$

Based on the competitive voting semantics [15], the detailed computation functions of the proposition-values and degree-of-belief values are given in [14]. Input- and rule-links are *alternative links*. Each of these links has a pair of *link weights* (u, v) and a *link-degree-of-belief* value denoted as deg[(name of the relation)]. The values propagated by these links will not be combined with other links. They are instead considered as possible alternative values computed individually.

The node value received by a node o $((t_o, f_o)$, deg$[o])$ from another node o_i $((t_i, f_i)$, deg$[o_i])$ via an input- or rule-link with link-weights of (u_i, v_i) and the link degree-of-belief value of deg[link] is given by:

$$(t_o, f_o) = \begin{cases} (1,0) \text{ if } (t_i \times u_i - f_i \times v_i) \geq 1 \\ (0,1) \text{ if } (t_i \times u_i - f_i \times v_i) \leq -1 \\ (0,0) \text{ otherwise} \end{cases}$$

$$deg[o] = \begin{cases} deg[o_i] & \text{if } deg[o_i] \leq deg[link] \text{ and } (t_o, f_o) \neq (0,0) \\ deg[link] & \text{if } deg[o_i] > deg[link] \text{ and } (t_o, f_o) \neq (0,0) \\ 0 & \text{otherwise} \end{cases}$$

When there are n inputs from rule-links and/or inheritance-links to this base node o as shown in the figure below, the network values from each input is computed individually. That is, for each node $o_i (0 < i \leq n)$, there is one input node value $((t_i, f_i), deg[i])$ from the incoming link computed using the above computation function.

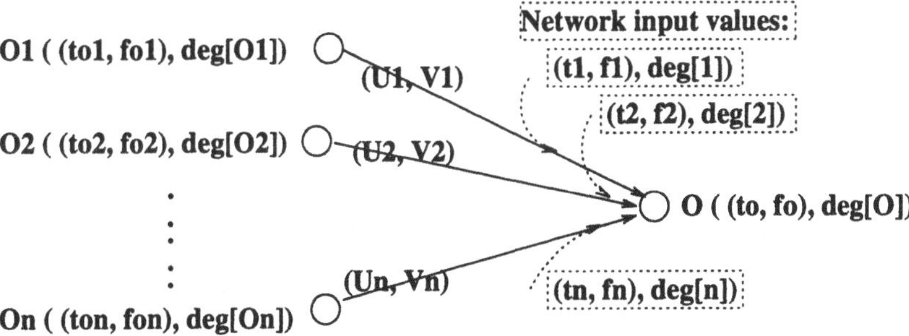

With the belief network's subsumptive assumption [13] that stronger beliefs always subsume weaker ones, the *selection function* below is then used to pick up the strongest input among these alternatives as the computed node value. This subsumptive nature is similar to the MAX operation in fuzzy set theory [27].

$$(t_o, f_o) = \begin{cases} (t_k, f_k) & \text{if } deg[k] > deg[i], 0 < k \leq n, k \neq i, \text{ for all } 0 < i \leq n \\ (t_j, f_j) & \text{if } (t_j, f_j) = (t_k, f_k), 0 < j \leq m, 0 < k \leq m, 1 < m \leq n, \\ & deg[j] = deg[k], deg[j] > deg[i], j \neq k \neq i, \text{ for all} \\ & 0 < i \leq n \\ (0,0) & \text{otherwise} \end{cases}$$

$$deg[o] = \begin{cases} deg[k] & \text{if } deg[k] \geq deg[i], 0 < k \leq n, k \neq i, \text{ for all } 0 < i \leq n \\ 0 & \text{otherwise} \end{cases}$$

If inputs to a base node o are given by combinative-links as well as rule-links, the input values from all combinative-links shall first be processed to yield at an input value. This input value is treated as one of the input node values and the same selection function above is used to determine the value of node o.

NLBN can represent classical logical expressions and other relations. Logical expressions are constructed by combinative-links. For example, a two input OR relation $a \vee b$ and a two input AND relation $c \wedge d$ are represented as:

where (2, 1/2) and (1/2, 2) are the corresponding link weights. Details and other logical expressions are described in [14].

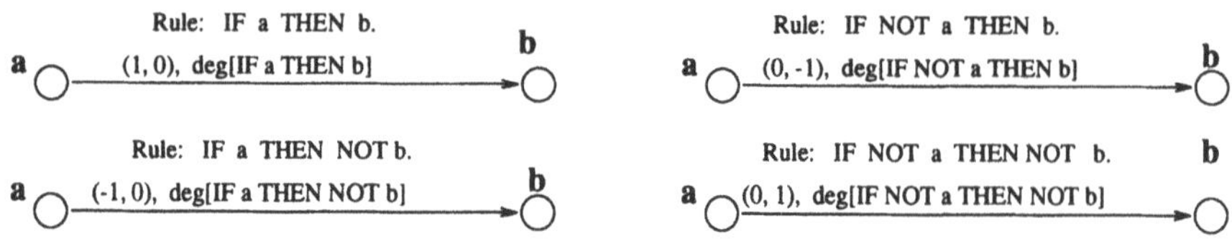

Fig. 1. Link weights for commonsense rules and inheritance relations.

Each defeasible IF-THEN rule in NLBN is represented by a *rule-link* from the condition base node to the conclusion base node. Their inferences are unidirectional. A rule "IF a THEN b" (denoted as $a \mapsto b$) has no hidden meaning of "IF NOT b THEN NOT a" (i.e. $\neg b \mapsto \neg a$) that would otherwise be associated with a rule expressed by a material implication. Typical link weights carried by rule-links are shown in Fig. 1. The corresponding truth tables for the IF-THEN rules are as follows:

Proposition-value of a	Proposition-value of b: IF a THEN b	IF a THEN NOT b	IF NOT a THEN b	IF NOT a THEN NOT b
(1, 0)	(1, 0)	(0, 1)	(0, 0)	(0, 0)
(0, 0)	(0, 0)	(0, 0)	(0, 0)	(0, 0)
(0, 1)	(0, 0)	(0, 0)	(1, 0)	(0, 1)

3 Flexible Mapping Functions

In an attempt to meet the four characteristics of conditional beliefs discussed in section 1, NLBN imposes the following two additional assumptions:

1. If a proposition can be derived from more than one IF-THEN rule, then the rule (or a set of agreeing rules) that gives the strongest conclusion subsumes all input conclusions from other rules. If there are opposite conclusions of the same degree, then the conclusion will be in a contradictory state.
2. Given any commonsense rule, the degree-of-belief of the conclusion depends on the degree of its condition. The stronger the condition, the stronger the conclusion. The mapping function for the conditions to their conclusions are *monotonic non-decreasing*, i.e. no stronger condition will give rise to a conclusion weaker than that of a weaker condition.

The computation functions for alternative-links in section 2 agree with the above conditions. Given a rule "IF a THEN b (deg[rule])", the rule mapping

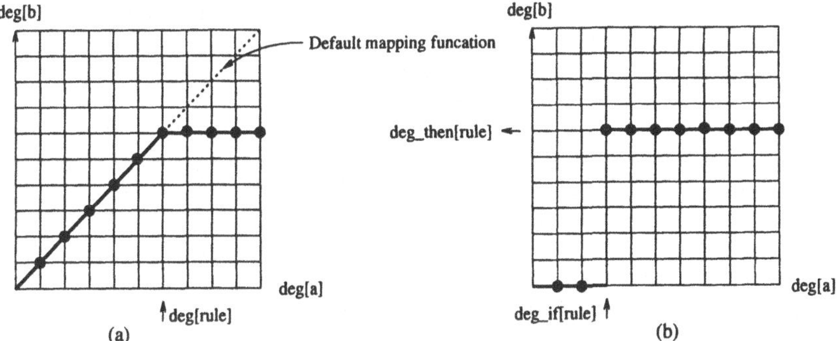

Fig. 2. Two types of rule mappings: (a) S-rule and (b) C-rule.

function given in section 2 is illustrated in Fig. 2(a). In this figure, the horizontal axis represents all increasing degrees of the rule condition deg[a] according to the TAO defined while the vertical axis represents the same set of ascending degrees for the conclusion deg[b]. The dotted diagonal line in this figure is the default mapping function and the value of deg[rule] puts a cap on it which is the maximum degree that is conveyed from the condition to its conclusion in the rule. We call this type of *simple* rule mapping a **S-rule** and the rule-links described so far are called *S-rule-links*. IF-THEN rules with this type of simple mappings are common in human reasoning.

Example 1. Simple mapping function: In a tennis tournament, a player may have the following commonsense rule:

IF *I hit a strong service* THEN *the return will be weak.* (normally)

This can be represented intuitively in NLBN by a S-rule with a mapping function similar to Fig. 2(a) where deg[rule]=normally. This representation includes semantics of "*if it is probable that I hit a strong service then the return will probably be weak*" with the conclusion degree linearly proportional to its condition degree up to and including "*if I normally hit a strong service then the return will normally be weak*". For any condition with a stronger belief such as "*I definitely hit a strong service*" the conclusion is capped by the deg[rule] as: *the return will normally be weak.* □

To allow for more flexible rule mapping functions we introduce a new type of rule-link:

Definition 1. (C-rules) A *controlled-rule-link* or *C-rule-link* is an alternative-link with two associated link degree-of-belief values: deg_if[rule] and deg_then[rule]. A deg_if[rule] is the starting rule degree for the condition while the conclusion of the rule is believed at deg_then[rule]. Any IF-THEN rule constructed using a *C-rule-link* is called a *C-rule*.

Given a C-rule "$a \mapsto b$ (deg_if[$a \mapsto b$], deg_then[$a \mapsto b$])" represented by a C-rule-link with a tuple of link-weights (u, v) from base node a to b, its network value is computed in the similar way as a S-rule in the previous section as follows:

$$(t_b, f_b) = \begin{cases} (1,0) \text{ if } (t_a \times u - f_a \times v) \geq 1 \text{ and } deg[a] \geq deg\_if[a \mapsto b] \\ (0,1) \text{ if } (t_a \times u - f_a \times v) \leq -1 \text{ and } deg[a] \geq deg\_if[a \mapsto b] \\ (0,0) \text{ otherwise} \end{cases}$$

$$deg[b] = \begin{cases} deg\_then[a \mapsto b] \text{ if } deg[a] \geq deg\_if[a \mapsto b] \text{ and } (t_b, f_b) \neq (0,0) \\ 0 \qquad\qquad\qquad\qquad \text{otherwise} \end{cases}$$

□

The mapping function of the example in the above definition is illustrated in Fig. 2(b) where the two rule degrees, deg_if[rule] and deg_then[rule], determine the boundary line of the mapping function for a C-rule. Any condition with a degree weaker than deg_if[rule] will give an unknown conclusion (with a deg[conclusion]=0). With this type of mapping functions, we can easily reduce or amplify the degrees of the conclusions.

Example 2. Restrained mapping function: A C-rule can be used to represent a rule with weak co-relations where the conclusion is always restrained to a weaker belief even if the condition is much strongly believed.

IF *I buy a lottery ticket* THEN *I will win.* (true, possibly) □

Example 3. Amplified mapping function: A C-rule can also model magnifying rule where the conclusion is always believed at a high degree even if the evidence for its condition is weak.

IF *my boyfriend dates another girl* THEN *he does not love me.* (probably, surely) □

More complex mapping functions can be achieved by compound rules in a *rule set*.

Definition 2. (Rule set) A *rule set*, or a *rule* for short, is a set of IF-THEN rules with the same link-weights linking any two base nodes in a NLBN. A rule set, which consists of m ($m > 0$) rules from base nodes a to b, is denoted as:

$$a \models\!\!\Rightarrow b \; (deg(a \models\!\!\Rightarrow b))$$

where $deg(a \models\!\!\Rightarrow b) = (deg_1, deg_2, \ldots, deg_m)$ and each deg_i ($0 < i \leq m$) is the (deg[rule]) for a S-rule or the (deg_if[rule], deg_then[rule]) for a C-rule. □

A special case is $m = 1$ where the rule set is a single S-rule or C-rule. When $m > 1$, a rule set represents a conditional belief with a compound mapping function constructed with more than one C-rule or a combination of C- and S-rules. According to the computation functions, when more than one S-rule are in a rule set, the S-rule with the strongest deg[rule] subsumes all other S-rules.

Example 4. Compound mapping functions:

IF *I love her* THEN *she will love me.* (possibly)
IF *I love her* THEN *she will love me.* (definitely, usually)

These rules form the following rule set in a NLBN:

I love her $\models\!\!\Rightarrow$ *she will love me.* ((possibly), (definitely, usually))

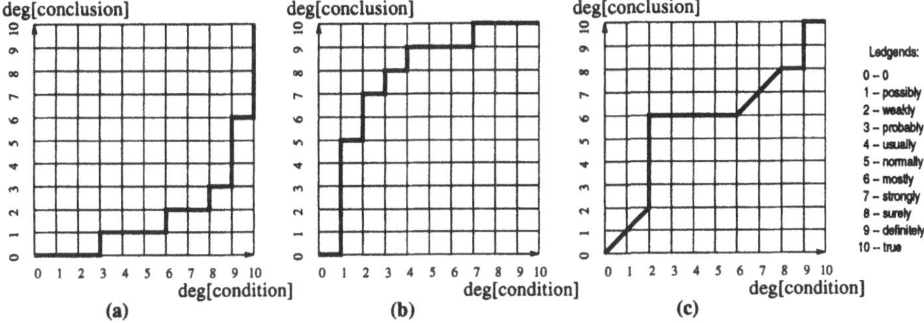

Fig. 3. Examples of compound IF-THEN rule mapping functions.

Three more compound mapping functions are shown in Fig. 3:

(a) shows a **concave** mapping function constructed by five C-rules:
condition $\models\!\!\Rightarrow$ *conclusion* ((probably, possibly), (mostly, weakly), (surely, probably), (definitely, mostly), (definitely, true))

(b) shows a **convex** mapping function of the following rule set:
condition $\models\!\!\Rightarrow$ *conclusion* ((possibly, normally), (weakly, strongly) (probably, surely), (usually, definitely), (strongly, true))

(c) represents a **free** mapping function of a rule set which consists of two C-rules and a S-rule:
condition $\models\!\!\Rightarrow$ *conclusion* ((weakly, mostly), (surely), (definitely, true)) □

4 Discussion

Modeling of conditional beliefs is an abstraction of the internal representations of the relations of the presented world, which is also another abstract entity [21]. It is therefore impossible to fulfill every aspect of commonsense conditional beliefs in a NLBN, let alone its limited symbolic representation. By selecting "relevant" characteristics from the view point of Artificial Intelligence, we recognize that human conditional beliefs are unidirectional, defeasible, have flexible mapping functions, and may be incomplete. The modeling of commonsense rules in NLBN was aimed at addressing these important issues.

In this paper, the concept of ***rule sets*** to represent more human-like conditional beliefs in a NLBN is studied. In a NLBN, acyclic conditional beliefs including contradictory ones (e.g. $a \mapsto b$ together with $a \mapsto \neg b$, or $\neg a \mapsto b$ with $\neg a \mapsto \neg b$) can be represented freely by rule sets as long as no closed loop is formed. By adopting the subsumptive computation functions defined, conclusions derived using these unidirectional inferencing conditionals are always defeasible by other stronger beliefs, either from other rules or from direct inputs.

We have defined two basic types of rules: S-rule and C-rule. With conditional beliefs represented by a set of these rules, any monotonic non-increasing mapping function from the condition to the conclusion of a rule in the TAO×TAO space can be defined (see examples in Fig. 3). If the total asymmetric order (TAO) for representing degrees of beliefs are not discrete values (e.g. real numbers, [0, 1] fuzzy measures, etc.), more complex mapping function descriptions and computations are necessary to handle their continuous transitions between specified belief values. Based on the subsumptive mapping philosophy of a NLBN, this may lead to similar results as the Falling Shadow Theory [26]. We are currently investigating into this area.

Acknowledgement

I would like to thank Norman Y. Foo of Sydney University for his invaluable comments during the conceptual formulation state of this approach. This research is partially supported by a Direct Grant and a Shaw College grant from the Chinese University of Hong Kong.

References

1. Ernest Wilcox Adams. *Logic of Conditionals : an Application of Probability to Deductive Logic*. D. Reidel, Dordrecht, 1975.
2. C. E. Alchourron, Peter Gärdenfors, and David Makinson. On the logic of theory change: Partial meet functions for contraction and revision. *Journal of Symbolic Logic*, 50:510–530, 1985.
3. Richard Boyd, Philip Gasper, and J. D. Trout, editors. *The Philosophy of Science*. MIT Press, Cambridge, Massachusetts, 1991.
4. Ronald J. Brachman and Hector J. Levesque, editors. *Readings in Knowledge Representation*. Morgan Kaufmann, San Mateo, California, 1985.

5. Bruce G. Buchanan and Edward H. Shortliffe. *Rule-Based Expert Systems — The MYCIN Experiments of the Stanford Heuristic Programming Project.* Addison-Wesley Publishing Company, Reading, Massachusetts, 1984.
6. Jon Doyle. A truth maintenance system. *Artificial Intelligence J.*, 12:231–272, 1979.
7. Peter Gärdenfors. *Knowledge in Flux : Modeling the Dynamics of Epistemic States.* MIT Press, Cambridge, Massachusetts, 1988.
8. Peter Gärdenfors and David Makinson. Nonmonotonic inferences based on expectations. *Artificial Intelligence J.*, 65:197–245, 1994.
9. Matehew L. Ginsberg, editor. *Readings in Nonmonotonic Reasoning.* Morgan Kaufmann, 1985.
10. Brian W. Kernighan and Dennis M. Ritchie. *The C Programming Language.* Prentice-Hall, Englewood Cliffs, New Jersey, 1978.
11. D. K. Lewis. *Counterfactuals.* Blackwell, Oxford, 1973.
12. Boon Toh Low. *Reasoning about Beliefs: An Inference Network Approach.* PhD thesis, Basser Department of Computer Science, University of Sydney, 1994.
13. Boon Toh Low. A subsumptive inference network for belief representation. In *proceedings of the Third Pacific Rim International Conference on Artificial Intelligence*, Beijing, 1994.
14. Boon Toh Low and Norman Y. Foo. A network formalism for commonsense reasoning. In *Proceedings of the Sixteenth Australian Computer Science Conference*, pages 425–434, Brisbane, 1993.
15. Boon Toh Low and Norman Y. Foo. Competitive voting semantics for neural-net decision functions. In *Proceedings of the Second Singapore International Conference on Intelligent Systems, SPICIS'94*, pages 225–230, 1994.
16. Witold Lukaszewicz. Two results on default logic. In *Proceedings of 9th IJCAI*, pages 459–461, Los Angeles, 1985.
17. John McCarthy. Circumscription: A form of non-monotonic reasoning. *Artificial Intelligence J.*, 13:27–39, 1980.
18. John McCarthy and Patrick J. Hayes. Some philosophical problems from the standpoint of artificial intelligence. In B. Meltxer and D. Mitchie, editors, *Machine Intelligence 4*, pages 463–502. Edinburgh University Press, 1969.
19. Drew McDermott. AI, logic and the frame problem. *Proceedings of the Frame Problem in Artificial Intelligence Workshop*, pages 105–118, 1987.
20. Donald Michie, editor. *Introductory Readings in Expert Systems.* Gordon and Breach, Science Publishers, New York, 1982.
21. George A. Miller. Trends and debates in cognitive psychology. *Cognition*, 10:215–225, 1981.
22. D. Nute. Defeasible reasoning and decision support systems. *Decision Support Systems*, 4:97–110, 1988.
23. R. Reiter. A logic for default reasoning. *Artificial Intelligence J.*, 13:81–132, 1980.
24. Abdul Satta and R. Goebel. Constraint satisfaction as hypothetical reasoning. In *Proceedings of AAAI'92*, Cancun, Mexico, 1992. AAAI Press.
25. Jude W. Shavlik and Thomas G. Dietterich, editors. *Readings in Machine Learning.* Morgan Kaufmann, San Mateo, California, 1990.
26. Pei Zhuang Wang. *Fuzzy Sets and Falling Shadows of Random Sets.* Beijing Normal University Press, 1985.
27. Lotfi A. Zadeh. Knowledge representation in fuzzy logic. *IEEE Transactions on Knowledge and Data Engineering*, 1(1):89–100, 1991.

Adaptive SEJONG-NET for On-Line Hangul Recognition

Hyeyoung Park[1], Kwanyong Lee[1], Hyeran Byun[1] and Yillbyung Lee[1 2]

[1] Department of Computer Science, Yonsei University, Seoul, Korea
[2] Center for Artificial Intelligence Research, Daejeon, Korea

Abstract. In this paper, a revised SEJONG-NET with adaptability for recognizing transformed on-line Hangul pattern is proposed. It is based on the structural characteristics of Hangul and the hypotheses on the processes of human Hangul recognition. Unlike the existing SEJONG-NET, the proposed model extracts the information about the orientation and the curvature of strokes in the lower layers. In the higher layers, it represents the information on graphemes as conceptual graphs, and detects a particular grapheme using the conceptual graph. The conceptual graph is composed of two kinds of nodes, concept nodes and relation nodes. The concept node has the orientation and curvature information, and the relation node describes the positional relations between two concept nodes. Through the computer simulations, we showed that the adaptive SEJONG-NET could recognize the transformed Hangul patterns after training the basic grapheme patterns, and also that untrained or severely deformed patterns can be efficiently recognized by creating a new graph or adjusting the values of the existing conceptual graphs. Hence, SEJONG-NET with adaptability can be considered as an efficient model for recognizing Hangul patterns with transformation.

1 Introduction

SEJONG-NET (<u>SE</u>lective <u>J</u>udgement <u>O</u>f <u>N</u>umerous <u>G</u>rapheme - neural <u>NET</u>work), inspired by the visual system of the vertebrates, is a neural network model to provide a comprehensive paradigm to explain visual character pattern recognition. This model has been designed originally for the recognition of on-line Hangul, and then modified to recognize Roman characters, Chinese radicals, and off-line Hangul[4, 5, 6, 7, 8, 9]. The basic characteristics of SEJONG-NET is that it has a hierarchical structure and processes not only static visual patterns but also dynamic visual patterns. The spatio-temporal information is processed in parallel through two separated paths respectively.

There are the overall structure and the functional process of SEJONG-NET in Figure 1 and Figure 2 respectively. The first layer, IN layer, represents a two dimensional input image with binary value. REC layer receives the information from IN layer and IN_1 layer, and represents the spatio-temporal information. The output of REC layer is propagated to the spatial information processing path(SSF layer, CSF layer) and the temporal information processing path(STF

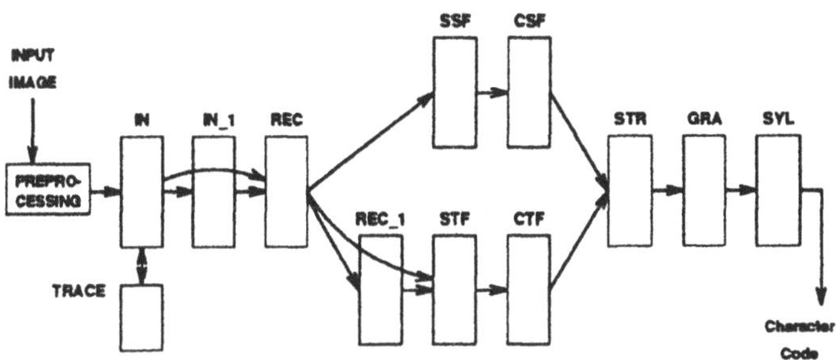

Fig. 1. Basic structure of SEJONG-NET

Feature)layer, CTF layer). STR layer combines the informations from the separated pathways, and then recognizes strokes. The sequence of strokes is searched and graphemes are detected in GRA layer. Finally SYL layer recognizes a syllable.

The basic model of SEJONG-NET for on-line Hangul recognition defines 7 primitive strokes and each input stroke of a character is mapped to one of them. In other words, all the existing SEJONG-NET models for Hangul recognition process a character stroke by stroke, and use automata for recognizing graphemes and syllables. Due to these processing mechanisms, the conventional models are very sensitive to the transformations of strokes.

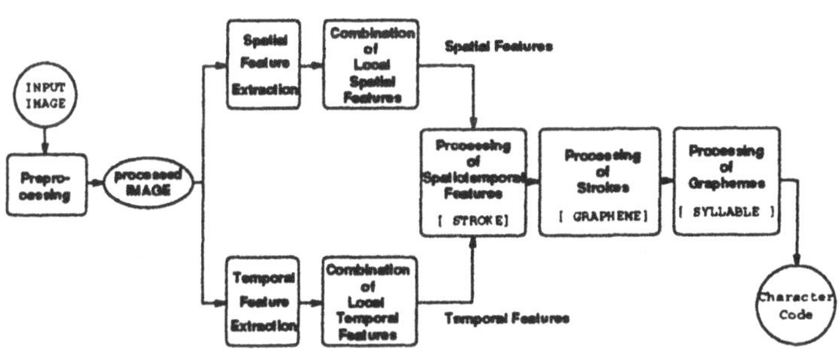

Fig. 2. Functional diagram of SEJONG-NET

In this paper, a revised SEJONG-NET model which can adapt oneself to the transformations of patterns is proposed. The model is based on the hypotheses on the processes of human Hangul recognition and the structural knowledge of Hangul.

2 Hypotheses on Hangul Recognition Process

For a new model, we take several hypotheses on the processing mechanism of Hangul recognition. Our hypotheses are based on our intuitions as well as the results of physiological and psychological experiments[1, 2, 3, 10, 11, 13, 14]. There are three basic hypotheses in the followings:

1. The recognition and learning process is done grapheme by grapheme. This hypothesis is supported by the result in [3], which shows that when human recognizes a Hangul character he first processes graphemes and then recognizes a complete character. And in the similar way, human learns a Hangul character through the combination of specific graphemes.
2. All graphemes can be represented by combinations of four orientation factors. In the existing models, a grapheme is described as a sequence of primitive strokes. In such a method, two same graphemes with different stroke sequence are regarded as different graphemes. However, this method can accept these graphemes as the same grapheme if they consist of the same stroke elements. In addition, orientation features are detected in primary visual cortex of human brain[13].
3. When human recognizes a Hangul character, he uses the temporal information as only secondary one. Since human usually recognizes the character image that had been written, not having been written, it is hard to think that the information of pen movement has the important role for character recognition. This hypothesis is supported by the fact that human can recognizes the grapheme image written by other direction although he learned a grapheme image written by only one direction. Hence in this paper we use temporal information only for segmenting a character image as a stream of individual strokes.

3 Structures and Functions

3.1 IN layer and TRACE layer

Each element of IN layer indicates the existence of visual stimulus at the corresponding point with binary values. TRACE layer has the information of sequence of input pixels. And IN_1 layer has the output pattern of IN layer before a unit of time, which is used for detecting the changes of stimulus. We show that the output pattern of IN layer for the Hangul character '시' in Figure 3.

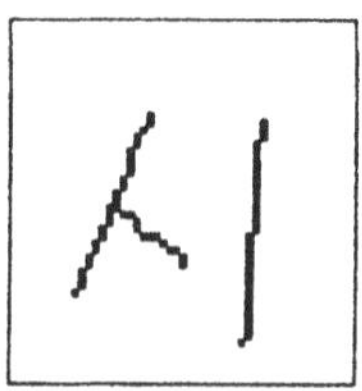

Fig. 3. IN layer for the Hangul character '시' [si]

3.2 REC layer

REC layer simulates the photoreceptor in the retina of the vertebrate animals. Namely, the point in which the latest stimulus exists has the largest output value and the other points have a stable value. These output values are computed by the following equation.

$$REC(t) = W_1 \times IN\_1(t) + W_2 \times (IN(t) - IN\_1(t)) \tag{1}$$

where W_1 and W_2 are real values between 0 and 1.

In the same manner of IN_1 layer, REC_1 layer has the output value which is equal to that of REC layer before one unit of time. The output of REC layer is transmitted to two separated paths for temporal and spatial processing.

3.3 STF layer

Each cell of STF layer is activated at the moment a stimuli comes out. This output pattern simulates the function of ON-OFF ganglion cell of the retina. The computational model is showed in the followings:

$$STF(t) = \begin{cases} 1 & \text{if } REC(t) - REC\_1(t) > 0 \\ 0 & \text{otherwise} \end{cases} \tag{2}$$

STF layer gives notice of the location of a new stimulus so that CTF layer can pay attention to the point.

3.4 CTF layer

As mentioned in the previous section, the temporal information is not very much important in the model. Hence CTF layer in the model detects the ending of a stroke and signals STR layer to start processing on the current stroke. In order to output, CTF layer compares the location of currently activated cell with that of previously activated cell in STF layer. If the two locations are not connected, then a stroke is ended before one unit of time and the next stroke is started from the current point.

3.5 SSF layer

The cells of SSF layer model after the simple cells and the complex cells in the primary visual cortex of the vertebrates which detect orientations[13]. SSF layer is designed for detecting four main orientation features($0°$, $45°$, $90°$, and $135°$) by using four 5×5 filters. Each filter represents a cell detecting the corresponding orientation and its pattern appeared in Figure 4 is the simplified one of the receptive field of the simple and complex cells. The weights of the filters have the value of -1,0 or 1, and cannot be changed by learning.

Figure 5 shows the output of SSF layer for '시'. There exist four planes corresponding to each orientation filter. In Figure 5, we can see that more than two planes can activate concurrently if the orientation is not exactly matched to a specific orientation filter. This fact indicates the system has the adaptability to the transformations caused by slantwise writing.

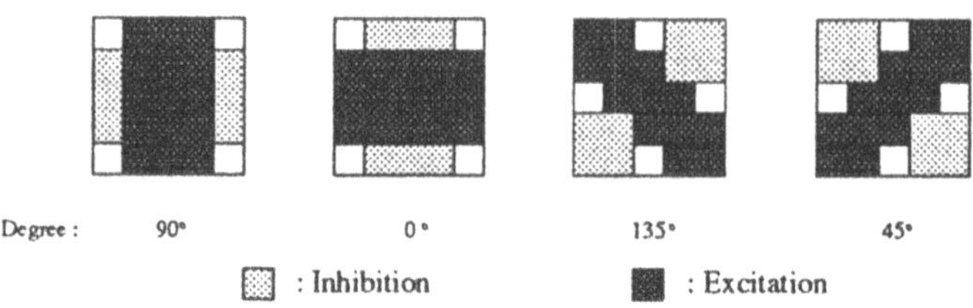

Fig. 4. The receptive field of SSF layer

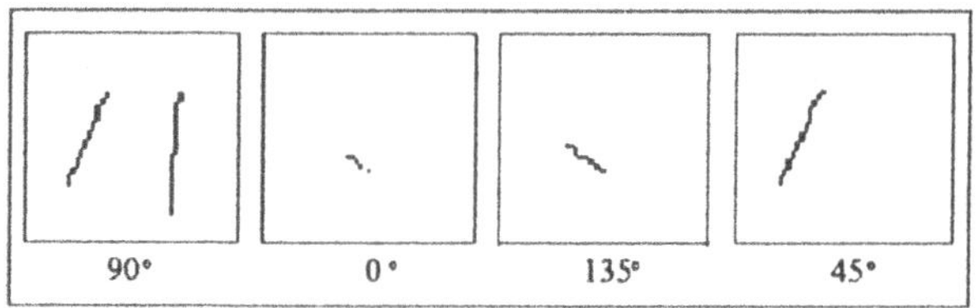

Fig. 5. The result of SSF layer for '시'

3.6 CSF layer

CSF layer plays the role of hypercomplex cells. The most important function of hypercomplex cells is the detection of the length and the curvature[10, 11, 13, 14]. In CSF layer, we designed the length detector by using inhibitory filters. For each plane of SSF layer, the model uses 2 inhibitory filters with 3×3 size to detect the starting point and the ending point respectively. The filters are put on an active position in the plane, and if the filtered activation value is greater than the threshold value, the point is taken for the starting point or the ending point. The filters are shown in Figure 6, where the location of fired cell is the point to be investigated, and the inhibition means that the weight value is -1. After finding the starting point and the ending point, we take the number of pixels between the starting and the ending point for the length of a stroke. And the sequence of pixels from the starting point to the ending point are regarded as an orientation object. The orientation object is treated as a basic processing element in the higher stage of this model.

To detect the curvature, the model uses 4 filters for each plane. There are two patterns of curvature for each orientation feature, and two filters for each curvature pattern. The filters used in CSF layer to detect curvature are shown in Figure 7. The curvature value of an orientation object is computed by subtraction the value of curvature2 from that of curvature1.

The output of CSF layer is a list of the orientation objects which have the information about length, curvature, and starting/ending point.

3.7 STR layer

STR layer, synchronized by CTF layer, generates a graph which describes the relation of the orientation objects. The structure of the graph is based on the

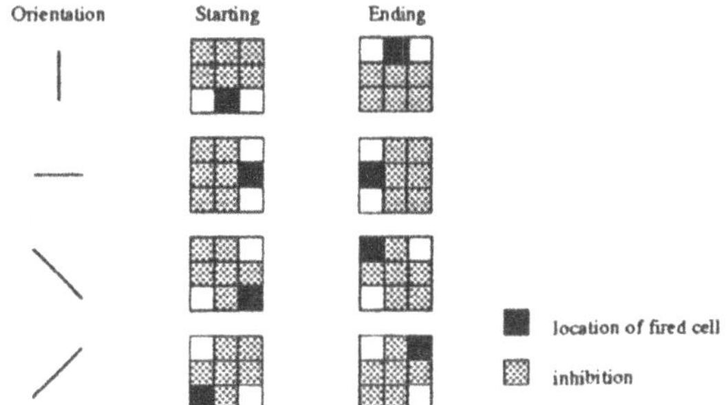

Fig. 6. The receptive field of the length detector in CSF layer

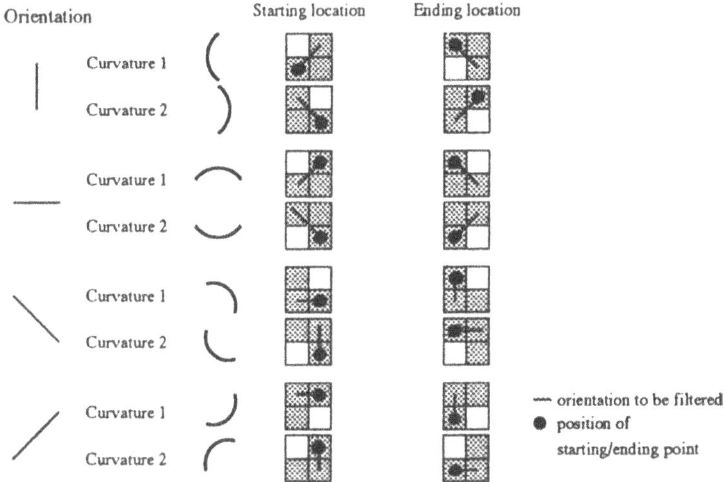

Fig. 7. The receptive field of the curvature detector in CSF layer

theory of conceptual graph[12]. The conceptual graph consists of two kinds of nodes, concept nodes and relation nodes, and directional arcs. In STR layer, a concept node stands for an orientation object and a relation node has the relational information between two concept nodes. To describe the relation of two concept nodes we use two kinds of information, location and contact. For the locational information, the system computes five values, namely *left, right, above, below* and *overlap*. For example, if one concept node is chosen as the pivot of computation, the left value stands for the portion of the other concept node which is in the left side of the pivot. Other location values are computed in the same way. The computational equation for left value is as follows, where m_x stands for x coordinates of the center of the pivot and P_i stands for a pixel in the other orientation object.

$$L = \sum_i \Phi(P_i) \tag{3}$$

where,

$$\Phi(P_i) = \begin{cases} 1 & \text{if } m_x > P_{i_x} \\ 0 & \text{otherwise} \end{cases}$$

For the contact information, the relation node has a 5×5 section of IN layer image on which it centers the contact point. Figure 8 shows the example of conceptual graphs for '시'. The conceptual graph generated in STR layer is used for matching the conceptual graphs on the graphemes in GRA layer.

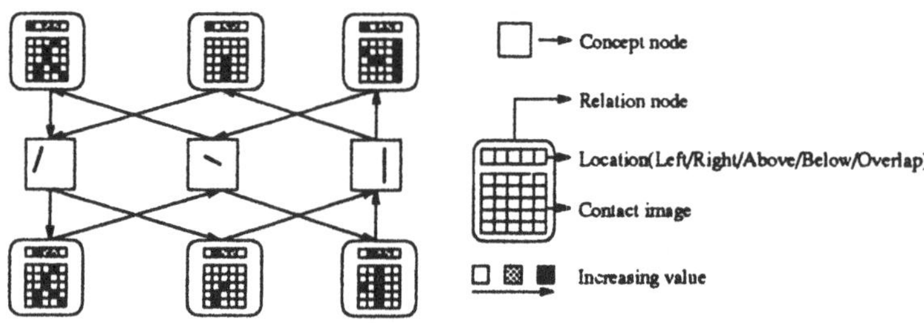

Fig. 8. Conceptual graph in STR layer for '시'

3.8 GRA layer

GRA layer detects a specific grapheme through comparing the conceptual graph of STR layer with the standard conceptual graphs, which represent the basic graphemes, 14 simple consonants, 10 simple vowels and 4 double vowels.

- simpe graphemes: 'ㄱ', 'ㄴ', 'ㄷ', 'ㄹ', 'ㅁ', 'ㅂ', 'ㅅ', 'ㅇ', 'ㅈ', 'ㅊ', 'ㅋ', 'ㅌ', 'ㅍ', 'ㅎ',
- simple consonants: 'ㅏ', 'ㅑ', 'ㅓ', 'ㅕ', 'ㅗ', 'ㅛ', 'ㅜ', 'ㅠ', 'ㅡ', 'ㅣ',
- 4 double vowels: 'ㅐ', 'ㅒ', 'ㅔ', 'ㅖ'.

The structure of the conceptual graphs of GRA layer is the same with that of STR layer. To detect a grapheme, GRA layer compares concept nodes and relation nodes in the standard conceptual graphs on graphemes with those in the conceptual graph of STR layer. The matching values between two nodes are computed by the following equation.

- Matching value for concept node
  - Concept = Orient + Curvature
  - Orient = A - MIN_i (| GO_i - SO_i |)
  - Curvature = B - | GC_i - SC_i |
    - GO_i,SO_i : orientation feature value(for GRA,STR)
    - GC_i,SC_i : curvature value(for GRA,STR)
    - A, B : constants

- Matching value of relation node

$$\text{Relation} = W_1 \times \text{Location} + W_2 \times \text{Contact}$$
$$\text{Location} = \sum_i |GL_i\text{-}\ SL_i\ |$$
$$\text{Contact} = \sum_i \sum_j GCO_{ij} \times LCO_{ij}$$

GL_i,SL_i : location feature value(for GRA,STR)

GCO_{jk},LCO_{jk} : the value of contact image point(for GRA,STR)

W_1, W_2 : weight values

In GRA layer, the values of the nodes of conceptual graphs are changable. In addition, a new conceptual graph can be added into the group of the standard conceptual graphs, too. During the learning process, at first the model computes the matching values of input grapheme patterns by using the standard grapheme patterns. If the value is greater than the threshold value, the values of the nodes of the corresponding conceptual graph in GRA layer are changed to absorb the input patterns into the conceptual graph. If not, a new conceptual graph is added. In this case, the new conceptual graph can be obtained from the conceptual graph generated in STR layer.

The computational equations for adjusting the values of nodes are as follows: In the equations, the variables are the same with those of the equations for computing matching values and $\alpha_i (i = 1, ..., 5)$ are constants.

- For concept nodes

$$GO_i = MAX_i(GO_i,SO_i)$$
$$GC_i = GC_i + \alpha_1 \times (SC_i\ \text{-}\ GC_i)$$

- For relation node.

$$GL_i = GL_i + \alpha_2 \times (SL_i\ \text{-}\ GL_i)$$
$$GCO_i = GCO_i + \alpha_3 \times SCO_i \times (SCO_i\ \text{-}\ GCO_i)$$
$$W_1 = W_1 + \alpha_4(\frac{Location}{Location+Contact} - W_1)$$
$$W_2 = W_2 + \alpha_5(\frac{Contact}{Location+Contact} - W_2)$$

3.9 SYL layer

SYL layer, the final output stage of the model, recognizes a Hangul character by combining the graphemes which are detected in GRA layer. We use the structural knowledge about Hangul characters such as the positional relations among graphemes in the process of finding the candidates of the character and choosing a specific character as a final result.

4 Computer Simulations and Results

The revised SEJONG-NET was implemented on SPARC station 10 (101MIPS) using C language. The data sets used in the simulations are as follows:

1. A set that consists of 14 simple consonants, 10 simple vowels, and 4 double vowels. for creating the standard conceptual graphs on the graphemes.
2. 10 sets of 28 graphemes for learning the standard conceptual graphs.

3. 4000 syllable characters(most frequently used 500 syllables × 8 persons).

We initialize the standard conceptual graphs using the basic 28 graphemes, and then train the nodes of the initialized conceptual graphs with slightly transformed patterns. In Figure 9 and Figure 10, there are the transformed patterns used for learning the standard conceptual graphs and the conceptual graph on the grapheme 'ㄱ' after learning. As shown in Figure 10, the value of the orientation features and the value of the relation node are varied to absorb the transformations of patterns.

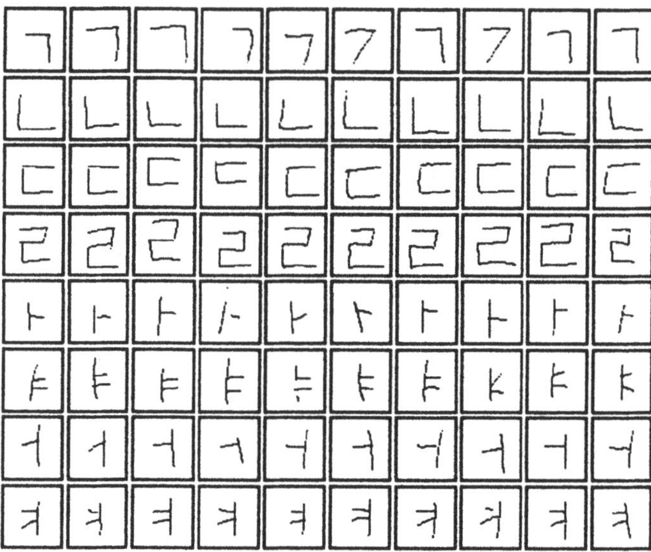

Fig. 9. The patterns used for the learning process

In Table 1, there is the result of recognition experiment for data set 3 after the learning process, and the example of character patterns used in the test process are shown in Figure 11. Unlike the learned patterns, the test patterns include the variations in the number and the sequence of storkes caused by the variety of writing patterns.

No. of patterns	No. Correct Reco.	No. Mis-reco.	Reco. Rate
4000	3412	588	85.3%

Table 1. Recognition result after the learning process

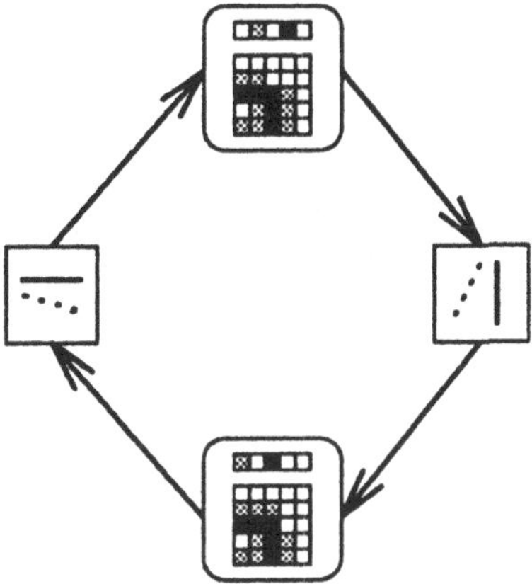

Fig. 10. Conceptual graph on the grapheme 'ㄱ' after the learning process

들	적	시	아	해	로	정	한	지	다
들	적	시	아	해	로	정	한	지	다
들	적	시	아	해	로	정	한	지	다
라	에	과	게	일	부	이	제	상	운
여	보	서	만	전	주	면	되	성	문
장	구	니	기	우	국	없	동	원	학
들	적	시	아	해	로	정	한	지	다
라	에	과	게	일	부	이	제	상	운
여	보	서	만	전	주	면	되	성	문
장	구	니	기	우	국	없	동	원	학

Fig. 11. The example of characters used in the test process

The main factor of mis-recognition is that the relation node was not learned enough to recognize the transformed patterns. Especially, in the case of 'ㅇ' and 'ㅎ', the mis-recognition rates were higher than that of other graphemes because these graphemes have more relation nodes and more various patterns in the contact image. Due to these facts, the overall recognition rate is not good, but it shows that the model can recognize the transformed patterns caused by continuous writing between strokes only through training standard grapheme patterns. Figure 12 shows the recognition example of the character '보' with continuous writing style.

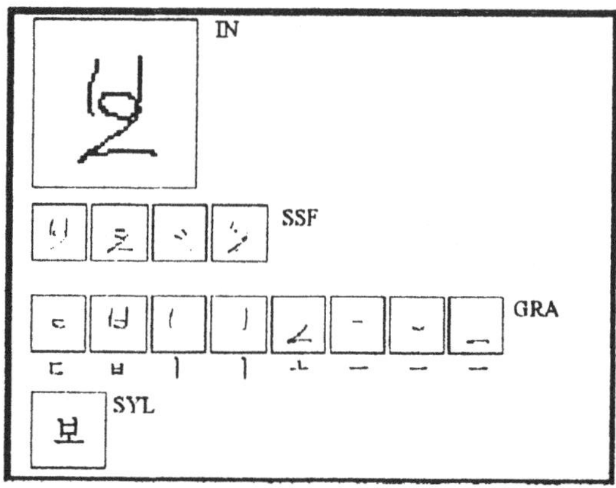

Fig. 12. The recognition example of the character with transformations

For the mis-recognized characters in Table 1, the model re-trains adaptively with 563 separated graphemes obtained from the mis-recognized characters. The number of the conceptual graphs newly created through the adaptive learning is 23. After the training on one accasion only, we test again with the same data used in Table 1, and get the result as Table 2. Although there exist mis-recognized characters as ever, we show that the revised model can improve the recognition performance through the adaptive learning.

No. of Patterns	No. Correct Reco.	No. Mis-reco.	Reco. Rate
4000	3816	184	95.4%

Table 2. Recognition rate after the adaptive learning

5 Conclusions

In the paper, we present the revised SEJONG-NET model with the adaptability to handle the transformed patterns of Hangul. From the experimental results, we can say that the model recognizes the various Hangul patterns which are transformed in the number of strokes or the sequence of stokes with the knowledge of only the standard grapheme patterns. And we also show that the model can increase its performance through adding the mechanism of adaptive learning. Hence the revised model can be considered as an efficient model for the recognition of Hangul pattern with the variations.

References

1. J.Kim, "A Review of Psychological Studies of Korean Letters and Syllables" *Proc. of Conference on Hangul and Korean Information Processing in Korea*, pp.114-119, 1989.
2. J.Kim and J.Kim,"Syllabic Processing and Letter Perception in Korean Word Recognition," Korean Journal of Experimental and Cognitive Psychology, Vol. 4, pp.36-51, 1992.
3. K.Do, "The Combination of Korean Letters in the Perception of Hangul," Korean Journal of Experimental and Cognitive Psychology, Vol. 4, pp.1-15, 1992.
4. Y.Lee and A.-Y.Chung, "Sejong-Net: A Dynamic Visual Pattern Recognition Neural Net," *Proc. of Int. Joint Conference on Neural Networks 90 WASH. DC*, Vol.1, pp.412-415, 1990
5. J.Cho, J.Kim, A.-Y.Chung and Y.Lee, "Sejong-Net: A Neural Net Model for Dynamic Character Recognition," *Proc. of Int. Conference on Fuzzy Logic and Neural Networks IIZUKA '90*, Vol.1, pp.315-318, 1990.7
6. J.Kim and Y.Lee, "Handwritten English Alphabet Recognition using SEJONG-NET," *Proc. of 1990 Fall Conference of SIG-AI of Korean Information Science Society*, pp.107-111, 1990 (in Korean)
7. S.Kim and Y.Lee, "On-line Recognition of Handwriting Chinese Character(Radical) using SEJONG-NET," *Proc. of 1991 Fall Conference of SIG-AI of KISS*, pp.25-29, 1991 (in Korean)
8. S.Lee, K.Lee and Y.Lee, "A Generalized Character Recognition using SEJONG-NET," *Proc. of the 2nd Pacific Rim Int. Conference on Artificial Intelligence*, Vol.2, pp.947-952, 1992
9. K.Lee and Y.Lee, "SEJONG-NET with Analysis-by-Synthesis," *Proc. of World Congress on Neural Networks- San Diego*, Vol.1, pp.649-657, 1994
10. Audice G. Leventhal, The Neural Basis of Visual Function, Macmillan Press, 1991
11. Dobbins, Zucker, and Cynader, "Endstopped neurons in the visual cortex as a substrate for calculating curvature," *Nature*, Vol.329, No.1, pp.438-441, 1987
12. John F.Sowa, CONCEPTUAL STRUCTURES: Information Processing in Mind and Machine, Addison-Wesley,1984
13. Kandel, Schwartz, and Jessell, PRINCIPLES OF NEURAL SCIENCE, Elsevier, 3rd Ed., 1991
14. Versavel, Orban, and Lagae, "Responses of Visual Cortical Neurons to Curved Stimulus and Chevrons," *Vision Research*, Vol.30, No.2, pp.235-248, 1990

A Unified Algebraic Structure for Uncertain Reasonings*

Xudong Luo and Chengqi Zhang

Department of Mathematics, Statistics and Computing Science
The University of New England, Armidale, NSW 2351, Australia
{xluo,chengqi}@neumann.une.edu.au

Abstract. This paper identifies an axiom foundation for uncertain reasonings in rule-based expert systems: a near topological algebra (NT-algebra for short), which holds some basic notions hidden behind the uncertain reasoning models in rule-based expert systems. In according with basic ways of topological connection in an inference network, an NT-algebraic structure has five basic operators, i.e. *AND*, *OR*, *NOT*, *Sequential* combination and *Parallel* combination, which obey some axioms. An NT-algebraic structure is defined on a near-degree space introduced by the authors, which is a special topological space. The continuities of real functions, of fuzzy functions and the functions in other sense can be uniformly considered in the framework of a near-degree space. This paper also proves that the EMYCIN's and PROSPECTOR's uncertain reasoning models correspond to good NT-algebras, respectively. Compared to other related works, the NT-algebra as an axiom foundation has the following characteristics: (1) various cases of assessments for uncertainties of both evidence and rules are put into a unified algebraic structure; and (2) major emphasis has been placed on the basic laws of the propagation for them in an inference network.

1 Introduction

In the real world, both evidence and rules may not always be certain. These facts have led the designers of expert systems to abandon the pursuit of logical completeness in favor of developing effective heuristic ways to exploit the fallible, but valuable, judgemental knowledge that human experts bring to particular classes of problems. Now based on the above reason, some uncertain reasoning models applied in rule-based expert systems have been proposed. Although they are quite different in appearance, what all of them simulate is an ability of human expert uncertain reasonings. These models imply that there should be a common structure to satisfy some necessary common conditions. Thus, it is possible to establish an axiom foundation for them.

If we have such an axiom, we can hold common notions in different models, develop the appropriate models for special applications, and examine the relationships among them, e.g. the transformation relationships between different

* This research is supported by a large grant from the Australian Research Council (A49530850).

models in a distributed expert system. In fact, some significant works in these areas have been done, but fail to provide satisfactory answers to the problem.

In this paper, an axiom foundation for uncertain reasonings in rule-based expert systems has been identified. Corresponding to the topological connection in an inference network in rule-based expert systems, there are five basic ways to propagate assessments for uncertainties of both evidence and rules. The formulae for five propagation ways satisfy some axiom abstracted from some common laws of uncertain reasonings of human beings. Thus, the operators corresponding to these five ways and a set of assessments for uncertainties can constitute an algebraic structure, called a near topological algebra (NT-algebra for short).

In the real life, uncertainties are probably assessed in terms of numbers, intervals, fuzzy numbers, fuzzy intervals, even general possibility distributions, and so on. All of them constitute a partial ordered structure, respectively. The operators in an NT-algebra are continuous with respect to each of their parameter. As a result, an NT-algebraic structure needs to be defined on a partial ordered structure, and on a sort of topological space, referred to as a near-degree space.

The remainder of the paper is organized as follows. Section 2 introduces the concepts of a near-degree space and of a continuous function on it, and explores its relationships to a metric space and to a topological space. Section 3 presents an algebraic structure, NT-algebra, as an axiom foundation for uncertain reasonings. Section 4 proves that the EMYCIN's [Sho et al.75, Mel80] and PROSPECTOR's [Dud et al.76] uncertain reasoning models correspond to a good NT-algebra, respectively. Section 5 compares our work with other research of a similar nature. Finally, Section 6 summarizes this paper.

2 The Concept of Near-Degree Space

In reality, the uncertainties of either evidence or rules may be assessed in terms of numbers, intervals, fuzzy numbers, fuzzy intervals, possibility distributions or elements in some partial ordered structure. Thus, in order to make an abstract study of uncertain reasonings, it is natural that the concept of the continuity of real functions, one of fuzzy functions and one of the functions in other cases, need to be placed under a uniform framework, which should not be too abstract to reveal appropriate characters. For this reason, we shall introduce the concept of a near-degree space which is a special sort of topological space. Oriented to the uncertain reasonings of human beings, rather than physical objects, the near-degree space should be different from the metric space. Evidently, in a sense, if the assessment for uncertainty of the proposition A is nearer to that of the proposition C than that of the proposition B is, then the near-degree between A and C should be greater than that between B and C. This particular rule is different from the rule of triangle inequality in the metric. Nevertheless, the difference-degree opposite to the near-degree should still satisfy the triangle inequality.

2.1 Near-Degree Space and N-Continuity

Definition 1 *Let L be a non-empty set and let $\preceq$ be a partial ordering on L^2. If there is a map $\sigma : L^2 \to [0,1]$ which satisfies: $\forall x, y, z \in L$*

1. $\sigma(x,x) = 1$;
2. $(x,z) \preceq (y,z) \Leftrightarrow \sigma(x,z) \leq \sigma(y,z)$;
3. $\sigma(x,z) \geq \sigma(y,x) + \sigma(z,y) - 1$.

then σ is called a near-degree on L with respect to $\preceq$, $\sigma' = 1 - \sigma$ is called a difference-degree on L with respect to $\preceq$, $(L, \sigma, \preceq)$ is called a near-degree space, and $\sigma(x,y)$ and $\sigma'(x,y)$ are called near-degree and difference-degree between x and y, respectively.

Clearly, a difference-degree satisfies the triangle inequality and a near-degree satisfies the commutative law.

Example 1. Suppose that we have the following matrixes:

$$C = (c_{ij})_{4\times 4} = \begin{pmatrix} 1\,3\,2\,4 \\ 3\,1\,2\,5 \\ 2\,1\,1\,6 \\ 4\,7\,8\,3 \end{pmatrix} \qquad D = (d_{ij})_{4\times 4} = \begin{pmatrix} 1 & 0.4 & 0.4 & 0.3 \\ 0.4 & 1 & 1 & 0.28 \\ 0.4 & 1 & 1 & 0.28 \\ 0.3 & 0.28 & 0.28 & 1 \end{pmatrix}$$

Let $L = \{a_1, a_2, a_3, a_4\}$, and let a partial ordering $\preceq$ be defined on L^2 by the matrix C, that is,$(a_i, a_j) \preceq (a_k, a_j) \Leftrightarrow c_{ij} \geq c_{kj}$, here c_{ij} is the ith row and jth column element of C and c_{kj} is the kth row and jth column element of C. It is easy to prove that a near-degree σ on L with respect to $\preceq$ can be defined by the matrix D: that is, $\sigma(a_i, a_j) = d_{ij}$,here d_{ij} is the ith row and jth column element of D, thus $(L, \sigma, \preceq)$ is a near-degree space.

Definition 2 *Let $(L, \sigma, \preceq)$ be a near-degree space.*

1. *Let $x \in L, \varepsilon \in (0,1)$, then the set $B_\sigma(x,\varepsilon) = \{y \in L | \sigma(x,y) > \varepsilon\}$ is called a ε-open ball with the center x.*
2. *A subset G of L is called a σ-open set $\Leftrightarrow \forall x \in G, \exists \varepsilon \in (0,1), B_\sigma(x,\varepsilon) \subset G$.*

If confusion does not occur, such an open ball is briefly denoted as $B(x,\varepsilon)$ and such a σ-open set is called an open set. The following theorem implies any open ball $B(x,\varepsilon)$ is an open set by the above definition.

Theorem 1. *$\forall y \in B(x,\varepsilon), \exists \varepsilon' \in (0,1)$ such that $B(y,\varepsilon') \subset B(x,\varepsilon)$.*

Proof. Let $\varepsilon' = \varepsilon + 1 - \sigma(x,y)$. $\forall z \in B(y,\varepsilon')$, we have $\sigma(y,z) > \varepsilon'$, thus, $\sigma(y,z) > \varepsilon + 1 - \sigma(x,y)$, that is, $\sigma(y,z) + \sigma(x,y) - 1 > \varepsilon$. By Definition 1 and considering a near-degree satisfies the commutative law, we have $\sigma(x,z) > \sigma(y,z) + \sigma(x,y) - 1$, thus, $\sigma(x,z) > \varepsilon$, namely, $z \in B(x,\varepsilon)$. Therefore, $B(y,\varepsilon) \subset B(x,\varepsilon)$. □

Definition 3 *Let $(L_1, \sigma_1, \preceq_1)$ and $(L_2, \sigma_2, \preceq_2)$ be two near-degree spaces, and $f : L_1 \to L_2$.*

1. *f is N-continuous at point $x \in L_1 \Leftrightarrow \forall \varepsilon \in (0,1), \exists \delta \in (0,1), \forall y \in L_1$, if $\sigma_1(x,y) > \delta$, then $\sigma_2(f(x), f(y)) > \varepsilon$.*
2. *f is N-continuous $\Leftrightarrow$ f is N-continuous at every point in L_1.*

If confusion does not occur, a N-continuous function is briefly said to be continuous.

Example 2. In Example 1, if a function $\varphi : L \to L$ is defined as:

$$a_1 \to a_2, a_2 \to a_2, a_3 \to a_3, a_4 \to a_3$$

then this function is continuous at point a_1. In fact, $\forall \varepsilon \in (0,1)$, let $\delta = 0.45$, if $\sigma(a_1, a_i) > \delta$, then $i = 1$, thus, $\sigma(\varphi(a_1), \varphi(a_i)) = \sigma(\varphi(a_1), \varphi(a_1)) = 1 > \varepsilon$.

Example 3. In Example 1, if a function $\varphi : L \to L$ is defined as:

$$a_1 \to a_1, a_2 \to a_3, a_3 \to a_4, a_4 \to a_1$$

then this function is not continuous at point a_2.In fact, let $\varepsilon = 0.4, \forall \delta \in (0,1)$, though $\sigma(a_2, a_3) = 1 > \delta, \sigma(\varphi(a_2), \varphi(a_3)) = \sigma(a_3, a_4) = 0.28 < \varepsilon$.

The following two theorems are similar to the corresponding ones on metric space.

Theorem 2. *Let $(L_1, \sigma_1, \preceq_1)$ and $(L_2, \sigma_2, \preceq_2)$ be two near-degree spaces, then the function $f : L_1 \to L_2$ is continuous $\Leftrightarrow$ if G is a σ_2-open set, then $f^{-1}[G]$ is a σ_1-open set.*

Proof. ($\Rightarrow$) Suppose that f is continuous and G is a σ_2-open set. If $f^{-1}[G] = \emptyset$, obviously it is a σ_1-open set. If $f^{-1}[G] \neq \emptyset$, then $\forall x \in f^{-1}[G], f(x) \in G$,thus $\exists \varepsilon \in (0,1)$, such that $B(f(x), \varepsilon) \subset G$. Since f is continuous at point x, that is, $\exists \delta \in (0,1)$, if $y \in B(x, \delta)$, then $f(y) \in B(f(x), \varepsilon) \subset G$, thus $y \in f^{-1}[G]$. As a result, $B(x, \delta) \subset f^{-1}[G]$, thus $f^{-1}[G]$ is a σ_1-open set.

($\Leftarrow$) Let $x \in L_1$ and $\varepsilon \in (0,1)$. By Theorem 1, $B(f(x), \varepsilon)$ is a σ_2-open set and it follows the assumption that $f^{-1}[B(f(x), \varepsilon)]$ is a σ_1-open set containing point x, thus there exists $\delta \in (0,1)$ such that $B(x, \delta) \subset f^{-1}[B(f(x), \varepsilon)]$, that is, $\forall y \in L_1$, if $\sigma(x,y) > \delta$, then $y \in B(x, \delta) \subset f^{-1}[B(f(x), \varepsilon)]$,thus $\sigma(f(x), f(y)) > \varepsilon$, that is, f is continuous at point x. □

Theorem 3. *Let $(L, \sigma, \preceq)$ be a near-degree space and let*

$$T_\sigma = \{G \subseteq L | G \text{ is a } \sigma\text{−open set}\}$$

then T_σ is a topology on L, called near-degree topology induced by σ. The space (L, T_σ) is still denoted as $(L, \sigma, \preceq)$.

Proof. (1) Clearly,$\emptyset$ and $L \in T_\sigma$. (2) If $G, H \in T_\sigma$, then $G \cap H \in T_\sigma$. In fact, if $G \cap H = \emptyset \in T_\sigma$; otherwise, let $x \in G \cap H$, then $\exists \varepsilon_1, \varepsilon_2 \in (0,1), B(x, \varepsilon_1) \subset G, B(x, \varepsilon_2) \subset H$. Thus,let $\varepsilon = \max\{\varepsilon_1, \varepsilon_2\}$, then $B(x, \varepsilon) \subset G \cap H$. As a result, $G \cap H \in T_\sigma$.(3) If $\mathcal{A} \subset T_\sigma$, then $\cup\mathcal{A} \in T_\sigma$. In fact, if $\cup\mathcal{A} = \emptyset \in T_\sigma$; otherwise, let $x \in \cup\mathcal{A}$, then $\exists G \in \mathcal{A}, x \in G$,thus $\exists \varepsilon \in (0,1), B(x, \varepsilon) \subset G \subset \cup\mathcal{A}$. As a result, $\cup\mathcal{A} \in T_\sigma$. □

This theorem implies that a near-degree space is a topological space.

2.2 A Near-Degree Space of Fuzzy Sets

In this subsection, we prove that the concept of a near-degree in fuzzy mathematics is a special case of the concept defined in Subsection 2.1 in a sense.

The definition of a near-degree of two fuzzy sets is as follows[Zha et al.81]:

Definition 4 *Let $\mathcal{L}(X)$ be denoted as the set of all fuzzy sets on a domain X. The function $\rho : \mathcal{L}^2(X) \to [0,1]$ is called a f-near-degree on $\mathcal{L}(X)$, if*

1. $\rho(\tilde{A}, \tilde{A}) = 1, \forall \tilde{A} \in \mathcal{L}(X)$;
2. $\rho(\tilde{A}, \tilde{B}) = \rho(\tilde{B}, \tilde{A}), \forall \tilde{A}, \tilde{B} \in \mathcal{L}(X)$;
3. $\forall \tilde{A}, \tilde{B}, \tilde{C} \in \mathcal{L}(X)$, *if* $\tilde{A} \subseteq \tilde{B} \subseteq \tilde{C}$,*then* $\rho(\tilde{A}, \tilde{C}) \leq \rho(\tilde{B}, \tilde{C})$.

The following theorem is almost obvious.

Theorem 4. *Let the map $\rho : \mathcal{L}^2(X) \to [0,1]$ be a f-near-degree on $\mathcal{L}(X)$. If $\forall \tilde{A}, \tilde{B}, \tilde{C} \in \mathcal{L}(X), \rho(\tilde{A}, \tilde{C}) \geq \rho(\tilde{A}, \tilde{B}) + \rho(\tilde{B}, \tilde{C}) - 1$, then $(\mathcal{L}(X), \rho, \preceq)$ is a near-degree space, here $\preceq$ is a partial-ordering on $\mathcal{L}(X)$, defined as $(\tilde{A}, \tilde{C}) \preceq (\tilde{B}, \tilde{C}) \Leftrightarrow \tilde{A} \subseteq \tilde{B} \subseteq \tilde{C}$.*

If there is no danger of misunderstanding, $(\mathcal{L}(X), \rho, \preceq)$ is briefly denoted as $(\mathcal{L}(X), \rho)$.

Example 4. The semantics such a linguistic term as *probable* and *very probable* can be provided by a trapezoid fuzzy number $\tilde{N} = (a, b, \alpha, \beta)$ defined by [Bon80]:

$$\mu_N(x) = \begin{cases} 0 & \text{if } x < a - \alpha \\ (\frac{1}{\alpha})(x - a + \alpha) & \text{if } x \in [a - \alpha, a] \\ 1 & \text{if } x \in [a, b] \\ (\frac{1}{\beta})(b + \beta - x) & \text{if } x \in [b, b + \beta] \\ 0 & \text{if } x > b + \beta \end{cases}$$

Let the set of all fuzzy numbers in the above form be denoted $\tilde{L}$, and define the map $\tilde{\sigma} : \tilde{L}^2 \to [0,1]$ as

$$\tilde{\sigma}(\tilde{m}, \tilde{n}) = 1 - \max\{|a - c|, |b - d|, |(a - \alpha) - (c - \gamma)|, |(b + \beta) - (d + \delta)|\}$$

here $\tilde{m} = (a, b, \alpha, \beta), \tilde{n} = (c, d, \gamma, \delta)$. We easily show that $\tilde{\sigma}$ is a f-near-degree on $\tilde{L}$, thus $(\tilde{L}, \tilde{\sigma})$ is a near-degree space. [Bon et al.86] gives the addition and subtraction operations on $\tilde{L}$ as follows:

$$\tilde{m} + \tilde{n} = (a + c, b + d, \alpha + \gamma, \beta + \delta)$$
$$\tilde{m} - \tilde{n} = (a - d, b - c, \alpha + \delta, \beta + \gamma)$$

For two operations above, when one parameter of them takes constant, both of them are continuous with respect to another parameter on the near-degree space (L, σ). In fact, let $\tilde{n}_0 = (c_0, d_0, \gamma_0, \delta_0)$ be a constant, we can easily verify

$$\tilde{\sigma}(\tilde{m} + \tilde{n}_0, \tilde{m}' + \tilde{n}_0) = \tilde{\sigma}(\tilde{m}, \tilde{m}')$$

here $\tilde{m}' = (a', b', \alpha', \beta')$, hence $\forall \varepsilon \in (0,1)$, let $\delta = \varepsilon$, if $\tilde{\sigma}(\tilde{m}, \tilde{m}') > \delta$, then $\tilde{\sigma}(\tilde{m} + \tilde{n}_0, \tilde{m}' + \tilde{n}_0) > \varepsilon$, that is, $\tilde{m} + \tilde{n}_0$ is continuous at any point $\tilde{m}$. Similar, in the case of subtraction operation.

This example implies how the concept of the continuity of fuzzy function is placed under the framework of a near-degree space.

2.3 The Near-Degree Space Induced by a Metric Space

The following obvious theorem gives a way in which a near-degree space can be induced by a metric space.

Theorem 5. *Suppose that (L, ρ) is a metric space. Let the function $g : [0, \infty) \to [0, 1)$ be a continuous and strictly increasing map, and $g(0) = 0$ and additionally define $g(\infty) \to 1$. And let $\sigma(x, y) = 1 - g(\rho(x, y))$, and a partial ordering $\preceq$ on L^2 is defined as $(x, z) \preceq (y, z) \Leftrightarrow \rho(x, z) \geq \rho(y, z)$. If*

$$\forall x, y, z \in L, g(\rho(x, z)) \leq g(\rho(x, y)) + g(\rho(y, z))$$

then $(L, \sigma, \preceq)$ is a near-degree space, said to be induced by (L, ρ), and g is called its induced function.

The following theorem implies how the conception of continuity on a metric space is placed in the framework of a near-degree space.

Theorem 6. *Let (L, ρ) be a metric space and let $(L, \sigma, \preceq)$ be a near-degree space induced by it. If the function $f : L \to L$ is continuous on (L, ρ), then it is also continuous on $(L, \sigma, \preceq)$.*

Proof. . Let the induced function of $(L, \sigma, \preceq)$ be g, that is,

$$\sigma(x, y) = 1 - g(\rho(x, y))$$

Suppose that $f : L \to L$ is continuous on (L, ρ). Thus,$\forall \varepsilon \in (0, 1)$, let $\varepsilon' = g^{-1}(1 - \varepsilon), \exists \delta' > 0$, if $\rho(x, y) < \delta'$, then $\rho(f(x), f(y)) < g^{-1}(1 - \varepsilon)$. Therefore, $\forall \varepsilon \in (0, 1)$, let $\delta = 1 - g(\delta')$, if $\sigma(x, y) > \delta$,then $\sigma(f(x), f(y)) > \varepsilon$, that is, f is continuous on $(L, \sigma, \preceq)$. □

3 The Definition of NT-Algebra

An NT-algebra is an algebraic structure defined on a partial ordered structure, with five operations which are continuous with respect to some of their parameters on a near-degree space. This algebraic structure is abstracted from uncertain reasonings, and reflects some common laws of assessments for uncertainty and of their propagation through an inference network.

3.1 Basic Definitions

Let $(L, \sigma, \preceq)$ be a near-degree space and let $(L, \leq_L, \bot, \top)$ be a partial ordered structure with the maximum element $\top$ and the minimum element $\bot$. The function f continued on $(L, \sigma, \preceq)$ is said to be continuous on L.

Definition 5 *The map $\varphi_I : L^2 \to L$ is called an I operation, if the following conditions hold:*

1. *φ_I is continuous on L for each parameter;*

2. φ_I *is monotonic and does not decrease for each parameter;*
3. $\forall x, y \in L, \varphi_I(x, y) = \varphi_I(y, x)$;
4. $\forall x \in L, \varphi_I(x, \top) = x$;
5. $\forall x, y, z \in L, \varphi_I(x, \varphi_I(y, z)) = \varphi_I(\varphi_I(x, y), z)$.

Definition 6 *The map* $\varphi_U : L^2 \to L$ *is called a U operation, if the following conditions hold:*

1. φ_U *is continuous on* L *for each parameter;*
2. φ_U *is monotonic and does not decrease for each parameter;*
3. $\forall x, y \in L, \varphi_U(x, y) = \varphi_U(y, x)$;
4. $\forall x \in L, \varphi_U(x, \perp) = x$;
5. $\forall x, y, z \in L, \varphi_U(x, \varphi_U(y, z)) = \varphi_U(\varphi_U(x, y), z)$.

Definition 7 *The map* $\varphi_C : L \to L$ *is called a C operation, if the following conditions hold:*

1. φ_C *is continuous on* L*;*
2. φ_C *decreases strictly;*
3. $\forall x \in L, \varphi_C(\varphi_C(x)) = x$.

Definition 8 *The map* $\varphi_S : L^{n+3} \to L$ *is called a S operation, if there are the units* $e_E, e_{rs_1}, \ldots, e_{rs_n}, e_H \in L$ *such that for any constants* $d_1, \ldots, d_n \in L$*, the following conditions hold:*

1. $\varphi_S(x, y_1, \ldots, y_n, e_E, e_H)$ *is continuous on* L *with respect to* x *and each* $y_i (1 \leq i \leq n)$*, respectively;*
2. $\varphi_S(x, d_1, \ldots, d_n, e_E, e_H)$ *is monotonic and does not decrease;*
3. $\varphi_S(e_E, y_1, \ldots, y_n, e_E, e_H) = e_H$;
4. $\varphi_S(x, e_{rs_1}, \ldots, e_{rs_n}, e_E, e_H) = e_H$.

Definition 9 *The map* $\varphi_P^m : L^{m+1} \to L$ *is called a P operation, if there is the unit* $e_0 \in L$ *such that the following conditions hold:*

1. $\varphi_P^m(x_1, \ldots, x_m, e_0)$ *is continuous for each parameter* $x_i (1 \leq i \leq m)$ *on* L*, respectively;*
2. $\varphi_P^m(x_1, \ldots, x_m, e_0)$ *is monotonic and does not decrease for each parameter* $x_i (1 \leq i \leq m)$*, respectively;*
3. $\varphi_P^m(e_0, x_2, \ldots, x_m, e_0) = \varphi_P^{m-1}(x_2, \ldots, x_m, e_0)$;
4. $\varphi_P^2(e_0, x_2, e_0) = x_2$;
5. $\varphi_P^m(x_1, \ldots, x_m, e_0) = \varphi_P^m(x_1', \ldots, x_m', e_0)$*, where* $x_1', \ldots, x_m'$*, is any permutation of* $x_1, \ldots, x_m$.

Definition 10 *The 9-tuple* $(L, \varphi_I, \varphi_U, \varphi_C, \varphi_S, \varphi_P^m, \leq_L, \perp, \top)$ *is called a near topological algebra on* $(L, \sigma, \preceq)$*, briefly called an NT-algebra on* L.

Definition 11 *If the following conditions hold:*

1. $\varphi_C(\varphi_U(\varphi_C(a), \varphi_C(b))) = \varphi_I(a, b)$

2. $\varphi_P^m(\varphi_S(a_1, b_1, \ldots, b_n, e_E, e_H), \ldots, \varphi_S(a_m, b_1 \ldots, b_n, e_E, e_H), e_H)$
$= \varphi_S(\varphi_P^m(a_1, \ldots, a_m, e_E), b_1, \ldots, b_n, e_E, e_H)$
3. $\varphi_P^m(x_1, \ldots, x_m, e_0) = \varphi_P^2(x_1, \varphi_P^{m-1}(x_2, \ldots, x_m, e_0), e_0)$

here besides e_E, e_H, e_0 are constants, others are any elements in L, then this NT-algebra is called a perfect NT-algebra. If the second condition above holds, then it is called a distributable NT-algebra. If the first and last conditions hold, then it is called a good NT-algebra.

3.2 Corresponding to a Model of Uncertain Reasoning

In this subsection, our discussion mainly refers to uncertain reasoning models like EMYCIN [Sho et al.75] and PROSPECTOR [Dud et al.76].

We have known that in a rule-based knowledge base, every rule is in a form of "*IF* E *THEN* H", that is, $E \rightarrow H$ where E is a Boolean combination of $E_1, \ldots, E_n$, which can be obtained by three ways: AND, OR and NOT. The three operators I, U and C are the operations of combining assessments for uncertainty of propositions combined by the three ways, respectively.

The two basic structures of an inference network are as follows:

$$E \rightarrow H_1 \rightarrow H_2 \rightarrow \ldots \rightarrow H_n$$

$$E_1 \rightarrow H$$
$$\nearrow \nwarrow$$
$$E_2 \ \ldots \ E_n$$

The procedure of uncertain reasoning is actually to propagate uncertainty through an inference network. How to propagate? Clearly, to answer this question is to make it clear the way of propagation for uncertainty along these two basic structures above. The operators S and P are their abstract descriptions.

So, an NT-algebra structure corresponds to an uncertain reasoning model.

3.3 The Relationships among Various Operations

In definition 11, we suggest three pieces of relationships. The first and last ones are easily understood. Now let us explain the second piece of relationship in the case $m = 2$. Suppose, now, that in a knowledge base there are three following pieces of rules: $E_1 \rightarrow E$, $E_2 \rightarrow E$ and $E \rightarrow H$. Let the value of strength of rule $E \rightarrow H$ be $(b_1, \ldots, b_n)$, the unit of E be e_E and the unit of H be e_H. Evidently, there are two ways of deriving the assessment for uncertainty of hypothesis H from the three rules above in an inference:

1. At the moment t_1, the known information enables us to derive E and the assessment, a_1, for its uncertainty from $E_1 \rightarrow E$, but does not enable us to derive E from $E_2 \rightarrow E$. Then, we continually infer to draw the hypothesis H and the assessment, $\varphi_S(a_1, b_1, \ldots, b_n, e_E, e_H)$, for its uncertainty from $E \rightarrow H$. Up to the moment $t_2 (> t_1)$, we get some of new information enabling us to derive E and the assessment, c_1, of its uncertainty from

$E_2 \to E$. In turn, again we derive the hypothesis H and another assessment, $\varphi_S(c_1, b_1, \ldots, b_n, e_E, e_H)$, for its uncertainty from $E \to H$. Finally, by the P operation, $\varphi_P^2(\varphi_S(a_1, b_1, \ldots, b_n, e_E, e_H), \varphi_S(c_1, b_1, \ldots, b_n, e_E, e_H), e_H)$ can be obtained. This value is the combined assessment for uncertainty of the hypothesis H from different sources. This is similar to the depth-first.

2. The known information, at same time, enables us to derive E and the two assessments, a_2 and c_2, for its uncertainty from $E_1 \to E$ and $E_2 \to E$, respectively. Later in the next we obtain the combined assessment, $\varphi_P^2(a_2, c_2, e_E)$, for the uncertainty of proposition E. Finally, we derive the hypothesis H and the assessment, $\varphi_S(\varphi_P^2(a_2, c_2, e_E), b_1, \ldots, b_n, e_E, e_H)$, for its uncertainty from $E \to H$. This is similar to the breadth-first.

Suppose that $a_1 = a_2 = a, c_1 = c_2 = c$. The final result of the assessment of the uncertainty of the hypothesis H may be independent of the two inference ways above. Formally,

$$\begin{aligned} &\varphi_P^2(\varphi_S(a, b_1, \ldots, b_n, e_E, e_H), \varphi_S(c, b_1, \ldots, b_n, e_E, e_H), e_H) \\ &= \varphi_S(\varphi_P^2(a, c, e_E), b_1, \ldots, b_n, e_E, e_H) \end{aligned}$$

In many cases, notably in the case of distributed expert systems, we need this assumption. Suppose that the information, for $E_2 \to E$, of one node expert system ES_1 is dependent upon another node expert system ES_2. If the obtained information is enough to derive E from $E_1 \to E$, needless to wait for ES_2 to send the information for using $E_2 \to E$, ES_1 can also continually reason to derive the hypothesis H from $E \to H$. Once ES_1 obtains the information for using $E_2 \to E$ from ES_2, it derives E, and then does H from $E \to H$ again. Of course, it is possible that the obtained information by ES_1 is enough for ES_1 to derive E both from $E_1 \to E$ and from $E_2 \to E$. Later in the next ES_1 derives the hypothesis H from $E \to H$. In the distributed expert systems, the uncertain reasoning model used by ES_1 should satisfy the above equality.

4 NT-Algebras of EMYCIN and PROSPECTOR

The readers may readily verify the following two theorems for themselves.

Theorem 7 (EMYCIN's NT-algebra). *Let*

1. $\varphi_I : [-1,1]^2 \to [-1,1]$ *be given by* $\varphi_I(x,y) = \min\{x,y\}$*;*
2. $\varphi_U : [-1,1]^2 \to [-1,1]$ *be given by* $\varphi_U(x,y) = \max\{x,y\}$*;*
3. $\varphi_C : [-1,1] \to [-1,1]$ *be given by* $\varphi_C(x) = -x$*;*
4. $\varphi_S : [-1,1]^4 \to [-1,1]$ *be given by* $\varphi_S(x, y, e_E, e_H) = y \times \max\{0, x\}$*;*
5. $\varphi_P^m : [-1,1]^{m+1} \to [-1,1]$ *be given recursively by*

$$\varphi_P^2(x_1, x_2, e_0) = \begin{cases} x_1 + x_2 - x_1 x_2 & \text{if } x_1, x_2 \geq 0 \\ \frac{x_1 + x_2}{1 - \min\{|x_1|, |x_2|\}} & \text{if } x_1 x_2 < 0 \\ x_1 + x_2 + x_1 x_2 & \text{if } x_1, x_2 < 0 \end{cases}$$

$$\varphi_P^m(x_1, \ldots, x_m, e_0) = \varphi_P^2(x_1, \varphi_P^{m-1}(x_2, \ldots, x_m), e_0)$$

Then $([-1,1],\varphi_I,\varphi_U,\varphi_C,\varphi_S,\varphi_P^m,\leq,-1,1)$ *is a good NT-algebra defined on the near-degree space* $([-1,1],\sigma,\preceq)$, *here* $\sigma(x,y)=1-|x-y|$ *and* $\preceq$ *is defined as* $(x,z)\preceq(y,z)\Leftrightarrow|x-z|\geq|y-z|$, *and* $e_E\equiv e_{rs}\equiv e_H\equiv e_0\equiv 0$.

Theorem 8 (PROSPECTOR's NT-algebra). *Let*

1. $\varphi_I:[0,1]^2\to[0,1]$ *be given by* $\varphi_I=\min\{x,y\}$;
2. $\varphi_U:[0,1]^2\to[0,1]$ *be given by* $\varphi_U=\max\{x,y\}$;
3. $\varphi_C:[0,1]\to[0,1]$ *be given by* $\varphi_C(x)=1-x$;
4. $\varphi_S:[0,1]^5\to[0,1]$ *be given by*

$$\varphi_S(x,y_1,y_2,e_E,e_H)=\begin{cases}\alpha+\frac{e_H-\alpha}{e_E}x & \text{if } 0\leq x<e_E\\ e_H+\frac{\beta-e_H}{1-e_E}(x-e_E) & \text{if } e_E\leq x\leq 1\end{cases}$$

where

$$\alpha=\frac{f(y_2)\times e_H}{(f(y_2)-1)\times e_H+1}$$
$$\beta=\frac{f(y_1)\times e_H}{(f(y_1)-1)\times e_H+1}$$

here $f:[0,1)\to[0,\infty)$ *is a 1-1 map increasing strictly and continually,* $f(0)=0$ *and* $f(1)\to\infty$;

5. $\varphi_P^m:[0,1]^{m+1}\to[0,1]$ *be given by*

$$\varphi_P^m(x_1,\ldots,x_m,e_0)=\frac{e_0'\times(\prod_{i=1}^m(\frac{x_i'}{e_0'}))}{1+e_0'\times(\prod_{i=1}^m(\frac{x_i'}{e_0'}))}$$

here $x_i'=\frac{x_i}{1-x_i}, i=1,\ldots,m, e_0'=\frac{e_0}{1-e_0}$

Then $([0,1],\varphi_I,\varphi_U,\varphi_C,\varphi_S,\varphi_P^m,\leq,0,1)$ *is a good NT-algebra defined on the near-degree space* $([0,1],\sigma,\preceq)$, *here* $\sigma(x,y)=1-|x-y|$ *and* $\preceq$ *is defined as* $(x,z)\preceq(y,z)\Leftrightarrow|x-z|\geq|y-z|$.

Note that, in the PROSPECTOR's uncertain reasoning model, the strength of a rule $E\to H$ is a pair (LS,LN), defined as

$$LS=\frac{P(E|H)}{P(E|\neg H)}$$
$$LN=\frac{P(\neg E|H)}{P(\neg E|\neg H)}$$

taking on values in $[0,\infty)$. From the two equations above, we easily get

$$P(H|E)=\frac{LS\times P(H)}{(LS-1)P(H)+1}$$
$$P(H|\neg E)=\frac{LN\times P(H)}{(LN-1)P(H)+1}$$

taking on values in $[0,1]$. Hence, we need α, β and a function $f:[0,1)\to[0,\infty)$ in φ_S, which satisfies $y_1=f^{-1}(LS), y_2=f^{-1}(LN)$. Thus for rule $E\to H$, $e_{rs_1}=e_{rs_2}=f^{-1}(1), e_E=P(E)$ and $e_H=P(H)$. Evidently, e_E, e_H, e_{rs_1} and e_{rs_n} can be different according to different rules. In the operation φ_P^m, for the rules:

$$E_1\to H, E_2\to H,\ldots,E_m\to H$$

the unit

$$e_0=\frac{P(H)}{1-P(H)}$$

Obviously, this unit can vary with hypothesis H.

5 Related Works

Finding a general framework for uncertain reasonings is an important issue in the study of uncertain reasonings. In this aspect, some researchers have done some work.

In the light of the model of the EMYCIN uncertain reasoning, Heckerman [Hec86] presented some pieces of axiom which the *Sequential* and *Parallel* combinations should satisfy. About the interval representation of uncertainty, Driakov presented in [Dri87] an axiom system which *AND*, *OR*, *NOT*, the *Sequential* and *Parallel* combinations should satisfy. In regard to the EMYCIN's uncertain reasoning model, in [Wan87] Wang suggested some descriptive conditions which operations of propagation for uncertainty through an inference network should satisfy. In a word, all of them considered the generality just suitable for some special cases. Although the work in [Zha92] is more general than those mentioned previously, Zhang is mainly concerned with parallel combinations.

In Zheng's Ph.D. dissertation [Zhe89], he suggested a uniform model for numerical uncertain reasonings. However, his model appears to abstract some considerations only in the assessments for the initial evidence and the final hypothesis in an inference network, but not in the propagation for the uncertainties of the initial evidence and the rules in an inference network. It is the latter which are most important.

In [Háj et al.90], Hájek et al. have studied of an algebraic structure corresponding to an uncertain reasoning model like EMYCIN's and PROSPECTOR's, but they have considered the parallel combination operation rather than the others, and their investigation does not present any ultimate foundations of uncertain reasoning in rule-based expert systems [Háj et al.91].

In short, this paper presents NT-algebra as an axiom foundation for uncertain reasonings in rule-based expert systems, in which various cases of assessments for uncertainties of evidence and rules as well as the basic laws of the propagation for them in an inference network are taken into account.

6 Summary and Conclusions

This paper introduced the concepts of a near-degree space, which is abstracted from the continuity of propagations for uncertainties in an uncertain reasoning. In this paper, we have proved that a near-degree space is a topological space, under the uniform framework of which the concepts of continuities of both real and fuzzy functions are placed.

This paper has presented an algebraic structure, NT-algebra, as an axiom foundation for uncertain reasonings in a rule-based expert system, which exposes some of the laws of uncertainty assessments and propagation in an inference network. In this paper, we also proved that the EMYCIN's and PROSPECTOR's uncertain reasoning models correspond to a good NT-algebra, respectively.

References

[Bon80] Bonissone,P.P.: A Fuzzy Set Based Linguistic Approach: Theory and Applications. Proceedings of the 1980 Winter Simulation Conference (Eds. Oren, J.I., Shub, C.M., Roth, P.F.) (1980) 99–111

[Bon et al.86] Bonissone, P.P. and Decker, K.S.: Selecting Uncertainty Calculi and Granularity: An Experiment in Trading-off Precision and Complexity. Uncertainty in Artificial Intelligence (Eds. Kanal, L.N. and Lemmer, J.F.), North Holland (1986) 217–247

[Dri87] Driakov, D.: A Calculus for Belief-Interval Representation of Uncertainty. Uncertainty in Knowledge-Based Systems, Springer-Verlag (1987) 205–216

[Dud et al.76] Duda, R.O., Hart, P.E. and Nillson, N.J.: Subjective Bayesian Methods for Rule-Based Inference Systems. AFIPS Conference Proceedings, AFIPS Press **45** (1976) 1075–1082

[Háj et al.90] Hájek, P. and Valdes, J.J.: Algebraic Foundations of Uncertainty Processing in Rule-Based Expert Systems (Group-Theoretic Approach). Computer and Artificial Intelligence **9:4** (1990) 325–344

[Háj et al.91] Hájek, P. and Valdes, J.J.: A Generalized Algebraic Approach to Uncertainty Processing in Rule-based Expert Systems (Dempsteroids). Computer and Artificial Intelligence **10:1** (1991) 29–42

[Hec86] Heckerman, O.: Probabilistic Interpretations for Mycin's Certainty Factors. Uncertainty in Artificial Intelligence (Eds. Kanal, L.N., Lemmer, J.F.), North Holland (1986) 167–196

[Mel80] Melle, W.V.: A Domain-Independent System that Aids in Constructing Knowledge-Based Consultation. Hpp-80-22, STAN-CS-80-820 (1980)

[Sho et al.75] Shortiffe, E.H. and Buchanan, B.G.: A Model of Inexact Reasoning in Medicine. Mathematics Biosciences **23** (1975) 351–379

[Wan87] Wang, Shenkang: An Application of Bases Formula in Expert System. Computer Research and Development **24:6** (1987) 55-56

[Zha et al.81] Zhao, Ruhua and Chen, Xiaojun: The Universal Definition of Near-Degree for the Fuzzy Subsets and the Grade of Imprecision. Journal of Xi'an Jiaotong University **15:6** (1981) 21-27

[Zha92] Zhang, Chengqi: Cooperation under Uncertainty in Distributed Expert Systems. Artificial Intelligence **56** (1992) 21–69

[Zhe89] Zheng, Fangqing: A Common Reasoning Model: The Theory and Method about Numeral Reasonings. Ph.D. Dissertation, Department of Computer Science, Jilin University, China (1989)

Exten: A System for Computing Default Logic Extensions

Allen P. Courtney*, Grigoris Antoniou** and Norman Y. Foo***

Abstract. This paper descirbes *Exten*, an object-oriented system for default reasoning. Its current functionality includes the computation of extensions for various default logics.

The efficiency of the system is strongly increased by applying pruning techniques to the search tree. We motivate and present these techniques, and demonstrate that they can cut down the size of the search tree significantly. Quite importantly, they complement very well the recently developed stratification method [4] which has proven to be powerful and has been implemented in our system.

Exten supports experimentation with default logics allowing the user to set various parameters. Also it has been designed to be open to future enhancements, which are supported by its object-oriented design. *Exten* is part of our long-term effort to develop an integrated toolkit for intelligent information management based on nonmonotonic reasoning and belief revision methods.

1 Introduction

Nonmonotonic reasoning provides mechanisms enabling knowledge systems to deal with incomplete information. One of the main approaches is default logic [16] which allows one to draw plausible conclusions based on default rules. Much work has been undertaken to study the properties of this formalism. Among other things, a series of variants have been introduced, such as [3, 7, 12, 13].

Default reasoning appears to be promising for applications, mainly because the basic concept of a default is simple and can be found in several fields. Nevertheless, work in nonmonotonic reasoning has neglected the development of operational systems for far too long (*Theorist* [15] being a notable exception), so its potential for applications has not been demonstrated yet. Only recently did the focus switch to implementations and applications [2, 8, 14, 5, 9, 17, 18].

This paper describes *Exten*, a system that computes extensions of default theories. In general, default logic implementations focus either on query evaluation

* Department of Computer Science, University of Sydney, NSW 2006, Australia, allenc@cs.usyd.edu.au

** School of Computing and Information Technology, Griffith University, QLD 4111, Australia, ga@cit.gu.edu.au

*** Department of Computer Science, University of Sydney, NSW 2006, Australia, norman@cs.usyd.edu.au

or on extension computation. Both problems have their merits. Query evaluation is more appropriate for the credulous interpretation where one is interested whether a formula is included in at least one extension of the default theory. On the other hand, it has been shown [19] that for the skeptical approach (which focuses on the intersection of all extensions of the theory) it can be necessary to compute all extensions. Moreover, often it is interesting to determine which alternative 'world views' are supported by the given knowledge. Our system in its current form computes extensions, and work is being undertaken to implement goal–driven query evaluation.

Exten is implemented in an object–oriented manner, therefore it is easily expandable. It computes extensions for several default logic variants, including Reiter's original logic [16], Justified [12] and Constrained Default Logic [7]. In this paper we focus on the computation of Reiter extensions.

The implementation is based on a forward–chaining approach, that means, we start with the set of facts and apply defaults as long as no more are applicable or an 'inconsistency' (failure) has occurred. The efficiency of the system is significantly improved by using tree–pruning techniques which will be motivated and described in section 3. The other basic efficiency–increasing technique used is stratification which was adapted from [4] and matches very well with the tree–pruning methods. Essentially, stratification is used to decompose the set of defaults into sets (strata) in such a way that extensions can be computed in a modular way. For the extension computation of every stratum we use the tree–pruning techniques mentioned before.

Section 4 gives some information on implementation aspects, including the user interface and the underlying classical theorem prover. Section 5 relates our work to some other approaches, while section 6 collects several points of current and future work. Even though our system is operational and reasonably efficient, it is just the starting point of our long–term effort to develop a flexible and powerful workbench for nonmonotonic reasoning and belief revision.

2 Forward–chaining default reasoning

We assume that the reader is familiar with the basics of predicate logic. A *default* δ has the form $\frac{\varphi:\psi_1,\ldots,\psi_n}{\chi}$ with closed first–order formulae φ, $\psi_1,\ldots,\psi_n$, χ $(n > 0)$. φ is the *prerequisite* $pre(\delta)$, $\psi_1,\ldots,\psi_n$ the *justifications* $just(\delta)$, and χ the *consequent* $cons(\delta)$ of δ. A *default theory* T is a pair (W, D) consisting of a set of formulae W (the set of facts) and a finite set of defaults D. A default of the form $\frac{\varphi:\chi}{\chi}$ is called *normal.*

Let $\delta = \frac{\varphi:\psi_1,\ldots,\psi_n}{\chi}$ be a default, and E a set of formulae. We say that δ *is applicable to* E iff φ is included in E, and $\neg\psi_1,\ldots,\neg\psi_n$ are not included in E.

Now we come to the formal foundation of a forward–chaining approach to default reasoning. Let $T = (W, D)$ be a default theory and $\Pi = (\delta_0,\ldots,\delta_m)$ a sequence of defaults from D without multiple occurrences. We denote by $\Pi[k]$ the initial segment of Π of length k, for $k \le m+1$.

- $In(\Pi) = Th(W \cup \{cons(\delta) \mid \delta \text{ occurs in } \Pi\})$.
- $Out(\Pi) = \{\neg\psi \mid \psi \in just(\delta), \delta \text{ occurs in } \Pi\}$.
- Π is a *process of* T iff δ_k is applicable to $In(\Pi[k])$, for all $k \leq m$.
- Π is *successful* iff $In(\Pi) \cap Out(\Pi) = \emptyset$, otherwise it is *failed*.
- Π is *closed* iff every $\delta \in D$ which is is applicable to $In(\Pi)$ already occurs in Π.

[1] shows that the original definition of extensions in default logic is equivalent to the following one: A set of formulae E is an *extension* of a default theory T iff there is a closed and successful process Π of T such that $E = In(\Pi)$.

The processes of a default theory T form a *process tree* [1]. The traversal of this tree gives us all extensions of T. A maximal path π corresponds either to a failed or to a closed and successful process of T (obviously it is unnecessary to expand a failed path π since all paths including π are failed, too).

3 Tree–pruning techniques

3.1 Exponential pruning

The definition of processes shows that there are potentially $n!$ possible processes, where n is the number of defaults in D. On the other hand, there are maximally 2^n possible extensions, so there is a huge discrepancy. Fortunately it is easy to prune the process tree in such a way that at most 2^n paths are constructed. The pruning is based on the following observation (for a proof see [6]).

1. Theorem *Let $\Pi = \Pi_1 \circ \Pi_2 \circ \delta \circ \Pi_3$ be a closed and successful process of T, and suppose that $pre(\delta) \in In(\Pi_1)$. Then $\Pi' = \Pi_1 \circ \delta \circ \Pi_2 \circ \Pi_3$ is a closed and successful process of T, too. By definition, $In(\Pi) = In(\Pi')$.*

Based on this result, the procedure for computing all extensions of a default theory using a so-called *exponentially pruned process tree* can be described as follows (the initial call is `Compute-Ext((), D, ∅)`). In the procedure below we have omitted the success checks (see also section 4).

```
PROCEDURE Compute-Ext(Π, Drest, Dout)

BEGIN
   NotClosed := false;
   M := {δ ∈Drest | pre(δ)∈In(Π)} = {δ1,...,δn};
   IF M = ∅ THEN
      IF IsClosed(Π, Dout) THEN
         ext := ext ∪ {In(Π)}
      FI
```

```
  ELSE
     FOR i := 1 TO n DO
        Drest := Drest - {δ_i};
        IF all ψ ∈ just(δ_i) are consistent with In(Π) THEN
           Compute-Ext(Π ∘ δ_i, Drest, Dout);
           NotClosed := true;
        FI;
        Dout := Dout ∪ {δ_i}
     END;
     IF NotClosed = false AND IsClosed(Π, Dout) THEN
        ext := ext ∪ {In(Π)}
     FI
  FI
END
```

The following remarks are in order. First, if a default δ_i is applicable at the current node of the process tree, then it is deleted from the set of available defaults *Drest*. Theorem 1 shows that by applying δ_i first, we obtain all extensions underneath the current node that include δ_i.

The same applies in case the prerequisite of δ_i 'is met', that is, $pre(\delta_i) \in In(\Pi)$, but δ_i is blocked in Π. Obviously, δ_i will remain blocked even if further defaults are applied since $In(\Pi)$ grows monotonically with Π, therefore we do not lose any extension by removing it from the set of available defaults.

The only catch is that when we are testing for the closure of a process, we must test the applicability of the 'dropped' defaults from *Dout*. Actually we are only forced to test whether these defaults are blocked; by construction we know that their prerequisite is met. If we find at least one default δ from *Dout* that is not blocked then we have to abandon the current path, backtrack and search for another path. Note that due to Theorem 1, we know that expansion of the current path (say by applying δ) can only lead to extensions that we have already constructed. The procedure above computes *unique extensions*.

Let us look at some examples[4]. First consider the default theory $T = (W, D)$, where $W = \emptyset$ and $D = \{\delta_1, \delta_2, \delta_3, \delta_4\}$ with

$$\delta_0 = \frac{true : a}{a}, \delta_1 = \frac{true : b}{b}, \delta_2 = \frac{true : c}{c}, \delta_3 = \frac{true : d}{d}.$$

The process tree with exponential pruning is found in Figure 1. To illustrate how the procedure works, let us discuss part of the generation of this tree.

First the leftmost path is generated, leading to an extension. Then we look for an alternative, so we have to backtrack by two stages; then we can apply δ_3 instead of δ_2. Note that, by definition of *Compute-Ext*, δ_2 has been removed from the set of available defaults (which currently is empty). But in order to be sure that the path 0–1–3 (corresponding to the process $(\delta_0, \delta_1, \delta_3)$) is closed

[4] All examples in this paper are normal theories for the sake of simplicity, but the pruning methods described apply to arbitrary default theories.

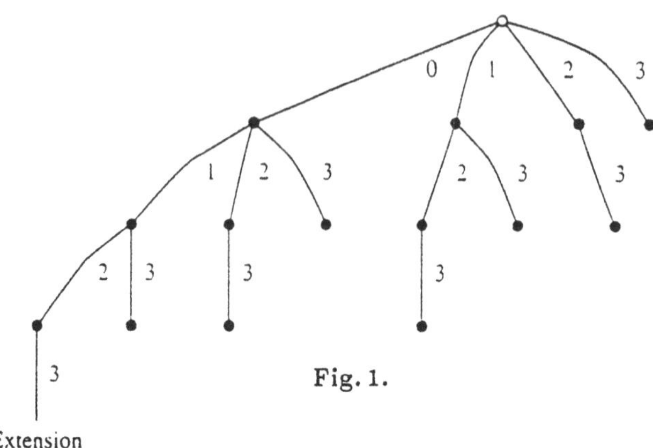

Fig. 1.

we have to check that δ_2 is blocked. In our case it is not blocked, so we have to abandon the current path and backtrack. Note that if we had not checked for the applicability of δ_2 (a default no longer in *Drest*), then we would have concluded that $Th(\{a, b, d\})$ is an extension which would have been wrong. Also we could have expanded the current path by applying δ_2, but then *we would not have obtained a new extension*, but rather the one that we already found.

This example shows that we have a long way to go to avoid the traversal of branches that cannot lead to new extensions. Before we present improvements let us consider another example to be used later. Let $T = (W, D)$, where $W = \{\neg a\}$ and $D = \{\delta_0, \delta_1, \delta_2, \delta_3\}$ with

$$\delta_0 = \frac{true : a}{a}, \delta_1 = \frac{c : b}{b}, \delta_2 = \frac{true : c}{c}, \delta_3 = \frac{true : d}{d}.$$

Figure 2 shows the process tree that is built by the procedure above, showing that T has the single extension $Th(\{\neg a, b, c, d\})$.

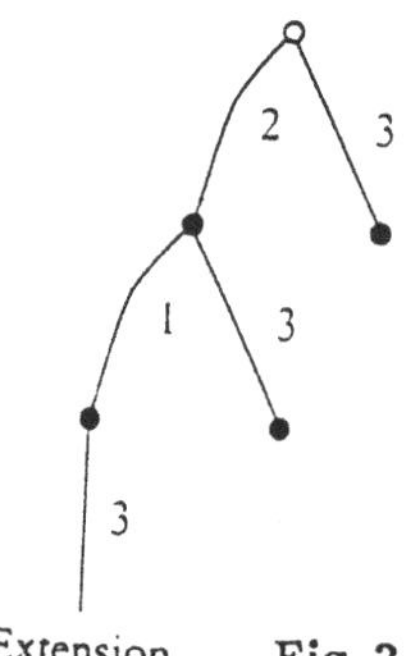

Fig. 2.

3.2 Final segment pruning

It is well known that in default logic, the set of generating defaults of one extension cannot be subset of the set of generating defaults of another extension. In this and the following subsection we describe methods which ensure that each extension has a default differentiating it from every *previous* extension. The following theorem delivers us such a distinguishing method for some cases (for a formal proof see [6]).

2. Theorem *Let $\pi = \pi_1 \circ \pi_2$ be a successful path of the exponentially pruned process tree, closed under the defaults currently available (that is, Drest). Further suppose that no* new *default was added to Dout during the construction of π_2. Then no new extensions can be found by expanding the process tree under π_1 following the procedure in subsection 3.1.*

Let us look at some examples. First consider the process tree from Figure 1. The process tree using the pruning method just described is tree 1) in Figure 3. Simply, the leftmost path has all defaults applied, therefore no new default was blocked and we may terminate the search by Theorem 2. Tree 2) in Figure 3 shows the pruned tree from Figure 2. In this example, δ_0 is blocked at the root. Defaults 2, 1 and 3 are applied leading to a closed and successful process. Of course, this path does block a default, namely δ_0. But note that it is not a *new* default that is blocked, ie it is not due to the path that δ_0 is blocked. Again Theorem 2 tells us that we can terminate the tree traversal because no further extension can be determined (in this case π_1 is empty).

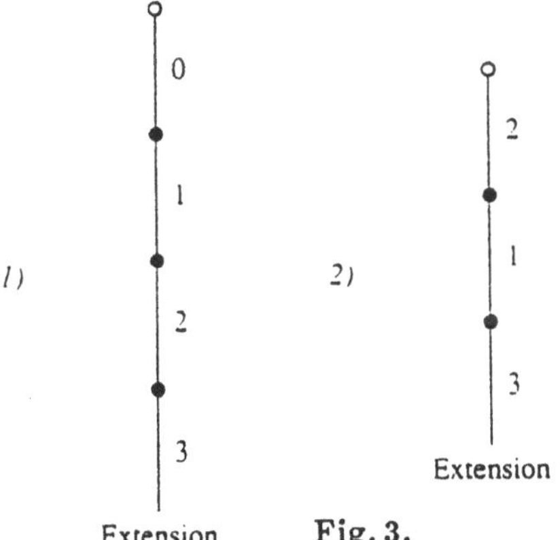

Fig. 3.

These examples used default theories with at most one extension. By no means need this be the case. Figure 4 shows the pruned process tree for the default theory $T = (W, D)$, where $W = \emptyset$ and $D = \{\delta_0, \delta_1, \delta_2, \delta_3\}$ with

$$\delta_0 = \frac{true : a}{a}, \delta_1 = \frac{true : \neg a}{\neg a}, \delta_2 = \frac{true : b}{b}, \delta_3 = \frac{true : c}{c}.$$

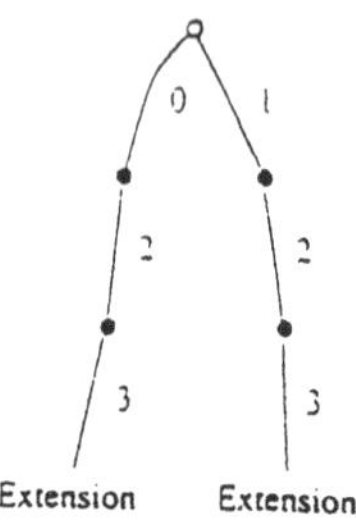

Fig. 4.

It is worth noting that the size of the process tree depends strongly on the initial ordering of defaults used. Figure 5 shows the process tree of the latter example if the initial ordering $(\delta_2, \delta_3, \delta_0, \delta_1)$ is used instead. Obviously the method of this subsection does not work very well here. A much better solution will be presented next, but we would like to point out that a syntactic preprocessing of the default theory may allow one to determine favourable initial orderings; this is clearly a question to be addressed in future research.

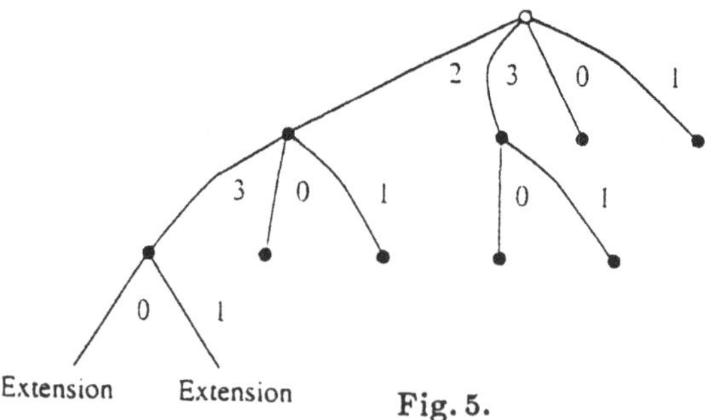

Fig. 5.

3.3 Goal pruning

We begin with a result that underlies the final pruning method we shall discuss (for a proof see [6]).

3. Theorem *Let π be a maximally successful path in the exponentially pruned process tree of the default theory $T = (W, D)$. Let M be the set of defaults in D (including those that have been removed) that are blocked or failed at the leaf of this path. Then every new extension computed after π must contain at least one default from M. M is called a* goal.

Note that here we have to consider the removed defaults as well, as opposed to Theorem 2. The reason is that whereas Theorem 2 affects only the part of the process tree *underneath the initial segment*, Theorem 3 affects all paths *constructed after* π, including those traversed after backtracking. Thus it has a *global effect* on the remaining process tree to be traversed, whilst Theorem 2 had a local effect underneath the initial segment. In this sense, final segment pruning is a special case of goal pruning.

The way we take advantage of Theorem 3 is straightforward. When we backtrack and try to determine further extensions, the usual method is to try all defaults that are applicable at that node and have not yet been tried. But if a maximally successful process has been determined, and $M = \{\delta_1, \ldots, \delta_n\}$, then it is sufficient to consider all *subtrees starting with one of the defaults* $\delta_1, \ldots, \delta_n$ (making combined use of theorems 1 and 3). Let us look at an example. Consider the default theory consisting of the defaults $\delta_0 = \frac{true:a}{a}, \delta_1 = \frac{true:b}{b}, \delta_2 = \frac{true:\neg a \wedge \neg b}{\neg a \wedge \neg b}$. Figure 6 shows the corresponding pruned process tree.

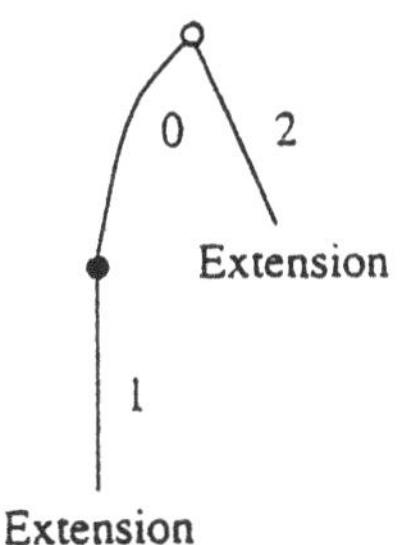

Fig. 6.

First δ_0 and δ_1 are applied, after which δ_2 is blocked. The set $\{\delta_2\}$ is the current goal. If we backtrack, $\{\delta_2\}$ is used as a goal but it is blocked. Therefore we backtrack to the root. If we were not using Theorem 3 we would consider both δ_1 and δ_2. But since $\{\delta_2\}$ is the current goal we only need to consider δ_2 which leads to the second extension of T.

Once several maximally successful paths have been determined, we have several goals, which are maintained in a set of goals $\{G_1, \ldots, G_k\}$. Theorem 3 tells us that every further extension will contain at least one element from every G_i. The way to achieve this is to use G_1 at the first stage, then subsequently G_2 etc, thus taking advantage of the information available. To keep the tree small,

Exten uses the heuristic which prefers shorter goals over longer ones.

Consider the default theory from Figure 5; Figure 7 shows the pruned tree using Theorem 3. The first maximally successful path found is 2-3-0, leading to a goal $\{\delta_1\}$. With simple backtracking we find the second maximally successful path 2-3-1, and have thus a second goal $\{\delta_0\}$. Note that δ_0 was not available (that means not in *Drest*), but still we can say that any further extension must include δ_0.

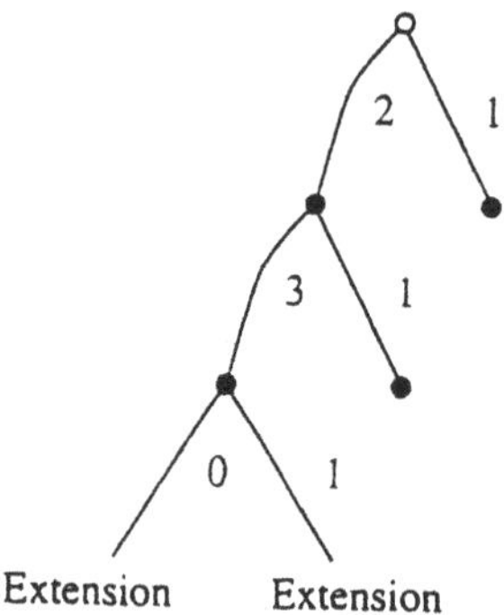

Fig. 7.

If we backtrack, we have two goals, $G_1 = \{\delta_1\}$ and $G_2 = \{\delta_0\}$. We use the first goal arbitrarily (both goals have the same length), and then try to apply δ_0. It is the only default in G_2 and blocked, therefore this path cannot lead to a new extension. We backtrack once again and repeat the same.

Note that the process tree has been reduced considerably. Still, it would have been preferable if the system could make use of the information that the defaults δ_0 and δ_1 block one another. Then one path would have been sufficient. This indicates that an initial static checking of the default theories may provide additional information for specific methods to prune the process tree further. We note that the methods described here are general–purpose in the sense that they apply to arbitrary default theories.

4 Some details on *Exten*

4.1 The user interface

Exten has a command line interface based around a small language, allowing the user to define or modify a default theory and to set various parameters (such as compute first n extensions or carry out success checks every m steps).

As for the system output, there are four levels of granularity. At the simplest level, only the extension is delivered. The second level describes the path (process) leading to the extension, to provide a means of explanation. On the third level, the entire (partial) process tree is displayed; this is done using the external program *Dot* [10]. Finally, the fourth mode offers a verbose trace of the calculation process by displaying additionally the defaults that were tested but were not applicable (of course, this information tends to be an overkill since the tree becomes excessively large).

4.2 The underlying theorem prover

Exten makes use of the recently developed theorem prover *Bluegum* [20], which is tableau–based and at present one of the most powerful classical theorem provers available. *Bluegum* was programmed in an object–oriented way in *C++*. We have incorporated some of the classes of *Blugum* into *Exten* to simplify the integration.

It has been pointed out [17] that tableaux offer a suitable basis for default reasoning, because of the duality of provability (closed tableau) and nonprovability (open tableau). This is particularly suitable for default reasoning, since the prerequisite of a default must be proven from the current In–set, while the negation of the justifications must *not* follow from In. theorem provers in computing extensions. Smaller tableaux can be built and combined together as appropriate to deliver the final result. This way we can avoid rebuilding parts of the tableau over and over again. For example, the set of facts W is involved in all attempted proofs, so it is reasonable to compute the (open) tableau associated with W once, and attempt to close it later on by adding default consequents and justifications or negations of prerequisites as appropriate. Currently we are working at realizing the idea just outlined.

5 Related work

In its present form *Exten* computes extensions of default logics. This contrasts much of the implementation work done elsewhere, for example [11, 18] which regards query evaluation. The focus of *Theorist* [15] was the explanation and prediction of formulae rather than the calculation of extensions. *Theorist* works with supernormal default theories and constraints, while our system can work with arbitrary theories.

As stated before the basic procedure used in our implementation is depth–first forward–chaining. This can be contrasted with the work of Risch and Schwind [17] where a backward–chaining approach is taken. There, starting from the set of defaults D, sets of maximally consistent sets of defaults are determined which then are decomposed into 'successful' subsets (the justifications of the defaults must be respected), and finally they are tested for being grounded (in the sense that the prerequisite of the defaults is provable). From inspection, it would seem that this algorithm is particularly suited to calculating extensions for theories with few consequent conflicts and short 'grounding chains'. In general, our algorithm tends to run faster, as tested on small default sets. It would be interesting to conduct a more substantial comparative study.

DeReS [5] is the system we are aware of that comes closest to *Exten*. It, too, is a system for computing extensions of default theories in different default logics, and it has proven capable of working with hundreds of defaults. Its main implementation technique is stratification which was developed as part of that system. Stratification is invaluable indeed, and we have integrated it in our system. The user interface of our system is more flexible than that of *DeReS* (in the version we had access to) in that it allows interactive changes to default theories easily and offers various parameters to be set, thus supporting experimentation. More significantly, *Exten* works for first order default theories, and uses pruning techniques in addition to stratification.

6 Current and future work

In this paper we described the algorithmic foundations and some other aspects of *Exten*, a system for computing default logic extensions. The design goals were

- to make the system flexible, in terms both of the manner in which the main algorithm could be used and the ease of implementation for additions to the workbench, and
- to make the system efficient through sensible data structures and process tree pruning.

We believe that these objectives have been met for several default logic variants. Still, the current system is just the beginning point for further enhancements. As we mentioned in the introduction, our ultimate goal is to develop a domain–independent toolkit which offers to the user various methods of nonmonotonic reasoning and belief revision. Points of current and future work include the following.

Another interesting idea is to carry out experiments to determine how our forward–chaining approach compares to backward–chaining algorithms like that of [17].

Further aspects we are currently working on include the addition of *structuring and modularity methods* on the representational level, and the study of the *dynamics of default reasoning*: The current state of the art of default logics is that extensions have to be recomputed from scratch once a modification, however slight, has been made. The application of belief revision techniques can help us maintain a large portion of conclusions that we have already drawn.

References

1. G. Antoniou. *Nonmonotonic Reasoning with Incomplete and Changing Information.* MIT Press 1996 (forthcoming)
2. R. Ben–Eliyahu and I. Niemela (eds.). *Applications and Implementations of Nonmonotonic Reasoning Systems.* Proceedings of the IJCAI-95 Workshop.

3. G. Brewka. Cumulative default logic: in defense of nonmonotonic inference rules. *Artificial Intelligence* 50,2 (1991): 183–205
4. P. Cholewinski. Stratified Default Logic. In *Proc. Computer Science Logic 1994*, Springer LNCS 933, 456-470
5. P. Cholewinski, W. Marek, A. Mikitiuk and M. Truszczynski. Experimenting with default logic. In *Proc. ICLP-95*, MIT Press 1995
6. A. P. Courtney. *Towards a Default Logic Workbench: Computing Extensions.* Honours Thesis, Basser Department of Computer Science, University of Sydney 1995
7. J.P. Delgrande, T. Schaub and W.K. Jackson. Alternative Approaches to default logic. *Artificial Intelligence* 70 (1994): 167–237
8. S.P. Engelson, R. Feldman, M. Koppel, A. Nerode and J.B. Remmel. Frost: A forward chaining rule ordering system for reasoning with nonmonotonic rule systems. In [2]
9. M. Hopkins. Orderings and Extensions. In *Proc. ESQUARU'93*, Springer 1993, LNAI 747
10. E. Koutsofinos and S.C. North. *Dot.* Bell Laboratories, *http://www.research.att.com/orgs/ssr/book/reuse*
11. T. Linke and T. Schaub. Lemma Handling in Default Logic Theorem Proving. In *Proc. Symbolic and Quantitative Approaches to Reasoning and Uncertainty*, Springer 1995, LNAI 946, 285–292
12. W. Lukaszewicz. Considerations of default logic: an alternative approach. *Computational Intelligence* 4,1(1988): 1–16
13. A. Mikitiuk and M. Truszczynski. Constrained and rational default logics. In *Proc. International Joint Conference on Artificial Intelligence* 1995
14. I. Niemela and P. Simmons. Evaluating an algorithm for default reasoning. In [2].
15. D. Poole. A Logical Framework for Default Reasoning. *Artificial Intelligence* 36 (1988): 27–47
16. R. Reiter. A logic for default reasoning. *Artificial Intelligence* 13(1980): 81–132
17. V. Risch and C. Schwind. Tableau-Based Characterization and Theorem Proving for Default Logic. *Journal of Automated Reasoning* 13 (1994): 223–242
18. T. Schaub. A new methodology for query-answering in default logics via structure-oriented theorem proving. *Journal of Automated Reasoning* 1995 (forthcoming)
19. K. Schlechta. Directly Sceptical Inheritance cannot Capture the Intersection of Extensions. In *Proc. GMD Workshop on Nonmonotonic Reasoning*, GMD 1989
20. K. Wallace. *Proof Truncation Techniques in Model Elimination Tableau-Based Theorem Proving.* Ph.D. Thesis, Department of Computer Science, University of Newcastle 1994

A Logic for Concurrent Events and Action Failure

David Morley[1] and Liz Sonenberg[2]

[1] Australian A. I. Institute Ltd., Level 6/171 LaTrobe St. Melbourne, 3000 Australia
[2] Dept. of Computer Science, University of Melbourne, Parkville, 3052 Australia

Abstract. When reasoning about agents interacting in a dynamic world, two problems present themselves: other events and actions may occur while an agent is acting; and an agent's actions may fail. We present a more expressive formalism for representing the different ways that events can occur together and extend a recently introduced logic of events to handle concurrent events. We apply the approach of Traverso and Spalazzi to handle actions and failure to obtain a logic that allows for concurrent events and admits reasoning with failure.

1 Introduction

Reasoning about the actions of autonomous agents has been a problem of continuing interest to researchers in AI. When agents are acting in a dynamic world, two significant problems arise:

Firstly, the agent will not be the only cause of change to the world. Many formalisms for reasoning about actions have been developed on the assumption that one agent is responsible for everything that happens; however, this assumption cannot be made in dynamic environments where the world is changing around the agent.

Secondly, although an agent may attempt an action, that action might not succeed. An agent has to be able to cope with the failure of its actions, or at the very least recognize failure.

Handling the second problem requires distinguishing an *event*, which may occur or not occur, from an *action* which, if attempted, may either succeed or fail. Explicit reasoning about failure is an essential component of inference in a dynamic environment, although absent from most formalisms. We address this in Sect. 4.

Handling the first problem requires a clear understanding of what an event is and what it means for events to occur concurrently. Our choice of of representation of events is motivated by the following:

Let a *behaviour* be a description of how the world changes over some time period. This may be as simple as a start state and an end state, or it may be a complete description of the state of the world at all intermediate times. In the situation calculus (McCarthy and Hayes 1969) an event can be viewed as the set of behaviours in which only it occurs and nothing else. Consider a scenario where an observer watches cars that pass through a particular section of a freeway. The event of a red car passing, e_{red}, is the set of those behaviours where exactly one car passes and that car is red. Similarly, we can have e_{white}.

This interpretation of events does not allow other events to occur at the same time. To accommodate this, situation calculus has been extended (e.g., Gelfond et al. 1991) with a *syntactic* operator for the composition of events, e.g., $e_{\text{red}} + e_{\text{white}}$ is identified with the set of behaviours where exactly one red car and one white car pass. However, this operator is not compositional in that there is no relationship between the interpretations of e_{red}, e_{white}, and $e_{\text{red}} + e_{\text{white}}$.

A different approach is for the event e_{red} to contain all behaviours where a red car passes, including those where other cars pass as well. The meaning of $e_{\text{red}} + e_{\text{white}}$ is then simply the intersection of the sets of behaviours associated with e_{red} and e_{white}. However, with this approach it is hard to identify the effects of an event on its own (Georgeff 1987) – there is no way of going from e_{red} to those behaviours where *only* a red car passes.

Another problem is that this definition of + does not give us the expressive precision we need. Consider the statement "a red car and a BMW pass" which would be written as $e_{\text{red}} + e_{\text{BMW}}$. The intersection of the sets associated with e_{red} and e_{BMW} includes behaviours where (i) two cars pass, one that is red and a *different* one that is a BMW, and (ii) a red BMW passes. These two cases have quite distinct meanings. The first meaning we will refer to as *concurrent composition* of two events – adding the effects of two different events. The second meaning we will refer to as *intersection* of two events – taking two descriptions of the *same* event and producing a more precise description. We use the term *co-occurrence* for the more ambiguous statement, which leaves the question of whether the events it refers to are (partially) the same unanswered. When describing the events that occur in a situation, if we mean concurrent composition but can only state co-occurrence, we may not be able to make the deductions we desire.

Therefore an approach to the representation of events is required in which it is possible to state that:

1. an event occurred without excluding the possible occurrence of other events;
2. an event occurred "alone" (with respect to some specified fluents);
3. two events co-occurred;
4. the concurrent composition of two events occurred; and
5. the intersection of two events occurred.

Importantly, the semantics of the operators used in representing these kinds of complex events should be compositional.

In Sect. 2 we take a recently introduced logic of events (Morley et al. 1995) and extend it to include the co-occurrence and concurrent composition operators, providing the desired expressive power. Section 3 provides formal semantics for the language. In Sect. 4 we exploit the approach to action failure that Traverso and Spalazzi (1995) use in the context of a process logic and apply it to our event logic. We show that the resultant action logic can then be viewed as generalizing that of Traverso and Spalazzi in Sect. 5.

2 A Logic of Events

In a previous paper (Morley et al. 1995), we discussed limitations of the popular Explanation Closure approach for handling the frame problem monotonically and proposed an alternative monotonic event logic that avoids these limitations. Concurrent events, being incidental to the emphasis in that paper on solving the frame problem, were not dealt with.

The key difference between the work of Morley et al. (1995) and previous approaches is in the semantics of events. Rather than a set of behaviours, an event is interpreted as a set of ***event instances.*** An event instance consists of a behaviour, stating how the world changes over the duration of the event – including changes due to other events – ***together with an indication of which changes are due to the event in question.*** Allowing changes due to other events satisfies our first expressiveness requirement.

Consider a behaviour where Fred and Mary are both drinking cups of coffee at the same time. We can distinguish two event instances, "Fred drinking coffee" and "Mary drinking coffee", which share this same behaviour. However, the two event instances are distinct, because the first instance includes as effects the changes in the level of coffee in Fred's cup whilst the second instance has the changes to Mary's cup.

What follows is an extension of that logic to incorporate concurrent events, with minor syntactic changes. To simplify the presentation, the language is untyped. However, in the use of the event language we are commonly dealing with propositions, p, q, etc., that denote propositional fluents, and events, e, e', etc., that denote sets of event instances.

Terms of the language, T, are constructed out of function symbols of various arities from $F = F_0 \cup F_1 \cup F_2 \cup ...$, variable symbols from V, and a selection of special constants and operators. T is defined to be the least set such that:

- $V \subset T$
- $F_0 \subset T$
- $\mathbf{e}, \mathbf{e}^0, \mathbf{e}^\perp \in T$
- $f(x_1, ..., x_n) \in T$ if $f \in F_n$ and $x_1, ..., x_n \in T$
- $\overline{e}, e \sqcap e', e + e', e \sqcup e', ee', e^* \in T$ if $e, e' \in T$
- $[p], [\overline{p}], [p^\perp], [p^\top] \in T$ if $p \in T$

Well formed formulas are constructed from terms using predicate symbols of various arities from $P = P_0 \cup P_1 \cup P_2 \cup ...$, the special predicates, fluent(x), event(x), OCC(e), $e \subseteq e'$, and $x = x'$, and the standard first order logical connectives and quantifiers.

Although the language is untyped, for brevity the abbreviations $\forall p.\phi$ and $\exists p.\phi$ will be used for $\forall p.(\text{fluent}(p) \rightarrow \phi)$ and $\exists p.(\text{fluent}(p) \wedge \phi)$ respectively. Quantification over events is similarly abbreviated as $\forall e.\phi$ and $\exists e.\phi$. As usual, free variables in sentences are implicitly universally quantified.

The special "type" predicates, fluent and event, are true of propositions and events respectively. The $\subseteq$ operator is the "more specific than" event relationship. For example, if e_{m} is the event of my depositing some money into my account and e_{m5} is the event of my depositing \$5 into my account, then $e_{\mathrm{m5}} \subseteq e_{\mathrm{m}}$. The $=$ operator is the equality relation. OCC(e) states that one of the event instances of e actually occurred, that is its behaviour correctly describes the changes to the world.

$\mathbf{e}$ is the "universal" event which includes all event instances. $\mathbf{e}^0$ consists all event instances of zero duration. $\mathbf{e}^{\perp}$ contains all event instances that have no effects. These can be thought of as "waiting" events.

$\overline{e}$ and $e \cap e'$ are standard set complement and intersection operators over events. Set intersection is used to further qualify an event. Thus if e_5 is the event of someone depositing \$5 into my account then $e_{\mathrm{m5}} = e_{\mathrm{m}} \cap e_5$. Similarly, $e_{\mathbf{red}} \cap e_{\mathrm{BMW}}$ means "a red BMW passes". $\mathbf{e}$ is the identity for intersection. Set union can be defined as $e_1 \cup e_2 \equiv \overline{\overline{e_1} \cap \overline{e_2}}$, with identity the "impossible" event, $\mathbf{e}^{\emptyset} \equiv \overline{\mathbf{e}}$, which has no instances.

If an event instance ends in a state that another starts with, the *concatenation* of the two event instances consists of concatenating the behaviours and combining the effects. The event ee' consists of all possible concatenations of event instances in e with event instances in e'. e^* denotes zero or more concatenations of e with itself. Thus if e is the event of running around a track once, then ee is the event of running around the track twice and e^* is the event of running around the track zero or more times. $\mathbf{e}^0$ is the identity for concatenation.

The *concurrent composition* of two event instances is defined for event instances with the same behaviour and *disjoint* effects. It takes the union of the effects of the two instances. For example, the concurrent composition of the "Mary drinking coffee" event instance with the "Fred drinking coffee" event instance is "Mary and Fred drinking coffee", which causes both cups to empty. The *concurrent composition* event $e + e'$ contains all possible concurrent compositions of event instances in e and e'. The event $e_{\mathbf{red}} + e_{\mathrm{BMW}}$ is "a red car passes and another car, a BMW, also passes". The event $e_{\mathrm{m5}} + e_5$ increases my bank balance by \$10. $\mathbf{e}^{\perp}$ is the identity for concurrent composition.

The *co-occurrence* event, $e \sqcup e'$, contains event instances that are formed from event instances in e and e' with matching behaviours by taking the union of their effects. For example, $e_{\mathrm{m5}} \sqcup e_5$ may increase my bank balance by \$5 or by \$10, since the events referred to may either be distinct or the same. The event $e \cap e'$ can be seen as the subset of $e \sqcup e'$ where the effects of the two instances are identical. The event $e + e'$ can be seen as the subset of $e \sqcup e'$ where the effects of the two instances were disjoint.

Propositions refer to sets of world states and are related to events via a number of operators. The event $[p]$ (not to be confused with a modal operator) contains all event instances where p remains true. The event $[\overline{p}]$ contains all event instances where p remains false.

$[p^{\perp}]$ is the set of all event instances where the truth of p is not *affected.* That is, the truth of p may change, but *not as an effect of the event.* As an example, during the "Fred drinking coffee" event instance above, the level of coffee in Mary's cup happens to change, but not as an effect of Fred drinking the coffee. Thus if p refers to Mary's cup being full, the "Fred drinking coffee" event instance is in $[p^{\perp}]$.

Conversely, $[p^{\top}]$ is the set of all event instances where if the truth of p changes, then that change *must be* an effect of the event. This provides the ability to state that an event occurred *alone*, meeting our second requirement. It also provides a means for solving the frame problem, outlined as follows:

Let p refer to the light being on, and e refer to the event of Fred switching the light on. e may include event instances where Fred turns the light on but then someone else turns the light off. Thus one cannot deduce that the light will end up being on just from OCC(e). However, the language is expressive enough for us to be able able to state that, as far as the light is concerned, this is the only event to occur. The event $e \cap [p^{\top}]$ contains only those instances where Fred's turning the light on is the *only* effect on the light. By stating OCC($e \cap [p^{\top}]$) one *can* deduce that the light will end up being on.

In contrast, the Explanation Closure approach (Schubert 1990) to solving the frame problem requires enumerating all events that could possibly affect the fluent and then stating that none of these other events occurred. These closure axioms introduce extra information that is not required in our approach and which can lead to unwanted deductions (Morley et al. 1995).

3 Semantics

The discrete time semantics presented here is based on world states. A *behaviour* is a finite sequence of world states. Thus if $w_1, ..., w_4$ are states then $\langle w_1 w_2 w_3 w_4 \rangle$ is a behaviour. Associated with any behaviour is the set of state *transitions* that are pairs of world states adjacent in that behaviour. Thus $\langle w_1 w_2 w_3 w_4 \rangle$ has transitions $\{w_1{:}w_2, w_2{:}w_3, w_3{:}w_4\}$. An *event instance* is identified as a behaviour plus some subset of the behaviour's transitions. Thus $\langle \langle w_1 w_2 w_3 w_4 \rangle, \{w_1{:}w_2, w_3{:}w_4\} \rangle$ is an event instance where the transition $w_2{:}w_3$ is incidental to the event.

The concatenation of two event instances is defined when the last behaviour state of one matches the first behaviour state of the other. It concatenates the behaviours (eliminating the common state) and takes the union of the effects. Thus the concatenation of $\langle \langle w_1 w_2 w_3 \rangle, \{w_1{:}w_2\} \rangle$ with $\langle \langle w_3 w_4 \rangle, \{w_3{:}w_4\} \rangle$ gives $\langle \langle w_1 w_2 w_3 w_4 \rangle, \{w_1{:}w_2, w_3{:}w_4\} \rangle$.

Events are interpreted as sets of event instances. An event e occurs, OCC(e), *with respect to an "actual" behaviour* if that behaviour matches the behaviour of one of the event instances in e. Thus any event containing the event instance $\langle \langle w_1 w_2 w_3 \rangle, \{w_1{:}w_2\} \rangle$ would be said to have occurred with respect to the behaviour $\langle w_1 w_2 w_3 \rangle$.

An *interpretation* $\mathcal{I}$ is a tuple $< \mathcal{W}, \mathcal{D}, \mathcal{F}, \mathcal{P} >$. $\mathcal{W}$ is a set of world states, from which we define:

- The set of all behaviours, finite non-empty sequences of states $\mathcal{B} = \mathcal{W}+$.
- Concatenation of behaviours, $\langle w_0 ... w_i \rangle \cdot \langle w'_0 ... w'_j \rangle = \langle w_0 ... w_i w'_1 ... w'_j \rangle$ defined when $w_i = w'_0$.

- The set of all transitions, $\mathcal{T} = \{w{:}w' \mid w, w' \in \mathcal{W}\}$.
- The transitions of a behaviour $tr(b) = \{w{:}w' \mid b = b' \cdot \langle ww' \rangle \cdot b''\}$
- The transitions that stay within some set, W, of world states, $tr^+(W) = \{w{:}w' \mid w, w' \in W\}$.
- The transitions that stay outside some set, W, of world states, $tr_-(W) = \{w{:}w' \mid w, w' \notin W\}$
- The transitions that stay within some set, W, or its complement, $tr^+_-(W) = tr^+(W) \cup tr_-(W)$
- The set of all event instances, $\mathcal{E} = \{\langle b, T \rangle \mid b \in \mathcal{B}, T \subseteq tr(b)\}$

Each term, x, needs to be assigned a meaning, $\mu(x) \in \mathcal{D}$. The domain, $\mathcal{D}$, is required to contain all sets of world states, $\mathcal{D}_P = 2^{\mathcal{W}}$, and all sets of event instances, $\mathcal{D}_E = 2^{\mathcal{E}}$. Propositions are interpreted as sets of world states, $\mu(p) \in \mathcal{D}_P$. Events are interpreted as sets of event instances, $\mu(e) \in \mathcal{D}_E$. Other terms map to other elements of the domain. $\mathcal{F}$ maps the function symbols of the language to functions over the domain: $\mathcal{F} : F_i \rightarrow (\mathcal{D}^i \rightarrow \mathcal{D})$. $\mathcal{P}$ maps the predicate symbols of the language to predicates over the domain: $\mathcal{P} : P_i \rightarrow (\mathcal{D}^i \rightarrow \{0, 1\})$.

$\mathcal{F}$, together with a variable assignment, $v : V \rightarrow \mathcal{D}$, defines a mapping $\mu(x)$ for any term x:

- $\mu(x) = v(x)$ for $x \in V$
- $\mu(x) = \mathcal{F}(x)()$ for $x \in F_0$
- $\mu(f(x_1, ..., x_n)) = \mathcal{F}(f)(\mu(x_1), ..., \mu(x_n))$ where $f \in F_n$
- $\mu(\mathbf{e}) = \mathcal{E}$
- $\mu(\mathbf{e}^0) = \{\langle\langle w \rangle, \emptyset\rangle \mid w \in \mathcal{W}\}$
- $\mu(\mathbf{e}^\perp) = \{\langle b, \emptyset \rangle \mid b \in \mathcal{B}\}$
- $\mu(e \sqcup e') = \{\langle b, T \cup T' \rangle \mid \langle b, T \rangle \in \mu(e),\ \langle b, T' \rangle \in \mu(e')\}$
- $\mu(e + e') = \{\langle b, T \cup T' \rangle \mid \langle b, T \rangle \in \mu(e),\ \langle b, T' \rangle \in \mu(e'),\ T \cap T' = \emptyset\}$
- $\mu(e \sqcap e') = \mu(e) \cap \mu(e') = \{\langle b, T \cup T' \rangle \mid \langle b, T \rangle \in \mu(e),\ \langle b, T' \rangle \in \mu(e'), \mathrm{T{=}T'}\}$
- $\mu(\overline{e}) = \mathcal{E} \setminus \mu(e)$
- $\mu(ee') = \{\langle b \cdot b', T \cup T' \rangle \mid \langle b, T \rangle \in \mu(e),\ \langle b', T' \rangle \in \mu(e')$ and $b \cdot b'$ defined $\}$
- $\mu(e^*) = \mu(\mathbf{e}^0) \cup \mu(e) \cup \mu(ee) \cup ...$
- $\mu([p]) = \{\langle b, T \rangle \mid tr(b) \subseteq tr^+(\mu(p))\}$
- $\mu([\overline{p}]) = \{\langle b, T \rangle \mid tr(b) \subseteq tr_-(\mu(p))\}$
- $\mu([p^\perp]) = \{\langle b, T \rangle \mid T \subseteq tr^+_-(\mu(p))\}$
- $\mu([p^\top]) = \{\langle b, T \rangle \mid (tr(b) \setminus T) \subseteq tr^+_-(\mu(p))\}$

The semantics of formulas with respect to an interpretation, $\mathcal{I}$, a variable assignment, v, and a behaviour, b, are given by:

- $\mathcal{I}, v, b \models r(x_1, ..., x_n)$ if and only if $\mathcal{P}(r)(\mu(x_1), ..., \mu(x_n)) = 1$ where $r \in P_n$
- $\mathcal{I}, v, b \models \mathrm{fluent}(x)$ if and only if $\mu(x) \in \mathcal{D}_P$
- $\mathcal{I}, v, b \models \mathrm{event}(x)$ if and only if $\mu(x) \in \mathcal{D}_E$
- $\mathcal{I}, v, b \models \mathrm{OCC}(e)$ if and only if there exists $\langle b, T \rangle \in \mu(e)$
- $\mathcal{I}, v, b \models e \subseteq e'$ if and only if $\mu(e) \subseteq \mu(e')$
- $\mathcal{I}, v, b \models x = x'$ if and only if $\mu(x) = \mu(x')$

plus the standard interpretations of quantifiers and logical connectives. If $\mathcal{I}, v, b \models x$ for all v, then we can omit v. For x containing no free variables, $\mathcal{I}, v, b \models x$ if and only if $\mathcal{I}, b \models x$. If $\mathcal{I}, v, b \models x$ for all b, then we can omit b. For b containing no references to the OCC predicate, $\mathcal{I}, v, b \models x$ if and only if $\mathcal{I}, v \models x$.

Note that with these semantics, if p logically implies q, i.e., $\mu(p) \subseteq \mu(q)$, and if an event instance causes p to become true, then unless q was already true, the event instance must cause q to become true as well. Thus we are able to deduce the ramifications of an event on q just by stating its effects on p. With careful choice of representation we believe causality can also be handled, but we do not go into the details in this paper.

4 Actions

Actions represent an agent's attempt to affect the world and may succeed or fail. In contrast an event can only occur or not occur. Thus an attempt by Mary to fire a gun is an action, which may succeed or fail. The action is related to but not the same as the event of Mary successfully firing the gun.

Giunchiglia et al. (1994) handle the potential failure of actions explicitly using a variant of process logic. An action is represented by two sets of behaviours: those in which the action succeeds and those in which it fails. Compound actions are constructed from constituent actions using conditional and repetition operators. Their logic does not however allow reasoning about concurrent actions, multiple agents, and so on.

Syntactically, we introduce actions using the "action type" predicate action(x) and use the abbreviations $\forall\alpha.\phi$ for $\forall\alpha.(\text{action}(\alpha) \rightarrow \phi)$ and $\exists\alpha.\phi$ for $\exists\alpha.(\text{action}(\alpha) \wedge \phi)$.

We then take a similar approach in that an action, α, is nothing more than a pair of events, the event of successful executions of the action, $S(\alpha)$, and the event of failed executions, $F(\alpha)$:

$$(S(\alpha) = S(\beta) \wedge F(\alpha) = F(\beta)) \leftrightarrow \alpha = \beta$$

We require that once an action succeeds or fails, it terminates. No successful or failed event instance for an action can be extended (by concatenating with another event instance of non-zero duration) into another event instance for that action (for brevity, $R(\alpha) \equiv S(\alpha) \cup F(\alpha)$ is defined to be the event of executing α either successfully or unsuccessfully):

$$(R(\alpha)\overline{\mathbf{e}^0}) \cap R(\alpha) = \mathbf{e}^\emptyset$$

Actions can be arbitrarily complex attempts to affect the world. Actions are described by providing axioms to constrain their success and failure events. For example, we would state that all successful event instances of a "load gun" action result in the gun being loaded.

As a slightly more complex example, consider an action of attempting to speak to Fred using the telephone. All successful event instances will have behaviours in which Fred answers the telephone. Thus the success of the "call Fred" action requires Fred's action of answering the telephone.

We also have the primitive action that always succeeds immediately, Σ, and the primitive action that always fails immediately, Φ:

$S(\Sigma) = \mathbf{e}^0$, $F(\Sigma) = \mathbf{e}^{\emptyset}$

$S(\Phi) = \mathbf{e}^{\emptyset}$, $F(\Phi) = \mathbf{e}^0$

Actions can be combined using various constructs for handling failure.

The conditional action $\alpha?\beta|\gamma$ first attempts α. If α succeeds it attempts β. If α fails it attempts γ. The success or failure of $\alpha?\beta|\gamma$ is determined by that of β or γ, whichever is attempted.

$S(\alpha?\beta|\gamma) = S(\alpha)S(\beta) \cup F(\alpha)S(\gamma)$

$F(\alpha?\beta|\gamma) = S(\alpha)F(\beta) \cup F(\alpha)F(\gamma)$

One application of the conditional is to allow an agent to explicitly handle failure of actions. Common uses of the conditional include $\alpha?\beta|\Phi$, where α is attempted and only if it succeeds is β attempted, and $\alpha?\Sigma|\beta$, where α is attempted and only if it fails is β attempted. These are abbreviated to $\alpha\&\beta$ and $\alpha|\beta$ respectively.

The repetition action while(α, β) alternately attempts α and β until one fails. If α fails, then while(α, β) succeeds. If β fails then while(α, β) fails. Thus while$(\alpha, \beta) = \alpha?(\beta\&\text{while}(\alpha, \beta))|\Sigma$.

$S(\text{while}(\alpha, \beta)) = (S(\alpha)S(\beta))^*F(\alpha)$

$F(\text{while}(\alpha, \beta)) = (S(\alpha)S(\beta))^*S(\alpha)F(\beta)$

The parallel action $\alpha \parallel \beta$ is the action that commences α and β at the same time, finishes when the longer of the two actions finishes, and is successful if and only if both sub-actions are successful. The semantics of the parallel operator is complicated by the fact that concurrent composition of events requires the matching of pairs of event instances with the same duration. Thus if the execution of α event instance is shorter than the corresponding execution of β, the execution of α must be padded-out with a waiting event, $\mathbf{e}^{\perp}$, before the concurrent composition is well-defined. Alternatively, if β is shorter, then it will need to be padded with a waiting event.

$S(\alpha \parallel \beta)=(S(\alpha)\mathbf{e}^{\perp} + S(\beta)) \cup (S(\alpha) + S(\beta)\mathbf{e}^{\perp})$

$F(\alpha \parallel \beta)=(R(\alpha)\mathbf{e}^{\perp} + F(\beta)) \cup (F(\alpha) + R(\beta)\mathbf{e}^{\perp})$

4.1 An Example Application

The logic presented here is suitable for describing the formal semantics of agent-oriented systems operating in a dynamic environment.

One such system is the Procedural Reasoning System, PRS, which provides a language for constructing reactive agents and which has been successfully applied to a number of real world applications (e.g., Georgeff and Ingrand 1990). Agents are provided with libraries of plans to guide their actions in particular circumstances. These plans can include goals such as $?p$, to test whether p is true, $!p$, to try to make p true, and $\hat{}p$ to wait until p is true.

As an example of reasoning about the semantics of PRS, actions can be associated with the various goals. The test goal, $?p$, is meant to succeed if and only if the proposition p is true at the start of the action: $S(?p) \subseteq [p]\mathbf{e}$ and $F(?p) \subseteq [\overline{p}]\mathbf{e}$. The achieve goal, $!p$, is meant to attempt to make p true and succeeds or fails based on whether p is in fact true at the end of the action. This translates to $S(!p) \subseteq \mathbf{e}[p]$, and $F(!p) \subseteq \mathbf{e}[\overline{p}]$. The wait goal, $\hat{}p$, is meant to wait ***without doing anything*** until p has become true. Like the achieve goal, successful executions involve events where p ends up being true. However, the logic allows us to state that the wait goal itself did not cause p to become true. $S(\hat{}p) \subseteq (\mathbf{e}[p]) \cap \mathbf{e}^{\perp}$ and $F(\hat{}p) = \mathbf{e}^{\emptyset}$.

The actions corresponding to goals can further be refined to describe various constraints imposed by implementation or by design issues. For example, $\hat{}p$ may be constrained to succeed as soon as p becomes true. These are useful in identifying correctness conditions for plans and identifying or stating hidden assumptions about plan execution, especially where multiple agents are involved.

5 Comparison with a Process Logic of Actions

The logic of Giunchiglia, et al. (1994) is reworked in a later paper (Traverso and Spalazzi 1995) where explicit sensing and planning actions are introduced. We will use this later presentation for comparison, ignoring the sensing and planning actions, which are incidental to the issues at hand.

Their logic includes ***propositions*** $p \in \mathcal{P}$, that refer to behaviours rather than states and correspond to our events, and ***tactics*** $\alpha \in \mathcal{T}$, that correspond to our actions. The ***modal operator*** $[\alpha]p$ is used to state (of a behaviour) that p is true after executing α, either successfully or unsuccessfully.

Propositions, p, are interpreted with respect to a structure, $\mathcal{U}$ and a behaviour. $\mathcal{U}$ consists of:

- a set of worlds $\mathcal{W}$, defining a set of behaviours $\mathcal{B} = \mathcal{W}+$;
- an assignment of sets of behaviours to propositions, $\rho : \mathcal{P} \to 2^{\mathcal{B}}$; and
- an assignment of meanings to tactics, $\mathcal{S} : \mathcal{T} \to 2^{\mathcal{B}}$ and $\mathcal{F} : \mathcal{T} \to 2^{\mathcal{B}}$, defining $\mathcal{R}(\alpha) = \mathcal{S}(\alpha) \cup \mathcal{F}(\alpha)$.

Given any $\mathcal{U}$, b, and p we can construct an interpretation, $\mathcal{I}(\mathcal{U})$ and well formed formula $\mathsf{x}(p) \to \mathrm{OCC}(\mathsf{e}(p))$ in our logic such that $\mathcal{U}, b \models p$ if and only if $\mathcal{I}, b \models \mathsf{x}(p) \to \mathrm{OCC}(\mathsf{e}(p))$. Thus one can view our logic as a generalisation of theirs.

The two notations share the same primitive tactics/actions, Σ and Φ, and the operators are generally minor syntactic variations. Each tactic, $\alpha \in \mathcal{T}$, can be mapped to an action:

$\mathsf{a}(\alpha) = \alpha$ for basic tactics, $\alpha \in \mathcal{T}_0$
$\mathsf{a}(\Sigma) = \Sigma$
$\mathsf{a}(\Phi) = \Phi$
$\mathsf{a}(\textbf{iffail } \alpha \textbf{ then } \beta \textbf{ else } \gamma) = \mathsf{a}(\alpha)?\mathsf{a}(\gamma)|\mathsf{a}(\beta)$
$\mathsf{a}(\alpha;\beta) = \mathsf{a}(\alpha)?\mathsf{a}(\beta)|\mathsf{a}(\beta)$
$\mathsf{a}(then(\alpha,\beta)) = \mathsf{a}(\alpha)\&\mathsf{a}(\beta)$
$\mathsf{a}(orelse(\alpha,\beta)) = \mathsf{a}(\alpha)|\mathsf{a}(\beta)$
$\mathsf{a}(repeat(\alpha)) = \mathrm{while}(\mathsf{a}(\alpha), \Sigma)$

Their logical connectives, $\neg p$ and $p \wedge q$, correspond to our event operators, $\overline{e}$ and $e \cap e'$. Their *chop* and $\mathcal{W}$ equate to our event concatenation and $\mathbf{e}^0$. We represent the event that corresponds to $[\alpha]p$ by a new constant, $e_{\alpha p}$. This contains all behaviours that when followed by an execution of α, result in a behaviour in p. Not only do we require $e_{\alpha p}R(\mathsf{a}(\alpha)) \subseteq \mathsf{e}(p)$, but also $e_{\alpha p}$ must contain *all* such behaviours. Therefore $\forall e'.(e'R(\mathsf{a}(\alpha)) \subseteq \mathsf{e}(p) \rightarrow e' \subseteq e_{\alpha p})$. Because of this, each of their propositions, p, must be mapped to an event term, $\mathsf{e}(p)$, plus a statement, $\mathsf{x}(p)$, that qualifies some of the event constants in $\mathsf{e}(p)$:

$\mathsf{e}(p) = e_p$, $\mathsf{x}(p) = true$ for basic propositions $p \in \mathcal{P}_0$
$\mathsf{e}(W) = \mathbf{e}^0$, $\mathsf{x}(W) = true$
$\mathsf{e}(Fail(\alpha)) = F(\mathsf{a}(\alpha))$, $\mathsf{x}(Fail(\alpha)) = true$
$\mathsf{e}(Succ(\alpha)) = S(\mathsf{a}(\alpha))$, $\mathsf{x}(Succ(\alpha)) = true$
$\mathsf{e}(\neg p) = \overline{\mathsf{e}(p)}$, $\mathsf{x}(\neg p) = \mathsf{x}(p)$
$\mathsf{e}(p \wedge q) = \mathsf{e}(p) \cap \mathsf{e}(q)$, $\mathsf{x}(p \wedge q) = \mathsf{x}(p) \wedge \mathsf{x}(q)$
$\mathsf{e}(p\ chop\ q) = \mathsf{e}(p)\mathsf{e}(q)$, $\mathsf{x}(p \wedge q) = \mathsf{x}(p) \wedge \mathsf{x}(q)$

The modal operator is somewhat trickier, with:

$\mathsf{e}([\alpha]p) = e_{\alpha p}$,
$\mathsf{x}([\alpha]p) = \mathsf{x}(p) \wedge (e_{\alpha p}R(\mathsf{a}(\alpha)) \subseteq \mathsf{e}(p)) \wedge (\forall e'.(e'R(\mathsf{a}(\alpha)) \subseteq \mathsf{e}(p) \rightarrow e' \subseteq e_{\alpha p}))$

We can now define $\mathcal{I}(\mathcal{U}) =< \mathcal{W}', \mathcal{D}', \mathcal{F}', \mathcal{P}' >$:

- We take the same set of world states, $\mathcal{W}' = \mathcal{W}$.
- The domain, $\mathcal{D}' = \mathcal{D}_P \cup \mathcal{D}_E \cup (\mathcal{D}_E \times \mathcal{D}_E)$, contains just propositions, events, and actions.
- The transformation introduces constants, e_p for each basic proposition $p \in \mathcal{P}_0$ and $e_{\alpha p}$ for each use $[\alpha]p$ of the modal operator. We need to assign sets of event instances to these terms – $\mathcal{F}(e_p)() = \{\langle b, tr(b)\rangle \mid b \in \rho(p)\}$ and $\mathcal{F}(e_{\alpha p})() = \{\langle b, tr(b)\rangle \mid \forall b' \in \mathcal{R}(\alpha).(b \cdot b' \in \rho(p))\}$. We define success and failure sets of event instance for each basic tactic α in $\mathcal{T}_0$ – $\mathcal{F}(S)(\alpha) = \{\langle b, tr(b)\rangle \mid b \in \mathcal{S}(\alpha)\}$ and $\mathcal{F}(F)(\alpha) = \{\langle b, tr(b)\rangle \mid b \in \mathcal{F}(\alpha)\}$. The success and failure sets of the primitive and compound actions are constrained by our action axioms.
- We need no predicate symbols.

Theorem 1. *If $p \in \mathcal{P}$ is a proposition in the logic of Traverso and Spalazzi (1995) without sensing and planning actions, then $\mathcal{U}, b \models p$ if and only if $\mathcal{I}(\mathcal{U}), b \models \mathsf{x}(p) \rightarrow \mathsf{OCC}(\mathsf{e}(p))$.*

Proof outline. The proof of the theorem uses the induction hypothesis that $\mathcal{U}, b \models p$ if and only if $\mathcal{I}, b \models \mathsf{x}(p) \rightarrow \mathsf{OCC}(\mathsf{e}(p))$ for p containing n or less operators, where $\mathcal{I} = \mathcal{I}(\mathcal{U})$.

The induction hypothesis is clearly true for $n = 0$.

There is insufficient space for the whole proof, so to illustrate we show the "only if" part of the proof for $[\alpha]p$:

Suppose $\mathcal{U}, b \models [\alpha]p$ where $[\alpha]p$ contains $n+1$ operators. From the definition this is the case if and only if $\mathcal{U}, b \cdot b' \models p$ for all $b' \in \mathcal{R}(\alpha)$. By the induction hypothesis we have

$$\mathcal{I}, b \cdot b' \models \mathsf{x}(p) \rightarrow \mathsf{OCC}(\mathsf{e}(p)) \text{ for all } b' \in \mathcal{R}(\alpha) \ . \tag{1}$$

Suppose the induction hypothesis is not true for $[\alpha]p$, that is $\mathcal{I}(\mathcal{U}), b \not\models \mathsf{x}([\alpha]p) \rightarrow \mathrm{OCC}(\mathsf{e}([\alpha]p))$. From the definition of $\mathsf{x}([\alpha]p)$ and $\mathsf{e}([\alpha]p)$ we must have

$$\mathcal{I} \models \mathsf{x}(p) \text{ and} \tag{2}$$

$$\mathcal{I} \models \forall e'.(e'R(\mathsf{a}(\alpha)) \subseteq \mathsf{e}(p) \rightarrow e' \subseteq e_{\alpha p}) \text{ and} \tag{3}$$

$$\mathcal{I}, b \not\models \mathrm{OCC}(e_{\alpha p}) \ . \tag{4}$$

From (1), (2), and modus ponens we deduce $\mathcal{I}, b \cdot b' \models \mathrm{OCC}(\mathsf{e}(p))$ for all $b' \in \mathcal{R}(\alpha)$.

This mean that $\{\langle b \cdot b', \emptyset \rangle\} \in \mu(\mathsf{e}(p))$ for all $b' \in \mathcal{R}(\alpha)$. So $\{\langle b \cdot b', tr(b \cdot b')\rangle \mid b' \in \mathcal{R}(\alpha)\} \subseteq \mu(\mathsf{e}(p))$. If we let $e_b = \{\langle b, \emptyset \rangle\}$ we can write this as $\mu(e_b R(\mathsf{a}(\alpha))) \subseteq \mu(\mathsf{e}(p))$. Thus

$$\mathcal{I} \models e_b R(\mathsf{a}(\alpha)) \subseteq \mathsf{e}(p) \ . \tag{5}$$

Letting e' in (3) equal e_b we get $\mathcal{I} \models e_b \subseteq e_{\alpha p}$. But if $\{\langle b, \emptyset \rangle\} \subseteq \mu(e_{\alpha p})$, then $\mathcal{I}, b \models \mathrm{OCC}(e_{\alpha p})$, contradicting (4), and refuting our denial of the induction hypothesis.

The treatment of the other operators is similar, thus the induction hypothesis holds for propositions with arbitrary numbers of operators.

□

6 Discussion

In contrast to the action logic of Traverso and Spalazzi (1995), the logic presented in this paper allows us to deal explicitly with concurrent events. Another work with similar aims to ours is Ferguson's interval-based temporal logic (1995) for use in planning, which supports the representation of concurrent events and action failure. Work which has features in common with our approach to events is that of Drakengren (1996), who also emphasizes compositionality. As this work was brought to our attention only recently, we cannot accommodate a detailed comparison in this paper.

Ferguson's "events" are similar to our event instances, but he cannot deal with events that do not occur. Our events (e.g., $e_{\mathbf{red}}$) are represented as event predicates (e.g., RED), rather than as first-order objects. For this reason, Ferguson cannot reason directly about properties of events in general. However, he can distinguish concurrent composition ($\exists e, e'.\mathrm{RED}(e) \wedge \mathrm{BMW}(e') \wedge e \neq e'$) from intersection ($\exists e.\mathrm{RED}(e) \wedge \mathrm{BMW}(e)$). Actions are introduced as first-order objects and are conditionally associated with the existence of a corresponding event if the attempt is successful. However, failure is treated solely as the non-existence of an event. Another limitation is that although actions are first-order objects, Ferguson cannot reason about compound actions, because actions are associated with event predicates rather than first-order objects.

In summary, the logic presented in this paper provides the ability to deal both with concurrent events and with the potential failure of actions, extending previous approaches to the individual issues. The logic provides a rich language of events and actions with clear correspondence to the underlying semantic relationships. The features of this logic make it ideally suited to reasoning about agents acting in dynamic, real-world environments.

7 Acknowledgments

This work was partly supported by the Cooperative Research Centre for Intelligent Decision Systems, Melbourne, Australia. The authors would also like to thank Michael Georgeff for insightful comments and helpful discussions.

References

Drakengren, T. 1996. Compositionality and the frame problem. Technical Report LiTH-IDA-R-96-4, Department of Computer and Information Science, Linköping University.

Ferguson, G. M. 1995. *Knowledge Representation and Reasoning for Mixed-Initiative Planning*. Ph.D. Dissertation, University of Rochester, Rochester, New York.

Gelfond, M., Lifschitz, V., and Rabinov, A. 1991. What are the limitations of the situation calculus? In Boyer, R., ed., *Automated Reasoning: Essays in Honor of Woody Bledsoe*. Dordrecht: Kluwer Academic Press. 167–179.

Georgeff, M. P., and Ingrand, F. F. 1990. Real-time reasoning: The monitoring and control of spacecraft systems. In *Proceedings of the Sixth IEEE Conference on Artificial Intelligence Applications.*

Georgeff, M. P. 1987. Actions, processes, and causality. In *Reasoning about Actions and Plans: Proceedings of the 1986 Workshop*, 99–122. Los Altos, California: Morgan Kaufmann.

Giunchiglia, F., Spalazzi, L., and Traverso, P. 1994. Planning with failure. In *Proceedings Second International Conference on AI Planning Systems (AIPS-94).*

McCarthy, J., and Hayes, P. J. 1969. Some philosophical problems from the standpoint of artificial intelligence. *Machine Intelligence* 4:463–502.

Morley, D. N., Sonenberg, E., and Georgeff, M. P. 1995. Saying you are there. In Yao, X., ed., *Proceedings Eighth Australian Joint Conference on AI (AI'95)*, 123–130. Singapore: World Scientific.

Schubert, L. 1990. Monotonic solution of the frame problem in the situation calculus. In Kyburg, H. E., Loui, R. P., and Carlson, G. N., eds., *Knowledge Representation and Defeasible Reasoning*, volume 5 of *Studies in Cognitive Science*. Kluwer Academic Press. 23–67.

Traverso, P., and Spalazzi, L. 1995. A logic for acting, sensing and planning. In *Proceedings of the Fourteenth International Joint Conference on Artificial Intelligence(IJCAI95)*, 1491–1497. Morgan Kaufmann.

Domain World Models Represented from Variable Viewpoints for ICAI Systems of High-School Chemistry

Tatsuhiro Konishi and Yukihiro Itoh

Department of Computer Science,
Shizuoka University

Abstract. Most of ICAI (Intelligent Computer Aided Instruction) systems for the natural sciences have each model of the domain world written in symbolic knowledge representation. In such symbolic models, the ways to represent objects in the domain worlds are decided on the basis of the designers' standpoints or viewpoints (what to omit in the models, what to make the primitive elements of the models, and so on). In this paper, we show that the world model of ICAI systems for many domains should be represented from variable viewpoints. Moreover we propose some methods to design and to handle the world model which can be represented from variable viewpoints, in the domain of the high-school chemistry. We show a basic viewpoint and three advanced viewpoints which are needed to solve 176 numerical exercises in a textbook of the domain. And we also report on our problem solving system with the world model.

Keywords: Intelligent CAI Systems, Domain World Models, Viewpoints

1 Introduction

When we design domain world models using a symbolic knowledge representation, we cannot avoid to establish some principles; for example, which property of the domain world should be written in the model, what should be primitives of the model, and so on. In this paper, we call the frameworks of knowledge representation derived from such principles "viewpoints" for the models. In intelligent CAI systems, the viewpoints influence the variation of exercises which they can teach, and the complexity or grain size of the method to solve the exercises.

Various methods to represent domain world models of ICAI systems are proposed by many researchers. Quantitative models are used in systems which don't have to handle naive logic directly [1]. Qualitative models are useful to explain phenomena to students [2,3]. But in most of qualitative models, parameters or landmarks are selected to suit to their task domains. As a result, their viewpoints seem to be decided in ad hoc ways, on a case by case basis. In this paper, we discuss the problem of "viewpoints" for ICAI systems. We show the necessity of the world model with variable viewpoints, and propose a method to manage viewpoints. Moreover, we introduce a problem solver which can select a valid viewpoint for each exercise of high-school chemistry, and reconstruct the domain world model from the viewpoint.

2 Fundamental Discussion

2.1 Various Viewpoints in Designing Domain World Models

In ICAI systems for natural sciences, domain knowledge should contain the domain world model, because such ICAI systems should be able to simulate scientific phenomena on the domain world. When we design domain world models for ICAI, we have to decide what to be represented and what to be omitted, considering what is essential in the subject and what should be taught to the students by the system. Moreover, we usually have to make some decision in symbolizing the domain world. We think that some principles used to make these decision fix a viewpoint. At least, the viewpoint contains the following types of principles, which are closely related with each other.

(1) the principles of omission
We usually omit the elements which have little influence upon the problem solving process or simulation of the phenomena, to simplify the world model. The major types of such omission are as follows:

(a) omission of a parameter
In general, parameters which have little influence upon the domain world, or of which the omission makes the problem simpler, are usually omitted. For example, frictional forces, or mass of strings in elementary dynamics, percentage of contained isotope in calculating atomic weight, and so on. Such types of omissions also occur when some objects are regarded as ideal ones; for example, an ideal gas, a rigid body, and so on. In such omission, the initial condition of exercise often shows which parameters should be omitted.

(b) omission of detailed value of a parameter
In qualitative models, some parameters are not omitted but represented only qualitatively. In such cases, the detailed continuous value of the parameter is omitted.

(c) omission of microscopic elements from macroscopic viewpoints
In several subjects such as chemistry or electromagnetics, macroscopic phenomena are regarded as the integration of huge numbers of microscopic phenomena. But in such subjects, microscopic elements of the world is often omitted in the world models. For example, we usually omit microscopic reactions and inverse reactions which cancel each other in the state of the chemical equilibrium, and regard such state as a stable one.

(2) the principles of the primitive elements of the representation
In designing the world models, we have to decide the grain size of primitive objects, and of the time. Such decisions are closely related with the above mentioned principles of omission.

(a) grain size of primitive objects in the world model
Objects can usually be represented in various grain sizes. For example, an electric cell can be represented either by a symbol, or by symbols representing its elements, such as electrodes, and electrolytes.

(b) grain size of time to represent behaviour of objects
The grain size of time is, in other words, the basic time step in the simulation. In quantitative simulations, the simulators calculate the changes of parameters in every time steps. In qualitative simulations, the time step seems to be not fixed, but almost settled by defining landmarks, because the changes which reach any landmarks are regarded as the basic steps of such simulations, and so width of intervals between the landmarks influences the length of time steps.

(3) the principles of the selection of properties to represent world status
In symbolic world models, status of the worlds are often represented as properties of objects. For example, the state that a ball is placed in front of a wall can be represented by the coordinates of the ball and the wall. But in this case, the width of the space between the ball and the wall can also represent the state. When we design symbolic world models, we have to decide a coherent method to represent such states.

2.2 The Necessity to Manage Variable Viewpoints in ICAI

As mentioned above, we have to establish principles on designing symbolic world model, but valid principles are not stable in a subject (moreover, even in an exercise). For examples:

- In circuitry, transient phenomena should be considered, or not.
- In circuitry, whether the behaviour of a circuit is represented using currents, or voltages.
- In dynamics, frictional forces, and mass of strings should be considered, or not.
- In physics, whether a phenomenon is analyzed by using only Newtonian physics, or also quantum physics.
- In chemistry, whether microscopic phenomena are considered.
- In chemistry, changes in reactions should be represented discretely, or continuously.

If we adopt a world model based on a fixed viewpoint for an ICAI system of such subjects, several problems must be found in the system. From the fixed principles of omission, many useless objects in an exercise cannot be omitted because they may be useful in some other exercises. But the structures of such models must become too complex to be understood by students. It is similar to the fixed grain size of primitives.

The problem of multiple viewpoints in ICAI would be similar to that of multiple domain ontologies in the field of knowledge engineering.

2.3 A Basic Method of Managing Variable Viewpoints

In order to manage variable viewpoints, we should develop following methods of:

- representation of the world model from multiple viewpoints
- selecting the valid viewpoint, and controlling the change of viewpoints
- problem solving on the basis of each viewpoint

But we think that it is too difficult to manage possible viewpoints.

(i) Difficulties of reasoning: Reasoning which uses symbolic knowledge is based on pattern matching. So the patterns representing the same fact should be unique, or should be able to be unified by simple procedures. But to manage multiple viewpoints, a lot of patterns are available to represent the same fact. As a result, we cannot construct problem solver.
(ii) Difficulties of changing viewpoints: To manage every viewpoint, we have to find coherent reasons to change viewpoints. But the reasons are so various that we cannot generalize them yet.

But we think that we don't have to manage so many viewpoints, because the viewpoints used for well-formed subjects can be restricted to some typical patterns. And the reasons to change the restricted patterns of viewpoints can be defined as some rules, because they are also restricted. In order to verify this idea, we have done a case study on a textbook, and found that many exercises can be solved by the approach comprehensively (The detail can be seen in 3.1).

On the other hand, another approach may be possible to manage multiple viewpoints which are reduced to some types: to define valid viewpoints for each exercise, and to design multiple knowledge representations and multiple inference engines for each viewpoint. In fact, when most of conventional ICAI systems have to handle another type of exercises, they are extended to use another type of knowledge representation and problem solver.

But in teaching students from multiple viewpoints, we think there are following two important points, which are difficult to cover in such an approach.

The first is that systems should be able to teach how to select the valid viewpoint for each exercise, because ability of such selection is essential in problem solving. In order to realize such training, systems should be able to explain and discuss the reason of the selection. Consequently, systems should have knowledge for viewpoint selection, or at least heuristics.

The second is that systems should be able to teach difference and commonness between world models represented from different viewpoints. Students should not only solve exercises using the model from the valid viewpoints, but also study which part of the model is useful in solving processes, and what is lack in the other models. In general, all relations between elements in a model and another model must be defined to support such studies. But it would be heavy. In the case that there are only small differences between models, we can define the common structure of the models, and also define differences between the common structure and each specific structure based on each viewpoint, instead of defining independent models. In this approach, it becomes easier to show students the relations between models.

It depends on the domain whether we can define such a common structure of models. For example, we can find a common structure for high-school chemistry (see chapter 3). We believe that we can define such common structures for many subjects in which the world consists of concepts that are relatively stable and limited. Most of elementary natural sciences seem to satisfy this condition. In this paper, we discuss only such domains.

In consequence, we adopt the basic approach as follows:

- reduce possible viewpoints to some typical ones of the domain.
- change viewpoints by using knowledge or heuristic.
- define the common structure of world models, and transform it for each viewpoint if needed. The transformation procedure is designed for each typical viewpoint.

3 The Method of Managing Variable Viewpoints in High-school Chemistry

3.1 Typical Viewpoints in High-school Chemistry

In high-school chemistry, behaviour of chemical systems can be usually represented on the basis of relations between reactants and products shown in chemical formulas. As far as managing such relations, we should consider only the initial states and results of reactions, and don't have to consider the details of intermediate states or process of the reactions. In the state after reactions, products are important but remaining reactants are not. Most of chemical reactions in this domain are irreversible. After the reactions, the state of the chemical system is regarded as stable, if microscopic changes are not so important. Considering these natures of this domain, we have proposed a representation of a world model from the following viewpoint. We call this model "the basic model".

a) Chemical materials are integrations of moleculars or atoms. In simulating the changes of such integrations, all of their contents are regarded as to be changed approximately, even if some moleculars or atoms are not changed strictly. (As a result, reactants remaining after reactions are omitted.) In other words, terms representing materials are always treated as universal one in the framework of predicate logic.
b) The basic time-step has enough length to finish a chemical reaction. In other words, details of intermediate states are not considered. Chemical reactions are represented discretely as conversion from / to three states: the initial state, the changing state, and the completed state.
c) When chemical systems are stable from macroscopic viewpoint, microscopic changes are omitted.

This viewpoint has several advantages as far as managing simple chemical reactions; numbers of symbols representing materials can be reduced, difficulty to represent continuous changes in symbolic way can be avoided, numbers of (microscopic) reactions in the model can be reduced, and so on. Moreover, there are only a few situations in which the viewpoint is invalid. In order to confirm it, we have done case study by using a textbook of high-school chemistry [8]. We picked up all exercises which makes students find some chemical values by calculation, and got 176 exercises. We found 144 of them can be solved by using the basic model.

It also became clear that the basic model is invalid for the following types of exercises.

- Exercises on titrations because remaining reactants should not be omitted.
- Exercises on velocity of chemical reactions because the intermediate state of reaction should be represented.
- Exercises on chemical equilibrium because the microscopic reactions should not be omitted in macroscopic stable states.

Consequently, we need to determine the following 3 types of viewpoints.

(1) In representing phenomena, terms representing materials are treated as universal one or not.
(2) The intermediate states of reactions are represented in the model or not.
(3) Microscopic changes in the macroscopic stable states are represented in the model or not.

Table 1 shows the numbers of exercises which need these changes of viewpoints on each chapter in the textbook used in our case study. It is confirmed that all of exercises which cannot be managed on the basic model can be solved by using these 3 types of viewpoints.

Table 1. Numbers of exercises to be solved from each viewpoint.

	Chapter 1 Structures of materials	Chapter 2 States of materials	Chapter 3 Changes of materials	Chapter 4 Inorganic compounds	Chapter 5 Organic compounds and high polymers	Total
From the Basic Model	36	51	36	13	8	144
From the Viewpoint(1)	7	1	4	1	3	16
From the Viewpoint(2)	0	0	3	0	0	3
From the Viewpoint(3)	0	0	13	0	0	13
Total	43	52	56	14	11	176

(The exercises are numerical ones in the textbook used in our case-study.)

As mentioned in Subsection 2.3, each world model which corresponds to different viewpoint should not be defined independently. They should be defined on the basis of the common structured model. Fortunately these 3 types of change of viewpoint can be realized as procedures adding some concepts and relations to the basic model (The outline is mentioned in Subsection 3.2). So we adopt the approach that the basic model is the common structure of the world model, and transform it to get the model from the three viewpoints.

3.2 A Method to Manage Variable Viewpoints

The Structure of the Basic Model.
The detailed structure of the basic model is mentioned in [7]. In this paper, we are going to show only the outline. The basic model consists of the following four elements.

a) Material-frames
Frames which represent materials or objects in the chemical world. They have several types of slots: "ako-slot" represents the classes to which the materials belong; and property-slots represent the properties of the materials (ex. mass, volume, mole, etc).

b) Phenomenon-frames
In the basic model, behaviour of the chemical world is represented discretely as the relations between *States of the world, Actions in the world, and Changes in the world* (Figure 1) *The States, the Actions, and the Changes* are represented by sets of simple-sentences, which are written in a verbal frame format. The verbal frames are called "Phenomenon-frames".

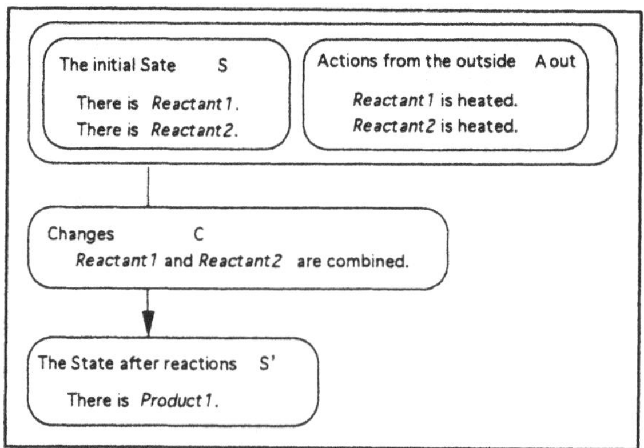

Fig. 1. The structure of the basic model.

c) Relation-frames (between phenomena)
Causal relations between Phenomenon-frames are represented by a simple frame format, called "Relation-frames". They have slots for causes and re-

sults in chemical reactions. For example, The relation that *Action-1* causes *Change-1* in *State-1* is represented as follows:
[Cause: (*State-1 Action-1*) Result: (*Change-1*)].

d) The Time-variable
The variable represents the time order of the *States and Changes.* A list of Phenomenon-frames are set in it.

Our system uses a kind of production-rules written in the format of the Relation-frame to simulate the chemical reactions. The rules are called "Chemical-reaction-knowledge (CRK)". Numerical relations in the phenomena are represented by the knowledge called " Numerical-relation-knowledge (NRK)".

Problem Solving Using the World Model.
The basic problem solving algorithm that doesn't contain changing viewpoints is as follows.

1) Conditions on the state of the chemical world in the exercise are given to the ploblem-solver, and it is asked how much a numerical property of a material in the world is.
2) Simulate chemical reactions from the given initial state by a kind of forward reasoning by using CRK.
3) Compare the result of the simulation to the given conditions. Unify the concepts in the given conditions with the concepts generated by simulation, and specify them. For example, if the given condition says that "the product is some salt of which the mass is 2 g." and the simulator finds that "$CaCl_2$ is generated by reactions.", then let the mass of the $CaCl_2$ be 2 g.
4) Pick up numerical relations from the result of the simulation and make simultaneous equations.
5) Find the asked value by solving the equations.

A Method to Control the Change of Viewpoints.
As mentioned in Subsection 2.3, our system control the change of viewpoints by using some heuristic rules. We call such rules "Viewpoint-rules". The viewpoint-rules has two-parts: Condition-part has conditions to select valid viewpoints, and Action-part has procedures to transform representations from the basic model into models corresponding to each viewpoint.

In general, we can point out some typical concepts which should be conceptualized from a certain viewpoint, but neglected from others. For example, reactants remaining after chemical reactions are such typical concepts from the viewpoint type (1) (mentioned in Subsection 3.1). Several numerical concepts can also be such concepts. Constant of chemical equilibrium can be represented in the model from the viewpoint (3), but cannot in basic model because microscopic reactions are omitted in it. We call such concepts "key concepts" of viewpoints. We use key concepts as triggers to change viewpoints. In our current method, the system change viewpoints when any key concepts are found in initial conditions of exercises. Such an approach may be incomplete for some domains, but enough to deal with the exercises which are appeared in the above mentioned case study. Table 2 shows key concepts of the viewpoints (1) - (3).

Table 2. Conditions of viewpoint rules.

Difference between initial conditions of exercise andthe basic model	Viewpoint to be selected
- The exercise says somereactants are remained after chemical reactions. - The exercise says another reactionwill occur after the first reaction but it cannot be simulated in the basic model.	Viewpoint(1)
- In the exercise, there are some key concepts such as "velocityof reactions", "intermediate states of reactions" and so on.	Viewpoint(2)
- In the exercise, there are some key concepts such as "constant of chemical equilibrium", "be in chemical equilibrium" and so on.	Viewpoint(3)

Key concepts can be found in the step 3) of the basic algorithm, by checking difference between the basic world model and initial conditions, because key concepts cannot be represented in the basic model. As a result, we extended the problem solving algorithm to perform changing viewpoints as follows:

1) Conditions on the state of the chemical world in the exercise are given to the ploblem-solver, and it is asked how much a numerical property of a material in the world is.
2) Simulate chemical reactions from the given initial state by a kind of forward reasoning by using CRK.
3) Compare the result of the simulation to the given conditions. If there are any concepts that cannot be matched to the result of the simulation in the initial condition, check viewpoint-rules. If any viewpoint rules are burnt, go to 4), otherwise go to 5).
4) Transform the world model by using procedure in the burnt rule. The outline of the method of transformation is mentioned in below. Go to 2) and simulate chemical reactions again.
5) Pick up numerical relations from the result of the simulation and make simultaneous equations.
6) Find the asked value by solving the equations.

The Typical Viewpoint (1): Representing Reactants Remaining after Reactions.

For this type of viewpoint, reactants remaining after reactions should be considered in the world model. In other words, the reactants must be divided into the reacting part and the other part. Figure 2 shows the outline of transformation for this type of viewpoint. The system generates two Material-frames (M2, M3) for each reactant (M1) in order to represent the subparts. The relation that M1 consists of M2 and M3 is generated as a Phenomenon-frame. The changes on M1 are transformed into changes on M2, and the fact that M3 is remaining after reaction is also generated. Moreover, some numerical relations are generated such as "the mass of M1 equals to the sum of M2 and M3" and so on.

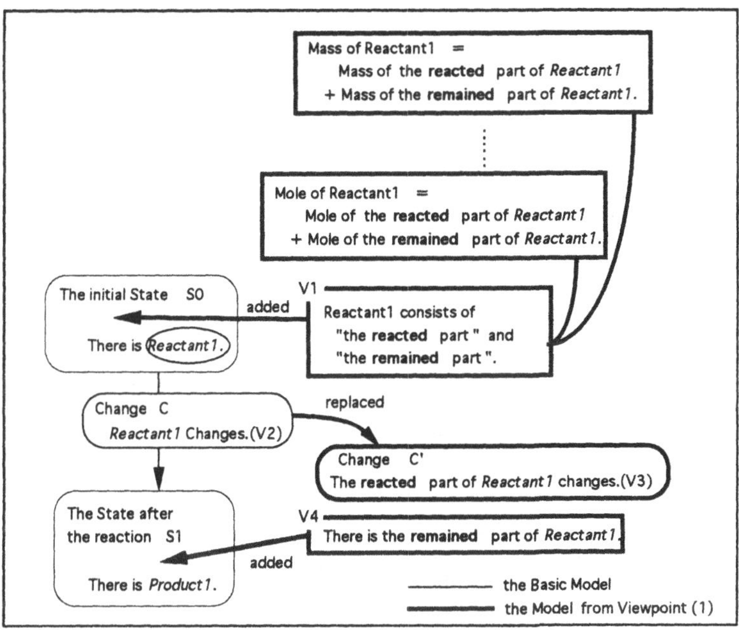

Fig. 2. Transformation into the model from viewpoint(1).

The Typical Viewpoint (2): Representing Intermediate States of Reactions.

For this type of viewpoint, intermediate states of reactions should be represented. Change must be divided into the part before the intermediate state and the part after it. Figure 3 shows the outline of transformation. The system generates a Phenomenon-frame of the intermediate state (S1/2) and inserts it between the initial state (S0) and the state after the reaction (S1). Two Phenomenon-frame representing the two parts of changes are generated (C1,C2) and inserted before / after the intermediate state. The time at the intermediate state is described in property-slot of S1/2. Similar transformations as for Viewpoint (1) have to be performed because reactants have not reacted completely in S1/2 yet. Moreover, some numerical relations are generated such as relations between mole of materials and velocity of reactions, etc.

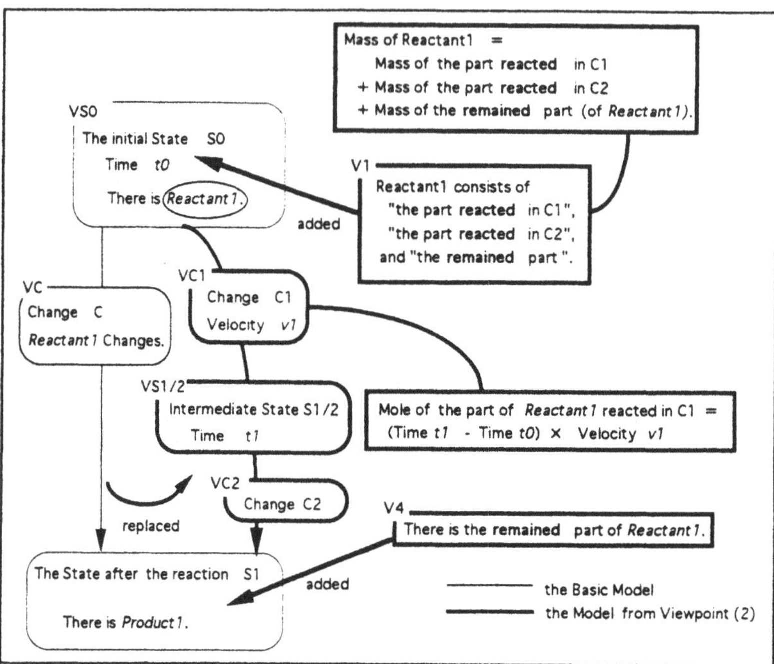

Fig. 3. Transformation into the model from viewpoint(2).

The Typical Viewpoint (3): Representing Microscopic Reactions in Macroscopic Stable States.

For this type of viewpoint, it should be represented that microscopic reactions are canceling with each other in stable states. In order to represent such actions, we have to extend the representation. We use a frame format called "Equilibrium-frame", which has slots for reaction and its inverse reaction. Constant of chemical equilibrium is also described in the frame. Figure 4 shows the outline of transformation. An Equilibrium-frame (E1) is generated and related with the stable state S. Microscopic reactions are simulated and the results are set in E1. The results are similar to the structure shown in Figure 3, but details are omitted. Numerical relations between Constant of chemical equilibrium, velocity of reactions, concentration of solutions, and so on are generated.

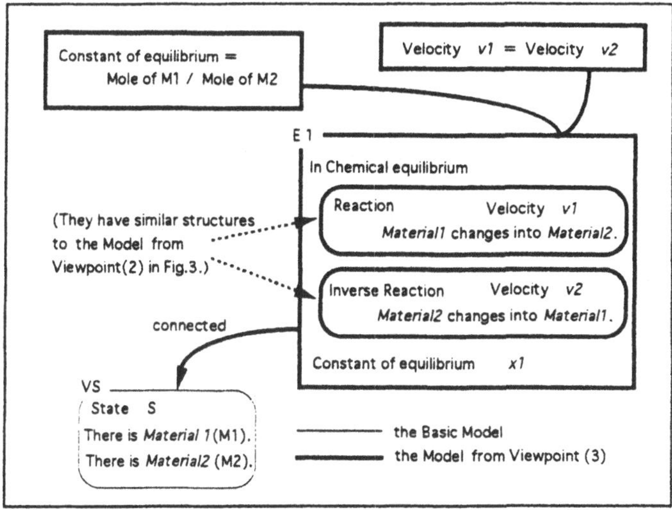

Fig. 4. Transformation into the model from viewpoint(3).

Transferring from Viewpoint (1)-(3) to Another.

In general, we may have to design transformation procedures from one of the typical viewpoint to another (such as from (1) to (2) or (3)). But in our problem solver, such additional procedures are not necessary, because of following reasons:

- The viewpoint (2) can serve the viewpoint (1), because it can represent reactants remaining after reactions. Therefore the transformation from the basic model to viewpoint (2) is designed to serve transformation to viewpoint (1) in our problem solver.
- In our case study, all exercises which need viewpoint (3) are concerned with concepts including time at intermediate states of reactions, such as velocity of reactions. So in our problem solver, the transformation to viewpoint (3) is designed to serve transformation to viewpoint (2).
- Consequently, we don't have to change viewpoints from (2) to (1), and also from (3) to (2) or (1).
- In our case study, there are no exercises which need transformation from viewpoint (1) to (2), (2) to (3), or (1) to (3). Therefore we don't implement such procedures of transformation. Moreover, we think it is not so difficult to design such procedures, because our transformation procedures from the basic model to the models of viewpoint (1)-(3) consist of sub-procedures rewriting the elements of the basic model, and the procedures to transform from viewpoint (1) to (2), from (1) to (3), and from (2) to (3) can be implemented by combining the sub-procedures.

4 Implementation

We constructed an experimental system which solves numerical exercises in high-school chemistry from variable viewpoints. Figure 5 shows the configuration of our system. The program is written in Common Lisp on UNIX Workstations. Figure 6 is an example of the result of problem solving by our system. A simple explanation generator makes the example from the knowledge representation. The generator is designed for Japanese, so we translated it for this paper. In this example, the system solves an exercise concerning velocity of a chemical reaction. At first the system simulates reactions on the basic model, but it could not identify the intermediate state written on the exercise. So the system changes viewpoint to the type (2).

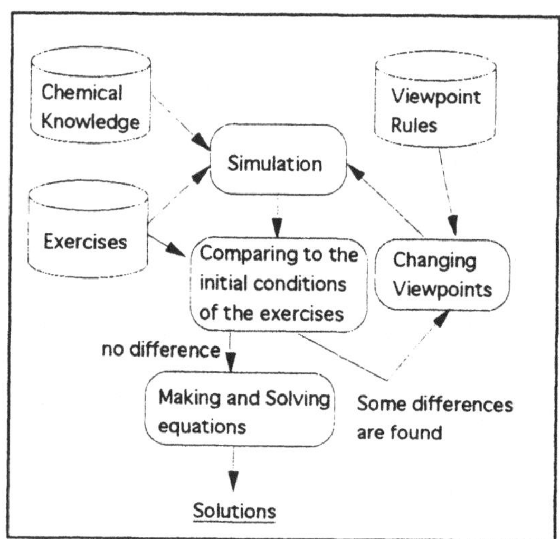

Fig. 5. Our problem solver.

Our current experimental system can solve 76 exercises which are picked up from the textbook used in our case study. In order to solve them, 36 CRK, 101 NRK and 95 knowledge of typical chemical materials are implemented. Some more knowledge should be implemented to solve remaining exercises, but we think they will not be so many.

問題：2N2O5 →4NO2 + O2の分解反応において、N2O5の濃度は、最初(時点TT1)0.072mol/l であり，10秒後(時点TT3)には0.054mol/l に変化した．この時のN2O5の分解速度を求めよ．

Question: In the chemical reaction "2N2O5 – >4NO2 + O2", the density of the N2O5 is 0.072mol/l before the reaction (TT1). Then 10 seconds later (TT3), it become 0.054mol/l. Find the velocity of the separation of theN2O5.

《解法》
<Problem Solving Process>

【 化学現象の再現 】
[result of simulating the chemical reaction]

「時点(TT1)においてN2O5が水中にあります」
N2O5 exists in the water solution at the moment "TT1".

　　ということから起こる変化を再現します．
　　Then simulate the change in the next step.

「N2O5が分解します」
The N2O5 is separated.

　　このことから変化後の状態を再現します．
　　Then simulate the state after the change.

「NO2が水中にあります」
「O2があります」
NO2 and O2 exist.

ここから、問題中に"時点(TT3)において残ったN2O5が水中にあります"と記述されているので反応の途中段階を考慮するように視点の変更を行います
Change the VIEWPOINT because it is mentioned in the question that N2O5 exists at "TT3" (10 seconds later from the start of the reaction), but the intermediate state is omitted in the result of the simulation.

【 化学現象の再現 】
[result of simulating the chemical reaction]

「時点(TT1)においてN2O5が水中にあります」
N2O5 exists in the water solution at the moment "TT1".

　　ということから起こる変化を再現します．
　　Then simulate the change in the next step.

「反応したN2O5が分解します」
A part of N2O5 is separated.

　　このことから変化後の状態を再現します．
　　Then simulate the state after the change.

「NO2が水中にあります」
「O2があります」
「1番目の反応で残ったN2O5が水中にあります」
NO2, O2, and N2O5 which hasn't reacted yet exist.

この結果、次のように解くことができます．
Solve the question on the basis of the chemical world model.

【 求解過程 】
[Calculating process]

1: 1番目の反応で残ったN2O5のモル濃度 = 0.054
(molar density of N2O5 which hasn't reacted yet) = 0.054
2: N2O5のモル濃度 = 0.072
(molar density of the N2O5 which exists at the beginning) = 0.072
3: 時点(TT3)の時刻 = 10
(The hour at TT3) = 10
4: 時点(TT1)の時刻 = 0
(The hour at TT1) = 0
5: N2O5の分解速度=
(N2O5のモル濃度
− 1番目の反応で残ったN2O5のモル濃度)
÷(時点(TT3)の時刻 − 時点(TT1)の時刻)
= 0.0018
(the velocity of the separation of the N2O5) =
{(molar density of N2O5 which hasn't reacted yet)
– (molar density of the N2O5 which exists at the beginning)}
/ {(The hour at TT3) – (The hour at TT1)}
= 0.0018

《 答 》N2O5の分解速度 = 0.0018 [mol/l·s]
Answer: (the velocity of the separation of the N2O5) = 0.0018 [mol/l·s]

Fig. 6. An example of solving an exercise with the viewpoint transformation.

5 Conclusion

On education of natural sciences, it is essential to train the ability of selecting effective viewpoint. So ICAI systems should know from which viewpoint its world model is represented, and it should be able to explain what kind of problems the viewpoint is effective. Our methods are also useful to train such an ability. So our future works will be designing and developing strategies to teach how to select viewpoints and mechanisms to teach the relation between problem solving processes and the structures of the world model based on viewpoints. Moreover, we have to evaluate our method not only in chemistry, but also another subjects.

References

[1] Woolf, B., Blegen, D., Jansen, J., and Verlop, A. "Teaching a complex industrial process", Proceedings of AAAI-86, pp.722–728, (1986)

[2] Forbus, K. and Falkenhainer, B. "Self-Explanatory Simulations: An Integration of qualitative and quantitative knowledge", Proceedings of AAAI-90, pp.380–387, (1990)

[3] Amador, F. D., Finkelstein, A., & Weld, D. S. "Real-time Self-Explanatory simulation. ", Proceedings of AAAI-93, pp.562–567, (1993)

[4] Wenger,E., "Artifical Intelligence and Tutoring Systems.", Morgan Kaufman. (1987)

[5] Sleeman,D.H. & Brown J.S., "Intelligent Tutoring Systems.", Academia Press. (1985)

[6] Konishi,T.,Itoh,Y.,Takagi,A.& Ohara.H, "The method for teaching how knowledge are constructed and simulation of the world for ICAI", Trans.IEICE,J73-D-II,No.7,pp.1007–1018.(in Japanese)(1990)

[7] Konishi,T., Itoh,Y. & Takagi,A., "A World Model for an ICAI System of High-school Chemistry in Japan.", Proc. of Internatinal Computer Symposium 94 (ICS'94), Vol.1, pp.343-350.(1994)

[8] "Koutou Gakkou Shinpen Kagaku." (a textbook of high-school chemistry), Daiichi Gakusyu sya (in Japanese) (1991)

Creating Theoretical Terms for Non-deterministic Actions

Rex Bing Hung Kwok
email: rkwok@cs.su.oz.au

Basser Department of Computer Science, Madsen Building F09, University of Sydney, NSW, 2006, Australia.

Abstract. Theoretical terms play a central role in many scientific theories and includes such terms as quark and lepton in physics. However, such terms do not refer to observables or the properties of observables. Due to their central role in many scientific theories, formalisations and implementations of scientific discovery should account for theoretical terms. Few methods have been developed within the field of Artificial Intelligence to account for such terms and little work on correctness has been done. This paper will define a formal method for creating theoretical terms based on observationally non-deterministic actions. Further, this paper will define a class of possible worlds models for which the method is provably correct.

1 Introduction

Many linguistic terms in scientific theories are theoretical and, as such, attempts to formalise or implement notions of scientific discovery should account for the occurrence of such terms. Theoretical terms refer to non-observable objects and the properties of such objects. For example, terms such as photon and quark in physics and covalent bond in chemistry do not refer to any observables. The field of artificial intelligence has seen a few methods which attempt to account for theoretical terms. These methods include inverse resolution [Mug89] and non-deterministic actions [SS89]. The process of resolution involves taking two clauses with a specific literal, which is negated in one clause but not in the other, and forming a resolvant clause which contains all the literals from both resolving clauses without the specific literal or its negation. With inverse resolution [Mug89] the process of resolution is inverted. Taking the resolvant clause and one of the initial resolving clauses, the aim is to come up with the second resolving clause; a process which is logically unsound. This can on occasion lead to the invention of new predicates. In general, a number of such inverse resolution problems are considered simultaneously and with a number of simplifying assumptions, an operator, called the W-operator, is defined. However, the process has been shown [Pag95] to create, in the propositional case, conservative extensions of theories; the enhanced theory with new terms cannot prove anything in the old language which was not provable before. The criterion for using the operator varies. Ling [Lin92] uses the W-operator when a theory becomes too large (there are too many clauses in a theory or a single clause contains too many literals) while Muggleton [MB88] uses the operator in conjunction with a procedure to decrease the size of a theory whenever possible; the rationale being an expression of Occam's razor that the smallest theory is the most accurate.

Using non-deterministic actions as an indication of hidden factors has a long history. A number of scientists, including Einstein, unhappy with the nondeterministic probabilistic predictions of quantum mechanical theory attempted to make the theory deterministic by assuming the existence of hidden variables. However, these attempts failed because quantum mechanical theory is inconsistent with the assumption of hidden variables. Despite this, Wilfred Sellars [Sel63] argues that, in general, theoretical terms may be used to explain why some observational phenomena do not have generalised laws within the observational framework. Sellars presents the example of the dissolution of gold in *aqua regia*. Although observationally identical, different samples of gold dissolve at different rates. One hypothesis is that gold has two different microscopic structures and the rate of dissolution is linearly proportional to the percentage of each micro-structure in a sample.

More recently, the idea of using theoretical terms to account for nondeterministic actions has been further developed by Shen and Simon [SS89] [She93]. Shen uses a framework consisting of an agent performing actions within an environment. Attached to each action, expressed as first order formulae, is a *condition* and a *prediction* for which the *prediction* is meant to be true after performing the action provided that the *condition* held prior to the action. The system which Shen develops analyses a sequence of actions and a sequence of observations such that observations are made as actions are performed. Procedures attempt to correct action predictions which contradict the observations. When an action behaves *non-deterministically* no correction can be made to the prediction and new predicates are created which are used to refine the action *condition* so that a number of distinct predictions can be made for the action. Constraints are generated by considering the actions performed prior to the instance of non-determinism so that new predicates are defined in terms of the differences in the observations and the history of actions leading up to the non-determinism. However, this is where the distinction between action and predicate becomes blurred. Within these definitions for new predicates, action symbols are used as predicate symbols. Furthermore, the definition of a non-deterministic action is not fully defined. An action is considered to have behaved non-deterministically when the same action performed on the 'same state' produces 'different consequences'. The notion of 'same state' is problematical because the notion of 'state' is absent from the framework. This is important because it may not be necessary, if not impossible, to establish exactly the same observational state in order to repeat an experiment and diagnose non-determinism. The problem here is in determining the observations affecting an action. Similarly, the notion of 'different consequences' is vague. Since actions tend to affect only a part of the world, any difference in observations upon repetition of an experiment does not indicate that the action is non-deterministic. The problem here is in defining the extent of action effects.

The primary concern of this paper is to consider whether the presence of theoretical factors can be provably diagnosed and to determine the assumptions which are necessary for such a diagnosis. The approach taken to this problem is to consider observationally non-deterministic actions. To a lesser extent, the number of theoretical terms created will also be investigated. This paper will adopt the basic idea of Shen to analyse a sequence of actions together with a sequence of observations. Within this framework a formal criterion for creating theoretical terms will be defined. A class of possible worlds models for events, based on the models developed by Foo [FZ93], will be defined over which the criterion for creating theoretical terms will be shown to be justified and correct. The aim of this paper is to present a foundational study of the creation of theoretical terms with a view to an eventual implementation. The framework for creating theoretical terms will be defined in the following section. In section three, a class of possible worlds structures will be defined and some results will be established about such a class. Section four will tie together the framework and the structures to show how and when the framework is correct.

2 The Framework

Adopting the ideas of Shen, the basis of the framework is an analysis of experimental results. From a set of actions, elements are chosen to compose a sequence of actions. Corresponding to this sequence is a sequence of observations consisting of an initial observation set and successive observations made after the performance of each action. Formally, an experimental framework is defined as follows:

Definition 2.1: An experimental framework, EF, is a quadruple $\langle A, L_o, H, O\rangle$ where
$A = \{\mathbf{a}_1, \mathbf{a}_2, \mathbf{a}_3, ...\}$ is a set of action symbols.
L_o is a first order language called the observational language.
$H = \langle h_1, h_2, ..., h_n\rangle$ is a sequence such that for every i, $h_i \in A$.
$O = \langle O_0, O_1, O_2, ..., O_n\rangle$ is a sequence such that for every i, O_i is a ground complete set of literals with respect to L_o.

With the above definition, the set A contains action names which denote the actions that can be performed. H is a sequence of action names which can be interpreted as a sequence of actions which have been performed; the index of the sequence being discrete time points. Matching this history sequence is a sequence of observations. Each element of the sequence O is a ground complete set of literals from the observational language L_o. The first element of O, O_0, is a set of initial observations while for any other index i, O_i represents the observations made after h_i has been performed.

In practice, it is impractical to diagnose an action as observationally nondeterministic by requiring exactly the same initial observational state to produce distinct results because an experimenter, typically, does not have control over all observational literals. The task of repeating an experiment becomes exceedingly difficult, if not impossible. Also, the factors affecting an action typically do not include all observations. Accepting that an action can be said to have been repeated when only a subset of observations are the same on multiple performances of an action, the extent and influence of the action would, similarly, be limited. As such, only a subset of observations after the performance of the action should be taken as being influenced by the action. For example, consider experiments in plant breeding about flower colour. Intuitively, the only factors influencing the flower colour of offspring would be the colours of the parent plants and the extent of these influences would only be the flower colour of the offspring. In repeating such experiments there should be no need to fix the time of day or the position of a certain butterfly in the world. Also, accepting that the factors affecting the experiment are the parent flower colours, the experiment should not be considered non-deterministic because after one experiment a thunderstorm followed while after another the sky was cloudless.

To account for the factors affecting an action and the extent of an action, attached to each action symbol in A is a set of sentences called the the prerequisite and a collection of sentence sets called the plausible results. Formally, this is defined as follows:

Definition 2.2: For each $\mathbf{a} \in A$ let
$P(\mathbf{a}) \in 2^{L_o}$
$R(\mathbf{a}) = \{R_1, R_2, ...\}$ such that each $R_i \in 2^{L_o}$

The prerequisite, $P(\mathbf{a})$, of an action is a set of sentences from the observational language while the plausible results, $R(\mathbf{a})$, is a set containing sets from the observational language. For instance, the prerequisite for a specific flower colour breeding experiment would be observational sentences denoting the colour of the parent plants while the result set would be a set of conceivable results — each result being a set of observational formulae describing the flower colour of offspring plants.

Combining the definitions of prerequisites and plausible results with the history and observation sequences, an action can be defined to have behaved non-deterministically when two different time points correspond with the same action symbol in the history while the observation sets prior to the actions satisfy the prerequisite and the resulting observations satisfy distinct plausible results. The degree of non-deterministic behaviour of an action is formally defined as follows:

Definition 2.3: $Furcation(\mathbf{a}, H, O) = \mid \{R \mid \exists t, R$ such that $O_{t-1} \models P(\mathbf{a})$ and $O_t \models R$ and $R \in R(\mathbf{a})\} \mid$

Each O_{t-1} satisfying the prerequisite in this definition can be interpreted as a 'reset state' for the action, **a**, as far as the agent is concerned. This is where the stipulation that each observational set is ground complete is used as the definition queries whether an observation set satisfies the prerequisites and the plausible results. As such, any formula from the prerequisites or the plausible results either satisfies or contradicts an observation set. The value of $Furcation(\mathbf{a}, H, O)$ is the number of distinct results which have been encountered on the performances of the action, satisfying the prerequisite, in the history. The criterion to create theoretical terms is that $Furcation(\mathbf{a}, H, O)$ is greater than one. Further, supposing that the furcation value is n, then $\lceil \log_2 n \rceil$ new propositional symbols will be created. Conjunctions of such propositions could be used to refine the prerequisite so that each prerequisite corresponds to at most one realised result for given history and observation sequences. Details of how this can be done are beyond the scope of this paper.

As an illustration of the framework consider the following blocks world scenario developed by Foo [Foo91]. In this two-dimensional world, there is a table and some blocks. Blocks either rest on the table or on top of other blocks. In addition, blocks may also be placed adjacently to each other and a block may actually rest straddled on two other blocks. The actions which can be performed in this world include placing blocks adjacently to each other, stacking a block on top of two adjacent blocks (forming a minimal three block pyramid consisting of two base blocks and an apex block), and an action which removes a base block from a pyramid. Formally, suppose that L_o is a first order language which contains parameters A, B, and C which represents blocks, predicate symbols $on(x, y)$, $table(x)$, and $adjacent(x, y)$ which represents that block x

is on block y, block x is on the table, and that block x is adjacent to block y respectively. Also, the action symbol set, A, contains **place_adjacent_**B_C **pyramid_stack_**A_B_C and **remove_support_**A_B_C where **place_adjacent_**B_C places block B adjacently to block C, **pyramid_stack_**A_B_C places block A on top of blocks B and C, and **remove_support_**A_B_C removes block B from the minimal pyramid formed by A, B, and C. To save space and focus attention on the important action in this example, only the prerequisite and plausible results of the **remove_support_**A_B_C action will be presented.

$P($ **remove_support_**$A\_B\_C)) = \{ \mathit{adjacent}(B, C), \mathit{on}(A, B), \mathit{on}(A, C), \mathit{table}(B), \mathit{table}(C)\}$
$R($**remove_support_**$A\_B\_C)) = \{\{ \mathit{table}(B), \mathit{table}(C), \mathit{on}(A, C)\}, \{ \mathit{table}(B), \mathit{table}(C), \mathit{table}(A)\}\}$

The prerequisite means that A, B, and C describe a three block pyramid while the plausible results contend that removing a base block of a pyramid can either leave the apex block balanced on the other base block or the apex can fall down on to the table.

Consider the following sample action history and observation sequences (for brevity only the positive literals are shown for each observation set):

$H = \langle$**remove_support_**A_B_C, **place_adjacent_**B_C, **pyramid_stack_**A_B_C, **remove_support_**$A\_B\_C\rangle$
$O = \langle\{ \mathit{table}(B), \mathit{table}(C), \mathit{adjacent}(B, C), \mathit{on}(A, B), \mathit{on}(A, C)\}$,
$\{ \mathit{table}(B), \mathit{table}(C), \mathit{table}(A)\}$,
$\{ \mathit{table}(B), \mathit{table}(C), \mathit{table}(A), \mathit{adjacent}(B, C)\}$,
$\{ \mathit{table}(B), \mathit{table}(C), \mathit{adjacent}(B, C), \mathit{on}(A, B), \mathit{on}(A, C)\}$,
$\{ \mathit{table}(B), \mathit{table}(C), \mathit{on}(A, C)\}\rangle$

These sequences give that $Furcation($**remove_support_**$A\_B\_C, H, O) = 2$ which means that one propositional symbol will be created. Pictorially, this observational non-determinism is shown in Figure 1. The intuitive understanding of the new proposition would be whether block B has more or less than half of block A resting on it. However, these issues stretch beyond the scope of this paper.

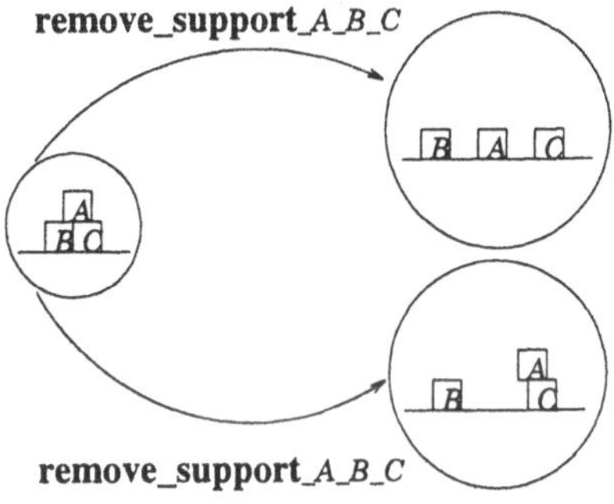

Fig. 1. The blocks world observational non-determinism.

3 Possible Worlds Structures for Events

The structures used in this paper are a refinement of the possible worlds semantics for events defined by Foo and Zhang [FZ93]. Such structures contain a set of possible worlds or states and a set of accessibility relations between worlds. Each accessibility relation describes how an action changes one state into one or more possible states. As such, there is no restriction that the relations be transitive, reflexive, or even symmetric. If the accessibility relations holds from an initial world to a resulting world then performing the action in the initial world can produce the resulting world. Also, as is standard in modal semantics, there is a domain and each n-ary relation is evaluated to hold true for certain n-ary tuples of domain elements in certain states. As a refinement to the set of relations in the structure, the relations are divided into two disjoint sets: the observational relations and the theoretical relations. In the following definition, as suggested the the subscripts, P_o and P_t correspond to the observational and theoretical relations respectively.

Definition 3.1: A possible worlds structure M is a quadruple (D, S, P, R) where

1. D is a set of domain elements
2. S is a set of states
3. P is a set of relations such that $P = P_o \cup P_t$ and $P_o \cap P_t = \emptyset$ and for each $p \in P$, given that p is an n-ary predicate, $p \subseteq D^n \times S$
4. R is a set of binary relations on $S \times S$

As an example of the valuation of predicates, consider the blocks world example presented in the previous section. Consider the initial observation set which indicates the presence of a three block pyramid. Within the domain, D, there are elements `A`, `B`, and `C` for the three blocks. Recall that blocks `B` and `C` rest adjacently on the table and that block `A` rests on both `B` and `C`. As such, if the pyramid were to exist in a state s, the valuation of the `on` relation would have (`A`, `B`, s), (`A`, `C`, s) $\in$ `on`; with the relation `table`, (`B`, s), (`C`, s) $\in$ `table` and for the relation `adjacent`, (`B`, `C`, s) $\in$ `adjacent`.

A simple notion of cause and effect can be defined in such structures to show how differences in the valuation of theoretical relations can become manifest in the valuation of observational relations via the accessibility relations. There is a cause and effect pair for an accessibility relation when every world in which the cause holds only leads to states, via the accessibility relation, in which the effect holds. Notice that this notion of cause and effect is relative to an accessibility relation. A notion of maximality can be defined on such cause and effect pairs by insisting that the cause should be as *small* as possible and that the effect should be as *large* as possible. Maximal cause and effects can then be partitioned with an equivalence relation which groups together those with the same causal observational content. From this, it can be shown that members of each partition have different theoretical causes if and only if they have different effects; in particular different observational effects. Causes and effects are defined as follows:

Definition 3.2: Suppose that M is a possible worlds structure and that $L(M)$ is the non-modal part of the language associated with the structure (a first order language).

Let C and E be sets of first order sentences from $L(M)$.
Define (C, E) to be a *cause-effect* pair in M under accessibility relation R_a if and only if for every $s, s' \in S$ if $M, s \models C$ and $(s, s') \in R_a$ then $M, s' \models E$

A cause-effect pair requires that every state entailing the causal set and every state accessible from that state, via the accessibility relation, entails every formula in the effect set. Such a definition allows an instance of triviality. There may be causal sets for which every state entailing the cause has no access to other worlds and as such any effect would form a cause-effect pair. This is a minor problem which can be fixed by stipulating that there is at least one pair of accessible worlds, one of which entails the cause and the other the effect. This problem, however, does not affect the work in this paper and will be neglected henceforth.

From the definition, the following observations can be made:

Observations 3.1: Suppose (C, E) is a cause-effect pair in M under R_a

1. If $C' \supseteq C$ then (C', E) is a cause-effect pair in M under R_a.
2. If $E' \subseteq E$ then (C, E') is a cause-effect pair in M under R_a.

These observations show that a cause-effect pair may contain sentences which are unnecessary to predict the same effect and that the effect set may be shrunk while maintaining the causal set. To maximise the predictions, for the least cause, it is possible to define a pre-order on cause-effect pairs to isolate the maximal pairs. The reason for seeking out such pairs, as noted in the introduction, is to isolate the factors which affect an action and the factors which are affected by an action. In the following definition the $<$ symbol will be overloaded, the intended interpretation of $<$, however, should be clear from the context. Further, to simplify the notation, for sets of first order sentences, Γ and Δ, $\Gamma \models \Delta$ means that for every possible worlds structure, M, and a state s in M, if s entails every formula in Γ, s also entails every formula in Δ.

Definition 3.3: For any sets of first order sentences, Γ and Δ, say that
$\Gamma < \Delta$ iff $\Delta \models \Gamma$ and $\Gamma \not\models \Delta$
$\Gamma = \Delta$ iff $\Delta \models \Gamma$ and $\Gamma \models \Delta$
$\Gamma \leq \Delta$ iff $\Gamma < \Delta$ or $\Gamma = \Delta$

Let (C, E) and (C', E') be cause-effect pairs in M under R_a.
Define $(C, E) \leq (C', E')$ iff either $(C' < C$ and $E \leq E')$ or $(E < E'$ and $C' \leq C)$.
Also, define $(C, E) = (C', E')$ iff $C = C'$ and $E = E'$

Since causes and effects are sets of first order sentences, the $\leq$ relation defined on such sets is simply the pre-order which the first order entailment relation defines. As an immediate consequence it can be shown that the $\leq$ relation defined on cause-effect pairs is a pre-order.

Lemma 3.1: Let $CE(M, R_a) = \{(C, E) \mid (C, E)$ is a cause-effect pair under R_a in $M\}$. Then $\leq$ defines a pre-order on $CE(M, R_a)$.

A notion of maximality can be extracted as follows:

Definition 3.4: Let $(C, E) \in CE(M, R_a)$. Say that (C, E) is *maximal* iff $\forall (C^{'}, E^{'}) \in CE(M, R_a)$ if $(C, E) \leq (C^{'}, E^{'})$ then $(C, E) = (C^{'}, E^{'})$. Further, let $MCE(M, R_a) = \{(C, E) \mid (C, E) \in CE(M, R_a)$ and (C, E) is maximal$\}$

This definition can be used to show that two maximal cause-effect pairs have different effects if and only if they have different causes.

Theorem 3.1: Let $(C, E), (C^{'}, E^{'}) \in MCE(M, R_a)$ then $(C \neq C^{'} \Leftrightarrow E \neq E^{'})$

The reason for the equivalence holding is that if either implication did not hold then a distinct cause-effect pair can be constructed which is strictly greater than the initial cause-effect pairs — contradicting their maximality. Consider two maximal cause-effect pairs which have different effects. If their causes are the same then the pair, consisting of the original cause and the set union of the original effects, would form a cause-effect pair which is strictly greater than either of the initial cause-effect pairs. This would contradict the initial premise that the cause-effect pairs are maximal. A similar argument can be used to show the converse. Note that the theorem can be established without assuming that the action is deterministic. All that is required is that there should exist maximal cause-effect pairs and this does not require the action to be deterministic. The result is important because it can be used to show how differences in the valuation of theoretical relations can become manifest through observationally non-deterministic actions. Consider two maximal cause-effect pairs with causes having the same observational content and differing effects. Since the effects are distinct, Theorem 3.1 implies that the causes are distinct and because the observational content of both causes are the same the difference can only be accounted for by the presence of theoretical relations within the causes. Formally, cause-effect pairs can be partitioned, according to the observational content of their causes, by the following relation:

Definition 3.5: Let $(C, E), (C^{'}, E^{'}) \in CE(M, R_a)$. Say that $(C, E) =_o (C^{'}, E^{'})$ iff for every formula, α, which contains only relations from P_o then $(C \models \alpha \Leftrightarrow C^{'} \models \alpha)$.

From the definition it can be shown that $=_o$ is equivalence relation on members of $CE(M, R_a)$.

Lemma 3.2: $=_o$ is an equivalence relation on $CE(M, R_a)$

The definition of equivalent observational causes on $CE(M, R_a)$ also, of course, defines an equivalence relation on the subset, $MCE(M, R_a)$, of maximal cause-effect pairs. Since $=_o$ is an equivalence relation, $=_o$ induces a partition on $MCE(M, R_a)$.

Definition 3.6: Suppose $(C, E) \in MCE(M, R_a)$.
Define $[(C, E)]_{=_o} = \{(C^{'}, E^{'}) \mid (C^{'}, E^{'}) \in MCE(M, R_a)$ and $(C, E) =_o (C^{'}, E^{'})\}$

There is now enough to show that any equivalence class from $MCE(M, R_a)$, having causes with the same observational content, with more than one element contains at least one theoretical relation.

Lemma 3.3: Suppose $(C, E), (C', E') \in MCE(M, R_a)$ and $(C, E) \neq (C', E')$ such that $[(C, E)]_{=_o} = [(C', E')]_{=_o}$ then there exists a $p \in P_t$ such that p occurs in C or C'.

This theorem shows how the presence of theoretical relations in causes can manifest itself in observational effects. Given an accessibility relation and two states which entail the observational content of a maximal cause-effect pair if the states accessible, from either initial state, entail different maximal effects then the theoretical content of the two initial states must have been different.

Another result that can be established concerns the number of theoretical factors within a cause for a finite propositional language. Without the linguistic restriction, however, the following preliminary result can be established about maximal cause-effect pairs.

Lemma 3.4: Let $(C, E), (C', E') \in MCE(M, R_a)$
If $(C, E) \neq (C', E')$ then $C \not\leq C'$ and $C' \not\leq C$ and $E \not\leq E'$ and $E' \not\leq E$

The lemma says that for any pair of distinct maximal cause-effect pairs, the consequence closure of the causes are never subsets of each other and, simultaneously, the consequence closures of the effects are never subsets of each other. The lemma follows, like Theorem 3.1, from the maximality assumption. If any of the conclusions are violated a cause-effect pair can be constructed which is strictly greater than the initial cause-effect pairs — contradicting their assumed maximality. This lemma is used to show the following theorem which sets the minimum number of theoretical propositional letters which occur in maximal cause-effect pairs.

Theorem 3.2: Let M be a possible worlds structure with a finite propositional language. Also, let $(C, E) \in MCE(M, R_a)$ for some accessibility relation R_a.
Let $n = \mid [(C, E)]_{=_o} \mid$
Let $k = \mid \{p \mid$ for some $(C', E') \in [(C, E)]_{=_o}$, p is a theoretical proposition occurring in $C'\} \mid$.
Then $k \geq \lceil \log_2 n \rceil$

This theorem shows that for an equivalence class of maximal cause-effect pairs, the number of theoretical propositions occurring in the causes of that class is at least the base two logarithm of the size of the class. To differentiate causes with the same observational content — using the fewest number of theoretical propositions — the constraint that no two causes should imply the other means that each cause should be complete with respect to the theoretical propositions used. Hence the fewest number of theoretical propositions required is the first integer greater than or equal to the base 2 logarithm of the size of the equivalence class.

This section has shown how possible worlds structures of actions can manifest theoretical factors through observational effects via accessibility relations. The main theorem, Theorem 3.1, has shown how maximal cause and effect pairs, with the same observational cause, have different effects if and only if the causes have some theoretical content. The vital half of the theorem is that different effects should imply different causes. Indeed, all that is necessary to gain this result is to consider *effect-maximal* cause-effect pairs and to partition such pairs based on the observational content of causes. However, from an experimental view point this is less convenient because the causes are not minimal and to repeat an experiment, more of the observational state needs to be fixed.

4 The Correctness of Creating Theoretical Terms

The procedural framework for creating theoretical terms can now be linked to the possible worlds structures to show when the framework is justified. Recall that the procedural framework contains a history sequence, H, and an observation sequence O. A possible worlds structure, M, is a model for such a framework when, among other constraints, the restriction of the structure to the domain elements and the observational relations at each state forms a realisation of the observational language of the framework, L_o. Also, for each action symbol, a, there should be a corresponding accessibility relation, R_a, within the structure. Most importantly, the should exist a sequence of states in M such that each state entails the corresponding observation set in O and that each successive pair of states is linked by an an accessibility relation which corresponds to the action symbol in H. Formally, this is defined as follows:

Definition 4.1: Let $EF = \langle A, L_o, H, O\rangle$ be an experimental framework and let $M = \langle D, P, S, R\rangle$ be a possible worlds structure of events. Suppose $H = \langle h_1, h_2, ..., h_n\rangle$ and $O = \langle O_0, O_1, O_2, ..., O_n\rangle$
Say that M is a model of EF iff

1. There is a bijection, ϕ, from A to R.
2. For every state, $s \in S$, the tuple $\langle D, P_{o,s}\rangle$, where $P_{o,s} = \{p' \mid p' = \{\langle d_1, d_2, ..., d_k\rangle \mid \langle d_1, d_2, ..., d_k, s\rangle \in p \text{ and } p \in P_o\}\}$, is a realisation of the observational language L_o.
3. $\exists s_0, s_1, ..., s_n \in S$ such that
   - for every $i, \alpha \in L_o$, if $0 \le i \le n$ and $O_i \models \alpha$ then $M, s_i \models \alpha$
   - for every i, if $1 \le i \le n$ then $(s_{i-1}, s_i) \in \phi(h_i)$

The first condition requires that for each action symbol there is a matching accessibility relation in the structure. The second condition requires that for each state, the combination of the domain, the observational relations and the valuation, restricted to the observational relations for that state, forms a realisation of the observational language, L_o. The final condition means that there is a sequence of states which match the observational history and that each successive pair of states is linked by an accessibility relation which matches the action symbol in the action history.

In the procedural framework, predicates are created when an action has a furcation factor greater than one. This relies on definitions of prerequisites and plausible results. Such notions coincide, in a possible worlds structure, with maximal cause-effect pairs.

Definition 4.2: Let $EF = \langle A, L_o, H, O \rangle$ be an experimental framework and let M be a model of EF. Suppose **a**$\in A$. Say that the prerequisite, $P(\mathbf{a})$, and the plausible results, $R(\mathbf{a})$, are *correct* in M iff there exists $(C, E) \in MCE(M, \phi(\mathbf{a}))$ such that

1. for every $\alpha \in L_o$ $(P(\mathbf{a}) \models \alpha \Leftrightarrow C \models \alpha)$
2. for every $R_i \in R(\mathbf{a})$ there exists $(C', E') \in [(C, E)]_{=_o}$ such that for every $\alpha \in L_o(R_i \models \alpha \Leftrightarrow E' \models \alpha)$

This definition requires that a prerequisite has an observational basis which forms an equivalence class of maximal cause-effect pairs in the model and, further, that for each plausible result, there is a maximal cause-effect pair within the equivalence class with an effect having the same observational content. In other words, this definition stipulates that the prerequisite and plausible results correspond to the observational fragment of an equivalence class of maximal cause-effect pairs having the same observational causes. Since all the causes have the same observational content, their observational fragments collapse to a single set — the prerequisite — while the effects, provided that they have observational differences, form the plausible results. Thus, from an agent viewpoint, an observationally non-deterministic action may be diagnosed as having theoretical factors. From this the following theorem can be established:

Theorem 4.1: Let EF be an experimental framework and M a model of EF. Let **a** be an action symbol and suppose that $P(\mathbf{a})$ and $R(\mathbf{a})$ is correct in M then if $Furcation(\mathbf{a}, H, O) \geq 2$ then there is an equivalence class of maximal cause-effect pairs, x in M under $\phi(\mathbf{a})$, such that there is a relation $p \in P_t$ which occurs in x.

This theorem shows that when the prerequisite and the plausible effects are correct, the criterion to create new predicates is true when there is a theoretical relation in the corresponding equivalence class of maximal cause-effect pairs in the model. The theorem holds because the correctness of the prerequisites and the plausible results together with a furcation factor greater than one implies that there is an equivalence class of maximal cause-effect pairs in the model of at least the size of the furcation factor. Since the size is greater than one, there must be at least one theoretical predicate among the causes of the equivalence class. Further, the following theorem can also be established:

Theorem 4.2 Let EF be an experimental framework and M a model of EF. Let **a** be an action symbol with $P(\mathbf{a})$ and $R(\mathbf{a})$ correct and suppose L_o is a finite propositional language. Suppose $k = \lceil \log_2(Furcation(\mathbf{a}, H, O)) \rceil$ (k propositional symbols are created) then there exists an equivalence class of maximal cause-effect pairs, x, in M under $\phi(\mathbf{a})$ and there exists $p_1, p_2, ..., p_k$ of distinct theoretical propositions which occur in the causes of x.

This theorem shows that in the finite propositional case, when k new propositional symbols are created there are at least k distinct theoretical propositions occurring in the formulae of some equivalence class of maximal cause-effect pairs. This theorem holds because the size of the equivalence class of maximal cause-effect pairs is greater than 2^{k-1} and, as such, there must be at least k distinct theoretical propositions present to differentiate each cause in the class.

5 Discussion and Conclusion

This paper has addressed the issue of creating new propositional symbols for observationally non-deterministic actions and defined a class of models for which the method is correct. A number of issues have been raised by this work which can be addressed in the future. In the framework proposed there are notions of prerequisites and plausible results which have their counterparts in the models. The learnability of such notions would be an interesting issue to pursue. Also, this paper has basically only addressed the issue of when new propositions are necessary. The issues of how new propositions can be incorporated into theories and in what sense theories containing theoretical terms are correct needs to be addressed. Further, this paper has approached the problem of theoretical terms from the perspective of the necessity for such terms. An equally valid perspective would be to consider theories which contain theoretical terms and to consider how experimental procedure may or may not corroborate such theories.

Finally, there are a number of classical developments in systems and automata theory [Boo67] [Zei76] that have analogues to the approach taken in this paper. For instance, the introduction of theoretical predicates is one way to understand the automaton-theoretic notion of state splitting. Current work involves examining a rapprochement of the work in this paper with established results in automata theory with a view to exploiting well known algorithms from the latter area.

References

[Boo67] Taylor L. Booth. *Sequential Machines and Automata Theory*. John Wiley & Sons, 1967.

[Foo91] N. Foo. How theories fail - a preliminary report. In *Proceedings of the National Conference on Information Technology*, 1991.

[FZ93] N. Foo and Y. Zhang. Possible worlds semantics for events. In *Proceedings of the 6th Australian Joint Conference on AI*. World Scientific, 1993.

[Lin92] X. C. Ling. Inventing necessary theoretical terms to overcome representation bias. In *Proceedings of Machine Learning 1992 Workshop on Inductive Learning*. Morgan Kaufman, 1992.

[MB88] Stephen Muggleton and Wray Buntine. Machine invention of first-order predicates by inverting resolution. In *Proceedings of the 5th International Machine Learning Workshop*, pages 339–352. Morgan Kaufman, 1988.

[Mug89] Stephen Muggleton. Inverting the resolution process. In J. E. Hayes and D. Michie, editors, *Machine intelligence 12*. 1989.

[Pag95] Maurice Pagnucco. Conjunctive versus disjunctive abduction - a pragmatic difference between abduction and inverse resolution. In *Poster Proceedings of the Eighth Australian Joint Conference on Artificial Intelligence*, pages 57–64, 1995.

[Sel63] W. Sellars. *Science, Perception and Reality*. Routledge and Kegan Paul, 1963.

[She93] W-M Shen. Discovery as automomous learning from the environment. In *Machine Learning, 12*, pages 145–165. Kluwer, 1993.

[SS89] Wei-Min Shen and Herbert A. Simon. Rule creation and rule learning through environmental exploration. In *Proceedings of the Eleventh International Joint Conference on Artificial Intelligence*. Morgan Kaufman, 1989.

[Zei76] B. P. Zeigler. *Theory of Modelling and Simulation*. Wiley, 1976.

Conservative Expansion Concepts for Default Theories

G. Antoniou*, C. K. MacNish** and N. Y. Foo***

Abstract. Conservative extensions of logical theories play an important role in software engineering. They provide a formal basis for program refinement and guarantee the integrity and transparency of modules and objects.

This paper studies conservative extension ideas in the context of default logic. In particular, we define several alternative concepts, study their properties, and derive interconnections among the concepts. The main result provides an interesting distinctive feature of Reiter's default logic over some well-known variants.

1 Introduction

The formal specification of software has been instrumental in improving the reliability of programs annd our understanding of the implementation process itself. The specification language Z [10] is typical of a number that have been developed for this purpose. An important aspect of this methodology is its view of what it means for one specification S' to be a refinement of another S. One interpretation of this relationship, for instance, is that S' is an implementation of S, so S' 'has more detail' than S. Influential work by Turski and Maibaum [11] advocated the idea that this be modelled in two steps: (i) regard S and S' as logical theories, and (ii) let S' be a conservative extension of S.

To anticipate the definitions below, recall that S' ($S \subseteq S'$) is a conservative extension of S if the formulae that follow from S' and can be expressed in the language of S are exactly those which follow from S. Intuitively, one can see that this captures the idea that while S' has more detail than S, the details are 'inessential' or 'non-corrupting'. More pertinent for modern software systems is the fact that this conservative extension criterion, as argued in [11], also guarantees the integrity of modularization and the transparency of objects in the object-oriented framework.

In knowledge representation the analog of a specification in the above sense is the knowledge base, often already conveniently expressed as a set of logical

* School of Computing and Information Technology, Griffith University, QLD 4111, Australia, ga@cit.gu.edu.au

** Department of Computer Science, University of Western Australia, WA 6907, Australia, kym@cs.uwa.edu.au

*** Basser Department of Computer Science, University of Sydney, NSW 2006, Australia, norman@cs.usyd.edu.au

formulae. The analog of a refinement (or its converse, an abstraction) has been largely ignored because the process of changing a knowledge base has hitherto been viewed as a belief revision or update. However, the increasing interest in ontologies and other pragmatic issues in knowledge representation suggests that the time is ripe to consider the analog of the refinement/abstraction process in knowledge bases. What makes our task both more difficult and interesting than that in classical software theory is that our knowledge bases are usually associated with a nonmonotonic inference engine. It is the interplay between the conservative extension property and nonmonotonicity, in particular default inference [9, 6, 4, 8], that we will investigate here. Our hope is that an understanding of this interplay will yield dividends for knowledge system design similar to those accrued for software engineering.

We define conservative expansion[4] concepts which correspond with the three main interpretations of default logics: the *skeptical approach* (the intersection of all extensions), the *credulous approach* (the union of all extensions), and the *choice approach* (specific extensions). All conservative expansion concepts introduced share the same basic idea: given logical languages Σ and Σ' with $\Sigma \subseteq \Sigma'$, a default theory T over Σ and a default theory T' over Σ' which includes T, T' is a conservative expansion of T if the conclusions over the restricted language Σ that can be drawn from T' are the same as the conclusions that can be drawn from T. What varies from concept to concept is what a conclusion is. The conservativity concepts make sense not only for Reiter's default logic [9] but for other extension-based nonmonotonic formalisms as well. These include default logic variants such as Justified Default Logic [6], Constrained Default Logic [4] and Rational Default Logic [8].

The main technical result of this paper concerns the relationship among the conservative expansion concepts. Apart from some straightforward results, the question of whether a conservative expansion according to the credulous approach is also a conservative expansion according to the skeptical approach turns out to be interesting, and sheds new light on the relationship between default logic variants: the property distinguishes Reiter's default logic from Justified, Constrained and Rational Default Logic. The reason for this difference is that the latter permit extensions which are 'nondistinct' in the sense that one extension may be a proper subset of another.

2 Technical preliminaries

We assume that the reader is familiar with the basics of predicate logic. We denote a signature (logical language) by Σ; if not stated otherwise, we work with an arbitrary but fixed signature. The formulae over Σ are denoted by For_Σ. The deductive closure of a set A of Σ-formulae is denoted $Th_\Sigma(A)$; we will often omit the subscript Σ when it is clear from the context. For signatures Σ and Σ' with $\Sigma \subseteq \Sigma'$, and a set of Σ'-formulae T', the *reduct* of T' wrt Σ is

[4] We talk here of conservative *expansions* rather than *extensions* to avoid misunderstandings with extensions of default theories.

the set of Σ–formulae in T', and is denoted by T'/Σ. The process of obtaining T'/Σ from T' is called *restriction*.

$\bigwedge A$ represents the conjunction of formulae in a finite set A.

A *default* δ has the form $\frac{\varphi:\psi_1,\ldots,\psi_n}{\chi}$ with closed first–order formulae φ, $\psi_1,\ldots,\psi_n$, χ $(n > 0)$. φ is the *prerequisite*, $pre(\delta)$, $\psi_1,\ldots,\psi_n$ the *justifications*, $just(\delta)$, and χ the *consequent*, $cons(\delta)$, of δ. A *default theory* T is a pair (W, D) consisting of a set of formulae W (the set of 'facts') and a countable set of defaults D. A default of the form $\frac{\varphi:\chi}{\chi}$ is called *normal*. If additionally φ is the formula *true* then we call the default *supernormal*. A default theory T is called *normal* if all defaults in D are normal. T is called *finite* if D is finite.

Let $\delta = \frac{\varphi:\psi_1,\ldots,\psi_n}{\chi}$ be a default and E a deductively closed set of formulae. We say that δ *is applicable to* E iff φ is included in E, and $\neg\psi_1,\ldots,\neg\psi_n$ are not included in E.

Let $T = (W, D)$ be a default theory and $\Pi = (\delta_0,\ \delta_1,\ldots)$ a finite or infinite sequence of defaults from D without multiple occurrences. We denote by $\Pi[k]$ the initial segment of Π of length k, provided the length of Π is at least k.

- $In(\Pi) = Th(W \cup \{cons(\delta) \mid \delta \text{ occurs in } \Pi\})$.
- $Out(\Pi) = \{\neg\psi \mid \psi \in just(\delta),\ \delta \text{ occurs in } \Pi\}$.

Π is called a *process of* T iff δ_k is applicable to $In(\Pi[k])$, for every k such that δ_k occurs in Π. Π is *successful* iff $In(\Pi) \cap Out(\Pi) = \emptyset$, otherwise it is *failed*. Π is *closed* iff every $\delta \in D$ which is applicable to $In(\Pi)$ already occurs in Π.

[1] shows that the original definition of extensions in default logic is equivalent to the following one: a set of formulae E is an *extension* of a default theory T iff there is a closed and successful process Π of T such that $E = In(\Pi)$. The set of all extensions of T is denoted by $ext(T)$.

We will also make use of *augmentations* [7] which are minimal sets of formulae, or *bases*, that generate individual extensions. In practice it is augmentations rather than extensions that we wish to manipulate, since the bases are finite and computable for finite default theories and decidable first–order subclasses. A set of formulae A is an *augmentation* of T iff A is a minimal set A' with

$$A' = W \cup \{\chi \mid \tfrac{\varphi:\psi_1,\ldots,\psi_n}{\chi} \in D,\ A' \vdash \varphi \text{ and } A \nvdash \neg\psi_1,\ldots,A \nvdash \neg\psi_n\}.$$

The set of all augmentations of T is denoted by $aug(T)$.

Theorem 1. *[7] Let T be a default theory. Then E is an extension of T iff $E = Th(A)$ where A is an augmentation of T.*

3 Three conservative expansion concepts

In classical logic, conservative extensions are defined in the following way. Let Σ and Σ' be signatures such that $\Sigma \subseteq \Sigma'$. A set of formulae Ax' over Σ' is a conservative extension of a set of formulae Ax over Σ if the following holds: for all Σ–formulae φ, $Ax' \models \varphi$ iff $Ax \models \varphi$.[5]

The idea of a conservative extension is that the extension of the logical language and the theory does not change the meaning of the logical symbols in the old language. In the following we formalize a similar idea for default logic. We do so by defining three concepts of conservative expansion which correspond to the three basic interpretations of default theories that have been proposed in the literature: the *skeptical approach* (inclusion of a formula in all extensions of a theory T), the *credulous approach* (inclusion of a formula in at least one extension of T), and the *choice approach* (restrict attention to one extension of T).

Definition 2 *Let Σ and Σ' be signatures such that $\Sigma \subseteq \Sigma'$. Let $T = (W, D)$ be a default theory over Σ, and $T' = (W', D')$ a default theory over Σ' such that $W \subseteq W'$ and $D \subseteq D'$.*

- *T' is a* Type 1 conservative expansion *of T iff:*

  $\bigcap_{E \in ext(T)} E = \bigcap_{E' \in ext(T')} E'/\Sigma$. [6]

- *T' is a* Type 2 conservative expansion *of T iff:*

  $\bigcup_{E \in ext(T)} E = \bigcup_{E' \in ext(T')} E'/\Sigma$.

- *T' is a* Type 3 conservative expansion *of T iff:*
  1. *$\forall E \in ext(T)\ \exists E' \in ext(T') : E = E'/\Sigma$, and*
  2. *$\forall E' \in ext(T') : E'/\Sigma \in ext(T)$.*

It should be noted that these definitions are meaningful for any variant of default logic (eg [4, 6, 8]). Unless stated otherwise we shall refer to Reiter's original version of default logic [9].

We now collect some simple results on the relationship between the concepts of conservative expansions introduced above. The first observation follows directly from the definitions.

Observation 3 *If T' is a Type 3 conservative expansion of T, then it is also a Type 1 and Type 2 conservative expansion of T.*

Next we show that Type 1 conservative expansions do not necessarily imply either of the other types. Consider the following example:

$$\Sigma = \Sigma' = \{p, q\}$$
$$W = W' = \emptyset$$

[5] Note that if Ax and Ax' are deductively closed the condition reduces to $Ax'/\Sigma = Ax$.

[6] We define / to have shorter scope than $\cap$ or $\cup$. Thus $\bigcap_{E' \in ext(T')} E'/\Sigma$ is read $\bigcap_{E' \in ext(T')}(E'/\Sigma)$.

$D = \{\frac{true:p}{p}\}$
$D' = \{\frac{true:p}{p}, \frac{true:p\wedge q}{p\wedge q}, \frac{true:p\wedge\neg q}{p\wedge\neg q}\}$.

The theory $T = (W, D)$ has the single extension $E = Th(\{p\})$, whilst the theory $T' = (W', D')$ has the extensions $E_1' = Th(\{p, q\})$ and $E_2' = Th(\{p, \neg q\})$. Obviously, $E_1' \cap E_2' = E$, so T' is a Type 1 conservative expansion of T, but this is neither true for Type 2 nor for Type 3.[7]

Observation 4 *A Type 1 conservative expansion of T is not necessarily a Type 2 or Type 3 conservative expansion of T.*

The question remains whether Type 2 conservative expansions imply any of the other types. This question requires a more detailed study which is provided in the following section.

4 Relationships between the credulous and the choice approaches

We begin with some refinements of the conservative expansion concepts that were introduced in the previous section. These refinements will be used in the subsequent investigation of the relationship between the conservative expansion concepts associated with the credulous and the choice approach. Our aim is first to work out those properties that are essential for the relationship between the conservative expansion approaches, and then to turn our attention to specific default logics.

Definition 5 *Let Σ and Σ' be signatures such that $\Sigma \subseteq \Sigma'$. Let $T = (W, D)$ be a default theory over Σ, and $T' = (W', D')$ be a default theory over Σ', such that $W \subseteq W'$ and $D \subseteq D'$.*

We define $\cap_E, \ldots, =_E$ as follows:

$$\begin{array}{lll}
\cap_E & \bigcap_{E\in ext(T)} E = \bigcap_{E'\in ext(T')} E'/\Sigma & \\
\cup_E & \bigcup_{E\in ext(T)} E = \bigcup_{E'\in ext(T')} E'/\Sigma & \\
\subseteq_E & \forall E \in ext(T)\ \exists E' \in ext(T'): & E \subseteq E'/\Sigma \\
\supseteq_E & \forall E' \in ext(T')\ \exists E \in ext(T): & E'/\Sigma \subseteq E \\
=_{E_R} & \forall E \in ext(T)\ \exists E' \in ext(T'): & E = E'/\Sigma \\
=_{E_L} & \forall E' \in ext(T')\ \exists E \in ext(T): & E'/\Sigma = E \\
=_E & =_{E_R} \text{ and } =_{E_L} &
\end{array}$$

Note that $\cap_E$, $\cup_E$ and $=_E$ are the conditions for Type 1, Type 2 and Type 3 expansions respectively.

[7] Note that D' contains only supernormal defaults, therefore the counter-example applies to all superclasses including normal defaults and general defaults.

4.1 Augmentations for conservative expansion concepts

In order to prove the relationship between Type 2 conservative expansions and types 1 and 3 (that is, between $\cup_E$, $\cap_E$ and $=_E$ in Definition 4.1) we require finite bases, or "augmentation" concepts, for intersections of extensions and restricted extensions. (Note that we cannot take intersections of augmentations directly as an approach to skeptical reasoning since the results would be syntax dependent.)

In the *skeptical approach* we believe formulae which are in the intersection $\bigcap_{E_i \in ext(T)} E_i$ or, from Theorem 2.1, in $\bigcap_{A_i \in aug(T)} Th(A_i)$. The following lemma shows the relationship between the intersection of augmentations and extensions.

Lemma 6. *Let T be a default theory. Then*

$$Th(\bigcap_{A_i \in aug(T)} A_i) \subseteq \bigcap_{A_i \in aug(T)} Th(A_i).$$

The reverse does not hold — for example, if we have $A_1 = \{p, p \rightarrow q\}$ and $A_2 = \{r, r \rightarrow q\}$, then $q \in Th(A_1) \cap Th(A_2)$ but $q \notin Th(A_1 \cap A_2)$.

Taking the intersection of augmentations is therefore not sufficient for skeptical reasoning. For finite default theories, a finite base for skeptical reasoning can be obtained, however, by taking the disjunction of the conjunctions of the augmentations. We define

$$\prod_{A_i \in aug(T)} A_i = \{\bigvee_i \bigwedge A_i\}.$$

Theorem 7. *Let T be a finite default theory. Then*

$$Th(\prod_{A_i \in aug(T)} A_i) = \bigcap_{A_i \in aug(T)} Th(A_i).$$

In the *credulous approach* we believe in formulae which are in the union $\bigcup_{E_i \in ext(T)} E_i$ or, from Theorem 2.1, in $\bigcup_{A_i \in aug(T)} Th(A_i)$. The following lemma shows the relationship between forming the union of augmentations and the union of extensions.

Lemma 8. *Let T be a default theory. Then*

$$\bigcup_{A_i \in aug(T)} Th(A_i) \subseteq Th(\bigcup_{A_i \in aug(T)} A_i).$$

The reverse does not hold — for example, if we have $\{p\} = A_1$ and $\{p \rightarrow q\} = A_2$, then $q \in Th(A_1 \cup A_2)$ but $q \notin Th(A_1) \cup Th(A_2)$.

Unlike skeptical reasoning, there is no augmentation concept for credulous reasoning. The reason is that the union of deductively closed sets may not be deductively closed. For example, a and b are elements of $Th(\{a\}) \cup Th(\{b\})$ but $a \wedge b$ is not.

We have shown that finite bases exist for the left-hand side of the skeptical conservative expansion concept $\cap_E$, while no such base exists for the left-hand side (and hence right-hand side) of the credulous concept $\cup_E$. We now concentrate on the right-hand side of $\cap_E$. Our aim is to find finite bases for restricted extensions and their intersections.

Looking firstly at restricted extensions, a finite base can be found by extending the idea of disjoining conjunctions, as used in Theorem 4.3, to disjunctive normal forms. We are then able to move the restriction operation inside the deductive closure.

Definition 9 *For a formula φ, define $dnf(\varphi)$ to be the disjunctive normal form of φ, and $dnf(\varphi)/\Sigma_{tr}$ to be the formula obtained by replacing each literal appearing in $dnf(\varphi)$ but not in the signature Σ with the formula true. This definition is extended to sets of formulae A in a natural way.*

The following theorem shows that $dnf(A')/\Sigma_{tr}$ provides the finite base we require.

Theorem 10. *Let T' be a finite default theory over Σ' and $\Sigma \subseteq \Sigma'$. Then $Th_{\Sigma'}(A')/\Sigma = Th_{\Sigma}(dnf(A')/\Sigma_{tr})$.*[8]

Corollary 11. *Let T' be a finite default theory over Σ' and $\Sigma \subseteq \Sigma'$. Then*

$$\bigcap_{A' \in aug(T')} Th_{\Sigma'}(A'_i)/\Sigma = Th_{\Sigma}(\prod_{A'_i \in aug(T')} dnf(A'_i)/\Sigma_{tr}).$$

Corollary 12. *Define T, T', Σ, Σ' as in Definition 4.1 with T, T' finite. Then condition $\cap_E$ is equivalent to the condition*

$$Th_{\Sigma}(\prod_{A_i \in aug(T)} A_i) = Th_{\Sigma}(\prod_{A'_i \in aug(T')} dnf(A'_i)/\Sigma_{tr}).$$

4.2 Relationship between conservative expansion concepts

We now have sufficient machinery to examine implications from $\cup_E$ to $=_E$ and $\cap_E$. We do so via the intermediate conditions $\subseteq_E$ and $\supseteq_E$.

Theorem 13. *Assume T, T' are finite and propositional default theories defined according to Definition 4.1. Then if $\cup_E$ holds, so do $\subseteq_E$ and $\supseteq_E$.*

Proof. Assume $\cup_E$ but not $\subseteq_E$. Then for any $E \in ext(T)$ there exists a set $E'_1 \in ext(T')$ such that:

(a) $E \cap E'_1/\Sigma$ is maximal w.r.t. set inclusion. (That is, there is no $E'_2 \in ext(T')$ such that $E \cap E'_1/\Sigma \subset E \cap E'_2/\Sigma$. Since T, T' are finite there is a finite number of extensions and therefore such a set must exist.)

[8] It is necessary to specify the language of closure (Th_{Σ}) to avoid tautologies from $\Sigma' - \Sigma$ on the r.h.s.

(b) For some formula $\alpha \in E$, $\alpha \notin E_1'/\Sigma$.

Since any extension is the deductive closure of a finite augmentation, it follows from Theorem 4.6 that E_1'/Σ is the deductive closure of a finite set (actually a single dnf formula). It then follows from Theorem 4.3 that $E \cap E_1'/\Sigma$ is the closure of a finite set. Let I be such a set. Since $I \cup \{\alpha\} \subseteq E$ and E is deductively closed, $\bigwedge(I \cup \{\alpha\}) \in E$. Since $\alpha \notin E_1'/\Sigma$ and $\alpha \in For_\Sigma$, $\alpha \notin E_1'$. Therefore, since E_1' is deductively closed, $\bigwedge(I \cup \{\alpha\}) \notin E_1'$. But every formula in E is included in some E'/Σ (by $\cup_E$), so there must be some theory $E_2' \in ext(T')$ such that $\bigwedge(I \cup \{\alpha\}) \in E_2'$ and hence $I \cup \{\alpha\} \subseteq E_2'$ and $I \cup \{\alpha\} \subseteq E_2'/\Sigma$. Finally $I \cup \{\alpha\} \subseteq E \cap E_2'/\Sigma$, and since $\alpha \notin E \cap E_1'/\Sigma$, $E \cap E_1'/\Sigma \subset E \cap E_2'/\Sigma$, contradicting the assumption that $E \cap E_1'/\Sigma$ is maximal.

Similarly, assume $\cup_E$ but not $\supseteq_E$. Then for some $E'/\Sigma \in ext(T')$ there exists a set $E_1 \in ext(T)$ such that:

(a) $E_1 \cap E'/\Sigma$ is maximal w.r.t. set inclusion.

(b) For some formula $\alpha \in E'/\Sigma$, $\alpha \notin E_1$.

It follows from Theorem 4.6 that E'/Σ is the deductive closure of a finite set, and from Theorem 4.3 that $E_1 \cap E'/\Sigma$ is the closure of a finite set. Let I be such a set. Since $I \cup \{\alpha\} \subseteq E'/\Sigma$ and $E'/\Sigma \subseteq E'$, $I \cup \{\alpha\} \subseteq E'$. Since E' is deductively closed, $\bigwedge(I \cup \{\alpha\}) \in E'$ and therefore $\bigwedge(I \cup \{\alpha\}) \in E'/\Sigma$. Since $\alpha \notin E_1$ and E_1 is deductively closed, $\bigwedge(I \cup \{\alpha\}) \notin E_1$. But, by $\cup_E$, every formula in E'/Σ is included in some $E \in ext(T)$, so there must be some theory $E_2 \in ext(T)$ such that $\bigwedge(I \cup \{\alpha\}) \in E_2$ and hence $I \cup \{\alpha\} \subseteq E_2$. Finally $I \cup \{\alpha\} \subseteq E_2 \cap E'/\Sigma$, and since $\alpha \notin E_1 \cap E'/\Sigma$, $E_1 \cap E'/\Sigma \subset E_2 \cap E'/\Sigma$, contradicting the assumption that $E_1 \cap E'/\Sigma$ is maximal. □

We now consider the conditions under which $\subseteq_E$ and $\supseteq_E$ lead to $=_{E_R}$ and $=_{E_L}$. This is based on the following two definitions.

Definition 14 (distinct extensions) *An extension relation ext is* distinct *w.r.t T if whenever $E \in ext(T)$ there is no $E' \in ext(T)$ such that $E' \subset E$.*

Definition 15 (distinct restricted extensions) *An extension relation ext is* distinct under restriction Σ *w.r.t. T' if, whenever $E \in ext(T')$, there is no $E' \in ext(T')$ such that $E'/\Sigma \subset E/\Sigma$.*

Before looking at which default logics satisfy these conditions, we show that the conditions give us the results we seek.

Theorem 16. *Let T and T' be default theories such that $\subseteq_E$ and $\supseteq_E$ hold. Then:*

(a) if ext is distinct w.r.t. T, $=_{E_R}$ holds.

(b) if ext is distinct under restriction Σ w.r.t. T', $=_{E_L}$ holds.

Proof. Assume $\subseteq_E$ and $\supseteq_E$.

(a) Assume *ext* is distinct w.r.t. T and not $=_{E_R}$. That is, for some $E_1 \in ext(T)$ there is no $E' \in ext(T')$ such that $E = E'/\Sigma$. From $\subseteq_E$ there exists $E' \in ext(T')$ such that $E_1 \subset E'/\Sigma$. But from $\supseteq_E$ there exists $E_2 \in ext(T)$ such that $E'/\Sigma \subseteq E_2$ and hence $E_1 \subset E_2$, contradicting the fact that *ext* is distinct.

(b) Similarly, assume ext is distinct under restriction Σ w.r.t. T', and not $=_{E_L}$. That is, for some $E_1' \in ext(T')$ there is no $E \in ext(T)$ such that $E_1'/\Sigma = E$. From $\supseteq_E$ there exists $E \in ext(T)$ such that $E_1'/\Sigma \subset E$. But from $\subseteq_E$ there exists $E_2' \in ext(T')$ such that $E \subseteq E_2'/\Sigma$ and hence $E_1'/\Sigma \subset E_2'/\Sigma$, contradicting the fact that ext is distinct under restriction Σ. □

The required result follows directly from Theorems 4.9 and 4.12 and Observation 3.2.

Corollary 17. *If T and T' are such that $\cup_E$ holds (and hence $\subseteq_E$ and $\supseteq_E$ hold), and if ext is distinct w.r.t. T and distinct under restriction Σ wrt T', then $=_E$ and $\cap_E$ hold.*

That is, if the distinction conditions hold, Type 2 conservative expansion implies both types 3 and 1.

4.3 Distinction and classes of default logics

Having defined the distinction properties for default logics and shown their importance, we now look at how the different default logics fare. We are particularly interested in whether the properties hold over classes of theories: we expect that in all cases it will be possible to find individual "pathological" examples for which the properties hold.

It is well-known that Reiter extensions are distinct for *all* theories T. This is not true for Justified, Constrained or Rational default logics. For Justified Default Logic, consider the theory $T' = (\emptyset, \{\frac{true:p}{q \wedge r}, \frac{true:\neg q}{r}\})$; T' has two extensions $E_1 = Th(\{q \wedge r\})$ and $E_2 = Th(\{r\})$ where $E_2 \subset E_1$. Similarly Constrained and Rational default logic extensions are not distinct, as illustrated by the theory $T' = (\emptyset, \{\frac{true:p}{q \wedge r}, \frac{true:\neg p}{r}\})$ which again has extensions $Th(\{q \wedge r\})$ and $Th(\{r\})$.

Lemma 18. *Reiter default logic has distinct extensions for any theory T. This is not true for Justified, Constrained and Rational default logic.*

Not surprisingly, the examples above violate $\cap_E$ and $=_E$ even though the satisfy $\subseteq_E$ and $\supseteq_E$ (and thus $\cup_E$). For Justified Default Logic, take $\Sigma = \Sigma' = \{p, q, r\}$, $T = (\emptyset, \frac{true:p}{q \wedge r}\})$ and $T' = (\emptyset, \{\frac{true:p}{q \wedge r}, \frac{true:\neg q}{r}\})$. T has the single extension $E = Th(\{q \wedge r\})$, and T' two extensions, $E_1 = Th(\{q \wedge r\})$ and $E_2 = Th(\{r\})$. Obviously, $\subseteq_E$ and $\supseteq_E$ hold, whereas $\cap_E$ and $=_E$ do not. The example for Constrained and Rational default logics works in a similar way.

The following theorem shows that Reiter's Default Logic is also well-behaved under restriction.

Theorem 19. *Let T and T' be default theories such that $\supseteq_E$ and $\subseteq_E$ hold. Then Reiter's extension relation is distinct under Σ w.r.t. T'.*

Proof. Assume to the contrary that there are $E_1', E_2' \in ext(T')$ with $E_1'/\Sigma \subset E_2'/\Sigma$. By $\supseteq_E$ there is $E \in ext(T)$ such that $E_2'/\Sigma \subseteq E$. Therefore $E_1'/\Sigma \subset E$. Now $E \not\subseteq E_1'$, otherwise $E \subseteq E_1'/\Sigma$. Let $E = In(\Pi)$ for a closed and successful process $\Pi = (\delta_0, \ldots, \delta_k)$ of T. Since $E \not\subseteq E'_1$ there must be a default δ_i which is not applicable to E'_1. Let i be minimal with this property. The minimality of i means that all defaults δ_j with $j < i$ are applicable to E'_1; since E'_1 is an extension of T' and $W \subseteq W'$, we conclude $In(\Pi[i]) \subseteq E'_1$. Since Π is a process of T we have $pre(\delta_i) \in In(\Pi[i]) \subseteq E'_1$.

In order that δ_i is not applicable to E'_1 there must be some $\psi \in just(\delta_i)$ such that $\neg\psi \in E'_1$. Note that δ_i is a default from D, therefore ψ and $\neg\psi$ are Σ-formulae. So we have $\neg\psi \in E'_1/\Sigma$. $E'_1/\Sigma \subset E$ therefore $\neg\psi \in E = In(\Pi)$. But then Π is not successful since $\neg\psi \in Out(\Pi)$ which is a contradiction. □

Corollary 20. *For Reiter's default logic, a conservative expansion of Type 2 is always a conservative expansion of Types 1 and 3. This is not true for Justified, Rational and Constrained default logic.*

Thus we see that Reiter's Default Logic exhibits more orderly behaviour with respect to expansion, providing another distinction between the original logic and more recently proposed variations.

5 A sufficient condition for conservative expansions

It is known that default logic behaves in a very volatile way when new facts or defaults are added. For example, the addition of the default $\frac{true:p}{\neg p}$ (where p is a new predicate symbol) destroys all previous extensions. Therefore we need rather strong conditions to ensure the property of a conservative expansion.

Theorem 21. *Let Σ and Σ' be signatures such that $\Sigma \subseteq \Sigma'$. Let $T = (W, D)$ and $T' = (W', D')$ be finite default theories over Σ and Σ' respectively, such that $W \subseteq W'$ and $D \subseteq D'$. T' is a Type 1, 2 and 3 conservative expansion of T if the following conditions are true:*

(a) All defaults in $D' - D$ are normal.

(b) $Th(W')/\Sigma = Th(W)$

(c) Predicates from Σ and W' do not occur in the consequents of the defaults in $D' - D$.

Proof. In the following we assume that both W and W' are consistent (if W is inconsistent then W' is inconsistent as well, and the claim is trivial; if W' is inconsistent and W consistent, then the condition (b) cannot be fulfilled).

Let $E = In(\Pi)$ be an extension of T, where $\Pi = (\delta_0, \ldots, \delta_n)$ is a closed and successful process of T. Let Π' be any closed process of T' which contains Π as its starting segment. Since Π is a closed process of T, Π' necessarily has the following form: $\Pi' = (\delta_0, \ldots, \delta_n, \gamma_0, \ldots, \gamma_m)$, where the γ_i are defaults from $D' - D$.

We show that Π' is a closed and successful process of T'; then $E' = In(\Pi')$ is an extension of T'. Since the consequents of the defaults γ_i do not include any symbols from Σ or W', and W' is consistent, it follows that $In(\Pi')/\Sigma = In(\Pi)$, that is, $E'/\Sigma = E$.

The success of Π' is shown as follows. Consider a formula $\neg\psi$ in $Out(\Pi')$. If it stems from a default δ_j in Π then $\psi \in For_\Sigma$. Since Π is successful, $\neg\psi \notin E$; by the property $E'/\Sigma = E$ we conclude that $\neg\psi \notin E' = In(\Pi')$. If, on the other hand, ψ stems from a default γ_i, then our claim follows from the observation that ψ is consistent with $In(\Pi'[n+i+1])$, ψ is included in $In(\Pi'[n+i+2])$ (since γ_i is normal), and all subsequent defaults are normal, so they cannot add to the In–set something that contradicts ψ (otherwise they would not have been applicable).

In the opposite direction, let $E' = In(\Pi')$ be an extension of T', for a closed and successful process $\Pi' = (\gamma_0, \ldots, \gamma_m)$ of T'. Let $\Pi = (\delta_0, \ldots, \delta_n)$ be the sequence of defaults from D which is obtained from Π' by deleting all defaults not in D; obviously, for every $i \in \{0, \ldots, n\}$ there is a number $pos(i)$ such that $\delta_i = \gamma_{pos(i)}$.

We note that $E'/\Sigma = In(\Pi')/\Sigma = In(\Pi)$ because of condition (c) and the consistency of W and W'. We conclude the proof by showing that Π is a closed and successful process of T, and thus that $E = In(\Pi)$ is an extension of T.

To prove that Π is a process we show that each default δ_i is applicable to $In(\Pi[i])$. Consider such a $\delta_i = \frac{\varphi:\psi_1,\ldots,\psi_k}{\chi}$, and suppose that δ_i is not applicable to $In(\Pi[i])$. One possible reason is that some ψ_l is inconsistent with $In(\Pi[i])$. But then ψ_l would be inconsistent with $In(\Pi')$ which contradicts the success of Π'. The only other possible reason for the inapplicability of δ_i is that $\varphi \notin In(\Pi[i])$. But since Π' is a process, we know that $\varphi \in In(\Pi'[pos(i)])$. By property (c) and by the construction of Π we know that $In(\Pi'[pos(i)])/\Sigma = In(\Pi[i])$. Since W is consistent we conclude that $\varphi \in In(\Pi[i])$ which is a contradiction to our assumption.

So Π is a process of T. Also, it is closed and successful because these properties are true of Π'. □

We note that the theorem above fails to hold if we omit any of the three conditions. The example preceding the theorem shows this for the case where we omit (a); it is easy to find counterexamples for the case where (b) or (c) is omitted. Also, similar results can be obtained in cases where all processes are successful. In Constrained Default Logic, for example, all constrained processes are successful (see [1]), therefore a similar result holds without requiring condition (a).

6 Conclusion and future work

In the previous sections we introduced several concepts of conservative expansions, and studied their properties and interconnections. One of the interesting aspects of our results is that we gave a new distinctive property of Reiter's original Default Logic compared with the most popular default logic variants.

The investigations of this paper can be expanded in several directions. For example, it will be interesting to determine the relationship between conservative expansions and stratification concepts [3]. It seems also interesting to study ways of restricting default theories. Finally we intend to investigate ways of refining default theories by modifying existing defaults, as opposed to the addition of defaults as done here.

This work is part of an ongoing research effort whose ultimate goal is the integration of default reasoning with software engineering methods, and in particular with object orientation, both with regard to the development process and to knowledge representation. To do so, we need to introduce and adapt concepts which have been proven important in software engineering — conservative extensions are one suc central concept.

References

1. G. Antoniou. *Nonmonotonic Reasoning with Incomplete and Changing Information.* MIT Press 1996 (forthcoming)
2. G. Antoniou, C.K. MacNish and N.Y. Foo. *Conservative Expansions of Default Theories.* Information Systems Research Report, University of Newcastle 1996
3. P. Cholewinski. Stratified default logic. In *Proc. Computer Science Logic 1994*, Springer LNCS 933, 456–470
4. J.P. Delgrande, T. Schaub and W.K. Jackson. Alternative approaches to default logic. *Artificial Intelligence* 70 (1994): 167–237
5. H. Ehrig and B. Mahr. *Fundamentals of Algebraic Specification Vol. 2.* Springer 1990
6. W. Lukaszewicz. Considerations of default logic: an alternative approach. *Computational Intelligence* 4,1(1988): 1–16
7. C. MacNish. Hierarchical default logic. In *Symbolic and Quantitative Approaches to Uncertainty: Proc. European Conference.* Springer-Verlag Lecture Notes in Computer Science 548, pp 246–253, 1991
8. A. Mikitiuk and M. Truszczynski. Constrained and rational default logics. In *Proc. International Joint Conference on Artificial Intelligence* 1995
9. R. Reiter. A logic for default reasoning. *Artificial Intelligence* 13(1980): 81–132
10. J.M. Spivey. *The Z Notation: A Reference Manual.* Prentice-Hall 1989.
11. W.M. Turski and T.S.E. Maibaum. *The Specification of Computer Programs.* Addison-Wesley, Reading Massachusetts, 1987

On Formation of Exception Hierarchy*

Kouzou Ohara**, Noboru Babaguchi and Tadahiro Kitahashi

The Institute of Scientific and Industrial Research, Osaka University,
8-1, Mihogaoka, Ibaraki, Osaka 567, Japan
Email : ohara@am.sanken.osaka-u.ac.jp

Abstract. In this paper, the rule specifying exceptions is discussed by using a representation original to the authors, the *exc-representation*, which can afford to express the hierarchy for exceptions. The hierarchy represents a kind of preference for incomplete knowledge in the inference. To form the rules, we focus on the contradiction derived by exceptions. Thus the rules to define the contradictions are of great importance in this paper. We devote the former half of this paper to discuss the definition of the exc-representation. We classify exceptions into the two types: the exceptions based on *general-specific relation* and the exceptions based on *co-existence relation.* For each type we define its representation. In the latter half, we propose a method to form the rules for each type. For the exceptions based on general-specific relation, our method is based on the inheritance rule on taxonomic hierarchy. For the co-existence relation, we produce the additional rules and predicates if necessary before forming the rules.

1 Introduction

In nonmonotonic logic, the abnormality theory(McCarthy 1986) is a typical one dealing with the exceptions. The theory is based on the viewpoint that an exception has some abnormality, and uses the *abnormal predicate* to represent the abnormality. In this theory, the exception is specified by a rule whose head is the abnormal predicate representing its abnormality, and whose body is itself. On the contrary the rule including the exception has the negation of the abnormal predicate in its body. As a result, the exception is excluded from the conclusion of the rule including it.

However, any rules concerned with the abnormal predicate should be given in advance by ourselves. It means that we have to know all exceptions for the rules. Whenever the new exceptional rule or fact is added to the rule set, we have to modify some rules concerned with it by ourselves. In a large scale knowledge system, such modification will be impossible.

An alternative method to represent the knowledge including exceptions uses nonmonotonic formalisms such as default logic(Reiter 1980), and autoepistemic

* This work was partly supported by a Grant-in-Aid for the Ministry of Education of Japan

** Research Fellow of the Japan Society for the Promotion of Science.

logic (Moore 1985). Unfortunately, however, these formalisms would give us no information about exceptions explicitly. The knowledge including exceptions is merely a kind of knowledge represented by such formalisms. In these formalisms, their attention to consistency in the rule set is interesting. Because the abnormality involved in an exception is exactly one of the sources deriving an inconsistency.

From the above discussion, we propose a method of forming the rule specifying exceptions based on the contradiction derived from them rather than their abnormality(Ohara et al. 1995a). In this paper, the exception of a rule is defined by instances satisfying predicates in its body and ones inconsistent with its head. Hence we describe the contradiction in terms of a logical formula, and consider the rules related to it.

We first classify exceptions into two types: the *exceptions based on general-specific relation* and the *exceptions based on co-existence relation.* This classification is based on the relation among a set of instances satisfying the body of the rule including exceptions and sets of ones satisfying the predicates inconsistent with its head. For each type, we define its own representation, which represents the hierarchy for exceptions, and propose a method of forming the rule expressed with it. For the exceptions of the former type, the method is based on the inheritance rule on taxonomic hierarchy(Genesereth and Nilsson 1987). For the latter type, we attempt to add some rules and predicates if necessary before forming the rule to describe a set of the exceptions.

2 Knowledge Representation

In this paper, we use the knowledge representation based on Horn clauses without function symbols. A fact is represented by a ground literal, and a piece of knowledge is represented by a logical formula. For example, we represent some complete knowledge including no exception as

$$Animal(x) \leftarrow Bird(x) \tag{1}$$
$$Bird(x) \leftarrow Penguin(x) \tag{2}$$
$$\overline{Fly}(x) \leftarrow Penguin(x) \tag{3}$$

where symbol $\leftarrow$ represents logical implication, and $\overline{Fly}$ is a predicate symbol which represent negation of " Fly ", that is, " $\overline{Fly}(x)$ " is a positive literal. We call such a rule the *complete-rule.*

On the other hand, we use a particular implication operator $\Leftarrow$ allowing exceptions for the incomplete knowledge including them. For example, the knowledge, " An animal can not normally fly ", " A bird can normally fly ", are represented as

$$\overline{Fly}(x) \Leftarrow Animal(x) \tag{4}$$
$$Fly(x) \Leftarrow Bird(x)\ . \tag{5}$$

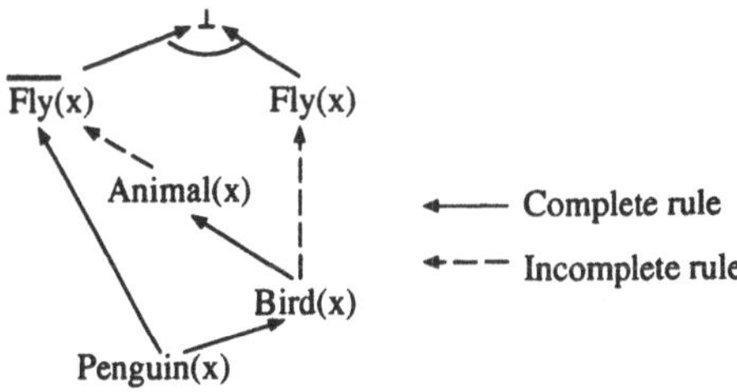

Fig. 1. Dependency graph for (1)~(6)

We call such a rule the *incomplete-rule*, and define its logical interpretation that " *an incomplete-rule entails its head if and only if its body is true, and the negation of its head is not proved* ". From this definition, we can interpret the incomplete-rule by nonmonotonic logics: default logic, autoepistemic logic, and so on. In the following, we call a set of the instances satisfying the body of a rule the *class* of the rule.

Since all literals are positive in Horn clauses, a particular complete-rule is required to define a contradiction. We call it the *restriction-rule*. For example, the following rule is a restriction-rule:

$$\bot \leftarrow Fly(x), \overline{Fly}(x) \tag{6}$$

where $\bot$ is a proposition representing a contradiction. This restriction-rule represents that " it is inconsistent that both $Fly(x)$ and $\overline{Fly}(x)$ hold at the same time". In the following, the head and the body of a rule r are denoted by *head*(r) and *body*(r), respectively.

Furthermore we introduce a graph expressing the dependency of predicates in rules. The graph is an AND/OR graph whose nodes are associated with predicates in rules, and whose branches are associated with directed links from the predicates in the body of a rule to the predicate of its head. This graph is called the *dependency graph*. In the graph, a solid arrow and a broken arrow denote the directed links corresponding to a complete-rule and an incomplete-rule, respectively. For example, the dependency graph for (1)~(6) is shown in Fig.1.

3 Exception Representation with Hierarchical Structure

3.1 Classification of Exceptions

Basically an exception is an instance which invalidates some rule. In other words, the exception does not satisfy the head of the rule although it satisfies its body. Hence a set of the exceptions of a rule is a subset of its class. Note that the exceptions satisfy the other predicates inconsistent with the head. For example, Tweety, which is a penguin, is an exception of (5). Because it satisfies $\overline{Fly}(x)$

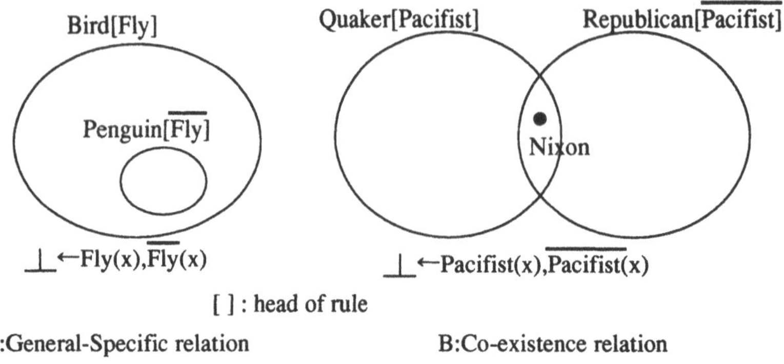

Fig. 2. Relationship among classes

inconsistent with the predicate $Fly(x)$ even if it is a bird. Since the *penguin* and the *bird* are the classes of (3) and (5), respectively, we can say that a set of exceptions is the intersection of classes of rules whose heads are inconsistent. In the following, we focus on the relationship among such classes, and define the two types of exceptions: the exception based on general-specific relation and the exception based on co-existence relation.

When a general-specific relation exists among the classes of rules with inconsistent heads, the elements of the specific class included by the general class are the exceptions of the incomplete-rule, whose body represents the general class, since the rule with more specific class is prioritized. We call such exceptions the *exceptions based on general-specific relation* (G-S type exceptions). For example, penguins are G-S type exceptions of (5), because the class of (5) *bird* is the general class for the class of (3) *penguin* (see Fig.2). In this paper, the general-specific relation is formally defined as follows.

Definition 1. For the two conjunctions of one or more predicates, $D1$ and $D2$, and some rule set which may be empty, Δ, if $D1$ is derived from $D2 \cup \Delta$, then $D1$ is more general than $D2$, or $D2$ is more specific than $D1$, it is represented as

$$D2 <_{\mathrm{gs}} D1 \ . \tag{7}$$

□

In the following, the relation among rules depends on the relation among their classes.

Now for G-S type exceptions, if the class of some incomplete-rule r_1 represents the exception of another incomplete-rule r_2, the exception of r_1 is "the exception of the exceptions of r_2". The relation "the exception of the exceptions"is regarded as a hierarchy. Similarly we can define a deeper level of the hierarchy "exception of exceptions of $\cdots$ ". We call such hierarchical structure for exceptions the *exception hierarchy*.

On the other hand, when there is no general-specific relation among the classes of the rules with inconsistent heads, and the classes only have some instances in common, we say that they are *co-existence relation*. In this case, the intersection of those classes is a set of the exceptions for all incomplete-rules concerned with those classes. The elements of the intersection are named as the *exceptions based on co-existence relation*(C-E type exceptions), and the conjunction expressing each class, that is, the body of each rule is named as the *constituent element*. Consider the following rules:

$$\bot \leftarrow Pacifist(x), \overline{Pacifist}(x) \tag{8}$$

$$Pacifist(x) \Leftarrow Quaker(x) \tag{9}$$

$$\overline{Pacifist}(x) \Leftarrow Republican(x) \tag{10}$$

$$Quaker(Nixon) \tag{11}$$

$$Republican(Nixon)\ . \tag{12}$$

In these rules, the classes of (9) and (10) are co-existence relation, and Nixon is a C-E type exception of both incomplete-rules, since Nixon is an element of the intersection of these classes. Both $Pacifist(x)$ and $\overline{Pacifist}(x)$ are the constituent elements (see Fig.2).

This example is a famous problem called Nixon Diamond(Lifschitz 1988) in nonmonotonic logic. Note that there is no preference between both incomplete-rules which are co-existence relation, and that we obtain different conclusions due to the order of evaluating them. For Nixon, if (9) is evaluated before (10), we obtain the conclusion that he is a pacifist. If we take the reverse order, the conclusion is that he is not a pacifist. It means that it is impossible for Nixon, or the C-E type exception to decide which of $Pacifist(x)$ or $\overline{Pacifist}(x)$ is false uniquely. Accordingly we consider that the C-E type exceptions should be excluded as exceptions from the entailment of all incomplete-rules whose classes include them. Similarly since it is impossible to define another class representing " exception of exceptions " in the set of C-E type exceptions, the exception hierarchy for them is always single, that is, " exception " only.

3.2 Exc-representation

In this section, we define the exception representation expressing the exception hierarchy. It is similar to the representation using the abnormal predicate by specifying exceptions explicitly with particular predicates, and to the formalisms such as hierarchic autoepistemic logic(Konolige 1988) and prioritized circumscription(McCarthy 1986) by giving the order of applying the incomplete knowledge in the inference. However it is different from them on the grounds that it could carry out the inference even if there is no preference among the some particular incomplete knowledge, like Nixon Diamond.

First of all, we consider the notation which express the exception of an incomplete-rule. For that purpose we introduce a symbol *exc* (the abbreviation of exception), and represent the exception of some incomplete-rule r as *exc-P*.

The P is *head*(r), and we call P the *core*. Similarly, the exception of $exc\text{-}P$ (that is, the exception of the exceptions of r) is represented as $exc^2\text{-}P$. Generally, we represent the exception of $exc^n\text{-}P$ as $exc^{n+1}\text{-}P$, and call n (or $n+1$) the *degree*, which represents the level of the exception hierarchy: the larger the degree is, the deeper the level is. A predicate with exc is named as the *exc-predicate*.

Next, we consider the representation specifying the exception included by an incomplete-rule. To specify it, we use exc-predicates as labels. The set of G-S type exceptions is the conclusion set of rules, which are more specific than the incomplete-rule including them and whose heads are inconsistent with its head. Accordingly we have only to label the exc-predicate, whose core is the head of the incomplete-rule, to those rules. For example, since the exceptions of (4) and the exceptions of the exceptions of it are the elements of the conclusion sets of (5) and (3) respectively, we represent these as

$$[exc\text{-}\overline{Fly}(x)]Fly(x) \Leftarrow Bird(x) \tag{13}$$

$$[exc^2\text{-}\overline{Fly}(x)]\overline{Fly}(x) \leftarrow Penguin(x)\ . \tag{14}$$

We call the rule with exc-predicates as labels the *exc-rule*, and call the part of the exc-rule without labels the *basic-rule* . Note that (14) does not have the exc-predicate $exc\text{-}Fly(x)$ as a label. We know the exception of the exc-rule by adding 1 to the degree of its label.

For C-E type exceptions, their set is represented by the conjunction of constituent elements as mentioned above. However there is no rule whose body is that conjunction in fact, because each conjunct is the body of some rule. Hence in this case, we use a particular basic-rule whose body is that conjunction and with no head. Remember the two matters about the C-E type exceptions: one is that they are the exceptions of all incomplete-rules with the constituent elements as their bodies, and the other is that their hierarchies are always single. Therefore the label part of the exc-rule for the C-E type exception consists of the exc-predicates whose cores are the heads of those incomplete-rules and whose degrees are all 1. For Nixon Diamond, we introduce the following exc-rule.

$$[exc\text{-}Pacifist(x), exc\text{-}\overline{Pacifist}(x)] \leftarrow Quaker(x), Republican(x) \tag{15}$$

We call the representation with exc the *exc-representation*. As mentioned above, the exc-rule for the G-S type exception is different from one for the C-E type exception. It means that the used exc-rule decides the type of the exception. Thus only for the inference with the C-E type exceptions such as Nixon Diamond, we can offer the particular entailment. For example, for the proof of the fact $Pacifist(Nixon)$ in Nixon Diamond we offer the following entailment:

$$Pacifist(Nixon)\langle\overline{Pacifist}(Nixon)\rangle\ . \tag{16}$$

It represents that " $Pacifist(Nixon)$ is true if $\overline{Pacifist}(Nixon)$ is false ".

In the existing nonmonotonic theories, only one inference strategy is applied to the incomplete knowledge including exceptions irrespective of their kinds mentioned above. In result, although they can derive a unique entailment by deciding the order of applying the knowledge in the inference for G-S type exceptions, for C-E type ones they can not derive it always. On the other hand, exc-representation can always derive it in any case by using the separate inference strategy for each type of exceptions. We would discuss the detail of the inference using the exc-representation on another occasion because it is not the main subject of this paper.

4 Method of Forming the Exc-rules

In this section, we discuss a method of forming the exc-rules. The basis of the exc-representation is to label the exc-predicate to the basic-rule. Since the core of the exc-predicate is the head of the incomplete-rule including the exception, we have only to acquire the degree and the basic-rule to describe the exc-rule. Especially for the C-E type exception, we have merely to acquire the basic-rule since the degree of the label in the exc-rule is always 1.

It is noted that the exception of some incomplete-rule satisfies the predicate inconsistent with its head. After all in the discussion about the exception of some incomplete-rule, all the related rules exist in the dependency graph whose top is the restriction-rule including the head of the incomplete-rule in its body. In the following, we call the set of rules in the dependency graph, whose top is the restriction-rule, the *Standard Rule Set, SRS.* The graph in Fig.1 represents a SRS. In the SRS, the restriction-rule is unique, and the rules whose heads are in the restriction-rule are very important; the other rules are used for checking the general-specific relation.

In addition, we assume that the input to the proposed methods is the output of a knowledge conversion procedure(Babaguchi et al. 1995), which convert the complete knowledge to the incomplete knowledge as a contradiction emerges. It means that the sources which derived the contradiction, rules or facts, surely exist in our input. This fact would guarantee the finite termination of the proposed methods.

4.1 G-S Type Exceptions

In this section, we discuss the method of forming the exc-rule for G-S type exceptions. The method is based on the inheritance rule in a taxonomic hierarchy (Genesereth and Nilsson 1987), "In a taxonomic hierarchy, a lower class inherits the property of a higher class unless there is no assertion to deny the inheritance". For example, " a penguin can not fly " is such assertion, because it denies that the penguin inherits the property " fly " which the bird has. Thus we can say that the lower (or more specific) class, which corresponds to the exception of the higher (or more general) class, has such assertion. It means that finding the class with the assertion in the order of generality allows us to specify the exception.

Fortunately the assertion to deny an inheritance corresponds to the basic-rule of an exc-rule. As mentioned above, the head of the basic-rule in an exc-rule is inconsistent with one of the incomplete-rule including the exception specified

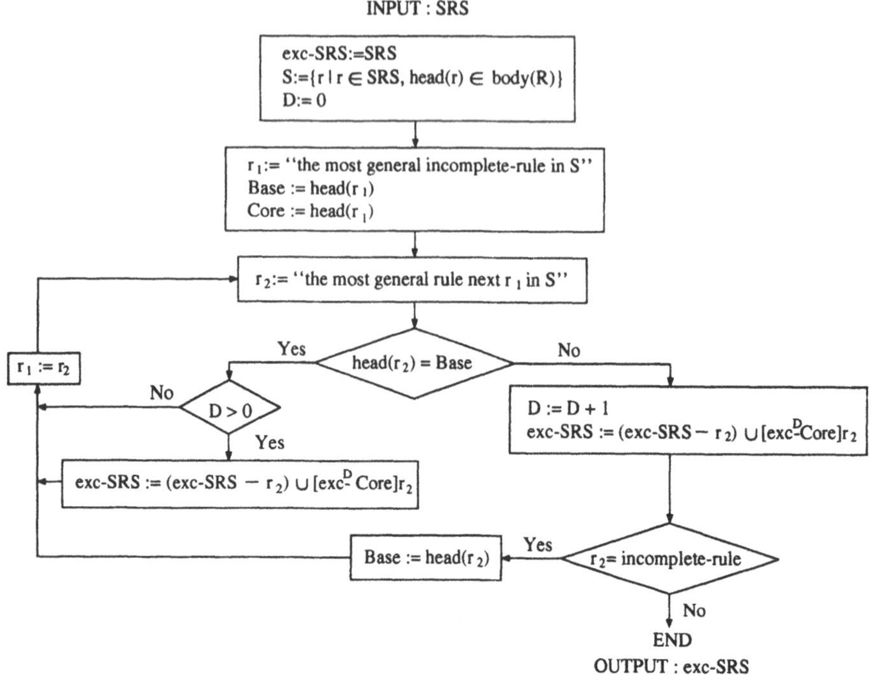

Fig. 3. Algorithm 1

by the exc-rule. Accordingly, only the rules whose heads are in the body of the restriction-rule have the possibility to be the basic-rules in SRS.

First, we find the most general incomplete-rule from among the rules with the previous possibility, and make its head both the *basic-predicate* and the *basic-core*. Next, in the order of generality we check whether the head of the other rule with the possibility matches with the current basic-predicate. Since the rule is exactly the basic-rule if they do not match, we labels to it the exc-predicate whose core is the basic-core and whose degree is 1. Furthermore if the obtained basic-rule is an incomplete-rule, we make its head a new basic-predicate, and repeat the same process: in the process the basic-core is not changed although the degree increases one by one. As a result, we can acquire the exception hierarchy, " the exception of the exceptions " , " the exception of the exceptions of $\cdots$ " .

This discussion is summarized as Algorithm1 in Fig.3. In Fig.3, the output exc-SRS is a rule set with exc-rules, and R is a unique restriction-rule in SRS. For example, let us apply the Algorithm1 to (1)~(6)(see Fig.4). First, the set S consists of (3), (4) and (5). In state1, since the general-specific relation in S is (3) $<_{gs}$ (5) $<_{gs}$ (4), r_1 is (4), both Base and Core are $\overline{Fly}(x)$, and r_2 is (5). Then as the $head(r_2)$ does not match with Base, we exclude (5) from exc-SRS, and add (13) to it. Since (5) is the incomplete-rule, in state2, new Base is $Fly(x)$, and new r_1 is (5). Then new r_2 is (3), whose head does not match with current Base.

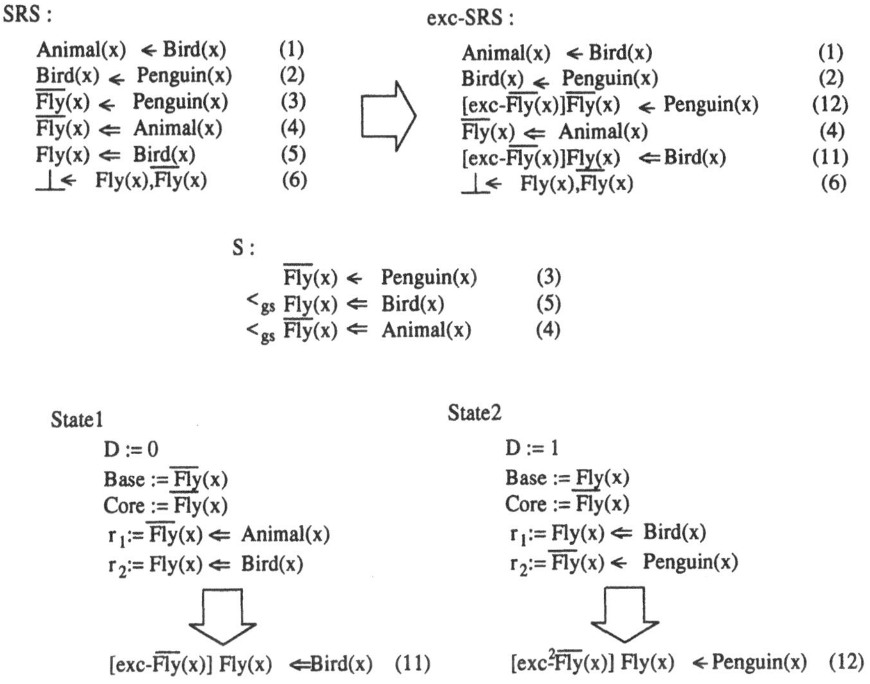

SRS :

$Animal(x) \leftarrow Bird(x)$	(1)
$Bird(x) \leftarrow Penguin(x)$	(2)
$\overline{Fly}(x) \leftarrow Penguin(x)$	(3)
$\overline{Fly}(x) \Leftarrow Animal(x)$	(4)
$Fly(x) \Leftarrow Bird(x)$	(5)
$\bot \leftarrow Fly(x), \overline{Fly}(x)$	(6)

exc-SRS :

$Animal(x) \leftarrow Bird(x)$	(1)
$Bird(x) \leftarrow Penguin(x)$	(2)
$[exc\text{-}\overline{Fly}(x)]\overline{Fly}(x) \leftarrow Penguin(x)$	(12)
$\overline{Fly}(x) \Leftarrow Animal(x)$	(4)
$[exc\text{-}\overline{Fly}(x)]Fly(x) \Leftarrow Bird(x)$	(11)
$\bot \leftarrow Fly(x), \overline{Fly}(x)$	(6)

S :

$\overline{Fly}(x) \leftarrow Penguin(x)$	(3)
$<_{gs} Fly(x) \Leftarrow Bird(x)$	(5)
$<_{gs} \overline{Fly}(x) \Leftarrow Animal(x)$	(4)

State1

$D := 0$
$Base := \overline{Fly}(x)$
$Core := Fly(x)$
$r_1 := \overline{Fly}(x) \Leftarrow Animal(x)$
$r_2 := Fly(x) \Leftarrow Bird(x)$

$[exc\text{-}\overline{Fly}(x)]\ Fly(x) \Leftarrow Bird(x)$ (11)

State2

$D := 1$
$Base := Fly(x)$
$Core := \overline{Fly}(x)$
$r_1 := Fly(x) \Leftarrow Bird(x)$
$r_2 := \overline{Fly}(x) \leftarrow Penguin(x)$

$[exc^2\text{-}\overline{Fly}(x)]\ Fly(x) \leftarrow Penguin(x)$ (12)

Fig. 4. Application of Algorithm1

Thus we exclude (3), and add (14). Since (3) is the complete-rule, Algorithm1 will terminate.

4.2 C-E Type Exceptions

For C-E type exceptions, the discussion is more simple. As mentioned in Sect.3.2, the basic-rule of the exc-rule representing the C-E type exceptions consists of the body only, which is the conjunction of the constituent elements. Each constituent element is the body of the rule whose head appears in the unique restriction-rule in SRS with the incomplete-rules including the exceptions. Furthermore each core of the exc-predicates in the label part of the exc-rule is the head of such incomplete-rule, and its degree is always 1. Therefore we can form the exc-rule from only the rules whose heads are in that restriction-rule.

Note that the number of rules whose heads are same predicate in the body of a restriction-rule is not always one. If there are two or more such rules, it is inappropriate that each body of them is regarded as a constituent element. Because the set represented by the conjunction of those bodies is more specific than the set of elements which may satisfy the common head. In fact, we should make the disjunction of those bodies a constituent element.

However, any disjunction is not permitted in the body of Horn clause. Thus

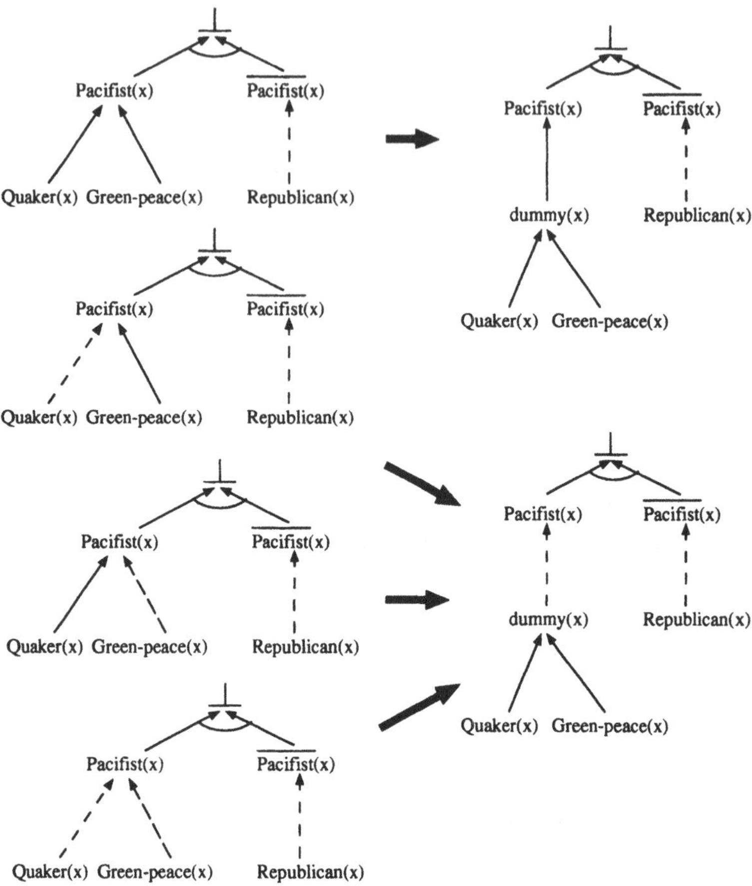

Fig. 5. Modification of the dependency graph

we need to introduce some additional predicates and rules. Suppose the additional predicate *dummy* whose arguments correspond to ones of a predicate r_1 in the body of the restriction-rule and the rules $R_{11}, R_{12}, \cdots, R_{1m}$ whose heads are r_1. We temporarily remove $R_{11}, \cdots, R_{1m}$ from SRS, and add m+1 additional rules to it instead of them: one of the added rules is a rule whose head is r_1 and whose body is *dummy*, and the others are ones whose heads are *dummy* and whose bodies are $body(R_{11}), \cdots, body(R_{1m})$, respectively. The later m rules must be the complete-rules, that is, the *dummy* represents the disjunction of the bodies of the removed rules. On the other hand, if all of the removed rules are complete-rules, the former rule is the complete-rule; otherwise it is the incomplete-rule.

An example of this modification is shown in Fig.5. In each graph in the left of Fig.5, the predicate $Pacifist(x)$ has two rules. Thus we remove the two rules, and add three additional rules. The rules whose heads are $dummy(x)$ are complete-rules. In the graph in the left top of Fig.5 since the removed rules are both complete-rules, the added rule whose body is $dummy(x)$ is a complete-rule. In the other graphs in the left of Fig.5, the added rules whose bodies are $dummy(x)$ are incomplete-rules since at least one of the removed rules is an incomplete-rule.

By applying this modification to each predicate in the body of the restriction-rule if necessary, each predicate has only one rule whose head is itself. Then we can form the exc-rule from those rules: the cores are the heads of the incomplete-rules whose heads are in the restriction-rule, and the body of the basic-rule is the conjunction of the bodies of the rules whose heads are in it. For the graph in the left bottom of Fig.5 the following exc-rule is formed:

$$[exc\text{-}Pacifist(x), exc\text{-}\overline{Pacifist}(x)] \leftarrow dummy(x), Republican(x) \ . \qquad (17)$$

Of course, we need to replace the removed rules after the formation.

5 Conclusion

In this paper, we discussed the formation of the rules expressing the exception hierarchy from the knowledge set including the incomplete knowledge. In the proposed method, the attention to the contradiction derived by the exception is allowed us to classify the exceptions, and to form the exc-rule using the restriction-rule. In result, we do not have to know any exception differently from abnormality theory although the exc-representation specifies them explicitly. We believe that the proposed method is a novel approach for specifying exceptions. For the exc-representation, we have already proposed an application to a logical database(Ohara et al. 1995b). Moreover the integration of our conversion procedure and the proposed method would offer the basic technology to the automatic maintenance for exceptions in the very large knowledge system.

The remaining problems are the following: applying our method to the practical knowledge base system, and evaluating its performance.

References

Babaguchi, N., Ohara, K., Katsurada, K., and Kitahashi, T. : Knowledge Conversion Initiated by Contradiction, Proc.9th Annual Conference of JSAI(1995)53–56

Genesereth, M.R. and Nilsson, N.J.: Logical Foundations of Artificial Intelligence, Morgan Kaufmann(1987)

Konolige, K. : Hierarchic Autoepistemic Theory for Nonmonotonic Reasoning: Preliminary Report, Proc.2nd Workshop on Non-monotonic Reasoning(1988)42–59

Lifschitz, V. : Benchmark Problems for Nonmonotonic Reasoning, Proc.2nd Workshop on Non-monotonic Reasoning(1988)202–219

McCarthy, J. : Applications of Circumscription to Formalizing Common-Sense Knowledge, Artif.Intell., Vol.28(1986)89–116

Moore, R. C. : Semantical Considerations on Non-Monotonic Logic, Artif.Intell., Vol.25(1985)75–94

Ohara, K., Babaguchi, N., and Kitahashi, T. : Acquiring Hierarchic Structure from Knowledge Including Exceptions, Proc.9th Annual Conference of JSAI(1995)61–64
Ohara, K., Babaguchi, N., and Kitahashi, T. : Relational Algebraic Representation for Query Procedure in Advanced Logical DataBase Handling Incomplete Knowledge, Trans.IPS.Japan, Vol.36, No.6(1995)1433–1440
Reiter, R. : A Logic for Default Reasoning, Artif.Intell., Vol.13, No.1/2(1980)81–132

Anytime Default Inference

Aditya K. Ghose[1], Randy Goebel[2]

[1] Knowledge Systems Group, Basser Department of Computer Science, University of Sydney, Syndey NSW 2006, Australia. aditya@cs.su.oz.au

[2] Department of Computing Science, University of Alberta, Edmonton, Alberta, Canada, T6G 2H1. goebel@cs.ualberta.ca

Abstract. *Default reasoning* plays a fundamental role in a variety of information processing applications. Default inference is inherently computationally hard and practical applications, specially time-bounded ones, may require that some notion of approximate inference be used. *Anytime algorithms* are a useful conceptualization of processes that may be prematurely terminated whenever necessary to return useful partial answers, with the quality of the answers improving in a well-defined manner with time. In his paper, we develop a repertoire of meaningful partial solutions for default inference problems and use these as the basis for specifying general classes of anytime default inference algorithms. We then present some of our earlier results on the connection between partial constraint satisfaction and default reasoning and exploit this connection to identify a large space of possible algorithms for default inference that may be defined based on partial constraint satisfaction techniques, which are inherently anytime in nature. The connection is useful because a number of existing techniques from the area of partial constraint satisfaction can be applied with little or no modification to default inference problems.

1 Introduction

Default reasoning plays a fundamental role in a variety of information processing applications. Default inference is inherently computationally hard [6] and practical applications, especially time-bounded ones, may require that some notion of approximate inference be used. Any approximation algorithm must provide useful partial results and the trade-offs involved must be clearly identified. Approximate default inference has received scant attention in the literature (the notable exception being the work of Cadoli and Schaerf [1] in which they improve on the complexity of reasoning with Reiter's default logic by using consequence relations that are sound and incomplete in one case and complete but unsound in the other). *Anytime algorithms* are a useful conceptualization of processes that may be prematurely terminated whenever necessary to return useful partial answers, with the quality of the answers improving in a well-defined manner with time. Dean and Boddy [2] define an anytime algorithm to be one which:

- Lends itself to preemptive scheduling techniques.
- Can be terminated at any time and will give some meaningful answer.

– Returns answers that improve in some well-behaved manner as a function of time.

In the rest of the paper, we shall informally refer to the process of an anytime algorithm progressively computing solutions of measurably improving quality as the *anytime progression*. Here, we shall develop a repertoire of meaningful partial solutions for default inference problems and use these as the basis for specifying general classes of anytime default inference algorithms. We then present some of our earlier results on the connection between partial constraint satisfaction and default reasoning and exploit this connection to identify a large space of possible algorithms for default inference that may be based on partial constraint satisfaction techniques, which are inherently anytime in nature. The connection is useful because a number of existing techniques from the area of partial constraint satisfaction can be applied with little or no modification to default inference problems and because tractable cases for partial constraint satisfaction suggest tractable default inference problems. A variety of formalizations of default inference exist in the literature. In this paper we shall consider default inference as formalized in PJ-default logic [3] or, equivalently, in the THEORIST system [10] (this variety of default reasoning has been variously referred to as *hypothetical reasoning*, *theory formation* or the *preferred subtheories* approach). This formalization improves over Reiter's default logic [12] by avoiding cases where Reiter's logic is too weak, preventing the derivation of "reasonable" conclusions (such as in the disjunctive default problem) as well as cases where Reiter's logic is too strong, permitting the derivation of unwanted conclusions (for a detailed discussion of these issues, see [3]). This approach has other useful properties as well, such as semi-monotonicity, the guaranteed existence of extensions, weak orthogonality of extensions and a constructive definition for extensions. We shall briefly outline PJ-default logic and the equivalent THEORIST-based approach below. Note that our discussion of a generalized framework for anytime default inference is independent of what formalism for default reasoning we commit to. The connection with partial constraint satisfaction applies only to this class of systems and will not hold for default reasoning systems which rely on a non-constructive definition of an extension, such as Reiter's default logic [12]. Note also that we shall restrict our attention to propositional default theories in this paper.

In general, a default theory is a pair (W, D) where W is a set of *facts* and D is a set of *default rules*. Default rules are of the form $\frac{\alpha:\beta}{\gamma}$ where α is referred to as the *prerequisite*, β as the *justification* and γ as the *consequent*. A default rule is *normal* if the justification is the same as the consequent. A default rule is *semi-normal* if the justification implies the consequent. In PJ-default logic, every default rule is prerequisite-free and semi-normal. Thus every PJ-default rule is of the form $\frac{:\beta}{\gamma}$ where $\beta \vdash \gamma$. In the following $Cn(X)$ represents the deductive closure of X.

Definition 1 [3]. Let (W,D) be a prerequisite-free semi-normal default theory. Define:
$E_0 = (E_{J_0}, E_{T_0}) = (Cn(W), Cn(W))$

$E_{i+1} = (E_{J_{i+1}}, E_{T_{i+1}}) = (Cn(E_{J_i} \cup \{\beta \wedge \gamma\}), Cn(E_{T_i} \cup \{\beta\}))$
where

$i \geq 0,$
$\frac{:(\beta \wedge \gamma)}{\beta} \in D,$
$\neg(\beta \wedge \gamma) \notin E_{J_i}.$

Then E is a PJ-extension for (W,D) iff
$E = (E_J, E_T) = (\bigcup_{i=0}^{\infty} E_{J_i}, \bigcup_{i=0}^{\infty} E_{T_i}).$

In the rest of the paper, we shall refer to the E_T part of a PJ-extension as an extension.

2 A general framework

The essence of an anytime algorithm is to exploit some measure of progress towards a goal, in order to estimate the quality of a current solution at any time during the computation of a solution. In this section, we shall establish a basic framework within which anytime algorithms for default inference may be defined and analyzed. There are three key elements in this framework. First, we need to define precisely the kinds of *default inference problems* we are interested in. Second, we need to specify some notion of *solution quality* since the anytime behaviour of an algorithm relies on a guarantee that solution quality improves with time. Third, we need a clear specification of the *semantics* of partial solutions generated by an anytime algorithm. We propose here a simple but useful set of nonmonotonic reasoning solutions, which provide us with a range of problem-solving behaviours over which anytime algorithms can be defined. We shall consider *solutions* to *default inference problems* in the following sense.

Definition 2. A *solution* for a default inference problem, given a default theory (W, D), is an answer to any of the following queries:

- *Coherence:* Compute an extension of (W, D).
- *Set-membership:* Determine if a given formula is an element of any extension of (W, D).
- *Set-entailment:* Determine if a given formula is an element of all extensions of (W, D).

Having defined the classes of default inference problems we are interested in, we now need to define an operative measure of solution quality. There is no single obvious answer to the question of how the quality of solutions to default inference problems may be measured. Different intuitions may apply to different default inference problems. The appropriate measure may also be contingent on the application domain. Consider, for instance the notion of solution quality being determined by distance from the exact solution. For coherence queries, such a measure makes sense. However, for set-membership and set-entailment queries, which have true/false solutions, the notion of distance from the exact solution is ill-defined. A measure thst can be defined for all three classes of queries is one that equates solution quality with the distance of the subproblem, for which the partial solution generated by an anytime algorithm is an exact one, to the full problem. This notion of distance can be defined in a variety of different ways, as we shall see below. Let the default theory under consideration be the *exact default theory.* Then, a partial solution is considered to improve over another one if the default theory for which the former is an exact solution is "closer" to the exact default theory than the default theory for which the latter is an exact solution. Thus, an anytime procedure proceeds by considering progressively less restricted versions of the exact default theory, such that, at the limit, it considers the exact default theory. The notion of distance of a default theory from the exact default theory is determined by the restriction strategy used. In general, we can conceive of two classes of restriction strategies:

- Language restriction strategies, in which the anytime algorithm considers progressively larger subsets of the language, following a priority relation defined on the language (thus more important subsets of the language are considered before less important ones). Given a restricted subset fo the language, the algorithm considers a restriction of the exact default theory insofar as it applies to the language subset being considered. In this paper, we shall focus on a specific case of langauge restriction, namely alphabet restriction, in which progressively larger subsets of the alphabet are considered. We shall call such strategies *α-partial strategies.*
- Theory restriction strategies, in which progressively larger subsets of the exact default theory are considered, following a priority relation defined on the default theory. In this paper, we shall focus on a specific case of theory restriction, namely default restriction, in which progressively larger subsets of the set of defaults are considered. We shall call such strategies *β-partial strategies.*

A partial solution may potentially fail to take into consideration the entire set of facts W in a default theory (W, D). Informally, we shall call a partial solution *W-preserving* only if it takes into account all the constraints imposed by W in a default theory (W, D). We shall be primarily interested in W-preserving solutions, but shall point out situations where useful classes of solutions can be W-preserving only in a limited sense.

To formalize α-partial solutions, we need to define a precise notion of what it means to *restrict* a default theory based on a set of propositional letters. In the following, $\mathcal{P}$ stands for the set of propositional letters in the language $\mathcal{L}$. $\lambda((W, D))$ refers to the set of propositional letters appearing in the default theory (W, D). $D_{\mathcal{P}}$ stands for the set of possible default theories (W, D) such that $\lambda((W, D)) \subseteq \mathcal{P}$. We shall assume that every element of W as well the justifications and consequents of every default rule in D is written in conjunctive normal form.

Definition 3. A *restriction* of a default theory is a function $\mathcal{R}$: $D_{\mathcal{P}} \times 2^{\mathcal{P}} \rightarrow D_{\mathcal{P}}$ such that $\lambda(R((W, D), S)) \subseteq S$ where $(W, D) \in D_{\mathcal{P}}$ and $S \in 2^{\mathcal{P}}$, where $\mathcal{R}$ can take one of the two following forms:

- If $\mathcal{R}$ is a *strong restriction*, then for every disjunction ϕ s.t. $\phi \in W$ or $\phi \in \beta$ where $\frac{:\beta}{\gamma} \in D$ or $\phi \in \gamma$ where $\frac{:\beta}{\gamma} \in D$, if $\phi = \alpha_1 \vee \alpha_2 \vee \ldots \vee \alpha_n$ and if there exists any α_i s.t. $\alpha_i \notin S$, if α_i is a positive literal or $\neg\alpha_i \notin S$, if α_i is a negative literal, then ϕ is replaced by $\top$ in $\mathcal{R}((W, D), S)$.
- If $\mathcal{R}$ is a *weak restriction*, then for every disjunction ϕ s.t. $\phi \in W$ or $\phi \in \beta$ where $\frac{:\beta}{\gamma} \in D$ or $\phi \in \gamma$ where $\frac{:\beta}{\gamma} \in D$, if $\phi = \alpha_1 \vee \alpha_2 \vee \ldots \vee \alpha_n$ and for every α_i s.t. $\alpha_i \notin S$, if α_i is a positive literal or $\neg\alpha_i \notin S$, if α_i is a negative literal, ϕ is replaced by $\alpha_1 \vee \alpha_2 \vee \ldots \alpha_{i-1} \vee \alpha_{i+1} \vee \ldots \vee \alpha_n$ in $\mathcal{R}((W, D), S)$.

Weak and strong restrictions reflect two distinct intuitions on what it means to consider a part of a theory that relates to a subset of the set of propositional letters appearing in a theory. Strong restrictions reflect the intuition that if a propositional letter, whose truth status we are indifferent to, appears in a disjunction, then the disjunction evaluates to true by virtue of our indifference sanctioning the assumption that the propositional letter (or its negation, if it appears in the disjunction in negated form) evaluates to true. Weak restrictions reflect the intuition that if a propositional letter appears in a disjunction (in positive or negated form), then we are interested in the portion of the disjunction that does not involve this propositional letter. It appears that there are no first principles argument for preferring one form of restriction over the other. An actual choice will probably be driven by application-specific considerations.

Definition 4. An *α-partial solution* with respect to a set $S \subseteq \mathcal{P}$ for a default inference problem given a default theory (W, D) is a *solution* for a default inference problem given a default theory $\mathcal{R}((W, D), S)$.

An α-partial solution is thus a solution which considers only those portions of the default theory which involve some subset of the set of propositional letters which appear in the original default theory. An *α-partial default inference procedure*, when prematurely terminated, would return an α-partial solution with respect to the subset of the propositional letters it has been able to consider this far. Such a procedure would return better solutions if it is stopped later, since it would be able to consider a larger subset of the set of propositional letters. A priority relation defined on $\lambda((W, D))$ could define the anytime progression, with higher priority propositional letters being considered before lower priority ones. α-partial procedures are *W-preserving* in a weak sense, since they only consider W restricted to the set of propositional letters of interest.

Definition 5. A *β-partial solution* to a default inference problem, given a default theory (W, D) is a *solution* for a default inference problem given a default theory (W', D') where either $W' \subseteq W$ or $D' \subseteq D$ or both.

Thus, a β-partial solution is one which looks at some subset of the default theory, while considering the entire set of propositional letters. Usually, only W-preserving solutions are of interest, so only subsets of D are considered. A *β-partial default inference procedure*, when prematurely terminated, would return a solution which respects some subset of D. Such a procedure would return better solutions if it is stopped later, since it would be able to consider a larger subset of the set of the set of defaults. A priority relation defined on (W, D) could define the anytime progression, with higher priority defaults being considered before lower priority ones.

2.1 Anytime procedures

In this section, we present a set of generalized procedures that return α and β-partial solutions to coherence, set-membership and set-entailment queries. These procedures lay the foundations on which actual strategy for partial solution computation should be based. The formal properties of these procedures, stated at the end of this section, explicate the precise nature of rationality guarantees that each of the two classes of partial solutions provide.

We assume that a procedure called COMPUTE-EXTENSION exists, which takes a default theory and a sequence of default rules and returns exactly one extension, obtained by attempting to fire each default rule in the sequence provided. The input sequence of propositional letters in the ALPHA class of algorithms determines the order in which these letters are considered. The input sequence of default rules in the BETA class of algorithms similarly determines the order in which progressively larger subsets of default rules are considered. Notice that the procedures defined in this section do not require any commitment to weak or strong restriction functions for default theories. That decision can be guided by application-specific considerations.

Algorithm 6. *ALPHA-COHERENCE*
Input: *A default theory (W,D), a logical variable INTERRUPT and a sequence* $< l_1, l_2, \ldots, l_n >$ *containing every element of* $\lambda((W, D))$.
Output: *A set of formulas EXTENSION and a set of propositional letters* $S \subseteq \lambda((W, D))$.

> $S = \{l_1\}$; $i = 1$
> *do while NOT(INTERRUPT) and* $S \subset \lambda((W, D))$
> $S = S \cup \{l_{i+1}\}$; $i = i + 1$.
>   *EXTENSION=COMPUTE-EXTENSION*($\mathcal{R}((W, D), S)$,
> $< d_1, d_2, \ldots, d_m >$)
>   *where* $< d_1, d_2, \ldots, d_m >$)
>   *is any arbitrary permutation of the elements of D*
> *return* $< EXTENSION, S >$
> *stop*

Algorithm 7. *ALPHA-SET-MEMBERSHIP*
Input: *A default theory (W,D), a logical variable INTERRUPT, a formula F and a sequence* $< l_1, l_2, \ldots, l_n >$ *containing every element of* $\lambda((W, D))$.
Output: *A logical variable IN-EXTENSION and a set of propositional letters* $S \subseteq \lambda((W, D))$.

$S = \{l_1\};\ i = 1$
do while NOT(INTERRUPT) and $S \subset \lambda((W, D))$
  $S = S \cup \{l_{i+1}\}; i = i + 1$
  for every permutation $< d_1, d_2, \ldots, d_m >)$ *of the elements of D*
    EXTENSION=COMPUTE-EXTENSION$(\mathcal{R}((W, D), S)$,
    $< d_1, d_2, \ldots, d_m >)$
    if $\{\neg F\} \cup$*EXTENSION is unsatisfiable then*
     return $< IN - EXTENSION{=}TRUE, S >$
     stop
return $< IN - EXTENSION{=}FALSE, S >$
stop

Algorithm 8. *ALPHA-SET-ENTAILMENT* **Input:** *A default theory (W,D), a logical variable INTERRUPT, a formula F and a sequence* $< l_1, l_2, \ldots, l_n >$ *containing every element of* $\lambda((W, D))$.
Output: *A logical variable IN-ALL-EXTENSIONS and a set of propositional letters* $S \subseteq \lambda((W, D))$.

$S = \{l_1\};\ i = 1$
do while NOT(INTERRUPT) and $S \subset \lambda((W, D))$
  $S = S \cup \{l_{i+1}\}; i = i + 1$
  IN-ALL-EXTENSIONS=TRUE
  for every permutation $< d_1, d_2, \ldots, d_m >)$ *of the elements of D*
    EXTENSION=COMPUTE-EXTENSION$(\mathcal{R}((W, D), S)$,
    $< d_1, d_2, \ldots, d_m >)$
    if $\{\neg F\} \cup$*EXTENSION is satisfiable then*
     IN-ALL-EXTENSIONS=FALSE
return $< IN - ALL - EXTENSIONS, S >$
stop

Algorithm 9. *BETA-COHERENCE*
Input: *A default theory (W,D), a logical variable INTERRUPT and a sequence* $< d_1, d_2, \ldots, d_n >$ *containing every element of D.*
Output: *A set of formulas EXTENSION and a set of default rules* $S \subseteq D$.

$S = \{d_1\};\ i = 1$
do while NOT(INTERRUPT) and $S \subset D$
  $S = S \cup \{d_{i+1}\};\ i = i + 1.$
  EXTENSION=COMPUTE-EXTENSION$((W, S)$,
  $< d_1, d_2, \ldots, d_m >)$
  where $< d_1, d_2, \ldots, d_m >)$ *is any*
  arbitrary permutation of the elements of S
return $< EXTENSION, S >$
stop

Similar procedures BETA-SET-MEMBERSHIP and BETA-SET-ENTAILMENT can also be defined.

We shall use the term *arbitrary termination* to denote the setting of the input variable INTERRUPT to TRUE at any point between start and completion of an anytime algorithm. $E(W, D)$ stands for the set of extensions of the default theory (W, D).

Theorem 10. *1. Let $< EXTENSION, S >$ be the output for some arbitrary termination of the algorithm ALPHA-COHERENCE, given a default theory (W, D) and a sequence $< l_1, l_2, \ldots, l_n >$ composed of every element of $\lambda((W, D))$. Then $EXTENSION \in E(\mathcal{R}((W, D), S))$.*

2. Let $< IN - EXTENSION, S >$ be the output for some arbitrary termination of the algorithm ALPHA-SET-MEMBERSHIP, given a default theory (W, D), a formula F and a sequence $< l_1, l_2, \ldots, l_n >$ composed of every element of $\lambda((W, D))$. Then $\exists e : (e \in E(\mathcal{R}((W, D), S))) \wedge (e \models F)$.

3. Let $< IN - ALL - EXTENSIONS, S >$ be the output for some arbitrary termination of the algorithm ALPHA-SET-ENTAILMENT, given a default theory (W, D), a formula F and a sequence $< l_1, l_2, \ldots, l_n >$ composed of every element of $\lambda((W, D))$. Then $\forall e : (e \in E(\mathcal{R}((W, D), S)))$ implies $e \models F$.

4. Let $< EXTENSION, S >$ be the output for some arbitrary termination of the algorithm BETA-COHERENCE, given a default theory (W, D) and a sequence $< d_1, d_2, \ldots, d_n >$ composed of every element of D. Then $EXTENSION \in E(W, S)$.

3 Mapping default theories to partial constraint satisfaction problems

Partial constraint satisfaction techniques [4] (or PCS techniques) were developed for handling overconstrained constraint satisfaction problems. In other words, when a constraint satisfaction problem admits no solution that satisfies all the specified constraints, a partial constraint satisfaction technique will enable us to identify the "best" partial solution, where the notion of "best" can be defined using a variety of metrics. For example, one notion of the "best" partial solution could be the solution that satisfies the maximal number of constraints. Partial constraint satisfaction with this metric is often termed as *maximal constraint satisfaction*. Given the difficulty of obtaining a priori guarantees on the existence of solutions that satisfy all constraints, it is clear that PCS techniques have a broader applicability than classical CSP techniques. PCS techniques are also suitable for solving problems in resource-bounded situations, such as when the time available for computing a solution is bounded. PCS techniques can help us identify solutions that are "good enough" or "close enough" to the complete solution in the available time. Formally, a partial constraint satisfaction problem specification consists of a finite set of variables $X = \{X_1, \ldots, X_n\}$, each associated with a domain of discrete values, $D_1, \ldots, D_n$, and a set of constraints $C = \{C_1, \ldots, C_m\}$. Each constraint is a relation defined on some subset of the set of variables. Formally, a constraint C_i consists of the *constraint-subset* $S_i = \{X_{i_1}, \ldots, X_{i_{j(i)}}\}$, where $S_j \subseteq X$, denoting the subset of the variables on which C_i is defined and the *relation* rel_i defined on S_i such that

$rel_i \subseteq D_{i_1} \times \ldots \times D_{i_{j(i)}}$. We shall define a solution of a maximal constraint satisfaction problem (or a *maximal solution*) to be an assignment of legal values (i.e. values from the respective domains) to each $X_i \in X$ such that the set of satisfied constraints $C' \subseteq C$ is such that there exists no C'' where $C' \subset C'' \subseteq C$ which is also satisfied by an assignment of legal values to all variables. In this paper, we shall consider a variant of the standard PCSP formulation, which we shall refer to as *prioritized-PCSP*. In addition to the standard PCSP specification described above, a prioritized-PCSP specification contains a partial order $\succeq$ defined on the set C of constraints. We say that a constraint c is *preferred* to a constraint c' iff $c \succeq c'$. If for some $c \in C$ there exists no $c' \in C$ such that $c' \succeq c$, then c is referred to as an *essential constraint*. All elements of C which are not essential constraints are referred to as *potential constraints*. Every solution to a prioritized-PCS problem must satisfy all essential constraints, although potential constraints may be violated. A solution s to a prioritized-PCSP is said to be *preferred* over another solution s' iff there exists a constraint c satisfied by s and a constraint c' satisfied by s' such that c is preferred to c' and there exists no c'' satisfied by s' and c''' satisfied by s such that c'' is preferred to c'''. A solution s is said to be *dominant* iff there exists no other solution s' such that s' is preferred over s. In this section, we shall summarize our previous work [5] on translations from PJ-default theories to prioritized-PCSP specifications. We shall then present results relating dominant maximal solutions of these translations to the corresponding PJ-default extensions.

Definition 11 [5]. Let $PCSP_{(W,D)}$ denote the translation of a PJ-default theory (W, D) to a prioritized-PCSP specification. $PCSP_{(W,D)}$ is a 4-tuple $< X_{(W,D)}, D_{(W,D)}, C_{(W,D)}, \succeq_{(W,D)} >$ where $X_{(W,D)}$ is the set of variables, $D_{(W,D)}$ is the set of domains for each of the variables, $C_{(W,D)}$ is the set of constraints and $\succeq_{(W,D)}$ is a partial order defined on $C_{(W,D)}$.

- $X_{(W,D)}$ =Herbrand-Base$(W \cup \{\alpha \mid \frac{:\alpha\wedge\beta}{\alpha} \in D\} \cup \{\beta \mid \frac{:\alpha\wedge\beta}{\alpha} \in D\})$.
- $D_{(W,D)} = \{D_1, \ldots, D_n\}$ where each $D_i = \{True, False\}$.
- $C_{(W,D)} = \{\Omega(x) \mid x \in W\} \cup \{\Omega(\alpha \wedge \beta) \mid \frac{:\alpha\wedge\beta}{\alpha} \in D\}$, where $\Omega(x)$ is as defined in Definition 2.
- $\forall c_1, c_2 \in C_{(W,D)}$, $c_1 \succeq_{(W,D)} c_2$ iff $c_1 = \Omega(x)$ s.t. $x \in W$ and $c_2 = \Omega(\alpha \wedge \beta)$ s.t. $\frac{:\alpha\wedge\beta}{\alpha} \in D$.

Theorem 12 [5]. *Let c_s denote the subset of $C_{(W,D)}$ that is satisfied by a dominant maximal solution of $PCSP_{(W,D)}$. Let $h_{c_s} = \{\alpha \mid \frac{:\alpha\wedge\beta}{\alpha} \in D, \Omega(\alpha \wedge \beta) \in c_s\}$. Then $Th(W \cup h_{c_s})$ is an extension for the PJ-default theory (W, D).*

4 Anytime strategies based on PCS techniques

In this section, we shall attempt to delineate the space of possible anytime procedures for default inference that may be based on PCS techniques. Two observations are of interest here:

- PCS techniques based on breadth-first backtrack search correspond directly to procedures for computing α-partial solutions. Progressively larger subsets of the set of variables (and hence, via our translation, of the set of propositional letters) are considered in progressively deeper breadth-first passes through the search tree. Arbitrary termination of such procedures will return solutions which are correct with respect to the set of variables (and hence, propositional letters) considered up to the most recent complete breadth-first pass through the search tree upto a certain depth.
- PCS techniques based on heuristic repair techniques, in the sense of [8], correspond directly to procedures for computing β-partial solutions. An initial assignment of values to variables (which must be consistent with essential constraints for W-preserving solutions) is repaired by progressively considering larger subsets of the set of potential constraints (and hence, progressively larger subsets of the default rules).

This does not preclude the possibility of using heuristic repair techniques for α-partial solutions or using breadth-first backtrack search for β-partial solutions. The correspondence would not be as direct, however. For brevity, we shall present only an instance of the first class of algorithms in detail. In the following, we define an algorithm for returning α-partial solutions to default inference problems. We define a single procedure for answering the three different kinds of queries by providing as input a variable QUERY which can take on any value from {COHERENCE, MEMBERSHIP, ENTAILMENT}. The algorithm calls a procedure PCS-BFS (for partial constraint satisfaction breadth first search). *INTERRUPT* operates as a global variable that the procedure PCS-BFS refers to. We assume that the variable *SearchFrontier* contains a set of pairs, where the first element of the pair is a partial solution (i.e., a set of variable assignments) and the second element is a set of constraints that this partial solution violates. We also assume that a procedure PCSP-Translate exists for translating a default theory into a PCSP specification. We assume that the priority relation on the constraints so generated, $\preceq$ partitions the set of constraints into two classes: C_W, the set of constraints obtained from the elements of W and C_D, the set of constraints obtained from the elements of D. *MaxConstraints* is the set of subsets of C_D that correspond to a maximal solution at any point. As before, the input variable sequence can be used to represent a priority relation on the set of propositional letters in the default theory. The variable QC (for query constraint) contains the translation of the formula $\neg F$ into a constraint in the same sense as described earlier.

Algorithm 13. *ALPHA-PCS*
Input: *A default theory* (W, D), *a formula* F, *a logical variable INTERRUPT, a variable QUERY, a sequence* $< v_1, v_2, \ldots, v_n >$ *containing every element of* $\lambda((W, D))$.
Output: *A 4-tuple < EXTENSION, MEMBER, ENTAILED, VARIABLES >. EXTENSION contains some element of E(W,D) in case QUERY=COHERENCE and NIL otherwise. MEMBER=TRUE in case QUERY=MEMBERSHIP and*

$\exists e : (e \in E(W,D)) \wedge (e \models F)$. Otherwise, MEMBER=FALSE. ENTAILED=TRUE in case QUERY=ENTAILMENT and $\forall e : e \in E(W,D) \rightarrow e \models F$. Otherwise, ENTAILED=FALSE. VARIABLES contains the set of propositional letters considered in computing the current solution.

```
PCSP=PCS-Translate((W,D))
QC=PCSP-Translate(({¬F},{}))
PCS-BFS({<{},{}>},{},<v1,v2,...,vn>,{}, QUERY, PCSP)
stop

procedure PCS-BFS(SearchFrontier, MaxConstraints, VariablesRemaining,
 VariablesDone, QUERY, PCSP, QC)
 If VariablesRemaining is the empty sequence then
  return <MaxConstraints, FALSE, FALSE, VariablesDone>
  stop
 else
  for NewAssignment=v1 = TRUE, v1 = FALSE, where v1 is the
  first element of the VariablesRemaining sequence
   for each <Soln, ViolatedConstraints> ∈ SearchFrontier
    If INTERRUPT then
     return <MaxConstraints, FALSE, FALSE, VariablesDone>
     stop
    else
     NewSoln= Soln ∪ NewAssignment
     If NewSoln violates no element of C_W then
      ViolatedConstraints=subset of C_D that NewSoln violates
      NewSearchFrontier=NewSearchFrontier ∪ <NewSoln, ViolatedConstraints>
  MaximalSolns= NewSearchFrontier
  -{<S,V> | ∃ <S',V'> ∈ NewSearchFrontier s.t. V' ⊂ V}
  MaxConstraints={c | c ⊆ C_D, there exists some s ∈ MaximalSolns s.t.
  s satisfies c and there is no c' s.t. c ⊂ c' ⊆ C_D s.t. s satisfies c'}
  If QUERY=MEMBERSHIP and there exists
  <Soln, ViolatedConstraints> ∈ MaximalSolns s.t. Soln violates QC then
   return <MaxConstraints, TRUE, FALSE, VariablesDone ∪{v1}>
   stop
  elseif QUERY=ENTAILMENT and for each
  <Soln, ViolatedConstraints> ∈ MaximalSolns, Soln violates QC then
   return <MaxConstraints, FALSE,TRUE, VariablesDone ∪{v1}>
   stop
  else
   PCS-BFS(NewSearchFrontier, MaxConstraints, <v2,v3,...,vn>,
   VariablesDone ∪{v1}, QUERY, PCSP, QC)
 stop
```

Notice that the algorithm above implicitly realizes a weak restriction function for default theories.

Theorem 14. *Let* $<$ *MaxConstraints, MEMBER, ENTAILED, VariablesDone* $>$ *be the output for some arbitrary termination of algorithm ALPHA-PCS, given a default theory* (W, D).

- $E(\mathcal{R}((W,D),S)) = \{Cn(W \cup d) \mid$ *d is the subset of D corresponding to some element* $c \in$ *MaxConstraints*$\}$.
- *If QUERY=MEMBERSHIP, then MEMBER=TRUE iff* $\exists e \in E(\mathcal{R}((\mathcal{W},\mathcal{D}),\mathcal{S}))$ *s.t.* $e \models F$ *where* F *is the query formula.*
- *If QUERY=ENTAILMENT, then ENTAILED=TRUE iff* $\forall e : (e \in E(\mathcal{R}((\mathcal{W},\mathcal{D}),\mathcal{S}))) \rightarrow (\rceil \models \mathcal{F})$, *where* F *is the query formula.*

References

1. Marco Cadoli and Marco Schaerf. Approximate inference in default logic and circumscription. In *Proc. of the Tenth European Conf. on AI*, pages 319–323, 1992.
2. T. Dean and M. Boddy. An analysis of time-dependent planning. In *Proc. of the Seventh National Conf. on AI*, pages 49–54, 1988.
3. J. P. Delgrande and W. K. Jackson. Default logic revisited. In *Proc. of the Second International Conference on the Principles of Knowledge Representation and Reasoning*, pages 118–127, 1991.
4. Eugene C. Freuder and Richard J. Wallace. Partial constraint staisfaction. *Artificial Intelligence*, 58(1-3):21–70, 1992.
5. Aditya K. Ghose, Abdul Sattar, and Randy Goebel. Default reasoning as partial constraint satisfaction. In *Proc. of the Sixth Australian Joint Conference on AI*, 1993.
6. H.A. Kautz and B. Selman. Hard problems for simple default logics. In *Proc. of the First International Conference on the Principles of Knowledge Representation and Reasoning*, pages 189–197, 1989.
7. Dekang Lin and Randy Goebel. Computing circumscription of ground theories with theorist. Technical Report TR89-26, Department of Computing Science, University of Alberta, Edmonton, Canada, October 1989.
8. Steven Minton, Mark D. Johnston, Andrew B. Philips, and Philip Laird. Minimizing conflicts: a heuristic repair method for constraint satisfaction and scheduling problems. *Artificial Intelligence*, 58(1-3):161–205, 1992.
9. David Poole. A logical framework for default reasoning. *Artificial Intelligence*, 36:27–47, 1988.
10. David Poole, Randy Goebel, and Romas Aleliunas. Theorist: a logical reasoning system for defaults and diagnosis. In N.J. Cercone and G. McCalla, editors, *The Knowledge Frontier: Essays in the Representation of Knowledge*, pages 331–352. Springer Verlag, 1987.
11. Teodor C. Przymusinski. An algorithm to computer circumscription. *Artificial Intelligence*, 38(1):49–73, 1989.
12. Raymond Reiter. A logic for default reasoning. *Artificial Intelligence*, 13(1 and 2):81–132, 1980.

Studying Properties of Classes of Default Logics – Preliminary Report

Grigoris Antoniou*, Tyrone O'Neill** and Joe Thurbon***

Abstract. The study of different variants of default logic reveales not only differences but also properties they share. For example, there seems to be a close relationship between semi-monotonicity and the guaranteed existence of extensions. Likewise, *formula-manipulating* default logics tend to violate the property of cumulativity. The problem is that currently such properties must be established separately for each approach.

This paper describes some steps towards the study of properties of *classes of default logics* by giving a rather general definition of what a default logic is. Essentially our approach is operational and restricts attention to purely formula-manipulating logics. We motivate our definition and demonstrate that it includes a variety of well-known default logics. Furthermore, we derive general results regarding the concepts of semi-monotonicity and cumulativity. As a benefit of the discussion we uncover that some design decisions of concrete default logics were not accidental as they may seem, but rather they were due to objective necessities.

1 Motivation

Default Logic [15] is one of the most prominent approaches to nonmonotonic reasoning, and appears to be the most promising for practical applications. Its main idea is to allow one to draw defeasible conclusions based on 'rules of thumb' (defaults). Reiter's original work has led to the development of a broad variety of default logic variants (eg [3, 5, 7, 8, 10, 13] which follow somewhat different even though similar intuitions as the original formalism, or seek to overcome some represenational deficiencies.

Despite the obvious differences between these approaches, still they follow similar basic design decisions, therefore they share common properties. For example, as Makinson points out [11], Reiter's default logic and its variants tend to violate the property of cumulativity. But how can we make this statement more formal? The current state of the art suggests that we study each variant of default logic separately.

* School of Computing and Information Technology, Griffith University, QLD 4111, Australia, ga@cit.gu.edu.au

** Basser Department of Computer Science, University of Sydney, NSW 2006, Australia, tyrone@cs.usyd.edu.au

*** Basser Department of Computer Science, University of Sydney, NSW 2006, Australia, joet@cs.usyd.edu.au

One of the authors had a similar problem when he was giving a seminar on Reiter's default logic. Somebody from the audience asked whether there was a relationship between semi–monotonicity and the guaranteed existence of extensions, as it is the case for normal default theories. At that time the only answer could be that these properties seem to come together *for that particular logic*. Later in this paper we shall prove a much more general result which establishes a relationship between both concepts for a *class of default logics*.

Our approach is to give a general definition of default logics, and then derive some properties for some subclasses. This task is consistent with work on nonomonotonic inference relations [9, 11] and nonmonotonic rule systems (NMRS) [12]. Our work is more specific than that on nonmonotonic inference relations in that we are only interested in default logics. In a subsequent section we show that nonmonotonic rule systems which manipulate classical formulae can be embedded into our framework, since they prove to be equivalent to Reiter's default logic (see section 3). Of course NMRS cover other nonmonotonic approaches which we disregard because we focus on default logics only.

The definition of default logics is given in an operational setting. Reasons for this decision include the technical simplicity of the presentation, the inclusion of most well–known variants of default logic, and that it is straightforward to give a prototype implementation, thus allowing one to carry out experiments with yet unknown variations of the general definition.

The properties we investigate closer are semi–monotonicity and cumulativity. In particular we show that the former property tends to 'come together' with the guaranteed existence of extensions. On the other hand, we show that we cannot expect any 'reasonable' *formula–manipulating* default logic to be cumulative, neither in the skeptical approach (intersection of all extensions) nor in the credulous approach (union of all extensions). This result justifies the study of default logics that manipulate more complex objects than usual defaults; such approaches include Cumulative Default Logic [3] which manipulates assrtions, L1 [4] which includes rules applied to defaults, and approaches based on conditionals (such as [6]). But if attention is restricted to prerequisite–free default theories, some default logics do satisfy cumulativity in the skeptical approach. Throughout the paper we assume that the reader is familiar with the notation and the basic notions of predicate logic.

2 A generic definition of default logics

In order to define a class of default logics we have to answer the question what constitutes a default logic. On the syntactical side everything is clear: A *default theory* contains a set W of first–order formulae (the *facts*) and a countable set D of defaults. Further ingredients of a default theory are regarded as extralogical and fixed (for example a priority ordering on defaults or a set of constraints). Technically, a *default* δ has the form $\frac{\varphi:\psi_1,\ldots,\psi_n}{\chi}$ with closed first–order formulae $\varphi, \psi_1, \ldots, \psi_n, \chi$; φ is the *prerequisite* $pre(\delta)$, $\psi_1, \ldots, \psi_n$ the *justifications* $just(\delta)$, and χ the consequent $cons(\delta)$ of the default.

The semantics of a default theory is given in the form of *extensions*; extensions are first–order theories consisting of W and the consequents of some defaults. The next question we are faced with is how to define extensions in a general setting. Traditionally, the extension concepts for specific variants of default logic have been given using fixed–points. In the following we adopt an alternative, operational view, which has been demonstrated to be equivalent with the fixed–point view for all well–known default logic formalisms [1]. The basic motivation for this approach is the necessity for an extension to be *grounded* in the given knowledge, as opposed to, say, autoepistemic logic [14] where we have more freedom to believe or not believe in some formulae.

To determine an extension, defaults are applied in some order; an extension is reached when a sequence of default applications cannot be expanded (no further defaults can be applied) and a success condition is satisfied. According to our definition, a default logic is determined by the following two relations: (i) an *applicability relation* which determines when a default can be applied; and (ii) a *success condition* which determines when an extension has been obtained. These relations are the parameters in the generic definition given below, and determine uniquely a specific default logic variant $\mathcal{DL}$.

Let $T = (W, D)$ be a default theory, and $\Pi = (\delta_0, \delta_1, \ldots)$ a finite or infinite sequence of defaults from D without repetitions[4], modelling an application order of default from D. We denote by $\Pi[k]$ the intial segment of Π of length k, provided that the length of Π is at least k. Slightly abusing the notation, often we interpret Π as a *set* of defaults in cases where the ordering is irrelevant.

With every sequence of defaults Π we associate a set of formulae $In(\Pi)$ which is the *current knowledge base* obtained after all defaults in Π have been applied. Formally, $In(\Pi)$ is defined to be $Th(W \cup \{cons(\delta) \mid \delta \text{ occurs in } \Pi\})$. Extensions are defined in the following way:

- Π is called a *process* of the default theory T iff δ_k is applicable to Π_k, for every k such that δ_k occurs in Π.
- Π is *successful* iff $SUC(\Pi, W, D)$ is true, otherwise it is *failed*.
- Π is *closed* iff every $\delta \in D$ which is applicable to Π already occurs in Π.
- E is an *extension* of T iff there is a closed and successful process Π of T such that $E = In(\Pi)$.

Note that this definition has two parameters, the relation SUC and the applicability relation. The success relation determines when a sequence of defaults has not caused an 'a posteriori inconsistency', which means that application of a default destroys the application of a previously applied one. In Reiter's original default theory, the success condition is $In(\Pi) \cap Out(\Pi) = \emptyset$, where $Out(\Pi)$ collects the negations of the justifications of defaults in Π (see [1]). We do not impose any conditions on SUC; this way we will determine which properties are essential to derive the results in subsequent sections. The only assumption we

[4] That mean, no default occurs in Π more than once.

make is that the *order* of the defaults in Π is irrelevant for the success conditions. Furthermore we note that some properties of SUC appear to be natural, for example:

- If $\Pi \subseteq \Pi'$ and Π' is successful, then Π is successful.
- If $\Pi \neq \emptyset$ and $In(\Pi)$ is inconsistent, then Π is failed.

Now we turn to the question of the applicability of a default. Let us first recall the situation in Reiter's default logic. There, a default $\frac{\varphi:\psi_1,\ldots,\psi_n}{\chi}$ is applicable to a set of formulae E wrt a set of formulae F iff $\varphi \in E$ and $F \not\models \neg\psi_1, \ldots, F \not\models \neg\psi_n$. We make two remarks:

1. It turns out that the sets E and F are collected from sequences of defaults; for example, the set E is usually $In(\Pi)$ for some process Π (see [1]). Therefore in our general context we define an applicability relation which has sequences (or sets) of defaults as its paramters instead of E and F.
2. The role of F is a kind of 'look ahead' which is used in the fixed-point definition of extensions. It allows one to separate the consistency checks from the derivability test for the prerequisite.

So, we introduce a relation $AP'(\delta, \Pi, \Pi', W)$ to express the fact that the default δ is applicable to Π wrt Π' in a default theory with facts W. Again, we do not impose any conditions on AP' other than that Π and Π' can be considered to be sets (the order of defaults is not essential). Some conditions appear to be natural but we omit them in order to be able to identify minimal sets of conditions that are required (by the proofs we give; we do not claim that there are not other proofs with less requirements) to derive properties of default logics. Natural properties of AP' include the following:

- If $In(\Pi')$ is inconsistent then $AP'(\delta, \Pi, \Pi', W)$ is always false.
- If for some $\psi \in just(\delta)$, $\{\psi\} \cup In(\Pi')$ is inconsistent, then $AP'(\delta, \Pi, \Pi', W)$ is false.
- If the $pre(\delta) \notin In(\Pi)$, then $AP'(\delta, \Pi, \Pi', W)$ is false.

The extension definition above is operational in the sense that no 'look ahead' or 'guessing' is required to determine the extensions; in this sense, the third argument of the relation AP' is not used (in fact, AP' has only introduced because it is needed for a proof later on.), since it is always equal the second argument (that means, the consistency check is carried out wrt the current state, ie Π). Therefore we define

$$AP(\delta, \Pi, W) \Leftrightarrow AP'(\delta, \Pi, \Pi, W).$$

We say that a default δ is *applicable* to a process Π of a default theory with facts W iff $AP(\delta, \Pi, W)$ is true.

3 Comparison with other approaches

First we summarize the discussion of the previous section:

- A default logic $\mathcal{DL}$ is determined by an applcability relation AP' and a success relation SUC.
- An extension is obtained as the In–set of a closed and successful process, that is of a process which cannot be expanded by applying further defaults and which satisfies the success condition of the default logic.

This definition covers well–known default logics such as Reiter's original Default Logic [15], Justified Default Logic (JDL) [10], Constrained Default Logic (CDL) [7], Prioritized Default Logic [5] and Rational Default Logic (RDL) [13]. For example, CDL is covered using the following definitions:

$AP'(\delta, \Pi, \Pi', W)$ iff $pre(\delta) \in In(\Pi)$ and $just(\delta) \cup \{cons(\delta)\} \cup Con(\Pi')$, where $Con(\Pi) = Th(W \cup cons(\Pi') \cup just(\Pi'))$.

$SUC(\Pi, W, D)$ is always true.

In summary, our definition includes all well–known *formula–manipulating* formalisms. Important variants not covered include Cumulative Default Logic [3] and Disjunctive Default Logic [8]. Note that both approaches are not purely formula–manipulating (the former manipulates assertions, the latter extends formulae by a special disjunction operator). In fact, it *is* possible to characterize them in an operational way similar to our definition, but we decided not to complicate our definitions just to cover these logics.

The nonmonotonic rule systems (NMRS) [12] are intended as computationally oriented systems which capture the desirable features of several well known nonmonotonic reasoning formalisms (general logic programming, default logics, deductive databases, pointwise circumscription, and truth maintenance systems). Formally, a *nonmonotonic rule system* $\mathcal{S}$ is a pair (U,N) where U is the object language (the set of all object level expressions) and N is a set of nonmonotonic rules. Rules r are of the form $\frac{\varphi_1,\ldots,\varphi_n:\psi_1,\ldots,\psi_m}{\chi}$, where $\{\varphi_1, \ldots, \varphi_n\}$ are the *premises* $prem(r)$, $\{\psi_1, \ldots, \psi_m\}$ the *constraints* $constr(r)$, and χ the *conclusion* $conc(r)$ of the rule r. These correspond closely to default preconditions, justifications, and consequents respectively.

Extensions of a NMRS are defined with respect to some I $\subseteq$ U; a set S is an extension of I (for a particular NMRS) iff S contains all and only the *S-consequences* of I. An S-consequence is any element of U occurring in some *S-deduction* from I. And an S-deduction of φ from I in (U,N) is a finite sequence $(\varphi_1, \ldots, \varphi_k)$ such that $\varphi_k = \varphi$ and, for all i $\leq$ k, at least one of the following conditions hold:

(1) φ is in I.

(2) φ is the conclusion of a rule r $\in$ N such that all the premises of r are included in $\{\varphi_1, \ldots, \varphi_k\}$ and all constraints of r are in U-S[5].

The set of S-consequences of I in (U,N) is denoted C_S(I). S is an *extension* of I iff C_S(I) = S.

It is known that NMRS include Reiter's default logic as a special case. In the following we show that when NMRS are restricted to the language of classical logic ($U = For$), the converse is true, too. We use the following syntactic translation: For a rule $r = \frac{\varphi_1,\ldots,\varphi_n:\psi_1,\ldots,\psi_m}{\chi}$ we define $df(r) = \frac{\varphi_1\wedge\ldots\wedge\varphi_n:\neg\psi_1,\ldots,\neg\psi_m}{\chi}$.

Default theories are closed under classical deduction, but the only closure in NMRS is under application of defaults; any 'background' inference, classical or otherwise, must be conducted through rules. In other words, if an extension of an NMRS is closed under classical deduction, then rules to that effect must be included in the rule set. Because of this difference between default logic and NMRS, one condition is required on NMRS before a translation between the two formalisms can proceed successfully:

- *Deductive Closure:* For the nonmonotonic rule system (For,N), N contains sufficient rules such that all extensions are deductively closed under first order classical deduction.

Theorem 1 *For any deductively closed set of formulae E, E is an extension of W $\subseteq$ For in the nonmonotonic rule system (For,N) satisfying the Deductive Closure condition iff E is an extension of the default theory T=(W,df(N)) in Reiter's default logic.*

Proof: Two points must be observed before we proceed with the proof. Firstly, when translating between default logic and NMRS, the conditions for applicability can be directly translated between default rules and NMRS rules. Second, instead of using the definition of a default theory extension introduced earlier in this paper, in this proof we use the equivalent original definition of Reiter [15]. An extension of a default theory T=(W,D) is a solution E to the fixed-point equation $E = \Lambda_T(E)$, where $\Lambda_T(E)$ is the *least* set of formulae E' satisfying the following three conditions: (i) E' contains W. (ii) E' is deductively closed. (iii) With respect to E, E' is closed under all applicable $\delta \in$ D.

Let E be an extension of W for the nonmonotonic formal system (For,N). First we show that E satisfies the conditions (i)-(iii); this shows $\Lambda_T(E) \subseteq E$ since $\Lambda_T(E)$ is defined to be the least such set. Any φ contained within W is clearly present in E due to condition (1); hence E satisfies condition (i). Satisfaction of condition (ii) follows directly from the Deductive Closure assumption. Suppose $\delta = df(r)$ is applicable to E. Then, $pre(\delta) \subseteq E$ and ψ is consistent with E, for every $\psi \in just(\delta)$. Since $\delta = df(r)$ we may construct an E-deduction consisting only of E-consequences already present in E

[5] Note that the constraints of a rule are interpreted as the negation of the justifications of defaults.

and terminating in $cons(\delta) = conc(r)$; since E is an extension (in the sense of NMRS), we conclude $cons(\delta) = conc(r) \in \Lambda_T(E)$, and E satisfies (iii). This shows $\Lambda_T(E) \subseteq E$.

Now let $\chi \in E$. If $\chi \in W$ then $\chi \in \Lambda_T(E)$. Otherwise there is an E-deduction $(\chi_1, \ldots, \chi_k)$ with $\chi_k = \chi$. We show by induction on i that $\chi_i \in \Lambda_T(E)$. If $\chi_i \in W$ this is trivial. Otherwise there is a rule r such that $conc(r) = \chi_i$, $prem(r) \subseteq \{\chi_1, \ldots, \chi_{i-1}\}$ and all constraints of r are in $For-S$. Using induction hypothesis we conclude $prem(r) \subseteq \Lambda_T(E)$. Then, by definition of $df(r)$, we know that $df(r)$ is applicable to $\Lambda_T(E)$ w.r.t. E. From the definition of $\Lambda_T(E)$ we finally get $\chi \in \Lambda_T(E)$.

Conversely, let E be an extension of the default theory T = (W,df(N)). We need to show that E is an extension of W in the NMRS (For,D); we do this by demonstrating that E corresponds exactly to those φ_i satisfying at least one of conditions (1) or (2) above. φ_i satisfying condition (1) are clearly present in E due to condition (i). To show that any φ_i satisfying condition (2) is in E, we use induction on i, the length of the E-deduction ending in φ_i. Suppose that $\varphi_1, \ldots, \varphi_{i-1}$ are all in E and that φ_i satisfies condition (2); φ_i satisfies (2) because of the presence in N of some applicable rule r of which φ_i is the conclusion; but since E satisfies (iii) and $df(r)$ is applicable, φ_i is in E. Because E is minimal with respect to conditions (i)-(iii), by the above it is also minimal with respect to (1) and (2); hence E is an extension for W of the nonmonotonic rule system (For,N). -

4 Existence of extensions, semi–monotonicity and successful processes

Existence of extensions means that every default theory has at least one extension. Semi–monotonicity is the following property: If E is an extension of $T = (W, D)$, then there is an extension E' of $T' = (W, D \cup D')$ such that $E \subseteq E'$. The following result follows trivially from the definitions.

Theorem 2 *If $SUC((), W, D)$ is always true, then semi–monotonicity implies the existence of extensions.*

For the following result on semi–monotonicity we have to restrict our attention to default logics which satisfy the following conditions:

1. $AP'(\delta, \Pi, \Pi_2, W)$ and $\Pi_1 \subseteq \Pi_2$ implies $AP'(\delta, \Pi, \Pi_1, W)$.
2. If $AP(\delta, \Pi, W)$ then there is a j such that $AP'(\delta, \Pi[i], \Pi, W)$, for all $i \geq j$ such that $\Pi[i]$ is defined.
3. If $\delta' \in \Pi$, $AP(\delta', \Pi[k], W)$ and $AP'(\delta, \Pi[l], \Pi, W)$ for some $l \leq k$, then $AP(\delta', \Pi[k] \cup \{\delta\}, W)$.

Property 1 says: the further the 'look ahead' (for the consistency check) is, the more difficult AP' is to satisfy. Property 2 says that if a default is applicable to a process then there is a stage after which this default is always applicable (in Reiter's default logic this happens once the prerequisite of the default has become part of the In–set; note that the consistency check is made wrt to the *whole* process Π). Property 3 says that when a default δ is added into a process Π at a stage k with look–ahead the entire process Π, then the applicability of subsequent defaults in the process is not affected (in Reiter's default logic: If the consistency checks are made wrt the entire Π instead of locally wrt $\Pi[k]$, then the defaults $\delta_k, \delta_{k+1}, \ldots$ in Π can still be applied even when δ has been inserted before them).

These conditions are natural, and are true for logics such as Reiter's default logic, Justified, Constrained and Rational Default Logic.

Theorem 3 *Let $\mathcal{DL}$ be a default logic such that its applicability relation AP' satisfies the conditions 1–3 shown above. If all processes in $\mathcal{DL}$ are successful, then the existence of extensions and semi–monotonicity are guaranteed.*

Proof: First we prove semi–monotonicity. Our task is to transform a closed process Π of the default theory $T = (W, D)$ to a closed process Π' of $T' = (W, D \cup D')$ by adding 'new' defaults from D'. In case Π is finite we simply expand Π by applying defaults from D' until a closed process of T' is reached[6].

When faced with an infinite Π we have the problem that there is no 'end' of Π where we can start adding new defaults. The solution to this problem is to 'weave' the new defaults into Π: After each default in Π we try to apply a default from D'. We must only take care not to destroy the applicability of defaults in Π which appear *after* the insertion point. Technically we use the relation AP' to look ahead to Π. We define a process $\Gamma = (\gamma_0, \gamma_1, \ldots)$ of T' as follows:

1. Let γ_{2i} be $\delta_k \in D'$ with k minimal such that $\delta_k \notin \{\gamma_0, \ldots, \gamma_{2i-1}\}$.
2. Let γ_{2i+1} be the first default $\gamma \in D' - \{\gamma_0, \ldots, \gamma_{2i}\}$ (referring to a fixed enumeration of D') such that $AP'(\gamma, \Gamma[2i+1], \Gamma[2i+1] \cup \Pi, W)$.

The definition of Γ implies the following properties (for all i):

- $\{\delta_0, \ldots, \delta_{i-1}\} \subseteq \{\gamma_0, \ldots, \gamma_{2i-1}\}$.
- $AP(\delta_i, \Gamma[2i], W)$ (follows from property 3).
- $AP(\gamma_{2i+1}, \Gamma[2i+1], W)$ (follows from property 1 and the definition of AP).

So Γ is a process of T' containing Π as a subsequence. We conclude the proof by showing that Γ is closed. Consider $\delta \in D'$ such that $AP(\delta, \Gamma, W)$. By property 2 above $AP'(\delta, \Gamma[i], \Gamma, W)$ is true for all $i \geq j$ (for some j). Having chosen the 'first default that...' (to ensure fairness) in case 2, we are sure that δ will eventually be selected at some stage, so $\delta \in \Gamma$, and Γ is closed. Since all process are successful, $In(\Gamma)$ is an extension of T' which contains $In(\Pi)$.

[6] In case of an infinite D' we have to proceed in a *fair* way; see [1] for more details.

The existence of extensions is shown in the same way: Simply expand the empty process to a closed process. —

Note that the conditions 1–3 were only used in the proof above for the case of infinite processes. The finite case is even simpler.

Corollary 4 *Let T be a finite default theory. If all processes of T in the default logic $\mathcal{DL}$ are successful then the existence of extensions and semi-monotonicity are guaranteed.*

Up to now we have not related SUC with AP'. If we do so we can give a very simple condition for all processes of the default logic $\mathcal{DL}$ represented by SUC and AP' to be successful.

Observation 5 *Suppose that $\mathcal{DL}$ is a default logic such that*

(a) $SUC((), W, D)$, *and*

(b) $SUC(\Pi, W, D)$ *and* $AP(\delta, \Pi, W)$ *implies* $SUC(\Pi \circ \delta, W, D)$.

Then all processes in $\mathcal{DL}$ are successful.

5 On the cumulativity of default logics

Cumulativity is the property that ensures the safe use of lemmas. To be precise:

- A default logic is *cumulative in the skeptical approach* if the following is true: If the formula φ is included in all extensions of a default theory (W, D), then for all formulae ψ, ψ is included in all extensions of (W, D) iff it is included in all extensions of $(W \cup \{\varphi\}, D)$.
- A default logic is *cumulative in the credulous approach* if the following is true: If the formula φ is included in an extension of a default theory (W, D), then for all formulae ψ, ψ is included in an extension of (W, D) iff it is included in an extension of $(W \cup \{\varphi\}, D)$.

5.1 A negative result

There is a wide–spread view that default logics which follow the basic design decisions of Reiter's original presentation will violate cumulativity; this can be found in [11], for example. Now we are ready to substantiate this view by a formal result. It says that under some simple and natural conditions, all default logics in our framework violate cumulativity. The conditions we have in mind are the following:

1. If for some $\psi \in just(\delta)$, $In(\Pi) \cup \{\psi\}$ is inconsistent, then $AP(\delta, \Pi, W)$ is false.
2. If $pre(\delta) \notin In(\Pi)$ then $AP(\delta, \Pi, W)$ is false.

3. For a normal default δ: If $pre(\delta) \in Th(W)$ and $just(\delta) \cup W$ is consistent, then $AP(\delta, \Pi, W)$ and $SUC((\delta), W, D)$.

The first two conditions are very natural and reflect the very idea of a default. The third condition is somewhat more controversial but is reasonable as well. It says that if we look at the first default, then the 'standard' default interpretation should lead to a successful process, provided the default is normal. The standard interpretation of a normal default reads as follows:

If φ is currently known, and if we may assume χ, then conclude χ.

The variety of default logics stems from the different interpretation of the informal terms 'currently known' and 'we may assume', because the current knowledge state is influenced by the previous application of other defaults. *But,* if we restrict attention to the first step and consider normal defaults (which assume exactly the conclusion they draw), then the condition is far less controversial. In fact, it is satisifed by DL, JDL, CDL and RDL[7].

Theorem 6 *Consider a default logic $\mathcal{DL}$ satisfying the conditions 1–3 above. Then $\mathcal{DL}$ is not cumulative in the skeptical or the credulous approach.*

Proof: Let $W = \emptyset$ and $D = \{\delta_0 = \frac{true:p}{p}, \delta_1 = \frac{p\vee q:\neg p}{\neg p}\}$. By condition 3, δ_0 is applicable to (), and (δ_0) is a successful process. By condition 1, $AP(\delta_1, (\delta_0), W)$ is false, so (δ_0) is closed and successful, and $E = Th(\{p\})$ an extension of (W, D). By condition 2, this is the only extension.

Now consider $W' = \{p \vee q\}$. By condition 3, (δ_0) is a successful process of (W', D); also it is closed using property 1. By the same arguments, (δ_1) is a closed and successful process of (W', D). So there are two extensions, $Th(\{p\})$ and $Th(\{\neg p, q\})$.

Violation of cumulativity in the skeptical approach follows from the observation that p is included in all extensions of (W, D) but not in all extensions of (W', D). Violation of the cumulativity in the credulous approach follows from the observation that $\neg p$ is included in an extension of (W', D) but not in an extension of (W, D). —

This result is a strong indication that if cumulativity is desired, we should turn attention to default logics which are not simply formula manipulating. Such approaches include Cumulative Default Logic which manipulates assertions and is cumulative in the skeptical appraoch, and Brewka's $L1$ [4] which uses inference rules acting on defaults and is cumulative both in the skeptical and the credulous approach [2].

---

[7] PDL violates this condition due to the priority relation. Also, preconstrained default logics may violate it as well. It is not difficult to see that such logics can be covered by weakening condition 3 to work for *some* cases only (for some priority relation or some sets of constraints). Then the proof of the following theorem goes through as well. We disregard this possibility to keep the conditions simple and intuitively clear.

5.2 A positive result

After the negative result of the previous subsection, we give here a positive counterpart. It says that if we restrict attention to prerequisite–free default theories (the prerequisite of all defaults is the formula *true*), there are cases of default logics (such as JDL and CDL) that satisfy cumulativity in the skeptical approach. Consider the class of default logics whose pre–requisite free theories satisfy the following conditions:

(a) If $\varphi \in \text{In}(\Pi)$ then $(AP(\delta, \Pi, W) \leftrightarrow (AP(\delta, \Pi, W \cup \{\varphi\}))$

(b) If $AP(\delta, \Pi, W)$ and $W' \subseteq W$ then $AP(\delta, \Pi, W')$

(c) All processes are successful.

Condition (a) is a weak condition which holds for all of the well known default logics. Condition (b) is appropriate only for prerequisite–free default theories. The third condition is strong but acceptable in the context of prerequisite–free defaults. The result we need is a direct consequence of the following theorem.

Theorem 7 *Let $\mathcal{DL}$ be a default logic satisfying conditions (a)–(c) above. Let T=(W,D) be a default theory such that D contains only prerequisite–free defaults. Let φ be a formula that is contained in all extensions of T, and consider the default theory T'=(W$\cup\{\varphi\}$,D). Then E is an extension of T iff E is an extension of T'.*

Proof: Since the In–Set of an extension Π is defined with respect to a particular default theory T=(W,D), in this proof we shall refer to such an In–Set as $In_T(\Pi)$.

Let E be an extension of T. Then there is a closed and successful process Π of T such that E=$In_T(\Pi)$. By condition (a) Π is a process of T'. By condition (c), Π is successful with respect to T'. Again by condition (1), only the defaults $\delta \in \Pi$ are applicable in T', hence Π is closed with respect to T'. Hence $In_{T'}(\Pi)$ is an extension of T.

Conversely, let E be an extension of T'. Then there is a closed and sucessful process Π' of T' such that E=$In_{T'}(\Pi')$. By condition (b), Π' is a process of T, and by condition (c) it is successful. Suppose for the purposes of *reductio ad absurdum* that Π' was not closed. Then, by condition (2), Π' can successfully be expanded to closed by adding to Π' one or more defaults $\delta \in$D (the limiting case being Π'=D). Let δ be the first of the defaults added to Π' in this expansion; then, by condition (1), $AP(\delta, \Pi', W \cup \{\varphi\})$ is true. But, because Π' is closed, $AP(\delta, \Pi', W \cup \{\varphi\})$ is false. Hence Π' is closed in T' and T, and E is an extension of T. —

Corollary 8 *Let $\mathcal{DL}$ be a default logic satisfying conditions (a)–(c) above. Let φ be a formula that is contained in every extension of a prerequisite–free default theory T=(W,D). Then, for every formula ψ, ψ is contained in all extensions of T iff ψ is contained in all extensions of T'=(W$\cup\{\varphi\}$),D).*

6 Conclusion and future work

This paper is a preliminary report on the study of properties of classes of default logics. We gave a definition of a default logic, discussed the motivation and compared it with existing concrete formalisms and with Nonmonotonic Rule Systems. Further we derived results which formalize some views that have been around in the literature for quite a while: (i) Default logics following Reiter's tradition tend to violate cumulativity. (ii) Default logics may satisfy cumulativity in the skeptical approach if we restrict attention to prerequisite–free defaults. (iii) The properties of semi–monotonicity and the existence of extensions tend to coincide for default logics.

We intend to continue this work. For example, we shall substantiate Makinson's claims that default logics tend to violate cautious monotony [11].

References

1. G. Antoniou. *Nonmonotonic Reasoning with Incomplete Information.* MIT Press 1996 (forthcoming)
2. G. Antoniou. Abstract properties for the choice provability relation in nonmonotonic logics. *Computers, Cognition and Artificial Intelligence* 12, 3 (1995)
3. G. Brewka. Cumulative default logic: in defense of nonmonotonic inference rules. *Artificial Intelligence* 50,2 (1991): 183–205
4. G. Brewka. *A Framework for Cumulative Default Logics.* TR–92–042, International Computer Science Institute, Berkeley 1992
5. G. Brewka. *Adding priorities and specificity to default logic.* Technical Report, GMD 1993
6. J.P. Delgrande. A first–order conditional logic for prototypical applications. *Artificial Intelligence* 33,1 (1987)
7. J.P. Delgrande, T. Schaub and W.K. Jackson. Alternative Approaches to default logic. *Artificial Intelligence* 70 (1994): 167–237
8. M. Gelfond, V. Lifschitz, H. Przymusinska and M. Truszczynski. Disjunctive Defaults. In *Proc. 2nd International Conference on Principles of Knowledge Representation and Reasoning,* Morgan Kaufmann 1991
9. S. Kraus, D. Lehmann and M. Magidor. Nonmonotonic Reasoning, Preferential Models and Cumulative Logics. *Artificial Intelligence* 44 (1990): 167–207
10. W. Lukaszewicz. Considerations of default logic: an alternative approach. *Computational Intelligence* 4,1(1988): 1–16
11. D. Makinson. General patterns in nonmonotonic reasoning. In *Handbook of Logic in Artificial Intelligence and Logic Programming* Vol. 3, Oxford University Press 1994
12. W. Marek, A. Nerode and J.B. Remmel. Nonmonotonic Rule Systems I. *Annals of Mathematics and Artificial Intelligence* (1990): 241–273
13. A. Mikitiuk and M. Truszczynski. Constrained and rational default logics. In *Proc. International Joint Conference on Artificial Intelligence* 1995
14. R.C. Moore. Semantical considerations on non–monotonic logic. *Artificial Intelligence* 25 (1985): 75–94
15. R. Reiter. A logic for default reasoning. *Artificial Intelligence* 13(1980): 81–132

Learning Cooperative Behavior in Multi-agent Environment

— a case study of choice of play-plans in soccer —

NODA Itsuki[1], MATSUBARA Hitoshi[1] and HIRAKI Kazuo[1]

Electrotechnical Laboratory, Tsukuba, Ibaraki 305, Japan

Abstract. *Soccer*, association football, is a typical team-game, and is considered as a standard problem of multi-agent system and cooperative computation. We are developing Soccer Server, a simulator of soccer, which provides a common test-bench to evaluate various multi-agent systems and cooperative algorithms. We are working on learning cooperative behavior in multi-agent environment using the server. In this article, we report a result of case study of learning selection of play-plans in multi-agent environment.

Keywords: Multi-agent System, Machine Learning, Neural Networks

1 Introduction

Soccer, the association football, is a typical team-game, in which each player is required to play cooperatively. Moreover, soccer is a real-time game in which situation changes dynamically. Because of those features, soccer can be considered as a standard problem of multi-agent systems and cooperative algorithms. We have developed Soccer Server, a simulator of soccer games, to provide a common test-bench to evaluate various multi-agent systems and cooperative algorithms. Using the server, a team of players written any kinds of programming system with facilities of UDP/IP can play a match with another team written another kind of systems.

We are working on learning cooperative behavior in multi-agent environment using the server. In this article, we show a result of learning of selection of play-plans in a simple situation of two-on-one in front of a goal on the server.

2 Soccer Game as a Standard Problem

From the standpoint of multi-agent systems, soccer (association football), which is just one of typical team sports, make a good example of problems in the real world that is moderately abstracted. Multi-agent systems provides us with research subjects such as cooperation protocol by distributed control and effective communication, while having advantages as follows:

- efficiency of cooperation

- adaptation
- robustness
- real-time

Soccer has the following characteristics:

- Robustness is more important than elaboration. A team should take a fail-safe strategies, because play-plans and strategies may fail by accidents.
- Adaptability is required for dynamic change of plans according to the operations of the opposing team.
- Team play is advantageous.
- A match is uninterrupted. Each player is required to plan in real-time, because it is difficult to make a whole plan before plays.
- As precise communication by language is not expected, effectiveness must be provided by combining simple signals with the situation.

These characteristics show that soccer is an appropriate example for evaluation of multi-agent systems. Various examples have been used to evaluate performance of multi-agent systems, but such examples are simple and small. Soccer is complex and large, so it is suitable to evaluate them in the large scale. Moreover, because soccer has a long history and is familiar to many people, there are many techniques and strategies that may be also useful for multi-agent systems. Recently, soccer has been used as an example on real robots as well as software simulators [1, 4, 3, 5]. Many of those experiments, however, have their own ways of setting, which makes it difficult to make a comparison among them. For satisfying the need for a common setting, we are developing *Soccer Server*[2]. Adaptation of this soccer server as a common setting makes it possible to compare various algorithms on multi-agent systems in the form of a game. Soccer Server is being used by many researchers, and was chosen as the official simulator for RoboCup 97, an international competition of robotic soccer held in IJCAI '97 at Nagoya.

3 Soccer Server

Soccer Server provides a virtual soccer field, in which players controlled by clients run and kick a ball. Figure 1 and Figure 2 show its window images.

Soccer Server consists of 3 modules: a field simulator module, a referee module and a message-board module (Figure 3). The field simulator module calculates movements of objects on the field and checks collisions among them. The referee module controls a game according to rules. The message-board module manages communication among clients.

A client connects with the server by a UDP socket. The server assigned a player to the client. Using the socket, the client sends commands to control its player and receives information from sensors of the player. Basically, each client can control only one player [1], so that the server connects with 22 clients at most [2]. All communication between the server and each client is done using by ASCII strings.

3.1 Simulator

The soccer field and all objects on it are 2-dimensional. The size of the field is decided according to the official size of rules of human soccer: The length is 105 and the width is 68. The width of goals is doubled, that is 14.64, because 2-dimensional simulation makes it difficult to get goals.

Simulation of movements is simplified. Movements of objects are simulated stepwise one by one. Noise is added to each movement according to the speed of the object. If a object overlaps another object, that is, collides with another object after its movement, the object is moved back until it does not overlap other objects. Then its velocity is multiplied by -0.1.

3.2 Protocol

All communication between the server and each client is done using by ASCII strings. An unit of communication is an S-expression. Protocols of communication between the server and a client is as follows.

Control Command A client can send the following commands to control its player.

- `(turn` *Moment*`)`
  Change the direction of the player according to *Moment*. *Moment* should be $-180 \sim 180$. Actual change of the direction is reduced when the player is moving fast.
- `(dash` *Power*`)`
  Increase the velocity of the player toward its direction according to *Power*. *Power* should be $-30 \sim 100$.
- `(kick` *Power Direction*`)`
  Kick the ball by *Power* to the *Direction* if the ball is near enough. *Power* should be $-30 \sim 100$, and *Direction* shoule be $-180 \sim 180$.
- `(say` *Message*`)`
  Broadcast *Message* to all players. *Message* is informed immediately to clients using a `(hear ...)` format described below.

Sensor Information A client gets two kinds of sensor information about the field from the server, visual and auditory information. The visual and auditory information are informed by **see** and **hear** messages respectively.

---

[1] Technically, it is easy to cheat the server. Therefore this is a gentleman's agreement.

[2] In order to test various kind of systems, we may permit a client controls multi-players when each control module of a player is separated logically from each other in the client.

- **(see** *Time ObjInfo ObjInfo* ...**)**
  Inform visual information. *Time* indicates the internal time(step-cycles of simulation). *ObjInfo* is information about a visible object, whose format is:
  (*ObjName Distance Direction*)
  ObjName ::= **(player** *Teamname UNum*) | **(goal** *Side*) | **(ball)**
  | **(flag [l|c|r] [t|b])** | **(line [l|c|r|t|b])**
  As the distance to a player increases, more information about the player is lost. Actually, *UNum* is lost in the case of farther than a certain distance, and *Teamname* is lost in the case of very far.
  This message is sent 2 times per second. (The frequency may be changed.)
- **(hear** *Time Direction Message*)
  Inform auditory information. This message is sent immediately when a client sends **(say** *Message*) command. *Direction* is the direction of the sender. *Time* indicates the current time.
  Judgements of the referee is also informed using this form. In this case, *Direction* is '**referee**'.

3.3 Coach Mode

In order to make it easy to set-up a certain situation, Soccer Server has a coach mode. In this mode, a special client called 'coach' can connect to the server, who can move any players and the ball. This mode is useful for learning and debugging client programs.

3.4 Implementation

Soccer Server is implemented using g++ and X-window system with Athena widget-set. Currently, I support SunOS 4.1.x, Solaris 2 and DEC OSF/1. I am planning to support other OSs and architectures.

Programs of the soccer server are available by FTP:

ftp://ci.etl.go.jp/pub/soccer/server/sserver-2.70.tar.gz

Home page of the soccer server is:

http://ci.etl.go.jp/~noda/soccer/server.html

We also have a mailing list about Robo-Cup:

rjl@csl.sony.co.jp

4 Learning Choice of Plan

4.1 Selection of Play in Soccer

In the case of dynamical environment like soccer, an agent must select a plan from many candidates reactively. Furthermore, in a multi-agent system, the agent

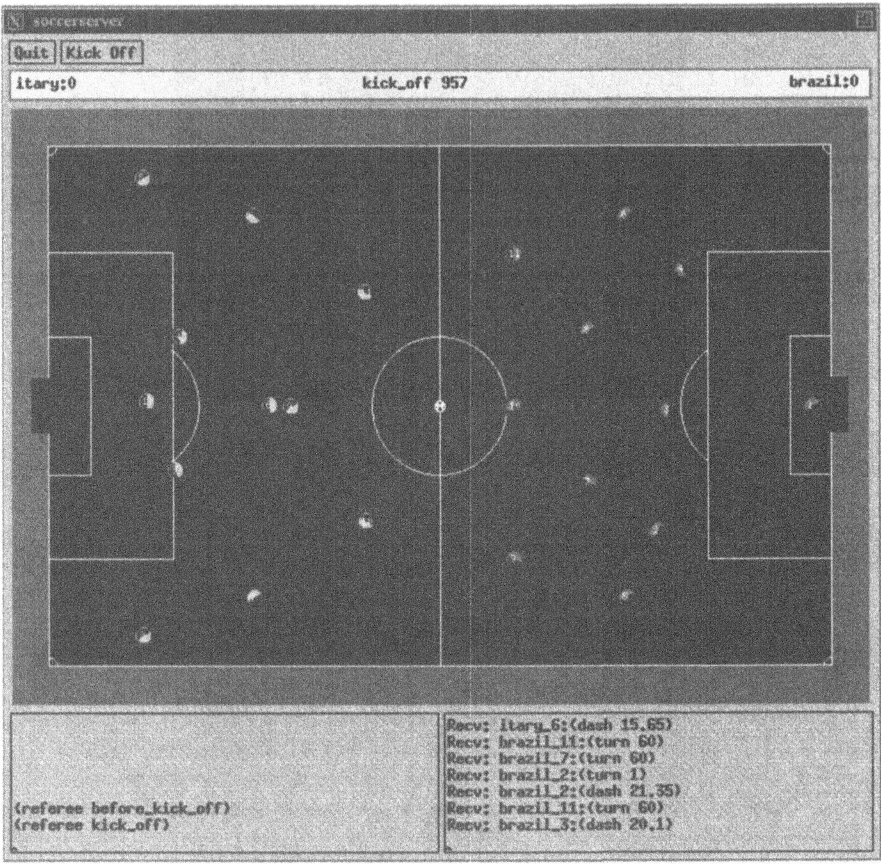

Fig. 1. Window Image of Soccer Server

must consider about behaviors and performances of other agents. In such case learning is necessary, because it is difficult to write down all rules to select plans in such complex environment.

Let's consider a situation that an offensive player attacks the opponent goal with a teammate against an opponent player (Figure 4). This is a simple but typical situation which requires cooperative play. The offensive player can shoot the ball to the goal directly, or can pass the ball to the teammate. Generally, reasonable rules to select these plans are as follows:

- If the opponent player cuts shoot-courses, the offensive player should pass the ball to the teammate.
- If the opponent player cuts pass-courses, the offensive player should shoot the ball directly.

However, it remains a problem how to define conditions of 'cutting-shoot-courses'

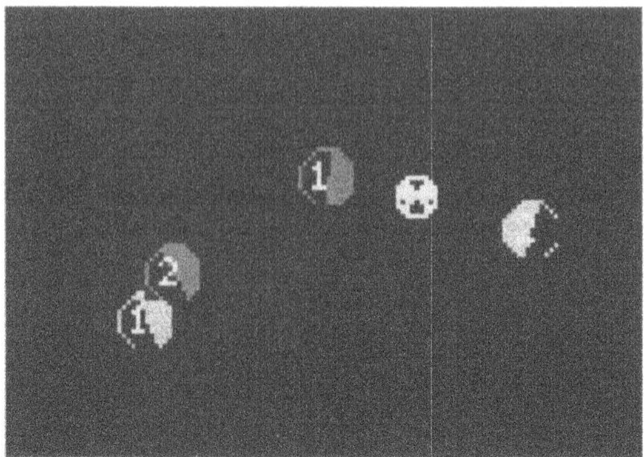

Fig. 2. Close-up of Players and a Ball

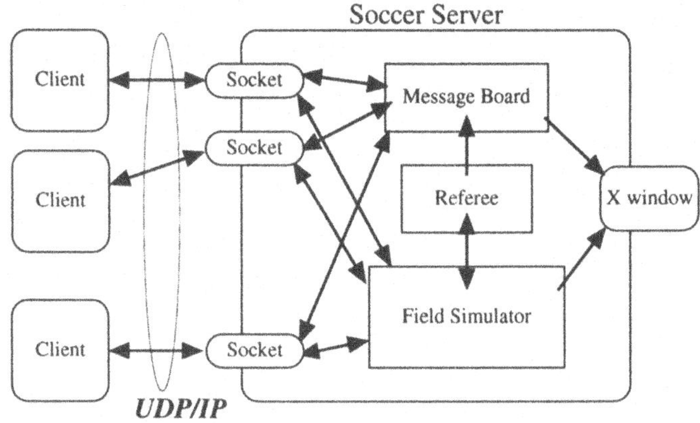

Fig. 3. Overview of Soccer Server

and 'cutting-pass-courses', which requires complex models of the players. In order to acquire such conditions and models, we applied learning by neural networks.

4.2 Experiment

We carried out an experiment as follows:

- The three players are set randomly in a penalty area.
- The opponent player is programed to keep the position between the ball and the goal.
- The teammate is programed to wait the pass and shoot the ball.
- The offensive player is programed as follows:

1. Collect information about positions of all objects (players, ball and goal).
2. Input the information to the neural network.
3. Receive the output of the network.
4. Choose one of 'pass' and 'shoot' plans according to the output of the neural networks.

- The neural network consists of 8 input-units, 30 hidden-units and 2 output-units. The network receives relative positions of the objects, and outputs two values, O_{pass} and O_{shoot}, which indicate expected success rate of pass and shoot plans. Initially, weights of connections in the network are set randomly, so that the network outputs arbitrary values before learning.
- The offensive player chooses pass or shoot plans according to the rate of O_{pass} and O_{shoot}: The probability of choosing the pass-plan is $O_{\text{pass}}/(O_{\text{pass}} + O_{\text{shoot}})$.
- A coach (teacher) informs 'nice' to all players when the offending team gets a goal, and 'fail' when the ball is out of the field or time is over.

Initially, we ran the players 1000 times with the initialized neural networks, and recorded data of situations that include positions of objects and final judgement of the coach ('pass' or 'fail'). Using the data, we trained the networks to output expected success rates of both plans correctly by the back-propagation method. Finally we ran again the players with the trained neural network.

Table 1 shows the rates of successes and failures of both plans before and after the learning. We can see that success rates of both plans are remarkably improved. Figure 5 shows changes of outputs of the neural networks for directions to the opponent player. In this graph, the curve of 'shoot' goes down when the opponent player is near to the goal. On the other hand, the curve of 'pass' goes down when the opponent player is in the side of the teammate. These responses implicitly reflect the rules to select plans described above: The area where the 'shoot'-curve goes down is the situation the opponent player cuts shoot-courses, while the area where the 'pass'-curve goes down is the situation the opponent player cuts pass-courses or marks the receiver. Because the network acquired such conditions suitably, the offensive team improved the success-rate.

Moreover, we found that the network also reflects models of other players suitably. Figure 6 shows changes of the output of 'shoot' for the distance and the direction of the opponent player. In this graph, the surface forms a valley along the direction of the goal, and the width of the bottom of the valley becomes narrow when the distance to the opponent player increases. This means that the opponent player has a fixed cover area, whose apparent angle becomes small when the opponent player is away from the offensive player.

5 Conclusion

In this article, we reported Soccer Server and an experiment of learning selection of play-plans on the server. The result of the experiment showed that simple learning technique of neural networks is useful to acquire models of other agents

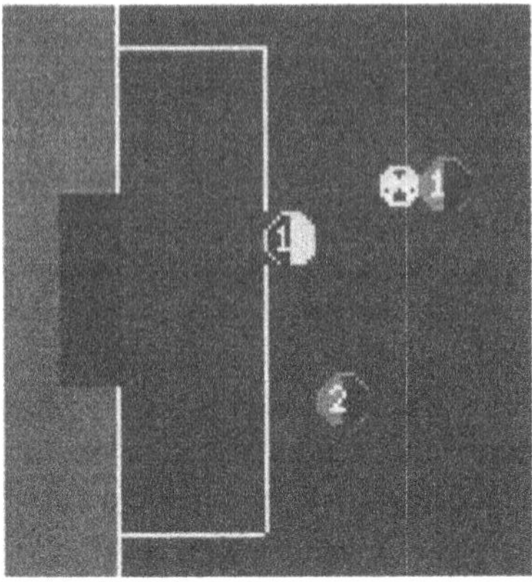

Fig. 4. A Situation of 2 on 1

Table 1. Success Rate of Shoot and Pass Plans

Before Learning			
	pass	shoot	total
nice	247(55.6%)	231(41.5%)	478(47.8%)
fail	197(44.4%)	325(58.5%)	522(52.2%)
total	444	556	1000
After Learning			
	pass	shoot	total
nice	327(74.3%)	353(63.0%)	680(68.0%)
fail	113(25.7%)	207(37.0%)	320(32.0%)
total	440	560	1000

and environment, and to improve the total performance. It is difficult to use acquired models directly for symbolic planning of sequences of plays, because such models are represented implicitly. It is also a problem that it is difficult to apply such neural networks to higher levels of decision making. However, these problems may be overcome by combining symbolic and neural planing using back-propagation as feedback[7, 6].

The experiment described in this article was done as a first step of a study of learning cooperative behavior. Cooperation was not a major part in this experiment. We, however, established the experiment to be easy to extend cooperative learning, and we are planning further experiment in which all players learn their mechanisms to select plans simultaneously.

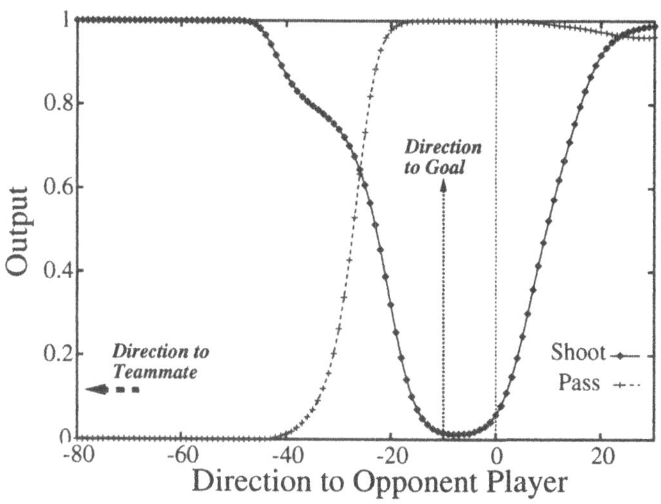

Fig. 5. Change of Network Output for Direction to Opponent Player

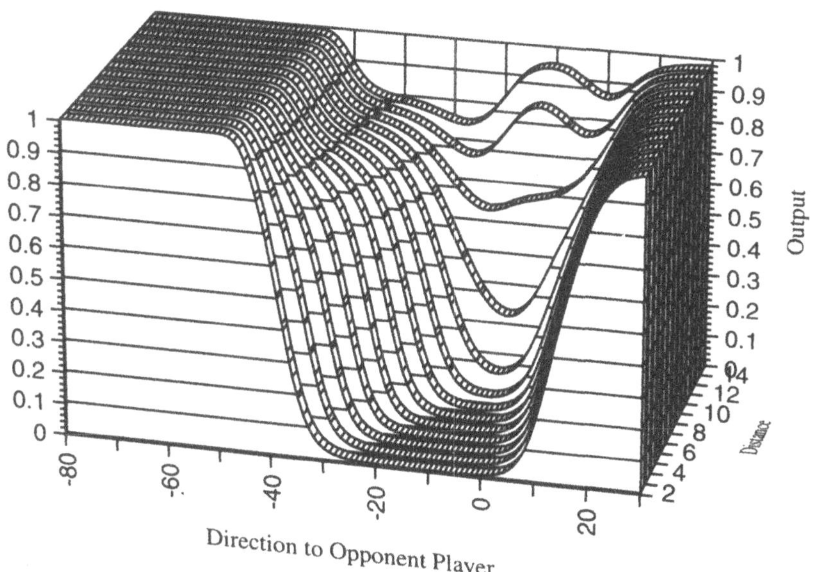

Fig. 6. Change of Shoot-Output for Distance and Direction to Opponent Player

References

1. Minoru Asada, Shoichi Noda, and Koh Hosoda. Non-physical intervention in robot learning based on lfe method. In *Proc. of Machine Learning Conference Workshop on Learning from Examples vs. Programming by Demonstration*, 1995.
2. Hiroaki Kitano, Minoru Asada, Yasuo Kuniyoshi, Itsuki Noda, and Eiichi Osawa. Robocup: The robot world cup intiative. In *Working Notes of IJCAI Workshop: Entertainment and AI/Alife*, pages 19–24, Aug. 1995.
3. M. K. Sahota. Reactive delivation: an architecture for real-time intelligent control in dynamic environments. In *Proc. of AAAI-94*, pages 1303–1308, 1994.
4. Mickael K. Sahota. Real-time intelligent behaviour in dynamic environments: Soccer-playing robots. matster thesis, Department of Computer Science, The University of British Columbia, Aug. 1993.
5. P. Stone and M. Veloso. Learning to pass or shoot: collaborate or do it yourself, 1995. unpublished manuscript.
6. J. Tani and N. Fukumura. Learning goal-directed sensory-based navigation of a mobile robot. *Neural Networks*, 7(3):553–563, 1994.
7. Yasuhiro Wada and Mitsuo Kawato. A neural network model for arm trajectory formation using forward and inverse dynamics models. *Neural Networks*, 6:919–932, 1993.

CiFi: An Intelligent Agent for Citation Finding on the World-Wide Web

Seng W. Loke, Andrew Davison and Leon Sterling

Department of Computer Science
The University of Melbourne
Parkville, Victoria 3052, Australia
email: {swloke,ad,leon}@cs.mu.oz.au

Abstract. The Web is an invaluable resource for finding citations and publications. This paper describes CiFi, a rule-based agent which autonomously finds citations on the Web, using multiple search strategies, and multiple Web-based information sources. CiFi performs heuristic-guided automated browsing, utilising the Lycos search engine to find starting points for browsing.

1 Introduction

The World-Wide Web is expanding at an exponential rate, and has become an important tool for information dissemination. Researchers are making their publications available on the Web from their home pages, university technical report pages, and technical report archives. Conference proceedings are appearing on the Web, and extensive bibliographic archives are already available on-line.

On-line citations, which often have links to the whole paper, are an invaluable resource for completing bibliography entries, and for obtaining papers. For example, a paper may have first been available as a technical report, but was later published in some conference proceedings. Because technical reports are less easily attainable, it is more useful to have the paper cited as published in the proceedings than as a technical report. Moreover, authors may want to look for papers on the Web, and cite their URLs[1], even when they can cite the papers as appearing in some hard-copy conference proceedings, or as technical reports. There is, therefore, a need to locate the desired citations or papers on the Web.

Intelligent software agents[4, 6], which perform tasks on behalf of the user, with a degree of autonomy and reasoning capability, are an important paradigm for information discovery and retrieval on the Web. The rapidly expanding Web, which makes browsing very time-consuming, has motivated the need for programs that automatically search for information.

Current approaches for information discovery on the Web include querying pre-computed indexes. The indices are generated by indexing agents that traverse the Web "off-line", indexing Web pages based on the words they contain. Keywords can be submitted to these search engines to recover links to documents

[1] URL stands for Uniform Resource Locator, which uniquely identifies a Web page.

indexed by the keywords. Inktomi[2], Alta Vista[3], and Lycos[4] are examples of this approach.

Indexing agents aim to index as much of the Web as possible. For instance, Lycos claims more than 90 percent coverage of the Web. However, search engines do not take the user directly to the specific piece of information sought, but to documents that possibly contain the required information. These documents become the starting points for browsing.

Our aim is twofold:

- To build an agent that is in the category of "concierge" [4]. This means that the user supplies only the author's name and the title of the paper, and delegates the search for the citation or HTML[5] paper to the agent. Our focus is on Computer Science (CS) technical publications.
- To investigate the use of logic programming rules for building an information retrieval agent which navigates over the Web guided by heuristics. To express the rules, we utilise the treatment of a Web page as a logic program module called *LogicWeb*, as introduced in [8]. A LogicWeb page or module is a Web page which has rules and facts.

In the rest of the paper, we first determine the effectiveness of Lycos and Alta Vista for finding citations by attempting a set of queries. Then, we describe a rule-based agent called CIFI which utilises the Lycos search engine, coupled with automated browsing.

§2 discusses searching for citations, or for the HTML version of papers using search engines and browsing. §3 describes the design and implementation of CIFI. In §4, we evaluate the current implementation of CIFI, discussing its efficacy and limitations. §5 reviews related work. Possible improvements and future extensions to CIFI are discussed in §6. §6 concludes.

2 Looking for Citations on the World-Wide Web

2.1 Querying Search Engines

In searching for a citation, an immediate approach is to use the author's name (i.e., first name and last name) and the title as search keywords. Lycos often returns the HTML paper as its first hit, provided the HTML version of the paper is available, and the title of the document is the title of the paper. However, there is greater chance of a citation to a paper existing on the Web than the actual paper itself.

A Lycos search is often less effective when only citations exist to a particular paper on the Web. In nine of the fifteen Lycos queries attempted, the first

[2] http://inktomi.berkeley.edu/

[3] http://www.altavista.digital.com/

[4] http://www.lycos.com/

[5] HTML stands for HyperText Markup Language, and is the standard language with which Web pages are written.

ten pages returned often contained the various keywords, but not the required citation. A fundamental reason for this is that the amount of page information kept in the Lycos index is insufficient.

Alta Vista employs full-content indexing which, together with its use of keyword proximity for document ranking, its large database, and its facility for stating that pages returned must contain particular keywords, makes it effective for retrieving pages containing a required citation. Alta Vista returned a page containing the paper citation among its first ten hits, often in the first place, for fourteen of the same fifteen queries used for Lycos above.

Although Alta Vista performs very impressively at the moment, search engines of its kind have some fundamental drawbacks:

- Keeping the index up-to-date is difficult, especially faced with the increasing size and growth rate of the Web. For instance, it may take several days for the index entry on a page to be added or updated. This means that a new page may contain a citation, but the old version, indexed by the search engine, does not. Alternatively, a page may have been moved or renamed since it was last indexed, so that the search engine returns an old URL. In general, search engines will always have problems returning timely information.
- Indexing on every (uncommon) word in a page means that the search engine's index will be huge.
- If the keywords (e.g., title and author name) happen to be quite common words, then many useless documents will be returned.
- It is often difficult to determine, from the information returned by the search engine, if a page contains the citation.
- The indexing agents do not index databases with their own search facilities (e.g., the *Unified Computer Science Technical Reports*[6] archive).

2.2 Querying Search Engines and Browsing

A solution to these drawbacks is to combine the search engine results with more extensive conventional browsing, guided by search heuristics tuned for finding citations.

Empirical evidence suggests that author's home pages, author's publications pages linked from author home pages, and departmental publications pages are the main sources of citations. Also, if the author's home page can be obtained, then the other types of pages can usually be found. For instance, the URL of the CS departmental page can usually be extracted from the URL of the author's home page.

Thus, our approach will use a search engine to find the author's home page and then use search heuristics like the one outlined above to guide browsing until the citation is found.

This method has the following advantages:

[6] http://www.cs.indiana.edu/cstr/search

- There is a degree of resilience to change, since it relies only on the home page being indexed. Changes inside the home page, or changes in the location and content of the publications pages can be accommodated, since these pages are accessed in real-time, instead of being found via indexed information.
- It does not rely on indexing on every (uncommon) word of a page. At the moment, search engines such as Alta Vista build indexes using the full text of a page. This approach is not scalable and will soon become impractical given the growth and volatility of the Web. It is more reasonable to expect an index to contain meta-information about, or a summary of, a page. The home page of an author can often be identified using information of this kind.
- Search engines generally do well in retrieving home pages given an author's first and last name. Also, the home page can often be identified easily among the other pages returned by a search. Search engines specialised for people's home pages can also be used[7].
- Browsing provides context, i.e., we know we are probably in a publications page if we followed a link labelled "publications" into the page. Context information of this kind help speed up the search.

CIFI also searches technical report archives, which are not indexed by search engines.

3 Design and Implementation of CIFI

A paper is uniquely identified by its author's name and title. CIFI takes, as input, the author's last name and given names (if available) and the title (which may be incomplete). It attempts to return the HTML version of the paper, or a citation of the paper, without further user intervention.

3.1 Alternative Strategies

CIFI uses a number of strategies to search the Web:

1. *Search the Web for the HTML version of the paper.* Words in the title and an author's name (last name and optionally, given names) are used as query keywords to Lycos.
2. *Search from the author's home page.* The author's name (last name and optionally, given names) are used as keywords to Lycos. Lycos returns a number of links which possibly point to the author's home page. These become starting points for further browsing.
3. *Search from the university CS department home page.* The CS department URL is extracted from the home page URL. The CS department home page is then explored for its technical report or publications page. If there are several possible home page links, several possible links to departmental home pages are extracted, and explored for publications.

[7] An example is the search engine *Ahoy!* (http://wednesday.cs.washington.edu:8080/).

4. *Search technical report archives.* Queries are sent to technical report search engines: the *Unified Computer Science Technical Reports* archive, and the *Networked Computer Science Technical Reports Library*[8].

If all the above strategies fail, then CIFI *sends an e-mail message* to the author, whose e-mail address is extracted from the home page, provided the home page is found.

3.2 Rules

Each of the strategies outlined in §3.1 is represented using rules. In addition, a second type of rule, *navigational rules*, are used to encode the actions to take when on a particular type of page (e.g., a home page).

In general, a citation is found using a page if: (a) the citation is on the page (the page type is first checked to see if it is likely to contain the citation), or (b) the citation is found using a page which is accessed via a link from the current page.

For example, if a home page does not contain publications details for the author, then a search is made for a link to the author's publications page.

Strategies developed for manual citation searches were used as the basis for the CIFI rules. We looked for common ways in which authors and CS departments make their technical reports and publications available on the Web, paying particular attention to the hypertext structure, and the labels and URLs used. The heuristics mostly relate to the selection of links during browsing, which rely on the type of the page.

In presenting the rules, we will assume the reader is acquainted with Prolog.

Accessing the Web from Prolog. In formulating the rules, Web pages are treated as logic program modules termed as LogicWeb pages [8]. Besides its HTML source, a LogicWeb page can have `link/2` facts representing out-links from the page, generated by parsing the page. A LogicWeb module can utilise the rules and facts of another by an operator similar to object-oriented message passing, denoted as `#>`. For example, the evaluation of the goal, `PageID#>Goal`, where `PageID` is the ID of a LogicWeb page and `Goal`, a goal, results in the evaluation of the goal `Goal` in `PageID`.

Heuristic-Free Search Rules. We first present rules for a heuristic-free search over a part of the Web. These rules describe a search of the Web exploring each page for the required citation, starting from a given page, until the citation is found:

```
fd_ctt_from(PageID,KeyWords,Citation) :-
    contains_ctt(PageID,KeyWords),
    extract_ctt(PageID,KeyWords,Citation).
fd_ctt_from(PageID,KeyWords,Citation) :-
```

[8] http://alvin.cs.cornell.edu/

```
    PageID#>link(Label,NextPageID),
    fd_ctt_from(NextPageID,KeyWords,Citation).
```

In the above, the predicate, `fd_ctt_from/3`, is true if the citation is found from the given page, identified by `PageID`. `PageID` is a term containing the URL of the page. `KeyWords` are the keywords (author name and title) entered by the user. `Citation` is a text fragment of the page containing the required citation.

The predicate `contains_ctt/2` determines if a page possibly contains the required citation, by checking to see if the page contains all the title keywords and the author's last name. The predicate `extract_ctt/3` extracts the required citation from the page.

In the second rule, the operator, `#>`, indicates the evaluation of the goal `link(Label,NextPageID)` (the `link/2` facts representing out-links from the page). The link goal retrieves an out-link from the page, and can be used to obtain different links through backtracking.

The second rule is not used if the first rule succeeds. Searching every page in this way is impractical, being much too expensive in time and computation.

Heuristic-Guided Search Rules. To minimise the search space, we employ link selection heuristics and page types. Only certain types of pages contain citations. For example, CS department home pages do not, but author home pages may. Also, only particular links will lead to a page containing citations. The above rules, augmented with heuristics and page types, become the following:

```
fd_ctt_from(PageType,PageID,KeyWords,Citation) :-
    is_a_pagetype_with_ctts(PageType),
    contains_ctt(PageID,KeyWords),
    extract_ctt(PageID,KeyWords,Citation).
fd_ctt_from(PageType,PageID,KeyWords,Citation) :-
    PageID#>link(Label,NextPageID),
    sat_link_criteria(PageType,link(Label,NextPageID),KeyWords,
                      NextPageType),
    fd_ctt_from(NextPageType,NextPageID,KeyWords,Citation).
```

`PageType` and `NextPageType` are page type identifiers indicating the current and the next context respectively. Examples of page types are: author home pages (called `auth_homepage`), CS department home pages (`cs_homepage`), the page of the first ten Lycos results using the title and author name as keywords (`lycos_auth_title_srch`), and the page of the first ten Lycos results using the author name as keywords (`lycos_auth_srch`).

The predicate `is_a_pagetype_with_ctts/1` determines if pages of the given page type could contain citations. This predicate ensures that only likely pages are checked for the required citation.

Link selection heuristics are applied in the predicate `sat_link_criteria/4`.

These rules describe a heuristic-guided search of a part of the Web in real-time.

Obtaining Starting Points and Link Selection. The predicate `sat_link_criteria/4` determines, given the page type and keywords, whether a link should be followed (i.e., whether the link satisfies some criteria described below), and the next page type to expect if the link is followed. Without this predicate, the search degenerates to exploring all links.

Relationships between a page type and its next page type(s) are expressed using `pt_related/2` facts. These relationships direct the search from one page type to another. Also, `cue_strings/2` facts are used to store strings that are looked for in the label of a link that would lead to each type of page. Below, we discuss link selection in different pages, giving several examples of these facts:

1. Lycos is queried using the author's name and keywords from the title. To determine which link, if any, in the Lycos results go to the HTML page, the label of the link is checked for all the title keywords. If they are all present, the link is likely to go to the paper.
2. The following checks are used to determine if a Lycos generated link goes to an author's home page:
   - If the label contains the author's name and the words "Home" (or "Personal") and "Page", then it is likely to go to the home page.
   - If the label contains parts of the author's name, or the phrase "Faculty Advisor", then the link is likely to go to the author's home page. In addition, the URL is inspected for the phrases "people", "Faculty", "researcher", "staff", "user", and "fac", or for the form:
     `<server-URL>/~<identifier>`
     For example, the following URL references a home page:
     `http://www.cs.mu.oz.au/~eas`
     The URL is parsed, and inspected in a Prolog predicate. The phrases above are stored in a fact.

   Since we want to look for the author's home page after this Lycos search, the relevant facts used by `sat_link_criteria/4` are:

   ```
   pt_related(lycos_auth_srch,auth_homepage).
   cue_strings(auth_homepage,["Home Page","Homepage",
               "Personal Page","Faculty Advisor"]).
   ```

   The fact `pt_related/2` above specifies the type of the next page to visit (i.e. `auth_homepage`) whenever on a `lycos_auth_srch` page. The strings to look for in a link to an author's home page is specified in the fact `cue_strings/2` above.
3. If the publications are not found on an author's home page, then a search is made for links and URLs containing the keywords "publications" or "papers". The check on the URLs ensures that even links with the label "here" like in "My publications are found *here.*" are examined. The facts used for link selection are:

   ```
   pt_related(auth_homepage,auth_pub_page).
   cue_strings(auth_pub_page,["Publications","Papers"]).
   ```

4. The CS department server's URL is extracted from the author's home page URL. For example, `http://www.cs.mu.oz.au/` is extracted from `http://-www.cs.mu.oz.au/~eas`. In the CS department home page, CiFi looks for link labels containing "technical report" or "publications". The motivation for this is that a CS department home page usually has a direct link to a technical report page, or to a publications page, with a link to the technical report page. This reasoning leads to the following `pt_related/2` and `cue_strings/2` facts:

```
pt_related(cs_homepage,cs_pub_page).
pt_related(cs_pub_page,cs_tr_page).
pt_related(cs_homepage,cs_tr_page).
cue_strings(cs_pub_page,["Publications"]).
cue_strings(cs_tr_page,["Technical Reports"]).
```

3.3 Extracting the Citation

The citation is extracted by sliding a window across the page, checking if the fragment contained in the window contains all the title keywords and the author's last name. A suitable frame size was chosen by measuring the sizes of several hundred citations.

Additional heuristics are employed to ensure what is extracted is indeed a citation. For example, a citation is often given as a bullet point, and a phrase like "selected publications" often precedes it.

3.4 Integrating Other Information Sources

As one of its search methods, CiFi sends queries to several technical report archive search engines. The results are checked for the citation required using a method like the one described above. Queries to search engines are constructed using the search engine URL appropriately appended with search keywords.

3.5 Current Implementation

CiFi is implemented in Prolog (with LogicWeb extensions[8]) for easier writing of rules, and the use of backtracking and pattern matching. The rules presented in §3.2 are a slight simplification of the actual Prolog clauses.

The program that interacts with the technical report archive search engines is also implemented in Prolog.

Lower-level text manipulation routines, such as that for extracting a citation, are written in C.

The Mosaic browser is used for Web access and display of results. The user interface is a CGI[9] form that accepts the author's last name, the author's given names, and title keywords (see Fig. 1(a)). Common words are filtered out. The citation, if found, is displayed on the browser (see Fig. 1(b)).

[9] CGI stands for Common Gateway Interface.

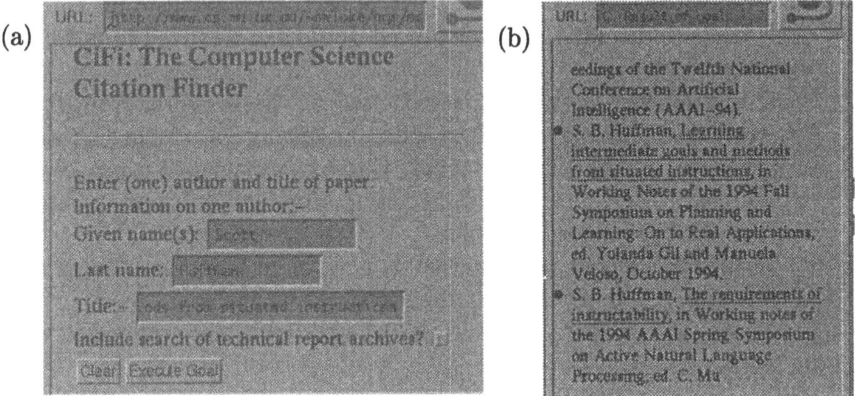

Fig. 1. (a) The interface to CIFI. (b) The result of a search. The required citation is the first citation in the displayed page fragment.

4 Evaluation

Thirty different citation searches were carried out, of which two-thirds were found. These citations were found mostly on authors' publications pages, authors' home pages, and departmental technical report pages. One citation was found by querying the technical report archives[10].

Failure cases indicate the following limitations of the current implementation:

- Insufficient keywords lead to failure or erroneous results. Including the given names of the author, and sufficient keywords from the title, helps to avoid problems.
- CIFI relies on Lycos to find the home page for an author. In several searches, the home page was not found among the first ten hits. Other home page databases on the Web could be employed, though we have not found one specialising in CS academics. We can also use indexes of personal home pages categorised by university[11], if the user can supply information on the affiliation of authors.
- The strategy used to look for the HTML copy of the paper, may only find a page containing its abstract. One way to deal with the problem is to examine the context surrounding the link for the word "abstract".
- We have not designed heuristics for departmental pages where the technical reports are classified by research groups or by year. For instance, such a format might allow a paper to be found based on its relation to words in the research group titles, or its year of publication.

[10] This is because technical report archives are searched last. Using technical report archives alone is inadequate, since they contain only technical reports of a limited number of participating institutions, and many publications are not technical reports.

[11] http://www.utexas.edu/world/personal/index.html

- One link with the paper title as its label actually pointed to an indirection node, because the page had been moved. Rules can be added to CiFi to deal with such cases.
- Some link labels to papers do not contain all the keywords from the title. For example, for the paper "Citescapes: Supporting Knowledge Construction on the Web", the link has the label "Citescapes Paper". Project or system names, like "Citescapes", could be distinguished in the keywords, and then be used alone to judge each link.
- If the title of a paper is misspelled in a citation, CiFi may fail to find it. Loose string matching could be used to avoid this problem.
- If a link to the (HTML) paper is part of a clickable map, the paper will not be found.

5 Related Work

5.1 Agents for Paper Search

A tool called WebFind for automatically searching for scientific papers was introduced in [9]. The main idea of WebFind is to use other information sources (non-Web) to help retrieve information from the Web. It uses the Melvyl database (a University of California library service) to find the institutional affiliations of an author of a paper, and employs NetFind to find the Internet address of a computer with that affiliation. It then uses this address to construct the URL of the affiliation's server. WebFind utilises heuristics to explore the server for the author's home page and publications page, in a similar way to CiFi's navigational rules. This tool is limited by the contents of the Melvyl database. In contrast to WebFind, CiFi looks for a citation to the paper which may, or may not, have a link to the actual paper. Also, the strategies that CiFi uses are a mixture of Web-based search engines and heuristics, without depending on external information sources.

BibAgent[10] semi-autonomously navigates over `ftp` directories (using the Alex file-system that integrates `ftp` directories) looking for a specified article. BibAgent examines `readme` files to aid its navigation, prioritises the directories to follow, and can retrieve the actual paper, or a completed bibliographic reference, from bibliographic files (e.g.,`.bib` files). BibAgent asks the user for traversal suggestions, and learns useful search paths for future use. In contrast to BibAgent, CiFi navigates over the Web, and searches Web pages for citations.

5.2 Browsing Agents

Browsing agents "surf the Web" on behalf of the user according to some criteria, or guide the user during browsing. Most of these perform more general searches, rather than targeting a particular domain, such as papers. Also, most learn user interests or permit user feedback. For instance, in [2], user feedback on intermediate search results is used to change the link selection heuristic, improving subsequent search results.

Fish-Search [3], traverses the Web looking for particular documents. The user specifies either keywords, a regular expression, or external filters that the contents of the document must match. Heuristic rules used to guide the search are handcoded-in and include: (1) after following a number of links in a given direction without finding relevant nodes, the search stops going in that direction; (2) links in relevant documents are traversed first before those of less relevant ones.

WebWatcher [1] uses a description of user interests to highlight interesting hyperlinks, and records hyperlinks to related pages. It also remembers the user's interests, based on the pages selected.

Letizia [7] is an agent that infers user interests from browsing behaviour, and explores links using a best-first search with heuristics utilising the inferred user interests. Based on its exploration, Letizia can recommend links to follow.

A case-based approach for information retrieval is taken in [5]. Past user feedback on example items allows it to suggest potentially relevant new items to the user.

CIFI does not require feedback, and does not learn from user interests because there is a specific target (e.g., a citation, or a HTML paper). Also, the required browsing behaviour can be specified using rules.

6 Conclusion and Future Work

The current implementation of CIFI demonstrates the feasibility of the rule-based approach for searching the Web. The experiments demonstrate the efficacy of CIFI, and point out its limitations.

Most of the limitations described in §4 are not fundamental, and can be addressed by extending the rule set or by the user supplying more keyword information.

Several extensions are possible:

- Even when CIFI fails to find a citation, it may provide useful information, such as the author's home page, and an explanation of why the search failed.
- More information sources can be added to the system. These include bibliography archives on the Web such as the *Computer Science Bibliography Glimpse Server*[12], and other CS technical report archives[13]. Knowledge of the format of search results returned by the above sites is needed to automatically collate and filter the results.
- Coauthors' home pages could be searched.
- CIFI should be able to autonomously reaccess a server that was previously too busy.
- The abstract and outline of each page in the Lycos search results can be used to help identify the author's home page.

[12] http://glimpse.cs.arizona.edu:1994/bib/

[13] Several technical report archives are listed in `http://liinwww.ira.uka.de/-bibliography/Techreports/others.html`

We will further explore the methodology of building an agent as an integration of distinctive logic modules. For example, search strategies in different modules can be composed together to form a particular collection of heuristics for a given task. Moreover, composition can be used to extend a set of rules.

This work explores the use of a "concierge" agent for finding citations on the Web. CIFI utilises a mixture of rule-based search heuristics and Web-based information sources to obtain its results. The navigational rules show that it is possible to exploit the unwritten conventions of the Web, and that Prolog backtracking search maps well to the Web-surfing task. Effort is required to acquire knowledge of the information sources, as well as the conventions. However, once the knowledge is attained and integrated into CIFI, it is usable in many ways, and can be extended. This approach should generalise to other categories of information, apart from citations.

References

1. R. Armstrong, D. Freitag, T. Joachims, and T. Mitchell. WebWatcher: A Learning Apprentice for the World-Wide Web. In *On-line Working Notes of the AAAI Spring Symposium Series on Information Gathering from Distributed, Heterogeneous Environments*, *http://www.isi.edu/sims/knoblock/sss95/mitchell.ps*, 1995.
2. M. Balabanovic and Y. Shoham. Learning Information Retrieval Agents: Experiments with Automated Web Browsing. In *On-line Working Notes of the AAAI Spring Symposium Series on Information Gathering from Distributed, Heterogeneous Environments*, *http://www.isi.edu/sims/knoblock/sss95/balabanovic.ps*, 1995.
3. P.M.E. De Bra and R.D.J. Post. Searching for Arbitrary Information in the WWW: the Fish-Search for Mosaic. *2nd International World-Wide Web Conference*, *http://www.ncsa.uiuc.edu/SDG/IT94/Proceedings/Searching/debra/article.html.*
4. O. Etzioni and D. Weld. Intelligent Agents on the Internet: Fact, Fiction, and Forecast. *IEEE Expert*, 10(4):44–49, August 1995.
5. K. Hammond, R. Burke, and C. Martin. A Case-Based Approach to Knowledge Navigation. *AAAI Workshop on Indexing and Reuse in Multimedia Systems*, pages 46–57, 1994.
6. S.R. Hedberg. Intelligent Agents: The First Harvest of Softbots Looks Promising. *IEEE Expert*, 10(4):6–9, August 1995.
7. H. Lieberman. Letizia: An Agent That Assists Web Browsing. *International Joint Conference on Artificial Intelligence, Montreal*, 1995.
8. S.W. Loke and A. Davison. Logic Programming with the World-Wide Web. *Proceedings of the 7th. ACM Conference on Hypertext (Hypertext '96).* ACM Press, pages 235–245, 1996.
9. A.E. Monge and C.P. Elkan. Integrating External Information Sources to Guide World-Wide Web Information Retrieval. *http://www-cse.ucsd.edu/users/amonge/Papers/ai96.ps.gz*, Submitted to AI'96.
10. D. Rus and D. Subramaniam. Information Retrieval, Information Structure, and Information Agents. Technical Report, Department of Computer Science, Dartmouth, PCS-TR96-255. To appear as Customising Multimedia Information Access in *ACM Computing Surveys*, February 1996.

Automatic Making of Sokoban Problems

Yoshio MURASE[1], Hitoshi MATSUBARA[2] and Yuzuru HIRAGA[1]

[1] University of Library and Information Science, 1-2 Kasuga, Tsukuba, Ibaraki, 305 JAPAN
[2] Electrotechnical Laboratory,
1-1-4 Umezono, Tsukuba, Ibaraki, 305 JAPAN

Abstract. This paper describes our program that makes *Sokoban* problems automatically. *Sokoban* is one of one-person puzzles invented in Japan. The program consists of three stages: generation, checking and evaluation. First, candidates for problems are generated randomly by a prototype and three templates . Second, unsolvable candidates are removed by the *Sokoban* solver. Finally trivial or uninteresting candidates are removed by the evaluator. The problems that the program made are judged good by human experts. Creation of art by computer is an important target of Artificial Intelligence. Our work can be characterized one of the attempts to create some arts by computers.

1 Introduction

This paper describes our program that makes *Sokoban* problems automatically. Our program consists of three stages: generation, checking and evaluation. First, candidates for problems are generated with a prototype and three templates at random. Second, unsolvable candidates are removed by our *Sokoban* solver. Finally trivial or uninteresting candidates are removed by our evaluator. The problems that our program made are judged good by human experts. Creation of art by computer is an important target of artificial intelligence. Our work can be characterized one of the attempts to create some arts by computers.

2 Sokoban

Sokoban is one of one-person puzzles invented in Japan at 1982. *Sokoban* is a Japanese word meaning a warehouse-keeper. The initial state of Fig.1 is an example of a problem. A "warehouse" consists of "walls" and "passways". The passway is a connected area of unit squares. A unit square can be occupied by either "warehouse-keeper", an "object", or can be empty. A number of squares (equally the number of objects) are designated as "goal areas". The objective of the puzzle is to operate the warehouse-keeper to push all objects to goal areas (see the goal state of Fig.1). In the later part of this paper we use the following items:

- : wall
- : goal area
- : object
- : warehouse-keeper
- : place where goal and object are overlapped

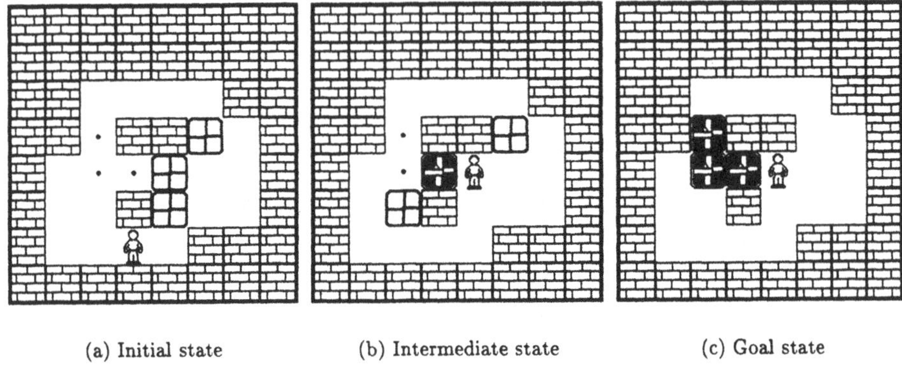

(a) Initial state (b) Intermediate state (c) Goal state

Fig. 1. An example of a Sokoban problem

There are two kinds of operations: MOVE and PUSH.

- MOVE: move the keeper one step toward four directions on the passway: up, down, right and left.
- PUSH: move an object one step forward by making the keeper push it from behind. The keeper can push only one object at a time.

While the rules are simple, the problems can get to be quite hard and interesting. *Sokoban* problems [Thinking Rabbit 1982, 1989] is one of the bestseller game softwares in Japan. *Xsokoban*[Myers 1995], a software of *Sokoban* on X-Windows, is played worldwide (in more than 20 countries so far).

Making good (or artistic) and interesting problems is a matter of expertise. Several human experts of *Sokoban* make good problems to be solved. Our objective is to make a program that makes good problems comparable to those of human experts.

Our program consists of three stages: generation, checking and evaluation. The latter sections describes these stages by showing an example. In this paper, we fix the size of warehouse 8×8 units and the number of objects to three. The actual program is capable of making larger and more complex *Sokoban* problems.

3 Generation

In this stage *Sokoban* problems are generated.

A generator is expected to keep the following conditions:

1. generate original problems.
2. generate problems that have solutions.
3. generate interesting problems.

It is impossible to keep the conditions completely, but we can improve possibility that good problems are generated by implementing several devices.

The generation stage starts from a prototype (Fig.2 (a)). In the following example we have chosen three templates (Fig.2 (b)).

Our program places the templates at random on the prototype. In the example, the first template is at the upper-left (Fig.2 (c)), the second is placed at the upper-right (Fig.2 (d)), and the third is placed at the lower-right (Fig.2 (e)).

The size of all templates shown in Fig.2 (b) is more than 2×2. If we use a template whose size is 1×3, it is likely that a lot of uninteresting problems will be generated. The position of the templates are chosen to overlap existing passways, so the generated passway is guaranteed to be connected.

Next, goal areas are chosen on the passway. Areas to where the keeper cannot push his object are marked GOAL_AVOID (Fig.3 (a)). Goal areas are chosen randomly avoiding GOAL_AVOID (Fig.3 (b)).

Then objects are placed on the passway. A "dead end area" is an area in the passway from which objects cannot be moved out of. Dead end must be removed from the candidates of the initial positions of objects provided that there are no goal areas within them.

Goal areas which are at corner are marked COR_GOAL (Fig.3 (c)). On the assumption that there is only one object, areas where the keeper can push the object from each goal area are calculated (Fig. 4). The calculated areas are marked GOAL_RANGE.

The first object is placed on an area that is in GOAL_RANGE areas and is not in COR_GOAL areas. New dead end areas (ADD_AVOID areas) are calculated. The second object is placed on an area that is in GOAL_RANGE areas and is not in COR_GOAL and is not in ADD_AVOID areas. New dead end areas are calculated. These steps are iterated until all the objects are placed.

In this example setting of objects are done as Fig.5. Finally the warehouse-keeper is placed on the passway at random. Fig.5 (f) is a generated problem in this example.

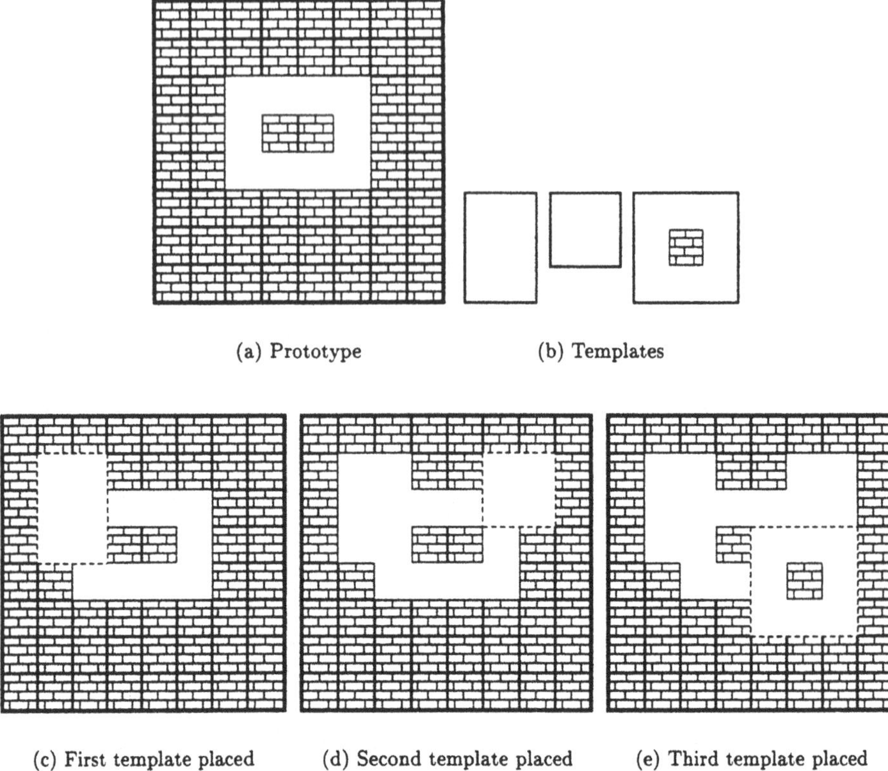

(a) Prototype (b) Templates

(c) First template placed (d) Second template placed (e) Third template placed

Fig. 2. Outline generation

4 Checking

Some of the problems generated by our program are solvable (i.e. the warehouse-keeper can push all the objects to the goal areas of the problem) while others are not. Unsolvable problems are *illegal* and must be rejected. Ueno et al. built an automatic *Sokoban* solver[Ueno, Nakayama and Hikita 1994]. which searches a solution sequence by best-first search. So it can sometimes solve problems that have long solution sequences, but it sometimes cannot solve problems that have short solution sequences. The best-first search is not adequate for checking solvability of generated problems. So we rewrote Ueno's solver into breadth-first search version. Our solver cannot solve problems that have long solution

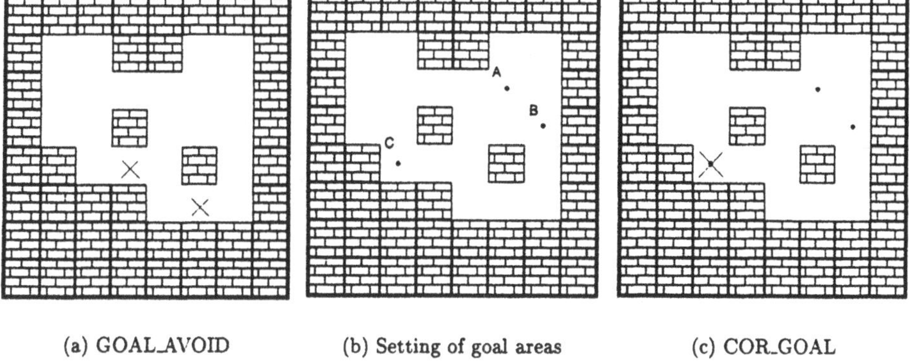

(a) GOAL_AVOID (b) Setting of goal areas (c) COR_GOAL

Fig. 3. Setting of goal areas

sequences but it can solve all problems that have short solution sequences.

Our program check all the generated problems by the new solver. If the new solver cannot solve a generated problem, it is removed from the candidate list. In average about half of the generated problems are removed at this stage (experimental data are shown later).

5 Evaluation

The remaining problems are all *legal*. But most of the problems are trivial and uninteresting. The evaluation program evaluates artistic values of the remaining problems. The evaluation criteria are:

1. length of solution sequence: if a problem has a very short solution sequence, it is trivial and is rejected. when the length of a solution sequence of a problem is less than seven, the problem is rejected.
2. the number of changes in directions of pushing in solution sequence: in interesting problems the keeper has to change the directions of pushing objects very often. if the number of the changes are less than four, it is trivial and must be removed.
3. the number of detours in solution sequence: if a solution sequence of a problem has no detours, it is uninteresting and is rejected.

The above criteria removes trivial or uninteresting problems from the candidate lists. In average four fifths of the remaining problems are removed.

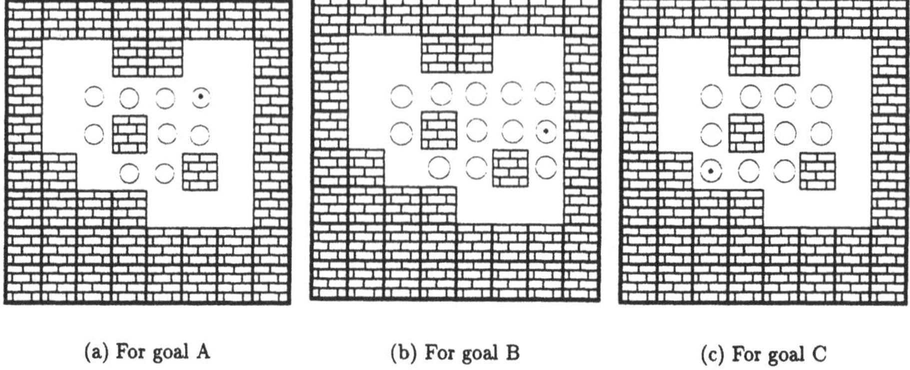

(a) For goal A (b) For goal B (c) For goal C

Fig. 4. Calculation of GOAL_RANGE

6 Problems that our program made

In this section we show four problems that our program made (see Fig.6). From the point of human experts' view, these problems have some artistic values.

We made experiments five hundred times with the prototype (Fig.2 (a)) and the templates set (Fig.2 (b)). The results are shown in Table 1. The generation stage failed seven times. About half of generated problems were unsolvable. Our programs outputted 44 problems as good problems, but "real" good problems which are evaluated good by human experts were fourteen out of them.

Table 1. Experimental data

# of generation failures		7
# of problems that have no solutions		245
solvable problems	removed	204
	outputted	44
# of trials		500
real good problems		14

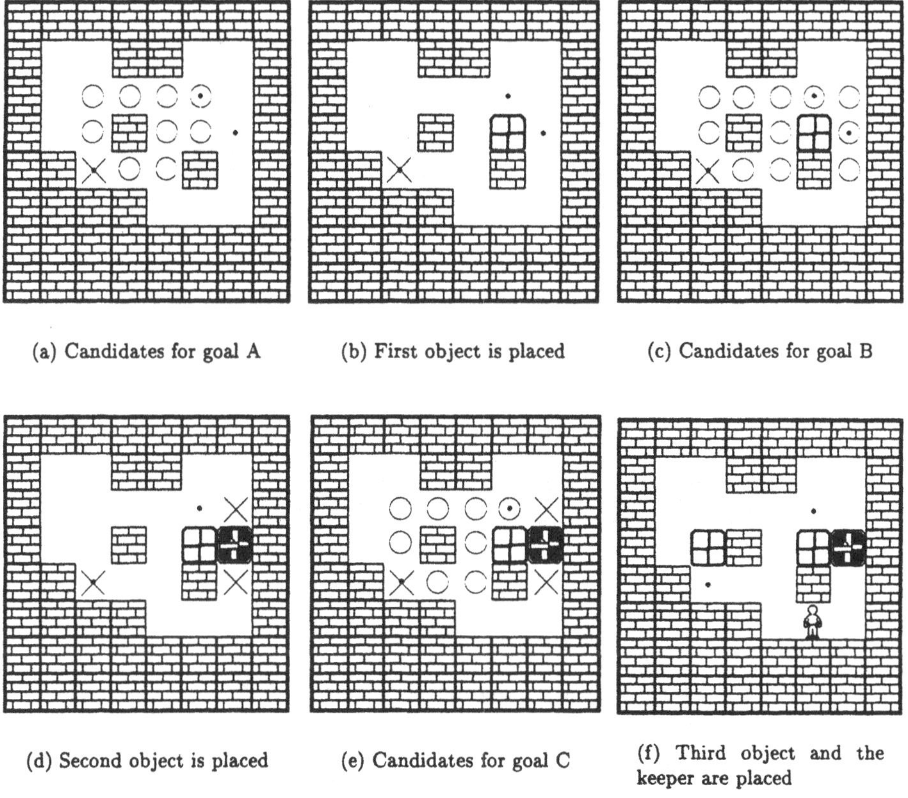

(a) Candidates for goal A
(b) First object is placed
(c) Candidates for goal B
(d) Second object is placed
(e) Candidates for goal C
(f) Third object and the keeper are placed

Fig. 5. Setting of the objects and the keeper

7 Concluding Remarks

We have built a program that makes *Sokoban* problems automatically [Murase 1996]. Some problems that our program made are judged good by human experts. Our program, however, has several drawbacks. For example, our program cannot make problems that have very long solution sequences. We have to revise our program to get more complex problems.

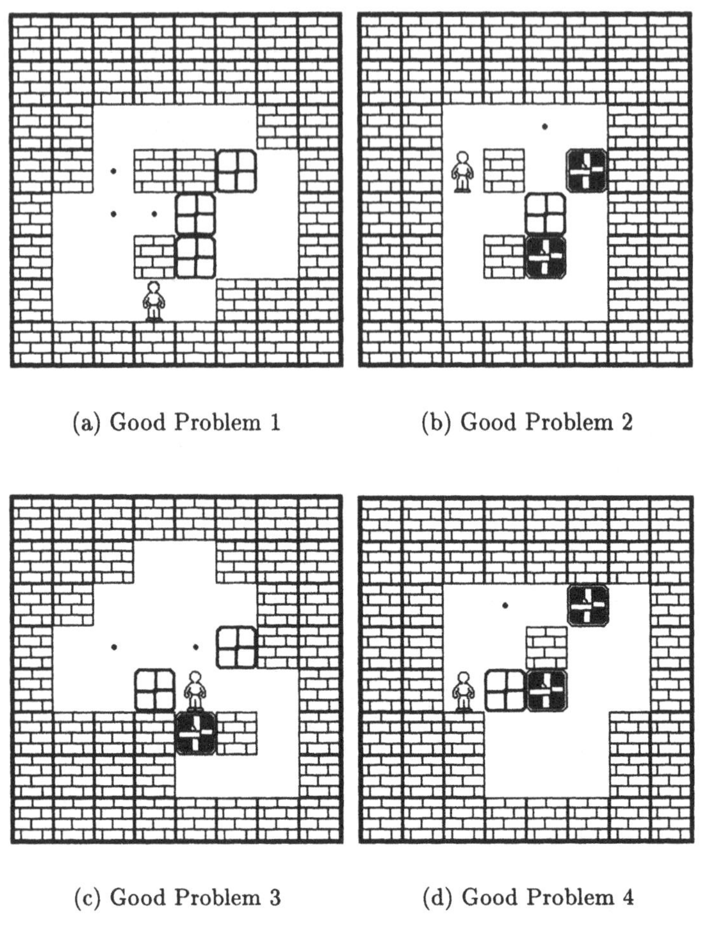

(a) Good Problem 1 (b) Good Problem 2

(c) Good Problem 3 (d) Good Problem 4

Fig. 6. Good problems

References

[Thinking Rabbit 1982, 1989] ThinkingRabbit: Sokoban problems 1,2, perfect (1982,1989)

[Myers 1995] A. Myers: XSokoban, http://clef.lcs.mit.edu/ andru/xsokoban.html (1995)

[Ueno, Nakayama and Hikita 1994] A.Ueno, K.Nakayama and T. Hikita: A program that solves *Sokoban* problems (in Japanese), bit, vol.26, no.12, pp.40-51 & vol.27, no.1, pp.92-100, Kyoritsu-shuppan, Tokyo (1994)

[Murase 1996] Y. Murase: An attempt of automatic creation of Sokoban problems (in Japanese), Bachelor Thesis of University of Library and Information Science, Tsukuba, Japan (1996)

Bringing About Rationality: Incorporating Plans Into a BDI Agent Architecture

Lawrence Cavedon[†] & Anand Rao[‡]

[†]Dept. of Computer Science, R.M.I.T.
GPO Box 2476V, Melbourne, Australia
cavedon@cs.rmit.edu.au

[‡]Australian Artificial Intelligence Institute
171 LaTrobe St., Melbourne, Australia
anand@aaii.oz.au

Abstract. Agents attempt to achieve their intentions through the use of plans, leading to further intentions corresponding to the actions and subgoals of those plans. We extend Rao and Georgeff's logic of belief, desire and intention with a logical representation of plans. This representation allows the specification of subgoals, using Segerberg's "bringing it about" modal operator. By using a plan library to semantically restrict an agent's intention-worlds, we define a framework that models the reasoning process of an intention-based autonomous agent. We show that this framework supports several desirable properties involving an agent's commitment to future intentions, based on its available plans.

1 Introduction

There has been much recent interest in the AI literature in logics of rationality (e.g. [3, 6, 9, 8, 11, 12]). Such logics provide frameworks within which the behaviour of intelligent agent systems can be formally specified. The main focus of the logics of rationality have been mental attitudes, such as *belief, desire, intention* and *goals*—these concepts are used to explain rational behaviour [1]. An important concept that has received somewhat less attention in this work is that of a *plan* (although see [6, 11, 12])—the plans available to an agent guides its choice of actions in achieving some goal or fulfilling a desire. In particular, the intentions of an agent are partially determined by its available plans.

Implementing an agent system that performs in some domain involves providing a *library* of plans that define methods for achieving certain goals. Such plans typically involve a *trigger* or *invocation condition* (this is the particular goal that the plan achieves) and a *body*. A plan body may be a sequence of actions; however, in more complex systems, a body will involve subgoals which are achieved prior to certain actions being performed.[2]

* The authors wish to thank the referees for several useful suggestions. This work was partially supported by the *Cooperative Research Centre for Intelligent Decision Systems*, Melbourne, Australia.

[2] For example, the goal of making a block *clear* may be a subgoal of *moving* it.

In agent systems that involve plan libraries and intention-based architectures (e.g. PRS [5]), the intentions of an agent interact with subgoals to produce new intentions. For example, if an agent intends to achieve ϕ and the chosen plan from its plan library tells it that ψ is a subgoal to achieving ϕ, then the agent should adopt the intention to achieve ψ. In order to tell the complete story of real agent systems, logics of rationality must therefore allow the logical representation of plans and capture the interaction between plans and intentions.

Reasoning about actions and intentions usually involves some variant of *dynamic logic*. However, we also need to be able to represent actions which "bring about" conditions if we are to satisfactorily model subgoals and their interaction with intentions. Segerberg [10] has defined an extension of dynamic logic which is extended with an operator δ that maps propositions to actions—$\delta\phi$ is a set of actions that "bring about", or *achieve*, ϕ. We show how this notion can be used to represent hierarchical plans. In particular, we extend Rao and Georgeff's logic of BDI (belief, desire and intention) in a way that allows us to formalise the interaction between plans and intentions. The resulting logical framework supports some interesting properties showing how an agent's intentions, and plans for satisfying those intentions, lead to the posting of further intentions involving the subgoals involved in those plans.

2 A Logic of BDI and Achievement

In this section, we present a summary of Rao and Georgeff's (henceforth *R&G*) logic of BDI augmented with (a modification of) Segerberg's logic of "bringing it about"—see [8, 9, 10] for further details. For simplicity, we restrict ourselves to the propositional case.

2.1 Beliefs, Desires and Intentions

R&G's logic of BDI is a multi-modal temporal logic. The core is a branching-time temporal logic based on Computation Tree Logic, specifically CTL* [4]. A *time-tree* is a forward-branching structure (i.e. each node has a single past and possibly multiple futures); a node in a time-tree is a *state* or *time-point* and each edge represents an event. A *path* is a (possibly infinite) sequence of edges through a time-tree and is represented by the sequence of states which it passes through (including those states at its beginning and end). The multiple paths emanating from a given state s represent the different possible futures which are achievable from s. Two modalities operate on path-formulas (i.e. formulas which are evaluated wrt paths): $opt(\phi)$ is true at s if ϕ holds on *some* path emanating from s, and indicates that ϕ is optionally true in the future of s; $inev(\phi)$ is true at s if ϕ holds on *all* paths emanating from s, and indicates that ϕ is inevitably true in the future of s. Other temporal operators are evaluated on paths: $\bigcirc\phi$ is true on path p if ϕ is true at the next state on p; $\mathsf{F}\phi$ is true on p if ϕ is true at *some* state in p; $\mathsf{G}\phi$ is true on p if ϕ is true at *all* states in p.

Figure 1 (taken from [9]) illustrates a time-tree. Examples of the different combinations of the temporal modalities (all of which evaluate to true at time-point t_1) are indicated at the right of the figure.

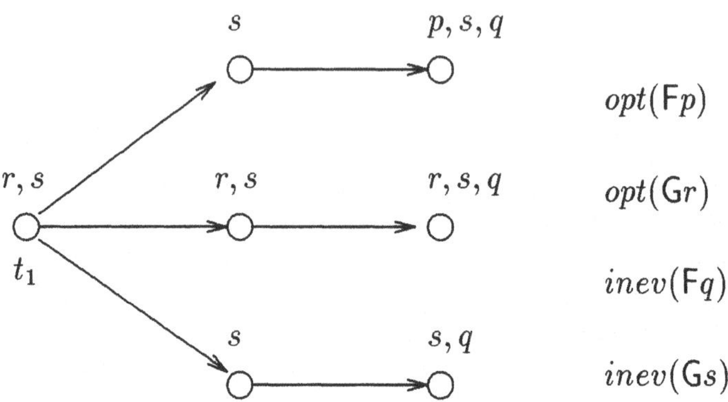

Fig. 1. Examples of the temporal modalities.

The BDI logic extends CTL* by adding a number of modalities, one each for belief, desire and intention. (For the purposes of the rest of this paper, we focus on intention and belief and ignore desire.) The semantics involves a possible-worlds framework, where each world is a CTL* time-tree. As usual, there is an accessibility relation associated with each modality BEL and INT, and a formula BEL(ϕ) (resp. INT(ϕ)) is true at a state s in world w if ϕ holds at state s in *every* world w' that is belief- (resp. intention-) accessible from w.

2.2 Bringing It About

Dynamic logic is a powerful framework for reasoning about actions and the effects they achieve, allowing formulas of the form $[\alpha]\phi$ and $\phi'[\alpha]\phi$, where α denotes a type of action and ϕ, ϕ' are standard propositional formulas. The first of these formulas is true at a state s if ϕ is true at every state which results after an execution of an action of type α; the second is true at a state s if $(\phi' \supset [\alpha]\phi)$ is true at s. Simple plans can be represented in the dynamic logic framework by the use of composition on actions—e.g. if α_1 and α_2 are action-types, then $\alpha_1;\alpha_2$ is the complex action-type consisting of the sequential composition of these two.[3]

However, to represent more complex, state-independent plans, we need to be able to refer to actions which "achieve" conditions. Segerberg [10] extends dynamic logic by introducing an operator δ for "bringing it about" (or "achieving") that a certain condition holds. For example, $\delta\phi$ denotes a set of actions

[3] For simplicity, we ignore parallel and non-deterministic actions and events here.

that achieve ϕ, i.e. make ϕ true. This allows us to represent plans as other than simply sequences of primitive actions. For example, a plan to open a door may first require an agent to ensure that the door is unlocked (which may involve the agent unlocking it) followed by a *turn*(*knob*) action. This is represented as follows: $[\delta\, unlocked(door); turn(knob)]opened(door)$. This simple plan is appropriate whether or not the door is unlocked in the initial state. Moreover, it corresponds to (a simple version of) the sort of plans found in implemented agent systems such as PRS.[4] We actually slightly modify the meaning of δ so that $\delta\phi$ denotes a set of *minimal* actions—minimal in the sense that ϕ is not achieved until the completion of the action—which achieve ϕ. We find that this modification is necessary for important technical reasons.[5]

An action-type is represented by a term of the logical language—there may be more than one action of this type.[6] An action is a transition between a pair of states—the semantic representation of a term (i.e. action-type) is a set of such transitions. The formula $do(\alpha)$ means that an action of type α is possibly executed at that point (i.e. along a path emanating from the state at which the formula is true).

2.3 Syntax and Semantics

In this section, we present the formal syntax and semantics of the BDI logic augmented with the achievement operator.

Definition 1. (Syntax) *The logical language consists of* terms *and* formulas. *Terms (which represent actions) are defined as follows:*

- *a primitive term (A denotes the set of these) is a term;*
- *if α_1 and α_2 are terms, then so too is $\alpha_1; \alpha_2$;*
- *if ϕ is a state formula (defined below) then $\delta\phi$ is a term.*

As in CTL, there are two types of formulas:* state formulas *(which are evaluated at a state in a time-tree) and* path formulas *(which are evaluated against a path in a time-tree). These are defined as follows:*

- *any propositional formula is a state formula;*
- *if ϕ and ϕ' are state formulas then so too are $\phi \vee \phi'$ and $\neg\phi$;*
- *if ϕ is a state formula then so too are* $\mathsf{BEL}(\phi)$ *and* $\mathsf{INT}(\phi)$*;*
- *if ψ is a path formula then $opt(\psi)$ and $inev(\psi)$ are state formulas;*
- *any state formula is also a path formula;*
- *if ψ and ψ' are path formulas then so too are $\psi \vee \psi'$, $\neg\psi$, $\bigcirc\psi$, $\mathsf{F}\psi$ and $\mathsf{G}\psi$;*
- *if α is a term then $do(\alpha)$ is a path formula;*
- *if α is a term and ϕ, ϕ' are state formulas then $[\alpha]\phi$ and $\phi'[\alpha]\phi$ are state formulas.*

---

[4] PRS's *achieve* operation, written $!\phi$, closely parallels the use of δ.

[5] Singh [11] considers Segerberg's δ operation problematic for the same reason.

[6] For convenience, we sometimes abuse the distinction between actions and action-types and (informally) refer to "the action α", where α is a term.

Definition 2. (Semantics) *An interpretation* $\mathcal{I}$ *is a tuple* $\langle W, T, <, \mathcal{B}, \mathcal{I}, \mathcal{V}, \Delta, \mathcal{A}\rangle$, *where:* W *is a set of worlds (i.e. time-trees);* T *is a set of states (i.e. time-points);* $<$ *is an ordering on states;*[7] $\mathcal{B}$ *and* $\mathcal{I}$ *are the belief- and intention-accessibility relations respectively; and* $\mathcal{V}$ *is an evaluation function mapping proposition symbols to* propositions, *represented as sets of world-state pairs.*[8] *The accessibility relations also relate world-state pairs to worlds: i.e.* $\mathcal{B} \subseteq W \times T \times W$ *(similarly for* $\mathcal{I}$*).*[9] *The notation* w_t *is used as an abbreviation to denote the world-state pair* $\langle w, t\rangle$. *The notation* $\mathcal{B}_t^w$ *is used to denote the set of worlds belief-accessible from* w_t *(similarly for intention-accessibility).*

$\mathcal{A}$ *maps each primitive term* α *to a set* S_α *of* actions, *i.e. a set of pairs of world-states. We require the following conditions, for all* $\langle w_s, w_t\rangle \in S_\alpha$*:*

- *(i) primitive actions consume exactly one time interval. Formally:* $w_s < w_t$ *and there is no* w_u *such that* $w_s < w_u < w_t$*;*
- *(ii) there is at most one possible outcome for each action emanating from a given state. Formally: if* $\langle w_s, w_{t'}\rangle \in S_\alpha$ *then* $w_t = w_{t'}$*;*
- *(iii) every transition has an associated action-type. Formally:* $\mathcal{A}$ *maps a primitive term to* every *pair satisfying (i); and*
- *(iv) each action is assigned to a unique action-type. Formally:* $S_\alpha \cap S_{\alpha'} = \emptyset$ *whenever* $\alpha \neq \alpha'$.

Δ *maps propositions (i.e. sets of world-state pairs) to sets of actions.* Δ *is assumed to satisfy the following constraints:*

- *(i)* ϕ *holds at the end of every action in* $\delta\phi$. *Formally: if* $\langle w_s, w_t\rangle \in \Delta(P)$ *then* $w_t \in P$*;*
- *(ii) "maximality": (a subaction of) every action that achieves* ϕ *is in* $\delta\phi$.[10] *Formally: for every proposition* P *and action* $\langle w_s, w_t\rangle$ *such that* $w_t \in P$, *there is some* $\langle w_s, w_{t'}\rangle$ $(w_s < w_{t'} \leq w_t)$[11] *such that* $\langle w_s, w_{t'}\rangle \in \Delta(P)$*; and*
- *(iii) all actions in* $\delta\phi$ *are* minimal *for achieving* ϕ, *in that* ϕ *does not become true before the end of the action. Formally: if* $\langle w_s, w_t\rangle \in \Delta(P)$ *then* $w_{s'} \notin P$, *for all* $w_s \leq w_{s'} < w_t$.

Finally, for non-primitive terms, we define $\mathcal{A}(\delta\phi) = \Delta(\mathcal{V}(\phi))$ *and* $\mathcal{A}(\alpha;\alpha') = \{\langle w_{t_1}, w_{t_3}\rangle \mid \langle w_{t_1}, w_{t_2}\rangle \in \mathcal{A}(\alpha)$ *and* $\langle w_{t_2}, w_{t_3}\rangle \in \mathcal{A}(\alpha')$ *(for some* w_{t_2}*)*$\}$.

Given an interpretation I, *world* w *and state* t, *the truth of formulas is defined as follows. (We define* $opt(\psi) \equiv \neg inev(\neg\psi)$ *and* $\mathsf{G}(\psi) \equiv \neg\mathsf{F}(\neg\psi)$*.)*

- $I, w_t \models \phi$ *iff* $w_t \in \mathcal{V}(\phi)$, *for* ϕ *an atomic formula;*
- $I, w_t \models \neg\phi$ *iff* $I, w_t \not\models \phi$*;*

---

[7] This ordering is required to be irreflexive, transitive and backward-linear.

[8] I.e. (state) formulas are evaluated with respect to a world and a state.

[9] Typically, these relations are required to satisfy certain conditions (e.g. reflexivity, transitivity).

[10] Segerberg's notion of maximality is different to this, mainly because all primitive terms in his language are of the form $\delta\phi$. Hence, Segerberg does not have to force actions to belong to some $\delta\phi$ since actions which do not cannot be referenced.

[11] $\langle w_s, w_{t'}\rangle$ is a "subaction" of $\langle w_s, w_t\rangle$ since it (possibly) ends before the latter.

- $I, w_t \models \phi_1 \vee \phi_2$ *iff* $I, w_t \models \phi_1$ *or* $I, w_t \models \phi_2$;
- $I, (w_{t_0}, w_{t_1}, ...) \models \phi$ *iff* $I, w_{t_0} \models \phi$, *for* ϕ *a state formula;*
- $I, (w_{t_0}, w_{t_1}, ...) \models \bigcirc\psi$ *iff* $I, (w_{t_1}, ...) \models \psi$;
- $I, (w_{t_0}, w_{t_1}, ...) \models \mathsf{F}\psi$ *iff* $\exists w_{t_k} \in \{w_{t_0}, w_{t_1}, ...\}$ *s.t.* $I, (w_{t_k}, w_{t_{k+1}}, ...) \models \psi$;
- $I, w_{t_0} \models inev(\psi)$ *iff* $\forall (w_{t_0}, w_{t_1}, ...)$, $I, (w_{t_0}, w_{t_1}, ...) \models \psi$;
- $I, w_t \models \mathsf{BEL}(\phi)$ *iff* $I, w'_t \models \phi$ *for all* $w' \in \mathcal{B}^w_t$;
- $I, w_t \models \mathsf{INT}(\phi)$ *iff* $I, w'_t \models \phi$ *for all* $w' \in \mathcal{I}^w_t$;
- $I, (w_{t_0}, w_{t_1}, ...) \models do(\alpha)$ *iff* $\exists w_{t_k} \in \{w_{t_0}, w_{t_1}, ...\}$ *s.t.* $\langle w_{t_0}, w_{t_k} \rangle \in \mathcal{A}(\alpha)$;
- $I, w_t \models [\alpha]\phi$ *iff* $I, w_{t'} \models \phi$ *for all* $\langle w_t, w_{t'} \rangle \in \mathcal{A}(\alpha)$;
- $I, w_t \models \phi'[\alpha]\phi$ *iff* $I, w_t \models \phi'$ *implies* $I, w_{t'} \models \phi$ *for all* $\langle w_t, w_{t'} \rangle \in \mathcal{A}(\alpha)$.

For convenience, we extend $\mathcal{V}$ *so that it applies to any state formula. For a non-atomic state formula* ϕ, *we define* $\mathcal{V}(\phi) = \{w_t \mid I, w_t \models \phi\}$.

Segerberg provides a sound and complete axiomatisation of his logic of "bringing it about" (as do *R&G* for their BDI logic). However, because of our modification to Segerberg's logic (i.e. in the maximality requirement), an axiomatisation of the above logic requires further investigation.

2.4 Modelling Rationality

Following the seminal work of Cohen and Levesque [3], *R&G* use their logic to formally model properties of rational behaviour. They do this by defining a number of conditions—both as axioms in the proof theory and as corresponding constraints on models—which a rational BDI agent is expected to satisfy. The posting of an intention is by way of a formula of the form $\mathsf{INT}(inev(\mathsf{F}\phi))$—i.e. the agent intends that ϕ will eventually become true, no matter what (i.e. in all possible futures).

The particular aspects of rationality that *R&G* are interested in are those relating the different attitudes. For example, an agent should believe that anything it intends is actually possible (this is called *intention-belief consistency*). More problematically, even when an agent believes ϕ inevitably follows from ψ, it should not necessarily intend ϕ whenever it intends ψ (this is called the *side-effect problem*). By requiring belief-accessible and intention-accessible worlds to overlap—i.e. $\mathsf{BEL}^w_t \cap \mathsf{INT}^w_t \neq \emptyset$—yet allowing them to otherwise vary, *R&G* are able to ensure that their framework imposes exactly those properties which are required and avoid the undesirable ones.[12] See [9] for more details.

3 Representing Plans and Plan Libraries

The "bringing it about" operator allows the logical representation of complex hierarchical plans. Consider the plans of an agent system such as PRS. A PRS

[12] Actually, there are some very (logically) non-standard behaviours of intention that *R&G*'s framework does not address, such as $\mathsf{INT}(\phi \wedge \psi) \supset \mathsf{INT}(\phi) \wedge \mathsf{INT}(\psi)$ being undesirable. We also ignore such issues here (although see [2, 6, 12]).

plan consists of a triggering condition ϕ and a body. A plan body π is a sequence of actions,[13] some of which are not directly specified but are a command to achieve some subgoal ψ. A plan of this form is represented in our logic as $[\pi]\phi$, where $\pi = \alpha_1; \ldots; \alpha_n$ (we assume plan bodies are finite). Further, any of these α_i may be of the form $\delta\psi$, which denotes an action that achieves the subgoal ψ. If a plan also involves a *precondition* ϕ', then its representation is of the form $\phi'[\pi]\phi$. For example, turning the key unlocks a door *if* the door is currently locked. This is modelled by a plan of the form $locked(door)[turn(key)]unlocked(door)$. Primitive plans (i.e. those which do not post subgoals) tend to be of this form. For the sake of abbreviation, we assume that *all* plans are of the form $\phi'[\pi]\phi$, writing $\mathsf{T}[\pi]\phi$ for $[\pi]\phi$, where T is logical truth (i.e. $I, w_t \models \mathsf{T}$ for all I, w_t).

An agent system incorporates a ***plan library***, i.e. a collection of plans for achieving the different goals (and subgoals) which may arise during the system's performance of the tasks it was designed to do. We assume here that all plans in the library of the system being modelled are represented in our logic, in the manner described above. Crucially, we assume that these plans are the *only* means available to an agent for addressing its goals—this is as it should be, since an agent can only call on its library of plans for methods that address its goals.[14] We need to ensure that our logical framework reflects this assumption: only plans can be used to specify actions which the agent performs in order to fulfil its intentions. Further, any actions in plans are assumed to be actions which the agent performs, not events outside the agent's control. Of course, an agent may *believe* that such an event would fulfil its intentions, but it should not *plan* such events or have the intention of using such events in order to achieve its goals. For example, an agent may believe a mighty hurricane could blow down the door and achieve *opened(door)*, but it should not *plan* for a hurricane to blow down the door if opening the door is its goal.[15]

In order to formally capture the constraint that plans provide the only means available to an agent system, we define the notion of a *plan world*, analogously to belief-/desire-/intention-worlds. However, we do not treat plans the same as the other attitudes. In particular, we take plans to be "static" entities (i.e. the same plan library is available at all worlds/states), so there is no associated accessibility relation.[16] Note that, rather than introducing plan-worlds, we could have imposed the restriction below on intention-worlds. However, the introduction of plan-worlds allows for greater flexibility in the modelling stage.[17]

---

[13] PRS plans are non-linear so a PRS plan-body could involve non-sequential actions.

[14] We are only concerned with deliberated behaviour here: e.g. an agent may incorporate a purely reactive component that does not perform means-end reasoning and therefore does not access a plan library.

[15] Of course, an agent may believe that a certain state is *inevitable*, given events outside its control. In this case, the agent may plan to do nothing except wait for its desired state to be brought about.

[16] Note that we *could* provide an accessibility relation and allow the availability of plans to vary across states and worlds—e.g. the plans available to the agent (as opposed to simply applicable) may depend on the situation in which the agent finds itself.

[17] For example, it is not clear that intentions arising from plans are the *only* intentions we want to allow.

The introduction of plans requires the addition of two new modalities: PLAN and OPLAN. PLAN(Φ) asserts that Φ is a plan available to the agent (i.e. a plan from its library). OPLAN is a bi-modal operator: OPLAN($\phi, \Phi_1 \wedge ... \wedge \Phi_n$) asserts that $\Phi_1 ... \Phi_n$ are the *only* plans available to the agent for achieving ϕ. OPLAN captures the limitations on an agent's choices for achieving its goals and is used to predict the future intentions of the agent. Plan worlds are similar to intention-worlds, with the restriction that *all* paths in a plan-world correspond to action-sequences from plans available to the agent (via its plan library).

Definition 3. *We extend the syntax of our language as follows. Let a* plan-formula *be a formula of the form* $[\pi']\phi'$ *or* $\phi''[\pi']\phi'$.

- *If* Φ *is a plan-formula, then* PLAN(Φ) *is a state formula;*
- *if* ϕ *is a state formula and* $\Phi_1, ..., \Phi_n$ *are plan formulas, then* OPLAN($\phi, \Phi_1 \wedge ... \wedge \Phi_n$) *is a state formula.*

The semantics is modified by adding another set $\mathcal{P}$ *of worlds to each interpretation* I*, such that* $\mathcal{P} \subseteq W$*. The worlds in* $\mathcal{P}$ *are called* plan worlds. *Given a term* π*, let* $\mathcal{A}_{\mathcal{P}}(\pi)$ *denote the action (i.e. set of tuples) to which* π *is mapped, restricted to worlds in* $\mathcal{P}$*—i.e.* $\mathcal{A}_{\mathcal{P}}(\pi) = \{\langle w_s, w_t\rangle \mid \langle w_s, w_t\rangle \in \mathcal{A}(\pi) \text{ and } w \in \mathcal{P}\}$.

Given a plan library $\mathcal{L}$ *(containing formulas of the form* $\phi'[\pi]\phi$[18]*), we require each interpretation to satisfy the following conditions:*

- *every plan in the plan library is true in every plan-world. Formally:* $\mathcal{A}_{\mathcal{P}}(\pi)\backslash_{\mathcal{V}(\phi')} \subseteq \mathcal{A}_{\mathcal{P}}(\delta\phi)$*, for every plan* $\phi'[\pi]\phi \in \mathcal{L}$*;*
- *the only way of achieving* ϕ *is by using a plan-body whose triggering condition* ϕ' *matches* ϕ.[19] *Formally:* $\mathcal{A}_{\mathcal{P}}(\delta\phi) \subseteq \bigcup\{\mathcal{A}_{\mathcal{P}}(\pi')\backslash_{\mathcal{V}(\phi'')} \mid \phi''[\pi']\phi' \in \mathcal{L} \text{ and } \mathcal{V}(\phi') \subseteq \mathcal{V}(\phi)\}$

where $S\backslash_{S_1} = \{\langle w_s, w_t\rangle \mid \langle w_s, w_t\rangle \in S \text{ and } w_s \in S_1\}$.[20]

The truth conditions for the new modalities are defined as follows:

- $I, w_t \models$ PLAN(Φ) *iff* $I, w' \models \Phi$ *for every* $w' \in \mathcal{P}$*;*
- $I, w_t \models$ OPLAN($\phi, \phi_1''[\pi_1']\phi_1' \wedge ... \wedge \phi_n''[\pi_n]\phi_n'$) *iff*
  (i) $I, w_t \models$ PLAN($\phi_1''[\pi_1']\phi_1'$) $\wedge ... \wedge$ PLAN($\phi_n''[\pi_n']\phi_n'$)*;*
  (ii) $\mathcal{V}(\phi_1') \subseteq \mathcal{V}(\phi)$ *and ... and* $\mathcal{V}(\phi_n') \subseteq \mathcal{V}(\phi)$*; and*
  (iii) $\mathcal{A}_{\mathcal{P}}(\delta\phi) \subseteq \bigcup_i\{\mathcal{A}_{\mathcal{P}}(\pi_i')\backslash_{\mathcal{V}(\phi_i'')}\}$.

The truth conditions of OPLAN can be described as follows: (i) each of the $\phi_i''[\pi_i']\phi_i'$ must indeed be a plan; (ii) each of the $\phi_i''[\pi_i']\phi_i'$ must be a plan for achieving ϕ (i.e. their triggering conditions must match ϕ); (iii) the union of these plans must encompass *all* ways of achieving ϕ. Note that these conditions taken together more or less reflect the conditions imposed on plan-worlds.[21]

---

[18] Recall that plans of the form $[\pi]\phi$ are written $\mathsf{T}[\pi]\phi$.

[19] I.e. in that $I \models \phi' \supset \phi$.

[20] I.e. $\mathcal{A}_{\mathcal{P}}(\pi)\backslash_{\mathcal{V}(\phi')}$ is the set of actions denoted by π, restricted to those whose first state supports ϕ'.

[21] We are currently investigating a semantic characterisation of OPLAN which is more closely related to Levesque's [7] characterisation of *only knowing*.

4 Plans and Intentions

R&G [9] define a number of conditions which ensure that the interaction between an agent's beliefs, desires and intentions satisfy certain properties which they consider to be necessary to rational behaviour. In this section, we examine some of the properties of our representation of plans and examine the interaction between an agent's intentions and its plans.

The conditions defined in [9] relate belief-, desire- and intention-worlds to each other. By similarly relating plan-worlds to intention-worlds, we are able to similarly ensure certain desired interactions between intentions and plans. In particular, we require every intention-world to be a plan-world.

Definition 4. *Every interpretation I is required to satisfy the following condition: for all world-state pairs w_t, $\mathcal{I}_t^w \subseteq \mathcal{P}$.*

The purpose of this restriction is to force an agent's intentions to be determined by its plans—in particular, effects are achieved only via plans from the agent's plan library. This is the behaviour we want—e.g. if an agent intends opening a door, it will not *intend* that a hurricane blow the door down (even if this is a real possibility) unless it has a plan for doing so.

The above semantic condition is formalised by the axiom $\mathsf{PLAN}(\Phi) \supset \mathsf{INT}(\Phi)$. Note that intending a plan Φ in no way involves the agent making a commitment to a particular choice of actions—i.e. the agent may never actually "choose" to perform the plan-body of Φ. The above axiom simply enforces the semantic requirement that intention-worlds contain action paths in which effects are only achieved by actions performed by the agent.[22]

The above simple semantic constraint ensures certain desirable properties in an agent's intentions. The first of these is that an agent uses its plans to satisfy an intention.[23]

Proposition 5. $\models \mathsf{INT}(inev(\bigcirc \mathsf{F}\phi)) \wedge \mathsf{OPLAN}(\phi, \phi_1'[\pi_1]\phi_1 \wedge \ldots \wedge \phi_n'[\pi_n]\phi_n)$
$\supset \mathsf{INT}(inev(\mathsf{F}(\phi_1' \wedge do(\pi_1)) \vee \ldots \vee \mathsf{F}(\phi_n' \wedge do(\pi_n))))$

This proposition states that if an agent has an intention to achieve ϕ in the future (i.e. it intends that ϕ inevitably becomes true), then it will also adopt the intention that it performs the body of one of its plans in order to achieve ϕ. The use of the $\bigcirc$ operator in the antecedent restricts the above result to intentions towards strictly future conditions—in particular, an agent may not intend to use a ϕ-achieving plan if ϕ already holds at the current time-point (which is to be expected). Note that a plan will only be executed if its precondition becomes true; however, that precondition may be empty (i.e. ϕ_i' may be T).

The above result is weaker than perhaps we would expect—in particular, we may expect the disjunction to take scope over the intention-operator, leading to a

[22] In fact, intending Φ—e.g. intending that whenever π were performed ϕ would become true—is possibly even intuitively meaningless, although there certainly seems to be nothing particularly problematic with holding such an intention.

[23] $\models$ denotes truth at all states in all worlds in all interpretations.

conclusion of the form $\mathsf{INT}(inev(\mathsf{F}(\phi'_1 \wedge do(\pi_1)))) \vee \ldots \vee \mathsf{INT}(inev(\mathsf{F}(\phi'_n \wedge do(\pi_n))))$. The difference between such a formula and the result in the proposition is that the latter involves no commitment to any plan—i.e. at the point at which the agent holds the intention towards ϕ, it only intends that it will achieve ϕ using (one of) its plans. The stronger result would imply a commitment to a particular plan—i.e. at each world, one of the disjuncts (each of which corresponds to a particular plan) would hold—a commitment which is made *at the point at which the intention towards ϕ is held.* The result of the proposition reflects the important notion of *delayed commitment*: the agent only commits to achieving its goal and only chooses a particular plan only when it must, and no earlier. For this reason, we believe that the (weaker) result of the proposition above is the preferred property.[24]

A second property relates to "achieve" actions. Consider a plan of the form $[\delta\psi; \alpha]\phi$: i.e. to achieve ϕ, first achieve ψ and then perform the action α. If the agent executes this plan body, then it will also achieve ψ and execute α: i.e. $\models do(\delta\psi; \alpha) \supset \mathsf{F}(\psi \wedge do(\alpha))$. In general, we have the following property.

Proposition 6.
$\models do(\alpha_0; \delta\psi_1; \alpha_1; \ldots; \delta\psi_n; \alpha_n) \supset do(\alpha_0) \wedge \mathsf{F}(\psi_1 \wedge do(\alpha_1) \wedge \ldots \wedge \mathsf{F}(\psi_n \wedge do(\alpha_n)))$[25]

While this property does not relate to intentions directly (i.e. the above implication holds at all worlds, not just plan- and intention-worlds), it combines with the previous proposition to provide the following property. (For purposes of abbreviation, we focus on a single plan.)

Proposition 7.
$$\models \mathsf{INT}(inev(\bigcirc\mathsf{F}\phi)) \wedge \mathsf{OPLAN}(\phi, \ldots \wedge \phi'_k[(\alpha_0; \delta\psi_1; \alpha_1; \ldots; \delta\psi_n; \alpha_n)]\phi_k \wedge \ldots)$$
$$\supset \mathsf{INT}(inev(\ldots \vee \mathsf{F}(\phi'_k \wedge do(\alpha_0) \wedge \mathsf{F}(\psi_1 \wedge do(\alpha_1) \wedge \ldots \wedge \mathsf{F}(\psi_n \wedge do(\alpha_n)))) \vee \ldots))$$

The "achieve ψ_i" actions in the plan for ϕ results in an indirect posting of intentions to achieve ψ_i, which is the sort of behaviour we would expect from the BDI architecture—i.e. plans lead to new intentions being adopted. Following from the earlier discussion, the intentions toward ψ_i are not of the form $\mathsf{INT}(inev(\psi_i))$ since there is a delayed commitment toward a specific plan. However, once the agent committed to using, say, the plan described in the above proposition to achieve the goal ϕ, then this would involve posting intentions towards the subgoals ψ_i. Note also if the plan mentioned in the proposition was the *only* ϕ-achieving plan available in the agent's plan library, then the agent would indeed adopt the intention to achieve each of the ψ_i—i.e. $\mathsf{INT}(inev(\mathsf{F}\psi_i))$ would be a consequence of $\mathsf{INT}(inev(\bigcirc\mathsf{F}\phi)) \wedge \mathsf{OPLAN}(\phi, \phi'_k[(\alpha_0; \delta\psi_1; \alpha_1; \ldots; \delta\psi_n; \alpha_n)]\phi_k)$, for each i. In the general case, however, at the point of having the intention to achieve ϕ, the strongest we can expect is for the agent to be committed towards

[24] Note that the stronger property would be supported if we used a *linear-time* rather than a branching-time logic (e.g. see [8]).

[25] For the fully general case, we allow any of the ψ_i to be T and any of the α_i to be the empty action.

using *some* plan for achieving ϕ—the commitment to a specific plan is delayed until necessary.[26]

There are clearly some desirable interactions between beliefs and plans. For example, we would expect $\mathsf{PLAN}(\Phi) \supset \mathsf{BEL}(\Phi)$ to be a theorem of the logic—if an agent has a plan for achieving ϕ then it should *believe* that the plan would achieve ϕ. This could be achieved by requiring all accessible belief-worlds to satisfy the first two constraints imposed on plan-worlds above.[27] As discussed earlier, the converse is *not* desired: even if an agent *believed* that an action α inevitably achieved ϕ, the agent should not ever adopt an intention towards doing α unless α is part of a plan (for achieving ϕ) in the agent's plan library.

5 Discussion

This paper reports initial work incorporating plans into a BDI logic. In particular, we have focussed on logically representing plans of the form found in agent systems such as PRS and modelling the interaction between an agent's available plans and the way in which these determine subsequent intentions of that agent. A primary concern has been to represent plans without reference to an agent's intentions and derive the properties of interaction between plans and intentions from separately imposed semantic and syntactic conditions. This is in contrast to the approaches of Wobcke [12] and Konolige and Pollack [6], both of whom explicitly incorporate intentions into their representation of plans. For example, Wobcke represents plans in the format $\mathsf{INT}(\phi) \wedge \mathsf{BEL}(\psi) \supset \mathsf{INT}(\phi')$; Konolige and Pollack define a representation $By(\alpha; \beta_1, ..., \beta_n)$ of plan-like structures which intuitively mean "the agent intends to achieve α by achieving β_1 and ... and β_n". By representing plans in a way that avoids explicit reference to intentions, we believe that our approach provides a more direct representation of the sort of plans found in implemented systems.[28]

While we argued that the results of the previous section, relating plans and intentions, were the desired ones, it would be interesting to further investigate the issue of commitment. In order to resolve a goal, an agent eventually chooses a plan from its library and *commits* to it. This roughly involves adopting intentions for further actions based on this particular plan—i.e. a subgoal ψ of such a plan will lead to the agent having an intention $\mathsf{INT}(inev(\mathsf{F}\psi))$. However, the notion of commitment is usually vaguely specified and not universally agreed on. An investigation of the formal properties of commitment to plans, within the logical framework defined here, will hopefully clarify the issue and take us closer to a comprehensive formal specification of intention-based agent systems.

Further investigation is also needed to determine whether certain plan libraries lead to an inconsistent framework—e.g. for the action sequences to satisfy the various restrictions on plan worlds, we need to ensure there are sufficient

---

[26] Again, using a linear-time logic would achieve the stronger result.

[27] Given $\mathsf{PLAN}(\Phi) \supset \mathsf{INT}(\Phi)$, this is captured by requiring $\mathsf{INT}(\Phi) \supset \mathsf{BEL}(\Phi)$.

[28] Singh's [11] representation also avoids explicit representation of intentions in plans.

plan bodies to achieve the conditions intended by an agent (recall that all intention worlds are plan worlds). In fact, this may lead to a characterisation of what constitutes an "adequate" collection of plans. The worlds framework itself introduces various characteristics. For example, the following is a consequence of the framework: $\models [\delta\phi]\psi \wedge \neg(\phi \supset \psi) \supset \mathsf{PLAN}([\delta\phi]\psi)$—if ψ always holds after achieving ϕ, then (unless ϕ implies ψ) the plan library *must* (explicitly) contain a plan to achieve ψ by achieving ϕ. Note that this does not relate to an agent's beliefs—it relates to all worlds—and so is analogous to the problem of logical omniscience in modal epistemic logics. It seems that we would need to move to a non-standard logic of intentions (e.g. [2, 12]) to address this particular issue.

There are other technical issues that require further investigation. One of these is a semantic characterisation of OPLAN based on Levesque's [7] notion of "only knowing". The proof-theoretic characterisation of δ also needs further research—since we have modified Segerberg's semantic conditions, particularly his condition ensuring maximality, the corresponding axiom schemas will also require modification. Other aspects of the framework to be investigated include: further properties of the interaction between plans, intentions and beliefs; extending the logical framework to a first-order language; and allowing more complex action descriptions (i.e. non-deterministic, parallel and failed actions).

References

1. M. E. Bratman. *Intentions, Plans, and Practical Reason.* Harvard University Press, Cambridge, MA, 1987.
2. L. Cavedon, L. Padgham, A. Rao, and E. A. Sonenberg. Revisiting rationality for agents with intentions. In *Eighth Australian Conference on AI*, 1995.
3. P. R. Cohen and H. J. Levesque. Intention is choice with commitment. *Artificial Intelligence*, 42(3), 1990.
4. E. A. Emerson. Temporal and modal logic. In J. van Leeuwen, editor, *Handbook of Theoretical Computer Science: Volume B.* Elsevier, Amsterdam, 1990.
5. M. P. Georgeff and F. F. Ingrand. Decision-making in an embedded reasoning system. In *IJCAI-89*, 1989.
6. K. Konolige and M. Pollack. A representationalist theory of intention. In *IJCAI-93*, 1993.
7. H. Levesque. All I know: A study in autoepistemic logic. *Artificial Intelligence*, 42, 1990.
8. A. S. Rao and M. P. Georgeff. Asymmetry thesis and side-effect problems in linear time and branching time intention logics. In *IJCAI-91*, 1991.
9. A. S. Rao and M. P. Georgeff. Modeling rational agents within a BDI-architecture. In *Second Int'l Conf. on Princ. of Knowledge Representation and Reasoning*, 1991.
10. K. Segerberg. Bringing it about. *Journal of Phil. Logic*, 18, 1989.
11. M. P. Singh. *Multiagent Systems: A Theoretical Framework for Intentions, Know-How, and Communications.* Springer Verlag, Heidelberg, Germany, 1994.
12. W. Wobcke. Plans and the revision of intentions. In *First Australian Workshop on Distributed AI*, 1995.

An Architecture for Autonomous Flying Vehicles: A Preliminary Report[†]

Lam-Fan Lee and Alex Kean
(llee@cs.ust.hk, kean@cs.ust.hk)

Department of Computer Science,
Hong Kong University of Science and Technology,
Clear Water Bay, Kowloon, Hong Kong

Abstract. This paper presents an architecture for task independent autonomous flying vehicles. First, we review the conventional architectures such as the model-and-planner, behavior-based, and the subsumption architectures. Second, we propose a strategic architecture, an adaptive composition of a set of strategic multi-agents, which could overcome many limitations of the existing architectures. Each strategy is designated to deal with a task and the composition of strategies tackle more complex task. The proposed strategic architecture maintains a uniform design for its low level control, high level planning, and multi-robot co-operative system thus facilitating strategies' composition and abstraction. This highly modular organization is hardware independent and increases the reusability of strategies. *Keywords:* Architecture, Multi-agent System, Planning.

1 Introduction

Research in autonomous flying vehicles is attracting attention (Lewis *et al.*, 1993; Baker *et al.*, 1992), chiefly due to its challenging new problems and its potential applications. These challenges include the difficulty in simultaneously coordinating multiple control points in an uncertain three dimensional environment, new research issues in three dimensional path planning and land covering problems, and the intricate interaction between task planning and path planning. In applications, these envisioned autonomous systems reduces the flight cost by reducing the size, weight, energy consumption, and considerable risks to human pilot. It is most suitable for routine works such as un-manned aerial map surveying and aerial monitoring of land traffic. It can potentially aid human operation in hazardous tasks such as forest fire fighting and high-sea or mountain terrain search-and-rescue operation.

Conventionally, building autonomous systems employs a bottom-up approach. We differ by using a top-down approach aiming at a more generic and flexible architecture. First, a generic and domain independent autonomous system architecture is designed. Hereon we shall call this architecture the *strategic architecture*. The strategic architecture is based on the strength of the existing architectures and complement known weakness with strategy from biological system. The strategic architecture is a decentralized, multi-layer and homogeneous structure of strategies. A *strategy* is a *program* performing a task and strategies can contribute or inhibit each other through sensor

[†] This research is supported by RGC grant HKUST 610/94E.

data-flow and definition-flow channels. Each strategy is designated for a purpose ranging from low level control, high level planning to multi-strategy cooperation. Explicit data and procedures communication between strategies is accomplished via message passing in a consultation-reply channel. A specific helicopter model and eventually the physical system will be built in order to demonstrate its feasibility and adaptability. In this preliminary report, we shall focus on describing the strategic architecture[1].

2 Evolution of Autonomous Systems Architecture

2.1 Model-and-Planner Approach

Robot planning, as described in (Sheu and Xue, 1993) and (Jones and Flynn, 1993), is to break down the whole decision process into four steps. First, the *sensor fusion* step constructs a complete internal world model of all anticipated sensor information. Second, the *task planning* step generates an optimal plan for a given goal based on the world model. Third, the *path planning* step finds a collision-free path in the world model for motion, and the *plan execution* step faithfully executes the optimal plan along the collision-free path. There can be no room for error or inconsistency in all these steps.

However, there are limitations with this approach. As Brooks (1991) has convincingly argued that constructing a complete world model by integrating all the sensor input is impractical and unnecessary. This leaves us with an incomplete world model which yield ineffective planning. Scaling up the system by augmenting the incomplete world model or extending the planners will inevitably increases the complexity of the system to become unmanageable. Moreover, information bottleneck arises when large number of sensor information are combined and used as a whole in the world model.

The dependency between steps indicates complete planning must occur prior to actions, thus, resulting in slow response time due to the time-consuming nature of planners. Consequently, any change in the world model forces a complete re-planning, no matter how small or localized the change has on the already planned action. The segregation of task and path planning steps, in that order, constrains the possibility of switching focus (or priority) between time-critical and path-critical task, or task with interwoven time and path criticality. One possible exception to the re-planning problem is the hierarchical approach by (Britanik and Marefat, 1995). This is an indication structural representation is essential, and structural flexibility is crucial.

Automating flying vehicles in a dynamic environment requires fast planning and re-planning, and real-time response in low level control. The autonomous system must be capable of scaling up without incurring information bottleneck, degrading the system response time. It is also not possible to completely characterize the world model of flying vehicles. For instant, airstream - a factor affecting flying vehicle's motion - is unpredictable, dynamically changing and chaotic nature.

2.2 Blackboard Architecture

The problem solving approach by the Blackboard Architecture (Nii, 1989) is via the co-operation of many knowledge sources, in a distributed manner. Each knowledge source

[1] The detailed description of the design and implementation is reported in (Lee, 1996).

consists of partitioned domain knowledge for solving a problem. A blackboard data structure is used to keep problem-solving state data. A problem is incrementally solved by the mechanism of knowledge sources responded to change in a centralized blackboard data structure. Scaling up the system is by adding new knowledge sources. Expanding the knowledge source in this distributed fashion does keep the increased complexity of the existing system manageable. The shortfall is that it lacks coordination between knowledge sources prior to and during actions. Consequently, different knowledge sources may corporate inconsistently. Moreover, high volume of competing access (multi-read and write) by knowledge sources to the centralized blackboard causes bottleneck problem.

Automated flying vehicle requires sizeable amount of sensor information from the environment, which may pose a bottleneck problem for the central blackboard. Control and planner must also act and react in a cooperative or competing manner.

2.3 Behavior-based Architecture

Brooks's (1991) behavior-based approach resolves the bottleneck problem and improves the response time by treating the environment as the blackboard, i.e. a reactive system. Robots are situated in the world and its perceptual and decision making process and actuation are not separable when reacting to the environment.

The system consists of a set of behaviors capable of executing in parallel. Each behavior reflexively respond to the sensors with action in a tight sensor-action loop. Furthermore, behaviors are flat in the sense that it is not possible to define higher order behaviors taking input from one and generating effect on the other behavior. In such, behaviors act without communication and coordination with others, giving rise to possible inconsistency like stuck in motion.

There is no explicit world model representation therefore there is no global planning. Consequently, there is no systematic method of establishing interaction between behaviors in a functional way, for instance, in a hierarchical arrangement. These limitations constrain the development of sophisticated behaviors for generic task resulting in hard-wiring behavior for each task. Furthermore, Mason (1993) points out that motor history, inborn information and expectation are necessary information in autonomous system, but are not available without explicit representation.

The Brooks' subsumption approach, described in (Jones and Flynn, 1993), resolves the inconsistency in behaviors by fusing competing behaviors' output with a pre-defined priority scheme. For instance, higher layer inhibits lower layer behavior's output. Again, an indication structural representation is essential. The behavior-based approach gains in response time even in uncertain environments by employing this tight sensor-action loop. Theoretically, its simplicity allows system scale up by constructing more behaviors. However, the exercise is usually *ad hoc* due to the lack of clear definition and homogeneity of behaviors. Clearly, behavior-based system's performance is highly correlated with the sensors' performance and limitations. For instance, Lewis *et al.* (1993) shows that delay in sensor information flow or sense failure degrades the response time, resulting in overall system degradation.

Tasks for flying vehicles, for instance establishing tilt angle for turning and balancing, involves changing requirement depending on different environmental factors.

It is economical to have generic behavior for generic task. Thus, task objectives must be explicitly represented and manipulated. Additionally, a unique requirement for autonomous flying vehicles is that it should exhibit "*plasticity*" in system degradation, in order to maintain acceptable safety criteria. Sensitivity of system performance on sensor failure should be minimized.

2.4 Multi-level Behavior-based Approach

The USC experimental autonomous flying vehicle system employs a task oriented, multi-level behavior-based approach (Lewis *et al.*, 1993). The system consists of four layers: low-, mid-, high-level behaviors and a sequencer in a unified framework. A high-level behavior performs its tasks using lower level behaviors and actuation occurs in the low-level behavior. The functions of behaviors vary in time and explicit communication between behaviors facilitate cooperation, compensating any possible delay in sensor information. This layering approach facilitates the construction of generic and sophisticated behaviors. The sequencer, acting as a manager, coordinates behaviors between levels and resolves possible conflicts between behaviors. The reliance on the quality of sensors is partially resolved by sending modulatory information between behaviors. However, changing requirement needs changing behavior definition. Thus, the system's versatility depends not only on sensor data-flow, but also definition-flow between behaviors. Furthermore, since the sequencer directly controls activities in several layers, it signals possible bottleneck problem.

3 The Strategic Architecture

The model-and-planner approach and the behavior-based architecture are the two extremes in a continuum of autonomous system architectures. The former approach generates a complete forethought plan for a goal prior to action whereas the latter relies on behaviors acting solely on sensor's information. The proposed *strategic architecture* bridges the two extremes by providing a homogeneous structure for behavior specification and interaction. The strategic architecture can be used to model variation of architecture that has characteristics that lies in the continuum between this two extremes.

3.1 Strategy

A *strategy* is an independent entity, designated to perform a whole or sub-task. It is a specialist similar to a knowledge source in the blackboard architecture. The collective workings of a set of strategies performs a task. A *primitive strategy* is a strategy directly couples with sensors and actuations, analog to low-level behaviors. Strategy contribute or inhibit each other through sensor data-flow and definition-flow channels. Explicit data and procedures communication between strategies is accomplished via message passing in a consultation-reply channel. Composition of strategies is defined by connecting the sensor data-flow, definition-flow and consultation-reply channels among a set of strategies, forming a larger and sophisticated strategy. Goal and static path planning, tracking, turns, rolling, and lateral cyclic control strategy are some examples.

3.2 Physical and Indirect Sensors

World information is captured by physical sensors and flows into targeted strategies. The data captured by the physical sensors is representative of some aspects of the physical world. However, physical sensors accuracy and reliability affect the overall system performance. To circumvent this dependency, we shall introduce a virtual sensor called *indirect sensor.* It is a virtual sensor combining data from multiple sensors, physical and indirect, and compute new information that reflect the characteristics of the physical world which cannot be captured by a physical sensor. Consistently, an indirect sensor is merely a designated strategy performing sensor filtering activity. This idea of extracting new information by transforming raw sensor input has an analog in biological system. For example, the mammal's visual cortex consists of different vision areas which contain different type of vision information (Young, 1991).

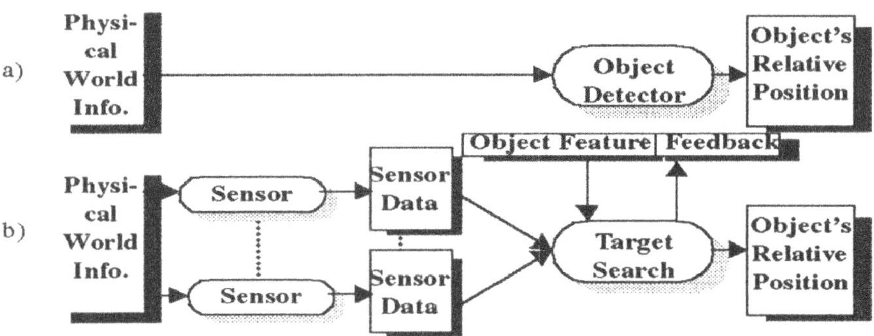

Fig. 1. Direct and Indirect Sensors

Strategy can reduce sensitivity to sensors information by using indirect sensor to provide redundancy in sensors information. For instance, combining a group of homogeneous low-accuracy physical sensors or fusion of different type of physical sensors. It can also be used to filter and recombine multiple sensors information, providing minimal and necessary information to strategies. Furthermore, allocating memory to indirect sensors facilitates recording sensor's history. Note that indirect sensors is a design to extract new information at the expense of response time with respect to physical sensors. The principle in designing an indirect sensor is typically driven by the need of the strategy that uses it. When an indirect sensor is serving a group of strategies, the indirect sensor is said to be task-oriented.

3.3 Consultation and Reply

A strategy may seek data or procedures from other specialized strategy in performing its task. For instance, a task planning strategy for an autonomous vehicle performs several tasks in different locations. It consults the path planning strategy for the sequence of optimal travelling locations. Such communication is achieved via the consultation-reply channel where data and procedures are transmitted via message passing. This communication channel is designed to address the need for cooperation between strategies. However, it can only be considered as an infrequently used channel because increasing communication between strategies can affects the overall system performance.

3.4 Definitions and Feedbacks

System's versatility depends on the ability of strategies adapting to the changes in task requirements (defined as definitions) on-the-fly caused by changes in the environment.

To facilitate definition passing, definition is type-less. For instance, a balancing strategy receive a change in definition to change from balancing at 0° to balancing at a tilted 15° angle. The change could be as simple as an on/off definition activating/deactivating a strategy or a temporal constraint to be satisfied. Common sense dictates the definition's complexity directly affects the performance of a strategy. As a principle, the differential in definition must be well defined and ordered. Thus, the balancing strategy is to perform a generic balancing task and the variability of definition influences the balancing behavior of the strategy.

The instigating strategy that changes the other strategy's definition receives a *feedback* in order to evaluate the effect of the change. The feedback is served as the input to a performance evaluation on the affected strategy by the instigating strategy. The definition and feedback tuple forms the control channel between strategies. Shared memory is the preferred method for the conceptual design and implementation, thus separating the strategy's execution and managing definition and feedback. Another option under investigation is to exploit message passing in object-oriented paradigm with parallel programming utilities.

3.5 Conflict Resolution in Definitions

Several strategies may compete to update the same strategy's definition. Four techniques to resolve this conflict are proposed. *Overriding* technique defines a total ordering of priority among competing strategies. This technique simulates inhibition behavior by strategy. For instance, safety monitoring strategy such as in obstacle avoidance, have higher priority in updating definition of motion strategy. *Sequencing* technique queue the updates in a FIFO order, resulting in the linearization of updates. If the definition is of numerical function type, such as aggregate, average, minimum or maximum, *function composition* is used to compose and evaluate the definition. Another alternative is to employ algebraic *constraints satisfaction* technique.

These techniques resides in the definition channel acting as a filter, independent of the strategy that updates or receives the definition. The complexity of the conflict resolution directly affects the strategy's performance. Time-critical strategy employs simplistic overriding or sequencing techniques whereas numerical function composition or constraint satisfaction techniques are appropriately used in sophisticated strategy at the expense of response time. It is intended these techniques will be turned into a strategy in our future design, consistent with other entities in the architecture.

Typical communication in a strategy with other entities is illustrated in figure 2. A strategy's definition is updated by higher layer strategies. Different updates is resolved

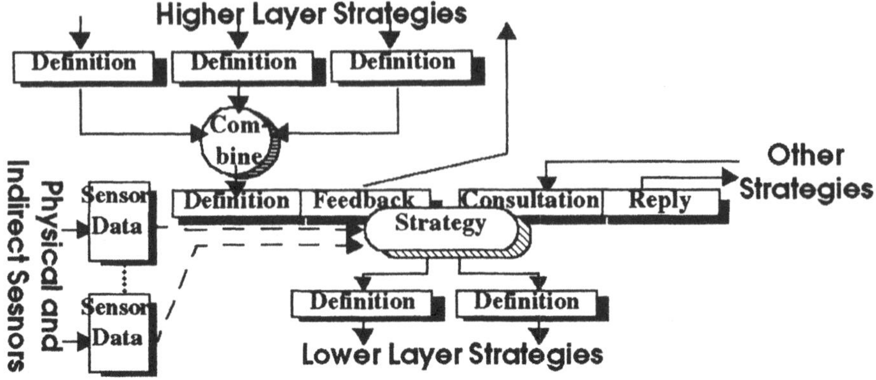

Fig. 2. A Strategic Architecture

by combining them into a single update in the definition. Physical sensors or indirect sensors feed sensor data into the strategy and explicit communication with other strategies is connected by the consultation-reply channel. The strategy can update the lower layer strategies' definitions in a similar fashion.

3.6 Strategy Composition

One of the advantages of the strategic architecture is its ease of composition. There are two kind of groupings: *functional* and *cross-functional* groupings. Functional grouping arranges strategies into layers demarcated by its functionality. Each layer in the hierarchy defines a functionality. For instance, defining an abstraction of tasks or an equivalent complexity class.

For our autonomous helicopter system, the basic control group is the lowest layer providing an interface to actuation. Next layer is the balancing control group performing reflex actions. For instance, the rolling strategy reactively maintains the cabin's banking angle and the anti-torque strategy continuously maintains the flight's direction. Maneuvers strategies, such as turning, is composed of strategies from the balancing control group. For instance, the rolling strategy is used to bank the helicopter into an optimal angle and rolling out when approaching the desired heading direction. Then, the anti-torque strategy is activated to fine tune the heading. These maneuvers strategies can further be used in more sophisticated strategies such as tracking and obstacle avoidance.

Cross-functional grouping embeds contributing strategies into a cross-layer strategic unit in tackling a task. Contributing strategies are strategies with different characteristics, such as response time, accuracy or response complexity, participating in tackling the task. For instance, the turns and anti-torque strategies are both responsible for the heading direction. Anti-torque strategy deals with finer direction movement by correcting the tail rotor pedals input; and the turns strategy deals with larger turn movement by combinations of other controls. Furthermore, rolling, tail-rotor pedal and lateral cyclic (LR) control strategy are also involved in the lateral motion. Thus, they are grouped

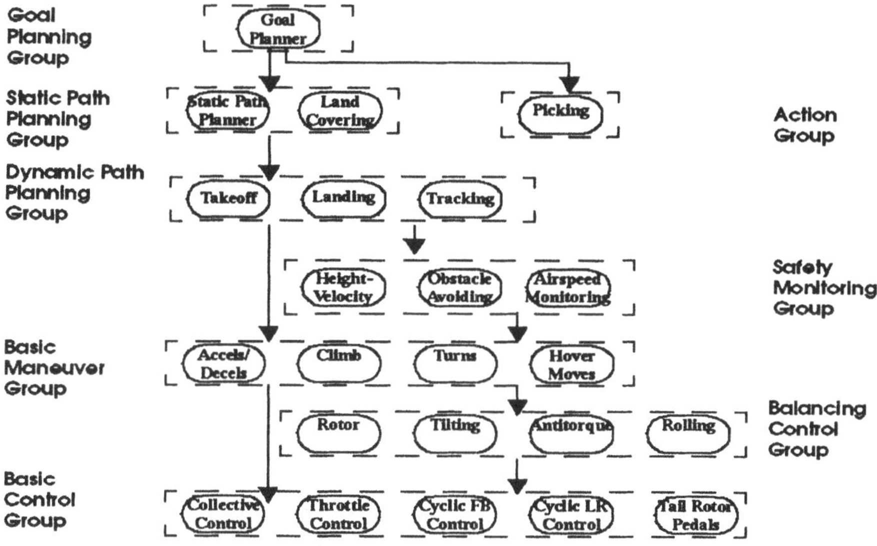

Fig. 3. Hierarchical Composition

into a lateral motion strategy unit. The grouping flexibility discussed provides the the strategic architecture modularity.

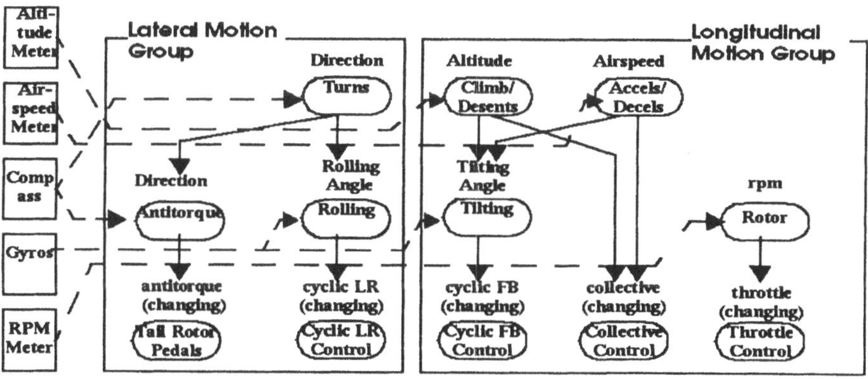

Fig. 4. Cross-functional Composition

4 Modelling Existing Architectures

The strategic architecture is the generalization of the model-and-planner and subsumption approaches and incorporating the flexible behavior-based architecture. Thus, we can model the existing architectures using the strategic architecture.

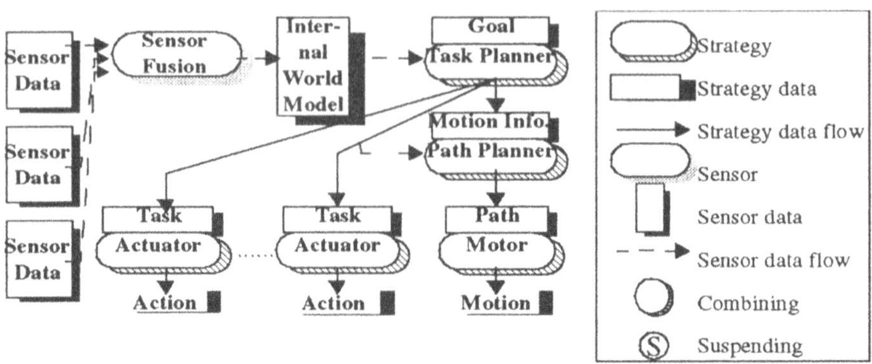

Fig. 5. The Model-and-Planner Approach

Figure 5 depicts the model-and-planner approach in which sensor fusion as an indirect sensor aggregating the sensor data and feeds it into the internal world model for task planning and path planning strategy. Given a goal, the task planning strategy defines a plan compose of a sequence of primitive actions carried out by activating each actuator sequentially. The specialized path planning strategy receives the same information from the internal world and the task planner. It plans and activates the motor primitive actions. Behavior-based approach (figure 6) is defined as a single layer of independent

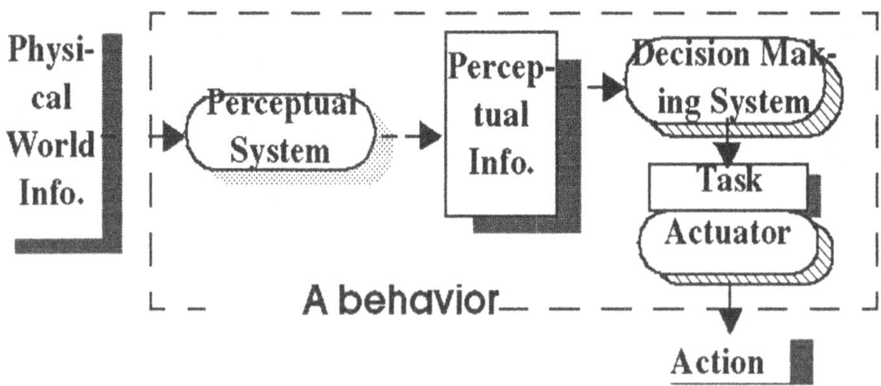

Fig. 6. The Behavior-based Architecture

behavior (strategy) with inseparable perceptual and decision making processes and actuator. No higher layer strategy coordinates among behaviors. A behavior-based system is a collection of all these independent unit of strategies. The subsumption approach, shown in Figure 7, is similar to the behavior-based architecture except that a behavior can inhibit other behavior over an actuator via the overriding technique in the definition channel.

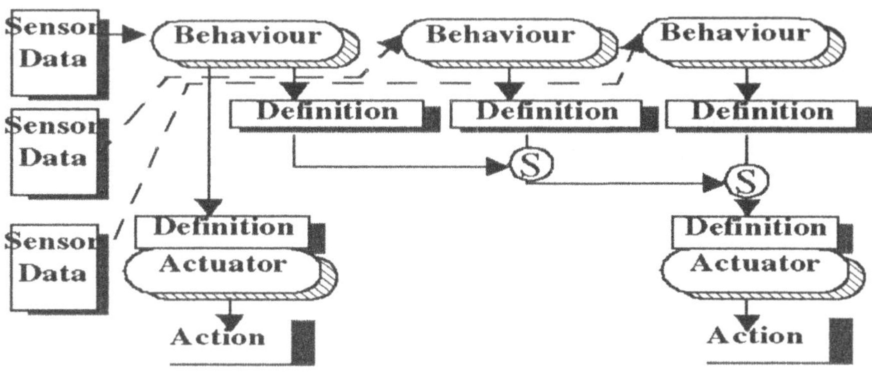

Fig. 7. The Subsumption Architecture

5 General Characteristics of Strategies

The strategic architecture's philosophy is to provide a homogeneous structure of representation for all strategies. The strategies can generally be ordered in a low to high layer fashion corresponding to the degree of a strategy's complexity. Lower layer strategies are characteristically time-critical, have shorter-term impact and need frequent updates on its definition. Higher layer strategies are less time-critical, have longer-term impact and its definitions are more stable. Additionally, higher layer strategies, for instance task planning strategies, are typically generic, hardware independent, and require more sophisticated sensor's information. Lower layer strategies such as rolling and tilting strategies are categorically dependent on its physical attributes and require less sophisticated sensor's information. Intuitively, higher layer strategies are of the similar characteristics to the model-and-planner approach and lower layer correspond to the behavior-based approach. However, the strategic architecture also permits the incorporation of architecture that falls between these two extremes.

6 Current Work

A preliminary design of an autonomous helicopter's strategic architecture is drafted and a simulation program is being built. Artificial sensors' data are used and the actuators' control signals are transformed into animation. The 3D graphics simulation is being built on an SGI machine based on McLean's (1990) mathematical model of helicopter's motion. The programming language is the objected-oriented language *C++* fitting the object oriented nature of the architecture. To increase its portability, the various communication channels, such as consultation and reply between strategies and the interface between the actual physical system and the simulation program, are encapsulated via the dynamic binding technique. This technique also enables the porting from one parallel programming scheme to another such as from PVM to multi-thread programming.

The drafted design has eight layers of strategies grouped according to its functionality (see figure 3). We shall summarize each layer briefly. The *basic control* strategies are the actuation strategies. These include the throttle, tail rotor controls and etc. The control's definitions are combined by aggregation to produce a single control signal for the actuation. The *balancing control* group has rotor, tilting, anti-torque and rolling strategies. These strategies are designed to support and simplify the basic maneuver strategies. Their definitions are numerical range such as the rate of change and the bank angle's range. *Basic maneuver* strategies are acceleration/deceleration, climbing, turning and hovering. These strategies have altitude and heading direction definitions and timing requirements. For example, the climbing strategy has three methods all require altitude and timing definitions. The change in these definition dictates which method is chosen. The cyclic-only method is used for rapid small gain in altitude; the collective-only method is used for smooth and small altitude gain; and the best-climbing method is used for large altitude gain (Padfield, 1992).

In the next layer, *safety monitoring* strategies and *dynamic path planning* strategies only make direct use of basic maneuver strategies, eliminating the need to interact with the lower layer control strategies. The safety monitoring strategies, such as obstacle avoidance, are strategically located in the middle of the whole structure because they are responsible for time-critical safety actions. Thus, they can override other strategies' use of maneuvers in the case of emergency. *Dynamic path planning* strategies are responsible for egocentric motion planning. They maintain the helicopter's spatial relationship with reference objects using sensor's information. For instance, the takeoff strategy relies on not only the absolute helicopter's altitude but also the relative distance from the ground. Similarly, the landing strategy maintains its stability by tracking its distance relative to the landing spot. Note that the reference object, in this case the ground, is changeable by updating the corresponding indirect sensor's definition. The tracking strategy performs general purpose tracking task.

Static path planning strategies plan the flight path with respect to the ground coordinate. An internal map is constructed using indirect sensors. The land covering strategy performs 2-dimensional land covering task (Iwano *et al.*, 1994) and we intend to generalize it to the 3-dimensional case. The *action* strategies is incorporated to handle task that is external to the helicopter. For instance, in forest fire fighting, an external bucket is connected tot he helicopter for loading and un-loading water. In the highest layer is the *goal planning* strategy, a general purpose task planner, that performs reasoning and problem solving. It recruits the lower layer strategies to execute its solution.

7 Conclusion

A strategic architecture is proposed to overcome the limitations of the existing architectures for autonomous system. It is a decentralized architecture consisting of layer-arranged homogeneous structure of strategies ranging from low level control, high level planning to multi-robot cooperative system[2]. Strategy composition can be functional or

[2] For instance, the decentralized control approach for distributed robot system (Laengle and Lueth, 1994).

cross-functional. Physical sensor and the introduction of indirect sensors enrich the sensor fusion process. The concept of definition and feedback channel allows the dynamic changes of strategy's requirement and conflict resolution techniques arbitrage competing updates by strategies. Explicit communication between strategies using consultation and reply channel completes the necessary interaction requirement. The strategic architecture covers the model-and-planner approach on one extreme and the behavior-based architecture one the other. Its flexibility and homogeneity will certainly lead to better design and implementation of autonomous systems.

Acknowledgment: We are grateful to Jane Mulligan (Department of Computer Science, University of British Columbia, Canada) for much of the idea of strategy programming.

References

1. Nelson C. Baker, Douglas C. MacKenzie, and Stephen A Ingalls. Development of an Autonomous Aerial Vehicle: A Case Study. *Journal of Applied Intelligence*, 2:271–297, 1992.
2. J. Britanik and M. Marefat. Hierarchical Plan Merging with Application to Process Planning. In *14th International Joint Conference on Artificial Intelligence*, pages 1677–1683, Montreal, Canada, 1995.
3. Rodney A. Brooks. Intelligence Without Reason. AI Memo No. 1293, Massachusetts Institute of Technology, 1991.
4. Kazuo Iwano, Prabhakar Raghavan, and Hisao Tamaki. The Traveling Cameraman Problem, with Applications to Automatic Optical Inspection (Extended Abstract). In *5th International Symposium on Algorithms and Computation*, pages 29–37, Beijing, China, 1994.
5. Joseph L. Jones and Anita M. Flynn. *Mobile robots: Inspiration to Implementation.* A.K. Peters, Wellesley, Massechusettes, 1993.
6. T. Laengle and T. C. Lueth. Decentralized Control of Distributed Intelligent Robots and Subsystems. In A. Crespo, editor, *Artificial Intelligence in Real Time Control*, pages 281–286. Pergamon, Oxford, UK, 1994.
7. Lam-Fan Lee. An Architecture for Autonomous Helicopters. Master's thesis, Department of Computer Science, Hong Kong University of Science & Technology, 1996. in preparation.
8. Anthony M. Lewis, Andrew H. Fagg, and George A. Bekey. The USC Autonomous Flying Vehicle: An Experiment in Real-Time Behavior-Based Control. In *IEEE International Conference on Robotics and Automation*, pages 422–449, Atlanta, Georgia, 1993.
9. Matthew T. Mason. Kicking the Sensing Habit. *AI Magazine*, 14(1), January 1993.
10. Donald McLean. *Automatic Flight Control Yystems.* Prentice Hall, New Jeysey, 1990.
11. Jane Mulligan. A Proposed Framework for Characterization of Robotics Systems. Technical Report 92-29, Department of Computer Science, University of British Columbia, 1992.
12. H. Penny Nii. Blackboard Systems. In Avron Barr, Paul R. Cohen, and Edward A. Feigenbaum, editors, *The Handbook of Artificial Intelligence*, volume 4, pages 1–82. Addison Wesley, 1989.
13. Randall R. Padfield. *Learning to Fly Helicopters.* TAB Books, Blue Ridge Summit, PA, 1992.
14. Phillip C-Y. Sheu and Q. Xue. *Intelligent Robotic Planning Systems.* World Scientific Publishing, Singapore, 1993.
15. Richard A. Young. Oh say, can you see? The Physiology of Vision. In *SPIE Vol. 1453 Human Vision, Visual Processing, and Digital Display II*, pages 92–123, San Jose, California, 1991.

Face Recognition Through Hough Transform for Irises Extraction and Projection Procedures for Parts Localization
- for Facial Caricaturing System PICASSO -

Yoshiaki SEGAWA †, Hiroshi SAKAI †, Toshio ENDOH ‡,
Kazuhito MURAKAMI †, Takashi TORIU ‡ and Hiroyasu KOSHIMIZU †

† School of Computer and Cognitive Sciences, Chukyo University
‡ Fujitsu Laboratories Ltd.

101 Tokodate, Kaizu-cho, Toyota, 470-03 JAPAN

Abstract In order to generate facial caricatures automatically, it is necessary to recognize facial parts in advance. Since it is difficult to realize the face recognition, the primal description of face has been provided manually so far also in our project PICASSO for facial caricaturing.

This paper presents a robust method to recognize human faces by detecting irises via Hough transform with a preprocessing based on a hierarchical binarization process and localizing parts-regions via projection process.

We experimented on this method with 30 face images and irises were successfully recognized for 29 images among them. Enforcing these results by employing a localizing procedure by means of projection process, a failure was quickly recovered and therefore the recognition rate of irises become 100%. In this paper, a procedure to extract other facial parts based on the information of irises were also proposed.

1. Introduction

We are developing PICASSO system for generating a facial caricature by computer[1]. Generally, when one draws a facial caricature he grasps the characteristic of the facial pattern, and emphasizes it. To generate a facial caricature by computer, it is necessary to get the positions and shapes of facial parts as a primal description of the face. Detection of the boundary of facial parts is an important step to get the primal description. We focus on iris extraction as the first step, because any person has almost the same shape of irises.

A. TOMONO and others have been proposed iris extraction method based on the least square method[2]. Since the method based on the least square method has the tendency to be affected by other facial parts, it is required to limit the processing region to extract irises. His method uses the zoomed-up image such that irises region occupies almost the whole image.

In this paper, we propose a method for extracting irises using Hough transform, which is not strongly affected by other facial parts. Hough transform was proposed by Hough and has been used for many applications[3]. However the application of Hough transform to this problem is not easy because the irises have less than 0.1% area in the whole face.

Then we propose a robust method for extracting irises by combining Hough transform with a preprocessing based on two-step thresholdings. We also propose a side procedure to evaluate the extracted irises. This procedure is realized by horizontal and vertical projections of the input image, and gives a evaluation information for the position of the detected irises. We also show experimentally the effectiveness of this method. Finally, we discuss a possible method for detecting other facial parts based on the information of the extracted irises.

2. The method for extracting irises[4]

2.1 Outline

The method we propose consists of main procedure (three processes); (1) preprocessing, (2) Hough transform, and (3) postprocessing and side procedure for evaluation of the main process (see Fig.1). In the preprocessing, the boundaries of irises are extracted, and then irises are extracted by using Hough transform. Since the irises have only 0.1% area in the whole face, it is necessary to remove other patterns in the preprocessing as much as possible. Then we adopt a strategy to narrow the processing region step by step.

In the preprocessing, first a median filter is operated to an input image to remove the noise. Then to extract the facial region, the image is binarized with a threshold such that the degree of coincidence between the out-most edges in the image and the region boundary of the binary image becomes highest[Appendix]. Next, in the facial region, the image is binarized again with a threshold such that the degree of coincidence between all edges in the image and the region boundary of the binary image becomes highest[5]. Then, to extract candidates for irises boundary, the largest connected region is removed as a hair region using a labeling process.

The candidates for iris pattern are extracted by applying Hough transform to the preprocessed image. Since Hough transform generates many candidates in general, a postprocessing is applied to determine the most probable pair of irises.

Concurrent to the above procedure, as the side procedures for irises recognition, vertical and horizontal projections are prepared for localizing the facial parts[4]. If the extracted pair of irises is out of the region of irises, the postprocessing in the main procedure must be executed again.

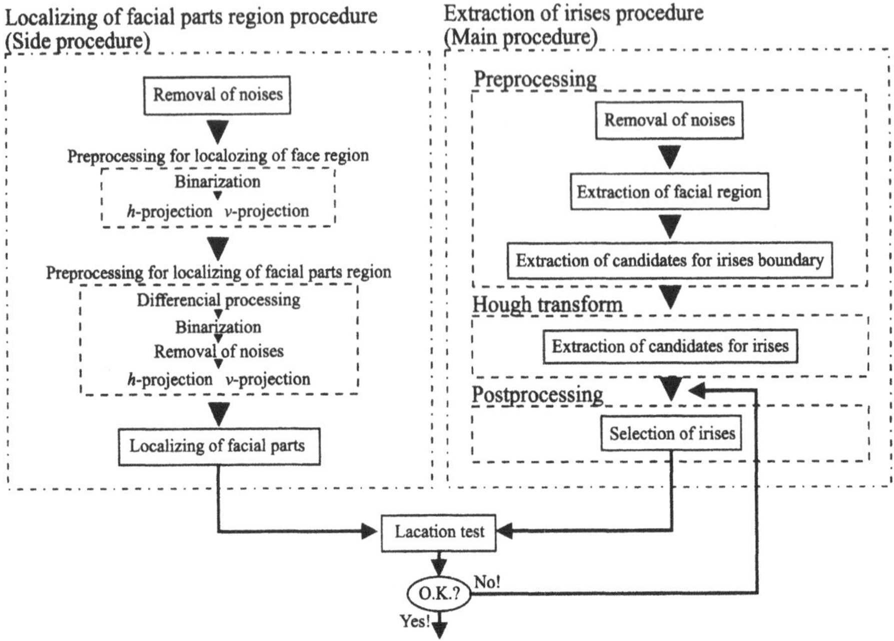

Fig.1. Flow chart of the recognition of facial parts

2.2 Preprocessor

(1) Median filtering In order to keep the edges clearer and to remove the noises, 5 ×5 median filter is applied to the original image.

(2) Extraction of facial region The image is binarized with a threshold such that the degree of coincidence between the out-most edges in the image and the region boundary of the binary image becomes highest. Let $I(x,y)$ be an original image and $J(x,y)$ be its differential image, and parameters s and t are the thresholds for binarizing $I(x,y)$ and $J(x,y)$, respectively. We find s and t such that the evaluation function $C(s,t)$ given by

$$C(s,t) = \frac{N(B_s \cap E_t)}{N(B_s \cup E_t)} \qquad (1)$$

is maximized. And we binarize $I(x,y)$ and $J(x,y)$ with these thresholds s and t. In eq.(1), $N(X)$ is the number of elements of the set X, B_s is the set of boundary pixels provided by thresholding $I(x,y)$ with s, and E_t is the set of the out-most edge pixels given by binarizing $J(x,y)$ with t. The out-most edges are defined as the exterior border of the extracted region by threshold t from $J(x,y)$.

The evaluation function $C(s,t)$ expresses the degree of coincidence between the boundary and the out-most edges.

In order to find s and t that maximize the evaluation function $C(s,t)$, it is not necessary actually to perform the image processing procedures such as binarization and edge detection for all combinations of the thresholds s and t. There is a method which reduces the order of computation to an order of the number of pixels as is shown in [5] and [Appendix].

(3) Extraction of candidates for irises boundary The original image $I(x,y)$ is binarized again in the same way of (2) except that the all edges on the inside of the facial region are used as E_t in eq.(1). Since it is not affected by the difference of gray values between the facial region and the background, the more proper threshold is selected to extract the facial parts.

The reason why a set of whole edges are used as E_t in eq.(1) is that the objective of this procedure is to extract irises.

And then, removing hair region, the rest are extracted as the candidates for irises boundary.

2.3 Hough transform for circle detection

First, we briefly describe the basic theory of Hough transform for circle detection.

The set of circles which have the same edge point (x_i,y_i) on their circumferences can be expressed by

$$(a - x_i)^2 + (b - y_i)^2 = r_0^2 \qquad (2).$$

Therefore, in order to detect some dominant circle from a noisy image, we first vote all possible parameters (a,b,r) for (x_i,y_i),i=1,2,3,$\cdots$. Since many corn's surfaces are accumulated in the parameter space, the highest crossing point can be easily detected as the dominant circle.

Then, if (a_0,b_0,r_0) is the detected parameter, the detected circle can be given by eq.(3) in image space.

$$(x - a_0)^2 + (y - b_0)^2 = r_0^2 \qquad (3)$$

In this paper, after the candidates for irises boundary are extracted, Hough transform for circle detection is applied to the candidates for irises boundary, and the candidates for irises are extracted.

Note that a kind of non-maximum suppression procedure is applied previously to the image to reduce computation cost. After that, candidate peaks for left and right irises are extracted independently from the corresponding left and right half region of the parameter space, respectively. The number of votes of the candidate peaks might be larger than or equal to a threshold.

2.4 Postprocessing

We present a method for selecting the best one from a number of left and right candidate pairs provided by the previous process.

The basic idea of this method is based on the following facts.

- Left and right irises are likely located to be horizontal.
- They are usually same in diameter.
- The previous process is likely to extract candidate circles at the outer region of the true irises.

The procedure of this method is realized by the following steps.

Step1. Let k be the maximum value of the votes, then the dominant circle be extracted here as the first candidate of iris.

Step2. Prepare a list for all possible left and right irises on condition that all counterparts are selected from the other side where the first candidate is extracted.

Step3. Delete any member of the list, in which the difference between vertical positions of right and left irises is greater than a threshold.

Step4. Delete any member of the list, in which the difference between radii of right and left irises is greater than a threshold.

Step5. First take a member from the list, in which the distance x_{lr} between right and left irises becomes minimum (x_{min}). Then, delete any member of the list, in which the distance x_{lr} must be satisfied by eq.(4).

$$x_{lr} \geq x_{\min} + \alpha \text{, where } \alpha \text{ is a clearance} \qquad (4)$$

Step6. Choose one pair of irises from the irises when more than one pair of irises are still remaining.

Step7. Decrement the parameter as $k = k - 1$, then go back to *Step2*.

2.5 Side procedures for evaluation

The following procedures are prepared to localize face region ($R^{(f)}$) and facial parts regions ($R^{(b)}$, $R^{(e)}$, $R^{(n)}$ and $R^{(m)}$).

(1) Binarization and projections After reducing random nise, input image is converted to binary image with a threshold given by discriminant analysis. Vertical and horizontal projections of the binary image, $p_i^{(v)}$, i=1,2,3,$\cdots$ and $p_j^{(h)}$, j=1,2,3,$\cdots$ are calculated.

(2) Localizing face region and facial parts region Projection $p_i^{(v)}$ and $p_j^{(h)}$ are utilized to detect face region $R^{(f)}$ by a simple thresholding process to these projections. The first and last points $i^{(l)}$ and $i^{(r)}$ satisfying $p_i^{(v)} > P^{(v)}$ are extracted as the leftmost and rightmost boundaries of the face region $R^{(f)}$. The first and last points $j^{(t)}$ and $j^{(b)}$ satisfing $p_j^{(h)} > P^{(h)}$ are also extracted as the top and bottom boundaries of $R^{(f)}$. Then, face region $R^{(f)}$ can be defined by eq.(5).

$$\text{for all } (i, j) \qquad i^{(l)} \leq i \leq i^{(r)}, \; j^{(t)} \leq j \leq j^{(b)} \qquad (5)$$

Within the face region $R^{(f)}$ defined by the previous procedure, projections $p_i^{(v)}$ and

$p_j^{(h)}$ are calculated again in order to avoid the disturbances caused by the background. Basing on these new projections, facial parts region $R^{(b)}$, $R^{(e)}$, $R^{(n)}$ and $R^{(m)}$ for eyebrows, eyes, nose, and mouth are extracted just in the same way as eq.(5) with thresholeds $P^{(b)}$, $P^{(e)}$, $P^{(n)}$, and $P^{(m)}$.

(3) Location tests The irises detected by Hough transform are tested here whether they are located inside of the eye region $R^{(e)}$ or not. If the condition is not satisfied, the candidates of irises are refined by using the information $R^{(e)}$ and the procedure for selection of irises given in 2-4 is repeatedly applied to these refined candidates.

3. Experiment and discussion

Each image was taken under the condition that the spot light was located in front of the face and the background was uniformly white. Each image is 640×480 in size and 8 bits in gray scale.

As a result, irises were successfully extracted for 29 images among 30 facial images. Figures 2～7 show the successive results of the processing procedure described before. The boundaries except for the boundary of irises was removed clearly. Consequently, no error boundary detection was happened in the processing. Applying Hough transform to the detected boundaries, irises were successfully extracted for the image even when a half iris is hidden by an eyelid. Fig.8 shows some typical examples of final results of extracted irises. These experiments demonstrated the proposed method works well for almost all faces.

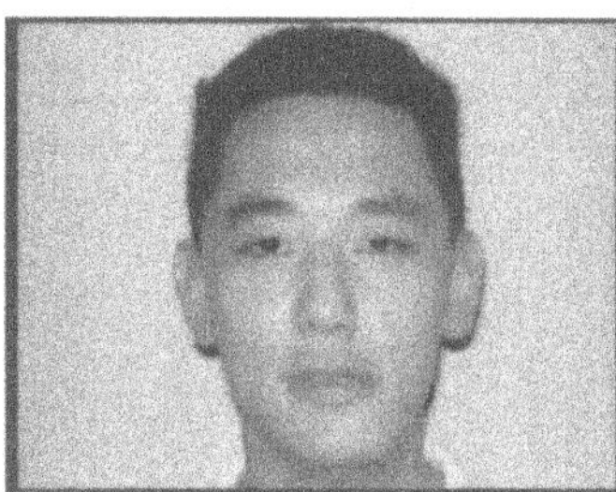

Fig. 2. Original image

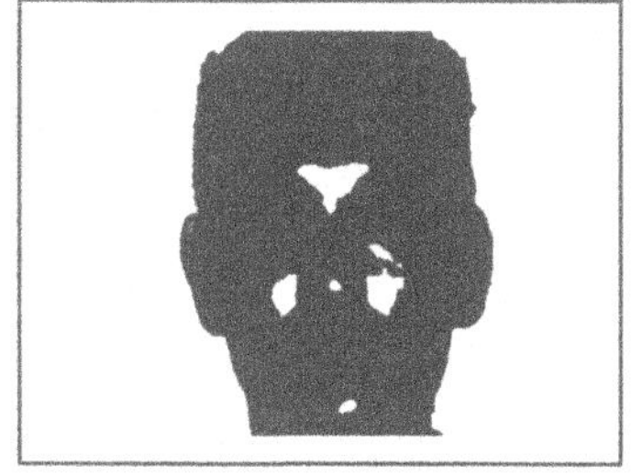

Fig. 3. Extracted facial region

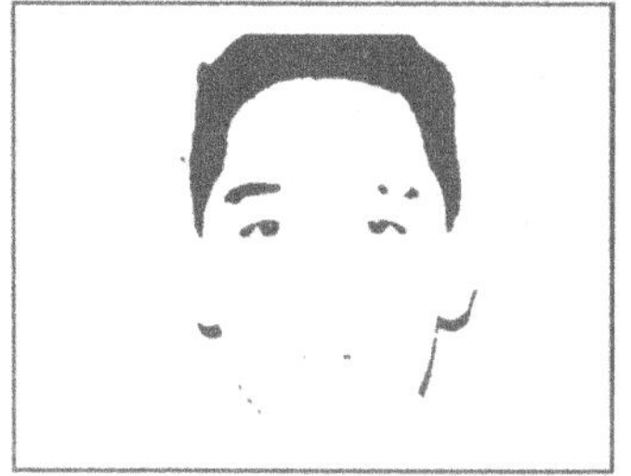

Fig. 4. Extracted facial parts

Fig. 5. Detected boundaries of facial parts

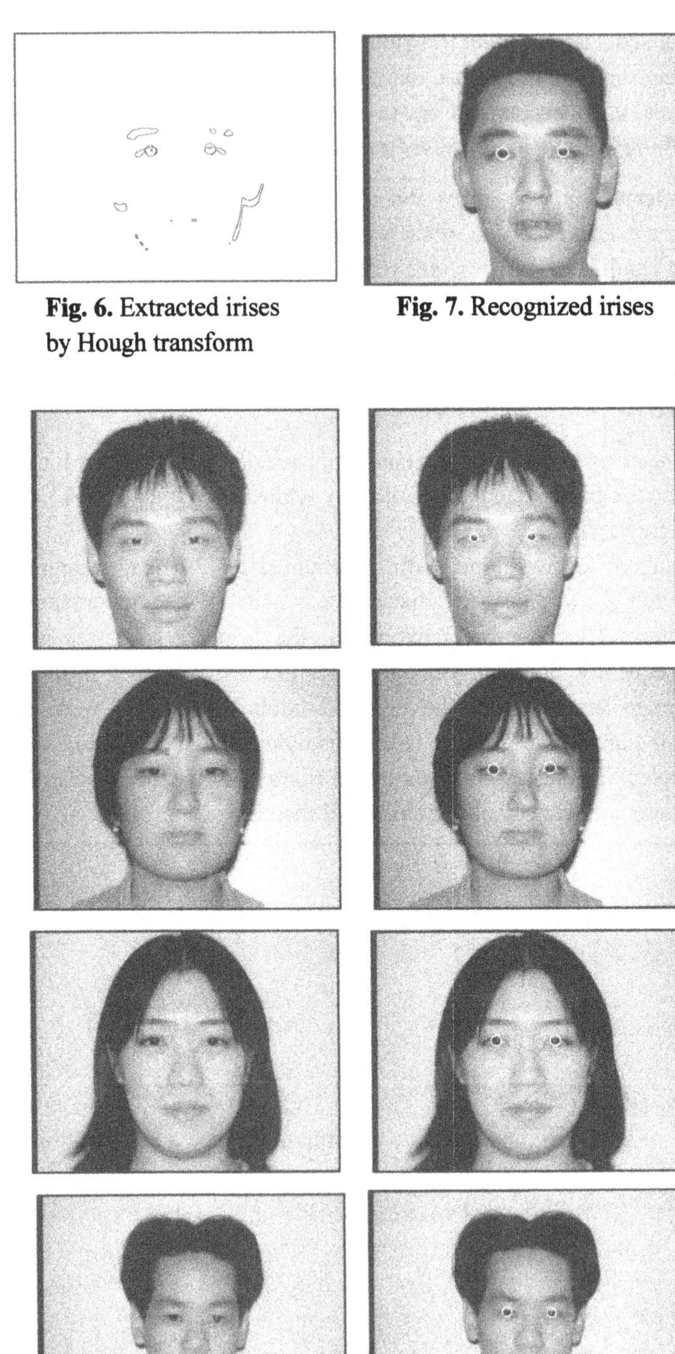

Fig. 6. Extracted irises by Hough transform

Fig. 7. Recognized irises

Fig. 8. Typical examples of final results of extracted irises

14 images included in the above 30 images were used for the side procedures. In the experiment, the recognition rate of face region $R^{(f)}$ became 100%, and the recognition rates of facial parts regions $R^{(b)}$, $R^{(e)}$, $R^{(n)}$ and $R^{(m)}$ became 86%, 100%, 100% and 86%, respectively. Fig.9 (a) and (b) show a result of successful example.

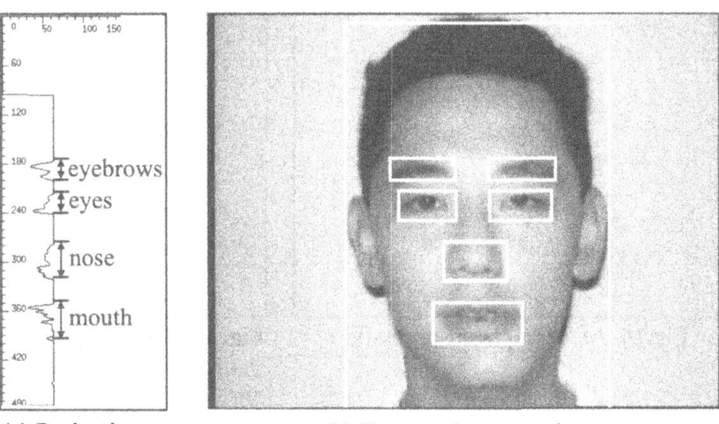

(a) Projection (b) Extracted parts regions

Fig.9. A experimental result of facial parts localization

In addition, we show an image given in Fig.10 which was failed in extraction of irises. In this case, because the boundary of right iris was not extracted as a smooth shape of arc, a circle was not detected around the right iris by Hough transform. And, as a result of postprocessor in subsection 2-4, a pair of tails of eyebrows were extracted as irises. Among 30 face images, this was only one example of failure.

It was experimentally known that this unsuccessful example was recovered by applying the information of eyebrow region $R^{(b)}$. In this case, since a pair of circles was not included in the region $R^{(b)}$, the postprocessing in the main procedure was executed again. As a result, all irises of all 30 image were perfectly extracted and it was finally known that the recognition rate of irises became 100%.

4. On recognition of other facial parts

The other facial parts except for irises, a nose, a mouth, etc., and the boundary of face and hair are necessary in primal description of face for PICASSO. Since irises can be extracted correctly, we can guess roughly the locations of other facial parts based on the information of irises. Therefore, as the regions of each facial parts can be extracted, the primal description of contour of each facial part can be realized by using the most suitable image processing for the respective facial part. And after the all facial parts are extracted, in order to adjust the expression to the scheme of PICASSO[1], the boundary of facial parts can be described with the specified number of boundary points by using resampling process. Thus, the generating primal description of face for facial caricaturing by PICASSO is completed by these processes.

Fig.11 is an example of facial caricatures generated by PICASSO, and the descriptions of these line drawings are of course provided by our method.

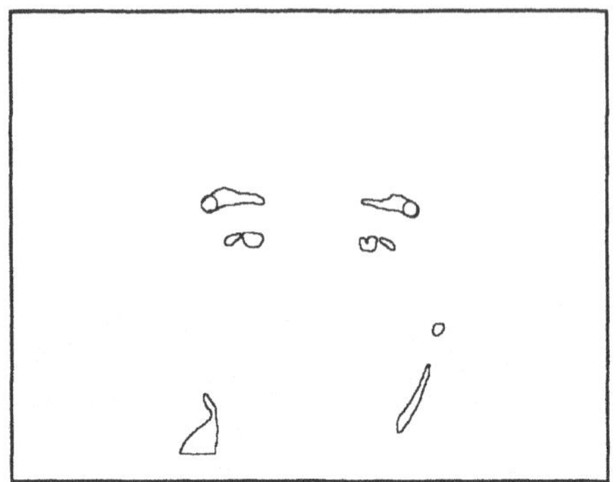

Fig.10. An example unsuccessful

Fig. 11. An example facial caricatures genarated by PICASSO

5. Summary

We have proposed a robust method to extract irises by using Hough transform for circle detection. And we have also proposed a preprocessing, which has features to narrow the processing region step by step. It consists of three processes; (1) removing noise in an input image by median filter, (2) extracting facial region by binarizing with a threshold such that the degree of coincidence between the out-most edges in the image and the region boundary of the binary image becomes highest, and (3) extracting candidates for the irises boundary by binarizing with a threshold such that the degree of coincidence between the all edges in the image and the region boundary of the binary image becomes highest. The preprocessing can remove the many patterns except irises, so that it enables Hough transform for circle detection to be applied exclusively to extracting irises. The Hough transform applied to candidates for the irises boundary can generate candidates for irises.

The candidates for irises are categorized to the candidates for the right iris and the left iris if they lie in the right side and the left side of the image, respectively. Reduction of candidates for irises is required because Hough transform generates many candidates in general. We have proposed a postprocessing to determine the most probable pair for irises among all pair of the left candidates and the right candidates.

The side procedures were also proposed in order to enforce the irises extraction. This procedures were based on projection processes which is robust for the existence of the noise in the image.

We have shown some experiments to extract irises by the proposed method from

30 facial images. Each image was photographed under the condition that the spot light was located in front of the face and background was uniformly white. As a result, irises were successfully extracted for 29 images. Combining the side procedures to the results, this unsuccessful extraction was easily recovered, and finally the recognition rate of irises became 100%. The photograph condition was sufficiently available for practical use, and the extraction for irises succeeded with high percentage.

It is a future work to extract other facial parts than irises using the information of extracted irises and to complete the primal description of face. And, more flexible applications of the side procedures should be examined to improve the performance of the face recognition.

[Acknowledgments]

We wish to express deep thanks to Grant-in-Aid of Scientific Research Promotion in Japan (No. 07207229, No. 07680415, No. 07780290) in 1995.

[References]

[1] K. Murakami, A. Nakamura, H. Koshimizu and F. Fukumura : "On Description of Facial Data in PICASSO for Facial Caricaturing System", PRU92-13, pp. 95-101 (May 1992).

[2] A. Tomono, F. Kishino and Y. Kobayashi : "Pupil Extraction Processing and Gaze Point Detection System Allowing Head Movement", IEICE Trans., Vol. J78-D-II, No. 3, pp. 636-646 (Mar. 1995).

[3] G. Chow and X. Li : "Toward a System for Automatic Facial Feature Detection", Pattern Recognition, Vol. 26, No. 12, pp. 1739-1755 (Dec. 1993).

[4] Y. Segawa, H. Sakai, T. Endoh, T. Toriu, K. Murakami and H. Koshimizu : "Extraction and Recognition of Facial Parts by Hough Transform", Proc. 1996 Anual Meating of IEICE (May 1996)

[5] T. Toriu, H. Iwase and T. Gotoh : "A Method for Threshold Selection Using Minimum Filtering", IEICE Trans., Vol. J72-D-II, No. 11, pp. 1800-1806 (Nov. 1989). Transaction: Systems and Computers in Japan, Vol. 21, No. 12, (1990).

[Appendix]

We describe a high-speed algorithm to obtain the thresholds s and t that maximize the objective function (1).

We define inter-pixel borders (vertical or horizontal) as the borders between two adjacent pixels, and define a region boundary as the boundary between regions and the background. Then, the necessary and sufficient condition that an inter-pixel border is on the region boundary of the binary image obtained by binarizing the original image with a threshold s is that the maximum value of two pixels on both sides of the border is equal to or greater than s, and also, the minimum value is smaller than s.

Accordingly, the total number of vertical or horizontal inter-pixel borders which are on the region boundary of the binary image for a threshold s is obtained by subtracting the cumulative histogram (accumulated from larger pixel values) for minimum value of two pixels on both sides of the border from that for the maximum value.

Next, we consider the case that E_t in equation (1) is a set of inter-pixel borders such that the absolute value of the difference of two pixels on both sides of the border is equal to or larger than a threshold t. We call these borders edges. The denominator of the formula (1) is equal to $N(B_s) + N(E_t) - N(B_s \cap E_t)$. Accordingly, the value of the objective function can be obtained from $N(B_s)$ the total number of inter-pixel borders constituting region boundary for the threshold s, $N(E_t)$ the total number of edges for the threshold t, and $N(B_s \cap E_t)$ the total number of inter-pixel borders constituting not only region boundary but also edges. Since edges are inter-pixel borders where the absolute value of the difference is equal to or larger than t, the total number of edges is obtained from the cumulative histogram for the absolute value of the difference. The total number of inter-pixel borders constituting the region boundary is obtained by the method mentioned above.

Then, as a basis of obtaining the total number of inter-pixel borders that are constituting not only the edges but also the region boundary, we consider a necessary and sufficient condition that an inter-pixel border belongs to not only the edges but also the region boundary. The condition is that the absolute value of the difference of two pixels on both sides of the borders is equal to or larger than t, the maximum value of those is equal to or larger than s, and the minimum value of those is smaller than s. Hence, the total number of the inter-pixel borders constituting not only the edges but also the region boundary is obtained by subtracting the number of the borders where the absolute value of the difference is equal to or larger than t and the minimum value is equal to or larger than s from the number of borders where the absolute value of difference is equal to or larger than t and maximum value is equal to or larger than s. This value can be calculated by subtracting 2-dimensional cumulative histogram (accumulated form larger values) for the absolute value of the difference and the minimum value from that for the absolute value of the difference and the maximum value. This calculation is performed for vertical borders and horizontal borders respectively, and the results are summed up.

Next, we consider the case that E_t in (1) is a set of out-most edges. The out-most edges consist of left-most edges, right-most edges, up-most edges, and down-most edges. The left-most edge is defined as the first edge that is found when one scans the image horizontally from the left end of the image. The right-most, up-most, and down-most edges are defined in the same way. As a preprocessing for calculating the value of the objective function, noticing left-most and right-most edges for example, we make such an image (left-right convex image) that at any pixel the value is the minimum of the maximum value of absolute values of differences at all inter-pixel borders located in the left-hand side of the pixel and the maximum value of absolute values of differences at all inter-pixel borders located in the right-hand side of the pixel.

Then, the necessary and sufficient condition that an inter-pixel border is left-most or right-most edge for a threshold t is that the border is on the region boundary when the left-right convex image is binarized with the threshold t. Therefore, the necessary and sufficient condition that an inter-pixel border belongs to both the region boundary and left-most or right-most edges is that the border is on the region boundary of the image obtained by binarizing the original image with the threshold s and also it is on the region boundary of the image obtained by binarizing the left-right convex image with the threshold t. This condition is equivalent to the condition that at that border the maximum value of two pixels on both sides of the border in the left-right convex image is equal to or larger than t, the minimum value of those is smaller than t, the maximum value of two pixels on both sides of the border in the original image is equal to or larger than s, and the minimum value of those is smaller than s. Consequently, the total number of inter-pixel borders that belong to not only the left-most or right-most edges but also the region boundary is obtained as follows. First, we calculate four 2-dimensional cumulative histograms H_1, H_2, H_3, and H_4. H_1 is the 2-dimensional cumulative histogram for the maximum value of two pixels on both sides of each border in the left-right convex image and the maximum value of those in the original image. H_2 is for maximum value in the left-right convex image and minimum value in the original image. H_3 is for minimum value in the left-right convex image and maximum value in the original image. H_4 is for minimum value in the left-right convex image and minimum value in the original image. Then, the total number of inter-pixel borders that belong to not only the left-most or right-most edges but also the region boundary is obtained as $(H_1 - H_2) - (H_3 - H_4)$. The total number of inter-pixel borders that belong to not only the up-most or down-most edges but also the region boundary is obtained in the same way. Using this, a method to obtain the value of the objective function (1) is easily constructed. In this method, to obtain the value of the objective function for all pairs of s and t, There is no necessity to perform image processing for binarizing the original image and detecting edges with all pairs of two thresholds s and t.

Extraction of Face Region and Features Based on Chromatic Properties of Human Faces

Tae-Woong Yoo and Il-Seok Oh
Department of Computer Science, Chonbuk National University
Deokjin-dong, Chonju, Chonbuk 560-756, Korea
email: isoh@moak.chonbuk.ac.kr

ABSTRACT

This paper presents a methodology to detect face region and some features, i.e., eyes and mouth, from color frontal face images as follows. Firstly we scissor face regions from many color face images and construct a face chromatic histogram in hue and saturation chromatic space. Secondly we use both the face symmetry information and chromatic histogram to detect the face region from the input image. Thirdly the locations of the eyes and mouth on the face region are determined by both detecting the intensity valley regions and using the positional relations of eyes and mouth in the face region. To support the methodology, this paper presents an implementation of the methodology. The results of the implementation show a high success rate.

1. Introduction

Many researches on human face image processing have been reported very widely [1, 2, 3, 4, 5, 6, 7, 8]. It is due to that more natural and intelligent interface between humans and computers becomes very important in computer community. For example, if a computer can detect the eye position and gazing direction of a pilot on flight simulator, it can assist the pilot's decision by displaying the region of the pilot's attention in high resolution. Similarly, the automatic control of cursor movement is possible by analysing a user face in the front of a computer.

In addition, face image processing is essential for the face recognition task which has many applications, such as entrance control system, face database retrieval, etc. [9]. Face detection and tracking from video sequence images are also necessary in VOD and multimedia applications [10].

Images used in face image processing are classified into two categories: grayscale and color images. Most existing researches have used grayscale images [1, 2, 3, 5, 6, 7, 8]. However, the color image provides more information than the grayscale image [11, 12, 13].

Chang and Huang extracted a face region and some features, i.e., eyes, mouth, and nostrils, by using color face images [4]. They used a fixed range in chromatic space for skin color to decide pixels on the face region. To extract nostrils, eyes, and mouth, they used a color thresholding technique.

Our approach is different from the Chang-Huang method in two aspects. Firstly, we use both face symmetricity information and chromatic information. Therefore our method does not fail in case that background has similar chromaticity as the face does. Secondly, we construct a face chromatic histogram and use it as a transformation function. Using this function, a face image is transformed into an image with confidence value for belonging to the face region. Compared with the Chang and Huang method, our approach in the paper can detect face regions more robustly since it operates in confidence value image.

The outline of this paper is as follows. Section 2 describes the construction of face chromatic histogram. Section 3 describes the extraction of face region. Section 4 describes the extraction of face features. Section 5 describes experimental results. Finally, Section 6 concludes the paper.

2. Construction of Face Chromatic Histogram

To extract a face region, we analyze the chromatic distribution of the face region. The result is represented by a histogram in chromatic space. To reduce the problem due to the chromatic variations of human faces, a histogram is constructed using many face images. In our experiment, 300 face images of similar aged people of the same race were used.

To construct a histogram, we first scissor the face region from each image. We convert the RGB representation into HSI representation using the formula (1). Note that I, S, and H in the formula stand for Intensity, Saturation, and Hue respectively. In HSI color model, chromatic (Hue and Saturation) and intensity components (Intensity) are separated. Therefore by removing the I component, the effect of illumination changes can be reduced [11].

$$
\begin{aligned}
I &= \frac{1}{3}(r+g+b) \\
S &= 1 - \frac{3}{(r+g+b)}[Min(r,g,b)] \\
H &= \cos^{-1}\left\{\frac{\frac{1}{2}[(r-g)+(r-b)]}{[(r-g)^2+(r-b)(g-b)]^{1/2}}\right\}
\end{aligned}
\tag{1}
$$

For histogram construction, we use only H and S components. For each pixel within the face region of a face image, we get the values of H and S and increment the corresponding bin of histogram. The following pseudo code describes this process formally:

```
initialize 2-D array HS to be 0;
for every face image I begin
  for each pixel P within face region of I begin
     h = hue_component(P);
     s = saturation_component(P);
     HS[h][s]++;
  end;
end;
```

The H and S axis must be quantized in proper levels. In our experiment, we quantize them into 32 levels. Figure 1(a) shows the histogram obtained experimentally in a bar graph. Figure 1(b) shows it in a grayscale image. From this histogram, we know that human face chromaticity is concentrated in the narrow region. This histogram will be used in Section 3 as a function that transforms the chromaticity of a pixel into confidence value for the pixel belonging to the face region.

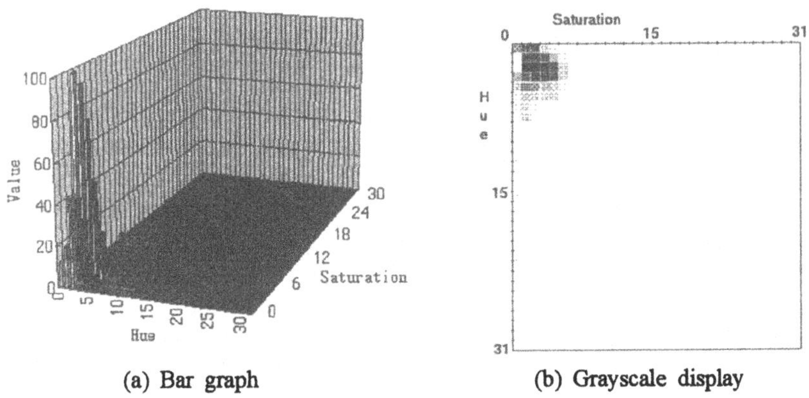

(a) Bar graph (b) Grayscale display

Fig. 1. Face chromatic histogram

3. Extraction of Face Region

To extract a face region, we use two kinds of information. The first is the symmetric information that comes from the physical characteristics of the face. In order to use symmetricity, we assume that the face image is frontal. The second is the chromatic information of the human face. The people of the same race have a similar skin color. Since the chromaticity of face colors is concentrated within a small region of chromatic space, the effective extraction of the face region is possible by using the chromatic information. The face chromatic histogram obtained experimentally in Section 2 supports this fact.

3.1 Detection of Symmetry

A symmetric point is determined for each scan line. The symmetric line of full images is detected by using them. At a scan line, pixels within 1/4 intervals in each of left and right directions from the center point are candidate for symmetric point. At each candidate point, we fold the scan line and compute the sum of differences of corresponding pixels. The candidate point resulting in the minimum summation value is determined as symmetric points of the scan line. Figure 2 shows the symmetric points for the hue and saturation component image.

(a) H image

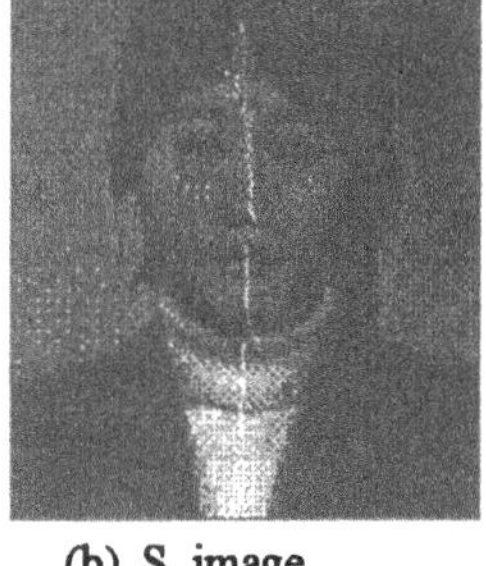

(b) S image

Fig. 2. Symmetric point image

In the symmetric point images, symmetric line is determined at a peak of vertical projection. Figure 4 shows the detected symmetric line.

3.2 Image Transformation Using Face Chromatic Histogram

We transform the chromatic value of each pixel into confidence value by using the face chromatic histogram. Following is a pseudo code describing the process:

```
for each pixel (x,y) of face image I begin
    h = hue_component(x,y);
    s = saturation_component(x,y);
    I[x][y] = HS[h][s];
end;
```

Figure 3 shows the transformed image. As expected, we can see that background and cloth regions have a low value while the pixels belonging to face region have high value.

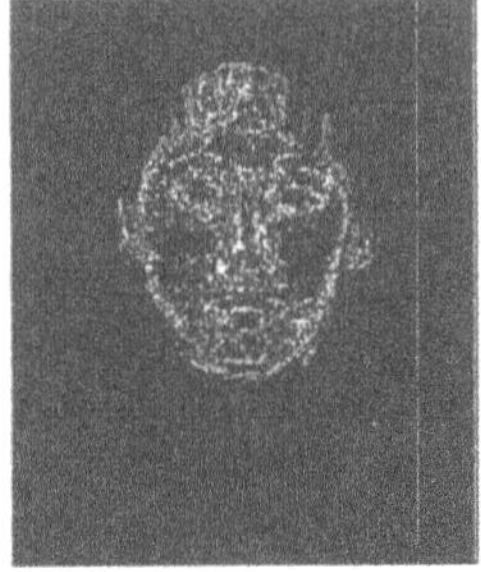

Fig. 3. Transformed image

3.3 Mask Operation

The face region is detected by applying an elliptical mask on the symmetric line of the transformed image. The mask has a fixed size, and its aspect ratio is 2:3 based on average length ratio of human faces. Applying the mask from top to bottom on the symmetric line, the face region is determined at the point where the mask sum is maximum. Figure 4 shows the detected face region.

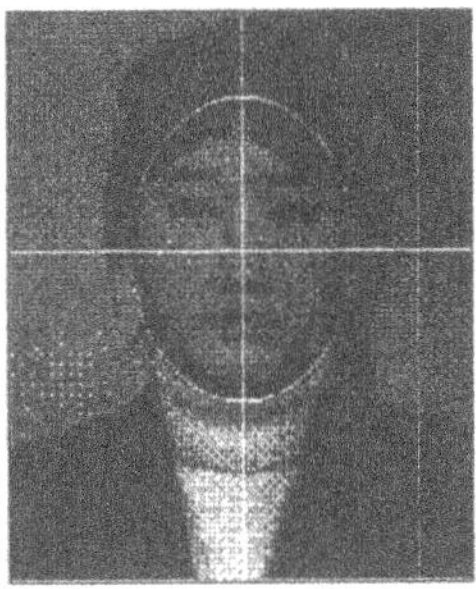

Fig. 4. Symmetric line and face region

Our method is different from Chang-Huang method [4] in two aspects. Firstly, we use both of symmetricity and chromaticity of human faces. Since we search for the face region only on symmetric line, correct detection is possible in the case that the background has similar chromaticity as the face does. In addition, it is computationally more efficient.

Secondly, a face chromatic histogram is constructed and used to transform a chromatic value into a confidence value for belonging to the face region. The Chang-Huang method also determines face region using skin color information [4]. But they convert the original image into binary image according to whether the chromatic value is within a fixed interval of skin color or not. They extract the face features from this binary image.

Obviously, their method does not operate properly in the case of face region pixel being out of the interval, and background or cloth region pixels being within the interval. Therefore our method can detect face regions more robustly since it operates on confidence value image.

4. Face Feature Extraction

Face features, that is, two eyes and a mouth in our method, are extracted within the face region detected in Section 3. Since their intensity is darker than the surrounding pixels, the intensity valley regions are extracted in I component image. Figure 5(a) shows the intensity valley regions extracted using the algorithm in [14]. It also shows a horizontal projection of the above half. In this projection, we determine the height of eye at the peak closer to the center line. At this height, a circular mask of fixed size is applied to count the surrounding black pixels and two positions with maximum number of black pixels are determined as eye pupil positions.

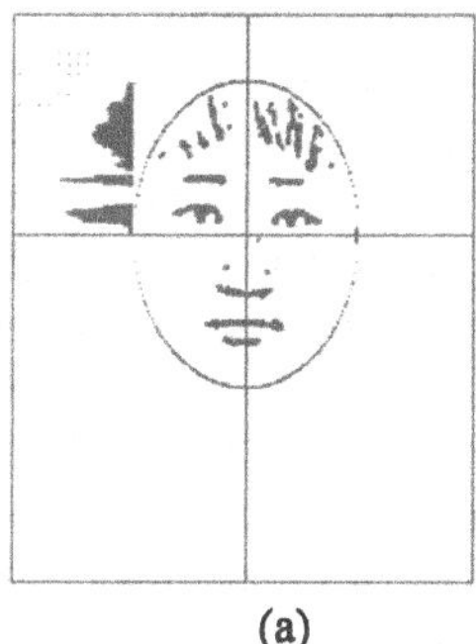

(a)

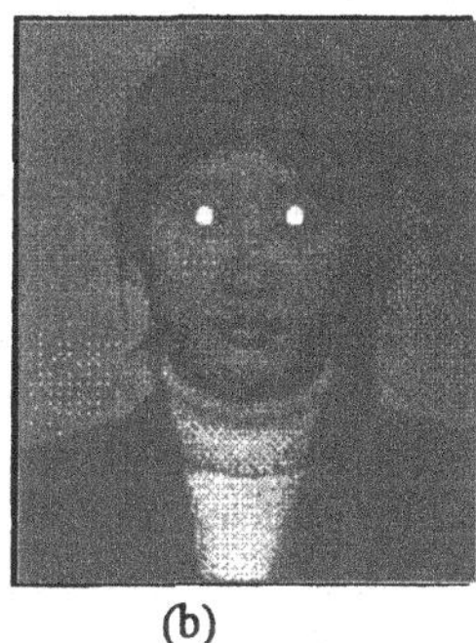

(b)

Fig. 5. Detection of eyes: (a) Intensity valley regions and horizontal projection, (b) Detected eye pupils

Using the eye position, the range where the mouth can appear is restricted as follows. Left and right eye positions are (x1,y) and (x2,y), respectively.

- x range : x1 ~ x2
- y range : (y+(x2-x1)) ~ (y+(x2-x1)×2)

Figure 6(a) shows this range and the horizontal projection. In this projection, the largest peak is determined as a mouth position (Figure 6(b)).

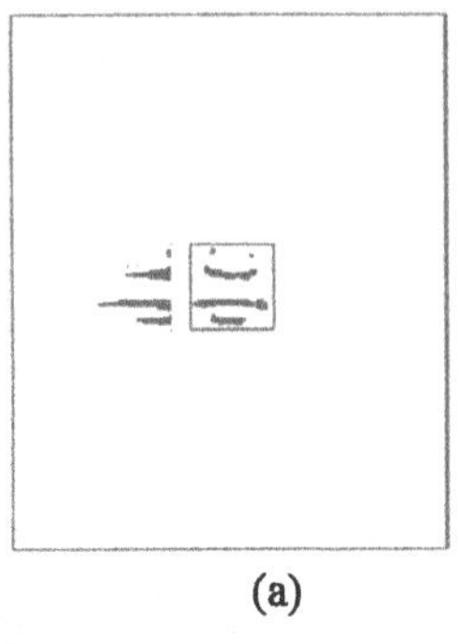

(a)

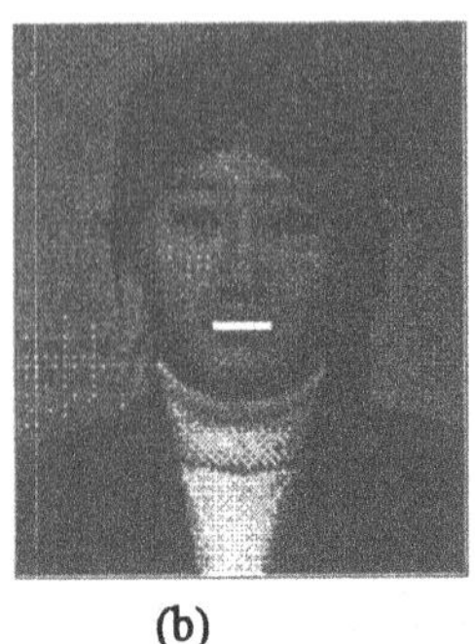

(b)

Fig. 6. Mouth detection: (a) Probable mouth range and horizontal projection, (b) Detected mouth

5. Experiment

Experiments were performed with both 265 face images without glass and 120 face images with glasses. The image resolution is 250×300. The images were acquired from university student cards. Since the photos are the ones acquired under the various illumination conditions, they are suitable for objective evaluation of algorithm performance. They all have the frontal faces.

The experimental results show high performance of face region and feature extraction. The method succeeds even if the clothes are similar to the face color. The success rate for the extraction of the symmetric line for the case of wearing glasses is similar to the case with no glasses as shown in Table 1 and Table 2. However, the success rate for face region extraction is lower if the subject is wearing glasses. The success rate for feature extraction is much lower. Figure 7 shows the results for some sample images.

Table 1. Performance for face images without glasses

number of image	symmetric line	face region	eyes	mouth	final
265	264	258	256	254	254
success rate	99.6%	97.4%	96.6%	95.8%	95.8%

Table 2. Performance for face images with glasses

number of image	symmetric line	face region	eyes	mouth	final
120	119	112	70	67	66
success rate	99.2%	93.3%	58.3%	55.8%	55%

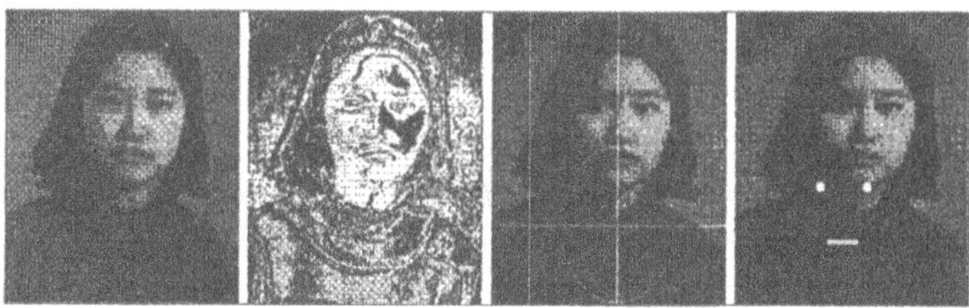

(a) Success for the image without glasses

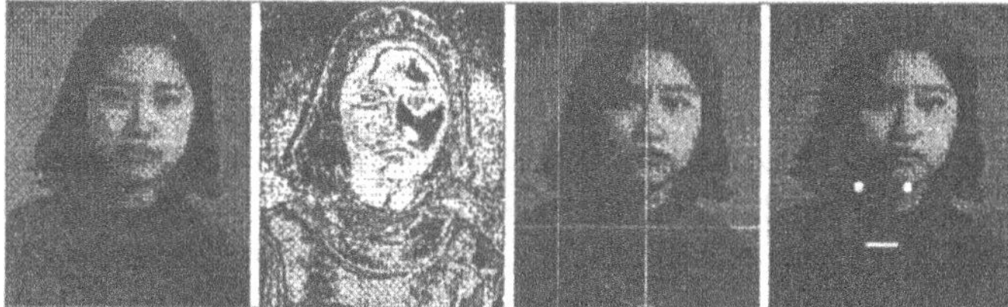

(b) Failure for the image without glasses

(c) Success for the image with glasses

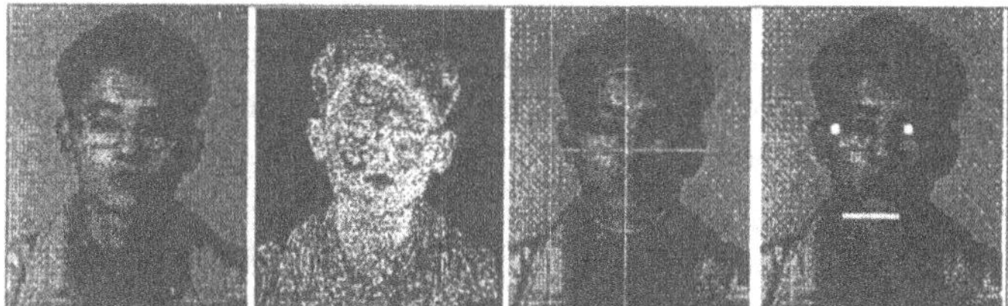

(d) Failure for the image with glasses

Fig. 7. Experimental images

6. Conclusions

We presented a methodology for extracting the face region and features from color frontal face images. A face chromatic histogram is constructed and used as a transformation function to obtain the confidence value for each pixel belonging to the face region.

As a future study, symmetric detection for the tilted face is required. Also the construction of face chromatic histogram for various races and ages is another research area.

REFERENCE

[1] R. Brunelli and T. Poggio, "Face recognition: features versus templates," *IEEE Transaction on Pattern Analysis and Machine Intelligence*, Vol. 15, No. 10, 1993, pp. 1042-1052.

[2] G. Chow and X. Li, "Towards a system for automatic facial feature detection," *Pattern Recognition*, Vol. 26, N0. 12, pp. 1739-1775.

[3] G. Gordon, "Face recognition based on depth maps and surface curvature," *SPIE Geometric Methods in Computer Vision*, Vol. 1570, 1991, pp. 234-246.

[4] T. C. Chang, T. S. Huang and C. Novak, "Facial feature extraction from color Images," *Proceeding of 12th International Conference on Pattern Recognition*, Vol. 2, 1994, pp. 39-43.

[5] Y. H. Kwon and N. V. Lobo, "Face detection using templates," *12th IAPR : International Conference on Pattern Recognition*, Vol. 1, 1994, pp. 764-767.

[6] C. L. Huang and C. W. Chen, "Human facial feature extraction for face interpretation and recognition," *ICPR'92*, 1992, pp. 204-207.

[7] B. Takacs and H. Wechsler, "Locating facial features using SOFM," *Proceeding of 12th International Conference on Pattern Recognition*, Vol. 2, 1994, pp. 55-60.

[8] X. Song, C. W. Lee, G. Xu and S. Tsuji, "Extracting facial features with partial feature template," *Asian Conference on Computer Vision '93*, November, 1993, pp. 751-754.

[9] J. K. Wu and A. D. Narasimhalu, "Identifying faces using multiple retrievals," *IEEE Multimedia*, Summer, 1994, pp. 27-38.

[10] S. W. Smoliar and H. Zhang, "Content-based video indexing and retrieval," *IEEE Multimedia*, Vol. 1, No. 2, Summer 1994, pp. 62-72.

[11] R. C. Gonzalez and R. E. Woods, *Digital Image Processing*, Addison Wesley, 1992.

[12] Y. Gong and M. Sakauchi, "Detection of regions matching specified chromatic features," *Computer Vision and Image Understanding*, Vol. 61, No. 2, 1995, pp. 263-269.

[13] M. J. Swain and D. H. Ballard, "Color Indexing," *International Journal Computer Vision*, Vol. 7, No. 1, 1991, pp. 11-32.

[14] I. S. Oh, S. M. Choi and T. W. Yoo, "Local comparison-based document image binarization preserving stroke connectivity," *Proceedings of Pacific Rim International Conference on Artificial Intelligence,* Beijing, 1994, pp. 939-942.

A Fast Pattern-Matching Algorithm Using Matching Candidates for Production Systems

Mitsunori Matsushita[1], Motohide Umano[2], Itsuo Hatono[2], and Hiroyuki Tamura[2]

[1] NTT Communication Science Laboratories, 1-2356, Take, Yokosuka-Shi, Kanagawa, Japan.
[2] Faculty of Engineering Science, Osaka University, 1-3, Machikaneyama-Cho, Toyonaka-Shi, Osaka, Japan.

Abstract. Several fast pattern matching algorithms have been proposed to improve the inference speed of production systems. In almost all of these algorithms, conditions in rules are represented using a dataflow network and working memory elements propagates this network as tokens. These algorithms are effective, but excessive constant testing is unavoidable when the working memory must be frequently updated.
This paper proposes a faster pattern matching algorithm for production systems. It uses an improved inference network employing matching candidates to circumvent the constant testing inherent in conventional networks. We classify constant-test nodes into inter-pattern test nodes and intra-pattern test nodes, a distinction not made in conventional networks. We then introduce memory nodes for matching candidates between these test nodes. This is done in order to exclude patterns that do not to be fired quickly. The ID3 algorithm is used to make an efficient inter-pattern test network that is capable of finding patterns in the rule conditions for working memory elements.

1 Introduction

Production systems are often used to make expert systems. Unfortunately, they spend too much time on the inference process. Some fast pattern matching algorithms have been proposed to quicken the inference process. In these algorithms, conditions in rules are represented using a dataflow network and a token of an element in working memory propagates the network. The Rete algorithm [1] is one of the most famous algorithms, and the TREAT algorithm[2] and the exclusive Rete algorithm[3] have also been proposed. These algorithms are effective, but some constant testing still cannot be avoided when the working memory is frequently updated.

We propose a fast matching algorithm using a dataflow network with the concept of matching candidates in order to avoid useless matching and hence useless testing. In the network, we classify constant-test nodes of the Rete network into inter-pattern test nodes and intra-pattern test nodes.

Inter-pattern test nodes are used to determine which condition patterns have the possibility of matching elements in the working memory, and intra-pattern test nodes are used to verify whether a specified condition pattern really matches these elements. We introduce memory nodes for matching candidates between these test nodes, which decreases the overhead of deletion and the change of tokens that remain is the network.

We apply the ID3 algorithm[4] to make an efficient inter-pattern test network that finds patterns in the rule conditions for working memory elements.

In this paper, we will first discuss the existing fast algorithms and their problem. We then introduce the proposed algorithm.

2 Conventional Methods and Their Problem

To produce results, a production system must repeat a sufficient number of recognition-action cycles, that is, matching conditions of rules with elements in working memory, selecting one of the several matched rules, and executing actions in the action part of the selected rule. If there are a lot of rules and working memory elements, the matching and processing operations take too long. Therefore, various approaches have been introduced to speed up inferencing.

2.1 The Rete Algorithm

The Rete algorithm translates conditions of rules into a discrimination network in the form of an augmented dataflow network. The pattern matchings that are overlapped in the recognition-action cycle can be omitted since the result of the last cycle is retained in the network. The following example may help.

- Ruleblock

```
(rule rb1
   (r1 if   ((class C1)(a1 =x)(a2 4)) ((class C2)(a1 =x)(a2 6))
       then (deposit (C4 (a1 8))))
   (r2 if   ((class C1)(a1 =x)(a2 4)) ((class C2)(a1 =x)(a2 7))
            ((class C3)(a1 6))
       then (deposit (C4 (a1 5)))) )
```

- Working memory

```
(working-memory wm1
   {((class C1)(a1 1)(a2 4)), ((class C2)(a1 1)(a2 6)),
    ((class C2)(a1 1)(a2 7)), ((class C3)(a1 7))        })
```

The rulebase rb1 consists of two rules r1 and r2, each of which includes 2 and 3 patterns as conditions respectively. An atom which has a symbol "=" in the head, e.g. =x, denotes a variable. And the working memory wm1 has four elements. A rule can fire if all patterns in the rule are matched with the working memory elements.

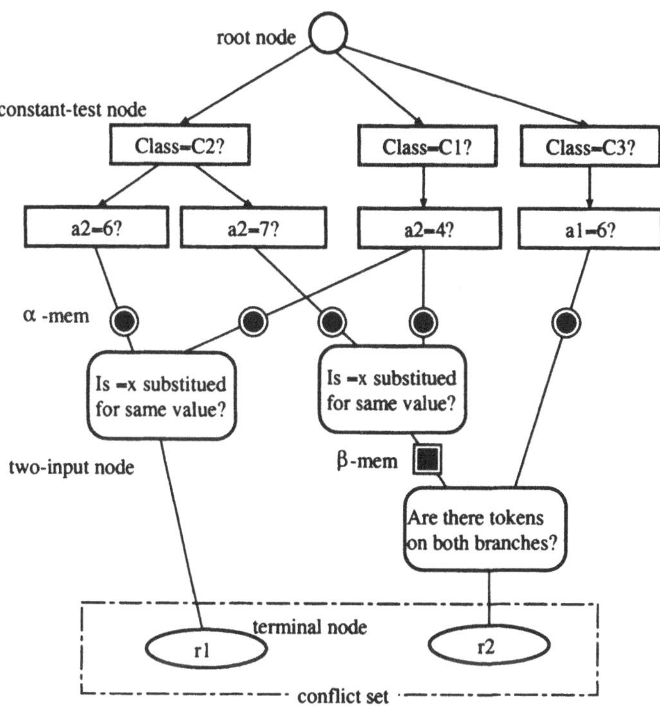

Fig. 1. Rete network sample

Figure 1 shows a network of the rulebase. Only the changed working memory elements are propagated from the root node and checked in each node in the network. We have 4 types of nodes in the network.

1. constant-test node
   It checks whether a constant attribute value of token satisfies a condition.

2. memory node
   It exists before two-input nodes and retains the token that passed constant-test nodes in the previous recognition-action cycle. A memory nodes that exists between two-input node and a constant-test node is called α-mem, and a node that exists between two-input nodes is called β-mem.

3. two-input node
   It checks whether a common variable is assigned the same constant in the condition part of a rule.

4. terminal node
   It corresponds to a rule.

The nodes of the same form that exist in the conditions of different rules are shared. First, we can avoid repeated identical matching operations. Second, a new token at a two-input node is matched to the token retained in the memory node in the previous recognition-action cycle. If the values of the variable are the same, the content of the memory node is appropriately updated and a new token is generated for propagation over the network. Matching results are retained in the network by every condition for the current working memory and are utilized for matching in the next cycle. This minimizes the matching of working memory elements that are not changed.

The effect of the Rete algorithm has been confirmed in various rules and adopted by many systems. However, it is not the best algorithm. Several better algorithms have been developed from it. For example, the TREAT algorithm generates two-input nodes dynamically to eliminate the overhead of updating memory at two-input nodes when the working memory is updated frequently. The exclusive Rete network utilizes the exclusiveness of the constant-test node of a network. The exclusiveness can also be applied to the TREAT network.

2.2 Matching in Conventional Methods

The problem with existing algorithms is explained below. We assume

$$\text{rule 1 : if } P_1 \ P_2 \cdots P_n \text{ then } \cdots$$

which is represented by the dataflow network in Fig.2.

If all condition patterns are matched but one pattern is not, this rule does not fire. In Fig.2, when tokens of working memory elements match $n-1$ condition patterns (P_1 to P_{n-1}) and they arrive at the α-mem's of their patterns, but no token arrives at the α-mem of pattern P_n, we see that the matching in the constant-test nodes toward the α-mem's of patterns (P_1 to P_{n-1}) was conducted in vain . Moreover, the processing in two-input nodes and β-mem after these α-mem's are also useless.

This is not so serious problem when the working memory is not updated so frequently because tokens arriving at α-mem's are nodes retained until the next recognition-action cycle. However, if the working memory is updated frequently, the overhead of updating increases in proportion to the number of the constant-test nodes that tokens pass through. This is true for not only the Rete algorithm but also the TREAT algorithm and the exclusive Rete algorithm.

3 A Fast Pattern-Matching Algorithm Using the Concept of Matching Candidates

The proposed inference algorithm uses a network that has memory nodes for matching candidates, where matching candidates means a token that only matches with a specific pattern in conditions but has no possibility of matching any other condition. By using this concept we can find easily rules that have patterns that

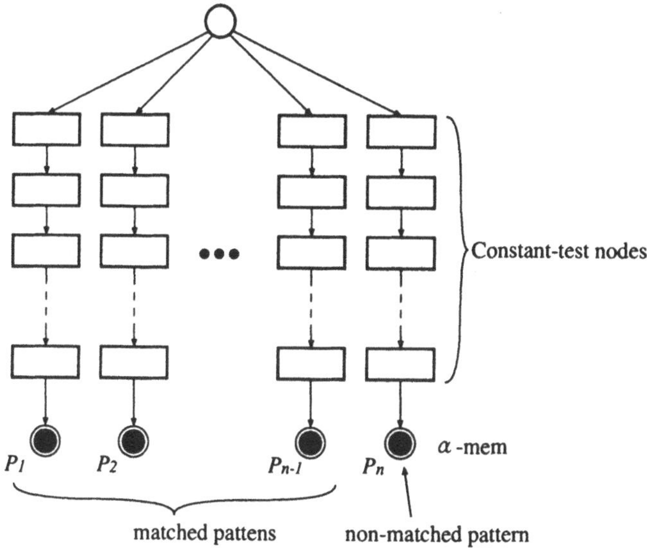

Fig. 2. Network representation of the rule conditions

do not match any token in working memory, and the pattern matching process of the rules that have no possibility at all of firing can be omitted. The proposed algorithm applies the concept of the matching candidates to conventional dataflow networks to reduce redundant matching processes. In this paper we apply this algorithm to the TREAT network, because we assume that working memory is updated frequently.

3.1 Detailed Proposed Algorithm

We use the following example.

```
(rule  (r1 if (=x b1 c1 d1) (a1 b2 =y d2) then ···)
       (r2 if (a2 b1 c2 d3) (a2 b2 c2 d3) then ···)
       (r3 if (a1 b2 =x d2)               then ···) )
```

This ruleblock has 3 rules that consist of 5 patterns, each of which has 4 attributes. In this example, =x and =y denote variables. The pattern matching process substitutes a value by

p1 : (=x b1 c1 d1)   p2 : (a1 b2 =y d2)   p3 : (a2 b1 c2 d3)

p4 : (a2 b2 c2 d3)   p5 : (a1 b2 =x d2)

which are referred to as pattern set P. This ruleblock is represented by the inference network using matching candidates as shown in Fig.3. This network consists of inter-pattern test nodes, memory nodes for matching candidates,

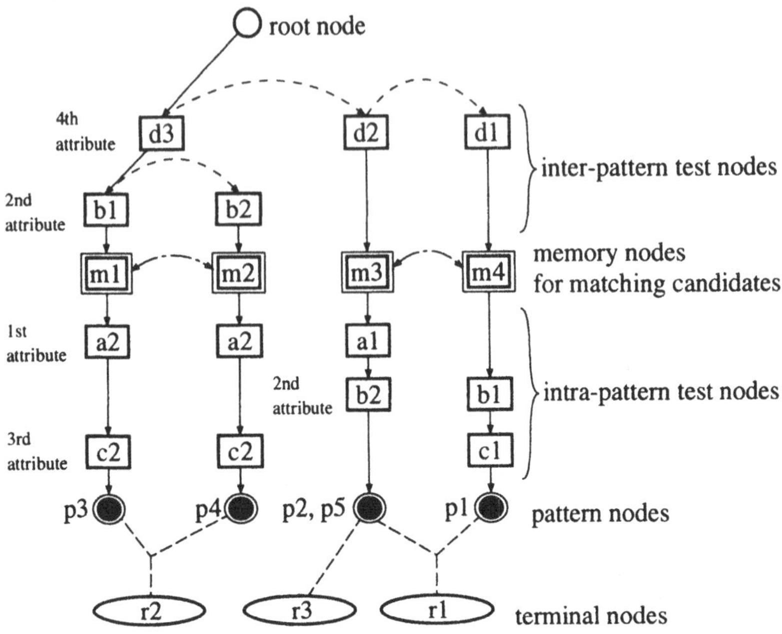

Fig. 3. Inference network using matching candidates

intra-pattern test nodes, and pattern nodes. Inference is executed by propagating updated working memory elements as tokens from the root node.

In this network, constant-test nodes are classified into inter-pattern test nodes and intra-pattern test nodes. Inter-pattern test nodes are used to specify the pattern that matches some token, while intra-pattern test nodes are used to check whether the remaining attributes match after the inter-pattern tests. Memory nodes for matching candidates lie between them. Since intra-pattern test nodes have no branches, a token arriving at a memory node for matching can only pass to a pattern node that follows the memory node. That is, it matches only the pattern of the conditions.

We describe the operations in each node.

1. Inter-pattern test node
   This node checks which attribute a token has based on characteristic attributes, where characteristic attributes are the attributes that make pattern - token matching faster.
   For example, in Fig.3, we check the fourth attributes first. If the attribute value is d3, we check the second attribute of the token. If the attribute value is b1, it has the possibility of matching pattern p3; if its value is b2, it has the possibility of matching pattern p4. If the value of the fourth attribute of the token is d2, it has the possibility of matching pattern p2 and p5, and if its value is d1, it may match pattern p1. In each node, if a token satisfies the

condition of the node, it then propagates to the output of the node, else it propagates to another node through an exclusion link (dotted lines in Fig.3). When the node has no links, no pattern matches the token of the working memory element. The exclusion link is the same as used in the exclusive Rete algorithm.

2. Memory node for matching candidates
This node retains the token that has passed the inter- pattern test nodes. A token arriving at one of these node never matches with the condition patterns that are chained to any other memory node for matching candidates. In the network, memory nodes of the condition patterns in the same rule are connected to each other by a link (the chained lines in Fig.3). If all memory nodes that are linked with a certain memory node do not have a token, it is known that no more matching processes are need and the token is retained for subsequent matching. If all memory nodes that are linked to the memory node have tokens, the token that arrived at the memory node is retained and a copy of the token is passed to the intra-pattern node connected to the memory node. In Fig.3, when memory nodes m2, m3, and m4 have tokens, copies of tokens in m3 and m4 are passed to the intra-pattern test nodes since the memory nodes m3 and m4 are connected to each other while a copy of the token in m2 does not go since memory node m1, connected to memory node m2, has no tokens.

3. Intra-pattern test node
These nodes test the attributes of the tokens that have not been tested in inter-pattern test nodes. A token that fails matching is deleted from the memory node as a matching candidate. If the token finally reaches a pattern node, its pattern is matched with the token. In Fig.3, a token (a1, b1, c1, d1) passes an inter-pattern test node and arrive at pattern node p1, while a token (a1 b2 c1 d1), which does not match the pattern in the second attribute, are deleted from memory node m4.

After all tokens in working memory are processed in intra-pattern test nodes, two-input nodes are dynamically constructed to check if the same variables in tokens hold the same value. The subsequent processes follow those of the TREAT algorithm. It is noted that the tokens of pattern nodes are deleted before the next recognition-action cycle.

In this algorithm, the more we reduce matching in inter-pattern test nodes, the more efficiently inference is executed. Thus we propose a method for making efficient inter-pattern test nodes using ID3 .

3.2 Method for Making Inter-Pattern Test Nodes Using ID3

ID3 yields a decision tree that can classify data with the fewest number of tests on average. We use the ID3 algorithm to make the inter-pattern test nodes from the condition patterns of rules. We use the an example of the set of condition

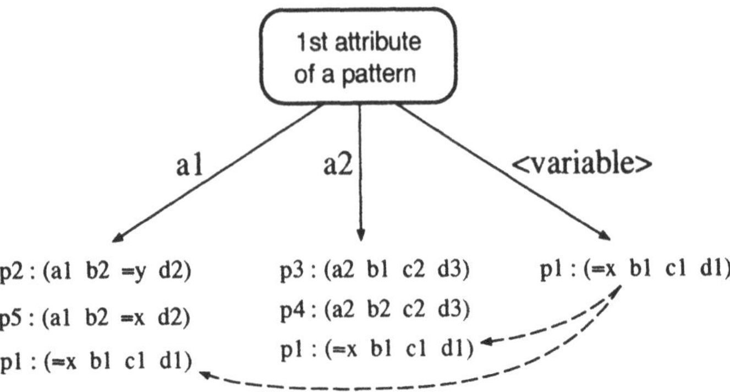

Fig. 4. First attribute classification of a pattern

patterns P in the ruleblock defined in the previous section. We have 4 attributes in these patterns for testing in the nodes.

If patterns in P are initially classified by the first attribute, they are tested by values a1 and a2 and the variables. Variables have the same behavior on matching even if they have different names, e.g., =x and =y. Therefore, they are treated as "<variable>". Since the first attribute of pattern p1 is a variable, it also matches values a1 and a2. A copy of p1 is then passed to the other nodes of branches a1 and a2, to ensure the exclusiveness of alternatives. This means that the branch of "<variable>" matches all values except a1 and a2. This constructs the sub-tree shown in Fig.4. Since we have a different number of variables in each pattern attribute, we have a different number of patterns in the sub-tree according to the attribute of test.

Next, we calculate the information amount for the case wherein the data are classified by the first attribute of the pattern. In ID3, data that have class names are not given to patterns. We give temporary class names in the form of patterns, where the class nodes, e.g., Group1 and Group2 form (a1 <variable> b2 d2) and (<variable> b1 c1 d1), respectively. The node of branch a1 is shown in Fig.5. The information amount $I(P_{\mathrm{a1}})$ of the node classified by value a1 is calculated as follows.

$$I(P_{\mathrm{a1}}) = -\frac{2}{3}\log_2\frac{2}{3} - \frac{1}{3}\log_2\frac{1}{3} = 0.918 \text{ (bit)} .$$

Similarly, information amounts $I(P_{\mathrm{a2}})$ and $I(P_{\mathrm{<variable>}})$ are calculated as

$$I(P_{\mathrm{a2}}) = 1.585 \text{ (bit)} , \quad I(P_{\mathrm{<variable>}}) = 0.0 \text{ (bit)} .$$

Therefore, the expected value of the information amount as classified by the first attribute is

$$E(\text{first attribute}, P) = \frac{3}{7} \times 0.918 + \frac{3}{7} \times 1.585 + \frac{1}{7} \times 0.0 = 1.073 \text{ (bit)} .$$

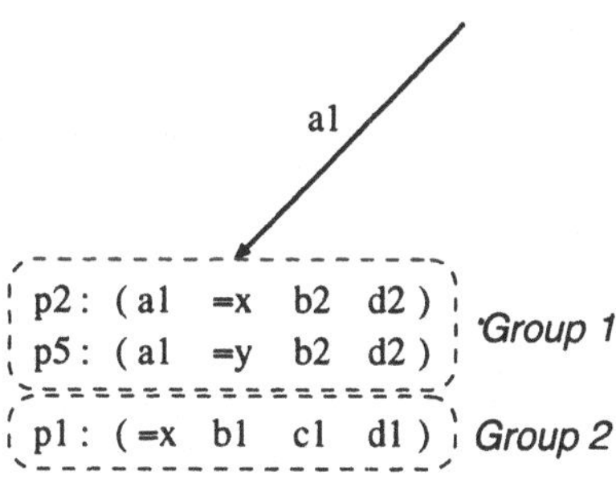

Fig. 5. Branch classification by attribute value a1

The expected the information amounts when classifying data P by the second, third, and fourth attributes of patterns are

$$E(\text{second attribute}, P) = 0.951 \text{ (bits)} \ ,$$
$$E(\text{third attribute}, P) = 0.973 \text{ (bits)} \ ,$$
$$E(\text{fourth attribute}, P) = 0.400 \text{ (bits)} \ .$$

The expected information amount is minimum if data P is classified by the fourth attribute. Thus we select the fourth attribute for the first test. This operation is repeated until only one class exists in one branch. The decision tree shown in Fig.6 is derived from the above examples.

Exclusive inter-pattern test nodes can be generated (see Fig.3) from this decision tree. Memory nodes for matching candidates in the same rule are connected with exclusive links.

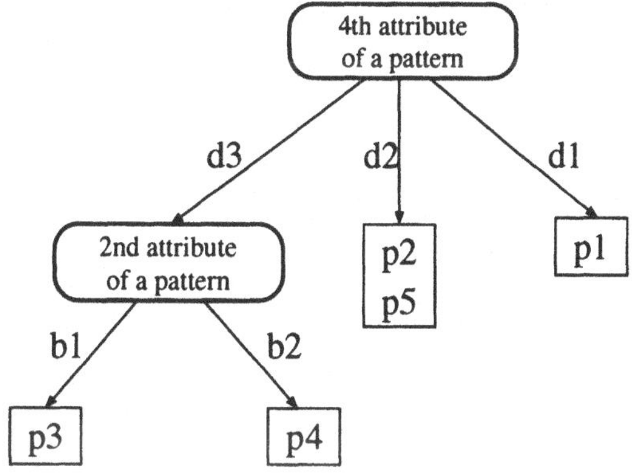

Fig. 6. Decision tree from a pattern

Exclusive links between inter-pattern test nodes are ordered by the number of patterns except for the link for "<variable>" which is set to the last term. Intra-pattern test nodes are the attributes that are not include in the inter-pattern test nodes.

All condition patterns have the same length in the example. For different pattern lengths, we first classify patterns by their length and then apply this algorithm. When the pattern contains a list as an element, the same process is repeated where the length of an atom is considered to be zero.

3.3 Performance Comparison

We compared the execution speeds of the proposed algorithm and the TREAT algorithm with exclusive links on the following four rulebases. The TREAT algorithm with exclusive links is used because we assume frequent updating of working memory.

1. rb1 : (15 rules, 15 patterns)
   This ruleblock describes a short comic story of Japan which tells how we can infer "A cooper can get money" from the fact "wind blows". It includes a very long inference chain and the historical information can be hardly used since working memory is updated frequently.

2. rb2 : (15 rules, 15 patterns)
   We add a condition pattern that always matches with a working memory element to check the effect of retaining tokens already matched. For example, the following rule is included in rb1 by adding two condition patterns (foo (bar)) and (bar (foo) bar).

   ```
   (r1  if   (blow wind) (foo (bar)) (bar (foo) bar)
        then (deposit (flit dust)) (delete (blow wind) 1))
   ```

   And we add two working memory elements (foo (bar)) and (bar (foo) bar). This means that the ratio of updating working memory is about 30%.

3. rb3 : (25rules, 45 patterns)
   This rulebase uses questions to determine what kind of stress is being felt.

4. rb4 : (18rules, 36 patterns)
   This rulebase evaluates the overhead of this method. This rulebase has no common patterns in conditions and cannot use the previous matching history. This means the dataflow provides no advantage.

Execution results are shown in Fig.7.

Rb1, rb2 and rb3 show that our method is 5% to 20% faster than the exclusive TREAT algorithm. Overhead of the network is the same as that of the exclusive TREAT algorithm (rb4). Therefore we conclude our algorithm is effective.

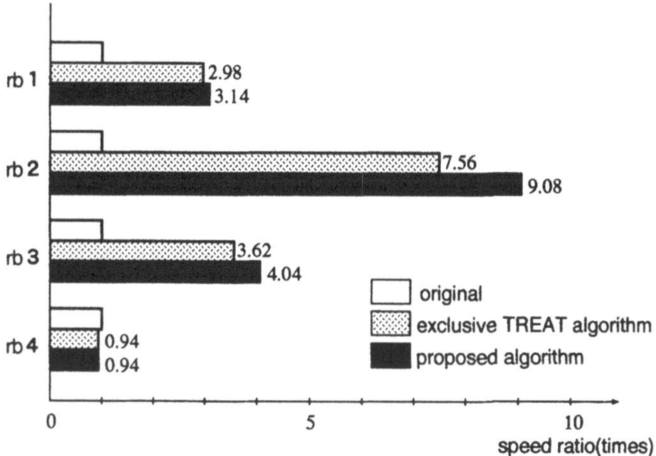

Fig. 7. Performance comparison of TREAT algorithm and proposed algorithm

4 Conclusion

This paper pinpointed the main inefficiency of conventional fast pattern matching algorithms, and proposed a new algorithm that uses matching candidates. This algorithm infers more quickly, especially when the working memory is updated frequently. The ID3 algorithm was adopted to more efficiently make inter-pattern test nodes. A leaf node of the decision tree corresponds to a memory node for matching candidates.

We implemented this algorithm using AKCL (Austin Kyoto Common Lisp) on SPARC station, SUN Microsystems.

References

1. Forgy, C. L.: Rete : A fast algorithm for the many pattern / many object pattern match problem. Artif. Intell. **19** (1982) 17–37
2. Miranker, D. P.: TREAT : A better match algorithm for AI production systems. AAAI-87 (1987) 42–47
3. Araya, S., Momohara, T., and Tamachi, T.: A fast pattern matching algorithm for production systems. Trans.IPS.Japan. **28** (1987) 768-775
4. Quinlan, J. R.: Discovering rules by induction from large collections of examples. Expert Systems in the Micro Electronics Age. Edinburgh University Press (1979)

Index

Springer-Verlag and the Environment

We at Springer-Verlag firmly believe that an international science publisher has a special obligation to the environment, and our corporate policies consistently reflect this conviction.

We also expect our business partners – paper mills, printers, packaging manufacturers, etc. – to commit themselves to using environmentally friendly materials and production processes.

The paper in this book is made from low- or no-chlorine pulp and is acid free, in conformance with international standards for paper permanency.

Lecture Notes in Artificial Intelligence (LNAI)

.Vol. 957: C. Castelfranchi, J.-P. Müller (Eds.), From Reaction to Cognition. Proceedings, 1993. VI, 252 pages. 1995.

Vol. 961: K.P. Jantke. S. Lange (Eds.), Algorithmic Learning for Knowledge-Based Systems. X, 511 pages. 1995.

Vol. 981: I. Wachsmuth, C.-R. Rollinger, W. Brauer (Eds.), KI-95: Advances in Artificial Intelligence. Proceedings, 1995. XII, 269 pages. 1995.

Vol. 984: J.-M. Haton, M. Keane, M. Manago (Eds.), Advances in Case-Based Reasoning. Proceedings, 1994. VIII, 307 pages. 1995.

Vol. 990: C. Pinto-Ferreira, N.J. Mamede (Eds.), Progress in Artificial Intelligence. Proceedings, 1995. XIV, 487 pages. 1995.

Vol. 991: J. Wainer, A. Carvalho (Eds.), Advances in Artificial Intelligence. Proceedings, 1995. XII, 342 pages. 1995.

Vol. 992: M. Gori, G. Soda (Eds.), Topics in Artificial Intelligence. Proceedings, 1995. XII, 451 pages. 1995.

Vol. 997: K. P. Jantke, T. Shinohara, T. Zeugmann (Eds.), Algorithmic Learning Theory. Proceedings, 1995. XV, 319 pages. 1995.

Vol. 1003: P. Pandurang Nayak, Automated Modeling of Physical Systems. XXI, 232 pages. 1995.

Vol. 1010: M. Veloso, A. Aamodt (Eds.), Case-Based Reasoning Research and Development. Proceedings, 1995. X, 576 pages. 1995.

Vol. 1011: T. Furuhashi (Ed.), Advances in Fuzzy Logic, Neural Networks and Genetic Algorithms. Proceedings, 1994. VIII, 223 pages. 1995.

Vol. 1020: I. D. Watson (Ed.), Progress in Case-Based Reasoning. Proceedings, 1995. VIII, 209 pages. 1995.

Vol. 1036: G. Adorni, M. Zock (Eds.), Trends in Natural Language Generation. Proceedings, 1993. IX, 382 pages. 1996.

Vol. 1037: M. Wooldridge, J.P. Müller, M. Tambe (Eds.), Intelligent Agents II. Proceedings, 1995. XVI, 437 pages, 1996.

Vol. 1038: W. Van de Velde, J.W. Perram (Eds.), Agents Breaking Away. Proceedings, 1996. XIV, 232 pages, 1996.

Vol. 1040: S. Wermter, E. Riloff, G. Scheler (Eds.), Connectionist, Statistical, and Symbolic Approaches to Learning for Natural Language Processing. IX, 468 pages. 1996.

Vol. 1042: G. Weiß, S. Sen (Eds.), Adaption and Learning in Multi-Agent Systems. Proceedings, 1995. X, 238 pages. 1996.

Vol. 1047: E. Hajnicz, Time Structures. IX, 244 pages. 1996.

Vol. 1050: R. Dyckhoff, H. Herre, P. Schroeder-Heister (Eds.), Extensions of Logic Programming. Proceedings, 1996. VIII, 318 pages. 1996.

Vol. 1053: P. Graf, Term Indexing. XVI, 284 pages. 1996.

Vol. 1056: A. Haddadi, Communication and Cooperation in Agent Systems. XIII, 148 pages. 1996.

Vol. 1069: J.W. Perram, J.-P. Müller (Eds.), Distributed Software Agents and Applications. Proceedings, 1994. VIII, 219 pages. 1996.

Vol. 1071: P. Miglioli, U. Moscato, D. Mundici, M. Ornaghi (Eds.), Theorem Proving with Analytic Tableaux and Related Methods. Proceedings, 1996. X, 330 pages. 1996.

Vol. 1076: N. Shadbolt, K. O'Hara, G. Schreiber (Eds.), Advances in Knowledge Acquisition. Proceedings, 1996. XII, 371 pages. 1996.

Vol. 1079: Z. W. Raś, M. Michalewicz (Eds.), Foundations of Intelligent Systems. Proceedings, 1996. XI, 664 pages. 1996.

Vol. 1081: G. McCalla (Ed.), Advances in Artificial Intelligence. Proceedings, 1996. XII, 459 pages. 1996.

Vol. 1082: N.R. Adam, B.K. Bhargava, M. Halem, Y. Yesha (Eds.), Digital Libraries. Proceedings, 1995. Approx. 310 pages. 1996.

Vol. 1083: K. Sparck Jones, J.R. Galliers, Evaluating Natural Language Processing Systems. XV, 228 pages. 1996.

Vol. 1085: D.M. Gabbay, H.J. Ohlbach (Eds.), Practical Reasoning. Proceedings, 1996. XV, 721 pages. 1996.

Vol. 1087: C. Zhang, D. Lukose (Eds.), Distributed Artificial Intelligence. Proceedings, 1995. VIII, 232 pages. 1996.

Vol. 1093: L. Dorst, M. van Lambalgen, F. Voorbraak (Eds.), Reasoning with Uncertainty in Robotics. Proceedings, 1995. VIII, 387 pages. 1996.

Vol. 1095: W. McCune, R. Padmanabhan, Automated Deduction in Equational Logic and Cubic Curves. X, 231 pages. 1996.

Vol. 1104: M.A. McRobbie, J.K. Slaney (Eds.), Automated Deduction – Cade-13. Proceedings, 1996. XV, 764 pages. 1996.

Vol. 1111: J. J. Alferes, L. Moniz Pereira, Reasoning with Logic Programming. XXI, 326 pages. 1996.

Vol. 1114: N. Foo, R. Goebel (Eds.), PRICAI'96: Topics in Artificial Intelligence. Proceedings, 1996. XXI, 658 pages. 1996.

Vol. 1115: P.W. Eklund, G. Ellis, G. Mann (Eds.), Conceptual Structures: Knowledge Representation as Interlingua. Proceedings, 1996. XIII, 321 pages. 1996.

Lecture Notes in Computer Science

Vol. 1083: K. Sparck Jones, J.R. Galliers, Evaluating Natural Language Processing Systems. XV, 228 pages. 1996. (Subseries LNAI).

Vol. 1084: W.H. Cunningham, S.T. McCormick, M. Queyranne (Eds.), Integer Programming and Combinatorial Optimization. Proceedings, 1996. X, 505 pages. 1996.

Vol. 1085: D.M. Gabbay, H.J. Ohlbach (Eds.), Practical Reasoning. Proceedings, 1996. XV, 721 pages. 1996. (Subseries LNAI).

Vol. 1086: C. Frasson, G. Gauthier, A. Lesgold (Eds.), Intelligent Tutoring Systems. Proceedings, 1996. XVII, 688 pages. 1996.

Vol. 1087: C. Zhang, D. Lukose (Eds.), Distributed Artificial Intelliegence. Proceedings, 1995. VIII, 232 pages. 1996. (Subseries LNAI).

Vol. 1088: A. Strohmeier (Ed.), Reliable Software Technologies – Ada-Europe '96. Proceedings, 1996. XI, 513 pages. 1996.

Vol. 1089: G. Ramalingam, Bounded Incremental Computation. XI, 190 pages. 1996.

Vol. 1090: J.-Y. Cai, C.K. Wong (Eds.), Computing and Combinatorics. Proceedings, 1996. X, 421 pages. 1996.

Vol. 1091: J. Billington, W. Reisig (Eds.), Application and Theory of Petri Nets 1996. Proceedings, 1996. VIII, 549 pages. 1996.

Vol. 1092: H. Kleine Büning (Ed.), Computer Science Logic. Proceedings, 1995. VIII, 487 pages. 1996.

Vol. 1093: L. Dorst, M. van Lambalgen, F. Voorbraak (Eds.), Reasoning with Uncertainty in Robotics. Proceedings, 1995. VIII, 387 pages. 1996. (Subseries LNAI).

Vol. 1095: W. McCune, R. Padmanabhan, Automated Deduction in Equational Logic and Cubic Curves. X, 231 pages. 1996. (Subseries LNAI).

Vol. 1096: T. Schäl, Workflow Management Systems for Process Organisations. XII, 200 pages. 1996.

Vol. 1097: R. Karlsson, A. Lingas (Eds.), Algorithm Theory – SWAT '96. Proceedings, 1996. IX, 453 pages. 1996.

Vol. 1098: P. Cointe (Ed.), ECOOP '96 – Object-Oriented Programming. Proceedings, 1996. XI, 502 pages. 1996.

Vol. 1099: F. Meyer auf der Heide, B. Monien (Eds.), Automata, Languages and Programming. Proceedings, 1996. XII, 681 pages. 1996.

Vol. 1100: B. Pfitzmann, Digital Signature Schemes. XVI, 396 pages. 1996.

Vol. 1101: M. Wirsing, M. Nivat (Eds.), Algebraic Methodology and Software Technology. Proceedings, 1996. XII, 641 pages. 1996.

Vol. 1102: R. Alur, T.A. Henzinger (Eds.), Computer Aided Verification. Proceedings, 1996. XII, 472 pages. 1996.

Vol. 1103: H. Ganzinger (Ed.), Rewriting Techniques and Applications. Proceedings, 1996. XI, 437 pages. 1996.

Vol. 1104: M.A. McRobbie, J.K. Slaney (Eds.), Automated Deduction – CADE-13. Proceedings, 1996. XV, 764 pages. 1996. (Subseries LNAI).

Vol. 1105: T.I. Ören, G.J. Klir (Eds.), Computer Aided Systems Theory – CAST '94. Proceedings, 1994. IX, 439 pages. 1996.

Vol. 1106: M. Jampel, E. Freuder, M. Maher (Eds.), Over-Constrained Systems. X, 309 pages. 1996.

Vol. 1107: J.-P. Briot, J.-M. Geib, A. Yonezawa (Eds.), Object-Based Parallel and Distributed Computation. Proceedings, 1995. X, 349 pages. 1996.

Vol. 1108: A. Díaz de Ilarraza Sánchez, I. Fernández de Castro (Eds.), Computer Aided Learning and Instruction in Science and Engineering. Proceedings, 1996. XIV, 480 pages. 1996.

Vol. 1109: N. Koblitz (Ed.), Advances in Cryptology – Crypto '96. Proceedings, 1996. XII, 417 pages. 1996.

Vol. 1110: O. Danvy, R. Glück, P. Thiemann (Eds.), Partial Evaluation. Proceedings, 1996. XII, 514 pages. 1996.

Vol. 1111: J.J. Alferes, L. Moniz Pereira, Reasoning with Logic Programming. XXI, 326 pages. 1996. (Subseries LNAI).

Vol. 1112: C. von der Malsburg, W. von Seelen, J.C. Vorbrüggen, B. Sendhoff (Eds.), Artificial Neural Networks – ICANN 96. Proceedings, 1996. XXV, 922 pages. 1996.

Vol. 1113: W. Penczek, A. Szałas (Eds.), Mathematical Foundations of Computer Science 1996. Proceedings, 1996. X, 592 pages. 1996.

Vol. 1114: N. Foo, R. Goebel (Eds.), PRICAI'96: Topics in Artificial Intelligence. Proceedings, 1996. XXI, 658 pages. 1996. (Subseries LNAI).

Vol. 1115: P.W. Eklund, G. Ellis, G. Mann (Eds.), Conceptual Structures: Knowledge REpresentation as Interlingua. Proceedings, 1996. XIII, 321 pages. 1996. (Subseries LNAI)

Vol. 1116: J. Hall (Ed.), Management of Telecommunication Systems and Services. XXI, 229 pages. 1996.

Vol. 1117: A. Ferreira, J. Rolim, Y. Saad, T. Yang (Eds.), Parallel Algorithms for Irregularly Structured Problems. Proceedings, 1996. IX, 358 pages. 1996.

Vol. 1120: M. Deza, R. Euler, I. Manoussakis (Eds.), Combinatorics and Computer Science. Proceedings, 1995. IX, 415 pages. 1996.